2015

北京统计年鉴

Beijing Statistical Yearbook

图书在版编目(CIP)数据

北京统计年鉴. 2015 ： 汉英对照 / 北京市统计局，国家统计局北京调查总队编. -- 北京：中国统计出版社，2015.7

ISBN 978-7-5037-7444-7

Ⅰ. ①北 Ⅱ. ①北 ②国 Ⅲ. ①统计资料－北京市－2015－年鉴－汉、英 Ⅳ. ①C832.1-54

中国版本图书馆CIP数据核字(2015)第127372号

北京统计年鉴-2015

作　　者/北京市统计局　国家统计局北京调查总队
责任编辑/郭　栋　李　冲
封面设计/高　立
出版发行/中国统计出版社
通信地址/北京市丰台区西三环南路甲6号　邮政编码/100073
电　　话/邮购（010）63376909　书店（010）68783171
网　　址/http://www.zgtjcbs.com
印　　刷/北京联兴盛业印刷有限公司
经　　销/新华书店
开　　本/880mm×1230mm　1/16
字　　数/1200千字
印　　张/37.75印张　彩插/1.5印张
版　　别/2015年9月第1版
版　　次/2015年9月第1次印刷
定　　价/350.00元

本书附同版本CD-ROM一张，光盘内容以书面文字为准。
如有印装差错，由本社发行部调换。

2014年，全市人民在党中央、国务院和市委、市政府的坚强领导下，积极落实稳增长、促改革、调结构、惠民生各项政策措施，着力疏解非首都功能、加快培育“高精尖”经济结构，全市经济持续健康发展，社会和谐稳定。

In 2014, under the firm leadership of Party Central Committee, the State Council and the Beijing Municipal Party Committee and Municipal Government, people of the Capital actively implemented various policies aiming to stabilize economic growth, promote innovation, adjust economic structure and benefit people's livelihood, emphasized on easing non-capital functions and accelerated the development of an innovation-oriented, technology-intensive and high-value economic structure, which exhibited a sustainable and healthy economic development as well as a harmonious and stable social environment.

2014年的北京 Beijing in 2014

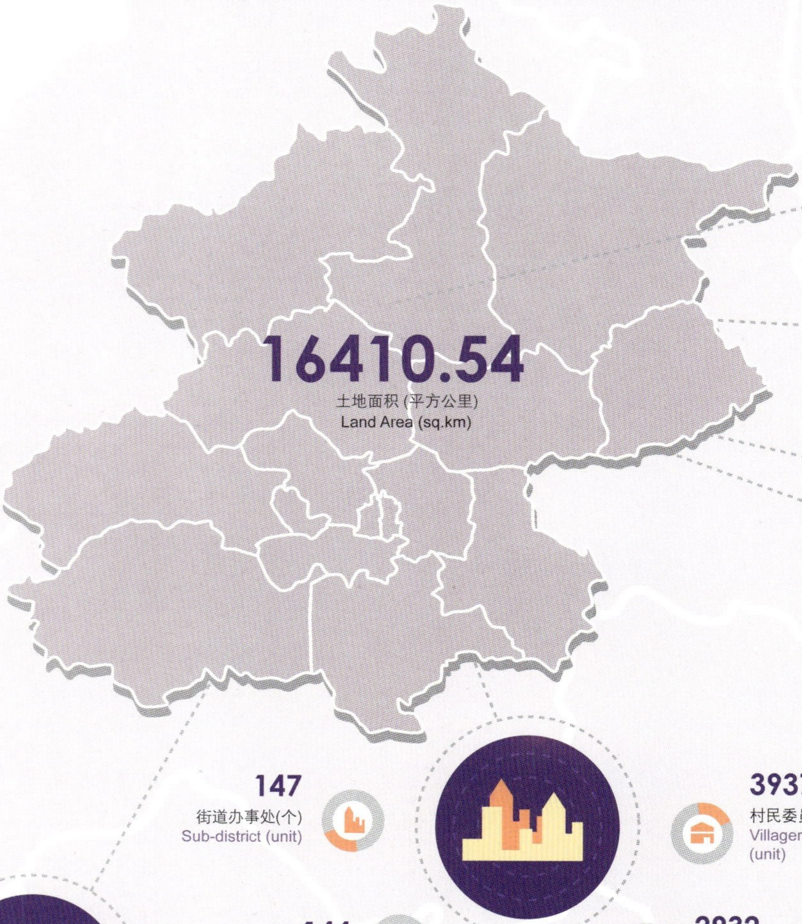

147
街道办事处(个)
Sub-district (unit)

3937
村民委员会(个)
Villagers' Committee (unit)

144
建制镇(个)
Designated Town (unit)

2932
社区居委会(个)
Community Neighborhood Committee (unit)

38
建制乡(个)
Designated Township (unit)

1311
人口密度(人/平方公里)
Density (person/sq.km)

2151.6
常住人口(万人)
Permanent Population (10000 persons)

818.7
常住外来人口(万人)
Permanent Migrant Population (10000 persons)

85.9
PM2.5年均浓度
(微克/立方米)
Annual Average Concentration of PM 2.5 (microgram/cubic meter)

15.9
人均公园绿地面积(平方米)
Per Capital Park Green Areas (square meter)

527
轨道交通运营线路长度(公里)
Length of Rail Transportation Lines in Operation (kilometer)

86.1
污水处理率(%)
Disposal Rate of Waste Water (%)

43910
城镇居民人均可支配收入(元)
Per Capita Annual Disposable Income of Urban Residents (yuan)

21330.8
地区生产总值(亿元)
Gross Domestic Product (100 million yuan)

16278
人均地区生产总值(美元)
Per Capita Gross Domestic Product (USD)

20226
农村居民人均纯收入(元)
Per Capita Net Income of Rural Residents (yuan)

77.9
第三产业比重(%)
Percentage of Tertiary Industry (%)

101.6
居民消费价格指数(%)
Consumer Price Index (%)

7562.3
全社会固定资产投资额(亿元)
Total Investment in Fixed Assets (100 million yuan)

4.93
每千常住人口
注册护士(人)
Number of Certified Nurses per 1000 Permanent Population (person)

9638.0
社会消费品零售总额(亿元)
Total Retail Sales of Consumer Goods (100 million yuan)

4.16
每千常住人口执业医师(人)
Number of Licensed Doctors per 1000 Permanent Population (person)

9.0
普通中学平均每一专任老师负担学生数(人)
Average Number of Students Taken Charge by Each Full-time Teacher in Ordinary Middle School (person)

5.95
研究与试验发展(R&D)经费内部支出相当于地区生产总值比例(%)
Internal R&D Expenditure as Percentage of GDP (%)

3136.0
技术合同成交总额(亿元)
Total Amount of Technological Contracts Signed (100 million yuan)

4027.2
地方公共财政预算收入(亿元)
Local Public Budgetary Financial Revenue (100 million yuan)

6.7
每十万常住人口
幼儿园数(个)
Number of Kindergartens per 100000 Permanent Population (unit)

14.4
小学平均每一专任老师负担学生数(人)
Average Number of Students Taken Charge by Each Full-Time Teacher in Primary School (Person)

0.8
每十万常住人口博物馆数(个)
Number of Museums per 100000 Permanent Population (unit)

4.5
每十万常住人口银幕数(块)
Number of Projection Screens per 100000 Permanent Population (piece)

北京一日 A Day in Beijing

每日创造
Daily Production

197658.6
地方财政收入
(万元/日)
Local Financial Revenue
(10000 yuan/day)

195828.7
地方财政支出
(万元/日)
Local Financial Expenditure
(10000 yuan/day)

9275.9
发电量
(万千瓦时/日)
Generating Capacity
(10000 kwh/day)

5937
汽车生产量
(辆/日)
Output of Motor Vehicles (unit/day)

492701
移动电话机生产量(台/日)
Output of Mobile Telephone (unit/day)

17078.3
海关出口总值
(万美元/日)
Total Value of Export at Customs
(USD 1000/day)

27825
微型计算机生产量
(台/日)
Production of Micro-computers (one/day)

4355.9
第一产业(万元/日)
Primary Industry (10000 yuan/day)

124515.1
第二产业(万元/日)
Secondary Industry (10000 yuan/day)

455535.3
第三产业(万元/日)
Tertiary Industry (10000 yuan/day)

584406.3
地区生产总值 (万元/日)
Gross Domestic Product (10000 yuan/day)

109506.3
国内旅游收入
(万元/日)
Domestic Tourism Income
(10000/day yuan/day)

1307
公共电汽车客运量
(万人次/日)
Passengers Carried by Buses and Trolley Buses
(10000 person-times/day)

1262.4
旅游外汇收入
(万美元/日)
Foreign Exchange Earnings from Tourism
(USD 10000/day)

928
轨道交通客运量
(万人次/日)
Passengers Carried by Rail Transit
(10000 person-times/day)

2014 年 Year

18.5
民航客运量
(万人次/日)
Civil Aviation Passenger Traffic (10000 person-times/day)

143.4
公路客运量
(万人次/日)
Highway Passenger Traffic
(10000 person-times/day)

34.5
铁路客运量
(万人次/日)
Railway Passenger Traffic
(10000 person-times/day)

304.1
特快专递业务量
(万件/日)
Business Volume of EMS
(10000/day)

3493
机动车销售量
(辆/日)
Sales of Automobiles
(unit/day)

① 人均地区生产总值(美元/人)
Per Capita Gross Domestic Product (USD/person)

年份	2010	2011	2012	2013	2014
人均地区生产总值	10910	12643	13857	15284	16278
比上年增长(%) Increase (%)	4.8	3.8	4.9	5.2	5.2

② 常住人口(万人)
Permanent Population (10000 persons)

年份	2010	2011	2012	2013	2014
常住人口	1961.9	2018.6	2069.3	2114.8	2151.6
比上年增长(%) Increase (%)	5.5	2.9	2.5	2.2	1.7

每日生活
Daily Life

570
常住出生人口
(人/日)
Birth Population
(Permanent Population)
(person/day)

287
常住死亡人口
(人/日)
Death Population
(Permanent Population)
(person/day)

466
登记结婚对数
(对/日)
Marriage Registered
(couple/day)

209
离婚对数
(对/日)
Registered Divorces
(couple/day)

120.3
城镇居民人均
可支配收入(元/日)
Per Capita Disposable
Income of Urban
Residents (yuan/day)

69797
住宅竣工面积
(平方米/日)
Completed Residential Floor
Space (square meter/day)

76.7
城镇居民人均
消费性支出(元/日)
Per Capita Consumption
Expenditures of Urban
Residents (yuan/day)

50972.6
吃类商品(万元/日)
Food
(10000 yuan/day)

21460.3
穿类商品(万元/日)
Clothing(10000 yuan/day)

175712.3
用类商品(万元/日)
Daily Supplies(10000 yuan/day)

15909.9
烧类商品(万元/日)
Fuel(10000 yuan/day)

264054.8
社会消费品零售总额 (万元/日)
Retail Sales of Consumer Goods
(10000 yuan/day)

381.1
污水处理量
(万立方米/日)
Disposal Volume of
Waste Water
(10000 cu.m/day)

55.4
农村居民人均
纯收入(元/日)
Per Capita Net
Income of Rural
Residents (yuan/day)

2.0
生活垃圾清运量
(万吨/日)
Domestic Waste Removed
and Transported
(10000 tons/day)

39.8
农村居民人均
生活消费支出(元/日)
Per Capita Living
Expenditures of Rural
Residents (yuan/day)

4637.3
城乡居民生活用电量
(万千瓦时/日)
Urban and Rural
Residential Electricity
Consumption
(10000 kwh/day)

346.6
居民家庭用天然气
(万立方米/日)
Natural Gas
for Living Use
(10000 cu.m/day)

141.8
居民家庭用自来水
(万立方米/日)
Tap Water
for Living Use
(10000 cu.m/day)

4459
电影放映场次
(场次/日)
Film Show Times
(Times/day)

43.2
医院诊疗人次
(万人次/日)
Hospital Visit
(10000 person-times/day)

2014
年 Year

3
■ 轨道交通运营线路长度(公里)
Operating Routes Length of
Rail Transit (km)
□ 轨道交通客运量(亿人次)
Passenger Traffic of Rail Transit
(100 million person-times)

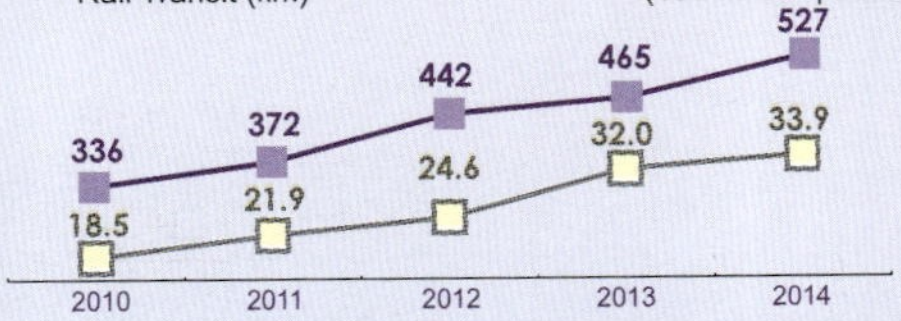

4
■ 公共电汽车运营线路长度(公里)
Operating Routes Length of
Buses and Trolley Buses (km)
□ 公共电汽车客运量(亿人次)
Passenger Traffic of Buses and Trolley
Buses (100 million person-times)

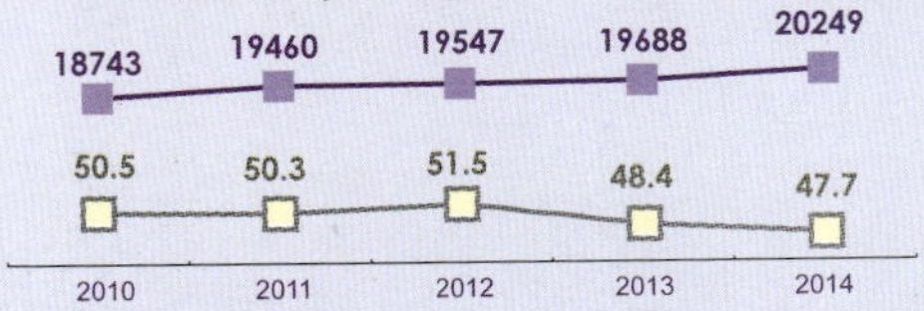

Stable Economic Situation as A Whole Continuous Improvement of Investment and Consumption Structure

地区生产总值总量突破2万亿元
GDP Hits Over RMB 2 Trillion

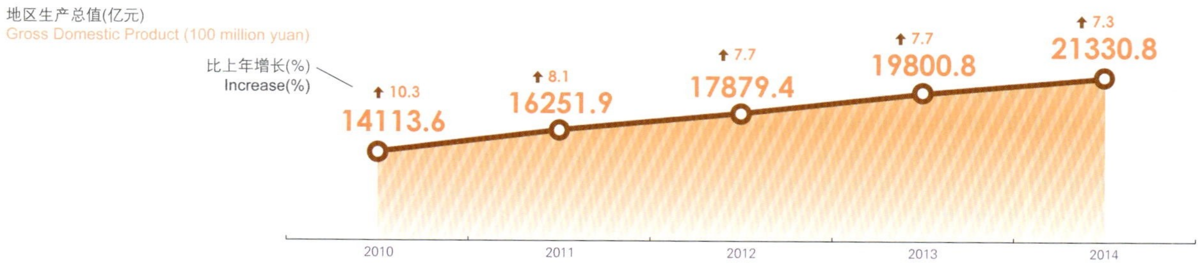

居民消费价格涨幅五年来最低
CPI Growth Rate is A Record Low in Recent 5 Years

城镇登记失业率处于低位
Registered Unemployment Rate in Urban Areas Stays at A Low Level

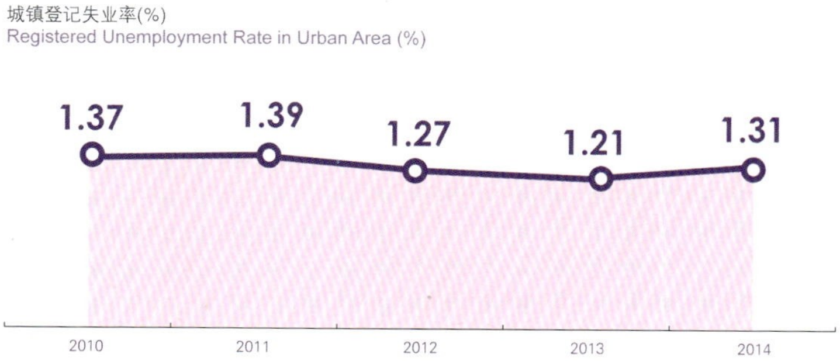

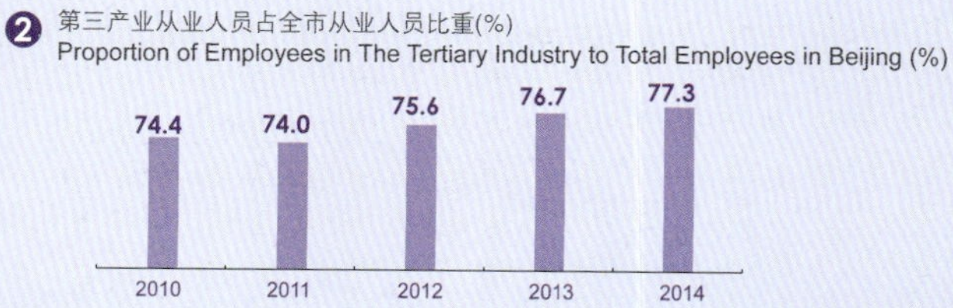

投资和消费结构继续优化
Continuous Improvement in Investment and Consumption Structure

民间投资(亿元)
Private Investment (100 million yuan)

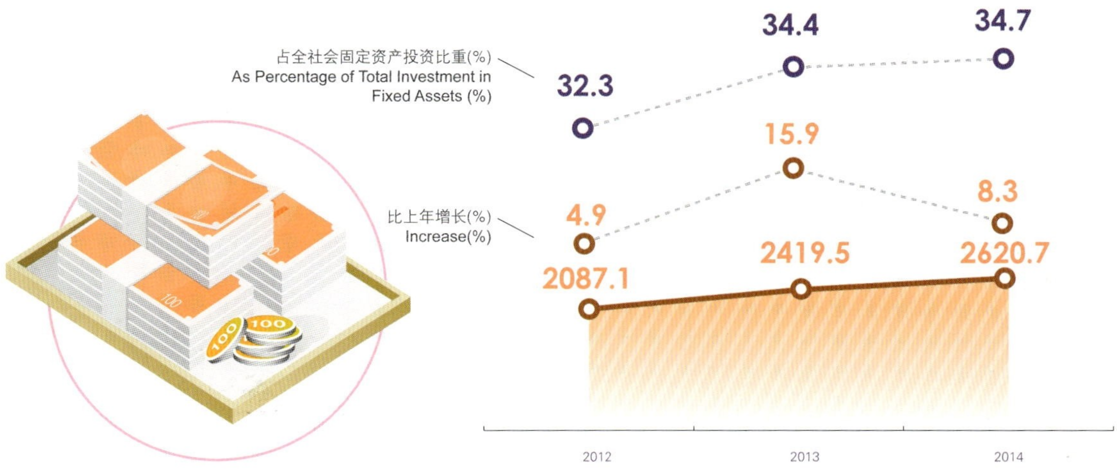

限额以上批发零售企业网上零售额(亿元)
Online Retail Sales of Wholesale and Retail Enterprises above Designated Size (100 million yuan)

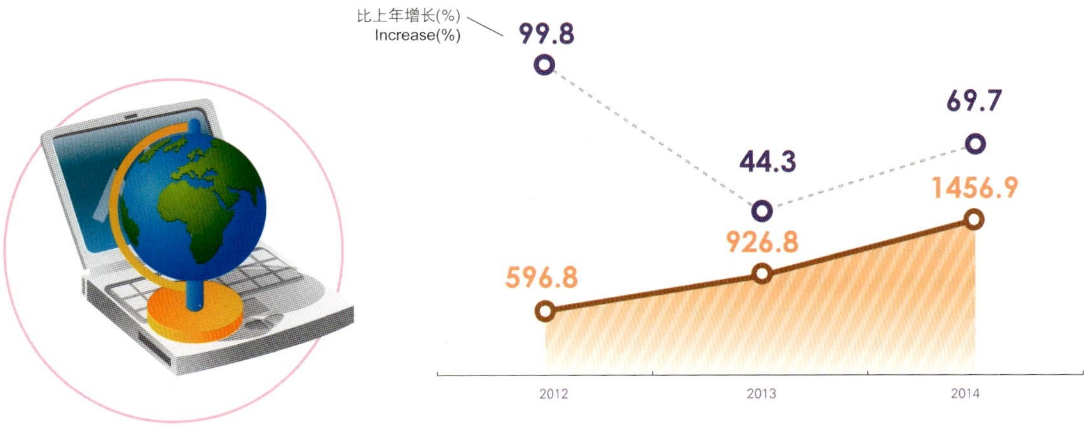

3 全社会固定资产投资(亿元)
Total Investment in Fixed Assets (100 million yuan)

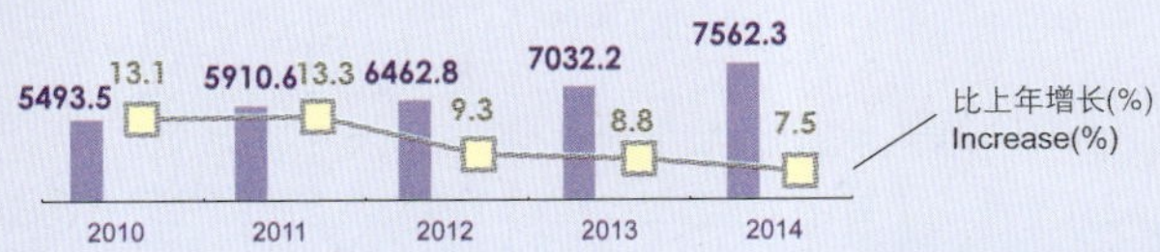

4 社会消费品零售总额(亿元)
Total Retail Sales of Consumer Goods (100 million yuan)

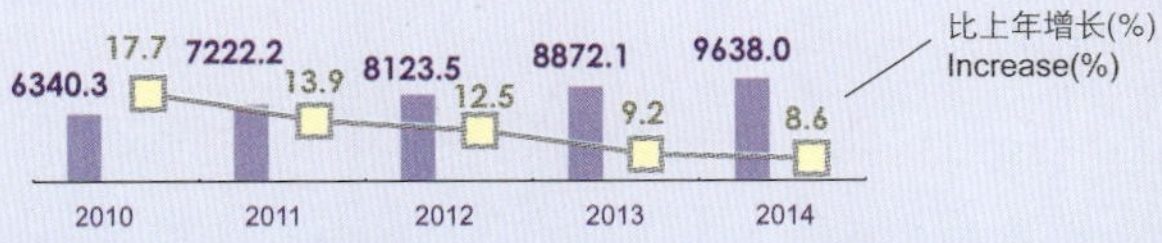

产业结构调整取得进展 新兴产业快速增长

Progress Has Been Made in Industrial Restructuring Emergin Industry Shows Rapid Growth

文化创意产业、信息产业等新兴产业占比提高
New Emerging Industries like Cultural Creative Industry and Information Industry Take Increasing Proportion

产业 Industry	占全市地区生产总值比重(%) Proportion to GDP (%) 2014	占全市地区生产总值比重(%) Proportion to GDP (%) 2013	新兴产业增加值(亿元) Added Value of New Emerging Industries (yuan 100 million) 2014	新兴产业增加值(亿元) Added Value of New Emerging Industries (yuan 100 million) 2013
文化创意产业 Cultural and Creative Industry	13.2	13.0	2826.3	2578.1
信息产业 Information Industry	14.9	14.4	3172.2	2855.2
高技术产业 High-tech Industry	22.2	21.7	4738.5	4291.5
现代服务业 Modern Service Industry	55.4	54.3	11820.0	10751.5
生产性服务业 Producer Services	52.5	51.1	11196.1	10127.7
信息服务业 Inforamtion Service	11.4	11.1	2434.1	2192.6

❶ 第三产业增加值(亿元)
Added Value of Tertiary Industry (100 million yuan)

❷ 信息传输、计算机服务和软件业增加值占全市地区生产总值比重(%)
Added Value of Information Transmission, Computer Service and Software Sectors as % of Beijing's GDP (%)
金融业增加值占全市地区生产总值比重(%)
Added Value of Finance Sector as % of Beijing's GDP (%)
房地产业增加值占全市地区生产总值比重(%)
Added Value of Real Estate Sector as % of Beijing's GDP (%)

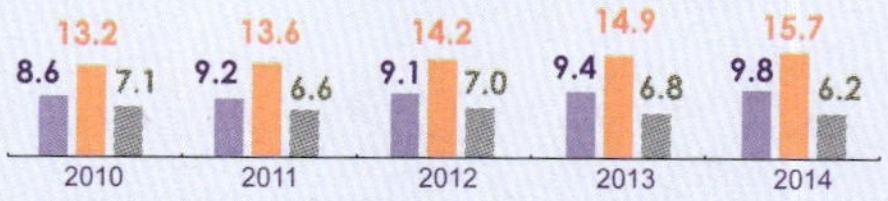

中关村示范区创新驱动发展
Innovation-driven Development in Zhongguancun Science Park

效益较快增长
Relatively Rapid Efficiency Growth

中关村示范区利润总额(亿元)
Total profits in Zhongguancun Science Park (100 million yuan)

创新成果丰富
Rich Innovative Achievements

中关村示范区专利申请数(件)
Patent Applications (unit)

中关村示范区专利授权数(件)
Patent Granted (unit)

中关村示范区获奖成果数(个)
Number of Prize-winning Achievements (unit)

③ 中关村国家自主创新示范区总收入(亿元)
Total Revenues of Zhongguancun Science Park (100 million yuan)

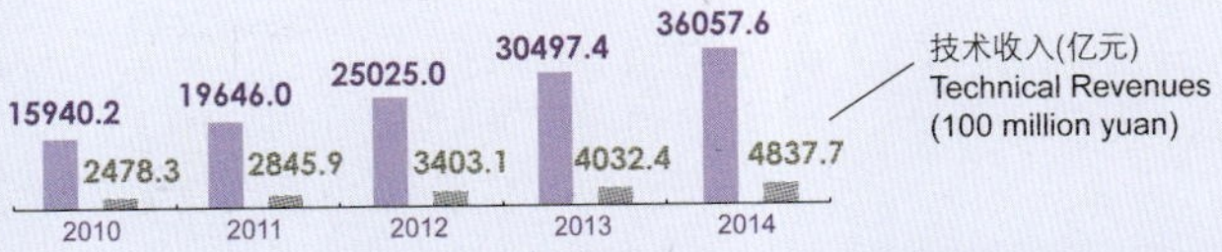

④ 中关村国家自主创新示范区实缴税费总额(亿元)
Total Taxes Paid of Zhongguancun Science Park (100 million yuan)

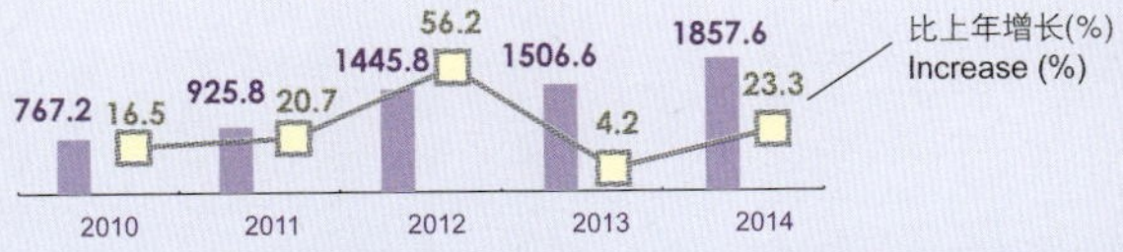

发展质量稳步提升 经济增长更加绿色、低碳

Stable Improvement in Development Quality More Green and Low-carbon Economic Growth

社会劳动生产率稳步提升
Stable Increase of Social Labor Productivity

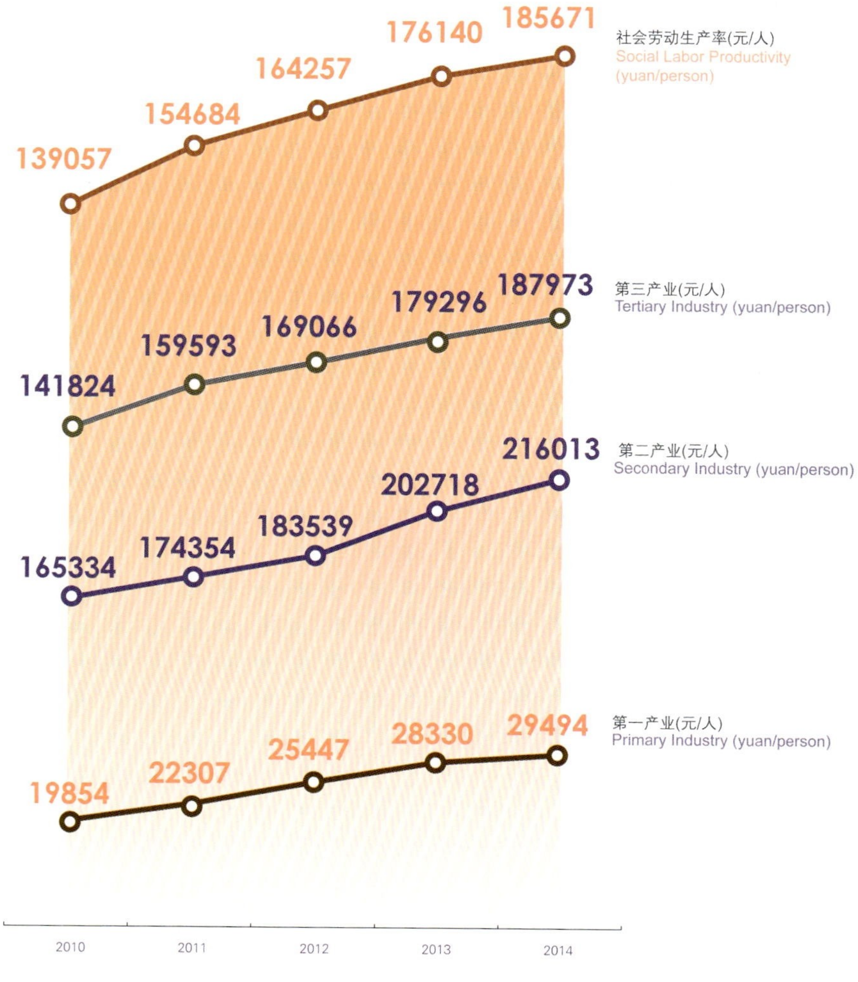

❶ 地方公共财政预算收入(亿元)
Revenue of Local Public Financial Budget (100 million yuan)

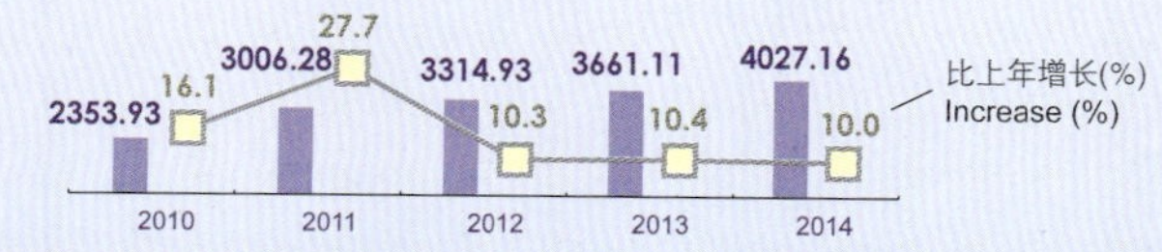

❷ 地方公共财政预算支出(亿元)
Expenditure of Local Public Financial Budget (100 million yuan)

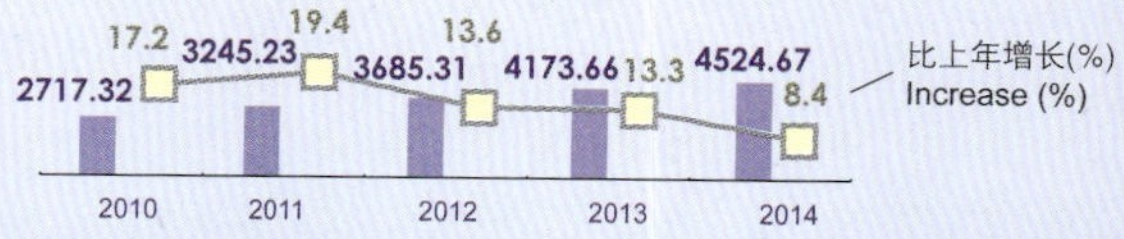

能源消费结构逐步改善
Gradual Improvement in Energy Consumption Structure

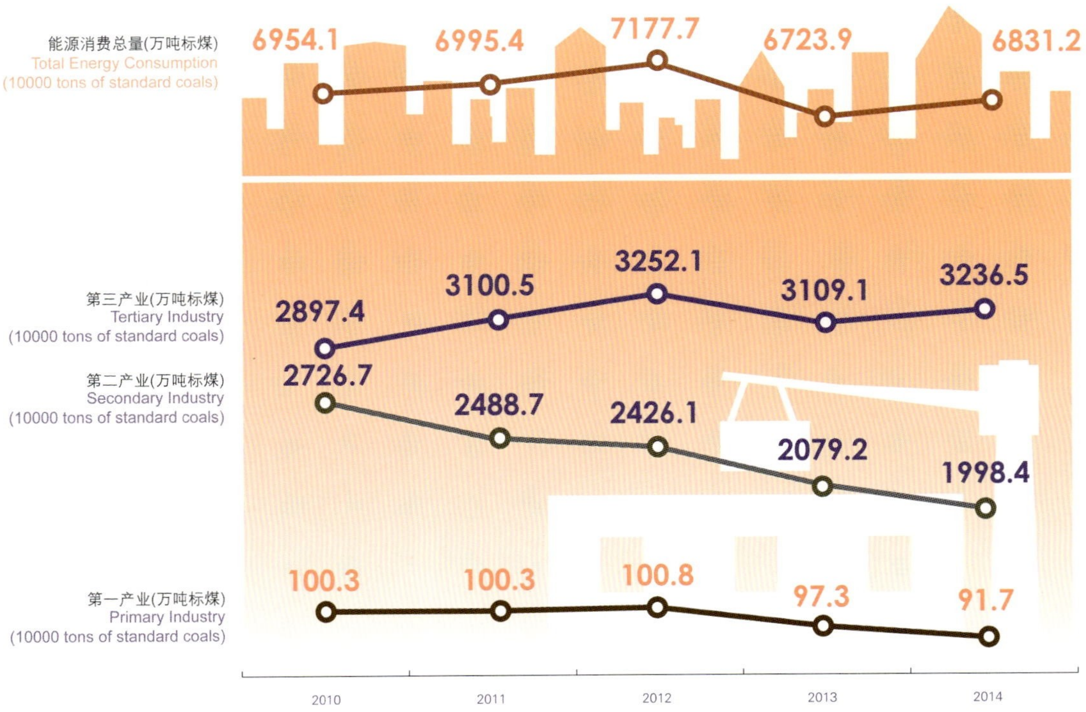

煤炭、天然气、石油占能源消费比重（%）
Proportion of Coal, Natural Gas and Petroleum Consumption to Total Energy Consumption (%)

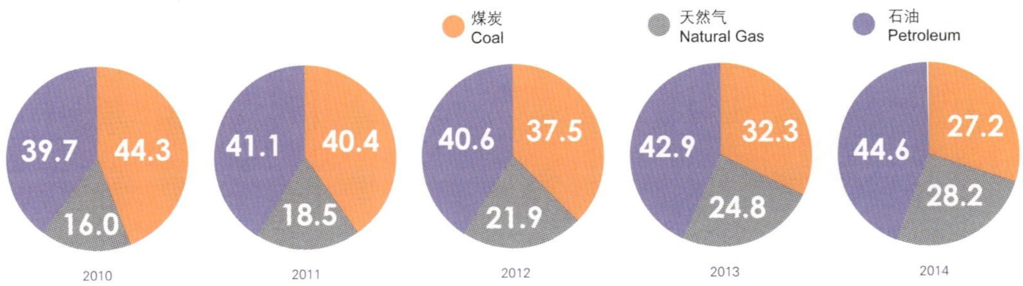

3 万元地区生产总值水耗(立方米)
Water Consumption in Regions with RMB 10,000 GDP (cubic meter)

4 万元地区生产总值能耗(吨标煤)
Energy Consumption in Regions with RMB 10,000 GDP (ton of standard coals)

对外交往活跃 境外投资与出境旅游热度高涨

Active Foreign Exchanges Boom of Overseas Investment and Outbound Tourism

境外中方实际投资快速增长

Rapid Increase of Actual Chinese Investment in Overseas Regions

中方实际投资额(万美元)
Actual Chinese Investment (USD 10000)

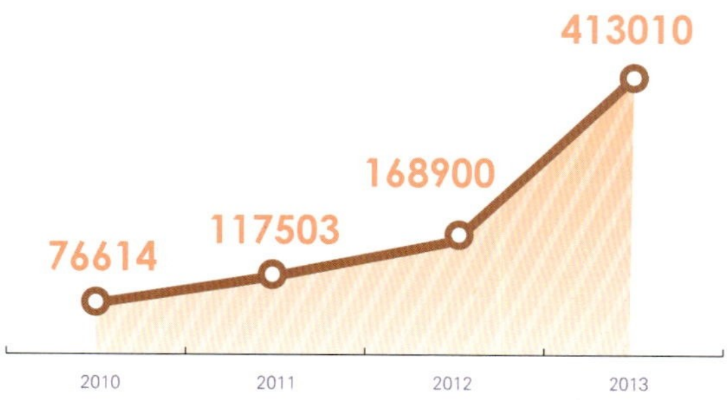

对外承包工程和劳务合作合同额(万美元)
Value of Foreign Contracted Projects and Contracts of Labor Service Cooperation (USD 10000)

对外承包工程和劳务合作在外人数(人)
Number of People Abroad Participating in Foreign Contracted Projects and Labor Service Cooperation (person)

❶ 实际利用外商投资(亿美元)
Actual Utilized Foreign Investment (USD 100 million)

❷ 对外承包工程完成营业额(亿美元)
Accomplished Turnover of Foreign Contracted Projects (USD 100 million)

出境游人数连续5年保持20%以上增速
Growth of Outbound Tourists Has Stayed at 20% and above for 5 Successive Years

旅行社组织出境旅游人数(万人次)
Outbound Tourists Organized by Travel Agencies (10000 person-time)

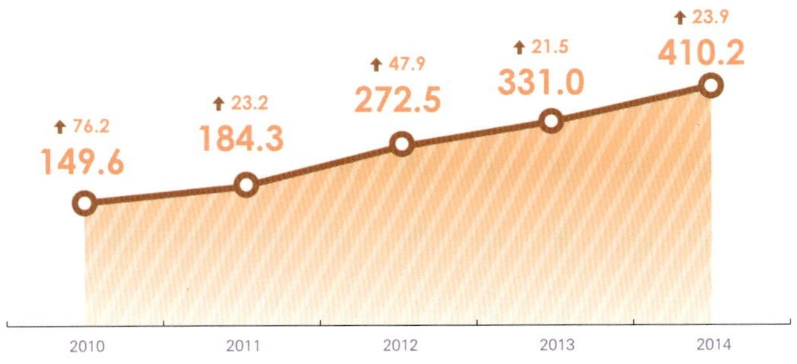

2014年旅行社组织出境游前5位国家及地区情况(万人次)
Top 5 Countries and Regions of Outbound Tourism Organized by Travel Agencies in 2014 (10,000 person-time)

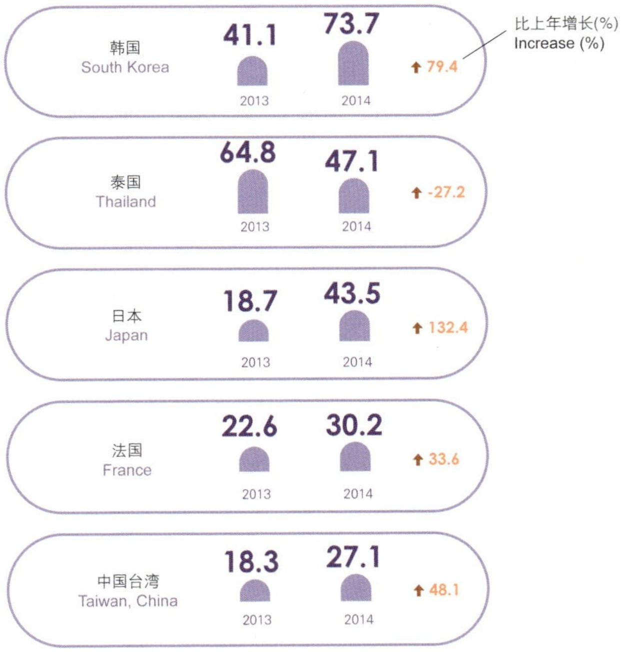

3 北京地区海关进口值(亿美元)
Customs Import in Beijing (USD 100 million)

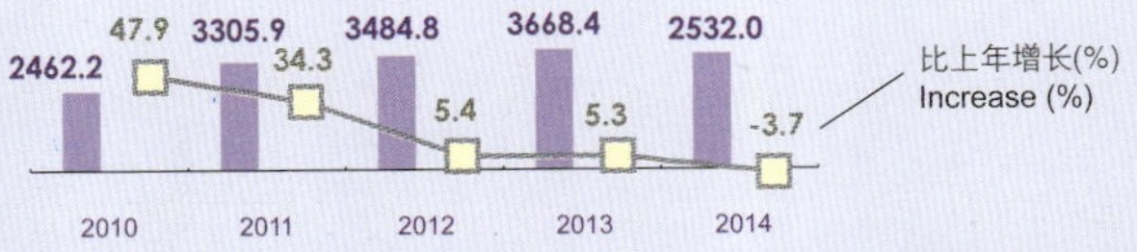

4 北京地区海关出口值(亿美元)
Customs Export in Beijing (USD 100 million)

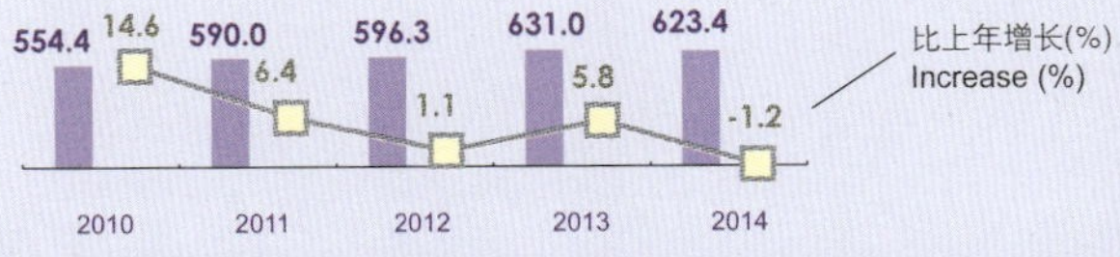

居民生活不断改善 惠民生支出持续增长

Gradual Improvement in People's Life Continuous Expenditure for the Benefit of People's Livelihood

居民收入与经济增长趋于同步
Residents' Income Becomes More Synchronized with Economic Growth

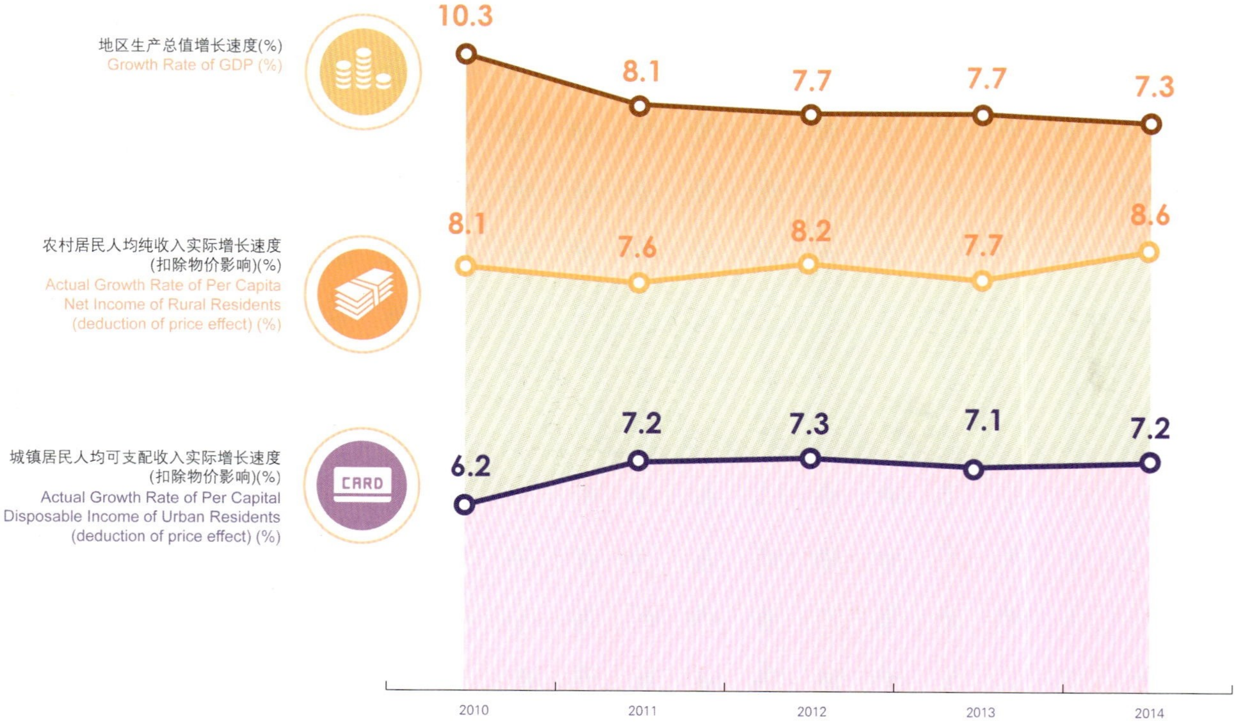

城乡居民收入比持续缩小
Gap Between Income in Urban and Rural Area Continues to Reduce

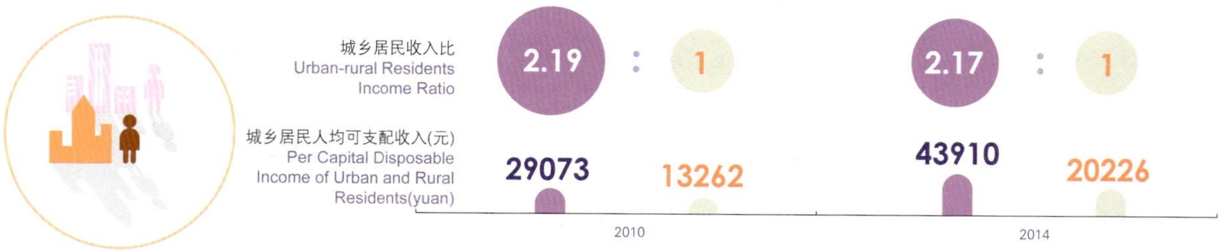

❶ 城镇居民人均可支配收入(元)
Per Capital Disposable Income of Urban Residents (yuan)

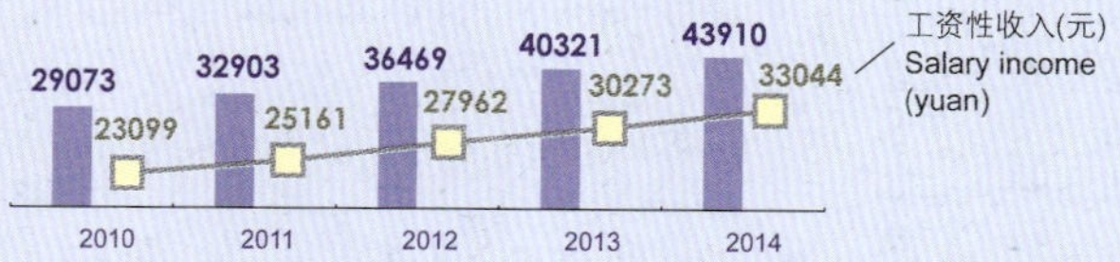

❷ 农村居民人均纯收入(元)
Per Capita Net Income of Rural Residents (yuan)

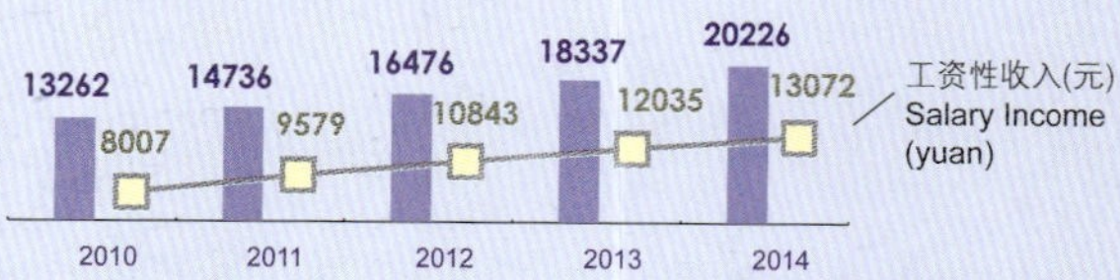

城乡居民消费结构不断改善
Continuous Improvement in Consumption Structure df Urban and Rural Residents

城镇居民消费支出结构
Consumption Expenditure Structure of Urban Residents

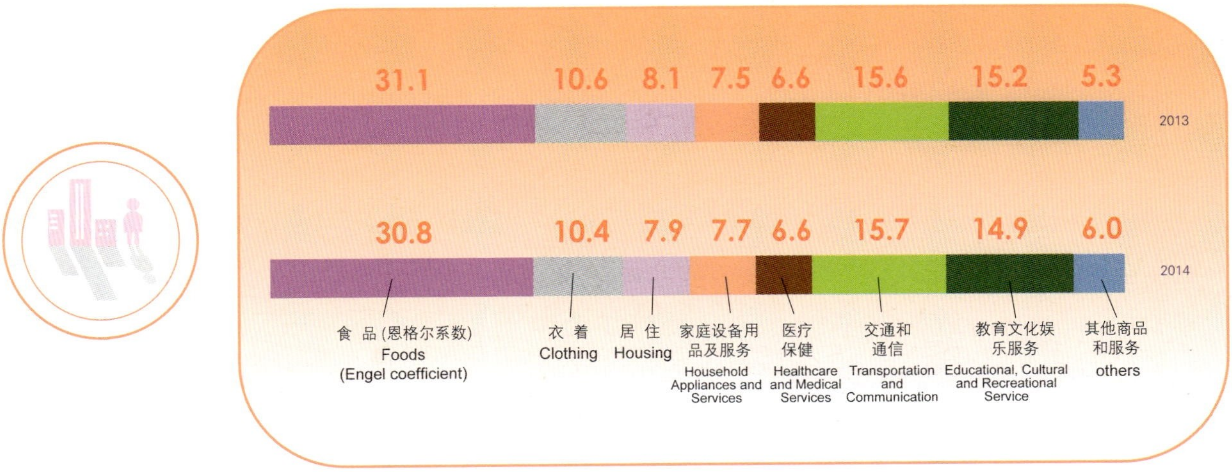

农村居民消费支出结构
Per Capital Consumption Expenditure Structure df Rural Residents

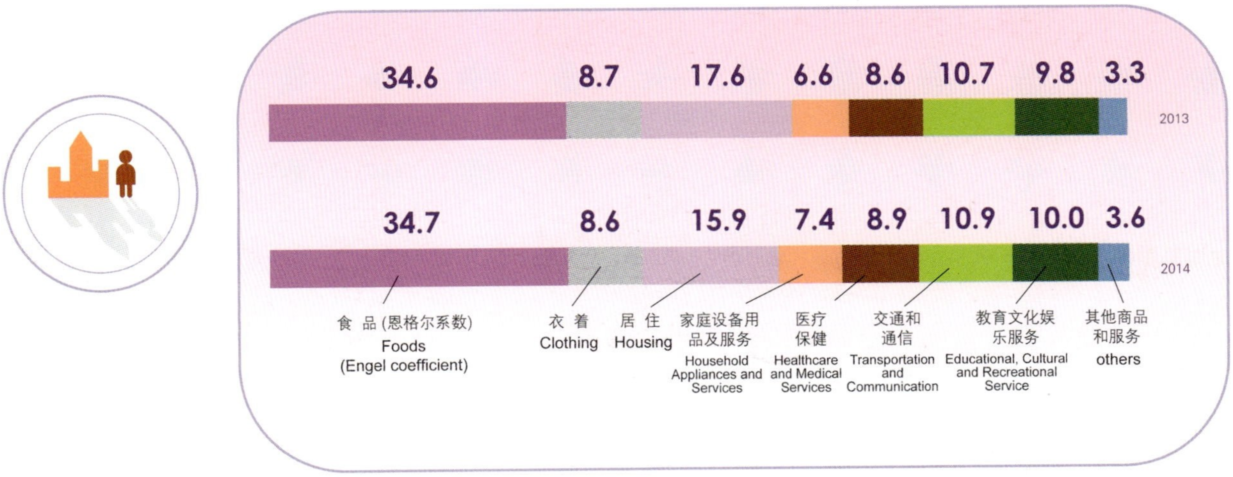

❸ 城镇居民人均消费性支出(元)
Per Capita Consumption Expenditure of Urban Residents (yuan)

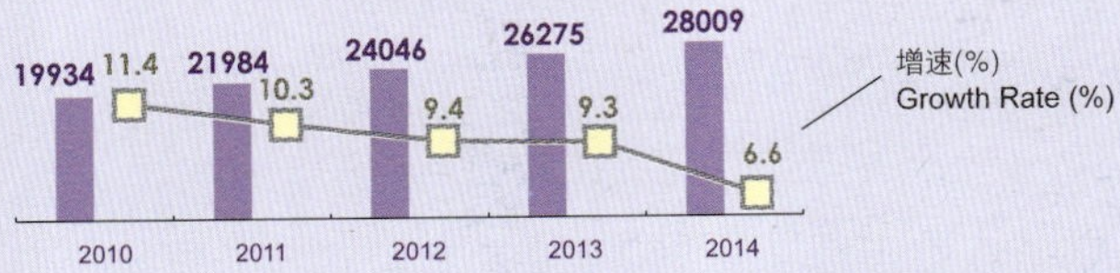

❹ 农村居民人均生活消费支出(元)
Per Capita Living Expenditure of Rural Residents (yuan)

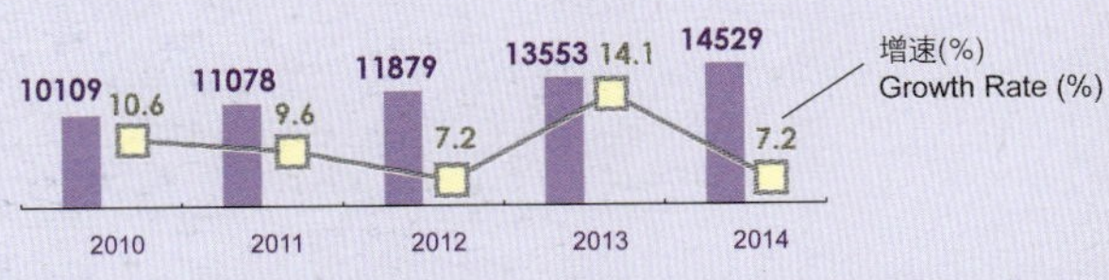

居民生活不断改善 惠民生支出持续增长

Gradual Improvement in People's Life Continuous Expenditure for the Benefit of People's Livelihood

财政支出继续向重点民生领域倾斜

Financial Expenditure Continues to Focus on Key Areas Related to People's Livelihood

地方公共财政预算支出(万元)
Expenditure of Local Public Financial Budget (10000 yuan)

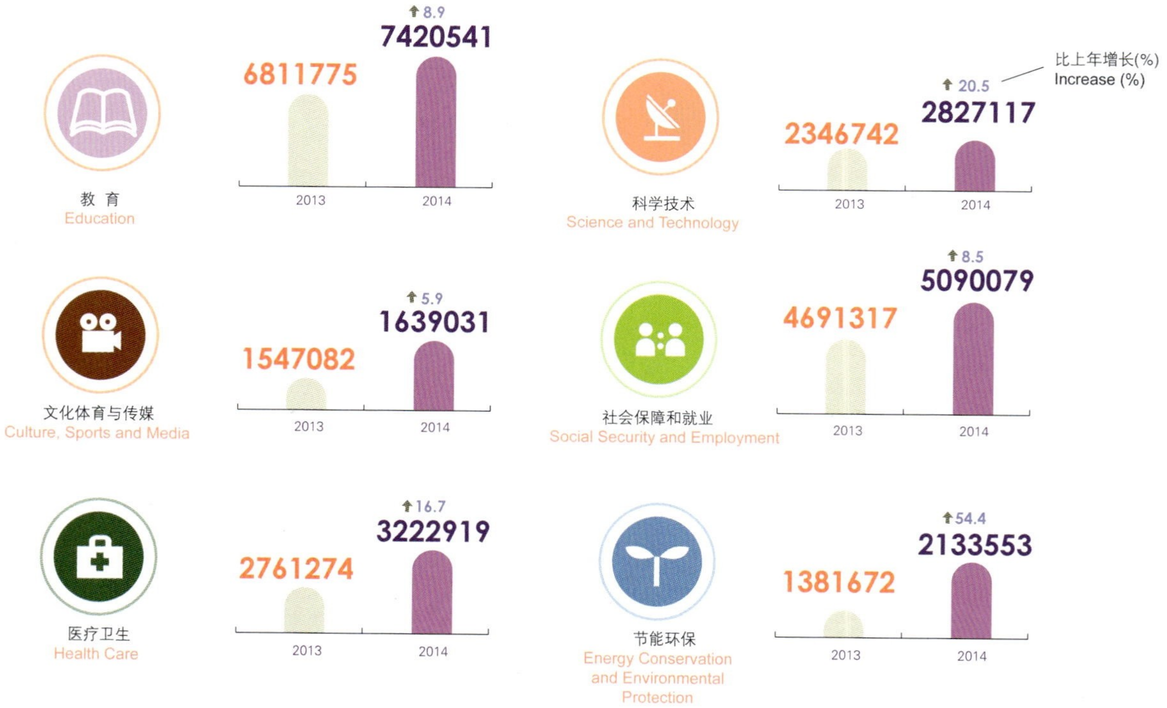

❶ 城镇居民人均可支配收入（高、低收入户）增速(名义增长)(%)
Growth Rate (nominal growth rate) of Per Capita Disposable Income of Urban Residents (residents with high and low income) (%)

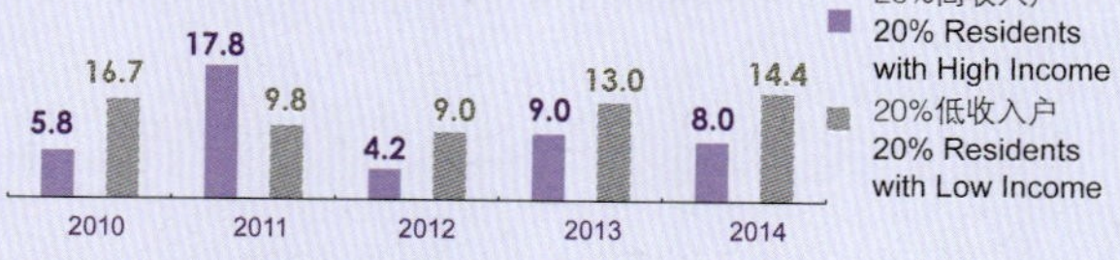

❷ 农村居民人均可支配收入（高、低收入户）增速(名义增长)(%)
Growth Rate (nominal growth rate) of Per Capita Disposable Income of Rural Residents (residents with high and low income) (%)

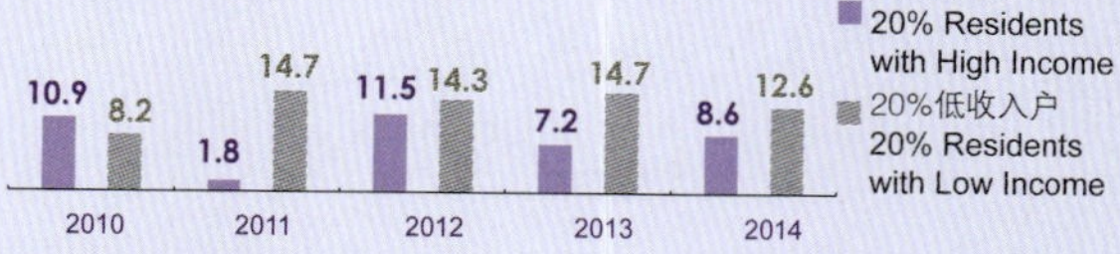

社会保障标准不断提高
Gradual Raise of Social Security Standard

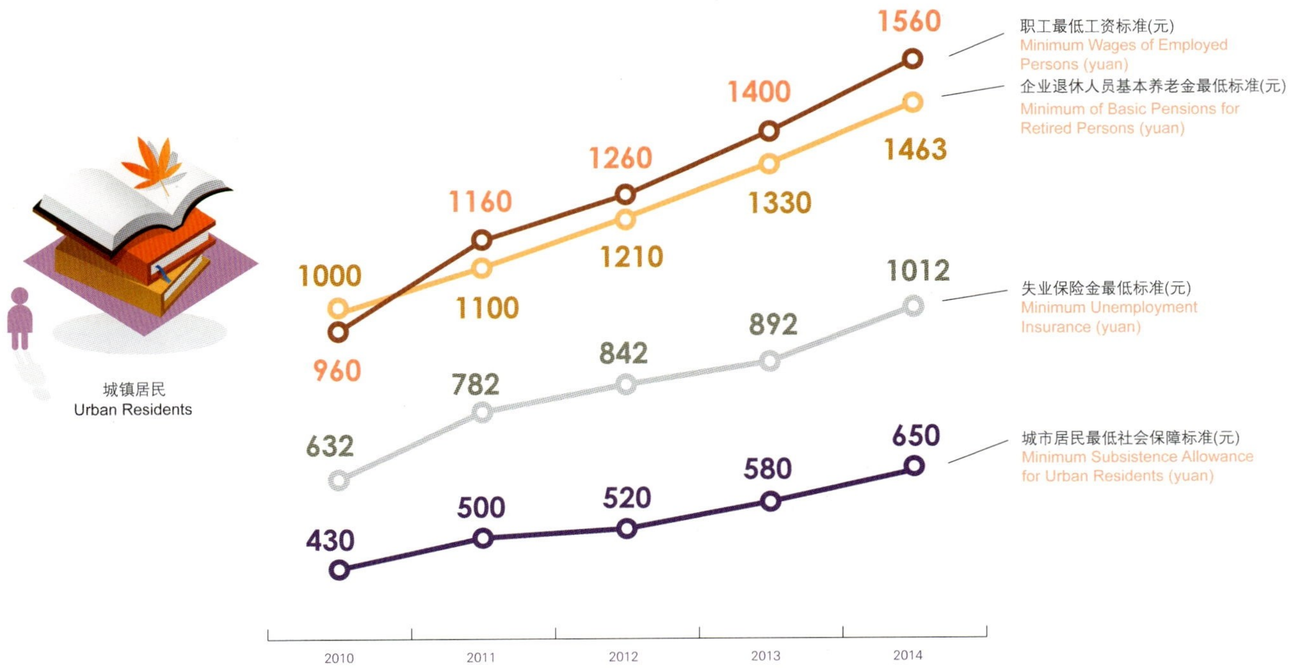

❸ 参加社会保险人数(万人)
Employed Persons Participating in Social Insurance (10000 persons)

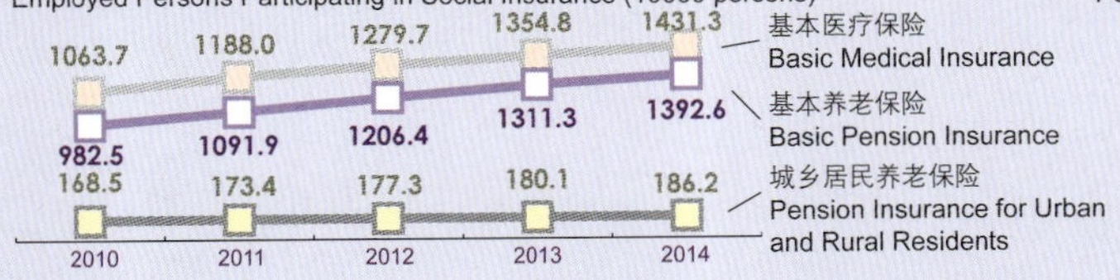

❹ 最低生活保障人数(万人)
Persons Receiving Minimum Substance Allowance (10000 persons)

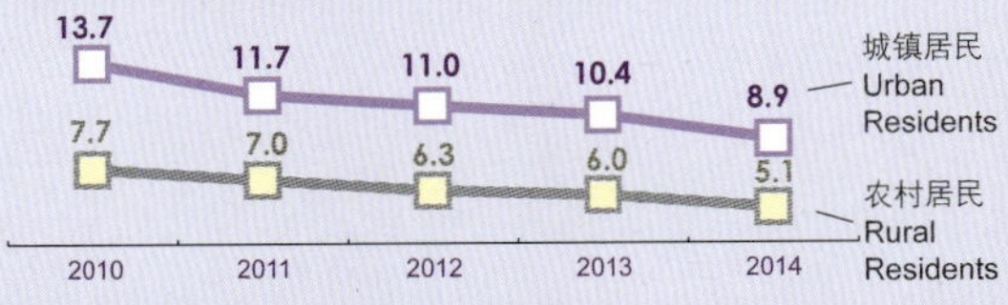

环境质量继续改善 主要污染物排放量明显减少

Continuous Environmental Improvement Emmission of Main Pollutants Shows Significant Decline

工业废水、废气、废物排放量全面下降
Emmission of Industrial Waste Water, Waste Gas and Waste Falls Comprehensively

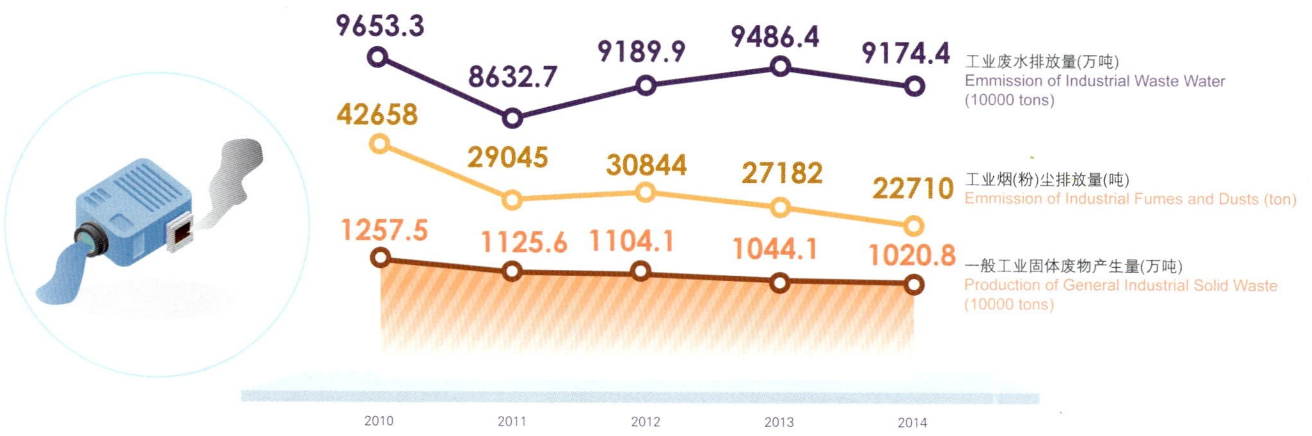

生活垃圾、生活污水处理能力不断增强
Ability to Dispose Household Garbage and Domestic Sewage Keeps Enhancing

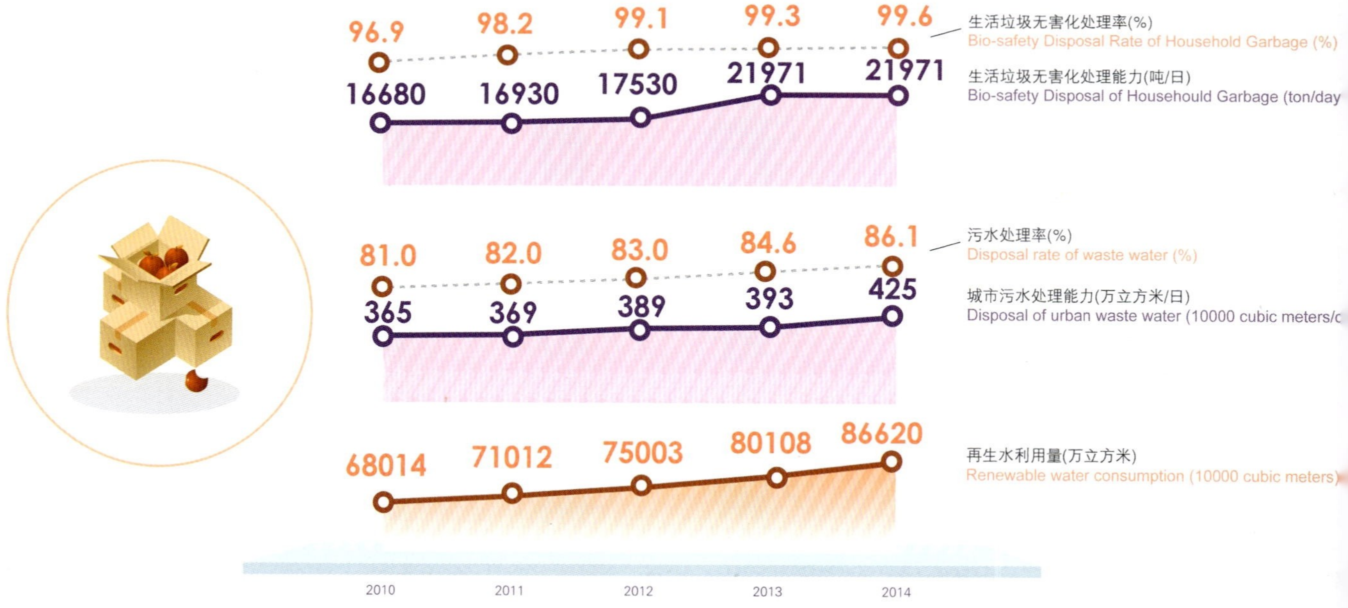

大气污染物浓度逐步降低
Concentration of Air Pollutants Gradually Decreases

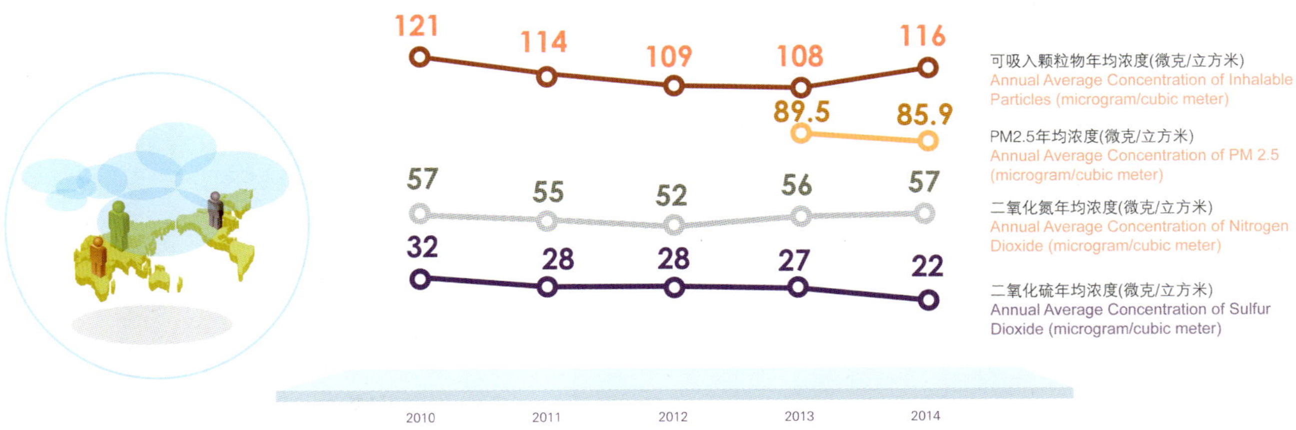

园林绿化成果持续巩固
Continuous Achievements in Landscaping

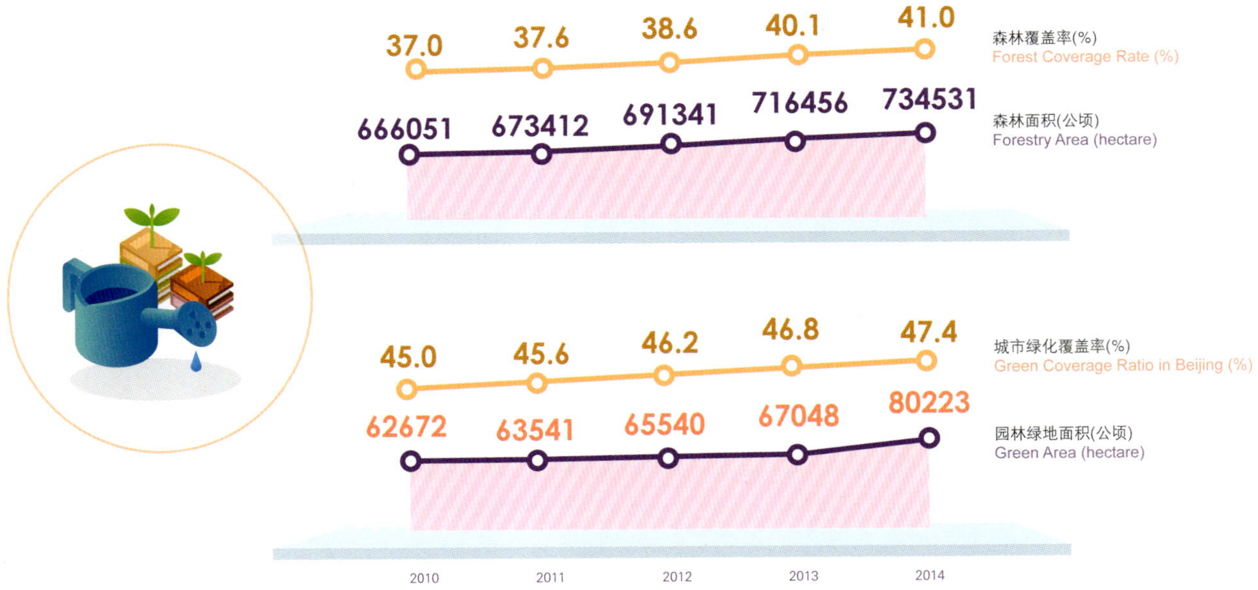

❸ 化学需氧量（COD）排放量(万吨)
COD Emmission (10000 tons)

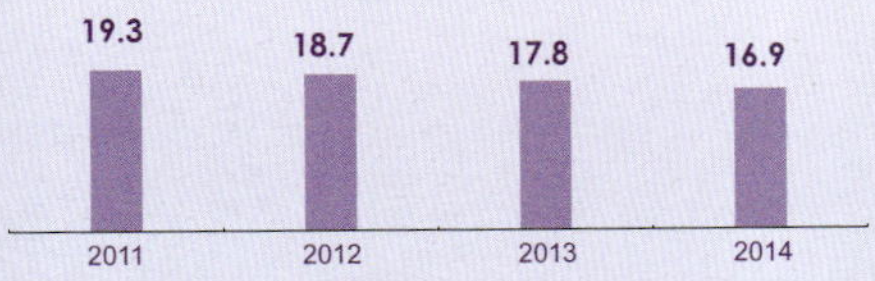

❹ 二氧化硫(SO_2)排放量(万吨)
SO_2 Emmission (10000 tons)

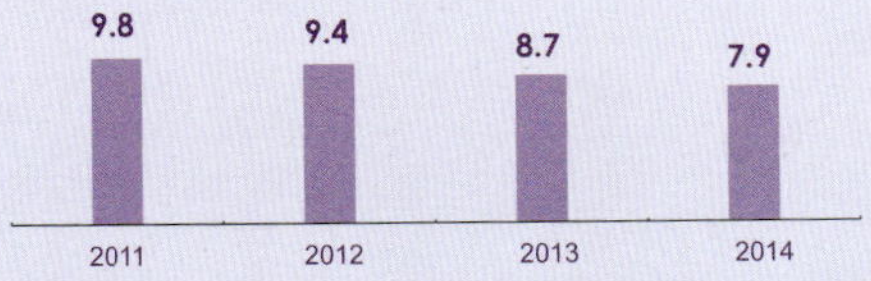

人口增长逐步放缓 产业升级引导就业结构改善

Slowdown in Population Increase Industrial Upgrading Leads to More Perfect Employment Structure

人口增量呈平稳下降趋势
Population Growth Shows Stable Decline

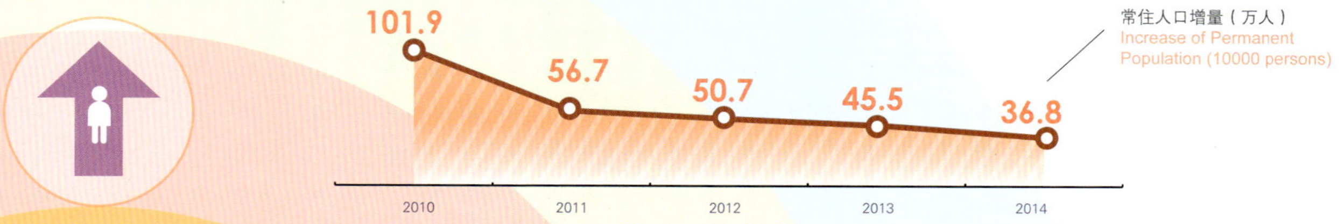

人口向城市发展新区集聚趋势进一步增强
Larger Population Moves to New Area of Urban Development

北京市各功能区人口比重分布 (%)
Ratio of Population in Each Functional Area of Beijing (%)

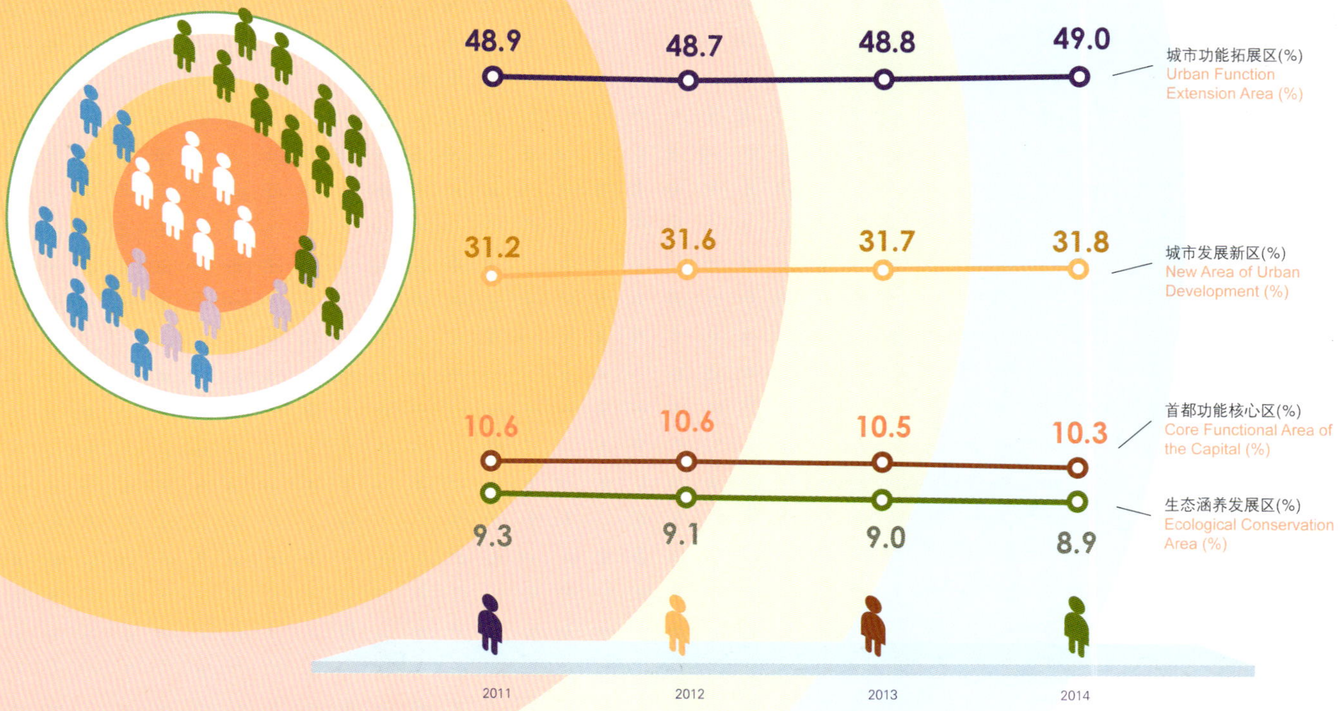

❶ 常住外来人口(万人)
Permanent Migrant Population (10000 persons)

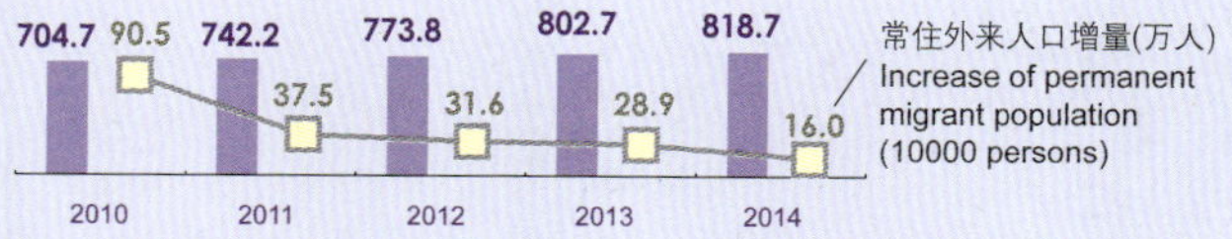

❷ 60岁及以上人口占常住人口比重(%)
Proportion of Population over 60 Years Old to Permanent Population (%)

65岁及以上人口占常住人口比重(%)
Proportion of Population over 65 Years Old to Permanent Population (%)

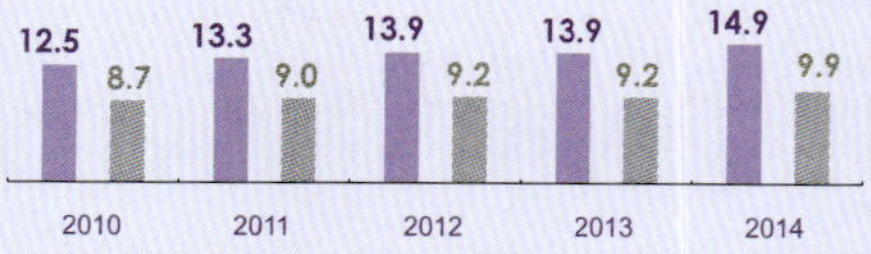

从业人员规模稳定增长
Employed Persons Increase Steadily

从业人员年末人数(万人)
Year-End Employed Persons (10000 persons)

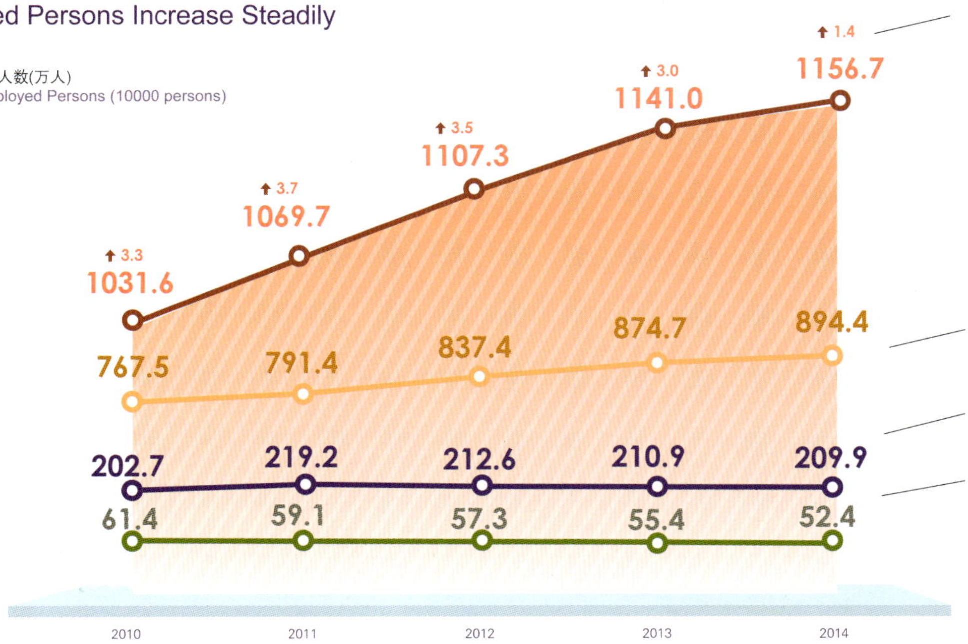

从业人员构成(%) (合计=100)
Annual Composition of Employed Persons (total = 100)

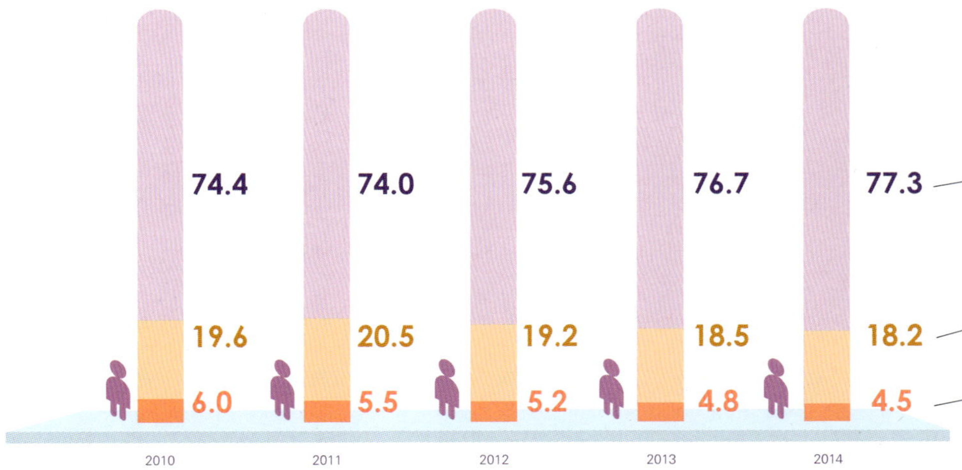

③ 城镇单位在岗职工人数(万人)
Number of Urban In-service Employees (10000 persons)

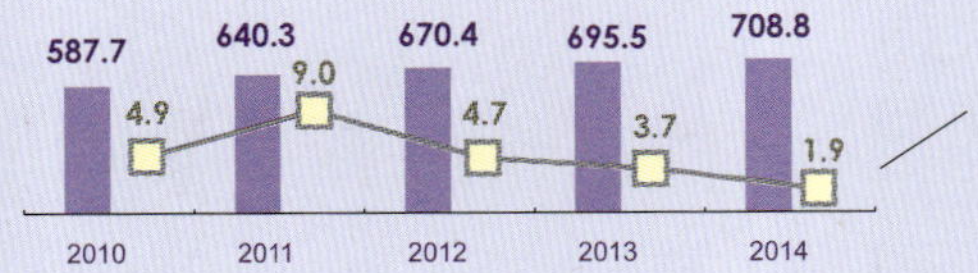

④ 城镇单位在岗职工平均工资(元)
Average Salary of Urban In-Service Employees (yuan)

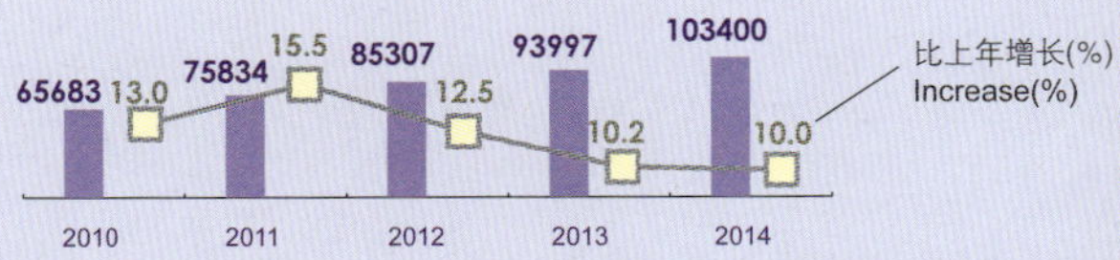

人口增长逐步放缓 产业升级引导就业结构改善

Slowdown in Population Increase Industrial Upgrading Leads to More Perfect Employment Structure

就业人口向更符合首都功能定位的行业聚集

Employed Population Moves to Industries Closer to Capital Functions

全市法人单位从业人员(万人)
Persons Employed by Legal Entities in Beijing (10000 persons)

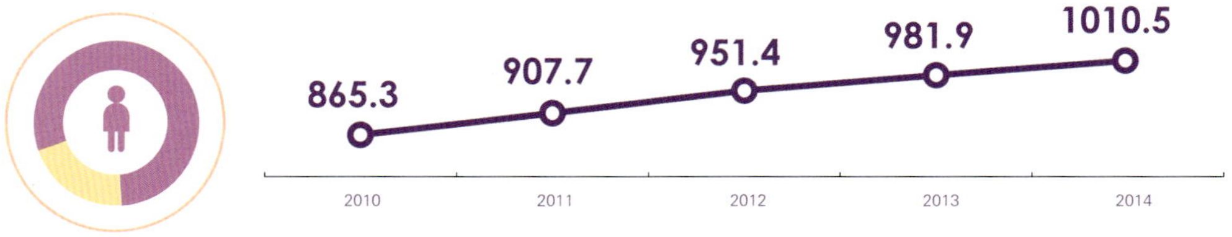

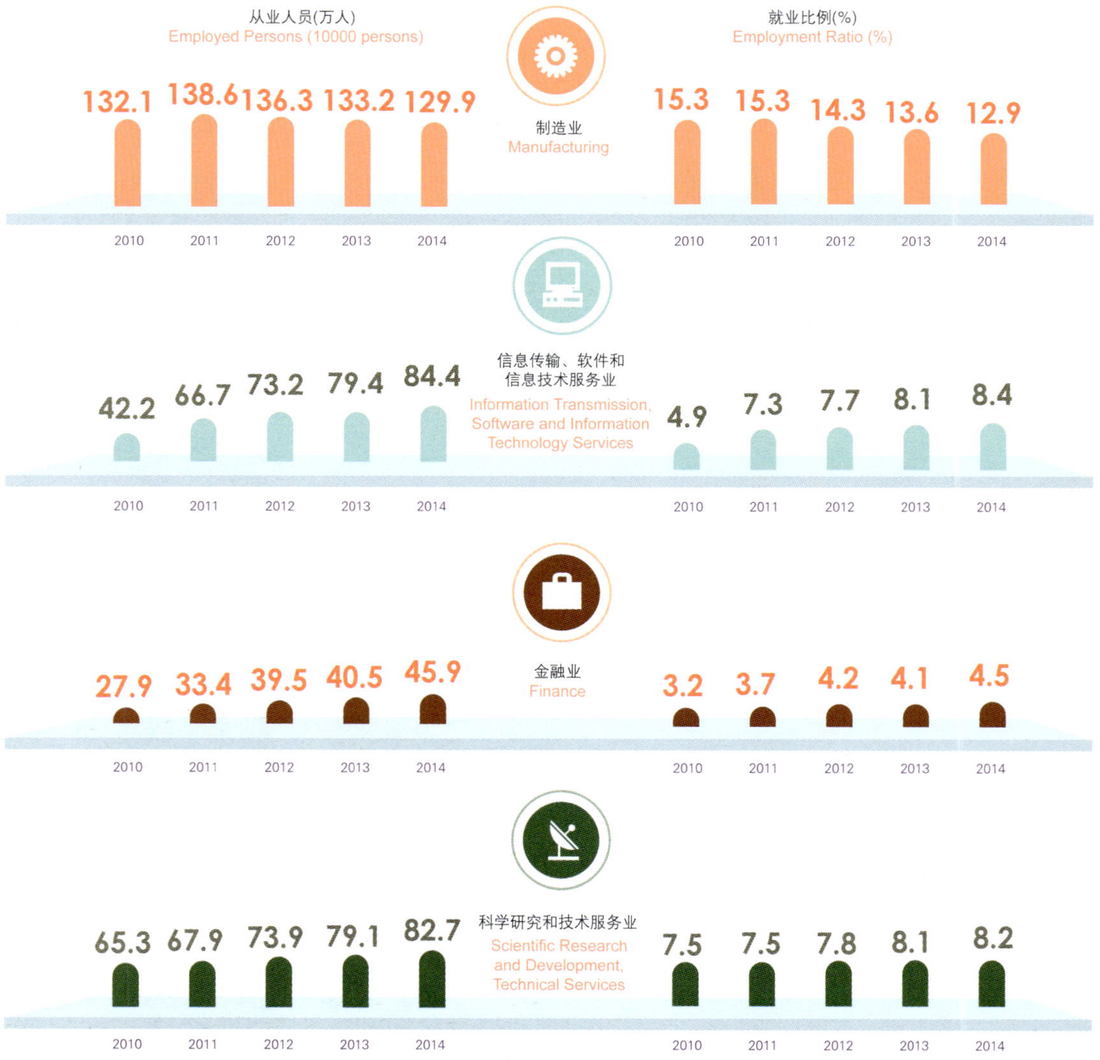

《北京统计年鉴—2015》
编辑委员会及编辑工作人员

使用指南

《北京统计年鉴》是一部按年连续出版的大型统计资料。本年鉴通过大量的统计数据，真实地记录了北京市一年来经济社会发展变化情况，是国内外各界人士了解北京、认识北京的重要资料工具书。

一、关于框架结构

（一）总体结构

《北京统计年鉴》整体框架基本保持稳定，彩页内容以图文并茂的形式反映一年来本地区经济社会发展主要特点和亮点；统计表是年鉴的主体内容，主要包括综合，国民经济核算，人口与就业，能源、资源和环境，全社会固定资产投资和房地产开发，财政与税收，价格指数，人民生活，城市公用事业，农业及农村经济，工业，建筑业，交通运输邮电，批发和零售业、住宿和餐饮业，对外经济贸易，旅游业，金融和保险，教育、文化，科技，卫生、体育，社会福利、社区、政法及其他，第三产业，开发区等章节，从多行业、多领域客观反映全市经济和社会发展情况。

（二）章节结构

章节设置：主要是参照统计制度，排列顺序具有一定的内在逻辑，大体为先综合指标、后分行业或分领域；先经济领域、后社会领域。

章节内结构：每一章节由简要说明、统计表和主要统计指标解释三部分组成。简要说明在每一章节首页，主要介绍该章节的主要内容、资料来源、统计范围、指标口径和历史数据调整方法；主要统计指标解释在每章节页尾，主要对本章节内所涉及的主要指标、计算方法等做简要解释；统计表是各章节的核心内容。

统计表排列：每一章节注重从反映该领域主要情况出发，编排统计表内容。统计表的排列顺序一般先是主要指标历史数据表，后为当年数据表。

二、关于使用要领

（一）年份

按照惯例，书名中标注的年份为出版年份，年鉴中统计表内所表示的最新数据则为上一年数据。例如，书名为《北京统计年鉴 2015》表示此本年鉴为 2015 年出版，年鉴中最新数据年份截至 2014 年。

统计表名中的“年份”大致会有三种标识方法，分别代表三种含义。一是统计表名为“****** (1978-2014年)”字样（其中，“******”代表该统计表反映的内容，下同），表示表内所列数据是从 1978 年到 2014 年；二是统计表名中未显示年份，表示表内所列数据为当年和上年两年数据；三是统计表名为“****** (2014 年)”，表示表内所列数据为 2014 年的数据。

（二）符号

统计表中常见符号如下：

\# ：代表表中的总量指标与分组指标呈依次缩进的格式。其中，有“#”号的分组指标表示其为总量指标的一部分；无“#”号的分组指标则反映全部分组指标数据之和为总指标数据。

‖ ：宾栏中的“‖”为分组符号，代表某个指标存在几种分组数据。

… ：表示该数据不足该表最小计量单位数。

空格：表示该项指标数据不详或没有数据。

*** ：表示为使个体数据得以保密，该数据不予公布。

（三）文字说明

文字说明包括使用指南、目录、简要说明、指标解释和表下注解。使用指南在目录之前，是对年鉴整体框架进行介绍，对主要调整内容进行说明；简要说明在每一章节首页，主要介绍该章节的主要内容、资料来源、统计范围、指标口径和历史数据调整方法等；统计表下的注释则是对部分统计指标口径、方法、范围等内容的说明。

（四）数据

一般情况下，每一章节的前几张表均为该专业或该领域核心指标的历史数据。历史数据如果按年份连续反映在一张表内的，一般是可以连续使用，但也需要留意表下的注释，以便对指标内涵有更详尽的了解；如果历史数据分成若干张表显示，则表示相关指标统计有过重大调整，需要分段反映。

此外，最新出版的年鉴上发布的部分历史数据会与以往年鉴上的数据有调整，存在差异，因此，在查询和使用历史数据时应以最新出版的年鉴为准。

（五）电子光盘

《北京统计年鉴》配有电子光盘，包括中文版和英文版两种语言的版本，辅助用户对数据进行加工处理。

（六）本年鉴中部分数据合计数或相对数由于计量单位取舍不同而产生的计算误差，均未作机械调整。

三、关于 2015 年版《北京统计年鉴》说明

与 2014 年版《北京统计年鉴》相比较，本年鉴在内容上主要做了如下修订：

1. 根据全国第三次经济普查结果及时更新相关数据。2013 年地区生产总值、社会消费品零售总额、能源消费总量、R&D 内部支出经费等数据已更新为全国第三次经济普查数据，其中 2009-2012 年社会消费品零售总额数据根据普查结果进行了修订。

2. 恢复由于第三次经济普查原因未在 2014 年年鉴中公布的数据。包括 2013 年规模以上中小微型企业主要指标、非公经济主要指标、收入法地区生产总值、能源平衡表、分行业能源消费总量和主要能源品种消费量等数据。

3. 根据国家行业划分新标准和最新三次产业划分规定调整有关指标内容。国民经济核算、新兴产业统计和相关指标按照新的行业标准进行了调整，并对地区生产总值三次产业 1978-2012 年的历史数据进行了修订。

4. 调整部分统计表内容。一是根据国家统计制度方法的变化，撤销了《企业景气指数》、《企业家信心指数》等统计表，并将《北京消费者信心指数》表调整到第十四章节中；二是根据部门统计制度变化撤销了《计划生育状况》表，并对《收养性单位情况》、《离婚、青少年刑事案犯情况》、《残疾人事业》等统计表中有关指标进行了调整。三是增加补充了部分指标，例如在《邮电业务主要指标》统计表中将“特快专递”指标更改为“快递业务总量”，数据口径由 EMS 快递业务量调整为全市快递业务总量；在《证券市场交易额情况》表中增加了“基金交易”指标；在《规模以上工业增加值》表中撤销“黑色金属制炼和延压加工业”指标，增加“铁路、船舶、航空航天和其他运输设备制造业”指标等。

5. 继续加强规范统一。针对年鉴中所有涉及统计分组的内容进行了统一规范，例如有关三次产业划分和行业划分存在交叉分组形式的统计表统一调整为“按产业分组”、“按国民经济行业分组”、“按重点行业分组”；有关中央、地方分组统一调整为“按隶属关系分组”；有关内资、外资企业分组统一调整为“按登记注册类型分组”等。此外，继续对简要说明、指标解释、表下注释以及英文翻译的一致性和准确性进行规范。

USER GUIDE

Beijing Statistical Yearbook is a large statistical book published continuously on a chronological basis. With a great deal of statistical data, this Yearbook gives a true reflection of the social and economic development and changes in Beijing over the past year. It serves as an important reference book for domestic and foreign personnel in all circles to understand and know Beijing.

I. Framework Structure

(I) Overall Structure

The overall structure of *Beijing Statistical Yearbook* remains basically stable. In color pages, main features and highlights about economic and social development of Beijing in this year have been presented with both illustration and pictures; statistical tables are the main part of this Yearbook, mainly including: General Survey; National Accounts; Population and Employment; Energy, Resources and Environmental Protection; Total Investment in Fixed Assets and Real Estate Development; Government Finance and Tax Revenues; Price Index; People's Livelihood; Public Utilities; Agriculture and Rural Economy; Industry; Construction; Transport, Post and Telecommunication Service; Wholesale and Retail Trade, Accomodation and Restaurants; Foreign Trade; Tourism; Finance and Insurance; Education and Culture; Science and Technology; Health Care and Sports; Social Welfare, Community, Plicies & Laws and Others; Tertiary Industry; and Development Zones, etc., reflecting the economic and social development situation across the city through multiple industries and fields.

(II) Structure of Chapters

Setting of chapters: The chapters are set in keeping with the statistical system, with certain inherent logic. Generally speaking, comprehensive indicators come first, followed by indicators in specific sectors and fileds. economic indicators cone before social indicators.

Internal structure of chapters: Each chapter is composed of the Brief Introduction, Statistical Tables and Explanatory Notes to Main Statistical Indicators. Brief Introduction appears on the first page of each chapter, mainly introducing the main content, source of data, statistical scope, indicator standards, method of adjustment to historical data in each chapter; Explanatory Notes to Main Statistical Indicators come on the last page of each chapter, mainly giving a brief explanation to the main indicators and calculation method, etc. involved in the chapter; Statistical Tables are the core content of each chapter.

Arrangement of statistical tables: In each chapter, statistical tables are arranged for the purpose of reflecting the main conditions in the field. Generally speaking, historical statistical tables come before current year statistical tables.

II. How to Use

(I) Years

Conventionally, the year indicated in the book is the year of publication. The latest data indicated in the statistical tables in this Yearbook are data in the previous years. For example, this book is titled *2015 Bejing Statistical Yearbook*, which means it will be published in 2015 while the lastest data in the book is from the end of 2014.

"Years" in the statistical tables are marked in three ways, each indicating a different meaning. Firstly, the statistical table is named "****** (1978-2014)" (of which, "******" represents the content reflected in the statistical table, the same below), indicating that the data listed in the table are those from 1978 to 2014; Secondly, the statistical table contains no years, indicating that the data listed in the table are those of the current year and the last two year; Thirdly, the statistical table is named "****** (2014)", indicating that the data listed in the table are those of 2014.

(II) Symbols

Symbols in statistical tables include:

#: means that the aggretate indicator and grouped indicators are indented. Grouped indicators marked with # are part of the aggregate indicator, while grouped indicators not marked with # indicate that the aggregate indicator is the sum of all group indicators.

||: means that there are multiple ways of grouping the indicators.

…: means that the figure is less than the minimum measurement unit of the table.

Blank: mean that the figure is unknown or unavailable.

***: means that the figure is not disclosed for secrecy reasons.

(III) Explanations

Explanations include User Guide, Table of Contents, Brief Introduction, Explanatory Notes to Main Statistical Indicators and notes under the tables. User Guide appears before the Table of Contents, giving an introduction to the overall framework of this Yearbook, and explaining the main adjustments; Brief Introduction appears on the first page of each chapter, giving an introduction to the chapter's main content, source of data, statistical scope, standards of indicators, adjustment method of historical data, etc; Notes under the statistical tables make an explanation on standard of some indicators, method and scope, etc.

(IV) Data

In general cases, the first tables in each chapter contain historical data of core indicators in the area or field. Generally speaking, historical data that are shown in one table continuously by year can be used continuously. But it is also necessary to refer to the notes under the table in order to have a full understanding of the connation of indicators; historical data that are shown in several tables indicate that there were major adjustments to relevant indicators, and they need to be reflected by sections.

In addition, some of the historical data in the latest yearbook may have been adjusted over data in previous yearbooks. Therefore, please refer to the latest yearbook when enquiring or using historical data.

(V) Electronic CD-ROM

Beijing Statistical Yearbook is provided with a CD-ROM, which containes Chinese and English versions of this Yearbook. The CD-ROM helps users in working with and processing the data.

(VI) The sum of some statistics or some relative numbers in this Yearbook might have certain calculation errors because of the choice of different units of measurement. All the statistics have not undergone mechanical adjustment.

III. About 2015 *Beijing Statistical Yearbook*

Compared with 2014 *Beijing Statistical Yearbook*, the following revisions have been made:

1. Relavant data has been timly updated according to results of the 3rd National Economic Census. GDP, retail sales of consumer goods, total energy consumption, internal R&D expenditures, etc. in 2013 have been updated as the data gained from the 3rd National Economic Census, of which retail sales of consumer goods from 2009 to 2012 have been revised according to consensus results.

2. Data not released in the 2014 yearbook due to the 3rd National Economic Census has been shown, which includes main indicators of micro-, small- and medium-sized enterprises above designated size, main indicators of non-public sectors of the economy above designated size, GDP by income approach, energy balance table, total energy consumption by sectors and consumption of main energy types in 2013.

3. Relevant indicators have been adjusted according to new standards for national sector classification and latest regulations on classifying the three industries. The data of national economic accounting and statistics on new emerging industries has been adjusted according to new sector standards. Historical data on GDP of the three industries from 1978 to 2012 has also been revised.

4. Information in statistical tables has been adjusted according to statistical method system. First, according to national statistic method system, statistical tables, such as *Business Climate Index* and *Entrepreneur Confidence Index*,

were cancelled and *Consumer Confidence Index in Beijing* was moved to Chapter 14; second, with reference to the revision of sector institutions, *Statistics on Family Planning* was cancelled and adjustment has been made to indicators in statistical tables like *Statistics on Adopting Institutions*, *Statistics for Divorce and Juvenile Criminal Cases* and *Basic Information on Undertakings for Disabled Persons*. Third, some indicators have been added according to times characters. For example, in *Main Indicators of Post and Telecommunication Service*, "EMS" was changed as "Total amount of delivery businesses" and its calculation basis was changed from amount of EMS into total amount of delivery businesses in Beijing; in *Amount of Transactions in Securities Market*, indicator of "fund transaction" was added; in *Added Value of Industries Above Designated Size*, indicator of "manufacture and pressing of ferrous metals" was cancelled and indicator of "manufacture of railway locomotives, building of ships and boats, manufacture of air and spacecrafts and other transportation equipments" is added.

5. Enhancement of standard unification continues. In this year, great efforts have been made to give unified regulations toward data related to statistical grouping in this Yearbook. For example, in statistical tables with the three industries and sectors classified by cross-grouping, the data was uniformly adjusted to be classified by "industries, national economic sectors and key sectors"; data classified by central and regional government was uniformly adjusted to be grouped by "affiliation"; and data classified by domestic and foreign enterprises was uniformly adjusted to be grouped by "registration type". Besides, regulations are continuouly made toward consistency and accuracy of Brief Introduction, Explanatory Notes on Statistical Indicators, notes under the table as well as english translation, etc.

目　　录
Contents

一、综合
GENERAL SURVEY

二、国民经济核算

NATIONAL ACCOUNTS

三、人口与就业
POPULATION AND EMPLOYMENT

四、能源、资源和环境

ENERGY, RESOURCES AND ENVIRONMENT

五、全社会固定资产投资和房地产开发

TOTAL INVESTMENT IN FIXED ASSETS AND REAL ESTATE DEVELOPMENT

六、财政与税收
GOVERNMENT FINANCE AND REVENUES

七、价格指数
PRICE INDEX

八、人民生活
PEOPLE'S LIFE

九、城市公用事业
PUBLIC UTILITIES

十、农业及农村经济
AGRICULTURE AND RURAL ECONOMY

十一、工业
INDUSTRY

十二、建筑业
CONSTRUCTION

十三、交通运输邮电
TRANSPORT, POST AND TELECOMMUNICATION SERVICES

十四、批发和零售业、住宿和餐饮业
WHOLESALE AND RETAIL TRADE, ACCOMMODATION AND RESTAURANTS

十五、对外经济贸易
FOREIGN ECONOMY AND TRADE

十六、旅游业
TOURISM

十七、金融和保险
FINANCE AND INSURANCE

十八、教育、文化
EDUCATION AND CULTURE

十九、科技

SCIENCE AND TECHNOLOGY

二十、卫生、体育
HEALTH CARE AND SPORTS

二十一、社会福利、社区、政法及其他
SOCIAL WELFARE, COMMUNITY, LAW AND OTHERS

二十二、第三产业
TERTIARY INDUSTRY

二十三、开发区
DVELOPMENT ZONES

01

综　合
GENERAL SURVEY

简要说明

一、本章资料的主要内容

本章主要包括北京市行政区划、法人及产业活动单位数、私营个体、非公经济、中小微型企业基本情况、全市社会经济发展的主要指标以及"十二五"时期监测指标等。

二、本章资料的数据来源

北京市行政区划情况来自北京市民政局；全市法人及产业活动单位情况来自北京市统计局；全市私营个体经济基本情况来自北京市工商行政管理局、北京市地方税务局、北京市国家税务局；非公经济数据和中小微型企业数据来自北京市统计局、国家统计局北京调查总队；全市社会经济主要指标及"十二五"时期主要监测指标资料由北京市统计局及国家统计局北京调查总队根据相关资料整理取得。

三、有关统计标准的变化说明

（一）《国民经济行业分类与代码》（GB/T 4754-2002版）与原（GB/T 4754-1994版）的主要框架结构变化：

增加的门类：a).信息传输、计算机服务和软件业 b).租赁和商务服务业 c).住宿和餐饮业 d).水利、环境和公共设施管理业 e).教育 f).国际组织

名称或范围进行调整的门类：a).农、林、牧、渔业 b).采矿业 c).制造业 d).交通运输、仓储和邮政业 e).批发和零售业 f).金融业 g).科学研究、技术服务和地质勘查业 h).居民服务和其他服务业 i).卫生、社会保障和社会福利业 j).文化、体育和娱乐业 k).公共管理和社会组织

取消的门类：a).地质勘查、水利管理 b).其它行业

（二）《国民经济行业分类》（GB/T 4754-2011版）与原（GB/T 4754-2002版）的主要框架结构变化：

门类名称调整：（1）"电力、燃气及水的生产和供应业"更名为"电力、热力、燃气及水生产和供应业"；（2）"信息传输、计算机服务和软件业"更名为"信息传输、软件和信息技术服务业"；（3）"科学研究、技术服务和地质勘查业"更名为"科学研究和技术服务业"；（4）"居民服务和其他服务业"更名为"居民服务、修理和其他服务业"；（5）"卫生、社会保障和社会福利业"更名为"卫生和社会工作"；（6）"公共管理和社会组织"更名为"公共管理、社会保障和社会组织"。

门类位次调整：（1）"批发和零售业"调至"建筑业"后面；（2）"住宿和餐饮业"调至"交通运输、仓储和邮政业"后面。

门类范围调整：A 农、林、牧、渔业；C 制造业；G 交通运输、仓储和邮政业；I 信息传输、软件和信息技术服务业；J 金融业；L 租赁和商务服务业；M 科学研究和技术服务业；O 居民服务、修理和其他服务业；P 教育；Q 卫生和社会工作；R 文化、体育和娱乐业；S 公共管理、社会保障和社会组织。

Brief Introduction

I. Main Content

Statistics in this chapter mainly show the basic information of administrative divisions of Beijing, number of corporate and industrial entities, non-public economy, small-, medium- and micro-sized enterprises,main indicators for social and economic development of the city, and monitoring indicators for the 12th Five-Year Plan, etc.

II. Source of Statistics

Statistics on administrative divisions of Beijing are from Beijing Municipal Bureau of Civil Affairs. Statistics on municipal corporate and industrial entities are from Beijing Municipal Bureau of Statistics. Statistics on private and self-employment economy in the city are from Beijing Administration for Industry and Commerce, Beijing Municipal Bureau of Local Tax and Beijing Municipal Bureau of State Tax. Statistics on non-public economy, small-, medium- and micro-sized enterprises are from National Bureau of Statistics Survey Office in Beijing and Beijing Municipal Bureau of Statistics. Statistics on social and economic indicators and main monitoring indicators for the 12th Five-Year Plan of the city are sorted out by Beijing Municipal Bureau of Statistics and National Bureau of Statistics Survey Office in Beijing on the basis of relevant statistics.

III. Adjustment to Historical Statistics According to New Industrial Standards

(I) Changes to the main framework of the *Classification and Codes of Sectors in National Economy* (GB/T 4754-2002) as compared with the previous version (GB/T 4754-1994):

Sectors added: a). information transmission, computer service and software, b). renting and leasing activities and business services, c). accommodation and restaurants, d). management of water conservancy, environment and public facilities, e). education, f). international organizations.

Sectors with name or range changed: a). agriculture, forestry, animal production and hunting, fishing, b). mining and quarrying, c). manufacturing, d). transport, storage and post, e). wholesale and retail trade, f). finance, g). scientific research, technical service, geological prospecting, h). resident service and other service, i). health care, social security, and social welfare, j). culture, sports and recreation, k). public administration and social organizations.

Sectors cancelled: a). geological prospecting, water conservancy management, b). other sectors.

（II）Compared with the previous (GB/T 4754-2002) version, the *Industrial Classification for National Economic Activities* (GB/T 4754-2011) mainly involves the following framework changes:

Changes to the name of category: (1) The "electric power, gas and water production and supply" is renamed "production and distribution of electricity,heating power, gas and water"; (2) the "information transmission, computer service and software" is renamed "information transmission, software and information technology services"; (3) the "scientific research, technical service and geological prospecting" is renamed "scientific research and development, technical services"; (4) the "resident service and other service" is renamed "resident services, repair and other services"; (5) the "health, social security and social welfare" is renamed "health care and social works"; (6) "public administration and social organization" is renamed "public administration, social security and social organizations".

Changes to the order of categories: (1) the "wholesale and retail trade" is put after the "construction"; (2) the "accommodation and restaurants" is put after the "transport, storage and post".

Changes to the scope of category: A. Agriculture, Forestry, Animal production and Hunting, Fishing; C. Manufacturing; G. Transport, Storage and Post; I. Information Transmission, Software and Information Technology Services; J. Finance; L. Renting and Leasing Activities and Business Services; M. Scientific Research and Development, Technical Service; O. Resident Services, Repair and Other Services; P. Education; Q. Health care and Social Works; R. Culture, Sports and Entertainment; S. Public Administration, Social Security and Social Organizations.

1-1 行政区划(2014年)
ADMINISTRATIVE DIVISIONS (2014)

单位：个 (unit)

地 区	District	街道办事处 Sub-district	建制镇 Designated Town	建制乡 Designated Township	社区居委会 Community Neighborhood Committee	村民委员会 Villagers' Committee
全 市	**Total**	**147**	**144**	**38**	**2932**	**3937**
首都功能核心区	**Core Functional Area of the Capital**	**32**			**444**	
东 城 区	Dongcheng District	17			187	
西 城 区	Xicheng District	15			257	
城市功能拓展区	**Urban Function Extension Area**	**71**	**9**	**22**	**1434**	**303**
朝 阳 区	Chaoyang District	24		19	408	154
丰 台 区	Fengtai District	16	2	3	305	65
石景山区	Shijingshan District	9			153	
海 淀 区	Haidian District	22	7		568	84
城市发展新区	**New Area of Urban Development**	**31**	**72**	**7**	**733**	**2189**
房 山 区	Fangshan District	8	14	6	130	459
通 州 区	Tongzhou District	4	10	1	111	475
顺 义 区	Shunyi District	6	19		99	426
昌 平 区	Changping District	5	15		211	302
大 兴 区	Daxing District	8	14		182	527
生态涵养发展区	**Ecological Conservation Area**	**13**	**63**	**9**	**321**	**1445**
门头沟区	Mentougou District	4	9		119	178
怀 柔 区	Huairou District	2	12	2	34	284
平 谷 区	Pinggu District	2	14	2	30	273
密 云 县	Miyun County	2	17	1	92	334
延 庆 县	Yanqing County	3	11	4	46	376

资料来源：北京市民政局。
Source: Beijing Municipal Bureau of Civil Affairs

1-2 规模(限额)以上法人单位基本情况(2014年)
NUMBER OF LEGAL ENTITIES ABOVE DESIGNATED SIZE (2014)

单位：个 (unit)

项目	Item	法人单位数合计 Total Number of Legal Entities	单产业法人 Single-industry Legal Entities	多产业法人 Multi-industry Legal Entities
合计	**Total**	**43640**	**36298**	**7342**
按登记注册类型分组	**By Registration Type**			
内资	Domestically-invested Enterprises	39533	33398	6135
国有	State-owned Enterprises	6285	5359	926
集体	Collectively-owned Enterprises	689	589	100
股份合作	Joint-equity Cooperative Enterprises	468	401	67
联营	Associated Enterprises	33	26	7
有限责任公司	Limited Liability Companies	14521	11928	2593
股份有限公司	Companies Limited by Shares	1217	838	379
私营	Private Enterprises	15937	13908	2029
其他	Others	383	349	34
港澳台商投资	Hong Kong, Macao and Taiwan-invested Enterprises	1564	1110	454
与港澳台商合资经营	Joint Ventures	491	371	120
与港澳台商合作经营	Cooperative Enterprises	119	103	16
港澳台商独资	Solely-funded Enterprises	922	622	300
港澳台商投资股份有限公司	Companies Limited by Shares	31	14	17
其他港澳台商投资	Others	1		1
外商投资	Foreign-invested Enterprises	2543	1790	753
中外合资经营	Joint Ventures	743	565	178
中外合作经营	Cooperative Enterprises	104	80	24
外资企业	Solely-funded Enterprises	1657	1124	533
外商投资股份有限公司	Companies Limited by Shares	36	20	16
其他外商投资	Others	3	1	2
按隶属关系分组	**By Affiliation**			
中央	Central	4529	3739	790
地方	Local	39111	32559	6552
按机构类型分组	**By Organization Type**			
企业	Enterprises	38334	31655	6679
事业单位	Institutions	3457	3172	285
机关	Government Agencies and Organizations	1138	845	293
社会团体	Social Organizations	245	172	73
其他机构	Others	466	454	12

注：本表为2014年年报规模(限额)以上法人单位数据。
Note: This table covers legal entities above designated size in the 2014 annual report.

1-3　国民经济各行业规模(限额)以上法人单位情况(2014年)
NUMBER OF LEGAL ENTITIES IN DIFFERENT SECTORS OF THE NATIONAL ECONOMY ABOVE DESIGNATED SIZE (2014)

单位: 个　　(unit)

行　业	Sector	法人单位数合计 Total Number of Legal Entities	单产业法人 Single-industry Legal Entities	多产业法人 Multi-industry Legal Entities
合　计	**Total**	**43640**	**36298**	**7342**
农、林、牧、渔业	**Agriculture, Forestry, Animal Production and Hunting, Fishing**			
采矿业	**Mining and Quarrying**	**24**	**18**	**6**
煤炭开采和洗选业	Mining and Washing of Coal	4	2	2
石油和天然气开采业	Extraction of Petroleum and Natural Gas	2		2
黑色金属矿采选业	Mining of Ferrous Metal Ores	7	6	1
有色金属矿采选业	Mining of Non-Ferrous Metal Ores			
非金属矿采选业	Mining and Processing of Nonmetal Ores	5	5	
开采辅助活动	Mining Support Service Activities	6	5	1
其他采矿业	Mining of Other Ores			
制造业	**Manufacturing**	**3557**	**2995**	**562**
农副食品加工业	Processing of Food from Agricultural Products	144	116	28
食品制造业	Manufacture of Foods	125	101	24
酒、饮料和精制茶制造业	Manufacture of Wine, Beverage and Refined Tea	42	29	13
烟草制品业	Manufacture of Cigarettes and Tobacco	1		1
纺织业	Manufacture of Textile	27	25	2
纺织服装、服饰业	Manufacture of Textile, Wearing Apparel and Ornament	141	105	36
皮革、毛皮、羽毛及其制品和制鞋业	Manufacture of Leather, Fur, Feather and Its Products, and Footwear	15	13	2
木材加工和木、竹、藤、棕、草制品业	Processing of Timbers, Manufacture of Wood, Bamboo, Rattan, Palm and Straw Products	16	14	2
家具制造业	Manufacture of Furniture	70	58	12
造纸和纸制品业	Manufacture of Paper and Paper Products	41	38	3
印刷和记录媒介复制业	Printing, Reproduction of Recording Media	118	111	7
文教、工美、体育和娱乐用品制造业	Manufacture of Articles for Culture, Education, Artwork, Sport and Entertainment Activities	35	28	7
石油加工、炼焦和核燃料加工业	Processing of Petroleum, Coking, Processing of Nucleus Fuels	23	20	3
化学原料和化学制品制造业	Manufacture of Chemical Raw Materials and Chemical Products	215	187	28
医药制造业	Manufacture of Medicines	193	160	33
化学纤维制造业	Manufacture of Chemical Fibres	3	2	1
橡胶和塑料制品业	Manufacture of Rubber and Plastics Products	124	108	16
非金属矿物制品业	Manufacture of Non-metallic Mineral Products	251	214	37
黑色金属冶炼和压延加工业	Manufacture and Pressing of Ferrous Metals	26	24	2

注: 1. 本表为2014年年报规模(限额)以上法人单位数据。
2. 本表行业划分执行2011年国民经济行业分类标准(GB/T 4754-2011)。

Note: a) This table covers legal entities above designated size in the 2014 annual report.
b) Sectors in this table are classified in accordance with the Standard for Classification of National Economic Sectors 2011 (GB/T 4754-2011).

1-3 续表 1 Continued

单位：个 (unit)

行业	Sector	法人单位数合计 Total Number of Legal Entities	单产业法人 Single-industry Legal Entities	多产业法人 Multi-industry Legal Entities
有色金属冶炼和压延加工业	Manufacture and Processing of Non-ferrous Metals	38	34	4
金属制品业	Manufacture of Fabricated Metal Products	228	198	30
通用设备制造业	Manufacture of General-Purpose Machinery	252	198	54
专用设备制造业	Manufacture of Special-Purpose Machinery	329	271	58
汽车制造业	Manufacture of Motor Vehicles	237	216	21
铁路、船舶、航空航天和其他运输设备制造业	Manufacture of Railway Locomotives, Building of Ships and Boats, Manufacture of Air and Spacecrafts and Other Transportation Equipments	74	66	8
电气机械和器材制造业	Manufacture of Electrical Machinery and Equipment	267	234	33
计算机、通信和其他电子设备制造业	Manufacture of Computers, Communication Equipment and Other Electronic Equipment	299	246	53
仪器仪表制造业	Manufacture of Measuring Instrument and Meter	176	139	37
其他制造业	Other Manufacturing	24	20	4
废弃资源综合利用业	Waste Rrecycling and Recovery	8	8	
金属制品、机械和设备修理业	Repair of Fabricated Metal Products, Machinery and Equipment	15	12	3
电力、热力、燃气及水生产和供应业	**Production and Distribution of Electricity, Heating Power, Gas and Water**	**105**	**83**	**22**
电力、热力生产和供应业	Production and Supply of Electric Power and Heat Power	63	51	12
燃气生产和供应业	Production and Distribution of Gas	22	17	5
水的生产和供应业	Production and Distribution of Water	20	15	5
建筑业	**Construction**	**3586**	**2846**	**740**
房屋建筑业	Construction of Building	649	396	253
土木工程建筑业	Civil Engineering Construction	584	436	148
建筑安装业	Construction Installation	864	726	138
建筑装饰和其他建筑业	Building Completion, Finishing and Other Construction	1489	1288	201
批发和零售业	**Wholesale and Retail Trade**	**8590**	**7074**	**1516**
批发业	Wholesale	5781	4980	801
零售业	Retail Trade	2809	2094	715
交通运输、仓储和邮政业	**Transport, Storage and Post**	**1002**	**778**	**224**
铁路运输业	Transport via Railway	15	10	5
道路运输业	Transport via Road	479	401	78
水上运输业	Water Transport	4	2	2
航空运输业	Air Transport	21	14	7
管道运输业	Transport via Pipeline	3	3	
装卸搬运和运输代理业	Loading, Unloading, Portage and Other Transport Services	341	233	108
仓储业	Storage	105	94	11
邮政业	Post	34	21	13
住宿和餐饮业	**Accommodation and Restaurants**	**3031**	**2417**	**614**
住宿业	Accommodation	1161	987	174
餐饮业	Restaurants	1870	1430	440
信息传输、软件和信息技术服务业	**Information Transmission, Software and Information Technology Services**	**2785**	**2227**	**558**
电信、广播电视和卫星传输服务	Telecommunications, Broadcasting, Television and Satellite Transmission Services	224	159	65
互联网和相关服务	Internet and Related Services	269	219	50
软件和信息技术服务业	Software and Information Technology Services	2292	1849	443

1-3 续表 2 Continued

单位：个 (unit)

行 业	Sector	法人单位数合计 Total Number of Legal Entities	单产业法人 Single-industry Legal Entities	多产业法人 Multi-industry Legal Entities
金融业	**Finance**	**2088**	**1794**	**294**
货币金融服务	Monetary Financial Services	637	553	84
资本市场服务	Capital Market Services	568	511	57
保险业	Insurance	511	397	114
其他金融业	Other Financial Services	372	333	39
房地产业	**Real Estate**	**4236**	**3581**	**655**
租赁和商务服务业	**Renting and Leasing Activities and Business Services**	**5339**	**4554**	**785**
租赁业	Renting and Leasing Activities	105	74	31
商务服务业	Business Services	5234	4480	754
科学研究和技术服务业	**Scientific Research and Development, Technical Services**	**3202**	**2736**	**466**
研究和试验发展	Research and Experimental Development	598	552	46
专业技术服务业	Professional Technique Services	1542	1244	298
科技推广和应用服务业	Technique Generalization and Application Services	1062	940	122
水利、环境和公共设施管理业	**Management of Water Conservancy, Environment and Public Facilities**	**534**	**478**	**56**
水利管理业	Management of Water Conservancy	39	35	4
生态保护和环境治理业	Ecological Protection and Environmental Control	62	51	11
公共设施管理业	Management of Public Facilities	433	392	41
居民服务、修理和其他服务业	**Resident Services, Repair and Other Services**	**477**	**400**	**77**
居民服务业	Resident Services	160	121	39
机动车、电子产品和日用产品修理业	Repair of Motor Vehicles, Electronics and Household Appliances	145	122	23
其他服务业	Other Services	172	157	15
教 育	**Education**	**1487**	**1356**	**131**
卫生和社会工作	**Health Care and Social Works**	**654**	**517**	**137**
卫 生	Health Care	609	474	135
社会工作	Social Work Activities	45	43	2
文化、体育和娱乐业	**Culture, Sports and Entertainment**	**1267**	**1142**	**125**
新闻和出版业	Journalism and Publishing	514	459	55
广播、电视、电影和影视录音制作业	Radio Broadcasting, Television, Movies, Videos and Sound Recording	228	206	22
文化艺术业	Cultures and Arts	250	236	14
体 育	Sports Activities	186	160	26
娱乐业	Entertainments	89	81	8
公共管理、社会保障和社会组织	**Public Administration, Social Security and Social Organizations**	**1676**	**1302**	**374**
中国共产党机关	Organs of Communist Party of China	49	43	6
国家机构	Organs of State	1265	974	291
人民政协、民主党派	Peole's Political Consultative Conference and Democratic Parties	25	24	1
社会保障	Social Security	9	9	
群众团体、社会团体和其他成员组织	Mass Communities, Social Organizations and Other Membership Organizations	283	210	73
基层群众自治组织	Grass Roots Self-Government Organization	45	42	3
国际组织	**International Organizations**			

1-4 规模(限额)以上企业法人单位情况(2014年)
NUMBER OF CORPORATE ENTERPRISES ABOVE DESIGNATED SIZE (2014)

单位：个 (unit)

项目	Item	法人单位合计 Total Number of Legal Entities	项目	Item	法人单位合计 Total Number of Legal Entities
合计	**Total**	**38334**	与港澳台商合资经营	Joint Ventures	491
按开业时间分	**By Openning Time**		与港澳台商合作经营	Cooperative Enterprises	119
1949年以前	Before 1949	36	港澳台商独资	Solely-funded Enterprises	921
1950-1965	From 1950 to 1965	277	港澳台商投资股份有限公司	Companies Limited by Shares	31
1966-1979	From 1966 to 1979	163	其他港澳台商投资	Others	1
1980-1989	From 1980 to 1989	1409	外商投资企业	Foreign-invested Enterprises	2540
1990年以后	After 1990	36449	中外合资经营	Joint Ventures	743
按登记注册类型分	**By Registration Type**		中外合作经营	Cooperative Enterprises	102
内资企业	Domestically-invested Enterprises	34231	外资企业	Solely-funded Enterprises	1656
国有企业	State-owned Enterprises	1662	外商投资股份有限公司	Companies Limited by Shares	36
集体企业	Collectively-owned Enterprises	596	其他外商投资	Other	3
股份合作企业	Joint-equity Cooperative Enterprises	461	**按控股情况分**	**By Share Holding Status**	
联营企业	Associated Enterprises	26	国有控股	State-owned Enterprises	7496
有限责任公司	Limited Liability Companies	14514	集体控股	Collectively-controlled Enterprises	1785
股份有限公司	Companies Limited by Shares	1217	私人控股	Privately-controlled Enterprises	24756
私营企业	Private Enterprises	15751	港澳台商控股	Hong Kong, Macao and Taiwan-controlled Enterprises	1413
其他内资企业	Other Domestically-invested Enterprises	4	外商控股	Foreign-controlled Enterprises	2307
港澳台商投资企业	Hong Kong, Macao and Taiwan-invested Enterprises	1563	其　他	Others	577

注：本表为2014年年报规模(限额)以上企业法人单位数据。
Note: This table covers legal entities above designated size in the 2014 annual report.

1-5 全市私营个体经济基本情况
STATISTICS FOR PRIVATE AND INDIVIDUAL ECONOMY

单位：万元 (10000 yuan)

项　目	Item	私营 Private 2014	2013	2014年为2013年% 2014 as % of 2013	个体 Individual 2014	2013	2014年为2013年% 2014 as % of 2013
工商登记注册*	**Registered at Administration for Industry and Commerce**						
户　数　（户）	Number of Business Entities (unit)	848099	673436	125.9	653319	664306	98.3
从业人员　（人）	Number of Employed Persons (person)	7255948	5278964	137.5	1029973	1123814	91.6
注册资本	Registered Capital	432893097	178551821	242.4	2180772	1854185	117.6
国税、地税入库税收合计	Taxes Put into Local and National Treasury	5753724	5043474	114.1	2015657	2360744	85.4

注：*为期末时点数。
资料来源：北京市工商行政管理局、北京市地方税务局、北京市国家税务局。
Note: Figures with * indicate the accumulative figures at end of the year.
Source: Beijing Administration for Industry and Commerce, Beijing Municipal Bureau of Local Taxation, Beijing Municipal Bureau of State Taxation.

1-6 规模以上非公经济主要指标(2013年)
MAIN INDICATORS OF NON-PUBLIC SECTORS OF THE ECONOMY ABOVE DESIGNATED SIZE (2013)

项目	Item	单位数 (个) Number of Enterprises (unit)	收入合计 (亿元) Total Income (100 million yuan)	利润总额 (亿元) Total Profits (100 million yuan)	应交税金合计 (亿元) Taxes Payable (100 million yuan)	从业人员平均人数 (万人) Average Number of Persons Employed (10000 persons)
合　计	**Total**	**28926**	**42287.6**	**3200.5**	**2001.0**	**335.4**
按登记注册类型分组	**Grouped by Registration Type**					
内　资	Domestic-funded	24875	21707.5	840.5	989.9	221.1
港澳台商投资	Hongkong, Macao and Taiwan-funded	1502	5246.4	532.1	314.7	40.8
外商投资	Foreign-funded	2549	15333.6	1827.9	696.4	73.6
按规模分	**Grouped by Size**					
大型企业	Large-sized Enterprises	867	18285.9	1384.7	791.3	117.2
中小微型企业	Mini-, Small-, Mediume-sized Enterprises	26185	22429.6	1519.9	985.4	201.7
中　型	Medium Size	5102	13623.5	1329.7	647.1	105.3
小　型	Small Size	15536	8013.1	263.9	297.1	89.4
微　型	Mini Size	5547	792.9	-73.7	41.2	7.0
按行业分组	**Grouped by Sector**					
#制造业	Manufacturing	2686	7659.5	515.3	362.4	63.0
建筑业	Construction	2817	1981.9	41.0	73.4	19.6
批发和零售业	Wholesale and Retail Trade	6007	17687.8	468.4	447.1	49.4
交通运输、仓储和邮政业	Transport, Storage and Post	758	815.0	26.6	28.5	16.4
住宿和餐饮业	Accommodation and Restaurants	2171	615.1	-2.9	44.0	26.9
信息传输、软件和信息技术服务业	Information Transmission,Software and Information Technology Services	2289	3401.7	1125.1	233.1	47.0
金融业	Finance	1222	1055.7	249.8	197.8	7.3
房地产业	Real estate	2923	2119.3	266.3	330.3	23.7
租赁和商务服务业	Renting and Leasing Activities and Business Services	4693	4780.5	339.7	172.2	42.9
科学研究和技术服务业	Scientific Research and Development, Technical Services	1955	1082.8	95.3	59.5	18.5
水利、环境和公共设施管理业	Management of Water Conservancy, Environment and Public Facilities	171	171.7	14.8	7.5	1.7
居民服务、修理和其他服务业	Resident Services, Repair and Other Services	344	137.2	2.3	8.2	6.6
教　育	Education	247	161.1	10.5	6.9	6.2
卫生和社会工作	Health Care and Social Works	124	69.1	4.7	1.4	1.9
文化、体育和娱乐业	Culture, Sports and Entertainment	389	146.5	12.5	10.5	2.7
公共管理和社会组织	Pulic Administration, Social Security and Social Organizations	99	172.5		…	0.4

注：1. 非公经济是指资产由我国私人控股、港澳台商控股、外商控股的“非公有控股”的企业法人单位，以及主要经费来源于私人、港澳台资和外资的非企业法人单位和个体工商户。私人、港澳台及外商控股是指由其绝对控股和相对控股的经济成分。本表不包含个体经营户数据。
2. 应交税金合计主要包括应交增值税、应交所得税、营业税金及附加和管理费用中的税金等。
3. 按规模分组中，各类型非公经济是指执行企业会计制度的非公企业数据，不包含执行事业会计制度的非公单位数据，因此，规模分组合计数不等于其他分组合计数。
4. 2013年，全市非公经济实现增加值7771.0亿元，其中第二产业增加值1985.9亿元，第三产业增加值5785.1亿元。

Note: a) Non-public economies mean enterprises as legal persons whose assets equity are held by non-public entities such as private, Hong Kong, Macao and Taiwan, and foreign businesses, as well as non-legal-person enterprises and self-employed entities whose main outlays come from private, Hong Kong, Macao and Taiwan, and foreign businesses. Economies with share held by private, Hong Kong, Macao and Taiwan, and foreign businesses mean economic elements with shares absolutely held by such businesses. This table excludes figures for self-employed entities.
b) Total Tax mainly includes payable VAT,payable income tax, business tax and surtax, and tax in management expenses, etc.
c) In the group by size, figures of various types of non-public sectors in the economy are those of non-public enterprises implementing enterprise accounting system, excluding those of non-public entities implementing public institution accounting system. Therefore, total amounts in the group by size are not equal to total amounts of other groups.
d) In 2013, non-public sectors of the economy in Beijing achieved added value of RMB 777.10 billion, of which the added value in the secondary industry reached RMB 198.59 billion and that in the tertiary industry hit RMB 578.51 billion.

1-7 规模以上非公经济主要指标(2014年)
MAIN INDICATORS OF NON-PUBLIC SECTORS OF THE ECONOMY ABOVE DESIGNATED SIZE (2014)

项 目	Item	单位数 (个) Number of Enterprises (unit)	收入合计 (亿元) Total Income (100 million yuan)	利润总额 (亿元) Total Profits (100 million yuan)	应交税金合计 (亿元) Taxes Payable (100 million yuan)	从业人员平均人数 (万人) Average Number of Persons Employed (10000 persons)
合 计	**Total**	**29388**	**48650.2**	**3958.1**	**2217.8**	**357.2**
按登记注册类型分组	**Grouped by Registration Type**					
内 资	Domestic-funded	25561	26148.6	1500.2	1202.9	242.4
港澳台商投资	Hongkong, Macao and Taiwan-funded	1458	6525.2	713.9	333.9	43.3
外商投资	Foreign-funded	2369	15976.4	1744.0	681.1	71.5
按规模分	**Grouped by Size**					
大型企业	Large-sized Enterprises	924	20569.8	1847.0	802.1	124.6
中小微型企业	Mini-, Small-, Mediume-sized Enterprises	26306	25140.7	1104.7	1061.5	211.6
中 型	Medium Size	5437	14081.4	691.9	629.2	114.4
小 型	Small Size	15713	9915.2	448.7	387.8	90.6
微 型	Mini Size	5156	1144.2	-35.9	44.5	6.6
按行业分组	**Grouped by Sector**					
#制造业	Manufacturing	2759	8172.4	525.8	376.2	62.5
建筑业	Construction	2757	2134.1	49.1	77.8	21.2
批发和零售业	Wholesale and Retail Trade	7096	21685.5	583.6	484.2	52.4
交通运输、仓储和邮政业	Transport, Storage and Post	719	927.2	32.9	25.3	16.9
住宿和餐饮业	Accommodation and Restaurants	2297	615.0	-18.9	42.5	25.8
信息传输、软件和信息技术服务业	Information Transmission,Software and Information Technology Services	2296	4104.7	1060.5	276.1	51.4
金融业	Finance	1511	2286.6	950.3	323.2	10.8
房地产业	Real estate	2701	2120.9	218.8	322.8	23.8
租赁和商务服务业	Renting and Leasing Activities and Business Services	3974	3939.2	373.8	169.7	50.9
科学研究和技术服务业	Scientific Research and Development, Technical Services	1826	1331.1	97.7	66.3	19.1
水利、环境和公共设施管理业	Management of Water Conservancy, Environment and Public Facilities	172	187.3	14.8	7.6	1.9
居民服务、修理和其他服务业	Resident Services, Repair and Other Services	356	137.3	2.0	7.7	7.0
教 育	Education	233	175.2	14.3	8.8	6.4
卫生和社会工作	Health Care and Social Works	151	91.9	5.5	2.0	2.4
文化、体育和娱乐业	Culture, Sports and Entertainment	399	183.8	18.6	11.6	2.8
公共管理和社会组织	Pulic Administration, Social Security and Social Organizations	105	266.9		0.7	0.4

注：1. 非公经济是指资产由我国私人控股、港澳台商控股、外商控股的"非公有控股"的企业法人单位，以及主要经费来源于私人、港澳台资和外资的非企业法人单位和个体工商户。私人、港澳台及外商控股是指由其绝对控股和相对控股的经济成分。本表不包含个体经营户数据。

2. 应交税金合计主要包括应交增值税、应交所得税、营业税金及附加和管理费用中的税金等。

3. 按规模分组中，各类型非公经济是指执行企业会计制度的非公企业数据，不包含执行事业会计制度的非公单位数据，因此，规模分组合计数不等于其他分组合计数。

4. 2014年，全市非公经济实现增加值8652.5亿元，其中第二产业增加值1952.1亿元，第三产业增加值6700.4亿元。

Note: a) Non-public economies mean enterprises as legal persons whose assets equity are held by non-public entities such as private, Hong Kong, Macao and Taiwan, and foreign businesses, as well as non-legal-person enterprises and self-employed entities whose main outlays come from private, Hong Kong, Macao and Taiwan, and foreign businesses. Economies with share held by private, Hong Kong, Macao and Taiwan, and foreign businesses mean economic elements with shares absolutely held by such businesses. This table excludes figures for self-employed entities.

b) Total Tax mainly includes payable VAT,payable income tax, business tax and surtax, and tax in management expenses, etc.

c) In the group by size, figures of various types of non-public sectors in the economy are those of non-public enterprises implementing enterprise accounting system, excluding those of non-public entities implementing public institution accounting system. Therefore, total amounts in the group by size are not equal to total amounts of other groups.

d) In 2014, non-public sectors of the economy in Beijing achieved added value of RMB 865.25 billion, of which the added value in the secondar industry reached RMB 195.21 billion and that in the tertiary industry hit RMB 670.04 billion.

1-8 规模以上中小微型企业主要指标(2013年)
MAIN INDICATORS OF MICRO- SMALL- AND MEDIUM-SIZED ENTERPRISES ABOVE DESIGNATED SIZE (2013)

项 目	Item	单位数 (个) Number of Enterprises (unit)	收入合计 (亿元) Total Income (100 million yuan)	利润总额 (亿元) Total Profits (100 million yuan)	应交税金合计 (亿元) Taxes Payable (100 million yuan)	从业人员平均人数 (万人) Average Number of Persons Employed (10000 persons)
合 计	**Total**	**34336**	**47418.0**	**3925.2**	**1898.0**	**296.1**
按规模分	**Grouped by Size**					
中 型	Medium Size	7795	32865.0	2355.9	1140.4	167.1
小 型	Small Size	19724	13214.0	774.8	463.2	119.4
微 型	Mini Size	6817	1339.0	794.5	294.5	9.6
按登记注册类型分	**Grouped by Registration Type**					
内 资	Domestic-funded	30721	40622.0	2761.1	1496.2	247.7
港澳台商投资	Hongkong, Macao and Taiwan-funded	1338	2276.7	134.2	130.5	18.8
外商投资	Foreign-funded	2277	4519.4	1029.9	271.2	29.6
按行业分	**Grouped by Sector**					
#制造业	Manufacturing	3372	6139.1	399.0	345.5	63.2
建筑业	Construction	3342	2246.9	70.9	81.9	23.3
批发和零售业	Wholesale and Retail Trade	7128	24847.6	409.0	375.0	35.2
交通运输、仓储和邮政业	Transport, Storage and Post	1026	889.9	27.2	23.5	14.9
住宿和餐饮业	Accommodation and Restaurants	2800	471.0	-25.4	33.3	24.0
信息传输、软件和信息技术服务业	Information Transmission,Software and Information Technology Services	2482	2068.6	1413.7	283.1	28.2
房地产业	Real estate	4114	2737.2	385.6	383.4	25.0
租赁和商务服务业	Renting and Leasing Activities and Business Services	5825	4408.5	935.6	216.2	51.1
科学研究和技术服务业	Scientific Research and Development, Technical Services	2552	1824.9	189.2	83.0	17.1
水利、环境和公共设施管理业	Management of Water Conservancy, Environment and Public Facilities	292	190.1	10.6	6.7	1.9
居民服务、修理和其他服务业	Resident Services, Repair and Other Services	363	121.3	3.2	6.7	3.0
卫生和社会工作	Health Care and Social Works	4	0.6	-0.2	…	…
文化、体育和娱乐业	Culture, Sports and Entertainment	931	510.5	65.6	32.4	6.5

注：1. 本表中的企业规模划型标准执行国家统计局《关于统计上大中小微型企业划分办法》(国统字〔2011〕75号)。按照国家统计局要求，铁路运输业、教育、卫生、自有房地产经营活动、金融业不划分规模，因此中小微数据不含这五个行业数据。

2. 行业划分执行2011年国民经济行业分类标准(GB/T 4754-2011)。

3. 2013年，全市中小微型企业实现增加值6617.1亿元，其中第二产业增加值1847.3亿元，第三产业增加值4769.8亿元。

Note: a) In this table, enterprise size is identified in accordance with the provisions stated in the Statistical Division Standards of Micro-, Small-, Medium- and Large-sized Enterprises released by the National Bureau of Statistics (G.T.Z. (2011) No. 75). According to requirements of National Bureau of Statistics, size division is unnecessary in sectors of railway transportation, education, health care, self-owned real estate operation and finance, so no data related to the five sectors is included in the table.

b) Sectors in this table are classified in accordance with the Standard for Classification of National Economic Sectors in 2011 (GB/T 4754-2011).

c) In 2013, micro-, small- and medium-sized enterprises in Beijing achieved added value of RMB 661.71 billion, of which added value in the secondary industry reached RMB 184.73 billion and that in the tertiary industry reached RMB 476.98 billion.

1-9 规模以上中小微型企业主要指标(2014年)
MAIN INDICATORS OF MICRO- SMALL- AND MEDIUM-SIZED ENTERPRISES ABOVE DESIGNATED SIZE (2014)

项 目	Item	单位数 (个) Number of Enterprises (unit)	收入合计 (亿元) Total Income (100 million yuan)	利润总额 (亿元) Total Profits (100 million yuan)	应交税金合计 (亿元) Taxes Payable (100 million yuan)	从业人员平均人数 (万人) Average Number of Persons Employed (10000 persons)
合 计	**Total**	**34014**	**50127.9**	**3751.7**	**1764.1**	**302.9**
按规模分	**Grouped by Size**					
中 型	Medium Size	8115	32232.1	1944.9	1112.2	175.1
小 型	Small Size	19572	14784.7	1078.1	561.2	118.7
微 型	Mini Size	6327	3111.1	728.7	90.7	9.2
按登记注册类型分	**Grouped by Registration Type**					
内 资	Domestic-funded	30698	43041.1	3094.5	1353.3	258.2
港澳台商投资	Hongkong, Macao and Taiwan-funded	1263	2458.9	209.6	145.1	17.9
外商投资	Foreign-funded	2053	4628.0	447.6	265.7	26.9
按行业分	**Grouped by Sector**					
#制造业	Manufacturing	3412	6424.4	481.4	360.1	62.1
建筑业	Construction	3244	2328.3	79.5	85.6	24.4
批发和零售业	Wholesale and Retail Trade	8240	25920.4	471.6	382.1	36.5
交通运输、仓储和邮政业	Transport, Storage and Post	944	1371.8	25.3	-7.0	15.0
住宿和餐饮业	Accommodation and Restaurants	2908	463.1	-31.7	33.0	22.2
信息传输、软件和信息技术服务业	Information Transmission,Software and Information Technology Services	2452	2300.6	663.4	93.4	29.0
房地产业	Real estate	3787	2698.2	362.2	384.1	24.1
租赁和商务服务业	Renting and Leasing Activities and Business Services	4975	4849.2	1358.9	259.8	57.7
科学研究和技术服务业	Scientific Research and Development, Technical Services	2357	2039.9	193.8	92.2	17.7
水利、环境和公共设施管理业	Management of Water Conservancy, Environment and Public Facilities	290	184.3	8.0	7.4	1.9
居民服务、修理和其他服务业	Resident Services, Repair and Other Services	363	112.1	2.3	5.9	3.1
卫生和社会工作	Health Care and Social Works	3	0.6	…	…	…
文化、体育和娱乐业	Culture, Sports and Entertainment	929	566.0	72.0	38.3	6.6

注：1. 本表中的企业规模划型标准执行国家统计局《关于统计上大中小微型企业划分办法》(国统字〔2011〕75号)。按照国家统计局要求，铁路运输业、教育、卫生、自有房地产经营活动、金融不划分规模，因此中小微数据不含这五个行业数据。
2. 行业划分执行2011年国民经济行业分类标准(GB/T 4754-2011)。
3. 2014年，全市中小微型企业实现增加值6906.5亿元，其中第二产业增加值1751.2亿元，第三产业增加值5155.3亿元。

Note: a) In this table, enterprise size is identified in accordance with the provisions stated in the Statistical Division Standards of Micro-, Small-, Medium- and Large-sized Enterprises released by the National Bureau of Statistics (G.T.Z. (2011) No. 75). According to requirements of National Bureau of Statistics, size division is unnecessary in sectors of railway transportation, education, health care, self-owned real estate operation and finance, so no data related to the five sectors is included in the table.
b) Sectors in this table are classified in accordance with the Standard for Classification of National Economic Sectors in 2011 (GB/T 4754-2011).
c) In 2014, micro-, small- and medium-sized enterprises in Beijing achieved added value of RMB 690.65 billion, of which added value in the secondary industry reached RMB 175.12 billion and that in the tertiary industry reached RMB 515.53 billion.

1-10 主要经济指标增长速度(1979-2014年)

单位：%

年 份 Year	地区生产总值比上年增长 YoY Growth Rate of Gross Domestic Product	全社会固定资产投资比上年增长 YoY Growth Rate of Fixed Asset Investment	房地产开发投资比上年增长 YoY Growth Rate of Real Estate Development Investment	地方公共财政预算收入比上年增长 YoY Growth Rate of Public Finance Budget Revenue	社会消费品零售总额比上年增长 YoY Growth Rate of Retail Sales of Consumer Goods	进出口总值比上年增长 YoY Growth Rate of Gross Value of Imports & Exports
1979	9.7	17.3			20.6	
1980	11.8	25.3			17.8	
1981	-0.5	10.2			12.6	
1982	7.4	5.5			6.6	
1983	16.4	32.9			14.6	
1984	17.4	29.2			22.5	16.3
1985	8.7	41.8			27.0	-8.6
1986	8.0	13.0			15.3	-6.0
1987	9.6	28.2			21.9	-12.7
1988	12.8	19.7			35.5	11.9
1989	4.4	-14.4			15.2	-4.3
1990	5.2	28.5			17.1	-17.4
1991	9.9	7.1	6.7		18.3	2.5
1992	11.3	38.5	40.4		23.2	3.1
1993	12.3	54.3	73.3		21.5	11.7
1994	13.7	58.1	70.4		25.4	3.5
1995	12.0	29.7	254.6		24.0	28.2
1996	9.0	4.2	-7.0		11.7	-20.8
1997	10.1	9.6	0.6		13.8	3.7
1998	9.5	20.2	14.3	20.0	13.7	0.4
1999	10.9	1.3	11.7	22.6	9.9	12.6
2000	11.8	10.8	23.9	22.7	9.9	43.8
2001	11.7	18.0	50.1	31.6	10.4	4.2
2002	11.5	18.5	26.2	25.9	9.5	2.0
2003	11.1	18.9	21.5	18.2	14.5	30.5
2004	14.1	17.2	22.5	29.7	14.4	38.1
2005	12.1	11.8	3.5	23.5	10.9	32.7
2006	13.0	19.3	12.8	21.5	13.2	25.9
2007	14.5	17.6	16.0	33.6	16.4	22.1
2008	9.1	-3.0	-4.4	23.1	21.1	40.8
2009	10.2	26.2	22.5	10.3	16.0	-20.9
2010	10.3	13.1	24.1	16.1	17.7	40.4
2011	8.1	13.3	10.1	27.7	13.9	29.1
2012	7.7	9.3	3.9	10.3	12.5	4.8
2013	7.7	8.8	10.5	10.4	9.2	5.4
2014	7.3	7.5	12.3	10.0	8.6	-3.4

注：1. 自2011年起全社会固定资产投资统计起点发生变化，但2011年全社会固定资产投资增长速度和房地产开发投资增长速度均按可比口径计算。
2. 2002-2004年地方公共财政预算收入增长速度是按可比口径计算。
3. 城镇居民人均可支配收入和农村居民人均纯收入实际增长速度是指扣除物价后的实际增长速度。
4. 2009-2013社会消费品零售总额增长速度据根据第三次全国经济普查数据进行了调整。

YOY GROWTH RATE OF MAIN INDICATORS (1979-2014)

(%)

农林牧渔业总产值比上年增长 YoY Growth Rate of Gross Output Value of Agriculture, Forestry, Animal Production and Hunting, Fishing	规模以上工业总产值比上年增长 YoY Growth Rate of Gross Output Value of Industrial Enterprises Above Designated Size	居民消费价格指数(上年=100) Consumer Price Index (Previous year=100)	城镇居民人均可支配收入 Per-capita Disposable Income of Urban Households 比上年名义增长 Nominal Growth Rate as Compared with That in the Last year	城镇居民人均可支配收入 Per-capita Disposable Income of Urban Households 比上年实际增长 Real Growth Rate as Compared with That in the Last year	农村居民人均纯收入 Per-capita Net Income of Rural Households 比上年名义增长 Normal Growth Rate as Compared with That in the Last year	农村居民人均纯收入 Per-capita Net Income of Rural Households 比上年实际增长 Real Growth Rate as Compared with That in the Last year
7.0		101.8	13.6	11.6	11.1	10.9
16.3		106.0	20.8	14.0	23.2	22.1
4.2		101.3	2.5	1.2	17.2	17.1
12.8		101.8	9.1	7.2	19.1	17.3
16.7		100.5	5.2	4.7	20.7	20.9
13.3		102.2	17.5	15.0	27.9	25.7
16.7	17.4	117.6	30.8	11.3	16.7	14.5
8.5	3.8	106.8	17.6	10.1	6.2	3.7
22.4	15.2	108.6	10.7	1.9	11.3	6.5
52.9	27.9	120.4	21.6	1.0	16.0	3.1
14.8	21.6	117.2	11.1	-5.2	15.8	2.2
16.2	3.8	105.4	11.9	6.2	5.4	2.1
9.0	16.7	111.9	14.2	2.1	9.6	1.7
10.5	17.8	109.9	15.8	5.4	10.3	2.0
18.8	35.7	119.0	39.4	17.1	18.2	5.1
43.7	35.1	124.9	43.5	14.9	30.6	9.1
13.9	-5.3	117.3	24.0	5.7	32.5	6.3
2.7	6.5	111.6	17.3	5.1	11.1	4.8
0.9	14.4	105.3	13.5	7.8	5.6	5.1
2.5	7.0	102.4	8.4	5.9	7.1	6.7
3.3	12.1	100.6	8.4	7.8	7.1	7.2
4.4	30.2	103.5	12.7	8.9	8.6	7.3
7.2	15.1	103.1	11.9	8.5	12.5	8.7
5.6	10.7	98.2	13.5	15.6	11.5	12.3
5.2	21.8	100.2	11.4	11.2	10.5	11.5
4.5	30.0	101.0	12.6	11.5	10.4	9.2
1.9	21.2	101.5	12.9	11.2	9.6	8.1
0.4	18.2	100.9	13.2	12.2	9.7	8.7
13.4	17.5	102.4	13.9	11.2	10.9	8.2
11.6	7.9	105.1	12.4	7.0	12.4	6.5
3.6	6.0	98.5	8.1	9.7	11.5	13.4
4.1	24.1	102.4	8.7	6.2	10.6	8.1
10.7	5.9	105.6	13.2	7.2	13.6	7.6
9.0	7.5	103.3	10.8	7.3	11.8	8.2
6.6	11.4	103.3	10.6	7.1	11.3	7.7
-0.4	6.2	101.6	8.9	7.2	10.3	8.6

Note: a) The statistical starting point for Fixed Asset Investment was changed in 2011. But the growth rates of Fixed Asset and Real Estate Development Investment in 2011 are calculated at comparable basis.

b) The growth rates of public finance budget revenue in 2002-2004 are calculated at comparable basis.

c) The growth rates of per-capita disposable income of urban households and per capita net income of rural households mean the real growth rate after the price influence is eliminated.

d) Data for YoY Growth Rate of Retail Sales of Consumer Goods of 2009-2013 were were revised acording to the third national economic census.

1-11 主要年份国民经济和社会发展总量与速度指标

项　　目		Item		1990	1995
人口与就业		**Population and Employment**			
人　口		**Population**			
年末全市常住人口	(万人)	Year-end Permanent Population	(10000 persons)	1086.0	1251.1
按性别分		By Sex			
男性人口		Male		545.0	627.0
女性人口		Female		541.0	624.1
按城乡分		By Urban Area and Rural Area			
城镇人口		Urban Population		798.0	946.2
乡村人口		Rural Population		288.0	304.9
年末户籍人口	(万人)	Year-end Registed Population	(10000 persons)	1032.2	1070.3
就　业		**Employment**			
从业人员年末人数	(万人)	Year-end Employed Persons	(10000 persons)	627.1	665.3
#城镇单位在岗职工人数		On-the-job Staff and Workers		454.9	470.9
年末实有城镇登记失业人员	(万人)	Registered Unemployed Persons in Urban Areas at Year End	(10000 persons)	1.7	2.2
宏观经济		**Macro Economy**			
国民经济核算		**National Accounts**			
地区生产总值	(亿元)	Gross Domestic Product	(100 million yuan)	500.8	1507.7
第一产业		Primary Industry		43.7	72.2
第二产业		Secondary Industry		262.0	643.6
第三产业		Tertiary Industry		195.1	791.9
人均地区生产总值	(元/人)	Per Capita Gross Domestic Product	(yuan/person)	4635	12690
固定资产投资		**Fixed Asset Investment**			
全社会固定资产投资	(亿元)	Total Fixed Asset Investment	(100 million yuan)	179.2	841.5
#房地产开发投资		Real Estate Development		22.5	352.8
#国有单位		State-Owned Entities		154.2	514.2
全社会房屋施工面积	(万平方米)	Floor Space of Houses under Construction	(10000 sq.m)	2864.9	5524.3
全社会房屋竣工面积	(万平方米)	Floor Space of Houses Completed	(10000 sq.m)	1081.2	1530.2
财　政		**Government Finance**			
地方财政收入	(亿元)	Local Finance Revenue	(100 million yuan)	74.0	115.3
#地方公共财政预算收入		Local Public Finance Budget Revenue			
地方财政支出	(亿元)	Local Finance Expenditure	(100 million yuan)	66.5	154.4
#地方公共财政预算支出		Local Public Finance Budget Expenditure			
价格指数(上年=100)		**Price Indices (Preceding Year=100)**			
居民消费价格指数	(%)	Consumer Price Index	(%)	105.4	117.3
商品零售价格指数	(%)	Retail Price Index	(%)	104.1	112.6
农产品生产价格指数	(%)	Farm Product Price Index	(%)	101.9	130.6
工业生产者出厂价格指数	(%)	Producer Price Index for Industrial Products	(%)	107.9	107.3
工业生产者购进价格指数	(%)	Purchase Price Index for Industrial Products	(%)	114.8	106.7
固定资产投资价格指数	(%)	Price Index of Investment in Fixed Asset	(%)		113.9
能源消费总量	**(万吨标准煤)**	**Total Energy Consumption**	**(10000 tons of SCE)**	**2709.7**	**3533.3**
产　业		**Industry**			
农村经济		**Rural Economy**			
耕地面积	(万公顷)	Cultivated Areas	(10000 hectare)	41.3	39.4
农林牧渔业总产值(现价)	(亿元)	Gross Output Value of Agriculture, Animal Production and Hunting, Fishing (at current prices)	(100 million yuan)	70.2	164.4
主要农产品产量	(万吨)	Yield of Agricultural and Sideline Products	(10000 tons)		
粮　食		Grain		264.6	259.8
蔬菜及食用菌		Vegetables and Edible Mushrooms		356.1	397.3
禽　蛋		Poultry Eggs		25.8	28.5
牛　奶		Milk		21.7	20.6
肉　类		Meat		26.8	39.8

注：1. 地区生产总值绝对值按现价计算，发展速度按可比价格计算；2006-2010年人均地区生产总值根据第六次人口普查数据进行修正。2013年地区生产总值为第三次全国经济普查数据；自2013年开始，地区生产总值三次产业分组口径根据国家统计局规定调整，并对2012年以前三次产业数据进行相应调整。
2. 2007年及以前在岗职工人数包括乡及乡以上独立核算法人单位，不包括乡镇企业、私营单位和个体工商户；2008年及以后包括乡镇企业。
3. 从2011年起，根据国家统计局相关规定，固定资产投资起点由50万元调整至500万元。

AGGREGATE INDICATORS AND SPEED INDICATORS ON NATIONAL ECONOMIC AND SOCIAL DEVELOPMENT IN KEY YEARS

总量指标 Aggregate Indicator					速度指标(%) Speed Indicator (%) 指 数(2014年为以下各年) Index (2014 as Percentage of the Following Year)					
2000	2005	2010	2013	2014	1990	1995	2000	2005	2010	2013
1363.6	1538.0	1961.9	2114.8	2151.6	198.1	172.0	157.8	139.9	109.7	101.7
710.9	778.7	1013.0	1090.7	1106.5	203.0	176.5	155.6	142.1	109.2	101.4
652.7	759.3	948.9	1024.1	1045.1	193.2	167.5	160.1	137.6	110.1	102.1
1057.4	1286.1	1686.4	1825.1	1859.0	233.0	196.5	175.8	144.5	110.2	101.9
306.2	251.9	275.5	289.7	292.6	101.6	96.0	95.6	116.2	106.2	101.0
1107.5	1180.7	1257.8	1316.3	1333.4	129.2	124.6	120.4	112.9	106.0	101.3
619.3	878.0	1031.6	1141.0	1156.7	184.5	173.9	186.8	131.7	112.1	101.4
434.2	448.4	587.7	695.5	708.8	155.8	150.5	163.2	158.1	120.6	101.9
3.3	10.6	7.7	6.8	8.8	525.1	400.5	264.2	83.0	113.5	128.8
3161.7	6969.5	14113.6	19800.8	21330.8	1164.6	665.8	408.7	230.8	134.5	107.3
77.3	86.2	122.7	159.6	159.0	131.8	126.3	117.9	114.8	107.3	100.0
1029.3	2017.2	3325.7	4292.6	4544.8	940.8	561.7	357.7	208.9	132.6	106.9
2055.1	4866.1	10665.2	15348.6	16627.0	1569.7	781.8	443.0	242.4	135.7	107.5
24127	45993	73856	94648	99995.0	588.7	370.3	250.9	164.0	120.5	105.2
1297.4	2827.2	5493.5	7032.2	7562.3	4220.0	898.7	582.9	267.5	137.7	107.5
522.1	1525.0	2901.1	3483.4	3911.3	17383.6	1108.6	749.1	256.5	134.8	112.3
765.8	897.7	1907.3	2382.0	2389.5	1549.6	464.7	312.0	266.2	125.3	100.3
6995.9	14096.2	15572.1	21526.0	21677.7	756.7	392.4	309.9	153.8	139.2	100.7
2358.2	4679.2	3908.4	3989.7	4967.5	459.4	324.6	210.6	106.2	127.1	124.5
398.4	1007.4	3810.9	5566.1	7214.5	9748.1	6259.4	1810.9	716.2	189.3	129.6
345.0	919.2	2353.9	3661.1	4027.2			1167.3	438.1	171.1	110.0
490.3	1137.3	4065.0	6039.4	7147.7	10745.3	4629.4	1457.7	628.5	175.8	118.4
443.0	1058.3	2717.3	4173.7	4524.7			1021.4	427.5	166.5	108.4
103.5	101.5	102.4	103.3	101.6						
98.9	99.7	100.4	99.8	99.1						
95.0	102.9	106.5	104.7	99.7						
102.5	101.3	102.2	97.4	99.1						
100.0	111.4	110.5	97.8	98.8						
101.0	100.7	102.5	99.9	100.0						
4144.0	**5521.9**	**6954.1**	**6723.9**	**6831.2**	**252.1**	**193.3**	**164.8**	**123.7**	**98.2**	**101.6**
32.9	23.3	22.4	22.1							
188.6	239.3	328.0	421.8	420.1	598.4	255.5	222.7	175.5	128.1	99.6
144.2	94.9	115.7	96.1	63.9	24.2	24.6	44.3	67.4	55.3	66.5
466.3	373.1	303.0	266.9	236.2	66.3	59.4	50.6	63.3	77.9	88.5
16.0	16.0	15.1	17.5	19.7	76.2	68.9	122.8	122.8	130.1	112.3
30.3	64.2	64.1	61.5	59.5	273.9	288.8	196.4	92.7	92.8	96.7
50.5	53.3	46.3	41.8	39.3	146.6	98.8	77.8	73.7	84.9	94.0

Note: a) Absolute values on GDP are calculated at current prices, whereas growth rates are calculated at comparable prices.Per Capita Gross Domestic Product from 2006 to 2010 were adjusted according to the 6th population census.Data of GDP for 2013 were collected from the third national economic censu; From 2013, The Gross Domestic Product of three industries were changed according to provisions of the National Bureau of Statistics, and the data on the three industries before 2012 was adjusted .

b) On-the-job staff and workers cover those in legal entities keeping separate accounts at and above the township level, excluding township enterprises, private entities and self-employed operators. On-the-job staff and workers in and after 2008 cover those in legal entities keeping separate accounts excluding private entities and self-employed operators.

c) From 2011, the starting point of fixed asset investment is changed from RMB 500,000 to RMB 5 million according to relevant regulations of National Bureau of Statistics.

1-11 续表 1

项目	Item	1990	1995
工业	**Industry**		
工业增加值(现价,规模以上) (亿元)	Added Value of Industry (at Current Prices, Above Designated Size) (100 million yuan)		473.1
工业总产值(现价,规模以上) (亿元)	Gross Output Value of Industry (at Current Prices, Above Designated Size) (100 million yuan)	625.9	1493.3
轻工业	Light Industry	262.2	472.2
重工业	Heavy Industry	363.7	1021.1
工业企业主要经济指标(规模以上)	Main Indicators of Industrial Enterprises (Above Designated Size)		
资产总计 (亿元)	Total Asset (100 million yuan)	498.3	2582.6
负债总额 (亿元)	Total Liability (100 million yuan)		1528.8
主营业务收入 (亿元)	Revenue from Main Businesses (100 million yuan)	610.5	1590.4
利润总额 (亿元)	Total Profit (100 million yuan)	48.9	85.3
建筑	**Construction**		
建筑业施工企业总产值 (亿元)	Gross Output Value (100 million yuan)	94.7	426.6
建筑业施工企业年末从业人员 (万人)	Year-end Employed Persons (10000 persons)	60.2	82.6
运输	**Transport**		
货物周转量 (亿吨公里)	Total Freight Turnover (100 million ton-km)	268.8	323.1
铁路	Railway	206.7	239.3
公路	Road	57.5	76.2
民航	Civil Aviation	4.5	7.5
管道	Pipeline	0.2	0.1
旅客周转量 (亿人公里)	Total Passenger Turnover (100 million passenger-km)	119.8	207.7
邮电	**Post and Telecommunication Services**		
邮电业务总量 (亿元)	Business Volume of Post and Telecommunications (100 million yuan)	11.9	56.1
固定电话用户 (万户)	Fixed Telephone Subscribers (10000 subscribers)	33.3	150.5
固定电话主线普及率 (线/百人)	Penetration Rate of Main Line (lines/100 persons)	3.1	12.0
移动电话用户 (万户)	Mobile Telephone Subscribers (10000 subscribers)	0.3	16.9
移动电话普及率 (户/百人)	Penetration Rate of Mobile Telephone (sets/100 persons)	0.03	1.4
商业	**Commerce**		
社会消费品零售总额 (亿元)	Retail Sales of Consumer Goods (100 million yuan)	345.1	950.4
对外经济贸易和旅游	**Foreign Trade and Tourism**		
北京地区进出口总值 (亿美元)	Total Value of Imports and Exports (USD 100 million)	236.4	370.4
进口值	Imports	192.3	267.9
出口值	Exports	44.1	102.5
实际利用外商直接投资额 (亿美元)	Paid-in Foreign Investment (USD 100 million)	2.8	14.0
接待入境旅游者人数 (万人次)	Inbound Tourists (10000 persons)	100.0	207.0
旅游外汇收入 (亿美元)	Foreign Exchange Earning from Tourism (USD 100 million)	6.6	21.8
金融保险	**Finance and Insurance**		
金融机构(含外资)本外币存款余额 (亿元)	Deposits of Financial Institutions (Including Foreign Institutions) (100 million yuan)		
金融机构(含外资)本外币贷款余额 (亿元)	Loans of Financial Institutions (Including Foreign Institutions) (100 million yuan)		
原保险保费收入 (亿元)	Premiums Revenue (100 million yuan)		

注：1. 工业增加值按生产法计算。
2. 邮电业务总量2000年及以前按1990年不变价格计算，2010年及以前按2000年不变价格计算,从2011年开始按2010年不变价计算。
3. 2013年社会消费品零售总额数据为第三次全国经济普查数据，2009-2012年数据根据第三次全国经济普查数据进行了修订。

1-11 Continued 1

总量指标 Aggregate Indicator					速度指标(%) Speed Indicator (%)					
					指 数(2014年为以下各年) Index (2014 as Percentage of the Following Year)					
2000	2005	2010	2013	2014	1990	1995	2000	2005	2010	2013
776.0	1627.0	2751.7	3432.1	3612.0						
2842.0	6946.2	13699.8	17370.9	18452.9	2948.2	1235.7	649.3	265.7	134.7	106.2
719.3	1164.9	2000.0	2541.5	2568.0	979.4	543.8	357.0	220.4	128.4	101.0
2122.7	5781.3	11699.8	14829.4	15884.9	4367.6	1555.7	748.3	274.8	135.8	107.1
4612.7	12829.8	22750.6	30800.7	33557.0	6734.3	1299.4	727.5	261.6	147.5	108.9
2676.4	4706.7	11548.1	16208.0	17137.6		1121.0	640.3	364.1	148.4	105.7
2821.4	7279.1	14807.1	18688.6	19776.7	3239.7	1243.5	701.0	271.7	133.6	105.8
127.1	413.5	1028.3	1282.9	1515.8	3097.4	1777.1	1192.7	366.6	147.4	118.2
812.5	1894.0	5196.0	7459.6	8209.8	8669.3	1924.5	1010.4	433.5	158.0	110.1
56.6	67.2	59.9	49.3	51.0	84.7	61.7	90.1	75.9	85.1	103.4
299.6	457.7	513.7	680.9	672.8	250.3	208.2	224.5	147.0	131.0	98.8
200.2	310.8	257.5	323.2	284.4	137.5	118.8	142.0	91.5	110.5	88.0
82.6	85.5	101.6	156.2	165.2	287.5	216.8	199.9	193.2	162.6	105.8
16.8	28.2	48.2	49.2	55.4	1239.7	738.8	330.2	196.6	114.8	112.6
0.04	33.3	106.4	152.3	167.9				504.8	157.9	110.2
314.0	838.1	1399.5	1498.8	1602.7	1337.8	771.7	510.4	191.2	114.5	106.9
214.7	413.0	1108.9	652.5	751.1	6317.5	1338.2	349.8	181.9	67.7	115.1
451.2	943.5	885.6	867.6	831.1	2496.2	552.1	184.2	88.1	93.8	95.8
33.1	61.3	45.1	41.0	39.3	1267.7	327.5	118.7	64.1	87.1	95.8
347.2	1459.8	2129.8	3373.8	4076.2			1174.0	279.2	191.4	120.8
25.5	94.9	108.6	159.5	232.2			910.5	244.7	213.8	145.5
1658.7	2911.7	6340.3	8872.1	9638.0	2792.8	1014.1	581.1	331.0	152.0	108.6
494.0	1255.1	3016.6	4299.4	4155.4	1757.4	1122.0	841.2	331.1	137.7	96.6
374.3	946.4	2462.2	3668.4	3532.0	1836.6	1318.6	943.6	373.2	143.4	96.3
119.7	308.7	554.4	631.0	623.4	1412.4	608.2	520.8	202.0	112.4	98.8
24.6	35.3	63.6	85.2	90.4	3264.4	644.5	367.8	256.4	142.1	106.1
282.1	362.9	490.1	450.1	427.5	427.5	206.5	151.5	117.8	87.2	95.0
27.7	36.2	50.4	47.9	46.1	701.3	211.2	166.5	127.3	91.4	96.1
11526.0	28969.9	66584.6	91660.5	100095.5			868.4	345.5	150.3	109.2
6407.9	15335.5	36479.6	47880.9	53650.6			837.3	349.8	147.1	112.0
93.4	498.2	966.5	994.4	1207.2			1291.9	242.3	124.9	121.4

Note: a) Added value of industry is calculated with the production approach.

b) Business volumes of post and telecommunications before and in 2000 were calculated at 1990's constant price, those before and in 2000 were calculated at 2000's constant price, and those since 2011 were calculated at 2010's constant price.

c) Data for Retail Sales of Consumer Goods of 2013 were collected from the third national economic census，and date for 2010-2012 were revised acording to the third national economic census.

1-11 续表 2

项目	Item	1990	1995
教育、文化、科技、卫生	**Education, Culture, Science and Technology and Health Care**		
教育	**Education**		
在校学生数 (万人)	Students Enrollment (10000 persons)		238.0
专任教师数 (万人)	Full-time Teachers (10000 persons)		17.7
文化	**Culture**		
公共图书馆总藏数 (万册、万件)	Collection of Public Libraries (10000 volumes)	2205	2629
科技	**Science and Technology**		
研究与试验发展经费内部支出 (亿元)	Expenditures on Research and Development (100 million yuan)		
技术合同成交总额 (亿元)	Volume of Technical Contract (100 million yuan)	20.3	41.2
专利授权量 (件)	Patent Grants (case)	2268	4025
卫生	**Health Care**		
卫生机构个数 (个)	Health Care Institutions (unit)	4953	4955
卫生机构病床数 (万张)	Beds at Health Care Institutions (10000 beds)	5.9	6.7
卫生技术人员数 (万人)	Medical Personnel (10000 persons)	11.2	11.6
#执业(助理)医师	Certified Doctors	5.1	5.4
注册护师(士)	Registered Nurses	3.5	3.7
生活与环境	**People's Living and Environment**		
婚姻	**Marriages and Divorces**		
登记结婚对数 (万对)	Number of Registered Marriages (10000 couples)	9.30	8.55
离婚对数 (万对)	Number of Divorces (10000 couples)	1.47	2.02
居住	**Housing**		
城镇居民人均住房建筑面积 (平方米)	Per Capita Living Space for Urban Residents (sq.m)		
农村居民人均住房面积 (平方米)	Per Capita Living Space for Rural Residents (sq.m)	20.62	24.74
生活	**People's Livelihood**		
城镇居民人均可支配收入 (元)	Per Capita Annual Disposable Income of Urban Residents (yuan)	1787	5868
农村居民人均纯收入 (元)	Per Capita Net Income of Rural Residents (yuan)	1297	3209
金融机构(含外资)储蓄存款余额 (亿元)	Saving Deposits of Financial Institutions (including foreign institutions) (100 million yuan)		
工资	**Wages**		
城镇单位在岗职工工资总额 (亿元)	Total Wage of On-the-job Staff and Workers (100 million yuan)	118.9	382.0
城镇单位在岗职工平均工资 (元)	Average Wage of On-the-job Staff and Workers (yuan)	2653	8144
市政建设	**Municipal Construction**		
全社会用电量 (亿千瓦时)	Total Electricity Consumption (100 million kwh)	150.5	222.6
自来水销售总量 (亿立方米)	Sales of Tap Water (100 million cu.m)	5.3	6.8
居民燃气用户 (万户)	Households with Access to Gas (10000 households)	176.1	219.8
城市公共交通客运量 (亿人次)	Passengers Carried by Urban Public Transport (100 million person-times)	33.5	37.2
环境	**Environment**		
城市绿化覆盖率 (%)	Urban Green Area Coverage (%)	28.0	32.7
污水处理率 (%)	Sewage Treatment Rate (%)	7.3	19.4

注：1. 北京地区用电量来源于北京市电力公司，2000年以前工业用电量不包含输配损失和发电企业自产自用电量。
2. 从2001年开始，有关职工的指标调整为在岗职工的指标。2007年及以前城镇单位在岗职工工资包括乡及乡以上独立核算法人单位，不包括乡镇企业、私营单位和个体工商户；2008年及以后包括乡镇企业。
3. 离婚对数包括在民政部门登记的对数和经法院调离和判离的对数。
4. 2010年及以前，本表中卫生机构数据都不包含村卫生室及驻京部队医院情况。2011年开始，包含村卫生室情况。2012年开始，卫生机构数、卫生技术人员数据中包含驻京部队医院，床位数不包含。

1-11 Continued 2

总量指标 Aggregate Indicator					速度指标(%) Speed Indicator (%)					
					指 数(2014为以下各年) Speed Indicator (2014 as Percentage of the Following Year)					
2000	2005	2010	2013	2014	1990	1995	2000	2005	2010	2013
229.9	226.4	330.0	373.6	377.5		158.6	164.2	166.7	114.4	101.0
16.7	17.5	20.7	21.6	22.5		127.5	134.8	129.0	109.0	104.0
3020	3626	4613	5316	5601	254.0	213.0	185.5	154.5	121.4	105.4
155.7	379.5	821.8	1185.0	1268.8			814.9	334.3	154.4	107.1
140.3	434.4	1579.5	2851.2	3136.0	15471.1	7617.2	2235.4	721.9	198.5	110.0
5905	10100	33511	62671	74661	3291.9	1854.9	1264.4	739.2	222.8	119.1
6176	4818	6539	10141	10265	207.2	207.2	166.2	213.1	157.0	101.2
7.1	7.9	9.3	10.4	11.0	186.0	164.0	154.1	138.9	118.2	105.5
11.6	12.0	17.1	23.0	24.3	217.6	209.5	210.3	202.6	142.0	105.7
5.2	5.1	6.6	8.6	9.0	175.9	165.6	173.7	177.0	135.8	104.4
4.0	4.3	6.7	10.1	10.6	307.2	289.1	266.1	247.5	157.7	105.5
8.02	9.66	13.81	16.37	17.00	182.8	198.8	212.0	176.0	123.1	103.9
2.66	3.42	4.40	6.46	7.64	517.7	378.7	286.9	223.0	173.6	118.2
	22.03	28.94	31.31	31.54				143.2	109.0	100.7
28.91	36.94	40.62	51.35	52.42	254.2	211.9	181.3	141.9	129.0	102.1
10350	17653	29073	40321	43910	2457.1	748.2	424.3	248.7	151.0	108.9
4687	7860	13262	18337	20226	1559.3	630.4	431.5	257.3	152.5	110.3
	8315.8	17585.2	23747.6	24855.7				298.9	141.3	104.7
695.5	1520.1	3789.1	6502.0	7293.3	6134.0	1909.3	1048.6	479.8	192.5	112.2
15726	34191	65683	93997	103400	3897.5	1269.6	657.5	302.4	157.4	110.0
384.4	570.5	809.9	913.1	937.0	622.7	421.0	243.8	164.2	115.7	102.6
7.5	7.2	8.9	9.8	10.3	196.1	152.3	137.2	144.4	115.9	105.3
291.9	462.6	634.2	737.4	846.0	480.4	384.9	289.8	182.9	133.4	114.7
40.7	51.8	69.0	80.5	81.6	243.8	219.6	200.6	157.6	118.3	101.4
36.5	42.0	45.0	46.8	47.4						
39.4	62.4	81.0	84.6	86.1						

Note: a) Figures on electricity eonsumption are provided by Beijing Electric Power Corporation. Before 2000, electricity consumption by industry excluded transmission and distribution losses and electricity generated and consumed by power generating enterprises.

b) From 2001, indicators related to the "staff and workers " have been changed to those of "on-the-job staff and workers". In and before 2007, figures on wages of urban on-the-job staff and workers covered corporate entities keeping separate accounts at and above the township level, excluding township enterprises, private entities and self-employed operators; in and after 2008, such figures included township enterprises.

c) Registered divorces include those registered with civil affair authorities and those mediated and ruled in courts.

d) From 2010, figures on health centers were emerged with other health institutions such as community health service centers (stations).From 2011,health care institutions included village health centers.

1-12 主要年份国民经济和社会发展结构指标
STRUCTURAL INDICATORS ON NATIONAL ECONOMIC AND SOCIAL DEVELOPMENT IN KEY YEARS

单位：% (%)

项目	Item	1990	1995	2000	2005	2010	2013	2014
人口与就业	**Population and Employment**							
常住人口	**Permanent Population**							
按性别分	By Sex							
男	Male	50.2	50.1	52.1	50.6	51.6	51.6	51.4
女	Female	49.8	49.9	47.9	49.4	48.4	48.4	48.6
按城乡分	By Urban Area and Rural Area							
城镇	Urban	73.5	75.6	77.5	83.6	86.0	86.3	86.4
乡村	Rural	26.5	24.4	22.5	16.4	14.0	13.7	13.6
就业	**Employment**							
从业人员年末人数	Year-end Employed Persons							
第一产业	Primary Industry	14.5	10.6	11.8	7.1	6.0	4.8	4.5
第二产业	Secondary Industry	44.9	40.7	33.6	26.3	19.6	18.5	18.2
第三产业	Tertiary Industry	40.6	48.7	54.6	66.6	74.4	76.7	77.3
宏观经济	**Macro Economy**							
国民经济核算	**National Accounts**							
地区生产总值	Gross Domestic Product							
第一产业	Primary Industry	8.7	4.8	2.4	1.2	0.9	0.8	0.7
第二产业	Secondary Industry	52.3	42.7	32.6	28.9	23.6	21.7	21.4
第三产业	Tertiary Industry	39.0	52.5	65.0	69.9	75.5	77.5	77.9
投资	**Investment**							
全社会固定资产投资	Fixed Asset Investment							
城镇	Urban	88.2	94.4	91.9	91.8	91.1	90.3	91.6
农村	Rural	9.7	4.8	6.5	8.2	8.9	9.7	8.4
资金来源结构	Source of Capital							
国家预算内资金	State Budgetary Appropriation	25.3	7.7	7.4	2.8	1.2	1.5	1.6
国内贷款	Domestic Loans	16.7	13.4	26.0	23.2	26.6	24.1	27.8
利用外资	Foreign Investment	11.2	20.5	3.6	1.6	0.5	0.2	0.3
债券、自筹和其他资金	Securities, Fundraising and Other Investment	46.8	58.4	63.0	72.4	71.6	74.2	70.3
财政	**Government Finance**							
地方公共财政预算收入主要税种	Main Taxes of Public Finance Budget Revenue							
#增值税	Value Added Tax			13.3	10.6	8.9	15.7	16.1
营业税	Business Tax			43.2	41.7	36.3	28.3	26.5
企业所得税	Corporate Income Tax			16.8	17.9	21.8	21.9	22.7
个人所得税	Private Income Tax			16.3	9.2	9.1	9.1	9.5
能源消费总量	**Energy Consumotion**							
第一产业	Primary Industry	3.9	3.4	2.5	1.6	1.4	1.5	1.3
第二产业	Secondary Industry	63.5	65.9	58.5	48.9	39.2	30.9	29.3
第三产业	Tertiary Industry	19.0	17.9	26.1	34.8	41.7	46.2	47.4
生活消费	Living Consumption	13.6	12.8	12.9	14.7	17.7	21.4	22.0

注：1. 自2012年开始，从业人员年末人数和能源消费总量三次产业分组口径根据国家统计局规定进行了调整。
2. 自2013年开始，地区生产总值三次产业分组口径根据国家统计局规定调整,并对2012年以前三次产业数据进行相应调整。
3. 2013年地区生产总值数据为第三次全国经济普查数据。

Note: a) From 2012, The grouping standards for Year-end Employed Persons and Energy Consumption of three industries were changed according to provisions of the National Bureau of Statistics.
b) From 2013, The Gross Domestic Product of three industries were changed according to provisions of the National Bureau of Statistics, and the data on the three industries before 2012 was adjusted .
c) Data for 2013 of Gross Domestic Productwere collected from the third national economic census.

1-12 续表 1 Continued 1

单位：% (%)

项 目	Item	1990	1995	2000	2005	2010	2013	2014
产 业	**Industry**							
农 业	**Agriculture**							
农林牧渔业产值结构	Structure of Gross Output Value of Agriculture							
农 业	Agriculture	55.6	52.8	46.7	38.0	47.0	40.4	36.9
林 业	Forestry	1.3	1.7	2.8	5.2	5.1	18.0	21.6
牧 业	Animal Production and Hunting	39.8	41.8	46.4	50.5	42.6	36.7	36.3
渔 业	Fishing	3.3	3.7	4.1	3.6	3.5	3.0	3.2
农林牧渔服务业	Service Activities for Agriculture, Forestry, Animal Production and Hunting, Fishing				2.7	1.8	1.9	2.0
工 业	**Industry**							
规模以上工业主要行业增加值结构	Structure of Added Value of Industry by Sector (Above Designated Size)							
#医药制造业	Manufacture of Medicines		1.6	3.6	3.0	5.6	7.4	7.8
汽车制造业	Manufacture of Motor Vehicles		9.4	3.7	8.7	16.6	21.3	20.1
计算机、通信和其他电子设备制造业	Manufacture of Computer, Communication Equipment and Other Electronic Equipment		9.9	24.7	16.7	8.7	8.9	8.4
电力、热力的生产和供应业	Production and Distribution of Electricity and Heating Power		7.0	6.4	11.8	14.9	17.5	18.9
建筑业	**Construction**							
建筑业总产值结构	Stucture of Gross Output Value of Construction							
#国有企业	State-owned Enterprises	68.7	69.1	44.8	27.4	6.3	5.1	3.5
集体企业	Collectively-owned Enterprises	31.3	26.4	21.7	4.7	2.0	1.7	1.6
港澳台商投资企业	Hong Kong, Macao and Taiwan-invested Enterprises		1.4	1.4	1.2	1.8	0.9	0.8
外商投资企业	Foreign-invested Enterprises		1.2	2.0	1.7	1.0	0.7	0.5
交通运输业	**Transport**							
货运量结构(按运输方式分)	Structure of Freignt (By Means of Transportation)							
铁 路	Railway	11.4	9.2	8.5	6.1	6.6	3.8	3.8
公 路	Road	87.5	90.4	91.2	92.4	85.1	87.1	86.1
民 航	Civil Aviation	0.04	0.05	0.1	0.2	0.5	0.5	0.5
管 道	Pipeline	1.0	0.3	0.2	1.2	7.7	8.6	9.6
客运量结构(按运输方式分)	Structure of Passenger (By Means of Transportation)							
铁 路	Railway	50.4	45.1	24.2	9.5	6.3	16.3	17.6
公 路	Road	46.7	47.7	70.7	85.3	89.7	73.9	73.0
民 航	Civil Aviation	2.9	7.2	5.1	5.2	4.0	9.8	9.4
国内贸易	**Domestic Trade**							
社会消费品零售总额结构	Structure Retail Sales of Consumer Goods							
吃类商品	Food	39.6	42.7	28.4	25.8	21.4	20.3	19.3
穿类商品	Clothing	13.2	14.6	12.0	9.7	8.8	8.8	8.1
用类商品	Daily Use Articles	44.8	40.8	56.2	56.5	62.4	64.4	66.5
烧类商品	Fuels	2.4	1.9	3.4	8.1	7.5	6.5	6.0
对外贸易	**Foreign Trade**							
地区出口商品结构	Structure of Export Commodities							
#一般贸易	General Trade		70.6	65.9	54.5	45.0	43.2	45.5
加工贸易	Processing Trade		21.3	29.6	39.6	42.1	40.5	35.9
地区进口商品结构	Structure of Import Commodities							
#一般贸易	General Trade		84.4	87.3	85.2	88.7	89.2	86.4
加工贸易	Processing Trade		5.2	3.5	8.2	5.9	5.6	7.1
国际旅游	**International Tourism**							
接待海外旅游人数结构	Structure of Inbound Tourist							
外国人	Foreigners	63.7	80.5	84.4	85.9	86.0	86.1	85.5
港澳台同胞	Compatriots from Hong Kong, Macao and Taiwan	34.6	17.6	15.6	14.1	14.0	13.9	14.5

注：2013年社会消费品零售总额数据为第三次全国经济普查数据，2009-2012年数据根据第三次全国经济普查数据进行了修订。

Note: Data for Retail Sales of Consumer Goods of 2013 were collected from the third national economic census，and data for 2010-2012 were revised acording to the third national economic census.

1-12 续表 2 Continued 2

单位：% (%)

项　　目	Item	1990	1995	2000	2005	2010	2013	2014
教育、科技、文化、卫生	**Education, Science and Technology, Culture, Health Care**							
教　育	**Education**							
在校学生结构	Structure of Students Enrollment							
#高等教育	Higher Education	8.3	9.0	14.0	46.2	49.5	50.4	51.1
中等教育	Secondary Education	32.5	41.0	48.7	29.7	22.1	18.9	17.3
小学教育	Primary Education	59.0	49.6	36.8	16.9	19.8	21.1	21.8
专任教师结构	Structure of Full-time Teachers							
#高等教育	Higher Education	24.6	22.7	22.2	32.7	35.9	32.2	31.6
中等教育	Secondary Education	38.3	38.6	40.5	33.6	29.1	31.5	31.9
小学教育	Primary Education	36.7	37.9	36.8	25.3	23.9	22.5	22.0
科　技	**Science and Technology**							
研究与试验发展(R&D)人员折合全时当量结构	Structure of R&D Personnel							
基础研究	Basic Research				12.9	15.2	14.8	15.9
应用研究	Applied Research				29.8	27.1	24.5	24.1
试验发展	Experimental Development				57.3	57.7	60.7	60.0
研究与试验发展(R&D)经费内部支出结构	Structure of Full-time and Non-full Time R&D Personnel							
基础研究	Basic Research				10.1	11.6	11.6	12.6
应用研究	Applied Research				27.8	26.4	21.8	21.7
试验发展	Experimental Development				53.1	62.0	66.6	65.8
卫　生	**Health Care**							
卫生技术人员结构	Structure of Medical Personnel							
#执业(助理)医师	Certified Doctors	45.6	46.7	44.6	42.2	38.5	37.4	36.9
注册护士	Registered Nurses	31.0	31.7	34.5	35.8	39.3	43.8	43.7
生活与环境	**People's Livelihood and Environment**							
生　活	**People's Livelihood**							
城镇居民消费结构	Consumption Structure of Urban Residents							
食品(恩格尔系数)	Food (Engel Coefficient)	54.2	48.5	36.3	31.8	32.1	31.1	30.8
衣　着	Clothing	14.8	15.1	8.9	8.9	10.4	10.6	10.4
居　住	Housing	3.5	4.5	6.9	7.9	7.9	8.1	7.9
家庭设备用品及服务	Household Appliances and Services	10.4	8.8	12.9	6.4	6.9	7.5	7.7
医疗保健	Health Care and Medical Services	1.4	2.9	6.9	9.8	6.7	6.6	6.6
交通和通信	Transport and Communications	1.5	4.7	7.1	14.7	17.2	15.6	15.7
教育文化娱乐服务	Education, Cultural and Entertainment Services	11.5	10.2	15.1	16.5	14.6	15.2	14.9
其他商品和服务	Qther Goods and Services	2.7	5.2	5.8	4.0	4.2	5.3	6.0
农村居民消费结构	Consumption Structure of Rural Residents							
食品(恩格尔系数)	Food (Engel Coefficient)	50.7	49.6	36.7	32.8	30.9	34.6	34.7
衣　着	Clothing	9.5	10.9	7.6	7.8	7.7	8.7	8.6
居　住	Housing	19.2	9.7	15.7	16.2	21.8	17.6	15.9
家庭设备用品及服务	Household Appliances and Services	8.0	7.6	7.3	6.2	5.6	6.6	7.4
医疗保健	Health Care and Medical Services	3.8	4.8	8.0	9.0	8.9	8.6	8.9
交通和通信	Transport and Communications	1.7	4.1	6.3	11.0	13.1	10.7	10.9
文教娱乐用品及服务	Education, Cultural and Entertainment Services	6.6	10.6	14.4	15.1	9.7	9.8	10.0
其他商品和服务	Qther Goods and Services	0.6	2.8	4.0	1.9	2.4	3.3	3.6
环　境	**Environment**							
林木绿化率	Green Area Coverage	28.3	36.3	42.0	50.5	53.0	57.4	58.4

1-13 国民经济和社会发展比例和效益指标
INDICATORS ON PROPORTIONS AND EFFICIENCY IN NATIONAL ECONOMIC AND SOCIAL DEVELOPMENT

项 目		Item		2014	2013
人口与就业		**Population and Employment**			
人 口		**Population**			
常住人口出生率	(‰)	Birth Rate of Permanent Population	(‰)	9.75	8.93
常住人口死亡率	(‰)	Death Rate of Permanent Population	(‰)	4.92	4.52
常住人口自然增长率	(‰)	Natural Growth Rate of Permanent Population	(‰)	4.83	4.41
就 业		**Employment**			
城镇登记失业率	(%)	Registered Unemployment Rate in Urban Areas	(%)	1.31	1.21
宏观经济		**Macro Economy**			
国民经济核算		**National Accounts**			
地区生产总值构成	(%)	Structure of Gross Domestic Product	(%)	100.0	100.0
第一产业		Primary Industry		0.7	0.8
第二产业		Secondary Industry		21.4	21.7
第三产业		Tertiary Industry		77.9	77.5
全社会劳动生产率	(元/人)	Overall Labor Productivity	(yuan/person)	185671	176140
第一产业		Primary Industry		29494	28330
第二产业		Secondary Industry		216013	202718
第三产业		Tertiary Industry		187973	179296
固定资产投资		**Fixed Asset Investment**			
全社会固定资产投资相当于地区生产总值比例	(%)	Proportion of Fixed Asset Investment to Gross Domestic Product	(%)	35.45	35.51
财 政		**Government Finance**			
地方财政收入相当于地区生产总值比例	(%)	Proportion of Local Finance Revenue to Gross Domestic Product	(%)	33.8	28.1
地方财政支出相当于地区生产总值比例	(%)	Proportion of Local Finance Expenditure to Gross Domestic Product	(%)	33.5	30.5
能源消费		**Energy Consumption**			
能源消费弹性系数		Energy Consumption Elasticity Coefficient		0.22	0.32
电力消费弹性系数		Electricity Consumption Elasticity Coefficient		0.37	0.51
万元地区生产总值能耗(可比价)	(吨标准煤)	Energy Consumption per 10000 yuan of GDP (Comparable Price)	(ton of SCE)	0.36	0.38
万元地区生产总值水耗(现价)	(立方米)	Water Consumption per 10000 yuan of GDP (Current Price)	(cu.m)	17.58	18.37
产 业		**Industry**			
规模以上工业企业效益		**Efficiency of Industrial Enterprises Above Designated Size**			
综合效益指数	(%)	General Efficiency Index	(%)	288.41	275.80
总资产贡献率	(%)	Total Asset Contribution Rate	(%)	8.23	7.79
资产保值增值率	(%)	Capital Maintenance and Appreciation Rate	(%)	112.32	105.93

注：本表有关地区生产总值、能源数据已根据2013年第三次全国经济普查数据进行了调整。
Note: In this table, Data of National Accounts, Energy Consumption for 2013 were adjusted acording to the third national economic census.

1-13 续表 Continued

项目		Item		2014	2013
资产负债率	(%)	Asset-liability Ratio	(%)	51.07	52.62
流动资产周转率	(次)	Turnover Rate of Working Capital	(time)	1.48	1.55
成本费用利润率	(%)	Ratio of Profits to Total Industrial Cost	(%)	8.11	7.24
全员劳动生产率	(元/人)	Overall Labor Productivity	(yuan/person)	309326	295513
产品销售率	(%)	Ratio of Sales to Gross Output Value	(%)	98.78	98.94
建筑业		**Construction**			
产值竣工率	(%)	Rate of Buildings Completed (by Output Value)	(%)	49.4	47.9
面积竣工率	(%)	Rate of Buildings Completed (by Floor Space)	(%)	16.4	18.2
邮电通信业		**Post and Communications**			
移动电话普及率	(户/百人)	Penetration Rate of Mobile Phone	(sets/100 persons)	232.2	159.5
固定电话主线普及率	(线/百人)	Penetration Rate of Main Line of Fixed Telephone	(line/100 persons)	39.3	41.0
国内贸易		**Domestic Trade**			
人均社会消费品零售总额	(元)	Per Capita Retail Sales of Consumer Goods	(yuan)	45181	42409
教育、科技、文化、卫生		**Education, Science and Technology, Culture and Health Care**			
教 育		**Education**			
学龄儿童入学率	(%)	Enrollment Rate of Children at School-Age	(%)	99.99	99.99
平均每一专任教师负担学生数		Average Number of Students Instructed by a Full-time Teacher			
#普通中学	(人)	Ordinary Secondary Education	(person)	9.0	9.5
小学学校	(人)	Primary Education	(person)	14.4	14.4
科 技		**Science and Technology**			
研究与试验发展经费内部支出相当于地区生产总值比例	(%)	Internal R&D Expenditures as % of GDP	(%)	5.95	5.98
文 化		**Culture**			
每万人拥有公共图书馆	(个)	Public Libraries per 10,000 persons	(library)	0.01	0.01
每万人拥有博物馆	(个)	Museums per 10,000 persons	(museum)	0.08	0.08
卫 生		**Health Care**			
婴儿死亡率	(‰)	Infant Mortality Rate	(‰)	2.33	2.33
孕产妇死亡率	(1/10万)	Maternal Mortality Rate	(1/100,000)	7.19	9.45
平均每千人口拥有执业医师数(常住人口)	(人)	Certified Doctors per 1,000 Persons (Permanent Resident)	(person)	4.16	4.06
家庭、生活、环境、灾害		**Household, Livelihood, Environment and Accidents**			
家 庭		**Household**			
少儿抚养比(常住人口)	(%)	Child-age Dependency Rate (Permanent Population)	(%)	12.34	11.64
老年抚养比(常住人口)	(%)	Old-age Dependency Rate (Permanent Population)	(%)	12.30	11.31
生 活		**Livelihood**			
城镇与农村居民收入比例(以农村居民收入为1)		Ratio of Urban Residents' Income to Rural Residents' Income (Rural Residents' Income = 1)		2.17	2.20
城镇居民人均住房建筑面积	(平方米)	Per Capita Living Space for Urban Residents	(sq.m)	31.54	31.31
农村居民人均住房面积	(平方米)	Per Capita Living Space for Rural Residents	(sq.m)	52.42	51.35
环境、灾害		**Environment and Accidents**			
人均公园绿地面积	(平方米)	Per Capita Park and Green Area	(sq.m)	15.9	15.7
平均每起火灾直接经济损失	(元)	Average Direct Losses per Fire Accident	(yuan)	15311	12496
平均每起交通事故直接经济损失	(元)	Average Direct Losses per Traffic Accident	(yuan)	9575	9158
重点食品安全监测抽检合格率	(%)	Up-to-standard Rate of Key Foods Security Monitor Spot Checks	(%)	98.39	98.35
药品抽验合格率	(%)	Up-to-standard Rate of Druy Spot Checks	(%)	99.88	99.88

1-14 北京一日
A DAY IN BEIJING

项 目		Item		2014	2013
每天创造的财富		**Daily Production**			
地区生产总值	(万元)	Gross Domestic Product	(10000 yuan)	584406.3	542487.9
第一产业		Primary Industry		4355.9	4373.7
第二产业		Secondary Industry		124515.1	117604.4
第三产业		Tertiary Industry		455535.3	420509.9
#批发和零售业		Wholesale and retail trade		66058.6	64129.9
信息传输、软件和信息技术服务业		Information transmission,software and information technology services		57038.4	50745.2
金融业		Finance		91992.1	80633.7
科学研究和技术服务业		Scientific research and development, technical services		45552.3	40349.9
地方财政收入	(万元)	Local Public Finance Budget Revenue	(10000 yuan)	197658.6	152495.4
地方财政支出	(万元)	Local Public Finance Budget Expenditure	(10000 yuan)	195828.7	165463.6
发电量	(万千瓦时)	Electricity Generated	(10000 kwh)	9275.9	9074.3
汽车生产量	(辆)	Output of Motor Vehicles	(vehicle)	5937	5584
移动电话机生产量	(台)	Output of Mobile Telephones	(set)	492701	514614
每天收入与消费量		**Daily Income and Consumption**			
城镇居民人均可支配收入	(元)	Per Capita Disposable Income of Urban Residents	(yuan)	120.3	110.5
城镇居民人均消费性支出	(元)	Per Capita Living Expenditures of Urban Residents	(yuan)	76.7	72.0
农村居民人均纯收入	(元)	Per Capita Net Income of Rural Residents	(yuan)	55.4	50.2
农村居民人均生活消费支出	(元)	Per Capita Living Expenditures of Rural Residents	(yuan)	39.8	37.1
城镇单位在岗职工平均工资	(元)	Average Wage of On-the-job Staff and Workers	(yuan)	283.3	257.5
社会消费品零售总额	(万元)	Retail Sales of Consumer Goods	(10000 yuan)	264054.8	243071.2
机动车销售量	(辆)	Sales of Motor Vehicles	(vehicle)	3493	3512
居民生活用电量	(万千瓦时)	Resident Electricity Use	(10000 kwh)	4637.3	4302.4
居民家庭用自来水	(万立方米)	Resident Tap Water Use	(10000 cu.m)	141.8	135.0
每天其他活动		**Other Daily Activities**			
地区出口值	(万美元)	Exports of Local Enterprises	(USD 10000)	17078.3	17287.0
旅游外汇收入	(万美元)	Foreign Exchange Earning from Tourism	(USD 10000)	1262.4	1313.6
国内旅游收入	(万元)	Domestic Tourism Earnings	(10000 yuan)	109506.3	100445.3
接待入境旅游人数	(人次)	Inbound Tourists	(person-time)	11711	12331
接待国内旅游者人数	(人次)	Domestic Tourists	(person-time)	704717	677776
市内公共交通客运量	(万人次)	Urban Public Transport Turnover	(10000 person-times)	2235.2	2204.9
每天人口和婚姻变动		**Daily Population and Marriage Changes**			
出生人口(常住人口)	(人)	Births (Permanent Residence)	(person)	570	512
死亡人口(常住人口)	(人)	Deaths (Permanent Residence)	(person)	287	259
登记结婚对数	(对)	Registered Marriages	(couple)	466	448
离婚对数	(对)	Divorces	(couple)	209	177

注：离婚对数包括在民政部门登记的对数和经法院调离和判离的对数。
Note: Divorces include those registered with civil affair authorities and those mediated and ruled in courts.

1-15 "十二五"时期经济社会发展主要监测指标
MAIN MONITORING INDICATORS OF SOCIAL AND ECONOMIC DEVELOPMENT IN THE TWELFTH FIVE-YEAR PLAN PERIOD

项目	Item	2014	2013
地区生产总值比上年增长 (%)	Growth Rate of GDP (%)	7.3	7.7
第三产业占地区生产总值比重 (%)	Tertiary Industry as % of GDP (%)	77.9	77.5
最终消费率 (%)	Final Consumption Rate (%)	62.5	61.4
地方公共财政预算收入比上年增长 (%)	Growth Rate of Local Public Finance Budget Revenue (%)	10.0	10.4
城镇居民人均可支配收入实际增长 (%)	Actual Growth Rate of Per-capita Disposable Income of Urban Residents (%)	7.2	7.1
农村居民人均纯收入实际增长 (%)	Actual Growth Rate of Per-capita Net Income of Rural Residents (%)	8.6	7.7
城镇登记失业率 (%)	Urban Registered Unemployment Rate (%)	1.31	1.21
65大类食品检验合格率 (%)	Up-to -standard Rate in Inspection on 65 Categories of Food (%)	97.46	97.41
#重点食品安全监测抽检合格率 (%)	Up-to-standard Rate of Key Foods Security	98.39	98.35
药品抽验合格率 (%)	Up-to-standard Rate of Drug Spot Checks (%)	99.88	99.88
全社会研究与试验发展经费支出占地区生产总值的比例 (%)	R&D Expenditure as % of GDP (%)	5.95	5.98
万元地区生产总值能耗降低 (%)	Decrease of Energy Consumption per 10000 yuan of GDP (%)	5.29	4.88
万元地区生产总值水耗降低 (%)	Decrease of Water Consumption per 10000 yuan of GDP (%)	3.93	5.87
林木绿化率 (%)	Green Area Coverage (%)	58.4	57.4

主要统计指标解释

法人单位　指有权拥有资产、承担负债，并独立从事社会经济活动（或与其他单位进行交易）的组织。法人单位应同时具备以下条件：（1）依法成立，有自己的名称、组织机构和场所，能够独立承担民事责任；（2）独立拥有（或授权使用）资产或者经费，承担负债，有权与其他单位签订合同；（3）具有包括资产负债表在内的账户，或者能够根据需要编制账户。

单产业法人　指仅包含一个产业活动单位的法人单位，该法人单位同时也是一个产业活动单位。

多产业法人　指由两个及以上产业活动单位组成的法人单位，这些产业活动单位接受法人单位的管理和控制。

登记注册类型　企业法人或企业产业活动单位的登记注册类型，按其在工商行政管理机关登记注册的类型填写。如企业登记注册类型发生变化，但未及时到工商部门变更登记，企业应根据变化后的实际情况填写。其他法人和产业活动单位的登记注册类型，按其主要经费来源和管理方式，根据实际情况，比照《企业登记注册类型与代码》填写。

国有企业　指企业全部资产归国家所有，并按《中华人民共和国企业法人登记管理条例》规定登记注册的非公司制的经济组织。不包括有限责任公司中的国有独资公司。

集体企业　指企业资产归集体所有，并按《中华人民共和国企业法人登记管理条例》规定登记注册的经济组织。

股份合作企业　指以合作制为基础，由企业职工共同出资入股，吸收一定比例的社会资产投资组建，实行自主经营，自负盈亏，共同劳动，民主管理，按劳分配与按股分红相结合的一种集体经济组织。

联营企业　指两个及两个以上相同或不同所有制性质的企业法人或事业单位法人，按自愿、平等、互利的原则，共同投资组成的经济组织称为联营企业。联营企业包括国有联营企业、集体联营企业、国有与集体联营企业和其他联营企业。

有限责任公司　指根据《中华人民共和国公司登记管理条例》规定登记注册，由两个以上，五十个以下的股东共同出资，每个股东以其所认缴的出资额对公司承担有限责任，公司以其全部资产对其债务承担责任的经济组织。有限责任公司包括国有独资公司、其他有限责任公司。

私营企业　指由自然人投资设立或由自然人控股，以雇佣劳动为基础的营利性经济组织。包括按照《公司法》、《合伙企业法》、《私营企业暂行条例》、《个人独资企业法》规定登记注册的私营独资企业、私营合伙企业、私营有限责任公司、私营股份有限公司和个人独资企业。

其他企业　指上述类型之外的其他内资经济组织。

港澳台商投资企业　指港澳台地区投资者依照中华人民共和国有关涉外经济的法律、法规成立的企业，包括与港澳台商合资经营企业、与港澳台商合作经营企业、港澳台商独资经营企业、港澳台商投资股份有限公司、其他港澳台商投资企业。

外商投资企业　指外国企业或外国人依照中华人民共和国有关涉外经济的法律、法规成立的企业，包括中外合资经营企业、中外合作经营企业、外资企业、外商投资股份有限公司、其他外商投资企业。

非公经济　指资产由我国私人控股、港澳台商控股、外商控股的“非公有控股”的企业法人单位，以及主要经费来源于私人、港澳台资和外资的非企业法人单位和个体工商户。其中，私人、港澳台及外商控股是指由其绝对控股和相对控股的经济成分。

Explanatory Notes on Main Statistical Indicators

Legal Entity refers to any organization that has the right to own assets and bear liabilities, and conducts social and economic activities independently (or conducts transactions with other entities). A business entity shall meet all of such conditions as: (1) established in accordance with law, having its own name, organization and site, capable of assuming civil responsibilities independently; (2) independently owning and using (or using under authorization) assets or outlays, assuming liabilities, having the right to sign contracts with other entities; (3) maintaining accounts including balance sheet, or capable of preparing accounts as needed.

Single-industry Legal Entity refers any business entity conducting only one industrial activity. Such business entity is also an industrial activity entity.

Multi-industry Legal Entity refers to any business entity composed of two or more industrial activity entities which are managed and controlled by the business entity.

Registration type of an enterprise as legal person or as industrial activity entity shall be completed according to the type registered at the administration for industry and commerce. In the event of any change in registration type, and no registration alteration is made with administration for industry and commerce in good time, the registration type shall be completed according to the actual situation. Registration type for other legal persons and industrial activity entities shall be completed according to the main source of outlays and management manner, pursuant to the actual conditions, and by referring to the *Type of Enterprise Registration and Code*.

State-owned Enterprise refers to non-corporation economic organizations where the entire assets are owned by the state and which have registered in accordance with the *Regulation of the People's Republic of China on the Management of Registration of Corporate Enterprises*, excluding solely state-funded corporations in limited liability companies.

Collectively-owned Enterprise refer to economic organizations where the assets are owned collectively and which have registered in accordance with the *Regulation of the People's Republic of China on the Management of Registration of Corporate Enterprises*.

Joint-equity Cooperative Enterprise refers to a form of collective economic organizations based on cooperative system, where capitals come mainly from employees as their shares, with certain proportion of capital from the public, where production is organized on the basis of independent operation, independent accounting for profits and losses, joint work, democratic management, and where the distribution system integrates distribution according to work with distribution according to capital share.

Associated Enterprise refers to organizations established by two or more corporate legal persons or institutional legal persons of the same or different ownership, through joint investment on the basis of equality, voluntary participation and mutual benefits. They include state-owned associated enterprises, collectively-owned associated enterprises, state-collective associated enterprises and other associated enterprises.

Limited Liability Company refers to organizations established with investment from 2-50 shareholders and registered in accordance with the *Regulation of the People's Republic of China on the Management of Registration of Corporations*, each shareholder bearing limited liability to the corporation depending on its share of investment, and the corporation bearing liability to its debt to the maximum of its total assets. Limited liability companies include solely state-funded limited liability companies and other limited liability companies.

Private Enterprise refers to profit-making organizations established by natural persons or controlled by natural persons using employed labor. Private enterprises include solely private-funded enterprises, private partnership enterprises, private limited liability companies, private companies limited by shares, and private-funded enterprises registered in accordance with provisions in the *Corporation Law*, *Partnership Enterprises Law*, *Interim Regulations on Private Enterprises* and *Sole Proprietorship Enterprise Law*.

Other Enterprise refers to domestically funded organizations other than those mentioned above.

Hong Kong, Macao and Taiwan-invested Enterprise refers to enterprises established by investors from Hong Kong, Macao and Taiwan in accordance with laws and rules of the People's Republic of China on foreign-related businesses. They include joint ventures with investors from Hong Kong, Macao and Taiwan, cooperative enterprises with investors from Hong Kong, Macao and Taiwan, enterprises wholly funded by investors from Hong Kong, Macao and Taiwan, companies limited by shares and funded by investors from Hong Kong, Macao and Taiwan, and other enterprises funded by investors from Hong Kong, Macao and Taiwan.

Foreign-invested Enterprise refers to enterprises

established by foreign enterprises or foreigners in accordance with laws and regulations of the People's Republic of China on foreign-related businesses. They include Sino-foreign joint ventures, Sino-foreign cooperative enterprises, foreign wholly-funded enterprises, foreign-funded companies limited by shares, and other foreign-funded enterprises.

Non-public Economy means enterprises as business entities whose shares are controlled by "non-public entities" and whose assets are controlled by individuals, investors from Hong Kong, Macao and Taiwan, and foreign investors, along with enterprises not as business entities and self-employed operators whose main funds are from individuals, investors from Hong Kong, Macao and Taiwan, and foreign investors. Here, enterprises controlled by individuals, investors from Hong Kong, Macao and Taiwan, and foreign investors mean economic sectors with absolute or relative control by such companies.

02

国民经济核算
NATIONAL ACCOUNTS

简 要 说 明

一、本章资料的主要内容

本章主要包括历年北京市地区生产总值、部分新兴产业增加值、各行业增加值、居民消费水平、全社会劳动生产率、三次产业的贡献率等资料。其中，地区生产总值是由北京市统计局根据统计资料、会计资料和部门财务资料采用不同方法核算的数据。

二、本章中关于历史数据调整的问题

本章中 1997–2008 年地区生产总值的数据及其分组资料，按照国家统一规定，根据“北京市第二次全国经济普查”和“北京市第二次全国农业普查”的数据结果进行了修正。

2006–2010 年人均地区生产总值数据根据全国第六次人口普查数据进行了修正。

2013 年数据为第三次全国经济普查数据。

三、有关统计标准的变化说明

（一）关于行业划分。根据国家统计局规定，执行《国民经济行业分类》GB/T 4754–2011 标准。

（二）关于三次产业划分。根据国家统计局《三次产业划分规定》（国统字[2012]108 号），对三次产业的范围进行了调整。第一产业是指农、林、牧、渔业（不含农、林、牧、渔服务业）；第二产业是指采矿业（不含开采辅助活动），制造业（不含金属制品、机械和设备修理业），电力、热力、燃气及水生产和供应业，建筑业；第三产业是指除第一产业、第二产业以外的其他行业。

Brief Introduction

I. Main Content

Statistics in this chapter include the GDP of Beijing, added value of some emerging sectors, added value of different sectors, residents' consumption level, total productivity, contribution rate of three industries in previous years. Among them, the GDP of Beijing is calculated by Beijing Municipal Bureau of Statistics using different measures according to statistical data, accounting data and financial data of different sectors.

II. Adjustment to Historical Statistics

Figures of GDP 1997-2008 and grouping data have been corrected in accordance with the national uniform regulation and the results of "the 2nd National Economic Census in Beijing" and "the 2nd National Agricultural Census in Beijing".

2006-2010 per-capita GDP figures were adjusted according to figures from the 6th national census.

The data of 2013 was adjusted to be the statistics for the 3rd National Economic Census.

Ⅲ. Explanation on Changes of Statistical Standards

(I) Industrial Classification. As regulated by National Bureau of Statistics, *Classification of National Economic Sectors* Standard GB/T 4754-2011 shall be adopted and accounting shall follow the standards.

(II) Classification of Three Industries. According to *Regulations on Three Industries Classification* (G.T.Z. [2012] No. 108) of National Bureau of Statistics, the scope of three industries has been adjusted. The primary industry refers to agriculture, forestry, animal production and hunting, fishing (excluding service activities for agriculture, forestry, animal production and hunting, fishing); secondary industry refers to mining and quarrying (excluding mining support service activities), manufacturing (excluding repair of fabricated metal products, machinery and equipment), production and distribution of electricity, heating power, gas and water and construction; the tertiary industry refers to others excluding the primary and secondary industries.

2-1 地区生产总值(1978-2014年)
GROSS DOMESTIC PRODUCT (1978-2014)

单位：亿元 (100 million yuan)

年份 Year	地区生产总值 Gross Domestic Product	按产业分组 By Three Industies 第一产业 Primary Industry	第二产业 Secondary Industry	第三产业 Tertiary Industry	按行业分组 By Sector #工业 Industry	#建筑业 Construction	人均地区生产总值(元/人) Per Capita Gross Domestic Product (yuan/person)	人均地区生产总值(美元/人) Per Capita Gross Domestic Product (USD/person)
1978	108.8	5.6	77.2	26.0	70.2	7.2	1257	797
1979	120.1	5.2	85.0	29.9	77.4	7.8	1358	908
1980	139.1	6.1	95.6	37.4	86.9	8.9	1544	1009
1981-1985	**950.9**	**61.9**	**588.4**	**300.6**	**515.5**	**73.9**		
1981	139.2	6.6	92.3	40.3	82.7	9.8	1526	895
1982	154.9	10.2	99.6	45.1	89.3	10.5	1671	883
1983	183.1	12.7	112.5	57.9	98.8	13.9	1943	983
1984	216.6	14.7	130.5	71.4	114.0	16.7	2262	972
1985	257.1	17.7	153.5	85.9	130.7	23.0	2643	900
1986-1990	**1978.7**	**162.1**	**1082.5**	**734.1**	**917.3**	**167.0**		
1986	284.9	19.0	165.6	100.3	141.2	24.6	2836	821
1987	326.8	24.2	182.2	120.4	154.5	28.1	3150	846
1988	410.2	36.9	220.9	152.4	189.5	31.8	3892	1046
1989	456.0	38.3	251.8	165.9	212.8	39.4	4269	1134
1990	500.8	43.7	262.0	195.1	219.3	43.1	4635	969
1991-1995	**4847.2**	**286.4**	**2213.0**	**2347.8**	**1833.5**	**386.9**		
1991	598.9	45.5	290.5	262.9	255.6	35.9	5494	1032
1992	709.1	48.7	344.7	315.7	293.0	52.9	6458	1171
1993	886.2	53.2	418.2	414.8	339.2	80.4	8006	1389
1994	1145.3	66.8	516.0	562.5	417.9	99.7	10240	1188
1995	1507.7	72.2	643.6	791.9	527.8	118.0	12690	1520
1996-2000	**12084.0**	**378.6**	**4263.3**	**7442.1**	**3450.5**	**827.2**		
1996	1789.2	73.4	712.3	1003.5	576.2	138.5	14254	1714
1997	2077.1	75.5	779.2	1222.4	635.9	145.9	16621	2005
1998	2377.2	76.1	838.0	1463.1	670.4	170.2	19128	2310
1999	2678.8	76.3	904.5	1698.0	724.0	183.3	21407	2586
2000	3161.7	77.3	1029.3	2055.1	844.0	189.3	24127	2915
2001-2005	**26032.9**	**412.4**	**7727.9**	**17892.6**	**6446.2**	**1313.5**		
2001	3708.0	78.6	1137.1	2492.3	938.8	203.6	26980	3260
2002	4315.0	80.5	1245.7	2988.8	1021.2	228.8	30730	3713
2003	5007.2	81.8	1482.4	3443.0	1224.5	262.7	34777	4202
2004	6033.2	85.3	1845.5	4102.4	1554.7	298.9	40916	4943
2005	6969.5	86.2	2017.2	4866.1	1707.0	319.5	45993	5615
2006-2010	**55346.2**	**535.7**	**13394.6**	**41415.9**	**11103.4**	**2467.7**		
2006	8117.8	85.4	2177.9	5854.5	1821.8	369.6	51722	6488
2007	9846.8	99.4	2493.9	7253.5	2082.8	426.6	60096	7903
2008	11115.0	111.4	2592.9	8410.7	2131.7	494.7	64491	9286
2009	12153.0	116.8	2804.2	9232.0	2303.1	552.4	66940	9799
2010	14113.6	122.7	3325.7	10665.2	2764.0	624.4	73856	10910
2011	16251.9	134.4	3678.0	12439.5	3048.8	703.7	81658	12643
2012	17879.4	148.1	3962.6	13768.7	3294.3	765.0	87475	13857
2013	19800.8	159.6	4292.6	15348.6	3566.4	831.6	94648	15284
2014	21330.8	159.0	4544.8	16627.0	3746.8	902.7	99995	16278

注：1. 本表数据按当年价格计算。2013年数据为第三次全国经济普查数据。
2. 2013年开始，地区生产总值行业划分执行《国民经济行业分类》GB/T 4754-2011标准。
3. 2013年开始，地区生产总值三次产业划分执行国家统计局《三次产业划分规定》(国统字[2012]108号)，并对本表1978-2012年以来三次产业数据进行相应调整。
4. 人均地区生产总值按年平均常住人口计算，2011年根据全国第六次人口普查数据对2006年至2010年人均地区生产总值进行了调整（下同）。

Note: a) Figures in this table are calculated at current year's prices.Data for 2013 were collected from the third national economic census.
b) Since 2013, GDP industrial classification has been subjected to Classification of National Economic Sectors Standard GB/T 4754-2011.
c) Since 2013, GDP three sector classification has been subject to Regulations on Three Industries Classification (G.T.Z. [2012] No. 108) issued by National Bureau of Statistics, according to which data on the three industries from 1978 to 2012 was adjusted in this table.
d) Per capita GDP is calculated at average permamnent population. In 2011,per capita GDP 2006-2010 were adjusted according to the 6th National Population Census (the same below).

2-2 地区生产总值指数(上年=100)(1978-2014年)
INDICES OF GROSS DOMESTIC PRODUCT (PRECEDING YEAR=100) (1978-2014)

单位：% (%)

年份 Year	地区生产总值 Gross Domestic Product	按产业分组 By Three Industies			按行业分组 By Sector		人均地区生产总值 Per Capita Gross Domestic Product
		第一产业 Primary Industry	第二产业 Secondary Industry	第三产业 Tertiary Industry	#工业 Industry	#建筑业 Construction	
1978	110.5	109.0	115.1	97.7	112.4	153.0	109.1
1979	109.7	105.0	109.2	113.2	110.1	108.4	107.4
1980	111.8	109.3	110.1	118.5	110.1	110.3	109.8
1981	99.5	109.1	96.3	106.0	95.3	106.4	98.3
1982	107.4	113.4	105.8	109.9	105.8	106.1	105.6
1983	116.4	107.5	113.6	124.2	111.5	132.3	114.5
1984	117.4	106.8	116.1	121.8	115.7	118.8	115.6
1985	108.7	106.3	111.0	104.4	109.1	124.7	106.9
1986	108.0	100.1	104.8	115.7	105.0	103.7	104.6
1987	109.6	113.4	105.6	116.7	105.5	106.3	106.1
1988	112.8	111.2	112.1	114.1	113.0	106.5	111.0
1989	104.4	101.1	108.9	97.3	108.4	112.2	103.1
1990	105.2	103.3	101.1	113.3	101.9	95.6	104.0
1991	109.9	103.7	107.5	114.5	112.6	81.6	108.9
1992	111.3	103.1	112.2	111.9	110.3	125.7	110.5
1993	112.3	103.2	113.0	113.1	110.5	128.5	111.4
1994	113.7	102.8	114.1	115.0	113.5	117.0	112.5
1995	112.0	92.0	107.7	120.5	107.7	107.6	105.4
1996	109.0	97.2	106.2	113.4	106.1	107.0	103.1
1997	110.1	102.9	108.1	113.2	108.7	105.1	110.6
1998	109.5	101.1	109.6	110.1	108.7	114.2	110.1
1999	110.9	102.8	112.0	110.6	112.8	108.0	110.1
2000	111.8	103.1	111.4	112.9	113.2	102.1	106.8
2001	111.7	103.7	109.5	113.1	110.2	106.6	106.5
2002	111.5	102.7	108.4	113.3	107.8	110.9	109.1
2003	111.1	98.9	112.0	111.2	112.2	110.7	108.3
2004	114.1	99.4	117.0	113.1	119.3	106.3	111.4
2005	112.1	98.1	110.1	113.4	110.9	106.3	109.1
2006	113.0	100.6	110.5	114.3	109.5	116.0	109.1
2007	114.5	102.2	112.7	115.4	113.1	110.9	109.7
2008	109.1	101.1	100.8	112.5	100.2	103.7	103.7
2009	110.2	104.6	110.4	110.2	108.8	118.5	104.6
2010	110.3	98.4	113.7	109.3	114.9	108.3	104.8
2011	108.1	100.9	106.7	108.7	107.5	102.9	103.8
2012	107.7	103.2	107.5	107.9	107.0	109.7	104.9
2013	107.7	103.0	108.1	107.6	107.8	109.7	105.2
2014	107.3	100.0	106.9	107.5	106.0	110.2	105.2

注：1. 本表数据按可比价格计算。
2. 2013年数据为第三次全国经济普查数据。

Note: a) Statistics in this table are calculated at comparable prices.
b) Data for 2013 were collected from the third national economic census.

2-3 地区生产总值指数(1978年=100)(1978-2014年)
INDICES OF GROSS DOMESTIC PRODUCT (YEAR OF 1978=100) (1978-2014)

单位：% (%)

年 份 Year	地区生产总值 Gross Domestic Product	按产业分组 By Three Industies 第一产业 Primary Industry	第二产业 Secondary Industry	第三产业 Tertiary Industry	按行业分组 By Sector #工业 Industry	#建筑业 Construction	人均地区生产总值 Per Capita Gross Domestic Product
1978	100.0	100.0	100.0	100.0	100.0	100.0	100.0
1979	109.7	105.0	109.2	113.2	110.1	108.4	107.4
1980	122.6	114.8	120.2	134.1	121.2	119.6	117.9
1981	122.0	125.2	115.8	142.2	115.5	127.2	115.9
1982	131.1	142.0	122.5	156.3	122.2	135.0	122.4
1983	152.6	152.6	139.2	194.1	136.3	178.6	140.2
1984	179.1	163.0	161.6	236.4	157.7	212.1	162.0
1985	194.7	173.3	179.3	246.8	172.0	264.5	173.2
1986	210.3	173.5	187.9	285.5	180.6	274.3	181.2
1987	230.4	196.7	198.5	333.2	190.6	291.6	192.2
1988	259.9	218.7	222.5	380.2	215.3	310.6	213.4
1989	271.4	221.1	242.3	369.9	233.4	348.5	220.0
1990	285.5	228.4	244.9	419.2	237.9	333.1	228.8
1991	313.8	236.9	263.3	479.9	267.8	271.8	249.1
1992	349.2	244.2	295.4	537.0	295.4	341.7	275.3
1993	392.2	252.0	333.8	607.4	326.4	439.1	306.7
1994	445.9	259.1	380.9	698.5	370.5	513.7	345.0
1995	499.4	238.4	410.2	841.7	399.0	552.8	363.7
1996	544.3	231.7	435.7	954.5	423.4	591.5	374.9
1997	599.3	238.4	471.0	1080.5	460.2	621.7	414.6
1998	656.2	241.0	516.2	1189.6	500.2	710.0	456.5
1999	727.7	247.7	578.1	1315.7	564.2	766.8	502.8
2000	813.6	255.4	644.0	1485.4	638.7	782.9	536.8
2001	908.8	264.8	705.2	1680.0	703.8	834.6	571.7
2002	1013.3	271.9	764.4	1903.4	758.7	925.6	623.9
2003	1125.8	268.9	856.1	2115.9	851.3	1024.6	676.0
2004	1284.5	267.3	1001.6	2393.1	1015.6	1089.1	753.1
2005	1440.3	262.2	1102.8	2714.9	1126.3	1157.7	821.5
2006	1627.5	263.8	1218.6	3102.0	1233.3	1342.9	896.3
2007	1863.3	269.6	1373.4	3580.0	1394.9	1489.3	983.2
2008	2033.0	272.6	1384.4	4027.6	1397.7	1544.4	1019.6
2009	2240.4	285.2	1528.7	4437.6	1520.8	1829.4	1066.5
2010	2471.2	280.6	1738.1	4850.3	1747.4	1981.2	1117.7
2011	2671.4	283.1	1854.6	5272.3	1878.5	2038.7	1160.2
2012	2877.1	292.2	1993.7	5688.8	2010.0	2236.5	1217.0
2013	3098.6	301.0	2155.2	6121.1	2166.8	2453.4	1280.3
2014	3324.8	301.0	2303.9	6580.2	2296.8	2703.6	1346.9

注：1. 本表数据按可比价格计算。
2. 2013年数据为第三次全国经济普查数据。

Note: a) Statistics in this table are calculated at comparable prices.
b) Data for 2013 were collected from the third national economic census.

2-4 地区生产总值构成(1978-2014年)
COMPOSITION OF GROSS DOMESTIC PRODUCT (1978-2014)

单位：% (%)

年 份 Year	地区生产总值 Gross Domestic Product	按产业分组 By Three Industies			按行业分组 By Sector	
		第一产业 Primary Industry	第二产业 Secondary Industry	第三产业 Tertiary Industry	#工业 Industry	#建筑业 Construction
1978	100.0	5.1	71.0	23.9	64.5	6.6
1979	100.0	4.3	70.8	24.9	64.4	6.5
1980	100.0	4.4	68.7	26.9	62.5	6.4
1981	100.0	4.7	66.3	29.0	59.4	7.1
1982	100.0	6.6	64.3	29.1	57.6	6.8
1983	100.0	6.9	61.4	31.7	53.9	7.6
1984	100.0	6.8	60.2	33.0	52.6	7.7
1985	100.0	6.9	59.7	33.4	50.8	9.0
1986	100.0	6.7	58.1	35.2	49.6	8.6
1987	100.0	7.4	55.8	36.8	47.3	8.6
1988	100.0	9.0	53.9	37.1	46.2	7.8
1989	100.0	8.4	55.2	36.4	46.7	8.6
1990	100.0	8.7	52.3	39.0	43.8	8.6
1991	100.0	7.6	48.5	43.9	42.7	6.0
1992	100.0	6.9	48.6	44.5	41.3	7.5
1993	100.0	6.0	47.2	46.8	38.3	9.0
1994	100.0	5.8	45.1	49.1	36.5	8.7
1995	100.0	4.8	42.7	52.5	35.0	7.8
1996	100.0	4.1	39.8	56.1	32.2	7.7
1997	100.0	3.6	37.5	58.9	30.6	7.0
1998	100.0	3.2	35.3	61.5	28.2	7.2
1999	100.0	2.8	33.8	63.4	27.0	6.9
2000	100.0	2.4	32.6	65.0	26.7	6.0
2001	100.0	2.1	30.7	67.2	25.3	5.5
2002	100.0	1.9	28.9	69.2	23.7	5.3
2003	100.0	1.6	29.6	68.8	24.5	5.2
2004	100.0	1.4	30.6	68.0	25.8	5.0
2005	100.0	1.2	28.9	69.9	24.5	4.6
2006	100.0	1.1	26.8	72.1	22.4	4.6
2007	100.0	1.0	25.3	73.7	21.2	4.3
2008	100.0	1.0	23.3	75.7	19.2	4.4
2009	100.0	1.0	23.1	75.9	19.0	4.5
2010	100.0	0.9	23.6	75.5	19.6	4.4
2011	100.0	0.8	22.6	76.6	18.8	4.3
2012	100.0	0.8	22.2	77.0	18.4	4.3
2013	100.0	0.8	21.7	77.5	18.0	4.2
2014	100.0	0.7	21.4	77.9	17.6	4.2

注：1. 2013年数据为第三次全国经济普查数据。
2. 2013年开始，地区生产总值行业划分执行《国民经济行业分类》GB/T 4754-2011标准。
3. 2013年开始，地区生产总值三次产业划分执行国家统计局《三次产业划分规定》(国统字[2012]108号)，并对本表1978-2012年以来三次产业数据进行相应调整。

Note: a) Data for 2013 were collected from the third national economic census.
b) Since 2013, GDP industrial classification has been subjected to Classification of National Economic Sectors Standard GB/T 4757-2011.
c) Since 2013, GDP three sector classification has been subject to Regulations on Three Industries Classification (G.T.Z. [2012] No. 108) issued by National Bureau of Statistics, according to which data on the three industries from 1978 to 2012 was adjusted in this table.

2-5 地区生产总值指数(2000年=100)(2000-2014年)
INDICES OF GROSS DOMESTIC PRODUCT (YEAR OF 2000=100) (2000-2014)

单位：% (%)

年 份 Year	地区生产总值 Gross Domestic Product	按产业分组 By Three Industies			按行业分组 By Sector		人均地区生产总值 Per Capita Gross Domestic Product
		第一产业 Primary Industry	第二产业 Secondary Industry	第三产业 Tertiary Industry	#工业 Industry	#建筑业 Construction	
2000	100.0	100.0	100.0	100.0	100.0	100.0	100.0
2001	111.7	103.7	109.5	113.1	110.2	106.6	106.5
2002	124.5	106.5	118.7	128.1	118.8	118.2	116.2
2003	138.3	105.3	132.9	142.4	133.3	130.8	125.9
2004	157.8	104.7	155.5	161.1	159.0	139.0	140.3
2005	176.9	102.7	171.2	182.8	176.3	147.8	153.0
2006	199.9	103.3	189.2	208.9	193.0	171.4	166.9
2007	228.9	105.6	213.2	241.1	218.3	190.1	183.1
2008	249.8	106.8	214.9	271.2	218.7	197.1	189.9
2009	275.3	111.7	237.3	298.8	238.0	233.5	198.6
2010	303.7	109.9	269.8	326.6	273.5	252.9	208.1
2011	328.3	110.9	287.9	355.0	294.0	260.2	216.0
2012	353.6	114.4	309.5	383.0	314.6	285.4	226.6
2013	380.8	117.8	334.6	412.1	339.1	313.1	238.4
2014	408.6	117.8	357.7	443.0	359.4	345.0	250.8

注：1. 本表数据按可比价格计算。
2. 2013年数据为第三次全国经济普查数据。

Note: a) Statistics in this table are calculated at comparable prices.
b) Data for 2013 were collected from the third national economic census.

2-6 按行业分地区生产总值
GROSS DOMESTIC PRODUCT BY SECTOR

单位：亿元 (100 million yuan)

项目	Item	2014	2013
地区生产总值	**Gross Domestic Product**	**21330.8**	**19800.8**
按产业分组	**By there industies**		
第一产业	Primary Industry	159.0	159.6
第二产业	Secondary Industry	4544.8	4292.6
第三产业	Tertiary Industry	16627.0	15348.6
按行业分组	**By Sector**		
农、林、牧、渔业	Agriculture, Forestry, Animal Production and Hunting, Fishing	161.3	161.8
采矿业	Mining and Quarrying	176.2	171.2
制造业	Manufacturing	2823.2	2745.2
电力、热力、燃气及水生产和供应业	Production and Distribution of Electricity,Heating Power, Gas and Water	747.4	650.0
建筑业	Construction	902.7	831.6
批发和零售业	Wholesale and Retail Trade	2411.1	2340.7
交通运输、仓储和邮政业	Transport, Storage and Post	948.1	871.8
住宿和餐饮业	Accommodation and Restaurants	363.8	374.8
信息传输、软件和信息技术服务业	Information Transmission,Software and Information Technology Services	2081.9	1852.2
金融业	Finance	3357.7	2943.1
房地产业	Real Estate	1329.2	1339.5
租赁和商务服务业	Renting and Leasing Activities and Business Services	1700.2	1566.5
科学研究和技术服务业	Scientific Research and Development, Technical Services	1662.7	1472.8
水利、环境和公共设施管理业	Management of Water Conservancy, Environment and Public Facilities	136.0	120.1
居民服务、修理和其他服务业	Resident Services, Repair and Other Services	155.0	139.9
教育	Education	859.0	770.5
卫生和社会工作	Health Care and Social Works	468.1	416.1
文化、体育和娱乐业	Culture, Sports and Entertainment	470.4	450.3
公共管理、社会保障和社会组织	Pulic Administration,Social Security and Social Organizations	576.8	582.7
国际组织	International Organizations		

注：1. 本表数据按当年价格计算。2013年数据为第三次全国经济普查数据。
2. 2013年开始，地区生产总值行业划分执行《国民经济行业分类》GB/T 4754-2011标准。
3. 2013年开始，地区生产总值三次产业划分执行国家统计局《三次产业划分规定》(国统字[2012]108号)。

Note: a) Figures in this table are calculated at current year's prices.Data for 2013 were collected from the third national economic census.
b) Since 2013, GDP industrial classification has been subjected to Classification of National Economic Sectors Standard GB/T 4754-2011.
c) Since 2013, GDP three sector classification has been subject to Regulations on Three Industries Classification (G.T.Z. [2012] No. 108) issued by National Bureau of Statistics.

2-7 按行业分地区生产总值指数(上年=100)
INDICES OF GROSE DOMESFIC PRODUCT BY SECTOR (PRECEDING YEAR=100)

单位：% (%)

项 目	Item	2014	2013
地区生产总值	**Gross Domestic Product**	**107.3**	**107.7**
按产业分组	**By Three Industies**		
第一产业	Primary Industry	100.0	103.0
第二产业	Secondary Industry	106.9	108.1
第三产业	Tertiary Industry	107.5	107.6
按行业分组	**By Sector**		
农、林、牧、渔业	Agriculture, Forestry, Animal Production and Hunting, Fishing	100.0	103.0
采矿业	Mining and Quarrying	98.2	103.1
制造业	Manufacturing	107.6	108.6
电力、热力、燃气及水生产和供应业	Production and Distribution of Electricity,Heating Power, Gas and Water	101.8	106.2
建筑业	Construction	110.2	109.7
批发和零售业	Wholesale and Retail Trade	105.0	106.5
交通运输、仓储和邮政业	Transport, Storage and Post	106.8	107.0
住宿和餐饮业	Accommodation and Restaurants	99.1	96.8
信息传输、软件和信息技术服务业	Information Transmission,Software and Information Technology Services	111.9	107.3
金融业	Finance	112.7	111.1
房地产业	Real Estate	97.8	103.4
租赁和商务服务业	Renting and Leasing Activities and Business Services	105.8	109.5
科学研究和技术服务业	Scientific Research and Development, Technical Services	111.1	111.3
水利、环境和公共设施管理业	Management of Water Conservancy, Environment and Public Facilities	111.4	105.4
居民服务、修理和其他服务业	Resident Services, Repair and Other Services	112.8	103.1
教 育	Education	109.7	106.9
卫生和社会工作	Health Care and Social Works	110.7	111.5
文化、体育和娱乐业	Culture, Sports and Entertainment	101.9	106.1
公共管理、社会保障和社会组织	Pulic Administration,Social Security and Social Organizations	97.4	102.2
国际组织	International Organizations		

注：1. 本表数据按可比价格计算。2013年数据为第三次全国经济普查数据。
2. 2013年开始，地区生产总值行业划分执行《国民经济行业分类》GB/T 4754-2011标准。
3. 2013年开始，地区生产总值三次产业划分执行国家统计局《三次产业划分规定》(国统字[2012]108号).

Note: a) Figures in this table are calculated at comparable prices.Data for 2013 were collected from the third national economic census.
b) Since 2013, GDP industrial classification has been subjected to Classification of National Economic Sectors Standard GB/T 4754-2011.
c) Since 2013, GDP three sector classification has been subject to Regulations on Three Industries Classification (G.T.Z. [2012] No. 108) issued by National Bureau of Statistics.

2-8 部分新兴产业增加值
ADDED VALUE OF SOME EMERGING INDUSTRIES

单位：亿元 (100 million yuan)

项 目	Item	2014	2013
地区生产总值	**Gross Domestic Product**	**21330.8**	**19800.8**
文化创意产业	**Cultural and Creative Industry**	**2826.3**	**2578.1**
文化艺术	Culture and Arts	115.6	96.7
新闻出版	Journalism and Publishing	239.7	241.4
广播、电视、电影	Radio Broadcasting, Television and Movies	200.3	191.1
软件、网络及计算机服务	Software, Internet and Computer Services	1605.2	1421.8
广告会展	Advertising and Exhibitions	220.2	206.0
艺术品交易	Artwork Trading	56.2	60.5
设计服务	Design Service	127.7	130.6
旅游、休闲娱乐	Tourism, Leisure and Entertainment	99.7	94.1
其他辅助服务	Other Auxiliary Service	161.7	135.9
信息产业	**Information Industry**	**3172.2**	**2855.2**
电子信息设备制造	Manufacture of Electronic Information Equipment	398.8	406.3
电子信息设备销售和租赁	Sales and Renting of Electronic Information Equipment	339.3	256.3
电子信息传输服务	Electronic Information Transmission Service	833.8	680.1
计算机服务和软件业	Computer Service and Software	1248.1	1172.1
其他信息相关服务	Other Information-related Service	352.2	340.4
高技术产业	**High-tech Industry**	**4738.5**	**4291.5**
医药制造业	Manufacture of Medicines	269.3	263.3
航空、航天器及设备制造业	Manufacture of Aircrafts and Spacecrafts	58.8	57.1
电子及通信设备制造业	Manufacture of Electronic and Communication Equipment	294.2	291.6
计算机及办公设备制造业	Manufacture of Computers and Office Equipments	50.9	56.5
医疗仪器设备及仪器仪表制造业	Manufacture of Medical Equipments and Meters	126.4	127.5
信息化学品制造业	Information Chemical Manufacturing	1.6	1.6
信息服务	Inforamtion Service	2194.8	1965.9
电子商务服务	E-commerce Services	31.6	25.5
检验检测服务	Examination and Inspection Service	92.3	86.8
专业技术服务业的高技术服务	High-tech Service in Professional Technology Service Sector	702.1	618.6
研发与设计服务	Research and Design Service	485.4	399.2
科技成果转化服务	Transformation Service on Technological Achievements	291.3	279.8
知识产权及相关法律服务	Intellectual Property and Relevant Legal Services	112.1	95.8
环境监测及治理服务	Environmental Monitoring and Governance Service	27.7	22.3
现代制造业	**Modern Manufacturing Industry**	**1744.6**	**1657.7**
电子类	Electronics	325.6	319.3
机电类	Electromechanical	342.7	312.3
交通类	Transport	750.8	708.6
医药类	Pharmaceutical	293.5	283.8
其他类	Other	32.0	33.7
现代服务业	**Modern Service Industry**	**11820.0**	**10751.5**
信息传输、软件和信息技术服务业	Information Transmission,Software and Information Technology Services	2081.9	1852.2
金融业	Finance	3357.7	2943.1
房地产业	Real Estate	1329.2	1339.5
商务服务业	Business Services	1602.3	1519.2
科学研究和技术服务业	Scientific Research and Development, Technical Services	1662.7	1472.8
环境管理业	Management of Environment	24.0	19.4
教 育	Education	859.0	770.5
卫 生	Health Care	432.8	384.5
文化、体育和娱乐业	Culture, Sports and Entertainment	470.4	450.3
生产性服务业	**Producer Services**	**11196.1**	**10127.7**
流通服务	Logistical Services	2393.6	2293.1
信息服务	Information Service	2081.9	1852.2
金融服务	Financial Service	3357.7	2943.1
商务服务	Business Service	1700.2	1566.5
科技服务	Scientific and Technological Services	1662.7	1472.8
信息服务业	**Inforamtion Service**	**2434.1**	**2192.6**
信息传输服务	Inforamtion Transmission Service	429.8	354.7
信息技术服务	Information Technology Service	1274.9	1190.7
信息内容服务	Information Content Service	729.4	647.2
物流业	**Logistics**	**790.2**	**713.6**
交通运输、邮政、仓储业	Transport, Post, Storage	615.9	541.1
流通加工、配送、包装业	Circulation and Processing, Delivery, Packaging	174.3	172.5

注：1. 本表数据按当年价格计算。2013年数据为第三次全国经济普查数据。
2. 新兴产业执行《国民经济行业分类》(GB/T4754-2011)。
3. 北京市从2013年开始执行国家高技术产业标准，包括高技术制造业和高技术服务业。

Note: a) Data in the table is calculated based on price in current year. Data in 2013 is the data from the third national economic census.
b) New emerging industries are subject to Classification of National Economic Sectors (GB/T4754-2011).
c) Beijing has implemented standards for national high-tech industries since 2013, industries on high-tech manufacturing and high-tech service are included.

2-9 收入法地区生产总值(1978-2014年)
GROSS DOMESTIC PRODUCT BY INCOME APPROACH (1978-2014)

单位：亿元 (100 million yuan)

年 份 Year	地区生产总值 Gross Domestic Product	劳动者报酬 Compensation for Labors	生产税净额 Net Taxes on Production	固定资产折旧 Depreciation of Fixed Assets	营业盈余 Operating Surplus
1978	108.8	37.1	16.5	11.5	43.7
1979	120.1	42.0	18.3	13.4	46.4
1980	139.1	48.9	21.0	15.4	53.8
1981-1985	**950.9**	**350.9**	**142.8**	**111.0**	**346.2**
1981	139.2	52.9	22.0	16.9	47.4
1982	154.9	57.4	23.2	17.7	56.6
1983	183.1	66.0	26.8	20.7	69.6
1984	216.6	79.1	31.8	25.4	80.3
1985	257.1	95.5	39.0	30.3	92.3
1986-1990	**1978.7**	**773.7**	**290.5**	**244.9**	**669.6**
1986	284.9	107.8	43.4	34.9	98.8
1987	326.8	125.4	48.0	40.9	112.5
1988	410.2	153.9	59.7	49.9	146.7
1989	456.0	179.3	66.5	57.1	153.1
1990	500.8	207.3	72.9	62.1	158.5
1991-1995	**4847.2**	**2102.6**	**717.3**	**608.1**	**1419.2**
1991	598.9	254.2	86.4	75.7	182.6
1992	709.1	304.7	103.3	89.5	211.6
1993	886.2	387.7	131.4	109.0	258.1
1994	1145.3	508.1	168.9	140.2	328.1
1995	1507.7	647.9	227.3	193.7	438.8
1996-2000	**12084.0**	**5112.5**	**1761.0**	**1664.8**	**3545.7**
1996	1789.2	760.9	264.9	236.9	526.5
1997	2077.1	880.1	302.6	275.0	619.4
1998	2377.2	1008.5	341.3	319.6	707.8
1999	2678.8	1135.3	388.1	375.3	780.1
2000	3161.7	1327.7	464.1	458.0	911.9
2001-2005	**26032.9**	**11244.4**	**3999.7**	**4091.6**	**6697.2**
2001	3708.0	1538.7	549.8	559.7	1059.8
2002	4315.0	1810.6	643.0	680.3	1181.1
2003	5007.2	2119.7	753.1	791.5	1342.9
2004	6033.2	2595.5	960.4	960.5	1516.8
2005	6969.5	3179.9	1093.4	1099.6	1596.6
2006-2010	**55346.2**	**26740.5**	**8959.8**	**7893.4**	**11752.5**
2006	8117.8	3657.3	1286.7	1268.3	1905.5
2007	9846.8	4405.8	1625.8	1383.0	2432.2
2008	11115.0	5615.8	1896.6	1608.4	1994.2
2009	12153.0	6141.6	1953.5	1707.7	2350.2
2010	14113.6	6920.0	2197.2	1926.0	3070.4
2011	16251.9	7992.4	2566.1	2155.8	3537.6
2012	17879.4	9102.6	2894.6	2269.6	3612.6
2013	19800.8	10238.6	3179.8	2386.2	3996.2
2014	21330.8	11118.4	3227.4	2418.7	4566.3

注：2013年数据为第三次全国经济普查数据。
Note: Data for 2013 were collected from the third national economic census.

2-10 收入法地区生产总值(2013年)
GROSS DOMESTIC PRODUCT BY INCOME APPROACH (2013)

单位：亿元 (100 million yuan)

项 目	Item	地区生产总值 Gross Regional Product	劳动者报酬 Renumeration of Labor	生产税净额 Net Production Tax	固定资产折旧 Depreciation of Fixed Asset	营业盈余 Operating Surplus
地区生产总值	**Gross Domestic Product**	**19800.8**	**10238.6**	**3179.8**	**2386.2**	**3996.2**
按产业分组	**By Three Industies**					
第一产业	Primary Industry	159.6	141.3	1.2	17.1	
第二产业	Secondary Industry	4292.6	1676.5	989.4	670.7	956.0
第三产业	Tertiary Industry	15348.6	8420.8	2189.2	1698.4	3040.2
按行业分组	**By Sector**					
农、林、牧、渔业	Agriculture, Forestry, Animal Production and Hunting, Fishing	161.8	142.7	1.5	17.6	
采矿业	Mining and Quarrying	171.2	73.3	61.9	22.7	13.3
制造业	Manufacturing	2745.2	1129.6	659.7	288.3	667.6
电力、热力、燃气及水生产和供应业	Production and Distribution of Electricity, Heating Power, Gas and Water	650.0	140.0	93.6	314.7	101.7
建筑业	Construction	831.6	395.5	213.4	53.9	168.8
批发和零售业	Wholesale and Retail Trade	2340.7	983.7	806.5	115.0	435.5
交通运输、仓储和邮政业	Transport, Storage and Post	871.8	532.6	70.6	292.0	-23.4
住宿和餐饮业	Accommodation and Restaurants	374.8	290.1	64.0	43.8	-23.1
信息传输、软件和信息技术服务业	Information Transmission,Software and Information Technology Services	1852.2	1035.3	192.8	193.9	430.2
金融业	Finance	2943.1	904.4	310.0	125.6	1603.1
房地产业	Real Estate	1339.5	339.3	314.5	363.5	322.2
租赁和商务服务业	Renting and Leasing Activities and Business Services	1566.5	1197.9	124.5	159.4	84.7
科学研究和技术服务业	Scientific Research and Development, Technical Services	1472.8	1017.3	161.4	147.5	146.6
水利、环境和公共设施管理业	Management of Water Conservancy, Environment and Public Facilities	120.1	82.7	9.4	13.7	14.3
居民服务、修理和其他服务业	Resident Services, Repair and Other Services	139.9	116.2	11.4	8.8	3.5
教 育	Education	770.5	654.0	14.6	82.0	19.9
卫生和社会工作	Health Care and Social Works	416.1	379.0	0.9	33.1	3.1
文化、体育和娱乐业	Culture, Sports and Entertainment	450.3	311.1	64.4	46.5	28.3
公共管理、社会保障和社会组织	Pulic Administration,Social Security and Social Organizations	582.7	513.9	4.6	64.2	
国际组织	International Organizations					

注：1. 2013年数据为第三次全国经济普查数据。
2. 2013年开始，地区生产总值行业划分执行《国民经济行业分类》GB/T 4754-2011标准。
3. 2013年开始，地区生产总值三次产业划分执行国家统计局《三次产业划分规定》(国统字[2012]108号)。

Note: a) Data for 2013 were collected from the third national economic census.
b) Since 2013, GDP industrial classification has been subjected to Classification of National Economic Sectors Standard GB/T 4754-2011.
c) Since 2013, GDP three sector classification has been subject to Regulations on Three Industries Classification (G.T.Z. [2012] No. 108) issued by National Bureau of Statistics.

2-11 收入法地区生产总值(2014年)
GROSS DOMESTIC PRODUCT BY INCOME APPROACH (2014)

单位：亿元 (100 million yuan)

项 目	Item	地区生产总值 Gross Regional Product	劳动者报酬 Renumeration of Labor	生产税净额 Net Production Tax	固定资产折旧 Depreciation of Fixed Asset	营业盈余 Operating Surplus
地区生产总值	**Gross Domestic Product**	**21330.8**	**11118.4**	**3227.4**	**2418.7**	**4566.3**
按产业分组	**By Three Industies**					
第一产业	Primary Industry	159.0	141.4	1.3	16.3	
第二产业	Secondary Industry	4544.8	1739.0	1048.6	665.0	1092.2
第三产业	Tertiary Industry	16627.0	9238.0	2177.5	1737.4	3474.1
按行业分组	**By Sector**					
农、林、牧、渔业	Agriculture, Forestry, Animal Production and Hunting, Fishing	161.3	142.9	1.5	16.9	
采矿业	Mining and Quarrying	176.2	131.5	49.0	41.3	-45.6
制造业	Manufacturing	2823.2	1097.2	677.1	269.0	779.9
电力、热力、燃气及水生产和供应业	Production and Distribution of Electricity, Heating Power, Gas and Water	747.4	145.6	102.9	322.4	176.5
建筑业	Construction	902.7	427.5	233.1	58.4	183.7
批发和零售业	Wholesale and Retail Trade	2411.1	1029.8	774.1	115.5	491.7
交通运输、仓储和邮政业	Transport, Storage and Post	948.1	652.4	67.4	290.5	-62.2
住宿和餐饮业	Accommodation and Restaurants	363.8	280.4	69.6	43.5	-29.7
信息传输、软件和信息技术服务业	Information Transmission,Software and Information Technology Services	2081.9	1159.1	170.1	222.8	529.9
金融业	Finance	3357.7	1102.8	439.4	135.1	1680.4
房地产业	Real Estate	1329.2	365.3	312.6	367.3	284.0
租赁和商务服务业	Renting and Leasing Activities and Business Services	1700.2	1259.8	115.9	152.1	172.4
科学研究和技术服务业	Scientific Research and Development, Technical Services	1662.7	1108.8	146.8	124.3	282.8
水利、环境和公共设施管理业	Management of Water Conservancy, Environment and Public Facilities	136.0	95.7	8.9	16.3	15.1
居民服务、修理和其他服务业	Resident Services, Repair and Other Services	155.0	125.6	17.0	8.9	3.5
教 育	Education	859.0	733.8	14.5	87.8	22.9
卫生和社会工作	Health Care and Social Works	468.1	427.7	0.6	34.1	5.7
文化、体育和娱乐业	Culture, Sports and Entertainment	470.4	321.9	23.6	49.6	75.3
公共管理、社会保障和社会组织	Pulic Administration,Social Security and Social Organizations	576.8	510.6	3.3	62.9	
国际组织	International Organizations					

2-12 支出法地区生产总值(1978-2014年)
GROSS DOMESTIC PRODUCT BY EXPENDITURE APPROACH (1978-2014)

单位：亿元 (100 million yuan)

年份 Year	地区生产总值 Gross Domestic Product	最终消费支出 Final Consumption Expenditure	居民消费 Households Consumption	政府消费 Government Consumption	资本形成总额 Gross Capital Formation	固定资本形成总额 Completed Fixed Assets	存货增加 Changes in Inventories	货物和服务净流出 Net Outflow of Goods and Services	最终消费率(消费率)(%) Final Consumption Rate (%)	资本形成率(投资率)(%) Capital Formation Rate (%)
1978	108.8	53.0	28.6	24.4	31.7	24.9	6.8	24.1	48.7	29.1
1979	120.1	55.4	31.5	23.9	37.0	29.1	7.9	27.7	46.1	30.8
1980	139.1	57.3	39.6	17.7	45.1	36.5	8.6	36.7	41.2	32.4
1981	139.2	61.8	44.2	17.6	50.5	40.2	10.3	26.9	44.4	36.3
1982	154.9	68.6	48.8	19.8	51.8	42.3	9.5	34.5	44.3	33.4
1983	183.1	77.6	54.6	23.0	62.9	56.1	6.8	42.6	42.4	34.4
1984	216.6	96.5	64.8	31.7	84.7	72.5	12.2	35.4	44.6	39.1
1985	257.1	127.1	88.7	38.4	150.6	102.7	47.9	-20.6	49.4	58.6
1986	284.9	161.1	109.9	51.2	178.8	116.0	62.8	-55.0	56.5	62.8
1987	326.8	181.5	124.3	57.2	201.2	148.6	52.6	-55.9	55.5	61.6
1988	410.2	222.6	161.9	60.7	251.1	177.7	73.4	-63.5	54.3	61.2
1989	456.0	244.0	176.1	67.9	271.5	151.9	119.6	-59.5	53.5	59.5
1990	500.8	269.7	194.1	75.6	296.5	195.0	101.5	-65.4	53.9	59.2
1991	598.9	302.6	225.7	76.9	327.3	208.8	118.5	-31.0	50.5	54.7
1992	709.1	341.5	260.7	80.8	414.6	289.0	125.6	-47.0	48.2	58.5
1993	886.2	445.6	354.9	90.7	535.0	445.5	89.5	-94.4	50.3	60.4
1994	1145.3	614.1	504.2	109.9	787.5	703.8	83.7	-256.3	53.6	68.8
1995	1507.7	844.2	672.8	171.4	1036.0	912.0	124.0	-372.5	56.0	68.7
1996	1789.2	1022.7	815.5	207.2	1034.8	949.6	85.2	-268.3	57.2	57.8
1997	2077.1	1215.5	927.0	288.5	1235.1	1040.1	195.0	-373.5	58.5	59.5
1998	2377.2	1335.5	988.5	347.0	1360.3	1249.4	110.9	-318.6	56.2	57.2
1999	2678.8	1510.4	1075.9	434.5	1533.9	1264.6	269.3	-365.5	56.4	57.3
2000	3161.7	1688.0	1155.8	532.2	1697.4	1400.4	297.0	-223.7	53.4	53.7
2001	3708.0	1911.7	1244.8	666.9	1936.5	1602.1	334.4	-140.2	51.6	52.2
2002	4315.0	2300.3	1528.0	772.3	2332.7	1951.9	380.8	-318.0	53.3	54.1
2003	5007.2	2636.5	1729.7	906.8	2737.8	2437.9	299.9	-367.1	52.7	54.7
2004	6033.2	3085.3	1979.5	1105.8	3167.5	2844.3	323.2	-219.6	51.1	52.5
2005	6969.5	3486.5	2221.8	1264.7	3580.9	3204.7	376.2	-97.9	50.0	51.4
2006	8117.8	4138.5	2587.6	1550.9	3936.7	3551.2	385.5	42.6	51.0	48.5
2007	9846.8	5108.7	3040.0	2068.7	4469.3	4022.6	446.7	268.8	51.9	45.4
2008	11115.0	6026.4	3466.5	2559.9	4722.9	3989.5	733.4	365.7	54.2	42.5
2009	12153.0	6930.4	3998.2	2932.2	5049.9	4435.0	614.9	172.7	57.0	41.6
2010	14113.6	8032.8	4774.0	3258.8	6059.7	5342.4	717.3	21.1	56.9	42.9
2011	16251.9	9488.2	5525.0	3963.2	6683.6	5953.9	729.7	80.1	58.4	41.1
2012	17879.4	10655.1	6203.3	4451.8	7409.6	7032.8	376.8	-185.3	59.6	41.4
2013	19800.8	12148.2	7099.9	5048.3	7989.6	7712.3	277.3	-337.0	61.4	40.3
2014	21330.8	13329.2	7691.6	5637.6	8309.4	7957.2	352.2	-307.8	62.5	39.0

注：1. 2013年数据为第三次全国经济普查数据。
2. 2011年根据全国第六次人口普查数据对2006年-2010年的数据进行了调整。

Note: a) Data for 2013 were collected from the third national economic census.
b) In 2011,Figures for 2006-2010 are revised according to the results of the Sixth National Population Census.

2-13 支出法地区生产总值
GROSS DOMESTIC PRODUCT BY EXPENDITURE APPROACH

单位：亿元 (100 million yuan)

项 目	Item	2014	2013	2014年为2013年% 2014 as % of 2013
地区生产总值	**Gross Domestic Product**	**21330.8**	**19800.8**	**107.3**
最终消费支出	**Final Consumption Expenditure**	**13329.2**	**12148.2**	**108.7**
居民消费	Households Consumption	7691.6	7099.9	106.8
城镇居民	Urban Resident	7094.6	6563.5	106.5
农村居民	Rural Resident	597.0	536.4	110.2
政府消费	Government Consumption	5637.6	5048.3	111.5
资本形成总额	**Gross Capital Formation**	**8309.4**	**7989.6**	**104.0**
固定资本形成总额	Completed Fixed Asset	7957.2	7712.3	103.0
存货增加	Changes in Inventories	352.2	277.3	127.4
货物和服务净流出	**Net Outflow of Goods and Services**	**-307.8**	**-337.0**	

注：1.发展速度按可比价格计算。
2.2013年数据为第三次全国经济普查数据。

Note: a) Development rate is calculated at comparable price.
b) Data for 2013 were collected from the third national economic census.

2-14 三大需求对地区生产总值增长的拉动(2001-2014年)
CONTRIBUTION OF THREE DEMANDS TO GROWTH OF GDP (2001-2014)

年 份 Year	最终消费支出 Final Consumption Expenditure		资本形成总额 Gross Capital Formation		货物和服务净流出 Net Outflow of Goods and Services	
	贡献率(%) Contribution Rate(%)	拉 动(百分点) Impetus (Percentage Points)	贡献率(%) Contribution Rate(%)	拉 动(百分点) Impetus (Percentage Points)	贡献率(%) Contribution Rate(%)	拉 动(百分点) Impetus (Percentage Points)
2001	32.4	3.8	43.2	5.1	24.4	2.8
2002	77.0	8.8	61.6	7.1	-38.6	-4.4
2003	40.7	4.5	66.3	7.4	-7.0	-0.8
2004	40.2	5.7	37.3	5.3	22.5	3.1
2005	37.2	4.5	45.7	5.5	17.1	2.1
2006	60.0	7.8	24.6	3.2	15.4	2.0
2007	61.1	8.9	21.0	3.0	17.9	2.6
2008	81.6	7.4	9.0	0.8	9.4	0.9
2009	76.4	7.8	39.0	4.0	-15.4	-1.6
2010	65.8	6.8	47.7	4.9	-13.5	-1.4
2011	83.4	6.8	12.7	1.0	3.9	0.3
2012	73.0	5.6	43.8	3.4	-16.8	-1.3
2013	68.4	5.3	37.3	2.9	-5.7	-0.5
2014	72.7	5.3	22.1	1.6	5.2	0.4

注：1. 三大需求指支出法地区生产总值的三大构成项目，即最终消费支出、资本形成总额、货物和服务净流出。
2. 贡献率指三大需求增量与支出法地区生产总值增量之比。
3. 拉动指地区生产总值增长速度与三大需求贡献率的乘积。
4. 本表数据按可比价格计算。
5. 根据全国第六次人口普查数据对2006年-2010年的数据进行了调整。2013年数据为第三次全国经济普查数据。

Note: a) Three demands of GDP by expenditure method are final consumption expenditure,gross capital formation and net outflow of goods and services.
b) Contribution rate of the three demands to GDP growth refers to the proportion of the increment of the each component of GDP by expenditure method to the increment of GDP.
c) Impetus of the three demands to GDP growth refers to the growth rate of GDP multiplied by the contribution share of the three demands.
d) Figures in this table are calculated at comparable prices.
e) Figures for 2006-2010 are revised according to the results of the Sixth National Population Census. Figures for 2013 were preliminary statistics.Data for 2013 were collected from the third national economic census.

2-15 居民消费水平(1978-2014年)
HOUSEHOLDS CONSUMPTION LEVEL (1978-2014)

年份 Year	居民消费水平(元) Level(yuan) 全市 All Households	城镇居民 Urban Households	农村居民 Rural Households	城乡消费水平对比(农村居民=1) Uban/Rural Consumption Ratio(Rural Households=1)	指数(1978年=100) Index(1978=100) 全市 All Households	城镇居民 Urban Households	农村居民 Rural Households	指数(上年=100) Index(Preceding=100) 全市 All Households	城镇居民 Urban Households	农村居民 Rural Households
1978	330	451	185	2.4	100.0	100.0	100.0	112.3	110.1	122.6
1979	356	464	221	2.1	117.5	114.5	120.8	117.5	114.5	120.8
1980	440	562	280	2.0	147.6	140.0	159.0	125.6	122.1	131.5
1981	485	590	338	1.7	160.3	144.8	189.4	108.6	103.6	119.2
1982	526	622	384	1.6	170.6	149.7	211.2	106.4	103.4	111.5
1983	579	674	432	1.6	175.4	151.2	222.6	102.8	101.0	105.4
1984	677	789	494	1.6	201.4	173.9	250.4	114.8	115.0	112.5
1985	912	1101	585	1.9	263.2	235.3	289.2	130.7	135.3	115.5
1986	1094	1284	749	1.7	312.9	272.0	365.8	118.9	115.6	126.5
1987	1198	1391	827	1.7	316.7	272.0	375.3	101.2	100.0	102.6
1988	1536	1779	1046	1.7	367.7	313.3	435.7	116.1	115.2	116.1
1989	1648	1874	1169	1.6	398.2	337.1	472.7	108.3	107.6	108.5
1990	1797	2045	1186	1.7	466.7	393.4	527.5	117.2	116.7	111.6
1991	2071	2330	1345	1.7	528.3	440.2	587.1	113.2	111.9	111.3
1992	2375	2696	1456	1.9	553.7	465.3	583.0	104.8	105.7	99.3
1993	3206	3743	1634	2.3	619.6	529.0	588.8	111.9	113.7	101.0
1994	4508	5307	2114	2.5	717.5	618.4	630.6	115.8	116.9	107.1
1995	5663	6497	3101	2.1	774.2	656.7	737.2	107.9	106.2	116.9
1996	6497	7477	3420	2.2	814.5	693.5	742.4	105.2	105.6	100.7
1997	7418	8594	3638	2.4	928.5	795.4	791.4	114.0	114.7	106.6
1998	7954	9195	3874	2.4	949.9	812.9	797.7	102.3	102.2	100.8
1999	8598	9916	4163	2.4	1025.9	876.3	855.1	108.0	107.8	107.2
2000	8820	10145	4277	2.4	1031.0	878.9	860.2	100.5	100.3	100.6
2001	9057	10301	4695	2.2	1026.9	865.7	915.3	99.6	98.5	106.4
2002	10882	12505	5020	2.5	1204.6	1026.7	952.8	117.3	118.6	104.1
2003	12014	13826	5275	2.6	1267.2	1082.1	954.7	105.2	105.4	100.2
2004	13425	15438	5713	2.7	1371.1	1169.8	1000.5	108.2	108.1	104.8
2005	14662	16478	6602	2.5	1442.4	1202.6	1105.6	105.2	102.8	110.5
2006	16487	18185	7580	2.4	1579.4	1292.8	1236.1	109.5	107.5	111.8
2007	18553	20320	8984	2.3	1691.5	1375.5	1389.4	107.1	106.4	112.4
2008	20113	21872	10375	2.1	1777.8	1436.0	1547.8	105.1	104.4	111.4
2009	22023	23812	11917	2.0	1928.9	1550.9	1742.8	108.5	108.0	112.6
2010	24982	26949	13392	2.0	2116.0	1696.7	1896.2	109.7	109.4	108.8
2011	27760	30037	13659	2.2	2243.0	1805.3	1835.5	106.0	106.4	96.8
2012	30350	32857	14664	2.2	2391.0	1922.6	1958.5	106.6	106.5	106.7
2013	33938	36375	18648	2.0	2548.8	2032.2	2326.7	106.6	105.7	118.8
2014	36057	38515	20506	1.9	2668.6	2119.6	2533.8	104.7	104.3	108.9

注：1. 2013年数据为第三次全国经济普查数据。
2. 2011年根据全国第六次人口普查数据对2006年-2010年的数据进行了调整。

Note: a) Data for 2013 were collected from the third national economic census.
b) In 2011,Figures for 2006-2010 are revised according to the results of the Sixth National Population Census.

2-16 社会劳动生产率(1978-2014年)
OVERALL LABOR PRODUCTIVITY (1978-2014)

单位：元/人 (yuan/person)

年 份 Year	社会劳动生产率 Overall Labor Productivity	第一产业 Primary Industry	第二产业 Secondary Industry	第三产业 Tertiary Industry
1978	2504	444	4484	1911
1979	2626	421	4556	2033
1980	2914	510	4750	2391
1981	2795	561	4316	2420
1982	2959	878	4437	2467
1983	3368	1094	4799	2998
1984	3909	1287	5347	3646
1985	4580	1671	6040	4268
1986	5002	1932	6331	4783
1987	5669	2569	6917	5501
1988	7046	4084	8309	6745
1989	7742	4270	9432	7140
1990	8203	4810	9564	7941
1991	9498	5014	10351	10145
1992	11051	5556	12282	11549
1993	13878	7112	14909	14644
1994	17728	9660	18709	18682
1995	22679	10042	23697	24647
1996	26997	10259	26824	30815
1997	31567	10523	30102	37337
1998	37202	10681	34657	44887
1999	43179	10452	40909	52038
2000	51082	10488	48506	61705
2001	59414	10909	53624	73303
2002	65974	11599	55217	83242
2003	72437	12556	64298	87043
2004	77478	13736	80484	84186
2005	80475	13937	86967	85035
2006	90313	13943	95417	96078
2007	105743	16403	109985	112658
2008	115565	17982	119077	123306
2009	122807	18658	137799	127602
2010	139057	19854	165334	141824
2011	154684	22307	174354	159593
2012	164257	25447	183539	169066
2013	176140	28330	202718	179296
2014	185671	29494	216013	187973

注：1．本表数据按当年价格计算。2013年数据为第三次全国经济普查数据。
2．2013年开始，地区生产总值三次产业划分执行国家统计局《三次产业划分规定》(国统字[2012]108号)，并对本表1978-2012年以来三次产业数据进行相应调整。

Note: a) Figures in this table are calculated at current year's prices.Data for 2013 were collected from the third national economic census.
b) Since 2013, GDP three sector classification has been subject to Regulations on Three Industries Classification (G.T.Z. [2012] No. 108) issued by National Bureau of Statistics, according to which data on the three industries from 1978 to 2012 was adjusted in this table.

2-17 三次产业贡献率(2001-2014年)
CONTRIBUTION RATE OF THREE INDUSTRIES TO THE INCREASE OF GDP (2001-2014)

单位：% (%)

年份 Year	地区生产总值 Gross Domestic Product	第一产业 Primary Industry	第二产业 Secondary Industry	第三产业 Tertiary Industry	#工业 Industry	#建筑业 Construction
2001	100.0	0.8	26.7	72.5	23.3	3.4
2002	100.0	0.5	23.4	76.1	18.0	5.4
2003	100.0	-0.2	33.4	66.8	28.0	5.4
2004	100.0	-0.1	37.9	62.2	35.4	2.5
2005	100.0	-0.3	26.9	73.4	24.1	2.8
2006	100.0	0.1	23.5	76.4	17.9	5.6
2007	100.0	0.2	24.9	74.9	21.4	3.5
2008	100.0	0.1	2.4	97.5	0.6	1.8
2009	100.0	0.4	26.5	73.1	18.6	7.9
2010	100.0	-0.1	34.4	65.7	30.7	3.7
2011	100.0	0.1	19.7	80.2	18.1	1.6
2012	100.0	0.3	22.9	76.8	17.6	5.3
2013	100.0	0.3	24.3	75.4	19.6	5.4
2014	100.0		21.7	78.3	16.0	6.1

注：1. 本表数据按可比价格计算。2013年数据为第三次全国经济普查数据。
2. 2013年开始，地区生产总值行业划分执行《国民经济行业分类》GB/T 4754-2011标准。
3. 2013年开始，地区生产总值三次产业划分执行国家统计局《三次产业划分规定》(国统字[2012]108号)。
4. 产业贡献率指各产业增加值增量与地区生产总值增量之比。

Note: a) Statistics in this table are calculated at comparable prices.Data for 2013 were collected from the third national economic census.
b) Since 2013, GDP industrial classification has been subjected to Classification of National Economic Sectors Standard GB/T 4754-2011.
c) Since 2013, GDP three sector classification has been subject to Regulations on Three Industries Classification (G.T.Z. [2012] No. 108) issued by National Bureau of Statistics.
d) Share of the contributions of the three industries to the increase of the GDP refers to the proportion of the increment of the value-added of each industry to the increment of GDP.

2-18 三次产业对地区生产总值增长的拉动(2001-2014年)
IMPETUS OF THREE INDUSTRIES TO GDP GROWTH (2001-2014)

单位：百分点 (Percentage Points)

年 份 Year	地区生产总值 Gross Domestic Product	第一产业 Primary Industry	第二产业 Secondary Industry	第三产业 Tertiary Industry	#工业 Industry
2001	11.7	0.1	3.1	8.5	2.7
2002	11.5	0.1	2.7	8.7	2.1
2003	11.1	…	3.7	7.4	3.1
2004	14.1	…	5.3	8.8	5.0
2005	12.1	…	3.2	8.9	2.9
2006	13.0	…	3.1	9.9	2.3
2007	14.5	…	3.6	10.9	3.1
2008	9.1	…	0.2	8.9	0.1
2009	10.2	…	2.7	7.5	1.9
2010	10.3	…	3.5	6.8	3.2
2011	8.1	…	1.6	6.5	1.5
2012	7.7	…	1.8	5.9	1.4
2013	7.7	…	1.9	5.8	1.5
2014	7.3	…	1.6	5.7	1.2

注：1. 本表数据按可比价格计算。2013年数据为第三次全国经济普查数据。
2. 2013年开始，地区生产总值行业划分执行《国民经济行业分类》GB/T 4754-2011标准。
3. 2013年开始，地区生产总值三次产业划分执行国家统计局《三次产业划分规定》(国统字[2012]108号)。
4. 三次产业拉动指地区生产总值增长速度与各产业贡献率之乘积。

Note: a) Statistics in this table are calculated at comparable prices.Data for 2013 were collected from the third national economic census.
b) Since 2013, GDP industrial classification has been subjected to Classification of National Economic Sectors Standard GB/T 4754-2011.
c) Since 2013, GDP three sector classification has been subject to Regulations on Three Industries Classification (G.T.Z. [2012] No. 108) issued by National Bureau of Statistics.
d) Contribution of the three industries to GDP growth refers to the growth rate of GDP multiplied by the industrial shares.

主要统计指标解释

地区生产总值 是按市场价格计算的地区生产总值的简称。它是一个地区所有常住单位在一定时期内生产活动的最终成果。地区生产总值有三种表现形式，即价值形态、收入形态和产品形态。从价值形态看，它是所有常住单位在一定时期内所生产的全部货物和服务价值超过同期投入的全部非固定资产货物和服务价值的差额，即所有常住单位的增加值之和；从收入形态看，它是所有常住单位在一定时期内所创造并分配给常住单位和非常住单位的初次分配收入之和；从产品形态看，它是最终使用的货物和服务减去进口货物和服务。在实际核算中，地区生产总值的三种表现形态表现为三种计算方法，即生产法、收入法和支出法。三种方法分别从不同的方面反映地区生产总值及其构成。

三次产业 根据社会生产活动历史发展的顺序对产业结构的划分，产品直接取自自然界的部门称为第一产业，对初级产品进行再加工的部门称为第二产业，为生产和消费提供各种服务的部门称为第三产业。它是世界上通用的产业结构分类，但各国的划分不尽一致。我国 2011 年版国民经济行业分类标准：第一产业是指农、林、牧、渔业（不含农、林、牧、渔服务业）；第二产业是指采矿业（不含开采辅助活动），制造业（不含金属制品、机械和设备修理业），电力、热力、燃气及水生产和供应业，建筑业；第三产业是指除第一产业、第二产业以外的其他行业。

最终消费率(消费率)

$$最终消费率(消费率)=\frac{最终消费支出}{地区生产总值}\times 100\%$$

资本形成率(投资率)

$$资本形成率(投资率)=\frac{资本形成总额}{地区生产总值}\times 100\%$$

部分新兴产业统计划分标准

1.**文化创意产业** 北京市文化创意产业指以创作、创造、创新为根本手段，以文化内容和创意成果为核心价值，以知识产权实现或消费为交易特征，为社会公众提供文化体验的具有内在联系的行业集群。北京市文化创意产业标准是在《国民经济行业分类》（GB/T 4754-2011）的基础上，根据文化创意活动的特点将行业分类中相关的类别重新进行的组合。适用于统计及政策管理中对文化创意相关活动的分类。内容上主要包括 9 大类，分别是文化艺术，新闻出版，广播、电视、电影，软件网络及计算机服务，广告会展，艺术品交易，设计服务，旅游、休闲娱乐，其他辅助服务。

2.**信息产业** 信息相关产业主要是指与电子信息相关联的各种活动的集合。信息产业标准是国家统计局在《国民经济行业分类》（GB/T 4754-2011）的基础上，参考了联合国的《全部经济活动的国际标准产业分类》，并结合我国的实际情况制定的。北京市从 2004 年开始执行国家信息产业统计标准。

3.**高技术产业** 高技术产业主要是指与高技术产品相关联的各种活动的集合。高技术产业标准是国家统计局在《国民经济行业分类》（GB/T 4754-2011）的基础上，根据高技术产业的特性，结合我国的实际情况制定的。北京市从 2013 年开始执行国家高技术产业统计标准。包括高技术制造业和高技术服务业。

4.**现代制造业** 现代制造业是指用现代科学技术武装起来的制造业，是现代科学技术与制造业相结合的产物。现代制造业是应用现代制造技术、现代生产组织系统和现代管理理念所进行的以现代集成制造为特征、知识密集为特色、高效制造为特点的技术含量高、附加值大、产业链长的产业组织体系。现代制造业产业标准是北京市统计局在《国民经济行业分类》（GB/T4754-2011）的基础上，根据现代制造业的特性，将符合基本要求的行业归并，结合北京市的实际情况制定的。北京市从 2005 年开始执行现代制造业统计标准。

5.**现代服务业** 现代服务业是相对于传统服务业而言，是适应现代人和现代城市发展的需求，而产生和发展起来的具有高技术含量和高文化含量的服务业。现代服务业有新服务领域、新服务模式、高文化品位和高技术含量的特征。现代服务业标准是北京市统计局在《国民经济行业分类》（GB/T4754-2011）的基础上，根据现代服务业的特性，将符合基本要求的行业归并，结合北京市的实际情况制定的。北京市从 2005 年开始执行现代服务业统计标准。

6．**生产性服务业** 指以市场化的中间投入服务为主导的行业，生产性服务业具有经营性和可贸易性的特点，不仅为制造业提供中间投入服务，也为第一产业和第三产业提供中间投入服务。北京市生产性服务业分类标准涉及《国民经济行业分类》（GB/T 4754-2011）中交通运输、仓储和邮政业，信息传输、软件和信息技术服务业，批发和零售业，金融业，租赁和商务服务业，科学研究和技术服务业 6 个行业门类。根据业务活动特点将生产性服务业划分为流通服务、信息服务、金融服务、商务服务、科技服务五大类别。

7．**信息服务业** 指以信息资源为基础，利用现代信息技术，对信息进行生产、收集、处理、输送、存储、传播、使用并提供信息产品和服务的产业。本分类涉及《国民经济行业分类》（GB/T 4754-2011）中信息传输、软件和信息技术服务业，文化、体育和娱乐业 2 个行业门类。根据信息服务业的概念和活动性质，将信息服务业划分为信息传输服务、信息技术服务和信息内容服务三大领域。

8．**物流业** 指为物品及其信息流动提供相关服务的经济活动。按照国家发改委、国家统计局、中国物流与采购联合会联合制定的《社会物流统计核算与报表制度（试行方案）》中的相关规定，物流业统计范围为：在工商登记注册时企业（单位）名称中具有“物流”、“配送”、“快运”、“储运”、“货运”等物流功能，且业务经营范围以配送、流通加工、包装、仓储、运输等物流业务为主的单位。

Explanatory Notes on Main Statistical Indicators

Gross Regional Product (GRP) is calculated at market prices. It represents the final results of all resident units in an area from their productive activities over a given period of time. It is expressed from three different perspectives respectively, namely value, income, and product. GRP from the value perspective refers to the total value of all goods and services produced by all resident units during a certain period of time, minus the total value of input of goods and services of the nature of non-fixed assets; in other words, it is the sum of added value of all resident units. GRP from the income perspective is the sum of primary incomes created by all resident units and distributed to resident and non-resident units. GRP from the product perspective means the finally used goods and services minus the imported goods and services. In actual national accounting, gross regional product is calculated in three methods, namely production method, income method and expenditure method, which reflect the gross regional product and its composition from different angles.

Three Industries means the division of industrial structure according to the historical sequence of social productive activities. The sector which receives products directly from nature is called the primary industry. The sector which re-processes primary products is called the secondary industry. The sector which offers various services for production and consumption is called the tertiary industry. This is a universal classification of industrial structure. However, the classification of three industries may vary in different countries. As stated in China's standards on Classification of Sectors in National Economy Version 2011: The primary industry refers to agriculture, forestry, animal production and hunting, fishing (excluding service activities for agriculture, forestry, animal production and hunting, fishing); secondary industry refers to mining and quarrying (excluding mining support service activities), manufacturing (excluding repair of fabricated metal products, machinery and equipment), production and distribution of electricity, heating power, gas and water and construction; the tertiary industry refers to others excluding the primary and secondary industries.

Final Consumption Rate (Consumption Rate)

Final Consumption Rate (Consumption Rate) = Final Consumption / GRP × 100%

Capital Formation Rate (Investment Rate)

Capital Formation Rate (Investment Rate) = Total Capital Formation /GRP ×100%

Statistical Classification of Some New Industries

1. Cultural and Creative Industry The cultural and creative industry in Beijing refers to an internally correlated cluster of sectors with invention, creation and innovation as fundamental means, cultural content and creative fruits as core value, realization or consumption of intellectual property rights as transaction features, which provide cultural experience for the public. It is a new combination of related sectors in the industrial classification according to the characteristics of cultural and creative activities on the basis of Classification of Sectors in National Economy (GB/T 4754-2011). It consists of 9 sectors, namely culture & art; press & publishing; broadcasting, television and film; software, internet and computer services; advertising and exhibition; artwork trading; design services; tourism, leisure and recreation; and other auxiliary services.

2. Information Industry Information industry mainly means the set of activities related to electronic information. It is classified by the National Bureau of Statistics on the basis of Classification of Sectors in National Economy (GB/T 4754-2011) by referring to the International Standard Classification of Industries for All Economic Activities of the United Nations and combining the actual situation of China. The national statistical standard for information industry was implemented in 2004 in Beijing.

3. High-tech Industry High-tech industry mainly means the set of activities related to high-tech products. It is classified by the National Bureau of Statistics on the basis of Classification of Sectors in National Economy (GB/T 4754-2011), taking into consideration the features of high-tech industry and combining the actual situation of China. The national statistical standard for information industry was implemented in 2013 in Beijing.

4. Modern Manufacturing Modern manufacturing industry mainly means the manufacturing industry equipped with modern science and technology. Modern manufacturing is an industrial organization system with large content of technology, great added value and long industrial chain, with features of modern integrated manufacturing, intensive knowledge, efficient manufacturing, using modern manufacturing technologies, modern production organization system and modern management concepts. It is a combination of modern science, technology and manufacturing. It is classified by the Beijing Municipal Bureau of Statistics on the basis of Classification of Sectors in National Economy (GB/T 4754-2011), taking into consideration the features of modern manufacturing industry, merging the sectors meeting basic requirements and combining the actual situation of Beijing. The statistical standard for information industry was implemented in 2005 in Beijing.

5. Modern Service Modern service is in contrast with conventional service. It is a service sector with great content of high technology and great content of culture, which has emerged and developed to meet the need of modern people and modern cities' development. Modern service industry has new service fields, new service modes, high cultural taste and great content of high technology. It is classified by the Beijing Municipal Bureau of Statistics on the basis of Classification of Sectors in National Economy (GB/T 4754-2011), taking into consideration the features of modern service industry, merging the sectors meeting basic requirements and combining the actual situation of Beijing. The statistical standard for modern service industry was implemented in 2005 in Beijing.

6. **Producer Service** means the sector dominated by intermediate input services. Producer service is operational and tradable. It offers intermediate input services for manufacturing industry, and for the primary and tertiary industries. The classification standard for producer service in Beijing involves 6 sectors in Classification of Sectors in National Economy (GB/T 4754-2011), namely transportation, warehousing and post; information transmission, software and information technical service; wholesale and retail trade; finance; leasing and business service; and scientific research and technical service. According to features of business activities, producer service is divided into 5 categories, namely circulation service, information service, financial service, business service and technical service.

7. **Information Service** means the sector producing, collecting, processing, delivering, storing, transmitting and using information, and providing information products and services on the basis of information resources and by using modern information technology. Information service involves two sectors in the Classification of Sectors in National Economy (GB/T 4754-2011, namely information transmission, software and information technical service; and culture, sports and recreation. According to the definition and features of activities of information service, it is divided into three areas, namely information transmission service, information technical service and information content service.

8. **Logistics** means economic activities offering relevant services for goods and information movement. According to relevant provisions in the Statistical Calculation and Reporting System (Trial) for Social Logistics developed jointly by the State Development and Reform Commission, the National Bureau of Statistics, and China Federation of Logistics and Procurement, the statistical scope of logistics covers: companies specializing in delivery, circulation processing, package, storage, transport and other logistical service, with their names registered for industry and commerce containing such terms as “logistics”, “delivery”, “fast transport”, “storage and transport”, “cargo transport”, etc.

03

人口与就业
POPULATION AND EMPLOYMENT

简要说明

一、本章资料的主要内容

本章人口部分包括历年北京市常住人口和户籍人口的分组资料；建国以来已开展的六次人口普查的北京市人口数据；1990 年以后的人口变动情况抽样调查数据；北京市计划生育数据。

本章劳动力部分包括北京市三次产业从业人员情况；法人单位从业人员及平均工资情况；城镇单位在岗职工人数及工资的分组情况；城镇登记失业情况等。

二、本章数据资料的来源

本章人口部分中，“户籍人口”数据来自于北京市公安局；“土地面积”数据来自于北京市国土资源局；计划生育情况来自于北京市卫生和计划生育委员会；其余资料均来自北京市统计局。

本章劳动力部分中，城镇登记失业情况由北京市人力资源和社会保障局提供，其他资料来源于北京市统计局。

三、有关统计标准的变化说明

（一）关于行业划分。根据国家统计局规定，自 2012 年开始执行《国民经济行业分类》（GB/T 4754-2011）标准。

（二）关于三次产业划分。根据国家统计局《三次产业划分规定》（国统字[2012]108 号），该规定对三次产业的范围进行了调整。其中第一产业是指农、林、牧、渔业（不含农、林、牧、渔服务业）；第二产业是指采矿业（不含开采辅助活动），制造业（不含金属制品、机械和设备修理业），电力、热力、燃气及水生产和供应业，建筑业；第三产业是指除第一产业、第二产业以外的其他行业。2012 年及以后开始执行此标准。

（三）关于统计上城乡划分标准

2008 年 7 月，国务院批复了国家统计局与民政部、住房城乡建设部、公安部、财政部、国土资源部、农业部共同制定的《关于统计上划分城乡的规定》（国函[2008]60 号文件和国家统计局令第 14 号），以后每年国家统计局都会出台《统计用区划代码和城乡分类代码》。本章中“城镇人口”和“乡村人口”的确定均执行当年的城乡分类标准。

Brief Introduction

I. Main Content

Population statistics in this chapter include classified data for permanent population and registered population in Beijing in previous years; statistics of population in Beijing from six national population censuses since the founding of the People's Republic of China; statistics from National Sample Survey on Population Changes after 1990 and statistics on family planning in Beijing.

Employment statistics in this chapter include information on employed persons in three industries in Beijing; employees and average wages in business entities; classified statistics for the number and wage of fully employed staff and workers in urban entities; registered unemployment in urban areas.

II. Source of Statistics

In the population section of this chapter, statistics on "registered population" are from Beijing Municipal Bureau of Public Security; statistics on "land area" are from Beijing Municipal Bureau of Land and Resources; family planning statistics are from Beijing Municipal Commission of Health and Family Planning; other statistics are from Beijing Municipal Bureau of Statistics.

In the employment section in this chapter, urban registered unemployment statistics are from Beijing Municipal Bureau of Human Resources and Social Security; other statistics are from Beijing Municipal Bureau of Statistics.

III. Changes in Relevant Statistical Standards

(I) Classification of Sectors. According to relevant provisions of the National Bureau of Statistics, the Standard for *Classification of National Economic Sectors* (GB/T 4754-2011) was implemented in 2012.

(II) Classification of Three Industries. According to the *Regulations on the Classification of the Three Industries (G.T.Z. [2012] No. 108)* issued by National Bureau of Statistics, the scope of three industries was changed. The primary industry refers to agriculture, forestry, animal production and hunting, fishing (excluding service for agriculture, forestry, animal production and hunting, fishing); the secondary industry refers to mining and quarrying (excluding mining support activities), manufacturing (excluding metal products, machinery and equipment repair), production and distribution of electricity, heating power, gas and water, and construction; the tertiary industry refers to sectors other than the primary and secondary industries. The *Regulations on the Classification of the Three Industries* (G.T.Z. [2012] No. 108) issued by National Bureau of Statistics came into effect in 2012.

(III) Urban-Rural Statistical Definition

In July 2008, the State Council approved the *Regulations on Urban-Rural Statistical Definition* (G.H. [2008] No. 60 and No. 14 Decree of National Bureau of Statistics) jointly developed by the National Bureau of Statistics, Ministry of Civil Affairs, Ministry of Housing and Urban-Rural Development, Ministry of Public Security, Ministry of Finance, Ministry of Land and Resources and Ministry of Agriculture. In the population section, new definition applies for the figures of "urban population" and "rural population".

3-1 六次人口普查人口基本情况
BASIC STATISTICS ON POPULATION CENSUS IN 1953, 1964, 1982, 1990, 2000 AND 2010

项 目	Item	1953	1964	1982	1990	2000	2010
常住人口 (万人)	**Permanent Population (10000 persons)**	**276.8**	**759.7**	**923.1**	**1081.9**	**1356.9**	**1961.2**
按性别分	**By Sex**						
男	Male	159.8	391.1	467.1	559.3	707.4	1012.6
女	Female	117.0	368.6	456.0	522.6	649.5	948.6
性别比(女=100)	Sex Ratio (Female=100)	136.5	106.1	102.4	107.0	108.9	106.8
按城乡分	**By Urban Area and Rural Area**						
城镇人口	Urban Population	205.8	425.8	597.0	794.5	1052.2	1685.9
乡村人口	Rural Population	71.0	333.9	326.1	287.4	304.7	275.3
家庭户规模 (人/户)	**Average Family Size (person/household)**			**3.7**	**3.2**	**2.9**	**2.5**
各年龄组人口比重 (%)	**Composition by Age Group (%)**						
0-14	Age 0-14	30.1	41.5	22.4	20.2	13.6	8.6
15-59	Age 15-59	64.3	51.9	69.1	69.7	73.9	78.9
60岁及以上	Age 60 and Above	5.6	6.6	8.5	10.1	12.5	12.5
#65岁及以上	Age 65 and Above	3.3	4.1	5.6	6.3	8.4	8.7
总抚养比 (%)	**Gross Dependency Ratio (%)**	**50.2**	**83.8**	**38.9**	**36.1**	**28.2**	**20.9**
老年抚养比	Old-age Dependency Ratio	5.0	7.5	7.8	8.6	10.8	10.5
少儿抚养比	Child Dependency Ratio	45.2	76.3	31.1	27.5	17.4	10.4
民族人口	**Population by Ethnic Group**						
汉 族 (万人)	Han Chinese (10000 persons)	260.0	731.2	890.8	1040.5	1298.4	1881.1
占常住人口比重 (%)	Percentage in Permanent Populatioı (%)	93.9	96.2	96.5	96.2	95.7	95.9
少数民族 (万人)	Ethnic Minority (10000 persons)	16.8	28.5	32.3	41.4	58.5	80.1
占常住人口比重 (%)	Percentage in Permanent Populatioı (%)	6.1	3.8	3.5	3.8	4.3	4.1
每十万人口拥有的各种受教育程度人口 (人)	**Population with Various Education Attainment Per 100000 Persons (person)**						
大专及以上	Junior College and Above		4359	4866	9300	16839	31499
高中和中专	Senior Secondary/Secondary Technical School		4513	17646	18978	23165	21220
初 中	Junior Secondary School		11768	29086	30551	34380	31396
小 学	Primary School		31883	26197	22579	16963	9956
文盲人口及文盲率	**Illiterate Population and Illiteracy Rate**						
文盲人口 (万人)	Illiterate Population (10000 persons)		168.9	114.7	94.3	57.8	33.3
文盲率 (%)	Illiteracy Rate (%)		34.2	16.0	10.9	4.9	1.9
平均受教育年限 (年)	**Average Education Years (year)**		**5.3**	**7.8**	**8.6**	**10.0**	**11.5**
平均预期寿命 (岁)	**Average Life Expectancy (year old)**			**71.9**	**72.9**	**76.1**	**80.2**

注：1. 1964年的文盲人口数为12周岁及以上文盲和半文盲人口，1982年、1990年、2000年、2010年的文盲人口数为15周岁及以上文盲和半文盲人口。文盲率是指15周岁及以上人口中，文盲人口和半文盲人口所占比重。

2. 本表与表3-2相同的指标数据不同，是因为本表数据为普查时点数，表3-2为年末时点数。1953年普查时点为7月1日零时；1964年普查时点为7月1日零时；1982年普查时点为7月1日零时；1990年普查时点为7月1日零时；2000年普查时点为11月1日零时；2010年普查时点为11月1日零时。

Note: a) Statistics on illiterate population covered the illiterate and semi-illiterate people at 12 and above in 1964, and those at 15 and above in 1982, 1990, 2000, and 2010. Illiteracy rate means the share of illiterate and semi-illiterate people in the population at 15 and above.

b) This table has the same indicators but different figures from 3-2, because this table uses the data at the time point of the census, while 3-2 uses the year end as the time point. The time point of the census in 1953 was 12 o'clock midnight, July 1st; the time point in 1964 was 12 o'clock midnight, July 1st; the time point in 1982 was 12 o'clock midnight, July 1st; the time point in 1990 was 12 o'clock midnight, July 1st; the time point in 2000 was 12 o'clock midnight, November 1st; the time point in 2010 was 12 o'clock midnight, November 1st.

3-2 常住人口(1978-2014年)
PERMANENT POPULATION (1978-2014)

年 份 Year	常住人口(万人) Permanent Population (10000 persons)	#常住外来人口 Permanent Migrant Population	按性别分 By Sex		按城乡分 By Urban Area and Rural Area		常住人口出生率(‰) Birth Rate (‰)	常住人口死亡率(‰) Death Rate (‰)	常住人口自然增长率(‰) Natural Growth Rate (‰)
			男 Male	女 Female	城镇人口 Urban Population	乡村人口 Rural Population			
1978	871.5	21.8	443.2	428.3	479.0	392.5	12.93	6.12	6.81
1979	897.1	26.5	454.6	442.5	510.3	386.8	13.67	5.92	7.75
1980	904.3	18.6	457.8	446.5	521.1	383.2	15.56	6.30	9.26
1981	919.2	18.4	465.9	453.3	533.3	385.9	16.93	6.02	10.91
1982	935.0	17.2	474.0	461.0	544.0	391.0	20.04	5.68	14.36
1983	950.0	16.8	483.0	467.0	557.0	393.0	15.63	5.49	10.14
1984	965.0	19.8	491.0	474.0	570.0	395.0	16.74	5.53	11.21
1985	981.0	23.1	500.0	481.0	586.0	395.0	15.45	5.75	9.70
1986	1028.0	56.8	524.0	504.0	621.0	407.0	15.82	4.47	11.35
1987	1047.0	59.0	525.0	522.0	637.0	410.0	17.29	5.40	11.89
1988	1061.0	59.8	534.0	527.0	650.0	411.0	14.43	5.08	9.35
1989	1075.0	53.9	538.0	537.0	664.0	411.0	12.84	5.35	7.49
1990	1086.0	53.8	545.0	541.0	798.0	288.0	13.04	5.81	7.23
1991	1094.0	54.5	547.0	547.0	808.0	286.0	8.03	5.82	2.21
1992	1102.0	57.1	554.0	548.0	819.0	283.0	9.22	6.11	3.11
1993	1112.0	60.8	559.0	553.0	831.0	281.0	9.35	6.16	3.19
1994	1125.0	63.2	564.0	561.0	846.0	279.0	8.96	5.76	3.20
1995	1251.1	180.8	627.0	624.1	946.2	304.9	7.92	5.12	2.80
1996	1259.4	181.7	639.0	620.4	957.9	301.5	8.02	5.34	2.68
1997	1240.0	154.5	628.7	611.3	948.3	291.7	7.91	6.02	1.89
1998	1245.6	154.1	630.6	615.0	957.7	287.9	6.00	5.30	0.70
1999	1257.2	157.4	636.4	620.8	971.7	285.5	6.50	5.60	0.90
2000	1363.6	256.1	710.9	652.7	1057.4	306.2	6.20	5.30	0.90
2001	1385.1	262.8	722.1	663.0	1081.2	303.9	6.10	5.30	0.80
2002	1423.2	286.9	743.1	680.1	1118.0	305.2	6.60	5.73	0.87
2003	1456.4	307.6	761.2	695.2	1151.3	305.1	5.06	5.15	-0.09
2004	1492.7	329.8	779.9	712.8	1187.2	305.5	6.13	5.39	0.74
2005	1538.0	357.3	778.7	759.3	1286.1	251.9	6.29	5.20	1.09
2006	1601.0	403.4	817.6	783.4	1350.2	250.8	6.22	4.94	1.28
2007	1676.0	462.7	850.8	825.2	1416.2	259.8	8.16	4.83	3.33
2008	1771.0	541.1	900.2	870.8	1503.6	267.4	7.89	4.59	3.30
2009	1860.0	614.2	949.8	910.2	1581.1	278.9	7.66	4.33	3.33
2010	1961.9	704.7	1013.0	948.9	1686.4	275.5	7.27	4.29	2.98
2011	2018.6	742.2	1040.7	977.9	1740.7	277.9	8.29	4.27	4.02
2012	2069.3	773.8	1068.1	1001.2	1783.7	285.6	9.05	4.31	4.74
2013	2114.8	802.7	1090.7	1024.1	1825.1	289.7	8.93	4.52	4.41
2014	2151.6	818.7	1106.5	1045.1	1859.0	292.6	9.75	4.92	4.83

注：1. 1978-1981年为户籍统计数，含暂住人口；1982-1989年数据是根据1982年、1990年两次人口普查数据调整的；1990年以后数据为人口变动情况抽样调查推算数，其中1995年、2005年为1%人口抽样调查推算数；2000年为第五次人口普查快速汇总推算数；2010年为第六次人口普查推算数。2006-2009年常住人口、出生率、死亡率等数据根据2010年人口普查数据进行了调整。

2. “按城乡分”栏包括的“城镇人口”和“乡村人口”，1978-1989年数据为户籍管理统计中的“非农业人口”和“农业人口”口径；1990-1999年数据是根据1990年、2000年两次人口普查数据调整的；2000年数据为国家统计局1999年发布的《关于统计上划分城乡的规定(试行)》中的“城镇人口”和“乡村人口”口径，2001-2005年数据为该口径的推算数；2006-2008年数据为国家统计局2006年发布的《关于统计上划分城乡的暂行规定》中的“城镇人口”和“乡村人口”口径的推算数；2009年以后数据为《国务院关于统计上划分城乡规定的批复》中的“城镇人口”和“乡村人口”口径的推算数。

Note: a) Statistics for 1978-1981 were figures of registered residents, including temporary residents; statistics for 1982-1989 were adjusted from population censuses in 1982 and 1990. Data after 1990 were estimated from sample surveys on population changes; data for 1995 and 2005 were estimated from sample surveys on 1% of the population. Data for 2000 were estimated from fast summarizing of the fifth population census. Data for 2010 were estimated from fast summarizing of the 6th population census. Data of permanant population, birth rate and death rate, etc. from 2006 to 2009 were adjusted from population census in 2010.

b) In classification by rural and urban areas, the "urban population" and "rural population" from 1978 to 1989 were non-agricultural population and agricultural population respectively in household registration. Data from 1990-1999 were adjusted from the population censuses conducted in 1990 and 2000, and those in 2000 were on the basis of statistical classification of rural and urban population stated in the Regulations on the Statistical Division of Rural and Urban Population (trial) issued by the State Statistical Bureau in 1999. Statistics from 2001 to 2005 were estimated on the same basis. Figures from 2006 to 2008 were the estimated figures of "urban population" and "rural population", of which the statistical range was provided in Provisional Regulations on Statistical Division of Rural and Urban Areas issued by the State Statistics Bureau in 2006. Figures after 2009 were the estimated figures of "urban population" and "ruralpopulation", of which the statistical range was provided in the Official Reply of the State Council Concerning the Statistical Division of Rural and Urban Areas.

3-3 常住人口总量(按区县分)(2014年)
TOTAL NUMBER OF PERMANENT POPULATION (BY DISTRICT) (2014)

单位：万人 (10000 persons)

地 区	District	常住人口 Permanent Population	#常住外来人口 Permanent Migrant Population	城镇人口 Urban Population	乡村人口 Rural Population
全 市	**Total**	**2151.6**	**818.7**	**1859.0**	**292.6**
首都功能核心区	**Core Funtional Area of the Capital**	**221.3**	**54.0**	**221.3**	
东城区	Dongcheng District	91.1	21.2	91.1	
西城区	Xicheng District	130.2	32.8	130.2	
城市功能拓展区	**Urban Function Extension Area**	**1055.0**	**436.4**	**1043.1**	**11.9**
朝阳区	Chaoyang District	392.2	179.8	389.7	2.5
丰台区	Fengtai District	230.0	85.1	228.6	1.4
石景山区	Shijingshan District	65.0	21.2	65.0	
海淀区	Haidian District	367.8	150.3	359.8	8.0
城市发展新区	**New Area of Urban Development**	**684.9**	**296.9**	**477.5**	**207.4**
房山区	Fangshan District	103.6	26.7	71.4	32.2
通州区	Tongzhou District	135.6	55.5	87.1	48.5
顺义区	Shunyi District	100.4	38.9	54.9	45.5
昌平区	Changping District	190.8	100.2	154.7	36.1
大兴区	Daxing District	154.5	75.6	109.4	45.1
生态涵养发展区	**Ecological Conservation Area**	**190.4**	**31.4**	**117.1**	**73.3**
门头沟区	Mentougou District	30.6	4.9	26.4	4.2
怀柔区	Huairou District	38.1	10.4	25.1	13.0
平谷区	Pinggu District	42.3	5.3	23.2	19.1
密云县	Miyun County	47.8	7.2	26.5	21.3
延庆县	Yanqing County	31.6	3.6	15.9	15.7

注：本表数据为人口抽样调查推算数据，为年末数。
Note: Figures in this table are estimated figures from sample survey on population in the end of year.

3-4 常住人口密度(按区县分)(2014年)
PERMANENT POPULATION DENSITY (BY DISTRICT) (2014)

地　　区	District	土地面积 (平方公里) Land Area (sq.km)	常住人口 (万人) Permanent Population (10000 persons)	常住人口密度 (人／平方公里) Permanent Population Density (person/sq.km)
全　　市	**Total**	**16410.54**	**2151.6**	**1311**
首都功能核心区	**Capital Core Functional Area**	**92.39**	**221.3**	**23953**
东 城 区	Dongcheng District	41.86	91.1	21763
西 城 区	Xicheng District	50.53	130.2	25767
城市功能拓展区	**Urban Function Extension Area**	**1275.93**	**1055.0**	**8268**
朝 阳 区	Chaoyang District	455.08	392.2	8618
丰 台 区	Fengtai District	305.80	230.0	7521
石景山区	Shijingshan District	84.32	65.0	7709
海 淀 区	Haidian District	430.73	367.8	8539
城市发展新区	**Urban Development New Area**	**6295.57**	**684.9**	**1088**
房 山 区	Fangshan District	1989.54	103.6	521
通 州 区	Tongzhou District	906.28	135.6	1496
顺 义 区	Shunyi District	1019.89	100.4	984
昌 平 区	Changping District	1343.54	190.8	1420
大 兴 区	Daxing District	1036.32	154.5	1491
生态涵养发展区	**Ecological Conservation Area**	**8746.65**	**190.4**	**218**
门头沟区	Mentougou District	1450.70	30.6	211
怀 柔 区	Huairou District	2122.62	38.1	179
平 谷 区	Pinggu District	950.13	42.3	445
密 云 县	Miyun County	2229.45	47.8	214
延 庆 县	Yanqing County	1993.75	31.6	158

注：本表常住人口数据为人口抽样调查数据推算数据，为年末数。
资料来源：本表“土地面积”由北京市国土资源局提供。
Note: Figures of permanent population in this table are estimated figures from the sample survey on population in the end of year.
Source: Figures of land area were provided by Beijing Municipal Bureau of Land Resources.

3-5 常住人口自然变动(按区县分)(2014年)
NATURAL CHANGE OF PERMANENT POPULATION (BY DISTRICT) (2014)

地 区	District	出生人数（人）Number of Births (person)	死亡人数（人）Number of Deaths (person)	自然增加人数（人）Natural Increase of Population (person)	出生率（‰）Birth Rate (‰)	死亡率（‰）Death Rate (‰)	自然增长率（‰）Natural Growth Rate (‰)
全 市	**Total**	**208090**	**104977**	**103113**	**9.75**	**4.92**	**4.83**
首都功能核心区	**Capital Core Functional Area**	**23789**	**16224**	**7565**	**10.75**	**7.33**	**3.42**
东城区	Dongcheng District	7651	7171	480	8.41	7.88	0.53
西城区	Xicheng District	16138	9053	7085	12.39	6.95	5.44
城市功能拓展区	**Urban Function Extension Area**	**91754**	**43743**	**48011**	**8.79**	**4.19**	**4.60**
朝阳区	Chaoyang District	34099	14370	19729	8.78	3.70	5.08
丰台区	Fengtai District	21512	10403	11109	9.43	4.56	4.87
石景山区	Shijingshan District	5547	3239	2308	8.57	5.01	3.56
海淀区	Haidian District	30596	15731	14865	8.44	4.34	4.10
城市发展新区	**Urban Development New Area**	**73324**	**30517**	**42807**	**10.81**	**4.50**	**6.31**
房山区	Fangshan District	12000	5785	6215	11.73	5.65	6.08
通州区	Tongzhou District	11837	5813	6024	8.83	4.33	4.50
顺义区	Shunyi District	11763	6551	5212	11.83	6.59	5.24
昌平区	Changping Ddistrict	20684	5993	14691	10.89	3.16	7.73
大兴区	Daxing District	17040	6375	10665	11.17	4.18	6.99
生态涵养发展区	**Ecological Conservation Area**	**19223**	**14493**	**4730**	**10.11**	**7.62**	**2.49**
门头沟区	Mentougou District	2201	2410	-209	7.22	7.90	-0.68
怀柔区	Huairou District	4939	2735	2204	12.93	7.16	5.77
平谷区	Pinggu District	4673	3060	1613	11.05	7.23	3.82
密云县	Miyun County	4608	3921	687	9.66	8.22	1.44
延庆县	Yanqing County	2802	2367	435	8.87	7.49	1.38

注：本表数据为人口抽样调查推算数据。
Note: Figures in this table are estimated figures from the sample survey on population.

3-6 常住人口年龄构成(2014年)
PERMANENT POPULATION BY AGE COMPOSITION (2014)

年龄组 Age Group	常住人口数(万人) Permanent Population (10000 persons)	比重(%) Percentage (%)
合 计 Total	**2151.6**	**100.0**
0-4	90.6	4.2
5-9	71.4	3.3
10-14	51.0	2.4
15-19	84.6	3.9
20-24	223.7	10.4
25-29	243.6	11.3
30-34	229.7	10.7
35-39	168.2	7.8
40-44	183.6	8.5
45-49	170.8	7.9
50-54	161.5	7.5
55-59	151.3	7.0
60-64	109.3	5.1
65-69	71.5	3.3
70-74	49.5	2.3
75-79	45.6	2.1
80-84	29.3	1.4
85岁及以上 85 and above	16.4	0.8

注：本表数据为人口抽样调查推算数据，为年末数。
Note: Figures in this table are estimated figures from the sample survey on population in the end of year.

3-7 常住人口受教育程度(2014年)
EDUCATION ATTAINMENT OF PERMANENT POPULATION (2014)

单位：人 (person)

项目	Item	调查人口合计 Total	男 Male	女 Female
6岁及以上人口	**Population at 6 and above**	**541394**	**271649**	**269745**
#小学	Primary School	57961	26640	31321
初中	Junior Secondary School	154393	83358	71035
普通高中	Senior Secondary School	83184	43418	39766
中职	Vocational School	35457	18277	17180
大学专科	Junior College	70316	34476	35840
大学本科	4-year Unversity Education	103236	48244	54992
研究生	Postgraduate	25556	14215	11341

注：本表数据为人口抽样调查样本数据。
Note: Figures in this table are sample figures from the sample survey on population.

3-8 常住人口家庭户规模(2014年)
FAMILY SIZE OF PERMANENT POPULATION (2014)

地区	Area	调查家庭总户数(户) Total Number of Households (household)	家庭户规模所占比重(%) Percentage of Various Sized Family (%) 一人户 One Person	二人户 Two Persons	三人户 Three Persons	四人户 Four Persons	五人及以上户 Five Persons and above
全市	**Total**	**197540**	**21.3**	**30.6**	**29.8**	**10.3**	**8.0**
城镇	Urban	165798	21.7	30.2	30.9	10.0	7.2
乡村	Rural	31742	19.2	32.7	24.0	12.0	12.1

注：本表数据为人口抽样调查样本数据。
Note: Figures in this table are sample figures from the sample survey on population.

3-9 户籍人口(1978-2014年)
REGISTERED POPULATION (1978-2014)

单位：万人 (10000 persons)

年份 Year	户籍户数(万户) Registered Households (10000 households)	户籍人口 Registered Population	#60岁及以上人口 Population at 60 and above	按性别分 By Sex		按户籍性质分 By Type of Household Register		户籍人口出生人数 Births of Registered Population	户籍人口死亡人数 Deaths of Registered Population	户籍人口自然增加人数 Natural Increase of Registered Population
				男 Male	女 Female	非农业户 Non-Agricultural	农业户 Agricultural			
1978	205.5	849.7		432.1	417.5	467.0	382.6	10.9	5.2	5.7
1979	214.6	870.6		441.1	429.4	495.2	375.4	11.8	5.1	6.7
1980	223.2	885.7		448.4	437.3	510.4	375.3	13.7	5.5	8.2
1981	234.8	900.8		456.6	444.2	522.6	378.2	15.1	5.4	9.7
1982	245.0	917.8		465.5	452.3	534.0	383.8	18.2	5.2	13.1
1983	255.1	933.2		474.7	458.5	547.1	386.0	14.5	5.1	9.4
1984	263.1	945.2		481.2	464.0	558.1	387.0	13.2	5.1	8.1
1985	274.1	957.9		488.0	469.9	572.5	385.4	11.8	5.2	6.6
1986	284.6	971.2		495.5	475.7	586.8	384.4	12.9	5.2	7.8
1987	299.4	988.0		504.1	483.9	601.0	387.0	16.9	5.3	11.6
1988	310.8	1001.2		510.4	490.8	614.3	387.0	15.3	5.5	9.8
1989	322.5	1021.1		520.3	500.8	630.6	390.5	19.0	5.7	13.3
1990	335.0	1032.2		525.3	507.0	640.2	392.1	14.0	6.3	7.7
1991	343.1	1039.5		528.5	511.1	648.4	391.2	9.2	5.7	3.5
1992	349.3	1044.9		530.8	514.1	656.3	388.6	8.3	6.2	2.2
1993	354.6	1051.2		533.9	517.3	668.7	382.5	7.9	6.3	1.6
1994	360.3	1061.8		538.9	522.8	683.8	377.9	8.5	6.3	2.2
1995	365.7	1070.3		543.0	527.3	696.9	373.5	8.5	6.2	2.3
1996	370.9	1077.7		546.8	530.9	709.7	368.0	7.8	6.7	1.2
1997	375.7	1085.5		550.4	535.1	722.7	362.9	7.6	6.7	0.9
1998	383.4	1091.5		552.6	538.9	733.6	357.8	6.7	7.5	-0.8
1999	390.3	1099.8		556.7	543.1	747.2	352.6	6.3	6.2	0.1
2000	397.9	1107.5		560.1	547.4	760.7	346.8	7.2	7.8	-0.5
2001	405.3	1122.3		567.3	555.0	780.2	342.2	6.0	5.3	0.7
2002	416.3	1136.3		574.7	561.6	806.9	329.4	6.0	5.2	0.8
2003	427.6	1148.8		581.0	567.9	830.8	318.0	4.5	5.8	-1.3
2004	439.8	1162.9		587.2	575.7	854.7	308.2	6.6	6.2	0.4
2005	451.7	1180.7		596.0	584.7	880.2	300.5	7.5	7.0	0.5
2006	463.7	1197.6		604.2	593.4	905.4	292.2	7.7	5.1	2.6
2007	473.0	1213.3	210.3	612.0	601.3	929.0	284.3	9.9	5.2	4.8
2008	481.2	1229.9	218.6	620.0	609.9	950.7	279.2	10.6	5.1	5.5
2009	488.7	1245.8	228.7	627.5	618.9	971.9	273.9	10.9	6.2	4.7
2010	496.1	1257.8	237.2	632.8	625.0	989.5	268.3	10.2	9.1	1.1
2011	503.1	1277.9	250.5	642.4	635.6	1013.8	264.2	12.5	5.3	7.2
2012	509.2	1297.5	266.1	651.7	645.8	1039.3	258.2	14.5	5.7	8.8
2013	516.2	1316.3	283.2	660.4	655.9	1065.0	251.4	13.6	5.7	7.9
2014	522.6	1333.4	301.0	668.3	665.1	1089.8	243.6	17.2	7.6	9.6

资料来源：北京市公安局。
Source: Beijing Municipal Bureau of Public Security.

3-10 户籍户数及人口数(按区县分)(2014年)
REGISTERED HOUSEHOLDS AND POPULATION (BY DISTRICT) (2014)

地区	District	户籍户数及人口 Registered Households and Population					
		户数(万户) Households (10000 households)			人口数(万人) Population (10000 persons)		
		合计 Total	非农业户 Non-Agricultural	农业户 Agricultural	合计 Total	非农业户 Non-Agricultural	农业户 Agricultural
全市	**Total**	**522.6**	**415.1**	**107.5**	**1333.4**	**1089.8**	**243.6**
首都功能核心区	**Capital Core Functional Area**	**82.5**	**82.5**		**240.9**	**240.9**	
东城区	Dongcheng District	34.6	34.6		98.0	98.0	
西城区	Xicheng District	47.9	47.9		142.9	142.9	
城市功能拓展区	**Urban Function Extension Area**	**212.1**	**198.9**	**13.2**	**593.4**	**566.3**	**27.1**
朝阳区	Chaoyang District	79.6	74.5	5.1	204.2	193.8	10.4
丰台区	Fengtai District	46.6	42.2	4.4	112.8	103.6	9.2
石景山区	Shijingshan District	14.4	14.4		38.0	38.0	
海淀区	Haidian District	71.6	67.8	3.7	238.5	230.9	7.5
城市发展新区	**Urban Development New Area**	**150.8**	**92.4**	**58.4**	**334.5**	**197.0**	**137.5**
房山区	Fangshan District	37.3	22.4	15.0	79.4	46.5	32.9
通州区	Tongzhou District	34.3	20.4	13.9	70.5	39.5	31.0
顺义区	Shunyi District	26.9	16.2	10.7	60.9	35.3	25.7
昌平区	Changping District	26.0	17.6	8.4	58.5	40.4	18.1
大兴区	Daxing District	26.3	15.9	10.4	65.1	35.3	29.8
生态涵养发展区	**Ecological Conservation Area**	**77.1**	**41.3**	**35.8**	**164.6**	**85.6**	**79.0**
门头沟区	Mentougou District	12.0	9.3	2.7	24.9	20.0	4.9
怀柔区	Huairou District	13.5	6.5	7.0	28.1	13.3	14.8
平谷区	Pinggu District	17.0	9.4	7.5	40.1	21.3	18.8
密云县	Miyun County	20.7	9.3	11.3	43.3	18.4	24.9
延庆县	Yanqing County	14.0	6.8	7.2	28.2	12.6	15.6

资料来源：北京市公安局。
Source: Beijing Municipal Bureau of Public Security.

3-11 户籍人口年龄构成(2014年)
AGE COMPOSITION OF REGISTERED POPULATION (2014)

年龄组 Age Group	户籍人口(万人) Registered Population (10000 persons)			占人口比重(%) Percentage (%)		
	合计 Total	男 Male	女 Female	合计 Total	男 Male	女 Female
合计 Total	**1333.4**	**668.3**	**665.1**	**100.0**	**50.1**	**49.9**
0-4	64.4	33.2	31.2	4.8	2.5	2.3
5-9	46.8	24.1	22.6	3.5	1.8	1.7
10-14	34.2	17.6	16.6	2.6	1.3	1.2
15-19	48.2	24.2	24.0	3.6	1.8	1.8
20-24	80.6	40.5	40.1	6.0	3.0	3.0
25-29	115.5	58.9	56.6	8.7	4.4	4.2
30-34	118.4	59.7	58.7	8.9	4.5	4.4
35-39	84.4	42.7	41.7	6.3	3.2	3.1
40-44	99.0	50.3	48.7	7.4	3.8	3.7
45-49	101.7	51.3	50.3	7.6	3.9	3.8
50-54	125.9	64.4	61.5	9.4	4.8	4.6
55-59	113.4	56.6	56.9	8.5	4.2	4.3
60-64	96.7	47.2	49.4	7.2	3.5	3.7
65-69	59.3	28.7	30.6	4.4	2.2	2.3
70-74	43.5	20.3	23.2	3.3	1.5	1.7
75-79	45.5	21.3	24.2	3.4	1.6	1.8
80-84	32.4	15.9	16.5	2.4	1.2	1.2
85-89	15.6	7.6	8.0	1.2	0.6	0.6
90岁及以上 90 and above	8.0	3.7	4.2	0.6	0.3	0.3

资料来源：北京市公安局。
Source: Beijing Municipal Bureau of Public Security.

3-12 户籍人口性别构成及性别比(按区县分)(2014年)
SEX COMPOSITION AND SEX RATIO OF REGISTERED POPULATION (BY DISTRICT) (2014)

地　　区	District	户籍人口(万人) Registered Population (10000 persons)			性别比 (女=100)
		合　计 Total	男 Male	女 Female	Sex Ratio (female=100)
全　　市	**Total**	**1333.4**	**668.3**	**665.1**	**100.5**
首都功能核心区	**Capital Core Functional Area**	**240.9**	**119.7**	**121.2**	**98.8**
东 城 区	Dongcheng District	98.0	48.4	49.6	97.6
西 城 区	Xicheng District	142.9	71.3	71.6	99.6
城市功能拓展区	**Urban Function Extension Area**	**593.4**	**298.8**	**294.6**	**101.4**
朝 阳 区	Chaoyang Dsitrict	204.2	102.3	101.9	100.5
丰 台 区	Fengtai District	112.8	57.1	55.6	102.8
石景山区	Shijingshan District	38.0	19.6	18.4	106.3
海 淀 区	Haidian District	238.5	119.7	118.7	100.9
城市发展新区	**Urban Development New Area**	**334.5**	**167.0**	**167.5**	**99.6**
房 山 区	Fangshan District	79.4	39.8	39.6	100.6
通 州 区	Tongzhou District	70.5	35.0	35.5	98.7
顺 义 区	Shunyi District	60.9	30.2	30.7	98.3
昌 平 区	Changping District	58.5	29.5	29.1	101.4
大 兴 区	Daxing District	65.1	32.4	32.7	99.3
生态涵养发展区	**Ecological Conservation Area**	**164.6**	**82.8**	**81.8**	**101.3**
门头沟区	Mentougou Dsitrict	24.9	12.7	12.2	104.4
怀 柔 区	Huairou District	28.1	14.1	14.0	100.3
平 谷 区	Pinggu District	40.1	20.2	19.9	101.3
密 云 县	Miyun County	43.3	21.6	21.7	100.0
延 庆 县	Yanqing County	28.2	14.2	14.0	102.0

资料来源：北京市公安局。
Source: Beijing Municipal Bureau of Public Security.

3-13 户籍人口变动情况
CHANGES OF REGISTERED POPULATION

单位：人 (person)

项　　目	Item	2014	2013
自然变动	**Natural Changes**		
自然增加	Natural Increase	95725	78673
非农业人口	Non-agricultural Population	104363	86948
农业人口	Agricultural Population	-8638	-8275
出　生	Births	171690	135925
非农业人口	Non-agricultural Population	155866	121743
农业人口	Agricultural Population	15824	14182
死　亡	Deaths	75965	57252
非农业人口	Non-agricultural Population	51503	34795
农业人口	Agricultural Population	24462	22457
机械变动	**Non-natural Changes**		
机械增加	Non-natural Increase	74654	109656
非农业人口	Non-agricultural Population	65021	99284
农业人口	Agricultural Population	9633	10372
市外迁入	Inflow	166600	198869
非农业人口	Non-agricultural Population	155749	186990
农业人口	Agricultural Population	10851	11879
迁往市外	Outflow	91946	89213
非农业人口	Non-agricultural Population	90728	87706
农业人口	Agricultural Population	1218	1507

资料来源：北京市公安局。
Source: Beijing Municipal Bureau of Public Security.

3-14 户籍人口自然变动情况(按区县分)
NATURAL CHANGES OF REGISTERED POPULATION (BY DISTRICT)

单位：人 (person)

地 区	District	出生人数 Number of Births		死亡人数 Number of Deaths		自然增加人数 Number of Natural Increase	
		2014	2013	2014	2013	2014	2013
全 市	**Total**	**171690**	**135925**	**75965**	**57252**	**95725**	**78673**
首都功能核心区	**Capital Core Functional Area**	**29789**	**23351**	**14508**	**9303**	**15281**	**14048**
东 城 区	Dongcheng District	11816	9426	6695	3884	5121	5542
西 城 区	Xicheng District	17973	13925	7813	5419	10160	8506
城市功能拓展区	**Urban Function Extension Area**	**73037**	**58501**	**26690**	**19046**	**46347**	**39455**
朝 阳 区	Chaoyang District	27504	22211	10602	7445	16902	14766
丰 台 区	Fengtai District	13559	10819	6291	4641	7268	6178
石景山区	Shijingshan District	4512	3549	2543	1506	1969	2043
海 淀 区	Haidian District	27462	21922	7254	5454	20208	16468
城市发展新区	**Urban Development New Area**	**49850**	**38863**	**22664**	**18197**	**27186**	**20666**
房 山 区	Fangshan District	10395	8201	5388	4576	5007	3625
通 州 区	Tongzhou District	10294	7993	5527	4155	4767	3838
顺 义 区	Shunyi District	9399	6670	4023	3629	5376	3041
昌 平 区	Changping District	8883	7240	3959	2723	4924	4517
大 兴 区	Daxing District	10879	8759	3767	3114	7112	5645
生态涵养发展区	**Ecological Conservation Area**	**19014**	**15210**	**12103**	**10706**	**6911**	**4504**
门头沟区	Mentougou District	2465	2050	2165	1491	300	559
怀 柔 区	Huairou District	3493	2694	1836	1887	1657	807
平 谷 区	Pinggu District	4962	4037	3224	2564	1738	1473
密 云 县	Miyun County	5047	3727	3095	2955	1952	772
延 庆 县	Yanqing County	3047	2702	1783	1809	1264	893

资料来源：北京市公安局。
Source: Beijing Municipal Bureau of Public Security.

3-15 三次产业从业人员年末人数及构成(1978-2014年)

EMPLOYED PERSONS IN THREE INDUSTRIES AND THEIR COMPOSITION (1978-2014)

年 份 Year	从业人员年末人数 (万人) Year-end Employed Persons (10000 persons)				构 成(%) (合计=100) Composition (%) (Total=100)		
		第一产业 Primary Industry	第二产业 Secondary Industry	第三产业 Tertiary Industry	第一产业 Primary Industry	第二产业 Secondary Industry	第三产业 Tertiary Industry
1978	444.1	125.9	177.9	140.3	28.3	40.1	31.6
1979	470.5	121.4	195.2	153.9	25.8	41.5	32.7
1980	484.2	118.0	207.3	158.9	24.4	42.8	32.8
1981	511.7	117.2	220.4	174.1	22.9	43.1	34.0
1982	535.2	115.1	228.6	191.5	21.5	42.7	35.8
1983	552.0	117.1	240.2	194.7	21.2	43.5	35.3
1984	556.2	111.3	247.9	197.0	20.0	44.6	35.4
1985	566.5	100.6	260.4	205.5	17.7	46.0	36.3
1986	572.7	96.1	262.7	213.9	16.8	45.9	37.3
1987	580.2	92.3	264.1	223.8	15.9	45.5	38.6
1988	584.1	88.4	267.6	228.1	15.1	45.8	39.1
1989	593.9	91.0	266.3	236.6	15.3	44.9	39.8
1990	627.1	90.7	281.6	254.8	14.5	44.9	40.6
1991	634.0	90.8	279.7	263.5	14.3	44.1	41.6
1992	649.3	84.5	281.6	283.2	13.0	43.4	43.6
1993	627.8	65.1	279.4	283.3	10.4	44.5	45.1
1994	664.3	73.2	272.2	318.9	11.0	41.0	48.0
1995	665.3	70.6	271.0	323.7	10.6	40.7	48.7
1996	660.2	72.5	260.1	327.6	11.0	39.4	49.6
1997	655.8	71.0	257.6	327.2	10.8	39.2	50.0
1998	622.2	71.5	226.0	324.7	11.5	36.3	52.2
1999	618.6	74.5	216.2	327.9	12.1	34.9	53.0
2000	619.3	72.9	208.2	338.2	11.8	33.6	54.6
2001	628.9	71.2	215.9	341.8	11.3	34.3	54.4
2002	679.2	67.6	235.3	376.3	10.0	34.6	55.4
2003	703.3	62.7	225.8	414.8	8.9	32.1	59.0
2004	854.1	61.5	232.8	559.8	7.2	27.3	65.5
2005	878.0	62.2	231.1	584.7	7.1	26.3	66.6
2006	919.7	60.3	225.4	634.0	6.6	24.5	68.9
2007	942.7	60.9	228.1	653.7	6.5	24.2	69.3
2008	980.9	63.0	207.4	710.5	6.4	21.2	72.4
2009	998.3	62.2	199.6	736.5	6.2	20.0	73.8
2010	1031.6	61.4	202.7	767.5	6.0	19.6	74.4
2011	1069.7	59.1	219.2	791.4	5.5	20.5	74.0
2012	1107.3	57.3	212.6	837.4	5.2	19.2	75.6
2013	1141.0	55.4	210.9	874.7	4.8	18.5	76.7
2014	1156.7	52.4	209.9	894.4	4.5	18.2	77.3

注：1. 2010年及以前，劳务派遣人员按照“谁发工资谁统计”的原则进行统计。2011年以后，劳务派遣人员按照“谁用工谁统计”的原则进行统计。

2. 自2012年开始，三次产业划分执行国家统计局《三次产业划分规定》(国统字〔2012〕108号)。

Note: a) In 2010 and before, dispatched personnel of labor service were calculated by "wage payers". After 2011, dispatched personnel of labor service were calculated by "employers".

b) Since 2012, the three industries have been classified according to the Regulations on the Classification of the Three Industries (G.T.Z. [2012] No. 108) issued by National Bureau of Statistics.

3-16 按登记注册类型分从业人员年末人数(1978-2014年)
YEAR-END EMPLOYED PERSONS BY TYPE OF REGISTRATION (1978-2014)

单位：万人 (10000 persons)

年份 Year	合计 Total	#城镇 Urban	#国有单位 State-owned Enterprises	#集体单位 Collectively-owned Enterprises	#联营单位 Associated Enterprises	#有限责任公司 Limited Liability Companies	#股份有限公司 Companies Limited by Shares	#外商投资 Foreign-invested	#港澳台商投资 Hong Kong, Macao and Taiwan-invested	#私营 Private Enterprises	#个体 Individual Economy
1978	444.1	291.6	240.9	50.7							
1979	470.5	311.9	254.2	57.8							
1980	484.2	326.8	269.4	57.1							0.3
1981	511.7	345.2	283.1	61.3							
1982	535.2	361.1	293.0	67.1							
1983	552.0	373.8	303.4	68.5							
1984	556.2	377.6	302.5	71.6				1.3			
1985	566.5	392.6	308.1	72.6				1.6			2.5
1986	572.7	400.5	324.4	71.1				2.4			2.6
1987	580.2	408.3	331.8	70.7				2.8			3.1
1988	584.1	413.9	336.4	69.9	0.2			3.4			3.5
1989	593.9	424.0	343.8	67.4	3.4			3.7			5.6
1990	627.1	461.2	357.9	86.8	5.1			4.6			6.3
1991	634.0	477.2	367.8	89.0	0.5			7.7	0.2		7.2
1992	649.3	490.6	371.5	90.5	0.4			11.4	0.2		14.0
1993	627.8	481.4	362.3	79.7	2.8			11.0	6.4		14.0
1994	664.3	492.7	363.5	73.3	3.5			15.0	9.4		20.9
1995	665.3	492.7	358.2	72.1	3.7			17.4	10.0		21.9
1996	660.2	495.7	355.1	68.6	3.4			20.7	10.1		22.9
1997	655.8	498.7	354.7	68.5	3.2			21.2	10.2		21.2
1998	622.2	463.2	308.1	51.0	5.2	13.7	10.8	21.2	13.1		20.1
1999	618.6	456.1	287.6	49.7	4.8	24.0	12.2	20.6	13.5		23.7
2000	619.3	456.3	266.2	48.3	4.0	34.2	14.0	23.8	14.2		24.4
2001	628.9	464.2	246.3	45.8	4.1	50.6	17.3	22.4	12.9		24.8
2002	679.2	513.6	224.8	36.8	4.1	85.0	27.1	29.2	17.0	4.8	33.1
2003	703.3	533.7	212.8	30.1	3.8	102.3	33.4	31.5	17.3	5.2	37.2
2004	854.1	682.7	199.5	28.2	3.5	134.5	37.9	45.0	18.3	134.2	45.7
2005	878.0	694.0	195.0	23.8	2.4	149.4	36.4	49.6	21.7	131.2	57.2
2006	919.7	734.2	189.3	18.8	2.1	165.1	35.5	57.3	23.5	154.8	65.6
2007	942.7	745.4	189.3	17.3	1.9	179.5	38.7	69.3	28.8	133.8	67.2
2008	980.9	813.7	187.8	24.8	2.2	196.4	46.4	72.9	33.5	159.6	65.1
2009	998.3	856.6	185.7	24.3	0.9	215.7	58.4	71.2	36.6	172.2	67.5
2010	1031.6	905.4	189.0	22.7	0.9	228.2	64.7	74.9	42.4	193.5	65.3
2011	1069.7	955.8	188.8	20.1	0.7	243.0	75.9	90.1	50.6	210.6	59.3
2012	1107.3	996.1	188.3	19.8	0.7	261.6	83.2	92.7	54.3	227.9	50.8
2013	1141.0	1073.0	189.5	17.5	0.7	278.0	85.4	96.1	56.1	265.9	64.8
2014	1156.7	1066.2	188.6	18.8	0.5	290.6	86.2	94.5	58.7	254.6	55.7

资料来源：表中2002-2013年私营从业人员数据来源于北京市工商行政管理局，2014年数据根据劳动工资年报全面调查和抽样调查推算得到；个体从业人员数据来源于北京市工商行政管理局。

Source: Figures of employed persons in private enterprises from 2002 to 2013 in this table were from Beijing Administration for Industry and Commerce. Figures in 2014 were calculated based on comprehensive and sample surveys in annual report on employee salary; and figures on self-employed individuals were from Beijing Administration for Industry and Commerce.

3-17 全市法人单位从业人员年末人数和平均工资
YEAR-END EMPLOYED PERSONS IN LEGAL ENTITIES AND AVERAGE WAGES

项目	Item	从业人员年末人数（万人）Year-end Employed Persons (10000 persons)		从业人员平均工资（元）Average Wage (yuan)	
		2014	2013	2014	2013
合计	**Total**	**1010.5**	**981.9**	**89804**	**82045**
按登记注册类型分	**By Registration Type**				
内资	Domestically-invested Enterprises	857.3	829.7	82566	75121
国有	State-owned Enterprises	188.6	189.5	102538	94173
集体	Collectively-owned Enterprises	18.8	17.5	45500	42502
股份合作	Joint-equity Cooperative Enterprises	6.6	6.8	42134	38149
联营	Associated Enterprises	0.5	0.7	69300	48850
有限责任公司	Limited Liability Companies	290.6	278.0	82562	74007
股份有限公司	Companies Limited by Shares	86.2	85.4	140914	125033
私营	Private Enterprises	254.6	239.6	52902	48027
其他	Others	11.4	12.2	60536	54442
港、澳、台商投资	Hong Kong, Macao and Taiwan-invested Enterprises	58.7	56.1	114991	104819
外商投资	Foreign-invested Enterprises	94.5	96.1	139490	128513
按国民经济行业分	**By Sector**				
农、林、牧、渔业	Agriculture, Forestry, Animal Production and Hunting, Fishing	4.2	3.9	45877	45286
采矿业	Mining and Quarrying	6.2	6.8	90010	82239
制造业	Manufacturing	129.9	133.2	72672	66218
电力、热力、燃气及水生产和供应业	Production and Distribution of Electricity, Heating Power, Gas and Water	8.6	9.1	110032	97934
建筑业	Construction	63.7	60.8	67422	60713
批发和零售业	Wholesale and Retail Trade	123.0	122.6	73290	66681
交通运输、仓储和邮政业	Transport, Storage and Post	66.6	65.5	74259	68379
住宿和餐饮业	Lodging and Catering Services	44.1	46.2	45417	41708
信息传输、软件和信息技术服务业	Information Transmission, Software and Information Technology Services	84.4	79.4	128507	119766
金融业	Financial Intermediation	45.9	40.5	217409	200529
房地产业	Real Estate	52.4	52.0	73859	69020
租赁和商务服务业	Leasing and Business Services	124.4	109.5	85663	81934
科学研究和技术服务业	Scientific Research and Development, Technical Services	82.7	79.1	107430	99072
水利、环境和公共设施管理业	Management of Water Conservancy, Environment and Public Facilities	11.8	11.4	63375	56201
居民服务、修理和其他服务业	Resident Service, Repair and Other Services	17.2	17.8	42239	39390
教育	Education	49.0	49.5	96190	85406
卫生和社会工作	Health Care and Social Works	26.9	26.1	121326	106907
文化、体育和娱乐业	Culture, Sports and Entertainment	22.8	23.0	104626	99851
公共管理、社会保障和社会组织	Public Management, Social Security and Social Organizations	46.7	45.5	76226	73552
国际组织	International Organizations				

注：行业划分执行2011年国民经济行业分类标准(GB/T 4754-2011)。
Note: Sectors in this table are classified in accordance with the Standard for Classification of National Economic Sectors 2011 (GB/T 4754-2011).

3-18 城镇单位在岗职工年末人数及工资总额(1978-2014年)
YEAR-END NUMBER AND WAGES OF FULLY EMPLOYED STAFF AND WORKERS IN URBAN ENTITIES (1978-2014)

年 份 Year	在岗职工年末人数(万人) Year-end Fully Employed Staff and Workers (10000 persons)	国有单位 State-owned	集体单位 Collectively-owned	其他单位 Others	在岗职工工资总额(亿元) Total Wages of Fully Employed Staff and Workers (100 million yuan)	国有单位 State-owned	集体单位 Collectively-owned	其他单位 Others
1978	291.6	240.9	50.7		18.7	16.2	2.5	
1979	311.9	254.2	57.7		22.4	19.4	3.0	
1980	326.5	269.4	57.1		26.9	23.3	3.6	
1981-1985					**183.7**	**153.7**	**29.6**	**0.4**
1981	344.4	283.1	61.3		28.3	24.2	4.1	
1982	360.1	293.0	67.1		30.5	25.9	4.6	
1983	371.9	303.4	68.5		33.8	28.5	5.3	
1984	375.4	302.5	71.6	1.3	40.4	33.7	6.6	0.1
1985	382.3	308.1	72.6	1.6	50.7	41.5	9.0	0.3
1986-1990					**421.1**	**349.7**	**64.4**	**7.0**
1986	397.9	324.4	71.1	2.4	58.0	48.5	9.1	0.4
1987	405.2	331.8	70.7	2.7	66.7	56.0	10.1	0.6
1988	410.4	336.4	69.9	4.1	81.2	68.1	12.1	1.0
1989	418.4	343.8	67.4	7.2	96.3	81.0	13.4	1.9
1990	454.9	357.9	86.8	10.2	118.9	96.1	19.7	3.1
1991-1995					**1198.1**	**950.3**	**156.6**	**91.2**
1991	470.0	367.8	89.0	13.2	132.2	106.1	21.5	4.6
1992	476.6	371.5	90.5	14.6	158.5	128.6	23.9	6.0
1993	467.3	362.3	79.6	25.4	218.9	176.6	28.5	13.8
1994	471.8	363.5	73.4	34.9	306.5	243.4	36.2	26.9
1995	470.9	358.2	72.1	40.6	382.0	295.6	46.5	39.9
1996-2000					**2825.4**	**1988.5**	**236.5**	**600.4**
1996	460.6	349.0	64.8	46.8	442.4	339.4	46.2	56.8
1997	465.3	348.7	65.0	51.6	514.8	383.6	53.8	77.4
1998	450.1	321.7	50.8	77.6	558.2	391.9	45.0	121.3
1999	438.0	303.0	49.6	85.4	614.5	420.0	44.8	149.7
2000	434.2	283.0	46.0	105.2	695.5	453.6	46.7	195.2
2001-2005					**5662.3**	**2872.7**	**184.6**	**2605.0**
2001	400.3	235.9	40.0	124.4	777.3	477.8	44.8	254.7
2002	434.2	212.6	32.7	188.9	950.9	508.8	40.0	402.1
2003	436.3	197.6	26.1	212.6	1098.9	565.5	35.0	498.4
2004	446.4	183.7	24.8	237.9	1315.1	625.7	34.0	655.4
2005	448.4	178.5	20.7	249.2	1520.1	694.9	30.8	794.4
2006-2010					**13890.4**	**4904.7**	**219.9**	**8765.8**
2006	453.1	172.9	16.4	263.8	1805.5	738.0	30.5	1037.0
2007	478.9	172.7	15.4	290.8	2194.3	862.4	31.2	1300.7
2008	526.1	171.0	22.7	332.4	2874.3	1008.8	48.2	1817.3
2009	560.4	170.9	22.4	367.1	3227.2	1074.3	53.3	2099.6
2010	587.7	175.1	21.1	391.5	3789.1	1221.2	56.7	2511.2
2011	640.3	177.1	18.7	444.5	4778.6	1421.1	62.3	3295.2
2012	670.4	177.3	18.6	474.5	5657.9	1582.5	71.6	4003.8
2013	695.5	178.4	16.5	500.6	6502.0	1724.7	70.2	4707.1
2014	708.8	177.7	17.8	513.3	7293.3	1884.5	81.5	5327.3

注：1. 2007年及以前城镇单位是指乡及乡以上独立核算法人单位，不包括乡镇企业、私营单位和个体工商户。2008年及以后城镇单位是指不包括私营单位和个体工商户的独立核算法人单位(下表同)。

2. 表中2000年及以前数据为职工口径，职工包括在岗职工和不在岗职工(下表同)。

Note: a) Urban entities in and before 2007 referred to legal entities with independent accounting at and above township level, excluding township enterprises, private entities and self-employed businesses. Urban entities in and after 2008 referred to legal entities with independent accounting excluding private entities and self-employed businesses (the same to the follow Tables).

b) Figures before 2001 were counted by the statistical range of employees including on-the-job and off-the-job ones (the same to the follow tables).

3-19 城镇单位在岗职工平均工资(1978-2014年)
AVERAGE WAGES OF FULLY EMPLOYED STAFF AND WORKERS IN URBAN ENTITIES (1978-2014)

单位：元 (yuan)

年份 Year	在岗职工平均工资 Average Wage of Fully Employed Staff and Workers	国有单位 State-owned Enterprises	集体单位 Collectively-owned Enterprises	其他单位 Others
1978	673	703	471	
1979	742	778	556	
1980	848	889	635	
1981	837	880	685	
1982	863	896	715	
1983	931	964	785	
1984	1086	1127	946	1170
1985	1343	1367	1231	1768
1986	1488	1530	1287	2080
1987	1670	1712	1449	2267
1988	2000	2048	1738	2661
1989	2312	2366	1992	2761
1990	2653	2713	2334	3243
1991	2877	2937	2504	3713
1992	3402	3500	2828	4289
1993	4780	4920	3834	5469
1994	6540	6695	5009	8179
1995	8144	8237	6516	10278
1996	9579	9645	7133	13851
1997	11019	10917	8259	15370
1998	12285	11971	8800	15989
1999	13778	13483	8928	17748
2000	15726	15483	9844	19165
2001	19155	19776	11063	20594
2002	21852	23754	11997	21432
2003	25312	28464	13580	23769
2004	29674	34009	13422	28026
2005	34191	39067	14695	32324
2006	40117	43298	17781	39513
2007	46507	50524	20379	45508
2008	54913	59361	20990	54983
2009	58140	63239	23553	57911
2010	65683	70320	26607	65755
2011	75834	81215	32469	75584
2012	85307	90456	38596	85234
2013	93997	97356	42482	94513
2014	103400	106097	45772	104473

3-20 城镇单位在岗职工年末人数
YEAR-END NUMBER OF FULLY EMPLOYED STAFF AND WORKERS IN URBAN ENTITIES

单位：人 (person)

项 目	Item	2014	2013	2014年为2013年% 2014 as % of 2013
合 计	**Total**	**7087922**	**6954597**	**101.9**
按登记注册类型分	**By Registration Type**			
内 资	Domestically-invested Enterprises	5654074	5524082	102.4
国 有	State-owned Enterprises	1777188	1783445	99.6
集 体	Collectively-owned Enterprises	177558	165345	107.4
股份合作	Joint-equity Cooperative Enterprises	61565	63766	96.5
联 营	Associated Enterprises	4174	6469	64.5
有限责任公司	Limited Liability Companies	2750957	2626320	104.7
股份有限公司	Companies Limited By Shares	787663	781099	100.8
其 他	Others	94969	97638	97.3
港、澳、台商投资	Hong Kong, Macao and Taiwan-invested Enterprises	556049	533924	104.1
外商投资	Foreign-invested Enterprises	877799	896591	97.9
按国民经济行业分	**By Sector**			
农、林、牧、渔业	Agriculture, Forestry, Animal Production and Hunting, Fishing	31839	30589	104.1
#农 业	Agriculture	8991	10974	81.9
采矿业	Mining and Quarrying	60871	67397	90.3
制造业	Manufacturing	974278	1007050	96.7
电力、热力、燃气及水生产和供应业	Production and Distribution of Electricity, Heating Power, Gas and Water	80364	85403	94.1
建筑业	Construction	428302	412088	103.9
批发和零售业	Wholesale and Retail Trade	679266	647356	104.9
批发业	Wholesale	380070	341847	111.2
零售业	Retail Trade	299196	305509	97.9
交通运输、仓储和邮政业	Transport, Storage and Post	589029	577387	102.0
#铁路运输业	Transport via Railway	110091	98182	112.1
道路运输业	Transport via Road	278198	269597	103.2
邮政业	Post	75790	77134	98.3
住宿和餐饮业	Lodging and Catering Services	261676	271133	96.5
住宿业	Lodging	126701	133707	94.8
餐饮业	Catering Services	134975	137426	98.2
信息传输、软件和信息技术服务业	Information Transmission, Software and Information Technology Services	597654	570199	104.8
金融业	Financial Intermediation	355455	321056	110.7
房地产业	Real Estate	381249	378727	100.7
租赁和商务服务业	Leasing and Business Services	676508	625960	108.1
租赁业	Leasing	18896	18147	104.1
商务服务业	Business Services	657612	607813	108.2
科学研究和技术服务业	Scientific Research and Development, Technical Services	554289	547380	101.3
水利、环境和公共设施管理业	Management of Water Conservancy, Environment and Public Facilities	94743	92830	102.1
居民服务、修理和其他服务业	Resident Services, Repair and Other Services	81363	85358	95.3
#居民服务业	Resident Services	27030	28886	93.6
教 育	Education	413158	415072	99.5
卫生和社会工作	Health Care and Social Works	239932	234651	102.3
#卫 生	Health Care	229295	223300	102.7
文化、体育和娱乐业	Culture, Sports and Entertainment	163532	170225	96.1
#文化艺术业	Cultures and Arts	31908	34937	91.3
体 育	Sports Activities	21595	22917	94.2
公共管理、社会保障和社会组织	Public Management, Social Security and Social Organizations	424414	414736	102.3

注：行业划分执行2011年国民经济行业分类标准(GB/T 4754-2011)。
Note: Sectors in this table are classified in accordance with the Standard for Classification of National Economic Sectors 2011 (GB/T 4754-2011).

3-21 城镇单位在岗职工工资总额
TOTAL WAGES OF FULLY EMPLOYED STAFF AND WORKERS IN URBAN ENTITIES

单位：万元 (10000 yuan)

项目	Item	2014	2013	2014年为2013年% 2014 as % of 2013
合计	**Total**	**72933475**	**65020386**	**112.2**
按登记注册类型分	**By Registration Type**			
内资	Domestically-invested Enterprises	54893951	48623030	112.9
国有	State-owned Enterprises	18844866	17247256	109.3
集体	Collectively-owned Enterprises	815114	702385	116.0
股份合作	Joint-equity Cooperative Enterprises	258467	241660	107.0
联营	Associated Enterprises	29717	31636	93.9
有限责任公司	Limited Liability Companies	22844292	19698696	116.0
股份有限公司	Companies Limited By Shares	11555570	10199839	113.3
其他	Others	545925	501558	108.8
港、澳、台商投资	Hong Kong, Macao and Taiwan-invested Enterprises	6257128	5454356	114.7
外商投资	Foreign-invested Enterprises	11782396	10943000	107.7
按国民经济行业分	**By Sector**			
农、林、牧、渔业	Agriculture, Forestry, Animal Production and Hunting, Fishing	161684	153878	105.1
#农业	Agriculture	40092	40314	99.4
采矿业	Mining and Quarrying	566759	559621	101.3
制造业	Manufacturing	7787615	7318327	106.4
电力、热力、燃气及水生产和供应业	Production and Distribution of Electricity, Heating Power, Gas and Water	985803	881792	111.8
建筑业	Construction	3298914	2867294	115.1
批发和零售业	Wholesale and Retail Trade	6215521	5444375	114.2
批发业	Wholesale	4382943	3704126	118.3
零售业	Retail Trade	1832578	1740249	105.3
交通运输、仓储和邮政业	Transport, Storage and Post	4534130	4077794	111.2
#铁路运输业	Transport via Railway	929446	834737	111.3
道路运输业	Transport via Road	1455206	1222995	119.0
邮政业	Post	577940	528828	109.3
住宿和餐饮业	Accommodation and Restaurants	1350865	1298478	104.0
住宿业	Accommodation	703362	692415	101.6
餐饮业	Restaurants	647503	606063	106.8
信息传输、软件和信息技术服务业	Information Transmission, Software and Information Technology Services	8628701	7601404	113.5
金融业	Finance	8857510	7414384	119.5
房地产业	Real Estate	3080021	2753756	111.8
租赁和商务服务业	Renting and Leasing Activities and Business Services	6739051	5908539	114.1
租赁业	Renting and Leasing Activities	128322	89477	143.4
商务服务业	Business Services	6610729	5819062	113.6
科学研究和技术服务业	Scientific Research and Development, Technical Services	6991615	6298432	111.0
水利、环境和公共设施管理业	Management of Water Conservancy, Environment and Public Facilities	618061	555050	111.4
居民服务、修理和其他服务业	Resident Services, Repair and Other Services	378141	377374	100.2
#居民服务业	Resident Services	127828	122159	104.6
教育	Education	4242184	3750880	113.1
卫生和社会工作	Health Care and Social Works	3023218	2574247	117.4
#卫生	Health Care	2962691	2515513	117.8
文化、体育和娱乐业	Culture, Sports and Entertainment	2038800	1955010	104.3
#文化艺术业	Cultures and Arts	291910	281876	103.6
体育	Sports Activities	157765	143288	110.1
公共管理、社会保障和社会组织	Public Management, Social Security and Social Organizations	3434882	3229751	106.4
国际组织	International Organizations			

注：行业划分执行2011年国民经济行业分类标准(GB/T 4754-2011)。
Note: Sectors in this table are classified in accordance with the Standard for Classification of National Economic Sectors 2011 (GB/T 4754-2011).

3-22 城镇单位在岗职工平均工资
AVERAGE WAGES OF FULLY EMPLOYED STAFF AND WORKERS IN URBAN ENTITIES

单位：元 (yuan)

项目	Item	2014	2013	2014年为2013年% 2014as % of 2013
合计	**Total**	**103400**	**93997**	**110.0**
按登记注册类型分	**By Registration Type**			
内资	Domestically-invested Enterprises	97602	88486	110.3
国有	State-owned Enterprises	106097	97356	109.0
集体	Collectively-owed Enterprises	45772	42482	107.7
股份合作	Joint-equity Cooperative Enterprises	41757	37960	110.0
联营	Associated Enterprises	70004	48109	145.5
有限责任公司	Limited Liability Companies	83932	75356	111.4
股份有限公司	Companies Limited By Shares	146981	131357	111.9
其他	Others	56947	51560	110.4
港、澳、台商投资	Hong Kong, Macao and Taiwan-invested Enterprises	113719	103059	110.3
外商投资	Foreign-invested Enterprises	134036	122538	109.4
按国民经济行业分	**By Sector**			
农、林、牧、渔业	Agriculture, Forestry, Animal Production and Hunting, Fishing	49798	48836	102.0
#农业	Agriculture	43357	35447	122.3
采矿业	Mining and Quarrying	90485	82729	109.4
制造业	Manufacturing	79077	71812	110.1
电力、热力、燃气及水生产和供应业	Production and Distribution of Electricity, Heating Power, Gas and Water	113363	100677	112.6
建筑业	Construction	78069	69525	112.3
批发和零售业	Wholesale and Retail Trade	90717	84535	107.3
批发业	Wholesale	114033	109711	103.9
零售业	Retail Trade	60924	56794	107.3
交通运输、仓储和邮政业	Transport, Storage and Post	78294	71958	108.8
#铁路运输业	Transport via Railway	90381	85481	105.7
道路运输业	Transport via Road	53038	46319	114.5
邮政业	Post	74983	69943	107.2
住宿和餐饮业	Accommodation and Restaurants	51164	47217	108.4
住宿业	Accommodation	54638	50502	108.2
餐饮业	Restaurants	47858	43951	108.9
信息传输、软件和信息技术服务业	Information Transmission, Software and Information Technology Service	146996	135346	108.6
金融业	Finance	253148	234497	108.0
房地产业	Real Estate	80407	73578	109.3
租赁和商务服务业	Renting and Leasing Activities and Business Services	102437	95525	107.2
租赁业	Renting and Leasing Activities	66313	51297	129.3
商务服务业	Business Services	103532	96809	106.9
科学研究和技术服务业	Scientific Research and Development, Technical Services	127304	116571	109.2
水利、环境和公共设施管理业	Management of Water Conservancy, Environment and Public Facilities	66184	59276	111.7
居民服务、修理和其他服务业	Resident Services, Repair and Other Services	46320	44023	105.2
#居民服务业	Resident Services	46997	41868	112.3
教育	Education	103198	91166	113.2
卫生和社会工作	Health Care and Social Works	128410	112293	114.4
#卫生	Health Care	131786	115402	114.2
文化、体育和娱乐业	Culture, Sports and Entertainment	123807	115062	107.6
#文化艺术业	Cultures and Arts	91373	81717	111.8
体育	Sports Activities	72194	61837	116.7
公共管理、社会保障和社会组织	Pulic Management,Social Security and Social Organizations	81288	78310	103.8
国际组织	International Organizations			

注：行业划分执行2011年国民经济行业分类标准(GB/T 4754-2011)。
Note: Sectors in this table are classified in accordance with the Standard for Classification of National Economic Sectors 2011 (GB/T 4754-2011).

3-23 国民经济各行业城镇单位在岗职工平均工资(2014年)
AVERAGE WAGES OF URBAN ENTITIES FULLY EMPLOYED STAFF AND WORKERS IN DIFFERENT SECTORS OF NATIONAL ECONOMY (2014)

单位：元 (yuan)

项　目	Item	平均工资 Average Wages	国有单位 State-owned	集体单位 Collectively-Owned	其他单位 Others
合　计	**Total**	**103400**	**106097**	**45772**	**104473**
农、林、牧、渔业	**Agriculture, Forestry, Animal Production and Hunting,Fishing**	**49798**	**59628**	**28906**	**48654**
#农、林、牧、渔服务业	Service Activities for Agriculture, Forestry, Animal Production and Hunting, Fishing	48216	73221	34379	35359
采矿业	**Mining and Quarrying**	**90485**		**67024**	**90756**
煤炭开采和洗选业	Mining and Washing of Coal	75324			75324
石油和天然气开采业	Extraction of Petroleum and Natural Gas	107443			107443
黑色金属矿采选业	Mining and Processing of Ferrous Metal Ores	81906		75022	82073
有色金属矿采选业	Mining and Processing of Non-Ferrous Metal Ores				
非金属矿采选业	Mining and Processing of Nonmetal Ores	54930		27694	64796
开采辅助活动	Mining Support Service Activities	109878			109878
其他采矿业	Mining of Other Ores	103833			103833
制造业	**Manufacturing**	**79077**	**96570**	**38662**	**79281**
农副食品加工业	Processing of Food from Agricultural Products	56948	51725	27900	57794
食品制造业	Manufacture of Foods	66247	46656	27119	66574
酒、饮料和精制茶制造业	Manufacture of Wine, Beverage and Refined Tea	70832	81493	29615	67916
烟草制品业	Manufacture of Cigarettes and Tobacco	200197	200197		
纺织业	Manufacture of Textile	48551	78102	29320	47860
纺织服装、服饰业	Manufacture of Textile, Wearing Apparel and Ornament	45788	45542	36548	46303
皮革、毛皮、羽毛及其制品和制鞋业	Manufacture of Leather, Fur, Feather and Its Products, and Footwear	45021	45769	71255	42211
木材加工和木、竹、藤、棕、草制品业	Processing of Timbers, Manufacture of Wood, Bamboo, Rattan, Palm and Straw Products	50455		26218	51482
家具制造业	Manufacture of Furniture	47607	55500	27938	47775
造纸和纸制品业	Manufacture of Paper and Paper Products	50717	51200	31334	53899
印刷和记录媒介复制业	Printing, Reproduction of Recording Media	61351	72090	50334	60091
文教、工美、体育和娱乐用品制造业	Manufacture of Articles for Culture, Education, Artwork, Sport and Entertainment Activities	50264	41151	39502	50942
石油加工、炼焦和核燃料加工业	Processing of Petroleum, Coking, Processing of Nucleus Fuels	81617	91364	24657	81697
化学原料和化学制品制造业	Manufacture of Chemical Raw Materials and Chemical Products	72454	92962	34504	72189
医药制造业	Manufacture of Medicines	124183	91060	38572	125534
化学纤维制造业	Manufacture of Chemical Fibers	55597			55597
橡胶和塑料制品业	Manufacture of Rubber and Plastics Products	51448	64847	44266	51765
非金属矿物制品业	Manufacture of Non-metallic Mineral Products	57439	58130	32725	58749
黑色金属冶炼和压延加工业	Manufacture and Pressing of Ferrous Metals	64463	60351	32737	65775

注：行业划分执行2011年国民经济行业分类标准(GB/T 4754-2011)。
Note: Sectors in this table are classified in accordance with the Standard for Classification of National Economic Sectors 2011 (GB/T 4754-2011).

3-23 续表 1 Continued 1

单位：元 (yuan)

行业	Sector	平均工资 Average Wages	国有单位 State-owned	集体单位 Collectively-Owned	其他单位 Others
有色金属冶炼和压延加工业	Manufacture and Pressing of Nonferrous Metals	66376	95580	33321	66920
金属制品业	Manufacture of Fabricated Metal Products	57054	49410	33981	59120
通用设备制造业	Manufacture of General-Purpose Machinery	78926	101331	38171	79688
专用设备制造业	Manufacture of Special-Purpose Machinery	83428	89748	45082	83784
汽车制造业	Manufacture of Motor Vehicles	80025	47733	42615	80279
铁路、船舶、航空航天和其他运输设备制造业	Manufacture of Railway Locomotives, Building of Ships and Boats, Manufacture of Air and Spacecrafts and Other Transportation Equipment	100650	135797	54119	86026
电气机械和器材制造业	Manufacture of Electrical Machinery and Equipment	83808	78270	38933	84707
计算机、通信和其他电子设备制造业	Manufacture of Computers, Communication Equipment and Other Electronic Equipment	96288	67498	39896	96640
仪器仪表制造业	Manufacture of Measuring Instruments and Meters	92608	77697	57320	93792
其他制造业	Other Manufacturing	97410	121551	29528	91515
废弃资源综合利用业	Waste Rrecycling and Recovery	63835	93957	32711	65257
金属制品、机械和设备修理业	Repair of Fabricated Metal Products, Machinery and Equipment	113421	45403	36539	115557
电力、热力、燃气及水生产和供应业	**Production and Distribution of Electricity, Heating Power, Gas and Water**	**113363**	**124831**	**34719**	**110229**
电力、热力生产和供应业	Production and Distribution of Electricity and Heating Power	121685	130213	34536	118879
燃气生产和供应业	Production and Distribution of Gas	99906	77989		102982
水的生产和供应业	Production and Distribution of Water	81920	78767	35600	82660
建筑业	**Construction**	**78069**	**82198**	**60562**	**78569**
房屋建筑业	Construction of Buildings	79593	68648	51204	82290
土木工程建筑业	Civil Engineering Construction	87995	96774	80593	87038
建筑安装业	Construction Installation	68782	48422	85897	68537
建筑装饰和其他建筑业	Building Completion, Finishing and Other Constructions	62963	78697	41596	62775
批发和零售业	**Wholesale and Retail Trade**	**90717**	**124417**	**44355**	**90048**
批发业	Wholesale	114033	154220	48799	112954
零售业	Retail Trade	60924	71569	40567	60977
交通运输、仓储和邮政业	**Transport, Storage and Post**	**78294**	**87456**	**32112**	**76809**
铁路运输业	Transport via Railway	90381	93781		80672
道路运输业	Transport via Road	53038	82183	22961	53152
水上运输业	Water Transport	190409			190409
航空运输业	Air Transport	162649	36167		162660
管道运输业	Transport via Pipeline	132199			132199
装卸搬运和运输代理业	Loading, Unloading, Portage and Other Transport Services	83113	69836	58666	84243
仓储业	Storage	66190	69700	35208	68066
邮政业	Post	74983	72486		76134
住宿和餐饮业	**Accommodation and Restaurants**	**51164**	**54742**	**43209**	**50852**
住宿业	Accommodation	54638	54762	47184	55197
餐饮业	Restaurants	47858	54463	33190	48031
信息传输、软件和信息技术服务业	**Information Transmission, Software and Information Technology Services**	**146996**	**134555**	**44270**	**147320**
电信、广播电视和卫星传输服务	Telecommunications, Broadcasting, Television and Satellite Transmission Services	152051	149720	50117	152198
互联网和相关服务	Internet and Related Services	125909	118296	31500	126109
软件和信息技术服务业	Software and Information Technology Services	149759	135263	43049	150118

3-23 续表 2 Continued 2

单位: 元 (yuan)

行 业	Sector	平均工资 Average Wages	国有单位 State-owned	集体单位 Collectively-Owned	其他单位 Others
金融业	**Finance**	**253148**	**198993**	**40727**	**254809**
货币金融服务	Monetary Financial Services	260206	211994		261765
资本市场服务	Capital Market Services	301178	145347	32317	309863
保险业	Insurance	190389	258264		189479
其他金融业	Other Financial Services	252627	218842	217400	252847
房地产业	**Real Estate**	**80407**	**76926**	**42997**	**82472**
租赁和商务服务业	**Renting and Leasing Activities and Business Services**	**102437**	**79744**	**32818**	**118135**
租赁业	Renting and Leasing Activities	66313	87793	34411	66470
商务服务业	Business Services	103532	79714	32800	120345
科学研究和技术服务业	**Scientific Research and Development, Technical Services**	**127304**	**138550**	**76650**	**121686**
研究和试验发展	Research and Experimental Development	135048	135577	83965	136894
专业技术服务业	Professional Technique Services	126123	143397	77999	122106
科技推广和应用服务业	Technique Generalization and Application Services	117999	145105	63848	114388
水利、环境和公共设施管理业	**Management of Water Conservancy, Environment and Public Facilities**	**66184**	**68018**	**31314**	**65685**
水利管理业	Management of Water Conservancy	83227	83959	50052	87836
生态保护和环境治理业	Ecological Protection and Environmental Control	104250	96882	16667	106601
公共设施管理业	Management of Public Facilities	61101	64888	29009	56679
居民服务、修理和其他服务业	**Resident Services, Repair and Other Services**	**46320**	**59808**	**31012**	**45259**
居民服务业	Resident Services	46997	56051	33200	45010
机动车、电子产品和日用产品修理业	Repair of Motor Vehicles, Electronics and Household Appliances	55807	61822	34032	57457
其他服务业	Other Services	40003	66985	26974	37856
教 育	**Education**	**103198**	**112309**	**70297**	**65890**
卫生和社会工作	**Health Care and Social Works**	**128410**	**138880**	**79633**	**74626**
卫 生	Health Care	131786	141078	85847	79396
社会工作	Social Works	56967	72505	36195	33532
文化、体育和娱乐业	**Culture, Sports and Entertainment**	**123807**	**139603**	**44474**	**97205**
新闻和出版业	Journalism and Publishing	136694	135109	70415	142689
广播、电视、电影和影视录音制作业	Radio Broadcasting, Television, Movies, Videos and Sound Recording	169001	203574	38154	105380
文化艺术业	Culture and Arts	91373	98825	32913	70704
体 育	Sports Activities	72194	98242	24913	61282
娱乐业	Entertainment	75071	100566	36984	71777
公共管理、社会保障和社会组织	**Public Management, Social Security and Social Organizations**	**81288**	**87259**	**42539**	**33868**
中国共产党机关	Organs of Communist Party of China	85210	85210		
国家机构	Organs of State	86558	86558		100500
人民政协、民主党派	Peole's Political Consultative Conference and Democratic Parties	107169	107169		
社会保障	Social Security	82942	82016	68222	108516
群众团体、社会团体和其他成员组织	Mass Communities, Social Organizations and Other Membership Organizations	102502	102974	52526	105101
基层群众自治组织	Grass Roots Self-Government Organization	19296		18609	19301
国际组织	**International Organizations**				

3-24 城镇登记失业率和城镇新增就业人数(1979-2014年)
REGISTERED UNEMPLOYED RATE IN URBAN AREA AND NEWLY EMPLOYED PERSONS IN URBAN AREA (1979-2014)

单位：万人 (10000 persons)

年 份 Year	年末实有登记失业人员 Year-end Number of Actual Registed Unemployed Persons	城镇登记失业率(%) Registered Unemployment Rate in Urban Area	城镇新增就业人数 Newly Employed Persons in Urban Area
1979	4.96	1.60	
1980	8.67	1.60	
1981	8.36	1.28	
1982	7.03	1.62	
1983	4.20	1.09	
1984	2.03	0.54	
1985	1.61	0.40	
1986	1.25	0.30	
1987	2.24	0.45	
1988	1.58	0.40	
1989	1.71	0.40	
1990	1.67	0.30	
1991	1.92	0.40	
1992	1.72	0.36	
1993	1.92	0.41	
1994	1.91	0.41	
1995	2.19	0.46	
1996	2.80	0.58	
1997	3.29	0.73	
1998	2.95	0.66	
1999	2.80	0.62	
2000	3.32	0.76	
2001	5.19	1.18	
2002	6.02	1.35	
2003	6.96	1.43	
2004	6.46	1.30	
2005	10.57	2.11	31.50
2006	10.40	1.98	34.39
2007	10.63	1.84	40.71
2008	10.33	1.82	41.97
2009	8.16	1.44	42.44
2010	7.73	1.37	44.64
2011	7.89	1.39	44.69
2012	7.20	1.27	43.89
2013	6.81	1.21	42.87
2014	8.77	1.31	42.65

注：2014年开始年末实有登记失业人员指标统计口径为全市口径，2014年以前为城镇口径。

资料来源：北京市人力资源和社会保障局。

Note: Since 2014, the year-end number of actual registered unemployed persons refers to the statistic of the whole city; while the number before 2014 refers to the statistic in urban and rural areas.

Source: Beijing Municipal Bureau of Human Resource and Social Security.

主要统计指标解释

户籍人口 指公民依照《中华人民共和国户口登记条例》已在其经常居住地的公安户籍管理机关登记了常住户口的人。

常住人口 指在某地区实际居住半年以上的人口。

常住外来人口 指不具有本市户籍户口，来自北京市行政区划以外的省、自治区、直辖市，且在京居住半年以上的人口。

出生率 指在一定时期内（通常为一年）出生人数与同期平均人数(或期中人数)之比，一般用千分比表示。计算公式:

$$出生率=\frac{年出生人数}{年平均人数}\times 1000‰$$

出生人数是指活产，即脱离母体时（不管怀孕月数），有过呼吸或其他生命现象的活婴儿总和。年平均人数是年初、年末人口数的平均数，也可用年中人口数代替。

死亡率 指在一定时期内（通常为一年）死亡人数与同期平均人数（或期中人数）之比，一般用千分比表示。计算公式:

$$死亡率=\frac{年死亡人数}{年平均人数}\times 1000‰$$

自然增长率 指在一定时期内（通常为一年）人口自然增加数（出生人数减死亡人数）与该时期内平均人数（或期中人数）之比，一般用千分比表示。计算公式:

$$自然增长率=\frac{年出生人数-年死亡人数}{年平均人数}\times 1000‰$$

人口自然增长率=人口出生率－人口死亡率

从业人员 指在各级国家机关、党政机关、社会团体及企业、事业单位中工作，取得工资或其他形式的劳动报酬的全部人员。包括：在岗职工、聘用的离退休人员以及在单位中工作的港澳台及外籍人员、兼职人员、借用的外单位人员和第二职业者。不包括本单位的不在岗职工。

在岗职工 指在本单位工作并由单位支付工资的人员，以及有工作岗位，但由于学习、病伤产假（六个月以内）等原因暂未工作，仍由单位支付工资的人员。

在岗职工工资总额 与“在岗职工”指标相对应，根据1990年1月1日的国家统计局令（一号）修订，指单位在报告期内直接支付给本单位在岗职工的劳动报酬总额。包括基础工资、职务工资、级别工资、工龄工资、计件工资、奖金、各种津贴和补贴、交通补贴、洗理费、书报费、旅游费、过节费、伙食补助、住房补贴、住房提租补贴、由单位从个人工资中直接为其代扣或代缴的个人所得税、房水电费以及住房公积金和社会保险基金个人缴纳部分等。

在岗职工平均工资 指企业、事业、机关等单位的在岗职工在一定时期内的人均劳动报酬。它表明一定时期在岗职工工资收入的高低程度，是反映在岗职工工资水平的主要指标。计算公式为:

$$\begin{matrix}在岗职工\\平均工资\end{matrix}=\frac{报告期实际支付的全部在岗职工工资总额}{报告期全部在岗职工平均人数}$$

从业人员平均工资 指企业、事业、机关等单位的从业人员在一定时期内的人均劳动报酬。计算公式为:

$$从业人员平均工资=\frac{报告期实际支付的全部从业人员劳动报酬总额}{报告期全部从业人员平均人数}$$

期末实有登记失业人员 指报告期末实有的登记失业人员总数，包括城镇登记失业人员和城市化建设地区的登记失业农民（失地农民）。

城镇登记失业率 指城镇登记失业人数与城镇从业人数和城镇登记失业人数二者之和的比。计算公式如下:

$$城镇登记失业率=\frac{年末实有登记失业人数}{城镇从业人数+年末实有登记失业人数}\times 100\%$$

Explanatory Notes on Main Statistical Indicators

Registered Population refers to persons who have registered their permanent residence with the public security register authority of their habitual residence according to the Households Registration Regulations of PRC.

Permanent Population refers to persons actually living for more than half a year at a place.

Permanent Migrant Population refers to persons who have no permanent residence registration in Beijing, come from other provinces, autonomous regions and municipalities, and have stayed in Beijing for more than half a year.

Birth Rate refers to the ratio of the number of births to the average population (or mid-period population) during a certain period of time (usually a year), which is often expressed in ‰. The following formula is used:

Birth Rate = Annual Number of Births/Annual Average Number of Population×1,000‰

Number of births refers to live births i.e. the births when babies had shown any vital phenomena regardless of the length of pregnancy. Annual average number of population is the average of the number of population at the beginning of the year and that at the end of the year. Sometimes it is substituted with the mid-year population.

Death Rate refers to the ratio of the number of deaths to the average population (or mid-period population) during a certain period of time (usually a year), which is often expressed in ‰. The following formula is used:

Death Rate= Annual Number of Deaths/Annual Average Number of Population×1,000‰

Natural Growth Rate refers to the ratio of the natural growth of population (births minus deaths) to the average population (or mid-period population) during a certain period of time (usually a year), which is often expressed in ‰. The following formula is used:

Natural Growth Rate of Population = (Annual Number of Births - Annual Number of Deaths)/Annual Average Number of Population×1,000‰

Natural Growth Rate of Population = Birth Rate - Death Rate

Employed Persons refer to all persons working in government agencies, Party and political organs, social groups, enterprises and public institutions at all levels, and receiving wages or labor remuneration in other forms. They include: fully employed staff and workers, retired persons employed, persons from Hong Kong, Macao, Taiwan and foreign countries who are employed, part-time employees, employees transferred from other entities, and employees with a second job. They exclude employees that are not on the job in the entity.

Fully Employed Staff and Workers refer to persons working in the entity and paid by the entity, as well as persons having a job in the entity, but not working temporarily due to study, illness, injury or maternity leaves (less than 6 months) and other reasons, and still paid by the entity.

Total Wages of Full-time Staff and Workers corresponds to the indicator Full-time Staff and Workers. The indicator was revised in accordance with No. 1 Decree of the National Bureau of Statistics dated January 1, 1990, referring to the total wages directly paid by an entity to full-time staff and workers of the entity during the reporting period. It consists of basic wage, position-based wage, post wage, wage of a rank, piece rate wage, bonus, allowances and subsidies, traffic subsidy, washing and haircutting allowance, books and newspaper allowance, travel benefit, festival bonus, food subsidy, housing subsidy, subsidy for incremental house rent, as well as personal income tax, water and electricity fees and the personally payable portion of housing accumulation fund and social security fund withheld directly by the employer from the employee's wage.

Average Wage of Full-time Staff and Workers refers to the per-capita labor remuneration of full-time staff and workers in enterprises, public institutions and government agencies within a given period of time. It shows the level of wage income of fully employed staff and workers within a given period of time, serving as a main indicator reflecting the level of wage of fully employed staff and workers. The following formula is used:

Average Wage of Full-time Staff and Workers = Total Wages of Full-time Staff and Workers Actually Paid in the Reporting Period / Total Number of Full-time Staff and Workers in the Reporting Period

Average Wage of Employed Persons refers to the per-capita labor remuneration of employed persons in enterprises and government agencies within a given period of time. The following formula is used:

Average Wage of Employed Persons = Total Wages of All Employed Persons Actually Paid in the Reporting Period / Total Number of Employed Persons in the Reporting Period

Number of Actual Registered Unemployed Persons in Urban Area at Year-end refers to the actual number of unemployed persons registered at the year end (including all unemployed persons receiving unemployment insurance benefit).

Period-end Actual Registered Unemployed Persons refer to the total number of actual unemployed persons registered at the end period, including unemployed persons registered in urban regions and the unemployed peasants registered in urbanization regions (land-lost peasants).

Registered Unemployment Rate in Urban Area refers to the ratio of urban registered unemployed persons to the sum of urban staff and workers and urban registered unemployed persons. The following formula is used:

Registered Unemployment Rate in Urban Area =Number of Actual Registered Unemployed Persons at Year-end / (Urban Employed Persons + Number of Actual Registered Unemployed Persons at Year-end) × 100%

04

能源、资源和环境
ENERGY, RESOURCES AND ENVIRONMENT

简要说明

一、本章资料的主要内容

本章包括的主要内容有：北京市能源生产量、能源消费量、万元地区生产总值能耗、能源消费的行业构成和品种构成、能源平衡表、能源消费弹性系数、人均及日均能源消费量和北京地区用电量情况；土地利用情况；气象情况、水资源情况、排水及节水情况；园林绿化及森林情况；大气环境、固体废物处置情况等环境保护资料。

二、本章资料的统计范围

本章能源部分统计范围为全社会口径。

三、本章资料的数据来源

本章能源部分由北京市统计局、国家统计局北京调查总队提供；土地利用情况由北京市国土资源局提供；气象资料由北京市气象局提供；水资源、排水及节水情况由北京市水务局提供；城市环境卫生由北京市市政市容管理委员会提供；环境保护资料由北京市环境保护局提供。

四、本章中关于历史数据调整的问题

本章中 2008 年能源消费数据为第二次经济普查数据，1995-2007 年的能源消费数据已根据北京市第二次全国经济普查的数据结果进行了修正。1997-2007 年的万元地区生产总值能耗及下降率、万元地区生产总值水耗及下降率、能源消费弹性系数、平均每万元地区生产总值能源消费量中使用的地区生产总值数据，已根据北京市第二次全国经济普查和北京市第二次全国农业普查的数据结果进行了修正。2013 年能源消费数据为第三次全国经济普查数据。

本章中人均生活用能、人均水资源按年平均常住人口计算；同时，根据北京市第六次全国人口普查的数据结果对2006-2010 年的人均指标数据进行了修正。

根据国家统计局能源核算统一要求，2013 年开始能源消费数据按照新口径核算。

五、有关统计标准的变化说明

（一）关于行业划分。根据国家统计局规定，自 2012 年开始执行《国民经济行业分类》GB/T 4754-2011 标准。

（二）关于三次产业划分。根据国家统计局《三次产业划分规定》（国统字[2012]108 号），对三次产业的范围进行了调整。其中第一产业是指农、林、牧、渔业（不含农、林、牧、渔服务业）；第二产业是指采矿业（不含开采辅助活动），制造业（不含金属制品、机械和设备修理业），电力、热力、燃气及水生产和供应业，建筑业；第三产业是指除第一产业、第二产业以外的其他行业。自 2012 年开始执行此规定。

六、全市能源统计的内容及能源消费量的测算方法

全市能源统计主要内容包括第二、三产业限额以上法人单位能源消费情况全面调查；限额以下法人单位能源消费情况抽样调查；农业生产能源消费统计；居民生活能源消费情况抽样调查；能源供应部门的能源供应情况等。

从全市范围看，各能源品种的生产量、供应量和消费量存在平衡关系。因此，在进行生产和居民生活的能源消费量测算时，根据全市各能源品种的生产量、供应量和供应结构进行平衡修正。

Brief Introduction

I. Main Content

This chapter consists of statistics for volume of energy production and energy consumption in Beijing, energy consumption per RMB 10,000 of GDP, energy consumption by sector and by type, energy balance sheet, energy consumption elasticity coefficient, per-capita and daily energy consumption and electricity consumption in Beijing; land utilization; meteorology, water resources, water drainage and water saving; landscaping and forest; atmospheric environment, solid waste disposal and other environmental protection data.

II. Scope of Statistics

In this chapter, statistics on energy cover the entire society.

III. Source of Statistics

Energy statistics are from Beijing Municipal Bureau of Statistics, and the NBS Survey Office in Beijing; statistics on land utilization are from Beijing Municipal Bureau of Land and Resources; meteorology statistics are from Beijing Municipal Bureau of Meteorology; water resources, water drainage and water saving statistics are from Beijing Water Authority; urban environment and sanitation statistics are from Beijing Municipal Commission of City Administration and Environment; other statistics on environmental protection are from Beijing Municipal Bureau of Environmental Protection.

IV. Adjustment to Historical Statistics

Total energy consumption figures of 2008 in this chapter are the results from the "second economic census". Statistics on total energy consumption from 1995 to 2007 are corrected based on the second national economic census in Beijing. Figures of GDP of Beijing used in the 1997-2007 energy consumption and decrease rate per RMB 10,000 of GDP, water consumption per RMB 10,000 of GDP and decrease rate, energy consumption elasticity coefficient, and energy consumption per RMB 10,000 of GDP by different energy have been corrected in accordance with results from the second economic census and the second agricultural census. Energy consumption figures of 2013 are the results from the 3rd national economic census.

In this chapter, the per-capita energy consumption for living, per-capita water resources are calculated by average permanent population; at the same time, per-capita figures from 2006 to 2010 have been corrected in accordance with the sixth national population census.

V. Changes in Relevant Statistical Standards

(I) Classification of Sectors. According to relevant provisions of the National Bureau of Statistics, the *Classification of National Economic Sectors* (Standard GB/T4754-2011) came into effect in 2012.

(II) Classification of Three Industries. According to the *Regulations on Three Industries Classification* (G.T.Z. [2012] No. 108) of National Bureau of Statistics, the scope of three industries has been adjusted. The primary industry refers to agriculture, forestry, animal production and hunting, fishing (excluding service activities for agriculture, forestry, animal production and hunting, fishing); secondary industry refers to mining and quarrying (excluding mining support service activities), manufacturing (excluding repair of fabricated metal products, machinery and equipment), production and distribution of electricity, heating power, gas and water and construction; the tertiary industry refers to others excluding the primary and secondary industries. The Provisions of the National Bureau of Statistics on *Regulations on Three Industries Classification* (G.T.Z. [2012] No. 108) came into effect in 2012.

According to requirements of National Bureau of Statistics on keeping unified energy statistical approach, the energy consumption has been calculated based on new approach since 2013.

VI. Content of Energy Statistics in Beijing and Calculation Method of Energy Consumption

Energy statistics in Beijing include complete survey on energy consumption in entities above designated size in the secondary and tertiary industries; sample survey on energy consumption in entities below designated size; statistics on energy consumption in agricultural production; sample survey on energy consumption in residents' living and energy supply in energy supply departments, etc.

In terms of the whole city, the volume of production, supply and consumption shall be balanced among all types of energy. Therefore, in the calculation of energy consumption in production and residents' living by using the above-mentioned method, a correction shall be made for balance according to the volume of production, supply and consumption of all types of energy in the city.

4-1 能源生产量(2000-2014年)
ENERGY PRODUCTION (2000-2014)

项目		Item		2000	2001	2002	2003	2004	2005	2006
一次能源	**(万吨标准煤)**	**Primary Energy**	**(10000 tons of SCE)**	**523.7**	**597.4**	**632.1**	**686.3**	**765.0**	**679.5**	**460.6**
#原 煤	(万吨)	Raw Coal	(10000 tons)	690.0	831.9	881.0	957.3	1067.9	945.2	642.1
二次能源	**(万吨标准煤)**	**Secondary Energy**	**(10000 tons of SCE)**	**2461.4**	**2362.0**	**2388.6**	**2470.5**	**2850.8**	**2832.1**	**2714.4**
#汽 油	(万吨)	Gasoline	(10000 tons)	146.2	146.7	154.1	151.4	169.8	156.5	159.3
煤 油	(万吨)	Kerosene	(10000 tons)					8.1	12.4	11.6
柴 油	(万吨)	Diesel Oil	(10000 tons)	183.9	186.7	174.1	170.2	180.7	176.8	185.9
燃料油	(万吨)	Fuel Oil	(10000 tons)	78.6	67.4	64.4	64.5	68.2	68.9	64.0
液化石油气	(万吨)	Liquefied Petroleum Gas	(10000 tons)	40.0	39.7	41.7	38.4	43.3	47.3	40.5
热 力	(万百万千焦)	Heat	(10 billion kilo-joules)	8758.8	8608.2	9064.0	9616.6	10973.9	11335.7	12181.6
电 力	(亿千瓦时)	Electricity	(100 million kwh)	180.7	174.5	180.3	188.3	200.4	209.8	209.7

4-1 续表 Continued

项目		Item		2007	2008	2009	2010	2011	2012	2013	2014
一次能源	**(万吨标准煤)**	**Primary Energy**	**(10000 tons of SCE)**	**466.1**	**414.2**	**475.7**	**481.1**	**482.0**	**501.8**	**541.7**	**514.0**
#原 煤	(万吨)	Raw Coal	(10000 tons)	648.8	578.5	641.3	500.1	500.1	493.1	500.1	457.5
二次能源	**(万吨标准煤)**	**Secondary Energy**	**(10000 tons of SCE)**	**2895.2**	**3213.3**	**3346.7**	**3457.3**	**3209.1**	**3267.2**	**3019.0**	**3333.2**
#汽 油	(万吨)	Gasoline	(10000 tons)	176.5	215.5	272.6	257.1	251.2	261.9	223.9	287.4
煤 油	(万吨)	Kerosene	(10000 tons)	36.4	85.2	111.6	116.1	126.4	132.9	99.4	152.3
柴 油	(万吨)	Diesel Oil	(10000 tons)	268.2	373.3	364.2	350.4	355.7	319.1	194.7	219.8
燃料油	(万吨)	Fuel Oil	(10000 tons)	41.9	42.1	29.6	34.9	21.4	24.0	16.9	4.7
液化石油气	(万吨)	Liquefied Petroleum Gas	(10000 tons)	66.2	50.0	40.3	32.9	30.2	35.0	28.1	32.1
热 力	(万百万千焦)	Heat	(10 billion kilo-joules)	12951.1	13846.2	14476.1	15710.9	15127.7	15632.4	14893.6	15055.4
电 力	(亿千瓦时)	Electricity	(100 million kwh)	224.4	244.9	242.0	263.3	257.3	284.7	326.7	351.6

注：2013年数据为第三次全国经济普查数据。

Note: Data for 2013 were collected from the third national economic census.

4-2 能源消费总量及万元地区生产总值能耗(1980-2014年)
TOTAL ENERGY CONSUMPTION AND ENERGY CONSUMPTION PER 10000 YUAN OF GDP (1980-2014)

单位：万吨标准煤 (10000 tons of SCE)

年份 Year	能源消费总量 Total Energy Consumption	第一产业 Primary Industry	第二产业 Secondary Industry	第三产业 Tertiary Industry	生活消费 Residential Consumption	万元地区生产总值能耗（吨标准煤） Energy Consumption per 10000 yuan of GDP (ton of SCE)	万元地区生产总值能耗下降率(%) Decrease Rate of Energy Consumption per 10000 yuan GDP(%)
1980	1907.7	66.8	1400.3	297.6	143.0	13.715	
1981	1902.6	53.3	1339.4	334.9	175.0	13.668	-0.23
1982	1920.4	55.7	1346.2	338.0	180.5	12.398	6.02
1983	1984.7	73.4	1379.4	313.6	218.3	10.839	11.22
1984	2144.1	85.8	1470.9	347.3	240.1	9.899	7.98
1985	2211.4	90.7	1488.3	351.6	280.8	8.601	5.12
1986	2400.0	95.7	1612.0	380.4	311.9	8.424	-0.49
1987	2475.8	89.0	1647.8	424.7	314.3	7.576	5.88
1988	2612.6	111.7	1748.1	412.2	340.6	6.369	6.45
1989	2653.2	114.4	1735.9	427.0	375.9	5.818	2.73
1990	2709.7	105.7	1720.1	515.3	368.6	5.411	2.92
1991	2872.0	126.7	1807.6	542.0	395.7	4.795	3.56
1992	2987.5	143.6	1888.1	552.4	403.4	4.213	6.54
1993	3264.6	133.6	2150.9	561.0	419.1	3.684	2.69
1994	3385.9	143.6	2234.1	574.8	433.4	2.956	8.78
1995	3533.3	120.4	2328.4	632.7	451.8	2.344	6.83
1996	3734.5	110.8	2477.0	698.1	448.6	2.087	2.75
1997	3719.2	95.7	2369.6	799.8	454.1	1.792	9.55
1998	3808.1	96.2	2400.5	856.4	455.0	1.603	6.49
1999	3906.6	86.9	2370.7	971.8	477.2	1.459	7.49
2000	4144.0	104.8	2424.8	1080.9	533.5	1.311	5.12
2001	4229.2	105.4	2366.6	1196.2	561.0	1.198	8.62
2002	4436.1	103.0	2414.6	1334.5	584.0	1.127	5.93
2003	4648.2	99.9	2476.7	1391.0	680.6	1.062	5.73
2004	5139.6	85.6	2664.2	1638.0	751.8	1.029	3.09
2005	5521.9	86.3	2702.5	1918.7	814.4	0.986 (0.792)	4.17
2006	5904.1	92.3	2773.1	2129.3	909.4	0.750	5.37
2007	6285.0	96.4	2793.8	2389.5	1005.3	0.697	7.02
2008	6327.1	96.9	2550.5	2610.5	1069.2	0.643	7.74
2009	6570.3	99.0	2544.2	2760.3	1166.8	0.606	5.76
2010	6954.1	100.3	2726.7	2897.4	1229.7	0.581 (0.493)	4.04
2011	6995.4	100.3	2488.7	3100.5	1305.9	0.458	6.95
2012	7177.7	100.8	2426.1	3252.1	1398.7	0.436	4.75
2013	6723.9	97.3	2079.2	3109.1	1438.3	0.380	4.88
2014	6831.2	91.7	1998.4	3236.5	1504.6	0.360	5.29

注：1. 本表能源消费量指标按等价值计算，万元地区生产总值能耗下降率按可比价计算。
2. 2000年及以前万元地区生产总值能耗按当年价格计算；2000年以后按可比价格计算，可比价格每五年调整一次基期，更换基期年份计算两个可比价数据，括号内数据按新基期价格计算。
3. 2013年数据为第三次全国经济普查数据。
4. 根据国家统计局能源核算统一要求，2013年开始能源消费数据按照新口径核算。

Note: a) Enery consumption in this table is at equivalent prices. Reduction rate of Energy Consumption per 10000 yuan of GDP is calculated at comparable prices.
b) Energy consumption per 10000 yuan of GDP before 2000 was calculated at the price of that year; figures after 2000 were calculated at comparable prices. The base period of comparable prices is changed every five years. Two figures at comparable prices were calculated for the year in which the base period is changed. Figures in brackets were calculated at the price of new base period.
c) Data for 2013 were collected from the third national economic census.
d) According to requirements of National Bureau of Statistics on keeping unified energy statistical approach, the energy consumption has been calculated based on new approach since 2013 .

4-3 按行业分能源消费总量
TOTAL ENERGY CONSUMPTION BY SECTOR

单位：万吨标准煤 (10000 tons of SCE)

项　　目	Item	2014	2013
能源消费总量	**Total Energy Consumption**	**6831.2**	**6723.9**
按产业分组	**By There Industies**		
第一产业	Primary Industry	91.7	97.3
第二产业	Secondary Industry	1998.4	2079.2
第三产业	Tertiary Industry	3236.5	3109.1
生活消费	Residential Consumption	1504.6	1438.3
按行业分组	**By Sector**		
#采矿业	Mining and Quarrying	22.2	22.0
制造业	Manufacturing	1332.8	1388.6
电力、热力、燃气及水生产和供应业	Production and Distribution of Electricity, Heating Pewer, Gas and Water	518.5	540.7
建筑业	Construction	124.9	127.9
批发和零售业	Wholesale and Retail Trade	194.2	189.9
交通运输、仓储和邮政业	Transport, Storage and Post	1204.2	1145.5
住宿和餐饮业	Accommodation and Restaurants	292.0	282.6
信息传输、软件和信息技术服务业	Information Transmission,Software and Information Technology Services	148.4	136.2
金融业	Finance	68.4	61.2
房地产业	Real Estate	374.9	377.0
租赁和商务服务业	Renting and Leasing Activities and Business Services	210.5	189.0
科学研究和技术服务业	Scientific Research and Development, Technical Services	159.8	160.8
水利、环境和公共设施管理业	Management of Water Conservancy, Environment and Public Facilities	61.5	53.5
居民服务、修理和其他服务业	Resident Services, Repair and Other Services	32.7	40.7
教　育	Education	220.5	208.2
卫生和社会工作	Healtlcare and Social Works	84.7	79.9
文化、体育和娱乐业	Culture, Sports and Entertainment	65.4	62.3
公共管理、社会保障和社会组织	Public Administration, Social Security and Social Organizations	119.3	122.3

注：1. 行业划分执行《国民经济行业分类》(GB/T 4754—2011)标准(下同)。
2. 2012年开始执行国家统计局《三次产业划分规定》，具体调整内容见本章简要说明(下同)。
3. 2013年数据为第三次全国经济普查数据。
4. 根据国家统计局能源核算统一要求，2013年开始能源消费数据按照新口径核算。

Note: a) Sectors in this table are classified in accordance with Standard for Classification of National Economic Sectors (GB/T 4754-2011) (the same below).
b) From 2012, Classification of Three Industires released by National Bureau of Statistics became effective. See brief introduction to this chapter for detailed changes (the same below).
c) Data for 2013 were collected from the third national economic census.
d) According to requirements of National Bureau of Statistics on keeping unified energy statistical approach, the energy consumption has been calculated based on new approach since 2013.

4-4 按三次产业分万元地区生产总值能耗及能耗下降率(2001−2014年)
ENERGY CONSUMPTION PER 10000 YUAN OF GDP AND DECREASE RATE BY THREE INDUSTRIES (2001-2014)

单位：吨标准煤 (ton of SCE)

年 份	万元地区生产总值能耗	按产业分组 By Three Industies			按主要行业分组 By Sector	
Year	Energy Consumption per 10000 yuan of GDP	第一产业 Primary Industry	第二产业 Secondary Industry	第三产业 Tertiary Industry	#工 业 Industry	#交通运输、仓储和邮政业 Transport, Storage and Post
2001	1.198	1.282	2.091	0.516	2.460	1.633
2002	1.127	1.220	1.968	0.508	2.318	1.675
2003	1.062	1.196	1.803	0.476	2.114	1.564
2004	1.029	1.031	1.658	0.496	1.898	1.929
2005	0.986	1.060	1.527	0.512	1.745	1.973
	(0.792)	(0.973)	(1.334)	(0.395)	(1.523)	(1.397)
2006	0.750	1.035	1.238	0.384	1.429	1.654
2007	0.697	1.058	1.107	0.373	1.271	1.794
2008	0.643	1.052	1.002	0.362	1.148	2.037
2009	0.606	1.028	0.906	0.348	1.038	2.040
2010	0.581	1.058	0.853	0.334	0.967	1.968
	(0.493)	(0.806)	(0.805)	(0.273)	(0.926)	(1.552)
2011	0.458	0.799	0.689	0.269	0.784	1.569
2012	0.436	0.778	0.624	0.262	0.716	1.529
2013	0.380	0.740	0.509	0.230	0.569	1.325
2014	0.360	0.697	0.458	0.223	0.516	1.304

注：1. 万元地区生产总值能耗按可比价格计算，可比价格每五年调整一次基期，更换基期年份计算两个可比价数据，括号内数据是按新基期价格计算。
2. 2013年数据为第三次全国经济普查数据。
3. 根据国家统计局能源核算统一要求，2013年开始能源消费数据按照新口径核算。

Note: a) Energy consumption per 10000 yuan of GDP were calculated at comparable prices. The base period of comparable prices is changed every five years. Two figures at comparable prices were calculated for the year in which the base period is changed. Figures in brackets were calculated at the price of new base period.
b) Data for 2013 were collected from the third national economic census.
c) According to requirements of National Bureau of Statistics on keeping unified energy statistical approach, the energy consumption has been calculated based on new approach since 2013 (same below).

4-4 续表 Continued

单位：% (%)

年 份 Year	万元地区生产总值能耗下降率 Decrease Rate of Energy Consumption per 10000 yuan GDP	按产业分组 By Three Industies			按主要行业分组 By Sector	
		第一产业 Primary Industry	第二产业 Secondary Industry	第三产业 Tertiary Industry	#工 业 Industry	#交通运输、仓储和邮政业 Transport, Storage and Post
2001	8.62	2.98	10.90	2.13	11.91	-14.90
2002	5.93	4.83	5.88	1.56	5.75	-2.60
2003	5.73	1.96	8.39	6.23	8.80	6.66
2004	3.09	13.79	8.04	-4.08	10.22	-23.40
2005	4.17	-2.80	7.89	-3.25	8.07	-2.24
2006	5.37	-6.35	7.15	2.87	6.17	-18.39
2007	7.02	-2.26	10.61	2.76	11.06	-8.47
2008	7.74	0.57	9.43	2.89	9.67	-13.56
2009	5.76	2.29	9.66	4.03	9.55	-0.16
2010	4.04	-2.96	5.74	3.96	6.88	3.52
2011	6.95	0.89	14.46	1.55	15.34	-1.11
2012	4.75	2.61	9.30	2.75	8.71	2.55
2013	4.88	3.87	7.50	2.90	7.72	0.36
2014	5.29	5.76	10.06	3.14	9.43	1.60

注：表内万元地区生产总值能耗下降率按可比价格计算。

Note: Energy consumption per 10000 yuan of GDP decrease rate is at comparable prices.

4-5 电力平衡表
ELECTRICITY BALANCE

单位：亿千瓦时 (100 million kwh)

项目	Item	2014	2013
可供本地区消费的能源量	**Total Energy Available for Local Consumption**	**577.77**	**584.90**
加工转换投入(-)产出(+)量	**Input(-) or Output(+) in Processing and Conversion**	**351.57**	**326.69**
火力发电	Thermal Power	351.57	326.69
供热	Heating		
煤炭洗选	Washing of Coal		
炼焦	Coking		
炼油及煤制油	Oil Refining and Coal to Liquid		
#油品再投入量(-)	Oil Product Re-input(-)		
制气	Gas Production		
#焦炭再投入量(-)	Coke Re-input(-)		
煤制品加工	Coal Product Processing		
回收能	**Energy Recycled**		
损失量	**Losses**	**59.94**	**59.86**
#运输和输配损失	In Transportation and Transmission		
终端消费量	**End-use Energy Consumption**	**873.47**	**848.84**
第一产业	Primary Industry	18.56	18.57
第二产业	Secondary Industry	260.77	261.67
工业	Industry	238.38	238.15
#用作原料、材料	Use as Materials		
建筑业	Construction	22.38	23.52
第三产业	Tertiary Industry	424.88	411.56
生活消费	Residential Consumption	169.26	157.04
城镇	Urban	145.74	134.74
乡村	Rural	23.52	22.30
平衡差额	Balance	-4.07	2.89
消费量合计	**Total Energy Consumption**	**933.41**	**908.70**

注：2013年数据为第三次全国经济普查数据。
Note: Data for 2013 were collected from the third national economic census.

4-6 综合能源平衡表(标准量)
COMPREHENSIVE ENERGY BALANCE (STANDARD VOLUME)

单位：万吨标准煤 (10000 tons of SCE)

项 目	Item	2014	2013
可供本地区消费的能源量	**Total Energy Available for Consumption**	**6818.29**	**6734.96**
加工转换投入(-)产出(+)量	**Input(-) or Output(+) in Processing and Conversion**	**-83.45**	**-84.31**
火力发电	Thermal Power		
供 热	Heating	-94.52	-95.80
煤炭洗选	Washing of Coal	-0.11	-0.25
炼 焦	Coking		
炼油及煤制油	Oil Refining and Coal to Liquid	300.81	271.61
#油品再投入量(-)	Oil Product Re-input(-)	-308.12	-277.77
制 气	Gas Production		
#焦炭再投入量(-)	Coke Re-input(-)		
煤制品加工	Coal Product Processing	-0.34	-0.88
回收能	**Energy Recycled**	**18.83**	**18.77**
损失量	**Losses**	**233.66**	**228.60**
#运输和输配损失	In Transportation and Transmission		
终端消费量	**End-use Energy Consumption**	**6514.12**	**6410.98**
第一产业	Primary Industry	91.69	97.31
第二产业	Secondary Industry	1681.25	1766.32
工 业	Industry	1556.40	1638.41
#用作原料、材料	Use as Materials	279.86	323.11
建筑业	Construction	124.85	127.91
第三产业	Tertiary Industry	3236.55	3109.04
生活消费	Residential Consumption	1504.63	1438.31
城 镇	Urban	1248.07	1199.04
乡 村	Rural	256.56	239.27
平衡差额	Balance	-12.94	11.07
消费量合计	**Total Energy Consumption**	**6831.23**	**6723.90**

注：2013年数据为第三次全国经济普查数据。
Note: Data for 2013 were collected from the third national economic census.

4-7 能源平衡表(实物量简表)(2013年)
ENERGY BALANCE (PHYSICAL VOLUME) (SIMPLE EDITION) (2013)

单位：万吨 (10000 tons)

项目	Item	原煤 Coal	洗精煤 Washed Coal	其他洗煤 Other Washed Coal	煤制品 Coal Products	煤矸石 Coal Slack	焦炭 Coke	焦炉煤气(亿立方米) Coking Gas (100 million cu.m)
可供本地区消费的能源量	**Total Energy Available for Local Consumption**	**2011.06**	**3.84**		**3.67**		**0.79**	
加工转换投入(-)产出(+)量	**Input(-) or Output(+) in Procesing and Conversion**	**-1158.55**	**-3.84**		**0.16**			
火力发电	Thermal Power	-631.97			-0.93			
供　热	Heating	-512.10			-17.47			
煤炭洗选	Washing of Coal	-14.47	8.50					
炼　焦	Coking							
炼油及煤制油	Oil Refining and Coal to Liquid							
#油品再投入量(-)	Oil Product Re-input(-)							
制　气	Gas Production							
#焦炭再投入量(-)	Coke Re-input(-)							
煤制品加工	Coal Product Processing		-12.34		18.55			
回收能	**Energy Recycled**							
损失量	**Losses**							
#运输和输配损失	In Transportation and Transmission							
终端消费量	**End-use Energy Consumption**	**853.16**			**3.83**		**0.79**	
第一产业	Primary Industry	41.41						
第二产业	Secondary Industry	290.23			0.75		0.78	
工　业	Industry	283.37			0.41		0.78	
#用作原料、材料	Use as Materials	0.08						
建筑业	Construction	6.86			0.34			
第三产业	Tertiary Industry	212.54			3.08		0.01	
生活消费	Residential Consumption	308.98						
城　镇	Urban	119.06						
乡　村	Rural	189.92						
平衡差额	Balance	-0.65						
消费量合计	**Total Energy Consumption**	**2011.71**	**12.34**		**22.23**		**0.79**	

注：2013年数据为第三次全国经济普查数据。

Note: Data for 2013 were collected from the third national economic census.

4-7 续表 1 Continued 1

单位：万吨 (10000 tons)

项 目	Item	高炉煤气（亿立方米）Blast Furnace Gas (100 million cu.m)	转炉煤气（亿立方米）Converter Gas (100 million cu.m)	其它煤气（亿立方米）Other Gas (100 million cu.m)	其它焦化产品 Other Carbonized Products	原油 Crude Oil	汽油 Gasoline	煤油 Kerosene
可供本地区消费的能源量	**Total Energy Available for Local Consumption**					**870.92**	**199.60**	**377.69**
加工转换投入(-)产出(+)量	**Input(-) or Output(+) in Procesing and Conversion**					**-870.03**	**223.87**	**99.38**
火力发电	Thermal Power							
供 热	Heating							
煤炭洗选	Washing of Coal							
炼 焦	Coking							
炼油及煤制油	Oil Refining and Coal to Liquid					-870.03	223.87	99.38
#油品再投入量(-)	Re-inputs of Oil Products							
制 气	Gas Production							
#焦炭再投入量(-)	Coke Re-input(-)							
煤制品加工	Coal Product Processing							
回收能	**Energy Recycled**							
损失量	**Losses**					**0.88**		
#运输和输配损失	In Transportation and Transmission							
终端消费量	**Final Consumption Industry**						**423.61**	**477.06**
第一产业	Primary Industry						5.28	
第二产业	Secondary Industry						22.63	0.08
工 业	Industry						15.57	0.08
#用作原料、材料	Use in Materials						0.13	0.03
建筑业	Construction						7.06	
第三产业	Tertiary Industry						119.71	476.98
生活消费	Residential Consumption						275.99	
城 镇	Urban						275.99	
乡 村	Rural							
平衡差额	Balance					0.01	-0.14	0.01
消费量合计	**Total Energy Consumption**					**870.92**	**423.61**	**477.06**

4-7 续表 2 Continued 2

单位：万吨 (10000 tons)

项目	Item	柴油 Diesel Oil	燃料油 Fuel Oil	石脑油 Naphtha	润滑油 Grease Oil	石蜡 Oilfin	溶剂油 Solvent Oil	石油沥青 Oil Asphalt	石油焦 Petroleum Coal
可供本地区消费的能源量	**Total Energy Available for Local Consumption**	**-0.90**	**-8.67**	**27.16**	**1.37**	**-5.71**	**0.35**	**10.37**	**-2.18**
加工转换投入(-)产出(+)量	**Input(-) or Output(+) in Procesing and Conversion**	**193.99**	**16.64**	**1.85**		**6.51**		**15.30**	**2.19**
火力发电	Thermal Power	-0.20							-3.69
供　热	Heating	-0.51	-0.28						-19.51
煤炭洗选	Washing of Coal								
炼　焦	Coking								
炼油及煤制油	Oil Refining and Coal to Liquid	194.70	16.93	101.04		6.51		15.30	25.39
#油品再投入量(-)	Oil Product Re-input(-)			-99.19					
制　气	Gas Production								
#焦炭再投入量(-)	Coke Re-input(-)								
煤制品加工	Coal Product Processing								
回收能	**Energy Recycled**								
损失量	**Losses**								
#运输和输配损失	In Transportation and Transmission								
终端消费量	**End-use Energy Consumption**	**193.19**	**8.01**	**28.76**	**1.37**	**0.77**	**0.35**	**25.37**	
第一产业	Primary Industry	3.66			0.10				
第二产业	Secondary Industry	42.80	5.77	28.76	1.27	0.77	0.35	25.37	
工　业	Industry	20.29	5.77	28.76	1.27	0.77	0.35	25.37	
#用作原料、材料	Use in Materials	0.23	3.69	28.76	1.27	0.77	0.35	25.37	
建筑业	Construction	22.51							
第三产业	Tertiary Industry	146.59	2.24						
生活消费	Residential Consumption	0.14							
城镇	Urban								
乡村	Rural	0.14							
平衡差额	Balance	-0.10	-0.04	0.25		0.03		0.30	0.01
消费量合计	**Total Energy Consumption**	**193.90**	**8.30**	**127.95**	**1.37**	**0.77**	**0.35**	**25.37**	**23.20**

4-7 续表 3 Continued 3

单位：万吨 (10000 tons)

项　目	Item	液化石油气 Liquefied Petroleum Gas	炼厂干气 Refinery Gas	其它石油制品 Other Petroleum Products	天然气（亿立方米） Natural Gas (100 million cu.m)	热力（万百万千焦） Heat (10000 million kilo-joule)	电力（亿千瓦时） Electricity (100 million kwh)	其它能源（万吨标准煤） Others (10000 tons of SCE)
可供本地区消费的能源量	**Total Energy Available for Local Consumption**	**17.17**		**-4.04**	**98.81**	**514.65**	**584.90**	**46.53**
加工转换投入(-)产出(+)量	**Input(-) or Output(+) in Procesing and Conversion**	**28.06**	**64.67**	**186.36**	**-44.17**	**14893.57**	**326.69**	**2.30**
火力发电	Thermal Power		-0.19	-0.73	-29.46		326.69	-16.47
供　热	Heating	-0.01	-2.47	-10.45	-14.71	14893.57		
煤炭洗选	Washing of Coal							
炼　焦	Coking							
炼油及煤制油	Oil Refining and Coal to Liquid	28.07	67.33	304.16				
#油品再投入量(-)	Oil Product Re-input(-)			-106.62				
制　气	Gas Production							
#焦炭再投入量(-)	Coke Re-input(-)							
煤制品加工	Coal Product Processing							
回收能	**Energy Recycled**							**18.77**
损失量	**Losses**	**3.88**			**3.83**		**59.86**	
#运输和输配损失	In Transportation and Transmission							
终端消费量	**Final Consumption Industry**	**41.34**	**62.67**	**182.43**	**50.82**	**15408.22**	**848.84**	**48.85**
第一产业	Primary Industry	0.06			0.01		18.57	
第二产业	Secondary Industry	2.55	62.67	182.43	10.54	4025.41	261.67	7.26
工　业	Industry	1.77	62.67	182.43	10.11	3913.07	238.15	6.89
#用作原料、材料	Use in Materials	0.23	1.91	181.09				
建筑业	Construction	0.78			0.43	112.34	23.52	0.37
第三产业	Tertiary Industry	18.03			28.33	7640.81	411.56	27.59
生活消费	Residential Consumption	20.70			11.94	3742.00	157.04	14.00
城　镇	Urban	12.25			11.60	3742.00	134.74	
乡　村	Rural	8.45			0.34		22.30	14.00
平衡差额	Balance	0.01	2.00	-0.11	-0.01		2.89	-0.02
消费量合计	**Total Energy Consumption**	**45.23**	**65.33**	**300.23**	**98.81**	**15408.22**	**908.70**	**65.31**

4-8 能源平衡表(实物量简表)(2014年)
ENERGY BALANCE (PHYSICAL VOLUME) (SIMPLE EDITION) (2014)

单位: 万吨 (10000 tons)

项 目	Item	原煤 Coal	洗精煤 Washed Coal	其他洗煤 Other Washed Coal	煤制品 Coal Products	煤矸石 Coal Slack	焦炭 Coke	焦炉煤气(亿立方米) Coking Gas (100 million cu.m)
可供本地区消费的能源量	**Total Energy Available for Local Consumption**	**1728.26**	**5.20**	**0.02**	**3.08**		**0.64**	
加工转换投入(-)产出(+)量	**Input(-) or Output(+) in Procesing and Conversion**	**-955.58**	**-5.13**		**0.35**			
火力发电	Thermal Power	-503.15			-0.59			
供 热	Heating	-444.56			-13.73			
煤炭洗选	Washing of Coal	-7.87	4.87					
炼 焦	Coking							
炼油及煤制油	Oil Refining and Coal to Liquid							
#油品再投入量(-)	Oil Product Re-input(-)							
制 气	Gas Production							
#焦炭再投入量(-)	Coke Re-input(-)							
煤制品加工	Coal Product Processing		-10.00		14.67			
回收能	**Energy Recycled**							
损失量	**Losses**							
#运输和输配损失	In Transportation and Transmission							
终端消费量	**End-use Energy Consumption**	**772.67**	**0.06**	**0.02**	**3.43**		**0.64**	
第一产业	Primary Industry	34.88						
第二产业	Secondary Industry	226.11	0.02		0.58		0.63	
工 业	Industry	220.28	0.02		0.24		0.63	
#用作原料、材料	Use as Materials				0.02			
建筑业	Construction	5.83			0.34			
第三产业	Tertiary Industry	218.23	0.04	0.02	2.85		0.01	
生活消费	Residential Consumption	293.45						
城 镇	Urban	114.12						
乡 村	Rural	179.34						
平衡差额	Balance	0.01	0.01					
消费量合计	**Total Energy Consumption**	**1728.25**	**10.05**	**0.02**	**17.75**		**0.64**	

4-8 续表 1 Continued 1

单位：万吨 (10000 tons)

项目	Item	高炉煤气（亿立方米）Blast Furnace Gas (100 million cu.m)	转炉煤气（亿立方米）Converter Gas (100 million cu.m)	其它煤气（亿立方米）Other Gas (100 million cu.m)	其它焦化产品 Other Carbonized Products	原油 Crude Oil	汽油 Gasoline	煤油 Kerosene
可供本地区消费的能源量	**Total Energy Available for Local Consumption**					**1034.61**	**153.19**	**355.27**
加工转换投入(-)产出(+)量	**Input(-) or Output(+) in Procesing and Conversion**					**-1033.31**	**287.42**	**152.31**
火力发电	Thermal Power							
供　热	Heating							
煤炭洗选	Washing of Coal							
炼　焦	Coking							
炼油及煤制油	Oil Refining and Coal to Liquid					-1033.31	287.42	152.31
#油品再投入量(-)	Re-inputs of Oil Products							
制　气	Gas Production							
#焦炭再投入量(-)	Coke Re-input(-)							
煤制品加工	Coal Product Processing							
回收能	**Energy Recycled**							
损失量	**Losses**					**1.31**		
#运输和输配损失	In Transportation and Transmission							
终端消费量	**Final Consumption Industry**						**440.62**	**507.58**
第一产业	Primary Industry						5.61	
第二产业	Secondary Industry						24.67	0.06
工　业	Industry						16.89	0.06
#用作原料、材料	Use in Materials							
建筑业	Construction						7.78	
第三产业	Tertiary Industry						126.08	507.52
生活消费	Residential Consumption						284.26	
城　镇	Urban						284.26	
乡　村	Rural							
平衡差额	Balance					-0.01	-0.01	
消费量合计	**Total Energy Consumption**					**1034.62**	**440.62**	**507.58**

4-8 续表 2 Continued 2

单位：万吨 (10000 tons)

项目	Item	柴油 Diesel Oil	燃料油 Fuel Oil	石脑油 Naphtha	润滑油 Grease Oil	石蜡 Oilfin	溶剂油 Solvent Oil	石油沥青 Oil Asphalt	石油焦 Petroleum Coal
可供本地区消费的能源量	**Total Energy Available for Local Consumption**	**-23.33**	**0.94**	**5.04**	**1.24**	**-10.41**	**0.08**	**6.83**	**-10.65**
加工转换投入(-)产出(+)量	**Input(-) or Output(+) in Procesing and Conversion**	**219.05**	**4.45**	**34.99**		**10.64**		**12.73**	**10.67**
火力发电	Thermal Power	-0.18							-6.33
供热	Heating	-0.56	-0.24						-19.44
煤炭洗选	Washing of Coal								
炼焦	Coking								
炼油及煤制油	Oil Refining and Coal to Liquid	219.80	4.69	124.97		10.64		12.73	36.45
#油品再投入量(-)	Oil Product Re-input(-)			-89.98					
制气	Gas Production								
#焦炭再投入量(-)	Coke Re-input(-)								
煤制品加工	Coal Product Processing								
回收能	**Energy Recycled**								
损失量	**Losses**								
#运输和输配损失	In Transportation and Transmission								
终端消费量	**End-use Energy Consumption**	**195.72**	**5.39**	**40.03**	**1.24**	**0.38**	**0.08**	**19.15**	
第一产业	Primary Industry	3.43							
第二产业	Secondary Industry	43.60	3.45	40.03	1.24	0.38	0.08	19.15	
工业	Industry	18.57	3.45	40.03	1.24	0.38	0.08	19.15	
#用作原料、材料	Use in Materials	0.26	0.57	40.03	1.24	0.38	0.08	19.15	
建筑业	Construction	25.03							
第三产业	Tertiary Industry	148.58	1.94						
生活消费	Residential Consumption	0.11							
城镇	Urban								
乡村	Rural	0.11							
平衡差额	Balance					-0.15		0.41	0.02
消费量合计	**Total Energy Consumption**	**196.46**	**5.63**	**130.01**	**1.24**	**0.38**	**0.08**	**19.15**	**25.77**

4-8 续表 3 Continued 3

单位：万吨 (10000 tons)

项目	Item	液化石油气 Liquefied Petroleum Gas	炼厂干气 Refinery Gas	其它石油制品 Other Petroleum Products	天然气（亿立方米） Natural Gas (100 million cu.m)	热力（万百万千焦） Heat (10000 million kilo-joule)	电力（亿千瓦时） Electricity (100 million kwh)	其它能源（万吨标准煤） Others (10000 tons of SCE)
可供本地区消费的能源量	**Total Energy Available for Local Consumption**	**16.29**		**4.54**	**113.70**	**1522.35**	**577.77**	**54.67**
加工转换投入(-)产出(+)量	**Input(-) or Output(+) in Procesing and Conversion**	**31.76**	**62.72**	**168.65**	**-56.49**	**15055.44**	**351.57**	**2.17**
火力发电	Thermal Power	-0.02	-0.09	-0.56	-37.89		351.57	-16.66
供热	Heating	-0.31	-0.76	-10.04	-18.60	15055.44		
煤炭洗选	Washing of Coal							
炼焦	Coking							
炼油及煤制油	Oil Refining and Coal to Liquid	32.08	63.57	323.54				
#油品再投入量(-)	Oil Product Re-input(-)			-144.29				
制气	Gas Production							
#焦炭再投入量(-)	Coke Re-input(-)							
煤制品加工	Coal Product Processing							
回收能	**Energy Recycled**							**18.83**
损失量	**Losses**	**2.00**			**4.79**		**59.94**	
#运输和输配损失	In Transportation and Transmission							
终端消费量	**Final Consumption Industry**	**48.04**	**57.27**	**181.51**	**52.42**	**16577.79**	**873.46**	**54.67**
第一产业	Primary Industry	0.06			0.01		18.56	
第二产业	Secondary Industry	2.22	57.27	181.51	10.35	3981.75	260.77	7.71
工业	Industry	1.81	57.27	181.51	10.13	3849.39	238.39	7.33
#用作原料、材料	Use in Materials	0.05	3.51	154.66				
建筑业	Construction	0.41			0.22	132.36	22.38	0.38
第三产业	Tertiary Industry	22.28			29.35	8574.04	424.87	30.04
生活消费	Residential Consumption	23.48			12.71	4022.00	169.26	16.92
城镇	Urban	13.12			12.26	4022.00	145.74	
乡村	Rural	10.36			0.45		23.52	16.92
平衡差额	Balance	-1.99	5.45	-8.32			-4.06	2.17
消费量合计	**Total Energy Consumption**	**50.37**	**58.12**	**336.40**	**113.70**	**16577.79**	**933.41**	**71.33**

4-9 能源平衡表(标准量简表)(2013年)
ENERGY BALANCE (STANDARD VOLUME) (SIMPLE EDITION) (2013)

单位：万吨标准煤 (10000 tons of SCE)

项　　目	Item	合计 Total	原煤 Coal	洗精煤 Washed Coal	其他洗煤 Other Washed Coal	煤制品 Coal Products	煤矸石 Coal Slack	焦炭 Coke	焦炉煤气 Coking Gas
可供本地区消费的能源量	**Total Energy Available for Local Consumption**	**6734.96**	**1560.69**	**3.34**		**2.23**		**0.77**	
加工转换投入(-)产出(+)量	**Input(-) or Output(+) in Proce -ssing and Transformation**	**-84.31**	**-919.04**	**-3.34**		**-0.18**			
火力发电	Thermal Power		-540.02			-0.60			
供　热	Heating	-95.80	-369.57			-11.24			
煤炭洗选	Washing of Coal	-0.25	-9.45	9.20					
炼　焦	Coking								
炼油及煤制油	Oil Refining and Coal to Liquid	271.61							
#油品再投入量(-)	Oil Product Re-input(-)	-277.77							
制　气	Gas Production								
#焦炭再投入量(-)	Coke Re-input(-)								
煤制品加工	Coal Product Processing	**-0.88**		-12.54		11.66			
回收能	**Energy Recycled**	**18.77**							
损失量	**Losses**	**228.60**							
#运输和输配损失	In Transportation and Transmission								
终端消费量	**Final Consumption Industry**	**6410.98**	**642.16**			**2.06**		**0.77**	
第一产业	Primary Industry	97.31	29.48						
第二产业	Secondary Industry	1766.32	206.84			0.41		0.76	
工　业	Industry	1638.41	201.87			0.22		0.76	
#用作原料、材料	Use as Materials	323.11	0.05						
建筑业	Construction	127.91	4.97			0.18			
第三产业	Tertiary Industry	3109.04	152.37			1.65		0.01	
生活消费	Residential Consumption	1438.31	253.47						
城　镇	Urban	1199.04	112.25						
乡　村	Rural	239.27	141.22						
平衡差额	Balance	11.07	-0.51			-0.01			
消费量合计	**Total Energy Consumption**	**6723.90**							

注：2013年数据为第三次全国经济普查数据。
Note: Data for 2013 were collected from the third national economic census.

4-9 续表 1 Continued 1

单位：万吨标准煤 (10000 tons of SCE)

项目	Item	高炉煤气(亿立方米) Furnace Gas (100 million cu.m)	转炉煤气(亿立方米) Converter Gas (100 million cu.m)	其它煤气 Other Gas	其它焦化产品 Other Carbonized Products	原油 Crude Oil	汽油 Gasoline	煤油 Kerosene
可供本地区消费的能源量	**Total Energy Available for Local Consumption**					**1244.20**	**293.69**	**555.73**
加工转换投入(-)产出(+)量	**Input(-) or Output(+) in Processing and Transformation**					**-1242.92**	**329.40**	**146.23**
火力发电	Thermal Power							
供　热	Heating							
煤炭洗选	Washing of Coal							
炼　焦	Coking							
炼油及煤制油	Oil Refining and Coal to Liquid					-1242.92	329.40	146.23
#油品再投入量(-)	Oil Product Re-input(-)							
制　气	Gas Production							
#焦炭再投入量(-)	Coke Re-input(-)							
煤制品加工	Coal Product Processing							
回收能	**Energy Recycled**							
损失量	**Losses**					**1.26**		
#运输和输配损失	In Transportation and Transmission							
终端消费量	**Final Consumption Industry**						**623.29**	**701.95**
第一产业	Primary Industry						7.77	
第二产业	Secondary Industry						33.30	0.12
工　业	Industry						22.91	0.12
#用作原料、材料	Use as Materials						0.19	0.04
建筑业	Construction						10.39	
第三产业	Tertiary Industry						176.13	701.83
生活消费	Residential Consumption						406.09	
城　镇	Urban						406.09	
乡　村	Rural							
平衡差额	Balance					0.02	-0.20	0.01
消费量合计	**Total Energy Consumption**							

4-9 续表 2 Continued 2

单位：万吨标准煤 (10000 tons of SCE)

项目	Item	柴油 Diesel Oil	燃料油 Fuel Oil	石脑油 Naphtha	润滑油 Grease Oil	石蜡 Oilfin	溶剂油 Solvent Oil	石油沥青 Oil Asphalt	石油焦 Petroleum Coal
可供本地区消费的能源量	**Total Energy Available for Local Consumption**	**-1.31**	**-12.39**	**40.73**	**1.93**	**-7.80**	**0.51**	**13.80**	**-2.38**
加工转换投入(-)产出(+)量	**Input(-) or Output(+) in Proce -ssing and Transformation**	**282.64**	**23.79**	**2.78**		**8.88**		**20.36**	**2.09**
火力发电	Thermal Power	-0.30	-0.01						-4.17
供 热	Heating	-0.76	-0.39						-22.05
煤炭洗选	Washing of Coal								
炼 焦	Coking								
炼油及煤制油	Oil Refining and Coal to Liquid	283.69	24.18	151.56		8.88		20.36	28.31
#油品再投入量(-)	Oil Product Re-input(-)			-148.78					
制 气	Gas Production								
#焦炭再投入量(-)	Coke Re-input(-)								
煤制品加工	Coal Product Processing								
回收能	**Energy Recycled**								
损失量	**Losses**								
#运输和输配损失	In Transportation and Transmission								
终端消费量	**Final Consumption Industry**	**281.47**	**11.46**	**43.14**	**1.93**	**1.05**	**0.51**	**33.76**	
第一产业	Primary Industry	5.33			0.14				
第二产业	Secondary Industry	62.36	8.25	43.14	1.79	1.05	0.51	33.76	
工 业	Industry	29.56	8.25	43.14	1.79	1.05	0.51	33.76	
#用作原料、材料	Use as Materials	0.33	5.27	43.14	1.79	1.05	0.51	33.76	
建筑业	Construction	32.80							
第三产业	Tertiary Industry	213.58	3.21						
生活消费	Residential Consumption	0.20							
城 镇	Urban								
乡 村	Rural	0.20							
平衡差额	Balance	-0.14	-0.06	0.37		0.03		0.40	-0.29
消费量合计	**Total Energy Consumption**								

4-9 续表 3 Continued 3

单位：万吨标准煤 (10000 tons of SCE)

项　目	Item	液化石油气 Liquefied Petroleum Gas	炼厂干气 Refinery Gas	其它石油制品 Other Petroleum Products	天然气 Natural Gas (100 million cu.m)	热力 Heat	电力 Electricity	其它能源 Others
可供本地区消费的能源量	**Total Energy Available for Local Consumption**	**29.44**		**11.12**	**1223.33**	**17.55**	**1713.22**	**46.53**
加工转换投入(-)产出(+)量	**Input(-) or Output(+) in Processing and Transformation**	**48.10**	**101.62**	**224.03**	**-575.80**	**507.87**	**956.90**	**2.30**
火力发电	Thermal Power		-0.30	-0.98	-394.05		956.90	-16.47
供　热	Heating	-0.02	-3.88	-14.00	-181.75	507.87		
煤炭洗选	Washing of Coal							
炼　焦	Coking							
炼油及煤制油	Oil Refining and Coal to Liquid	48.12	105.80	368.00				
#油品再投入量(-)	Oil Product Re-input(-)			-128.99				
制　气	Gas Production							
#焦炭再投入量(-)	Coke Re-input(-)							
煤制品加工	Coal Product Processing							
回收能	**Energy Recycled**							**18.77**
损失量	**Losses**	**6.65**			**45.35**		**175.34**	
#运输和输配损失	In Transportation and Transmission							
终端消费量	**Final Consumption Industry**	**70.86**	**98.48**	**235.29**	**602.18**	**525.42**	**2486.33**	**48.85**
第一产业	Primary Industry	0.10			0.09		54.41	
第二产业	Secondary Industry	4.37	98.48	235.29	124.89	137.27	766.45	7.26
工　业	Industry	3.03	98.48	235.29	119.76	133.44	697.55	6.89
#用作原料、材料	Use as Materials	0.39	3.00	233.56				
建筑业	Construction	1.34			5.13	3.83	68.90	0.37
第三产业	Tertiary Industry	30.91			335.70	260.55	1205.50	27.59
生活消费	Residential Consumption	35.48			141.50	127.60	459.97	14.00
城　镇	Urban	20.99			137.44	127.60	394.67	
乡　村	Rural	14.49			4.06		65.31	14.00
平衡差额	Balance	0.03	3.14	-0.14			8.45	-0.02
消费量合计	**Total Energy Consumption**							

4-10 能源平衡表(标准量简表)(2014年)
ENERGY BALANCE (STANDARD VOLUME) (SIMPLE EDITION) (2014)

单位：万吨标准煤 (10000 tons of SCE)

项目	Item	合计 Total	原煤 Coal	洗精煤 Washed Coal	其他洗煤 Other Washed Coal	煤制品 Coal Products	煤矸石 Coal Slack	焦炭 Coke	焦炉煤气 Coking Gas
可供本地区消费的能源量	**Total Energy Available for Local Consumption**	**6818.29**	**1384.27**	**4.97**	**0.01**	**1.72**		**0.62**	
加工转换投入(-)产出(+)量	**Input(-) or Output(+) in Processing and Transformation**	**-83.45**	**-782.66**	**-4.90**		**0.54**			
火力发电	Thermal Power		-450.07			-0.37			
供热	Heating	-94.52	-327.52			-8.61			
煤炭洗选	Washing of Coal	-0.11	-5.07	4.96					
炼焦	Coking								
炼油及煤制油	Oil Refining and Coal to Liquid	300.81							
#油品再投入量(-)	Oil Product Re-input(-)	-308.12							
制气	Gas Production								
#焦炭再投入量(-)	Coke Re-input(-)								
煤制品加工	Coal Product Processing	-0.34		-9.86		9.53			
回收能	**Energy Recycled**	**18.83**							
损失量	**Losses**	**233.66**							
#运输和输配损失	In Transportation and Transmission								
终端消费量	**Final Consumption Industry**	**6514.12**	**601.60**	**0.05**	**0.01**	**2.26**		**0.62**	
第一产业	Primary Industry	91.69	24.93						
第二产业	Secondary Industry	1681.25	162.47	0.02		0.38		0.61	
工业	Industry	1556.40	158.21	0.02		0.16		0.61	
#用作原料、材料	Use as Materials	279.85				0.01			
建筑业	Construction	124.85	4.26			0.22			
第三产业	Tertiary Industry	3236.55	157.67	0.03	0.01	1.88		0.01	
生活消费	Residential Consumption	1504.63	256.53						
城镇	Urban	1248.07	107.59						
乡村	Rural	256.56	148.94						
平衡差额	Balance	-12.94	0.01	0.02					
消费量合计	**Total Energy Consumption**	**6831.23**							

注：从2010年起，热力调整为按当量热值计算，电力仍然按等价热值计算。
Note: From 2010, heating power is calculated as equivalent heat value. Electrivity is still calculated in equivalent caloricity.

4-10 续表 1 Continued 1

单位：万吨标准煤 (10000 tons of SCE)

项目	Item	高炉煤气（亿立方米） Furnace Gas (100 million cu.m)	转炉煤气（亿立方米） Converter Gas (100 million cu.m)	其它煤气 Other Gas	其它焦化产品 Other Carbonized Products	原油 Crude Oil	汽油 Gaso-line	煤油 Kero-sene
可供本地区消费的能源量	**Total Energy Available for Local Consumption**					**1478.05**	**225.40**	**522.75**
加工转换投入(-)产出(+)量	**Input(-) or Output(+) in Proce-ssing and Transformation**					**-1476.18**	**422.92**	**224.11**
火力发电	Thermal Power							
供　热	Heating							
煤炭洗选	Washing of Coal							
炼　焦	Coking							
炼油及煤制油	Oil Refining and Coal to Liquid					-1476.18	422.92	224.11
#油品再投入量(-)	Oil Product Re-input(-)							
制　气	Gas Production							
#焦炭再投入量(-)	Coke Re-input(-)							
煤制品加工	Coal Product Processing							
回收能	**Energy Recycled**							
损失量	**Losses**					**1.87**		
#运输和输配损失	In Transportation and Transmission							
终端消费量	**Final Consumption Industry**						**648.32**	**746.85**
第一产业	Primary Industry						8.25	
第二产业	Secondary Industry						36.29	0.08
工　业	Industry						24.84	0.08
#用作原料、材料	Use as Materials							
建筑业	Construction						11.45	
第三产业	Tertiary Industry						185.51	746.77
生活消费	Residential Consumption						418.27	
城　镇	Urban						418.27	
乡　村	Rural							
平衡差额	Balance							0.01
消费量合计	**Total Energy Consumption**							

4-10 续表 2 Continued 2

单位：万吨标准煤 (10000 tons of SCE)

项　目	Item	柴油 Diesel Oil	燃料油 Fuel Oil	石脑油 Naphtha	润滑油 Grease Oil	石蜡 Oilfin	溶剂油 Solvent Oil	石油沥青 Oil Asphalt	石油焦 Petroleum Coal
可供本地区消费的能源量	**Total Energy Available for Local Consumption**	**-33.99**	**1.34**	**7.56**	**1.75**	**-14.20**	**0.12**	**9.08**	**-11.62**
加工转换投入(-)产出(+)量	**Input(-) or Output(+) in Processing and Transformation**	**319.18**	**6.36**	**52.49**		**14.52**		**16.93**	**12.69**
火力发电	Thermal Power	-0.27							-6.93
供　热	Heating	-0.82	-0.35						-21.32
煤炭洗选	Washing of Coal								
炼　焦	Coking								
炼油及煤制油	Oil Refining and Coal to Liquid	320.27	6.71	187.46		14.52		16.93	40.94
#油品再投入量(-)	Oil Product Re-input(-)			-134.97					
制　气	Gas Production								
#焦炭再投入量(-)	Coke Re-input(-)								
煤制品加工	Coal Product Processing								
回收能	**Energy Recycled**								
损失量	**Losses**								
#运输和输配损失	In Transportation and Transmission								
终端消费量	**Final Consumption Industry**	**285.17**	**7.70**	**60.05**	**1.76**	**0.52**	**0.12**	**25.48**	
第一产业	Primary Industry	5.00							
第二产业	Secondary Industry	63.52	4.93	60.05	1.76	0.52	0.12	25.48	
工　业	Industry	27.05	4.93	60.05	1.76	0.52	0.12	25.48	
#用作原料、材料	Use as Materials	0.38	0.82	60.05	1.76	0.52	0.12	25.48	
建筑业	Construction	36.47							
第三产业	Tertiary Industry	216.50	2.77						
生活消费	Residential Consumption	0.15							
城　镇	Urban								
乡　村	Rural	0.15							
平衡差额	Balance	0.02			-0.01	-0.20		0.53	1.07
消费量合计	**Total Energy Consumption**								

4-10 续表 3 Continued 3

单位：万吨标准煤 (10000 tons of SCE)

项目	Item	液化石油气 Liquefied Petroleum Gas	炼厂干气 Refinery Gas	其它石油制品 Other Petroleum Products	天然气 Natural Gas (100 million cu.m)	热力 Heat	电力 Electricity	其它能源 Others
可供本地区消费的能源量	**Total Energy Available for Local Consumption**	**27.93**		**6.35**	**1440.53**	**51.91**	**1658.98**	**54.67**
加工转换投入(-)产出(+)量	**Input(-) or Output(+) in Processing and Transformation**	**54.44**	**98.55**	**200.94**	**-768.35**	**513.39**	**1009.46**	**2.17**
火力发电	Thermal Power	-0.03	-0.14	-0.74	-534.23		1009.46	-16.66
供热	Heating	-0.53	-1.20	-13.42	-234.12	513.39		
煤炭洗选	Washing of Coal							
炼焦	Coking							
炼油及煤制油	Oil Refining and Coal to Liquid	55.00	99.89	388.25				
#油品再投入量(-)	Oil Product Re-input(-)			-173.14				
制气	Gas Production							
#焦炭再投入量(-)	Coke Re-input(-)							
煤制品加工	Coal Product Processing							
回收能	**Energy Recycled**							**18.83**
损失量	**Losses**	**3.43**			**56.25**		**172.11**	
#运输和输配损失	In Transportation and Transmission							
终端消费量	**Final Consumption Industry**	**82.36**	**89.99**	**217.25**	**615.92**	**565.30**	**2508.02**	**54.66**
第一产业	Primary Industry	0.11			0.11		53.30	
第二产业	Secondary Industry	3.80	89.99	217.25	121.66	135.78	748.74	7.71
工业	Industry	3.10	89.99	217.25	119.08	131.27	684.47	7.33
#用作原料、材料	Use as Materials	0.09	5.51	185.11				
建筑业	Construction	0.70			2.58	4.51	64.27	0.38
第三产业	Tertiary Industry	38.20			344.82	292.37	1219.97	30.03
生活消费	Residential Consumption	40.25			149.33	137.15	486.01	16.92
城镇	Urban	22.50			144.10	137.15	418.47	
乡村	Rural	17.76			5.24		67.54	16.92
平衡差额	Balance	-3.42	8.56	-9.96	0.01		-11.69	2.18
消费量合计	**Total Energy Consumption**							

4-11 分行业能源消费总量和主要能源品种消费量(2013年)

单位：万吨

项目	Item	能源消费总量(万吨标准煤) Total Energy Consumption (10000 tons of SCE)	煤炭 Coal
合计	**Total**	**6723.89**	**2019.23**
农、林、牧、渔业	Agriculture, Forestry, Animal Production and Hunting, Fishing	97.31	41.41
采矿业	Mining and Quarrying	22.04	2.10
煤炭开采和洗选业	Mining and Washing of Coal	6.17	1.00
石油和天然气开采业	Extraction of Petroleum and Natural Gas	0.01	
黑色金属矿采选业	Mining of Ferrous Metal Ores	13.43	1.05
有色金属矿采选业	Mining of Non-ferrous Metal Ores	0.01	
非金属矿采选业	Mining and Processing of Nonmetal Ores	2.04	0.05
开采辅助活动	Mining Support Service Activities	0.38	
其他采矿业	Mining of Other Ores n.e.c		
制造业	Manufacturing	1388.55	262.83
农副食品加工业	Processing of Food from Agricultural Products	26.86	13.02
食品制造业	Manufacture of Foods	30.34	6.46
酒、饮料和精制茶制造业	Manufacture of Wine, Beverage and Refined Tea	34.92	25.48
烟草制品业	Manufacture of Cigarettes and Tobacco	2.28	
纺织业	Manufacture of Textile	6.37	3.00
纺织服装、服饰业	Manufacture of Textile Wearing Apparel and Ornament	15.21	7.42
皮革、毛皮、羽毛及其制品和制鞋业	Manufacture of Leather, Fur, Feather and Its Products, and Footwear	1.19	0.19
木材加工和木、竹、藤、棕、草制品业	Processing of Timbers, Manufacture of Wood, Bamboo, Rattan, Palm, and Straw Products	6.21	0.52
家具制造业	Manufacture of Furniture	7.90	1.70
造纸和纸制品业	Manufacture of Paper and Paper Products	11.18	4.67
印刷和记录媒介复制业	Printing, Reproduction of Recording Media	25.21	2.10
文教、工美、体育和娱乐用品制造业	Manufacture of Articles for Culture, Education, Artwork, Sport and Entertainment Activities	4.94	1.50
石油加工、炼焦和核燃料加工业	Processing of Petroleum, Coking, Processing of Nucleus Fuel	468.50	0.79
化学原料和化学制品制造业	Manufacture of Chemical Raw Materials and Chemical Products	113.08	18.11
医药制造业	Manufacture of Medicines	32.13	9.07
化学纤维制造业	Manufacture of Chemical Fibers	0.99	0.02
橡胶和塑料制品业	Manufacture of Rubber and Plastics Products	29.67	5.78
非金属矿物制品业	Manufacture of Non-Metallic Mineral Products	203.33	129.09

注：1. 各行业能源消费总量为各行业终端消费量与各行业分摊的损失量和加工转换损失量之和，不等于分品种能源消费量(标准煤)的合计。
2. 2013年数据为第三次全国经济普查数据。

CONSUMPTION OF TOTAL ENERGY AND MAIN ENERGY VARIETIES BY SECTOR (2013)

(10000 tons)

焦炭 Coke	汽油 Gasoline	煤油 Kerosene	柴油 Diesel Oil	燃料油 Fuel Oil	液化石油气 Liquefied Petroleum Gas	天然气（亿立方米） Natural Gas (100 million cu.m)	热力（万百万千焦） Heat (10 billion kilo-joule)	电力（亿千瓦时） Electricity (100 million kwh)
0.79	**423.61**	**477.06**	**193.90**	**8.30**	**45.23**	**98.81**	**15408.22**	**908.70**
	5.28		3.66		0.06	0.01		18.57
0.03	0.12		2.27			0.06	71.17	4.75
	0.04		0.05				1.31	1.79
	0.05		1.08			0.06	68.91	2.75
0.03			1.12				0.86	0.11
	0.03		0.02				0.09	0.10
0.75	14.33	0.08	16.88	5.77	1.71	9.05	3639.36	176.28
	0.42		0.36	0.01	0.06	0.15	50.70	4.36
	0.45		0.54		0.14	0.44	97.11	5.30
	0.27		0.28		0.01	0.11	51.62	4.38
	0.01					0.12		0.29
	0.12		0.03		0.01	0.02	12.67	1.13
	0.62		0.16		0.03	0.02	35.10	2.43
	0.06		0.01		0.01		3.37	0.28
	0.16		0.07		0.01		0.81	1.51
	0.49		0.09	0.01	0.03	0.01	11.79	1.77
	0.30		0.14		0.02	0.07	7.90	2.07
	0.78	0.01	0.18		0.04	0.21	55.25	6.09
	0.16		0.03		0.02	0.02	18.35	0.93
	0.07		0.12		0.02	1.94	1127.01	15.23
	0.67		0.71	3.66	0.25	0.20	1033.73	14.25
	0.51		0.28		0.03	0.35	121.39	5.48
	0.01					0.03	0.71	0.19
	0.47		0.17		0.08	0.07	83.82	7.10
0.04	0.93		9.62	2.08	0.07	0.81	35.42	21.01

Note: a) Total energy consumption in each sector is the end consumption of each sector plus losses shared by each sector and losses from processing in each sector, but not equal to sum of consumption (SCE equivalent) of all sorts of energy.

b) Data for 2013 were collected from the third national economic census.

4-11 续表

单位：万吨

项　　目	Item	能源消费总量(万吨标准煤) Total Energy Consumption (10000 tons of SCE)	煤　炭 Coal
黑色金属冶炼及压延加工业	Manufacture and Pressing of Ferrous Metals	27.63	0.66
有色金属冶炼及压延加工业	Manufacture and Pressing of Non-Ferrous Metals	5.74	0.45
金属制品业	Manufacture of Fabricated Metal Products	35.61	4.85
通用设备制造业	Manufacture of General-purpose Machinery	30.94	2.99
专用设备制造业	Manufacture of Special-purpose Machinery	24.28	3.19
汽车制造业	Manufacture of Motor Vehicles	100.13	4.13
铁路、船舶、航空航天和其他运输设备制造业	Manufacture of Railway Locomotives, Building of Ships and Boats, Manufacture of Air and Spacecrafts and Other Transportation Equipment	17.49	10.99
电气机械和器材制造业	Manufacture of Electrical Machinery and Equipment	21.56	2.24
计算机、通讯和其他电子设备制造业	Manufacture of Computer, Communication Equipment and Other Electronic Equipment	86.54	0.82
仪器仪表制造业	Manufacture of Measuring Instruments and Meters	7.72	0.64
其他制造业	Other Manufacturing	4.98	2.21
废弃资源综合利用业	Waste recycling and recovery	1.12	0.14
金属制品、机械和设备修理业	Repair of Fabricated Metal Products, Machinery and Equipment	4.50	0.60
电力、燃气及水的生产和供应业	Production and Distribution of Electricity, Gas and Water	540.72	1181.08
电力、热力生产和供应业	Production and Supply of Electric Power and Heat Power	449.68	1180.72
燃气生产和供应业	Production and Distribution of Gas	56.25	0.01
水的生产和供应业	Production and Distribution of Water	34.79	0.35
建筑业	Construction	127.91	7.20
批发和零售业	Wholesale and Retail Trade	189.91	8.66
交通运输、仓储和邮政业	Transport, Storage and Post	1145.52	15.94
住宿和餐饮业	Accommodation and Restaurants	282.56	30.19
信息传输、软件和信息技术服务业	Information transmission,software and information technology services	136.19	1.17
金融业	Finance	61.22	1.09
房地产业	Real Estate Trade	376.99	60.22
租赁和商务服务业	Renting and Leasing Activities and Business Services	188.98	14.22
科学研究和技术服务业	Scientific Research and Development, Technical Services	160.81	12.81
水利、环境和公共设施管理业	Water, Environment and Municipal Engineering Conservancy	53.50	6.35
居民服务、修理和其他服务业	Resident services, repair and other services	40.70	15.37
教　育	Education	208.19	24.32
卫生和社会工作	Healthcare and Social Works	79.89	8.75
文化、体育和娱乐业	Culture, Sports and Entertainment	62.25	2.02
公共管理、社会保障和社会组织	Public Administration, Social Security and Social Organizations	122.34	14.52
生活消费	Residential Consumption	1438.31	308.98
城　镇	Urban	1199.04	119.06
乡　村	Rural	239.27	189.92

4-11 Continued

(10000 tons)

焦 炭 Coke	汽 油 Gasoline	煤 油 Kerosene	柴 油 Diesel Oil	燃料油 Fuel Oil	液 化 石油气 Liquefied Petroleum Gas	天然气 (亿立方米) Natural Gas (100 million cu.m)	热 力 (万百万千焦) Heat (10 billion kilo-joule)	电 力 (亿千瓦时) Electricity (100 million kwh)
0.69	0.11		0.24		0.01	0.88	2.62	5.29
0.01	0.09		0.03		0.01	0.02	10.09	1.59
	1.19		0.47	0.01	0.45	0.41	40.26	7.73
	1.04	0.01	0.41		0.17	0.15	122.65	6.84
	1.08		0.35		0.03	0.13	102.13	5.05
	1.77	0.01	1.24		0.12	2.26	139.08	20.31
0.01	0.21		0.21		0.01	0.05	117.85	2.49
	0.92		0.10		0.04	0.09	82.46	4.69
	0.63		0.30		0.01	0.27	194.98	25.48
	0.56		0.03		0.01	0.05	47.02	1.42
	0.09		0.10		0.02	0.02	30.70	0.89
	0.03		0.05			0.02	0.57	0.22
	0.11	0.05	0.56			0.13	2.20	0.48
	1.13		1.85	0.28	3.95	48.99	202.54	116.98
	0.67		1.69	0.28	0.05	44.67	169.82	105.21
	0.26		0.06		3.89	4.25	7.20	0.87
	0.20		0.10		0.01	0.07	25.52	10.90
	7.06		22.51		0.78	0.43	112.34	23.52
	22.82	0.01	4.48	0.01	0.52	0.60	647.47	38.78
	45.40	476.51	124.28	1.60	0.35	2.35	603.86	44.64
0.01	1.58		0.72	0.02	15.06	5.62	601.01	48.03
	3.80		0.53		0.06	0.16	234.87	40.44
	2.77		0.18		0.04	0.12	303.87	15.07
	4.52		1.01	0.60	0.21	7.56	1214.89	64.77
	11.22		4.64	0.01	0.29	1.93	633.28	37.33
	9.13	0.46	3.11		0.15	2.39	631.05	28.06
	2.13		3.65		0.16	0.46	38.64	11.21
	1.43		0.73		0.15	0.92	40.89	4.78
	3.66		1.65		0.38	3.76	1335.64	29.88
	0.96		0.42		0.20	1.16	375.17	14.33
	1.88		0.32		0.12	0.57	284.88	13.67
	8.40		0.87	0.01	0.34	0.73	695.29	20.57
	275.99		0.14		20.70	11.94	3742.00	157.04
	275.99				12.25	11.60	3742.00	134.74
			0.14		8.45	0.34		22.30

4-12 分行业能源消费总量和主要能源品种消费量(2014年)

单位：万吨

项　目	Item	能源消费总量(万吨标准煤) Total Energy Consumption (10000 tons of SCE)	煤　炭 Coal
合　计	**Total**	**6831.22**	**1736.54**
农、林、牧、渔业	Agriculture, Forestry, Animal Production and Hunting, Fishing	91.69	34.88
采矿业	Mining and Quarrying	22.21	1.90
煤炭开采和洗选业	Mining and Washing of Coal	5.53	0.94
石油和天然气开采业	Extraction of Petroleum and Natural Gas	0.01	
黑色金属矿采选业	Mining of Ferrous Metal Ores	15.22	0.93
有色金属矿采选业	Mining of Non-ferrous Metal Ores	0.01	
非金属矿采选业	Mining and Processing of Nonmetal Ores	1.22	0.03
开采辅助活动	Mining Support Service Activities	0.22	
其他采矿业	Mining of Other Ores n.e.c		
制造业	Manufacturing	1332.76	214.13
农副食品加工业	Processing of Food from Agricultural Products	26.16	12.14
食品制造业	Manufacture of Foods	30.02	7.22
酒、饮料和精制茶制造业	Manufacture of Wine, Beverage and Refined Tea	31.10	20.32
烟草制品业	Manufacture of Cigarettes and Tobacco	1.99	
纺织业	Manufacture of Textile	5.49	2.52
纺织服装、服饰业	Manufacture of Textile Wearing Apparel and Ornament	14.34	6.74
皮革、毛皮、羽毛及其制品和制鞋业	Manufacture of Leather, Fur, Feather and Its Products, and Footwear	1.14	0.19
木材加工和木、竹、藤、棕、草制品业	Processing of Timbers, Manufacture of Wood, Bamboo, Rattan, Palm, and Straw Products	5.56	0.59
家具制造业	Manufacture of Furniture	7.65	1.40
造纸和纸制品业	Manufacture of Paper and Paper Products	11.69	5.06
印刷和记录媒介复制业	Printing, Reproduction of Recording Media	24.47	2.19
文教、工美、体育和娱乐用品制造业	Manufacture of Articles for Culture, Education, Artwork, Sport and Entertainment Activities	4.39	1.16
石油加工、炼焦和核燃料加工业	Processing of Petroleum, Coking, Processing of Nucleus Fuel	477.21	0.67
化学原料和化学制品制造业	Manufacture of Chemical Raw Materials and Chemical Products	97.66	12.70
医药制造业	Manufacture of Medicines	32.30	7.53
化学纤维制造业	Manufacture of Chemical Fibers	1.30	0.02
橡胶和塑料制品业	Manufacture of Rubber and Plastics Products	27.39	4.05
非金属矿物制品业	Manufacture of Non-Metallic Mineral Products	168.30	100.88

注：各行业能源消费总量为各行业终端消费量与各行业分摊的损失量和加工转换损失量之和，不等于分品种能源消费量(标准煤)的合计。

CONSUMPTION OF TOTAL ENERGY AND MAIN ENERGY VARIETIES BY SECTOR (2014)

(10000 tons)

焦 炭 Coke	汽 油 Gasoline	煤 油 Kerosene	柴 油 Diesel Oil	燃料油 Fuel Oil	液 化 石油气 Liquefied Petroleum Gas	天然气 (亿立方米) Natural Gas (100 million cu.m)	热 力 (万百万千焦) Heat (10 billion kilo-joule)	电 力 (亿千瓦时) Electricity (100 million kwh)
0.64	**440.62**	**507.58**	**196.46**	**5.63**	**50.37**	**113.70**	**16577.79**	**933.41**
	5.61		3.43		0.06	0.01		18.56
0.01	0.13		1.52		0.04	0.01	13.85	6.19
	0.03		0.06		0.04		1.40	1.60
	0.06		0.85			0.01	12.17	4.43
0.01	0.01		0.56				0.14	0.12
	0.03		0.05				0.14	0.04
0.62	15.73	0.05	16.08	3.45	1.70	9.70	3680.41	174.29
	0.44		0.35	0.01	0.06	0.14	54.22	4.40
	0.49		0.58		0.13	0.42	86.68	5.26
	0.26		0.26		0.01	0.18	51.48	4.13
						0.10		0.28
	0.14		0.03		0.01	0.02	10.56	0.97
	0.67		0.14		0.03	0.03	40.27	2.23
	0.06		0.01				3.80	0.26
	0.18		0.10		0.01		0.53	1.38
	0.54		0.11	0.01	0.03	0.02	12.94	1.74
	0.35		0.17		0.02	0.07	9.07	2.12
	0.90		0.21		0.04	0.18	62.21	5.84
	0.19		0.05		0.02	0.02	19.08	0.80
	0.07		0.17		0.08	2.74	1132.17	17.25
	0.75		0.72	0.54	0.19	0.19	928.36	13.58
	0.52		0.23		0.04	0.36	146.15	5.82
	0.02					0.03		0.30
	0.54		0.25		0.13	0.12	78.71	6.60
0.01	0.99		8.74	2.83	0.08	0.81	39.33	18.45

Note: Total energy consumption in each sector is the end consumption of each sector plus losses shared by each sector and losses from processing in each sector, but not equal to sum of consumption (SCE equivalent) of all sorts of energy.

4-12 续表

单位：万吨

项目	Item	能源消费总量（万吨标准煤）Total Energy Consumption (10000 tons of SCE)	煤炭 Coal
黑色金属冶炼及压延加工业	Manufacture and Pressing of Ferrous Metals	24.78	0.58
有色金属冶炼及压延加工业	Manufacture and Pressing of Non-Ferrous Metals	5.26	0.25
金属制品业	Manufacture of Fabricated Metal Products	34.37	4.67
通用设备制造业	Manufacture of General-purpose Machinery	30.35	3.36
专用设备制造业	Manufacture of Special-purpose Machinery	23.59	2.39
汽车制造业	Manufacture of Motor Vehicles	102.63	1.47
铁路、船舶、航空航天和其他运输设备制造业	Manufacture of Railway Locomotives, Building of Ships and Boats, Manufacture of Air and Spacecrafts and Other Transportation Equipment	17.12	9.42
电气机械和器材制造业	Manufacture of Electrical Machinery and Equipment	22.09	2.91
计算机、通讯和其他电子设备制造业	Manufacture of Computer, Communication Equipment and Other Electronic Equipment	85.90	0.88
仪器仪表制造业	Manufacture of Measuring Instruments and Meters	8.07	0.62
其他制造业	Other Manufacturing	5.54	1.53
废弃资源综合利用业	Waste recycling and recovery	1.10	0.14
金属制品、机械和设备修理业	Repair of Fabricated Metal Products, Machinery and Equipment	3.80	0.53
电力、热力、燃气及水生产和供应业	Production and Distribution of Electricity, Heating Power, Gas and Water	518.54	964.88
电力、热力生产和供应业	Production and Supply of Electric Power and Heat Power	417.76	964.51
燃气生产和供应业	Production and Distribution of Gas	63.89	0.01
水的生产和供应业	Production and Distribution of Water	36.89	0.36
建筑业	Construction	124.85	6.17
批发和零售业	Wholesale and Retail Trade	194.18	6.66
交通运输、仓储和邮政业	Transport, Storage and Post	1204.15	16.09
住宿和餐饮业	Accommodation and Restaurants	292.04	19.71
信息传输、软件和信息技术服务业	Information transmission,software and information technology services	148.40	0.85
金融业	Finance	68.41	1.06
房地产业	Real Estate Trade	374.91	63.23
租赁和商务服务业	Renting and Leasing Activities and Business Services	210.51	26.83
科学研究和技术服务业	Scientific Research and Development, Technical Services	159.81	14.54
水利、环境和公共设施管理业	Water, Environment and Municipal Engineering Conservancy	61.52	7.28
居民服务、修理和其他服务业	Resident services, repair and other services	32.69	13.75
教 育	Education	220.52	24.60
卫生和社会工作	Healthcare and Social Works	84.70	10.56
文化、体育和娱乐业	Culture, Sports and Entertainment	65.44	1.87
公共管理、社会保障和社会组织	Public Administration, Social Security and Social Organizations	119.26	14.10
生活消费	Residential Consumption	1504.63	293.45
城 镇	Urban	1248.07	114.12
乡 村	Rural	256.56	179.33

4-12 Continued

(10000 tons)

焦 炭 Coke	汽 油 Gasoline	煤 油 Kerosene	柴 油 Diesel Oil	燃料油 Fuel Oil	液 化 石油气 Liquefied Petroleum Gas	天然气 (亿立方米) Natural Gas (100 million cu.m)	热 力 (万百万千焦) Heat (10 billion kilo-joule)	电 力 (亿千瓦时) Electricity (100 million kwh)
0.60	0.11		0.31		0.01	0.81	2.16	4.73
	0.10		0.04		0.04	0.02	12.86	1.45
	1.31		0.49		0.41	0.37	57.05	7.44
	1.18	0.01	0.46		0.13	0.15	136.71	6.46
	1.19		0.30		0.04	0.12	124.70	4.84
	1.99	0.01	1.23		0.11	2.22	158.63	22.20
0.01	0.23		0.20		0.01	0.04	119.21	2.66
	0.98		0.10		0.04	0.08	96.43	4.61
	0.69		0.42		0.01	0.27	207.24	25.52
	0.57		0.03		0.01	0.05	55.24	1.46
	0.10		0.12		0.01	0.02	29.38	0.79
	0.03		0.04			0.02	0.85	0.22
	0.14	0.03	0.22	0.06		0.10	4.39	0.50
	1.02		1.71	0.24	2.40	61.70	155.13	117.84
	0.57		1.55	0.24	0.38	56.44	120.00	105.23
	0.26		0.06		2.00	5.16	7.60	0.87
	0.19		0.09		0.02	0.10	27.53	11.74
	7.78		25.03		0.41	0.22	132.36	22.38
	23.35		3.88	0.01	0.42	0.64	723.09	40.50
	46.45	507.07	126.56	1.88	0.32	3.17	615.33	45.02
0.01	1.53		0.61	0.02	19.42	6.11	660.90	49.90
	4.41		0.42		0.06	0.16	279.95	44.71
	2.78		0.41		0.04	0.22	329.91	17.07
	4.59		1.63		0.15	7.82	1202.76	63.50
	13.62		5.47	0.01	0.20	2.26	766.57	37.75
	10.75	0.46	0.86		0.14	2.33	724.50	27.37
	2.85		4.69		0.21	0.42	49.50	13.04
	1.69		1.04	0.01	0.08	0.29	72.31	4.42
	3.24		1.51		0.49	3.64	1587.26	31.62
	0.95		0.37		0.25	1.06	404.97	15.68
	2.14		0.32		0.11	0.50	343.06	14.63
	7.73		0.81	0.01	0.39	0.73	813.93	19.68
	284.27		0.11		23.48	12.71	4022.00	169.26
	284.27				13.12	12.26	4022.00	145.74
			0.11		10.36	0.45		23.52

4-13 能源消费弹性系数(2000-2014年)
ELASTICITY COEFFICIENT OF ENERGY CONSUMPTION (2000-2014)

项 目 Item	能源消费比上年增长 (%) Growth of Energy Consumption over the Previous Year	电力消费比上年增长(%) Growth of Electricity Consumption over the Previous Year	地区生产总值比上年增长(%) Growth of Gross Domestic Product(GDP) over the Previous Year	能源消费弹性系数 Elasticity Coefficient of Energy Consumption	电力消费弹性系数 Elasticity Coefficient of Electricity Consumption
2000	6.08	9.53	11.8	0.51	0.81
2001	2.06	5.68	11.7	0.18	0.49
2002	4.89	9.54	11.5	0.43	0.83
2003	4.78	5.71	11.1	0.43	0.51
2004	10.57	10.60	14.1	0.75	0.75
2005	7.44	11.16	12.1	0.61	0.92
2006	6.92	9.16	13.0	0.53	0.71
2007	6.45	9.06	14.5	0.45	0.63
2008	0.67	4.90	9.1	0.07	0.54
2009	3.84	7.15	10.2	0.38	0.70
2010	5.84	9.49	10.3	0.57	0.92
2011	0.59	2.74	8.1	0.07	0.34
2012	2.61	6.82	7.7	0.34	0.88
2013	2.44	3.95	7.7	0.32	0.51
2014	1.60	2.72	7.3	0.22	0.37

注：1. 地区生产总值增长速度按可比价计算。
2. 2013年数据为第三次全国经济普查数据。
3. 根据国家统计局能源核算统一要求，2013年开始能源消费数据按照新口径核算。

Note: a) The groth rates of GDP are calculated at comparable prices.
b) Data for 2013 were collected from the third national economic census.
c) According to requirements of National Bureau of Statistics on keeping unified energy statistical approach, the energy consumption has been calculated based on new approach since 2013.

4-14 平均每万元地区生产总值能源消费量(2001-2014年)
ENERGY CONSUMPTION PER 10000 YUAN OF GROSS DOMESTIC PRODUCT (2001-2014)

项 目 Item	能源总消费量 (吨标准煤) Total (ton of SCE)	煤 炭 (吨) Coal (ton)	电 力 (千瓦时) Electricity (kwh)	石 油 (吨) Petroleum (ton)
2001	1.20	0.77	1127.91	0.23
2002	1.13	0.66	1108.09	0.25
2003	1.06	0.63	1053.83	0.22
2004	1.03	0.59	1021.65	0.20
2005	0.99	0.55	1012.86	0.20
	(0.79)	(0.44)	(813.60)	(0.16)
2006	0.75	0.39	786.01	0.15
2007	0.70	0.33	748.74	0.15
2008	0.64	0.28	719.84	0.14
2009	0.61	0.25	700.03	0.13
2010	0.58	0.22	694.69	0.12
	(0.49)	(0.19)	(588.72)	(0.10)
2011	0.46	0.15	559.28	0.10
2012	0.44	0.14	554.57	0.09
2013	0.38	0.11	513.11	0.08
2014	0.36	0.09	491.30	0.08

注：1. 本表中每万元地区生产总值能源消费量按可比价格计算，可比价格每五年调整一次基期，更换基期年份计算两个可比价数据，括号内数据是按新基期价格计算。
2. 2013年数据为第三次全国经济普查数据。
3. 根据国家统计局能源核算统一要求，2013年开始能源消费数据按照新口径核算。

Note: a) Energy consumption per 10000 yuan of GDP were calculated at comparable prices. The base period of comparable prices is changed every five years. Two figures at comparable prices were calculated for the year in which the base period is changed. Figures in brackets were calculated at the price of new base period.
b) Data for 2013 were collected from the third national economic census.
c) According to requirements of National Bureau of Statistics on keeping unified energy statistical approach, the energy consumption has been calculated based on new approach since 2013.

4-15 人均生活用能源(2000-2014年)
PER CAPITA ENERGY CONSUMPTION FOR NON-PRODUCTIVE PURPOSE (2000-2014)

年 份 Year	合 计 (千克标准煤) Total (kg of SCE)	煤 炭 (千克) Coal (kg)	电 力 (千瓦时) Electricity (kwh)	液化石油气 (千克) Liquefied Petroleum Gas(kg)	天然气 (立方米) Natural Gas (cu.m)	汽 油 (升) Gasoline (liter)
2000	407.1	223.6	363.6	13.7	16.4	31.4
2001	408.2	209.6	392.5	13.1	18.7	38.4
2002	415.8	156.0	445.8	16.3	24.1	50.7
2003	472.7	187.8	488.2	20.2	28.4	61.8
2004	509.8	167.6	546.2	22.2	32.9	72.2
2005	537.4	154.1	586.8	20.8	37.4	93.5
2006	579.4	169.9	610.8	15.2	53.5	113.5
2007	613.5	169.1	651.1	16.8	54.8	136.5
2008	620.4	148.4	674.8	12.8	53.1	153.8
2009	642.7	150.7	709.4	12.5	54.3	162.1
2010	643.5	145.9	729.1	11.3	53.1	164.9
2011	656.1	140.5	727.2	10.7	52.7	167.6
2012	684.3	133.2	791.8	9.3	56.5	174.4
2013	687.5	147.7	750.6	9.9	57.1	180.7
2014	705.3	137.6	793.5	11.0	59.6	182.5

注：1. 本表人均生活用能源按常住人口年平均数计算。2006-2010年数据根据全国第六次人口普查进行了修正。
2. 2013年数据为第三次全国经济普查数据。
3. 根据国家统计局能源核算统一要求，2013年开始能源消费数据按照新口径核算。

Note: a) Per-capita energy consumption for non-productive prupose is calculated by average permanent population. Figures for 2006-2010 have been revised in accordance with the 6th national population census.
b) Data for 2013 were collected from the third national economic census.
c) According to requirements of National Bureau of Statistics on keeping unified energy statistical approach, the energy consumption has been calculated based on new approach since 2013.

4-16 主要能源日均消费量(2000-2014年)
DAILY CONSUMPTION OF MAIN ENERGY VARIETIES(2000-2014)

年份 Year	合计 (万吨标准煤) Total (10000 tons of SCE)	煤炭 (吨) Coal (ton)	焦炭 (吨) Coke (ton)	原油 (吨) Crude Oil (ton)	汽油 (吨) Gasoline (ton)	煤油 (吨) Kerosene (ton)	柴油 (吨) Diesel Oil (ton)	燃料油 (吨) Fuel Oil (ton)	电力 (万千瓦时) Electricity (10000 kwh)	天然气 (万立方米) Natural Gas (10000 cu.m)
2000	11.3	76598.4	12270.5	20620.2	3046.4	3213.1	2303.3	2448.1	10297.8	352.5
2001	11.6	74331.5	11769.9	19191.8	3997.3	3542.5	2972.6	2147.9	10912.3	457.5
2002	12.2	70726.0	10353.4	20501.4	4380.8	3978.1	3145.2	1950.7	11953.4	569.9
2003	12.7	75274.0	12008.2	19909.6	4772.6	3778.1	3194.5	1811.0	12635.6	580.8
2004	14.0	80404.4	12451.6	22114.8	5420.8	4994.5	3603.8	1830.6	13937.2	737.7
2005	15.1	84081.4	10887.7	21906.8	6444.7	5187.9	3859.2	1804.9	15535.3	877.8
2006	16.2	83717.0	9551.2	21811.5	7620.8	6407.1	4862.7	1316.4	16958.6	1113.7
2007	17.2	81771.8	9813.4	26052.3	8896.4	7591.8	5260.8	1174.0	18495.6	1277.8
2008	17.3	75073.8	6363.4	30513.7	9314.2	8699.5	6207.7	699.5	19349.7	1658.5
2009	18.0	73005.5	5807.4	31861.1	9961.9	9367.9	6580.3	1161.6	20790.4	1901.4
2010	19.1	72181.1	6039.7	30583.3	10178.9	10757.0	6504.4	1826.8	22764.4	2048.8
2011	19.2	64809.3	911.8	30276.2	10679.2	11503.6	6605.8	2045.2	23388.5	2015.3
2012	19.6	62018.9	881.7	29392.6	11363.4	12112.8	5896.7	2135.5	24916.4	2515.6
2013	18.4	55321.3	21.7	23860.7	11605.7	13070.1	5312.2	227.3	24896.0	2707.2
2014	18.7	47576.5	17.5	28345.6	12071.7	13906.3	5382.5	154.3	25572.9	3115.0

注：1. 2013年数据为第三次全国经济普查数据。
2. 根据国家统计局能源核算统一要求，2013年开始能源消费数据按照新口径核算。

Note: a) Data for 2013 were collected from the third national economic census.
b) According to requirements of National Bureau of Statistics on keeping unified energy statistical approach, the energy consumption has been calculated based on new approach since 2013.

4-17 全社会用电量(1978-2014年)
TOTAL ELECTRICITY CONSUMPTION IN BEIJING (1978-2014)

单位：万千瓦时 (10000 kwh)

年份 Year	全社会用电量 Electricity Consumption	第一产业 Primary Industry	第二产业 Secondary Industry	工业 Industry	建筑业 Construction	第三产业 Tertiary Industry	城乡居民生活用电 Residential Electricity Consumption	城市 Urban	乡村 Rural
1978	735000	48993	570621	570621		94555	20831	11022	9809
1979	802317	52134	620262	620262		107437	22484	11495	10989
1980	854638	65283	648496	648496		116947	23912	12441	11471
1981	867153	80027	643976	643976		121883	21267	9452	11815
1982	925700	104842	657060	657060		139403	24395	10820	13575
1983	956293	92601	687937	687937		151290	24465	12320	12145
1984	1029420	105234	716653	716653		177455	30078	16025	14053
1985	1106255	111110	746324	746324		210622	38199	22479	15720
1986	1181155	105688	851519	835725	15794	175090	48858	31008	17850
1987	1285023	77909	923797	899760	24037	224747	58570	35063	23507
1988	1378574	83809	970885	943383	27502	248446	75434	48624	26810
1989	1421817	100151	979216	949629	29587	258067	84383	56120	28263
1990	1504785	93049	1014037	986356	27681	302775	94924	65262	29662
1991	1613977	93256	1061207	1032064	29143	348769	110745	77575	33170
1992	1759611	101985	1155514	1123835	31679	375874	126238	88621	37617
1993	1924978	107010	1243115	1206001	37114	429835	145018	103579	41439
1994	2054504	101134	1307898	1262961	44937	479679	165791	119025	46766
1995	2225922	102099	1403864	1341398	62466	538936	181022	130897	50125
1996	2443709	111904	1496968	1422590	74378	617286	217551	158474	59077
1997	2636078	120444	1529201	1449129	80072	721774	264659	196641	68018
1998	2762080	108267	1548485	1457149	91336	811283	294045	220543	73502
1999	2972629	121242	1581977	1478523	103454	912834	356576	276642	79934
2000	3844266	130865	2172604	2066892	105712	1064322	476475	385396	91079
2001	3999415	131811	2105819	1978673	127146	1222471	539314	439058	100256
2002	4399637	137370	2293735	2145292	148443	1342490	626042	517386	108656
2003	4676056	107372	2418419	2250525	167894	1447344	702921	574623	128298
2004	5131804	104234	2593504	2391414	202090	1628731	805335	647474	157861
2005	5705364	114308	2795753	2605832	189921	1906093	889210	706405	182805
2006	6115719	122550	2943550	2744127	199423	2090888	958731	768884	189847
2007	6670089	133557	3091374	2881807	209567	2378399	1066759	862604	204155
2008	6897189	136065	2943893	2763399	180494	2654140	1163091	949878	213213
2009	7391465	157310	3027974	2853018	174956	2918229	1287952	982720	305232
2010	8099029	168992	3278682	3081364	197319	3258009	1393346	951811	441535
2011	8217055	170368	3109174	2894464	214708	3490143	1447370	945588	501782
2012	8742835	181391	3209078	2980645	228430	3734022	1618344	1370932	247412
2013	9131113	185749	3345854	3110626	235229	4029145	1570365	1347401	222964
2014	9370485	185633	3352904	3129060	223846	4139319	1692629	1457398	235231

注：1. 1985年以前农、林、牧、渔和水利业用电量中，只包含农业排灌、农副业和社队企业的用电量。
2. 1980年以前的城市居民用电量以全市市政用电量的 1/10计算。
3. 2000年以前工业用电量不包含输配损失和发电企业自产自用电量。

资料来源：北京市电力公司。

Note: a) Before 1985, electricity consumption by agriculture, forestry, animal production and hunting, fishing and water conservancy only included the electricity consumption by farming irrigation, agricultural and sideline products, and village enterprises.
b) Before 1980, electricity consumption by urban residents was one-tenth of the total electricity consumption by municipal administration in Beijing.
c) Before 2000, electricity consumption by industry excluded transmission and distribution losses and electricity generated and consumed by power generating enterprises.

Source: Beijing Electric Power Corporation.

4-18 主要土地利用状况(2009-2013年)
LAND UTILIZATION (2009-2013)

单位：公顷 (hectare)

年 份 Year	耕地面积 Arable Land	园地面积 Garden Plot	林地面积 Forest Land	草地面积 Grass Land	城镇村及工矿用地面积 Land for Urban, Rural,Industrial and Mining Use	交通运输用地面积 Land for Transportation	水域及水利设施用地面积 Water Areas and Land for Water Conservancy Facilities
2009	227170.43	141617.22	743696.19	84843.14	284791.79	44446.42	80235.85
2010	223779.38	139298.50	742018.50	85827.05	290782.01	45335.78	79774.99
2011	221956.16	138072.99	740730.87	85651.69	295116.72	45452.68	79380.05
2012	220856.16	137117.72	739633.48	85491.29	297758.79	46327.98	79088.32
2013	221157.28	135573.37	738036.45	85348.82	300847.83	46626.41	78739.52

注：表中2009年数据为第二次全国土地调查数据，2010-2013年为各年土地变更调查数据。

资料来源：北京市国土资源局。

Note: Statistics for 2009 were from the 2nd National Land Survey, and statistics for 2010-2013 were survey data of land changed.

Source: Beijing Municipal Bureau of Land Resources.

4-19 水资源情况(2001-2014年)

单位：亿立方米

项　目	Item	2001	2002	2003	2004
全年水资源总量	**Total Volume of Water Resource in the Year**	**19.2**	**16.1**	**18.4**	**21.4**
地表水资源量	Volume of Surface Water Resource	7.8	5.3	6.1	8.2
地下水资源量	Volume of Underground Water Resource	15.7	14.7	14.8	16.5
人均水资源(立方米)	**Per-capita Water Resource(cu.m)**	**139.7**	**114.7**	**127.8**	**145.1**
全年供水(用水)总量	**Total Volume of Water Supplied (Consumed) in the Year**	**38.9**	**34.6**	**35.8**	**34.6**
按来源分	By Source				
地表水	Surface Water	11.7	10.4	8.3	5.7
地下水	Underground Water	27.2	24.2	25.4	26.8
再生水	Recycled Water			2.1	2.0
南水北调	Water Transit from South to North				
应急供水	Emergent Water Supply				
按用途分	By Purpose				
农业用水	Water Used by Agriculture	17.4	15.5	13.8	13.5
工业用水	Water Used by Industry	9.2	7.5	8.4	7.7
生活用水	Domestic Water	12.0	10.8	13.0	12.8
环境用水	Water for the Environment	0.3	0.8	0.6	0.6
万元地区生产总值水耗(立方米)	**Water Consumption per 10000 yuan GDP (cu.m)**	**104.91**	**80.19**	**71.50**	**57.35**
万元地区生产总值水耗下降率(%)	**Decrease Rate of Water Consumption per 10000 yuan GDP (%)**	**13.79**	**20.22**	**6.91**	**15.29**

注：1. 万元地区生产总值水耗按现价计算，下降率按可比价计算，如按可比价计算，2014年万元地区生产总值水耗为19.73立方米。
2. 本表人均水资源按常住人口年平均数计算。2006-2010年数据根据全国第六次人口普查进行了修正。
3. 2013年万元地区生产总值水耗及下降率数据为第三次全国经济普查数据。

资料来源：除人均数据和万元地区生产总值水耗以外其它数据来自北京市水务局。

STATISTICS FOR WATER RESOURCES (2001-2014)

(100 million cu.m)

2005	2006	2007	2008	2009	2010	2011	2012	2013	2014
23.2	**22.1**	**23.8**	**34.2**	**21.8**	**23.1**	**26.8**	**39.5**	**24.8**	**20.3**
7.6	6.7	7.6	12.8	6.8	7.2	9.2	18.0	9.4	6.5
15.6	15.4	16.2	21.4	15.1	15.9	17.6	21.6	15.4	13.8
153.1	**140.6**	**145.3**	**198.5**	**120.3**	**120.8**	**134.7**	**193.3**	**118.6**	**94.9**
34.5	**34.3**	**34.8**	**35.1**	**35.5**	**35.2**	**36.0**	**35.9**	**36.4**	**37.5**
6.4	5.7	5.0	4.7	3.8	3.9	4.8	4.4	3.9	7.7
23.1	22.2	21.6	20.5	19.7	19.1	18.8	18.3	17.9	17.5
2.6	3.6	5.0	6.0	6.5	6.8	7.0	7.5	8.0	8.6
			0.7	2.6	2.6	2.6	2.8	3.5	0.8
2.5	2.8	3.2	3.2	2.9	2.9	2.7	2.9	3.0	2.8
13.2	12.8	12.4	12.0	12.0	11.4	10.9	9.3	9.1	8.2
6.8	6.2	5.8	5.2	5.2	5.1	5.0	4.9	5.1	5.1
13.4	13.7	13.9	14.7	14.7	14.8	15.6	16.0	16.2	17.0
1.1	1.6	2.7	3.2	3.6	4.0	4.5	5.7	5.9	7.2
49.50	**42.25**	**35.34**	**31.58**	**29.92**	**24.94**	**22.13**	**20.07**	**18.37**	**17.58**
11.07	**12.01**	**11.38**	**7.56**	**8.12**	**10.14**	**5.49**	**7.38**	**5.87**	**3.93**

Note: a) Water consumption per 10000 yuan GDP is at current prices,and decrease rate is at comparable prices.Caculated at comparable prices, the water consumption per 10000 yuan GDP in 2014 is 19.73 cubic metres.

b) Per-capita water resource are calculated by average permanent population.Per-capita figures 2006-2010 have been corrected in accordance with the Sixth Population Census.

c) Water consumption per 10000 yuan GDP and Decrease Rate of Water Consumption for 2013 is were collected from the third national economic census.

Source: Except for per-capita figures and water consumption per 10000 yuan GDP,other figures are from Beijing Water Authority.

4-20 气象情况(1978-2014年)
METEOROLOGY (1978-2014)

年 份 Year	降水量 (毫米) Precipitation (mm)	平均气温(℃) Average Temperature (℃)	最高 Highest	最低 Lowest	日照时数(时) Hours of Sunshine (hours)	平均风速(米/秒) Average Wind Speed (meter/second)	平均气压(百帕) Average Air Pressure (100 pa)	大风日数(日) Days of Strong Wind (day)	雨日数(日) Days of Rain (day)
1978	664.8	11.6	37.5	-14.4	2865.4	2.6	1012.8	35	64
1979	718.4	11.1	35.9	-15.4	2667.4	2.5	1012.2	33	63
1980	380.7	11.0	35.1	-15.4	2920.8	2.5	1012.7	29	83
1981	393.2	12.3	38.1	-14.0	2803.9	2.5	1010.8	15	92
1982	544.4	12.8	37.3	-14.3	2825.1	2.6	1010.5	26	92
1983	489.9	13.0	37.2	-15.0	2844.3	2.4	1010.3	29	100
1984	488.8	11.9	36.1	-14.9	2767.6	2.4	1010.6	18	90
1985	721.0	11.5	35.1	-15.2	2511.9	2.2	1010.4	12	104
1986	665.3	12.1	38.5	-15.4	2804.1	2.3	1010.7	21	96
1987	683.9	12.3	36.1	-15.5	2631.9	2.4	1010.3	23	102
1988	673.3	12.7	38.1	-13.2	2558.1	2.4	1010.8	17	96
1989	442.2	13.2	35.8	-11.0	2626.2	1.9	1011.1	3	78
1990	697.3	12.7	37.5	-14.8	2325.0	1.9	1010.6	12	113
1991	747.9	12.5	35.7	-12.6	2536.6	2.1	1010.8	8	98
1992	541.5	12.8	37.5	-8.7	2712.5	2.2	1011.0	6	100
1993	506.7	13.0	35.8	-13.0	2669.8	2.6	1010.8	12	91
1994	813.2	13.7	37.2	-11.5	2470.5	2.5	1010.1	9	92
1995	572.5	13.3	35.0	-9.2	2519.1	2.6	1010.3	16	89
1996	700.9	12.7	36.0	-10.0	2418.7	2.6	1011.0	16	103
1997	430.9	13.1	38.2	-14.0	2596.5	2.5	1012.9	11	76
1998	731.7	13.1	37.2	-14.2	2420.7	2.3	1012.5	10	93
1999	266.9	13.1	41.9	-12.2	2594.0	2.4	1012.5	7	86
2000	371.1	12.8	39.4	-15.0	2667.2	2.5	1012.7	10	83
2001	338.9	12.9	39.6	-17.0	2611.7	2.4	1012.9	10	78
2002	370.4	13.2	41.1	-12.8	2588.4	2.3	1012.7	15	84
2003	444.9	12.9	37.6	-15.0	2260.2	2.5	1013.3	6	93
2004	483.5	13.5	38.9	-12.9	2515.4	2.4	1012.6	12	94
2005	410.7	13.2	38.9	-11.5	2576.1	2.4	1012.8	5	79
2006	318.0	13.4	37.3	-14.7	2192.7	2.2	1012.5	5	86
2007	483.9	14.0	37.3	-11.7	2351.1	2.2	1012.6	5	78
2008	626.3	13.4	36.3	-13.5	2391.4	2.2	1012.6	8	100
2009	480.6	13.3	39.6	-12.2	2511.8	2.2	1011.9	15	86
2010	522.5	12.6	40.6	-16.7	2382.9	2.3	1012.2	14	88
2011	720.6	13.4	35.9	-11.6	2485.7	2.2	1013.2	3	82
2012	733.2	12.9	38.0	-13.7	2450.2	2.2	1012.2	3	85
2013	578.9	12.8	38.2	-14.1	2371.1	2.1	1012.2	3	71
2014	461.5	14.1	41.1	-11.2	2344.1	2.1	1013.0	8	77

资料来源：北京市气象局。
Source: Beijing Municipal Bureau of Meteorology.

4-21 气　象(2014年)
METEOROLOGY (2014)

月　份 Month	降水量 (毫米) Precipitation (mm)	平均气温(℃) Average Temperature (℃)	日照时数(时) Hours of Sunshine (hours)	平均风速(米/秒) Average Wind Speed (meter/second)	平均气压(百帕) Average Air Pressure (100 pa)	大风日数(日) Days of Strong Wind (day)	雨日数(日) Days of Rain (day)
全　年　Total	**461.5**	**14.1**	**2344.1**	**2.1**	**1013.0**	**8**	**77**
1		-0.6	192.4	1.9	1022.1	1	
2	4.8	-0.4	107.9	2.0	1024.5		4
3	0.9	10.1	233.8	2.4	1015.7		2
4	20.8	17.1	231.1	2.2	1012.4		9
5	33.7	22.2	274.1	2.8	1003.4	4	8
6	91.8	25.1	237.1	2.0	1001.9	1	14
7	119.8	28.1	174.4	2.1	1000.4		9
8	50.1	26.3	224.9	1.8	1004.4		13
9	127.6	21.0	157.3	1.8	1010.6		8
10	12.0	14.0	122.9	1.6	1016.5		7
11		6.4	167.2	1.9	1019.8		3
12		-0.5	221.0	2.5	1023.8	2	

注：1. 无霜期217天。
　　2. 年极端最高气温41.1℃，出现日期5月29日。
　　3. 年极端最低气温-11.2℃，出现日期2月11日。
资料来源：北京市气象局。
Note: a) Annual frost-free period is217 days.
　　b) Annual utmost highest air temperature is41.1℃, seen on the 29th of May.
　　c) Annual utmost lowest air temperature is -11.2℃, seen on the 11th of February.
Source: Beijing Municipal Bureau of Meteorology.

4-22 污水处理及环境卫生(1978-2014年)
SEWAGE DISPOSAL AND ENVIRONMENTAL SANITATION (1978-2014)

年份 Year	污水管道长度(公里) Length of Sewage Pipes (km)	污水处理能力(万立方米/日) Sewage Treatment Capacity (10000 cu.m/day)	污水处理率(%) Sewage Treatment Rate (%)	再生水利用量(万立方米) Volume of Recycled Water Used (10000 cu.m)	生活垃圾无害化处理能力(吨/日) Harmless Disposal Capacity of Domestic Waste (ton/day)	生活垃圾产生量(万吨) Output of Domestic Garbage (10000 tons)	生活垃圾清运量(万吨) Domestic Waste Removed and Transported (10000 tons)	生活垃圾无害化处理率(%) Rate of Harmless Disposal of Domestic Waste (%)	粪便清运量(万吨) Excrement Removed and Transported (10000 tons)
1978	290	23	7.6				107.20		88.9
1979	309	23	10.2				128.00		89.4
1980	334	23	9.4				147.00		95.1
1981	347	25	10.8				174.00		97.6
1982	365	25	10.9				204.70		99.3
1983	411	25	10.2				221.40		99.5
1984	568	25	10.0				235.40		98.8
1985	706	25	10.0				248.10		142.2
1986	747	26	8.9				274.40		167.5
1987	805	26	7.7				298.30		181.0
1988	770	26	7.4				319.90		190.0
1989	860	26	6.6				337.00		196.0
1990	904	30	7.3				384.10		210.0
1991	968	30	6.6				397.10		210.3
1992	1036	5	1.2				430.90		216.0
1993	1064	5	3.1				446.30		220.6
1994	1122	25	9.6				467.20		238.1
1995	1065	59	19.4				483.90		258.4
1996	1597	59	21.2				483.00		268.0
1997	1635	59	22.0				490.00		279.0
1998	1712	59	22.5				495.10		295.6
1999	1754	59	25.0				505.00		298.0
2000	1852	129	39.4		6550		295.56	56.4	274.0
2001	2163	144	42.0		6750		309.27	82.2	301.0
2002	2658	181	45.0		8750		321.35	86.4	311.7
2003	2903	215	50.1		9400		361.36	91.3	268.0
2004	2909	255	53.9		10050	495.46	405.86	93.8	175.0
2005	2521	324	62.4	23816	10350	536.93	454.59	96.0	171.7
2006	3398	331	73.2	36088	10350	585.13	538.32	92.5	175.7
2007	4357	348	76.2	49501	10350	619.49	600.93	95.7	189.1
2008	4458	329	78.9	60000	12148	672.82	656.61	97.7	206.8
2009	4495	356	80.3	64999	13680	669.13	656.12	98.2	211.2
2010	4479	365	81.0	68014	16680	634.86	632.98	96.9	194.4
2011	4765	369	82.0	71012	16930	634.35	634.35	98.2	207.5
2012	5735	389	83.0	75003	17530	648.31	648.31	99.1	207.2
2013	6363	393	84.6	80108	21971	671.69	671.69	99.3	220.7
2014	6536	425	86.1	86620	21971	733.84	733.84	99.6	216.1

注：1. 污水处理能力等指标1992年及以后为污水无害化处理情况，1992年以前为污水简易处理情况。
2. 生活垃圾无害化处理率按清运量计算。

资料来源：北京市水务局、北京市市政市容管理委员会。

Note: a) Disposal capacity and other indicators in and after 1992 were about harmless disposal, and those before 1992 were about simple disposal.
b) The harmless disposal rate of domestic waste is calculated with the volume of waste cleared and transported.

Source: Beijing Water Authority，Beijing Municipal Commission of City Administration and Environment.

4-23 排水及节水
WATER DRAINAGE AND SAVING

项　目		Item		2014	2013
排　水		**Water Drainage**			
污水处理能力	(万立方米/日)	Sewage Treatment Capacity	(10000cu.m/day)	425	393
#二三级	(万立方米/日)	Grade-II and III Treatment	(10000cu.m/day)	425	393
污水年处理量	(万立方米)	Annual Treatment Volume of Sewage	(10000 cu.m)	139107	131401
#污水厂	(万立方米)	Treated by Sewage Treatment Plants	(10000 cu.m)	136531	128745.7
#二三级	(万立方米)	Grade-II and III Treatment	(10000 cu.m)	136531	128745.7
污水处理率	(%)	Sewage Treatment Rate	(%)	86.1	84.6
#集中处理率	(%)	Rate of Concentrated Treatment	(%)	86.1	84.6
污水排放总量	(万立方米)	Total Volume of Sewage Drainage	(10000 cu.m)	161548	155317
排水管道长度	(公里)	Length of Drainage Pipelines	(km)	14290	13505
污水管	(公里)	Sewage Pipes	(km)	6536	6363
雨水管	(公里)	Rain Pipes	(km)	5555	5038
雨污合流管	(公里)	Rain-sewage Sewer	(km)	2198	2104
再生水利用量	(万立方米)	Volume of Recycled Water Used	(10000 cu.m)	86620	80108
节　水		**Water Saving**			
节水量	(万立方米)	Volume Saved	(10000 cu.m)	12024	11322
节水措施	(项)	Water Saving Measures Implemented	(unit)	127	207

资料来源：北京市水务局。
Source: Beijing Water Authority.

4-24 环境卫生
MUNICIPAL ENVIRONMENT AND SANITATION

项　目		Item		2014	2013
工作量		**Work Load**			
清扫街道面积	(万平方米／日)	Area of Cleaned Streets	(10000 sq.m/day)	15104	14234
生活垃圾无害化处理能力	(吨/日)	Harmless Disposal Capacity of Domestic Waste	(ton/day)	21971	21971
生活垃圾产生量	(万吨)	Output of Domestic Waste	(10000 tons)	733.8	671.7
生活垃圾清运量	(万吨)	Domestic Waste Removed and Transported	(10000 tons)	733.8	671.7
生活垃圾无害化处理量	(万吨)	Volume of Harmless Disposal of Domestic Waste	(10000 tons)	730.8	667.0
生活垃圾无害化处理率	(%)	Rate of Harmless Disposal of Domestic Waste	(%)	99.6	99.3
(按清运量计算)		(Calculated by Volume of Waste Cleared and Transported)			
餐余垃圾处理量	(万吨)	Kitchen Waste Removed and Transported	(10000 tons)	24.3	20.0
粪便清运量	(万吨)	Excrement Removed and Transported	(10000 tons)	216.1	220.7
环卫机械数量	**(辆)**	**Number of Environmental Sanitation Machinery**	**(unit)**	**10255**	**9797**
环卫设施		**Environmental Sanitation Facilities**			
公共厕所	(座)	Public Lavatories	(unit)	5429	5563

资料来源：北京市市政市容管理委员会。
Source: Beijing Municipal Commission of City Administration and Environment.

4-25 环境保护(2000-2014年)
ENVIRONMENTAL PROTECTION (2000-2014)

年份 Year	可吸入颗粒物年日均值(毫克/立方米) Daily Average of Inspiratory Particulate Matter in the Year (mg/cu.m)	二氧化硫年日均值(毫克/立方米) Daily Average of Sulfur Dioxide in the Year (mg/cu.m)	二氧化氮年日均值(毫克/立方米) Daily Average of Nitrogen Dioxide (mg/cu.m)	化学需氧量(COD)排放量(万吨) COD Emission Volume (10000 tons)	二氧化硫(SO2)排放量(万吨) SO2 Emission Volume (10000 tons)	区域环境噪声平均值(分贝) Average Value of Noises in Regional Environment (db)	道路交通干线噪声平均值(分贝) Average Value of Noises in Road Transportation (db)
2000	0.162	0.071	0.071	17.9	22.4	53.9	71.0
2001	0.165	0.064	0.071	17.0	20.1	53.9	69.6
2002	0.166	0.067	0.076	15.3	19.2	53.5	69.5
2003	0.141	0.061	0.072	13.4	18.3	53.6	69.7
2004	0.149	0.055	0.071	13.0	19.1	53.8	69.6
2005	0.142	0.050	0.066	11.6	19.1	53.2	69.5
2006	0.161	0.053	0.066	11.0	17.6	53.9	69.7
2007	0.148	0.047	0.066	10.7	15.2	54.0	69.9
2008	0.122	0.036	0.049	10.1	12.3	53.6	69.6
2009	0.121	0.034	0.053	9.9	11.9	54.1	69.7
2010	0.121	0.032	0.057	9.2	11.5	54.1	70.0
2011	0.114	0.028	0.055	19.3	9.8	53.7	69.6
2012	0.109	0.028	0.052	18.7	9.4	54.0	69.2
2013	0.108	0.027	0.056	17.8	8.7	53.9	69.1
2014	0.116	0.022	0.057	16.9	7.9	53.6	69.1

注：化学需氧量(COD)排放量和二氧化硫排放量(SO2)指标自2011年起调整统计口径和核算方法。
资料来源：北京市环境保护局。
Note: From 2011, statistical standard and calculation method are adjusted for COD emission volume and SO2 emission volume.
Source: Beijing Municipal Bureau of Environmental Protection.

4-26 环境保护
ENVIRONMENTAL PROTECTION

项　目		Item		2014	2013
水环境		Water Environment			
废水排放总量	(万吨)	Total Discharge of Sewage	(10000 tons)	150713.57	144579.93
#工业废水排放量		Industrial Waste Water Discharge Volume		9174.35	9486.42
化学需氧量(COD)排放量	(吨)	COD Emission Volume	(ton)	168840	178475
#工业废水中COD排放量		Emission of COD in Industrial Waster Water		6050	6055
氨氮排放量	(吨)	Ammonia Nitrogen Discharge		18951	19704
#工业废水中氨氮排放量		Ammonia Nitrogen Discharge in Industrial Waster Water	(ton)	328	330
大气环境		Atmosphere Environment			
二氧化硫(SO2)排放量	(吨)	SO2 Emission Volume	(ton)	78906	87042
#工业二氧化硫排放量		Emission of Industrial SO2		40347	52041
氮氧化物排放量	(吨)	Smoke and Dust Emission	(ton)	150955	166329
#工业氮氧化物排放量		Emission of Industrial Smoke and Dust		64400	75297
烟(粉)尘排放量	(吨)	Smoke and Dust Emission	(ton)	57372	59286
#工业烟(粉)尘排放量		Emission of Industrial Smoke and Dust		22710	27182
固体废物		Solid Waste			
一般工业固体废物产生量	(万吨)	General Industrial Solid Waste Generated	(10000 tons)	1020.76	1044.12
一般工业固体废物综合利用量	(万吨)	General Industrial Solid Waste Recycled	(10000 tons)	894.98	904.46
一般工业固体废物处置量	(万吨)	General Industrial Solid Waste Disposed	(10000 tons)	125.92	140.16
危险废物产生量	(吨)	Hazardous Wastes Generated	(ton)	148278	132177
危险废物综合利用量	(吨)	Hazardous Wastes Recycled	(ton)	82056	57879
危险废物处置量	(吨)	Hazardous Wastes Disposed	(ton)	66071	68125.7
生态环境		Ecological Environment			
自然保护区个数	(个)	Number of Nature Reserves	(unit)	20	20
#国家级自然保护区		State-level Nature Reserves		2	2
自然保护区面积	(万公顷)	Area of Nature Reserves	(10000 hectares)	13.79	13.41

数据来源：北京市环境保护局。
Source: Beijing Municipal Bureau of Environmental Protection.

4-27 园林绿化及森林情况(1978-2014年)

年份 Year	年末公园绿地面积 (公顷) Green Land and Park (year-end) (hectare)	人均公园绿地面积 (平方米/人) Per Capita Green Land and Park (sq.m/person)	城市绿化覆盖率 (%) Green Land Coverage (%)	林木绿化率 (%) Forest Coverage (%)	年末园林绿地面积 (公顷) Green Area (year-end) (hectare)
1978	2693	5.07	22.30		
1979	2693	5.07	22.30		
1980	2746	5.14	20.10	16.6	
1981	2751	5.14	20.10	16.6	
1982	2779	5.14	20.10	16.6	
1983	2823	5.14	20.10	16.6	
1984	2878	5.14	20.10	16.6	
1985	3263	4.94	22.10	16.6	
1986	3606	5.07	22.86	16.6	
1987	3570	5.07	22.90	16.6	
1988	4074	5.80	25.00	16.6	
1989	6910	6.00	26.00	16.6	
1990	7110	6.14	28.00	28.3	
1991	4279	6.41	28.43	28.3	
1992	4213	6.65	30.33	28.3	
1993	4452	7.76	31.33	28.3	
1994	5221	7.89	32.39	28.3	
1995	5017	7.48	32.68	36.3	
1996	5147	7.54	33.24	36.3	
1997	5408	7.80	34.22	36.3	
1998	6351	9.00	35.60	36.3	
1999	6457	9.10	36.30	36.3	
2000	7140	9.66	36.50	42.0	26680
2001	7554	10.07	38.78	44.0	30224
2002	7907	10.66	40.57	45.5	32572
2003	9115	11.43	40.87	47.5	38475
2004	10446	11.45	41.91	49.5	36755
2005	11365	12.00	42.00	50.5	38877
2006	11788	12.00	42.50	51.0	45495
2007	12101	12.60	43.00	51.6	46320
2008	12316	13.60	43.50	52.1	46993
2009	18070	14.50	44.40	52.6	61695
2010	19020	15.00	45.00	53.0	62672
2011	19728	15.30	45.60	54.0	63541
2012	21178	15.50	46.20	55.5	65540
2013	22215	15.70	46.80	57.4	67048
2014	28798	15.90	47.40	58.4	80223

资料来源：北京市园林绿化局。

STATISTICS FOR LANDSCAPING AND FORESTS (1978-2014)

森林面积 (公顷) Forest Area (hectare)	森林覆盖率 (%) Forest Coverage Rate (%)	活立木蓄积量 (万立方米) Total Stock of Standing Trees (10000 cu.m)	森林蓄积量 (万立方米) Forest Stock (10000 cu.m)	森林火灾次数 (次) Number of Forest Fires (unit)	森林火灾经济损失 (万元) Economic Loss of Forest Fires (10000 yuan)
619243.2		1521.4	1295.3	9	11.4
626006.3	35.9	1521.4	1295.3	13	96.7
636565.7	36.5	1559.5	1368.9	8	28.1
641368.3	36.5	1574.0	1394.4		
658914.1	36.7	1810.3	1406.2	2	…
666050.7	37.0	1854.7	1435.4	4	1.4
673411.8	37.6	1899.4	1468.7	3	1.7
691341.1	38.6	1943.3	1499.0	1	
716456.1	40.1	1993.4	1536.8		
734530.6	41.0	2109.1	1669.9	1	

Source: Beijing Municipal Bureau of Landscape and Forestry.

主要统计指标解释

能源生产量 能源生产量是反映能源生产规模、构成、生产成果的重要指标。按能源的成因分为一次能源（亦称天然能源）生产量和二次能源（亦称人工能源）生产量。

一次能源生产量 指报告期内生产一次能源的企业将自然界现存的能源资源经过开采而产出的合格产品，主要包括原煤、原油、天然气、水电等。

二次能源生产量 指报告期内将一次能源经过各种加工转换设备生产出的另一种形式的各种合格的能源产品。如火电、热力、洗煤、焦炭、各种石油制品、焦炉煤气、其他煤气等。

能源消费总量 指一定地域（行政或地理区域）内，国民经济各行业和居民家庭在一定时期所消费的各种能源的总和。能源消费总量包括终端能源消费量、能源加工转换损失量、能源运输和管理过程的损失量三部分。

能源消费总量（等价值） 是电力、热力按等价热值计算的能源消费总量。等价热值是能源统计中经常使用的一个热值概念，是指加工转换产出的某种二次能源所投入的一次能源的量，即获得一个度量单位的某种二次能源所消耗的以热值表示的一次能源。

能源加工转换投入产出量 能源具有由一种能量形式转换为另一种能量形式及耗用过程中可用一种能源替代另一种能源的特征。为提高能源的利用价值和效率，对能源进行加工、转换，产出适合生产和生活需要的更高级的能源产品。在加工转换投入(-)产出(+)量中，“-”表示能源加工转换的投入量，“+”表示二次能源的产出量。

投入量 是指为生产二次能源产品，所投入到能源加工转换设备的各种能源数量。在表中以负数表示。

产出量 是指各种能源（一次能源或少量再投入的二次能源）经过加工转换后，产出的各种二次能源产品（包括不作为能源使用的副产品，联产品）数量。

加工转换损失量 是指在能源加工、转换过程中损失的能量（能源），即能源加工、转换过程中投入的能源和产出的二次能源之间的差额。

损失量 指能源在经营管理和生产、输送、分配、储存等过程中发生的损失以及由于自然因素等原因造成的损失数量。不包括加工转换损失量。

终端消费量 是指能源消费环节的最后一个环节的能源消费，包括直接用作燃料、原材料和动力的各种能源的消费。它们的消费过程体现了能源消费的终止，不会再重新作为能源投入使用。终端消费量不包括用于能源加工转换投入量、加工转换损失量和损失量。

能源消费弹性系数 指能源消费总量增长率与地区生产总值增长率的比值。

电力消费弹性系数 指电力消费量增长率与地区生产总值增长率的比值。

平均每万元地区生产总值能源消费量 能源总消费量或分品种能源消费量与地区生产总值之比。

人均生活用能量 指用于生活消费的各种能源数量与人口总数之比。

日均能源消费量 指各品种能源消费量与当年实际天数之比。

垃圾无害化处理能力 指垃圾无害化处理场（厂）按工艺设计每天所能处理生活垃圾的数量。垃圾无害化处理场（厂）必须是按照有关技术、环境、卫生标准和规范进行设计、建设、运行、维护和管理的各种生活垃圾处理设施，主要包括卫生填埋场、堆肥厂和焚烧厂等。

水资源总量 指降水形成的地表和地下水总量，不包括过境水量。

排水管道长度 指所有排水总管、干管、支管、检查井及连接井进出口等长度之和。计算时应按单管计算，即在同一条街道上如有两条或两条以上并排的排水管道时，应按每条排水管道的长度相加计算。

污水处理能力 指污水处理厂（或处理装置）每昼夜处理污水量的设计能力。

按污水处理的程度，一般可分为一级处理、二级处理和三级处理。

一级处理是以沉淀为主体的处理工艺。指去除污水中的漂浮物和悬浮物的净化过程，主要为沉淀。

二级处理是以生物处理为主体的处理工艺。指污水经一级处理后，用生物处理方法继续除去污水中胶体和溶解性有机物的净化过程。

三级处理也称高级处理或深度处理。指进一步去除二级处理不能完全去除的污水中的污染物的处理工艺。

污水处理量 指污水处理厂和处理装置实际处理的污水量。包括物理处理量、生物处理量和化学处理量。

污水处理率 指污水处理量与污水排放总量的比率。计算公式：

$$\text{污水处理率} = \frac{\text{污水处理量}}{\text{污水排放总量}} \times 100\%$$

生活垃圾清运量 指报告期内收集和运送到各垃圾处理场（厂）的垃圾的数量。

粪便清运量 指报告期内收集和运送到各粪便处理场（厂）的粪便的数量。

生活垃圾无害化处理量 指报告期内简易处理场和各种垃圾无害化处理场（厂）处理垃圾的总量。垃圾简易处理量指垃圾简易填埋场所处理的垃圾总量。垃圾无害化处理量指垃圾无害化处理场（厂）所处理的垃圾总量。

生活垃圾无害化处理率 指报告期垃圾无害化处理量与垃圾产生量的比率。计算公式：

$$垃圾无害化处理率=\frac{垃圾无害化处理量}{垃圾产生量}\times 100\%$$

在统计时，如果生活垃圾产生量不易取得，可用清运量代替。

化学需氧量（COD）排放量 指工业废水中 COD 排放量与生活污水中 COD 排放量之和。指用化学氧化剂氧化水中有机污染物时所需的氧量。COD 值越高，表示水中有机污染物污染越重。

二氧化硫（SO_2）排放量 指报告期内工业 SO_2 排放量与生活 SO_2 排放量之和。

工业固体废物综合利用量 指报告期内企业通过回收、加工、循环、交换等方式，从固体废物中提取或者使其转化为可以利用的资源、能源和其他原材料的固体废物量（包括当年利用的往年工业固体废物贮存量）。如用做农业肥料、生产建筑材料、筑路等。

公园绿地 指向公众开放，以游憩为主要功能，兼具生态、美化、防灾等作用，其绿地率达到 65%以上，配有多种乔灌木及地被植物，有一定设施和艺术布局的绿地。包括公园、社区公园、街旁绿地、其他公园绿地。人均公园绿地面积计算口径为户籍非农业人口。

绿化覆盖率 指报告期末区域内绿化覆盖面积与区域面积的比率。

计算公式：

$$绿化覆盖率=\frac{区域内绿化覆盖面积}{区域面积}\times 100\%$$

森林面积 指由乔木树种构成，郁闭度 0.20 以上(含 0.20)的林地或冠幅宽度 10 米以上的林带的面积，即有林地面积。它是反映森林资源总面积的重要指标。森林面积包括天然起源和人工起源的针叶林面积、阔叶林面积、针阔混交林面积和竹林面积。

活立木蓄积量 指一定范围土地上全部树木蓄积的总量，包括森林蓄积、疏林蓄积、散生木蓄积和四旁树蓄积。

森林蓄积量 指一定森林面积上存在着的林木树干部分的总材积，以立方米为计量单位。

森林火灾次数 指发生在城市市区外的一切森林、林木和林地的火灾次数，包括森林火警、一般灾害、重大灾害和特大灾害。

Explanatory Notes on Main Statistical Indicators

Energy Production is an important indicator reflecting the size, composition and results of energy production. By the cause of formation, it consists of the production of primary energy (also known as natural energy) and that of secondary energy (also known as artificial energy).

Production of Primary Energy means up-to-grade products produced by primary energy producers in the reporting period through extraction of existing energy in the nature, mainly including raw coal, crude oil, natural gas, hydroelectricity, etc.

Production of Secondary Energy means various up-to-grade energy products in another form that are made from primary energy with various processing and converting equipment in the reporting period, including thermal power, heating power, washed coal, coke, various petroleum products, coke oven gas and other gases, etc.

Total Energy Consumption means the total consumption of various energies by national economic sectors and resident households in a specific region (administrative or geographic). Total energy consumption can be divided into three parts: end-use energy consumption, loss during energy processing and conversion and loss during energy transport and management.

Total Energy Consumption (in Equivalent Caloricity) means the total consumption of electric power and heating power calculated in equivalent caloricity. Equivalent caloricity is a caloricity concept frequently used in statistics of energy. It means the quantity of primary energy input for a secondary energy produced through processing and conversion, i.e. the primary energy in terms of caloricity which is consumed to produce one measuring unit of a secondary energy.

Input and Output of Energy Processing and Conversion One form of energy can be converted into another form of energy. And in consumption, one sort of energy can be replaced with another. In order to improve the energy use value and efficiency, energy is processed and converted to produce energy products at higher levels which are suitable for productive and living needs. In the processing and conversion input (-) and output (+), "-" means the input for energy processing and conversion. And "+" means the output from energy processing and conversion.

Input means the volume of energy put into the energy processing and converting equipment in order to produce secondary energy products.

Output means the volume of secondary energy products (including byproducts and multi-products that cannot be used as energy) from processing and conversion of energy sources (primary energy or a small amount of secondary energy re-input).

Loss during Processing and Conversion means the energy lost in the processing and conversion of energy, namely the difference between the energy input and the secondary energy output during energy processing and conversion.

Energy Loss means the loss of energy during operation, management, production, transportation, distribution and storage, as well as the loss due to natural factors and other reasons. It excludes the loss during processing and conversion.

End-use Energy Consumption means the energy consumption in the last section of energy consumption, including the consumption of various energy sources used as fuel, raw materials and power. Such consumption represents the end of energy consumption, and the energy will not be put into use again as energy. End-use energy consumption does not include the input for energy processing and conversion, loss during the processing and conversion of energy, and energy loss.

Elasticity Coefficient of Energy Consumption means the ratio of growth rate of total energy consumption to the growth rate of GDP.

Elasticity Coefficient of Electric Power Consumption means the ratio of growth rate of electric power consumption to the growth rate of GDP.

Average Energy Consumption per RMB 10000 of GDP means the ratio of total energy consumption or energy consumption by variety to GDP.

Per-capital Energy Consumption by Households means the ratio of quantity of energy consumed by households to the total population.

Daily Energy Consumption means the ratio of energy consumption to the actual days in the same year.

Harmless Disposal Capacity of Waste means the daily quantity of domestic waste that can be disposed at harmless disposal facilities (sites) according to the process designed. Harmless disposal facilities (sites) must be domestic waste disposal facilities, including landfills, manure yards, incineration facilities and so on, which are designed, built, operated and managed in accordance with relevant technological, environmental, and sanitary standards and criterion.

Total Water Resources means the total volume of surface water and underground water caused by rainfall, excluding passing-by water.

Length of Sewage Pipes means the total length of all main drainage pipes, trunk pipes, branch pipes, access manholes, and connector well entrances and exits, and so on. The length of single pipes shall be included, i.e. if there are two or more drainage pipes parallel on a street, the length of every pipe shall be included.

Sewage Treatment Capacity means the designed capacity of sewage disposal day and night for a sewage disposal plant (or facility).

In terms of extent, sewage disposal consists of primary disposal, secondary disposal and tertiary disposal.

Primary Disposal is a disposal process focusing on precipitation. It means a purification process removing the floating and suspended substances in sewage, mostly precipitation.

Secondary Disposal is a disposal process focusing on biological disposal. It means a purification process further removing the colloids and resolvable organic substances in sewage after the process of primary disposal.

Tertiary Disposal is also known as senior or deep disposal. It means a disposal process further removing any pollutants that cannot be removed completely in the process of secondary disposal.

Volume of Sewage Treated means the volume of sewage actually disposed by sewage disposal plants and facilities, consisting of physical volume, biological volume and chemical volume of waste water disposed.

Sewage Treatment Rate means the ratio of sewage disposed to the total discharge of sewage. The formula is:

Sewage Disposal Rate = Volume of Sewage Disposed / Total Discharge of Sewage × 100%

Domestic Waste Removed and Transported means the quantity of waste collected and transported to waste treatment sites (plants) in the reporting period.

Excrement Removed and Transported means the quantity of excrement collected and transported to waste treatment sites (plants) in the reporting period.

Volume of Harmless Disposal of Domestic Waste means the total volume of waste disposed by simple disposal sites and harmless waste disposal sits (plants) in the reporting period. Simple disposal of waste means the total volume of waste by simple landfills. Harmless waste disposal means the total volume of waste disposed by harmless waste disposal sites (plants).

Rate of Harmless Disposal of Domestic Waste means the ratio of harmless waste disposal to the waste produced in the reporting period. The formula is:

Rate of Harmless Disposal of Domestic Waste = Harmless Waste Disposal / Waste Produced × 100%

In practical statistics, if it is hard to get figures on the volume of domestic waste produced, the volume removed and transported may be used.

COD Emission Volume means the sum of COD emission in industrial sewage and in domestic waste water. It means the amount of oxygen required when chemical oxidants are used to oxidize organic pollutants in water. A higher value of COD corresponds to more serious pollution by organic pollutants.

SO_2 Emission Volume means the sum of industrial SO_2 emission and domestic SO_2 emission in the reporting period.

Industrial Solid Waste Utilized means the volume of solid wastes from which useful materials can be extracted or which can be converted into usable resources, energy or other materials by means of reclamation, processing, recycling and exchange (including utilizing in the year the stocks of industrial solid wastes of the previous year). Examples of such utilizations include fertilizers, building materials and road materials.

Green Land and Parks means the green land open to the public, with main function of recreation, together with ecological, landscaping and disaster preventing functions, and with more than 65% green coverage, provided with multiple arbors, shrubs and ground-cover plants, along with certain facilities and artistic layouts. They include parks, community parks, street-side green land and other green land in gardens. Per capita area of green land is calculated on the basis of non-agricultural household population.

Green Land Coverage means the ratio of area of green land in a region to the total area of the region in the reporting period. The formula is:

Green Land Coverage = Area of Green Land in a Region / Total Area of the Region × 100%

Forest Area means the area of forest where arbor trees grow with canopy density above 0.2 (and at 0.2) or forest area with crown width more than 10m, i.e. the area of land with forest. It is an important indicator reflecting the total area of forest resources. Forest Area includes the area of coniferous forest, broad leaf forest, mixed coniferous-broad-leaf forest and bamboo forest from both natural and artificial origins.

Total Stock of Standing Trees mean the total stock of all trees on specific area of land, including trees in forest, trees in sparse forest, scattered trees and trees planted by the side of villages, farm houses and along roads and rivers.

Forest Stock means the total volume of timber of forest tree trunks growing on specific area of forest, which are measured in cubic meters.

Number of Forest Fires means the number of all fires occurring in forests, woods, woodlands outside the urban districts, including forest fires, general fires, severe fires and fire disasters.

05

全社会固定资产投资和房地产开发

TOTAL INVESTMENT IN FIXED ASSETS AND REAL ESTATE DEVELOPMENT

简要说明

一、本章资料的主要内容

本章资料包括历年北京市全社会固定资产投资、房地产开发的主要分组数据、保障性安居工程建设等情况。

二、本章资料的统计范围

1996 年及以前固定资产投资统计起点为 5 万元以上，1996 年以后调整为 50 万元及以上，从 2011 年开始调整为 500 万元及以上。

三、有关统计标准的变化说明

（一）关于行业划分。根据国家统计局规定，自 2012 年开始执行《国民经济行业分类》（GB/T 4754-2011）标准。

（二）关于三次产业划分。根据国家统计局《三次产业划分规定》（国统字[2012]108 号），该规定对三次产业的范围进行了调整。其中第一产业是指农、林、牧、渔业（不含农、林、牧、渔服务业）；第二产业是指采矿业（不含开采辅助活动），制造业（不含金属制品、机械和设备修理业），电力、热力、燃气及水生产和供应业，建筑业；第三产业是指除第一产业、第二产业以外的其他行业。自 2012 年开始执行此规定。

四、本章资料的数据来源

本章资料来源于北京市统计局、国家统计局北京调查总队。

五、本章的统计调查方法

除农户固定资产投资统计采用抽样调查方法外，其他均为全面调查。

Brief Introduction

I. Main Content

Statistics in this chapter include figures on fixed assets investment in Beijing and its main grouped figures as well as figures on government-subsidized housing projects.

II. Scope of Statistics

Before and in 1996, the threshold of fixed assets statistics was over RMB 50,000; after 1996, it was increased to RMB 500,000 and above; since 2011, the figure has been set at RMB 5 million and above.

III. Changes in Relevant Statistical Standards

(I) Classification of Sectors. According to relevant provisions of the National Bureau of Statistics, the Standard for Classification of National Economic Sectors (GB/T 4754-2011) came into effect in 2012.

(II) Classification of Three Industries. According to the Regulations on the Classification of the Three Industries (G.T.Z. [2012] No. 108) issued by National Bureau of Statistics, the scope of three industries has been adjusted. The primary industry refers to agriculture, forestry, animal production and hunting, fishing (excluding services for a agriculture, forestry, animal production and hunting, fishing); the secondary industry refers to mining (excluding mining support activities), manufacturing (excluding metal products, machinery and equipment repair), production and distribution of electricity, heating power, gas and water, and construction; the tertiary industry refers to sectors other than the primary and secondary industries. The Regulations on the Classification of the Three Industries (G.T.Z. [2012] No. 108) issued by National Bureau of Statistics came into effect in 2012.

IV. Source of Statistics

Statistics in this chapter are from the Beijing Municipal Bureau of Statistics and NBS Survey Office in Beijing.

V. Method of Statistical Survey

Sample survey is used for the statistics on investment of rural households in fixed assets. For other statistics, the complete survey is conducted.

5-1 全社会固定资产投资和增长速度情况(1978-2014年)
TOTAL INVESTMENT IN FIXED ASSETS AND GROWTH RATE (1978-2014)

单位：亿元 (100 million yuan)

年份 Year	全社会固定资产投资 Total Investment in Fixed Assets	城镇固定资产投资 Investment in Urban Fixed Assets	#房地产开发投资 Investment in Real Estate Development	农村固定资产投资 Investment in Rural Fixed Assets	#基础设施投资 Infrastructure Investment	#建筑安装投资 Construction and Installation Investment	新增固定资产 Incremental Fixed Assets
1978	22.6	22.6			5.4		16.9
1979	26.5	26.5			5.8		21.2
1980	33.2	33.2			6.0		23.2
1981-1985	**286.8**	**234.4**		**50.8**	**40.6**		**184.4**
1981	36.6	31.4		5.2	5.8		30.9
1982	38.6	34.5		4.1	6.1		26.3
1983	51.3	38.5		12.8	6.7		32.5
1984	66.3	52.2		14.1	8.8		47.1
1985	94.0	77.8		14.6	13.2		47.6
1986-1990	**724.1**	**634.9**	**22.5**	**76.5**	**117.9**		**417.4**
1986	106.2	94.5		10.4	14.5		58.5
1987	136.2	121.4		12.7	22.1		79.9
1988	163.0	138.7		21.3	23.2		77.3
1989	139.5	122.2		14.7	26.5		79.6
1990	179.2	158.1	22.5	17.4	31.6		122.1
1991-1995	**2358.7**	**2181.5**	**568.4**	**154.1**	**494.9**	**1297.1**	**1229.1**
1991	192.0	168.4	24.0	21.0	35.2	107.3	139.0
1992	266.0	234.7	33.7	27.2	58.8	136.2	157.8
1993	410.4	376.6	58.4	30.0	91.4	232.0	201.6
1994	648.8	607.4	99.5	35.7	153.4	362.6	356.0
1995	841.5	794.4	352.8	40.2	156.1	459.0	374.7
1996-2000	**5461.7**	**5063.8**	**1979.5**	**322.7**	**1382.1**	**3069.5**	**4051.2**
1996	876.9	825.6	328.2	43.6	188.8	515.8	592.5
1997	961.2	912.4	330.3	40.6	218.3	546.2	637.9
1998	1155.6	1060.3	377.4	75.8	320.4	626.9	759.3
1999	1170.6	1072.9	421.5	78.2	302.7	679.1	949.5
2000	1297.4	1192.6	522.1	84.5	351.9	701.5	1112.0
2001-2005	**10857.4**	**10033.6**	**5974.0**	**755.4**	**2260.0**	**5926.2**	**6897.4**
2001	1530.5	1417.1	783.8	93.7	356.4	801.6	1177.0
2002	1814.3	1688.2	989.4	102.5	411.9	964.9	1251.0
2003	2157.1	1999.9	1202.5	132.1	417.8	1151.3	1165.9
2004	2528.3	2333.0	1473.3	195.3	463.2	1438.9	1455.1
2005	2827.2	2595.4	1525.0	231.8	610.7	1569.5	1848.4
2006-2010	**21538.5**	**19678.6**	**10863.2**	**1859.9**	**6137.3**	**9860.6**	**11666.8**
2006	3371.5	3086.3	1719.9	285.2	935.3	1836.0	1972.1
2007	3966.6	3656.7	1995.8	309.9	1175.8	2117.9	2004.9
2008	3848.5	3554.8	1908.7	293.7	1160.7	1798.8	2666.8
2009	4858.4	4378.2	2337.7	480.2	1462.0	1983.0	2457.2
2010	5493.5 (5218.3)	5002.6	2901.1	490.9	1403.5	2124.9	2565.8
2011	5910.6	5463.9	3036.3	446.7	1400.2	2585.3	2382.0
2012	6462.8	5853.1	3153.4	609.8	1789.2	3076.6	2570.4
2013	7032.2	6352.6	3483.4	679.6	1785.7	3482.2	3163.8
2014	7562.3	6926.6	3911.3	635.7	2018.1	3468.1	3887.3

注：1. 根据国家统计局有关规定，从2004年起，全社会固定资产投资中不包括零星购置投资。
2. 2004年起,新增固定资产、基础设施投资、建筑安装投资中包含农村投资。
3. 根据国家统计局有关规定，2011年起投资统计起点调整为500万元，为便于比较2010年的相应数据也作了调整，未加括号的为原口径数，括号内为调整后的数据，当年固定资产投资等增长速度均按可比口径计算。

Note: a) According to related regulations of National Bureau of Statistics, since 2004, total investment in fixed assets has not included investment in acquiring minor items.
b) Since 2004, rural investment has been counted in incremental fixed assets, infrastructure investment, construction and installation investment.
c) Since 2011, the statistical threshold of investment has been adjusted to RMB 5 million according to the related regulations of National Bureau of Statistics. For comparison, relevant figures in 2010 were adjusted accordingly. Figures with no brackets are based on the former standard. Figures in brackets are data after adjustment. Growth rates of fixed assets investment in respective years are calculated in comparable terms.

5-1 续表 Continued

单位：% (%)

年份 Year	全社会固定资产投资比上年增长 Growth rate of Total Investment in Fixed Assets	城镇固定资产投资 Growth rate of Investment in Urban Fixed Assets	#房地产开发投资 Growth rate of Investment in Real Estate Development	农村固定资产投资 Growth rate of Investment in Rural Fixed Assets	#基础设施投资 Growth rate of Infrastructure Investment	#建筑安装投资 Growth rate of Construction and Installation Investment
1978						
1979	17.3	17.3			7.4	
1980	25.3	25.3			3.4	
1981-1985	**18.8**	**11.7**			**10.3**	
1981	10.2	-5.4			-3.3	
1982	5.5	9.9		-21.2	5.2	
1983	32.9	11.6		212.2	9.8	
1984	29.2	35.6		10.2	31.3	
1985	41.8	49.0		3.5	50.0	
1986-1990	**14.8**	**16.8**		**1.5**	**20.0**	
1986	13.0	21.5		-28.8	9.8	
1987	28.2	28.5		22.1	52.4	
1988	19.7	14.3		67.7	5.0	
1989	-14.4	-11.9		-31.0	14.2	
1990	28.5	29.4		18.4	19.2	
1991-1995	**34.2**	**36.0**	**59.9**	**19.7**	**40.8**	
1991	7.1	6.5	6.7	20.7	11.4	
1992	38.5	39.4	40.4	29.5	67.0	26.9
1993	54.3	60.5	73.3	10.3	55.4	70.3
1994	58.1	61.3	70.4	19.0	67.8	56.3
1995	29.7	30.8	254.6	12.6	1.8	26.6
1996-2000	**8.9**	**8.2**	**3.9**	**16.2**	**19.7**	**9.9**
1996	4.2	3.9	-7.0	8.5	20.9	12.4
1997	9.6	10.5	0.6	-6.9	15.6	5.9
1998	20.2	16.2	14.3	86.7	46.8	14.8
1999	1.3	1.2	11.7	3.2	-5.5	8.3
2000	10.8	11.2	23.9	8.1	16.3	3.3
2001-2005	**17.7**	**17.9**	**29.0**	**20.1**	**8.5**	**18.0**
2001	18.0	18.8	50.1	10.9	1.3	14.3
2002	18.5	19.1	26.2	9.4	15.6	20.4
2003	18.9	18.5	21.5	28.9	1.4	19.3
2004	17.2	16.7	22.5	47.8	10.9	25.0
2005	11.8	11.2	3.5	18.7	31.8	9.1
2006-2010	**14.4**	**14.2**	**12.0**	**16.2**	**24.2**	**7.7**
2006	19.3	18.9	12.8	23.0	53.2	17.0
2007	17.6	18.5	16.0	8.7	25.7	15.4
2008	-3.0	-2.8	-4.4	-5.2	-1.3	-15.1
2009	26.2	23.2	22.5	63.5	26.0	10.2
2010	13.1	14.3	24.1	2.2	-4.0	7.2
2011	13.3	14.8	10.1	-2.9	0.3	22.4
2012	9.3	7.1	3.9	36.5	27.8	19.0
2013	8.8	8.5	10.5	11.5	-0.2	13.2
2014	7.5	9.0	12.3	-6.5	13.0	-0.4

5-2 按登记注册类型分全社会固定资产投资(1978-2014年)
TOTAL INVESTMENT IN FIXED ASSETS BY REGISTRATION TYPE (1978-2014)

单位：亿元　　　　(100 million yuan)

年 份 Year	全社会固定资产投资 Total Investment in Fixed Assets	国 有 State-owned	集 体 Collectively-owned	股份制 Joint-stock	港澳台商 Hong Kong, Macao and Taiwan	外 商 Foreign	私营个体 Private	其 他 Others
1978	22.6							
1979	26.5							
1980	33.2							
1981-1985	**286.8**	**223.8**	**22.6**				**40.4**	
1981	36.6	30.1	1.3				5.2	
1982	38.6	33.0	1.5				4.1	
1983	51.3	37.1	1.4				12.8	
1984	66.3	50.0	2.2				14.1	
1985	94.0	73.6	16.2				4.2	
1986-1990	**724.1**	**609.6**	**83.1**				**31.4**	
1986	106.2	88.7	13.3				4.2	
1987	136.2	115.8	15.2				5.2	
1988	163.0	133.2	21.4				8.4	
1989	139.5	117.7	15.1				6.7	
1990	179.2	154.2	18.1				6.9	
1991-1995	**2358.7**	**1764.2**	**188.7**				**24.8**	
1991	192.0	165.0	20.2				6.8	
1992	266.0	230.1	27.3				8.6	
1993	410.4	340.1	37.4				2.0	
1994	648.8	514.8	44.6				3.1	
1995	841.5	514.2	59.2				4.3	
1996-2000	**5461.7**	**3380.8**	**261.8**				**155.3**	
1996	876.9	545.7	57.6				4.8	
1997	961.2	605.7	54.7				4.0	
1998	1155.6	727.9	48.7				30.9	
1999	1170.6	735.7	55.8				36.1	
2000	1297.4	765.8	45.0				79.5	
2001-2005	**10857.4**	**3922.4**	**303.3**				**809.4**	
2001	1530.5	752.6	45.8				110.9	
2002	1814.3	771.5	53.9				150.6	
2003	2157.1	745.1	62.4				201.3	
2004	2528.3	755.5	69.5	1063.8	204.5	198.8	176.4	59.8
2005	2827.2	897.7	71.7	1211.8	164.1	274.1	170.2	37.6
2006-2010	**21538.5**	**8162.9**	**398.0**	**9206.8**	**903.8**	**1480.8**	**1121.2**	**265.0**
2006	3371.5	1207.2	69.3	1384.5	180.9	315.9	174.9	38.8
2007	3966.6	1343.0	80.4	1679.0	236.4	378.9	209.0	39.9
2008	3848.5	1388.6	66.8	1688.5	145.3	274.9	242.2	42.2
2009	4858.4	2316.8	68.9	1728.5	172.2	273.0	233.0	66.0
2010	5493.5	1907.3	112.6	2726.3	169.0	238.1	262.1	78.1
2011	5910.6	1903.3	99.4	3053.2	224.1	266.8	278.4	85.4
2012	6462.8	2248.2	106.8	3280.9	208.8	300.2	231.7	86.1
2013	7032.2	2382.0	151.4	3318.4	464.2	321.7	317.0	77.5
2014	7562.3	2389.5	151.4	3944.0	380.7	255.9	366.1	74.7

注：1. 根据国家统计局有关规定，从2004年起，全社会固定资产投资中不包括零星购置投资。
2. 国有包括登记注册类型为国有、国有联营及国有独资公司的单位。
3. 集体包括登记注册类型为集体和集体联营的单位。

Note: a) According to related regulations of National Bureau of Statistics, since 2004, total investment in fixed assets has not included investment in acquiring minor items.
b) State-owned units include state-owned enterprises, state-owned associated enterprises and wholly state-owned enterprises.
c) Collectively-owned units include collectively-owned enterprises and collectively-owned associated enterprises.

5-3 按产业分全社会固定资产投资(1978-2014年)
INVESTMENT IN FIXED ASSETS BY INDUSTRY (1978-2014)

单位：亿元 (100 million yuan)

年份 Year	全社会固定资产投资 Total Investment in Fixed Assets	第一产业 Primary Industry	第二产业 Secondary Industry	第三产业 Tertiary Industry
1978	22.6	1.4	10.8	10.4
1979	26.5	1.0	12.0	13.5
1980	33.2	0.7	15.7	16.8
1981-1985	**286.8**	**5.9**	**98.1**	**130.4**
1981	36.6	0.6	13.6	17.2
1982	38.6	1.2	15.4	17.9
1983	51.3	1.2	16.4	20.9
1984	66.3	1.3	20.3	30.6
1985	94.0	1.6	32.4	43.8
1986-1990	**724.1**	**9.4**	**218.8**	**384.2**
1986	106.2	1.5	41.4	51.6
1987	136.2	1.6	46.9	72.9
1988	163.0	2.0	48.8	87.9
1989	139.5	1.9	38.4	81.9
1990	179.2	2.4	43.3	89.9
1991-1995	**2358.7**	**15.5**	**624.1**	**973.5**
1991	192.0	2.7	51.3	90.4
1992	266.0	3.9	82.9	114.2
1993	410.4	2.1	150.4	165.7
1994	648.8	3.7	185.8	318.4
1995	841.5	3.1	153.7	284.8
1996-2000	**5461.7**	**9.9**	**914.3**	**2160.2**
1996	876.9	2.8	174.9	319.7
1997	961.2	0.9	201.1	380.1
1998	1155.6	1.5	201.7	479.7
1999	1170.6	1.7	179.4	470.4
2000	1297.4	3.0	157.2	510.3
2001-2005	**10857.4**	**63.4**	**1410.6**	**9383.4**
2001	1530.5	8.4	154.2	1367.9
2002	1814.3	7.5	185.0	1621.8
2003	2157.1	21.0	260.7	1875.4
2004	2528.3	14.6	401.0	2112.7
2005	2827.2	11.9	409.7	2405.6
2006-2010	**21538.5**	**159.9**	**2172.8**	**19205.8**
2006	3371.5	14.5	363.2	2993.8
2007	3966.6	16.7	484.1	3465.8
2008	3848.5	28.1	386.0	3434.4
2009	4858.4	57.4	411.4	4389.5
2010	5493.5	43.2	528.1	4922.3
2011	5910.6	47.2	762.2	5101.3
2012	6462.8	145.4	719.8	5597.5
2013	7032.2	175.5	755.0	6101.7
2014	7562.3	163.9	716.8	6681.6

注：1. 根据国家统计局有关规定，从2004年起，全社会固定资产投资中不包括零星购置投资。
2. 2000年及以前按产业划分中，不含房地产开发投资及农村投资。2000年以后含房地产开发投资及农村固定资产投资。
3. 自2012年起，三次产业划分执行国家统计局《三次产业划分规定》(国统字〔2012〕108号)。

Note: a) According to related regulations of National Bureau of Statistics, since 2004, total investment in fixed assets has not included investment in acquiring minor items.

b) Data of investment in fixed assets grouped by industry excluded investment in real estate development and rural investment in 2000 and before. After 2000, data of investment in fixed assets included investment in real estate development and rural fixed assets.

c) Since 2012, the three industries have been classified according to the Regulations on the Classification of the Three Industries (G.T.Z. [2012] No. 108) issued by National Bureau of Statistics.

5-4 全社会固定资产投资资金来源情况(1978-2014年)
TOTAL INVESTMENT IN FIXED ASSETS BY SOURCE OF FUNDS (1978-2014)

单位：亿元 (100 million yuan)

年份 Year	上年末结余资金 Surplus Funds by the End of the Previous Year	本年资金来源小计 Subtotal of Funds at Current Year	国家预算内资金 State Budgets	国内贷款 Domestic Loans	债券 Bonds	利用外资 Foreign Investment	自筹资金 Self-raised Funds	其他资金 Others
1978		22.5	16.9					
1979		26.5	19.2					
1980		33.2	18.5					
1981		31.4	15.4					
1982		34.5	14.1					
1983		38.5	16.0					
1984		52.2	22.5					
1985		77.8	30.4					
1986		94.5	33.0					
1987		126.2	43.1					
1988		149.4	37.4					
1989		123.1	35.0	12.8		18.2	44.5	12.6
1990		136.2	34.4	22.8		15.2	52.3	11.5
1991		151.1	35.5	28.2		13.9	65.5	8.0
1992		216.7	42.2	40.1		14.9	109.9	9.6
1993	54.3	425.2	47.1	79.2	1.6	28.0	205.2	64.1
1994	71.1	695.7	64.1	91.5	0.8	96.9	331.2	111.2
1995	200.8	915.8	70.3	122.7	1.1	187.3	339.8	194.6
1996	204.9	926.1	76.7	152.8	1.0	161.2	330.5	203.9
1997	183.1	1016.7	86.3	194.3		139.2	383.4	213.5
1998	207.1	1140.1	98.4	223.8	17.0	132.1	450.2	218.6
1999	212.1	1183.8	136.2	262.2	1.4	82.7	461.3	240.0
2000	293.1	1439.1	107.0	373.8	0.6	51.5	505.6	400.6
2001	325.5	1796.8	136.7	429.4	2.5	35.6	595.6	597.0
2002	433.2	2075.3	108.5	543.8	1.9	41.5	672.8	706.8
2003	542.7	2674.0	78.4	755.2		52.6	887.9	899.9
2004	654.6	3712.8	118.6	804.7		120.5	1245.7	1423.3
2005	924.4	4553.7	128.8	1055.8		70.9	1452.8	1845.4
2006	1043.8	4927.3	126.4	1347.5	32.7	76.2	1532.2	1812.3
2007	1202.2	6193.0	102.2	1513.3	22.4	82.8	2195.6	2276.7
2008	1469.5	5184.7	104.2	1394.2	35.5	80.0	2016.4	1554.5
2009	1321.7	8702.2	118.1	3038.5	17.5	39.3	2441.3	3047.4
2010	2109.1	8327.8	99.5	2218.7	4.3	43.8	3209.1	2752.4
2011	2341.4	8235.4	71.7	1853.6	85.4	29.8	3588.6	2606.3
2012	2830.7	9156.0	156.1	2186.3	12.7	24.9	3478.4	3297.6
2013	3133.1	10580.3	159.6	2554.1	0.8	23.5	4295.2	3547.2
2014	3586.5	10208.7	161.7	2841.0	8.0	33.3	4347.9	2816.8

注：1978-1992年不含房地产开发和农村投资；1993-2003年不含农村投资。

Note: Figures from 1978 to 1992 did not include investment in real estate development and rural investment; figures from 1993 to 2003 did not include rural investment.

5-5 全社会基础设施投资(1978-2014年)

单位：亿元

年份 Year	基础设施投资 Infrastructure Investment	#能源 Energy	电力 Electricity	供热 Heating	供气 Gas	供水 Water	#公共服务业 Public Services	#园林绿化 Landscaping	#环境卫生 Environmental Sanitation	#市政工程管理 Municipal Project Management
1978	5.4	1.4	0.7				0.6			
1979	5.8	1.1	0.4				1.3			
1980	6.0	0.9	0.6				2.3			
1981-1985	**40.6**	**9.4**	**5.4**				**11.2**			
1981	5.8	1.3	0.6				2.0			
1982	6.1	1.4	0.9				1.9			
1983	6.7	1.5	0.9				1.9			
1984	8.8	1.4	0.7				3.0			
1985	13.2	3.8	2.3				2.5			
1986-1990	**117.9**	**39.8**	**21.1**				**25.3**			
1986	14.5	4.8	2.3				2.1			
1987	22.1	8.0	4.1				3.1			
1988	23.2	8.8	4.1				5.3			
1989	26.5	9.2	5.2				6.6			
1990	31.6	9.0	5.3				8.3			
1991-1995	**494.9**	**134.1**	**84.6**	**12.3**	**15.2**	**22.0**	**62.9**	**2.9**		**57.3**
1991	35.2	12.4	6.4	2.0	1.3	2.7	7.5	0.3		6.8
1992	58.8	17.7	9.0	4.0	2.6	2.1	8.2	0.4		7.2
1993	91.4	19.3	11.4	1.4	2.6	3.9	4.1	1.6		1.7
1994	153.4	38.0	22.7	2.5	5.0	7.8	27.2	0.3		26.5
1995	156.1	46.7	35.1	2.4	3.7	5.5	15.9	0.3		15.1
1996-2000	**1382.1**	**363.4**	**239.7**	**45.2**	**41.4**	**37.1**	**321.0**	**14.2**	**27.1**	**275.9**
1996	188.8	59.2	48.2	3.4	4.1	3.5	29.1	2.3	0.1	25.4
1997	218.3	75.6	52.1	10.3	7.8	5.4	24.3	1.7	2.8	19.8
1998	320.4	85.1	54.2	14.2	6.7	10.0	38.0	3.0	1.9	33.1
1999	302.7	90.3	58.6	11.2	10.3	10.2	75.0	5.4	2.9	64.7
2000	351.9	53.2	26.6	6.1	12.5	8.0	154.6	1.8	19.4	132.9
2001-2005	**2260.0**	**301.7**	**165.2**	**52.7**	**53.9**	**29.9**	**668.6**	**23.1**	**79.9**	**511.4**
2001	356.4	40.8	19.3	7.2	11.0	3.3	114.6	6.7	22.4	85.4
2002	411.9	49.5	26.0	7.2	13.2	3.0	101.6	3.5	17.0	81.1
2003	417.8	36.1	10.6	11.3	10.8	3.4	152.8	1.9	17.0	103.6
2004	463.2	73.0	39.3	14.8	6.9	12.0	139.3	5.5	16.3	100.8
2005	610.7	102.3	70.0	12.2	12.0	8.1	160.3	5.5	7.2	140.6
2006-2010	**6137.3**	**780.3**	**443.6**	**176.9**	**57.6**	**102.1**	**1640.0**	**44.8**	**349.4**	**1117.7**
2006	935.3	113.4	72.8	18.7	11.0	10.9	265.3	3.4	55.4	194.8
2007	1175.8	200.2	121.0	43.0	11.2	25.0	289.5	8.0	75.7	187.3
2008	1160.7	144.1	88.4	25.9	8.1	21.7	291.6	8.0	82.2	188.7
2009	1462.0	165.4	88.9	40.1	10.5	25.8	434.5	15.9	77.7	314.0
2010	1403.5	157.2	72.5	49.2	16.8	18.7	359.1	9.5	58.4	232.9
2011	1400.2	171.1	90.1	25.3	17.0	38.8	379.4	8.1	40.5	267.8
2012	1789.2	231.9	106.3	64.8	27.3	33.5	508.1	22.0	23.5	361.6
2013	1785.7	270.2	133.7	53.6	38.1	44.8	451.3	18.2	53.6	318.3
2014	2018.1	352.7	149.1	81.4	21.3	100.9	502.5	67.7	35.9	366.6

注：2004年及以后基础设施投资包括农村基础设施投资。

TOTAL INVESTMENT IN INFRASTRUCTURE (1978-2014)

(100 million yuan)

#交通运输 Transportation	#铁路 Railway	#公路 Road	#城市公共交通业 Urban Public Transportation	#航空 Aviation	#邮政电信 Post & Telecommunications	邮政 Post	电信 Telecommunications	基础设施投资占全社会固定资产投资比重(%) Infrastructure Investment as Percentage of Total Investment in Fixed Assets (%)
1.7	0.8	0.4		0.5	0.4			23.9
1.7	0.4	0.4		0.8	0.4			21.9
2.3	1.1	0.7		0.5	0.5			17.9
11.1	**3.9**	**5.5**		**1.7**	**5.2**			
1.8	0.6	0.9		0.3	0.4			15.8
1.9	0.8	0.8		0.3	0.4			15.8
2.6	1.2	1.0		0.4	0.6			13.1
2.3	0.7	1.3		0.3	1.1			13.3
2.6	0.7	1.6		0.4	2.7			14.0
28.3	**5.0**	**19.3**		**4.0**	**20.3**			
3.1	1.0	1.5		0.6	3.5			13.7
6.6	1.2	4.0		1.3	3.2			16.2
4.7	1.4	3.0		0.4	3.0			14.2
5.2	0.7	3.9		0.6	5.2			19.0
8.7	0.7	6.9		1.1	5.4			17.6
123.0	**50.8**	**30.6**	**22.4**	**4.6**	**137.3**	**9.5**	**127.8**	
9.3	0.8	5.6	2.3	0.5	5.8	5.0	0.8	18.3
20.1	4.7	10.7	4.0	0.7	12.3	1.1	11.2	22.1
29.4	11.2	4.7	4.7	1.1	24.2	1.7	22.5	22.3
30.0	13.6	3.6	5.7	1.0	48.6	0.9	47.7	23.6
34.2	20.5	6.0	5.7	1.3	46.4	0.8	45.6	18.6
337.4	**26.0**	**131.3**	**80.0**	**3.2**	**299.6**	**6.0**	**293.6**	
54.0	11.7	15.8	6.0	1.2	44.1	0.9	43.2	21.5
51.2	6.0	11.1	9.1	0.2	60.3	2.1	58.2	22.7
104.6	8.0	42.1	24.4		77.5	1.8	75.7	27.7
63.0		30.1	20.7		54.0	0.4	53.6	25.9
64.6	0.3	32.2	19.8	1.8	63.7	0.8	62.9	27.1
766.2	**23.2**	**294.0**	**302.8**	**137.6**	**384.0**	**6.2**	**377.9**	
104.4	1.5	52.8	45.1	2.0	84.8	2.2	82.6	23.3
159.7	1.4	107.0	44.6	1.4	78.7	1.6	77.1	22.7
129.2	9.3	55.3	48.8	15.8	82.2	0.9	81.3	19.4
148.8	7.2	38.2	51.1	52.3	68.5	1.0	67.5	18.3
224.1	3.9	40.7	113.2	66.2	69.9	0.5	69.4	21.6
3010.9	**358.7**	**732.8**	**1456.7**	**457.7**	**462.9**	**8.2**	**454.4**	
439.6	25.1	140.6	201.0	72.2	72.3	1.2	71.1	27.7
548.0	65.7	189.6	202.4	87.5	84.8	…	84.7	29.6
604.2	75.9	170.5	215.8	141.8	86.7	0.3	86.3	30.2
698.6	114.9	134.8	426.7	21.9	124.9	3.3	121.5	30.1
720.5	77.1	97.3	410.8	134.3	94.2	3.4	90.8	25.5
680.7	43.6	107.7	351.3	176.6	82.3	2.7	79.6	23.7
712.0	43.0	98.2	391.0	178.1	122.0	4.6	117.4	27.7
664.5	36.9	127.5	310.9	162.5	132.9	3.5	129.4	25.4
756.5	9.0	84.6	491.6	166.0	127.3	0.1	127.2	26.7

Note: Investment in infrastructure in and after 2004 includes that in rural infrastructure investment.

5-6 全社会基础设施投资(2014年)
TOTAL INVESTMENT IN INFRASTRUCTURE (2014)

项目	Item	投资额（万元） Investment (10000 yuan) 全市 Beijing Municipality	#城镇 Urban	比重(%) Percentage (%) 全市 Beijing Municipality	#城镇 Urban
合计	**Total**	**20181371**	**17033754**	**100.0**	**100.0**
能源	**Energy**	**3526910**	**3392141**	**17.5**	**19.9**
电力	Electricity	1490662	1429153	7.4	8.4
供热	Heating	814248	805408	4.0	4.7
供气	Gas	213092	205345	1.1	1.2
供水	Water	1008908	952235	5.0	5.6
公共服务业	**Public Services**	**5025198**	**4189085**	**24.9**	**24.6**
园林绿化	Landscaping	677499	571859	3.4	3.4
环境卫生	Environmental Sanitation	359039	232621	1.8	1.4
市政工程管理	Municipal Project Management	3666353	3235940	18.2	19.0
其他公共服务业	Others	322307	148665	1.6	0.9
交通运输	**Transportation**	**7565114**	**7402678**	**37.5**	**43.5**
铁路	Railway	90028	88895	0.4	0.5
公路	Road	845550	693902	4.2	4.1
管道运输	Pipeline	51951	51951	0.3	0.3
城市公共交通业	Urban Public Transportation	4915982	4906936	24.4	28.8
#公交电汽车客运	Buses and Electirc Cars	381474	381474	1.9	2.2
出租汽车	Taxis	104269	100089	0.5	0.6
航空	Aviation	1659914	1659914	8.2	9.7
其他	Others	1689	1080		
邮政电信	**Post and Telecommunications**	**1273193**	**1264693**	**6.3**	**7.4**
邮政	Post	1056	1056		
电信	Telecommunications	1272137	1263637	6.3	7.4
其他	**Others**	**2790956**	**785157**	**13.8**	**4.6**
#水利	Water Conservancy	1450038	759234	7.2	4.5

5-7 全社会固定资产投资及新增固定资产(按行业分)(2014年)
TOTAL INVESTMENT IN FIXED ASSETS AND ITS INCREMENTAL FIXED ASSETS (GROUPED BY SECTOR) (2014)

单位：万元 (10000 yuan)

项目	Item	投资额 Investment			新增固定资产 Incremental Fixed Assets		
		合计 Total	中央 Central	地方 Local	合计 Total	中央 Central	地方 Local
合计	**Total**	**75622723**	**8691272**	**66931451**	**38873180**	**6177027**	**32696153**
农、林、牧、渔业	**Agriculture, Forestry, Animal Production and Hunting, Fishing**	**1605804**	**1272**	**1604532**	**913170**	**12990**	**900180**
农业	Agriculture	168037	288	167749	116080	12006	104074
林业	Forestry	1347133		1347133	738615		738615
畜牧业	Animal Production and Hunting	19875		19875	8027		8027
渔业	Fishing	400		400			
农、林、牧、渔服务业	Service Activities for Agriculture, Forestry, Animal Production and Hunting, Fishing	70359	984	69375	50448	984	49464
采矿业	**Mining and Quarrying**	**81125**	**6106**	**75019**	**136157**		**136157**
煤炭开采和洗选业	Mining and Washing of Coal	12854		12854	21485		21485
黑色金属矿采选业	Mining of Ferrous Metal Ores	62165		62165	114672		114672
制造业	**Manufacturing**	**3506487**	**315953**	**3190534**	**5287104**	**396854**	**4890250**
农副食品加工业	Processing of Food from Agricultural Products	43211		43211	25011		25011
食品制造业	Manufacture of Foods	107788	1461	106327	79697	38149	41548
酒、饮料和精制茶制造业	Manufacture of Wines, Beverage and Refined Tea	47104		47104	10984		10984
烟草制品业	Manufacture of Cigarettes and Tobacco	17166	17166				
纺织业	Manufacture of Textile	3014		3014	2609		2609
纺织服装、服饰业	Manufacture of Textile Wearing Apparel and Ornament	35182		35182	8630		8630
皮革、毛皮、羽毛及其制品和制鞋业	Manufacture of Leather, Fur, Feather and Its Products, and Footwear						
木材加工及木、竹藤、棕、草制品	Processing of Timbers, Manufacture of Wood, Bamboo, Rattan, Palm and Straw Products						
家具制造业	Manufacture of Furniture	34592		34592	14237		14237
造纸及纸制品业	Manufacture of Paper and Paper Products	22661		22661	9494		9494
印刷和记录媒介复制业	Printing, Reproduction of Recording Media	46421	5317	41104	22536	7461	15075
文教、工美、体育和娱乐用品制造业	Manufacture of Articles for Culture, Education, Artwork, Sport and Entertainment Activities	28230		28230	5347		5347
石油加工、炼焦及核燃料加工业	Processing of Petroleum, Coking, Processing of Nucleus Fuel	41824	40805	1019	15708	11435	4273
化学原料及化学制品制造业	Manufacture of Chemical Raw Materials and Chemical Products	177426	87723	89703	182404	141149	41255
医药制造业	Manufacture of Medicines	456228	75203	381025	229210	25515	203695
化学纤维制造业	Manufacture of Chemical Fibers	110		110	95		95
橡胶和塑料制品业	Manufacture of Rubber and Plastic Products	31885		31885	6852		6852
非金属矿物制品业	Manufacture of Non-metallic Mineral Products	48328	1722	46606	79425		79425
黑色金属冶炼及压延加工业	Manufacture and Pressing of Ferrous Metals	5281		5281	4021		4021
有色金属冶炼及压延加工业	Manufacture and Pressing of Non-ferrous Metals	1839		1839	6260		6260
金属制品业	Manufacture of Fabricated Metal Products	32262	8128	24134	76615	45225	31390
通用设备制造业	Manufacture of General-Purpose Machinery	47327		47327	33627		33627

注：1. 本表分行业数据不含农户投资。
2. 行业划分执行2011年国民经济行业分类标准(GB/T 4754-2011)。

Note: a) The figures of grouping exclude investment of rural households.
b) Sectors are classified in accordance with the Standard for Classification of National Economic Sectors 2011 (GB/T 4754-2011).

5-7 续表 1 Continued 1

单位：万元 (10000 yuan)

项　目	Item	投资额 Investment			新增固定资产 Incremental Fixed Assets		
		合计 Total	中央 Central	地方 Local	合计 Total	中央 Central	地方 Local
专用设备制造业	Manufacture of Special-Purpose Machinery	234253	11985	222268	130110	1000	129110
汽车制造业	Manufacture of Motor Vehicles	1308073	14746	1293327	1594242	23447	1570795
铁路、船舶、航空航天和其他运输设备制造业	Manufacture of Railway Locomotives, Building of Ships and Boats, Manufacture of Air and Spacecrafts and Other Transportation Equipment	67423	30764	36659	65843	65843	
电气机械及器材制造业	Manufacture of Electrical Machinery and Equipment	95610		95610	37973		37973
计算机、通信和其他电子设备制造业	Manufacture of Computer, Communication Equipment and Other Electronic Equipment	494829	18072	476757	2579338	6736	2572602
仪器仪表制造业	Manufacture of Measuring Instrument and Meter	63140	200	62940	29768	10160	19608
其他制造业	Other Manufacturing	10881	2052	8829	31252	14918	16334
废弃资源综合利用业	Waste Recycling and Recovery	3790		3790			
金属制品、机械和设备修理业	Repair of Fabricated Metal Products, Machinery and Equipment	609	609		5816	5816	
电力、热力、燃气及水生产和供应业	**Production and Distribution of Electricity, Heating Power, Gas and Water**	**3531451**	**316706**	**3214745**	**2474564**	**107**	**2474457**
电力、热力的生产和供应业	Production and Supply of Electric Power and Heat Power	2309451	316706	1992745	2031452	107	2031345
燃气生产和供应业	Production and Distribution of Gas	213092		213092	223890		223890
水的生产和供应业	Production and Distribution of Water	1008908		1008908	219222		219222
建筑业	**Construction**	**45758**	**4775**	**40983**	**32637**	**4775**	**27862**
房屋建筑业	Construction of Building	6735	4000	2735	4000	4000	
土木工程建筑业	Civil Engineering Construction	14221		14221	17577		17577
建筑安装业	Construction Installation	8276		8276	5725		5725
建筑装饰和其他建筑业	Building Completion, Finishing and Other Construction	16526	775	15751	5335	775	4560
批发和零售业	**Wholesale and Retail Trade**	**333440**	**18697**	**314743**	**163526**		**163526**
批发业	Wholesale	184975	18697	166278	17193		17193
零售业	Retail Trade	148465		148465	146333		146333
交通运输、仓储和邮政业	**Transport, Storage and Post**	**7758017**	**1860701**	**5897316**	**3121016**	**1793120**	**1327896**
铁路运输业	Transport via Railway	96278	95145	1133	51778	50645	1133
道路运输业	Transport via Road	5773838	2262	5771576	1242623	10800	1231823
水上运输业	Water Transport						
航空运输业	Air Transport	1659914	1652254	7660	1204721	1204721	
管道运输业	Transport via Pipeline	51951	51951		511715	511715	
装卸搬运和运输代理业	Loading, Unloading, Portage and Other Transport Services	1689		1689	1080		1080
仓储业	Storage	173291	58033	115258	99452	5592	93860
邮政业	Post	1056	1056		9647	9647	
住宿和餐饮业	**Accommodation and Restaurants**	**647985**	**78269**	**569716**	**569920**	**267771**	**302149**
住宿业	Accommodation	635048	78269	556779	563112	267771	295341
餐饮业	Restaurants	12937		12937	6808		6808
信息传输、软件和信息技术服务业	**Information Transmission, Software and Information Technology Services**	**1834411**	**325392**	**1509019**	**1347106**	**63867**	**1283239**
电信、广播电视和卫星传输服务	Telecommunications, Broadcasting, Television and Satellite Transmission Services	997455	121321	876134	828006	1628	826378
互联网和相关服务	Internet and Related Services	299514		299514	197421		197421
软件和信息技术服务业	Software and Information Technology Services	537442	204071	333371	321679	62239	259440
金融业	**Finance**	**545367**	**382124**	**163243**	**238285**	**201908**	**36377**
货币金融服务	Monetary Financial Services	267799	253207	14592	213076	199121	13955
资本市场服务	Capital Market Services	2971		2971			
保险业	Insurance	270931	126636	144295	25209	2787	22422
其他金融业	Other Financial Services	3666	2281	1385			

5-7 续表 2 Continued 2

单位：万元 (10000 yuan)

项　目	Item	投资额 Investment			新增固定资产 Incremental Fixed Assets		
		合计 Total	中央 Central	地方 Local	合计 Total	中央 Central	地方 Local
房地产业	**Real Estate**	**43543854**	**3090072**	**40453782**	**17175208**	**1820570**	**15354638**
租赁和商务服务业	**Renting and Leasing Activities Business Services**	**475457**	**36289**	**439168**	**584115**	**15669**	**568446**
租赁业	Renting and Leasing Activities	17751	5187	12564	13134		13134
商务服务业	Business Services	457706	31102	426604	570981	15669	555312
科学研究和技术服务业	**Scientific Research and Ddevelopment, Technical Services**	**1424812**	**831027**	**593785**	**382144**	**217151**	**164993**
研究与试验发展	Research and Experimental Development	672268	502181	170087	124711	93935	30776
专业技术服务业	Professional Technique Services	322859	182883	139976	97061	300	96761
科技推广和应用服务业	Technique Generalization and Application Services	429685	145963	283722	160372	122916	37456
水利、环境和公共设施管理业	**Management of Water Conservancy, Environment and Public Facilities**	**6036439**	**8597**	**6027842**	**2916633**	**129958**	**2786675**
水利管理业	Management of Water Conservancy	1539658	863	1538795	429678		429678
生态保护和环境治理业	Ecological Protection and Environmental Control	85214		85214	24310		24310
公共设施管理业	Management of Public Facilities	4411567	7734	4403833	2462645	129958	2332687
居民服务、修理和其他服务业	**Resident Services, Repair and Other Services**	**115086**	**957**	**114129**	**45303**	**957**	**44346**
居民服务业	Resident Services	9689		9689	8270		8270
机动车、电子产品和日用产品修理业	Repair of Motor Vehicles, Electronics and Household Applicances	13051		13051	6923		6923
其他服务业	Other Services	92346	957	91389	30110	957	29153
教　育	**Education**	**1559828**	**888467**	**671361**	**996942**	**329049**	**667893**
卫生和社会工作	**Health Care and Social Works**	**670285**	**112652**	**557633**	**877701**	**352703**	**524998**
卫　生	Health Care	597592	112652	484940	779194	352703	426491
社会工作	Social Work activities	72693		72693	98507		98507
文化、体育和娱乐业	**Culture, Sports and Entertainment**	**920122**	**307982**	**612140**	**384655**	**148445**	**236210**
新闻出版业	Journalism and Publishing	59789	56193	3596	67147	50944	16203
广播、电视、电影和影视录音制作业	Radio Broadcasting, Television,Movies, Videos and Sound Recording	191440	110347	81093	108012	72955	35057
文化艺术业	Culture and Arts	314949	140230	174719	175575	24546	151029
体　育	Sports Activities	73973	1212	72761	30259		30259
娱乐业	Entertainment	279971		279971	3662		3662
公共管理、社会保障和社会组织	**Public Management, Social Security and Social Organizations**	**479057**	**105234**	**373823**	**744659**	**421133**	**323526**
中国共产党机关	Organs of Communist Party of China	11951	11430	521	132985	129179	3806
国家机构	Organs of State	318575	16006	302569	284222		284222
社会保障	Social Security	64884	53202	11682	213668	202844	10824
群众团体、社会团体和其他成员组织	Mass Communities, Social Organizations and Other Membership Organizations	83258	24596	58662	113784	89110	24674
基层群众自治组织	Grass Roots Self-government Organizations	389		389			

5-8 全社会房屋建筑施工及竣工面积(1978-2014年) FLOOR SPACE OF BUILDINGS UNDER CONSTRUCTION AND COMPLETED (1978-2014)

单位：万平方米 (10000 sq.m)

年 份 Year	施工面积 Floor Space of Buildings under Construction	#住 宅 Residential Buildings	竣工面积 Floor Space of Buildings Completed	#住 宅 Residential Buildings	中 央 Central	地 方 Local
1978	956.3	456.8	407.0	190.4	158.7	248.3
1979	1340.6	780.2	537.6	304.9	235.2	302.4
1980	1704.1	1037.0	648.4	396.9	315.8	332.6
1981-1985			**3941.6**	**2383.4**	**1723.2**	**2218.4**
1981	1875.8	1189.9	726.9	462.6	327.2	399.7
1982	1938.6	1210.1	728.3	463.8	303.7	424.6
1983	1952.1	1163.6	775.5	514.0	312.3	463.2
1984	2351.9	1327.1	818.7	437.6	352.7	466.0
1985	2802.7	1599.2	892.2	505.4	427.3	464.9
1986-1990			**5142.4**	**2939.9**	**2635.1**	**2507.3**
1986	2760.7	1557.4	906.5	532.7	424.5	482.0
1987	2578.0	1273.2	1042.2	608.9	507.8	534.4
1988	2642.2	1226.2	1065.6	623.5	499.6	566.0
1989	2450.8	1167.8	1046.9	601.8	565.8	481.1
1990	2864.9	1561.9	1081.2	573.0	637.4	443.8
1991-1995			**6206.7**	**3707.2**	**1869.2**	**4337.5**
1991	2818.0	1612.0	1036.4	601.8	396.2	640.2
1992	3126.8	1784.7	1111.4	681.2	399.3	712.1
1993	3607.5	1866.4	1158.0	654.8	320.5	837.5
1994	4460.9	2315.1	1370.7	832.1	366.8	1003.9
1995	5524.3	2897.6	1530.2	937.3	386.4	1143.8
1996-2000			**9644.3**	**5979.9**	**2726.7**	**6917.6**
1996	5633.2	2696.9	1517.5	870.4	452.0	1065.5
1997	5819.4	2881.3	1625.7	996.8	492.2	1133.5
1998	6496.1	3473.7	1821.5	1093.1	508.4	1313.1
1999	6556.5	3754.8	2321.4	1519.9	655.3	1666.1
2000	6995.9	4083.3	2358.2	1499.7	618.8	1739.4
2001-2005			**17781.6**	**11992.2**	**1733.0**	**16048.6**
2001	8203.3	5226.4	2554.6	1804.9	490.6	2064.0
2002	9697.7	6193.3	3121.8	2191.4	441.8	2680.0
2003	11262.2	7011.3	3222.8	2322.3	242.1	2980.7
2004	13121.9	7513.1	4203.2	2649.5	301.9	3901.3
2005	14096.2	8043.2	4679.2	3024.1	256.6	4422.6
2006-2010			**20059.1**	**10993.8**	**2002.6**	**18056.4**
2006	14069.2	7113.0	4191.0	2391.6	388.6	3802.4
2007	14146.7	6788.8	3866.4	2098.0	399.6	3466.8
2008	14145.3	6656.3	3840.7	1871.1	496.8	3343.9
2009	14380.6	7058.4	4252.6	2369.6	388.4	3864.2
2010	15572.1	7932.9	3908.4	2263.5	329.2	3579.1
2011	18065.2	8817.1	4032.9	2121.8	425.5	3607.4
2012	20045.4	9217.8	3723.5	1992.5	216.9	3506.6
2013	21526.0	9469.0	3989.7	2154.8	255.2	3734.4
2014	21677.7	8978.3	4967.5	2547.6	541.4	4426.1

注：2007年及以前，表中数据不包含农村农户房屋施工和竣工面积。

Note: Figures in and before 2007 excluded floor space of buildings under construction and completed in rural areas.

5-9 全社会房屋建筑施工及竣工面积
FLOOR SPACE OF BUILDINGS UNDER CONSTRUCTION AND COMPLETED

单位：万平方米 (10000 sq.m)

项　目	Item	2014	2013	占竣工面积比重(%) Proportion in Completed Floor Space (%)	
				2014	2013
施工总面积	**Floor Space of Buildings under Construction**	**21677.7**	**21526.0**		
竣工总面积	**Floor Space of Buildings Completed**	**4967.5**	**3989.7**	**100.0**	**100.0**
按隶属关系分	**By Affiliation**				
中　央	Central	541.4	255.2	10.9	6.4
地　方	Local	4426.1	3734.4	89.1	93.6
#国　有	State-owned	764.5	692.0	15.4	17.3
集　体	Collectively-owned	234.8	34.7	4.7	0.9
按功能区分	**By Functional Zone**				
首都功能核心区	Core Functional Area of the Capital	94.4	93.4	1.9	2.3
城市功能拓展区	Urban Function Extension Area	1831.4	1137.8	36.9	28.5
城市发展新区	New Area of Urban Development	2380.8	2181.9	47.9	54.7
生态涵养发展区	Ecological Conservation Area	661.0	576.6	13.3	14.5

5-10 房地产开发面积(1990-2014年)

单位：万平方米

年份 Year	商品房施工面积 Floor Space of Commercial Buildings under Construction	#本年新开工面积 Floor Space of Buildings Newly Started Construction in Current Year	住宅 Residential Houses	#经济适用房 Affordable Houses	#公寓别墅 Apartments & Villas	办公楼(写字楼) Office Buildings	商业、非公益用房及其他 Buildings for Commercial Use, Non-public Buildings and Others	商品房竣工面积 Floor Space of Comnmercial Buildings Completed	住宅 Residential Houses	#经济适用房 Affordable Houses	#公寓别墅 Apartments & Villas
1990	774.0	249.1	643.4			17.4	41.2	271.6	226.5		
1991	815.1	317.6	692.1			2.1	57.6	275.2	240.4		
1992	1021.1	508.6	865.4			7.6	54.8	331.4	300.8		
1993	1262.0	524.8	887.6					356.4	280.6		
1994	1593.2	659.4	1107.6					445.7	385.6		
1995	2810.2	1012.2	1728.7		334.8	462.7	252.6	653.0	506.3		55.6
1996	2824.6	578.7	1520.7		316.8	638.7	283.9	663.4	470.8		43.3
1997	2869.6	848.4	1541.1		335.7	637.7	260.8	682.3	478.3		99.8
1998	3499.1	1193.4	2107.2		368.3	590.7	297.7	842.8	588.7		57.0
1999	3784.0	1061.8	2447.9	301.4	390.7	484.4	281.3	1208.5	908.3	114.1	93.2
2000	4455.0	1676.9	2971.6	296.6	537.8	449.1	281.3	1365.6	1013.7	184.9	164.2
2001	5966.7	2789.8	4349.6	563.1	494.4	495.5	330.6	1707.4	1393.4	214.0	150.8
2002	7510.7	3206.0	5397.5	660.2	550.8	672.5	400.3	2384.4	1926.2	228.4	161.9
2003	9070.7	3433.8	6352.9	802.5	705.0	901.3	557.7	2593.7	2080.8	322.8	127.9
2004	9931.3	3054.3	6759.4	793.2	776.0	1122.4	641.8	3067.0	2343.9	298.8	153.2
2005	10748.5	2965.9	7283.4	783.4	1023.5	1209.8	809.2	3770.9	2841.4	325.6	342.7
2006	10483.5	3179.4	6311.3	551.9	913.8	1245.8	1403.0	3193.9	2193.3	270.1	255.6
2007	10438.6	2557.4	5914.5	440.1	1009.2	1364.6	1482.1	2891.7	1854.0	188.6	239.6
2008	10014.3	2337.2	5538.2	544.9	954.7	1287.2	1429.8	2558.0	1399.3	101.1	233.0
2009	9719.1	2246.6	5551.9	628.7	840.9	1132.2	1323.4	2678.6	1613.2	98.2	213.7
2010	10300.9	2974.2	6176.0	572.7	830.0	1054.8	1229.3	2386.7	1498.5	144.6	183.2
2011	12065.4	4246.1	7168.1	444.8	754.8	1422.7	1187.5	2245.2	1316.1	74.6	133.0
2012	13122.5	3224.2	7510.4	435.1	642.2	1711.9	1236.9	2390.9	1522.7	188.5	135.1
2013	13886.9	3577.5	7406.9	310.5	530.1	2114.1	4365.9	2666.4	1692.0	95.7	133.5
2014	13641.5	2502.8	6999.7	328.0	485.4	2277.1	4364.7	3054.1	1804.3	101.4	52.5

注：1. 2005年及以前的商品房销售面积为竣工后的全部商品房销售面积，2006年及以后为期房与现房销售面积之和。
2. 2010年起，商品房销售面积中包含定向安置房数据。
3. 2012年及以前商业、非公益用房及其他只包括商业及服务性等营业性用房。自2013年起包括：厂房、仓库、商业营业用房、服务业用房、教育用房、文化体育用房、医疗用房、科研用房及其他用房。

STATISTICS FOR FLOOR SPACE OF REAL ESTATE DEVELOPENT (1990-2014)

(10000 sq.m)

办公楼(写字楼) Office Buildings	商业、非公益用房及其他 Buildings for Commercial Use, Non-public Buildings and Others	商品房销售面积 Floor Space of Commercial Buildings Sold	住宅 Residential Houses	#经济适用房 Affordable Houses	#公寓别墅 Apartments & Villas	办公楼(写字楼) Office Buildings	商业、非公益用房及其他 Buildings for Commercial Use, Non-public Buildings and Others	年末商品房待售面积 Floor Space of Vacant Commercial Buildings at the Year End	#住宅 Residential Houses	#一年以内 Less than One Year	#三年以上 Over Three Years
9.7	13.3	142.2									
0.9	10.9	154.0	152.5								
2.7	8.3	159.1	153.0								
		182.0	182.0								
		168.6	149.0			17.2	1.1				
27.9	43.5	191.9	180.0		16.7	4.0	4.5	81.5			
79.0	38.3	215.3	183.1		24.9	13.7	14.4	214.8	179.6		
80.9	42.4	290.9	256.2		53.5	18.8	8.0	298.3	258.9		
92.3	69.8	409.2	377.0		40.0	23.2	7.0	334.8	262.9		
108.8	43.1	544.4	484.7	45.8	55.1	48.0	6.8	624.3	529.1		
97.2	48.7	956.9	898.2	166.5	107.6	41.2	6.1	627.4	515.1		
98.0	48.2	1205.0	1127.5	185.2	120.8	49.8	17.4	774.0	634.1	429.4	84.6
97.4	82.9	1708.3	1604.4	220.7	153.6	44.0	32.9	919.0	763.2	557.9	96.4
94.0	117.5	1895.8	1771.1	320.0	131.9	38.1	50.8	1123.4	896.9	745.5	109.8
153.9	225.3	2472.0	2285.8	306.3	172.7	92.5	60.2	1044.1	723.8	744.4	72.9
287.8	180.9	2803.2	2566.0	304.0	302.1	131.2	66.9	1374.2	799.7	993.5	75.8
304.4	289.2	2607.6	2205.0	176.3	276.9	260.3	108.6	1039.7	494.1	628.3	106.9
314.8	315.1	2176.6	1731.5	100.1	319.3	265.7	134.8	1136.2	411.8	697.2	203.1
364.6	313.1	1335.4	1031.4	108.3	164.6	139.4	112.4	1438.3	522.7	945.1	209.8
316.6	322.4	2362.3	1880.5	82.2	339.8	255.8	157.1	1351.4	426.8	768.0	229.9
198.4	271.9	1639.5	1201.4	49.5	175.9	208.1	142.1	1482.7	511.9	810.4	239.7
245.2	232.4	1440.0	1035.0	39.4	93.3	211.4	108.7	1792.6	699.8	1021.5	298.3
226.8	240.1	1943.7	1483.4	85.9	116.9	253.5	114.0	1911.8	789.5	958.7	309.0
273.1	701.3	1903.1	1363.7	106.6	87.8	317.9	221.5	1861.4	829.3	922.3	337.7
387.5	862.3	1459.0	1141.3	56.2	48.2	136.8	180.9	2065.7	864.8	1121.4	374.2

Note: a) Floor space of commercial buildings sold in 2005 and before was the floor space of completed commercial buildings, and after 2006, the figure is the sum of completed commercial buildings and those under construction.

b) Since 2010, the floor space of completed commercial buildings has included figures of targeted resettlement buildings.

c) In and Before 2012, buildings for commercial use, non-public buildings and others only included business and commercial buildings. Since 2013, it has included: factory buildings, warehouses, commercial buildings, buildings for service industy, education buildings, cultural and sports buildings, medical buildings, scientific research buildings and others.

5-11 房地产开发情况(1990-2014年)
STATISTICS FOR REAL ESTATE DEVELOPENT (1990-2014)

年 份 Year	房地产开发企业个数(个) Number of Real Estate Development Enterprises (unit)	房地产开发投资额(亿元) Investment in Real Estate Development (100 million yuan)	#土 地购置费 Land Purchase Cost	按用途分 By Purpose of Investment 住 宅 Residential Buildings	写字楼(办公楼) Office Buildings	商业、非公益用房及其他 Buildings for Commercial Use, Non-public Buildings and Others	按投资构成分 By Investment Structure #建筑安装工程 Construction and Installation Projects	#设备工器具购置 Purchase of Equipment, Tools and Devices
1990		22.5		12.3			18.4	
1991-1995		**568.4**		**264.8**			**341.9**	
1991	40	24.0		14.0			16.8	
1992	42	33.7		20.0			20.7	
1993	74	58.4	2.5	38.1			43.4	0.4
1994	81	99.5	4.0	50.3			69.3	0.9
1995	623	352.8	52.4	142.4	71.5	35.2	191.7	8.4
1996-2000		**1979.5**	**161.5**	**950.7**	**351.5**	**161.3**	**1280.6**	**95.5**
1996	554	328.2	15.0	124.9	84.2	35.2	222.0	17.0
1997	601	330.3	23.9	132.9	91.1	29.2	208.0	19.8
1998	585	377.4	28.4	168.0	78.5	36.1	250.7	20.7
1999	716	421.5	36.6	236.6	52.5	30.2	278.6	16.8
2000	893	522.1	57.6	288.3	45.2	30.6	321.3	21.2
2001-2005		**5974.0**	**993.6**	**3239.5**	**696.1**	**368.3**	**3498.9**	**137.8**
2001	1142	783.8	115.6	464.2	72.0	41.7	438.0	22.3
2002	1508	989.4	149.2	586.7	97.3	57.6	572.7	31.5
2003	1546	1202.5	213.2	633.0	142.7	61.3	716.2	24.3
2004	2704	1473.3	275.8	776.0	187.9	94.8	872.1	35.4
2005	3123	1525.0	239.8	779.5	196.2	112.9	881.8	42.3
2006-2010		**10863.2**	**3642.0**	**5211.5**	**1055.2**	**1270.8**	**4550.5**	**255.0**
2006	2882	1719.9	477.9	863.6	216.7	226.0	953.2	55.5
2007	2688	1995.8	644.7	991.7	242.2	267.4	1015.3	58.9
2008	3433	1908.7	639.0	940.6	170.5	240.4	829.6	48.6
2009	3171	2337.7	587.7	906.6	166.7	200.7	841.6	45.7
2010	3190	2901.1	1292.7	1509.0	259.1	336.3	910.8	46.3
2011	3069	3036.3	1301.2	1778.3	363.8	296.7	1235.1	38.5
2012	2960	3153.4	1102.7	1628.0	384.8	275.9	1383.1	65.7
2013	2927	3483.4	1159.5	1724.6	611.7	1147.1	1510.0	53.0
2014	2810	3911.3	1561.2	1962.0	750.2	1199.1	1601.9	47.3

注：2012年及以前商业、非公益用房及其他只包括商业及服务性等营业性用房。自2013年起包括：厂房、仓库、商业营业用房、服务业用房、教育用房、文化体育用房、医疗用房、科研用房及其他用房。

Note: In and Before 2012, buildings for commercial use, non-public buildings and others only included business and commercial buildings. Since 2013, it has included: factory buildings, warehouses, commercial buildings, buildings for service industy, education buildings, cultural and sports buildings, medical buildings, scientific research buildings and others.

5-12 房地产开发企业经营情况(2014年)
REAL ESTATE DEVELOPMENT ENTERPRISES (2014)

项　目	Item	企业单位个数(个) Number of Enterprises (unit)	实收资本合计(万元) Paid-in Capital (10000 yuan)	资产总计(万元) Total Assets (10000 yuan)	主营业务收入(万元) Main Business Income (10000 yuan)	利润总额(万元) Total Profits (10000 yuan)	年末从业人员(人) Number of Staff at the Year End (person)
合　计	**Total**	**2810**	**58759573**	**439214511**	**37577821**	**6741672**	**93044**
按企业登记注册类型分	**By Registration Type**						
内资企业	Domestically-Funded Enterprises	2559	48265322	385118586	33591167	5824740	80134
国有企业	State-owned Enterprises	115	8002057	31683178	2408184	733470	5604
集体企业	Collectively-owned Enterprises	19	70150	1454370	40547	26340	330
私营企业	Private Enterprises	572	2303159	23566787	1504795	-135684	9683
股份合作企业	Joint-equity Cooperative Enterprises	1	5000	12800		-718	50
股份有限公司	Companies Limited by Shares	62	5197912	36939759	2350937	874526	3701
有限责任公司	Limited Liability Companies	1790	32687044	291461692	27286704	4326806	60766
港澳台商投资企业	Hong Kong, Macao and Taiwan-invested Enterprises	149	7052374	33367020	2700766	487961	7817
港澳台合资经营	Joint Ventures	54	2381710	8477002	1071480	210365	2071
港澳台合作经营	Cooperative	56	1305568	7980697	353493	-16037	2870
港澳台商独资企业	Solely-funded Enterprises	39	3365096	16909321	1275793	293633	2876
港澳台商投资股份有限公司	Companies Limited by Shares						
外商投资企业	Foreign-invested Enterprises	102	3441877	20728905	1285888	428971	5093
中外合资经营	Joint Ventures	40	1249261	6631944	496561	219611	1470
中外合作经营	Cooperative	37	618614	4075228	465408	88841	1511
外资(独资)企业	Solely-funded Enterprises	22	1233424	5938972	294122	91952	1634
外商投资股份有限公司	Companies Limited by Shares	3	340578	4082761	29797	28567	478
按隶属关系分	**By Affiliation**						
中　央	Central	108	5556514	32648394	3307939	1140264	4337
地　方	Local	2702	53203059	406566117	34269882	5601409	88707
按资质等级分	**By Qualification Grade**						
一　级	First-grade	111	9097527	96214485	7044147	2408372	13303
二　级	Second-grade	190	6560248	60332063	6141456	1105301	12989
三　级	Third-grade	237	4171490	37116424	3525935	202842	8574
四　级	Fourth-grade	1200	16617193	133517428	10894744	1382210	32794
暂　定	Provisional	563	13621547	78106317	8406116	1459276	15209
其　他	Others	509	8691567	33927794	1565423	183671	10175
按营业状况分	**By Operating Condition**						
营　业	Operating	2637	57832702	434972168	37438592	6706503	92264
停　业	Closed	158	700799	3540545	112513	-17187	701
筹　建	In Preparation						
当年关闭	Closed in the Current Year	5	21000	110961	26716	54269	
当年破产	Bankrupted in the Current Year						
其　他	Others	10	205072	590837		-1913	79

5-13 房地产开发企业开发建设情况(2014年)
DEVELOPMENT OF REAL ESTATE ENTERPRISES (2014)

单位：万元、平方米 (10000 yuan,sq.m)

项目	Item	全市合计 Total	#国有企业 State-owned	#三资企业 Foreign Funded	按隶属关系分 By Affiliation 中央 Central	地方 Local
计划总投资	**Total Planned Investment**	**220006115**	**11947645**	**18491887**	**13585455**	**206420660**
开始建设至本年度累计	**Accumulative Investment Completed**					
完成投资	**from Beginning to the End of This Year**	**165790600**	**9165364**	**14058697**	**10766397**	**155024203**
本年完成投资合计	**Investment Completed in the Current Year**	**39113411**	**1463493**	**1954507**	**2123046**	**36990365**
#土地购置费	Land Purchase Cost	15612239	226532	480043	886435	14725804
本年完成投资按用途分	**Grouped by Purpose of Investment**					
住宅	Residential Buildings	19620321	457644	590328	1282022	18338299
#普通住房	Ordinary Residential Houses					
别墅、高档公寓	Villas, High-end Apartments	1637493		333998	18016	1619477
办公楼(写字楼)	Office Buildings	7502347	161053	267662	304493	7197854
商业、非公益用房及其他	Buildings for Commercial Use, Non-public Buildings and Others	11990743	844796	1096517	536531	11454212
本年购置土地面积	**Land Space Purchased in Current Year**	**6732011**	**153997**	**39655**	**287198**	**6444813**

5-14 保障性安居工程建设情况
CONSTRUCTION OF GOVERNMENT-SUBSIDIZED HOUSING PROJECTS

单位：亿元、万平方米 (100 million yuan,10000 sq.m)

项目	Item	2014	2013	2014年为2013年% 2014 as % of 2013
完成投资额	**Investment Completed**	**639.0**	**729.7**	**87.6**
经济适用房	Affordable Houses	36.7	45.5	80.7
限价房	Price-capped Houses	131.9	112.3	117.4
公租(廉租)房	Public Rental (Low-rent) Houses	85.0	77.9	109.1
定向安置房	Targeted Resettlement Houses	385.4	494.0	78.0
施工面积	**Floor Space Under Construction**	**4368.0**	**4857.1**	**89.9**
经济适用房	Affordable Housing	328.0	380.7	86.2
限价房	Price-capped Housing	607.6	599.2	101.4
公租(廉租)房	Public Rental (Low-rent) Housing	381.7	352.2	108.4
定向安置房	Resettlement Housing	3050.8	3525.0	86.5
竣工面积	**Floor Space Completed**	**1201.6**	**1079.2**	**111.3**
经济适用房	Affordable Houses	116.4	115.3	101.0
限价房	Price-capped Houses	217.7	196.2	111.0
公租(廉租)房	Public Rental (Low-rent) Houses	55.7	78.0	71.4
定向安置房	Targeted Resettlement Houses	811.9	689.7	117.7
本年新开工面积	**Floor Space Newly Started in the Year**	**509.5**	**964.9**	**52.8**
经济适用房	Affordable Houses	56.5	57.9	97.6
限价房	Price-capped Houses	177.4	101.2	175.3
公租(廉租)房	Public Rental (Low-rent) Houses	75.9	119.5	63.5
定向安置房	Targeted Resettlement Houses	199.8	686.3	29.1

主要统计指标解释

全社会固定资产投资 包括城镇固定资产投资（含房地产开发投资）和农村固定资产投资。

城镇固定资产投资 是指城镇各种登记注册类型的企业、事业、行政单位及个体户进行的计划总投资在500万元及以上的建设项目投资。镇及镇以上各级政府及主管部门直接领导、管理的建设项目和企事业单位的投资均为城镇固定资产投资。

农村固定资产投资 农村投资统计以投资项目建设地址所在的地域为界定农村投资统计的范围，即农村投资是指各种投资主体建设的建设项目地址在农村区域范围内的、以满足农村居民生产、生活需要为主要目的的各种投资活动。农村固定资产投资包括农户和非农户固定资产投资。

新增固定资产投资 是指报告期内交付使用的固定资产价值。包括本年内建成投入生产或交付使用的工程投资和达到固定资产标准的设备、工具、器具的投资及有关应摊入的费用。属于增加固定资产价值的其他建设费用，应随同交付使用的工程一并计入新增固定资产。

基础设施投资 是指能够为企业提供作为中间投入用于生产的基本需求；能够为消费者提供所需的基本消费服务；能够为社区提供用于改善不利的外部环境的服务等建设的投资，包括固定资产投资中用于市政工程、电信工程、公共设施和水利环保等建设的投资。

上年末结余资金 是指上年资金来源中没有形成固定资产投资额而结余的资金。包括尚未用到工程上去的材料价值、未开始安装的需要安装设备价值及结存的现金和银行存款等。

本年资金来源小计 是指固定资产投资单位在报告期收到的，用于固定资产投资的各种货币资金。包括国家预算内资金、国内贷款、债券、利用外资、自筹资金和其他资金。

国家预算内资金 分为财政拨款和财政安排的贷款两部分。包括中央财政的基本建设基金(分经营性基金和非经营性基金两部分)、专项支出(如煤代油专项等)、收回再贷、贴息资金，财政安排的挖潜改造和新产品试制支出、城建支出、商业部门简易建筑支出、不发达地区发展基金等资金中用于固定资产投资的资金；地方财政中由国家统筹安排的资金等。

国内贷款 是指报告期固定资产投资项目单位向银行及非银行金融机构借入的用于固定资产投资的各种国内借款，包括银行利用自有资金及吸收存款发放的贷款、上级主管部门拨入的国内贷款、国家专项贷款(包括煤代油贷款、劳改煤矿专项贷款等)，地方财政专项资金安排的贷款、国内储备贷款、周转贷款等。

利用外资 是指报告期收到的用于固定资产建造和购置投资的境外资金(包括设备、材料、技术在内)。包括外商直接投资、对外借款(外国政府贷款、国际金融组织贷款、出口信贷、外国银行商业贷款、对外发行债券和股票)及外商其他投资(包括利用外商投资收益在国内进行固定资产再投资活动的资金)。不包括我国自有外汇资金(包括国家外汇、地方外汇、留成外汇、调剂外汇和国内银行自有资金发行的外汇贷款等)。

自筹资金 指固定资产投资单位报告期收到的，由各地区、各部门及企业、事业单位筹集用于固定资产投资的预算外资金，包括中央各部门、各级地方和企业、事业单位的自有资金。

其他资金来源 是指在报告期收到的除以上各种资金之外其他用于固定资产投资的资金。包括社会集资、个人资金、无偿捐赠的资金及其他单位拨入的资金等。

住宅建设投资 是指专供居住使用的房屋，包括职工家属宿舍、职工单身宿舍、学生宿舍和经济适用房等房屋建造的投资，不包括购置的商品住宅。

建筑安装工程投资（建筑安装工作量） 是指各种房屋、建筑物的建造工程，各种设备、装置的安装工程，又称建筑安装工作量。建筑工程投资必须经过兴工动料，通过施工活动才能实现。在安装工程中，不包括被安装设备本身价值。

设备工器具购置 是指建设单位或企、事业单位购置或自制的，达到固定资产标准的设备、工具、器具的价值。

房地产开发投资 指从本年1月1日起至本年最后一天止完成的全部用于房屋建设工程和土地开发工程的投资额，以及公益性建筑和土地购置费等投资。

土地购置费 通过各种方式取得土地使用权而支付的费用（包括开发补偿费）。土地购置费包括:（1）通过“划拨”方式取得的土地使用权所支付的土地补偿费、附着物和青苗补偿费、安置补偿费及土地征收管理费等；竣工后计入新增固定资产。（2）通过“出让”方式（包括协议出让、招、拍、挂出让）取得的土地使用权所支付的费用；竣工后不计入新增固定资产。土地购置费按当期实际发生额计入投资。土地购置费为分期付款的，应分期计入投资。

经济适用住房 指政府提供政策优惠，限定套型面积和销售价格，按照合理标准建设，面向城镇低收入住房困难家庭供应的具有保障性质的政策性住房。

限价商品住房 指政府控制土地出让价格，限定销售价格和套型面积，向城镇中等收入家庭供应的普通商品住房。

公共租赁住房 指政府提供财政投入和政策支持，限定套型建筑面积标准，按照合理标准组织建设，或通过长期租赁等方式筹集，按照当地政府规定的供应标准，面向城镇中等偏下收入住房困难家庭、新就业职工和有稳定职业并在城镇居住一定年限的外来务工人员供应的保障性住房。

廉租住房 指政府提供财政投入和政策支持，限定套型建筑面积标准，按照合理标准组织建设，或通过购买、改建和租赁等方式筹集，按照当地政府规定的供应标准，面向城镇低收入住房困难家庭供应的具有保障性质的住房。

房屋施工面积 是指报告期内施工的全部房屋建筑面积。包括本期新开工的面积和上年开工跨入本期继续施工房屋面积，以及上期已停建在本期恢复施工的房屋面积。本期竣工和本期施工后又停建、缓建的房屋面积仍包括在施工面积中，多层建筑应填各层建筑面积之和。

房屋竣工面积 是指报告期内房屋建筑按照设计要求已全部完工，达到住人和使用条件，经验收鉴定合格（或达到竣工验收标准），可正式移交使用的各栋房屋建筑面积的总和。

待售面积 指报告期末已竣工的可供销售或出租的商品房屋建筑面积中，尚未销售或出租的商品房屋建筑面积，包括以前年度竣工和本期竣工的房屋面积，但不包括报告期已竣工的拆迁还建，统建代建，公共配套建筑、房地产公司自用及周转房等不可销售或出租的房屋面积。

Explanatory Notes on Main Statistical Indicators

Total Investment in Fixed Assets includes urban investment in fixed assets (including the investment in real estate development) and rural investment in fixed assets.

Investment in Urban Fixed Assets refers to investment in construction projects with a total planned investment over RMB 5,000,000 (inclusive) by enterprises with various types of registration, institutions, administrative units and individuals in urban areas. The investment in construction projects under the direct leadership and management of government agencies at and above town levels and investment by enterprises and public institutions are also calculated in investment in urban fixed assets.

Investment in Rural Fixed Assets refers to all investment activities that are conducted in rural areas to meet the production and living needs of the rural residents. Investment in rural fixed assets consists of investment in fixed assets by rural and non-rural households.

Incremental Fixed Assets Investment means the value of fixed assets put into use in the reporting period, including investment in projects completed and put into use within the year, and investment in equipment, tools and appliances that reach the standard of fixed assets, together with expenses incurred in these activities. Other construction costs adding value to fixed assets shall be calculated in the incremental fixed assets together with the projects put into use.

Infrastructure Investment refers to investment that provides intermediate inputs for enterprise to meet their basic production needs, provides consumers with basic consumer services needed, or provides communities with services for improving external environment, which includes the investment in municipal projects, telecom projects, public facilities, water conservancy and environmental protection.

Surplus Funds by the Year End of the Previous Year refers to the fund in the previous year that was not included in the investment in fixed assets, including the value of materials not yet used for projects, value of equipment to be installed, and balance of cash and bank deposits.

Subtotal of Funds at Current Year refers to monetary capital received by investors that was used for investment in fixed assets, including funds from state budgetary funds, domestic loans, bonds, foreign investment, self-raised funds and other funds.

State Budgets consists of budgetary appropriation and government loans. More specifically, it consists of infrastructure fund from the central government (operating fund and non-operating fund), earmarked expenditures (e.g. expenditures on replacing oil with coal), refinancing, discount interest funds, expenditures on technical updates, transformation and new products promotion, expenses on urban construction, expenses on temporary construction from business departments, development funds for less developed areas, as well as local budgetary funds transferred from the central budget.

Domestic Loans refer to loans of various forms borrowed by fixed assets investment project entities from banks and non-bank financial institutions for the purpose of investment in fixed assets during the reporting period, including loans issued by banks from their equity funds and deposits, loans appropriated by higher authorities, special loans allocated by the central government (including loans for replacing oil with coal, and special loans for labor camp coal mines), loans arranged by local government from special funds, domestic reserve loans and revolving loans.

Foreign Investment refers to foreign funds received during the reporting period for the investment in construction and purchase of fixed assets (including equipment, materials and technologies), including foreign direct investment, foreign loans (loans from foreign governments and international financial institutions, export credit, commercial loans from foreign banks, issued bonds and stocks overseas), and other foreign investments (including funds for domestic re-investment in fixed assets by earnings from foreign investment). It does not include foreign exchanges owned by China (foreign exchanges owned by the central and local governments, foreign exchanges retained, foreign exchange swap, loans in foreign exchanges issued by the domestic banks with their own funds, etc.).

Self-raised Funds refer to non-budgetary funds for investment in fixed assets received during the reporting period by different regions, departments, enterprises and public institutions, including self-owned funds of central departments, local authorities, enterprises and public institutions.

Other Funds refer to funds for investment in fixed assets received from sources other than those listed above, including social funds, personal funds, donated funds and funds transferred from other institutions.

Investment in Construction of Residential Buildings refer to the investment in houses specially used for residence, including employee family's dormitories, single employees' dormitories, student dormitories, and affordable houses, excluding purchased commercial residences.

Construction and Installation Investment (Workload of Construction and Installation) refers to the investment in construction projects of various houses and buildings, and installation projects of various equipment and devices, also known as the workload of construction and installation. It can only be realized through construction work and consumption of materials. For installation projects, the value of equipment installed is not included.

Purchase of Equipment, Tools and Devices refers to the

value of equipment, tools and devices purchased or made by construction companies, enterprises or public institutions, which reach the specified amount of fixed assets.

Real Estate Development Investment refers to all investment used for housing projects and land development projects, together with public welfare buildings and land purchase costs spent from January 1st to the last day of the year.

Land Purchase Cost refers to expenses on acquiring the land use right, including development compensation. It includes: (1) Expenses on land use right by allocation, including land compensation fees, compensation fees for its attached objects and crops; after completion, these expanses will be included in incremental fixed assets. (2) Expenses on land use right by transfer, including fees for agreement transfer, bid invitation, auction and listing; after completion, these expanses will not be included in incremental fixed assets. Land purchase expense shall be accounted according to actual amount paid. If paid by installment, it should be included in investment by stages.

Affordable Houses refer to government-subsidized houses that are supplied to urban low-income households and built in line with reasonable standards, limited size and fixed pricing.

Price-capped Houses refer to ordinary commercial houses with limited size and fixed pricing that are supplied to middle-income urban households, and their land transfer price is controlled by the government.

Public Rental Houses refer to government-subsidized houses that are built in line with reasonable standards and limited size, and can be rented by lower middle-income urban households with housing difficulties, new employees and migrant workers with stable jobs and have lived in the urban area for a certain period.

Low-rent Houses refer to government-subsidized houses that are built in line with reasonable standards and limited size, with funds raised by purchasing, reconstruction or leasing, and can be rented by low-income urban households with housing difficulties.

Floor Space of Buildings under Construction refers to the total floor space of all houses and buildings under construction during the reference period, including floor space of newly started buildings in current period, floor space of construction extended from the previous period to the current period, and floor space of construction suspended during the previous period and resumed in the current period. Floor space of construction completed in the current period, and floor space of construction started and then suspended in the current period are also included in the floor space under construction. For multi-storey buildings, the sum of floor space of all floors shall be calculated.

Floor Space of Buildings Completed refers to the total floor space of all houses and buildings fully completed as required in the design plan during the reference period, which have been examined as qualified for living and use, and can be handed over and put into use.

Floor Space of Vacant Commercial Buildings refers to total floor space of commercial buildings for sale or for renting by the end of the reference period. It consists of the floor space of completed buildings in previous years and in the current year, but does not include relocated houses or buildings of unified construction or agent contract, as well as houses not for sale or renting such as public facilities, houses used by real estate companies and temporary houses.

06

财政与税收
GOVERNMENT FINANCE AND REVENUES

简要说明

一、本章资料的主要内容

本章资料包括北京市财政收支情况，北京市国税、地税税收(费)收入情况。其中财政收支包括历年财政收入、支出及相当于地区生产总值比例等情况；税收（费）收入包括国税、地税税收（费）收入分组情况。

二、本章资料的数据来源

本章财政收支数据由北京市财政局提供；税收（费）数据由北京市国家税务局、北京市地方税务局提供。

Brief Introduction

I. Main Content

Statistics in this chapter include fiscal revenues and expenditures, and state and local tax revenues of Beijing Municipality. Figures of fiscal revenues and expenditures include fiscal revenues, expenditures and their proportions to GDP of Beijing in previous years; figures of tax revenues include the grouped figures of state and local tax revenues.

II. Source of Data

Data of fiscal revenues and expenditures are from Beijing Municipal Bureau of Finance; data of tax revenues are from Beijing Municipal Bureau of State Tax and Beijing Municipal Bureau of Local Tax.

6-1 地方财政收支(1978-2014年)
LOCAL FISCAL REVENUE AND EXPENDITURE (1978-2014)

单位：亿元 (100 million yuan)

年 份 Year	地方财政收入 Local Financial Revenue	#地方公共财政预算收入 Local Public Budgetary Revenue	税收收入 Tax Revenue	#增值税 Value-added Tax	#营业税 Operation Tax	#个人所得税 Individual Income Tax	#企业所得税 Company Income Tax	#城市维护建设税 Urban Maintenance and Construction Tax	非税收入 Non-tax Revenue	#政府性基金预算收入 Governmental Fund Budgetary Revenue
1978	50.46		18.25							
1979	47.75		19.41							
1980	51.29		21.22							
1981-1985	**234.27**		**191.96**	**8.34**	**11.46**	**0.61**	**43.77**	**2.16**		
1981	49.12		24.22			0.02	1.76			
1982	47.25		25.81	0.05		0.05	1.43			
1983	39.84		38.03	1.30		0.07	11.70			
1984	45.62		43.91	2.20	1.23	0.13	12.70			
1985	52.44		59.99	4.79	10.23	0.34	16.18	2.16		
1986-1990	**337.13**		**397.96**	**65.02**	**103.00**	**7.29**	**116.89**	**16.67**		
1986	60.34		60.83	7.61	13.19	0.97	20.46	2.51		
1987	63.62		67.77	9.09	15.42	1.54	21.87	2.70		
1988	68.11		84.04	15.10	21.11	1.23	27.70	3.37		
1989	71.05		91.09	16.75	25.33	1.53	24.31	3.74		
1990	74.01		94.23	16.47	27.95	2.02	22.55	4.35		
1991-1995	**456.48**		**643.24**	**136.88**	**228.80**	**35.46**	**105.24**	**34.07**		
1991	77.02		100.58	19.53	30.78	2.56	20.59	4.77		
1992	80.25		110.54	22.29	35.86	3.15	19.08	5.13		
1993	84.10		148.19	42.30	52.07	4.30	14.20	6.57		
1994	99.85		120.53	25.54	45.63	9.24	21.70	7.18		
1995	115.26		163.40	27.22	64.46	16.21	29.67	10.42		
1996-2000	**1341.65**		**1397.26**	**185.46**	**570.06**	**190.18**	**223.71**	**70.84**		
1996	150.90		201.32	29.53	81.61	22.67	37.22	11.36		
1997	209.91	182.32	235.82	32.67	97.54	28.76	41.05	12.74	-53.50	27.59
1998	262.01	229.45	272.23	37.58	113.00	36.49	41.42	14.12	-42.78	32.56
1999	320.44	281.37	315.10	39.72	128.86	45.88	45.99	15.27	-33.74	39.07
2000	398.39	345.00	372.79	45.96	149.05	56.38	58.03	17.35	-27.79	53.39
2001-2005	**3611.96**	**3244.40**	**3216.46**	**367.43**	**1389.75**	**355.88**	**566.23**	**147.84**	**27.94**	**367.57**
2001	507.68	454.17	475.00	59.00	181.35	79.52	86.07	20.53	-20.83	53.51
2002	600.96	533.99	539.87	66.69	227.79	61.29	100.00	24.91	-5.88	66.97
2003	665.94	592.54	588.96	75.26	263.69	57.21	93.70	28.85	3.58	73.40
2004	830.03	744.49	726.50	68.88	333.16	73.34	121.70	34.72	17.99	85.55
2005	1007.35	919.21	886.13	97.60	383.76	84.52	164.76	38.83	33.08	88.14
2006-2010	**11889.54**	**8827.85**	**8453.62**	**800.72**	**3321.83**	**801.97**	**1965.28**	**317.03**	**374.23**	**3061.69**
2006	1235.78	1117.15	1076.82	117.80	460.99	102.28	213.86	45.17	40.33	118.63
2007	1882.04	1492.64	1435.67	134.84	601.06	135.20	309.34	56.63	56.97	389.40
2008	2282.04	1837.32	1775.58	158.34	651.78	171.33	497.52	63.95	61.75	444.71
2009	2678.77	2026.81	1913.97	179.73	752.60	177.84	430.42	71.28	112.84	651.96
2010	3810.91	2353.93	2251.59	210.01	855.40	215.33	513.09	80.00	102.34	1456.98
2011	4359.10	3006.28	2854.63	237.76	1071.51	272.90	683.71	145.65	151.65	1352.82
2012	4573.72	3314.93	3124.75	314.00	1152.74	281.49	752.47	160.34	190.18	1197.92
2013	5566.08	3661.11	3514.52	574.89	1034.79	333.84	802.12	177.41	146.59	1841.76
2014	7214.54	4027.16	3861.29	646.69	1068.64	383.52	915.84	187.24	165.87	3122.91

注：1. 地方财政收支数为决算数。
2. 2011年开始，原指标“地方一般预算收入”和“地方一般预算支出”更名为“地方公共财政预算收入”和“地方公共财政预算支出”(下同)。
3. 自2012年开始，地方财政收支包含三部分内容，即地方财政公共预算收支、政府性基金预算收支和国有资本经营预算收支(下同)，历史数据仅包含前两部分内容。

资料来源：北京市财政局。

Note: a) Local government revenue and expenditures are final accounts.
b) Since 2011, "local general budgetary revenue" and "local general budgetary expenditure" are renamed as "local public budgetary revenue" and "local public budgetary expenditure" (the same below).
c) Since 2012, local financial revenue has included three parts: local public budgetary financial revenue and expenditures, governmental fund budgetary revenue and expenditures and budgetary revenue and expenditures of state-owned capital operation(the same below). Historical data only includes the first two parts.

Source: Beijing Municipal Bureau of Finance.

6-1 续表

单位：亿元

年份 Year	地方财政支出 Local Government Expenditures	#地方公共财政预算支出 Local Public Budgetary Expenditures	#一般公共服务 General Public Service	#教育 Education	#科学技术 Science and Technology	#文化体育与传媒 Culture, Sports and Media	#社会保障和就业 Social Security and Employment
1978	20.38						
1979	20.06						
1980	14.87						
1981-1985	**111.40**						
1981	14.85						
1982	16.80						
1983	19.61						
1984	27.15						
1985	32.99						
1986-1990	**272.89**						
1986	44.27						
1987	49.67						
1988	52.93						
1989	59.50						
1990	66.52						
1991-1995	**473.64**						
1991	67.98						
1992	71.74						
1993	80.99						
1994	98.53						
1995	154.40						
1996-2000	**1646.07**						
1996	187.45						
1997	262.20	236.39					
1998	307.55	280.68					
1999	398.53	355.19					
2000	490.34	443.00					
2001-2005	**4219.74**	**3878.85**					
2001	614.92	559.11					
2002	683.98	628.35					
2003	809.39	734.80					
2004	974.17	898.28					
2005	1137.28	1058.31					
2006-2010	**12765.99**	**9942.31**	**987.56**	**1604.40**	**578.30**	**309.36**	**1048.02**
2006	1411.58	1296.84	159.95	209.21	70.14	40.51	149.22
2007	2067.65	1649.50	179.56	263.00	90.74	53.62	179.28
2008	2400.93	1959.29	196.27	316.30	112.19	61.11	209.33
2009	2820.86	2319.37	212.21	365.67	126.31	74.75	234.29
2010	4064.97	2717.32	239.57	450.22	178.92	79.36	275.90
2011	4574.94	3245.23	261.38	520.08	183.07	87.01	354.88
2012	4866.43	3685.31	286.57	628.65	199.94	141.37	424.31
2013	6039.42	4173.66	297.12	681.18	234.67	154.71	469.13
2014	7147.75	4524.67	272.23	742.05	282.71	163.90	509.01

6-1 continued

(100 million yuan)

#医疗卫生与计划生育 Healthcare	#节能环保 Energy Conservation and Environmental Protection	#交通运输 Transportation	#城乡社区事务 Urban and Rural Community Affairs	#农林水 Agriculture, Forestry and Water Conservancy	#政府性基金预算支出 Governmental Fund Budgetary Expenditure
718.40	**199.77**	**422.53**	**1182.65**	**613.55**	**2823.69**
100.95	20.14	7.05	153.26	88.62	114.74
118.95	29.27	33.09	187.43	102.51	418.15
145.05	35.47	80.35	199.84	121.77	441.64
166.63	54.04	147.07	347.82	142.01	501.50
186.82	60.85	154.99	294.30	158.64	1347.65
225.49	94.51	199.12	339.27	187.34	1329.71
256.06	113.54	243.76	430.76	222.69	1118.45
276.13	138.17	231.79	510.67	297.62	1798.81
322.29	213.36	214.55	567.40	343.67	2559.09

6-2 地方财政收支增长速度及相当于地区生产总值比例(1978-2014年)
GROWTH RATE OF LOCAL GOVERNMENT REVENUE AND EXPENDITURES AND THEIR SHARE IN GDP (1978-2014)

单位：% (%)

年 份 Year	增长速度(上年=100) Growth Rate (Previous Year=100)				相当于地区生产总值比例 Proportion in GDP			
	地方财政收入 Local Financial Revenue	#地方公共财政预算收入 Local Public Budgetary Revenue	地方财政支出 Local Financial Expenditures	#地方公共财政预算支出 Local Public Budgetary Expenditures	地方财政收入 Local Government Revenue	#地方公共财政预算收入 Local Public Budgetary Revenue	地方财政支出 Local Government Expenditures	#地方公共财政预算支出 Local Public Budgetary Expenditures
1978	18.0		27.6		46.4		18.7	
1979	-5.4		-1.6		39.8		16.7	
1980	7.4		-25.9		36.9		10.7	
1981-1985					**24.6**		**11.7**	
1981	-4.2		-0.1		35.3		10.7	
1982	-3.8		13.1		30.5		10.8	
1983	-15.7		16.7		21.8		10.7	
1984	14.5		38.4		21.1		12.5	
1985	14.9		21.5		20.4		12.8	
1986-1990					**17.0**		**13.8**	
1986	15.1		34.2		21.2		15.5	
1987	5.4		12.2		19.5		15.2	
1988	7.1		6.6		16.6		12.9	
1989	4.3		12.4		15.6		13.0	
1990	4.2		11.8		14.8		13.3	
1991-1995					**9.4**		**9.8**	
1991	4.1		2.2		12.9		11.4	
1992	4.2		5.5		11.3		10.1	
1993	4.8		12.9		9.5		9.1	
1994	9.9		21.7		8.7		8.6	
1995	21.8		56.7		7.6		10.2	
1996-2000					**11.1**		**13.6**	
1996	30.9		21.4		8.4		10.5	
1997	25.5		39.9		10.1	8.8	12.6	11.4
1998	24.8	20.0	17.4	18.7	11.0	9.7	12.9	11.8
1999	22.3	22.6	29.6	26.5	12.0	10.5	14.9	13.3
2000	24.3	22.7	23.0	24.7	12.6	10.9	15.5	14.0
2001-2005					**13.9**	**12.5**	**16.2**	**14.9**
2001	27.4	31.6	25.4	26.2	13.7	12.2	16.6	15.1
2002	25.8	25.9	11.2	12.4	13.9	12.4	15.9	14.6
2003	17.2	18.2	18.3	16.9	13.3	11.8	16.2	14.7
2004	28.3	29.7	20.4	22.3	13.8	12.3	16.1	14.9
2005	21.4	23.5	16.7	17.8	14.5	13.2	16.3	15.2
2006-2010					**21.5**	**16.0**	**23.1**	**18.0**
2006	22.7	21.5	24.1	22.5	15.2	13.8	17.4	16.0
2007	52.3	33.6	46.5	27.2	19.1	15.2	21.0	16.8
2008	21.3	23.1	16.1	18.8	20.5	16.5	21.6	17.6
2009	17.4	10.3	17.5	18.4	22.0	16.7	23.2	19.1
2010	42.3	16.1	44.1	17.2	27.0	16.7	28.8	19.3
2011	14.4	27.7	12.5	19.4	26.8	18.5	28.2	20.0
2012	4.9	10.3	6.4	13.6	25.6	18.5	27.2	20.6
2013	21.7	10.4	24.1	13.3	28.5	18.8	31.0	21.4
2014	29.6	10.0	18.4	8.4	33.8	18.9	33.5	21.2

注：2002-2004年地方财政收入增长速度按可比口径计算。
资料来源：北京市财政局。
Note: The growth rate of local government revenue in 2002-2004 is calculated at comparable figures.
Source: Beijing Municipal Bureau of Finance.

6-3 地方财政收入
LOCAL FINANCIAL REVENUE

项　目	Item	绝对数(万元) Absolute Value (10000 yuan) 2014	2013	2014年为2013年% 2014 as % of 2013	构　成(%) Composition (%) 2014	2013
合　计	**Total**	**72145371**	**55660805**	**129.6**	**100.0**	**100.0**
地方公共财政预算收入	**Local Public Budgetary Revenue**	**40271609**	**36611097**	**110.0**	**55.8**	**65.8**
#增值税	Value-added Tax	6466927	5748900	112.5	9.0	10.3
营业税	Business Tax	10686441	10347918	103.3	14.8	18.6
个人所得税	Personal Income Tax	3835236	3338449	114.9	5.3	6.0
城市维护建设税	Urban Maintenance and Construction Tax	1872354	1774052	105.5	2.6	3.2
固定资产投资方向调节税	Tax on the Adjustment of the Investment in the Fixed Assets					
耕地占用税	Arable Land Occupation Tax	46892	89964	52.1	0.1	0.2
企业所得税	Company Income Tax	9158440	8021152	114.2	12.7	14.4
国有资本经营收入	Operation Income of State-owned Assets	-947864	-602398			
罚没收入	Income of Fines and Confiscations	386713	344880	112.1	0.5	0.6
行政事业性收费收入	Administrative Fees	538976	416928	129.3	0.7	0.7
政府性基金预算收入	**Government Fund Budgetary Revenue**	**31229135**	**18417585**	**169.6**	**43.3**	**33.1**
国有资本经营预算收入	**Budgetary Revenue of State-owned Capital Operation**	**644627**	**632123**	**102.0**	**0.9**	**1.1**

资料来源：北京市财政局。
Source: Beijing Finance Bureau.

6-4 地方财政支出
LOCAL FINANCIAL EXPENDITURE

项　目	Item	绝对数(万元) Absolute Value (10000 yuan) 2014	2013	2014年为2013年% 2014 as % of 2013	构　成(%) Composition (%) 2014	2013
合　计	**Total**	**71477458**	**60394197**	**118.4**	**100.0**	**100.0**
地方公共财政预算支出	**Local Public Budgetary Expenditures**	**45246690**	**41736563**	**108.4**	**63.3**	**69.1**
#一般公共服务	General Public Service	2722329	2971203	91.6	3.8	4.9
教　育	Education	7420541	6811775	108.9	10.4	11.3
科学技术	Science and Technology	2827117	2346742	120.5	4.0	3.9
文化体育与传媒	Culture, Sports and Media	1639031	1547082	105.9	2.3	2.6
社会保障和就业	Social Security and Employment	5090079	4691317	108.5	7.1	7.8
医疗卫生与计划生育	Healthcare	3222919	2761274	116.7	4.5	4.6
节能环保	Energy Conservation and Environmental Protection	2133553	1381672	154.4	3.0	2.3
交通运输	Transportation	2145513	2317948	92.6	3.0	3.8
城乡社区事务	Urban and Rural Community Affairs	5673982	5106691	111.1	7.9	8.5
农林水事务	Agriculture, Forestry and Water Conservancy	3436680	2976191	115.5	4.8	4.9
政府性基金支出合计	**Total Expenditures of Governmental Funds**	**25590902**	**17988141**	**142.3**	**35.8**	**29.8**
国有资本经营预算支出	**Budgetary Expenditure of State-owned Capital Operation**	**639866**	**669493**	**95.6**	**0.9**	**1.1**

资料来源：北京市财政局。
Source: Beijing Municipal Bureau of Finance.

6-5 地税税费收入分税种、分行业完成情况(2007-2014年)
LOCAL TAX REVENUE BY CATEGORY AND INDUSTRY (2007-2014)

单位: 亿元 (100 million yuan)

项目	Item	2007	2008	2009	2010	2011	2012	2013	2014
地税税费收入	**Local Tax Revenue**	**1366.14**	**1578.02**	**1771.87**	**2104.89**	**2666.6**	**2865.25**	**3061.60**	**3387.80**
按税种分	**By Category**								
#营业税	Business Tax	601.06	651.78	749.90	855.40	1071.51	1152.74	1032.35	1067.92
企业所得税	Coporate Income Tax	150.64	161.06	142.24	173.18	210.52	221.02	258.07	333.91
个人所得税	Personal Income Tax	308.24	409.62	436.49	536.27	681.27	703.48	834.47	958.79
按行业分	**By Sector**								
第一产业	Primary Industry	1.66	2.05	2.57	3.67	3.90	4.94	4.98	7.74
第二产业	Secondary Industry	198.90	216.00	209.91	235.20	303.14	326.20	348.54	388.51
#制造业	Manufacturing	74.52	94.87	88.62	101.75	138.36	150.45	160.70	179.36
电力、燃气及水的生产和供应业	Production and Distribution of Electricity, Gas and Water	12.00	14.96	15.46	15.69	19.37	21.18	25.20	28.94
建筑业	Construction	108.51	97.19	98.64	109.88	134.37	144.65	153.99	171.73
第三产业	Tertiary Industry	1165.57	1359.97	1559.39	1866.00	2359.58	2534.11	2708.14	2991.56
#交通、运输、仓储及邮政业	Transport, Storage and Post	37.78	45.90	46.43	51.41	63.95	60.58	38.14	40.47
信息传输、计算机服务和软件业	Information Transmission, Computer Servicesand Software	64.63	82.03	85.87	98.02	125.48	132.76	123.65	141.82
批发和零售业	Wholesale and Retail Trade	66.80	85.20	89.24	111.40	159.35	169.30	188.84	206.15
金融业	Finance	142.17	211.13	228.57	276.40	366.35	446.67	477.99	599.52
房地产业	Real Estate	317.19	282.32	371.28	437.40	520.36	525.44	659.25	734.16

资料来源：北京市地方税务局。
Source: Beijing Municipal Bureau of Local Taxation.

6-6 国税税收收入分税种、分行业完成情况(2007-2014年)
STATE TAX REVENUE BY CATEGORY AND INDUSTRY (2007-2014)

单位: 亿元 (100 million yuan)

项目	Item	2007	2008	2009	2010	2011	2012	2013	2014
国税税收收入	**State Tax Revenue**	**3030.6**	**3861.7**	**4561.1**	**4346.8**	**5332.5**	**6339.4**	**7470.9**	**8325.2**
按税种分	**By Category**								
#增值税	Value-added Tax	574.1	652.4	749.7	868.3	961.7	1096.0	1456.3	1659.8
营业税	Business Tax	196.6	225.3	160.6	145.4	161.3	191.3	203.7	80.7
企业所得税	Corporate Income Tax	1874.9	2526.3	3116.5	2642.0	3506.5	3609.4	5024.4	5757.3
按行业分	**By Sector**								
第一产业	Primary Industry	0.4	1.0	4.0	5.8	0.7	0.3	2.6	0.9
第二产业	Secondary Industry	684.8	602.6	627.8	779.1	881.1	843.8	1069.3	1159.4
#制造业	Manufacturing	402.4	419.3	563.6	623.2	709.2	764.6	832.0	889.5
电力、燃气及水的生产和供应业	Production and Distribution of Electricity, Gas and Water	76.4	124.1	84.3	105.2	103.5	131.0	261.4	194.1
建筑业	Construction	7.4	14.6	20.4	30.1	45.3	54.8	57.0	50.9
第三产业	Tertiary Industry	2345.4	3258.1	3929.3	3561.9	4450.8	5495.3	6399.0	7164.8
#交通、运输、仓储及邮政业	Transport, Storage and Post	151.6	173.2	134.2	157.9	209.2	212.1	245.1	242.6
信息传输、计算机服务和软件业	Information Transmission, Computer Services and Software	116.6	126.2	208.4	30.8	105.9	245.9	373.2	296.2
批发和零售业	Wholesale and Retail Trade	719.2	842.8	820.5	1081.6	1410.8	1314.6	1451.0	1474.0
金融业	Finance	1090.5	1768.6	2396.0	1831.2	2158.0	3034.0	3500.2	4153.2
房地产业	Real Estate	67.3	106.3	77.0	107.6	122.3	111.6	157.0	156.9

资料来源：北京市国家税务局。
Source: Beijing Municipal Bureau of State Taxation.

主要统计指标解释

财政部分

地方财政收入 指国家财政参与社会产品分配所得的收入，是实现国家职能的财力保证。包括地方公共财政预算收入、政府性基金预算收入和国有资本经营预算收入。

地方公共财政预算收入 是通过一定的形式和程序，由各级财政部门组织并纳入预算管理的各项收入。

政府性基金预算收入 是按规定收取，转入或通过当年财政安排，由财政管理并具有指定用途的政府性基金预算收入等。

国有资本经营预算 是指国家以所有者身份取得国有资本收益，并对所得收益进行分配而发生的各项收支预算，是政府预算的重要组成部分。

税收收入 包括增值税、营业税、企业所得税、个人所得税、资源税、城市维护建设税、房产税、印花税、城镇土地使用税、土地增值税、车船税、耕地占用税、契税等。

非税收收入 包括专项收入、行政事业性收费、罚没收入和其他收入。

地方财政支出 是以国家为主体，以财政的事权为依据进行的一种财政资金分配活动，集中反映了国家的职能活动范围及其所发生的耗费，包括地方公共财政预算支出和基金预算支出。

地方公共财政预算支出 是各级财政部门对集中的一般预算收入有计划地分配和使用而安排的支出。

政府性基金预算支出 是各级财政部门用基金预算收入安排的支出。

一般公共服务支出 指政府提供基本公共管理与服务的支出，包括人大事务、政协事务、政府办公厅（室）及相关机构事务、发展与改革事务、统计信息事务、财政事务、税收事务、审计事务、海关事务、人力资源事务、纪检监察事务、人口与计划生育事务、 商贸事务、知识产权事务、工商行政管理事务、国土资源事务、 海洋管理事务、 测绘事务、地震事务、气象事务、民族事务、宗教事务、港澳台侨事务、档案事务、共产党事务、民主党派事务及工商联事务、群众团体事务、彩票事务等。

教育支出 指政府教育事务支出，包括教育行政管理、学前教育、小学教育、初中教育、普通高中教育、普通高等教育、初等职业教育、中专教育、技校教育、职业高中教育、高等职业教育、广播电视教育、留学生教育、特殊教育、干部继续教育、教育机关服务等。

科学技术支出 指用于科学技术方面的支出，包括科学技术管理事务、基础研究、应用研究、技术研究与开发、科技条件与服务、社会科学、科学技术普及、科技交流与合作等。

文化教育与传媒支出 指政府在文化、文物、体育、广播影视、新闻出版等方面的支出。

社会保障和就业支出 指政府在社会保障与就业方面的支出，包括社会保障和就业管理事务、民政管理事务、财政对社会保险基金的补助、补充全国社会保障基金、行政事业单位离退休、企业改革补助、就业补助、抚恤、退役安置、社会福利、残疾人事业、城市居民最低生活保障、其他城镇社会救济、农村社会救济、自然灾害生活救助、红十字事务等。

医疗卫生与计划生育支出 指政府医疗卫生与计划生育管理方面的支出。

节能环保支出 指政府环境保护支出，包括环境保护管理事务支出、环境监测与监察支出、污染治理支出、自然生态保护支出、天然林保护工程支出、退耕还林支出、风沙荒漠治理支出、退牧还草支出、已垦草原退耕还草、能源节约利用、污染减排、可再生能源和资源综合利用等支出。

交通运输支出 指政府交通运输和邮政业方面的支出，包括公路运输支出、水路运输支出、铁路运输支出、民用航空运输支出、邮政业支出等。

城乡社区事务支出 指政府城乡社区事务支出，包括城乡社区管理事务支出、城乡社区规划与管理支出、城乡社区公共设施支出、城乡社区住宅支出、城乡社区环境卫生支出、建设市场管理与监督支出等。

农林水事务支出 指政府农林水事务支出，包括农业支出、林业支出、水利支出、扶贫支出、农业综合开发支出等。

税收部分

税费收入 指由各级地方税务局征缴的各项税收收入和罚没收入。包括营业税、企业所得税、个人所得税、资源税、房产税、契税、城市维护建设税等。

税收收入 指由各级国家税务局征缴的各项税收收入。包括增值税、消费税、营业税、企业所得税、个人所得税、城市维护建设税等。

营业税 是对在中华人民共和国境内提供应税劳务、转让无形资产或者销售不动产的单位和个人，就其取得营业额征收的一种税。

企业所得税 是对中国境内全部企业的生产经营所得和其他所得征收的一种税。

增值税 指以商品或劳务销售额为计税依据并实行扣除已征税款制度的一种流转税。

个人所得税 是对个人（自然人）取得的各项应税所得征收的一种税。

Explanatory Notes on Main Statistical Indicators

Finance

Local Financial Revenue refers to the revenue for the national finance through participating in the distribution of social products. It is the financial guarantee to ensure the functions and powers of the government. The local financial revenue includes local public budgetary revenue, governmental fund budgetary revenue and budget of state-owned capital operation.

Local Public Budgetary Revenue refers to the revenue organized by finance authorities at all levels in certain form and through certain procedures and involved in budgetary management.

Governmental Fund Budgetary Revenue refers to governmental fund budgetary revenues collected, transferred or allocated by government finance in the current year in accordance with regulations, and regulated by government finance and used for specific purpose.

Budget of State-owned Capital Operation refers to the state-owned capital income of the country as the owner and all kinds of income and expenditure budgets resulted from the allocation of the income. It is an important part of governmental budget.

Tax Revenue includes value-added tax, business tax, corporate income tax, individual income tax, resource tax, urban maintenance and construction tax, house property tax, stamp tax, urban land use tax, land appreciation tax, tax on vehicles and boat operation, farm land occupation tax, deed tax, etc.

Non-tax Revenue includes special program receipts, charge of administrative and institutional units, income of fines and confiscation, and other non-tax revenues.

Local Government Expenditure refers to the allocation of financial funds by the state based on the financial administration, which demonstrates the scope of government functioning and the expenditures incurred. It includes local public budgetary expenditure and fund budgetary expenditure.

Local Public Budgetary Expenditure refers to the expenditure arranged by finance authorities at all levels from the general budgetary revenue according to the planned distribution .

Governmental Fund Budgetary Expenditure refers to the expenditure arranged by finance authorities at all levels according to the fund budget revenue.

Expenditure for General Public Services refers to the spending on the basic public management and services provided by the government, including the expenses on affairs of Beijing Municipal People's Congress, CPC Beijing Municipal Committee, General Office of Beijing Municipal Government and relative institutions, development and reform, statistical information, finance, taxation, audit, customs, human resources, discipline inspection and supervision, population and family planning, commerce and trade, intellectual property, administration for industry and commerce, land and resources, oceanic administration, surveying and mapping, earthquake, weather, ethnics, religions, Hong Kong, Macao, Taiwan, and Overseas Chinese, archive administration, Chinese Communist Party, democratic parties, federation of industry and commerce, mass organizations, and lottery, etc.

Expenditure for Education refers to the spending of government on education, including the expenses on the administration of education, pre-school education, primary education, junior high school education, senior high school education, general higher education, primary vocational education, secondary vocational education, technical school education, vocational senior high school education and higher vocational education, radio and television education, overseas student education, special education, continuing education for management personnel, and services for education authorities, etc.

Expenditure for Science and Technology refers to the spending on science and technology (S&T), including the expense on the administration of S&T, basic research, applied research, research and development, conditions and services of S&T, popularization of social science and S&T, exchanges and cooperation of S&T, etc.

Expenditure for Cultural Education and Media refers to the spending on culture, cultural relics, sports, radio, films, television, press and publication, etc.

Expenditure for Social Security and Employment refers to the spending on social security and employment, including the expenses on social security and employment administration affairs, civil affairs, budgetary subsidy on the social insurance funds, subsidy on National Social Security Fund, subsidy on retirees of administrative and institutional units, subsidy on enterprise reform, subsidy on employment, pension, reemployment of ex-serviceman, social welfare, the handicapped undertakings, subsistence allowances for urban residents, other urban social relief, rural social relief, relief for natural disasters, affairs of Red Cross, etc.

Expenditure for Health Care and Family Planning refers to the spending of government on health care and family planning.

Expenditure for Energy Conservation and Environmental Protection refers to the spending of government on environmental protection, including the expenses on administration of environmental protection, environment monitoring and supervision, pollution control, natural and ecological protection, projects of natural forest protection, reforestation, control of sand storms, returning pasture and grazing land to grassland, energy conservation and utilization, emission reduction, comprehensive utilization of renewable energy and resources, etc.

Expenditure for Transportation refers to the spending of government on transportation and postal services, including the expenses on highway transportation, waterway transportation, railway transportation, civil aviation transportation and postal services, etc.

Expenditure for Urban and Rural Community Affairs refers to the spending of government on urban and rural community affairs, including the expenses on administration of urban and rural communities, planning and management of urban and rural communities, public facilities in urban and rural communities, residential houses in urban and rural communities, sanitation in urban and rural communities, management and supervision of construction markets, etc.

Expenditure for Agriculture, Forestry and Water Conservancy Affairs refers to the spending of government on agriculture affairs, forestry affairs, water conservancy affairs, poverty alleviation and comprehensive agricultural development, etc.

Taxes

Local Tax Revenue refers to the revenue of taxes, fines and confiscations levied and collected by local tax bureaus at all levels, including business tax, corporate income tax, personal income tax, resource tax, house property tax, deed tax, urban maintenance and construction tax, etc.

State Tax Revenue refers to the revenue of taxes levied and collected by state tax bureaus at all levels, including value-added tax, excise tax, business tax, corporate income tax, individual income tax, urban maintenance and construction tax, etc.

Business Tax is a kind of tax levied against the business income of entities and individuals providing taxable labor services, transferring intangible assets or selling real estate within the territory of PRC.

Corporate Income Tax is a sort of tax levied against income of China domestic enterprises from their production and operation and other income.

Value-Added Tax is a sort of commodity turnover tax based on commodity and service sales, with a system of deduction of tax levied.

Personal Income Tax is a sort of tax levied against taxable income earned by individuals (natural persons).

07

价格指数
PRICE INDEX

简要说明

一、本章资料的主要内容

本章价格指数资料，反映生产、流通、消费与投资的价格变动趋势和变动幅度。主要包括居民消费价格指数；商品零售价格指数；农产品生产者价格指数；工业生产者出厂价格指数；工业生产者购进价格指数；固定资产投资价格指数；住宅销售价格指数。

二、本章资料的数据来源

本章资料由国家统计局北京调查总队、北京市统计局提供。

三、调查方法

（一）居民消费价格指数和商品零售价格指数

编制居民消费价格指数、商品零售价格指数的资料采用抽样调查和重点调查相结合的方法取得，即在全市选择不同的区域，按照布局合理的原则抽选价格调查点，由国家确定调查商品和服务项目，在此基础上按照消费量大、价格变动趋势有较强代表性的原则选择调查样本，对其市场价格进行定期调查，以样本推算总体。现将指数编制过程按下列几个步骤进行说明。

抽选价格调查点。按照布局合理等原则，将不同区域各种类型的商场、农贸市场、服务网点分别按销售额、成交额和经营规模为标志，从高到低排队，依据所需调查点的数量进行等距抽样。

选择代表规格品。代表商品和服务项目由国家确定，代表规格品由各省市按照有关原则选择。选择原则：（1）消费量较大；（2）价格变动趋势和变动程度有较强的代表性，即选中规格品的价格变动特征与未选中规格品之间价格变动的相关性愈高愈好；（3）选中的规格品之间，性质相隔愈远愈好，价格变动特征的相关性愈低愈好；选中的工业消费品必须是合格产品，产品包装上有注册商标、产地、规格等级等标识。

目前，居民消费价格调查按用途划分为 8 大类，262 个基本分类，国家规定大城市调查规格品数量应在 600 种左右，北京市由于编制分收入层居民消费价格指数，代表规格品数量增加到 1626 种。商品零售价格指数划分为 16 个大类，229 个基本分类，北京市代表规格品数量为 1276 种。

价格资料的采集。采取定人、定点、定时直接调查的方法采集价格资料。

权数资料来源与计算。居民消费价格指数的权数根据城市居民家庭生活消费支出调查资料整理计算。商品零售价格指数的权数根据商业统计中社会消费品零售总额计算。

（二）工业生产者出厂价格指数和工业生产者购进价格指数

工业生产者出厂价格是工业品第一次出售时的出厂价格。该项调查采用重点调查与典型调查相结合的调查方法。重点调查对象为选中的全年主营业务收入 2000 万元及以上的工业法人样本单位及部分生产特定产品的全年主营业务收入 2000 万元以下的工业法人样本单位。

工业生产者购进价格是工业企业作为中间投入的价格。调查对象从填报工业生产者出厂价格的企业中选择。

选择代表企业的原则：（1）按工业行业选择调查企业，各中类行业原则上都要有调查企业；（2）大型企业应尽量都选择占相当大比重企业；（3）选择生产正常、稳定的企业作为调查对象；（4）选择企业时要兼顾不同所有制形式。

选择代表产品的原则：（1）按工业行业选择代表产品；（2）选择对国计民生影响大的产品；（3）选择生产较为稳定的产品；（4）选择有发展前景的产品；（5）选择具有地方特色的产品。

除了以上原则及方法外，工业生产者购进价格调查还要考虑到特殊性，即调查企业要填报其生产中消耗的主要原材料、燃料、动力，不填报消耗较少、在生产投入中比重较小的原材料、燃料、动力。

权数的确定。编制工业生产者出厂价格指数所用的权数，用工业品销售产值算。计算资料来自于经济普查的工业数据。若近期没有经济普查，采用工业统计年度资料计算。编制工业生产者购进价格指数所用的权数来自工业部门各种物质消耗额，计算资料为经济普查资料结合一次性产品调查数据。权数一般五年更换一次。

（三）固定资产投资价格指数

固定资产投资价格调查采用重点调查与典型调查相结合的方法。固定资产投资价格调查所涉及的价格是构成固定资产投资额实体的实际购进价格（或结算价格）。调查的内容包括构成当年建筑工程实体的钢材、木材、水泥、地方建筑材料、电料、化工材料等主要建筑材料价格；投入的劳动力价格（单位工资）和各种施工机械使用费用；设备工器具购置和其他费用投资价格。

选择建筑安装工程调查点的原则：（1）样本单位应具有一定覆盖面；（2）投资经济活动代表性强；（3）兼顾不同经济类型；（4）选择重点工程；（5）兼顾不同工程类别。

选择其他费用调查点的原则：在选择其他费用调查点时，所遵循的原则与建筑安装工程调查点的原则基本相同，特别是要注意选择那些投资额大的工程。但由于其他费用不易取得，所以在实际操作过程中，应同时在建设单位、施工单位开展重点调查，并辅以典型调查（从有关管理部门取得资料）。

权数的确定。固定资产投资价格指数的计算权数是建筑安装工程、设备工器具购置和其他费用三者前三年投资完成额的平均比重。

（四）住宅销售价格指数是反映住宅销售价格总水平变动趋势和程度的相对数。包括新建住宅销售价格指数和二手住宅销售价格指数。

新建住宅销售价格的调查方法：目前我国住宅销售价格调查在 70 个大中城市开展。新建住宅销售价格、面积、金额等资料直接采用当地房地产管理部门的网签数据。新建住宅的网签数据内容主要包括：住宅在建项目（楼盘）名称、项目地址、幢号、总层数、所在层数、住宅结构、建筑面积、成交总价（合同金额）、签约时间等。

二手住宅销售价格的调查方法：二手住宅销售价格调查为非全面调查，采用重点调查与典型调查相结合的方法，按照房地产经纪机构上报、房地产管理部门提供与调查员实地调查相结合的方式收集基础数据。

（五）农产品生产者价格指数

农产品生产者价格调查采取抽样调查和重点调查相结合的调查方法。抽取 300 个农产品生产和出售的农业生产经营单位及行政村作为调查对象。对一些区域性比较强的农产品采取在主产区主观选样的方法选择农业生产经营单位及行政村作为调查对象。

被调查单位及行政村在辅助调查员的指导下将在报告期出售的农产品的名称、出售数量、价格、金额即时记入农产品生产者价格调查台账，并上报，由市级超级汇总。由于北京市林业产品（树苗）产值比重较少，不足 1%，根据国家统计局统计制度要求，不需要进行林业产品生产者价格调查。

Brief Introduction

I. Main Content

Price indexes in this chapter reflect the trend and rate of changes in prices of production, circulation, consumption and investment, mainly consisting of consumer price index (CPI), retail price index (RPI), producer price index for farm products, producer price index for industrial products (PPI); purchasing price index for industrial products; price index for investment in fixed assets; and selling price index for residential houses.

II. Source of Statistics

Statistics in this chapter are from NBS Survey Office in Beijing and Beijing Municipal Bureau of Statistics.

III. Survey Methods

1. Consumer Price Index (CPI) and Retail Price Index (RPI)

Data for compilation of the consumer price index and retail price index are collected through a combination of sample surveys and surveys of key units. Different areas are selected across the city as the sample areas and representative commodities with large amount of consumption and price changes are selected as the sample commodities in reasonable layout. Commodity and service items are identified by the central government. Regular surveys are conducted to collect data on their market prices. General indexes are inferred on the basis of the sample data. The process of CPI development is described as the following steps.

The selection of price survey sites: By adopting the principle of reasonable layout, an equidistant sampling is conducted for department stores, agricultural product trade markets and service outlets in different types and in different areas by their sales value, transaction value and operational scale, which will be ranked in a descending order based on the number of survey sites required.

The selection of representative commodities: Representative commodity and service items are determined by the country. Representative commodities are selected by provinces and cities according to relevant principles. Principles for selection: (1) large quantity of consumption; (2) strongly representative trend and extent of price changes, which means the characteristics of price changes of selected commodities shall be highly correlated with price changes of those that are not selected; (3) selected commodities shall be different in their nature and least correlated in the characteristics of price changes between each other; the selected industrial products must be qualified products, with registered trademark, origin, specifications, grade and other marks on the their package.

At present, data are collected over 600 specifications each month under 262 basic headings in 8 categories in the consumer price surveys. In Beijing, due to the development of CPI by income class, representative commodities have increased to 1626 specifications. Retail price index consists of 16 categories, 229 basic headings and 1276 specifications of representative commodities.

Method of data collection: Price data are collected through direct surveys by designated personnel at designated sites on periodic basis.

Source and calculation of the weights: CPI weights are calculated according to survey information on living expenditures of urban residents. RPI weights are calculated according to the total retail sales of commodities.

2. Producer Price Index for Industrial Products (PPI); Purchasing Price Index for Industrial Products

The producer price index for industrial products refers to the producer's price of industrial products when sold for the first time. The survey program is a combination of the key units' survey and typical units' survey methods. Key units refer to industrial enterprises with annual turnover from primary activities at and above RMB 20 million. Typical units refer to the industrial enterprises with annual revenue from the primary activities below RMB 20 million.

Purchasing price for Industrial Products refers to the price of intermediate inputs of industrial enterprise. Enterprises for survey are selected among those that have submitted the ex-factory prices of industrial products.

Principles for selecting the representative enterprises: (1) enterprises to be covered in the survey are selected by industrial sectors. In principle, every branch should have enterprises selected; (2) all (or a majority of) large-sized enterprises should be selected; (3) enterprises selected should be those with normal and stable production; (4) enterprises selected should include those with different ownerships.

Principles for selecting representative products: (1) representative products are be selected by industrial sectors; (2) the selected products should have significant impact on the national economy and people's livelihood; (3) the production of the goods selected should be relatively more stable; (4) the prospects of the goods selected should be promising; (5) the products selected shall represent the localities.

In addition to the above-mentioned principles, a special condition shall be taken into account in the survey of producer price index for industrial products. Namely, enterprises under survey shall report main raw materials, fuel and power consumed in production.

Determination of weights: Weights used for compiling producer price index for industrial products (PPI) are calculated according to sales value of industrial products. Data for calculation are industrial data from economic census. If no economic census is conducted recently, data from annual industrial statistics will be used. Weights for compiling the purchasing price index for industrial products are from consumption value of different materials. Data for calculation are data from economic census combined with data from primary product survey; the weights are changed every five years.

3. Price Index for Investment in Fixed Assets

A combined method of key survey and typical survey is used for the collection of data on prices of investment in fixed assets. The prices collected in the surveys of investment in fixed assets are the actual purchasing prices (or settlement prices) of entities of investment in fixed assets. The survey covers the prices of main construction materials that constitute the architectural engineering entities in the year, such as steel, timber, cement, local construction materials, electric parts and chemical materials in construction projects; prices of labor input (wages) and costs of use of construction machines; purchasing price of equipment, tools and devices as well as other expenditures.

Principles for selecting survey sites of construction and installation projects: (1) the sample unit shall have certain coverage; (2) the economic activity of investment should have strong representativeness; (3) different types of registration should be considered; (4) key projects shall be selected; (5) attention should be given to various types of projects.

Principles for selecting survey sites of other expenditures: in the selection of survey sites of other expenditures, the same principles shall be followed as in the selection of survey sites of building and installation projects. Especially projects with larger amount of investment shall be selected. Since it is not easy to obtain data on other expenditures, during the actual data operations, survey on key builders and construction units is to be conducted concurrently with survey on typical units (with information from administration units).

Determination of weights. Weights used for calculating the fixed assets investment price index are determined according to the average proportion of investment amount of construction and installation projects, purchase of equipment, tools and instruments and other expenditures completed in the previous three years.

4. Selling Price Index for Residential Houses is a relative number reflecting the trend and extent of overall level of house selling prices. It includes selling price index for new houses and second-hand houses.

Survey method of new house selling price:

At present, real estate price survey is conducted in 70 medium and large-sized cities across the country. For new houses, selling price, area, amount and other data are taken directly from the online data recorded by local real estate authorities. Online data of new house transaction mainly consist of the name of construction project in process, project location, building number, total number of floors, floor number, house structure, building area, total price of transaction (contractual amount), and date of contract signing, etc.

Survey method of second-hand house selling price: Survey of second-house selling price is incomplete survey conducted with the combined method of key survey and typical survey. Basic data are collected in a combined manner of reporting by real estate broker agencies, providing by real estate authorities and field survey by investigators.

5. Producer Price Index for Farm Products

A combined method of sample survey and key survey was used for the survey of producer prices of farm products. 300 entities and administrative villages producing and selling agricultural products are sampled. For some regional agricultural products, data on farm entities and administrative villages are collected with the method of subjective sampling in main production areas.

Under the instruction of assistant investigators, the surveyed entities and administrative villages will record the name, quantity, price and amount of farm products sold during the reporting period onto the log book and report them for summarization at the municipal level.

As the production of forestry products (saplings) in Beijing is relatively small, taking no more than 1%, so no survey on producer price for forestry products is conducted according to statistical requirements of National Bureau of Statistics.

7-1 各种价格指数(1978-2014年)
PRICE INDEXES (1978-2014)

(上年=100) (preceding year=100)

年份 Year	居民消费价格指数 Consumer Price Index	商品零售价格指数 Retail Price Index	农产品生产者价格指数 Producer Price Index for Farm Products	工业生产者出厂价格指数 Producer Price Index for Industrial Products (PPI)	工业生产者购进价格指数 Purchasing Price Index for Industrial Products	固定资产投资价格指数 Price Index for Investment in Fixed Assets
1978	100.6	100.6				
1979	101.8	101.8	109.5			
1980	106.0	106.7	105.5			
1981	101.3	101.4	109.4			
1982	101.8	102.0	101.9			
1983	100.5	100.6	101.8			
1984	102.2	102.1	102.3			
1985	117.6	118.6	117.6			
1986	106.8	106.7	108.1			
1987	108.6	108.7	116.1			
1988	120.4	121.9	123.2			
1989	117.2	118.5	106.8			
1990	105.4	104.1	101.9	107.9	114.8	
1991	111.9	108.5	101.7	105.8	111.7	107.3
1992	109.9	108.3	102.4	100.9	103.3	112.2
1993	119.0	116.9	107.0	121.8	133.2	126.6
1994	124.9	117.9	133.4	112.9	118.7	116.2
1995	117.3	112.6	130.6	107.3	106.7	113.9
1996	111.6	107.3	101.5	100.7	100.3	108.2
1997	105.3	103.8	92.8	101.1	103.4	102.7
1998	102.4	98.3	93.6	95.1	98.1	100.8
1999	100.6	98.8	97.5	97.7	95.8	99.9
2000	103.5	98.9	95.0	102.5	100.0	101.0
2001	103.1	98.8	102.0	99.4	100.5	100.6
2002	98.2	98.4	92.4	96.6	97.1	100.4
2003	100.2	98.2	102.5	101.5	104.7	102.2
2004	101.0	99.2	106.2	103.0	114.2	104.3
2005	101.5	99.7	102.9	101.3	111.4	100.7
2006	100.9	100.2	99.1	99.1	105.5	100.4
2007	102.4	100.8	114.4	99.7	105.0	102.8
2008	105.1	104.4	112.3	103.3	115.8	107.8
2009	98.5	97.8	98.3	94.4	88.6	97.1
2010	102.4	100.4	106.5	102.2	110.5	102.5
2011	105.6	103.2	110.7	102.3	108.4	105.7
2012	103.3	100.6	104.7	98.4	98.7	101.3
2013	103.3	99.8	104.7	97.4	97.8	99.9
2014	101.6	99.1	99.7	99.1	98.8	100.0

注：1. 从2011年开始"工业品出厂价格指数"更名为工业生产者出厂价格指数，"原材料、燃料、动力购进价格指数"更名为工业生产者购进价格指数"(下同)。
2. 从2013年起，农产品生产价格指数调整为农产品生产者价格指数。

Note: a) From 2011 ,the "Ex-factory Price Index for Manufactured Products" has been renamed as "Producer Price Index for Industrial Products (PPI), and the "Purchasing Price Index for Raw Materials, Fuels and Power" has been renamed as "Purchasing Price Index for Industrial Products" (the same below).
b) From 2013,the "Producer Price Index For Agricultural Products" has been renamed as "Producer Price Index For Farm Products".

7-2 各种价格定基指数(1978-2014年)
FIXED-BASE PRICE INDEXES (1978-2014)

年 份 Year	居民消费价格指数 Consumer Price Index (1978=100)	商品零售价格指数 Retail Price Index (1978=100)	工业生产者出厂价格指数 Producer Price Index for Industrial Products (1990=100)	工业生产者购进价格指数 Purchasing Price Index for Industrial Products (1990=100)	固定资产投资价格指数 Price Index for Investment in Fixed Assets (1990=100)
1978	100.0	100.0			
1979	101.8	101.8			
1980	107.9	108.6			
1981	109.3	110.1			
1982	111.3	112.3			
1983	111.8	113.0			
1984	114.3	115.4			
1985	134.4	136.8			
1986	143.5	145.9			
1987	155.8	158.6			
1988	187.6	193.3			
1989	219.9	229.1			
1990	231.8	238.5	100.0	100.0	100.0
1991	259.4	258.8	105.8	111.7	107.3
1992	285.1	280.3	106.8	115.4	120.4
1993	339.3	327.7	130.0	153.7	152.4
1994	423.8	386.4	146.8	182.4	177.1
1995	497.1	435.1	157.5	194.7	201.7
1996	554.8	466.9	158.6	195.2	218.3
1997	584.2	484.6	160.4	201.9	224.2
1998	598.2	476.4	152.5	198.0	226.0
1999	601.8	470.7	149.0	189.7	225.7
2000	622.9	465.5	152.7	189.7	228.0
2001	642.2	459.9	151.8	190.7	229.4
2002	630.6	452.5	146.6	185.1	230.3
2003	631.9	444.4	148.8	193.8	235.3
2004	638.2	440.8	153.3	221.4	245.5
2005	647.8	439.5	155.3	246.6	247.2
2006	653.6	440.4	153.9	260.2	248.2
2007	669.3	443.9	153.5	273.3	255.1
2008	703.4	463.4	158.6	316.3	275.0
2009	692.8	453.2	149.8	280.3	266.9
2010	709.4	455.0	153.1	309.7	273.6
2011	749.1	469.6	156.6	335.7	289.2
2012	773.8	472.4	154.1	331.3	293.0
2013	799.3	471.5	150.1	324.0	292.7
2014	812.1	467.3	148.7	320.1	292.7

7-3 八大类居民消费价格指数(1978-2014年)

(上年=100)

年份 Year	居民消费价格指数 Consumer Price Index	#服务项目价格指数 Price Index of Services	食品 Food	#粮食 Grain	#油脂 Oil or Fat	#肉禽及其制品 Meat, Poultry and Their Processed Products	#水产品 Aquatic Products
1978	100.6	100.0	101.2	100.0	100.0		100.6
1979	101.8	101.2	102.2	100.0	100.0		107.2
1980	106.0	95.5	108.2	100.0	100.0		131.3
1981	101.3	100.4	102.9	100.0	100.0		100.0
1982	101.8	100.1	104.2	100.0	100.0		100.0
1983	100.5	100.3	101.5	100.0	100.0		100.0
1984	102.2	103.1	102.8	99.3	100.6		106.6
1985	117.6	108.1	126.6	104.6	116.3		235.3
1986	106.8	107.9	109.6	103.6	132.4		129.7
1987	108.6	107.6	111.3	104.6	103.5		116.1
1988	120.4	106.0	123.9	114.4	120.7		144.9
1989	117.2	104.6	112.5	109.5	129.2		114.5
1990	105.4	118.2	103.7	104.5	101.9		101.7
1991	111.9	142.9	111.2	132.2	137.4		102.0
1992	109.9	122.8	111.5	134.3	110.9		101.8
1993	119.0	133.8	120.7	134.6	111.8		109.3
1994	124.9	136.1	126.7	144.0	133.8	138.2	125.6
1995	117.3	128.3	121.1	135.2	109.0	123.2	111.1
1996	111.6	120.0	107.7	112.2	90.8	101.5	104.5
1997	105.3	117.5	102.2	96.8	100.7	107.0	109.7
1998	102.4	121.3	97.1	96.4	103.3	93.2	94.8
1999	100.6	107.9	97.7	97.9	99.4	92.3	95.5
2000	103.5	116.2	97.9	91.4	85.8	98.4	107.3
2001	103.1	115.9	101.5	95.0	87.5	102.6	96.9
2002	98.2	99.4	98.0	98.5	94.7	98.9	95.7
2003	100.2	100.7	103.2	99.1	114.1	100.9	102.5
2004	101.0	101.8	104.8	120.6	117.0	110.1	107.1
2005	101.5	101.3	104.9	104.6	98.0	103.8	104.7
2006	100.9	101.2	102.8	101.6	101.5	99.4	101.9
2007	102.4	101.3	109.2	107.4	117.3	128.7	108.8
2008	105.1	99.9	116.1	108.9	121.3	125.1	120.1
2009	98.5	94.8	102.4	105.6	83.9	95.2	104.5
2010	102.4	103.7	105.5	109.6	100.9	101.2	110.6
2011	105.6	106.4	110.6	110.8	114.2	121.8	109.5
2012	103.3	104.2	106.6	102.6	104.5	106.7	104.8
2013	103.3	105.5	104.7	104.4	99.8	106.7	103.4
2014	101.6	102.5	103.2	102.2	96.9	99.9	106.1

CONSUMER PRICE INDEX FOR EIGHT CATEGORIES (1978-2014)

(preceding year=100)

#鲜 菜 Fresh Vegetables	#鲜 果 Fresh Fruits	烟酒及用品 Tobacco, Liquor and Related Articles	衣 着 Clothing	家庭设备用品及维修服务 Household Facilities, Articles and Repair Services	医疗保健和个人用品 Healthcare and Personal Articles	交 通和通信 Transportation and Communication	娱乐教育文化用品及服务 Recreational, Educational, Cultural Articles and Services	居 住 Residence
114.5	101.6		100.0		100.4		100.1	
100.2	99.5		99.3		103.7		104.5	
114.1	106.7		99.5		101.5		100.8	
111.4	100.8		99.4		101.4		100.3	
104.7	94.3		96.7		101.4		100.1	
104.9	119.1		97.0		103.0		98.1	
106.8	112.1		101.2		107.4		100.0	
162.0	148.6		103.0		106.5		101.6	
106.7	121.4		101.3		102.2		100.8	
118.4	124.0		104.0		103.1		103.5	
133.5	124.4		125.1		131.5		114.4	
105.1	112.0		126.2		119.5		133.1	
107.1	98.6		110.3		111.0		93.5	
118.4	111.1		105.7		105.0		94.4	
115.1	104.6		103.3		114.8		92.8	
114.5	109.2		109.2		115.1		99.7	
128.5	114.9		124.7	112.7	113.2	104.9	118.7	124.1
124.3	129.5		117.5	108.3	102.6	100.3	100.8	113.2
113.7	104.6		119.1	104.6	110.1	102.1	110.1	129.2
95.0	94.0		102.9	105.4	105.2	100.3	98.1	121.2
93.9	89.5		105.9	97.5	108.6	99.0	97.8	104.7
106.2	101.4		99.4	96.5	115.8	98.3	98.8	101.0
98.4	88.4		102.6	96.3	113.5	92.3	97.8	117.9
100.2	101.5	101.5	100.4	97.0	98.7	100.8	114.2	104.2
84.7	94.5	100.6	95.9	97.0	100.2	99.5	96.6	101.9
145.4	111.4	100.2	97.1	97.7	100.1	97.8	98.3	101.6
95.0	104.1	101.2	98.9	96.9	99.2	95.7	101.5	101.4
111.9	111.0	100.0	100.1	99.7	98.0	97.5	99.7	105.9
112.8	112.0	99.9	99.7	101.2	101.1	99.3	98.7	101.4
109.9	100.8	101.8	100.0	100.4	100.3	95.7	99.2	103.5
108.1	112.9	106.0	99.1	104.4	102.0	97.6	98.0	103.0
111.9	109.4	102.2	98.4	100.3	99.9	95.9	97.6	89.8
124.0	112.3	101.1	98.4	99.4	101.5	100.8	99.4	105.0
97.3	112.1	102.5	102.7	104.2	103.7	101.5	99.7	108.5
114.5	101.6	102.2	100.9	102.8	101.5	99.1	102.3	103.9
108.7	107.2	100.1	101.5	101.7	100.2	99.0	103.9	105.6
94.4	117.1	99.7	100.4	100.3	99.9	99.2	103.2	101.4

7-4 多基期居民消费价格指数(2014年)
CONSUMER PRICE INDEX WITH MULTIPLE BASE PERIODS (2014)

项 目	Item	1978=100	1980=100	1990=100	2000=100	2005=100	2010=100
居民消费价格指数	**Consumer Price Index**	**812.1**	**752.5**	**350.2**	**130.4**	**125.4**	**114.5**
#服务项目价格指数	**Price Index of Services**	**3144.6**	**3136.5**	**1350.3**	**144.4**	**120.7**	**119.9**
食 品	**Food**	**1310.8**	**1186.9**	**475.4**	**202.6**	**179.4**	**127.4**
#粮 食	Grain	1255.5	1255.5	850.5	195.3	166.9	121.3
油 脂	Oil and Fat	780.0	780.0	306.4	153.0	141.2	115.4
肉禽及其制品	Meat, Poultry and Their Processed Products	1562.7	1264.5	542.8	249.9	213.5	138.6
水产品	Aquatic Products	3264.6	2318.9	364.3	206.2	193.9	125.9
菜	Vegetables	3093.9	2737.2	753.0	268.9	212.0	116.0
#鲜 菜	Fresh Vegetables	3384.4	2962.1	736.0	278.7	212.5	114.3
干菜及菜制品	Dried Vegetables and Vegetable Products	893.0	860.4	413.7	173.6	184.7	133.0
调味品	Flavoring	1041.7	1072.5	528.3	150.8	143.2	115.8
干鲜瓜果	Dried and Fresh Melons and Fruits	1505.6	1407.1	386.1	237.9	200.6	133.4
烟酒及用品	**Tobacco, Liquor and Related Articles**	**451.5**	**451.5**	**206.1**	**120.7**	**116.5**	**104.6**
衣着	**Clothing**	**354.6**	**362.7**	**217.0**	**93.5**	**101.0**	**105.6**
#服 装	Garments	369.9	381.6	223.9	94.2	101.6	105.4
衣着材料	Clothing Materials	316.6	317.8	223.9	121.1	129.1	124.6
鞋袜帽	Footwear, Hosiery and Hats	369.7	375.2	219.2	88.5	97.5	104.9
家庭设备用品及维修服务	**Household Facilities, Articles and Repair Services**	**302.6**	**300.9**	**158.5**	**102.6**	**115.6**	**109.2**
医疗保健和个人用品	**Healthcare and Personal Articles**	**675.4**	**620.9**	**275.4**	**106.4**	**110.4**	**105.4**
交通和通信	**Transportation and Communication**	**104.4**	**104.4**	**88.0**	**81.1**	**88.5**	**98.8**
娱乐教育文化用品及服务	**Recreational, Educational, Cultural Commodities and Services**	**234.7**	**229.2**	**120.9**	**111.7**	**101.6**	**109.4**
居 住	**Residence**	**730.2**	**981.6**	**719.5**	**142.4**	**123.0**	**120.7**
#住房租金	House Rent	2002.5	3166.3	3141.1	160.6	140.5	122.7
水、电、燃料	Water, Electricity, and Fuels	780.7	780.7	643.8	171.2	115.7	108.7

7-5 居民消费价格分类指数(2014年)
CONSUMER PRICE INDEX BY CATEGORY (2014)

项　　目	Item	2013 =100	项　　目	Item	2013 =100
居民消费价格指数	**Consumer Price Index**	**101.6**	**医疗保健和个人用品**	**Healthcare and Personal Articles**	**99.9**
#非食品价格指数	Non-food Price Index	**101.0**	医疗保健	Health Care	101.1
#服务项目价格指数	Price Index for Services	**102.5**	医疗器具及用品	Medical Apparatus and Supplies	100.9
#消费品价格指数	Price Index for Consumer Goods	**101.0**	中药材及中成药	Traditional Chinese Medicial Materials and Chinese Patent Drugs	102.6
食　品	**Food**	**103.2**			
粮　食	Grain	102.2			
淀粉及制品	Starches and Their Processed Products	104.6	西　药	Western Medicines	99.9
干豆类及豆制品	Beans and Their Processed Products	106.1	保健器具及用品	Healthcare Appliances and Articles	103.5
油　脂	Oil and Fat	96.9	医疗保健服务	Healthcare Services	100.0
肉禽及其制品	Meat, Poultry and Their Processed Products	99.9	个人用品及服务	Personal Articles and Services	97.7
			化妆美容用品	Cosmetics	97.2
蛋	Eggs	109.5	清洁类化妆品	Cosmetics for Cleaning	99.4
水产品	Aquatic Products	106.1	个人饰品	Personal Accessories	92.7
菜	Vegetables	96.3	个人服务	Personal Services	104.5
调味品	Flavoring	101.6	**交通和通信**	**Transportation and Communication**	**99.2**
糖	Sugar	100.4	交　通	Transportation	100.0
茶及饮料	Tea and Beverages	101.0	交通工具	Vehicles	98.1
干鲜瓜果	Dried and Fresh Melons and Fruits	111.7	车用燃料及零配件	Fuels and Vehicle Parts	97.2
			车辆使用及维修费	Fees for Use and Maintenance of Vehicles	103.9
糕点饼干面包	Cake, Biscuits and Bread	102.4			
液体乳及乳制品	Liquid Milk and Dairy Products	108.8	市区公共交通费	Incity Public Traffic	103.0
在外用膳食品	Foods Eaten Externally	103.3	城市间交通费	Intercity Traffic	102.0
其他食品	Other Foods	102.9	通　信	Communication	97.4
烟酒及用品	**Tobacco, Liquor and Related Articles**	**99.7**	通信工具	Communication Devices	77.9
			通信服务	Communication Services	99.7
烟　草	Tobacco	100.8	**娱乐教育文化用品及服务**	**Recreational, Educational, Cultural Articles and Related Services**	**103.2**
酒	Liquor	98.6			
衣　着	**Clothing**	**100.4**	文娱用耐用消费品及服务	Durable Consumer Goods for Cultural and Recreation Use and Services	91.1
服　装	Garments	100.0			
衣着材料	Clothing Materials	101.9	教　育	Education	106.4
鞋袜帽	Footwear, Hosiery and Hats	100.9	文化娱乐类	Culture and Entertainment	101.9
衣着加工服务费	Clothing Processing Services	105.8	旅　游	Tourism	104.5
家庭设备用品及维修服务	**Households Facilities, Articles and Repairing Services**	**100.3**	**居　住**	**Residence**	**101.4**
			建房及装修材料	Building and Decoration Materials	100.1
耐用消费品	Durable Consumer Goods	99.1			
室内装饰品	Interior Decorations	98.2	住房租金	House Rent	101.3
床上用品	Bedding	95.0	自有住房	Private Housing	101.3
家庭日用杂品	Daily Groceries for Households	99.9	水、电、燃料	Water, Electricity and Fuels	103.1
家庭服务及加工维修服务	Households Services and Maintenance Services	110.0			

7-6 商品零售价格分类指数(2014年)
RETAIL PRICE INDEX BY CATEGORY (2014)

项目	Item	2013 =100
商品零售价格指数	**Retail Price Index**	**99.1**
食品	**Food**	**103.3**
粮食	Grain	102.2
淀粉及制品	Starches and Their Processed Products	104.6
干豆类及豆制品	Beans and Their Processed Products	106.1
油脂	Oil and Fat	96.9
肉禽及其制品	Meat, Poultry and Their Processed Products	99.9
食用畜肉及副产品	Meat and Sideline Products	100.0
禽	Pourtry	99.1
加工肉禽	Processed Meat and Poultry	100.0
蛋	Eggs	109.5
水产品	Aquatic Products	106.1
鱼	Fish	102.0
其他水产品	Other Aquatic Products	110.4
菜	Vegetables	96.3
调味品	Flavoring	101.6
糖	Sugar	100.4
干鲜瓜果	Dried and Fresh Melons and Fruits	111.7
糕点饼干面包	Cake, Biscuits and Bread	102.4
液体乳及乳制品	Liquid Milk and Dairy Products	108.8
在外用膳食品	Foods Eaten Externally	103.3
其他食品	Other Foods	102.9
饮料、烟酒	**Beverages, Tobacco and Liquor**	**100.3**
茶及饮料	Tea and Beverages	101.0
茶叶	Tea	101.5
饮料	Beverages	100.5
烟草	Tobacco	100.8
酒	Liquor	98.6
服装、鞋帽	**Garments, Footwear, and Hats**	**100.3**
服装	Garments	100.0
男式服装	Clothing for Men	99.3
女式服装	Clothing for Women	100.5
儿童服装	Clothing for Children	100.8
鞋袜帽	Footwear, Hosiery and Hats	100.9
鞋	Shoes	100.9
袜子	Hosiery	100.9
帽子	Hats	103.7
其他	Others	101.0
纺织品	**Textiles**	**95.9**
衣着材料	Clothing Materials	101.9
床上用品	Bedding	94.9
家用电器及音像器材	**Household Appliances, and Audio Equipment**	**94.7**
家庭设备	Household Appliances	96.9
文娱用耐用消费品	Durable Consumer Goods for Cultural and Recreation Use	91.2
专业音响器材	Professional Audio Equipment	97.4
文化办公用品	**Cultural and Office Ariticles**	**93.6**
日用品	**Domestic Commodities**	**99.7**
日用百货	General Merchandise	100.5
日用杂品	Groceries for Daily Use	98.0
洗涤用品	Washing Products	100.0
其他日用品	Other Domestic Commodities	99.6
体育娱乐用品	**Sports and Entertainment Articles**	**101.6**
体育用品	Sports Articles	101.5
娱乐用品	Entertainment Articles	101.8
交通、通信用品	**Transportation and Communication Articles**	**95.5**
交通运输机械	Transportation Machinery	97.4
通信器材	Communication Devices	80.6
家具	**Furnitures**	**101.6**
化妆品	**Cosmetics**	**98.2**
金银珠宝	**Gold, Silver and Jewelry**	**88.5**
中西药品及医疗保健用品	**Traditional Chinese and Western Medicines and Healthcare Articles**	**101.5**
医疗器具及用品	Medical Apparatus and Articles	100.9
中药材及中成药	Traditional Chinese Medicial Materials and Chinese Patent Drugs	102.6
西药	Western Medicines	99.9
保健器具及用品	Healthcare Apparatus and Articles	103.5
书报杂志及电子出版物	**Books, Newspapers, Magazines and Electronic Publications**	**102.6**
教材及参考书	Teaching Materials and Reference Books	101.6
书报杂志	Books and Magazines	104.5
电子音像制品	Electronic Publications	99.7
燃料	**Fuels**	**97.8**
煤炭及制品	Coal and Coal Products	99.3
石油及制品	Petroleum and Related Products	97.7
建筑材料及五金电料	**Building Materials and Hardware**	**99.7**
建筑装璜材料	Building and Decoration Materials	99.6
五金电料	Hardware	100.6

7-7 农产品生产者价格指数
PRODUCER PRICE INDEX FOR FARM PRODUCTS

(上年=100) (preceding year=100)

项　　目	Item	2014	2013
总指数	**General Index**	**99.7**	**104.7**
农业产品	Agricultural Products	100.1	105.5
#粮　食	Grain	102.3	102.9
蔬菜及食用菌	Vegetable and Edible Fungus	97.1	107.0
林业产品	Forestry Products		111.3
畜牧业产品	Animal Husbandry Products	99.5	104.2
#肉　牛	Beef Cattle	104.2	113.1
肉　羊	Mutton Sheep	100.8	106.0
奶产品	Milk Products	110.6	111.3
猪	Hogs	89.9	98.3
肉禽(毛重)	Poultry (Gross Weight)	100.8	104.4
禽　蛋	Eggs	106.6	105.1
渔业产品	Fishing	97.5	99.0

注：从2013年起，农产品生产价格指数调整为农产品生产者价格指数。
Note: From 2013,the "Producer Price Index For Agricultural Products" has been renamed as "Producer Price Index For Farm Products".

7-8 工业生产者出厂价格及购进价格指数(2000-2014年)

(上年=100)

年 份 Year	工业生产者出厂价格指数 Producer Price Index for Industrial Products (PPI)	轻工业 Light Industry	重工业 Heavy Industry	生产资料 Means of Production	生活资料 Comsumer Goods	工业生产者购进价格指数 Purchasing Price Index for Industrial Products	燃料、动力类 Fuels and Power
2000	102.5	98.0	104.2	103.4	98.8	100.0	104.3
2001	99.4	99.6	99.4	99.4	99.6	100.5	101.7
2002	96.6	97.6	96.4	96.4	97.9	97.1	102.3
2003	101.5	98.0	104.5	102.2	99.1	104.7	109.6
2004	103.0	100.2	105.3	103.7	100.6	114.2	120.0
2005	101.3	98.7	103.3	101.9	99.1	111.4	117.1
2006	99.1	97.9	99.6	99.0	99.3	105.5	113.1
2007	99.7	100.7	99.2	99.3	101.3	105.0	105.1
2008	103.3	101.8	104.0	103.8	101.3	115.8	132.3
2009	94.4	96.2	93.6	93.3	99.1	88.6	85.1
2010	102.2	98.7	103.8	102.7	100.3	110.5	121.3
2011	102.3	104.6	102.0	102.5	101.6	108.4	117.8
2012	98.4	101.1	98.0	97.8	101.0	98.7	99.0
2013	97.4	100.7	96.9	96.7	100.5	97.8	96.4
2014	99.1	100.8	98.8	98.7	100.9	98.8	99.4

PRODUCER PRICE INDEX AND PURCHASING PRICE INDEX FOR INDUSTRIAL PRODUCTS (2000-2014)

(preceding year=100)

黑色金属材料类 Ferrous Metal Materials	有色金属材料和电线类 Nonferrous Metal Materials and Electric Wires	化工原料类 Chemical Raw Materials	木材及纸浆类 Timber and Paper Pulp	建筑材料及非金属矿类 Construction Materials and Nonmetal Ores	其他工业原材料及半成品类 Other Industrial Materials and Semi-finished Products	农副产品类 Agricultural Products	纺织原料类 Textile Raw Materials
100.5	106.9	103.4	94.8	101.9	98.4	94.5	91.5
100.3	97.9	97.6	98.3	99.5	98.8	103.5	100.6
96.4	96.1	99.3	102.5	97.6	92.3	93.6	97.8
110.9	101.4	107.3	100.6	99.0	95.2	114.3	98.1
124.5	120.9	111.1	100.7	105.8	103.8	122.3	102.8
108.3	123.3	114.9	103.6	101.8	102.8	96.3	106.2
96.7	138.3	104.1	100.3	99.4	98.0	101.3	100.9
115.6	112.2	106.7	101.7	103.5	95.3	138.6	99.2
128.5	97.9	108.3	108.5	115.2	94.9	132.6	101.5
79.8	81.1	82.3	97.0	99.4	95.3	88.2	97.6
115.4	121.6	111.7	104.2	102.7	99.0	106.6	102.8
112.7	115.2	112.7	105.7	103.0	98.9	128.8	108.2
92.2	96.7	102.5	99.0	93.9	98.8	98.5	100.8
94.6	92.1	98.6	98.4	94.2	98.9	102.2	99.6
95.3	95.3	99.2	99.9	96.8	98.9	97.5	100.7

7-9 工业生产者出厂价格指数
PRODUCER PRICE INDEX FOR INDUSTRIAL PRODUCTS

(上年=100) (preceding year=100)

项 目	Item	2014	2013
总指数	**General Index**	**99.1**	**97.4**
按轻、重工业分	**By Light Industry and Heavy Industry**		
轻工业	Light Industry	100.8	100.7
以农产品为原料	Using Farming Products as Raw Materials	101.4	102.0
以非农产品为原料	Using Non-agricultural Products as Raw Materials	100.1	99.0
重工业	Heavy Industry	98.8	96.9
采 掘	Excavation	84.3	87.7
原 料	Raw Materials	104.6	99.6
加 工	Processing	97.3	96.3
按生产、生活资料分	**By Capital Goods and Living Goods**		
生产资料	Means of Production	98.7	96.7
采 掘	Excavation	84.3	87.7
原 料	Raw Materials	104.6	99.6
加 工	Processing	97.0	95.9
生活资料	Living Goods	100.9	100.5
食 品	Foods	103.7	102.9
衣 着	Clothing	98.2	97.7
一般日用品	Articles for Daily Use	100.4	99.1
耐用消费品	Durable Consumer Goods	99.3	99.8

7-10 工业生产者出厂价格指数(按行业分)
PRODUCER PRICE INDEX FOR INDUSTRIAL PRODUCTS (BY SECTOR)

(上年=100) (preceding year=100)

项　　目	Item	2014	2013
总指数	**General Index**	**99.1**	**97.4**
煤炭开采和洗选业	Mining and Washing of Coal	84.5	86.8
黑色金属矿采选业	Mining and Processing of Ferrous Metal Ores	77.4	99.1
非金属矿采选业	Mining and Processing of Nonmetal Ores	104.4	100.0
农副食品加工业	Processing of Food from Agriculture Products	100.0	105.8
食品制造业	Manufacture of Foods	104.5	101.6
酒、饮料和精制茶制造业	Manufacture of Wines, Beverage and Refined Tea	103.2	101.4
烟草制品业	Manufacture of Cigarettes and Tobacco	109.7	100.1
纺织业	Manufacture of Textile	96.7	96.8
纺织服装、服饰业	Manufacture of Textile Wearing Apparel and Ornament	99.8	99.3
皮革、毛皮、羽毛及其制品和制鞋业	Manufacture of Leather, Fur, Feather and Its Products, and Footwear	100.5	100.4
木材加工和木、竹、藤、棕、草制品业	Processing of Timbers, Manufacture of Wood, Bamboo, Rattan, Palm and Straw Products	99.8	100.1
家具制造业	Manufacture of Furniture	101.1	102.4
造纸和纸制品业	Manufacture of Paper and Paper Products	96.7	97.7
印刷和记录媒介复制业	Printing, Reproduction of Recording Media	99.6	99.6
文教、工美、体育和娱乐用品制造业	Manufacture of Articles for Culture, Education, Artwork, Sports and Entertainment Activity	100.1	97.1
石油加工、炼焦和核燃料加工业	Processing of Petroleum, Coking, Processing of Nucleus Fuel	97.5	98.0
化学原料和化学制品制造业	Manufacture of Chemical Raw Material and Chemical Products	98.6	99.0
医药制造业	Manufacture of Medicines	103.5	99.6
化学纤维制造业	Manufacture of Chemical Fibres	100.1	99.8
橡胶和塑料制品业	Manufacture of Rubber and Plastics Products	99.1	98.0
非金属矿物制品业	Manufacture of Non-Metallic Mineral Products	98.8	98.0
黑色金属冶炼和压延加工业	Manufacture and Processing of Ferrous Metals	94.1	92.1
有色金属冶炼和压延加工业	Manufacture and processing of Non-Ferrous Metals	96.8	89.2
金属制品业	Manufacture of Fabricated Metal Products	96.2	96.9
通用设备制造业	Manufacture of General-Purpose Machinery	99.2	98.7
专用设备制造业	Manufacture of Special-Purpose Machinery	98.9	100.0
汽车制造业	Manufacture of Motor Vehicles	99.8	99.2
铁路、船舶、航空航天和其他运输设备制造业	Manufacture of Railway Locomotives, Building of Ships and Boats, Manufacture of Air and Spacecrafts and Other Transportation Equipments	97.7	98.2
电气机械和器材制造业	Manufacture of Electrical Machinery and Equipment	99.6	97.8
计算机、通信和其他电子设备制造业	Manufacture of Computer, Communication Equipment and Other Electronic Equipment	93.8	92.4
仪器仪表制造业	Manufacture of Measuring Instrument and Meter	99.8	99.3
其他制造业	Other Manufacturing	100.3	100.7
废弃资源综合利用业	Waste Recycling and Recovery	86.8	98.5
金属制品、机械和设备修理业	Repair of Fabricated Metal Products, Machinery and Equipment	101.5	103.4
电力、热力生产和供应业	Production and Supply of Electricity and Heating Power	108.9	100.2
燃气生产和供应业	Production and Distribution of Gas	108.8	104.8
水的生产和供应业	Production and Distribution of Water	109.8	100.0

注：根据国家统计局规定，2012年起执行2011年国民经济行业分类标准(GB/T 4754-2011)。

Note: According to provisions of the National Bureau of Statistics, since 2012, sectors have been classified in accordance with the Standard for Classification of National Economic Sectors 2011(GB/T 4754-2011).

7-11 工业生产者购进价格指数
PURCHASING PRICE INDEX FOR INDUSTRIAL PRODUCTS

(上年=100) (previous year=100)

项　　目	Item	2014	2013
总指数	**General Index**	**98.8**	**97.8**
燃料、动力类	Fuels and Power	99.4	96.4
黑色金属材料类	Ferrous Metal Materials	95.3	94.6
#钢　材	Steel Products	94.7	94.3
其　他	Others	97.6	95.9
有色金属材料和电线类	Nonferrous Metal Materials and Electric Wires	95.3	92.1
化工原料类	Chemical Raw Materials	99.2	98.6
木材及纸浆类	Timber and Paper Pulp	99.9	98.4
建筑材料及非金属矿类	Construction Materials and Nonmetal Ores	96.8	94.2
其他工业原材料及半成品类	Other Industrial Materials and Semi-finished Products	98.9	98.9
农副产品类	Agricultural Products	97.5	102.2
纺织原料类	Textile Raw Materials	100.7	99.6

7-12 固定资产投资价格指数(2014年)
PRICE INDEX FOR INVESTMENT IN FIXED ASSETS (2014)

项　　目	Item	1992 =100	1993 =100	1994 =100	2000 =100	2004 =100	2005 =100	2006 =100	2007 =100	2008 =100	2009 =100	2010 =100	2011 =100	2012 =100	2013 =100
总指数	**General Index**	**243.2**	**192.2**	**165.3**	**128.3**	**119.3**	**118.4**	**118.0**	**114.8**	**106.5**	**109.6**	**107.0**	**101.2**	**99.9**	**100.0**
建筑安装、装饰工程	Construction, Installation and Decoration Projects	294.6	224.6	187.4	137.3	119.1	118.4	118.9	114.0	102.1	108.3	104.1	94.9	95.8	98.5
人工费	Labor Cost	1032.5	730.1	504.7	221.5	190.6	183.3	176.1	165.9	152.0	145.9	137.2	122.9	112.0	105.3
材料费	Cost of Materials	232.0	172.0	146.3	125.9	107.8	108.0	109.6	105.4	93.3	101.7	97.9	89.0	92.2	97.0
机械使用费	Cost of Machinery Use				124.3	120.9	120.9	119.3	117.4	111.6	110.8	109.0	105.4	102.2	100.9
设备、工器具购置	Purchase of Equipment, Tools and Instruments	103.6	90.0	88.3	70.7	85.3	86.6	87.0	88.0	89.7	92.7	93.5	94.6	97.1	99.4
其他费用	Others	211.8	173.5	140.5	132.9	129.2	126.8	124.6	121.9	116.3	115.4	113.2	108.8	104.6	101.7

7-13 住宅销售价格指数(2014年各月)

SELLING PRICE INDEX OF RESIDENTIAL HOUSES (EACH MONTH OF 2014)

(上年同月=100) (same month of previous year=100)

项目	Item	1月 Jan.	2月 Feb.	3月 Mar.	4月 Apr.	5月 May	6月 Jun.
新建住宅	**New Residential Houses**	**114.7**	**112.2**	**110.3**	**108.9**	**107.7**	**106.4**
#新建商品住宅	New Commercial Residential Houses	118.8	115.5	113.0	111.2	109.7	108.0
90平方米及以下	90sq.m and below	119.9	116.1	113.3	111.3	110.1	108.2
90-144平方米	90-144sq.m	118.2	115.3	112.8	111.1	109.5	107.8
144平方米以上	Above 144sq.m	118.4	115.3	113.0	111.2	109.6	108.0
二手住宅	**Second-hand Residential Houses**	**118.4**	**115.9**	**112.6**	**110.2**	**107.4**	**104.7**
90平方米及以下	90sq.m and below	119.0	116.0	112.6	110.2	107.4	104.7
90-144平方米	90-144sq.m	118.6	116.3	113.2	110.7	107.8	104.9
144平方米以上	Above 144sq.m	116.4	114.9	111.9	109.8	107.1	104.6

7-13 续表 Continued

(上年同月=100) (same month of previous year=100)

项目	Item	7月 Jul.	8月 Aug.	9月 Sep.	10月 Oct.	11月 Nov.	12月 Dec.
新建住宅	**New Residential Houses**	**104**	**102.1**	**100.4**	**98.7**	**97.9**	**97.3**
#新建商品住宅	New Commercial Residential Houses	104.9	102.6	100.4	98.3	97.4	96.6
90平方米及以下	90sq.m and below	104.4	101.8	99.4	96.8	96.1	94.2
90-144平方米	90-144sq.m	104.4	102.1	99.9	97.4	96.5	95.1
144平方米以上	Above 144sq.m	105.8	103.6	101.7	100.4	99.2	99.7
二手住宅	**Second-hand Residential Houses**	**102.4**	**100.4**	**97.6**	**96.8**	**96.3**	**95.9**
90平方米及以下	90sq.m and below	102.3	100.2	97.3	96.5	96.0	95.9
90-144平方米	90-144sq.m	102.7	100.6	97.7	96.8	96.5	95.8
144平方米以上	Above 144sq.m	102.4	100.5	98.1	97.5	96.9	96.0

主要统计指标解释

居民消费价格指数　是度量消费商品及服务项目价格水平随着时间而变动的相对数，反映居民家庭购买的消费品及服务价格水平的变动情况。居民消费价格指数变动率通常被用来作为反映通货膨胀（或紧缩）程度的指标。

商品零售价格指数　是度量工业、商业、餐饮业和其他零售企业向城乡居民、机关团体出售生活消费品和办公用品价格水平随着时间而变动的相对数，反映市场商品零售价格的变动程度。

工业生产者出厂价格指数　是反映全部工业产品出厂价格总水平变动程度的相对数。其中包括工业企业售给商业、外贸、物资部门的产品，还包括售给工业和其他部门的生产资料以及直接售给居民的生活消费品。通过工业生产者价格指数能观察工业产品出厂价格变动对工业总产值的影响。

工业生产者购进价格指数　是反映全部工业原材料、燃料、动力购进价格总水平变动程度的相对数。用其可以观察和研究工业企业原材料价格变动对生产的影响，以及企业对原材料涨价的消化能力和承受能力，为制定价格政策提供依据。

固定资产投资价格指数　是反映固定资产投资额价格变动程度的相对数。固定资产投资额由建筑安装装饰工程投资完成额，设备、工器具购置投资完成额和其他费用投资完成额三部分组成。编制固定资产投资价格指数可以准确地反映固定资产投资中涉及的各类商品和取费项目价格变动幅度，消除按现价计算的固定资产投资指标中的价格变动因素，真实地反映固定资产投资的规模、速度、结构和效益，为国家科学地制定、检查固定资产投资计划，提高宏观调控水平，为完善国民经济核算体系提供科学、可靠的依据。

住宅销售价格指数　是反映住宅销售价格总水平变动趋势和程度的相对数。包括新建住宅销售价格指数和二手住宅销售价格指数。

农产品生产者价格指数　是指农产品生产者价格总水平变动程度的相对数。农产品生产者价格是指农产品生产者第一次出售其产品时的单位产品价格。

Explanatory Notes on Main Statistical Indicators

Consumer Price Index (CPI) is a relative number measuring the changes in prices of consumer goods and service purchased by consumers over time. CPI is usually used for reflecting the level of inflation (or deflation).

Retail Price Index is a relative number measuring the changes in prices of consumer goods and office supplies provided by industrial, commercial, restaurants and other retail businesses over time. It reflects the extent of changes in retail prices of commodities in the market.

Producer Price Index for Industrial Products (PPI) is a relative number reflecting the degree of changes in general producer prices of all industrial products, including products sold by industrial enterprises to commercial, foreign trade and materials companies, as well as production materials sold to industrial and other enterprises, and consumer goods directly sold to consumers. It can be used to analyze the impact of producer prices of industrial products on gross industrial output value.

Purchasing Price Index for Industrial Products is a relative number reflecting the degree of changes in the overall level of prices of all industrial materials, fuels and power. It can be used to observe and analyze the effect of changes in prices of raw materials in industrial enterprises on their production, as well as the enterprises' capacity of digesting and bearing the rising prices of raw materials, thus providing basis for formulating price policies.

Price Index for Investment in Fixed Assets is a relative number reflecting the degree of changes in prices of investment in fixed assets. The investment in fixed assets consists of three components, i.e. the investment in construction and installation, the investment in purchasing equipment and instrument, and the investment in other items. Removing the factor of price change in the aggregates of investment at current prices, this indicator shows the changes in the prices of commodities and fees involved in the investment of fixed assets, and can be used to observe the actual size, growth, structure, and efficiency of investment in fixed assets and provides reliable and scientific basis for government planning on and examination of fixed assets investment, thus to improve overall adjustment and controlling skill, and further improve the national accounting system.

Selling Price Index of Residential Houses is a relative number reflecting the trend and degree of changes in the overall level of house selling prices, including newly built residential house selling price index and second-hand house selling price index.

Producer Price Index for Farm **Products** is a relative number reflecting the degree of changes in the overall production prices of farm products. Producer price of farm products refers to the price of unit product at which the producers of farm products sell their products for the first time.

08

北京统计年鉴2015　BEIJING STATISTICAL YEARBOOK

人民生活
PEOPLE'S LIFE

简要说明

一、本章资料的主要内容

本章资料反映北京市居民生活现状及变化情况，分为城镇居民生活和农村居民生活两部分。调查内容主要包括家庭基本情况、家庭收入和消费支出情况、主要商品购买数量及支出金额、居住状况和耐用消费品拥有量等。

二、本章资料的数据来源

城乡居民生活状况的数据来源于国家统计局北京调查总队、北京市统计局。

三、本章资料的调查方法

城乡居民生活状况调查方法和方案由国家统计局统一制定，采用抽样调查的方法，按对全市及分区县居民主要收支指标有代表性的原则在全市城乡住户中抽取样本，并按一定的周期对样本进行轮换以保证其代表性。对抽中的住户采用日记账和问卷相结合的方式采集数据。

四、本章资料的调查范围

城镇住户调查的口径范围：2000-2003 年为 1000 户城市居民，覆盖城八区；2004-2006 年为 2000 户城市居民，覆盖城八区；2007 年为 3000 户城镇居民，覆盖所有区县；2008-2012 年为 5000 户城镇居民，覆盖所有区县。

农村住户调查的口径范围：2000-2002 年为 2710 户，覆盖 14 个郊区县；2003 年为 2670 户（石景山区全部农民转居民，40 个样本取消），覆盖 13 个郊区县；2004-2012 年为 3000 户，覆盖 13 个郊区县。

城乡住户调查一体化：2013 年，根据国家统计局实施城乡住户调查一体化改革的要求和《住户收支与生活状况调查方案》的有关规定，国家统计局北京调查总队、北京市统计局对全市城乡住户进行了统一的样本抽取，城乡住户调查样本量共计 10000 户。

五、五等分组的含义

要客观的反映不同收入层次家庭的收支及生活状况，必须按不同收入水平进行分组来观察和分析。“五等分组”即城镇住户按人均可支配收入、农村住户按人均纯收入从低到高排队分别分成五等份，即低收入组、中低收入组、中等收入组、中高收入组和高收入组五部分，各组的户数均占总户数的 20%。通过对调查户的分组，可以分别计算各组人均收入、消费性支出的情况，以观察不同收入组之间的差距和存在的问题。

Brief Introduction

I. Main Content

Statistics in this chapter reflect the living conditions of residents in Beijing and their changes, consisting of two parts, one for urban residents, and the other for rural residents. Figures include the basic family situation, household income and expenditures in cash, purchase quantity and expenditures of main commodities, housing conditions and number of durable consumer goods in possession.

II. Source of Statistics

Statistics on the living conditions of urban and rural residents are from NBS Survey Office in Beijing, and Beijing Municipal Bureau of Statistics.

Ⅲ. Method of Survey

Methods and plans of survey for living conditions of urban and rural residents are designated by National Bureau of Statistics. The method of sampling survey is adopted to take samples across Beijing Municipality following the principle of selecting representative residents in terms of major income and expenditure indicators. Samples are changed in certain periods to ensure their representativeness. For selected residents, statistics are gathered through journals and questionnaires.

IV. Scope of Survey

Scope of survey for urban residents: In 2000-2003, the survey covered 1,000 urban households in 8 urban districts; in 2004-2006, covered 2,000 urban households in 8 urban districts; in 2007 covered 3,000 urban households in all districts and counties; in 2008-2012, covered 5,000 households in all districts and counties.

Scope of survey for rural residents: In 2000-2002, the survey covered 2,710 households in 14 suburban districts and counties; in 2003, covered 2,670 households (All rural residents became urban residents in Shijingshan District, so 40 samples were cancelled.) in 13 suburban districts and counties; in 2004-2012 covered 3,000 households in 13 suburban districts and counties.

Integration of survey on urban and rural residents. In 2013, according to the requirements of the National Bureau of Statistics on carrying out integrated reforms of urban and rural resident survey, and Survey Plan on Income and Expenditure, and Living Conditions of Households, the NBS Survey Office in Beijing and Beijing Municipal Bureau of Statistics took a total of 10,000 samples of urban and rural residents in an integrated way.

V. Meaning of Five-level Grouping

It is necessary to have groups at different levels for observation and analysis to reflect the income and payment and living conditions of households at different income levels. "Five-level grouping" means that urban households are divided into five groups in a low-to-high order regarding the per capita disposable income, while rural households are grouped by net per capita income. These five groups are the low-income, middle-low-income, middle-income, middle-high-income and high-income groups. The number of households in each group accounts for 20% of the total. Through grouping of the households under survey, we can calculate the per capital income and consumptive expenditures of each group so as to observe the differences between different income groups and existing problems.

8-1 人民生活基本情况(1978-2014年)
PEOPLE'S LIFE (1978-2014)

年份 Year	城镇居民家庭基本情况 Basic Information on Urban Household Lives							
	人均家庭总收入(元) Per Capita Total Income (Yuan)	人均可支配收入(元) Per Capita Disposable Income (Yuan)	人均可支配收入实际增长(%) Actual Growth Rate of Per Capita Disposable Income (%)	人均消费性支出(元) Per Capita Living Expenditures (Yuan)	#食品 Foods	城镇居民家庭恩格尔系数(%) Engel Coefficient of Urban Households (%)	每一城镇就业者负担人数(人) Dependents Per Urban Employee (person)	城镇居民人均住房建筑面积(平方米) Per Capita Floor Space of Houses in Urban Areas (sq.m)
1978	450.2	365.4		359.9	211.2	58.7	1.86	
1979	491.5	415.0	11.6	408.7	236.7	57.9	1.83	
1980	599.4	501.4	14.0	490.4	271.0	55.3	1.80	
1981	619.6	514.1	1.2	511.4	295.1	57.7	1.72	
1982	668.1	561.1	7.2	534.8	317.6	59.3	1.66	
1983	716.6	590.5	4.7	574.1	337.7	58.8	1.65	
1984	837.7	693.7	15.0	666.8	379.1	56.8	1.63	
1985	1158.8	907.7	11.3	923.3	466.9	50.6	1.66	
1986	1317.3	1067.5	10.1	1067.4	543.4	50.9	1.66	
1987	1413.2	1181.9	1.9	1147.6	605.0	52.7	1.65	
1988	1767.7	1437.0	1.0	1455.6	743.4	51.1	1.71	
1989	1899.6	1597.1	-5.2	1520.4	841.3	55.3	1.52	
1990	2067.3	1787.1	6.2	1646.1	892.2	54.2	1.52	
1991	2359.9	2040.4	2.1	1860.2	1016.8	54.7	1.47	
1992	2813.1	2363.7	5.4	2134.7	1126.3	52.8	1.43	
1993	3935.4	3296.0	17.1	2939.6	1404.7	47.8	1.42	
1994	5585.9	4731.2	14.9	4134.1	1919.0	46.4	1.41	
1995	6748.7	5868.4	5.7	5019.8	2436.5	48.5	1.41	
1996	7945.8	6885.5	5.1	5729.5	2671.5	46.6	1.41	
1997	8741.7	7813.1	7.8	6531.8	2854.4	43.7	1.43	
1998	10098.2	8472.0	5.9	6970.8	2865.7	41.1	1.40	
1999	10654.8	9182.8	7.8	7498.5	2959.2	39.5	1.41	
2000	12560.3	10349.7	8.9	8493.5	3083.4	36.3	1.41	
2001	13768.8	11577.8	8.5	8922.7	3229.3	36.2	1.39	
2002	13253.3	12463.9	15.6	10285.8	3472.5	33.8	1.41	19.22
2003	14959.3	13882.6	11.2	11123.8	3522.7	31.7	1.39	19.71
2004	17116.5	15637.8	11.5	12200.4	3925.5	32.2	1.44	21.49
2005	19533.3	17653.0	11.2	13244.2	4215.6	31.8	1.39	22.03
2006	22417.0	19978.0	12.2	14825.0	4561.0	30.8	1.40	23.65
2007	24576.0	21989.0	11.2	15330.0	4934.0	32.2	1.40	24.77
2008	27678.0	24725.0	7.0	16460.0	5562.0	33.8	1.40	26.90
2009	30674.0	26738.0	9.7	17893.0	5936.0	33.2	1.40	27.69
2010	33360.0	29073.0	6.2	19934.0	6393.0	32.1	1.40	28.94
2011	37124.0	32903.0	7.2	21984.0	6905.0	31.4	1.50	29.38
2012	41103.0	36469.0	7.3	24046.0	7535.0	31.3	1.40	29.26
2013	45274.0	40321.0	7.1	26275.0	8170.0	31.1	1.50	31.31
2014	49730.0	43910.0	7.2	28009.0	8632.0	30.8	1.50	31.54

8-1 续表 Continued

年 份 Year	农村居民家庭基本情况 Basic Information on Rural Households Lives								居民储蓄存款余额(亿元) Balance of Deposits (100 million yuan)	人均储蓄(元) Per Capita Deposits (Yuan)
	人均纯收入(元) Per Capita Net Income (Yuan)	人均纯收入实际增长(%) Actual Growth Rate of Per Capita Net Income (%)	人均总支出(元) Per Capita Total Expenditures (Yuan)	人均生活消费支出(元) Per Capita Living Expenditures (Yuan)	#食品 Foods	农村居民家庭恩格尔系数(%) Engel Coefficient of Rural Households (%)	每一农村劳动力负担人数(人) Dependents Per Rural Labor Force (person)	农村居民人均住房面积(平方米) Per Capita Living Space of Rural Residents (sq.m)		
1978	224.8		219.0	185.4	116.7	63.2	2.15	9.20	9.33	110
1979	250.0	10.9	235.0	204.7	131.1	63.9	2.16	9.67	11.07	127
1980	308.1	22.1	290.0	256.8	140.2	54.1	2.13	10.09	14.39	162
1981	361.4	17.1	350.5	307.2	160.6	52.3	2.14	12.35	17.39	193
1982	430.2	17.3	411.2	345.5	181.1	52.4	1.97	13.01	21.77	237
1983	519.5	20.9	498.5	384.4	193.8	50.4	1.82	14.24	29.81	319
1984	664.2	25.7	559.3	435.0	222.5	51.1	1.79	14.22	38.82	411
1985	775.1	14.5	726.0	510.0	240.5	47.1	1.64	16.48	51.70	540
1986	823.1	3.7	857.0	645.3	292.4	45.3	1.66	17.41	68.58	706
1987	916.4	6.5	943.0	705.5	340.9	48.3	1.64	18.38	92.90	940
1988	1062.6	3.1	1246.0	883.3	407.9	46.2	1.63	19.23	111.60	1115
1989	1230.7	2.2	1356.0	976.3	484.3	49.6	1.62	20.09	162.01	1587
1990	1297.1	2.1	1372.0	980.7	497.0	50.7	1.61	20.62	226.62	2196
1991	1422.3	1.7	1585.0	1100.1	537.0	48.8	1.59	21.92	299.23	2879
1992	1568.8	2.0	1684.0	1179.0	573.8	48.7	1.58	22.67	389.79	3730
1993	1854.8	5.1	1714.0	1308.9	611.7	46.8	1.51	23.70	562.54	5351
1994	2422.1	9.1	2175.0	1676.5	824.8	49.2	1.49	24.42	853.21	8036
1995	3208.5	6.3	3080.0	2433.0	1206.0	49.6	1.47	24.74	1253.95	11716
1996	3562.7	4.8	3272.0	2655.5	1233.1	46.4	1.45	25.74	1706.98	15839
1997	3762.4	5.1	3379.0	2795.4	1248.4	44.7	1.48	27.39	1975.26	18197
1998	4028.9	6.7	3617.0	2945.5	1241.9	42.2	1.44	27.64	2287.19	20955
1999	4316.4	7.2	3938.0	3132.5	1253.5	40.0	1.43	28.65	2680.66	24374
2000	4687.0	7.3	4517.9	3441.4	1263.6	36.7	1.51	28.91	2923.21	26395
2001	5274.3	8.7	5098.8	3871.5	1353.2	34.9	1.52	31.01	3536.32	31510
2002	5880.1	12.3	5548.7	4206.0	1386.6	33.0	1.48	32.58	4389.69	38631
2003	6496.3	11.5	5886.6	4655.3	1475.6	31.7	1.45	33.95	5293.53	46079
2004	7172.1	9.2	6275.2	4886.4	1592.3	32.6	1.46	34.21	6122.35	52647
2005	7860.0	8.1	7181.2	5515.0	1807.0	32.8	1.45	36.94	7477.59	49346
2006	8620.0	8.7	7935.0	6061.0	1937.0	32.0	1.42	39.10	8703.29	55453
2007	9559.0	8.2	8866.0	6828.0	2190.0	32.1	1.40	39.54	9113.49	55621
2008	10747.0	6.5	10166.0	7656.0	2629.0	34.3	1.40	39.40	11869.91	68871
2009	11986.0	13.4	11814.0	9141.0	2961.0	32.4	1.39	39.42	14566.30	80233
2010	13262.0	8.1	12805.0	10109.0	3121.0	30.9	1.39	40.62	16876.30	88314
2011	14736.0	7.6	14503.0	11078.0	3593.0	32.4	1.38	48.63	18924.64	95087
2012	16476.0	8.2	15196.0	11879.0	3945.0	33.2	1.40	49.08	21419.28	104794
2013	18337.0	7.7	16994.0	13553.0	4696.0	34.6	1.49	51.35	22929.60	109604
2014	20226.0	8.6	18011.0	14529.0	5043.0	34.7	1.50	52.42	24004.40	112528

注：1. 本表中“居民储蓄存款余额”为中资金融机构人民币储蓄存款余额。
2. 本表中计算“人均储蓄”使用的人口标准:2004年及以前年份使用北京市户籍人口，2005年开始使用北京市年平均常住人口。
3. 2011年农村居民人均纯收入及其分组数据按国家统计局方案进行了口径调整，2011年增长速度为同口径增速。

资料来源：表中“居民储蓄存款余额”数据来自中国人民银行营业管理部。

Note: a) In this table, the "balance of deposits" is the balance of deposits in RMB for domestic-funded financial institutions.
b) Population figures used for "per capital deposits" in this table are the population for residents registered in Beijing before 2004, and since 2005, the figures are the annual permanent residents population in Beijing.
c) Since 2011, coverage of figures for per capita net income of rural households and their grouping are adjusted in accordance with plans of the National Bureau of Statistics. Growth rate in 2011 are figures with the same coverage.

Source: Figures of Balance of Deposits in the table are from the Banking Administration Department of the People's Bank of China.

8-2 城镇居民家庭基本情况(按收入水平分)(2014年)
BASIC DATA ON URBAN HOUSEHOLDS (BY INCOME LEVEL) (2014)

项目	Item	全市平均 Average	低收入户20% Low Income 20%	中低收入户20% Medium-Low Income 20%
平均每户家庭人口 (人)	Average Population Per Household (person)	2.6	3.0	2.9
平均每户就业人口数 (人)	Average Empolyee Per Household (person)	1.3	1.4	1.4
平均每一就业者负担人数 (人)	Dependents Per Employee Person (person)	1.5	1.9	1.5
平均每人年可支配收入 (元)	Per Capita Annual Disposable Income (yuan)	43910	21180	31512
平均每人年消费性支出 (元)	Per Capita Annual Living Expenditures (yuan)	28009	16744	21061

8-2 续表 Continued

项目	Item	中等收入户20% Medium Income 20%	中高收入户20% Medium-High Income 20%	高收入户20% High Income 20%
平均每户家庭人口 (人)	Average Population Per Household (person)	2.5	2.5	2.2
平均每户就业人口数 (人)	Average Empolyee Per Household (person)	1.2	1.2	1.3
平均每一就业者负担人数 (人)	Dependents Per Employee Person (person)	1.4	1.3	1.1
平均每人年可支配收入 (元)	Per Capita Annual Disposable Income (yuan)	38637	48246	77667
平均每人年消费性支出 (元)	Per Capita Annual Living Expenditures (yuan)	25640	29922	45389

8-3 城镇居民家庭人均收入(2014年)
PER CAPITA ANNUAL INCOME OF URBAN HOUSEHOLDS (2014)

单位：元 (yuan)

项目	Item	全市平均 Average	低收入户20% Low Income 20%	中低收入户20% Medium-Low Income 20%	中等收入户20% Medium Income 20%	中高收入户20% Medium-High Income 20%	高收入户20% High Income 20%	2014年为2013年% 2014 as % of 2013
家庭总收入	**Total Income of Households**	**49730**	**24553**	**35144**	**43058**	**54117**	**89539**	**109.8**
#可支配收入	Annual Disposable Income	43910	21180	31512	38637	48246	77667	108.9
工资性收入	Wage Income	33044	15397	19792	22767	34425	67696	109.2
工资及补贴收入	Wage and Subsidies	31679	14655	19453	21980	33370	64008	109.4
其他劳动收入	Other Income from Work	1365	742	339	787	1055	3688	104.4
经营净收入	Business Income	1670	776	1062	1397	589	5364	112.3
财产性收入	Property Income	653	242	415	298	441	1822	113.6
利息收入	Interest Income	161	38	145	73	103	599	111.8
股息与红利收入	Dividend Income	87	28	11	61	92	436	177.6
保险收益	Insurance Proceeds	11			23	1	30	73.3
其他投资收入	Other Income from Investment	22	…		…	…	7	129.4
出租房屋收入	House Rent Income	342	104	259	141	245	736	104.6
其他财产性收入	Other Property Income	30	72		…		14	130.4
转移性收入	Transfer Income	14363	8138	13875	18596	18662	14657	111.0
#养老金或离退休金	Pensions or retirement payments	13129	7142	13015	17643	17426	12631	110.1
社会救济收入	Social Relief Income	24	95	16				133.3
辞退金	Dismissal Income	34					119	106.3
保险收入	Insurance Income	4	19					66.7
#失业保险金	Unemployment Insurance Income	4	19					66.7
赡养收入	Alimony Income	99	61	48	116	104	206	77.3
捐赠收入	Donation Income	221	131	140	121	160	464	102.8
提取住房公积金	Money Drawing from Public Reserve Fund for Housing	142	5	7	31	189	432	58.4
记账补贴	Account Subsidy	636	584	594	641	629	761	218.6
出售财物收入	**Income from Property Sales**	**23**	**…**	**5**	**5**	**2**	**102**	**持平**
借贷收入	**Loan Income**	**2755**	**2598**	**2057**	**2080**	**2079**	**6892**	**42.1**

注：城镇居民人均可支配收入实际增长7.2%。
Note: Real growth rate of the per capita annual disposable income is 7.2%.

8-4 城镇居民家庭人均总支出(2014年)
PER CAPITA ANNUAL EXPENDITURES OF URBAN HOUSEHOLDS (2014)

单位：元 (yuan)

项目	Item	全市平均 Average	低收入户20% Low Income 20%	中低收入户20% Medium-Low Income 20%	中等收入户20% Medium Income 20%	中高收入户20% Medium-High Income 20%	高收入户20% High Income 20%	2014年为2013年% 2014 as % of 2013
家庭总支出	**Total Expenditures of Households**	**35836**	**21221**	**25882**	**31871**	**37532**	**61878**	**108.5**
消费性支出	Living Expenditures	28009	16744	21061	25640	29922	45389	106.6
#服务性消费支出	Service Living Expenditures	9197	5158	6604	7949	10138	15780	110.7
购房与建房支出	Expenditures for Purchasing and Building Houses	628	760	352	625	4	2056	230.0
购房	Purchasing Houses	617	719	350	625		2056	228.5
建房	Building Houses	11	41	2		4		366.7
转移性支出	Transfer Expenditures	2519	942	1404	2088	2680	5458	110.9
缴纳个人所得税	Individual Income Tax	582	29	40	288	400	2305	119.8
捐赠支出	Donation Expenditures	1458	737	1028	1475	1560	2090	112.6
购买彩票	Lottery Expenditures	3	5	1	3	7	7	50.0
赡养支出	Alimony Expenditures	237	59	150	94	458	687	94.0
各种非储蓄性保险支出	Non-depositing Insurance Expenditures	204	103	177	195	208	284	106.8
#车辆保险支出	Automotive Insurance	105	45	59	85	92	237	持平
其他转移性支出	Others	35	9	8	33	47	85	83.3
财产性支出	Property Expenditures	77	16	67	25	84	169	202.6
社会保障支出	Social Security Expenditures	4603	2759	2998	3493	4842	8806	110.2
个人交纳的养老基金	Contribution to Pensions	1774	1234	1257	1376	1721	3266	109.6
个人交纳的住房公积金	Contribution to Public Reserve Fund for Housing	2214	1022	1280	1661	2506	4488	111.3
个人交纳的医疗基金	Contribution to Medical Funds	556	454	418	415	551	949	110.1
个人交纳的失业基金	Contribution to Unemployment Funds	53	41	37	39	53	97	110.4
其他社会保障支出	Others	6	8	6	2	11	6	35.3
借贷支出	**Credit Expenditures**	**2665**	**1186**	**1917**	**2442**	**2293**	**5149**	**22.5**
#存入储蓄款	Deposits	2203	906	1673	2123	1823	4041	19.8
归还借款	Repayment of Loans	29	7	2	62	66	21	72.5
储蓄性保险支出	Depositing Insurance Costs	105	54	53	74	181	158	86.8
购买有价证券	Purchase of Securities	37	1	28	38	42	59	31.9
归还住房贷款	Repayment of Housing Loan	256	169	134	85	117	807	81.5
归还汽车贷款	Repayment of Automobile Loans	6			52	5		54.5

8-5 城镇居民家庭人均消费性支出(2014年)
PER CAPITA ANNUAL LIVING EXPENDITURES OF URBAN HOUSEHOLDS (2014)

单位：元 (yuan)

项目	Item	全市平均 Average	低收入户20% Low Income 20%	中低收入户20% Medium-Low Income 20%	中等收入户20% Medium Income 20%	中高收入户20% Medium-High Income 20%	高收入户20% High Income 20%	2014年为2013年% 2014 as % of 2013
消费性支出	**Living Expenditures**	**28009**	**16744**	**21061**	**25640**	**29922**	**45389**	**106.6**
食　品	Foods	8632	6181	7249	8019	9365	12018	105.7
衣　着	Clothing	2903	1589	2129	2610	2902	5163	103.9
居　住	Housing	2202	1542	1502	1843	2186	3933	103.6
家庭设备用品及服务	Household Appliances and Services	2143	1272	1635	1743	2205	3821	108.6
医疗保健	Health care and Medical Services	1862	1135	1660	1985	2006	2444	108.4
交通和通信	Transportation and Communication	4407	2096	3024	4422	4259	7912	107.3
教育文化娱乐服务	Educational, Cultural and Recreational Services	4170	2227	2779	3838	4986	6680	104.6
其他商品和服务	Other Goods and Services	1690	702	1083	1180	2013	3418	120.6

注：城镇居民人均消费性支出实际增长4.9%。
Note: Real growth rate of the per capita living expenditures is 4.9%.

8-6 城镇居民家庭人均消费性支出构成(2014年)
COMPOSITION OF ANNUAL LIVING EXPENDITURES OF URBAN HOUSEHOLDS (2014)

单位：% (%)

项目	Item	全市平均 Average	低收入户20% Low Income 20%	中低收入户20% Medium-Low Income 20%	中等收入户20% Medium Income 20%	中高收入户20% Medium-High Income 20%	高收入户20% High Income 20%
消费性支出	**Living Expenditures**	**100.0**	**100.0**	**100.0**	**100.0**	**100.0**	**100.0**
食　品（恩格尔系数）	Foods (Engel Coefficient)	30.8	36.9	34.4	31.3	31.3	26.5
衣　着	Clothing	10.4	9.5	10.1	10.2	9.7	11.4
居　住	Housing	7.9	9.2	7.1	7.2	7.3	8.7
家庭设备用品及服务	Household Appliances and Services	7.7	7.6	7.8	6.8	7.4	8.4
医疗保健	Healthcare and Medical Services	6.6	6.8	7.9	7.7	6.7	5.4
交通和通信	Transportation and Communication	15.7	12.5	14.4	17.2	14.2	17.4
教育文化娱乐服务	Educational, Cultural and Recreational Services	14.9	13.3	13.2	15.0	16.7	14.7
其他商品和服务	Other Goods and Services	6.0	4.2	5.1	4.6	6.7	7.5

8-7 城镇居民家庭人均食品支出(2014年)
PER CAPITA ANNUAL EXPENDITURES ON FOOD OF URBAN HOUSEHOLDS (2014)

单位：元 (yuan)

项目	Item	全市平均 Average	低收入户20% Low Income 20%	中低收入户20% Medium-Low Income 20%	中等收入户20% Medium Income 20%	中高收入户20% Medium-High Income 20%	高收入户20% High Income 20%
食品	**Foods**	**8632**	**6181**	**7249**	**8019**	**9365**	**12018**
粮油类	Grain and Oil	830	714	751	832	862	986
肉禽蛋及水产品类	Meat, Poultry and Aqnatio Products	1722	1375	1465	1751	1891	2062
蔬菜类	Vegetables	596	517	534	599	633	674
调味品	Flavoring	156	129	138	157	166	184
糖烟酒饮料类	Sugar, Tabacco and Beverage	1273	845	982	1241	1298	1940
干鲜瓜果类	Nuts, Fresh Melons and Fruits	864	683	720	831	946	1102
糕点、奶及奶制品	Cake, Milk and Dairy Products	757	572	653	697	837	1014
其他食品	Others	157	114	134	140	149	241
饮食服务	Catering Services	2277	1232	1872	1771	2583	3815

8-8 城镇居民家庭人均衣着、居住支出(2014年)
PER CAPITA ANNUAL EXPENDIATURES ON CLOTHING AND HOUSING OF URBAN HOUSEHOLDS (2014)

单位：元 (yuan)

项目	Item	全市平均 Average	低收入户20% Low Income 20%	中低收入户20% Medium-Low Income 20%	中等收入户20% Medium Income 20%	中高收入户20% Medium-High Income 20%	高收入户20% High Income 20%
衣着	**Clothing**	**2903**	**1589**	**2129**	**2610**	**2902**	**5163**
服装	Garments	1967	1058	1426	1758	2064	3405
衣着材料	Clothing Materials	16	12	12	13	12	35
鞋类	Footwear	789	460	605	736	716	1420
其他衣着用品	Others	120	53	79	96	99	281
衣着加工服务费	Service Fees for Clothing Processing	11	6	7	7	11	22
居住	**Housing**	**2202**	**1542**	**1502**	**1843**	**2186**	**3933**
住房	Housing	1141	794	652	758	1020	2587
#租赁房房租	Renting	603	244	319	526	341	1671
住房装潢支出	Decoration	450	496	239	178	590	790
维修用建筑材料	Building Materials for Maintenance	80	45	78	51	81	123
水电燃料及其他	Water, Electricity, Fuels and Others	880	648	705	952	939	1077
#水费	Water	143	106	102	157	149	181
电费	Electricity	344	239	268	416	366	405
燃料	Fuels	151	120	158	160	145	174
#罐装液化石油气	Bottled LPG	15	17	17	20	9	16
管道液化石油气	Pipeline LPG	2	1	1	2	4	1
管道天然气	Pipeline Natural Gas	127	93	128	129	120	152
居住服务费	Residential Service Fees	181	100	145	133	227	269

8-9 城镇居民家庭人均家庭设备用品及服务、医疗保健、交通和通信支出(2014年)

PER CAPITA ANNUAL EXPENDITURE ON HOUSEHOLDS APPLICANCES AND SERVICES, HEALTH CARE AND MEDICAL SERVICES, TRANSPORTATION AND COMMUNICATION OF URBAN HOUSEHOLDS (2014)

单位：元 (yuan)

项目	Item	全市平均 Average	低收入户20% Low Income 20%	中低收入户20% Medium-Low Income 20%	中等收入户20% Medium Income 20%	中高收入户20% Medium-High Income 20%	高收入户20% High Income 20%
家庭设备用品及服务	**Household Applicances and Services**	**2143**	**1272**	**1635**	**1743**	**2205**	**3821**
耐用消费品	Durable Consumer Goods	873	496	754	673	892	1528
家具	Furniture	353	222	306	215	378	656
家庭设备	Household Appliances	520	274	448	458	514	872
室内装饰品	Interior Decorations	79	42	44	63	66	187
床上用品	Bedding	223	113	159	233	213	389
家庭日用杂品	Daily Groceries for Households	774	537	603	673	794	1231
家具材料	Furnitures	20	3	2	7	82	10
家庭服务	Household Services	174	81	73	94	158	476
医疗保健	**Healthcare and Medical Services**	**1862**	**1135**	**1660**	**1985**	**2006**	**2444**
医疗器具	Medical Apparatus	36	35	41	26	35	44
保健器具	Healthcare Apparatus	29	20	25	21	39	41
药品费	Medicine Fees	430	374	438	441	415	461
滋补保健品	Healthcare Products	370	153	181	399	308	813
医疗费	Medical Expenses	997	553	975	1098	1209	1085
其他医疗保健支出	Others						
交通和通信	**Transportation and Communication**	**4407**	**2096**	**3024**	**4422**	**4259**	**7912**
交通	Transportation	3193	1281	1950	3429	2999	6198
家庭交通工具	Vehiles for Households	875	169	471	1484	638	1575
车辆用燃料及零配件	Fuels and Vehicle Parts	945	343	576	794	1031	1876
交通工具服务支出	Expenditure on Vehicle Services	442	226	233	451	470	797
交通费	Transportation Expenses	931	543	670	700	860	1950
通信	Communication	1214	815	1074	993	1260	1714
通信工具	Communication Devices	359	233	328	291	392	493
通信服务	Communication Services	855	582	746	702	868	1221

8-10 城镇居民家庭人均教育文化娱乐服务、其他商品和服务支出(2014年)

PER CAPITA ANNUAL EXPENDITURES ON EDUCATIONAL, CULTURAL, RECREATIONAL SERVICES AND OTHER GOODS AND SERVICES OF URBAN HOUSEHOLDS (2014)

单位：元 (yuan)

项目	Item	全市平均 Average	低收入户20% Low Income 20%	中低收入户20% Medium-Low Income 20%	中等收入户20% Medium Income 20%	中高收入户20% Medium-High Income 20%	高收入户20% High Income 20%
教育文化娱乐服务	**Educational, Cultural and Recreational Services**	**4170**	**2227**	**2779**	**3838**	**4986**	**6680**
文化娱乐用品	Cultural and Recreational Articles	926	450	672	781	1058	1562
文化娱乐服务	Cultural and Recreational Services	2238	946	1458	2076	2510	3976
教育	Education	1006	831	649	981	1418	1142
教材	Teaching Materials	29	18	37	29	27	32
教育费用	Educational Expenses	977	813	612	952	1391	1110
#非义务教育学杂费	#Tuition for Non-compulsory Education	90	222	61	40	54	94
义务教育学杂费	Tuition for Compulsory Education	27	25	18	18	41	38
成人教育费	Tuition for Adult Education	209	56	58	193	276	453
培训班	Training Courses	330	283	263	277	551	286
其他商品和服务	**Other Goods and Services**	**1690**	**702**	**1083**	**1180**	**2013**	**3418**
其他商品	Other Goods	1222	454	751	928	1451	2442
其他服务	Other Services	468	248	332	252	562	976

8-11 城镇居民家庭每百户主要耐用消费品拥有量(1978-2014年)
NUMBER OF MAIN DURABLE CONSUMER GOODS PER 100 URBAN HOUSEHOLDS (1978-2014)

年 份 Year	淋浴热水器(台) Shower Heaters (unit)	洗衣机(台) Washing Machines (unit)	彩色电视机(台) Color TV Sets (unit)	电冰箱(台) Refrige-rators (unit)	照相机(架) Cameras (unit)	空调器(台) Air Conditioners (unit)	计算机(台) Computers (unit)	移动电话(部) Mobile Phones (unit)	家用汽车(辆) Motor Vehicles (unit)
1978					8				
1979		…			10				
1980		2		…	11				
1981		12	2	2	13				
1982		19	2	3	17				
1983		29	4	7	21				
1984		42	8	15	29				
1985		58	32	42	35				
1986		76	51	62	47				
1987		83	58	72	56				
1988		86	70	81	60				
1989		90	81	89	62				
1990		93	91	96	67				
1991		93	97	102	73	…			
1992	17	96	101	101	77	1			
1993	23	100	107	101	82	2			
1994	39	103	112	104	85	5			
1995	45	100	114	104	87	12			
1996	52	101	119	105	87	14			
1997	58	101	124	104	88	27	12	1	1
1998	65	102	133	105	95	34	15	3	1
1999	67	100	141	103	95	50	24	13	3
2000	74	103	146	107	96	70	32	28	3
2001	78	102	149	107	101	90	45	62	3
2002	84	99	148	102	100	107	56	94	4
2003	85	99	147	100	103	119	68	134	7
2004	94	102	151	103	100	136	79	165	13
2005	97	105	153	104	109	147	89	190	14
2006	98	107	155	105	113	157	96	206	18
2007	99	102	147	108	99	157	92	207	20
2008	95	99	134	103	82	152	86	191	23
2009	98	100	138	104	89	163	97	213	30
2010	98	100	140	103	92	169	104	221	34
2011	97	100	138	103	85	171	104	215	38
2012	99	101	141	103	90	179	112	226	42
2013	99	100	140	103	85	180	110	225	43
2014	99	101	141	104	88	186	114	229	45

8-12 城镇居民家庭每百户主要耐用消费品拥有量(2014年)
NUMBER OF MAIN DURABLE CONSUMER GOODS PER 100 URBAN HOUSEHOLDS (2014)

项目		Item		全市平均 Average	低收入户20% Low Income 20%	中低收入户20% Medium-Low Income 20%	中等收入户20% Medium Income 20%	中高收入户20% Medium-High Income 20%	高收入户20% High Income 20%
洗衣机	(台)	Washing Machines	(unit)	101	98	92	98	101	106
电冰箱	(台)	Refrigerators	(unit)	104	103	100	102	102	108
微波炉	(台)	Microwave Ovens	(unit)	87	87	85	89	92	84
空调器	(台)	Air Conditioners	(unit)	186	164	158	166	176	199
淋浴热水器	(台)	Showers	(unit)	99	97	93	94	102	106
消毒碗柜	(台)	Disinfectors	(unit)	6	6	5	5	7	6
洗碗机	(台)	Dishwashers	(unit)	2	1	…	2	3	3
摩托车	(辆)	Motorcyles	(unit)	2	3	2	3	3	1
助力车	(辆)	Powered Bicycles	(unit)	12	14	14	12	13	11
家用汽车	(辆)	Motor Vehicles	(unit)	45	33	31	38	49	58
移动电话	(部)	Mobile Phones	(unit)	229	225	221	217	234	234
#接入互联网的移动电话	(部)	Mobile Phones Accessed to the Internet	(unit)	104	108	110	82	104	122
彩色电视机	(台)	Color TV Sets	(unit)	141	122	126	137	143	150
#接入有线电视网络的电视机	(台)	TV Sets Accessed to Cable TV Network	(unit)	116	109	111	114	127	117
计算机	(台)	Computers	(unit)	114	93	101	93	115	125
#接入互联网的计算机	(台)	Computers Accessed to the Internet	(unit)	105	88	91	81	98	112
组合音响	(套)	Audio Systems	(set)	11	6	7	10	13	15
摄像机	(架)	Video Cameras	(unit)	25	10	21	21	31	36
照相机	(架)	Cameras	(unit)	88	63	79	74	85	93
健身器材	(套)	Fitness Equipment	(set)	11	6	7	13	10	16

8-13 城镇居民家庭居住构成情况(2014)
COMPOSITION OF HOUSING CONDITIONS FOR URBAN HOUSEHOLDS (2014)

项 目	Item	构成(%) Composition (%)
房屋产权情况	**Housing Property Right**	**100.0**
租赁公房	Public Houses Rented	11.3
租赁私房	Private Houses Rented	8.4
原有私房	Private Houses Formerly Owned	9.4
房改私房	Private Houses from Housing Reform	31.1
商品房	Commercial Houses	37.6
借用房	Borrowed Houses	1.7
其 他	Others	0.5
住宅建筑式样	**Style of House Construction**	**100.0**
单栋住宅	Individual Storied Buildings	0.5
四居室	Four-bedroom	4.0
三居室	Three-bedroom	24.0
二居室	Two-bedroom	50.4
一居室	One-bedroom	9.7
普通楼房	Ordinary Storied Buildings	8.6
平房及其他	Single-story Buildings and Others	2.8
饮水情况	**Water Drinking**	**100.0**
自来水	Tap Water	98.6
矿泉水	Mineral Water	
纯净水	Purified Water	1.4
井、河水	Well Water and River Water	
其 他	Others	
用水情况	**Water Using**	**100.0**
独用自来水	Tap Water for Separate Use	98.4
公用自来水	Public Tap Water	1.6
井、河水	Well Water and River Water	
其 他	Others	
卫生设备拥有情况	**Possession of Sanitary Equipment**	**100.0**
无卫生设备	No Sanitary Equipment	8.0
有厕所浴室	Having Bathrooms and Lavatories	90.2
有厕所无浴室	Having Lavatories and No Bathroom	0.4
公 用	Public Sanitary Equipment	1.4
炊用燃料使用情况	**Using of Cooking Fuels**	**100.0**
煤 炭	Coal	
罐装液化石油气	Bottled LPG	11.8
管道液化石油气	Pipeline LPG	0.9
管道煤气	Pipeline Gas	
管道天然气	Pipeline Natural Gas	86.6
柴 油	Diesel Oil	
其他燃料	Others	0.7

8-14 全市国有土地上房屋总量情况(2007-2014年)

STATISTICS FOR HOUSES ON STATE-OWNED LAND (2007-2014)

单位：万平方米 (10000 sq.m)

项 目	Item	2007	2008	2009	2010	2011	2012	2013	2014
年末实有房屋建筑面积	Floor Space of Houses (year-end)	66918	70993	74715	77772	80986	83510	88219	88219
年末实有住宅建筑面积	Floor Space of Residential Buildings (year-end)	37981	39852	41756	43431	44113	45627	47610	47610

注：统计范围为全市国有土地上的全部房屋，其中2007-2010年数据为根据房屋初始备案登记信息调整修订后的数据，2011年以后为房屋全生命周期平台年末时点数据。

数据来源：北京市住房和城乡建设委员会。

Note: These statistics covered all houses on state-owned land of Beijing, of which figures after 2011 were year-end figures on life-cycle platform, and figures of 2007-2010 were adjusted and revised according to the original house registration information.

Source: Beijing Municipal Commission of Housing and Urban-Rural Development.

8-15 农村居民家庭基本情况(按收入水平分)(2014年)

BASIC DATA ON RURAL HOUSEHOLDS (BY INCOME LEVEL) (2014)

项 目	Item	全市平均 Average	低收入户20% Low Income 20%	中低收入户20% Low-Medium Income 20%	中等收入户20% Medium Income 20%	中高收入户20% Medium-High Income 20%	高收入户20% High Income 20%
平均每户常住人口 (人)	Permanent Population Per Household (person)	2.99	3.10	3.13	3.16	2.98	2.76
平均每户整半劳动力 (个)	Full/Semi Labor Force Per Household (person)	2.00	1.84	2.11	2.14	1.98	2.02
平均每一劳动力负担人口 (人)	Dependents Per Labor Force (person)	1.50	1.69	1.48	1.48	1.51	1.36
人均生产性固定资产原值 (元)	Original Value of Per Capita Productive Fixed Assets (Yuan)	5783	13968	3731	1474	2422	2412
人均住房面积 (平方米)	Per Capita Living Space (sq.m)	52.42	50.06	50.06	45.85	52.37	61.21
人均总收入 (元)	Per Capita Total Income (Yuan)	22268	13359	16525	20449	25197	36324
#现金收入 (元)	Cash Income (Yuan)	22179	13332	16415	20403	25093	36205
人均纯收入 (元)	Per Capita Net Income (Yuan)	20226	9068	15349	19730	24594	34796
人均生活消费支出 (元)	Per Capita Annual Living Expenditures (Yuan)	14529	10927	11845	13612	15485	21912
#现金支出 (元)	Cash Expenditures (Yuan)	14377	10851	11737	13494	15310	21820
平均每个劳动力创造纯收入 (元)	Average Net Income Created by Each Labor Force (Yuan)	25405	13351	21283	26711	29319	36804
农村居民家庭恩格尔系数 (%)	Engel Coefficient of Rural Households (%)	34.7	32.9	35.1	35.9	36.8	32.7

8-16 农村居民家庭人均纯收入(2014年)
PER CAPITA ANNUAL NET INCOME OF RURAL HOUSEHOLDS (2014)

单位：元 (yuan)

项目	Item	全市平均 Average	低收入户20% Low Income 20%	中低收入户20% Low-Medium Income 20%	中等收入户20% Medium Income 20%	中高收入户20% Medium-High Income 20%	高收入户20% High Income 20%	2014年为2013年% 2014 as % of 2013
纯收入	**Net Income**	**20226**	**9068**	**15349**	**19730**	**24594**	**34796**	**110.3**
生产性收入	**Productive Income**	**13939**	**5681**	**11625**	**14880**	**17366**	**23107**	**108.3**
工资性收入	Wage Income	13072	5338	10699	14157	16532	21430	108.6
家庭经营纯收入	Net Income from Family Business	867	343	926	723	834	1677	104.1
第一产业收入	From Primary Industry	258	180	283	251	88	450	96.3
#牧业收入	From Animal Husbandry	48	-15	25	16	14	151	
第二产业收入	From Secondary Industry	59	-101	78	37	147	194	151.3
第三产业收入	From Tertiary Industry	550	264	565	435	599	1033	104.6
#交通运输业收入	From Transportation	305	406	354	263	199	179	121.5
非生产性收入	**Non-productive Income**	**6287**	**3387**	**3724**	**4850**	**7228**	**11689**	**115.0**
转移性收入	Transfer Income	3835	2646	2519	3398	4206	6076	111.3
财产性收入	Property Income	2452	741	1205	1452	3022	5613	121.3

注：农村居民人均纯收入实际增长8.6%。
Note: Real growth rate of the per capita annual net income of rural households is 8.6%.

8-17 农村居民家庭人均生活消费支出(2014年)
PER CAPITA ANNUAL LIVING EXPENDITURES OF RURAL HOUSEHOLDS (2014)

单位：元 (yuan)

项目	Item	全市平均 Average	低收入户20% Low Income 20%	中低收入户20% Low-Medium Income 20%	中等收入户20% Medium Income 20%	中高收入户20% Medium-High Income 20%	高收入户20% High Income 20%	2014年为2013年% 2014 as % of 2013
生活消费支出	**Living Expenditures**	**14529**	**10927**	**11845**	**13612**	**15485**	**21912**	**107.2**
食品	Foods	5043	3596	4163	4890	5700	7163	107.4
衣着	Clothing	1251	658	877	1279	1439	2165	106.6
居住	Housing	2310	2809	2378	2083	1983	2786	96.8
家庭设备用品及服务	Household Applicaneas and Services	1069	750	733	844	1275	1600	119.0
医疗保健	Healthcare and Medical Services	1289	1095	1092	892	1302	2079	110.5
交通和通讯	Transportation and Communication	1583	928	1132	1704	1636	2444	109.0
文教娱乐用品及服务	Cultural, Educational and Recreational Articles and Services	1454	910	1174	1401	1574	2534	109.2
其他商品及服务	Other Commodities and Services	530	181	296	519	576	1141	118.0

注：农村居民人均生活消费支出实际增长5.5%。
Note: Real growth rate of the per capita annual living expen ditures of rural households is 5.5%.

8-18 农村居民家庭人均生活消费支出构成(2014年)
COMPOSITION OF PER CAPITA ANNUAL LIVING EXPENDITURES OF RURAL HOUSEHOLDS (2014)

单位：% (%)

项目	Item	全市平均 Average	低收入户20% Low Income 20%	中低收入户20% Medium-Low Income 20%	中等收入户20% Medium Income 20%	中高收入户20% Medium-High Income 20%	高收入户20% High Income 20%
生活消费支出	**Living Expenditures**	**100.0**	**100.0**	**100.0**	**100.0**	**100.0**	**100.0**
食 品（恩格尔系数）	Foods (Engel Coefficient)	34.7	32.9	35.1	35.9	36.8	32.7
衣 着	Clothing	8.6	6.0	7.4	9.4	9.3	9.9
居 住	Housing	15.9	25.7	20.1	15.3	12.8	12.7
家庭设备用品及服务	Household Applicaneas and Services	7.4	6.9	6.2	6.2	8.2	7.3
医疗保健	Health care and Medical Services	8.9	10.0	9.2	6.6	8.4	9.5
交通和通讯	Transportation and Communication	10.9	8.5	9.6	12.5	10.6	11.1
文教娱乐用品及服务	Educational, Cultural and Recreational Services	10.0	8.3	9.9	10.3	10.2	11.6
其他商品及服务	Other Goods and Services	3.6	1.7	2.5	3.8	3.7	5.2

8-19 农村居民家庭人均食品、衣着、居住、家庭设备用品及服务支出(2014年)
PER CAPITA ANNUAL EXPENDIATURES ON FOOD, CLOTHING, HOUSING, HOUSEHOLD FACILITIES, ARTICLES AND SERVICES OF RURAL HOUSEHOLDS (2014)

单位：元 (yuan)

项目	Item	全市平均 Average	低收入户20% Low Income 20%	中低收入户20% Low-Medium Income 20%	中等收入户20% Medium Income 20%	中高收入户20% Medium-High Income 20%	高收入户20% High Income 20%
食 品	**Foods**	**5043**	**3596**	**4163**	**4890**	**5700**	**7163**
#谷 物	Grain	397	381	361	382	418	454
蔬菜及制品	Vegetables and Related Products	437	334	340	410	511	566
肉、禽、蛋、奶及制品	Meat, Poultry, Egg, Milk and Related Products	1254	926	1088	1163	1571	1682
衣 着	**Clothing**	**1251**	**658**	**877**	**1279**	**1439**	**2165**
#服 装	Garments	792	416	555	783	900	1464
居 住	**Housing**	**2310**	**2809**	**2378**	**2083**	**1983**	**2786**
#住 房	Housing	966	1711	1165	827	639	978
燃 料	Fuels	691	636	692	661	649	842
家庭设备用品及服务	**Household Applicaneas and Services**	**1069**	**750**	**733**	**844**	**1275**	**1600**
#耐用消费品	Durable Consumer Goods	501	422	335	431	616	862
家庭日用杂品	Daily Groceries for Households	354	238	266	277	401	464

8-20 农村居民家庭人均医疗保健、交通和通讯、文教娱乐用品及服务、其他商品及服务支出(2014年)

PER CAPITA ANNUAL EXPENDIATURES ON HEALTH CARE AND MEDICAL SERVICES, CULTURAL, EDUCATIONAL AND RECREATION ARTICLES AND SERVICES AND OTHER COMMODITIES AND SERVICES OF RURAL HOUSEHOLDS (2014)

单位：元 (yuan)

项目	Item	全市平均 Average	低收入户20% Low Income 20%	中低收入户20% Low-Medium Income 20%	中等收入户20% Medium Income 20%	中高收入户20% Medium-High Income 20%	高收入户20% High Income 20%
医疗保健	**Health care and Medical Services**	**1289**	**1095**	**1092**	**892**	**1302**	**2079**
#药品	Medicines	465	452	430	356	440	600
医疗费	Medical Expenses	742	611	607	496	753	1281
交通和通讯	**Transportation and Communication**	**1583**	**928**	**1132**	**1704**	**1636**	**2444**
#交通工具	Vehicles	254	147	98	433	216	186
通讯工具	Communication Devices	164	92	111	162	198	304
通讯费	Communication Fees	332	242	311	318	346	453
文教娱乐用品及服务	**Cultural, Educational and Recreational Articles and Services**	**1454**	**910**	**1174**	**1401**	**1574**	**2534**
#文娱用机电消费品	Mechanical and Electrical Consumer Goods for Cultural and Recreational Use	203	121	169	186	290	370
书报杂志	Books, Newspapers and Magazines	17	6	15	23	17	31
学杂费	Tuition and Incidentals	287	251	281	306	295	404
文娱费	Recreation	629	340	477	561	688	1213
其他商品及服务	**Other Commodities and Services**	**530**	**181**	**296**	**519**	**576**	**1141**
#服务性支出	Services Expenditures	123	47	69	121	130	273

8-21 农村居民家庭人均粮食收支情况(2014年)
PER CAPITA GRAIN BALANCE OF RURAL HOUSEHOLDS (2014)

单位：公斤 (kg)

项目	Item	全市平均 Average	低收入户20% Low Income 20%	中低收入户20% Low-Medium Income 20%	中等收入户20% Medium Income 20%	中高收入户20% Medium-High Income 20%	高收入户20% High Income 20%
年内粮食收入实物量	**Grain Collected in the Year**	**267.5**	**305.8**	**186.2**	**183.4**	**143.9**	**284.1**
家庭经营生产	Household-based Production	61.9	109.2	72.2	57.1	29.2	25.3
购买	Purchased	205.6	196.6	114.0	126.3	114.7	258.8
年内粮食消费及出售量	**Grain Consumed and Sold in the Year**	**255.8**	**307.0**	**167.0**	**199.9**	**128.7**	**260.3**
生活用粮	Grain for Domestic Use	98.2	101.3	93.0	95.2	98.7	102.4
#稻谷	Rice	35.1	35.6	35.5	37.3	34.4	35.0
小麦	Wheat	47.7	49.3	43.3	45.0	47.8	50.5
出售粮食	Grain Sold	59.2	113.1	63.6	85.7	28.8	8.3
其他	Others	98.4	92.6	10.4	19.0	1.2	149.6

8-22 农村居民家庭主要食品人均消费量(2014年)
PER CAPITA CONSUMPTION OF MAJOR FOODS OF RURAL HOUSEHOLDS (2014)

项目		Item		全市平均 Average	低收入户20% Low Income 20%	中低收入户20% Low-Medium Income 20%	中等收入户20% Medium Income 20%	中高收入户20% Medium-High Income 20%	高收入户20% High Income 20%
粮食	(公斤)	Grain	(kg)	98.2	101.3	92.9	95.2	98.7	102.4
豆类及豆制品	(公斤)	Bean Products	(kg)	7.3	7.2	7.6	6.7	7.6	7.3
蔬菜及菜制品	(公斤)	Vegetables	(kg)	101.8	92.2	90.4	96.9	112.0	115.3
植物油	(公斤)	Vegetable Oil	(kg)	9.5	8.7	9.0	9.6	9.7	11.5
猪肉	(公斤)	Pork	(kg)	15.4	13.6	14.2	14.7	17.4	17.3
牛羊肉	(公斤)	Beef and Mutt	(kg)	4.9	3.2	3.9	4.5	6.3	7.0
家禽	(公斤)	Poultry	(kg)	5.1	4.2	4.5	5.0	6.0	6.4
蛋类及其制品	(公斤)	Eggs	(kg)	11.6	10.4	10.6	11.7	12.4	13.5
奶及奶制品	(公斤)	Milk and Diar	(kg)	19.3	13.3	17.3	16.3	25.4	27.0
水产品	(公斤)	Aquatic Produ	(kg)	6.4	4.8	5.3	5.9	7.3	9.6
食糖	(公斤)	Sugar	(kg)	0.9	0.9	0.9	0.7	0.8	0.8
酒类	(公斤)	Liquor	(kg)	17.9	15.8	17.6	20.1	18.6	19.5
茶叶	(公斤)	Tea	(kg)	0.7	0.5	0.6	0.7	0.7	0.9
干鲜瓜果	(公斤)	Melons and Fr	(kg)	52.6	40.7	45.6	53.4	56.6	68.6

8-23 农村居民家庭每百户主要耐用消费品拥有量(1978-2014年)
NUMBER OF MAIN DURABLE CONSUMER GOODS PER 100 RURAL HOUSEHOLDS (1978-2014)

年 份 Year	移动电话 (部) Mobile Phones (unit)	空调机 (台) Air Conditioners (unit)	彩 色 电视机 (台) Color TV Sets (unit)	家 用 计算机 (台) Computers (unit)	照相机 (架) Cameras (unit)	洗衣机 (台) Washing Machines (unit)	电冰箱 (台) Refrige-rators (unit)	家用汽车 (辆) Motor Vehicles (unit)
1978								
1979								
1980								
1981								
1982								
1983								
1984								
1985			7		2	23	2	
1986			12		4	39	5	
1987			15		5	48	9	
1988			20		7	56	14	
1989			25		8	61	19	
1990			29		8	63	23	
1991			42		11	69	36	
1992			46		14	73	40	
1993			56		15	76	47	
1994		1	65		17	80	53	
1995		2	74		21	81	63	
1996		2	79		21	83	67	
1997		3	85		25	84	72	
1998		5	92		26	85	75	
1999		9	101		29	86	81	
2000	14	20	107	7	26	85	84	3
2001	30	27	112	12	29	91	86	5
2002	52	35	116	16	32	94	91	6
2003	77	39	116	22	32	94	94	6
2004	102	47	119	27	35	96	96	8
2005	139	63	129	36	37	97	100	10
2006	161	72	131	41	38	97	100	10
2007	182	78	134	46	37	99	104	11
2008	201	89	137	52	39	101	104	12
2009	212	98	138	58	42	101	105	12
2010	224	107	139	64	42	103	107	16
2011	231	108	134	63	37	99	104	19
2012	235	113	136	67	37	99	103	21
2013	221	123	132	74	32	95	102	34
2014	222	127	132	75	32	97	103	35

8-24 农村居民家庭每百户主要耐用消费品拥有量(2014年)
NUMBER OF MAIN DURABLE CONSUMER GOODS PER 100 RURAL HOUSEHOLDS (2014)

项目		Item		全市平均 Average	低收入户20% Low Income 20%	中低收入户20% Low-Medium Income 20%	中等收入户20% Medium Income 20%	中高收入户20% Medium-High Income 20%	高收入户20% High Income 20%
洗衣机	(台)	Washing Machines	(unit)	97	91	101	97	97	98
电冰箱	(台)	Refrigerators	(unit)	103	99	104	105	104	104
摩托车	(辆)	Motorcycles	(unit)	11	12	12	11	10	8
家用汽车	(辆)	Motor Vehicles	(unit)	35	22	32	30	38	48
彩色电视机	(台)	Color TV Sets	(unit)	132	126	136	133	136	133
照相机	(架)	Cameras	(unit)	32	17	26	29	40	47
抽油烟机	(台)	Smoke Exhausters	(unit)	75	58	72	74	82	87
微波炉	(台)	Microwave Ovens	(unit)	61	43	54	68	63	77
热水器	(台)	Water Heaters	(unit)	96	92	94	96	96	97
固定电话	(部)	Fixed-line Telephones	(unit)	79	71	80	73	78	84
移动电话	(部)	Mobile Phones	(unit)	222	200	232	237	233	220
#接入互联网	(部)	Accessed to the Internet	(unit)	88	67	94	95	99	106
家用计算机	(台)	Computers	(unit)	75	54	77	81	80	92
#接入互联网	(部)	Accessed to the Internet	(unit)	59	41	63	70	67	73
空调机	(台)	Air Conditioners	(unit)	127	98	120	121	142	150

8-25 农村居民家庭居住情况(2014年)
LIVING CONDITIONS OF RURAL HOUSEHOLDS (2014)

项目		Item		2014
年内建房户数比重	(%)	**Households with Newly Built Houses within the Year**	(%)	**1.3**
户均住房价值	(元)	**Housing Value Per Household**	(Yuan)	**997642**
住房类型		**Type of Housing**		**100.0**
楼房面积占比重	(%)	Storied Buildings	(%)	19.6
砖瓦平房面积占比重	(%)	Single-storey Brick-and-Tile Housing	(%)	80.4
其他面积占比重	(%)	Others	(%)	
饮用水来源情况		**Source of Drinking Water**		**100.0**
自来水户数占比重	(%)	Tap Water Users	(%)	100.0
深井水户数占比重	(%)	Deep-well Water Users	(%)	
浅井水户数占比重	(%)	Shallow-well Water Users	(%)	
住房卫生设备使用情况		**Use of Sanitation Facilities**		**100.0**
无厕所户数占比重	(%)	Households Without Washroom	(%)	1.4
使用旱厕户数占比重	(%)	Households Using Dry Toilet	(%)	19.1
使用卫生厕所户数占比重	(%)	Households Using Sanitary Washroom	(%)	79.5
炊事使用的主要能源		**Main Energy Used in Cooking**		**100.0**
使用液化气的户数占比重	(%)	Households Using LPG	(%)	91.8
使用煤炭的户数占比重	(%)	Households Using Coal	(%)	0.7
使用柴草的户数占比重	(%)	Households Using Firewood	(%)	2.6
使用电的户数占比重	(%)	Households Using Electricity	(%)	4.0
使用其他燃料的户数占比重	(%)	Households Using Other Fuels	(%)	0.9
住宅外道路路面状况		**Pavement Conditions of Roads Outside Houses**		**100.0**
水泥或柏油路面的户数占比重	(%)	Cement or Tar-coated Surface	(%)	91.9
沙石或石板等硬质路面的户数占比重	(%)	Hard Surface Paved with Sand and Stones or Slates	(%)	7.8
其它路面的户数占比重	(%)	Other Pavements	(%)	0.3

主要统计指标解释

城镇部分

平均每一就业者负担人数 是由家庭人口数与离退休人口数之差，再除以就业人口数计算得到的。计算公式为:

$$平均每一就业者负担人数=\frac{(家庭人口数-离退休人口数)}{就业人口数}$$

家庭总收入 指调查户中生活在一起的所有家庭成员在调查期得到的工资性收入、经营净收入、财产性收入、转移性收入的总和，不包括出售财物和借贷收入。收入的统计标准以实际发生的数额为准，无论收入是补发还是预发，只要是调查期得到的都应如实计算。

可支配收入 指调查户可用于最终消费支出和其他非义务性支出以及储蓄的总和，即居民家庭可以用来自由支配的收入。它是家庭总收入扣除交纳的个人所得税、个人交纳的社会保障支出以及调查户的记账补贴后的收入。计算公式为:

可支配收入＝家庭总收入－交纳个人所得税－个人交纳的社会保障支出－记账补贴

工资性收入 指就业人员通过各种途径得到的全部劳动报酬，包括所从事主要职业的工资以及从事第二职业、其他兼职和零星劳动得到的其他劳动收入。

工资及补贴收入 指劳动者从工作单位得到的全部劳动报酬和各种福利。

其他劳动收入 指家庭成员从事第二职业、兼职、零星劳动等劳动所得的报酬。

经营净收入 指家庭成员从事生产经营活动所获得的净收入，是全部生产经营收入中扣除生产成本和税金（但不扣除个人所得税）后所得的收入。如当期收入小于生产费用的开支，冲减成本后直接计入即可。

财产性收入 指家庭拥有的动产(如银行存款、有价证券)、不动产(如房屋、土地等)所获得的收入。包括出让财产使用权所获得的利息、租金、专利收入；财产营运所获得的红利收入、财产增值收益等。不包括出售财物获得的收入。

保险收益 指家庭参加储蓄性保险，扣除缴纳的保险本金后，所获得的保险净收益。不包括保险责任人对保险人给予的保险理赔收入。

其他投资收入 指家庭从事股票、保险以外的投资行为所获得的投资收益。如出售艺术品、邮票等收藏品超过原购买价的那部分收入；如投资各种经营活动（自己不参与经营）所获得的利润；财产转让溢价部分收入，包括出售住房增值部分的收入。

转移性收入 指国家、单位、社会团体对居民家庭的各种转移支付和居民家庭间的收入转移。包括政府对个人收入转移的离退休金、失业救济金、赔偿等；单位对个人收入转移的辞退金、保险理赔、住房公积金、家庭间的赠送和赡养等。

保险收入 指参加保险的住户得到的保险收入，包括从保险公司得到的保险理赔款以及其他责任赔款。如人身意外事故赔偿、财产损失赔偿和住院医疗赔偿等。不包括人寿保险返回的年金。

出售财物收入 指调查户出售家庭财物所得到的收入。由于出售财物是家庭财产从实物形态转为货币形态，家庭财产总量不变，因此不计入可支配收入中。

借贷收入 指家庭资产不发生增减的周转性非生产经营性收入。包括提取银行存款、借入款、收回借出款、兑售有价证券、收回投资本金、贷款等。

家庭总支出 指家庭除借贷支出以外的全部实际支出。包括消费性支出、购房与建房支出、转移性支出、财产性支出、社会保障支出。支出统计是以实际购得的商品或服务的总价值填报，不论其付款方式是一次付清、分期付款、还是赊购，只要商品或服务已被消费就要按其总价值计量。如果采用分期付款或赊购形式，则要在借贷收入类相应的项目填入实付款与总的应付款的差额。

消费性支出 指调查户用于满足家庭日常生活消费需要的全部支出，包括食品、衣着、居住、家庭设备用品及服务、医疗保健、交通和通信、教育文化娱乐服务、其他商品和服务等八大类。包括用于赠送的商品或服务。消费性支出构成是按照商品或服务的用途进行分类，如果消费支出的目的与用途不一致时，必须按照用途归入相应类内。

服务性消费支出 指调查户用于本家庭支付社会提供的各种文化和生活方面的非商品性服务费用。包括为别人付款的服务。服务消费与商品消费不同，其特点在于其劳动过程和消费过程在时间与空间上的统一。

购房与建房支出 指调查户购买住房、建房时的全部支出。

转移性支出 指调查户对国家、单位、住户、个人的转移支付。包括交纳的税款、捐赠和赡养支出等。

财产性支出 指家庭购买或维护财产所支付的利息等有关费用。

社会保障支出 指调查户家庭成员参加国家法律、法规规定的社会保障项目中由个人交纳的保障支出。不包括职工所在单位交纳的那部分社会保障金。

人均住房建筑面积 指调查户现住房的总建筑面积。现住房计算总建筑面积时以房屋产权证或租赁证为准，建筑面积也可按使用面积×1.333 计算得出。应扣除住房中专门用于出租的建筑面积。

农村部分

平均每一劳动力负担人口 是由调查户常住人口除以整半劳动力计算得到的。计算公式为:

$$平均每一劳动力负担人口=\frac{调查户常住人口}{整半劳动力}$$

农村居民家庭整半劳动力 指农村常住居民家庭成员中有劳动能力并经常参加实际劳动的人员。是生产的基本要素指标之一，是发展生产增加农民家庭收入的重要源泉。按规定，农村男18周岁至50周岁、女18周岁至45周岁为整劳动力；男16周岁至17周岁、51周岁到60周岁，女16周岁到17周岁、46周岁至55周岁为半劳动力。农民家庭整半劳动力既包括在上述规定劳动年龄内和在劳动年龄以外有劳动能力并经常参加实际劳动的男女整半劳动力，也包括农民家庭常住人员中属于职工的劳动力。但不包括在劳动年龄内已丧失劳动能力的人员。

农村居民家庭总收入 指报告期内农村住户和住户成员以各种来源渠道得到的收入总和。按收入的性质分为工资性收入、家庭经营性收入、财产性收入和转移性收入。

纯收入 指农村住户当年从各个来源得到的总收入相应地扣除所发生的费用后的收入总和。纯收入主要用于再生产投入和当年生活消费支出，也可用于储蓄和各种非义务性支出。“农民人均纯收入”是按人口平均的纯收入水平，反映的是一个地区或一个农户农村居民的平均收入水平。计算方法:

纯收入＝总收入－家庭经营费用支出－税费支出－生产性固定资产折旧－农村内部亲友赠送收入

农村居民家庭生活消费支出 指农村住户用于物质生活和精神生活方面的支出。包括食品、衣着、居住、家庭设备用品及服务、医疗保健、交通和通讯、文化教育娱乐用品及服务、其他商品和服务等消费支出。

恩格尔系数 随着家庭和个人收入增加，收入中用于食品方面的支出比例将逐渐减小，这一定律被称为恩格尔定律，反映这一定律的系数被称为恩格尔系数。计算公式为:

$$恩格尔系数=\frac{食品支出总额}{家庭或个人消费支出总额}\times 100\%$$

Explanatory Notes on Main Statistical Indicators

Urban Households

Dependents Per Employed Person refers to the difference between the total number of persons and the number of retired persons in an urban household, which is divided by the number of employed persons in an urban household. The following formula is used:

Dependents Per Urban Employee = (total number of persons - the number of retired persons in an urban household) / the number of employed persons in the household

Total Income of Household refers to the sum of wage income; net business income; income from properties; and income from transfers of members of the households. Income from selling of properties and income from borrowing are not included. Income is calculated on actual basis. Any income paid in the survey period, no matter it is repaid or prepaid, should be included.

Disposable Income refers to the actual income at the disposal of members of the households, which can be used for final consumption, other non-compulsory expenditures and savings. This equals to total income minus income tax, personal contribution to social security and subsidies for keeping accounts in a sampled household. The following formula is used:

Disposable Income = Total Income of Household – Personal Income Tax - Personal Contribution to Social Security - Subsidies for Keeping Accounts for a Sampled Household

Wage Income refers to income earned by employed persons through all channels, including other earnings from main job, second job, part-time job, and casual work.

Wages and Subsidies refers to all rewards and welfares received by an employee from the employer.

Other Income from Work refers to the rewards received by family members from any second job, part-time job, and casual work.

Business Income refers to the net income of family members from productive and operating activities. It is the income of all productive and operating income deducting the production cost and tax. If the income in the period is smaller than the production cost, the difference is counted in the "Other Expenditure on Lending".

Property Income refers to the income earned from personal estates (such as bank deposits, securities) and real estates (such as house and land) owned by households, including the interest, rent, and patent income gained from transfer of use right of any property; bonus from property operation and property premium; it does not include the income from selling of any property.

Insurance Proceeds refers to the net proceeds of insurance gained by households for participating in depositing insurance after the paid insurance principal is deducted, excluding the income of insurance claim paid by the responsible person under the insurance program.

Other Income from Investment refers to the return of investment earned by households from investment activities other than stock transactions and insurance, such as income from selling artworks, stamps and other collections in excess of their original purchase costs; any profit from investment in operating activities (without personally participating in the operation); premium from property transfer, including the added value earned from house sales.

Transfer Income refers to various transfer payment from the nation, enterprises, companies, and social groups to households, along with income transfer between households, including such government's transfer of personal income as retirement pension, unemployment relief payment, and compensations; transfer of personal income from enterprises and companies such as dismissal pay, insurance claim, public housing funds, and donation and support between households.

Insurance Income refers to the insurance income obtained by households participating in insurance programs, including any claim payment and other agreed compensation from an insurance company, such as compensation for personal incidence, compensation for property loss, and compensation for hospitalization costs, excluding annuity paid from life insurance.

Income from Property Sales refers to the income received by the sampled household for selling any household properties. As the sale of household property is a conversion of physical form of household property to monetary form, and the total amount of household properties remains unchanged, the income from selling property is not included in the disposable income.

Loan Income refers to the non-productive and non-operating income which causes no change in the amount of household property, including withdrawal of bank deposits, borrowings, lending repaid, conversion and sale of securities, returned principal of investment, loans, etc.

Household Expenditures refers to all expenditures of households except credit expenditures. It includes expenditure on consumption; on purchasing or building houses; on transfers; on properties; and on social security. Expenditure is calculated with the total value of goods and services actually purchased. Whether they are purchased with lump-sum payment, installment, or on credit basis, the goods and services are measured at their total value so long as they are consumed. In the case of installment or credit-based purchase, the difference between the actually made payment and the payables shall be counted in the relevant item of income from borrowing and lending.

Living Expenditures refers to total expenditures of households for consumption in daily life, including eight major categories, i.e. expenditures on foods, clothing, housing, household articles, appliances and services, healthcare and medical services, transportation and communication, recreational, educational and cultural services; and other goods and services. It includes any good or service for donation. Components of consumption expenditures are classified according to the purpose of goods and services. In the event of any discrepancy in the aim and purpose of consumption expenditures, it must be involved in relevant category according to the purpose of goods and services.

Service Living Expenditures refers to expenditure of households on various kinds of non-commercial services provided by society, including services paid for other persons. Not like commodity consumption, service consumption is completed in a consistent period and space.

Expenditures for Purchasing and Building Houses refers to all expenditures for purchase and construction of houses by the sampled households.

Transfer Expenditures refers to the transfer payment made by the sampled households to the State, enterprises and companies, households and individuals, including tax payment, donation and support payments, etc.

Property Expenditures refers to relevant costs including interest paid by the sampled households for purchasing or maintaining properties.

Social Security Expenditures refers to the personal payment made by members of the sampled family for any social security program stated in national laws and regulations, excluding the payment made by employers for social security.

Building Area of Current Houses refers to the total building area of house resided by the surveyed households, which is calculated on the basis of the property ownership certificate or lease certificate. The building area can also be calculated as the usable floor space multiplied by 1.333, which shall deduct the building area of the house specially used for lease.

Rural Households

Dependents Per Labour Force refers to the number of permanent population in the sampled household divided by the number of full/semi labourers. It is calculated with the following formula:

Dependents Per Laborer = Number of Permanent Population in the Sampled Households / Number of Full/Semi laborers

Full/Semi Labour Force in Rural Households refers to persons among permanent family members in rural households who are capable of working and work frequently. This is one of the indicators for basic production elements, and an important source for production development and increase of farmer's household income. As stated in regulations, rural males aged 18-50 and females aged 18-45 are full labours. Males aged 16-17 and 51-60 and females aged 16-17 and 46-55 are semi labor force. Full/Semi Labour Force in Rural Households includes the male and female full/semi labour force within the above-mentioned range age as well as those beyond such range of ages who are capable of working and work frequently; also include labourers among permanent members in rural households who are employees. But it exclude persons who are within the range of labour age but incapable of working.

Total Income of Rural Households refers to the total income earned from various sources by the rural households and their members during the reporting period, and by the nature of income. It consists of income from wages and salaries, income from household operations, income from properties and transfer income.

Net Income refers to the total income of rural households from all sources minus all corresponding expenses. Net income is mainly used as input for reinvestment in production and as consumption expenditure of the year, and also used for savings and non-compulsory expenses of various forms. "Per capita net income of farmers" is the level of net income averaged by population, reflecting the average income level of rural households in a given area. The following formula is used:

Net Income = Total Income - Household Operation Expenses - Taxes and Fees Paid - Taxes and Fees - Depreciation of Fixed Assets for Production – Income from Donation by Relatives and Friends in Rural Areas

Living Expenditures of Rural Households refers to spending by rural households on material life and cultural life, including consumption spending on food, clothes, housing, household appliance and service, medical service and health care, transport and communication, cultural, educational and entertainment supplies and services, other goods and services.

Engel's Coefficient Along with the increase in household and personal income, a gradually smaller portion of income is used for purchase of food. This law is called Engel's law, and the coefficient reflecting such law is called Engel's Coefficient. The following formula is used:

$$\text{Engels Coefficient} = \frac{\text{expenditure on food}}{\text{total consumption expenditure}} \times 100\%$$

09

城市公用事业
PUBLIC UTILITIES

简要说明

一、本章资料的主要内容

本章资料反映北京市城市公用事业的综合水平，主要内容包括四部分:

1. 历年城市公用事业基本情况;
2. 水、气、热等供应及消费情况;
3. 城市公交、出租车情况;
4. 市政主要设施情况。

二、本章资料的数据来源

本章城市供热、供气情况由北京市市政市容管理委员会提供；自来水情况由北京市水务局提供；城市公交、出租车情况由北京市交通委员会提供；道路及市政主要设施情况由北京市交通委员会、北京市公安交通管理局、北京市路灯管理中心提供。

Brief Introduction

I. Main Content

Statistics in this chapter show the overall level of urban public utilities in Beijing, which consist of four parts:

1. Basic statistics for urban public utilities in previous years;
2. Water, gas and heating supply and consumption;
3. Urban public transport and taxi services;
4. Main public facilities.

II. Source of Data

Data on urban heating and gas supply were provided by Beijing Municipal Commission of City Administration and Environment; data on tap water were provided by Beijing Water Authority; data on urban public transport and taxi services were provided by Beijing Municipal Commission of Transport; data on roads and main public facilities were provided by Beijing Municipal Commission of Transport, Beijing Traffic Management Bureau and Street Lighting Administration Center Of Beijing.

9-1 公路、城市道路及桥梁(1978-2014年)
HIGHWAYS, URBAN ROADS AND BRIDGES (1978-2014)

年份 Year	境内道路总里程(公里) Total Length of Highways and Roads (km)	公路里程(公里) Total Length of Highways (km)	#高速公路 Express-ways	城市道路里程(公里) Length of Urban Roads (km)	#快速路 Rapid Roads	#主干路 Trunk Roads	城市道路面积(万平方米) Area of Urban Roads (10000 sq.m)	城市道路桥梁(座) Number of Bridges (unit)	#立交桥 Overpasses
1978		6562		2078			1611	351	2
1979		7278		2131			1618	348	2
1980		7487		2185			1664	351	6
1981		7566		2234			1742	342	8
1982		7683		2671			2098	408	9
1983		8058		2820			2265	431	10
1984		8271		2928			2393	440	11
1985		8482		2979			2485	460	16
1986		8995		3038			2559	479	16
1987		9103		3087			2631	510	22
1988		9124		3151			2701	522	23
1989		9371		3235			2815	552	27
1990		9648	35	3276			2905	562	33
1991		10259	63	3308			3134	569	40
1992		10827	71	3189			3212	595	55
1993		11260	99	3285			3398	596	64
1994		11532	112	3316			3470	616	75
1995		11811	113	3194			3494	582	84
1996		12084	114	3665			3807	646	133
1997		12306	144	3637			4061	693	140
1998		12498	190	3721			4214	715	138
1999		12825	230	3753			4353	787	141
2000		13600	268	4126			4921	834	149
2001		13891	335	4312			6062	891	160
2002		14359	463	5444			7645	1051	180
2003	18942	14453	499	3055			5345	848	119
2004	19010	14630	525	4067	219	834	6417	949	271
2005	19015	14696	548	4073	239	922	7437	964	304
2006	25377	20503	625	4419	232	955	7258	1079	376
2007	25765	20754	628	4460	236	960	7632	1230	377
2008	26921	20340	777	6186	242	755	8941	1738	381
2009	27436	20755	884	6247	242	805	9179	1765	393
2010	27907	21114	903	6355	263	874	9395	1855	411
2011	28446	21347	912	6258	263	861	9164	1885	418
2012	28585	21492	923	6271	263	865	9236	1950	413
2013	28808	21673	923	6295	269	953	9611	1998	414
2014	29209	21849	982	6426	383	965	10002	2042	422

注：1. 境内道路总里程为全市道路和公路里程之和(剔除道路、公路交叉重复部分)。
2. 道路及桥梁1978年-1981年统计范围为城八区及通县；1982年-2002年统计范围为城八区及14个县城；2003年-2010年统计范围为城八区和北京经济技术开发区。2011年起城市道路及其附属设施统计范围为城六区。
3. 2008年道路数据为北京市城市道路普查数据。

资料来源：北京市交通委员会。

Note: a) Total length of highways and roads means the sum of roads and highways across the city (excluding intersections of roads and highways)
b) Statistics for roads and bridges covered 8 urban districts and Tongzhou County in 1978-1981; the coverage was extended to 8 urban districts and 14 counties in 1982-2002; in 2003-2010, the coverage included 8 central urban districts and Beijing Economic-Technological Development Zone; since 2011, statistics for urban roads and the auxiliary facilities have been confined to 6 urban districts.
c) Statistics for roads and highways in 2008 were from Beijing Urban Road Census.

Source: Beijing Municipal Commission of Transport.

9-2 城市公共交通(1978-2014年)

年份 Year	公共交通运营线路条数(条) Number of Operating Public Transport Routes (line)	公共电汽车 Buses and Trolley Buses	轨道交通 Rail Transit	公共交通运营线路长度(公里) Length of Operating Public Transport Lines (km)	公共电汽车 Buses and Trolley Buses	轨道交通 Rail Transit	公共交通运营车辆(辆) Number of Operating Public Transport Vehicles in Operation (vehicle)
1978	119	118	1	1427	1403	24	2743
1979	121	120	1	1469	1446	24	2997
1980	123	122	1	1479	1455	24	3113
1981	127	126	1	1525	1501	24	3375
1982	139	138	1	1678	1654	24	3620
1983	151	150	1	1820	1797	24	3907
1984	164	162	2	1939	1899	40	4221
1985	191	189	2	2312	2272	40	4583
1986	200	198	2	2574	2534	40	4576
1987	194	192	2	2382	2342	40	4776
1988	199	197	2	2445	2405	40	4787
1989	207	205	2	2525	2485	40	4890
1990	216	214	2	2654	2614	40	5160
1991	223	221	2	2755	2715	40	5182
1992	262	260	2	3379	3338	42	5223
1993	268	266	2	3532	3491	42	5213
1994	284	282	2	4117	4075	42	5319
1995	300	298	2	4538	4497	42	5367
1996	399	397	2	7317	7276	42	6828
1997	667	665	2	14011	13969	42	10479
1998	690	688	2	14929	14888	42	10819
1999	750	748	2	16566	16513	54	12509
2000	682	680	2	15639	15585	54	14191
2001	555	553	2	13180	13126	54	15420
2002	592	589	3	15835	15760	75	17580
2003	620	616	4	16131	16017	114	17445
2004	621	617	4	15247	15133	114	19343
2005	626	622	4	18328	18214	114	19471
2006	624	620	4	18582	18468	114	20489
2007	649	644	5	17495	17353	142	20525
2008	679	671	8	18057	17857	200	23221
2009	701	692	9	18498	18270	228	23730
2010	727	713	14	19079	18743	336	24011
2011	764	749	15	19832	19460	372	24478
2012	795	779	16	19989	19547	442	25831
2013	830	813	17	20153	19688	465	27590
2014	895	877	18	20776	20249	527	28331

注：自2006年5月1日起，公共电汽车、轨道交通售票采取刷卡方式，并陆续进行了票制票价改革，客运量统计口径方法相应调整，因此与历史数据不可比。

资料来源：本表2005年及以后数据来源于北京市交通委员会。

URBAN PUBLIC TRANSPORT (1978-2014)

		公共交通			出租小汽车 Taxis Service	
公共电汽车 Buses and Trolley Buses	轨道交通 Rail Transit	客运量（万人次） Passengers Carried by Public Transport (10000 person-times)	公共电汽车 Buses and Trolley Buses	轨道交通 Rail Transit	运营车辆（辆） Operating Vehicles (vehicle)	客运量（万人次） Passenger Traffic (10000 persons)
2627	116	172559	169465	3094		
2889	108	205703	200918	4785		
3001	112	236998	231477	5521		
3259	116	263944	257478	6466		
3500	120	284175	276922	7253		
3753	154	302501	294301	8200		
4037	184	324437	314132	10305		
4398	185	335227	321264	13963		
4371	205	328770	312990	15780		
4524	252	330417	311190	19227		
4535	252	337094	306396	30698		
4587	303	306435	275383	31052		
4857	303	334673	296495	38178		
4877	305	344525	307438	37087		
4900	323	348770	305959	42811		
4890	323	335378	286268	49110		
4984	335	353289	299993	53296		
4984	383	371579	315777	55802		
6427	401	349847	305433	44414		
10044	435	391182	346676	44507		
10382	437	418825	372494	46331		
12018	491	426706	378483	48223		
13604	587	406691	363213	43478		
14803	617	449720	402850	46870		
16939	641	492122	443880	48242		
16753	692	426628	379380	47248		
18451	892	499830	439130	60700		
18503	968	517769	449793	67976	66000	65000
19522	967	468225	397919	70306	66646	64121
19395	1130	488138	422645	65493	66646	64111
21507	1714	592523	470863	121660	66646	69000
21716	2014	658785	516517	142268	66646	68000
21548	2463	689788	505144	184645	66646	69000
21628	2850	722552	503272	219280	66646	69600
22146	3685	761578	515416	246162	66646	69862
23592	3998	804775	484306	320469	67046	69946
23667	4664	815849	477180	338668	67546	66828

Note: From May 1, 2006, buses, trolley buses and rail transit tickets were sold by card swiping. Ticket system and prices were also reformed successively. The statistical coverage and methods for passenger traffic were adjusted accordingly, so these figures were incomparable with historical data.

Source: From 2005, data in this table were provided by Beijing Municipal Commission of Transport.

9-3 城市供水、供气及供热(1978-2014年)

URBAN WATER SUPPLY, GAS SUPPLY AND HEAT SUPPLY (1978-2014)

年份 Year	全市集中供热管道长度(公里) Total Length of Pipelines for Centralized Heating (km)	全市集中供热面积(万平方米) Centralized Heating Area in Beijing (10000 sq.m)	#住宅 Residence	煤气销售量(万立方米) Sales Volume of Coal Gas (10000 cu.m)	液化石油气销售量(吨) Sales Volume of Liquefied Petroleum Gas (ton)	天然气销售量(万立方米) Sales Volume of Natural Gas (10000 cu.m)
1978				32687	97255	
1979				32113	114350	
1980				34935	128990	
1981				36309	134771	
1982				36748	149805	
1983				37319	150058	
1984				38710	156421	
1985				41678	169720	
1986				44542	182239	
1987				47594	178205	
1988				49595	177112	287
1989				56056	175814	1805
1990		3702		59508	172688	3544
1991		4560		66111	174326	5062
1992		5281		73615	174694	6040
1993		5730		80163	177065	6702
1994		7056		80409	173105	7623
1995		7537		85201	177637	11003
1996		7838		88356	185304	13504
1997		8399		76429	172879	16565
1998		9102		68998	174464	32619
1999		9992		61846	188450	64833
2000		10860		46719	190571	95919
2001		14729		33960	182188	150585
2002		18172		21077	234680	176504
2003		25108		23991	311657	208837
2004		28150	18962	17714	431660	250326
2005	6272	31736	22218	16776	356551	294279
2006	7013	34977	23158	9763	415268	389202
2007	10424	37203	23697		319631	441327
2008	11948	42501	26738		289576	578626
2009	12156	44240	27694		332693	645356
2010	12224	46715	32305		299392	677009
2011	11734	50794	34563		394437	726229
2012	11031	52555	35104		379371	883385
2013	11192	54591	36806		453546	956852
2014	12038	56786	38085		531556	1088999

注：1. 2006年6月开始全市煤气家庭用户已全部置换为天然气用户，因此2007年以后煤气销售量无数据。

2. 自2012年起，自来水数据口径调整为城镇公共供水。

资料来源：北京市市政市容管理委员会、北京市水务局。

Note: a) Since June 2006, all households using coal gas have started to use natual gas. Therefore, there are no data on coal gas sales volume since 2007

b) Relevant figures of tap water for 2012 were changed to cover urban public water supply.

Source: Beijing Municipal Commission of City Administration and Environment and Beijing Water Authority.

9-3 续表 Continued

年 份 Year	居 民 燃气用户 (万户) Gas Using Households (10000 households)	自来水综合 生产能力 (万立方米/日) Gereral Production Capacity of Tap Water (10000 cu.m/day)	自来水供水 管线长度 (公里) Length of Tap Water Supply Pipelines (km)	自 来 水 销售总量 (万立方米) Total Sales Volume of Tap Water (10000 cu.m)
1978	65.2	134	2926	32664
1979	76.7	151	3083	36232
1980	80.3	163	3272	38933
1981	85.1	167	3435	41634
1982	88.0	164	4216	41136
1983	90.9	166	4452	42778
1984	96.9	167	4622	43716
1985	102.3	176	4927	45601
1986	153.6	188	5079	46695
1987	160.9	185	5257	47680
1988	165.4	189	5550	50059
1989	172.6	206	5647	50145
1990	176.1	215	5770	52718
1991	184.7	221	5947	56107
1992	192.4	226	6130	58704
1993	197.5	234	6367	60794
1994	210.3	242	6727	67977
1995	219.8	264	6907	67877
1996	188.1	266	6907	69684
1997	243.0	302	6339	79046
1998	254.4	330	6989	75969
1999	259.8	357	7179	78098
2000	291.9	367	7610	75364
2001	310.0	371	8146	69807
2002	336.4	428	8555	79322
2003	406.0	429	9278	71583
2004	438.6	399	9981	82986
2005	462.6	348	9831	71600
2006	540.2	373	11899	74970
2007	556.4	391	13133	77778
2008	591.0	404	14118	80792
2009	600.0	424	14791	86881
2010	634.2	445	16144	89185
2011	644.1	473	16963	94622
2012	713.5	411	14029	93826
2013	737.4	444	14495	98178
2014	846.0	503	14994	103402

9-4 全市集中供热
CENTRALIZED HEATING SUPPLY

项目	Item	2014	2013	2014年为2013年% 2014 as % of 2013
供热面积 （万平方米）	**Total Area of Heating Supply (10000 sq.m)**	**56786**	**54591**	**104.0**
#住宅	Residence	38085	36806	103.5
供热能力 （兆瓦）	**Heating Supply Capacity (megawatt)**	**40445**	**38585**	**104.8**
热电厂供热	Heating from Thermal Power Plants	7509	7199	104.3
锅炉房供热	Heating from Boiler Houses	32936	31386	104.9
供热总量 （万吉焦）	**Total Heating Supply (10000 giga joules)**	**35300**	**33960**	**103.9**
热电厂供热	Heating from Thermal Power Plants	5518	5268	104.7
锅炉房供热	Heating from Boiler Houses	29782	28692	103.8
供热管道长度 （公里）	**Length of Pipelines (km)**	**12038**	**11192**	**107.6**

资料来源：北京市市政市容管理委员会。
Source: Beijing Municipal Commission of City Administration and Environment.

9-5 液化石油气及天然气
LIQUEFIED PETROLEUM GAS AND NATURAL GAS

项目	Item	2014	2013	2014年为2013年% 2014 as % of 2013
液化石油气	**Liquefied Petroleum Gas**			
供气总量 （吨）	Gas Supply (ton)	546293	472980	115.5
销售气量 （吨）	Gas Sales (ton)	531556	453546	117.2
#家庭用量 （吨）	Domestic Consumption (ton)	234779	202468	116.0
家庭用户 （万户）	Domestic Consumers (10000 households)	278.2	190.5	146.0
天然气	**Natural Gas**			
供气总量 （万立方米）	Gas Supply (10000 cu.m)	1136874	994222	114.3
销售气量 （万立方米）	Gas Sales (10000 cu.m)	1088999	956852	113.8
#家庭用量 （万立方米）	Domestic Consumption (10000 cu.m)	126503	119406	105.9
家庭用户 （万户）	Domestic Consumers (10000 households)	567.8	546.9	103.8
居民燃气用户 （万户）	**Household Gas Users (10000 households)**	**846.0**	**737.4**	**114.7**

注：本表天然气、液化石油气用量中包含燕山石化用气量。
资料来源：北京市市政市容管理委员会、中国石化集团北京燕山石化有限公司。
Note: Data on natural gas consumption and liquefied petroleum gas consumption in this table include the consumption of Yanshan Petrochemical.
Source: Beijing Municipal Commission of City Administration and Environment, and SINOPEC Beijing Yanshan Petrochemical Co., Ltd.

9-6 自来水及自备水源
TAP WATER AND SELF-PROVIDED SOURCES OF WATER

项目		Item		2014	2013
自来水		**Tap Water**			
综合生产能力	(万立方米/日)	General Production Capacity	(10000cu.m/day)	503	444
供水管道长度	(公里)	Length of Water Supply Pipelines	(km)	14994	14495
销售总量	(万立方米)	Total Sales Volume	(10000 cu.m)	103402	98178
#生产运营用	(万立方米)	For Production Use	(10000 cu.m)	12661	12161
公共服务用	(万立方米)	For Public Service Use	(10000 cu.m)	37865	36045
居民家庭用	(万立方米)	For Domestic Use	(10000 cu.m)	51739	49268
自备井水		**Self-provided Well Water**			
用水量	(万立方米)	Consumption	(10000 cu.m)	59373	69634
#生产运营用	(万立方米)	For Production Use	(10000 cu.m)	14811	15705
公共服务用	(万立方米)	For Public Service Use	(10000 cu.m)	18130	19158
居民家庭用	(万立方米)	For Domestic Use	(10000 cu.m)	19378	26854

注：自来水数据口径为城镇公共供水。2013年起自备井水相关数据的填报范围调整为市区、卫星城、中心镇、一般建制镇，不含农业。
资料来源：北京市水务局。

Note: Statistical basis for tap water is urban public water supply. Since 2013, statistical scope for the data on self-provided well water were changed to cover urban area, satellite city, central town, town with general organizational structure, except agriculture.
Source: Beijing Water Authority.

9-7 公共交通及客运出租小轿车
PUBLIC TRANSPORT AND TAXI SERVICES

项目		Item		2014	2013
公共交通		**Public Transportation**			
运营车辆	(辆)	Operating Vehicles	(unit)	28331	27590
公共电汽车	(辆)	Buses and Trolley Buses	(unit)	23667	23592
轨道交通	(辆)	Rail Transit	(unit)	4664	3998
运营线路条数	(条)	Number of Operating Routes	(line)	895	830
公共电汽车	(条)	Buses and Trolley Buses	(line)	877	813
轨道交通	(条)	Rail Transit	(line)	18	17
运营线路长度	(公里)	Length of Operating Routes	(km)	20776	20153
公共电汽车	(公里)	Buses and Trolley Buses	(km)	20249	19688
轨道交通	(公里)	Rail Transit	(km)	527	465
客运量	(万人次)	Passenger Traffic	(10000 person-times)	815849	804775
公共电汽车	(万人次)	Buses and Trolley Buses	(10000 person-times)	477180	484306
轨道交通	(万人次)	Rail Transit	(10000 person-times)	338668	320469
客运出租小轿车		**Taxi Services**			
年末运营车辆	(辆)	Vehicles in Operation (year-end)	(unit)	67546	67046
客运量	(万人次)	Passenger Traffic	(10000 person-times)	66828	69946

资料来源：北京市交通委员会。
Source: Beijing Municipal Commission of Transport.

9-8 市政设施情况
BASIC STATISTICS FOR MUNICIPAL FACILITIES

项　目		Item		2014	2013
境内道路总里程	(公里)	Total Length of Highways and Roads	(km)	29209	28808
高速公路里程	(公里)	Length of Expressways	(km)	982	923
城市道路里程	(公里)	Length of Urban Roads	(km)	6426	6295
#快速路	(公里)	Rapid Roads	(km)	383	269
#主干路	(公里)	Trunk Roads	(km)	965	953
城市道路面积	(万平方米)	Coverage of Urban Roads	(10000 sq.m)	10002	9611
#铺装步道	(万平方米)	Paved Roads	(10000 sq.m)	1667	1639
城市道路立交桥数	(座)	Number of Overpasses in City	(unit)	422	414
城市过街天桥数	(座)	Number of Pedestrain Overpasses in City	(unit)	528	520
城市地下通道数	(座)	Number of Underpasses in City	(unit)	211	211
备案停车场个数	(个)	Number of Parking Lots Recorded	(unit)	6448	5964
备案停车场车位总数	(个)	Total Capacity of Parking Lots Recorded	(unit)	1757718	1574126
路口电视监视点位	(台)	TV Monitors at Crossings	(unit)	1235	1235
城六区照明线路长度	(公里)	Length of Lighting Lines in 6 Urban District	(km)	6407	6194

注：1. 本表统计范围为城六区。
　　2. 表中"备案停车场个数"和"备案停车场车位总数"为原指标"经营性停车场个数"和"经营性停车场车位总数"。
资料来源：北京市交通委员会、北京市公安交通管理局、北京市路灯管理中心。

Note: a) Data in this table covers 6 urban districts .
　　b) In the table, the "Parking Lots Recorded" and "Total Capacity of Parking Lots Recorded" are the original indicators "Operational Parking Lots" and "Total Capacity of Operational Parking Lots".

Source: Beijing Municipal Communission of Transport, Beijing Administration for Public Security & Traffic, Beijing Street Lamp Administration Center.

主要统计指标解释

自来水综合生产能力 指按供水设施取水、净化、送水、出厂输水干管等环节实际测定计算的综合生产能力。不包括供水高峰阶段，超负荷增加的生产能力。计算时，以四个环节中最薄弱的环节为主确定能力。

自来水供水管道长度 指从送水泵至用户水表之间所有管道的长度。不包括新安装尚未使用的管道。

生产运营用水 指在城市范围内生产、运营的农、林、牧、渔业、工业、建筑业、交通运输业等单位在生产、运营过程中的用水。

公共服务用水 指为城市社会公共生活服务的用水。包括行政事业单位、部队营区和公共设施服务、社会服务业、批发零售贸易业、旅馆饮食业以及社会服务业等单位的用水。

居民家庭用水 指城市范围内所有居民家庭的日常生活用水。包括城市居民家庭、农民家庭、公共供水站用水。

公共交通年末运营车辆 指公交企业（单位）用于运营业务的全部车辆数。

运营线路总长度 指全部运营线路长度之和。计算公式：

$$运营线路长度 = \sum 各条运营线路长度$$

$$= \sum\left[\begin{pmatrix}上行起点至终点里程 + 下行起点至终点里程 \\ + 上下行终点掉头里程\end{pmatrix}\right]$$

公路里程 指公路的长度，凡达到《公路工程技术标准（JTGB01-2003)》规定的技术等级的公路，均统计公路里程，包括大、中城市的郊区公路里程，公路通过城镇（指县城、集镇）街道的里程和公路桥梁长度、隧道长度、渡口的宽度以及分期修建的公路已验收交付使用的里程。国道、省道、县道、乡道和专用公路中新增的人工修建的、路基宽度在4.5米以上的等外路里程也纳入公路里程统计。按技术等级公路可分为高速公路、一级公路、二级公路、三级公路、四级公路和等外公路。

道路里程 指道路长度和与道路相通的桥梁、隧道的长度，按车行道中心线计算。城市道路由车行道和人行道两部分组成。在统计时只统计路面宽度在3.5米（含3.5米）以上的各种铺装道路，包括开放型工业区和住宅区道路在内。

道路面积 指道路面积和与道路相通的广场、桥梁、隧道的面积（统计时，将人行道面积单独统计）。人行道面积按道路两侧面积相加计算。包括步行街和广场，不含人车混行的道路。

Explanatory Notes on Main Statistical Indicators

General Production Capacity of Tap Water means the comprehensive production capacity of water facilities calculated by on-site measurement, including capacity of the water in-taking, treatment, transmission and delivery; while overloaded capacity during water supply peak hours are not included. Calculation of the capacity was mainly dependent upon the weakest link of the whole production process.

Length of Tap Water Supply Pipelines means the length of all pipes linking between the water outlet pumps and users' water meters, excluding the ones newly installed and not yet put into use.

Water for Production Use means the water used for production and operation of business entities within the city, covering sectors including agriculture, forestry, animal production and hunting, fishing, industry, construction, transportation, etc.

Water for Public Service Use means the water used for urban public services, including water supply for administrative and public institutions, military units, public facilities, social services, wholesale and retail trades, hotels and catering, and social service organizations.

Water for Domestic Use means the water used for daily life of all households in urban area, including the water used for urban residents, rural households, and public water supply stations.

Year-end Public Transport Vehicles in Operation means the number of all vehicles used for operational businesses in public transit enterprises (institutions).

Total Length of Public Transport Routes means the sum of all lines in operation. It is calculated with the formula:

Length of Public Transit Lines = ∑ Length of all lines in operation = ∑ [(mileage from the upward starting point to the end point + mileage from the downward starting point to the end point + mileage of double back from upward and downward end points)]

Total Length of Highways means the length of highways. Such statistics apply for any highway reaching the technical grade stated in *Highway Engineering Technical Standards (JTGB01-2003)*, including the mileage of highways in suburbs of middle and large cities, mileage of highways passing through streets in towns (counties and townships), length of highway bridges, length of tunnels, width of ferries, and mileage of highways constructed in several phases and put into use. The mileage of non-graded new highways built manually onto national highways, provincial highways, county highways, township highways and special highways, with roadbed width of 4.5m and above, are also incorporated. In terms of technical grade, highways fall into expressways, first-grade highways, second-grade highways, third-grade highways, fourth-grade highways, and non-graded highways.

Length of Highways and Roads means the length of roads and bridges and tunnels connecting with roads, calculated by the central lines of carriage ways. Urban roads consist of carriageways and sidewalks. Statistics only cover paved roads with width of pavement above 3.5m (including 3.5m), roads in open industrial zones and residential zones included.

Area of Roads means the area of roads and the area of squares, bridges and tunnels connecting to the roads (the area of sidewalks is calculated separately). The area of sidewalks is the sum of area on both sides of roads, including pedestrian streets and squares, excluding roads passable for both pedestrians and vehicles.

10

农业及农村经济
AGRICULTURE AND RURAL ECONOMY

简要说明

一、本章资料的主要内容

本章资料反映北京市农业生产和农村经济基本情况，主要包括农村基层组织情况、农村地区人口、从业人员、耕地、农林牧渔业产值及主要农产品生产情况、设施农业、农业观光园、民俗旅游、农村固定资产投资、乡镇企业情况、农村经济收入与分配情况等。

二、本章资料的统计范围

农林牧渔业统计范围包括辖区内全部农林牧渔业生产单位、非农行业单位附属的农林牧渔业生产活动单位以及农户的农业生产活动。军委系统的农林牧渔业生产（除军马外）也应包括在内，但不包括农业科学试验机构进行的农业生产。

1. 农业：指各种农作物的种植活动。包括谷物、豆类、薯类、棉花、油料、糖料、麻类、烟叶、蔬菜、食用菌及花卉盆景园艺产品、水果、坚果、饲料和香料作物、药材及其它作物的种植。

2. 林业：包括林木的栽培(不包括茶园、桑园和果园的栽培、管理和收获等活动)、木材和竹材的采运、林产品的采集。

3. 畜牧业：包括牲畜饲养和放牧、家禽饲养以及野生动物的捕猎和饲养。

4. 渔业：分为淡水养殖和海水养殖，包括水生动物和海藻类植物的养殖和捕捞。

农村社会经济统计范围包括所有乡镇辖区内的社会经济活动。

三、本章资料的数据来源

乡镇企业数据由北京市经济和信息化委员会提供。农村经济收入分配数据由北京市农村经济研究中心农村合作经济经营管理站提供，耕地数据由北京市国土资源局提供，林业数据由北京市园林绿化局提供，水产品数据由北京市农业局提供，农村基层组织资料由北京市民政局提供。其余资料均由北京市统计局、国家统计局北京调查总队提供。

四、本章资料的调查方法和核算方法

根据农业生产特点，农林牧渔业总产值的核算采用“产品法”计算，即用产品产量乘以价格求出各种产品的产值，按产品产值类别分别汇总，计算出农林牧渔各业的产值，各业相加为农林牧渔业总产值。

(1)农业：包括谷物和其他作物；蔬菜、食用菌及花卉盆景园艺产品；水果、坚果、饲料、香料；中药材。

(2)林业：包括林木的培育和种植；木材、竹材采运；林产品的采集。

(3)牧业：包括除渔业养殖以外的一切动物饲养和放牧以及野生动物的捕猎和饲养。

(4)渔业：包括水生动物和海藻类植物的养殖和捕捞。

(5)服务业：产值等于农林牧渔服务业营业收入。

1957 年以前的农业总产值中包括了厩肥和农民自给性手工业（如农民自制衣服、鞋、袜，自己从事粮食初步加工等）。1958 年及以后的林业产值中增加了村及村以下竹木采伐产值；牧业中取消了厩肥产值；副业中取消了农民自给性手工业产值；渔业中增加了海洋捕捞水产品产值。1980 年及以后的农业总产值，在副业中增加了农民家庭兼营工业商品部分的产值。从 1984 年起村及村以下办工业产值划归工业。从 1993 年起，取消副业，将野生动物的捕猎划入牧业，野生植物采集和农民家庭兼营商品性工业划归农业。从 2003 年起按照新的《国民经济行业分类》标准取消了“其它农业”；将农林牧渔服务业产值纳入农林牧渔业总产值中；从农林牧渔业总产值中取消了“家庭兼营商品性工业”；将村以上木材和竹材的采运划入了林业；产值计算采用生产者价格，即生产者第一次出售农产品的价格。2004 年国家统计局报表制度规定农林牧渔业总产值增加按可比价计算的产值及发展速度（计算方法：用现价产值的中类数据除以中类缩减指数求得各中类的可比价产值，各中类相加得大类的可比价产值，最后用大类数据相加得农业可比价总产值，可比价产值除以上年现价产值得发展速度）。从 2005 年起，取消了按 1990 年价格计算的农业产值。由于 2006 年农业普查后对农业生产历史数据进行了修订，新修订的农业产值数据只到大类，如果按大类缩减计算农业可比价总产值不符合国家报表制度要求，故 2005 年及以前年度没有按可比价计算的发展速度。2010 年起，根据新的《统计用产品分类目录》将原林业产值中的核桃、栗子、白果、松子等干果产值调整至农业产值中，为同口径对比，将 2009 年年报数据也作了相应调整。

主要粮食播种面积数据通过卫星遥感测量方法取得,粮食产量数据通过抽样调查方法取得。农林牧渔业生产统计采取全面调查方法，村级起报。

五、本章中关于历史数据调整的问题

根据 2006 年第二次农业普查结果，北京市统计局、国家统计局北京调查总队按照国务院农普办要求，依照国际通用做法，已对 1997—2005 年的相关指标历史数据进行了修订。

Brief Introduction

I. Main Content

Statistics in this chapter show basic situation of agricultural production and rural economy in Beijing, mainly consisting of statistics for rural grass-root organizations, population and employment, arable land, output of agriculture, forestry, animal production and hunting, fishing, production of main agricultural products, facility agriculture, agricultural sightseeing gardens, folk-custom tourism, investment in fixed assets in rural areas, township enterprises, income and distribution of rural economy.

II. Scope of Statistics

Statistics on agriculture, forestry, animal production and hunting, fishing cover all related producing entities, producers affiliated to non-agricultural departments, as well as farmers' agricultural production activities. Production by the military commission system shall also be included (except for army horse breeding), but the production by scientific testing agencies is not included.

1. Agriculture: It refers to the growing of various agricultural crops, including grains, beans, potatoes, cotton, oil plants, sugar plants, fiber plants, tobacco leaves, vegetables, edible fungus, flower bonsai and gardening products, fruits, nuts, feedstuff, and spice crops, herbs, and other crops.

2. Forestry: It includes tree planting (except for the cultivation, management and harvest of tea gardens, mulberry fields, and orchards), the logging of timber and bamboo, and the collection of forestry products.

3. Animal production and hunting: It includes the breeding and grazing of livestock, poultry agriculture, as well as hunting and breeding of wildlife.

4. Fishing: It falls into two parts: freshwater agriculture and mariculture, including the cultivation and fishing for aquatic animals and algae.

Statistics for social and economic development in rural areas cover social and economic activities of all villages and towns within the jurisdiction.

III. Source of Statistics

Statistics on township enterprises were provided by Beijing Municipal Commission of Economy and Information Technology. Statistics on income distribution in rural economy were provided by the Operation and Management Station of Rural Cooperative Economy, Beijing Research Center for Rural Economy. Statistics on arable land were provided by Beijing Municipal Bureau of Land and Resources. Forestry statistics were provided by Beijing Municipal Bureau of Landscape and Forestry. Statistics on aquatic products were provided by Beijing Municipal Bureau of Agriculture. Statistics on rural basic organization were provided by Beijing Municipal Bureau of civil Affairs. All other statistics were provided by Beijing Municipal Bureau of Statistics and National Bureau of Statistics Survey Office in Beijing.

IV. Method for Survey and Counting

Based on agricultural production characteristics, the gross output value of agriculture, forestry, animal production and hunting, fishing was calculated by the "product approach"--that is to multiply production volume by the unit price, so as to get output value of each product, then sum it up by category, namely agriculture, forestry, animal production and hunting, fishing; and the sum total of these categories will be gross output value of the whole sector.

(1) Agriculture: including cereal and other crops; vegetables, edible mushrooms, flower bonsai and gardening products; fruits, nuts, beverage, spices, and herbs.

(2) Forestry: including the cultivation and planting of forest trees; logging of timber and bamboo; and collection of forestry products.

(3) Animal production and hunting: including the breeding and grazing of animals other than fish breeding, as well as hunting and breeding of wildlife.

(4) Fishing: including cultivation and catching of aquatic animals and seaweed plants.

(5) Service: the output value equals the operating income of services in support of agriculture, forestry, animal production and hunting, fishing.

Prior to 1957, China's gross agricultural output value included the output of barnyard manure and handicraft products for self-consumption (e.g. clothes, shoes, socks, and primary grain processing by peasants). Since 1958, output value of bamboo and timber logging by villages and units subordinated to villages has been included in the statistics of forestry; output value of barnyard manure has been excluded from animal production and hunting statistics; subsistence handicrafts has been excluded from sideline products output value; and the output value of aquatic products by marine fishing has been added to fishing. Since 1980, the output value of industrial commodities operated by rural households has been included in the output value of sideline products. Since 1984, industrial output value produced by villages and units subordinated to villages has been added in the sector of industry. In 1993, the group "sideline products" was cancelled; the hunting of wild animals has been classified as animal production and hunting, and the gathering of wild plants and commercial industrial businesses run by rural households have been included in agriculture. A new Standard for *Classification of National Economic Sectors* was introduced in 2003. According to the new classification, the group "other agricultural activities" was cancelled; the output value of services in support of agriculture, forestry, animal production and hunting, fishing is included in the gross output value of agriculture; the value of industrial output by households is excluded; output value of wood and bamboo logging is included in forestry statistics; the output value is calculated at the producer's price, namely the price at which producers sell their agricultural products for the first time; the 2004 Reporting System of National Bureau of Statistics states that, for incremental gross output value of agriculture, forestry, animal production and hunting, fishing, the output value and growth rate shall be calculated at comparable prices (calculation method: use the output value of groups at present prices to divide the groups' deflator, so as to get the output value at comparable prices; then add up the groups' output value to get the whole division's output value at comparable prices; in the end, add up all divisions' output value to get the gross output value at comparable prices for agriculture sector and divide the output value at comparable prices by the output value at current prices in the previous year to get the growth rate). Since 2005, the practice of using prices of 1990 as reference numbers to calculate agricultural output value has been cancelled. As historical data of agricultural production were revised after the agricultural census in 2006, revised agricultural production output value figures were presented only in divisions; and it does not meet the requirements of national reporting system to calculate the gross agricultural output value at comparable prices by divisions' deflator. Therefore, there were no figures of growth rate at comparable prices in and prior to 2005. Since 2010, the output value of nuts such as walnuts, chestnuts, gingkoes and pine nuts formerly included in forestry has been added in the output value of framing according to the new *Catalog on Statistical Product Classification*. In order to conduct same-caliber comparison, data in the 2009 annual report have also been adjusted accordingly.

Data on the sown area of major grain were collected by satellite remote sensing; data on grain yield were gathered through sampling survey; and the production figures on agriculture, forestry, animal production and hunting, fishing sectors were added up by complete survey, starting from the village level.

V. Adjustments to Historical Statistics

Based on results of the second agricultural census 2006, Beijing Municipal Bureau of Statistics and NBS Survey Office in Beijing revised related historical statistics during 1997-2005 as required by the Agricultural Census Office of the State Council and in accordance with the international practice.

10-1 农村基本情况(1978-2014年)
BASIC STATISTICS FOR RURAL AREAS (1978-2014)

年份 Year	乡政府 (个) Township Governments (unit)	镇政府 (个) Town Governments (unit)	村民委员会 (个) Villagers' Committees (unit)	乡镇及行政村常住户数 (万户) Number of Permanent Households in Towns and Administrative Villages (10000 households)	乡镇及行政村常住人口 (万人) Permanent Population in Towns and Administrative Villages (10000 persons)	乡镇及行政村从业人员 (万人) Employed Persons in Towns and Administrative Villages (10000 persons)
1978				91.9	382.1	165.3
1979				92.9	374.7	165.1
1980				95.0	374.3	167.4
1981				98.9	377.6	172.9
1982				103.2	381.8	179.4
1983				106.6	384.0	184.6
1984				108.9	385.6	188.9
1985	350	15	4394	111.8	387.2	190.0
1986	327	15	4400	113.1	386.9	189.5
1987	324	14	4326	115.7	388.9	189.8
1988	321	13	4111	118.6	389.6	189.2
1989	322	14	4483	121.5	390.0	186.1
1990	252	77	4481	124.5	392.0	184.3
1991	209	77	4480	125.5	390.7	182.1
1992	209	77	4229	126.2	387.6	178.7
1993	192	81	4476	126.5	382.4	176.0
1994	174	92	4464	124.9	376.0	171.6
1995	166	100	4355	125.0	371.5	163.6
1996	166	100	4357	124.6	368.9	164.2
1997	132	108	4348	124.6	365.3	161.2
1998	126	105	4032	125.9	364.4	161.0
1999	125	103	4040	125.9	363.9	165.3
2000	70	142	4039	126.8	363.7	165.8
2001	52	139	4010	127.6	361.6	165.3
2002	51	141	4005	128.0	357.6	165.6
2003	45	142	3985	131.1	360.6	169.6
2004	42	142	3985	132.8	359.9	171.4
2005	43	142	3953	142.2	381.8	184.0
2006	41	142	3957	143.6	501.6	316.9
2007	41	142	3955	176.9	510.0	313.4
2008	40	142	3951	189.8	547.4	321.3
2009	40	142	3950	203.8	572.5	338.7
2010	40	142	3943	216.0	589.4	347.8
2011	38	144	3941	212.4	574.8	338.3
2012	38	144	3940	215.2	582.5	341.7
2013	38	144	3938	221.9	599.5	353.5
2014	38	144	3937	225.2	606.9	357.0

注：1. 从业人员指标1998年以前为乡村劳动力。
2. 乡政府个数、镇政府个数、村民委员会个数由北京市民政局提供。
3. 2006年乡镇及行政村人口和从业人员为农业普查数据；2007年以后乡镇及行政村人口和从业人员为农业普查口径，包含居住半年以上外来人口。
4. 2006年乡镇及行政村户数为农业普查数据，为自然户口径；2007年以后为居住一年以上的户口径。

Note: a) Employed persons before 1998 were rural labor force.
b) Numbers of township governments, town governments, villagers' committees are provided by Beijing Municipal Bureau of Civil Affairs.
c) Population and employed persons in towns and administrative villages were agriculture census data in 2006. Statistical range of agriculture census data have covered population and employed persons in towns and administrative villages since 2007 including migrant population residing for over 6 months.
d) Number of households in towns and administrative villages in 2006 was from agricultural census, using natural households as the caliber; since 2007, the caliber was changed into households residing for over a year.

10-2 农业生产条件(1978-2014年)
CONDITIONS FOR AGRICULTURAL PRODUCTION (1978-2014)

年份 Year	年末实有耕地面积(万公顷) Actual Area of Arable Land (year-end) (10000 hectares)	有效灌溉面积(千公顷) Effective Irrigation Area (1000 hectares)	农业机械总动力(万千瓦) Total Power of Agricultural Machinery (10000 kw)	农村用电量(万千瓦小时) Rural Electricity Consumption (10000 kwh)	化肥施用量(万吨) Consumption of Chemical Fertilizers (10000 tons)
1978	42.9	341.7	189.4	58802	11.6
1979	42.7	340.8	212.2	63124	11.3
1980	42.6	340.3	234.6	76753	12.3
1981	42.5	341.3	244.8	91844	11.2
1982	42.4	339.4	242.2	96961	12.0
1983	42.3	343.3	261.8	104608	12.0
1984	42.2	342.6	290.8	119289	10.7
1985	42.1	338.4	320.4	126830	8.2
1986	41.9	337.9	345.5	180640	9.1
1987	41.8	337.9	388.4	159450	10.0
1988	41.6	338.1	399.7	163986	10.6
1989	41.4	338.4	423.9	128414	11.8
1990	41.3	335.1	416.2	122711	14.4
1991	41.1	328.7	384.8	111347	14.4
1992	40.9	331.1	399.8	143963	14.4
1993	40.6	314.7	450.5	169911	14.9
1994	40.2	323.4	459.2	172042	19.8
1995	39.4	292.4	468.1	201731	18.8
1996	34.4	301.9	468.4	275871	18.9
1997	34.2	323.3	433.2	301655	19.7
1998	34.1	323.7	415.5	290859	19.3
1999	33.8	322.1	410.4	330069	19.0
2000	32.9	322.7	399.2	572257	17.9
2001	29.2	322.7	394.9	619806	15.7
2002	27.5	219.7	381.8	414248	14.9
2003	26.0	178.9	366.9	427266	14.3
2004	23.6	186.7	340.3	383954	14.5
2005	23.3	181.5	337.7	421680	14.8
2006	23.3	181.5	325.5	416459	14.8
2007	23.2	173.6	300.5	411238	14.0
2008	23.2	171.8	267.0	427377	13.6
2009	22.7	165.2	271.5	439099	13.8
2010	22.4	162.6	276.0	443774	13.7
2011	22.2	163.1	265.2	454009	13.8
2012	22.1	159.2	241.1	473121	13.7
2013	22.1	154.4	207.7	485320	12.8
2014		158.3	195.8	505559	11.6

注：1. 化肥施用量为折纯量。
2. 2003年以前农村用电量由原北京市供电局提供。
3. 农业机械总动力数据由北京市农业局提供。
4. 1991-2001年有效灌溉面积由北京市水务局提供。

Note: a) Data on consumption of chemical fertilizers were net amount.
b) Figures of rural electricity consumption before 2003 were provided by the former Beijing Electric Power Supply Bureau.
c) Figures of total power of agricultural machinery were provided by Beijing Municipal Bureau of Agriculture.
d) Figures of irrigated area 1991-2001 were provided by Beijing Water Authority.

10-3 农作物播种面积和造林面积(1978-2014年)
SOWN AND AFFORESTATION AREA (1978-2014)

年 份 Year	农作物播种面积(万公顷) Sown Area (10000 hectares)	#粮食作物 Grain Crops	#玉米 Corn	#小麦 Wheat	#油料 Oil-bearing Crops	#蔬菜及食用菌 Vegetables and Edible Mushrooms	#瓜类及草莓 Melons & Strawberries	#饲料 Forage	造林面积(万公顷) Afforestation Area (10000 hectares)
1978	69.1	56.1	16.9	19.2	3.3	5.6	0.2	2.0	1.4
1979	67.7	56.0	18.2	19.7	3.0	5.4	0.3	2.0	1.6
1980	65.7	54.9	19.7	18.8	2.8	5.1	0.4	1.8	2.4
1981	64.4	53.0	19.8	18.4	2.7	5.5	0.6	1.7	2.7
1982	64.2	52.7	19.7	18.1	2.4	5.9	0.8	1.6	2.8
1983	63.8	53.0	20.1	18.7	1.9	5.7	0.5	1.5	3.3
1984	63.3	52.3	20.6	19.5	1.8	5.8	0.7	1.5	3.2
1985	61.8	51.1	21.7	19.1	2.0	5.4	0.9	1.3	3.0
1986	60.5	49.9	21.6	18.5	2.0	5.8	1.1	1.0	1.5
1987	59.8	49.5	22.3	18.3	1.6	6.0	0.9	1.1	2.0
1988	59.5	48.8	22.2	18.6	1.5	6.3	1.0	1.2	1.6
1989	58.9	48.3	21.9	18.5	1.3	6.8	0.8	1.1	0.8
1990	59.0	48.4	22.4	18.8	1.2	7.0	0.6	1.1	1.3
1991	59.0	48.3	22.3	19.2	1.2	7.3	0.5	1.0	1.5
1992	58.5	47.7	22.4	19.2	1.2	7.5	0.5	0.8	1.5
1993	56.5	45.6	21.8	17.8	1.3	7.8	0.5	0.7	4.8
1994	55.1	43.0	20.6	16.4	1.2	9.1	0.6	0.6	5.5
1995	55.3	43.4	20.8	17.2	1.2	9.1	0.5		4.7
1996	53.8	42.7	20.8	17.1	1.1	8.8	0.5	0.5	4.0
1997	53.6	42.5	20.6	17.1	1.0	8.9	0.5	0.5	3.8
1998	53.5	42.3	20.8	17.1	1.0	9.0	0.5	0.5	3.7
1999	52.6	41.0	19.8	16.8	1.0	9.2	0.5	0.5	3.0
2000	45.4	30.8	13.6	12.2	1.5	10.4	0.8	1.2	2.6
2001	38.0	21.4	10.0	7.3	1.4	11.3	0.9	1.9	3.2
2002	33.5	16.9	8.7	4.7	1.6	11.5	0.9	1.8	4.8
2003	30.1	14.1	7.5	3.6	1.4	10.8	0.9	1.9	4.7
2004	30.4	15.4	9.4	3.9	1.1	9.1	0.8	2.8	3.2
2005	30.8	19.2	12.0	5.3	0.9	7.9	0.8	1.5	1.2
2006	32.0	22.0	13.6	6.3	0.7	7.1	0.9	0.6	1.3
2007	29.5	19.7	13.9	4.1	0.7	7.0	0.9	0.4	1.1
2008	32.2	22.6	14.6	6.4	0.7	6.8	0.8	0.4	0.9
2009	32.0	22.6	15.1	6.1	0.6	6.8	0.8	0.4	1.8
2010	31.7	22.3	15.0	6.2	0.5	6.8	0.8	0.5	1.4
2011	30.3	20.9	14.1	5.8	0.5	6.7	0.8	0.5	2.1
2012	28.3	19.4	13.2	5.2	0.5	6.4	0.8	0.3	3.6
2013	24.2	15.9	11.4	3.6	0.3	6.2	0.7	0.2	4.4
2014	20.0	12.0	8.9	2.4	0.3	5.7	0.6	0.3	2.3

注：1．蔬菜播种面积2006年为农业普查衔接数据，1997年-2005年为历史修订数据。

2．造林面积2009年以前为人工造林面积，2009年起调整为荒山荒(沙)地造林面积，包括人工造林、无林地和疏林地新封面积。

Note: a) Figures of vegetable sown area in 2006 were from agricultural census, and figures in 1997-2005 were historically revised data.

b) Afforestation area before 2009 was artificial afforestation area, and after 2009 it became barren mountains and barren (sand) afforestation area, including the area of artificial forests, non-forest land and newly enclosed forest land.

10-4 农林牧渔业总产值(1978-2014年)

GROSS OUTPUT VALUE OF AGRICULTURE, FORESTRY, ANIMAL PRODUCTION AND HUNTING, FISHING (1978-2014)

年份 Year	农林牧渔业总产值(亿元) Gross Output Value of Agriculture, Forestry, Animal Production and Hunting, Fishing (RMB 100 million)	农业 Agriculture	林业 Forestry	牧业 Animal Production and Hunting	渔业 Fishing	农林牧渔服务业 Related Service Industry	农林牧渔业总产值比上年增长(%) Growth Rate (%) 按现价计算 Calculated at Current Price	按可比价计算 Calculated at Comparable Price
1978	11.5	8.9	0.2	2.4	0.01			
1979	12.3	8.8	0.2	3.3	0.02		7.0	
1980	14.3	9.8	0.5	3.9	0.05		16.3	
1981-1985	**99.4**	**64.6**	**3.9**	**30.1**	**0.8**			
1981	14.9	10.1	0.7	4.1	0.05		4.2	
1982	16.8	11.3	0.7	4.7	0.05		12.8	
1983	19.6	12.7	0.8	6.0	0.1		16.7	
1984	22.2	14.4	0.9	6.7	0.2		13.3	
1985	25.9	16.1	0.8	8.6	0.4		16.7	
1986-1990	**245.7**	**142.1**	**4.1**	**91.6**	**7.9**			
1986	28.1	17.2	0.8	9.4	0.7		8.5	
1987	34.4	20.3	0.8	12.3	1.0		22.4	
1988	52.6	31.4	0.9	18.6	1.7		52.9	
1989	60.4	34.2	0.7	23.3	2.2		14.8	
1990	70.2	39.0	0.9	28.0	2.3		16.2	
1991-1995	**570.1**	**293.2**	**11.2**	**244.6**	**21.1**			
1991	76.5	39.6	1.5	32.8	2.6		9.0	
1992	84.5	43.2	1.6	36.3	3.4		10.5	
1993	100.4	51.1	2.3	42.7	4.3		18.8	
1994	144.3	72.5	3.1	64.0	4.7		43.7	
1995	164.4	86.8	2.7	68.8	6.1		13.9	
1996-2000	**883.4**	**441.8**	**18.2**	**388.5**	**34.9**			
1996	168.9	89.2	2.8	71.1	5.8		2.7	
1997	170.5	86.8	2.9	74.6	6.2		0.9	
1998	174.8	88.3	3.2	75.8	7.5		2.5	
1999	180.6	89.4	4.1	79.5	7.6		3.3	
2000	188.6	88.1	5.2	87.5	7.8		4.4	
2001-2005	**1114.6**	**423.2**	**57.0**	**567.3**	**45.6**			
2001	202.2	84.7	9.0	99.3	9.2		7.2	
2002	213.5	83.5	11.9	108.6	9.5		5.6	
2003	224.7	80.9	12.3	114.3	9.3	7.9	5.2	
2004	234.9	83.1	11.4	124.3	8.9	7.2	4.5	
2005	239.3	91.0	12.4	120.8	8.7	6.4	1.9	
2006-2010	**1459.4**	**648.4**	**87.1**	**643.7**	**51.5**	**28.7**		
2006	240.2	104.5	14.8	105.1	9.8	6.0	0.4	0.9
2007	272.3	115.5	17.8	122.4	10.1	6.5	13.4	0.8
2008	303.9	128.1	20.5	140.5	9.8	5.0	11.6	0.8
2009	315.0	146.1	17.2	136.1	10.3	5.3	3.6	5.5
2010	328.0	154.2	16.8	139.6	11.5	5.9	4.1	-1.7
2011	363.1	163.4	18.9	162.7	11.5	6.6	10.7	0.9
2012	395.7	166.3	54.8	154.2	13.0	7.5	9.0	2.9
2013	421.8	170.4	75.9	154.8	12.8	8.0	6.6	2.1
2014	420.1	155.1	90.7	152.7	13.2	8.4	-0.4	持平

注：1.农林牧渔业总产值绝对数按现价计算，从2003年起执行新《国民经济行业分类标准》，农林牧渔业总产值中含农林牧渔服务业产值。
2.2003年以后，计算农林牧渔业总产值使用的价格从农产品综合平均价调整为农产品生产价格。
3.2006年为与农业普查衔接的数据，1997-2005年为历史修订数据。
4.2010年按照新的《统计用产品分类目录》，将原归属林业产值的核桃、板栗等林产品调整至农业产值，并对2009年数据作了调整。

Note: a) The absolute number of agricultural gross output value are calculated at current prices. In the year of 2003, new Standard for Classification of National Economic Sectors was implemented, and gross output value of agriculture, forestry, animal production and hunting, fishing has included the output value of services for agriculture, forestry, animal production and hunting, fishing.

b) After 2003, the prices used for calculating the output value of agriculture, forestry, animal production and hunting, fishing have been changed from comprehensive average price of agricultural products to production price of agricultural products.

c) Figures for 2006 were from agricultural census, and figures in 1997-2005 were historically revised data.

d) Output value of forestry productions such as walnuts and chestnuts was transferred to that of the agriculture sector in 2010 according to the new Catalog of Product Classification Used for Statistics. Figures of 2009 were adjusted accordingly.

10-5 主要农业产品产量(1978-2014年)
OUTPUT OF MAJOR AGRICULTURAL PRODUCTS (1978-2014)

单位：万吨 (10000 tons)

年 份 Year	粮 食 Grain	油 料 Oil-bearing Crops	蔬菜及食用菌 Vegetables and Edible Mushroom	干鲜果品 Nuts and Fresh Fruits	牛 奶 Milk	肉 类 Meat	#猪牛羊肉 Pork, Beef and Mutton	禽蛋产量 Poultry and Eggs	水产品 Aquatic Products
1978	186.0	2.6	164.5	17.5	5.4	11.9	11.9	2.1	0.2
1979	172.8	2.6	181.3	15.8	6.0	13.1	13.1	3.1	0.3
1980	186.0	3.1	175.9	15.9	6.8	15.1	15.1	3.4	0.4
1981-1985	**1004.8**	**13.1**	**1002.2**	**86.7**	**53.3**	**69.0**	**69.0**	**44.3**	**4.0**
1981	180.7	2.2	172.8	15.6	7.6	13.2	13.2	3.7	0.4
1982	185.5	2.3	208.3	13.8	8.9	13.9	13.9	5.4	0.4
1983	201.5	2.1	199.1	18.2	10.6	14.9	14.9	8.9	0.6
1984	217.4	2.6	218.0	20.2	12.6	13.4	13.4	12.2	1.0
1985	219.7	3.9	204.0	18.9	13.5	13.6	13.6	14.1	1.6
1986-1990	**1181.9**	**15.2**	**1422.2**	**119.3**	**89.7**	**90.8**	**78.3**	**103.8**	**18.8**
1986	216.5	3.0	222.7	18.7	14.6	13.3	13.3	14.7	2.2
1987	227.0	3.3	241.1	22.5	15.5	12.9	12.9	16.8	3.0
1988	234.6	3.0	271.3	23.8	18.0	14.5	14.5	21.8	3.9
1989	239.2	2.8	331.0	26.7	19.9	23.3	17.2	24.7	4.6
1990	264.6	3.1	356.1	27.6	21.7	26.8	20.4	25.8	5.1
1991-1995	**1354.7**	**17.6**	**1915.9**	**198.5**	**113.7**	**180.7**	**134.0**	**139.3**	**34.7**
1991	279.7	3.3	368.4	29.3	23.9	33.9	24.8	27.9	5.6
1992	281.9	3.4	381.4	34.0	24.5	35.9	27.3	30.0	6.4
1993	284.1	3.8	418.8	39.6	22.5	36.7	28.2	31.4	7.0
1994	249.2	3.8	350.0	48.8	22.2	34.4	24.8	31.2	7.6
1995	259.8	3.3	397.3	46.8	20.6	39.8	28.9	28.5	8.1
1996-2000	**1059.4**	**15.0**	**2101.9**	**291.8**	**120.2**	**218.1**	**146.5**	**98.2**	**38.2**
1996	237.4	2.9	403.2	51.3	21.0	38.2	27.3	24.7	7.8
1997	237.5	2.7	408.8	54.8	22.2	39.9	27.8	23.8	7.7
1998	239.3	2.8	403.8	59.5	22.7	43.4	30.3	17.9	7.6
1999	201.0	2.8	419.8	60.2	24.0	46.1	30.2	15.8	7.6
2000	144.2	3.8	466.3	66.0	30.3	50.5	30.9	16.0	7.5
2001-2005	**410.3**	**18.5**	**2302.3**	**419.5**	**295.5**	**287.8**	**169.1**	**78.9**	**35.0**
2001	104.9	4.3	491.0	71.9	42.9	55.9	33.0	15.6	7.4
2002	82.3	4.6	507.4	78.7	55.1	60.9	35.2	15.2	7.4
2003	58.0	3.3	486.7	84.1	63.3	60.6	35.2	16.2	7.1
2004	70.2	2.9	444.1	90.9	70.0	57.4	34.0	15.9	6.7
2005	94.9	2.5	373.1	93.9	64.2	53.3	31.7	16.0	6.4
2006-2010	**577.3**	**10.0**	**1622.7**	**445.3**	**322.1**	**231.7**	**135.0**	**76.5**	**29.6**
2006	109.2	2.2	341.2	88.7	61.9	45.3	26.9	15.2	5.4
2007	102.1	2.2	340.1	91.1	62.2	47.9	27.1	15.6	6.0
2008	125.5	2.2	321.3	89.8	66.4	45.1	25.9	15.2	6.1
2009	124.8	1.8	317.1	90.3	67.4	47.2	27.6	15.4	5.8
2010	115.7	1.6	303.0	85.4	64.1	46.3	27.5	15.1	6.3
2011	121.8	1.4	296.9	87.8	64.0	44.4	27.6	15.1	6.1
2012	113.8	1.3	279.9	84.3	65.1	43.2	27.3	15.2	6.4
2013	96.1	1.0	266.9	79.5	61.5	41.8	27.9	17.5	6.4
2014	63.9	0.7	236.2	74.5	59.5	39.3	26.9	19.7	6.8

注：1. 蔬菜、干鲜果品、猪牛羊肉产量2006年为农业普查衔接数据，1997年-2005年为历史修订数据。
2. 肉类产量1988年及以前为猪牛羊肉产量。
3. 2006年及以前水产品产量为淡水鱼产量，2007年以后含远洋捕捞量。水产品数据由北京市农业局提供。

Note: a) Figures of output for vegetables, nuts and fresh fruits, pork, beef and mutton in 2006 were from agricultural census, and figures in 1997-2005 were historically revised data.
b) Output of meat in and before 1988 was the output of pork, beef and mutton.
c) Output of aquatic products was output of fresh water fish in and before 2006, and long-range fishing has been included since 2007. Figures of aquatic products were provided by Beijing Municipal Bureau of Agriculture.

10-6 平均每一从业人员创造农、林、牧、渔业产值(1990-2014年)
AVERAGE OUTPUT VALUE OF AGRICULTURE, FORESTRY, ANIMAL PRODUCTION AND HUNTING, FISHING CREATED BY EACH PERSON (1990-2014)

单位：元 (Yuan)

年 份 Year	农林牧渔业总产值 Total Output Value of Agriculture, Forestry, Animal Production and Hunting, Fishing	#农 业 Agriculture	#林 业 Forestry	#畜牧业 Animal Production and Hunting	#渔 业 Fishing
1990	8507	5537	1540	54837	22729
1991	9523	5722	2807	68268	26442
1992	11329	6678	3826	78905	33689
1993	13859	8271	4558	92901	39518
1994	21002	12461	6507	139136	39182
1995	25110	15760	5750	156332	47266
1996	25250	15504	6741	173404	53133
1997	26101	15605	6886	169541	56211
1998	25817	15653	7724	124279	68379
1999	25396	15621	8398	101869	63684
2000	27061	16454	8416	99481	65223
2001	29772	16838	12287	109151	76321
2002	33313	18193	15209	116799	86784
2003	37770	19579	14634	129862	92879
2004	40569	20934	12376	153518	98619
2005	40834	22700	12496	156911	96184
2006	36559	21147	17398	166889	195867
2007	44276	25892	19324	177359	126998
2008	49175	28405	22031	212910	122318
2009	51750	33061	18507	215008	128750
2010	54579	35130	17886	228814	164441
2011	62556	38613	20344	285988	155637
2012	70258	40585	59852	282916	175234
2013	77516	43643	81323	294659	179937
2014	81816	42790	98094	313314	199704

注：1. 2006年从业人员为农普数据，2007年以后为农业普查口径，含居住半年以上的外来人口。
2. 2006年农林牧渔业总产值及分行业产值为与农业普查衔接的数据，1997-2005年为历史修订数据。
3. 2010年按照新的《统计用产品分类目录》，将原归属林业产值的核桃、板栗等林产品调整至农业产值，并对2009年数据作了调整。

Note: a) Figures of employed persons in 2006 were from agriculture census. These figures are from agriculture census and include migrant population who have resided for over half a year since 2007.
b) Figures of output value for agriculture, forestry, animal production and hunting, fishing in 2006 were from agricultural census, and figures in 1997-2005 were historically revised data.
c) Output value of forestry, such as walnuts and chestnuts, was transferred to the agriculture sector in 2010 according to the new Catalog of Product Classification Used for Statistics. Figures in 2009 were adjusted accordingly.

10-7 耕地面积(2009-2013年)
ARABLE LAND AREA (2009-2013)

单位：公顷 (hectare)

项　　目	Item	2009	2010	2011	2012	2013
年初耕地总资源	**Total Arable Land Resources at the Beginning of the Year**		**227170.4**	**223779.4**	**221956.2**	**220856.2**
年内增加	**Increase in the Year**		**11.1**	**521.5**	**545.4**	**1776.4**
#土地整理	Land Consolidation				429.6	1748.7
土地复垦	Land Rehabilitation					
土地开发	Land Development			4.8		
农业结构调整	Agricultural Structure Adjustment			489.8	42.8	
其　他	Others		11.1	26.9	73.1	27.6
年内减少	**Decrease in the Year**		**3402.1**	**2344.7**	**1645.4**	**1475.2**
#建设占用	Occupied by Construction		3038.2	1917.0	1302.3	1310.6
灾害损毁	Disaster Damage				172.9	1.3
生态退耕	Farmland Converted for Ecological Preservation					
农业结构调整	Agricultural Structure Adjustment		321.0	412.7	83.6	163.4
其　他	Others		43.0	15.0	86.7	
年末耕地面积	**Total Arable Land Resources at the End of the Year**	**227170.43**	**223779.4**	**221956.2**	**220856.2**	**221157.3**
水　田	Paddy Field	2240.49	2207.9	2155.2	2121.1	2059.7
水浇地	Irrigable Land	171983.18	169205.7	167694.0	166562.7	167208.6
其　他	Others	52946.76	52365.7	52107.0	52172.4	51889.0

注：表中2009年耕地面积相关数据为第二次全国土地调查数据，2010-2013年为各年土地变更调查数据。
资料来源：北京市国土资源局。

Note: Related statistics for Arable land area in 2009 were from the 2nd National Land Survey, and statistics for 2010-2013 were survey data of land changed.

Source: Beijing Municipal Bureau of Land and Resources.

10-8 农村固定资产投资情况(2014年)
INVESTMENT IN FIXED ASSETS IN RURAL AREAS (2014)

单位：万元、万平方米 (10000 yuan, 10000 sq.m)

项目	Item	合计 Total	非农户 Non-Agricultural	农户 Agricultural
本年固定资产投资完成额	**Investment in Fixed Assets Completed in the Year**	**6356772**	**5848834**	**507938**
按投资方向分	**By Use of Funds**			
农、林、牧、渔业	Agriculture, Forestry, Animal Production and Hunting, Fishing	1603289	1570378	32911
采矿业	Mining and Quarrying	12081	12081	
制造业	Manufacturing	429601	429463	138
电力、热力、燃气及水生产和供应业	Production and Distribution of Electricity, Heating Power, Gas and Water	134769	134769	
建筑业	Construction	29022	26309	2713
批发和零售业	Wholesale and Retail Trade	93044	87474	5570
交通运输、仓储和邮政业	Transport, Storage and Post	238575	234075	4500
住宿和餐饮业	Accommodation and Restaurants	51603	48958	2645
信息传输、软件和信息技术服务业	Information Transmission, Software and Information Technology Services	12758	12758	
金融业	Finance			
房地产业	Real Estate	1470129	1011092	459037
租赁和商务服务业	Renting and Leasing Activities and and Business Services	154820	154820	
科学研究和技术服务业	Scientific Research and Development, Technical Services	11024	11024	
水利、环境和公共设施管理业	Management of Water Conservancy, Environment and Public Facilities	1528569	1528569	
居民服务、修理和其他服务业	Resident Services, Repair and Other Services	4251	3827	424
教育	Education	148437	148437	
卫生和社会工作	Healthcare and Social Works	56484	56484	
文化、体育和娱乐业	Culture, Sports and Entertainment	348571	348571	
公共管理、社会保障和社会组织	Public Management, Social Security and Social Organizations	29745	29745	
上年末结余资金	**Balance by the End of Last Year**	**738412**	**738412**	
本年资金来源小计	**Total Source of Funds in the Year**	**5877378**	**5369440**	**507938**
国家资金	State Funds	28193	28193	
国内贷款	Domestic Loan	546832	546832	
债券	Bonds			
利用外资	Foreign Funds	18182	18182	
自筹资金	Self-raised Funds	4954627	4446689	507938
其他资金	Other Funds	329544	329544	
本年施工房屋面积	**Floor Space of Buildings under Construction in the Current Year**	**2382**	**1954**	**428**
#住 宅	Residential Buildings	1115	714	401
本年竣工房屋面积	**Floor Space of Buildings Completed in the Current Year**	**880**	**474**	**406**
#住 宅	Residential Buildings	589	209	380
本年竣工房屋投资完成额	**Investment of Buildings Completed in the Current Year**	**460290**		**460290**
#住 宅	Residential Buildings	436124		436124
本年新增固定资产	**Original Value of Incremental Fixed Assets in the Current Year**	**4598162**	**4115827**	**482335**

注：1. 本表非农户固定资产投资为全面调查；农户固定资产投资为抽样调查。
2. 行业划分执行2011年国民经济行业分类标准(GB/T 4754-2011)。

Note: a) Figures of Investment by non-agricultural households in fixed assets in this table are from comprehensive survey; investment by agricultural households in fixed assets is from sample survey.
b) Sectors are classified in accordance with the Standard for Classification of National Economic Sectors 2011 (GB/T 4754-2011).

10-9 农业生产条件
PRODUCTIVE CONDITIONS OF AGRICULTURE

项目		Item		2014	2013	2014年为2013年% 2014 as % of 2013
主要农业机械拥有量		**Possession of Major Agricultural Machinery**				
农业机械总动力	(万千瓦)	Total Power of Agricultural Machinery	(10000 kw)	195.8	207.7	94.2
大中型拖拉机	(混合台)	Large and Medium-sized Tractors	(unit)	6649	6461	102.9
小型拖拉机	(台)	Mini Tractors	(unit)	1973	2421	81.5
机引农具	(台)	Tractor-propelled Farm Tools	(unit)	13451	14406	93.4
机动喷雾器	(部)	Motorized Sprayers	(unit)	20884	22205	94.1
联合收割机	(台)	Combine Harvesters	(unit)	2088	2172	96.1
机动脱粒机	(台)	Motorized Shellers	(unit)	3941	4066	96.9
米面加工机	(台)	Processing Machines of Rice and Flour	(unit)	4158	4067	102.2
机动挤奶器	(台)	Motorized Milkers	(unit)	2056	1727	119.1
饲料粉碎机	(台)	Fodder Grinders	(unit)	3869	3912	98.9
载重汽车	(辆)	Motor Trucks	(unit)	1696	2320	73.1
农业机械作业面积		**Operation Area of Agricultural Machinery**				
机耕面积	(公顷)	Cultivated Area by Machinery	(hectare)	13007	72603	17.9
占全部耕地面积比重	(%)	Share in the Total Arable Land	(%)	89.9	87.8	
机播面积	(公顷)	Sown Area by Machinery	(hectare)	112854	147491	76.5
占播种面积比重	(%)	Share in the Total Sown Area	(%)	94.2	66.8	
机收面积	(公顷)	Harvest Area by Machinery	(hectare)	94636	128629	73.6
占收获面积比重	(%)	Share in the Total Harvest Area	(%)	77.8	56.3	
农村用电量及小水电		**Rural Electricity Consumption and Small Hydropower Stations**				
农村用电量	(万千瓦小时)	Rural Electricity Consumption	(10000 kwh)	50559	485320	104.2
农田水利		**Irrigation and Water Conservancy**				
排灌用动力机械	(台)	Irrigation Machinery	(unit)	40024	39694	100.8
排灌用动力机械动力	(万千瓦)	Power of Irrigation Machinery	(10000 kw)	45.1	43.9	102.6
机(电)井	(眼)	Motor-pumped Wells	(unit)	32586	32586	100.0
#已配套	(眼)	Completed Sets	(unit)	30645	30645	100.0
扬水站(固定机电排灌站)	(处)	Pumping Stations (Drainage and Irrigation Stations with Fixed Machinery)	(unit)	1573	1573	100.0
有效灌溉面积	(公顷)	Effective Irrigation Area	(hectare)	158299.6	154420.5	102.5
化肥施用量(折纯)		**Consumption of Chemical Fertilizers (converted into net amount)**				
化肥施用量	(吨)	Consumption of Chemical Fertilizers	(ton)	116398	127809	91.1
#氮　肥	(吨)	Nitrogenous Fertilizers	(ton)	53678	59373	90.4
磷　肥	(吨)	Phosphate Fertilizers	(ton)	6673	7415	90.0
钾　肥	(吨)	Potash Fertilizers	(ton)	6026	6722	89.7

注：1．农村小水电站是指乡村两级小水电站实有数。
2．主要农业机械拥有量、农业机械作业面积、排灌动力机械数据由北京市农业局提供。
3．机(电)井、扬水站数据由北京市水务局提供。

Note: a) Figures of rural small hydropower stations refer to actual number of small hydropower stations at township and village level.
b) Figures of possession of major agricultural machinery, operation area of agricultural machinery and irrigation machinery are provided by Beijing Municipal Bureau of Agriculture.
c) Figures of motor-pumped wells and pumping stations are provided by Beijing Water Authority.

10-10 农林牧渔业总产值
GROSS OUTPUT VALUE OF AGRICULTURE, FORESTRY, ANIMAL PRODUCTION AND HUNTING, FISHING

单位：万元 (10000 yuan)

项目	Item	总产值 Gross Output Value 2014	2013	2014年为2013年% 2014 as % of 2013
合计	**Total**	**4200672.4**	**4217827.9**	**99.6**
农业	**Agriclture**	**1551014.9**	**1704065.2**	**91.0**
谷物	Cereal	138057.6	207507.1	66.5
豆类	Beans	4043.5	5287.5	76.5
经济作物	Cash Crops	5988.4	8488.3	70.5
蔬菜、食用菌	Vegetables and Edible Mushromms	650456.8	688039.0	94.5
水果（含瓜果类）	Fruits (including melons)	551942.2	565617.8	97.6
其他	Others	200526.4	229125.5	87.5
林业	**Forestry**	**906852.3**	**758857.3**	**119.5**
牧业	**Animal Production and Hunting**	**1526589.6**	**1547519.2**	**98.6**
牲畜饲养	Animal Breeding	455134.6	446670.6	101.9
养猪	Hogs	475438.7	540726.6	87.9
家禽饲养	Poultry	517795.8	483513.8	107.1
#禽蛋	Poultry Eggs	273770.1	227924.5	120.1
其他	Others	78220.5	76608.2	102.1
渔业	**Fishing**	**132024.0**	**127809.5**	**103.3**
农林牧渔服务业	**Services for Farming, Forestry, Animal Production and Hunting, Fishing**	**84191.6**	**79576.7**	**105.8**

10-11 主要农作物播种面积及产量
SOWN AREA AND OUTPUT OF MAJOR CROPS

项目	Item	2014 播种面积（公顷） Sown Areas (hectare)	2014 单产（公斤/公顷） Output Per Unit (kg/hectare)	2014 总产量（吨） Total Output (ton)	2013 播种面积（公顷） Sown Areas (hectare)	2013 单产（公斤/公顷） Output Per Unit (kg/hectare)	2013 总产量（吨） Total Output (ton)
粮食	**Grain**	**120174.1**	**5320.4**	**639369.1**	**158911.1**	**6049.0**	**961259.8**
按季节分	By Season						
夏粮	Summer Grain	23614.8	5174.5	122195.7	36241.3	5170.3	187377.3
秋粮	Autumn Grain	96559.3	5356.0	517173.4	122669.7	6308.7	773882.5
按品种分	Grouped by Variety						
稻谷	Rice	182.8	6943.1	1269.2	188.9	6913.2	1305.9
冬小麦	Winter Wheat	23550.6	5177.7	121937.9	36196.4	5172.1	187213.2
玉米	Corn	88619.0	5646.5	500382.8	114486.4	6567.0	751832.2
薯类	Tubers	1306.3	5220.6	6819.5	1436.9	5412.0	7776.5
大豆	Soybeans	4143.1	1457.6	6039.0	4110.1	1960.1	8056.1
棉花	**Cotton**	**104.3**	**1026.5**	**107.1**	**140.9**	**1071.0**	**150.9**
油料	**Oil-bearing Crops**	**2590.6**	**2597.7**	**6729.6**	**3418.0**	**2856.1**	**9762.1**
#花生	Peanuts	2198.7	2767.4	6084.7	3024.9	3003.3	9084.7
药材	**Medical Materials**	**2741.9**	**639.2**	**1752.6**	**2260.9**	**850.4**	**1922.7**
蔬菜及食用菌	**Vegetables and Edible Mushrooms**	**57481.9**	**41084.9**	**2361634.5**	**61984.7**	**43052.4**	**2668593.0**
瓜类及草莓	**Melons & Strawberries**	**6476.1**	**38855.8**	**251632.9**	**6953.5**	**42763.0**	**297352.4**
#西瓜	Watermelons	5607.8	40894.1	229326.0	5777.3	46387.8	267996.1
饲料	**Forage**	**3359.9**			**2250.9**		
#牧草	Forage Grass	301.4			363.8		
花卉	**Flowers**	**3813.7**			**3833.9**		

10-12 林业及干鲜果品生产
FORESTRY, NUTS AND FRESH FRUIT PRODUCTION

项目		Item		2014	2013	2014年为2013年% 2014 as % of 2013
林业生产		**Forestry**				
造林面积	(公顷)	Afforestation Area	(hectare)	22937	43823	52.3
#人工造林面积	(公顷)	Artificial Afforestation Area	(hectare)	22937	30808	74.5
#平原造林面积	(公顷)	Afforestation Area on the Plain	(hectare)	23600	24284	97.2
育苗面积	(公顷)	Seedling Growing Area	(hectare)	13052	17736	73.6
#本年新育	(公顷)	Newly Growing in the Current Year	(hectare)	2600	1643	158.2
果类生产		**Fruits**				
干鲜果总产量	(吨)	Output of Nuts and Fresh Fruit	(ton)	745147	795071	93.7
干 果	(吨)	Nuts	(ton)	32250	53936	59.8
#核 桃	(吨)	Walnuts	(ton)	9280	12280	75.6
板 栗	(吨)	Chinese Chestnuts	(ton)	19853	35782	55.5
鲜 果	(吨)	Fresh Fruits	(ton)	712897	741135	96.2
#苹 果	(吨)	Apples	(ton)	75015	87330	85.9
梨	(吨)	Pears	(ton)	132822	147628	90.0
葡 萄	(吨)	Grapes	(ton)	34360	36709	93.6
柿 子	(吨)	Persimmons	(ton)	41613	43036	96.7
桃	(吨)	Peaches	(ton)	367617	358519	102.5
年末实有果园面积	**(公顷)**	**Actual Orchard Area (year-end)**	**(hectare)**	**57524**	**60183**	**95.6**

资料来源：林业生产数据由北京市园林绿化局提供。
Source: Figures of forestry are from Beijing Municipal Bureau of Landscape and Forestry.

10-13 牲畜饲养及畜产品产量
LIVESTOCK BREEDING AND OUTPUT

项目		Item		2014	2013	2014年为2013年% 2014 as % of 2013
畜禽存栏		**Amount of Livestock and Poultry on Hand**				
大牲畜	(万头)	Large Animals	(10000 heads)	20.32	21.09	96.3
#牛	(万头)	Cattle and Buffaloes	(10000 heads)	19.68	20.35	96.7
猪	(万头)	Hogs	(10000 heads)	179.60	189.23	94.9
羊	(万只)	Sheep	(10000 units)	68.35	59.47	114.9
山 羊	(万只)	Goats	(10000 units)	17.19	15.80	108.8
绵 羊	(万只)	Sheep	(10000 units)	51.16	43.67	117.2
家 禽	(万只)	Poultry	(10000 units)	2544.58	2524.88	100.8
#产蛋鸡	(万只)	Hens	(10000 units)	1678.44	1628.83	103.0
肉 鸡	(万只)	Chickens	(10000 units)	584.64	582.57	100.4
鸭	(万只)	Ducks	(10000 units)	273.48	289.25	94.5
兔	(万只)	Rabbits	(10000 units)	4.28	6.00	71.3
畜禽出栏		**Amount of Livestock and Poultry Marketed**				
牛	(万头)	Cattle	(10000 heads)	9.20	11.24	81.9
猪	(万头)	Hogs	(10000 heads)	305.76	314.39	97.3
羊	(万只)	Sheep	(10000 units)	68.67	70.77	97.0
畜禽产品产量		**Output of Livestock and Poultry Products**				
肉类产量	(万吨)	Output of Meat	(10000 tons)	39.32	41.80	94.1
#猪 肉	(万吨)	Pork	(10000 tons)	24.01	24.63	97.5
牛 肉	(万吨)	Beef	(10000 tons)	1.70	2.05	82.9
羊 肉	(万吨)	Mutton	(10000 tons)	1.17	1.20	97.5
牛奶产量	(万吨)	Output of Milk	(10000 tons)	59.48	61.46	96.8
禽 蛋	(万吨)	Poultry Eggs	(10000 tons)	19.65	17.50	112.3
#鸡 蛋	(万吨)	Eggs	(10000 tons)	19.32	17.12	112.9
蜂 蜜	(吨)	Honey	(ton)	2321	2757	84.2

10-14 水产品生产
AQUATIC PRODUCTS

项目	Item	2014	2013	2014年为2013年% 2014 as % of 2013
渔业水域面积 (公顷)	**Area of Fishery Waters (hectare)**	**25463**	**21276**	**119.7**
#淡水养殖面积 (公顷)	Freshwater Agriculture (hectare)	3924	4221	93.0
#池塘 (公顷)	Puddles and Ponds (hectare)	3850	4143	92.9
水产品产量 (吨)	**Output of Aquatic Products (ton)**	**68184**	**63610**	**107.2**
#淡水鱼产量 (吨)	Output of Freshwater Fish (ton)	54962	56603	97.1
#大水库 (吨)	Large Reservoirs (ton)	2339	2264	103.3
中、小水库 (吨)	Medium and Small Reservoirs (ton)	1752	1427	122.8
池塘 (吨)	Puddles and Ponds (ton)	44181	47837	92.4

资料来源：北京市农业局。
Source: Beijing Municipal Bureau of Agriculture.

10-15 农业观光园、民俗旅游、种业和设施农业(2010-2014年)
AGRICULTURAL SIGHTSEEING GARDENS, FOLK-CUSTOM TOURISM, BREEDING OF SEEDS AND FACILITY AGRICULTURE (2010-2014)

项目	Item	2010	2011	2012	2013	2014
农业观光园	**Agricultural Sightseeing Gardens**					
农业观光园个数 (个)	Number of Agricultural Sightseeing Gardens (unit)	1303	1300	1283	1299	1301
高峰期从业人员 (人)	Employed Persons in Peak Production Period (person)	42561	46038	48906	50406	47088
接待人次 (万人次)	Visits Received (10000 person-times)	1774.9	1842.9	1939.9	1944.4	1911.2
经营总收入 (亿元)	Total Operating Income (100 million yuan)	17.80	21.72	26.88	27.36	24.92
民俗旅游	**Folk-Custom Tourism Receiption**					
从事民俗旅游实际经营接待户 (户)	Number of Actual Operating Households in Folk-Custom Tourism Receiption (household)	7979	8396	8367	8530	8863
高峰期从业人员 (人)	Employed Persons in Peak Production Period of the Term (person)	16856	18232	18705	19578	21493
民俗旅游接待人次 (万人次)	Number of Visits Received by Folk-Custom Tourism (10000 person-times)	1553.6	1668.9	1695.8	1806.5	1914.2
民俗旅游总收入 (亿元)	Total Income of Folk-Custom Tourism (100 million yuan)	7.35	8.68	9.05	10.20	11.25
种业	**Seed Industry**					
种业收入 (亿元)	Income (100 million yuan)	14.57	18.12	16.09	13.98	14.04
#销往外埠收入 (亿元)	Sales to Other Areas (100 million yuan)	8.05	11.68	9.70	8.23	7.95
#牧业收入 (亿元)	Income from Animal Production and Hunting (100 million yuan)	12.13	15.09	13.63	12.59	12.51
设施农业	**Facility Agriculture**					
设施农业实际利用占地面积 (公顷)	Actual Area Utilized by Facility Agriculture (hectare)	18323	18616	19059	18852	18232
设施农业播种面积 (公顷)	Sown Area of Facility Agriculture (hectare)	36811	38006	37797	38763	38115
设施农业收入 (亿元)	Income of Facility Agriculture (100 million yuan)	40.72	45.58	51.98	57.32	51.27

10-16 农业观光园
STATISTICS FOR AGRICULTURAL SIGHTSEEING GARDENS

项目		Item		2014	2013	2014年为2013年% 2014 as % of 2013
农业观光园个数	(个)	Number of Agricultural Sightseeing Gardens	(unit)	1301	1299	100.2
高峰期从业人员	(人)	Employed Persons in Peak Production Period	(person)	47088	50406	93.4
接待人次	(万人次)	Visits Received	(10000 person-times)	1911.2	1944.4	98.3
经营总收入	(万元)	Total Operating Income	(10000 yuan)	249154.7	273600.0	91.1

10-17 民俗旅游
STATISTICS FOR FOLK-CUSTOM TOURISM

项目		Item		2014	2013	2014年为2013年% 2014 as % of 2013
从事民俗旅游实际经营接待户	(户)	Number of Actual Operating Households in Folk-Custom Tourism Receiption	(household)	8863	8530	103.9
高峰期从业人员	(人)	Number of Employed Persons at the End of the Term	(person)	21493	19578	109.8
民俗旅游接待人次	(万人次)	Number of Visits Received by Folk-Custom Tourism	(10000 person-times)	1914.2	1806.5	106.0
民俗旅游总收入	(万元)	Total Income of Folk-Custom Tourism	(10000 yuan)	112543.0	101958.7	110.4

注：从2014年起，将民俗旅游中期末从业人员调整为高峰期从业人员。
Note: From 2014, employed persons of folk-custom tourism in late period are changed as the persons in peak production period.

10-18 种业生产
STATISTICS FOR PRODUCTION OF SEED INDUSTRY

项目	Item	产量 Output 2014	2013	2014年为2013年% 2014 as % of 2013	收入(万元) Income (10000 yuan) 2014	2013	2014年为2013年% 2014 as % of 2013
合计	**Total**				**140354.0**	**139807.6**	**100.4**
农业	**Agriculture**				**6429.2**	**5547.2**	**115.9**
#小麦种 (公斤)	Wheat Seeds (kg)	1470993	4434263	33.2	429.7	850.5	50.5
玉米种 (公斤)	Corn Seeds (kg)	493627	486735	101.4	339.4	290.8	116.7
蔬菜种 (公斤)	Vegetable Seeds (kg)	165130	91055	181.4	1642.2	1290.1	127.3
林业	**Forestry**				**5925.7**	**5443.3**	**108.9**
#树苗 (百株)	Saplings (100 units)	9274.0	13939.0	66.5	5925.6	5443.3	108.9
牧业	**Animal Production and Hunting**				**125111.4**	**125936.0**	**99.3**
#种猪 (头)	Boars (head)	210746	261970	80.4	45354.3	57225.0	79.3
种雏禽 (万只)	Breeding Birds (10000 units)	2903.9	3037.4	95.6	20618.6	19227.6	107.2
种蛋 (万枚)	Breeding Eggs (10000 units)	43720.6	35556.2	123.0	49008.1	39700.3	123.4
渔业	**Fishing**				**2887.7**	**2881.1**	**100.2**
#种鱼苗 (万尾)	Breeding Fish Fry (10000 units)	7048.8	5939.5	118.7	2552.7	2564.3	99.5

10-19 设施农业(2014年)
FACILITY AGRICULTURE (2014)

项　目	Item	设施农业播种面积（公顷） Sown Area of Facility Agriculture (hectare)	设施农业产量（吨） Output of Facility Agriculture (ton)	设施农业收入（万元） Income of Facility Agriculture (10000 yuan)
合　计	**Total**	**38115**		**512718.9**
温　室	**Greenhousse**	**22073**		**371842.0**
蔬菜及食用菌	Vegetables and Edible Mushrooms	19906	706691	274335.6
花卉苗木	Flowers and Saplings	814		30715.8
#切　花	Cut Flowers	176	2669	4801.6
盆　花	Potted Flowers	619	6854	25767.2
瓜果类	Melons	772	19817	46546.3
园林水果	Fruits	394	4054	12952.2
其　它	Others	187		7292.1
大　棚	**Greenhouse Garden**	**12448**		**116194.1**
蔬菜及食用菌	Vegetables and Edible Mushrooms	9565	330227	76855.8
花卉苗木	Flowers and Sapling	156		4674.2
#切　花	Cut Flowers	35	562	592.9
盆　花	Potted Flowers	106	1521	4047.3
瓜果类	Melons	2477	115254	31103.6
园林水果	Fruits	182	1483	2028.5
其　它	Other	68		1532.0
中小棚	**Medium and Small Shed**	**3594**		**24682.8**
蔬菜及食用菌	Vegetables and Edible Mushrooms	1541	46689	10284.7
花卉苗木	Flowers and Sapling	29		712.2
#切　花	Cut Flowers	2	23	31.2
盆　花	Potted Flowers	12	278	371.4
瓜果类	Melons	1931	57922	11096.7
园林水果	Fruits	4	56	77.2
其　它	Other	88		2512.0

注：切花产量的计量单位是万枝，盆花产量的计量单位是万盆。
Note: Cut flowers output are measured in 10000 ones; and potted flowers, 10000 pots.

10-20 乡镇企业各业基本情况(2014年)
BASIC STATISTICS FOR TOWN AND TOWNSHIP ENTERPRISES IN DIFFERENT SECTORS (2014)

项目	Item	企业个数(个) Number of Enterprises (unit)		从业人员(人) Employed Persons (person)		总收入(万元) Total Income (10000 yuan)		利润总额(万元) Total Profits (10000 yuan)	
		数量 Number	构成(%) Composition (%)	数量 Number	构成(%) Composition (%)	数量 Number	构成(%) Composition (%)	数量 Number	构成(%) Composition (%)
合计	**Total**	**139809**	**100.0**	**1073852**	**100.0**	**55452169**	**100.0**	**3008559**	**100.0**
农业	Agriculture	2656	1.9	12765	1.2	602759	1.0	33605	1.1
工业	Industry	75412	53.9	665110	61.9	28558419	51.5	1663880	55.3
建筑业	Construction	4978	3.6	102695	9.6	5646202	10.2	236325	7.9
交通运输业	Transportation	8238	5.9	37648	3.5	4164487	7.5	307409	10.2
批发零售业	Wholesale and Retail Trade	23438	16.8	70656	6.6	8970422	16.2	274161	9.1
住宿及餐饮业	Lodging and Catering Services	8089	5.8	46346	4.3	1393410	2.5	92720	3.1
居民服务、其它服务和娱乐业	Household Services, Other Services and Entertainment	15323	11.0	121358	11.3	3699133	6.7	301175	10.0
其他	Others	1675	1.2	17277	1.6	2399337	4.3	99284	3.3

资料来源：北京市经济和信息化委员会。

Source: Beijing Municipal Commission of Economy and Information Technology.

10-21 农村经济收入与分配
INCOME AND DISTRIBUTION OF RURAL ECONOMY

单位：万元 (10000 yuan)

项目	Item	2014	2013	2014年为2013年% 2014 as % of 2013
营业收入	**Operation Income**	**54363139.5**	**50911573.0**	**106.8**
农业	Agriculture	1145991.6	1168971.8	98.0
#粮食	Grain	267984.7	310323.2	86.4
林业	Forestry	269242.3	243406.7	110.6
牧业	Animal Production and Hunting	1248455.6	1207972.1	103.4
渔业	Fishing	112345.1	111721.3	100.6
工业	Industry	15098140.0	14366190.6	105.1
建筑业	Construction	6663592.5	6150834.4	108.3
交通运输业	Transportation	3110454.1	3038449.7	102.4
商业、饮食业	Commerce and Catering	10976478.2	10345381.6	106.1
服务业	Services	11557852.0	10369376.8	111.5
其他	Others	4180588.1	3909268.0	106.9
营业成本	**Operation Costs**	**48312777.2**	**45241887.0**	**106.8**
农业	Agriculture	1126818.9	1146066.6	98.3
#粮食	Grain	265478.3	308073.3	86.2
林业	Forestry	266010.2	239624.5	111.0
牧业	Animal Production and Hunting	1235995.5	1191249.3	103.8
渔业	Fishing	108983.3	108011.4	100.9
工业	Industry	13299656.1	12589806.6	105.6
建筑业	Construction	5957220.8	5478480.8	108.7
交通运输业	Transportation	3003249.9	2931553.0	102.4
商业、饮食业	Commerce and Catering	9910009.5	9418878.3	105.2
服务业	Services	9739446.0	8687548.2	112.1
其他	Others	3665387.0	3450668.3	106.2
营业利润	**Operating Profits**	**1347589.5**	**1372018.5**	**98.2**
利润总额	**Total Profits**	**1975759.0**	**1895094.3**	**104.3**
税后利润	**After-tax Profits**	**1711218.4**	**1651419.5**	**103.6**
可供分配的利润	**Profits Available for Distribution**	**2207386.9**	**1888185.0**	**116.9**
未分配利润	**Undistributed Profits**	**1520704.5**	**1258879.2**	**120.8**

资料来源：北京市农村经济研究中心农村合作经济经营管理站。
Source: Operation and Management Station for Rural Cooperative Economy of Beijing Rural Economy Research Center.

10-22 乡镇企业出口供货情况
GOODS SUPPLIES FOR EXPORT OF TOWN AND TOWNSHIP ENTERPRISES

单位：万元 (10000 yuan)

项目	Item	2014	2013
合计	**Total**	**1138012**	**1210724**
化工	Chemical Products	53636	57063
机械	Machinery	19159	203836
矿产	Mineral Products	10610	11288
轻工	Light Industry	172077	183072
食品	Food	123357	131239
土产畜产	Local and Livestock Products	26552	28248
纺织服装	Textile and Garments	386901	411622
工艺品	Artworks	27761	29535
其他	Others	317959	154821

资料来源：北京市经济和信息化委员会。
Source: Beijing Municipal Commission of Economy and Information Technology.

主要统计指标解释

农林牧渔业总产值 是以货币表现的农林牧渔业的全部产品总量和对农林牧渔业生产活动进行的各种支持性服务活动的价值。

耕地 指种植农作物的土地，包括熟地，新开发、复垦、整理地，休闲地（含轮歇地、轮作地）；以种植农作物（含蔬菜）为主，间有零星果树、桑树或其他树木的土地；平均每年能保证收获一季的已垦滩地和海涂。耕地中包括南方宽度<1.0米、北方宽度<小于2.0米固定的沟、渠、路和地坎(埂)；临时种植药材、草皮、花卉、苗木等的耕地，以及其他临时改变用途的耕地。

农作物播种面积 指实际播种或移植有农作物的面积。凡是实际种植有农作物的面积，不论种植在耕地上还是种植在非耕地上，均包括在农作物播种面积中。在播种季节基本结束后，因遭灾而重新改种和补种的农作物面积，也包括在内。

有效灌溉面积 指具有一定的水源，地块比较平整，灌溉工程或设备已经配套，在一般年景下当年能够进行正常灌溉的耕地面积。

设施农业 指以工厂化生产方式，建造人工设施，改变气候条件，提高农作物抵御自然灾害的能力，改良生物特性，使作物实现错季或反季节生产，达到农作物均衡生产的目的。

农业机械总动力 指主要用于农、林、牧、渔业的各种动力机械的动力总和。包括耕作机械、排灌机械、收获机械、农用运输机械、植物保护机械、牧业机械、渔业机械和其他农用机械[内燃机按引擎马力折成瓦（特）计算，电动机按功率折成瓦（特）计算]。不包括专门用于乡、镇、村、组办工业、基本建设、非农业运输、科学实验和教学等非农业生产方面用的动力机械与作业机械。

农村用电量 指本年度内，扣除在农村中的国有经济工业交通、基建等单位的用电量以后的农村生产和生活的全年用电总量（计量单位千瓦小时，按全年累计数统计），即包括国家电网供电，也包括农村自办电站供电量。

农用化肥施用量 指本年度内实际用于农业生产的化学肥料数量，包括氮肥、磷肥、钾肥和复合肥。施用量要求按折纯量计算数量，即各类化学肥料的实际施用数量按其含氮、含五氧化二磷、含氧化钾的比例折成百分之百计算。

折纯量＝实物量×某种化肥有效成份含量的百分比

乡镇及行政村单位常住户数 指长期（一年以上）居住在乡镇（不包括城关镇）行政管理区域内的住户，还包括居住在城关镇所辖行政村范围内的农村住户。户口不在本地而在本地居住一年及以上的住户也包括在本地农村住户内；有本地户口，但举家外出谋生一年以上的住户，无论是否保留承包耕地都不包括在本地农村住户范围内。不包括乡村地区内的国有经济的机关、团体、学校、企业、事业单位的集体户。

乡镇及行政村常住人口 指乡村地区常住居民户数中的常住人口数，即经常在家或在家居住6个月以上，而且经济和生活与本户连成一体的人口。外出从业人员在外居住时间虽然在6个月以上，但收入主要带回家中，经济与本户连为一体，仍视为家庭常住人口；在家居住，生活和本户连成一体的国家职工、退休人员也为家庭常住人口。但是现役军人、中专及以上（走读生除外）的在校学生、以及常年在外（不包括探亲、看病等）且已有稳定的职业与居住场所的外出从业人员，不应当作家庭常住人口。

乡镇及行政村从业人员 指全部乡镇及行政村人口中16岁以上实际参加生产经营活动并取得实物或货币收入的人员，既包括劳动年龄内经常参加劳动的人员，也包括超过劳动年龄但经常参加劳动的人员。但不包括户口在家的在外学生、现役军人和丧失劳动能力的人，也不包括待业人员和家务劳动者。从业人员按从事主业时间最长（时间相同按收入）分为农业从业人员，工业从业人员，建筑业从业人员，交通运输仓储及邮政业从业人员，信息传输、计算机服务和软件业，批发与零售业从业人员，住宿和餐饮业从业人员，其它从业人员。

Explanatory Notes on Main Statistical Indicators

Gross Output Value of Agriculture, Forestry, Animal Production and Hunting, Fishing refers to the monetary value of all products of agriculture, forestry, animal production and hunting, fishing, as well as the monetary value of services provided in support of all the above-mentioned sectors.

Arable Land refers to the land suitable for growing crops, including cultivated land; any land newly opened up, reclaimed and cultivated; fallow land (including swidden and rotated land); land mostly for growing crops (including vegetables), supplemented by mulberry trees, fruit trees, and other trees; cultivated bottomland and shallows that can secure an average of one harvest annually. Arable land includes furrows, ditches, paths and field ridges less than 1m wide in the southern part of China, or less than 2m wide in the northern part. It also covers arable land that is temporarily for growing medicinal materials, turf, flowers, nursery stock and other uses.

Sown Area refers to the area of all lands actually sown or transplanted with crops, including both the cultivated and non-cultivated land. Area of lands re-planted after seedtime has passed due to natural disasters is also included.

Effective Irrigation Area refers to the area of arable lands that can be effectively irrigated in a normal harvest year, i.e. relatively level land, with certain water sources and complete sets of irrigation facilities.

Facility Agriculture means to produce in an industrialized manner, put in place facilities of manual intervention, change climate conditions, increase the crops' capability to resist natural disasters, and improve the crops' biological property, so as to stagger harvest seasons, create anti-season production, and achieve balanced production of crops.

Total Power of Agricultural Machinery refers to the total power of motive power machines used in agriculture, forestry, animal production and hunting, fishing sectors, including machinery for ploughing, irrigation and drainage, harvesting, agricultural transport, plant protection, animal production and hunting, fishing and other farm machinery (The horsepower of internal combustion engines is converted into watts, and the output of electric motors is also converted into watts). Motive power machines and operating machines exclusively used for non-agricultural production activities, such as industrial operations run by counties, towns, villages and teams, capital construction, non-agricultural transport, scientific experiments and teaching, are not included.

Rural Electricity Consumption refers to the total rural production and rural residents' electricity consumption in the whole year (unit of measurement: kilowatt-hour; the data representing accumulative usage of the year), deducting the consumption by entities like state-owned industry, transport, and infrastructure construction. The data cover both power supplies by the State Grid and by the rural self-run power stations.

Consumption of Chemical Fertilizers refers to the total quantity of chemical fertilizers applied in agricultural production within the year, including nitrogenous fertilizer, phosphate fertilizer, potash fertilizer, and compound fertilizer. The amount of chemical fertilizers applied is calculated in terms of net amount, that is, to use the gross weight of the respective fertilizers in calculating the quantity of effective ingredients (e.g. nitrogen content in nitrogenous fertilizer, phosphorous pent oxide content in phosphate fertilizer, and potassium oxide content in potash fertilizer).

Net Amount = Physical Quantity× Content (%) of Effective Ingredients in Certain Chemical Fertilizer

Number of Resident Households in Towns and Administrative Villages refers to households living in the administrative areas of towns and villages (excluding township government premises) on a long-term basis (more than one year), including those living in administrative villages within township government premises. Households with non-local household registration but having been living locally for more than one year are also counted as local rural households; while households with local household registration but left to make a living elsewhere for more than one year, with or without contract lands, are not counted as local rural households. Collective households of state-owned organs, groups, schools, enterprises, and public institutions, as well as households living in grouped commercial residential quarters in rural areas are not included.

Permanent Population in Towns and Administrative Villages refers to the population of permanent households in rural areas, namely those who stay home regularly or live at home for more than 6 months with their economic life and livelihood incorporated into the household. Migrant workers who live away from home for more than 6 months but taking most of their earnings back home, with their economic life still incorporated into the household, are also counted as permanent population of the household; state employees and retirees who live locally with their life incorporated into the household are also considered permanent population. But soldiers in active service, enrolled students (externs excluded) in technical secondary schools or above, as well as migrant workers who lived away from home for years (excluding those who travel to visit their families or to seek medical care) with a stable job and residence elsewhere, are not regarded as permanent population.

Employ Persons in Towns and Administrative Villages refer to persons aged above 16 in all towns and administrative villages, who actually participate in productive and operating activities and earn incomes in kind or cash, including persons within the range of labor age and regularly participating in labor, and persons beyond the range of labor age but regularly participating in labor; while local registered students who left home for education, soldiers in active service, and people who lost the ability to work are not included, neither are the people waiting for employment or domestic workers. In terms of the length of employment period (or in terms of income if the employment periods are identical), employment falls into the following categories: agriculture, industry, construction, transportation, storage and post, information transmission, software and information technology services, wholesale and retail trade, accommodation and restaurants, and other sectors.

11

北京统计年鉴2015　BEIJING STATISTICAL YEARBOOK

工　业
INDUSTRY

简要说明

一、本章统计的主要内容

本章资料反映北京市工业方面的基本情况，主要包括按登记注册类型、轻重工业、企业规模、工业行业大类等分组的主要经济指标数据，还包括国有控股工业企业、股份制工业企业、港澳台及外商投资工业企业、大中型工业企业的主要经济指标数据。

具体指标包括单位数、工业总产值、工业增加值、资产总计、负债合计、主营业务收入、主营业务成本、主营业务税金及附加、利润总额、应交增值税、总资产贡献率、资产负债率、成本费用利润率、主要工业产品产量等。

二、本章资料的统计范围

1984 年以前农村的村及村以下办工业归属农业，1984 年以后划归工业。

1999 年以前，工业的统计范围按隶属关系划分为乡及乡以上独立核算工业企业和非独立核算生产单位、村办工业、城镇合作工业、农村合作工业、城镇个体工业、农村个体工业六大部分（1984 年以前村办工业不在工业统计范围内）。

2000 年-2006 年，工业统计调查范围由按隶属关系划分，改变为按企业规模划分。2000 年至 2006 年，分为全部国有及年主营业务收入在 500 万元及以上非国有工业企业（简称“规模以上”）和年主营业务收入在 500 万元以下非国有工业企业和全部个体经营工业单位（简称“规模以下”）两部分。

2007 年-2010 年，分为年主营业务收入在 500 万元及以上法人工业企业（简称“规模以上”）和年主营业务收入在 500 万元以下法人工业企业和全部个体经营工业单位（简称“规模以下”）两部分。

2011 年及以后，分为年主营业务收入在 2000 万元及以上法人工业企业（简称“规模以上”）和年主营业务收入在 2000 万元以下法人工业企业和全部个体经营工业单位（简称“规模以下”）两部分。

三、数据来源和调查方法

本章工业企业统计数据来源于北京市统计局、国家统计局北京调查总队。其中，规模以上数据为全面调查，规模以下数据为抽样调查。

四、有关统计标准的变化说明

（一）关于行业划分：本章资料中工业行业分类 2002-2011 年期间执行 2002 年《国民经济行业分类标准》(GB/T 4754-2002)划分标准，2012 年开始执行 2011 年《国民经济行业分类》(GB/T 4754-2011)划分标准;

（二）关于企业标准划分: 2010 年以前企业大中小型划分执行《统计上大中小型企业划分办法（暂行）》标准，自 2011 年开始，大中小微型企业划分标准执行国家统计局《关于统计上大中小微型企业划分办法》（国统字[2011]75 号）。

五、本章中关于历史数据调整的问题

按照国家统计局统一要求和统一方法，规模以上工业总产值及增加值历史资料已根据“北京市第一次全国经济普查”的结果采用“趋势离差法”进行了修正。调整历史区间为 1993 年至 2003 年。2004 年为第一次经济普查数据，2008 年为第二次经济普查数据，2013 年为第三次经济普查数据。

Brief Introduction

I. Main Content

Data in this chapter show the basic situation of industry in Beijing, including: major economic indicators grouped by type of registration, light or heavy industry, enterprise scale, and industrial sector. and also includes main economic indicators for state-holding industrial enterprises, industrial enterprises limited by shares, Hong Kong, Macao, Taiwan and foreign-invested enterprises, and the large and medium-sized industrial enterprises.

Indicators include: unit number, gross industrial output value, industrial added value, total assets, total liabilities, main business income, main business cost, main business tax and surtax, total profits, payable VAT, contribution rate to total assets, asset-liability ratio, cost-profit ratio, and output of main industrial products, etc.

II. Scope of Statistics

Prior to 1984, the rural industrial production run by villages and units subordinated to villages was classified as agriculture. Since 1984, it has been grouped into industry.

Before 1999, industrial statistics coverage was divided into six parts by registration type, i.e. industrial enterprises at the township-level and above with and without independent accounting, village-run industry, urban cooperative industry, rural cooperative industry, urban individual operated industry, and rural individual operated industry (village-run industry was not included in the industrial statistics before 1984).

2000-2006, the scope of industrial statistics was grouped by enterprise scale instead of registration type. From 2000 to 2006, industrial enterprises fell into two classes. One class includes all state-owned enterprises and non-state-owned ones with annual main business income of RMB 5 million and above ("above designated size"), while the other class covers all individual operations and non-state-owned enterprises with annual main business income below RMB 5 million ("below designated size").

2007-2010, industrial enterprises fell into two classes. One includes corporate industrial enterprises with main business income of RMB 5 million and above ("above designated size"), the other includes corporate industrial enterprises with main business income below RMB 5 million and all individual operations ("below designated size").

In and after 2011, industrial enterprises fell into two classes. One includes corporate industrial enterprises with main business income of RMB 20 million and above ("above designated size"), the other includes corporate industrial enterprises with main business income below RMB 20 million and all individual operations ("below designated size").

III. Source of Data and Methods of Survey

Data on industrial enterprises in this chapter were provided by Beijing Municipal Bureau of Statistics and NBS Survey Office in Beijing. Data on industrial enterprises above designated size were gathered through complete survey, and data on those below designated size were obtained through sampling survey.

IV. Changes in Relevant Statistical Standards

(I) Classification of Industrial Sectors: In this chapter, classification of industrial sectors during 2002-2011 was based on the *Standard for Classification of National Economic Sectors 2002* (GB/T 4754-2002). *Standard for Classification of National Economic Sectors 2011* (GB/T 4754-2011) began to be enforced in 2012;

(II) Classification of Enterprises: Before 2010, small, medium and large-sized enterprises were classified by standards of *Measures for Statistical Classification of Small, Medium and Large-sized Enterprises (Temporary)*. Since 2011, the classification of micro, small, medium and large-sized enterprises has been in line with standards of Circular by National Bureau of Statistics on Printing and Issuing the *Measures for Statistical Classification of Micro, Small, Medium and Large-sized Enterprises* (G.T.Z. [2011] No. 75).

V. About the Adjustment to Historical Data

In accordance with the unified requirements and methods of the National Bureau of Statistics, data on total output value and added value of industrial enterprises above designated size were based on results from the "first national economic census in Beijing" after revision through the "trend deviation method". The time span of the revised data is from 1993 to 2003. The first economic census was carried out in 2004 and the second in 2008, and the third in 2013.

11-1 规模以上工业总产值(1984-2014年)
GROSS OUTPUT VALUE OF INDUSTRY ABOVE DESIGNATED SIZE (1984-2014)

单位：亿元 (100 million yuan)

年份 Year	合计 Total	轻工业 Light Industry	重工业 Heavy Industry	#大中型工业 Medium and Large-sized Industry
1984	276.2	118.0	158.2	178.7
1985	324.2	135.8	188.4	213.7
1986-1990	**2448.3**	**1039.7**	**1408.6**	**1691.2**
1986	336.5	140.8	195.7	231.6
1987	387.6	160.1	227.5	272.1
1988	495.6	212.5	283.1	345.4
1989	602.7	264.1	338.6	408.3
1990	625.9	262.2	363.7	433.8
1991-1995	**5826.7**	**1936.6**	**3890.1**	**3770.8**
1991	730.2	298.1	432.1	507.4
1992	860.0	306.5	553.5	587.4
1993	1166.6	361.9	804.7	747.6
1994	1576.6	497.9	1078.7	990.7
1995	1493.3	472.2	1021.1	937.7
1996-2000	**10382.8**	**3026.2**	**7356.6**	**5765.7**
1996	1590.6	509.1	1081.5	962.3
1997	1819.7	577.8	1241.9	999.6
1998	1947.0	598.2	1348.8	1059.8
1999	2183.5	621.8	1561.7	1090.9
2000	2842.0	719.3	2122.7	1653.1
2001-2005	**23980.6**	**4911.1**	**19069.5**	**16858.4**
2001	3270.1	842.4	2427.7	2298.4
2002	3620.2	882.4	2737.8	2434.7
2003	4410.8	936.7	3474.1	3183.9
2004	5733.3	1084.7	4648.6	3699.3
2005	6946.2	1164.9	5781.3	5242.1
2006-2010	**53010.4**	**8204.7**	**44805.7**	**40357.2**
2006	8210.0	1258.2	6951.8	6237.9
2007	9648.4	1505.5	8142.9	7365.9
2008	10413.1	1674.3	8738.8	7898.9
2009	11039.1	1766.7	9272.4	8349.3
2010	13699.8	2000.0	11699.8	10505.3
2011	14513.6	2227.2	12286.4	11289.3
2012	15596.2	2402.1	13194.1	12239.6
2013	17370.9	2541.5	14829.4	13941.3
2014	18452.9	2568.0	15884.9	15039.5

注：1. 工业总产值按现价计算。
2. 规模以上工业：2000年以前各年为乡及乡以上工业口径；2000-2006年调整为全部国有及年主营业务收入在500万元及以上非国有工业口径；2007年-2010年调整为年主营业务收入500万元及以上的全部法人工业企业；2011年及以后调整为年主营业务收入2000万元及以上的全部法人工业企业(下同)。
3. 自2011年开始，大中型企业划分标准执行国家统计局《关于统计上大中小微型企业划分办法》(国统字[2011]75号)(下同)。

Note: a) Gross output value is calculated at current prices.
b) Data on industry above designated size covered enterprises at and above the township level before 2000, 2000-2006 covered all State-owned enterprises and non-State-owned enterprises with main business income of over RMB 5 million annually, 2007-2010 covered all corporate industrial enterprises with main business income of over RMB 5 million annually, and from 2011 covered all corporate industrial enterprises with main business income over RMB 20 million (the same below).
c) Since 2011, Division standards of medium and large-sized enterprises complies with Statistical Division Standards of Micro, Small, Medium and Large-sized Enterprises issued by National Bureau of Statistics (G.T.Z. [2011] No. 75) (the same below).

11-2 规模以上工业企业主要指标(1978-2014年)
MAIN INDICATORS FOR INDUSTRIAL ENTERPRISES ABOVE DESIGNATED SIZE (1978-2014)

年 份 Year	企业单位个数 (个) Number of Enterprises (unit)	从业人员平均人数 (万人) Average Number of Employed Persons (10000 persons)	资产总计 (万元) Total Assets (10000 yuan)	负债合计 (万元) Total Liabilities (10000 yuan)	固定资产原价 (万元) Original Value of Fixed Assets (10000 yuan)	主营业务收入 (万元) Main Business Income (10000 yuan)	利润总额 (万元) Total Profits (10000 yuan)	利税总额 (万元) Total Taxes & Profits (10000 yuan)
1978	4225	114.79			1305271	1098279	370551	501588
1979	3746	116.79	1417223		1371335	1186497	414344	554895
1980	3733	140.91	1547267		1495083	1987967	453147	604241
1981-1985						**12561630**	**2404751**	**3383077**
1981	3778	152.90	1650869		1622035	2054862	440753	599452
1982	3867	158.70	1748915		1750727	2183458	440000	604372
1983	4011	161.98	1846698		1886857	2408893	469364	642437
1984	4291	165.50	2003625		2045344	2728866	505249	707360
1985	4458	165.63	2338194		2337082	3175551	549385	829456
1986-1990						**24054442**	**2924045**	**4825016**
1986	5461	169.85	2720485		2627346	3385055	523961	813979
1987	5746	170.52	3147157		3008917	3935004	570760	885303
1988	5932	170.54	3607173		3412765	5032042	701574	1081370
1989	6175		4343353		3890267	5597829	638385	1087017
1990	6272	173.46	4982746		4382462	6104512	489365	957347
1991-1995						**57731437**	**4241285**	**8051832**
1991	6344	172.39	5672894		5052285	7271529	583381	1106009
1992	6205	175.48	6409037		5754181	8526860	748098	1347058
1993	10320	167.90	15209851		9986886	12822058	1095165	1811556
1994	10889	179.50	19692285		9648050	13207344	961715	1857476
1995	10712	176.16	25826309	15287699	13900296	15903646	852926	1929733
1996-2000						**103617473**	**3188809**	**8655552**
1996	16905	166.63	28755517	17220941	16319878	15801389	330539	1225314
1997	19387	157.52	34083006	20496564	18503218	17070867	405129	1405499
1998	18089	167.11	40129028	24839166	22213387	20345380	484460	1617338
1999	19682	161.10	42540707	25863159	23121446	22186280	697807	1846310
2000	16027	145.60	46127325	26763977	25316408	28213557	1270874	2561091
2001-2005						**233471075**	**13486920**	**23453788**
2001	4356	108.02	44482243	24595592	25036546	30068965	1369794	2795203
2002	4551	107.56	47429487	25278299	26554117	31827790	1655153	3219863
2003	4019	100.81	51779832	27511740	27559571	38856527	2352909	4189859
2004	6872	113.60	120495094	41430793	39221838	59926564	3974076	6417537
2005	6301	117.06	128298350	47067350	44340413	72791229	4134988	6831326
2006-2010						**576103251**	**35550064**	**57599572**
2006	6400	117.36	142444009	55423362	50306165	89141630	5311453	8479249
2007	6398	119.25	162155043	65083476	58148433	104401683	6956067	10552194
2008	7206	123.38	168024206	80850104	65745860	112758173	5569968	9379138
2009	6891	120.41	195407033	98746128	70836396	121730618	7429216	12699472
2010	6885	124.15	227505774	115480740	79360648	148071147	10283360	16489519
2011	3740	117.87	253217462	126486073	86208174	157533565	11294991	18061726
2012	3692	120.15	286131557	148372202	102771932	169051357	12678868	20104385
2013	3641	116.14	308007299	162079598	107885887	186886314	12828840	21252443
2014	3686	116.55	335570497	171375654	115329380	197766666	15157524	24078630

注：规模以上指:2000年以前统计范围为独立核算工业企业；2000-2006年为全部国有及年主营业务收入500万元及以上非国有企业；2007年-2010年调整为年主营业务收入500万元及以上的全部法人工业企业；2011年及以后调整为年主营业务收入2000万元及以上的全部法人工业企业。

Note: "Above designated size" covered industrial enterprises with independent accounting system before 2000; 2000-2006, covered all State-owned enterprises and non-State-owned enterprises with main business income of and over RMB 5 million annually; 2007-2010 covered all corporate industrial enterprises with main business income of and over RMB 5 million annually; from 2011, covered all corporate industrial enterprises with main business income over RMB 20 million.

11-3 规模以上工业增加值(1993-2014年)

单位：亿元

年 份 Year	增加值 Added Value of Industry	轻工业 Light Industry	重工业 Heavy Industry	#计算机、通信和其他电子设备制造业 Manufacture of Computers, Communication Equipment and Other Electronic Equipment	#汽车制造业 Manufacture of Motor Vehicles	#电力、热力生产和供应业 Production and Supply of Electricity and Heating Power	#铁路、船舶、航空航天和其他运输设备制造业 Manufacture of Railway Locomotives, Building of Ships Manufacture Air and Spacecrafts and Other Transportation Equipment
1993	304.1	98.3	205.8	22.6	28.4	4.6	
1994	374.6	138.0	236.6	30.9	29.7	9.5	
1995	473.1	112.3	360.8	46.7	44.4	33.0	
1996-2000	**3058.8**	**981.7**	**2077.1**	**622.0**	**180.7**	**170.4**	
1996	500.2	168.8	331.4	66.6	38.1	-12.1	
1997	558.0	170.1	387.9	75.7	58.0	45.8	
1998	588.2	197.2	391.0	133.8	30.0	41.5	
1999	636.5	200.6	435.9	154.5	25.6	45.4	
2000	776.0	245.0	531.0	191.4	29.0	49.8	
2001-2005	**6153.4**	**1549.4**	**4604.0**	**1078.7**	**505.4**	**564.2**	
2001	866.3	265.2	601.0	203.6	39.0	52.4	
2002	960.7	306.6	654.1	177.8	54.8	66.6	
2003	1174.7	304.8	869.9	228.3	126.0	78.3	
2004	1524.7	332.6	1192.1	197.5	144.2	174.4	
2005	1627.0	340.2	1286.8	271.5	141.4	192.5	
2006-2010	**11071.1**	**2366.2**	**8704.9**	**1423.7**	**1329.5**	**1705.0**	
2006	1840.2	370.1	1470.1	329.7	155.1	254.6	
2007	2159.4	427.6	1731.9	363.6	194.9	355.2	
2008	2037.6	482.3	1555.3	289.4	211.1	358.4	
2009	2282.2	529.4	1752.8	201.2	310.6	327.3	
2010	2751.7	556.8	2194.8	239.8	457.8	409.5	
2011	2899.1	619.2	2279.9	204.5	562.1	448.8	
2012	3033.3	681.3	2352.0	243.6	512.6	536.0	53.5
2013	3432.1	749.7	2682.4	304.4	732.3	602.3	71.7
2014	3612.0	766.6	2845.3	305.1	726.2	682.0	96.9

注：1. 本表增加值均按生产法计算，2004年以前数据为根据全国第一次经济普查数据调整后的数据。

2. 2012年开始行业划分执行2011年国民经济行业分类标准(GB/T 4754-2011)；表中2012年前，汽车制造业为原“交通运输设备制造业”数据，计算机、通信和其它电子设备制造业为原“通信设备、计算机及其他电子设备制造业”的数据。

ADDED VALUE OF INDUSTRY ABOVE DESIGNATED SIZE (1993-2014)

(100 million yuan)

#化学原料和化学制品制造业 Manufacture of Chemical Raw Materials and Chemical Products	#通用设备制造业 Manufacture of General-Purpose Machinery	#专用设备制造业 Manufacture of Special-Purpose Machinery	#电气机械和器材制造业 Manufacture of Electrical Machinery and Equipment	#仪器仪表制造业 Manufacture of Measuring Instruments and Meters	#医药制造业 Manufacture of Medicines	#非金属矿物制品业 Manufacture of Non-Metallic Mineral Products	#石油加工、炼焦和核燃料加工业 Processing of Petroleum, Coking, Processing of Nuclear Fuel
15.5	13.0	10.0	10.1	3.2	5.5	14.8	12.5
19.7	15.9	26.4	11.6	4.5	5.3	21.2	14.2
28.9	17.2	12.1	9.8	9.0	7.5	17.7	45.9
136.2	**73.1**	**114.5**	**99.5**	**52.6**	**90.3**	**139.4**	**194.5**
26.0	18.1	16.9	15.4	10.6	11.8	28.4	37.9
21.4	13.2	19.3	17.3	7.5	15.6	25.7	42.3
25.3	17.5	22.9	21.0	10.9	12.6	30.9	31.4
24.0	8.2	22.9	19.0	11.1	22.7	19.6	42.3
39.5	16.1	32.5	26.8	12.4	27.6	34.8	40.6
381.2	**200.8**	**263.7**	**257.8**	**142.2**	**225.4**	**230.1**	**215.6**
44.1	25.7	29.2	36.5	17.0	31.0	34.4	35.8
55.3	25.5	56.3	38.7	19.0	47.2	47.2	53.9
76.3	36.6	49.8	54.9	21.6	53.2	48.5	29.6
141.8	56.5	67.7	65.1	38.3	44.7	52.0	19.7
63.7	56.5	60.7	62.6	46.4	49.3	48.0	76.6
331.2	**495.2**	**526.7**	**497.0**	**313.6**	**543.0**	**333.5**	**461.6**
56.9	72.6	86.6	57.1	57.2	57.0	53.5	49.6
72.6	84.7	84.7	85.8	70.6	81.6	52.7	56.9
60.5	99.1	111.9	92.9	58.7	115.3	55.2	-2.3
57.1	97.4	112.3	126.4	61.0	135.8	85.8	172.5
84.1	141.4	131.2	134.8	66.1	153.3	86.3	184.9
77.7	153.1	139.8	137.1	63.6	184.2	80.7	122.8
56.1	130.2	130.4	124.8	59.6	222.2	79.5	126.2
55.8	125.0	158.1	135.4	64.9	254.2	80.5	98.2
62.3	147.3	132.6	145.5	68.2	283.1	75.0	151.3

Note: a) Added value in this table is calculated with production method. Figures before 2004 are adjusted according to the national first economic census.

b) The Standard for Classification of National Economic Sectors 2011 (GB/T 4754-2011) became effective in 2012; in this table,figures of " manufacture of motor vehicles" in 2012 were figures of the former "manufacture of transportation equipment", and figures of "manufacture of computers, communication equipment and other electronic equipment" were figures of the former "manufacture of communication equipment, computers and other electronic equipment".

11-4 规模以上工业产品产量(1978-2014年)
OUTPUT OF INDUSTRIAL PRODUCTS ABOVE DESIGNATED SIZE (1978-2014)

年份 Year	布(万米) Cloth (10000 m)	机制纸及纸板(万吨) Machine-made Paper and Paperboard (10000 tons)	饮料酒(万千升) Alcoholic Beverage (10000 kl)	乳制品(万吨) Dairy Products (10000 tons)	家用电冰箱(万台) Household Refrigerators (10000 units)	照相机(万台) Camera (10000 units)	家具(万件) Furniture (10000 pieces)	原煤(万吨) Raw Coal (10000 tons)	原油加工量(万吨) Crude Oil Processed (10000 tons)	乙稀(万吨) Ethylene (10000 tons)	发电量(万千瓦时) Electricity Generation (10000 kwh)
1978	25436	12.1	8.4			0.5	137.8	818.7			990750
1979	27297	13.9	9.9		2.0	0.7	171.3	711.1			1042870
1980	28940	14.0	11.6		2.6	1.0	200.2	791.0	591.1		1065060
1981-1985	**142080**	**86.9**	**87.3**	**2.0**	**41.6**	**25.7**	**1348.4**	**4269.1**	**2811.3**	**132.3**	**5101356**
1981	28635	14.5	13.4		3.1	4.2	217.7	788.7	533.5	24.7	993071
1982	29758	15.8	14.9	0.2	4.5	0.9	243.5	811.3	533.5	25.6	1003446
1983	30068	17.1	17.4	0.3	6.4	2.8	254.2	840.5	563.8	27.3	1028826
1984	27621	18.9	20.3	0.6	10.3	5.3	297.9	884.3	589.4	26.9	1038842
1985	25998	20.6	21.3	0.9	17.3	12.5	335.1	944.3	591.1	27.8	1037171
1986-1990	**153032**	**120.5**	**131.4**	**4.7**	**96.4**	**74.6**	**2096.6**	**4745.3**	**3210.5**	**141.8**	**5656282**
1986	27503	21.9	21.5	0.7	18.1	15.9	303.8	917.2	619.0	25.3	1043208
1987	29738	24.1	22.7	0.8	19.4	16.5	283.0	899.8	640.2	27.0	1057493
1988	32262	23.3	23.9	1.0	23.6	15.8	347.1	906.0	645.0	30.3	1110758
1989	32271	25.8	28.7	1.0	24.7	13.5	572.1	1016.8	651.9	29.1	1191269
1990	31258	25.4	34.6	1.2	10.7	12.9	590.6	1005.5	654.4	30.1	1253554
1991-1995	**133994**	**116.5**	**347.3**	**5.9**	**27.0**	**450.8**	**3261.0**	**4851.0**	**3269.9**	**172.2**	**6772732**
1991	31497	27.2	43.8	1.3	7.1	5.4	602.0	996.5	653.4	31.1	1318000
1992	29717	22.6	56.6	1.2	9.1	4.2	570.0	1015.2	662.5	32.8	1423000
1993	26816	19.1	72.6	1.6	4.2	39.3	729.0	835.4	664.0	27.2	1410900
1994	21440	21.0	83.1	0.3	6.6	158.8	605.0	1008.5	642.0	28.1	1298718
1995	24524	26.6	91.2	1.5		243.1	755.0	995.4	648.0	53.0	1322114
1996-2000	**96005**	**70.0**	**436.6**	**7.3**	**15.9**	**706.5**	**1986.8**	**4360.0**	**3336.5**	**306.0**	**7330814**
1996	22585	15.3	102.2	1.2	6.3	234.3	510.6	1013.7	633.6	57.5	1415555
1997	25185	18.1	...	1.7	...	157.7	469.4	1011.7	657.0	58.0	1464302
1998	21299	13.1		0.9	0.3	177.7	348.5	989.5	602.3	57.0	1566621
1999	14753	13.0	148.8	1.4	5.8	81.6	386.2	792.1	701.9	68.0	1431772
2000	12183	10.6	185.6	2.1	3.6	55.2	272.1	553.0	741.7	65.5	1452564
2001-2005	**38411**	**59.5**	**700.9**	**119.7**	**189.7**	**685.0**	**2036.9**	**4359.5**	**3624.5**	**430.7**	**8369923**
2001	11353	8.8	135.8	3.7	5.9	61.3	370.6	690.2	647.9	54.3	1326588
2002	10314	6.2	138.7	1.4	16.2	220.7	368.3	880.9	695.2	90.4	1419754
2003	8393	7.9	132.8	1.3	22.8	238.3	323.8	822.6	701.1	88.8	1451197
2004	4081	19.6	148.0	56.4	63.1	116.8	567.7	1067.9	783.4	98.2	2038933
2005	4270	17.0	145.6	56.9	81.7	47.9	406.5	897.9	796.9	99.0	2133451
2006-2010	**4508**	**64.0**	**906.9**	**270.8**	**447.0**	**189.1**	**3765.4**	**2971.5**	**5143.2**	**455.6**	**11960020**
2006	930	14.0	170.8	63.5	74.1	49.2	893.4	629.2	828.9	99.1	2136918
2007	536	10.4	189.1	57.9	73.1	34.7	638.8	633.3	915.0	90.9	2278658
2008	1583	14.9	180.0	44.9	79.0	49.0	690.9	567.7	1114.6	85.4	2431255
2009	965	14.1	181.1	52.2	128.7	27.1	719.4	641.3	1161.3	84.1	2424839
2010	495	10.6	185.8	52.3	92.1	29.2	822.8	500.0	1123.4	96.2	2688350
2011	339	10.0	187.0	58.6	73.5	26.6	750.2	500.1	1103.1	89.6	2628331
2012	351	11.3	191.7	56.6	80.4	18.2	720.1	493.1	1075.0	84.0	2908214
2013	361	10.0	198.0	58.5	83.7	17.9	995.9	500.1	881.6	72.3	3312116
2014	361	6.6	187.4	60.6		6.6	674.7	457.5	1051.1	77.6	3385699

11-4 续表 Continued

年 份 Year	粗 钢 (万吨) Crude Steel (10000 tons)	钢 材 (万吨) Rolled Steel (10000 tons)	水 泥 (万吨) Cement (10000 tons)	交 流 电动机 (万千瓦) Alternator (10000 kw)	汽 车 (万辆) Motor Vehicles (10000 units)	#轿 车 Sedan Cars	移动通信手持机 (万台) Mobile Phones (10000 units)	微型计算机设 备 (万台) Micro-Computers (10000 units)	数控金属切削机床 (台) CNC Metal Cutting Lathe (unit)	显示器 (万台) Displays (10000 units)	集 成 电 路 (亿块) IC (100 million units)
1978	191.0	116.8	191.5	152.5	1.8						
1979	196.5	137.5	196.9	179.7	2.4						
1980	200.9	152.1	217.4	142.7	2.8						
1981-1985	**1114.2**	**907.9**	**1355.7**	**713.0**	**17.2**			**2.0**			
1981	190.3	149.5	225.7	104.0	2.7						
1982	200.4	159.4	249.1	123.3	2.8						
1983	214.1	177.9	270.8	148.3	3.1			0.3			
1984	241.7	200.1	291.6	165.4	3.6			1.2			
1985	267.7	221.0	318.5	172.0	5.0			0.5			
1986-1990	**1837.8**	**1556.7**	**1649.3**	**889.7**	**39.5**			**6.9**			
1986	303.6	255.5	310.5	178.4	5.8			0.5			
1987	335.5	283.4	319.6	196.4	7.4			0.9			
1988	369.0	314.9	334.3	199.5	9.0			3.0			
1989	386.0	327.9	345.9	163.8	8.5			1.3			
1990	443.7	375.0	339.0	151.6	8.8			1.2			
1991-1995	**3411.0**	**2613.9**	**2364.7**	**824.3**	**70.8**			**32.3**			
1991	499.7	402.9	377.6	156.7	11.0			1.7			
1992	575.0	438.3	403.0	174.9	13.8			3.0			
1993	702.7	525.3	477.9	162.3	13.4			4.1			
1994	828.7	617.6	531.7	165.0	14.7			4.3			
1995	804.9	629.8	574.2	165.4	17.9			19.2			
1996-2000	**3937.5**	**3343.3**	**3758.9**	**753.3**	**57.7**			**686.6**	**2238**		**5.4**
1996	794.7	654.3	666.0	151.9	13.4			28.1	326		0.5
1997	801.7	652.4	700.9	148.7	11.0			59.8	433		0.6
1998	803.2	676.1	762.0	149.7	8.5			160.9	430		0.6
1999	734.5	663.8	803.0	142.0	12.3	1.0		180.0	481		1.3
2000	803.4	696.7	827.0	161.0	12.5	0.5	1549.6	257.8	568		2.4
2001-2005	**4113.3**	**4096.9**	**4963.3**	**1169.8**	**179.6**	**45.7**	**21081.2**	**2407.0**	**5783**		**33.0**
2001	824.9	727.3	809.0	175.1	14.3	0.5	2163.4	339.7	1004		2.1
2002	816.9	750.0	884.0	199.3	18.1	0.7	2280.1	415.7	912		2.5
2003	816.4	785.0	882.0	253.1	34.7	7.3	3334.5	469.3	1188		4.7
2004	827.5	868.3	1204.5	279.4	53.9	15.0	4172.1	532.7	1024		11.1
2005	827.6	966.3	1183.8	262.9	58.6	22.2	9131.1	649.6	1655		12.6
2006-2010	**2988.1**	**4267.1**	**5443.8**	**1160.6**	**492.9**	**191.6**	**106256.6**	**4052.3**	**23256**	**3205.7**	**90.2**
2006	818.1	1016.3	1269.4	269.0	68.3	27.0	14068.0	736.1	1875	680.7	11.8
2007	810.8	1030.4	1167.3	281.9	70.7	20.3	22719.9	843.3	2382	513.6	15.7
2008	466.8	656.8	880.8	259.7	76.6	28.3	20725.5	691.7	3108	478.1	19.1
2009	464.9	769.6	1077.4	159.0	127.1	53.8	21355.3	842.7	6125	655.6	18.3
2010	427.5	794.0	1049.0	191.1	150.3	62.2	27388.0	938.6	9766	877.8	25.3
2011	2.9	287.0	911.5	146.0	150.5	67.1	25962.3	1083.7	12537	851.4	32.0
2012	2.6	253.8	874.5	117.1	167.0	78.5	19949.3	1074.5	13332	796.9	31.9
2013	2.3	221.8	868.4	145.4	203.8	94.5	18783.4	1106.9	6983	305.3	38.4
2014	2.1	195.0	703.1	115.0	216.7	118.6	17983.6	1015.6	13890	548.1	54.3

11-5 规模以上工业企业主要经济指标(2014年)

单位：万元

项　目	Item	企业单位个数(个) Number of Enterprises (unit)	#亏损企业 Loss-Suffering Enterprises	工业总产值(当年价格) Gross Output Value of Industry (at current year's prices)	工业增加值 Added Value of Industry	工业销售产值(当年价格) Sales Value of Industry (at current)	#出口交货值 Delivery Value of Exports
合　计	**Total**	**3686**	**684**	**184528984**	**36119531**	**182282093**	**14268774**
按隶属关系分组	**By Affiliation**						
中央企业	Central Enterprises	238	35	66335419	12080649	65908552	526425
地方企业	Local Enterprises	3448	649	118193565	24038882	116373541	13742348
按登记注册类型分组	**By Registration Type**						
内资企业	Domestically-Invested Enterprises	2834	495	112021231	21400353	110522824	3294544
国有企业	State-owned Enterprises	81	15	34574780	6031856	34448335	22669
集体企业	Collectively-owned Enterprises	45	12	315318	106485	312246	5850
股份合作企业	Joint-equity Cooperative Enterprises	60	9	877087	107217	884117	23466
联营企业	Associated Enterprises						
有限责任公司	Limited Liability Companies	1264	262	43545672	8339352	43030157	1828945
股份有限公司	Companies Limited by Shares	240	44	22664424	4498251	22275952	971099
私营企业	Private Enterprises	1143	153	10041078	2316653	9569372	442515
其他企业	Others	1		***	***	***	***
港澳台商投资企业	Hong Kong, Macao and Taiwan-invested Enterprises	209	50	18105818	2349904	17537926	1777347
港澳台合资经营	Joint Ventures	105	19	4462121	1242767	4394090	783092
港澳台合作经营	Cooperatives	6	2	37071	16751	37202	
港澳台商独资企业	Solely-funded Enterprises	87	29	12654918	961927	12187359	863160
港澳台商投资股份有限公司	Companies Limited by Shares	11		951708	128459	919275	131095
外商投资企业	Foreign-invested Enterprises	643	139	54401935	12369275	54221343	9196882
中外合资经营	Joint Ventures	245	49	35180739	8126161	35123884	6590860
中外合作经营	Cooperatives	11	3	211575	100413	218229	35813
外资(独资)企业	Solely-funded Enterprises	376	84	18235755	3925154	18104901	2514482
外商投资股份有限公司	Companies Limited by Shares	11	3	773867	217546	774329	55727
按城乡分组	**By urban and rural regions**						
#农村企业	Rural Enterprises	77	17	1173159	207367	1170804	20445
按控股类型分组	**By holding types**						
#国有控股	State-holding Enterprises	765	174	106747664	21183125	106003753	2780059
集体控股	Collectively-holding Enterprises	125	22	3039685	596954	2948160	148567
私人控股	Private-holding Enterprises	2061	315	24836486	5921108	24044721	1025054
港澳台控股	Hong Kong, Macao, and Taiwan-holding Enterprises	154	45	15451953	1530315	14955172	1347844
外商控股	Foreign-Investor-holding Enterprises	555	121	34070663	6835313	33950478	8950083
按轻重工业分组	**By light and heavy industries**						
轻工业	Light Industry	1259	259	25680273	7666166	25099323	1608049
重工业	Heavy Industry	2427	425	158848711	28453366	157182771	12660724
按规模分组	**By size**						
#大中型企业	Medium and Large-sized Enterprises	748	137	150395400	30140259	148721905	12588508

注：1. 工业增加值按生产法计算。
2. 应交税金合计包括应交增值税、应交所得税、营业税金及附加和管理费用中的税金。

MAIN ECONOMIC INDICATORS OF INDUSTRIAL ENTERPRISES ABOVE DESIGNATED SIZE (2014)

(10000 yuan)

平均用工人数(人) Average Number of Employed Persons (person)	资产负债 Assets and Liabilities						
	资产总计 Total Assets	流动资产合计 Total Current Assets	#存货 Inventories	#产成品 Finished Products	#应收账款 Accounts Receivable (Net)	固定资产合计 Total Fixed Assets	固定资产原价 Total Original Value of Fixed Assets
1167685	**335570497**	**140424729**	**22962586**	**7650639**	**35791072**	**62778442**	**115329380**
198052	149351575	39922867	4758366	1249405	8013594	29612887	59939935
969633	186218922	100501861	18204221	6401234	27777478	33165555	55389445
777242	264651243	96695434	14748156	4905540	24300571	50620477	91891914
52956	113911074	23160536	1246755	147954	2757933	20432393	39892491
7539	420788	302356	91471	46468	62347	78888	158004
9107	587092	438605	109289	56085	147344	96359	162971
379724	90314448	42089916	7220759	2378555	12658687	23222088	39527575
176442	46324416	21420733	3749563	1288032	5453607	4949593	9269370
151446	13091774	9282314	2329993	988395	3220630	1840480	2880827
28	***	***	***	***	***	***	***
100186	20579699	13398840	2663378	857971	3354064	3108269	6210467
45284	5124026	3192919	567119	232497	992144	1274922	3317794
953	160406	145112	9012	3714	15489	12187	24623
46744	11595412	7411965	1391514	587403	1270697	1727635	2676866
7205	3699855	2648844	695734	34358	1075735	93526	191185
290257	50339555	30330454	5551053	1887128	8136436	9049695	17226998
138942	31457107	18027659	2959469	908605	3575967	5164569	8636988
6268	286553	212018	-8201	5829	58748	61749	154388
134732	16730993	11474283	2505302	926945	4355098	3532268	7824594
10315	1864902	616495	94483	45748	146624	291110	611028
15224	1196274	940534	229941	83500	448619	176380	341022
500883	244008987	80888751	10599818	3133843	16160660	50425583	92616730
28027	3682095	2774036	632824	194282	1177354	396242	703026
336345	44410921	27638581	5876045	2226665	9305327	4602903	7204013
74907	15511672	9875399	1874779	713429	2040574	2229699	3620045
222763	27161912	18638108	3905737	1357668	6971209	5056735	11054203
363518	37730012	22468313	5363616	2385593	4823391	6969035	12955532
804167	297840485	117956415	17598970	5265046	30967681	55809406	102373847
840908	284503770	108045472	15635960	4843892	24964596	56234140	103959001

Note: a) Added value of industry is calculated with production method.
b) Total tax payable mainly includes VAT payable, income tax payable, business tax and surtax, and tax in management expenses.

11-5 续表

单位：万元

项目	Item	资产负债 Assets and Liabilities 负债合计 Total Liabilities	#流动负债合计 Total Current Liabilities	#应付账款 Accounts Receivable	所有者权益合计 Total Owner's Equity	#实收资本 Paid-up Capital
合　计	**Total**	**171375654**	**112548697**	**38275019**	**163891012**	**69116104**
按隶属关系分组	**By Affiliation**					
中央企业	Central Enterprises	**73860857**	**37768946**	**10011808**	**75490718**	**29843084**
地方企业	Local Enterprises	97514797	74779751	28263211	88400295	39273020
按登记注册类型分组	**By Registration Type**					
内资企业	Domestially-Invested Enterprises	**133084379**	**79402915**	**22988739**	**131273238**	**53688965**
国有企业	State-owned Enterprises	54006193	20817860	3596936	59904880	20922153
集体企业	Collectively-owned Enterprises	262075	227045	70092	158713	36479
股份合作企业	Joint-equity Cooperative Enterprises	376247	354629	172880	210846	98017
联营企业	Associated Enterprises					
有限责任公司	Limited Liability Companies	52710088	36942301	12133716	37604360	22422695
股份有限公司	Companies Limited by Shares	18319017	14098289	4314909	27716539	7634920
私营企业	Private Enterprises	7409821	6962230	2700056	5677187	2574408
其他企业	Others	***	***	***	***	***
港澳台商投资企业	Hong Kong, Macao and Taiwan-invested Enterprises	11752128	10697042	4842916	8827571	4063627
港澳台合资经营	Joint Ventures	2476240	2228916	790698	2647786	1595446
港澳台合作经营	Cooperatives	11047	11047	3866	149359	39379
港澳台商独资企业	Solely-funded Enterprises	7274100	6760611	3292521	4321312	1486830
港澳台商投资股份有限公司	Companies Limited by Shares	1990741	1696469	755831	1709114	941972
外商投资企业	Foreign-invested Enterprises	26539148	22448740	10443364	23790204	11363512
中外合资经营	Joint Ventures	16525969	13644930	6077051	14931138	6077348
中外合作经营	Cooperatives	153699	143737	58776	132854	158547
外资(独资)企业	Solely-funded Enterprises	9199744	8134290	4193564	7521045	4502446
外商投资股份有限公司	Companies Limited by Shares	659736	525783	113973	1205166	625170
按城乡分组	**By urban and rural regions**					
#农村企业	Rural Enterprises	795877	721841	351869	400397	157678
按控股类型分组	**By holding types**					
#国有控股	State-holding Enterprises	124036910	70031330	19727427	119972077	51140870
集体控股	Collectively-holding Enterprises	1974760	1778978	946096	1707336	581077
私人控股	Private-holding Enterprises	21120456	18736525	6775018	22996839	8253897
港澳台控股	Hong Kong, Macao, and Taiwan-holding Enterprises	9596539	8859806	4051410	5915133	2234735
外商控股	Foreign-Investor-holding Enterprises	14262643	12782326	6672653	12889066	6732744
按轻重工业分组	**By light and heavy industries**					
轻工业	Light Industry	18631065	16070967	4523398	19098947	8592109
重工业	Heavy Industry	152744589	96477730	33751621	144792066	60523995
按规模分组	**By size**					
#大中型企业	Medium and Large-sized Enterprises	144556355	88386686	28632741	139947415	56894159

11-5 Continued

(10000 yuan)

损益 Profits and Losses								应交税金合计 Total Tax			
营业收入 Business Income	#主营业务收入 Main Business Income	营业成本 Business Cost	#主营业务成本 Main Business Cost	销售费用 Sales Expenses	管理费用 Management Expenses	财务费用 Financial Expenses	利润总额 Total Profits	应交税金合计 Total Tax	#营业税金及附加 Business Tax and Surtax	#主营业务税金及附加 Main Business Tax and Surtax	#应交增值税 Value Added Tax Payable
201794110	**197766666**	**170121159**	**166994443**	**8675519**	**9191424**	**2144861**	**15157524**	**11436589**	**3067618**	**3051352**	**5615607**
68791838	**67640226**	**62228341**	**61254753**	**457850**	**1573346**	**1028285**	**5479152**	**3832099**	**1268089**	**1262805**	**1827371**
133002272	130126441	107892819	105739690	8217669	7618078	1116576	9678373	7604490	1799529	1788548	3788236
121086161	**118683701**	**104997732**	**103166274**	**3238617**	**5778778**	**1863612**	**9113002**	**6323381**	**1692830**	**1677353**	**3300377**
34751236	34595852	31832518	31731193	140071	319598	755884	4104199	1929678	431130	430095	1026017
332854	320901	266642	260733	15831	35130	10	17849	25336	3964	3733	17178
951411	939504	851814	850142	34562	33828	4304	29736	27297	2742	2741	18235
49258285	48051805	43513299	42573334	1211353	2840516	752992	2249191	1816960	195932	185846	1139307
25290070	24444277	20293256	19622115	1163244	1649389	269397	2041490	2044074	1011966	1008486	784825
10499661	10328717	8237863	8126419	673483	900239	80973	670440	480006	47092	46447	314791
***	***	***	***	***	***	***	***	***	***	***	***
22194107	21662031	19167654	18721159	1345290	897832	83756	970510	695798	65596	65081	435265
4922305	4690632	3826840	3618124	280327	270557	30109	517757	321406	29757	29606	169498
54531	54225	41598	41389	4291	6975	-36	1320	4815	384	384	3324
16036025	15870909	14310774	14198120	1006147	536637	-2547	396811	317661	27308	26944	219328
1181247	1046265	988441	863525	54525	83663	56230	54623	51916	8147	8147	43115
58513842	57420934	45955774	45107010	4091613	2514814	197493	5074012	4417410	1309192	1308919	1879965
36498260	36045647	28890364	28569376	1827927	1383844	98087	3667221	3191272	1207810	1207708	1161132
422336	416070	364993	357730	41037	20600	-3059	-1333	23293	1978	1978	18059
20720726	20112941	16035519	15535159	2143388	1033992	82864	1351191	1155160	94552	94387	664608
872521	846276	664898	644745	79261	76378	19600	56935	47686	4853	4847	36166
1273808	1230471	1065899	1038913	35464	73123	4176	106160	70511	5282	5263	34488
113981233	111807499	99312004	97634598	2438405	4081217	1698204	9372714	7376847	2705394	2692307	3138617
3171859	3119570	2550682	2531017	168072	245716	9498	233166	145855	16436	15582	91050
26548951	26046840	20009651	19656372	1933848	2394680	294946	2251506	1408284	142306	140933	908649
19356096	18988003	17087743	16794184	1141600	704473	32178	619977	480764	45701	45326	306097
38296601	37370486	30794838	30014679	2973981	1735479	104913	2660389	2006483	156112	155848	1159628
29805005	28983246	20366041	19771815	4441954	2322174	236476	2399925	2558703	583498	580599	1442742
171989105	168783420	149755118	147222628	4233565	6869250	1908385	12757599	8877886	2484120	2470753	4172865
163631110	160397750	138236952	135660661	7136735	6436166	1844530	13034993	9844200	2913664	2901997	4641494

11-6 规模以上工业企业主要经济指标(按行业分)(2014年)

单位：万元

项　目	Item	企业单位个数(个) Number of Enterprises (unit)	#亏损企业 Loss-Suffering Enterprises	工业总产值(当年价格) Gross Output Value of Industry (at current year's prices)	工业增加值 Added Value of Industry
合计	**Total**	**3686**	**684**	**184528984**	**36119531**
煤炭开采和洗选业	Mining and Washing of Coal	4		5491992	304987
石油和天然气开采业	Extraction of Petroleum and Natural Gas	2	***	***	***
黑色金属矿采选业	Mining and Processing of Ferrous Metal Ores	7		1316681	116056
非金属矿采选业	Mining and Processing of Nonmetal Ores	5		23348	10886
开采辅助活动	Mining Support Service Activities	6	1	2029296	1085338
农副食品加工业	Processing of Food from Agricultural Products	144	38	3825018	532388
食品制造业	Manufacture of Foods	125	32	2789079	390499
酒、饮料和精制茶制造业	Manufacture of Wines, Beverage and Refined Tea	42	11	1919525	550854
烟草制品业	Manufacture of Cigarettes and Tobacco	1	***	***	***
纺织业	Manufacture of Textile	27	4	206051	32488
纺织服装、服饰业	Manufacture of Textile Wearing Apparel and Ornament	141	35	1379236	559481
皮革、毛皮、羽毛及其制品和制鞋业	Manufacture of Leather, Fur, Feather and Its Products, and Footwear	15	3	111189	25896
木材加工和木、竹、藤、棕、草制品业	Processing of Timbers, Manufacture of Wood, Bamboo, Rattan, Palm, and Straw Products	16	3	135018	23401
家具制造业	Manufacture of Furniture	70	13	798476	185339
造纸和纸制品业	Manufacture of Paper and Paper Products	41	12	644423	221096
印刷和记录媒介复制业	Printing, Reproduction of Recording Media	118	27	1230727	522334
文教、工美、体育和娱乐用品制造业	Manufacture of Articles for Culture, Education, Artwork, Sport and Entertainment Activities	35	9	830143	32379
石油加工、炼焦和核燃料加工业	Processing of Petroleum, Coking, Processing of Mucleus Fuels	23	1	8453806	1513100
化学原料和化学制品制造业	Manufacture of Chemical Raw Materials and Chemical Products	215	44	3520728	623228
医药制造业	Manufacture of Medicines	193	25	6690347	2831080
化学纤维制造业	Manufacture of Chemical Fibres	3	***	***	***
橡胶和塑料制品业	Manufacture of Rubber and Plastics Products	124	25	1128322	295822
非金属矿物制品业	Manufacture of Non-metallic Mineral Products	251	48	4880385	750441
黑色金属冶炼和压延加工业	Manufacture and Pressing of Ferrous Metals	26	8	1338253	102292
有色金属冶炼和压延加工业	Manufacture and Pressing of Non-ferrous Metals	38	4	686892	90458
金属制品业	Manufacture of Fabricated Metal Products	228	45	3062268	635495
通用设备制造业	Manufacture of General-purpose Machinery	252	44	5505967	1473050
专用设备制造业	Manufacture of Special-purpose Machinery	329	53	5903160	1326336
汽车制造业	Manufacture of Motor Vehicles	237	41	36476369	7262437
铁路、船舶、航空航天和其他运输设备制造业	Manufacture of Railway Locomotives, Building of Ships and Boats, Manufacture of Air and Spacecrafts and Other Transportation Equipment	74	6	3815408	968593.6
电气机械和器材制造业	Manufacture of Electrical Machinery and Equipment	267	40	7375878	1455022
计算机、通信和其他电子设备制造业	Manufacture of Computers, Communication Equipment and Other Electronic Equipment	299	62	24244643	3050912
仪器仪表制造业	Manufacture of Measuring Instruments and Meters	176	18	2573411	681523
其他制造业	Other Manufacturing	24	3	523436	157282
废弃资源综合利用业	Waste Recycling and Recovery	8	5	76471	13391
金属制品、机械和设备修理业	Repair of Fabricated Metal Products, Machinery and Equipment	15	1	382012	161357
电力、热力生产和供应业	Production and Distribution of Electricity and Heating Power	63	18	40869661	6819739
燃气生产和供应业	Production and Distribution of Gas	22	3	2988642	483064
水的生产和供应业	Production and Distribution of Water	20	2	613411	304301

注：1. 行业划分执行2011年国民经济行业分类标准(GB/T 4754-2011)。
2. 应交税金合计包括应交增值税、应交所得税、营业税金及附加和管理费用中的税金。

MAIN ECONOMIC INDICATORS OF INDUSTRIAL ENTERPRISES ABOVE DESIGNATED SIZE (BY SECTOR) (2014)

(10000 yuan)

工 业 销售产值 (当年价格) Sales Value of Industry (at current year's prices)	#出口交货值 Delivery Value of Exports	平均用工人数(人) Average Number of Employed Persons (person)	资产负债 Assets and Liabilities: 资产总计 Total Assets	流动资产合计 Total Current Assets	#存货 Inventories	#产成品 Finished Products	#应收账款 Accounts Receivable	固定资产合计 Total Fixed Assets	固定资产原价 Total Original Value of Fixed Assets
182282093	**14268774**	**1167685**	**335570497**	**140424729**	**22962586**	**7650639**	**35791072**	**62778442**	**115329380**
5478195	117539	13961	3071628	1918941	149170	148144	580422	54508	196383
***	***	2009	***	***	***	***	***	***	***
1316032		25598	21247871	6714689	278883	43049	1492434	3980819	5811507
19392		409	67711	41169	4995	4393	15931	8610	10834
2029296	190028	21019	4958487	2462069	296845	6596	854660	1213880	2529914
3757399	100084	34115	3878152	2679549	541316	277116	405761	466905	776593
2764594	145393	53272	3425544	2130538	408140	190820	482715	718982	1309226
1939771	14159	28161	4196516	1669685	267790	88364	124965	617131	1323853
***	***	922	***	***	***	***	***	***	***
216906	29021	4628	571015	363172	61702	38766	74773	101941	166378
1260652	243381	45404	1661225	1284947	591936	371268	242666	215543	371343
109874	17842	2199	101100	83246	43091	19524	21669	8689	16687
135828	10208	2633	171495	97778	20036	4614	25826	50478	98800
784341	54817	15445	929166	605611	170751	78131	150430	173182	259349
641614	52194	5948	597684	371783	97475	29876	128145	159634	353494
1228303	11027	25484	2044328	1146792	260374	106020	246319	634013	1497200
853294	62702	6868	895368	723238	363817	199113	127964	84499	150759
8398458		14031	2725934	1101106	639989	230853	162285	829473	2786294
3423208	109960	35555	5268425	3245945	516600	227388	832699	1129836	2522637
6413928	92180	72780	10359697	6193772	1537629	612074	1485820	1570311	2438361
***	***	572	***	***	***	***	***	***	***
1121812	103257	20651	1759639	850065	196244	103144	277214	300427	572408
4863115	122846	55607	9369033	6862301	912756	243602	3326736	1080970	2100604
1335940	127673	7437	3856477	585661	209853	74773	155911	525304	827240
650971	136872	5800	737689	497038	149652	49164	153508	118244	189553
3037213	206331	42397	5221470	3256296	853843	333402	800566	798866	1377251
5343680	797856	57256	8983941	6500055	1894247	573628	1750173	1124425	2047688
5817569	713898	72785	14586184	9581691	1866747	559220	2759265	1073104	1794889
36418374	626085	142515	32767138	17838118	2446233	1040306	4717389	6139243	9128067
3567187	62587	36392	6018410	4436977	1557427	164806	1445060	1027109	1273658
7155958	506604	57418	11492623	8843171	1764277	499977	4007105	677975	1408200
23548493	9365251	127396	28565227	17120996	3483243	1118398	4132195	4380565	9156529
2556176	124858	33029	4627691	3412809	874461	155763	1141902	402565	650305
507787	25253	7133	1172316	687473	127339	32003	209105	282607	479803
76706	343	836	94693	37604	5825	2226	2890	46830	63334
372137	76468	7703	495447	269479	95808	4813	105022	190374	349835
40868572		59705	126076039	22618603	126837	916	2796856	27534700	53858104
2988642		11908	4509837	1348946	12538	7502	411564	1450171	2009520
610787		10704	7264111	2477098	16475	547	112661	3110787	4772500

Note: a) Sectors in this table are classified in accordance with the Standard for Classification of National Economic Sectors 2011 (GB/T 4754-2011).
b) Total tax payable mainly includes VAT payable, income tax payable, business tax and surtax, and tax in management expenses.

11-6 续表

单位：万元

项目	Item	资产负债 Assets and Liabilities 负债合计 Total Liabilities	#流动负债合计 Total Current Liabilities	#应付账款 Accounts Payable	所有者权益合计 Total Owner's Equity
合计	**Total**	**171375654**	**112548697**	**38275019**	**163891012**
煤炭开采和洗选业	Mining and Washing of Coal	1597542	1418176	788835	1474086
石油和天然气开采业	Extraction of Petroleum and Natural Gas	***	***	***	***
黑色金属矿采选业	Mining and Processing of Ferrous Metal Ores	12360947	4980333	904992	8886923
非金属矿采选业	Mining and Processing of Nonmetal Ores	34785	34785	7202	32925
开采辅助活动	Mining Support Service Activities	1889229	1691464	569929	3069257
农副食品加工业	Processing of Food from Agricultural Products	2290176	1961726	312485	1587977
食品制造业	Manufacture of Foods	2170397	2035096	660204	1255147
酒、饮料和精制茶制造业	Manufacture of Wines, Beverage and Refined Tea	1735960	1580184	357907	2460556
烟草制品业	Manufacture of Cigarettes and Tobacco	***	***	***	***
纺织业	Manufacture of Textile	290887	205150	59306	280129
纺织服装、服饰业	Manufacture of Textile Wearing Apparel and Ornament	984375	924565	283382	676851
皮革、毛皮、羽毛及其制品和制鞋业	Manufacture of Leather, Fur, Feather and Its Products, and Footwear	67244	66020	13319	33856
木材加工和木、竹、藤、棕、草制品业	Processing of Timbers, Manufacture of Wood, Bamboo, Rattan, Palm, and Straw Products	103681	99581	23781	67814
家具制造业	Manufacture of Furniture	514933	470684	120193	414233
造纸和纸制品业	Manufacture of Paper and Paper Products	301031	282537	98120	296653
印刷和记录媒介复制业	Printing, Reproduction of Recording Media	856314	746715	282951	1188014
文教、工美、体育和娱乐用品制造业	Manufacture of Articles for Culture, Education, Artwork, Sport and Entertainment Activities	565480	531796	260851	329888
石油加工、炼焦和核燃料加工业	Processing of Petroleum, Coking, Processing of Mucleus Fuels	1516928	1487190	379502	1209006
化学原料和化学制品制造业	Manufacture of Chemical Raw Materials and Chemical Products	2757198	2528773	558410	2511227
医药制造业	Manufacture of Medicines	4599731	3898685	1116826	5759966
化学纤维制造业	Manufacture of Chemical Fibres	***	***	***	***
橡胶和塑料制品业	Manufacture of Rubber and Plastics Products	865928	668444	211931	594648
非金属矿物制品业	Manufacture of Non-metallic Mineral Products	5742890	5454999	2349259	3626143
黑色金属冶炼和压延加工业	Manufacture and Pressing of Ferrous Metals	1278606	445598	230680	2577871
有色金属冶炼和压延加工业	Manufacture and Pressing of Non-ferrous Metals	319482	292532	112296	418207
金属制品业	Manufacture of Fabricated Metal Products	2859325	2493382	801902	2362146
通用设备制造业	Manufacture of General-purpose Machinery	4153953	3812176	1297720	4829630
专用设备制造业	Manufacture of Special-purpose Machinery	7791593	6336000	2244938	6794591
汽车制造业	Manufacture of Motor Vehicles	18746044	15537768	8044294	14021094
铁路、船舶、航空航天和其他运输设备制造业	Manufacture of Railway Locomotives, Building of Ships and Boats, Manufacture of Air and Spacecrafts and Other Transportation Equipment	3940266	3640828	1334983	2078144
电气机械和器材制造业	Manufacture of Electrical Machinery and Equipment	6722706	6312763	2550683	4769917
计算机、通信和其他电子设备制造业	Manufacture of Computers, Communication Equipment and Other Electronic Equipment	14456595	12103159	5688116	14108632
仪器仪表制造业	Manufacture of Measuring Instruments and Meters	2254671	2078460	880303	2373020
其他制造业	Other Manufacturing	407330	282918	131869	764986
废弃资源综合利用业	Waste Recycling and Recovery	67750	44031	4485	26943
金属制品、机械和设备修理业	Repair of Fabricated Metal Products, Machinery and Equipment	244958	242798	59939	246081
电力、热力生产和供应业	Production and Distribution of Electricity and Heating Power	61158589	25279293	5205541	64917451
燃气生产和供应业	Production and Distribution of Gas	1481480	1175780	170739	3028357
水的生产和供应业	Production and Distribution of Water	3427248	1118447	59823	3836863

11-6 Continued

(10000 yuan)

#实收资本 Paid-up Capital	损益 Profits and Losses: 营业收入 Business Income	#主营业务收入 Main Business Income	营业成本 Business Cost	#主营业务成本 Main Business Cost	销售费用 Sales Expenses	管理费用 Management Expenses	财务费用 Financial Expenses	利润总额 Total Profits	应交税金合计 Total Tax Payable	#营业税金及附加 Business Tax and Surtax	#主营业务税金及附加 Main Business Tax and Surtax	#应交增值税 Value Added Tax Payable
69116104	**201794110**	**197766666**	**170121159**	**166994443**	**8675519**	**9191424**	**2144861**	**15157524**	**11436589**	**3067618**	**3051352**	**5615607**
691325	5514667	5488906	5376139	5371443	9216	51781	7212	99380	85000	20612	20594	56485
***	***	***	***	***	***	***	***	***	***	***	***	***
2873054	3754500	3587761	3725872	3559188	9084	168352	259235	218117	96645	15201	13880	70102
13150	30543	29831	20970	20582	297	5507	182	8689	3821	500	468	1755
2693319	1815679	1811851	1625999	1625554	9360	88539	26505	23116	78309	30445	29841	20791
634608	4357455	4323505	3684610	3665323	267944	187470	45650	156333	204371	90827	90809	79661
1070338	4761732	4663987	3160815	3072060	1121221	260382	19524	170996	312032	26399	26085	224278
800371	2188028	2085172	1609868	1526691	362285	132916	6545	79794	232336	84901	84746	115035
***	***	***	***	***	***	***	***	***	***	***	***	***
217344	380245	372547	328377	325734	8058	29392	6995	12858	13207	2122	1851	7848
304468	1466430	1431743	997458	970852	229829	139624	11273	100314	108542	9697	9586	78671
12563	126707	124905	106592	104930	5688	6135	876	7169	6033	434	434	3589
71874	150846	144127	129932	124099	8191	10859	838	1431	6795	657	520	5585
218571	786066	771232	619382	609959	64924	64406	6979	33908	38796	3913	3791	26913
182667	765021	749340	609576	598757	23420	35193	594	93076	56740	3356	3225	26613
702369	1384408	1310553	1045935	996667	43393	168344	833	122841	110028	9825	9400	70681
227019	998092	979612	918724	913511	27989	47851	10233	-475	17905	2780	2214	12154
87531	9411608	8827155	8282669	7705798	62436	147748	25930	154929	1009472	733296	732266	230574
1750150	3762352	3673159	3062737	2992018	285332	303699	57339	274527	185967	18857	18729	117965
1836668	6855598	6626299	3256104	3061726	1835777	655425	103106	1125810	805041	65390	65149	538696
***	***	***	***	***	***	***	***	***	***	***	***	***
363352	1390434	1341234	1178312	1142653	43595	96065	12726	62112	62129	6516	6329	38443
1578572	5527267	5395978	4722823	4626306	227070	358531	72650	179391	178559	26936	26235	109864
876153	1435124	1416745	1325490	1310475	51288	37318	24338	16382	13473	2070	1940	10890
146655	847976	743947	756241	658488	12987	43609	4063	29200	25779	10024	9983	8877
1169164	3625111	3430665	3063926	2913485	103654	276919	36423	147448	129498	20803	19862	75763
1953029	5987845	5852872	4598589	4518159	322267	467574	42921	557450	384579	31551	31287	231247
2850728	6800516	6550560	5081275	4926609	396695	732564	97687	753399	367588	43992	43245	218654
5687452	37793594	36921815	31165303	30523882	1341074	1400437	26479	3180988	2975012	1234307	1233715	975111
845704	3920857	3865492	3152456	3113613	66655	303173	30407	361870	162197	13356	12689	98936
2825476	7909140	7742663	6272574	6131098	394982	562438	83484	603639	393455	32288	32130	248265
6744365	28447408	28155056	25101434	24885634	1039961	1444663	56683	988411	580394	57157	54963	328024
771289	3068130	3023490	2182207	2163584	218283	354260	12736	357033	201799	18644	18037	126967
286246	567283	552893	392608	381684	18866	80003	489	79036	37949	3223	3223	20671
19351	76995	76457	72609	72241	285	6423	676	571	3879	353	333	3049
168304	387797	377533	278843	273952	5687	75133	7317	29421	24076	1507	1496	13707
24249723	41015205	40915292	38599915	38537443	8870	206000	988773	4516327	1932403	173783	172537	1202423
799293	3036963	2996932	2770128	2746023	32698	125251	23446	308316	170352	16261	15464	128492
3093079	800623	788152	584484	577923	3341	58875	16458	239190	73404	3034	2309	12991

11-7 规模以上工业企业主要经济效益指标(2014年)

单位：%

项　　目	Item	工业经济效益综合指数 Aggregate Index of Industrial Economic Efficiency	企业亏损面 Loss-Suffering Enterprises as % of Total	总资产贡献率 Contribution Rate of Total Assets	资产保值增值率 Rate of Assets Preservation and Appreciation
合　　计	**Total**	**288.41**	**18.56**	**8.23**	**112.32**
按隶属关系分组	**By Affiliation**				
中央企业	Central Enterprises	472.00	14.71	6.62	108.60
地方企业	Local Enterprises	251.98	18.82	9.56	115.71
按登记注册类型分组	**By Registration Type**				
内资企业	Domestically-funded Enterprises	262.02	17.47	6.39	112.95
国有企业	State-owned Enterprises	803.23	18.52	5.67	108.80
集体企业	Collectively-Owned Enterprises	175.64	26.67	9.80	105.23
股份合作企业	Joint-equity Cooperative Enterprises	161.44	15.00	9.14	111.53
联营企业	Associated Enterprises				
有限责任公司	Limited Liability Companies	212.79	20.73	5.15	109.64
股份有限公司	Company Limited by Shares	260.26	18.33	9.86	127.74
私营企业	Private Enterprises	188.62	13.39	9.21	117.76
其他企业	Others	225.09		9.62	216.24
港澳台商投资企业	Hong Kong, Macao and Taiwan-invested Enterprises	241.13	23.92	9.19	160.65
港澳台合资经营	Joint Ventures	304.97	18.10	16.53	143.33
港澳台合作经营	Cooperatives	163.35	33.33	2.97	94.93
港澳台商独资企业	Solely-funded Enterprises	234.25	33.33	7.78	260.87
港澳台商投资股份有限公司	Companies Limited by Shares	176.44		4.20	93.20
外商投资企业	Foreign-invested Enterprises	385.33	21.62	17.20	98.30
中外合资经营	Joint Ventures	499.37	20.00	21.01	114.07
中外合作经营	Cooperatives	166.19	27.27	6.72	94.72
外资(独资)企业	Solely-funded Enterprises	280.58	22.34	12.41	82.27
外商投资股份有限公司	Companies Limited by Shares	208.25	27.27	5.43	65.81
按城乡分组	**By urban and rural regions**				
#农村企业	Rural Enterprises	195.94	22.08	13.10	108.59
按控股类型分组	**By holding types**				
#国有控股	State-holding Enterprises	357.86	22.75	7.32	110.35
集体控股	Collectively-holding Enterprises	227.64	17.60	9.82	107.49
私人控股	Private-holding Enterprises	210.15	15.28	8.86	127.04
港澳台控股	Hong Kong, Macao, and Taiwan-holding Enterprises	225.78	29.22	8.44	195.42
外商控股	Foreign-Investor-holding Enterprises	299.62	21.80	14.70	91.65
按轻重工业分组	**By light and heavy industries**				
轻工业	Light Industry	239.45	20.57	13.01	111.37
重工业	Heavy Industry	313.92	17.51	7.62	112.45
按规模分组	**By size**				
#大中型企业	Medium and Large-sized Enterprises	320.80	18.32	8.31	110.15

MAIN INDICATORS OF ECONOMIC BENEFITS OF INDUSTRIAL ENTERPRISES ABOVE DESIGNATED SIZE (2014)

(%)

资产负债率 Assets-Liabilities Ratio	流动资产周转率(次) Turnover of Current Assets (times)	成本费用利润率 Ratio of Profits to Costs	全员劳动生产率(元/人) Overall Labor Productivity (Yuan/person)	产品销售率 Sales Rate of Products	增加值率 Value-added Rate	人均销售收入(元) Sales Revenue Per Capita (Yuan)	流动比率(倍) Liquidity Ratio (times)	速动比率(倍) Quick Ratio (times)
51.07	**1.48**	**8.11**	**309326**	**98.78**	**19.57**	**1693665**	**1.25**	**1.04**
49.45	1.81	8.52	609974	99.36	18.21	3415276	1.06	0.93
52.37	1.35	7.89	247917	98.46	20.34	1342017	1.34	1.10
50.29	1.28	7.99	275337	98.66	19.10	1526985	1.22	1.03
47.41	1.55	12.46	1139032	99.63	17.45	6532943	1.11	1.05
62.28	1.08	5.73	141246	99.03	33.77	425655	1.33	0.93
64.09	2.06	3.22	117730	100.80	12.22	1031628	1.24	0.93
58.36	1.23	4.75	219616	98.82	19.15	1265440	1.14	0.94
39.55	1.12	8.99	254942	98.29	19.85	1385400	1.52	1.25
56.60	1.24	6.85	152969	95.30	23.07	682007	1.33	1.00
56.78	2.30	3.84	192416	92.09	18.76	944607	1.74	1.16
57.11	1.81	4.61	234554	96.86	12.98	2162181	1.25	1.00
48.33	1.70	12.33	274438	98.48	27.85	1035825	1.43	1.18
6.89	0.36	2.51	175769	100.35	45.19	568997	13.14	12.32
62.73	2.60	2.52	205786	96.31	7.60	3395282	1.10	0.89
53.81	0.36	5.16	178292	96.59	13.50	1452137	1.56	1.15
52.72	1.97	9.77	426149	99.67	22.74	1978279	1.35	1.10
52.53	2.18	11.50	584860	99.84	23.10	2594295	1.32	1.10
53.64	1.94	-0.32	160200	103.15	47.46	663800	1.48	1.53
54.99	1.75	7.19	291331	99.28	21.52	1492811	1.41	1.10
35.38	0.99	6.94	210903	100.06	28.11	820432	1.17	0.99
66.53	1.43	9.22	136211	99.80	17.68	808244	1.30	0.98
50.83	1.45	8.85	422916	99.30	19.84	2232208	1.16	1.00
53.63	1.11	7.89	212993	96.99	19.64	1113059	1.56	1.20
47.56	1.00	9.27	176043	96.81	23.84	774408	1.48	1.16
61.87	2.28	3.32	204295	96.78	9.90	2534877	1.11	0.90
52.51	1.99	7.64	306842	99.65	20.06	1677589	1.46	1.15
49.38	1.36	8.96	210888	97.74	29.85	797299	1.40	1.06
51.28	1.50	7.96	353824	98.95	17.91	2098860	1.22	1.04
50.81	1.56	8.63	358425	98.89	20.04	1907435	1.22	1.05

11-8 规模以上国有控股工业企业主要经济指标(2014年)

单位：万元

项目	Item	企业单位个数(个) Number of Enterprises (unit)	#亏损企业 Loss-Suffering Enterprises	工业总产值(当年价格) Gross Output Value of Industry (at current year's prices)	工业增加值 Added Value of Industry	工业销售产值(当年价格) Sales Value of Industry (at current year's prices)
合计	**Total**	**765**	**174**	**106747664**	**21183125**	**106003753**
按隶属关系分组	**By Affiliation**					
中央企业	Central Enterprises	229	33	66156271	12070285	65722706
地方企业	Local Enterprises	536	141	40591393	9112840	40281047
按轻重工业分组	**By light and heavy industries**					
轻工业	Light Industry	195	41	6750979	2266890	6644426
重工业	Heavy Industry	570	133	99996685	18916235	99359327
按规模分组	**By size**					
#大中型企业	Medium and Large-sized Enterprises	273	61	94894140	19769545	94317146

11-8 续表

单位：万元

项目	Item	资产负债 Assets and Liabilities					营业收入 Business Income
		负债合计 Total Liabilities	#流动负债合计 Total Current Liabilities	#应付账款 Accounts Payable	所有者权益合计 Total Owner's Equity	#实收资本 Paid-up Capital	
合计	**Total**	**124036910**	**70031330**	**19727427**	**119972077**	**51140870**	**113981233**
按隶属关系分组	**By Affiliation**						
中央企业	Central Enterprises	73221908	37277018	9873205	75088766	29746638	68351921
地方企业	Local Enterprises	50815002	32754312	9854222	44883311	21394232	45629313
按轻重工业分组	**By light and heavy industries**						
轻工业	Light Industry	6697739	5013845	998145	8525537	3200005	7909990
重工业	Heavy Industry	117339171	65017485	18729282	111446540	47940865	106071243
按规模分组	**By size**						
#大中型企业	Medium and Large-sized Enterprises	114512496	61922191	16748771	113231951	46552550	100619115

MAIN ECONOMIC INDICATORS OF STATE-HOLDING INDUSTRIAL ENTERPRISES ABOVE DESIGNATED SIZE (2014)

(10000 yuan)

#出口交货值 Delivery Value of Exports	平均用工人数(人) Average Number of Employed Persons (person)	资产负债 Assets and Liabilities: 资产总计 Total Assets	流动资产合计 Total Current Assets	#存货 Inventories	#产成品 Finished Products	#应收账款 Accounts Receivable	固定资产合计 Total Fixed Assets	固定资产原价 Total Original Value of Fixed Assets
2780059	**500883**	**244008987**	**80888751**	**10599818**	**3133843**	**16160660**	**50425583**	**92616730**
503335	193468	148310674	39371936	4690960	1224859	7903949	29567694	59846650
2276724	307415	95698313	41516815	5908858	1908984	8256711	20857888	32770080
102857	93416	15223276	7961399	1788600	720997	1162816	3128684	6014507
2677202	407467	228785711	72927352	8811218	2412846	14997844	47296899	86602223
2620026	431777	227744447	71355295	8655944	2345326	13306335	47896097	88331171

11-8 Continued

(10000 yuan)

损益 Profits and Losses: #主营业务收入 Main Business Income	营业成本 Business Cost	#主营业务成本 Main Business Cost	销售费用 Sales Expenses	管理费用 Management Expenses	财务费用 Financial Expenses	利润总额 Total Profits	应交税金合计 Total Tax Payable	#营业税金及附加 Business Tax and Surtax	#主营业务税金及附加 Main Business Tax and Surtax	#应交增值税 Value Added Tax Payable
111807499	**99312004**	**97634598**	**2438405**	**4081217**	**1698204**	**9372714**	**7376847**	**2705394**	**2692307**	**3138617**
67268982	61851857	60940304	439933	1538644	1012262	5459764	3813591	1266425	1261140	1814527
44538517	37460147	36694295	1998472	2542573	685942	3912949	3563256	1438969	1431167	1324090
7702254	5765348	5633768	610562	688343	57524	654019	963143	441154	439591	388698
104105245	93546656	92000830	1827843	3392874	1640680	8718694	6413704	2264240	2252716	2749919
98788031	87370539	85935542	2177127	3386993	1552986	8725741	6939623	2660909	2650951	2877582

11-9 规模以上国有控股工业企业主要经济指标(按行业分)(2014年)

单位：万元

项 目	Item	企业单位个数(个) Number of Enterprises (unit)	#亏损企业 Loss-Suffering Enterprises	工业总产值(当年价格) Gross Output Value of Industry (at current year's prices)	工业增加值 Added Value of Industry
合 计	**Total**	**765**	**174**	**106747664**	**21183125**
煤炭开采和洗选业	Mining and Washing of Coal	4		5491992	304987
石油和天然气开采业	Extraction of Petroleum and Natural Gas	2	***	***	***
黑色金属矿采选业	Mining and Processing of Ferrous Metal Ores	4		1248959	93534
非金属矿采选业	Mining and processing of nonmetal ores	1	***	***	***
开采辅助活动	Mining Support Service Activities	3	***	***	***
农副食品加工业	Processing of Food from Agricultural Products	26	9	1813070	292086
食品制造业	Manufacture of Foods	15	5	549874	111077
酒、饮料和精制茶制造业	Manufacture of Wines, Beverage and Refined Tea	8	2	597305	214939
烟草制品业	Manufacture of Cigarettes and Tobacco	1	***	***	***
纺织业	Manufacture of Textile	11	3	57793	6252
纺织服装、服饰业	Manufacture of Textile Wearing Apparel and Ornament	6	1	40912	6841
皮革、毛皮、羽毛及其制品和制鞋业	Manufacture of Leather, Fur, Feather and Its Products, and Footwear	2	***	***	***
木材加工和木、竹、藤、棕、草制品业	Processing of Timbers, Manufacture of Wood, Bamboo, Rattan, Palm, and Straw Products	1	***	***	***
家具制造业	Manufacture of Furniture	4	2	57470	14759
造纸和纸制品业	Manufacture of Paper and Paper Products	4	2	25401	544
印刷和记录媒介复制业	Printing, Reproduction of Recording Media	33	7	593976	289279
文教、工美、体育和娱乐用品制造业	Manufacture of Articles for Culture, Education, Artwork, Sport and Entertainment Activities	7	2	94674	-5522
石油加工、炼焦和核燃料加工业	Processing of Petroleum, Coking, Processing of Mucleus Fuels	8	1	7673520	1437363
化学原料和化学制品制造业	Manufacture of Chemical Raw Materials and Chemical Products	36	12	1339563	29602.05
医药制造业	Manufacture of Medicines	33	1	1430380	622177
化学纤维制造业	Manufacture of Chemical Fibres	2	***	***	***
橡胶和塑料制品业	Manufacture of Rubber and Plastics Products	13	2	173001	36435
非金属矿物制品业	Manufacture of Non-metallic Mineral Products	59	19	1519919	211482
黑色金属冶炼和压延加工业	Manufacture and Pressing of Ferrous Metals	5	4	817974	24452
有色金属冶炼和压延加工业	Manufacture and Pressing of Non-ferrous Metals	10	2	354680	41827
金属制品业	Manufacture of Fabricated Metal Products	34	12	1134486	152347
通用设备制造业	Manufacture of General-purpose Machinery	45	16	940950	199276
专用设备制造业	Manufacture of Special-purpose Machinery	64	10	1724306	358857
汽车制造业	Manufacture of Motor Vehicles	42	13	23507614	5368304
铁路、船舶、航空航天和其他运输设备制造业	Manufacture of Railway Locomotives, Building of Ships and Boats, Manufacture of Air and Spacecrafts and Other Transportation Equipment	35	5	3265380	806738
电气机械和器材制造业	Manufacture of Electrical Machinery and Equipment	29	7	1931336	163696
计算机、通信和其他电子设备制造业	Manufacture of Computers, Communication Equipment and Other Electronic Equipment	77	13	4337617	1161883
仪器仪表制造业	Manufacture of Measuring Instruments and Meters	48	6	847222	181771
其他制造业	Other Manufacturing	11	1	462520	139991
废弃资源综合利用业	Waste Recycling and Recovery	2	***	***	***
金属制品、机械和设备修理业	Repair of Fabricated Metal Products, Machinery and Equipment	4		306700	121977
电力、热力生产和供应业	Production and Distribution of Electricity and Heating Power	47	13	40682920	6825782
燃气生产和供应业	Production and Distribution of Gas	13	1	505640	68289
水的生产和供应业	Production and Distribution of Water	16	1	578755	290366

注：1. 行业划分执行2011年国民经济行业分类标准(GB/T 4754-2011)。
2. 应交税金合计包括应交增值税、应交所得税、营业税金及附加和管理费用中的税金。

MAIN ECONOMIC INDICATORS OF STATE-OWNED AND STATE-CONTROLLED INDUSTIRAL ENTERPRISES ABOVE DESIGNATED SIZE (BY SECTOR) (2014)

(10000 yuan)

工业销售产值(当年价格) Sales Value of Industry (at current year's prices)	#出口交货值 Delivery Value of Exports	平均用工人数(人) Average Number of Employed Persons (person)	资产负债 Assets and Liabilities						
			资产总计 Total Assets	流动资产合计 Total Current Assets	#存货 Inventories	#产成品 Finished Products	#应收账款 Accounts Receivable	固定资产合计 Total Fixed Assets	固定资产原价 Total Original Value of Fixed Assets
106003753	**2780059**	**500883**	**244008987**	**80888751**	**10599818**	**3133843**	**16160660**	**50425583**	**92616730**
5478195	117539	13961	3071628	1918941	149170	148144	580422	54508	196383
***	***	2009	***	***	***	***	***	***	***
1250665		24339	21161425	6668174	267869	40879	1486219	3944483	5757448
***	***	69	***	***	***	***	***	***	***
***	***	19777	***	***	***	***	***	***	***
1757006	9392	12490	2072974	1546738	274562	176161	123086	196825	308781
546108	5715	9763	695165	308744	68163	35952	97414	138496	223347
599780	3851	11529	2596829	977009	128543	36496	30277	199432	518401
***	***	922	***	***	***	***	***	***	***
67068	9293	2497	361618	211835	28098	18959	20244	75364	101857
44491	14909	1765	68354	44088	22290	11656	11905	16901	26834
***	***	427	***	***	***	***	***	***	***
***	***	147	***	***	***	***	***	***	***
55821	2483	1719	140834	72346	19976	13899	14101	29321	46668
28549		379	62658	40249	11168	3722	15358	12767	20828
600093	112	12177	1060080	591861	110863	55888	117358	321805	856177
107201	6206	2047	473395	390535	225574	125833	84430	40074	62835
7618938		12468	2539648	956286	598205	221838	131495	807680	2745247
1297969	2637	11428	2753018	1596089	203054	94940	245546	621004	1570067
1392505	6110	19550	3455531	1923437	582586	185466	370238	567846	895172
***	***	528	***	***	***	***	***	***	***
170945	36118	4270	287268	173291	43861	27594	36775	72362	125112
1506762	29963	21413	3855191	2738809	236560	90499	1134288	538672	1021433
811951	76477	3451	3470999	290084	100632	42443	38950	479817	698509
325319	87566	2827	408903	281776	87768	25402	77127	84033	127514
1123876	139302	14986	2199533	1068496	261045	83646	220993	445897	705349
912498	68483	15407	2403291	1694578	655070	125557	348116	235877	452500
1693941	49686	25222	4061616	2946950	813499	266450	952737	449733	778716
23473498	373163	83933	24268021	12150383	1563955	670932	1560560	4559687	6528504
3029221	60280	31376	5082595	3758536	1407222	124119	1156526	968688	1172039
1894172	74257	9340	4285363	3360287	694010	81766	1750538	117392	255984
4223331	1299102	35108	10679870	5740561	1050791	321666	1294095	2426821	4470971
851911	8807	10189	1266433	981637	298586	57124	278290	115135	197477
446016	5124	5940	1069959	617518	115854	27800	185779	260492	449760
***	***	287	***	***	***	***	***	***	***
299653	74897	6851	370139	178049	77623	165	71356	173447	319665
40693607		56622	125760878	22445116	94716	3	2762360	27458658	53744863
505640		3581	562434	326962	8752	6586	39215	214872	323981
576263		10089	7175567	2439939	9908	22	102640	3087594	4732035

Note: a) Sectors in this table are classified in accordance with the Standard for Classification of National Economic Sectors 2011 (GB/T 4754-2011).
b) Total tax payable mainly includes VAT payable, income tax payable, business tax and surtax, and tax in management expenses.

11-9 续表

单位：万元

项目	Item	资产负债 Assets and Liabilities			
		负债合计 Total Liabilities	#流动负债合计 Total Current Liabilities	#应付账款 Accounts Payable	所有者权益合计 Total Owner's Equity
合计	**Total**	**124036910**	**70031330**	**19727427**	**119972077**
煤炭开采和洗选业	Mining and Washing of Coal	1597542	1418176	788835	1474086
石油和天然气开采业	Extraction of Petroleum and Natural Gas	***	***	***	***
黑色金属矿采选业	Mining and Processing of Ferrous Metal Ores	12314262	4936428	897168	8847164
非金属矿采选业	Mining and processing of nonmetal ores	***	***	***	***
开采辅助活动	Mining Support Service Activities	***	***	***	***
农副食品加工业	Processing of Food from Agricultural Products	1307476	1100012	86273	765498
食品制造业	Manufacture of Foods	438599	378338	116399	256567
酒、饮料和精制茶制造业	Manufacture of Wines, Beverage and Refined Tea	798932	678246	26549	1797897
烟草制品业	Manufacture of Cigarettes and Tobacco	***	***	***	***
纺织业	Manufacture of Textile	183066	99436	15347	178553
纺织服装、服饰业	Manufacture of Textile Wearing Apparel and Ornament	63730	63493	9591	4624
皮革、毛皮、羽毛及其制品和制鞋业	Manufacture of Leather, Fur, Feather and Its Products, and Footwear	***	***	***	***
木材加工和木、竹、藤、棕、草制品业	Processing of Timbers, Manufacture of Wood, Bamboo, Rattan, Palm, and Straw Products	***	***	***	***
家具制造业	Manufacture of Furniture	76967	55306	16808	63867
造纸和纸制品业	Manufacture of Paper and Paper Products	24881	17886	7512	37777
印刷和记录媒介复制业	Printing, Reproduction of Recording Media	364281	310739	102774	695799
文教、工美、体育和娱乐用品制造业	Manufacture of Articles for Culture, Education, Artwork, Sport and Entertainment Activities	323106	296073	201535	150288
石油加工、炼焦和核燃料加工业	Processing of Petroleum, Coking, Processing of Mucleus Fuels	1457425	1427941	349604	1082223
化学原料和化学制品制造业	Manufacture of Chemical Raw Materials and Chemical Products	1651398	1493465	227886	1101620
医药制造业	Manufacture of Medicines	1162232	826839	201266	2293298
化学纤维制造业	Manufacture of Chemical Fibres	***	***	***	***
橡胶和塑料制品业	Manufacture of Rubber and Plastics Products	162366	158352	22527	124902
非金属矿物制品业	Manufacture of Non-metallic Mineral Products	2323562	2226924	724578	1531629
黑色金属冶炼和压延加工业	Manufacture and Pressing of Ferrous Metals	1068065	257140	137787	2402935
有色金属冶炼和压延加工业	Manufacture and Pressing of Non-ferrous Metals	124624	104978	49192	284280
金属制品业	Manufacture of Fabricated Metal Products	1118670	917267	330681	1080863
通用设备制造业	Manufacture of General-purpose Machinery	1398569	1303831	300334	1004722
专用设备制造业	Manufacture of Special-purpose Machinery	2658369	2213194	826163	1403247
汽车制造业	Manufacture of Motor Vehicles	13767001	10941927	4913280	10501020
铁路、船舶、航空航天和其他运输设备制造业	Manufacture of Railway Locomotives, Building of Ships and Boats, Manufacture of Air and Spacecrafts and Other Transportation Equipment	3530401	3252820	1129482	1552195
电气机械和器材制造业	Manufacture of Electrical Machinery and Equipment	2809097	2669091	1026606	1476266
计算机、通信和其他电子设备制造业	Manufacture of Computers, Communication Equipment and Other Electronic Equipment	5071589	3629698	999954	5608281
仪器仪表制造业	Manufacture of Measuring Instruments and Meters	694600	597869	208091	571834
其他制造业	Other Manufacturing	363496	245561	122638	706463
废弃资源综合利用业	Waste Recycling and Recovery	***	***	***	***
金属制品、机械和设备修理业	Repair of Fabricated Metal Products, Machinery and Equipment	202836	202651	41069	167303
电力、热力生产和供应业	Production and Distribution of Electricity and Heating Power	60907393	25089223	5149754	64853486
燃气生产和供应业	Production and Distribution of Gas	276913	256993	51504	285521
水的生产和供应业	Production and Distribution of Water	3391524	1094280	55920	3784043

11-9 Continued

(10000 yuan)

#实收资本 Paid-up Capital	损益 Profits and Losses: 营业收入 Business Income	#主营业务收入 Main Business Income	营业成本 Business Cost	#主营业务成本 Main Business Cost	销售费用 Sales Expenses	管理费用 Management Expenses	财务费用 Financial Expenses	利润总额 Total Profits	应交税金合计 Total Tax Payable	#营业税金及附加 Business Tax and Surtax	#主营业务税金及附加 Main Business Tax and Surtax	#应交增值税 Value Added Tax Payable
51140870	**113981233**	**111807499**	**99312004**	**97634598**	**2438405**	**4081217**	**1698204**	**9372714**	**7376847**	**2705394**	**2692307**	**3138617**
691325	5514667	5488906	5376139	5371443	9216	51781	7212	99380	85000	20612	20594	56485
***	***	***	***	***	***	***	***	***	***	***	***	***
2870989	3687633	3529619	3673347	3513635	7770	159667	258535	216169	88807	12940	11619	65147
***	***	***	***	***	***	***	***	***	***	***	***	***
***	***	***	***	***	***	***	***	***	***	***	***	***
199367	2226954	2218659	1855864	1853664	146665	71943	21318	63133	165134	88598	88593	59505
199834	640038	627199	486074	474246	96943	35199	5492	4594	24157	2289	2289	19101
108235	693391	660317	543105	519794	68369	41963	-603	57793	120734	67914	67759	42080
***	***	***	***	***	***	***	***	***	***	***	***	***
158187	142874	135709	116146	113708	1932	20375	4764	1922	5950	1467	1199	3160
49305	66609	64659	69611	68936	1309	6066	2072	4983	2573	361	358	1840
***	***	***	***	***	***	***	***	***	***	***	***	***
***	***	***	***	***	***	***	***	***	***	***	***	***
27945	74436	69784	53624	51249	12440	7065	-64	1085	6448	774	653	4914
10417	98826	97373	94865	94440	836	3435	-199	-880	1878	167	89	1002
443441	720662	660541	515167	475307	12946	110059	-2203	82518	70434	6421	5997	42714
137839	155174	151373	127986	126997	14126	15783	6104	-9312	5775	884	865	3898
63184	8499173	7915642	7450825	6874423	41324	134938	24890	112767	980158	729135	728107	216507
1107449	1397805	1344467	1304689	1263566	28121	142901	46451	102953	30732	3089	2996	21510
677003	1454712	1437053	792402	783000	203303	182723	16905	309877	166344	14978	14803	108134
***	***	***	***	***	***	***	***	***	***	***	***	***
82648	303241	281841	264794	250330	7767	23405	2078	8109	11206	1541	1473	6209
750806	1827842	1774742	1581461	1539425	68935	139838	31495	80213	54969	8611	8012	31974
793025	859388	843202	829940	815328	33436	17793	20806	-24106	-6719	560	476	2524
85635	452819	352545	403516	308891	6331	23783	1188	13132	17219	9252	9211	4231
542885	1474745	1369651	1300894	1220224	27462	110527	9562	36519	34733	7485	7001	17614
603623	1083622	1056441	898084	881230	35050	110444	10928	25855	65928	6667	6423	49650
860007	1996331	1955544	1548925	1527414	93824	232774	18337	129298	105598	14228	13551	67851
4248558	23893562	23467099	18844745	18597170	1124117	939783	3516	2328558	2449306	1204268	1203877	704899
659755	3283774	3235917	2720078	2685019	33789	238452	28132	259480	105606	9604	8939	68538
1201509	2020754	1953044	1744218	1682070	98832	126995	54611	24599	55764	4379	4312	52287
3580876	5156392	5075156	4067992	4019227	183904	495782	79161	424270	170450	19882	17961	96370
258193	954712	938064	763942	756524	36674	107440	3413	69412	48824	5695	5326	33659
255295	502546	489933	346283	336562	14856	72234	-810	74811	34707	2699	2699	18755
***	***	***	***	***	***	***	***	***	***	***	***	***
142393	307543	297875	232954	228314	1443	62620	6806	8872	14463	812	802	7804
24207293	40824850	40725759	38408576	38346456	4895	188673	984672	4506565	1929479	173277	172031	1201992
190638	532432	506665	509511	496349	5285	33002	-2024	36155	31753	2540	2110	18829
3067020	765166	752852	562084	555554	1647	52445	15392	236662	71124	2630	1906	11331

11-10 规模以上股份制工业企业主要经济指标(2014年)

单位：万元

项目	Item	企业单位个数(个) Number of Enterprises (unit)	#亏损企业 Loss-Suffering Enterprises	工业总产值(当年价格) Gross Output Value of Industry (at current year's prices)	工业增加值 Added Value of Industry	工业销售产值(当年价格) Sales Value of Industry (at current year's prices)	#出口交货值 Delivery Value of Exports
合　计	**Total**	**1504**	**306**	**66210096**	**12837603**	**65306109**	**2800045**
按隶属关系分组	**By Affiliation**						
中央企业	Central Enterprises	183	29	31861049	5813771	31558517	413569
地方企业	Local Enterprises	1321	277	34349047	7023832	33747592	2386475
按轻重工业分组	**By Light and Heavy Industries**						
轻工业	Light Industry	435	91	9184076	2718110	8986537	162457
重工业	Heavy Industry	1069	215	57026020	10119493	56319572	2637587
按规模分组	**By Size**						
#大中型企业	Medium and Large-sized Enterprises	349	74	48656367	10220886	48060141	2438677

11-10 续表

单位：万元

项目	Item	固定资产原价 Total Original Value of Fixed Assets	资产负债 Assets and Liabilities: 负债合计 Total Liabilities	#流动负债合计 Total Current Liabilities	#应付账款 Accounts Payable	所有者权益合计 Total Owner's Equity	#实收资本 Paid-up Capital
合　计	**Total**	**48796945**	**71029105**	**51040590**	**16448624**	**65320898**	**30057614**
按隶属关系分组	**By Affiliation**						
中央企业	Central Enterprises	19462159	20260281	17242244	6400923	16456099	8336782
地方企业	Local Enterprises	29334786	50768824	33798346	10047701	48864799	21720832
按轻重工业分组	**By Light and Heavy Industries**						
轻工业	Light Industry	6382570	8848051	7116156	1646707	9302059	4069825
重工业	Heavy Industry	42414375	62181054	43924434	14801917	56018839	25987789
按规模分组	**By Size**						
#大中型企业	Medium and Large-sized Enterprises	43448370	57104662	38385890	11400565	52285701	23755259

注：应交税金合计包括应交增值税、应交所得税、营业税金及附加和管理费用中的税金。

MAIN ECONOMIC INDICATORS OF SHARE-HOLDING INDUSTRIAL ENTERPRISES ABOVE DESIGNATED SIZE (2014)

(10000 yuan)

平均用工人数(人) Average Number of Employed Persons (person)	资产负债 Assets and Liabilities					
	资产总计 Total Assets	流动资产合计 Total Current Assets	#存货 Inventories	#产成品 Finished Products	#应收账款 Accounts Receivable	固定资产合计 Total Fixed Assets
556166	**136638864**	**63510649**	**10970322**	**3666586**	**18112295**	**28171682**
151780	36716381	17617813	3545329	1124223	5200533	9066660
404386	99922483	45892836	7424994	2542364	12911762	19105021
131301	18150110	10544909	2354653	1067684	1858245	3624633
424865	118488753	52965740	8615669	2598903	16254049	24547049
415634	109390363	46870308	7344254	2270917	12563276	25008391

11-10 Continued

(10000 yuan)

损益 Profits and Losses								应交税金合计 Total Tax Payable			
营业收入 Business Income	#主营业务收入 Main Business Income	营业成本 Business Cost	#主营业务成本 Main Business Cost	销售费用 Sales Expenses	管理费用 Management Expenses	财务费用 Financial Expenses	利润总额 Total Profits		#营业税金及附加 Business Tax and Surtax	#主营业务税金及附加 Main Business Tax and Surtax	#应交增值税 Value Added Tax Payable
74548355	**72496082**	**63806555**	**62195449**	**2374597**	**4489905**	**1022389**	**4290681**	**3861034**	**1207899**	**1194332**	**1924131**
34053470	33082416	30623535	29792274	383381	1243470	240717	1202948	1875298	866413	861713	785750
40494885	39413666	33183020	32403174	1991216	3246434	781672	3087733	1985736	341486	332620	1138381
10447583	10251902	7493463	7383708	988656	948758	99032	1155256	834167	174505	172071	464759
64100773	62244180	56313092	54811740	1385941	3541147	923357	3135425	3026867	1033393	1022261	1459372
54838743	53222233	46848029	45542866	1799829	3183775	871010	3337394	3150079	1134635	1124231	1490397

Note: Total tax payable mainly includes VAT payable, income tax payable, business tax and surtax, and tax in management expenses.

11-11 规模以上股份制工业企业主要经济指标(按行业分)(2014年)

单位：万元

项目	Item	企业单位个数(个) Number of Enterprises (unit)	#亏损企业 Loss-Suffering Enterprises	工业总产值(当年价格) Gross Output Value of Industry (at current year's prices)	工业增加值 Added Value of Industry
合计	**Total**	**1504**	**306**	**66210096**	**12837603**
煤炭开采和洗选业	Mining and Washing of Coal	4		5491992	304987
石油和天然气开采业	Extraction of Petroleum and Natural Gas	2	***	***	***
黑色金属矿采选业	Mining and Processing of Ferrous Metal Ores	5		1275159	100670
非金属矿采选业	Mining and Processing of Nonmetal Ores	2	***	***	***
开采辅助活动	Mining Support Service Activities	3	***	***	***
农副食品加工业	Processing of Food from Agricultural Products	62	17	2091709	370655
食品制造业	Manufacture of Foods	35	10	513841	132613
酒、饮料和精制茶制造业	Manufacture of Wines, Beverage and Refined Tea	12	5	153504	76840
纺织业	Manufacture of Textile	15	4	102169	12056
纺织服装、服饰业	Manufacture of Textile Wearing Apparel and Ornament	32	6	445662	205474
皮革、毛皮、羽毛及其制品和制鞋业	Manufacture of Leather, Fur, Feather and Its Products, and Footwear	4	1	20899	1671
木材加工和木、竹、藤、棕、草制品业	Processing of Timbers, Manufacture of Wood, Bamboo, Rattan, Palm, and Straw Products	6	2	34078	9697
家具制造业	Manufacture of Furniture	18	3	142375	38866
造纸和纸制品业	Manufacture of Paper and Paper Products	15	4	84977	10305
印刷和记录媒介复制业	Printing, Reproduction of Recording Media	37	9	580485	278832
文教、工美、体育和娱乐用品制造业	Manufacture of Articles for Culture, Education, Artwork, Sport and Entertainment Activities	14	4	718185	6654
石油加工、炼焦和核燃料加工业	Processing of Petroleum, Coking, Processing of Mucleus Fuels	11	1	7608430	1417762
化学原料和化学制品制造业	Manufacture of Chemical Raw Materials and Chemical Products	82	17	1584239	157305
医药制造业	Manufacture of Medicines	88	11	2685576	1141072
化学纤维制造业	Manufacture of Chemical Fibres	2	***	***	***
橡胶和塑料制品业	Manufacture of Rubber and Plastics Products	36	9	316252	48088
非金属矿物制品业	Manufacture of Non-metallic Mineral Products	133	33	3304004	444660
黑色金属冶炼和压延加工业	Manufacture and Pressing of Ferrous Metals	14	7	910204	52908
有色金属冶炼和压延加工业	Manufacture and Pressing of Non-ferrous Metals	15	3	488189	57956
金属制品业	Manufacture of Fabricated Metal Products	85	21	1594179	310591
通用设备制造业	Manufacture of General-purpose Machinery	88	22	1111852	339273
专用设备制造业	Manufacture of Special-purpose Machinery	136	18	3551775	685895
汽车制造业	Manufacture of Motor Vehicles	71	22	6028434	447153
铁路、船舶、航空航天和其他运输设备制造业	Manufacture of Railway Locomotives, Building of Ships and Boats, Manufacture of Air and Spacecrafts and Other Transportation Equipment	44	5	2003055	453786
电气机械和器材制造业	Manufacture of Electrical Machinery and Equipment	113	18	4040365	564491
计算机、通信和其他电子设备制造业	Manufacture of Computers, Communication Equipment and Other Electronic Equipment	145	30	5155602	1257967
仪器仪表制造业	Manufacture of Measuring Instruments and Meters	86	10	1387874	411295
其他制造业	Other Manufacturing	13	1	485010	146244
废弃资源综合利用业	Waste Recycling and Recovery	4	2	49888	13464
金属制品、机械和设备修理业	Repair of Fabricated Metal Products, Machinery and Equipment	8		58127	24626
电力、热力生产和供应业	Production and Distribution of Electricity and Heating Power	38	9	9124387	1762752
燃气生产和供应业	Production and Distribution of Gas	12	1	401986	79703
水的生产和供应业	Production and Distribution of Water	14	1	557046	271988

注：1．行业划分执行2011年国民经济行业分类标准(GB/T 4754-2011)。
2．应交税金合计包括应交增值税、应交所得税、营业税金及附加和管理费用中的税金。

MAIN ECONOMIC INDICATORS OF SHARE-HOLDING INDUSTRIAL ENTERPRISES ABOVE DESIGNATED SIZE (BY SECTOR) (2014)

(10000 yuan)

工业销售产值(当年价格) Sales Value of Industry (at current year's prices)	#出口交货值 Delivery Value of Exports	平均用工人数(人) Average Number of Employed Persons (person)	资产负债 Assets and Liabilities: 资产总计 Total Assets	流动资产合计 Total Current Assets	#存货 Inventories	#产成品 Finished Products	#应收账款 Accounts Receivable	固定资产合计 Total Fixed Assets
65306109	**2800045**	**556166**	**136638864**	**63510649**	**10970322**	**3666586**	**18112295**	**28171682**
5478195	117539	13961	3071628	1918941	149170	148144	580422	54508
***	***	2009	***	***	***	***	***	***
1275788		24631	21193870	6686446	271156	41037	1486955	3955387
***	***	213	***	***	***	***	***	***
***	***	19777	***	***	***	***	***	***
2028522	3285	16192	2973144	2075743	297753	169222	252570	265683
501783	38555	10833	865090	602332	116415	35531	95995	129689
155263	1687	3539	481791	275160	93571	47376	32226	107972
106821	7930	2798	457923	282220	43882	29760	38800	79437
400869	33054	13949	681178	490693	214162	156109	104900	96256
21649	6152	363	10327	9419	4920	1761	2051	908
34400		1153	65706	42274	8508	1299	11527	12676
137915	3075	3457	229117	133743	49867	27266	23165	49971
87396	1499	1863	100426	45629	14806	7063	19577	24636
575242	3437	10839	951044	541460	123837	54420	84531	294093
722741	5014	3910	702598	561878	305405	161504	90354	68279
7565231		12531	2499971	940520	575476	207588	133575	789198
1540439	13647	16078	2954294	1860605	247878	111521	342249	528479
2644447	15079	35909	5848945	3224504	740844	259948	652407	986817
***	***	528	***	***	***	***	***	***
309660	36913	6285	904505	288835	76748	43542	64281	109427
3308709	75513	36707	6916983	5102740	579770	168725	2405620	753276
902392	82346	5594	3594493	368206	136399	59371	54601	511011
448301	90875	3811	532454	336485	113451	36052	94564	95774
1550424	127250	20713	2819148	1556904	447419	131481	384281	521682
1048839	50425	19921	3289010	2022398	542924	172719	612329	381154
3495249	213157	39633	9742866	6220132	1224745	393729	1688068	643235
6034087	366254	54171	8140294	3436443	628530	282197	1167249	1503238
1864757	61514	23326	3691548	2747550	727725	93006	1182618	452350
3882455	51872	26999	6365035	4777587	817611	247629	2417480	342809
5061272	1162462	47755	15261273	6978977	1365502	445160	1886636	2458733
1374159	24775	18576	2817451	2001399	555474	95854	620131	234064
469077	6856	5965	1121169	659038	118992	28084	200584	262749
50527	343	556	85019	33519	4832	1625	1047	41670
56352		883	133558	75667	25393	414	27697	25396
9109139		39058	14797880	2352907	56344	758	400003	7689269
401986		2162	364389	231416	1786	13	36891	106780
554740		9518	7064969	2365199	9539	22	102638	3044764

Note: a) Sectors in this table are classified in accordance with the Standard for Classification of National Economic Sectors 2011 (GB/T 4754-2011).
b) Total tax payable mainly includes VAT payable, income tax payable, business tax and surtax, and tax in management expenses.

11-11 续表

单位：万元

项目	Item	资产负债 Assets and Liabilities 固定资产原价 Total Original Value of Fixed Assets	负债合计 Total Liabilities	#流动负债合计 Total Current Liabilities	#应付账款 Accounts Payable	所有者权益合计 Total Owner's Equity
合 计	**Total**	**48796945**	**71029105**	**51040590**	**16448624**	**65320898**
煤炭开采和洗选业	Mining and Washing of Coal	196383	1597542	1418176	788835	1474086
石油和天然气开采业	Extraction of Petroleum and Natural Gas	***	***	***	***	***
黑色金属矿采选业	Mining and Processing of Ferrous Metal Ores	5772311	12328968	4951134	897796	8864902
非金属矿采选业	Mining and Processing of Nonmetal Ores	***	***	***	***	***
开采辅助活动	Mining Support Service Activities	***	***	***	***	***
农副食品加工业	Processing of Food from Agricultural Products	410503	1698187	1416979	144085	1274957
食品制造业	Manufacture of Foods	200464	661926	603026	104340	203164
酒、饮料和精制茶制造业	Manufacture of Wines, Beverage and Refined Tea	159300	299913	293832	73587	181878
纺织业	Manufacture of Textile	111905	222539	138909	42138	235384
纺织服装、服饰业	Manufacture of Textile Wearing Apparel and Ornament	154711	341537	325392	97810	339642
皮革、毛皮、羽毛及其制品和制鞋业	Manufacture of Leather, Fur, Feather and Its Products, and Footwear	2014	7461	7461	-1117	2866
木材加工和木、竹、藤、棕、草制品业	Processing of Timbers, Manufacture of Wood, Bamboo, Rattan, Palm, and Straw Products	26412	43776	42676	10698	21930
家具制造业	Manufacture of Furniture	77156	123132	97768	33470	105985
造纸和纸制品业	Manufacture of Paper and Paper Products	40387	63415	62007	27420	37011
印刷和记录媒介复制业	Printing, Reproduction of Recording Media	719501	331111	304439	112013	619933
文教、工美、体育和娱乐用品制造业	Manufacture of Articles for Culture, Education, Artwork, Sport and Entertainment Activities	121525	454865	421738	221044	247733
石油加工、炼焦和核燃料加工业	Processing of Petroleum, Coking, Processing of Mucleus Fuels	2723488	1441730	1411992	346998	1058242
化学原料和化学制品制造业	Manufacture of Chemical Raw Materials and Chemical Products	1450084	1704614	1601204	259358	1249680
医药制造业	Manufacture of Medicines	1480065	2272366	1886298	472028	3576579
化学纤维制造业	Manufacture of Chemical Fibres	***	***	***	***	***
橡胶和塑料制品业	Manufacture of Rubber and Plastics Products	195570	454916	270351	50085	160729
非金属矿物制品业	Manufacture of Non-metallic Mineral Products	1395877	4265000	4010834	1603788	2651983
黑色金属冶炼和压延加工业	Manufacture and Pressing of Ferrous Metals	769975	1150548	339046	160770	2443945
有色金属冶炼和压延加工业	Manufacture and Pressing of Non-ferrous Metals	149546	210215	186191	63212	322239
金属制品业	Manufacture of Fabricated Metal Products	816321	1455437	1245884	452330	1363710
通用设备制造业	Manufacture of General-purpose Machinery	621270	1501441	1353692	359717	1787569
专用设备制造业	Manufacture of Special-purpose Machinery	1027452	5111649	3893645	1440791	4631216
汽车制造业	Manufacture of Motor Vehicles	2004652	4729439	3742710	1746432	3410855
铁路、船舶、航空航天和其他运输设备制造业	Manufacture of Railway Locomotives, Building of Ships and Boats, Manufacture of Air and Spacecrafts and Other Transportation Equipment	766930	2365276	2243101	963676	1326272
电气机械和器材制造业	Manufacture of Electrical Machinery and Equipment	600772	4192720	3961794	1438950	2172315
计算机、通信和其他电子设备制造业	Manufacture of Computers, Communication Equipment and Other Electronic Equipment	3872178	5856364	4415794	1306957	9404909
仪器仪表制造业	Manufacture of Measuring Instruments and Meters	371195	1246727	1168278	421492	1570724
其他制造业	Other Manufacturing	452921	379865	259828	126933	741305
废弃资源综合利用业	Waste Recycling and Recovery	56459	59445	35746	579	25574
金属制品、机械和设备修理业	Repair of Fabricated Metal Products, Machinery and Equipment	35616	49783	49403	28977	83776
电力、热力生产和供应业	Production and Distribution of Electricity and Heating	1.4E+07	8540753	5934882	1966410	6257127
燃气生产和供应业	Production and Distribution of Gas	137015	235984	228083	54117	128405
水的生产和供应业	Production and Distribution of Water	4651089	3342996	1048402	55958	3721973

11-11 Continued

(10000 yuan)

#实收资本 Paid-up Capital	损益 Profits and Losses								应交税金合计 Total Tax Payable	#营业税金及附加 Business Tax and Surtax	#主营业务税金及附加 Main Business Tax and Surtax	#应交增值税 Value Added Tax Payable
	营业收入 Business Income	#主营业务收入 Main Business Income	营业成本 Business Cost	#主营业务成本 Main Business Cost	销售费用 Sales Expenses	管理费用 Management Expenses	财务费用 Financial Expenses	利润总额 Total Profits				
30057614	**74548355**	**72496082**	**63806555**	**62195449**	**2374597**	**4489905**	**1022389**	**4290681**	**3861034**	**1207899**	**1194332**	**1924131**
691325	5514667	5488906	5376139	5371443	9216	51781	7212	99380	85000	20612	20594	56485
***	***	***	***	***	***	***	***	***	***	***	***	***
2872444	3713354	3551962	3694441	3531612	8089	162872	258716	216678	91267	13927	12606	66384
***	***	***	***	***	***	***	***	***	***	***	***	***
***	***	***	***	***	***	***	***	***	***	***	***	***
425647	2503001	2482003	2037088	2027488	162166	116748	32247	133264	172132	88812	88798	61002
161272	561423	552561	415737	407688	62036	38591	12845	32068	39481	2861	2549	24086
119107	215480	212193	157792	156521	8629	18433	5618	-5240	46505	32355	32308	12139
186724	242164	235683	206124	204701	3346	23936	5072	4497	7488	1600	1329	4175
147713	527756	521399	305086	303198	104966	61586	4165	64102	51498	4611	4607	35712
3538	22267	22259	19561	19560	1412	1141	199	55	652	51	51	547
17557	49565	43024	39440	33614	2536	5680	476	1076	2779	301	164	2265
60299	165948	161297	130704	128335	16889	12522	1149	4651	11985	1207	1086	8822
29311	125088	121090	113029	109456	3570	8926	556	-864	2660	201	201	2093
375458	638910	617469	458228	450030	13403	88274	-1799	80355	63609	4934	4536	37976
199076	860081	842408	804302	799422	20539	35856	8886	-3083	11118	1868	1302	7350
40231	8423510	7839615	7384927	6808372	38084	131611	23798	110774	976137	728967	727940	213386
1129261	1668771	1611196	1472338	1426207	64339	161229	40154	160573	48724	4212	4121	33507
1046359	2734041	2685821	1366916	1333947	480420	322445	17199	704138	318408	25612	25388	202833
***	***	***	***	***	***	***	***	***	***	***	***	***
136752	485190	455181	440721	419652	11279	29770	9397	-3223	14266	2055	1868	8648
1103831	3824548	3730319	3321259	3243025	131302	247647	56394	93861	100569	19076	18392	61388
809614	958042	940109	909638	894639	35423	26590	23174	-18738	-1629	1055	925	5979
103455	586096	485822	524644	428958	8152	28421	3335	19717	20466	9362	9320	5945
668870	1796417	1724209	1522691	1477069	33403	139432	16321	85634	55852	9999	9514	28534
842476	1271122	1233448	970701	947668	63891	151302	19552	78222	80739	7560	7376	54229
1993062	3844566	3739910	2925363	2841859	186137	367033	67763	507964	192690	27253	26718	111925
1657682	6730383	6422804	6051891	5852740	207722	447434	9599	80241	218423	66655	66264	109407
703316	2125361	2084138	1742676	1713415	42748	190652	23085	120126	91545	7439	6771	57059
1297983	4165045	4134385	3396551	3381993	223127	325414	59054	166074	144189	14965	14890	101603
3918187	6318826	6237110	4881162	4833217	304714	698815	82990	491877	252475	27984	26127	155929
469574	1573874	1548324	1094336	1082124	93468	207663	7062	210848	110914	10313	9858	70502
271035	524931	512318	360885	351165	16580	73565	-253	78047	35817	2944	2944	19205
17650	50418	50283	44588	44424	285	5651	407	3062	3104	274	274	2362
46233	60396	58217	35631	34627	4483	10302	712	14435	6086	436	426	3999
2606327	9258078	9192839	9045054	9002877	6000	149042	172919	438752	407892	33272	32211	296526
110889	426820	404840	377779	365650	4579	17865	-674	31658	26521	1985	1709	15850
3030514	744262	731953	549203	543355	209	46959	15575	235673	69503	2482	1758	10326

11-12 规模以上港澳台及外商投资工业企业主要经济指标(2014年)

单位：万元

项目	Item	企业单位个数(个) Number of Enterprises (unit)	#亏损企业 Loss-Suffering Enterprises	工业总产值(当年价格) Gross Output Value of Industry (at current year's prices)	工业增加值 Added Value of Industry	工业销售产值(当年价格) Sales Value of Industry (at current year's prices)	#出口交货值 Delivery Value of Exports
合　计	**Total**	**852**	**189**	**72507753**	**14719179**	**71759269**	**10974229**
按隶属关系分组	**By Affiliation**						
中央企业	Central Enterprises	11		1138414	424014	1146001	95072
地方企业	Local Enterprises	841	189	71369340	14295165	70613268	10879158
按轻重工业分组	**By Light and Heavy Industries**						
轻工业	Light Industry	311	85	11042345	3253976	10817724	1231408
重工业	Heavy Industry	541	104	61465409	11465202	60941546	9742821
按规模分组	**By Size**						
#大中型企业	Medium and Large-sized Enterprises	265	51	64482435	12999825	63797606	9933425

11-12 续表

单位：万元

项目	Item	资产负债 Assets and Liabilities					
		固定资产原价 Total Original Value of Fixed Assets	负债合计 Total Liabilities	#流动负债合计 Total Current Liabilities	#应付账款 Accounts Payable	所有者权益合计 Total Owner's Equity	#实收资本 Paid-up Capital
合　计	**Total**	**23437466**	**38291276**	**33145782**	**15286280**	**32617774**	**15427139**
按隶属关系分组	**By Affiliation**						
中央企业	Central Enterprises	1789642	1029769	844144	191341	1566681	852997
地方企业	Local Enterprises	21647824	37261507	32301638	15094939	31051093	14574141
按轻重工业分组	**By Light and Heavy Industries**						
轻工业	Light Industry	4170886	6061007	5664413	2017903	5678400	3388626
重工业	Heavy Industry	19266579	32230269	27481370	13268377	26939374	12038513
按规模分组	**By Size**						
#大中型企业	Medium and Large-sized Enterprises	20089784	32078499	27811958	13189450	26298675	11919584

MAIN ECONOMIC INDICATORS OF HONGKONG, MACAO, TAIWAN AND FOREIGN-INVESTED INDUSTRIAL ENTERPRISES ABOVE DESIGNATED SIZE (2014)

(10000 yuan)

平均用工人数(人) Average Number of Employed Persons	资产负债 Assets and Liabilities					
	资产总计 Total Assets	流动资产合计 Total Current Assets	#存货 Inventories	#产成品 Finished Products	#应收账款 Accounts Receivable	固定资产合计 Total Fixed Assets
390443	**70919253**	**43729294**	**8214431**	**2745099**	**11490500**	**12157964**
11856	2596451	830160	121926	23393	264270	710316
378587	68322803	42899134	8092505	2721706	11226231	11447648
140477	11739407	7582453	1800667	840105	2051193	2015034
249966	59179846	36146842	6413764	1904994	9439307	10142930
319810	58377174	36084995	6474282	2142396	9016147	10414294

11-12 Continued

(10000 yuan)

损益 Profits and Losses								应交税金合计 Total Tax Payable	#营业税金及附加 Business Tax and Surtax	#主营业务税金及附加 Main Business Tax and Surtax	#应交增值税 Value Added Tax Payable
营业收入 Business Income	#主营业务收入 Main Business Income	营业成本 Business Cost	#主营业务成本 Main Business Cost	销售费用 Sales Expenses	管理费用 Management Expenses	财务费用 Financial Expenses	利润总额 Total Profits				
80707949	**79082965**	**65123428**	**63828168**	**5436903**	**3412647**	**281248**	**6044522**	**5113208**	**1374788**	**1374000**	**2315230**
1374312	1291684	1038487	968861	18607	113488	30507	241250	117290	5947	5947	55702
79333637	77791281	64084941	62859308	5418296	3299158	250741	5803272	4995918	1368841	1368053	2259528
13650802	13149732	8659267	8263476	2993558	909877	109435	867437	1096959	104171	104046	728621
67057147	65933233	56464161	55564692	2443345	2502770	171814	5177085	4016250	1270617	1269954	1586608
71508976	70075970	57795641	56642562	4939570	2718810	199455	5294835	4606209	1332780	1332280	2023719

11-13 规模以上港澳台及外商投资工业企业主要经济指标(按行业分)(2014年)

单位：万元

项目	Item	企业单位个数(个) Number of Enterprises (unit)	#亏损企业 Loss-Suffering Enterprises	工业总产值(当年价格) Gross Output Value of Industry (at current year's prices)	工业增加值 Added Value of Industry
合计	**Total**	**852**	**189**	**72507753**	**14719179**
开采辅助活动	Mining Support Service Activities	3	***	***	***
农副食品加工业	Processing of Food from Agricultural Products	27	12	671624	82211
食品制造业	Manufacture of Foods	45	15	1926515	183564
酒、饮料和精制茶制造业	Manufacture of Wines, Beverage and Refined Tea	23	6	1281842	316560
纺织业	Manufacture of Textile	6		75640	15329
纺织服装、服饰业	Manufacture of Textile Wearing Apparel and Ornament	28	13	329952	124858
皮革、毛皮、羽毛及其制品和制鞋业	Manufacture of Leather, Fur, Feather and Its Products, and Footwear	3	***	***	***
木材加工和木、竹、藤、棕、草制品业	Processing of Timbers, Manufacture of Wood, Bamboo, Rattan, Palm, and Straw Products	1	***	***	***
家具制造业	Manufacture of Furniture	14	4	311448	52988
造纸和纸制品业	Manufacture of Paper and Paper Products	14	5	503934	195478
印刷和记录媒介复制业	Printing, Reproduction of Recording Media	17	1	229419	95106
文教、工美、体育和娱乐用品制造业	Manufacture of Articles for Culture, Education, Artwork, Sport and Entertainment Activities	10	1	54899	15399
石油加工、炼焦和核燃料加工业	Processing of Petroleum, Coking, Processing of Mucleus Fuels	3	***	***	***
化学原料和化学制品制造业	Manufacture of Chemical Raw Materials and Chemical Products	43	13	1030982	320983
医药制造业	Manufacture of Medicines	37	7	3304428	1448053
橡胶和塑料制品业	Manufacture of Rubber and Plastics Products	27	7	390116	134427
非金属矿物制品业	Manufacture of Non-metallic Mineral Products	26	7	543946	175845
黑色金属冶炼和压延加工业	Manufacture and Pressing of Ferrous Metals	4		387437	46054
有色金属冶炼和压延加工业	Manufacture and Pressing of Non-ferrous Metals	3	***	***	***
金属制品业	Manufacture of Fabricated Metal Products	40	11	752675	199715
通用设备制造业	Manufacture of General-purpose Machinery	86	14	3348129	783442
专用设备制造业	Manufacture of Special-purpose Machinery	86	23	1588793	401683
汽车制造业	Manufacture of Motor Vehicles	117	11	29977210	6724328
铁路、船舶、航空航天和其他运输设备制造业	Manufacture of Railway Locomotives, Building of Ships and Boats, Manufacture of Air and Spacecrafts and Other Transportation Equipment	8		234530	50911
电气机械和器材制造业	Manufacture of Electrical Machinery and Equipment	46	11	2358676	682735
计算机、通信和其他电子设备制造业	Manufacture of Computers, Communication Equipment and Other Electronic Equipment	75	19	18356161	1578640
仪器仪表制造业	Manufacture of Measuring Instruments and Meters	38	3	837678	179531
其他制造业	Other Manufacturing	6	1	23952	7193
废弃资源综合利用业	Waste recycling and recovery	1	***	***	***
金属制品、机械和设备修理业	Repair of Fabricated Metal Products, Machinery and Equipment	4		301720	122254
电力、热力生产和供应业	Production and Distribution of Electricity and Heating Power	4		726635	258306
燃气生产和供应业	Production and Distribution of Gas	6	1	2468665	415649
水的生产和供应业	Production and Distribution of Water	1	***	***	***

注：1. 行业划分执行2011年国民经济行业分类标准(GB/T 4754-2011)。
2. 应交税金合计包括应交增值税、应交所得税、营业税金及附加和管理费用中的税金。

FOREIGN-INVESTED INDUSTRIAL ENTERPRISES ABOVE DESIGNATED SIZE (BY SECTOR) (2014)

(10000 yuan)

工业销售产值(当年价格) Sales Value of Industry (at current year's prices)	#出口交货值 Delivery Value of Exports	平均用工人数(人) Average Number of Employed Persons (person)	资产负债 Assets and Liabilities: 资产总计 Total Assets	流动资产合计 Total Current Assets	#存货 Inventories	#产成品 Finished Products	#应收账款 Accounts Receivable	固定资产合计 Total Fixed Assets
71759269	**10974229**	**390443**	**70919253**	**43729294**	**8214431**	**2745099**	**11490500**	**12157964**
***	***	1242	***	***	***	***	***	***
677589	68384	9151	467018	291873	120641	35972	79655	117809
1917222	100345	34347	2210061	1309261	216685	134982	325315	511494
1304282	10208	15853	1432537	631408	105258	33400	80315	340465
81280	20103	1299	89582	63135	11753	5208	28646	19776
303659	167881	12433	345167	290448	120983	67327	39132	34556
***	***	844	***	***	***	***	***	***
***	***	151	***	***	***	***	***	***
307212	32532	4391	243171	173253	51682	27371	57069	42334
498306	50433	3232	399394	269665	71460	18861	87771	105818
227755	5504	4383	302600	184792	34781	17288	54505	91179
74696	38501	1873	117973	105980	46286	32366	17862	9098
***	***	1133	***	***	***	***	***	***
987013	54563	9659	1268639	720123	117839	52867	233344	409376
3098494	69941	26660	3446891	2374265	654043	312422	626055	343738
394304	57943	7747	405970	269903	54558	24857	109560	103893
537833	32596	7939	795367	550327	166153	25643	215996	157470
390508	42185	1332	227717	189931	68015	13694	90327	9372
***	***	324	***	***	***	***	***	***
776440	61788	8764	1275017	851202	175758	54901	230040	171115
3390603	655271	25979	4474354	3579424	1111196	283756	843346	600468
1571625	434690	17693	3214165	2160215	346557	91075	678543	262767
29965755	253025	82356	24205957	14113601	1747369	721288	3419018	4550284
236031	1060	988	196184	182679	43432	15082	78052	11187
2377880	447134	17179	3617437	2932486	651700	110853	1227676	213332
17790674	8171343	68363	12111279	9199942	1917231	610193	1952593	1830318
841166	83086	7912	1121960	919984	219020	33175	350127	76700
22920	16183	653	13119	9355	4571	2296	1618	2949
***	***	126	***	***	***	***	***	***
295817	76468	6552	338205	173160	62249	2086	70153	163755
730992		1362	3854713	600590	15223		109624	639948
2468665		8126	3917008	1009340	3897	774	373171	1227924
***	***	397	***	***	***	***	***	***

Note: a) Sectors in this table are classified in accordance with the Standard for Classification of National Economic Sectors 2011 (GB/T 4754-2011).
b) Total tax payable mainly includes VAT payable, income tax payable, business tax and surtax, and tax in management expenses.

11-13 续表

单位：万元

项目	Item	资产负债 Assets and Liabilities 固定资产原价 Total Original Value of Fixed Assets	负债合计 Total Liabilities	#流动负债合计 Total Current Liabilities	#应付账款 Accounts Payable	所有者权益合计 Total Owner's Equity
合计	**Total**	**23437466**	**38291276**	**33145782**	**15286280**	**32617774**
开采辅助活动	Mining Support Service Activities	***	***	***	***	***
农副食品加工业	Processing of Food from Agricultural Products	231429	329548	314602	105056	137470
食品制造业	Manufacture of Foods	994118	1305122	1234613	477417	904939
酒、饮料和精制茶制造业	Manufacture of Wines, Beverage and Refined Tea	727630	820978	791321	264626	611559
纺织业	Manufacture of Textile	50381	54975	54975	12820	34607
纺织服装、服饰业	Manufacture of Textile Wearing Apparel and Ornament	76969	235122	222428	65305	110045
皮革、毛皮、羽毛及其制品和制鞋业	Manufacture of Leather, Fur, Feather and Its Products, and Footwear	***	***	***	***	***
木材加工和木、竹、藤、棕、草制品业	Processing of Timbers, Manufacture of Wood, Bamboo, Rattan, Palm, and Straw Products	***	***	***	***	***
家具制造业	Manufacture of Furniture	64385	134050	132050	23481	109121
造纸和纸制品业	Manufacture of Paper and Paper Products	273212	177394	174894	60137	222000
印刷和记录媒介复制业	Printing, Reproduction of Recording Media	222983	97453	80847	31892	205147
文教、工美、体育和娱乐用品制造业	Manufacture of Articles for Culture, Education, Artwork, Sport and Entertainment Activities	17122	55208	54699	20056	62766
石油加工、炼焦和核燃料加工业	Processing of Petroleum, Coking, Processing of Mucleus Fuels	***	***	***	***	***
化学原料和化学制品制造业	Manufacture of Chemical Raw Materials and Chemical Products	741827	505691	412224	121643	762947
医药制造业	Manufacture of Medicines	629713	1691413	1490461	493678	1755478
橡胶和塑料制品业	Manufacture of Rubber and Plastics Products	226686	169359	167831	73367	226407
非金属矿物制品业	Manufacture of Non-metallic Mineral Products	377223	424657	416885	136567	370710
黑色金属冶炼和压延加工业	Manufacture and Pressing of Ferrous Metals	49798	104700	83193	64997	123017
有色金属冶炼和压延加工业	Manufacture and Pressing of Non-ferrous Metals	***	***	***	***	***
金属制品业	Manufacture of Fabricated Metal Products	369264	608709	490808	127864	666307
通用设备制造业	Manufacture of General-purpose Machinery	1205034	2052823	1880399	728134	2421531
专用设备制造业	Manufacture of Special-purpose Machinery	469309	1877782	1697085	554167	1336383
汽车制造业	Manufacture of Motor Vehicles	6989829	13721620	11518778	6172394	10484337
铁路、船舶、航空航天和其他运输设备制造业	Manufacture of Railway Locomotives, Building of Ships and Boats, Manufacture of Air and Spacecrafts and Other Transportation Equipment	22010	128475	128413	67989	67709
电气机械和器材制造业	Manufacture of Electrical Machinery and Equipment	614290	1716584	1558521	808348	1900853
计算机、通信和其他电子设备制造业	Manufacture of Computers, Communication Equipment and Other Electronic Equipment	5139203	8102865	7224993	4183212	4008414
仪器仪表制造业	Manufacture of Measuring Instruments and Meters	157921	638229	614519	340425	483732
其他制造业	Other Manufacturing	6909	6409	6405	2074	6710
废弃资源综合利用业	Waste recycling and recovery	***	***	***	***	***
金属制品、机械和设备修理业	Repair of Fabricated Metal Products, Machinery and Equipment	310926	187492	187451	27179	150713
电力、热力生产和供应业	Production and Distribution of Electricity and Heating Power	1595001	1514582	978713	87092	2340130
燃气生产和供应业	Production and Distribution of Gas	1676659	1188973	903193	112649	2728035
水的生产和供应业	Production and Distribution of Water	***	***	***	***	***

11-13 Continued

(10000 yuan)

#实收资本 Paid-up Capital	损益 Profits and Losses 营业收入 Business Income	#主营业务收入 Main Business Income	营业成本 Business Cost	#主营业务成本 Main Business Cost	销售费用 Sales Expenses	管理费用 Manage-ment Expenses	财务费用 Financial Expenses	利润总额 Total Profits	应交税金合计 Total Tax Payable	#营业税金及附加 Business Tax and Surtax	#主营业务税金及附加 Main Business Tax and Surtax	#应交增值税 Value Added Tax Payable
15427139	**80707949**	**79082965**	**65123428**	**63828168**	**5436903**	**3412647**	**281248**	**6044522**	**5113208**	**1374788**	**1374000**	**2315230**
***	***	***	***	***	***	***	***	***	***	***	***	***
135789	757291	746179	651743	643111	60531	43180	8115	-5860	18020	1485	1484	11321
830461	3810675	3722845	2439187	2358993	1020756	194203	3702	123686	252063	21977	21976	185291
673888	1451987	1385159	1029652	970564	288009	84699	6887	25721	111579	19143	19143	71985
25835	106994	105781	95607	94388	2565	4084	1884	7578	4609	412	412	2861
76354	363579	338706	291866	268203	33637	28596	3647	7822	18622	1850	1743	13332
***	***	***	***	***	***	***	***	***	***	***	***	***
***	***	***	***	***	***	***	***	***	***	***	***	***
40079	245475	236830	175599	169470	32681	23663	1996	9088	8891	1111	1111	6487
138206	531330	522284	395445	388627	18746	21433	-651	93837	51776	2851	2851	23283
118989	252183	247249	188039	186453	13289	20925	-312	30165	18783	1608	1608	11913
10824	77164	76796	62687	62508	4346	6962	241	2728	5452	649	649	3826
***	***	***	***	***	***	***	***	***	***	***	***	***
442262	1031894	1022505	679957	673928	173154	78565	9772	76866	99861	11377	11377	57905
624568	3441888	3265352	1486207	1328019	1266373	243866	80536	316474	428669	35348	35331	297424
132012	460534	444312	368126	355504	21990	38950	884	28135	26476	2618	2618	16627
217360	575438	565039	457923	452908	26118	45198	7028	36404	45660	4167	4167	29856
58636	429157	429123	372143	372143	14111	9099	792	34621	14091	781	781	4321
***	***	***	***	***	***	***	***	***	***	***	***	***
286276	989264	905171	818581	738985	45154	74274	12632	39751	48820	5555	5555	32497
935861	3741202	3670030	2937631	2889618	196247	225514	18373	355015	240574	17790	17790	138281
515124	2104589	1970617	1571965	1505786	136629	234467	22057	173016	119730	10458	10452	71271
3975639	30637877	30083445	24747513	24312218	1121266	926239	13782	3083887	2739549	1166327	1166321	854012
20584	297282	296088	219049	218907	12096	12443	-1285	54071	28012	1353	1353	11874
1059067	2773732	2654304	2108432	1992625	117173	155521	12704	381773	203497	13271	13198	114317
2613590	21333531	21141452	19675349	19518108	676738	625005	-27272	416733	277318	23780	23612	139436
181561	1094422	1083334	817662	813426	95650	80941	3240	106326	65055	5497	5496	39873
6745	24126	24100	19422	19393	1560	2422	253	452	497	109	109	286
***	***	***	***	***	***	***	***	***	***	***	***	***
120471	306553	298468	232035	228149	8	60762	6520	10775	15683	908	908	8239
1352591	731303	727114	512411	510624		30575	66081	314821	93692	4485	4485	40352
600695	2485922	2471268	2243324	2232162	25366	91808	25469	273439	138843	13597	13189	109831
***	***	***	***	***	***	***	***	***	***	***	***	***

11-14 大中型工业企业主要经济指标(2014年)

单位：万元

项目	Item	企业单位个数(个) Number of Enterprises (unit)	#亏损企业 Loss-Suffering Enterprises	工业总产值(当年价格) Gross Output Value of Industry (at current year's prices)	工业增加值 Added Value of Industry
合计	**Total**	**748**	**137**	**150395400**	**30140260**
按隶属关系分组	**By Affiliation**				
中央工业	Central Enterprises	103	14	59052787	11446521
地方工业	Local Enterprises	645	123	91342612	18693738
按登记注册类型分组	**By Registration Type**				
内资企业	Domestially-Invested Enterprises	483	86	85912965	17140435
国有企业	State-owned Enterprises	34	4	34084127	5882129
集体企业	Collectively-owned Enterprises	4		93391	48183
股份合作企业	Joint-equity Cooperative Enterprises	2	***	***	***
联营企业	Associated Enterprises				
有限责任公司	Limited Liability Companies	241	54	27819486	6114723
股份有限公司	Companies Limited by Shares	108	20	20836881	4106163
私营企业	Private Enterprises	94	7	2995125	934104
港澳台商投资企业	Hong Kong, Macao and Taiwan-invested Enterprises	70	15	16117342	1867440
港澳台合资经营	Joint Ventures	37	7	3495291	947273
港澳台合作经营	Cooperatives	1	***	***	***
港澳台商独资企业	Solely-funded Enterprises	24	7	11747567	809833
港澳台商投资股份有限公司	Companies Limited by Shares	8		867723	108047
外商投资企业	Foreign-invested Enterprises	195	36	48365093	11132385
中外合资经营	Joint Ventures	81	9	33045622	7707701
中外合作经营	Cooperatives	4	2	177352	99860
外资(独资)企业	Solely-funded Enterprises	104	22	14435956	3122526
外商投资股份有限公司	Companies Limited by Shares	6	3	706163	202297.34
按城乡分组	**By Urban and Rural Regions**				
#农村企业	Rural Enterprises	12	4	799808	130176
按轻重工业分组	**By Light and Heavy Industries**				
轻工业	Light Industry	275	59	17710106	5634927
重工业	Heavy Industry	473	78	132685294	24505332
按规模分组	**By Size**				
#大型企业	Medium and Large-sized Enterprises	164	31	119939196	22652103

MAIN ECONOMIC INDICATORS OF LOCAL MEDIUM AND LARGE-SIZED INDUSTRIAL ENTERPRISES (2014)

(10000 yuan)

工业销售产值(当年价格) Sales Value of Industry (at current year's prices)	#出口交货值 Delivery Value of Exports	平均用工人数(人) Average Number of Employed Persons (person)	资产负债 Assets and Liabilities: 资产总计 Total Assets	流动资产合计 Total Current Assets	#存货 Inventories	#产成品 Finished Products	#应收账款 Accounts Receivable	固定资产合计 Total Fixed Assets
148721904	**12588507**	**840908**	**284503769**	**108045472**	**15635961**	**4843892**	**24964596**	**56234139**
58674576	476396	178241	143754166	35798925	3820340	839201	6773010	29125649
90047328	12112111	662667	140749603	72246547	11815621	4004691	18191586	27108491
84924299	2655082	521098	226126595	71960477	9161679	2701496	15948449	45819846
33977553	19903	47002	112843351	22571003	1147046	116593	2590365	20136810
96769		2884	110654	78717	14980	2809	8706	25950
***	***	2864	***	***	***	***	***	***
27578068	1590867	259600	70863878	28372194	4221470	1239218	8155010	20454654
20482074	847811	156034	38526486	18498114	3122783	1031698	4408266	4553737
2702329	184133	52714	3679570	2370067	629357	289515	771544	620573
15601207	1552746	82550	17443108	11111650	2197475	652663	2747573	2747214
3448368	646606	35736	3670919	2160406	390903	139807	718045	1065898
***	***	424	***	***	***	***	***	***
11299274	775045	39517	10318083	6481813	1158525	479691	1012316	1595122
846944	131095	6873	3452323	2467772	647599	32948	1016188	86069
48196399	8380680	237260	40934066	24973345	4276807	1489732	6268574	7667079
33003811	6264632	118350	26150179	15702011	2435566	747213	2974710	4525858
183077	30203	5540	238226	185064	-16876	2840	51873	45152
14304967	2036982	103958	12786858	8530308	1779029	700000	3126204	2832294
704543	48864	9412	1758804	555961	79089	39679	115788	263775
799856	7136	7057	641100	535940	94933	26124	321269	77301
17279214	1065915	247897	25964233	14416136	3173763	1392822	2821128	4997503
131442691	11522592	593011	258539537	93629336	12462198	3451070	22143468	51236636
118756536	10668149	519539	235154330	78945998	9537191	3125469	14499241	47921484

11-14 续表

单位：万元

项目	Item	资产负债 Assets and Liabilities 固定资产原价 Total Original Value of Fixed Assets	负债合计 Total Liabilities	#流动负债合计 Total Current Liabilities	#应付账款 Accounts Payable	所有者权益合计 Total Owner's Equity	#实收资本 Paid-up Capital
合　计	**Total**	**103959001**	**144556355**	**88386686**	**28632741**	**139947415**	**56894159**
按隶属关系分组	**By Affiliation**						
中央工业	Central Enterprises	58777515	70522606	34621637	8453127	73231561	28434776
地方工业	Local Enterprises	45181486	74033749	53765049	20179615	66715854	28459383
按登记注册类型分组	**By Registration Type**						
内资企业	Domestially-Invested Enterprises	83869217	112477856	60574728	15443292	113648740	44974575
国有企业	State-owned Enterprises	39352324	53469870	20438393	3471518	59373481	20691682
集体企业	Collectively-owned Enterprises	66098	43770	40990	7097	66883	12880
股份合作企业	Joint-equity Cooperative Enterprises	***	***	***	***	***	***
联营企业	Associated Enterprises						
有限责任公司	Limited Liability Companies	34794341	40675613	25885113	7587777	30188265	17572487
股份有限公司	Companies Limited by Shares	8654028	16429049	12500777	3812787	22097436	6182772
私营企业	Private Enterprises	961880	1831596	1686484	551373	1847974	500754
港澳台商投资企业	Hong Kong, Macao and Taiwan-invested Enterprises	5489363	10194042	9241850	4268111	7249066	3291559
港澳台合资经营	Joint Ventures	2904705	1787671	1587231	616243	1883247	1242871
港澳台合作经营	Cooperatives	***	***	***	***	***	***
港澳台商独资企业	Solely-funded Enterprises	2405455	6565042	6107563	2985095	3753041	1141199
港澳台商投资股份有限公司	Companies Limited by Shares	178224	1839774	1545502	665690	1612549	905722
外商投资企业	Foreign-invested Enterprises	14600421	21884457	18570109	8921338	19049609	8628025
中外合资经营	Joint Ventures	7475998	13851077	11643944	5532017	12299103	4514411
中外合作经营	Cooperatives	118095	122976	113362	47621	115249	145207
外资(独资)企业	Solely-funded Enterprises	6432076	7301073	6335253	3243742	5485785	3365759
外商投资股份有限公司	Companies Limited by Shares	574252	609332	477549	97959	1149472	602648
按城乡分组	**By Urban and Rural Regions**						
#农村企业	Rural Enterprises	146392	466607	435664	235559	174492	57184
按轻重工业分组	**By Light and Heavy Industries**						
轻工业	Light Industry	9372755	12377508	10311359	2669764	13586724	5337442
重工业	Heavy Industry	94586246	132178846	78075327	25962977	126360691	51556718
按规模分组	**By Size**						
#大型企业	Medium and Large-sized Enterprises	88941135	120207853	67865629	20948251	114946477	45822116

注：应交税金合计包括应交增值税、应交所得税、营业税金及附加和管理费用中的税金。

11-14 Continued

(10000 yuan)

损益 Profits and Losses								应交税金合计 Total Tax Payable	#营业税金及附加 Business Tax and Surtax	#主营业务税金及附加 Main Business Tax and Surtax	#应交增值税 Value Added Tax Payable
营业收入 Business Income	#主营业务收入 Main Business Income	营业成本 Business Cost	#主营业务成本 Main Business Cost	销售费用 Sales Expenses	管理费用 Management Expenses	财务费用 Financial Expenses	利润总额 Total Profits				
163631110	**160397751**	**138236953**	**135660661**	**7136735**	**6436166**	**1844529**	**13034993**	**9844200**	**2913664**	**2901997**	**4641494**
60738088	59759198	54794796	53943124	361012	1336070	993376	5185070	3661913	1249149	1245103	1721505
102893022	100638553	83442157	81717537	6775722	5100096	851154	7849923	6182287	1664516	1656894	2919989
92122134	90321781	80441312	79018099	2197165	3717356	1645075	7740158	5237991	1580884	1569717	2617775
34149034	34018579	31370424	31279976	105039	249705	755169	4062472	1890974	426932	426350	1003154
99534	92579	69795	64832	5994	14141	-709	8102	13903	2033	2033	10216
***	***	***	***	***	***	***	***	***	***	***	***
31883865	30983303	28320884	27574162	767287	1834487	632526	1435928	1221268	136586	129482	770985
22954878	22238930	18527144	17968704	1032542	1349288	238484	1901466	1928811	998048	994749	719413
2942863	2897224	2104625	2082153	267855	260282	19534	317134	173563	16534	16352	106798
19822902	19327457	17299807	16878352	1202910	728377	80508	762102	555552	53910	53439	353265
3858587	3641228	3046709	2847691	183038	187034	29042	393042	242383	22915	22808	121374
***	***	***	***	***	***	***	***	***	***	***	***
14859425	14714367	13319781	13221309	971160	464139	-2579	321810	264504	23037	22673	190429
1098268	965241	928203	804237	47578	76778	54046	47356	48120	7903	7903	40976
51686075	50748513	40495834	39764210	3736660	1990433	118947	4532734	4050657	1278870	1278842	1670454
34153593	33755636	27041113	26763756	1706317	1177625	21208	3443285	3050004	1195252	1195229	1072352
386972	380967	334504	327372	40016	14735	-3702	980	21735	1848	1848	17046
16352828	15840731	12515177	12085080	1914950	730487	83677	1036727	935769	77263	77263	548157
792682	771179	605041	588002	75376	67586	17763	51742	43149	4508	4502	32899
858014	833443	723607	703165	22519	40323	2547	73544	45195	3069	3069	20351
20719645	20055274	13273017	12783252	3806210	1570677	173761	1802083	2074150	538718	536468	1138682
142911466	140342476	124963936	122877409	3330525	4865488	1670769	11232910	7770050	2374947	2365529	3502812
128859304	126986233	111249318	109745384	5013525	3894686	1515264	9692374	7544072	2473264	2465506	3407742

Note: Total tax payable mainly includes VAT payable, income tax payable, business tax and surtax, and tax in management expenses.

11-15 大中型工业企业主要经济指标(按行业分)(2014年)

单位：万元

项目	Item	企业单位个数(个) Number of Enterprises (unit)	#亏损企业 Loss-Suffering Enterprises	工业总产值(当年价格) Gross Output Value of Industry (at current year's prices)	工业增加值 Added Value of Industry
合计	**Total**	**748**	**137**	**150395400**	**30140260**
煤炭开采和洗选业	Mining and Washing of Coal	1	***	***	***
石油和天然气开采业	Extraction of Petroleum and Natural Gas	2	***	***	***
黑色金属矿采选业	Mining and Processing of Ferrous Metal Ores	6		1290480	108920
开采辅助活动	Mining Support Service Activities	4	1	1998988	1065429
农副食品加工业	Processing of Food from Agricultural Products	30	7	2411634	423050
食品制造业	Manufacture of Foods	41	14	2113913	236226
酒、饮料和精制茶制造业	Manufacture of Wines, Beverage and Refined Tea	14	3	1688518	460185
烟草制品业	Manufacture of Cigarettes and Tobacco	1	***	***	***
纺织业	Manufacture of Textile	2	***	***	***
纺织服装、服饰业	Manufacture of Textile Wearing Apparel and Ornament	41	17	842903	400597
皮革、毛皮、羽毛及其制品和制鞋业	Manufacture of Leather, Fur, Feather and Its Products, and Footwear	3	***	***	***
木材加工和木、竹、藤、棕、草制品业	Processing of Timbers, Manufacture of Wood, Bamboo, Rattan, Palm, and Straw Products	2	***	***	***
家具制造业	Manufacture of Furniture	9	1	453825	118328
造纸和纸制品业	Manufacture of Paper and Paper Products	6	1	431154	169168
印刷和记录媒介复制业	Printing, Reproduction of Recording Media	18	2	628182	277456
文教、工美、体育和娱乐用品制造业	Manufacture of Articles for Culture, Education, Artwork, Sport and Entertainment Activities	3	***	***	***
石油加工、炼焦和核燃料加工业	Processing of Petroleum, Coking, Processing of Mucleus Fuels	5	1	7750355	1464138
化学原料和化学制品制造业	Manufacture of Chemical Raw Materials and Chemical Products	23	6	1606954	326064
医药制造业	Manufacture of Medicines	51	4	5255075	2284205
化学纤维制造业	Manufacture of Chemical fibres	1	***	***	***
橡胶和塑料制品业	Manufacture of Rubber and Plastics Products	15	2	497192	171394
非金属矿物制品业	Manufacture of Non-metallic Mineral Products	39	9	2848814	487028
黑色金属冶炼和压延加工业	Manufacture and Pressing of Ferrous Metals	6	2	913546	44065
有色金属冶炼和压延加工业	Manufacture and Pressing of Non-ferrous Metals	5	1	293146	51795
金属制品业	Manufacture of Fabricated Metal Products	29	8	1517608	281415
通用设备制造业	Manufacture of General-purpose Machinery	44	7	3761797	1079474
专用设备制造业	Manufacture of Special-purpose Machinery	54	9	3559332	728327
汽车制造业	Manufacture of Motor Vehicles	71	9	33895832	6836323
铁路、船舶、航空航天和其他运输设备制造业	Manufacture of Railway Locomotives, Building of Ships and Boats, Manufacture of Air and Spacecrafts and Other Transportation Equipment	22	3	3158932	763528
电气机械和器材制造业	Manufacture of Electrical Machinery and Equipment	46	5	5255944	1028403
计算机、通信和其他电子设备制造业	Manufacture of Computers, Communication Equipment and Other Electronic Equipment	81	14	21374576	2488593
仪器仪表制造业	Manufacture of Measuring Instrument and Meter	29	2	1242559	340322
其他制造业	Other Manufacturing	7	1	439290	135420
金属制品、机械和设备修理业	Repair of Fabricated Metal Products, Machinery and Equipment	1	***	***	***
电力、热力生产和供应业	Production and Distribution of Electricity and Heating Power	29	7	40144453	6775721
燃气生产和供应业	Production and Distribution of Gas	3		***	***
水的生产和供应业	Production and Distribution of Water	4		512005	249494

注：1. 行业划分执行2011年国民经济行业分类标准(GB/T 4754-2011)。
2. 应交税金合计包括应交增值税、应交所得税、营业税金及附加和管理费用中的税金。

MAIN ECONOMIC INDICATORS OF MEDIUM AND LARGE-SIZED INDUSTRIAL ENTERPRISES (BY SECTOR) (2014)

(10000 yuan)

工 业 销售产值 (当年价格) Sales Value of Industry (at current year's prices)	#出 口 交货值 Delivery Value of Exports	平 均 用工人数 (人) Average Number of Employed Persons (person)	资 产 负 债 Assets and Liabilities: 资 产 总 计 Total Assets	流动资产 合 计 Total Current Assets	#存 货 Inventories	#产成品 Finished Products	#应收账款 Accounts Receivable	固定资产 合 计 Total Fixed Assets	固定资产 原 价 Total Original Value of Fixed Assets
148721904	**12588507**	**840908**	**284503769**	**108045472**	**15635961**	**4843892**	**24964596**	**56234139**	**103959001**
***	***	13578	***	***	***	***	***	***	***
***	***	2009	***	***	***	***	***	***	***
1290909		25306	21215426	6696417	275596	42891	1491698	3969914	5796644
1998988	190028	20756	4887496	2402149	295381	6596	837785	1207076	2520125
2358528	29501	23711	3010537	2082264	358464	205746	238210	309294	511683
2103261	94095	43393	2399616	1408479	237094	133374	310841	553781	981148
1708321	13830	24565	3516101	1315128	182811	43286	82035	473194	1077764
***	***	922	***	***	***	***	***	***	***
***	***	1119	***	***	***	***	***	***	***
760104	179708	31358	945650	697187	323766	220603	120620	148347	244832
***	***	1194	***	***	***	***	***	***	***
***	***	1432	***	***	***	***	***	***	***
443853	29424	8760	490504	276275	66092	33395	74116	114596	158062
422400	19617	2538	284050	190715	61465	14973	40314	68739	192736
639934	7303	13286	976333	522786	122379	55475	97115	330095	836329
***	***	2365	***	***	***	***	***	***	***
7708127		13077	2585886	1007578	582000	205862	142195	796402	2732911
1558779	35046	19881	2980329	1838875	192985	86505	383502	586361	1599385
5049744	62258	53134	7956763	4619257	1216213	502433	1067447	1178224	1775512
***	***	448	***	***	***	***	***	***	***
492845	71865	10680	417474	241678	64403	34057	96493	111082	221243
2857123	90718	32734	5985963	4141296	600285	134358	1852503	663423	1255825
906255	115714	5494	3577723	343848	136616	54838	57128	503904	765416
260702	96294	2902	385506	263387	82750	27897	77723	62225	96332
1502087	150903	20479	2899483	1604459	378790	103524	313569	467390	734769
3601672	620872	34244	5956151	4318543	1276059	381601	1061064	768028	1449279
3546826	519143	42603	9963396	6095633	1064524	336062	1536838	626844	1112935
33873392	540627	122822	30638861	16248230	2043072	890106	4048530	5805913	8594812
2930165	52761	30076	4816019	3578870	1343263	92955	1088661	920822	1108646
5132158	435234	34080	7815626	5991542	1118588	232401	2935952	418950	943768
20780640	8953984	99687	21101250	13754974	2704967	816899	3137482	4070337	8617498
1248573	40661	15422	1990441	1470107	398544	73321	482798	178009	316650
423202	5122	5483	1048995	598298	110607	25452	179280	258882	446085
***	***	6464	***	***	***	***	***	***	***
40143827		56277	122197339	21717242	109842	758	2556219	26641826	52315119
***	***	10365	***	***	***	***	***	***	***
512005		8264	6760477	2220074	8604	22	101274	2953008	4497783

Note: a) Sectors in this table are classified in accordance with the Standard for Classification of National Economic Sectors 2011 (GB/T 4754-2011).
b) Total tax payable mainly includes VAT payable, income tax payable, business tax and surtax, and tax in management expenses.

11-15 续表

单位：万元

项目	Item	资产负债 Assets and Liabilities 负债合计 Total Liabilities	#流动负债合计 Total Current Liabilities	#应付账款 Accounts Payable	所有者权益合计 Total Owner's Equity
合计	**Total**	**144556355**	**88386686**	**28632741**	**139947415**
煤炭开采和洗选业	Mining and Washing of Coal	***	***	***	***
石油和天然气开采业	Extraction of Petroleum and Natural Gas	***	***	***	***
黑色金属矿采选业	Mining and Processing of Ferrous Metal Ores	12346241	4965627	904364	8869184
开采辅助活动	Mining Support Service Activities	1867882	1682493	568951	3019614
农副食品加工业	Processing of Food from Agricultural Products	1693705	1413485	170486	1316832
食品制造业	Manufacture of Foods	1541890	1453258	526197	857726
酒、饮料和精制茶制造业	Manufacture of Wines, Beverage and Refined Tea	1427670	1278110	268990	2088431
烟草制品业	Manufacture of Cigarettes and Tobacco	***	***	***	***
纺织业	Manufacture of Textile	***	***	***	***
纺织服装、服饰业	Manufacture of Textile Wearing Apparel and Ornament	479675	453694	140343	465975
皮革、毛皮、羽毛及其制品和制鞋业	Manufacture of Leather, Fur, Feather and Its Products, and Footwear	***	***	***	***
木材加工和木、竹、藤、棕、草制品业	Processing of Timbers, Manufacture of Wood, Bamboo, Rattan, Palm, and Straw Products	***	***	***	***
家具制造业	Manufacture of Furniture	259282	220110	45830	231223
造纸和纸制品业	Manufacture of Paper and Paper Products	151062	150531	46475	132988
印刷和记录媒介复制业	Printing, Reproduction of Recording Media	329675	301150	113074	646658
文教、工美、体育和娱乐用品制造业	Manufacture of Articles for Culture, Education, Artwork, Sport and Entertainment Activities	***	***	***	***
石油加工、炼焦和核燃料加工业	Processing of Petroleum, Coking, Processing of Mucleus Fuels	1448798	1419314	354934	1137087
化学原料和化学制品制造业	Manufacture of Chemical Raw Materials and Chemical Products	1564464	1460765	193669	1415866
医药制造业	Manufacture of Medicines	3612249	3046332	797087	4344514
化学纤维制造业	Manufacture of Chemical fibres	***	***	***	***
橡胶和塑料制品业	Manufacture of Rubber and Plastics Products	250227	241183	77998	167247
非金属矿物制品业	Manufacture of Non-metallic Mineral Products	3314831	3091003	1185705	2671132
黑色金属冶炼和压延加工业	Manufacture and Pressing of Ferrous Metals	1113152	302264	163532	2464571
有色金属冶炼和压延加工业	Manufacture and Pressing of Non-ferrous Metals	114891	95782	53974	270615
金属制品业	Manufacture of Fabricated Metal Products	1435786	1146888	369372	1463697
通用设备制造业	Manufacture of General-purpose Machinery	2491805	2273829	764210	3464346
专用设备制造业	Manufacture of Special-purpose Machinery	5086393	3996296	1396195	4877002
汽车制造业	Manufacture of Motor Vehicles	17433700	14291595	7240445	13205161
铁路、船舶、航空航天和其他运输设备制造业	Manufacture of Railway Locomotives, Building of Ships and Boats, Manufacture of Air and Spacecrafts and Other Transportation Equipment	3384713	3124992	1037024	1431306
电气机械和器材制造业	Manufacture of Electrical Machinery and Equipment	4612737	4309997	1651435	3202889
计算机、通信和其他电子设备制造业	Manufacture of Computers, Communication Equipment and Other Electronic Equipment	12259486	10056520	4810002	8841764
仪器仪表制造业	Manufacture of Measuring Instrument and Meter	899115	836732	328346	1091326
其他制造业	Other Manufacturing	354374	236687	117865	694621
金属制品、机械和设备修理业	Repair of Fabricated Metal Products, Machinery and Equipment	***	***	***	***
电力、热力生产和供应业	Production and Distribution of Electricity and Heating Power	58939733	23780303	4968032	63257606
燃气生产和供应业	Production and Distribution of Gas	***	***	***	***
水的生产和供应业	Production and Distribution of Water	3210387	944069	47831	3550091

11-15 Continued

(10000 yuan)

#实收资本 Paid-up Capital	损益 Profits and Losses 营业收入 Business Income	#主营业务收入 Main Business Income	营业成本 Business Cost	#主营业务成本 Main Business Cost	销售费用 Sales Expenses	管理费用 Management Expenses	财务费用 Financial Expenses	利润总额 Total Profits	应交税金合计 Total Tax Payable	#营业税金及附加 Business Tax and Surtax	#主营业务税金及附加 Main Business Tax and Surtax	#应交增值税 Value Added Tax Payable
56894159	**163631110**	**160397751**	**138236953**	**135660661**	**7136735**	**6436166**	**1844529**	**13034993**	**9844200**	**2913664**	**2901997**	**4641494**
***	***	***	***	***	***	***	***	***	***	***	***	***
***	***	***	***	***	***	***	***	***	***	***	***	***
2871599	3728778	3565418	3704778	3541210	8765	165148	259055	217608	94185	14213	12892	68865
2655032	1784078	1780250	1615776	1615331	8575	79455	25493	13461	77201	29579	28975	20791
467942	2737790	2718632	2203838	2195775	199652	127543	34293	141682	184388	89778	89763	68315
770224	4006982	3914348	2558079	2473083	1069134	200596	9059	143695	271847	23187	22875	197001
544267	1891149	1793858	1375660	1295271	344467	112482	5004	61142	207796	79184	79056	103399
***	***	***	***	***	***	***	***	***	***	***	***	***
***	***	***	***	***	***	***	***	***	***	***	***	***
182127	858506	831891	511762	490775	174602	93118	6119	82404	76821	6743	6636	54542
***	***	***	***	***	***	***	***	***	***	***	***	***
***	***	***	***	***	***	***	***	***	***	***	***	***
62982	398608	387222	293586	285355	46045	35587	4447	23931	23122	2531	2439	16438
54088	452675	440967	325893	316172	17841	17841	202	89949	46659	2714	2714	20514
374079	694956	644081	530820	492585	20606	96364	-1428	46856	60032	5099	4767	40985
***	***	***	***	***	***	***	***	***	***	***	***	***
45041	8632074	8049105	7538256	6962472	55966	133654	23459	144227	996095	731621	730593	221999
1075498	1660516	1616184	1304226	1270125	178279	154566	35074	208074	99651	11984	11922	66266
1190444	5435087	5228241	2461063	2283973	1614912	478654	100474	881771	661569	54944	54749	446878
***	***	***	***	***	***	***	***	***	***	***	***	***
78353	527325	517482	417196	409713	16848	43701	3792	44513	31087	2961	2960	18503
929961	3358686	3257274	2833752	2752640	123213	224232	51826	127856	119126	20512	20015	76772
840291	983573	966724	922084	907171	45560	27373	23764	-22312	-3306	1186	1077	4904
54613	304555	300043	251924	249617	7201	21020	883	17253	16040	9270	9270	3403
604690	1835048	1728393	1517057	1437187	47790	156262	21223	99977	63767	10610	10379	35188
1214810	3909140	3807391	2991587	2925382	207071	255414	26979	434956	270387	21426	21296	159512
1805086	4028894	3817709	3047009	2907206	235700	411148	78641	504646	201305	24804	24640	120380
5281562	34980473	34222161	28717126	28166347	1286252	1252590	29296	3015453	2866747	1226561	1226165	912187
564368	3191072	3165152	2629705	2615240	36037	218776	24682	277467	111128	8827	8730	67334
1822738	5556455	5424570	4400721	4284809	300953	345426	57330	466527	286464	22226	22224	180487
5339517	25100627	24855347	22459541	22274327	897195	1062597	50990	783835	422970	41444	39587	222742
300874	1510061	1491287	1073377	1062825	114589	140556	6359	217890	109360	9337	9140	68202
251517	469522	460016	321558	314631	14291	66926	-916	72294	33346	2555	2555	18020
***	***	***	***	***	***	***	***	***	***	***	***	***
23240400	40272702	40182223	37907717	37848640	6646	169507	899195	4333141	1875986	169709	168465	1175045
***	***	***	***	***	***	***	***	***	***	***	***	***
2916133	698181	689335	505062	501720	109	39259	16780	230517	67563	2316	1691	10292

11-16 规模以上工业企业主要工业产品生产能力
PRODUCTION CAPACITY OF MAIN INDUSTRIAL PRODUCTS IN INDUSTRIAL ENTERPRISES ABOVE DESIGNATED SIZE

主要工业产品名称		Name of Main Industrial Products		2014	2013
原油加工能力	(吨)	Crude Oil Processing Capacity	(ton)	11500000	14000000
硅酸盐水泥熟料	(吨)	Portland Cement Chamotte	(ton)	6266000	6690000
发电设备容量总计	(万千瓦)	Total Capacity of Power Generation Equipment	(10000 KW)	1555	787
火电设备容量	(万千瓦)	Capacity of Thermal Power Equipment	(10000 KW)	782	674
水电设备容量	(万千瓦)	Capacity of Hydropower Equipment	(10000 KW)	98	98
风电设备容量	(万千瓦)	Capacity of Wind Power Equipment	(10000 KW)	15	15
原　煤	(吨)	Raw Coal	(ton)	5200000	5200000
卷　烟	(万支)	Cigarette	(10000 units)	4185000	4347000
棉纺锭	(锭)	Knitting Spindles (Ring Spindle Spinning)	(unit)		19360
气流纺锭	(头)	Air Spinning Spindles (Rotating-cup Spinning)	(unit)	1656	1656
棉布织机	(台)	Cotton Cloth Weaver	(unit)	66	66
水　泥	(吨)	Cement	(ton)	8350000	9740000
钢　材	(吨)	Rolled Steel	(ton)	1764694	1789316
金属切削机床	(台)	Metal-Cutting Machine Tools	(unit)	24524	23579
汽　车	(辆)	Motor Vehicles	(unit)	2277500	2078500
#基本型乘用车(轿车	(辆)	Basic-type Passenger Vehicles (Sedans)	(unit)	1069000	902000
家用电冰箱	(台)	Household Refrigerators	(unit)		1500000
移动通信手持机(手机)	(台)	Mobile Communication Handsets (Mobile Phones	(unit)	63540000	149560318
微型计算机设备	(台)	Micro-computers	(unit)	20138300	20325104

11-17 主要工业产品产量
OUTPUT OF MAIN INDUSTRIAL PRODUCTS

工业产品名称		Name of Main Industrial Product		2014	2013
单晶硅	(千克)	Monocrystalline Silicon	(kg)	122372.8	148918.1
中成药	(万吨)	Finished Traditional Chinese Herbal Medicines	(10000 tons)	4.4	4.0
沥青和改性沥青防水卷材	(万平方米)	Asphalt and Modified Asphalt Waterproof Roll Materials	(10000 sq.m)	6653.6	6428.0
纤维增强塑料制品	(万吨)	Fiber-reinforced Plastic Products	(10000 tons)	3.2	2.1
耐火材料制品	(万吨)	Products Made from Fire-resistant Materials	(10000 tons)	50.3	50.9
冷轧薄宽钢带	(万吨)	Cold-rolled Thin Broad Steel Bands	(10000 tons)	106.4	111.4
单一稀土金属	(千克)	Single Rare Earth Metals	(kg)	272553.0	136799.0
发动机	(万千瓦)	Engines	(10000 KW)	12616.3	11482.8
气动元件	(万件)	Pneumatic Components	(10000 units)	20645.6	19373.4
数控金属切削机床	(台)	Digital Metal Cutting Tools	(unit)	13890	6983
机床数控装置	(套)	CNC Units of Lathe	(unit)	61072	87114
工业电炉	(台)	Industrial Electric Cookers	(unit)	161	137
环境污染防治专用设备	(台套)	Special Equipment for Prevention and Control of Environmental Pollution	(set)	79645	100223
汽　车	(万辆)	Automobiles	(10000 units)	216.7	203.8
#基本型成用车(轿车)	(万辆)	#Including: Basic-type Passenger Vehicles (Sedans)	(10000 units)	118.6	94.5
运动型多用途乘用车(SUV)	(万辆)	Sport Utility Vehicles (SUV)	(10000 units)	33.4	32.9
载货汽车	(万辆)	Freight Trucks	(10000 units)	51.2	62.5
改装汽车	(万辆)	Refitted Automobiles	(10000 units)	1.9	1.6
风力发电机组	(万千瓦)	Wind Power Generator Units	(10000 KW)	439.4	411.6
锂离子电池	(万只)	Lithiums Ion Batteries	(10000 units)	5509.6	7832.1
移动通信手持机(手机)	(万台)	Mobile Communication Handsets (Mobile Phones)	(10000 units)	17983.6	18783.4
微型计算机设备	(万台)	Micro-computer Equipment	(10000 units)	1015.6	1106.9
服务器	(台)	Servers	(unit)	164099	117397
液晶显示模组	(万套)	Liquid Crystal Display Modules	(10000 sets)	7616.5	659.0
显示器	(万台)	Displays	(10000 units)	548.1	305.3
集成电路	(亿块)	Integrated Circuits	(100 million pieces)	54.3	38.4
彩色电视机	(万台)	Color TV Sets	(10000 units)	193.6	100.0

11-18 规模以上高技术制造业主要经济指标(2014年)
MAIN ECONOMIC INDICATORS OF HIGH-TECH MANUFACTURING ENTERPRISES ABOVE DESIGNATED SIZE (2014)

单位：亿元 (100 million yuan)

项 目	Item	工业总产值 Gross Output Value of Industry	主营业务收入 Main Business Income	利润总额 Total Profits	应交税金 Tax Payable
合 计	**Total**	**3716.0**	**4156.7**	**277.0**	**173.8**
按登记注册类型分组	**By Registration Type**				
内 资	Domestially-Invested Enterprises				
国 有	State-owned Enterprises	64.0	64.6	6.3	2.2
集 体	Collectively-owned Enterprises	1.3	1.6	0.0	0.1
股份合作企业	Joint-equity Cooperative Enterprises	3.9	4.2	0.1	0.2
联营企业	Associated Enterprises				
有限责任公司	Limited Liability Companies	742.0	791.9	89.1	40.7
股份有限公司	Companies Limited by Shares	325.8	408.7	63.4	32.7
私营企业	Private Enterprises	186.4	191.9	25.5	14.1
其 他	Others				
港澳台商投资	Hong Kong, Macao and Taiwan-invested Enterprises	1059.3	1328.0	24.4	14.9
外商投资	Foreign-invested Enterprises	1333.3	1366.0	68.3	68.9
按高技术领域分组	**By Field of High Technology**				
信息化学品制造	Information Chemical Manufacturing	4.9	5.2	-0.4	0.1
医药制造业	Manufacture of Medicines	669.0	662.6	112.6	80.5
航空、航天器及设备制造业	Manufacture of Aircrafts and Spacecrafts	178.4	183.8	14.2	5.0
电子及通信设备制造业	Manufacture of Electronic Equipment and Communication Equipment	2122.2	2198.2	93.7	52.5
计算机及办公设备制造业	Manufacture of Computers and Office Equipments	369.3	690.0	3.7	7.0
医疗仪器设备及仪器仪表制造业	Manufacture of Medical Equipments and Meters	372.1	416.9	53.1	28.7

注：应交税金合计包括应交增值税、应交所得税、营业税金及附加和管理费用中的税金。
Note: Total tax payable mainly includes VAT payable, income tax payable, business tax and surtax, and tax in management expenses.

11-19 规模以下工业主要指标(2014年)
MAJOR INDICATORS FOR INDUSTRIAL ENTERPRISES BELOW DESIGNATED SIZE (2014)

项 目	Item	单位个数(个) Number of Enterprises (unit)	从业人员平均人数(人) Average Number of Employed Persons (person)	工业总产值(当年价格，万元) Gross Output Value (at year's current prices, 10000 yuan)
合 计	**Total**	**27134**	**258156**	**7322175**
法人工业企业	Corporate Industrial Enterprises	18885	220257	6795681
个体经营工业单位	Individual Operated Business	8249	37899	526494

注：规模以下工业企业指年主营业务收入2000万元以下的法人工业企业和全部个体经营工业单位。
Note: Industrial enterprises below designed size refers to corperate industrial enterprises with main business income below RMB 20 million and all individual operated business.

主要统计指标解释

工业　指从事自然资源的开采，对采掘品和农产品进行加工和再加工的物质生产部门。具体包括：（1）对自然资源的开采，如采矿、晒盐、森林采伐等（但不包括禽兽捕猎和水产捕捞）；（2）对农副产品的加工、再加工，如粮油加工、食品加工、扎花、纺织、制革等；（3）对采掘品的加工、再加工，如炼铁、炼钢、化工生产、石油加工、机器制造、木材加工等，以及电力、自来水、煤气的生产和供应等；（4）对工业品的修理、翻新，如机器设备的修理。

轻工业　指主要提供生活消费品和制作手工工具的工业。按其所使用的原料不同，可分为两大类：（1）以农业为原料的轻工业，是指直接或间接以农产品为基本原料的轻工业。主要包括食品制造、饮料制造、烟草加工、纺织、缝纫、皮革和毛皮制作、造纸以及印刷等工业；（2）以非农产品为原料的轻工业，是指以工业品为原料的轻工业。主要包括文教体育用品、化学药品制造、合成纤维制造、日用化学制品、日用玻璃制品、日用金属制品、手工工具制造、医疗器械制造、文化和办公用机械制造等工业。

重工业　是指为国民经济各部门提供物质技术基础的主要生产资料的工业。按其生产性质和产品用途，可以分为下列三类：（1）采掘（伐）工业，是指对自然资源的开采，包括石油开采、煤炭开采、金属矿开采、非金属矿开采和木材采伐等工业；（2）原材料工业，指向国民经济各部门提供基本材料、动力和燃料的工业。包括金属冶炼及加工、炼焦及焦炭化学、化工原料、水泥、人造板以及电力、石油和煤炭加工等工业；（3）加工工业，是指对工业原材料进行再加工制造的工业。包括装备国民经济各部门的机械设备制造工业、金属结构、水泥制品等工业，以及为农业提供的生产资料如化肥、农药等工业。

根据上述划分原则，修理业中以重工业产品为修理作业对象的划为重工业，反之划为轻工业。

工业总产值　指工业企业在报告期内生产的以货币形式表现的工业最终产品和提供工业劳务活动的总价值量。它包括：在本企业内不再进行加工，经检验、包装入库（规定不需包装的产品除外）的成品价值，对外加工费收入，自制半成品、在制品期末期初差额价值。工业总产值采用“工厂法”计算，即以工业企业作为一个整体，按企业生产活动的最终成果来计算。

工业增加值　是指工业企业在报告期内以货币形式表现的工业生产活动的最终成果，反映企业生产过程中新创造的价值。

工业销售产值　是以货币形式表现的，工业企业在报告期内销售的本企业生产的工业产品或提供工业性劳务价值的总价值量。包括企业在报告期内实际销售（包括本期生产和非本期生产）的全部成品、半成品的总价值，报告期内完成的对外承接的工业品加工的加工费收入，对外工业品修理作业可获取的加工费收入和对内非工业部门提供的加工修理、设备安装等收入。已销售的成品、半成品不论是本期生产的、还是非本期生产的，只要是本期销售出去的均包括在内。企业为本单位基本建设部门、生活福利部门等提供的产品和工业性作业及自制设备也应视同销售，这部分也应作为销售统计。

资产总计　指企业过去的交易或者事项形成的、由企业拥有或者控制的、预期会给企业带来经济利益的资源。资产一般按流动性分为流动资产和非流动资产。其中流动资产可分为货币资金、交易性金融资产、应收票据、应收账款、预付款项、其他应收款、存货等；非流动资产可分为长期股权投资、固定资产、无形资产及其他非流动资产等。

（1）流动资产合计　资产满足以下条件之一应归为流动资产：①预计在一个正常营业周期中变现、出售或耗用，主要包括存货、应收账款等；②主要为交易目的而持有；③预计在资产负债表日起一年内（含一年）变现；④自资产负债表日起一年内，交换其他资产或清偿负债的能力不受限制的现金或现金等价物。包括货币资金、应收票据、应收账款、存货等项目。

（2）固定资产合计　指企业为生产商品、提供劳务、出租或经营管理而持有的，使用寿命超过一个会计年度的有形资产。包括使用期限超过一年的房屋、建筑物、机器、机械、运输工具以及其他与生产、经营有关的设备、器具、工具等。固定资产合计是时点指标，表示固定资产经过扣减折旧、减值准备等后的期末余额。

负债合计　指企业过去的交易或者事项形成的，预期会导致经济利益流出企业的现时义务。负债一般按偿还期长短分为流动负债和非流动负债。

（1）流动负债合计　负债满足下列条件之一的应归为流动负债：①预计在一个正常营业周期中清偿；②主要为交易目的而持有；③自资产负债表日起一年内到期应予清偿；④企业无权自主地将清偿推迟至资产负债表日后一年以上。包括短期借款、应付票据、应付账款、应付职工薪酬、应交税费等项目。

（2）非流动负债合计　指流动负债之外的负债。包括长期借款、应付债券等。

所有者权益合计　指企业资产扣除负债后由所有者享有的剩余权益。公司的所有者权益又称股东权益。包括实收资本、资本公积、盈余公积、未分配利润等。

实收资本 指企业各投资者实际投入的资本（或股本）总额，包括货币、实物、无形资产等各种形式的投入。实收资本按投资主体可分为国家资本、集体资本、法人资本、个人资本、港澳台资本和外商资本。

主营业务收入 指企业确认的销售商品、提供劳务等主营业务的收入。

主营业务成本 指企业经营主要业务所发生的成本总额。

主营业务税金及附加 指企业经营主要业务应负担的营业税、消费税、城市维护建设税、教育费附加等。

营业利润 指企业从事生产经营活动所取得的利润。

利润总额 指企业在一定会计期间的经营成果，是生产经营过程中各种收入扣除各种耗费后的盈余，反映企业在报告期内实现的亏盈总额。

应交增值税 指企业按税法规定，从事货物销售或提供加工、修理修配劳务等增加货物价值的活动本期应交纳的税金。

应交增值税=销项税额-（进项税额-进项税额转出）-出口抵减内销产品应纳税额-减免税款+出口退税

应交增值税不含期初未抵扣税额。

工业产品销售率 指报告期工业销售产值与工业总产值之比。计算公式：

$$工业产品销售率(\%)=\frac{报告期现价工业销售产值}{报告期现价工业总产值}\times 100\%$$

工业增加值率 指报告期工业增加值占工业总产值的比重，反映降低中间消耗的经济效益。计算公式：

$$工业增加率(\%)=\frac{报告期现价工业增加值}{报告期现价工业总产值}\times 100\%$$

工业成本费用利润率 指在一定时期内实现的利润与成本费用之比，是反映工业生产成本及费用投入的经济效益指标，同时也是反映降低成本的经济效益的指标。计算公式：

$$工业成本费用利润率(\%)=\frac{利润总额}{成本费用总额}\times 100\%$$

工业全员劳动生产率 指根据产品的价值量指标计算的平均每一个职工在单位时间内创造的工业生产最终成果。是考核企业经济活动的重要指标，是企业生产技术水平、经济管理水平、职工技术熟练程度和劳动积极性的综合表现。

$$工业全员劳动生产率（元/人）=\frac{工业增加值（现价）}{平均用工人数}$$

平均用工人数 指报告期企业平均实际拥有的、参与本企业生产经营活动的人员数。

流动资产周转次数 指在一定时期内流动资产完成的周转次数，反映流动资产的周转速度。计算公式：

$$流动资产周转次数(次)=\frac{产品销售收入}{流动资产平均余额}$$

流动比率 是反映企业每百元流动负债中，有多少元流动资产作后盾。计算公式：

$$流动比率(倍)=\frac{流动资产总额}{流动负债总额}$$

速动比率 是衡量企业流动资产中可以立即用于偿付流动负债的能力。计算公式：

$$速动比率(倍)=\frac{流动资产总额-存货}{流动负债总额}$$

资产负债率 反映在企业资产总额中有多少资产是通过借债而得的，也可以用于衡量企业利用债权人提供资金进行经营活动的能力以及企业在清算时保护债权人利益的程度。计算公式：

$$资产负债率=\frac{负债总额}{资产总额}\times 100\%$$

总资产贡献率 反映企业全部资产的获利能力，是企业经营业绩和管理水平的集中体现，是评价和考核企业盈利能力的核心指标。计算公式为：

$$总资产贡献率=(利润总额+税金总额+利息支出)\div 平均资产总额\times 100\%$$

其中：税金总额为主营业务税金及附加、管理费用中的税金与应交增值税之和；平均资产总额为期初期末资产总计的算术平均值。

资本保值增值率 反映企业净资产的变动状况，是企业发展能力的集中体现。计算公式为：

$$资本保值增值率=\frac{报告期期末所有者权益}{上年同期期末所有者权益}\times 100\%$$

高技术制造业 是指国民经济行业中R&D投入强度相对较高的制造业行业，根据国家统计局《高技术产业（制造业）分类（2013）》标准界定。

Explanatory Notes on Main Statistical Indicators

Industry refers to the material production sector which is engaged in extraction of natural resources and processing and reprocessing of minerals and agricultural products, including (1) extraction of natural resources, such as mining, salt production, logging (but not including animal hunting and fishing); (2) processing and reprocessing of agricultural products, such as grain and oil processing, food processing, embroidery, textile manufacturing and leather making; (3) processing and reprocessing of mining products, such as iron making, steel making, chemical production, petroleum processing, machine building, timber processing; and production and supply of electric power, tap water and gas; (4) repair and refurbishment of industrial products, such as the repair of machinery equipment.

Light Industry refers to the industries that produce consumer goods and hand tools. It falls into two categories, based on different raw materials:

(1) Industries basing the raw materials on agriculture, which directly or indirectly use farm products as basic raw materials, mainly include the manufacture of foods and beverages, tobacco processing, textile manufacturing, tailoring, fur and leather manufacturing, paper making, printing, etc.

(2) Industries using non-agricultural products as raw materials, which means the manufactured goods are used as raw materials, mainly include the manufacture of cultural, educational articles and sports goods, chemical medicines, synthetic fiber, daily chemical products, glass products for daily use, metal products for daily use, hand tools, medical appliances and instruments, as well as stationery and office machinery.

Heavy Industry refers to the industries that provide material and technical foundation as key means of production for various sectors of the national economy. It falls into the following three categories according to the purpose of production or the use of products:

(1) Mining, quarrying and logging industry refers to the industry that extracts natural resources, including the extraction of petroleum, coal, metal and non-metal ores and logging.

(2) Raw material industry refers to the industry that provides various sectors of the national economy with basic materials, fuels and power. It includes smelting and processing of metals, coking and coke chemistry, chemical materials, cement, artificial boards, as well as power generation, petroleum refining and coal processing.

(3) Processing industry refers to the industry that reprocesses raw materials. It includes machine manufacturing, which equips various sectors of the national economy, metal structure, cement products, and chemical fertilizer and pesticide industry that provide means of production for agriculture.

According to the above principle of classification, the repair services for products of heavy industry are classified as heavy industry, while the repair services for products of light industry are classified as light industry.

Gross Output Value of Industry is the total value in monetary terms for final industrial products and industrial labor service provided by industrial enterprises during the reporting period. It includes the value of the finished products, which will not be further processed in the enterprises and have been inspected, packed and put in storage (except for products required not to be packed), the revenue from processing products for others, the value of semi-finished products, and the price spread between the finished products and products at the initial stage. The gross industrial output value is calculated with “factory method”; that is, to take an industrial enterprise as a whole. It calculates the final products created by the enterprise.

Added Value of Industry refers to the final results of industrial production by industrial enterprises in monetary terms during the reporting period. It shows the newly created value generated in production by the enterprises.

Sales Value of Industry refers to the total value of industrial products sold or labor service provided by an industrial enterprise during the reporting period in monetary terms. It includes the total value of all finished and semi-finished products actually sold by the enterprise (including products produced in current period and noncurrent period), revenue from processing products for others, repairing industrial products for others, as well as processing, repairing, and installing equipment for internal non-industrial departments in the reporting period. All finished and semi-finished products sold in the current period will be counted, regardless of whether they were produced in the current period or not. The value of products, industrial work and home-built equipment provided by the enterprise for its capital construction department and welfare department will also be included in the industrial sales value.

Total Assets refer to resources formed by previous transactions or matters of an enterprise, owned or controlled by the enterprise, and expected to bring economic benefits to the enterprise. Classified by the liquidity, assets fall into current assets and non-current assets. Current assets include monetary capital, tradable financial assets, notes receivable, accounts receivable, prepayment, other receivables, and inventory, etc.; while non-current assets include long-term equity investment, fixed assets, intangible assets, and other non-current assets, etc.

(1) Total Current Assets Assets that meet any of the following requirements are considered current assets: a. assets expected to be cashed in, sold or consumed in a normal operating cycle, which mainly includes inventory and accounts receivable, etc.; b. assets held mainly for transaction; c. assets expected to be cashed in within one year (including one year) from the balance sheet date; d. cash or cash equivalents with unrestricted capacity of exchanging for other assets or paying off debts within one year from the balance sheet date, which include monetary capital, notes receivable, accounts receivable, inventory, etc.

(2) Total Fixed Assets refer to tangible assets held by an enterprise for producing commodities, rendering labor services, leasing or management, with service life exceeding one fiscal year, which include houses and buildings, apparatus, machinery, means of transport, as well as other equipment, instruments and tools related to production and operation, which have a service life exceeding one year. Total Fixed Assets is a time point indicator, showing the ending balance of fixed assets after deduction and discount, and impairment provision, etc.

Total Liabilities refer to the present obligations formed by previous transactions or matters of an enterprise, expected to lead the flow of economic benefits out of the enterprise. By the term of payment, liabilities generally include current liabilities and non-current liabilities.

(1) Total Current liabilities Liabilities that meet any of the following requirements are considered current liabilities: a. assets expected to be paid off within one normal operating cycle; b. assets held mostly for the purpose of transaction; c. assets expected to be due and paid off within one year from the balance sheet date; d. assets that the enterprise has no right to delay the payment to more than one year after the balance sheet date on its own. They include short-term loans, notes payable, accounts payable, wages payable, taxes and fees payable, etc.

(2) Total Non-current Liabilities refer to liabilities other than current liabilities, including long-term borrowings and bonds payable, etc.

Total Owner's Equity refers to the remaining equity of assets in an enterprise held by owners after deducting the liabilities. Owner's equity of a company is also called shareholders' equity, including paid-up capital, capital reserves, operating surplus reserves and non-distributed profits, etc.

Paid-up Capital refers to the total capital (or equity) actually contributed by investors to an enterprise, including input in various forms, such as monetary investment, physical investment and intangible assets. Categorized by investors, paid-up capital includes state capital, collective capital, legal person's capital, personal capital, capital from Hong Kong, Macao and Taiwan, and foreign capital.

Main Business Income refers to the income from main business of selling commodities and rendering services recognized by the enterprise.

Main Business Cost refers to the total cost incurred by the enterprise during its operation of main business.

Main Business Tax and Surtax refers to the business tax, excise tax, urban maintenance and construction tax, educational surcharge to be levied against the main business operated by an enterprise.

Operating Profits refer to the profits reaped by an enterprise from its productive and operating activities.

Total Profits refer to the operating results of an enterprise during certain accounting period, representing the surplus of various incomes from production and operation deducting various expenses, reflecting the total gains and losses realized by the enterprise during the reporting period.

VAT Payable refer to the tax payable by an enterprise in current period according to provisions in Law of Tax for its activities of adding value to goods, such as selling the goods, providing labor service for processing, repair and replacement.

VAT Payable = Output Tax – (Input Tax – Transfer-out of Input Tax) – Tax Payable Deducted by Export from Output Tax of Domestically Sold Products – Tax Concession + Export Rebate

VAT Payable excludes the taxes not deducted at the beginning of the period.

Sales Rate of Industrial Products refers to the ratio of industrial sales output to the gross output value of industry during the reporting period. The following formula is used:

Sales Rate of Industrial Products (%) = Sales Value of Industry at Present Value During the Reporting Period / Gross Output Value of Industry at Present Value During the Reporting Period × 100%

Rate of Industrial Added Value refers to the ratio of added value of industry to the gross output value of industry during the reporting period. It indicates the economic benefits from reduction of intermediate consumption. The following formula is used:

Rate of Industrial Added Value = Added Value of Industry at Present Value During the Reporting Period / Gross Output Value of Industry at Present Value During the Reporting Period × 100%

Rate of Profits to Total Industrial Costs refers to the ratio of profits realized in a given period to the total costs in the same period, which reflects the economic efficiency of industrial production input. The following formula is used:

Rate of Profits to Total Industrial Cost (%) = (Total Profits/ Total Costs) ×100%

Overall Labor Productivity of Industry refers to the average final result of industrial production created by each employee within a unit time, measured with the value of products. It is an important indicator evaluating the economic activities of an enterprise, and it reflects the level of production technology and economic management of the enterprise, employees' skills, as well as enthusiasm for work.

Overall Labor Productivity of Industry (RMB/person) = Added Value of Industry (at present value) / Average Number of Employees

Turnover of Current Assets refer to the number of times for current assets turnover within a given period of time. It reflects the turnover velocity of current assets. The following formula is used:

Turnover of Current Assets (No. of times) = Product Sales Income / Average Balance of Current Assets

Liquidity Ratio reflects how many current assets are backing up every RMB 100 of current liabilities in an enterprise. The following formula is used:

Liquidity Ratio (times) = Total Current Assets / Total Current Liabilities

Quick Ratio indicates the capacity of an enterprise's current assets for paying off current liabilities immediately. The following formula is used:

Quick Ratio (times) = (Total Current Assets – Inventory) / Total Current Liabilities

Assets-liabilities Ratio reflects how many assets—out of the total assets of the enterprise, are obtained by borrowing. It can be used to evaluate the enterprise's capability of operating by using the funds provided by creditors, and to what extent the enterprise will be able to protect the creditors' interests in the case of liquidation. The following formula is used:

Assets-liabilities Ratio = Total Liabilities / Total Assets × 100%

Contribution Rate of Total Assets indicates the profitability of all assets in an enterprise, reflecting the operating performance and management of the enterprise. It serves as a core indicator evaluating the enterprise's profitability. The following formula is used:

Total Assets Contribution rate = (Total Profit + Total Tax + Total Interest Expenses) / Average Total Assets × 100%

Note: the total tax is the sum of main business tax and surtax, tax in management expenses, and VAT payable; average total assets are represented by the arithmetic average of total assets at the beginning and the end of the period.

Rate of Assets Preservation and Appreciation reflects the changes in the net assets of an enterprise. It reflects the growth potential of the enterprise. The following formula is used:

Capital Preservation and Appreciation Rate = Owner's Equity at the End of the Reporting Period / Owner's Equity at the End of the Same Period in the Previous Year × 100%

High-tech Manufacturing Sector refers to all sectors in the high-tech industry other than software development.

12

建筑业
CONSTRUCTION

简要说明

一、本章资料的主要内容

本章资料主要反映北京市建筑业企业基本情况和生产经营情况。主要指标包括企业个数、从业人员、建筑业总产值、建筑业企业房屋建筑面积、利润、税金等。

二、本章资料的统计范围

建筑业统计范围从 2004 年起，由原具有建筑业资质等级四级及四级以上的独立核算的建筑业企业调整为具有施工总承包、专业承包资质的所有法人建筑业企业。

三、本章资料的数据来源及调查方法

本章建筑业企业统计数据根据国家统计局制定的《建筑业统计报表制度》整理汇总。建筑业统计数据采取全面调查的方法。资料由北京市统计局、国家统计局北京调查总队提供。

四、有关统计标准的变化说明

本章资料中建筑业行业分类 2002-2011 年期间执行 2002 年《国民经济行业分类标准》(GB/T 4754-2002)划分标准，2012 年开始执行 2011 年《国民经济行业分类》(GB/T 4754-2011)划分标准。

五、本章中关于历史数据调整的问题

由于 2004 年开展了“北京市第一次全国经济普查”，按照国家统计局统一要求和统一方法，历史资料要根据普查结果进行修正。本章中 1993 至 2003 年的建筑业总产值数据采用“趋势离差法”进行了调整，2004 年为第一次经济普查数据，2008 年为第二次经济普查数据，2013 年为第三次经济普查数据。

Brief Introduction

I. Main Content

Data in this chapter reflect the basic situation and operation of construction enterprises in Beijing. Main indicators include number of enterprises, employees, total output value of the construction sector, as well as floor space, profits, and tax of construction enterprises.

II. Scope of Statistics

Since 2004, data on construction sector, which previously covered construction enterprises with independent accounting at or above Level-4 in construction qualifications, have been adjusted to cover all construction enterprises with qualifications of general and specialized contracting.

III. Source of Data and Methods of Survey

Data on construction enterprises in this chapter were gathered based on *Statistical Statement System for Construction Sector* developed by the National Bureau of Statistics. The figures were gained through complete survey, and were provided by Beijing Municipal Bureau of Statistics and NBS Survey Office in Beijing.

IV. Changes in Relevant Statistical Standards

In this chapter, classification of construction sectors during 2002-2011 was based on the *Standard for Classification of National Economic Sectors 2002* (GB/T 4754-2002). *Standard for Classification of National Economic Sectors 2011* (GB/T 4754-2011) began to be enforced in 2012.

V. About the Adjustment to Historical Data

As “The First National Economic Census in Beijing” was conducted in 2004, in accordance with the principles of unified requirements and methods by the National Bureau of Statistics, historical data must be revised on basis of the census result. Data of total output value of construction sector during 1993-2003 were revised by “trend deviation method”. The first economic census was in 2004, and the second was in 2008, and the third was in 2013.

12-1 建筑业企业基本情况(1978-2014年)
BASIC STATISTICS FOR ENTERPRISES IN THE CONSTRUCTION INDUSTRY (1978-2014)

年份 Year	建筑施工企业单位数(个) Construction Enterprises (unit)	建筑施工企业年末从业人员(万人) Employed Persons (year-end) (10000 persons)	建筑施工企业总产值(亿元) Gross Output Value (100 million yuan)	主营业务收入(亿元) Main Business Income (100 million yuan)	建筑施工企业利润总额(亿元) Total Profits (100 million yuan)	建筑施工企业房屋建筑面积(万平方米) Floor Space of Buildings (10000 sq.m) 施工面积 Floor Space under Construction	竣工面积 Floor Space Completed
1978	64	25.4	10.5		0.7		
1979	70	26.4	12.7		0.9		
1980	71	27.8	14.7		1.5		
1981	71	27.0	14.5		1.6		
1982	91	30.7	17.3		1.7		
1983	116	37.2	22.6		2.5		
1984	2765	53.0	33.4		3.2		
1985	2549	63.9	43.9		3.9		
1986	2361	61.3	51.3		3.3		
1987	2292	64.4	67.0		4.1		
1988	1659	64.2	81.6		3.9		
1989	1545	60.0	89.0		3.8		
1990	994	60.2	94.7		3.4		
1991	922	60.3	99.6		2.8	2495	1172
1992	976	62.7	122.6		3.1	2774	1227
1993	1098	75.9	215.5	205.5	6.1	3499	1428
1994	1259	73.4	336.0	289.4	9.4	4035	1437
1995	1332	82.6	426.6	337.6	7.8	4602	1593
1996	1292	82.5	494.7	431.3	8.9	5328	1967
1997	1297	80.3	556.4	481.1	10.4	5801	2117
1998	1482	75.6	678.6	579.3	12.4	6525	2225
1999	1588	62.0	750.6	645.8	13.6	6824	2632
2000	1697	56.6	812.5	706.8	16.4	7247	2809
2001	1811	57.8	1055.4	906.9	18.7	8919	3198
2002	2122	57.0	1211.3	1094.0	24.7	10241	3827
2003	2419	59.1	1521.2	1329.9	31.5	12160	4486
2004	2623	51.2	1659.8	1936.0	40.0	14424	5258
2005	2752	67.2	1894.0	2206.9	67.3	15418	4862
2006	2800	66.9	2167.9	2666.2	112.8	16202	4786
2007	2845	51.7	2576.8	3351.3	115.7	18225	4946
2008	3527	47.0	3066.2	3856.8	84.5	19537	4803
2009	3556	56.2	4059.7	5081.1	217.4	22721	5225
2010	3594	59.9	5196.0	6545.0	265.2	29440	5933
2011	3667	49.6	6046.3	7565.9	219.6	36507	6456
2012	3572	49.2	6588.3	8125.2	293.0	41660	8414
2013	3522	49.3	7459.6	9404.3	385.8	49259	8950
2014	3426	51.0	8209.8	10492.2	473.2	56477	9275

注：1. 1996-2003年全部指标的统计口径为四级及四级以上的法人建筑施工企业。
2. 2004年开始全部指标的统计口径为建筑施工总承包、专业承包的建筑业企业。
3. 建筑施工企业房屋建筑面积包括在本市和外省完成的施工、竣工面积。

Note: a) Data from 1996 to 2003 covers the corporate construction enterprises at Grade IV and above.
b) Data from 2004 covers general contracting and specialized contracting construction enterprises.
c) Data on floor space covers buildings under construction and completed in Beijing and other provinces.and outside the city.

12-2 建筑业施工企业基本情况(2014年)
BASIC STATISTICS FOR CONSTRUCTION ENTERPRISES (2014)

项目	Item	总产值 (万元) Gross Output Value (10000 yuan)	年末从业人员 (人) Employed Persons (year-end) (person)	签订合同额 (万元) Value of Contract Signed (10000 yuan)	竣工产值 (万元) Output Value of Completion (10000 yuan)
合　计	**Total**	**82097957**	**510464**	**212418540**	**40580704**
按企业登记注册类型分	**By Registration Type**				
内资企业	Domestically-funded Enterprises	81050084	498420	209294541	39901906
国有企业	State-owned Enterprises	2849259	25765	8305861	3099487
集体企业	Collectively-owned Enterprises	1347434	17159	1819819	941650
股份合作企业	Joint-equity Cooperative Enterprises	406998	6928	520341	376373
联营企业	Associate Enterprises	1694	3	418	1694
有限责任公司	Limited Liability Companies	63423006	322491	174838520	29751168
股份有限公司	Companies Limited by Shares	6597523	16251	14187874	1916675
私营企业	Private Enterprises	6424171	109823	9621709	3814858
其他企业	Others				
港、澳、台商投资企业	Hong Kong, Macao and Taiwan-invested Enterprises	653094	6143	1499269	487169
外商投资企业	Foreign-invested Enterprises	394778	5901	1624730	191629
按隶属关系分	**By Affiliation**				
中　央	Central	44854508	178412	136972368	19339792
地　方	Local	37243449	332052	75446172	21240911
按行业分	**By Sector**				
房屋建筑业	Construction of Buildings	43188968	199843	122949593	23352557
土木工程建筑业	Civil Engineering Construction	25272524	125151	64904895	10764503
建筑安装业	Construction Installation	6761269	96498	14631145	2722643
建筑装饰和其他建筑业	Building Decoration and Other Construction	6875195	88972	9932908	3741002

注：1. 统计范围为施工总承包、专业承包的法人建筑业企业（下表同）。
2. 行业划分执行2011年国民经济行业分类标准(GB/T 4754-2011)。

Note: a) Statistics covers general contracting and specialized contracting corporate construction enterprises(same as the following table).
b) Sectors in this table are classified in accordance with the Standard for Classification of National Economic Sectors in 2011(GB/T 4754-2011).

12-3 建筑业施工企业主要财务指标(2014年)

单位：万元

项目	Item	企业单位个数(个) Number of Enterprises (unit)	资产负债 Assets and Liabilities						
			资产总计 Total Assets	流动资产合计 Total Current Assets	#应收账款 Accounts Receivable	固定资产合计 Total Fixed Assets	固定资产原价 Total Original Value of Fixed Assets	负债合计 Total Liabilities	#流动负债合计 Total Current Liabilities
合计	**Total**	**3426**	**179093098**	**123118125**	**26738746**	**5099668**	**8267704**	**126323348**	**111189006**
按企业登记注册类型分	**By Registration Type**								
内资企业	Domestically-funded Enterprises	3343	177316605	121495492	26216715	5028235	8151568	124975097	109877552
国有企业	State-owned Enterprises	87	9371743	6918924	1179553	414518	826538	5902003	5215007
集体企业	Collectively-owned Enterprises	110	1812602	1447736	150386	82563	140561	1466836	1450586
股份合作企业	Joint-Equity Cooperative Enterprises	61	487312	431733	52989	33330	66716	312655	301825
联营企业	Associate Enterprises	1	***	***	***	***	***	***	***
有限责任公司	Limited Liability Companies	1198	109341509	88213803	21218482	3491591	5651789	90115772	83800293
股份有限公司	Companies Limited by Shares	56	47685346	17240240	1727708	404517	535606	21918265	14033217
私营企业	Private Enterprises	1830	8617289	7242254	1886971	601714	930320	5259247	5076304
其他企业	Others								
港、澳、台商投资企业	Hong Kong, Macao and Taiwan- invested Enterprises	42	751237	725585	184729	20697	39665	619538	604462
外商投资企业	Foreign-invested Enterprises	41	1025256	897047	337302	50736	76471	728713	706992
按隶属关系分	**By Affiliation**								
中　央	Central	197	124424101	77171422	15320581	2677596	4354661	84073585	71690401
地　方	Local	3229	54668997	45946703	11418165	2422072	3913043	42249763	39498605
按国民经济行业分	**By Sector**								
房屋建筑业	Construction of Buildings	611	76663145	59040710	14967393	1715007	3010650	58072252	51597058
土木工程建筑业	Civil Engineering Construction	566	81959005	46850074	7414893	1806310	3306229	53207217	45059171
建筑安装业	Construction Installation	814	10250802	8600163	2046210	594211	793811	7611297	7422962
建筑装饰和其他建筑业	Building Decoration and Other Construction	1435	10220146	8627178	2310250	984140	1157014	7432582	7109814

注：1. 行业划分执行2011年国民经济行业分类标准(GB/T 4754-2011)。
2. 应交税金合计包括应交增值税、应交所得税、营业税金及附加和管理费用中的税金。

MAIN FINANCIAL INDICATORS OF CONSTRUCTION ENTERPRISES (2014)

(10000 yuan)

			损益 Profits and Loss							应交税金合计		
#应付账款 Accounts Payable	所有者权益合计 Total Owner's Equity	#实收资本 Paid-up Capital	营业收入 Business Income	#主营业务收入 Main Business Income	营业成本 Business Cost	#主营业务成本 Main Business Cost	管理费用 Management Expenses	财务费用 Financial Expenses	利润总额 Total Profits	应交税金合计 Total Taxes Payable	#营业税金及附加 Business Tax and Surtax	#主营业务税金及附加 Main Business Tax and Surtax
39884691	**52769750**	**24613753**	**105591478**	**104922480**	**96491260**	**96025806**	**3644108**	**754754**	**4731726**	**3314317**	**2500247**	**2474244**
39403008	52341508	24337300	103516350	102870005	94630026	94180646	3545042	751125	4695612	3245331	2453967	2428202
1700004	3469740	1557556	6035041	5996538	5608832	5580718	203868	-2901	226235	174652	112595	112110
339077	345766	189338	1454451	1444080	1291225	1286348	93833	-2908	54897	54720	42728	42391
49607	174657	102769	445050	434359	396254	386667	18600	1989	16177	18907	14506	14290
***	***	***	***	***	***	***	***	***	***	***	***	***
32965104	19225738	11861514	81509859	81043295	74848548	74518894	2443752	484627	2439569	2534518	1963676	1941876
2505640	25767081	7897407	6321122	6302408	5823094	5805896	259377	252185	1820792	166843	82525	81413
1843556	3358043	2728216	7750409	7648907	6661727	6601778	525554	18133	137940	295677	237924	236108
158511	131699	125835	961708	947136	880111	868336	46128	962	1065	33066	24632	24558
323171	296543	150619	1113421	1105339	981124	976825	52938	2667	35049	35919	21648	21483
26603961	40350516	16305966	62576203	62400113	57971621	57859702	1660302	457989	3790174	1815829	1287370	1272445
13280729	12419234	8307787	43015275	42522367	38519639	38166104	1983806	296765	941553	1498488	1212877	1201799
22357980	18590894	9009117	50970421	50666285	47141664	46919107	1379213	415734	2038039	1556833	1167353	1158321
13006745	28751788	11833743	35945609	35762434	32944890	32829796	1241334	289583	2240179	1084656	818942	813587
2577653	2639504	1786034	9830231	9727495	8720034	8641022	532575	7686	257879	336916	257620	255400
1942313	2787564	1984860	8845217	8766267	7684672	7635882	490986	41751	195629	335912	256332	246937

Note: a) Sectors in this table are classified in accordance with the Standard for Classification of National Economic Sectors 2011 (GB/T 4754-2011).
b) Total tax payable mainly includes VAT payable, income tax payable, business tax and surtax, and tax in management expenses.

12-3 续表 Continued

项目	Item	#应交所得税 Income Tax Payable (10000 yuan)	#应交增值税 Value Added Tax Payable	流动比率(倍) Current Ratio (times)	速动比率(倍) Quick Ratio (times)	资产负债率(%) Assets-Liabilities Ratio (%)	资本金利润率(%) Capital-Profit Ratio (%)
合计	**Total**	**666347**	**92312**	**1.11**	**0.93**	**70.5**	**19.2**
按企业登记注册类型分	**By Registration Type**						
内资企业	Domestically-funded Enterprises	651401	85547	1.11	0.93	70.5	19.3
国有企业	State-owned Enterprises	36466	21548	1.33	0.97	63.0	14.5
集体企业	Collectively-owned Enterprises	10478	286	1.00	0.64	80.9	29.0
股份合作企业	Joint-Equity Cooperative Enterprises	3826	391	1.43	0.99	64.2	15.7
联营企业	Associate Enterprises			2.5	2.33	39.9	0.3
有限责任公司	Limited Liability Companies	485525	48138	1.05	0.87	82.4	20.6
股份有限公司	Companies Limited by Shares	75936	4186	1.23	1.16	46.0	23.1
私营企业	Private Enterprises	39170	10997	1.43	1.19	61.0	5.1
其他企业	Others						
港、澳、台商投资企业	Hong Kong, Macao and Taiwan-invested Enterprises	5049	2779	1.20	0.97	82.5	0.8
外商投资企业	Foreign-invested Enterprises	9897	3986	1.27	1.06	71.1	23.3
按隶属关系分	**By Affiliation**						
中央	Central	458704	44459	1.08	0.93	67.6	23.2
地方	Local	207643	47853	1.16	0.93	77.3	11.3
按国民经济行业分	**Grouped by Sector**						
房屋建筑业	Construction of Buildings	357601	7322	1.14	0.94	75.7	22.6
土木工程建筑业	Civil Engineering Construction	209573	39326	1.04	0.89	64.9	18.9
建筑安装业	Construction Installation	51641	20033	1.16	0.96	74.3	14.4
建筑装饰和其他建筑业	Building Decoration and Other Construction	47532	25632	1.21	1.05	72.7	9.9

12-4 建筑业施工企业竣工率
PROJECT COMPLETION RATE OF CONSTRUCTION ENTERPRISES

单位：% (%)

项 目	Item	产值竣工率 Completion Rate by Output Value		面积竣工率 Completion Rate by Floor Space	
		2014	2013	2014	2013
合 计	**Total**	**49.4**	**47.9**	**16.4**	**18.2**
按企业登记注册类型分	**By Registration Type**				
内资企业	Domestically-funded Enterprises	49.2	47.8	16.4	18.2
国有企业	State-owned Enterprises	108.8	75.4	26.1	19.0
集体企业	Collectively-owned Enterprises	69.9	47.7	32.1	21.4
股份合作企业	Joint-equity Cooperative Enterprises	92.5	63.0	49.5	29.2
联营企业	Associate Enterprises				
有限责任公司	Limited Liability Companies	46.9	45.8		18.1
股份有限公司	Companies Limited by Shares	29.1	32.4	12.2	15.1
私营企业	Private Enterprises	59.4	63.3		26.3
其他企业	Others				
港、澳、台商投资企业	Hong Kong, Macao and Taiwan-invested Enterprises	74.6	60.9	8.9	6.0
外商投资企业	Foreign-invested Enterprises	48.5	49.6	20.5	38.3
按隶属关系分	**By Affiliation Relationship**				
中 央	Central	43.1	43.9	13.5	16.6
地 方	Local	57.0	52.5	22.2	21.0
按国民经济行业分	**By Sector**				
房屋建筑业	Construction of Buildings	54.1	58.0	16.2	18.5
土木工程建筑业	Civil Engineering Construction	42.6	30.0	23.3	9.9
建筑安装业	Construction Installation	40.3	45.1	15.2	17.2
建筑装饰和其他建筑业	Building Completion, Finishing and Other Construction	54.4	49.3	0.1	1.0

注：行业划分执行2011年国民经济行业分类标准(GB/T 4754-2011)。
Note: Sectors in this table are classified in accordance with the Standard for Classification of National Economic Sectors in 2011 (GB/T 4754-2011).

主要统计指标解释

建筑业总产值 是以货币表现的建筑业企业在一定时期内生产的建筑产品和服务的总和。它包括建筑工程产值、设备安装工程产值、其他产值三部分内容。

(1)**建筑工程产值** 指列入建筑工程预(概)算内的各种工程价值。

(2)**安装工程产值** 指为设备安装而发生的安装工程费用，在设备安装产值中，不得包括被安装设备本身价值。

(3)**其他产值** 建筑业总产值中除建筑工程、安装工程以外的产值，包括房屋构筑物修理产值、非标准设备制造产值、总包企业向分包企业收取的管理费，以及不能明确划分的施工活动所完成的产值。

年末从业人员 指年末最后一日24小时在本单位工作，并取得工资或其他形式劳动报酬的人员数。该指标为时点指标，不包括最后一日当天及以前与单位解除劳动合同关系的人员，是在岗职工、劳务派遣人员及其他从业人员之和。

房屋施工面积 指报告期内施过工的全部房屋建筑面积，包括：本期新开工的房屋面积、上期施工跨入本期继续施工的房屋面积、上期停缓建本期复工的房屋面积、本期开工又停缓建和本期竣工的房屋面积。

房屋竣工面积 指在报告期内房屋建筑按照设计要求已全部完工，达到了住人和使用条件，经检查验收鉴定合格或达到竣工验收标准，可正式移交使用的房屋建筑面积。

签订合同额 指建筑业企业在报告期直接同建设单位签订合同的总价款和以前年度同建设单位签定合同的未完工程跨入本年度继续施工工程合同的总价款余额。

主营业务收入 指企业确认的销售商品、提供劳务等主营业务的收入。

主营业务成本 指企业经营主要业务所发生的成本总额。

主营业务税金及附加 指企业经营主要业务应负担的营业税、消费税、城市维护建设税、教育费附加等。

主营业务利润 指企业经营主要业务实现的利润。

利润总额 指企业在一定会计期间的经营成果，是生产经营过程中各种收入扣除各种耗费后的盈余，反映企业在报告期内实现的亏盈总额。

Explanatory Notes on Main Statistical Indicators

Gross Output Value of Construction refers to total of construction products and services, expressed in money terms, completed by construction and installation enterprises during a given period of time. It includes: output value of construction works, output value of installation works and other output value.

(1) Output Value of Construction Works means the value of works involved in project budgets.

(2) Output Value of Installation Works means the costs of installation works incurred for equipment installation. Output value of equipment installation does not include the value of installed equipment itself.

(3) Other Output Value means, of the total output value of construction, the output value other than that of construction and installations works. It includes the repair output value of houses and structures, manufacturing output value of non-standard equipment, management charges collected by general contracting enterprises from subcontracting enterprises, as well as the output value of construction activities falling in no specific categories.

Year-end Employed Persons refers to the number of employed persons who work during the 24 hours of the last day in a year and acquire wage or other forms of labor income. This time-spot index, which does not include persons who terminate their labor contracts at or before the last day of the year, is the sum of fully employed persons, dispatched personnel of labor service and other employed persons.

House Construction Area means the building area of all houses in the reporting period, including: the area of houses newly started in current period, area of houses built in the previous period and continued in current period, area of houses suspended in the previous period and restarted in current period, area of houses started and suspended in current period, and area of houses completed in current period.

Area of Houses Completed means the area of houses and buildings entirely completed in line with requirements of design, meeting conditions of living and use, satisfactorily accepted by relevant authorities or reaching standards for completion inspection and officially delivered and used in the reporting period.

Value of Signed Contracts means total price of contracts signed directly between construction and installation enterprises and builders in the reporting period and the balance of total price of contracts signed with builders in previous year and continued the implementation in the current year.

Main Business Income means the income recognized by an enterprise from main business such as sale of commodities and rendering of service.

Main Business Cost means the total cost incurred in an enterprise for the operation of main business.

Main Business Tax and Surtax means the sales tax, excise, urban maintenance and construction tax, educational surcharge, etc. to be paid by an enterprise for the operation of main business.

Main Business Profit means the profit reaped by an enterprise in its operation of main business.

Total Profits mean the operating result of an enterprise in certain accounting period. It is the surplus of all revenues deducting all costs in its production and operation, reflecting its total profit and loss realized in the reporting period.

13

交通运输邮电

TRANSPORT, POST AND TELECOMMUNICATON SERVICES

简要说明

一、本章资料的主要内容

本章资料反映北京市交通运输业和邮政电信业发展的基本状况。

交通运输业资料主要包括：铁路、公路、民航、管道四种运输方式的线路条数、里程、总运量及周转量、主要技术经济指标（不含管道）；机动车拥有情况。

邮政电信业资料主要包括：邮电业务完成情况、邮政电信发展水平等资料。

二、各部分资料的调查范围及数据来源

1. 铁路资料：主要是国家铁路运营情况，不含地方铁路、合资铁路和军用铁路及由厂矿企事业单位自建的铁路专用线和专用铁道，资料来源于北京铁路局。

2. 公路资料：(1)公路里程为年末通车里程数，不含在建和未正式投入使用的公路里程；(2)公路运输统计范围包括在北京市注册从事公路货运的全部企事业单位和私人(包括个体联户)，资料来源于北京市交通委员会。

3. 管道运输资料：包括输送原油、成品油、天然气以及其他气体的管线长度、输送能力及完成的运输量。管道运输统计数据主要来源于中石油北京天然气管道有限公司和中国石油化工股份有限公司北京燕山分公司所属的管道运输企业，由两家集团公司分别负责收集审核本部门统计数据。

4. 民航运输资料：不包括在京运输飞行的外省市及外国航空公司。统计范围为各航空公司从事国内运输、港澳台运输、国际运输的定期航班航线条数及里程、运输量等。2009年及以前数据主要来源于中国国际航空公司、新华航空有限责任公司，2010年起为北京地区的民航运输法人单位。

5. 邮政电信资料：包括邮政和电信运营企业为社会公众提供的各类邮政和电信服务，不含专用网业务资料。邮电业务量按业务种类分为邮政业务量和电信业务量。数据主要来源于北京市邮政公司、中国联合网络通信有限公司北京市分公司、中国移动通信集团北京有限公司、中国铁通集团有限公司北京分公司、中国电信股份有限公司北京分公司。

6. 民用汽车拥有量资料：民用汽车指在公安交通管理部门已注册登记领有民用车辆牌照的全部汽车数量。民用汽车根据汽车结构分为载客汽车、载货汽车及其他汽车；根据汽车所有者不同分为私人汽车、单位汽车。民用汽车数据来自于北京市公安局公安交通管理局。

Brief Introduction

I. Main Content

Figures in this chapter show the basic situation of development of transport, post and telecommunication in Beijing.

Transportation statistics include the number of lines, mileage, total volume of transport, turnover and main technological and economic indicators (excluding pipelines) for four transport modes, i.e. railway, highway, civil aviation, and pipeline,; and number of motor vehicles.

Post and telecommunication statistics include: performance of post and telecom services, development level of post and telecommunication sector, and so on.

II. Scope of Survey and Source of Data

1. Data on railways: including the operation of national railways, excluding local railways, railways built by joint ventures, military railways, and dedicated lines and railways built by factories, mines, enterprises and public institutions. These data are from Beijing Railway Bureau.

2. Data on highways: (1) highway mileage covers highways open to traffic at the year end, excluding those under construction and not put into use; (2) highway transport statistics cover all enterprises and public institutions as well as individuals (including self-employed) registered in Beijing for highway cargo transportation. These data are from Beijing Municipal Commission of Transport.

3. Data on pipeline transport: including the length, capacity and completed traffic of pipelines for transport of crude oil, refined oil, natural gas, and other gases. These data are mainly from Beijing Natural Gas Pipelines Co., Ltd. of Sinopec and CNPC. Statistical data on the pipelines transportation business affiliated to Beijing Yanshan Branch were collected and reviewed by the two corporations mentioned above respectively.

4. Data on civil aviation: excluding non-local and foreign airlines flying and operating in Beijing. Statistics consist of the number, mileage, and traffic volume of regular flight lines for domestic transport, transport from and to Hong Kong, Macao and Taiwan, and international transport. Data for 2009 and earlier are sourced from Air China and Xinhua Airline; from 2010, from corporate entities of civil aviation transport in Beijing area.

5. Data on post and telecommunication: including those on postal and telecom services offered by post and telecom operators, excluding data on services of dedicated networks. Business volume falls into two categories, namely postal service and telecommunication service. Data are mainly sourced from Beijing Post and Telecom Company, Beijing Branch of China Unicom, China Mobile Beijing Company, Beijing Branch of China Tietong, and Beijing Branch of China Telecom.

6. Data on number of civil automobiles: civil automobiles refer to all vehicles registered with traffic administration and granted license plates. In terms of automobile structure, civil automobiles consist of passenger automobiles, cargo automobiles, and so on; in terms of ownership, they include private and company ones. These data are sourced from Beijing Traffic Management Bureau.

13-1 交通运输邮电业基本情况(1978-2014年)
TRANSPORT, POST AND TELECOMMUNICATION (1978-2014)

年份 Year	铁路里程(公里) Railway Mileage (km)	公路里程(公里) Highway Mileage (km)	客运量(万人) Passenger Traffic (10000 persons)	铁路 Railway	公路 Highway	民航 Civil Aviation	货运量(万吨) Freight Traffic (10000 tons)	铁路 Railway	公路 Highway	民航 Civil Aviation	管道 Pipeline
1978	699	6562	4431	2264	2120	47	7394	3370	4023	1	
1979	700	7278	4777	2504	2220	53	7764	3485	4277	2	
1980	707	7487	5285	2762	2465	58	7571	3356	4213	2	
1981-1985			**33230**	**17688**	**15058**	**484**	**45456**	**15425**	**29063**	**14**	**954**
1981	858	7566	5877	2982	2824	71	8546	3046	5498	2	
1982	858	7683	6215	3205	2931	79	9097	3065	5812	2	218
1983	860	8058	6662	3546	3038	78	9403	3152	6016	3	232
1984	864	8271	7273	3877	3287	109	9671	3133	6301	3	234
1985	876	8482	7203	4078	2978	147	8739	3029	5436	4	270
1986-1990			**38506**	**21290**	**16160**	**1056**	**121771**	**15518**	**104929**	**41**	**1283**
1986	876	8995	7337	4106	3059	172	22121	3030	18794	6	291
1987	876	9103	7763	4418	3117	228	23068	3125	19734	8	201
1988	876	9124	8491	4782	3460	249	24749	3168	21308	9	264
1989	876	9371	7434	4214	3034	186	25184	3144	21767	8	265
1990	876	9648	7480	3770	3490	220	26648	3051	23326	10	262
1991-1995			**40918**	**20615**	**18010**	**2292**	**147385**	**14923**	**131956**	**79**	**427**
1991	876	10259	7704	4036	3378	289	26804	2983	23739	11	71
1992	875	10827	8158	4196	3593	369	27707	2912	24700	14	80
1993	875	11260	7607	4374	2781	452	29865	3048	26730	17	70
1994	875	11532	8537	3992	4008	537	30825	3006	27700	19	99
1995	875	11811	8913	4017	4250	646	32184	2974	29087	17	106
1996-2000			**62554**	**19683**	**38888**	**3983**	**154376**	**13491**	**140455**	**125**	**304**
1996	922	12084	8801	3650	4395	756	32907	2851	29960	18	78
1997	924	12306	9263	3613	4902	748	32351	2883	29360	20	87
1998	924	12498	11228	3762	6704	762	30127	2563	27490	22	52
1999	997	12825	14866	4201	9878	788	28275	2583	25635	30	27
2000	997	13600	18396	4458	13009	929	30717	2612	28010	35	60
2001-2005			**191964**	**25350**	**157061**	**9553**	**156702**	**11053**	**144049**	**277**	**1323**
2001	987	13891	22469	4750	16630	1090	30607	2505	28007	38	57
2002	987	14359	28384	5032	22103	1249	30961	2348	28375	44	194
2003	964	14453	30520	4352	24940	1228	30925	2265	28361	45	254
2004	964	14630	49750	5437	41463	2850	31700	1959	29256	73	412
2005	966	14696	60841	5779	51925	3137	32509	1976	30050	77	406
2006-2010			**435377**	**37892**	**376377**	**21107**	**121931**	**8820**	**106451**	**508**	**6151**
2006	962	20503	12276	6269	2482	3525	33547	1956	30953	89	549
2007	962	20754	20040	6915	9275	3850	20770	1925	17872	98	875
2008	956	20340	128525	7644	117118	3763	21885	1733	18689	93	1369
2009	956	20755	133872	8161	121373	4339	22017	1635	18753	98	1531
2010	956	21114	140663	8903	126130	5630	23712	1572	20184	130	1827
2011	1067	21347	145773	9755	129918	6100	26849	1380	23276	132	2061
2012	1115	21492	149037	10315	132333	6389	28650	1232	24925	134	2359
2013	1116	21673	71056	11588	52481	6988	28294	1078	24651	136	2429
2014	1124	21849	71715	12609	52354	6752	29518	1132	25416	149	2821

注：1. 铁路数据为北京市市辖范围，2005年以前取自北京铁路分局，2005年及以后取自北京铁路局。
2. 从2006年开始，公路里程包括村道数据。
3. 2006-2007年公路客运量为持有道路运输经营许可证的客运车辆发生的旅客运输量；从2008年开始，公路客运量根据交通运输部《公路水路运输量专项调查方案》调整旅客运输量统计口径,调整后包括旅游客运、省际客运企业、郊区客运和市郊公交的运输量。2013年公路客运量、公路旅客周转量按照《交通运输部办公厅关于印发公路水路运输量统计试行方案(2014)的通知》，统计范围调整为省际客运、旅游客运和郊区客运，市郊公交不再纳入客运量统计。
4. 从2007年开始,公路货物运输为营业性运量。
5. 民航统计范围为北京地区的民航运输法人单位，不包括在京运输飞行的外省市及外国航空公司。

Note: a) Railway figures are statistics within Beijing's jurisdiction. Figures for years before 2005 were from Beijing Railway Branch, those in and after 2005 were from Beijing Railway Bureau.
b) From 2006, road mileage includes figures of rural roads.
c) In 2006 and 2007, highway passenger traffic refered to numbers of passengers traveled by vehicles with road transportation permit ; From 2008, highway passenger traffic refers to passengers travelled for tourism, cross-provincial, suburban and peri-urban purposes, in line with the adjustments made in Special Survey Program for Highway and Water Way Transportation Volume by the Ministry of Traffic and Transportation. In 2013, according to the Notice by the General Office of the Ministry of Transport on Printing and Issuing Provisional Plan for Counting Highway and Water Way Transportation Volume,the statistical scope of highway passenger traffic and highway passenger turnover was changed to inter-provincial, tourist and suburban transport, and suburban buses are no longer counted.
d) From 2007, highway freight traffic refers to freight for operational purpose.
e) Civil aviation covers legal entities of civil aviation registered in Beijing, excluding airlines of other provinces and other countries with transport and flight in Beijing.

13-1 续表 1 Continued 1

年份 Year	旅客周转量(万人公里) Total Passenger Turnover (10000 passengers-km)	铁路 Railway	公路 Highway	民航 Civil Aviation	货物周转量(万吨公里) Total Freight Turnover (10000 ton-km)	铁路 Railway	公路 Highway	民航 Civil Aviation	管道 Pipeline
1978			59367				92247		
1979			64033				97616		
1980			73692				93899		
1981-1985			**498768**				**540035**		
1981			81879				93254		
1982	755815	641550	90092	24173	3451037	3329450	106767	13530	1290
1983	853655	723200	103742	26713	3794223	3666600	110118	16099	1406
1984	968481	821431	113871	33179	4309798	4171789	115740	20896	1373
1985	1089919	936300	109184	44435	4719663	4576400	114156	27437	1670
1986-1990	**6333894**	**2608550**	**649210**	**3076133**	**13703344**	**11007906**	**2496086**	**191715**	**7637**
1986	1133620	496288	119065	518267	2569579	2133836	405645	28281	1817
1987	1281763	534720	133735	613308	2792589	2282106	471393	37966	1124
1988	1503508	588947	141625	772936	2887270	2344684	498391	42612	1583
1989	1216981	521263	122435	573283	2765660	2179878	546022	38194	1566
1990	1198022	467332	132350	598339	2688246	2067402	574635	44662	1547
1991-1995	**8690001**	**2645880**	**842807**	**5201314**	**15220745**	**11382191**	**3488944**	**346841**	**2769**
1991	1383465	506431	139041	737993	2799731	2153176	591187	54929	439
1992	1666810	531574	161735	973501	2938746	2230406	642200	65614	527
1993	1656130	551392	127461	977277	3143512	2301941	767790	73216	565
1994	1906718	547488	180030	1179200	3107722	2303265	725740	78142	575
1995	2076879	508995	234540	1333344	3231034	2393403	762027	74940	663
1996-2000	**12752549**	**2649587**	**1744526**	**8358436**	**14987253**	**10458031**	**3918017**	**609517**	**1688**
1996	2219196	459514	250488	1509194	3176234	2311011	784888	79983	352
1997	2272177	477538	261204	1533435	3129097	2263274	769190	96202	431
1998	2419787	505554	304592	1609641	2846652	1952602	783237	110470	343
1999	2701471	579759	400597	1721115	2838857	1929269	754264	155171	153
2000	3139918	627222	527645	1985051	2996414	2001875	826438	167691	410
2001-2005	**27318106**	**3454437**	**5282581**	**18581088**	**18786284**	**12470145**	**4130198**	**1121536**	**1064404**
2001	3462571	677146	529776	2255649	3159848	2167201	826437	165832	378
2002	3961623	642676	603510	2715437	3405498	2213728	835873	195792	160105
2003	3933077	619631	693100	2620346	3620777	2409620	789952	208058	213147
2004	7580057	738956	1582441	5258660	4022791	2571459	822992	270182	358158
2005	8380778	776028	1873754	5730996	4577370	3108137	854944	281672	332617
2006-2010	**53738139**	**4632513**	**10259436**	**38846188**	**22812698**	**12714298**	**4414583**	**1906235**	**3777583**
2006	8254536	890691	791947	6571898	4231243	2625719	885991	335693	383840
2007	9603464	908438	1474249	7220776	4490390	2684862	792883	376074	636572
2008	10419977	902281	2409604	7108091	4542168	2535249	840878	356744	809297
2009	11464758	935596	2677144	7852018	4412317	2293902	878887	355257	884271
2010	13995404	995507	2906492	10093405	5136580	2574567	1015944	482467	1063602
2011	15286501	1086609	3036655	11163237	6169272	3113203	1323259	474856	1257955
2012	15957877	1163833	3047757	11746287	6383052	3076143	1397736	489845	1419328
2013	14987719	1179555	1360831	12447333	6809063	3231824	1561929	491861	1523448
2014	16027249	1356313	1382967	13287969	6728238	2843623	1651938	553661	1679016

13-1 续表 2 Continued 2

年份 Year	机动车拥有量（万辆） Possession of Motor Vehicles (10000 units)	#民用汽车拥有量 Possession of Civil Motor Vehicles	#私人 Private	邮电业务总量（万元） Business Volume of Post and Telecommunications Service (10000 yuan)	年末固定电话用户数（万户） Number of Fixed Telephone Subscribers (10000 subscribers)	年末移动电话用户数（万户） Number of Mobile Phone Subscribers (10000 subscribers)	固定电话主线普及率（线/百人） Popularization Rate of Landline Telephones (lines/100 persons)	移动电话普及率（户/百人） Popularization Rate of Mobile Phones (subscribers/100 persons)	互联网宽带接入用户数（万户） Subscribers of Broad Band Internet (10000 subscribers)
1978		6.1		24114	7.3		0.8		
1979		7.0		26724	7.8		0.9		
1980		8.1		30047	8.4		0.9		
1981-1985				**204839**					
1981		8.9		31907	9.2		1.0		
1982		9.3		34777	9.8		1.1		
1983		9.8		38525	10.9		1.2		
1984		12.1		45629	12.1		1.3		
1985		16.0		54002	13.6		1.4		
1986-1990				**434582**					
1986		18.6		62079	16.5		1.6		
1987		19.3	0.7	71152	19.5		1.9		
1988		22.2	1.3	84331	23.8		2.2		
1989		24.8	2.4	98124	27.8		2.6		
1990		27.1	2.8	118896	33.3	0.3	3.1	0.03	
1991-1995				**1664508**					
1991		29.7	3.5	157418	39.5	0.7	3.6	0.1	
1992		34.1	4.9	215769	48.0	1.2	4.4	0.1	
1993		41.6	6.7	311251	66.5	3.2	6.0	0.3	
1994		48.1	8.5	418774	100.4	7.7	8.9	0.7	
1995		58.9	12.8	561296	150.5	16.9	12.0	1.4	
1996-2000				**6756754**					
1996		62.2	17.4	729022	195.7	31.0	15.5	2.5	
1997		78.4	29.8	930137	251.2	62.0	20.3	5.0	
1998		89.8	40.7	1290967	313.3	104.2	25.1	8.4	
1999		95.1	44.7	1659133	376.3	186.2	29.9	14.8	
2000	157.8	104.1	49.4	2147496	451.2	347.2	33.1	25.5	
2001-2005				**15331552**					
2001	169.9	114.5	62.4	2182782	525.7	629.4	38.0	45.4	
2002	189.9	133.9	81.1	2540454	585.5	919.5	41.1	64.6	
2003	212.4	163.1	107.1	3040327	682.7	1109.0	46.9	76.1	
2004	229.6	187.1	129.8	3438376	847.4	1340.7	56.8	89.8	
2005	258.3	214.6	154.0	4129614	943.5	1459.8	61.3	94.9	228.9
2006-2010				**40044606**					
2006	287.6	244.1	181.0	5046014	905.2	1571.1	56.5	98.1	281.2
2007	312.8	277.8	212.1	6726273	914.5	1598.3	54.6	95.4	347.2
2008	350.4	318.1	248.3	8008147	884.9	1616.2	50.0	91.3	382.7
2009	401.9	372.1	300.3	9175072	893.1	1825.4	48.0	98.1	451.7
2010	480.9	452.9	374.4	11089100 (4284217)	885.6	2129.8	45.1	108.6	545.6
2011	498.3	473.2	389.7	4878792	883.9	2575.9	43.8	127.6	523.4
2012	520.0	495.7	407.5	5464681	883.1	3168.0	42.7	153.1	572.0
2013	543.7	518.9	426.5	6524689	867.6	3373.8	41.0	159.5	534.7
2014	559.1	532.4	437.2	7511309	831.1	4076.2	39.3	232.2	552.7

注：1. 邮电业务总量2000年及以前按1990年不变价格计算，2001-2010年按2000年不变价格计算，2011年开始按2010年不变价格计算。表内2010年邮电业务总量是按2000年价格计算,()内数据是按2010年价格计算。

2. 2006-2010年主线普及率和移动电话普及率根据第六次人口普查数据进行了调整。

Note: a) Business volume of post and telecommunications before 2000 was calculated at 1990's constant prices; that of 2001-2010 was calculated at 2000's constant prices; and from 2011, the volume was calculated at 2010's constant prices. In this table, the volume of post and telecommunication service in 2010 was calculated at 2000's price, and figures in () were calculated at 2010's price.

b) Data of popularization rate of landline telephones and mobile phones for 2006-2010 were adjusted based on the results from the 6th population census .

13-2 社会客货运总量(换算周转量)
PASSENGER AND FREIGHT TRAFFIC (CONVERTED TURNOVER)

单位：万吨公里 (10000 tons-km)

项目	Item	2014	2013	2014年为2013年% 2014 as % of 2013	构成(%) Composition(%)	
					2014	2013
运输总量	**Total**	**9399252.6**	**9281235.4**	**101.3**	**100.0**	**100.0**
铁路	Railway	4199936.8	4411379.5	95.2	44.7	47.5
公路	Highway	1790234.7	1698012.1	105.4	19.0	18.3
民航	Civil Aviation	1730065.0	1648395.7	105.0	18.4	17.8
管道	Pipeline	1679016.1	1523448.1	110.2	17.9	16.4

13-3 运输线路
TRANSPORTATION ROUTES

项目	Item	条数(条) Number (line)		长度(公里) Length (km)	
		2014	2013	2014	2013
铁路	Railway	56	55	1123.6	1115.5
公路	Highway	10372	10289	21849	21673.3
民航	Civil Aviation				
#中国国际航空公司	Air China	322	298		
中国新华航空有限责任公司	China Xinhua Airlines	370	331		
管道	Pipeline	17	17	3825.5	3825.5

注：铁路长度为营业里程，管道长度为管输里程。
Note: Railway length refers to operating mileage, and pipeline length refers to transportation mileage.

13-4 铁路、民航主要技术经济指标

MAIN TECHNICAL AND ECONOMIC INDICATORS OF RAILWAY AND CIVIL AVIATION

项目	Item	2014	2013	2014年为2013年% 2014 as % of 2013
铁路	**Railway**			
内燃机车每万吨公里耗柴油（千克）	Diesel Consumption of Diesel Locomotives per 10 000 Ton-km (kg)	34.4	34.5	99.7
电力机车每万吨公里耗电（千瓦小时）	Electricity Consumption of Electric Locomotives per 10000 Ton-km (kwh)	100.3	95.4	105.1
民航	**Civil Aviation**			
每吨公里耗航空油（千克）	Aviation-oil Consumption per Ton-km (kg)	0.29	0.29	98.9

13-5 机动车拥有量

NUMBER OF CIVIL MOTOR VEHICLES

单位：万辆 (10000 units)

项目	Item	2014	2013	2014年为2013年% 2014 as % of 2013
机动车	**Motor Vehicles**	**559.1**	**543.7**	**102.8**
#民用汽车	Civil Automobiles	532.4	518.9	102.6
#载货汽车	Trucks	28.9	25.7	112.5
载客汽车	Passanger Vehicles	496.9	486.1	102.2
#私人汽车	Private Cars	437.2	426.5	102.5
#轿车	Sedans	316.5	311.0	101.8

资料来源：北京市公安局公安交通管理局。

Source: Beijing Traffic Management Bureau.

13-6 邮电业务主要指标
MAIN INDICATORS OF POST AND TELECOMMUNICATION SERVICE

项目		Item		2014	2013	2014年为2013年% 2014 as % of 2013
邮电业务总量	**(万元)**	**Business Volume of Post and Telecommunications**	**(10000 yuan)**	**7511308.7**	**6524689**	**115.1**
邮政业务量		Post		637602	584585	109.1
电信业务量		Telecommunications		6873707	5940104	115.7
邮电业务		**Total Amount of Post and Telecommunication Businesses**				
函　件	(万件)	Letters	(10000 pcs)	66091	71559	92.4
包　件	(万件)	Parcels	(10000 pcs)	500	582	85.9
特快专递业务量	(万件)	Express Mail Services	(10000 pcs)	111012	81818	135.7
汇　票	(万件)	Money Orders	(10000 pcs)	440	620	70.9
订销报纸(累计)	(万份)	Newspapers Subscribed	(10000 copies)	72504	81970	88.5
订销杂志(累计)	(万份)	Magazines Subscribed	(10000 copies)	3858	4695	82.2
邮政储蓄期末余额	(亿元)	Post Savings Deposit Balance	(100 million yuan)	764.1	748.8	102.0
长途电话通话量(固定)	(亿分钟)	Long-distance Calls (Fixed-line Telephone)	(100 million minutes)	42.4	42.2	100.6
本地电话通话量(固定)	(亿次)	Local Calls (Fixed-line Telephone)	(100 million times)	99.0	131.0	75.6
移动电话通话量	(亿分钟)	Calls of Mobile Phones	(100 million minutes)	1587.5	1536.0	103.4
移动短信业务量	(亿条)	Short Message Services	(100 million messages)	453.4	459.0	98.8
年末移动电话用户	(万户)	Mobile Phone Subscribers	(10000 subscribers)	4076.2	3373.8	120.8
#3G移动电话用户数	(万户)	3G Mobile Phone Subscribers	(10000 subscribers)	1928.8	1461.0	132.0
年末固定电话用户	(万户)	Fixed Telephone Subscribers	(10000 subscribers)	831.1	867.6	95.8
#住宅电话用户	(万户)	Household Telephone Subscribers	(10000 subscribers)	501.0	525.8	95.3
长途光缆纤芯长度	(芯公里)	Fiber Core Length of Long-distance Optic Cables	(core-km)	180670.0	180658.7	持平
长途电话交换机容量	(万路端)	Capacity of Long-distance Telephone Exchanges	(10000 roadheads)	53.8	56.6	95.1
局用交换机容量	(万门)	Capacity of Office Telephone Exchanges	(10000 units)	1514.5	1678.4	90.2
移动电话交换机容量	(万户)	Capacity of Mobile Phone Exchanges	(10000 subscribers)	4910	4820	101.9
固定电话主线普及率	(线/百人)	Popularization Rate of Fixed-line Telephone	(lines/100 persons)	39.3	41.0	
移动电话普及率	(户/百人)	Popularization Rate of Mobile Phones	(subscribers/100 persons)	232.2	159.5	
固定互联网宽带接入用户数	(万户)	Subscribers of Broad Band Internet	(10000 subscribers)	552.7	534.7	103.4
互联网上网人数	(万人)	Number of Internet Users	(10000 persons)	1593.0	1556.0	102.4

注：1. 邮电业务总量为2010年不变价计算。
2. "互联网上网人数"来源于中国互联网络信息中心（CNNIC）发布的《中国互联网络发展状况统计报告》。
3. 从2013年开始，特快专递业务量填报范围扩大为取得快递业务经营许可企业及其备案分支机构。

Note: a) Business volume of post and telecommunications is calculated based on constant price in 2010.
b) "Number of Internet Users" was sourced from the Statistical Report on Internet Development in China issued by CNNIC.
c) Since 2013, enterprises permitted to conduct express delivery businesses and their filed branches are required to submit the business volume of Express Mail Services.

主要统计指标解释

货（客）运量 指在一定时期内，各种运输工具实际运送的货物（旅客）数量。是反映运输业为国民经济和人民生活服务的数量指标，也是制定和检查运输生产计划，研究运输发展规模和速度的重要指标。货运按吨计算，客运按人计算。货物不论运输距离长短，货物类别，均按实际重量统计；旅客不论行程远近或票价多少，均按一人一次作为客运量统计。半价票、小孩票也按一人统计。

货物（旅客）周转量 指在一定时期内，由各种运输工具运送的货物（旅客）数量与其相应运输距离的乘积之总和，是反映运输业生产总成果的重要指标，也是编制和检查运输生产计划、计算运输效率、劳动生产率以及核算运输单位的主要基础资料。计算货物周转量通常按发出站与到达站之间的最短距离，也就是计费距离计算。

邮电业务总量 是以货币形式表示的邮政电信企业为社会提供各类邮政通信服务的总数量。计算公式为：

$$\text{邮电业务总量}=\sum\left(\text{各类邮政通信业务量}\times\text{不变单价}\right)+\text{出租代维及其他业务收入}$$

函件 是指邮政部门为用户传递以书面信息为主的邮件，包括信件、印刷品和邮送广告。

包件 指符合包裹准寄范围，通过邮政渠道寄递的物品。包括国内普通包裹、国内快递包裹、国际及港澳台包裹。

长途电话交换机容量 是指用于接入长途电话网的电话交换机的设备额定容量。

局用交换机容量 是指安装在本地电信企业内用于接续本地固定电话的电话交换机容量。包括现用和备用的人工或自动交换机（含远端模块）的全部容量，包括接入网设备容量。

移动电话交换机容量 分为 GSM、CDMA 两种。指移动电话交换机根据一定话务模型和交换机处理能力计算出来的最大同时服务用户的数量。

主线普及率 是指报告期行政区域常住人口中，平均每百人拥有的固定电话主线数。计算公式为：

$$\text{主线普及率}=\frac{\text{电话主线数(本地电话用户)}}{\text{行政区域常住人口数}}$$

移动电话普及率 是指报告期行政区域常住人口中，平均每百人拥有的移动电话的用户数。计算公式为：

$$\text{移动电话普及率}=\frac{\text{移动电话用户总数}}{\text{行政区域常住人口数}}$$

固定互联网宽带接入用户数 指报告期末在电信企业登记注册，通过 xDSL、FTTx+LAN 以及其他宽带接入方式和普通专线接入公众互联网的用户。

Explanatory Notes on Main Statistical Indicators

Freight (Passenger) Traffic refers to the volume of freight (passenger) transported with various means during a certain period of time. It is a quantitative measure to show how the transport industry serves the national economy and people's life, and is also an important indicator for preparing and reviewing transport plan and studying the development scale and speed of the transport industry. Freight transport is calculated in tons and passenger traffic is calculated in the number of persons. Regardless of the types or traveling distance of freight, freight transport is calculated in the actual weight of goods: and regardless of the traveling distance or ticket price, passenger traffic is calculated following the principle that one person can be counted only once in one travel. The passenger who travels with a half-price ticket or a child ticket is also calculated as one person.

Freight (Passenger) Turnover refers to the sum of the transported cargo (passengers) multiplied by the transport distance during a certain period of time. This is an important indicator to show the total results of the transport industry, and also serves as main basic data for preparing and reviewing transport plans and measuring transport efficiency, labor productivity and the transport unit. Freight Turnover is usually calculated by the shortest distance between the departure station and the arrival station, namely the charging distance.

Business Volume of Post and Telecommunications refers to the total amount of post and telecommunication services, expressed in monetary terms, provided by the post and telecommunication sectors for the society. The formula is as follows:

Business Volume of Post and Telecommunications

=∑(Transactions of Post and Telecommunication Service x Constant Price) + Income from Leasing, Maintenance and other Services

Correspondences mean mails mainly in the form of written information delivered by postal authorities, including letters, prints and delivered advertisements.

Parcels means articles permitted for mailing, and mailed through postal channels, including domestic express parcels,

international parcels, and parcels from and to Hong Kong, Macao and Taiwan.

Capacity of Long-distance Phone Exchanges means the rated capacity of phone exchangers used for connecting to the long-distance phone network.

Capacity of Local Exchanges means the capacity of phone exchangers installed in local telecom businesses and used for linking local fixed telephones. It is the sum of all capacity of existing and backup manual or automatic exchangers (with far-end modules), including the capacity of network access equipment.

Capacity of Mobile Phone Exchanges, divided into GSM and CDMA, means the maximum number of users receiving services simultaneously from mobile phone exchangers, calculated from certain traffic model and exchanger processing capacity.

Popularization Rate of Fixed-line Telephones means the average number of main lines of fixed-line telephones owned per one hundred persons of permanent population in administrative areas in the reporting period. It is calculated with the following formula:

Popularization Rate of Landline= Number of Main Lines of Telephone (Local Phone Users) / Number of Permanent Population in Administrative Areas

Popularization Rate of Mobile Phones means the average number of mobile phones owned per 100 persons among permanent population in administrative areas in the reporting period. It is calculated with the following formula:

Popularization Rate of Mobile Phones = Total Number of Mobile Phone Users / Permanent Population in Administrative Areas

Subscribers of Broadband Internet means subscribers registered at telecom companies to connect with public Internet through xDSL, FTTx+LAN as well as other broadband connections and general special lines at the end of reporting period.

14

批发和零售业、住宿和餐饮业

WHOLESALE AND RETAIL TRADE, ACCOMMODATION AND RESTAURANTS

简要说明

一、本章资料的主要内容

本章资料反映北京市商品流通市场发展及批发和零售业、住宿和餐饮业经营情况。主要内容有社会消费品零售总额；批发和零售业商品购进、销售、库存总值、商品分类销售情况及主要商品销售情况；住宿业和餐饮业经营情况；机动车销售情况；限额以上批发和零售业、住宿业和餐饮业财务状况；连锁企业基本情况；商品交易市场基本情况、成交额；北京消费者信心指数。

二、本章的统计范围

社会消费品零售总额指标于1993年、1997年和2003年做了较大调整。1993年起不再包括对农民的农业生产资料；1997年起不再包括居民购买住房；2003年起不再包括由各种经济类型的制造业法人企业、产业活动单位直接售给城乡居民（包括本企业职工）和社会集团的商品以及农民对非农业居民的零售额。

限额以上批发和零售业、住宿业和餐饮业统计限额标准：2008年以前，批发业为年销售额2000万元及以上；零售业为年销售额500万元及以上；住宿业为星级饭店和星级以外年营业收入500万元及以上；餐饮业为年营业额200万元及以上。2008年调整后，批发业为年主营业务收入2000万元及以上；零售业为年主营收入500万元及以上；住宿业为星级饭店和星级以外年主营业务收入200万元及以上；餐饮业为年主营业务收入200万元及以上。

北京消费者信心指数调查范围覆盖全市16个区县。

三、本章的资料来源

本章资料中所有资料均由北京市统计局、国家统计局北京调查总队提供。

四、本章的统计调查方法

限额以上批发和零售业、住宿和餐饮业单位采用全面调查的方法；连锁企业、商品交易市场采取全数调查；限额以下批发和零售业、住宿和餐饮业法人单位及个体户采用抽样调查方法。

北京消费者信心指数调查采用计算机辅助电话方式调查，调查对象为居住在北京市半年以上18-65周岁的城乡居民。

五、有关统计标准的变化说明

2010年以前企业大中小型划分执行2003年《统计上大中小型企业划分办法（暂行）》标准；自2011年开始，大中微型企业划分标准执行国家统计局《关于统计上大中小微型企业划分办法》（国统字[2011]75号）。

六、本章中关于历史数据调整的问题

按照国家统计局统一要求和统一方法，本章中1978年至2003年的社会消费品零售总额数据，根据第一次经济普查结果，采用“速度推算法”进行了修正，2004年数据为第一次经济普查数据；2005-2007年数据根据第二次经济普查结果，采用“趋势离差法”进行了修正，2008年数据为第二次经济普查数据；2009-2012年数据根据第三次经济普查结果进行了修正，2013年数据为第三次经济普查数据。

Brief Introduction

I. Main Content

Statistics in this chapter show the development of commodity circulation market and the operations of wholesale and retail trades, accommodation and restaurants. Figures mainly include retail sales of consumer goods, total value of commodity purchase, sales and inventory in wholesale and retail trades, sales of commodities by category, and sales of main commodities; operation situation of accommodation and restaurants; sales of mobile vehicles; financial status of wholesale, retail, accommodation and restaurants enterprises above designated size; basic situation of chain businesses; basic situation and turnover of commodity transaction markets, and trading volume of main commodities; and settlement of consumer complaints; and consumer confidence index.

II. Scope of Statistics

Major adjustments were made to the indicators of Retail Sales of Consumer Goods for 1993, 1997 and 2003. From 1993, the indicator did not cover agricultural means of production for farmers any longer; from 1997, it did not cover houses bought by residents any longer; from 2003, it did not cover goods sold by corporate manufacturing enterprises and industrial activity entities of various economic types to urban and rural residents (including enterprises' own employees) and social groups as well as retail sales by farmers to non-agricultural residents any longer.

As for standards for wholesale and retail trades, accommodation and restaurants above designated size, before 2008, for wholesale trades, the standard was annual sales of RMB 20 million and above; for retail trades, annual sales of RMB 5 million and above; for accommodation, star-rated hotels and non-star-rated hotels with annual turnover of RMB 5 million and above; for restaurants, annual turnover of RMB 2 million and above. After adjustments were made in 2008, the designated size is, for whole sale trades, annual sales of RMB 20 million and above; for retail trades, annual sales of RMB 5 million and above; for accommodation, star-rated hotels and non-star-rated hotels with annual main business income of RMB 2 million and above; for restaurants, annual main business income of RMB 2 million and above.

Survey of consumer confidence index covers 16 districts and counties in the City.

III. Source of Data

Data in settlement are all sourced from Beijing Municipal Bureau of Statistics and NBS Survey Office in Beijing.

IV. Survey Methodology

The method of comprehensive survey was used for statistics of wholesale and retail trades, accommodation, and restaurants service enterprises above designated size; complete enumeration was used for chain businesses, and commodity trading markets; sample survey was used for wholesale and retail trades, accommodation, and restaurants corporate enterprises below designated size as well as self-employed businesses.

Statistics on consumer confidence index were obtained through computer-aided phone calls to urban and rural residents at 18-65 who have been living in Beijing for more than half a year.

V. Changes in Relevant Statistical Standards

Before 2010，the classification of small, medium and large-sized enterprises should comply with the standard of *Measures for Statistical Classification of Small, Medium and Large-sized Enterprises (Temporary)* 2003. Since 2011, the classification of micro, small, medium and large-sized enterprises has been in line with standards of Circular by National Bureau of Statistics on Printing and Issuing the *Measures for Statistical Classification of Micro, Small, Medium and Large-sized Enterprises* (G.T.Z. [2011] No. 75).

VI. Adjustment to Historical Data

In accordance with the unified requirements and methods put forward by the National Bureau of Statistics, data for 1978-2003 on retail sales of consumer goods were adjusted with the "speed calculation method" according to the first economic census results in 2004. Data for 2004 are gathered from the first economic census. Data for 2005-2007 were revised with the "trend deviation method" in accordance with the second economic census results in 2008. Data for 2008 are gathered from the second economic census. Data for 2009-2012 were revised with the "trend deviation method" in accordance with the third economic census results in 2013. Data for 2013 were gathered from the third economic census.

14-1 历年社会消费品零售总额(1978-2014年)
TOTAL RETAIL SALES OF CONSUMER GOODS (1978-2014)

单位：亿元 (100 million yuan)

年份 Year	社会消费品零售总额 Total Retail Sales of Consumer Goods	按商品类别分 By Category of Commodity			
		吃类商品 Food	穿类商品 Clothing	用类商品 Daily Supplies	烧类商品 Fuels
1978	44.2	18.0	8.9	16.0	1.3
1979	53.3	20.8	11.3	19.7	1.5
1980	62.8	24.9	13.4	22.9	1.6
1981-1985	**472.7**	**180.9**	**85.1**	**196.2**	**10.5**
1981	70.7	28.0	14.5	26.5	1.7
1982	75.4	29.7	13.7	30.3	1.7
1983	86.4	34.0	15.7	34.8	1.9
1984	105.8	39.6	18.7	45.2	2.3
1985	134.4	49.6	22.5	59.4	2.9
1986-1990	**1239.8**	**494.9**	**166.7**	**551.8**	**26.4**
1986	155.0	60.7	22.8	68.0	3.5
1987	188.9	77.4	27.4	80.2	3.9
1988	256.0	100.6	36.0	114.9	4.5
1989	294.8	119.4	34.9	134.1	6.4
1990	345.1	136.8	45.6	154.6	8.1
1991-1995	**3239.5**	**1261.4**	**481.3**	**1422.2**	**74.6**
1991	408.3	158.2	53.7	187.6	8.8
1992	503.0	193.6	66.9	230.5	12.0
1993	611.2	220.7	96.5	277.6	16.4
1994	766.6	283.2	125.3	338.6	19.5
1995	950.4	405.7	138.9	387.9	17.9
1996-2000	**6811.7**	**2177.0**	**858.9**	**3576.5**	**199.3**
1996	1061.6	427.5	152.5	461.8	19.8
1997	1208.5	447.9	161.6	565.6	33.4
1998	1373.6	399.8	167.2	764.2	42.4
1999	1509.3	430.4	178.8	852.9	47.2
2000	1658.7	471.4	198.8	932.0	56.5
2001-2005	**11671.8**	**3061.2**	**1218.6**	**6722.7**	**669.3**
2001	1831.4	528.7	221.9	1016.9	63.9
2002	2005.2	540.2	219.9	1167.4	77.7
2003	2296.9	596.4	252.3	1356.4	91.8
2004	2626.6	644.9	242.1	1538.3	201.3
2005	2911.7	751.0	282.4	1643.7	234.6
2006-2010	**23503.8**	**5388.2**	**2126.1**	**14130.0**	**1859.5**
2006	3295.3	818.8	314.7	1852.6	309.2
2007	3835.2	940.4	359.3	2205.2	330.3
2008	4645.5	1073.3	411.7	2799.4	361.1
2009	5387.5	1201.0	482.2	3319.6	384.7
2010	6340.3	1354.7	558.2	3953.2	474.2
2011	7222.2	1636.6	712.7	4310.0	562.9
2012	8123.5	1759.9	769.3	4999.5	594.8
2013	8872.1	1804.7	777.1	5711.1	579.2
2014	9638.0	1860.5	783.3	6413.5	580.7

注：1978-2003年社会消费品零售额按2004年第一次经济普查数据进行了修订，2004年为第一次经济普查数据，2005-2007年数据按第二次经济普查进行了修订，2008年数据为第二次经济普查数据；2009-2012年数据根据第三次全国经济普查数据进行了修订，2013年数据为第三次全国经济普查数据。

Note: Retail sales of consumer goods for 1978-2003 were revised according to the first economic cencus in 2004. Figures for 2004 were gathered from the first economic census. Figures for 2005-2007 were revised based on the results of the second economic census. Figures for 2008 were gathered from the second economic census.Data for 2009-2012 were revised acording to the third national economic census; and data for 2013 were collected from the third national economic census.

14-2 社会消费品零售总额(2010-2014年)
TOTAL RETAIL SALES OF CONSUMER GOODS (2010-2014)

单位：亿元 (100 million yuan)

项 目	Item	2010	2011	2012	2013	2014	2014年为2013年% 2014 as % of 2013
社会消费品零售总额	**Total Retail Sales of Consumer Goods**	**6340.3**	**7222.2**	**8123.5**	**8872.1**	**9638.0**	**108.6**
按商品类别分	**By Category of Commodity**						
吃类商品	Food	1354.7	1636.6	1759.9	1804.7	1860.5	103.1
穿类商品	Clothing	558.2	712.7	769.3	777.1	783.3	100.8
用类商品	Daily Supplies	3953.2	4310.0	4999.5	5711.1	6413.5	112.3
烧类商品	Fuels	474.2	562.9	594.8	579.2	580.7	100.3
按销售单位所在地分	**By Location of Seller**						
城 镇	Urban	6238.0	7106.1	7995.1	8721.0	9471.5	108.6
农 村	Rural	102.3	116.1	128.4	151.1	166.5	110.2
按消费品形态分	**By Form of Consumer Goods**						
餐饮收入	Food and Beverage Income	678.5	817.8	880.2	836.1	829.7	99.2
商品零售	Retail Sales of Commodities	5661.8	6404.4	7243.3	8036.0	8808.3	109.6

注：2010年-2012年数据根据第三次全国经济普查进行了修订，2013年数据为第三次全国经济普查数据。

Note: Data for 2010-2012 were revised acording to the third national economic census; and data for 2013 were collected from the third national economic census.

14-3 按登记注册类型分限额以上批发和零售企业商品零售额(2014年)
RETAIL SALES OF GOODS IN WHOLESALE AND RETAIL ENTERPRISES ABOVE DESIGNATED SIZE BY REGISTRATION TYPE (2014)

单位：万元 (10000 yuan)

项 目	Item	合计 Total Sales	批发业 Wholesale	零售业 Retail Trade
总 计	**Total**	**79774062**	**8472656**	**71301406**
内资企业	Domestic Funded Enterprises	62688363	6118595	56569768
#国有	State-owned Enterprises	1311594	80977	1230617
集体	Collectively-owned Enterprises	416976	8638	408337
股份有限公司	Companies Limited by Shares	9291289	1288017	8003272
港澳台商投资企业	Hong Kong, Macao and Taiwan-invested Enterprises	5239846	541031	4698814
外商投资企业	Foreign-invested Enterprises	11845854	1813030	10032824

注：本表统计范围为限额以上批发和零售业法人单位、产业活动单位和个体经营户。

Note: Figures in this table cover legal entities in wholesale and retail trade above designated size, activity entities and individual entities .

14-4 批发和零售业商品购进、销售、库存情况
TOTAL VALUE OF PURCHASES, SALES AND INVENTORY OF COMMODITIES IN WHOLESALE AND RETAIL TRADE

单位：万元 (10000 yuan)

项目	Item	2014	2013	2014年为2013年% 2014 as % of 2013
商品购进额	**Total Purchases of Commodities**	**598222733**	**576922435**	**103.7**
市内购进	In the City	146762720	130171085	112.7
市外购进	From Outside Beijing	357719468	361457940	99.0
进口	Imported	93740545	85293410	109.9
商品销售额	**Total Sales of Commodities**	**665129727**	**619044895**	**107.4**
批发额	**Wholesale**	**577053329**	**538675930**	**107.1**
市内批发	In the City	146860106	133833421	109.7
市外批发	To Outside Beijing	403390728	383679144	105.1
出口	Exported	26802495	21163365	126.6
零售额	**Retail**	**88076398**	**80368965**	**109.6**
期末商品库存额	**Inventory (Year-end)**	**56129381**	**49672018**	**113.0**

注：本表统计范围为批发和零售业法人单位、产业活动单位和个体经营;2013年数据为第三次全国经济普查数据。
Note: Figures in this table cover legal entities in wholesale and retail trade above designated size, activity entities and individual entities; and data for 2013 were collected from the third national economic census.

14-5 限额以上批发和零售业商品购进、销售、库存情况(2014年)
TOTAL VALUE OF PURCHASES, SALES AND INVENTORY IN WHOLESALE AND RETAIL ENTERPRISES ABOVE DESIGNATED SIZE (2014)

单位：万元 (10000 yuan)

项目	Item	合计 Total Sales	批发业 Wholesale	零售业 Retail
商品购进额	**Total Purchases of Commodities**	**570130307**	**489890931**	**80239376**
市内购进	In the City	130725512	91040268	39685244
市外购进	From Outside Beijing	346650850	307999368	38651483
进口	Imported	92753946	90851296	1902650
商品销售额	**Total Sales of Commodities**	**600655245**	**512669802**	**87985443**
批发额	**Wholesale**	**520881183**	**504197146**	**16684036**
市内批发	In the City	131609469	123699763	7909706
市外批发	To Outside Beijing	362594916	354119056	8475860
出口	Exported	26676798	26378327	298471
零售额	**Retail**	**79774062**	**8472656**	**71301406**
期末商品库存额	**Inventory (Year-end)**	**54229553**	**46941952**	**7287602**

注：本表统计范围为限额以上批发和零售业法人单位、产业活动单位和个体经营户。
Note: Figures in this table cover legal entities in wholesale and retail trade above designated size, activity entities and individual entities.

14-6 限额以上批发和零售业商品销售类值(2014年)
SALES BY CATEGORY FOR WHOLESALE AND RETAIL ENTERPRISES ABOVE DESIGNATED SIZE (2014)

单位：万元 (10000 yuan)

项 目	Item	商品销售额 Total Sales	批发额 Wholesale	零售额 Retail
合 计	**Total**	**600655245**	**520881183**	**79774062**
粮油、食品类	Cereal, Oil and Food	20119989	14651306	5468684
#粮油类	Cereal and Oil	9895037	9167886	727150
肉禽蛋类	Meat, Poultry and Eggs	1845225	1090991	754234
饮料类	Beverages	3679229	3090262	588967
烟酒类	Tobacco and Liquor	9598969	8427632	1171337
服装鞋帽、针、纺织品类	Clothing, Shoes, Hats and Textiles	11549578	4858109	6691469
服装类	Clothing	7671776	2539967	5131809
鞋帽类	Shoes and Hats	2407417	1216323	1191094
针、纺织品类	Knitwear and Textiles	1470385	1101818	368567
化妆品类	Cosmetics	2713584	1100164	1613420
金银珠宝类	Gold, Silver and Jewelry	14152512	9896781	4255731
日用品类	Articles for Daily Use	7881774	4602204	3279570
#儿童玩具类	Children's Toys	209702	80993	128709
五金、电料类	Hardware and Electrical Materials	1561204	1419376	141828
体育、娱乐用品类	Sports and Recreation Goods	5534675	4569414	965261
书报、杂志类	Newspapers and Magazines	2144593	983713	1160880
电子出版物及音像制品类	E-Journals and Video Products	524640	268093	256547
家用电器和音像器材类	Household Appliances and Audiovisual Products	15419143	11676481	3742662
中西药品类	Traditional Chinese and Western Medicines	16768437	8846808	7921628
#西药类	Western Medicines	11775563	6404717	5370846
中草药及中成药类	Chinese Herbal Medicines and Chinese Patent Medicines	2838873	1218244	1620629
文化、办公用品类	Cultural and Office Goods	24593072	19434558	5158514
家具类	Furniture	1027566	145292	882274
通讯器材类	Communication Devices	49377909	39328829	10049080
煤炭及制品类	Coal and Coal Products	27049169	27044545	4625
木材及制品类	Wood and Wooden Products	2133715	2133715	
石油及制品类	Petroleum and Its Products	68110447	62637334	5473113
化工材料及制品类	Raw Chemical Materials	71872205	71872205	
#化肥类	Fertilizer	11973038	11973038	
金属材料类	Metal Materials	101872737	101872737	
建筑及装潢材料类	Building and Decoration Materials	3948463	3688697	259766
机电产品及设备类	Electric-mechanic Products and Equipment	27587519	27013449	574070
#农机类	Agricultural Machinery	286847	286847	
汽车类	Automobiles	84403229	65964441	18438788
种子饲料类	Seed and Feedstuff	1751396	1751396	
棉麻类	Cotton and Hemp	3582101	3581940	161
其他类	Others	21697391	20021704	1675687

注：本表统计范围为限额以上批发和零售业法人单位、产业活动单位和个体经营户。
Note: Figures in this table cover legal entities in wholesale and retail trade above designated size, activity entities and individual entities .

14-7 限额以上批发和零售业商品销售情况(2014年)
COMMODITY SALES OF WHOLESALE AND RETAIL ENTERPRISES ABOVE DESIGNATED SIZE (2014)

项目		Item		商品销售量 Total Sales	批发量 Wholesale Volume	零售量 Retail Volume
大米(稻米)	(百公斤)	Rice	(100 kg)	26020433	23604113	2416320
白面(小麦面)	(百公斤)	Flour (Wheat Flour)	(100 kg)	8728860	7959060	769800
杂　粮	(百公斤)	Coarse Cereals	(100 kg)	81997183	81764801	232382
食用植物油	(百公斤)	Edible Vegetable Oil	(100 kg)	37679735	36584286	1095450
猪　肉	(百公斤)	Pork	(100 kg)	2649103	1887039	762064
牛　肉	(百公斤)	Beef	(100 kg)	494128	369247	124881
羊　肉	(百公斤)	Mutton	(100 kg)	171030	92496	78534
禽　肉	(百公斤)	Poultry	(100 kg)	1980713	1758789	221924
鲜　蛋	(百公斤)	Fresh Eggs	(100 kg)	655790	188309	467480
鲜　菜	(百公斤)	Fresh Vegetable	(100 kg)	5356	1884	3472
鲜瓜果	(百公斤)	Fresh Melons and Fruits	(100 kg)	5483	2540	2943
水产品	(百公斤)	Aquatic Products	(100 kg)	2123	1714	408
食　糖	(百公斤)	Sugar	(100 kg)	33376	33012	364
卷　烟	(万支)	Cigarettes	(10000 units)	10359470	9940208	419262
酒	(百升)	Wine	(100 liter)	61977849	60313411	1664438
#白　酒	(百升)	Distillate Spirit	(100 liter)	4660344	3713553	946790
啤　酒	(百升)	Beer	(100 liter)	56619086	56168966	450119
茶　叶	(百公斤)	Tea	(100 kg)	97280	55220	42060
各种服装	(百件)	Clothing	(100 units)	5516434	3732033	1784401
鞋	(百双)	Shoes	(100 pairs)	1092800	738065	354735
数码照相机	(台)	Digital Cameras	(unit)	11307463	10495604	811859
自行车	(辆)	Bicycles	(unit)	504624	373197	131427
彩色电视机	(台)	Color TV Sets	(unit)	7903492	5204786	2698706
数码摄像机	(台)	Digital Video Cameras	(unit)	1166825	1037309	129516
家用电风扇	(台)	Household Electrical Fans	(unit)	1135044	856202	278842
电冰箱（家用电冰箱）	(台)	Household Refrigerators	(unit)	2846513	2056095	790418
洗衣机（家用洗衣机）	(台)	Household Washing Machines	(unit)	5712924	4901858	811066
家用空调器（房间空调器）	(台)	Household Air Conditioners (Room Air Conditioners)	(unit)	6830044	5747281	1082763
微波炉	(台)	Microwave Ovens	(unit)	1255863	914303	341560
热水淋浴器	(台)	Showers	(unit)	983787	477255	506532
吸尘器	(台)	Vacuum Cleaners	(unit)	1602947	1354785	248162
抽油烟机	(台)	Range Hoods	(unit)	631531	380983	250548
电脑（微型计算机）	(台)	Computers (Micro Computers)	(unit)	19056739	13541349	5515390
移动电话机	(部)	Mobile Phones	(unit)	279819887	230963724	48856163
煤　炭	(吨)	Coal	(ton)	486291190	486253143	38047
汽　油	(吨)	Gasoline	(ton)	11618387	7274392	4343995
煤　油	(吨)	Kerosene	(ton)	17279174	17279136	38
柴　油	(吨)	Diesel	(ton)	16181290	15219243	962047
钢　材	(吨)	Steel Products	(ton)	152513177	152511534	1643
水　泥	(吨)	Cement	(ton)	36453299	36276599	176700
汽　车	(辆)	Motor Vehicles	(unit)	2766150	2055661	710489
#轿　车	(辆)	Sedan Cars	(unit)	1609518	1026919	582599
化学肥料	(吨)	Chemical Fertilizers	(ton)	83292973	83292973	
化学农药	(吨)	Chemical Pesticides	(ton)	104007	104007	
铜	(吨)	Copper	(ton)	4187977	4187977	
铝	(吨)	Aluminium	(ton)	4898014	4898014	

注：本表统计范围为限额以上批发和零售业法人单位、产业活动单位和个体经营户。

Note: Figures in this table cover legal entities in wholesale and retail trade above designated size, activity entities and individual entities .

14-8 机动车销售情况(2001-2014年)
SALES OF MOTOR VEHICLES (2001-2014)

单位：万辆 (10000 units)

项目	Item	2001	2002	2003	2004	2005	2006	2007	2008	2009	2010	2011	2012	2013	2014
机动车销售量	**Sales of Motor Vehicles**	**22.9**	**26.0**	**40.8**	**44.7**	**57.0**	**71.4**	**79.8**	**87.8**	**114.8**	**143.2**	**79.7**	**128.5**	**128.2**	**127.5**
#轿车	Sedan Cars	11.4	15.1	25.2	27.2	38.0	46.2	52.7	54.5	70.6	92.4	49.0	83.2	80.5	74.2
新车	**New Vehicles**	**16.4**	**17.7**	**29.3**	**30.4**	**37.2**	**39.1**	**44.3**	**49.3**	**70.2**	**91.6**	**40.0**	**58.6**	**58.5**	**54.2**
#轿车	Sedan Cars	10.0	12.0	19.7	20.6	27.7	30.3	34.8	34.9	50.6	66.6	26.2	39.4	37.9	32.0
旧车	**Second-hand Vehicles**	**6.6**	**8.3**	**11.5**	**14.3**	**19.8**	**32.3**	**35.5**	**38.5**	**44.6**	**51.6**	**39.7**	**69.9**	**69.7**	**73.3**
#轿车	Sedan Cars	1.4	3.0	5.6	6.6	10.2	15.9	17.9	19.5	19.9	25.8	22.8	43.8	42.6	42.2

资料来源：北京市工商行政管理局。
Source: Beijing Administration For Industry & Commerce.

14-9 限额以上住宿和餐饮业经营情况(2014年)
STATISTICS FOR ACCOMMODATION AND RESTAURANTS ABOVE DESIGNATED SIZE (2014)

项目	Item	合计 Total	住宿业 Accommodation Industry	餐饮业 Catering Industry
客房数 (间)	**Number of Rooms (room)**	**251734**	**244789**	**6945**
床位数 (个)	**Number of Beds (unit)**	**420600**	**408442**	**12158**
餐位数 (位)	**Number of s (table)**	**1550791**	**347989**	**1202802**
营业额 (万元)	**Turnover (10000 yuan)**	**9727779**	**4316782**	**5410997**
客房收入	Income from Rooms	2348921	2311070	37851
餐费收入	Income from Money	6337840	1189117	5148723
商品销售额	Sales of Commodities	137367	46526	90841
其他收入	Other Incomes	903652	770070	133582

注：本表统计范围为限额以上住宿和餐饮业法人单位、产业活动单位和个体经营户。
Note:This table covers legal entities in accommodation and restaurants above designated size, activity entities and individual entities .

14-10 限额以上批发和零售企业财务状况(2014年)

单位：万元

项目	Item	企业单位个数(个) Number of Enterprises (unit)	资产总计 Total Assets	流动资产合计 Total Current Assets
合计	**Total**	**8589**	**357230450**	**263863656**
按隶属关系分	**By Affiliation**			
中央	Central	496	154847735	110305165
地方	Local	8093	202382715	153558490
按企业登记注册类型分	**By Registration Type**			
内资	Domestically-invested Enterprises	7993	287812446	210017601
国有	State-owned Enterprises	275	31121518	22058159
集体	Collectively-owned Enterprises	90	1164001	708868
股份合作	Joint-equity Cooperative Enterprises	80	728066	491273
联营	Associate Enterprises	8	23866	21562
有限责任公司	Limited Liability Companies	2714	183098160	140758741
股份有限公司	Companies Limited by Shares	136	40222858	19491078
私营	Private Enterprises	4689	31453713	26487707
其他	Other	1	***	***
港澳台商投资	Hong Kong, Macao and Taiwan-invested Enterprises	224	12179691	9262856
外商投资	Foreign-invested Enterprises	372	57238313	44583199
按国民经济行业分	**By Sector**			
批发业	**Wholesale**	**5780**	**315443628**	**232081225**
农、林、牧产品批发	Wholesale of Agriculture, Forestry and Animal Production and Hunting Products	106	18258961	9710053
食品、饮料及烟草制品批发	Wholesale of Foods, Beverage and Tobaccos	444	13663365	10829615
纺织、服装及家庭日用品批发	Wholesale of Textile, Clothes and Household Commodities	514	14730932	11239426
文化、体育用品及器材批发	Wholesale of Cultural and Sports Goods and Equipment	278	9102891	6439498
医药及医疗器材批发	Wholesale of Medicine and Medical Devices	427	10719472	8349486
矿产品、建材及化工产品批发	Wholesale of Mineral Products, Building Materials, and Chemical Products	1751	134617733	94166526
机械设备、五金交电及电子产品批发	Wholesale of Mechanical Equipment, Hardware and Electronic Products	2059	81861108	64081287
贸易经纪与代理	Trade Broker and Agent	84	25763669	23636058
其他批发	Others	117	6725496	3629275
零售业	**Retail**	**2809**	**41786822**	**31782431**
综合零售	Integrated Retail	224	11961425	7936878
食品、饮料及烟草制品专门零售	Special Retails of Foods, Beverage and Tobacoos	119	878380	657018
纺织、服装及日用品专门零售	Special Retail of Textile, Clothing and Domestic Commodities	228	1795748	1419496
文化、体育用品及器材专门零售	Special Retail of Cultural and Sports Goods and Equipment	196	2664534	2344035
医药及医疗器材专门零售	Special Retail of Medicine and Medical Devices	438	5292501	3533677
汽车、摩托车、燃料及零配件专门零售	Special Retail of Automobiles, Motorcycles, Fuels and Their Accessories	790	9823376	7747882
家用电器及电子产品专门零售	Special Retail of Household Electrical Appliances and Electronic Products	504	6419658	5800017
五金、家具及室内装修材料专门零售	Special Retail of Hardware, Furniture and Indoor Decoration Materials	119	748008	584201
货摊、无店铺及其他零售业	Stand Retail, Retail Without Shops and Other Retail	191	2203193	1759229
按规模划分	**By Size**			
#大中型企业	Medium-and Large-sized Enterprises	3231	304620049	219930900

注：1. 限额以上批发和零售企业是指年主营业务收入2000万元及以上批发业和年主营业务收入500万元及以上的零售业法人企业。
2. 行业划分执行2011年国民经济行业分类标准(GB/T 4754-2011)。
3. 自2011年开始，大中型企业划分标准执行国家统计局《关于统计上大中小微型企业划分办法》(国统字[2011]75号)(下同)。

FINANCIAL STATUS OF WHOLESALE AND RETAIL ENTERPRISES ABOVE DESIGNATED SIZE (2014)

(10000 yuan)

资产负债 Assets and Liabilities							
#应收账款 Accounts Receivable	固定资产合计 Total Fixed Assets	固定资产原价 Total Original Value of Fixed Assets	负债合计 Total Liabilities	#流动负债合计 Total Current Liabilities	#应付账款 Accounts Payable	所有者权益合计 Total Owner's Equity	#实收资本 Paid-up Capital
45103740	**9348460**	**14971316**	**258062964**	**230994353**	**68227812**	**99166739**	**51502280**
21540418	2424820	3660239	116283727	101544945	31768274	38564008	21741245
23563322	6923640	11311078	141779237	129449408	36459538	60602731	29761036
38676827	7882677	11945936	215249510	190540089	55289057	72562188	42004380
2794410	963150	1405932	21689766	18486257	2578636	9431752	4364976
43715	78250	128990	908926	633425	152404	255075	63424
27155	44246	53265	741982	741011	38493	-13916	59541
4086	1392	3363	19450	19450	15508	4416	2453
27409929	4881725	7180233	144032461	131805669	42821221	39064951	27327583
1977116	1060566	1739323	23684853	15664902	3296497	16538005	5148569
6420351	853297	1434778	24171268	23188570	6385832	7282445	5037835
***	***	***	***	***	***	***	***
1266398	388971	701745	8335183	7300826	2308441	3844508	1917102
5160515	1076811	2323636	34478271	33153438	10630314	22760043	7580798
41405720	**6437787**	**10061345**	**225883640**	**200247544**	**60276552**	**89560039**	**45572256**
638168	275563	376218	12431657	10845848	1270120	5827304	3064655
1506697	543372	811639	10047289	9554549	1254378	3616076	1743053
1566922	321958	501489	9373722	9182802	3629006	5357262	2899181
1177389	306533	477827	6833715	5350467	922003	2269177	1395868
2863772	235576	432511	7490768	7052040	3394727	3228704	1527585
15816389	3020220	4316061	98068051	84338116	20001871	36549682	22593547
9454490	1489919	2790926	52840031	48796293	13523126	29021077	10596660
7865816	184973	255356	22658404	22036962	15825479	3105265	1534538
516076	59675	99319	6140003	3090467	455843	585493	217169
3698020	**2910673**	**4909972**	**32179323**	**30746809**	**7951261**	**9606700**	**5930024**
265824	1224340	2159816	7994261	7254432	2367729	3966365	1655581
37957	154248	236325	380454	371790	146127	497926	168922
218039	119650	213318	1567475	1479047	657435	228273	404954
135612	149669	206832	2022296	1918574	593124	642238	332620
1505854	91750	162080	4213855	4075086	1237214	1078646	435394
463233	936984	1531062	7774283	7518650	603535	2049093	1732575
651230	89514	154016	4763617	4734859	779790	1656042	639879
104024	87825	139752	581681	559083	98063	166327	190403
316249	56692	106772	2881402	2835288	1468245	-678209	369697
38042077	7250675	12124307	219491880	193913445	57430667	85128169	40012055

Note: a) Wholesale and retail enterprises above designated size refer to wholesale enterprises with an annual main business income of RMB 20 million or above and retail enterprises of RMB 5 million or above.

b) Sectors in this table are classified in accordance with the Standard for Classification of National Economic Sectors 2011 (GB/T 4754-2011).

c) Since 2011, Division standards of medium and large-sized enterprises complies with Statistical Division Standards of Micro, Small, Medium and Large-sized Enterprises issued by National Bureau of Statistics (G.T.Z. [2011] No. 75) (the same below).

14-10 续表

单位：万元

项目	Item	损益 营业收入 Business Income	#主营业务收入 Main Business Income	营业成本 Business Cost	#主营业务成本 Main Business Cost
合计	**Total**	**515965426**	**506767557**	**478798730**	**472977165**
按隶属关系分	**By Affiliation**				
中央	Central	197259639	193421914	190657169	187455712
地方	Local	318705787	313345643	288141561	285521453
按企业登记注册类型分	**By Registration Type**				
内资	Domestically-invested Enterprises	403382605	396520488	383229034	378448703
国有	State-owned Enterprises	44113571	43930383	42037706	41992250
集体	Collectively-owned Enterprises	1071709	1047244	994626	990927
股份合作	Joint-equity Cooperative Enterprises	824904	822573	793590	793278
联营	Associate Enterprises	60427	60390	54849	54849
有限责任公司	Limited Liability Companies	268533046	262797033	256774435	252234278
股份有限公司	Companies Limited by Shares	37097884	36602620	34984510	34899087
私营	Private Enterprises	51675639	51255150	47584280	47478995
其他	Other	***	***	***	***
港澳台商投资	Hong Kong, Macao and Taiwan-invested Enterprises	17110304	16875924	14198261	14138185
外商投资	Foreign-invested Enterprises	95472518	93371145	81371435	80390278
按国民经济行业分	**By Sector**				
批发业	**Wholesale**	**439269563**	**431766167**	**411430543**	**405909620**
农、林、牧产品批发	Wholesale of Agriculture, Forestry and Animal Poduction and Hunting Products	10479753	10407266	10103187	10084450
食品、饮料及烟草制品批发	Wholesale of Foods, Beverage and Tobaccos	17896150	17091951	15430845	14737679
纺织、服装及家庭日用品批发	Wholesale of Textile, Clothes and Household Commodities	23616549	23405561	20256192	20126535
文化、体育用品及器材批发	Wholesale of Cultural and Sports Goods and Equipment	13413406	13273316	12454284	12414774
医药及医疗器材批发	Wholesale of Medicine and Medical Devices	14172726	13961109	12301559	12217405
矿产品、建材及化工产品批发	Wholesale of Mineral Products, Building Materials, and Chemical Products	228080278	226622590	223493163	222240232
机械设备、五金交电及电子产品批发	Wholesale of Mechanical Equipment, Hardware and Electronic Products	120387612	115883094	107132612	103850198
贸易经纪与代理	Trade Broker and Agent	5866950	5775883	5252343	5234012
其他批发	Others	5356141	5345396	5006358	5004336
零售业	**Retail**	**76695863**	**75001390**	**67368187**	**67067545**
综合零售	Integrated Retail	15529617	14588526	12443525	12404722
食品、饮料及烟草制品专门零售	Special Retails of Foods, Beverage and Tobacoos	1298998	1243544	779836	769636
纺织、服装及日用品专门零售	Special Retail of Textile, Clothing and Domestic Commodities	2632615	2559198	1699341	1687585
文化、体育用品及器材专门零售	Special Retail of Cultural and Sports Goods and Equipment	3293934	3241888	2864985	2846991
医药及医疗器材专门零售	Special Retail of Medicine and Medical Devices	5247177	5217005	4558288	4554461
汽车、摩托车、燃料及零配件专门零售	Special Retail of Automobiles, Motorcycles, Fuels and Their Accessories	24303319	23985784	22743757	22628820
家用电器及电子产品专门零售	Special Retail of Household Electrical Appliances and Electronic Products	15109846	14976286	13864229	13828822
五金、家具及室内装修材料专门零售	Special Retail of Hardware, Furniture and Indoor Decoration Materials	751900	731383	509450	508110
货摊、无店铺及其他零售业	Stand Retail, Retail Without Shops and Other Retail	8528457	8457775	7904776	7838399
按规模划分	**By Size**				
#大中型企业	Medium-and Large-sized Enterprises	441002306	432327523	408983650	403491586

注：应交税金合计包括应交增值税、应交所得税、营业税金及附加和管理费用中的税金。

14-10 Continued

(10000 yuan)

Profits and Losses				应交税金合计 Total Tax Payable	#营业税金及附加 Business Tax and Surcharges	#主营业务税金及附加 Business Tax and Surtax	#应交增值税 Value Added Tax Payable	#应交所得税 Income Tax Payable
销售费用 Sales Expenses	管理费用 Management Expenses	财务费用 Financial Expenses	利润总额 Total Profits					
19420653	**8874589**	**2090554**	**10124902**	**7648204**	**949034**	**896424**	**4051093**	**2395582**
2553233	1668463	806543	2964057	1799141	238175	224815	753592	716742
16867420	7206126	1284012	7160845	5849063	710859	671609	3297501	1678840
9947420	5361865	2166908	4903952	4176938	663319	616989	2046324	1282399
617339	495399	221676	1119985	575663	156364	152643	156549	239584
38905	32864	11665	5151	13288	2710	2117	8356	845
14702	15968	11824	-10901	6329	692	662	4975	507
5299	1100	150	711	1740	148	146	1429	148
5921797	2868164	1357605	3009139	2500814	326239	306643	1194729	856296
1168260	462024	274178	491258	306080	90534	72206	127781	67917
2180618	1486338	289810	288730	773025	86631	82573	552505	117103
***	***	***	***	***	***	***	***	***
1684519	613532	102065	586896	656605	66333	63157	404005	176213
7788714	2899192	-178418	4634054	2814661	219382	216278	1600764	936969
13656814	**6610954**	**1750129**	**8693420**	**5857299**	**667516**	**637136**	**2973845**	**2012970**
155744	142330	205668	286500	114479	11588	9853	59637	36563
1590842	368090	17459	896237	677643	167187	166383	326900	172376
2286585	646383	-6656	572501	656081	57167	56236	456077	131090
547812	260502	118126	84381	182506	16464	16391	95381	63836
961592	404971	47497	542072	371160	32104	31540	213679	118292
1841873	1344273	1225809	949341	944351	155293	137797	410668	299210
6026025	3208549	149188	4655223	2671566	200064	192058	1370294	1030044
152166	156491	-34693	545589	156878	20787	20362	9044	119290
94175	79366	27732	161575	82634	6863	6517	32167	42269
5763840	**2263635**	**340426**	**1431482**	**1790906**	**281518**	**259288**	**1077247**	**382612**
1899393	655905	70665	550067	595985	135268	120824	297957	144256
353692	78825	3581	78021	113084	10374	9703	74537	26761
704174	206103	10039	-1126	152042	21117	19002	115291	12731
225469	142219	14731	60634	58205	9504	9169	30023	16863
308887	190504	87239	190040	176443	15869	15593	120625	37205
806424	494649	163160	91482	290830	36328	33319	190343	53102
743020	266281	-7859	550364	280159	35503	34676	185328	54887
146087	58362	5196	26312	42439	7093	6552	24568	9149
576695	170787	-6327	-114312	81720	10462	10451	38576	27658
17674614	7606753	1771543	8068562	6092376	811362	761741	3298744	1762047

Note: Total tax payable mainly includes VAT payable, income tax payable, business tax and surtax, and tax in management expenses.

14-11 限额以上住宿业企业财务状况(2014年)

单位：万元

项目	Item	企业单位个数(个) Number of Enterprises (unit)	资产负债 Assets and Liabilities 资产总计 Total Assets	流动资产合计 Total Current Assets	#应收账款 Accounts Receivable	固定资产合计 Total Fixed Assets	固定资产原价 Total Original Value of Fixed Assets	负债合计 Total Liabilities	#流动负债合计 Total Current Liabilities	#应付账款 Accounts Payable
合　计	**Total**	**1161**	**12401680**	**4235080**	**166385**	**4854118**	**8240768**	**9407954**	**6451354**	**415254**
按隶属关系分	**By Affiliation**									
中　央	Central	195	1991907	562086	24867	1028090	1825809	1131804	805949	69757
地　方	Local	966	10409773	3672994	141518	3826027	6414959	8276150	5645405	345497
按登记注册类型分	**By Registration Type**									
内　资	Domestically-invested Enterprises	1094	9014595	3045974	135296	3738744	5698139	7210210	5269300	354217
国　有	State-owned Enterprises	252	2406827	641741	21148	1301802	1825726	1681398	1135549	67083
集　体	Collectively-owned Enterprises	49	323103	94894	3530	185254	291843	223073	122207	7966
股份合作	Joint-equity Cooperative Enterprises	28	99661	40449	3597	30960	66064	75771	64416	5412
联　营	Associate Enterprises	2	***	***	***	***	***	***	***	***
有限责任公司	Limited Liability Companies	421	4999601	1646999	86696	1962539	3075978	4017606	3001017	174404
股份有限公司	Companies Limited by Shares	9	323953	162864	1889	71043	112965	296881	228507	32131
私　营	Private Enterprises	333	857190	456318	19014	186543	320945	908446	710969	66658
其　他	Others									
港澳台商投资	Hong Kong, Macao and Taiwan-invested Enterprises	37	2298543	765809	22732	659016	1558993	1416158	838600	41381
外商投资	Foreign-invested Enterprises	30	1088542	423298	8358	456358	983636	781586	343454	19656
按行业类别分	**By Sector Type**									
旅游饭店	Tourism Hotels	643	10501804	3501870	127240	4474946	7616629	8192224	5443278	345132
一般旅馆	Common Inns	486	1789585	701316	38429	357725	587946	1090537	909023	62786
其他住宿服务	Other Accomodation Services	32	110291	31895	716	21446	36193	125193	99052	7336

注：1. 限额以上住宿业企业是指年主营业务收入200万元及以上的住宿业法人企业。
2. 应交税金合计包括应交增值税、应交所得税、营业税金及附加和管理费用中的税金。

FINANCIAL STATUS OF ACCOMMODATION ENTERPRISES ABOVE DESIGNATED SIZE (2014)

(10000 yuan)

		损益 Profits and Losses								应交税金合计				
所有者权益合计 Total Owner's Equity	#实收资本 Paid-up Capital	营业收入 Business Income	#主营业务收入 Main Business Income	营业成本 Business Cost	#主营业务成本 Main Business Cost	销售费用 Sales Expenses	管理费用 Management Expenses	财务费用 Financial Expenses	利润总额 Total Profits	应交税金合计 Total Tax Payable	营业税金及附加 Business Tax and Surcharges	#主营业务税金及附加 Main Business Tax and Surtax	#应交增值税 Value Added Tax Payable	#应交所得税 Income Tax Payable
2993726	**3633466**	**3438789**	**3405588**	**907069**	**900286**	**1095440**	**1226440**	**191473**	**-108418**	**316746**	**190787**	**190230**	**2360**	**50542**
860103	777637	687144	682202	195313	194056	204543	249558	5794	-4470	60891	37271	37078	730	8403
2133623	2855829	2751645	2723386	711756	706231	890897	976882	185680	-103948	255854	153516	153152	1630	42140
1804385	2444723	2497906	2468215	654836	648251	883180	917316	144675	-207334	202799	136497	135939	1899	19201
725429	784100	688192	680889	187150	185425	226048	273093	20415	-42495	55639	37448	37157	839	4065
100031	51164	103020	102200	16495	16495	46160	32535	384	1980	9624	5682	5676	23	1071
23890	17182	33047	32997	8885	8881	11994	9793	854	381	2595	1804	1793	22	442
***	***	***	***	***	***	***	***	***	***	***	***	***	***	***
981995	1440312	1259749	1241434	319074	314920	444523	464419	96240	-118544	106754	68737	68512	899	12419
27072	43840	44473	42080	28264	28262	6525	13679	6645	-12120	4065	2441	2439	41	176
-51256	104204	364466	363654	93703	93004	146803	121093	20087	-36069	23838	20103	20081	75	1027
882386	860531	615448	614389	183470	183283	140804	195763	27354	59582	69335	33974	33973	375	17110
306956	328212	325434	322985	68763	68752	71456	113361	19445	39334	44612	20317	20317	86	14231
2309580	3013994	2743756	2723641	698772	695086	859344	1023029	166242	-108566	262727	152574	152190	1907	40961
699048	604075	664385	651489	198259	195183	224548	190811	19482	11160	51963	36486	36312	337	9536
-14902	15397	30648	30458	10038	10018	11548	12601	5750	-11013	2055	1728	1728	116	45

Note: a) Accommodation enterprises above designated size refer to corporate enterprises with an annual main business income of RMB 2 million or above.

b) Total tax payable mainly includes VAT payable, income tax payable, business tax and surtax, and tax in management expenses.

14-12 限额以上餐饮业企业财务状况(2014年)

单位：万元

项目	Item	企业单位个数(个) Number of Enterprises (unit)	资产负债 Assets and Liabilities 资产总计 Total Assets	流动资产合计 Total Current Assets	#应收账款 Accounts Receivable	固定资产合计 Total Fixed Assets	固定资产原价 Total Original Value of Fixed Assets	负债合计 Total Liabilities	#流动负债合计 Total Current Liabilities	#应付账款 Accounts Payable
合计	**Total**	**1868**	**4261019**	**2310980**	**134308**	**602484**	**1176231**	**3540778**	**3112476**	**599511**
按隶属关系分	**By Affiliation**									
中央	Central	16	83125	65666	3049	6037	21545	59831	59811	19567
地方	Local	1852	4177893	2245313	131259	596447	1154686	3480948	3052665	579944
按登记注册类型分	**By Registration Type**									
内资	Domestically-invested Enterprises	1724	3145480	1791127	115791	397944	781451	2779064	2397054	473490
国有	State-owned Enterprises	30	40906	26981	952	7708	17792	24400	19149	3004
集体	Collectively-owned Enterprises	30	12798	5337	859	4628	7865	11884	11595	3238
股份合作	Joint-equity Cooperative Enterprise	47	25021	18112	535	3188	6224	22913	21798	1619
联营	Associated Enterprises									
有限责任公司	Limited Liability Companies	476	1422721	760131	55481	171754	333059	1343311	1085272	169330
股份有限公司	Companies Limited by Shares	29	569614	298961	3037	78442	137205	291090	230351	101782
私营	Private Enterprises	1112	1074420	681605	54927	132224	279307	1085467	1028890	194519
其他	Others									
港澳台商投资	Hong Kong, Macao and Taiwan-invested Enterprises	66	503145	325456	8828	66238	118330	315622	287509	54151
外商投资	Foreign-invested Enterprises	78	612394	194396	9689	138302	276450	446092	427913	71870
按行业类别分	**By Sector Type**									
正餐	Dinner	1646	3116399	1797475	99233	422868	836325	2652663	2436177	475475
快餐	Fast Food	130	649334	282194	12824	143523	273145	426826	399840	82520
饮料及冷饮	Beverage and Cold Drink	28	371486	157109	10177	21977	37886	345355	171865	20009
其他餐饮业	Others	64	123800	74202	12074	14116	28876	115934	104594	21508

注：1. 限额以上餐饮业企业是指年主营业务收入200万元及以上的餐饮业法人企业。
2. 应交税金合计包括应交增值税、应交所得税、营业税金及附加和管理费用中的税金。

FINANCIAL STATUS OF RESTAURANTS ENTERPRISES ABOVE DESIGNATED SIZE (2014)

(10000 yuan)

		损益 Profits and Losses								应交				
所有者权益合计 Total Owner's Equity	#实收资本 Paid-up Capital	营业收入 Business Income	#主营业务收入 Main Business Income	营业成本 Business Cost	#主营业务成本 Main Business Cost	销售费用 Sales Expenses	管理费用 Management Expenses	财务费用 Financial Expenses	利润总额 Total Profits	税金合计 Total Tax Payable	#营业税金及附加 Business Tax and Surtax	#主营业务税金及附加 Main Business Tax and Surcharges	#应交增值税 Value Added Tax Payable	#应交所得税 Income Tax Payable
720240	**855483**	**5345038**	**5286163**	**2236349**	**2220538**	**2206049**	**646012**	**50475**	**-77749**	**341003**	**282089**	**280945**	**9849**	**40653**
23295	9722	112818	108629	40246	38990	45694	17650	-210	3492	7582	5667	5458	97	1642
696945	845762	5232220	5177535	2196103	2181549	2160355	628362	50685	-81242	333421	276422	275487	9752	39011
366416	557374	3276688	3239308	1393149	1384492	1335795	438824	43037	-98003	209313	175566	174482	4027	23102
16507	7150	48717	43076	20292	19003	17977	6894	117	1420	3568	2675	2403	289	486
914	1823	22032	22015	10936	10936	7483	2582	63	-256	1325	1209	1209	8	96
2108	2242	37566	37527	19766	19765	13001	3010	203	-464	2200	2094	2092	1	48
79410	209796	1359296	1340108	552805	547085	579182	180445	11508	-26646	91775	72606	72100	1263	14771
278525	134589	184537	182168	62325	61521	82653	31880	12368	-14472	13096	8802	8797	842	2116
-11047	201775	1624541	1614414	727026	726181	635498	214014	18778	-57585	97348	88180	87881	1623	5587
187522	112742	716750	715620	248708	248271	331282	73786	3515	16690	49671	36974	36973	1835	9817
166302	185368	1351599	1331235	594492	587776	538972	133402	3923	3564	82019	69549	69491	3988	7734
463736	645956	3529214	3500168	1475394	1468820	1427688	470718	42995	-79641	231555	191806	191206	3188	29729
222508	155929	1399979	1370447	570436	561884	612803	134511	4188	5951	81781	71070	70528	3888	5724
26130	28769	195536	195275	63424	63424	94546	19506	1642	6521	14814	9501	9501	536	4564
7865	24829	220310	220274	127096	126411	71012	21277	1650	-10580	12852	9712	9710	2236	637

Note: a) Restaurants enterprises above designated size refer to corporate enterprises with an annual main business income of RMB 2 million or abov

b)Total tax payable mainly includes VAT payable, income tax payable, business tax and surtax, and tax in management expenses.

14-13 连锁企业基本情况(2001-2014年)
STATISTICS FOR CHAIN ENTERPRISES (2001-2014)

年 份 Year	连锁总店 (个) Number of General Chain Stores (unit)	门店总数 (个) Number of Chain Stores (unit)	从业人员年末人数 (人) Number of Employed Persons Year-end (person)	营业面积 (平方米) Operational Area (sq.m)	商品销售总额 (营业额) (万元) Total Sales of Commodities (Turnover) (10000 yuan)	#零售额 Retail Sales
2001	129	2123	139470	1605808	4831168	2186540
2002	146	3523	109089	2356266	6621975	6487185
2003	153	4519	132030	3405562	8404232	7601221
2004	196	5432	153942	3783507	8603560	8337829
2005	188	5973	166598	4376383	10612658	9507168
2006	205	6730	170007	5546003	11229026	9514297
2007	210	7645	185114	6677266	13890913	11573838
2008	240	8611	223954	6745802	15720473	12954839
2009	240	8928	218024	6995047	17366414	13816796
2010	234	9299	228292	7268786	21329783	16255496
2011	233	9845	280798	7953891	25742536	19507890
2012	220	10014	287975	8339674	26758403	20140433
2013	241	11111	299445	9026207	27834646	21495798
2014	243	11433	279567	9252645	28173728	21100845

14-14 连锁企业基本情况(按登记注册类型、经营业态分)(2014年)
STATISTICS FOR CHAIN ENTERPRISES (BY REGISTRATION TYPE OF ENTERPRISES AND OPERATION FORMS) (2014)

项目	Item	门店总数 (个) Number of Chain Stores (unit)	从业人员年末人数 (人) Year-end Employed Persons (person)	营业面积 (平方米) Operational Area (sq.m)	商品销售额(营业额) (万元) Total sales of Commodities (10000 yuan)	#零售额 Retail Sales
合计	**Total**	**11433**	**279567**	**9252645**	**28173728**	**21100845**
按登记注册类型分	**By Registration Type**					
内资	Domestically-invested Enterprises	7672	180057	7085410	22774465	16075274
国有	State-owned Enterprises	84	1386	20028	48041	44268
集体	Collectively-owned Enterprises	296	1147	82968	89278.9	83478.4
股份合作	Joint-equity Cooperative Enterprises	7	149	5410	3245	3245
联营	Associate Enterprises	5	29	928	813.7	813.7
有限责任公司	Limited Liability Companies	3462	90488	3423194	8313210	6338334
股份有限公司	Companies Limited by Shares	1747	54308	2847577	13177395	8525062
私营	Private Enterprises	2071	32550	705305	1142483	1080073
其他	Others					
港、澳、台商投资	Hong Kong, Macao and Taiwan-invested Enterprises	1516	31845	501686	1243676	1054536
外商投资	Foreign-invested Enterprises	2245	67665	1665549	4155587	3971036
按经营业态分	**By Operation Form**					
零售业态	**Retail**	**7433**	**160142**	**7348063**	**25419413**	**18462101**
便利店	Convenient Stores	1075	5537	121411	270812	263681
折扣店	Discount Stores	9	705	85664	156877	156877
超市	Supermarkets	1484	54687	2204636	5145037	3496646
大型超市	Large Supermarkets	172	27010	1244542	2508650	2334619
仓储会员店	Warehouse Club Stores	7	2427	134877	343614	343614
百货店	Department Stores	66	15141	1743364	3206092	3203004
专业店	Specialty Stores	2287	28840	1184233	5019705	4294822
加油站	Gas Stations	691	8247	350956	7806667	3474688
专卖店	Boutiques	1631	16534	205988	743105	675295
家居建材商店	Furniture and Building Material Stores	11	1014	72392	218854	218854
餐饮业态	**Chain Catering Enterprises**	**3871**	**116075**	**1895382**	**2651971**	**2636754**
中式正餐	Chinese Dinner	645	47368	979996	828574	826306
中式快餐	Chinese Fast Food	1273	20388	278738	540297	530865
外国风味正餐	Exotic Dinner	569	15554	220576	410353	410254
外国风味快餐	Exotic Fast Food	956	28548	342611	698805	695386
茶馆	Teahouses	9	45	910	365	365
咖啡店	Cafés	388	3622	68247	160653	160653
其他	Others	31	550	4304	12924	12924
住宿业态	**Chain Accomodation Enterprises**	**129**	**3350**	**9200**	**102344**	**1991**
旅游饭店	Tourism Hotels	60	1715	3548	53212	510
一般旅馆	Common Inns	69	1635	5652	49132	1481

14-15 商品交易市场基本情况(2014年)
STATISTICS FOR COMMODITY TRANSACTION MARKETS (2014)

项 目	Item	市场数量(个) Number of Markets (unit)	摊位数(个) Number of Booths (unit)	成交额(亿元) Turnover (100 million yuan)
全市合计	**Total**	**728**	**253087**	**3511.4**
按经营方式分	**By Business Practice**			
批发市场	Wholesale Market	133	94316	2207.2
零售市场	Retail Market	595	158771	1304.3
按经营环境分	**By Business Environment**			
露天式	Open-air	145	59557	1423.5
封闭式	Closed	542	171881	1743.9
其 他	Others	41	21649	344.0
按市场地理环境分	**By Market Place**			
二环以内	Inside the Second Ring Road	54	14994	56.4
二环至三环以内	Between the Second and Third Ring Road	93	37494	88.8
三环到四环以内	Between the Third and Fourth Ring Road	105	49144	1256.7
四环至五环以内	Between the Fourth and Fifth Ring Road	91	33680	1182.2
五环至六环以内	Between the Fifth and Sixth Ring Road	166	47549	618.7
六环以外	Outside the Sixth Ring Road	219	70226	308.6
按功能区分	**By Functional Area**			
首都功能核心区	Core Functional Area of the Capital	91	37672	123.7
城市功能拓展区	Urban Function Extension Area	301	112451	2575.7
城市发展新区	New Area of Urban Development	239	74152	714.9
生态涵养发展区	Ecological Conservation Area	97	28812	97.1

14-16 亿元及以上商品交易市场基本情况(2014年)
STATISTICS FOR COMMODITY TRANSACTION MARKETS OVER RMB 100 MILLION (2014)

项 目	Item	市场数量(个) Number of markets (unit)	总摊位数(个) Number of Booths (unit)	#出租摊位数 Number of Booths on Lease	成交额(亿元) Turnover (100 million yuan)
全市合计	**Total**	**131**	**122894**	**108167**	**3390.3**
按经营方式分	**By Business Practice**				
批发市场	Wholesale Market	57	73359	61297	2182.5
零售市场	Retail Market	74	49535	46870	1207.8
按经营环境分	**By Business Environment**				
露天式	Open-air	20	23886	14816	1399.1
封闭式	Closed	102	84816	79836	1657.6
其 他	Others	9	14192	13515	333.5
按市场地理环境分	**By Market Place**				
二环以内	Inside the Second Ring Road	8	8168	7944	47.4
二环至三环以内	Between the Second and Third Ring Road	13	18492	17680	69.2
三环到四环以内	Between the Third and Fourth Ring Road	34	32374	31332	1236.7
四环至五环以内	Between the Fourth and Fifth Ring Road	20	19599	18432	1171.4
五环至六环以内	Between the Fifth and Sixth Ring Road	25	19506	18034	594.8
六环以外	Outside the Sixth Ring Road	31	24755	14745	270.8
按功能区分	**By Functional Area**				
首都功能核心区	Core Functional Area of the Capital	17	22549	21736	107.2
城市功能拓展区	Urban Function Extension Area	67	62161	58912	2526.5
城市发展新区	New Area of Urban Development	29	27966	19939	676.1
生态涵养发展区	Ecological Conservation Area	18	10218	7580	80.5

14-17 商品交易市场经营情况(2014年)
STATISTICS FOR COMMODITY TRANSACTION MARKETS (2014)

项目	Item	市场数量(个) Number of Markets (unit)	出租摊位数(个) Number of Booths (unit)	营业面积(万平方米) Operating Area (10,000 sq.m)	成交额(亿元) Turnover (100 million yuan)
合计	**Total**	**728**	**214002**	**1322.9**	**3511.4**
综合市场	**Comprehensive Markets**	**363**	**104509**	**572.5**	**1722.0**
生产资料综合市场	Comprehensive Market of Capital Goods	1	310	6.0	0.9
工业消费品综合市场	Comprehensive Market of Industrial Consumer Goods	54	23392	52.6	97.1
农产品综合市场	Comprehensive Market of Agricultural Products	213	52439	362.3	1425.7
其他综合市场	Other Comprehensive Markets	95	28368	151.6	198.3
专业市场	**Specialized Markets**	**365**	**109493**	**750.4**	**1789.4**
生产资料市场	**Market of Capital Goods**	**36**	**7616**	**65.9**	**75.9**
农业生产用具市场	Market of Agricultural Production Tools				
农用生产资料市场	Market of Agricultural Production Means				
煤炭市场	Coal Market				
木材市场	Timber Market	2	349	6.0	1.0
建材市场	Building Material Market	30	6337	46.3	48.2
化工材料及制品市场	Chemical Material and Product Market				
金属材料市场	Metal Material Market	2	398	8.2	3.5
机械设备市场	Mechanical Equipment Market	1	262	3.3	13.5
其他生产资料市场	Other Markets of Capital Goods	1	270	2.1	9.7
农产品市场	**Agricultural Product Market**	**52**	**15139**	**102.5**	**439.8**
粮油市场	Foodstuff and Oil Market	5	2282	22.2	179.2
肉禽蛋市场	Meat, Poultry and Egg Market	4	357	1.5	3.8
水产品市场	Aquatic Product Market	3	2010	7.6	104.3
蔬菜市场	Vegetable Market	15	3004	19.4	16.7
干鲜果品市场	Dried and Fresh Fruit Market	3	1191	27.1	15.8
棉麻土畜、烟叶市场	Cotton, Linen, Local and Livestock Product, and Tobacco Leaf Market				
其他农产品市场	Other Agricultural Product Markets	22	6295	24.7	120.0
食品、饮料及烟酒市场	**Food, Beverage, Tobacco and Wine Market**	**15**	**1699**	**8.2**	**4.3**
食品饮料市场	Food and Beverage Market	4	199	1.0	0.4
茶叶市场	Tea Market	6	998	5.4	3.7
烟酒市场	Tobacco and Wine Market				
其他食品饮料及烟酒市场	Other Food, Beverage, Tobacco and Wine Markets	5	502	2.3	0.3
纺织、服装、鞋帽市场	**Textile, Costume, Shoe and Hat Market**	**70**	**34610**	**219.1**	**61.0**
布料及纺织品市场	Cloth and Textile Market	8	1918	7.9	2.5
服装市场	Clothing Market	52	27499	73.4	51.3
鞋帽市场	Shoe and Hat Market	1	712	2.0	0.5
其他纺织服装鞋帽市场	Other Textile, Costume, Shoe and Cap Markets	9	4481	135.8	6.8
日用品及文化用品市场	**Domestic Commodity and Cultural Article Market**	**15**	**9261**	**19.6**	**50.2**
小商品市场	Small Commodity Market	7	7560	11.2	31.1

14-17 续表 Continued

项 目	Item	市场数量(个) Number of Markets (unit)	出租摊位数(个) Number of Booths (unit)	营业面积(万平方米) Operating Area (10000 sq.m)	成交额(亿元) Turnover (100 million yuan)
箱包市场	Case and Bag Market				
玩具市场	Toy Market				
文具市场	Stationary Market	1	843	4.3	15.8
图书、报刊杂志市场	Book, Newspaper, and Magazine Market	1	174	1.2	2.4
音像制品及电子出版物市场	Audiovisual Product and E-journal Market	1	14	0.8	0.2
体育用品市场	Sports Good Market				
其他日用品及文化用品市场	Other Domestic Commodity and Cultural Article Market	5	670	2.0	0.7
黄金、珠宝、玉器等首饰市场	**Market of Gold, Jewelry, and Jade**	**13**	**3273**	**11.5**	**24.9**
电器、通讯器材、电子设备市场	**Market of Electrical Appliances, Communication Devices, and Electronic Equipment**	**20**	**5635**	**18.7**	**88.2**
家电市场	Household Appliance Market	2	99	0.2	0.2
通讯器材市场	Communication Device Market	6	1050	3.2	1.9
照相、摄像器材市场	Photographic and Camera Shooting Equipment Market	2	364	2.0	3.9
计算机及辅助设备市场	Computer and Supporting Equipment Market	6	3088	12.0	69.9
其他电器、通讯器材、电子设备市场	Other Electrical Appliance, Communication Device and Electronic Equipment Market	4	1034	2.3	12.3
医药、医疗用品及器材市场	**Medicine, Medial Article and Equipment Market**				
中药材市场	Chinese Herb Market				
其他医药、医疗用品及器材市场	Other Medicine, Medial Article and Equipment Market				
家具、五金及装饰材料市场	**Furniture, Hardware, and Decoration Material Market**	**72**	**14412**	**133.7**	**135.0**
家具市场	Furniture Market	30	5135	59.5	53.2
装饰材料市场	Decoration Materials Market	20	4615	35.7	36.9
灯具市场	Lamp and Lantern Market	4	753	10.0	2.8
厨具、盥洗设备市场	Kitchen and Washroom Equipment Market				
五金材料市场	Hardware Market	11	2152	10.4	4.0
其他装修市场	Other Decoration Market	7	1757	18.1	38.1
汽车、摩托车及零配件市场	**Automobile, Autobike, and Part and Fitting Market**	**23**	**6058**	**106.2**	**891.0**
汽车市场	Automobile Market	10	1491	69.1	826.7
摩托车市场	Autobike Market				
机动车零配件市场	Automobile Part and Fitting Market	13	4567	37.0	64.3
花、鸟、鱼、虫市场	**Flower, Bird, Fish and Insect Market**	**15**	**1862**	**6.0**	**1.4**
花卉市场	Flower Market	14	1627	5.2	1.3
鸟市场	Bird Market				
观赏鱼市场	Fish Market				
其他花鸟鱼虫市场	Other Flower, Bird, Fish and Insect Market	1	235	0.8	0.0
旧货市场	**Secondhand Goods Market**	**13**	**7678**	**13.0**	**7.5**
古玩、古董、字画市场	Curio, Antique, Calligraphy and Painting Market	6	1705	7.2	0.8
邮票、硬币市场	Stamp and Coin Market	1	887	0.8	0.7
其他旧货市场	Other Secondhand Goods Market	6	5086	5.0	5.9
其他专业市场	**Other Specialized Markets**	**21**	**2250**	**46.1**	**10.2**

14-18 北京消费者信心指数(2014年)
BEIJING CONSUMER CONFIDENCE INDEX (2014)

项 目	Item	一季度 First Quarter	二季度 Second Quarter	三季度 Third Quarter	四季度 Fourth Quarter
消费者信心指数	**Consumer Confidence Index**	**102.6**	**105.9**	**105.0**	**108.0**
消费者满意指数	**Consumer Satisfaction Index**	**104.6**	**107.4**	**107.1**	**109.6**
就业状况满意指数	Index of Satisfaction with Employment Status	118.8	120.7	121.3	123.6
家庭收入状况满意指数	Index of Satisfaction with Household Income Status	94.6	100.1	97.0	100.0
耐用消费品购买时机满意指数	Index of Satisfaction with Durable Consumer Goods	100.3	101.4	102.9	105.3
消费者预期指数	**Consumer Expectation Index**	**101.3**	**104.9**	**103.6**	**107.0**
就业状况预期指数	Index of Expectation for Employment Status	105.1	108.4	108.0	111.3
家庭收入状况预期指数	Index of Expectation for Household Income Status	97.4	101.4	99.1	102.6

主要统计指标解释

社会消费品零售总额 指企业（单位、个体户）通过交易直接售给个人、社会集团非生产、非经营用的实物商品金额，以及提供餐饮服务所取得的收入金额。个人包括城乡居民和入境人员，社会集团包括机关、社会团体、部队、学校、企事业单位、居委会或村委会等。

批发和零售业单位 指在流通环节从事商品批发活动和零售活动的单位。

商品购进额 指从本企业（单位）以外的单位和个人购进(包括从国外直接进口)作为转卖或加工后转卖的商品金额（含增值税）。本指标反映批发和零售业从国内外市场上购进商品的总量。

商品销售额 指对本企业以外的单位和个人出售的商品金额（包括售给本单位消费用的商品，含增值税）。本指标反映批发和零售业在国内市场上销售商品以及出口商品的总量。

期末商品库存额 对于批发和零售业法人企业和个体经营户，是指取得所有权的全部商品金额（含增值税）；对于批发和零售业产业活动单位，是指期末实际在库且归属法人具有所有权的全部商品金额（含增值税）。这个指标反映批发和零售业的商品库存情况，以及对市场商品供应的保证程度。

连锁总店（总部） 负责连锁企业资源（商号、商誉、经营模式、服务标准、管理模式等）的开发、配置、控制或使用等功能的企业核心管理机构。连锁经营是指经营同类商品或服务，使用统一商号的若干店铺，在同一总店（总部）的管理下，采取统一采购或特许经营等方式,实现规模效益的组织形式，包括直营连锁、特许连锁和自愿连锁三种形式。直营连锁是指连锁店铺由连锁公司全资或控股开设，在总部的直接控制下，开展统一经营的连锁经营形式；特许连锁是指拥有注册商标、企业标志、专利、专有技术等经营资源的企业（特许人），以合同形式将其拥有的经营资源许可其他经营者（被特许人）使用，被特许人按合同约定在统一的经营模式下开展经营，并向特许人支付特许经营费用的连锁经营形式；自愿连锁是指若干个店铺或企业自愿组合起来，在不改变各自资产所有权关系的情况下，以同一个品牌形象面对消费者，以共同进货为纽带开展的连锁经营形式。

连锁门店 在连锁企业经营管理的基础上，按照总店（总部）的指示和服务规范要求，承担日常销售业务的店铺，称连锁门店，包括直营店（控股店）和加盟店。

（1）直营店（控股店） 是指由连锁企业总部投资开设，按连锁经营管理模式，由总部统一管理的店铺。

（2）加盟店 是指在特许连锁中，被特许人获得特许人授权后，使用其商标、商号、经营模式、专利和专有技术等经营资源建立的店铺，也包括自愿连锁的成员店。

门店总数 指该连锁企业所拥有的全部门店（包括直营店和加盟店）数量。其中，总店（如果总公司有门店的话）作为一个直营店处理。此外，有的地区分出控股店，控股店按直营店统计。

餐饮业企业 指在一定场所，专门从事对食物进行现场烹饪、调制，并出售给顾客主要供现场消费服务活动的企业。如各种饭馆、中西餐厅、酒馆、茶馆和火车餐车、车站食堂、飞机场餐厅等。

住宿业企业 指有偿为顾客提供临时住宿服务活动的单位。如旅游饭店、宾馆、酒店和旅馆、旅店等。

商品交易市场 指经有关部门和组织批准设立，有固定场所、设施，有经营管理部门和监管人员，若干市场经营者入内，常年或实际开业三个月以上，集中、公开、独立地进行生活消费品、生产资料等现货商品交易以及提供相关服务的交易场所，包括各类消费品市场，生产资料市场等。

消费者信心指数 是综合反映并量化消费者对当前经济形势评价和对经济前景、收入水平、收入预期以及消费心理状态的主观感受，是预测经济走势和消费趋向的一个先行指标，是监测经济周期变化不可缺少的依据。消费者信心指数由消费者满意指数和消费者预期指数构成。其中消费者满意指数反映了消费者对当前经济生活的评价；消费者预期指数反映了消费者对未来一段时期经济发展变化的预期。

指数值的含义：指数取值介于 0 和 200 之间，100 为指数强弱临界点。指数超过 100，表明消费者信心处于强信心区，数值由 100 趋近 200，表明消费者信心逐渐增强；反之，指数小于 100 时，表示消费者信心处于弱信心区，数值由 100 趋近 0，表明消费者信心逐渐减弱。

Explanatory Notes on Main Statistical Indicators

Total Retail Sales of Consumer Goods refer to the total prices of physical commodities sold by enterprises (entities or self-employed businesses) through transaction directly to individuals and social groups to be used for non-productive and non-operating purposes, combined with the amount of income from provision of food and beverage services. Individuals include urban and rural residents and persons entering China. Social groups include government agencies, social organizations, armies, schools, enterprises and public institutions, residents' committee or villagers' committee, and so on.

Wholesale and Retail Entities refer to entities engaged in commodity wholesale and retail activities in circulation.

Total Purchases of Commodities refer to the total value (including value added tax) of purchases (including direct imports from foreign countries) of commodities by the enterprises (entities) from other entities or individuals for the purpose of re-selling, either with or without further processing of the commodities purchased. This indicator is used to show the total value of purchases of retail and wholesale commodities from domestic and overseas markets.

Total Sales of Commodities refer to value of commodities sold by the enterprises to other entities and individuals (including the commodities consumed by the enterprises themselves, including value added tax). This indicator is used to show the total value of wholesale and retail commodities sold in domestic markets and exported.

Inventory (year-end) refers to, for wholesale and retail enterprises and self-employed businesses, the value of all commodities with ownership gained (VAT included); for wholesale and retail entities, refer to the value of all commodities with ownership, actually in storage at the end of a period, and owned by the legal person (VAT included). This indicator shows the commodity inventory in wholesale and retail trades, and to what extent the commodities will be supplied to the market.

General Chain Store (Headquarters) means the core management organization in an enterprise, responsible for the development, deployment, control or use of resources (trade name, goodwill, operating model, service standards and management model, etc.) of the chain enterprise. Chain operation means an organization form in which several stores using unified trade name merchandise the same commodities or provide the same services through uniform purchase or franchise operation under the management of the same general store (headquarters) to achieve benefits of scale. Chain operation falls into direct-sale chain, franchised chain and voluntary chain. Direct-sale chain is a form of chain operation that chain stores are wholly funded or controlled by chain companies, carrying out uniform operation under the direct control of headquarters; franchised chain is a form of chain operation that any enterprise (the franchiser) owning operating resources, such as trademarks, logos, patents and proprietary technologies, authorize such operating resources to any other operator (the franchisee) by contract, and the franchisee operates under uniform operating model as stated in the contract, and pays franchise fees to the franchiser; voluntary chain is a form of chain operation that several stores or enterprises combine together voluntarily to face consumers with the same brand image without changing their own asset ownership relations, and link together through joint purchase.

Chain Stores Based on the operation and management of chain enterprises, stores carrying out daily sales business by following the general store's (headquarters) instruction and required service standards are called chained stores. They include direct-sale stores (controlled stores) and franchise stores.

(1) Direct-sale Stores (Controlled Stores) refer to stores opened with funds from the headquarters of chain enterprises, using the chain operation and management model, and under the uniform management of the headquarters.

(2) Franchised Stores refer to, in franchise chains, stores established after the franchisee is authorized by the franchiser to use its trademark, trade name, operating mode, patent and proprietary technologies and other operating resources. Voluntary chain members are also included.

Total Number of Stores refers to the number of all stores owned by the chain enterprises (including direct-sale stores and franchised stores). The general store (if the parent company has stores) is regarded as a direct-sale store. In addition, controlled stores are considered separately in some areas, which are regarded as direct-sale stores.

Restaurants Enterprises refer to enterprises specialized in cooking and seasoning food which is sold to clients for on-site consumption at a specific site, such as various restaurants, Chinese food and Western food restaurants, pubs, teahouses, dining compartments on trains, canteens at railway stations, and restaurants at airports.

Accommodation Enterprises refer to entities providing clients with temporary accommodation services, such as tourist hotels, guesthouses, rest houses and inns.

Commodity Transaction Markets refer to transaction sites approved by competent authorities and organizations, with fixed places and facilities. There are operation management departments and regulating personnel in the markets, where several operators stay over years or open for over three months, conducting transactions of on-hand commodities such as living consumables and capital goods, and offering relevant services in a concentrated, open and independent manner. Commodity transaction markets include various markets of consumer goods and capital good market, etc.

Consumer Confidence Index is an indicator reflecting and quantifying the consumers' evaluation on current economic situation, and their personal feeling about the economic prospects, income level, income expectation, and psychological state of consumption. It serves as a leading indicator predicting the trend of economy tendency of consumption, and an essential basis for monitoring the changes in economic cycle and other conditions as well as expectation on the economic prospects in the future. Consumer Confidence Index consists of consumer satisfaction index and consumer expectation index, and the latter one reflects consumers' evaluation on current economic life; consumer expectation index reflects consumers' expectation on the development and changes in the economic prospect in the future.

Indexes range from 0 to 200. 100 represents a critical point between strong and weak confidence. An index greater than 100 indicates the consumers' confidence is strong. An index going toward 200 from 100 shows the consumers' confidence is becoming gradually strong; in contrary, an index smaller than 100 means the consumers' confidence is weak. When the indexes go toward 0 from 100, it means the consumers' confidence is weakening gradually.

对外经济贸易
FOREIGN ECONOMY AND TRADE

简要说明

一、本章资料的主要内容

本章资料主要反映北京市对外经济贸易的发展状况，包括对外贸易、利用外资、对外经济合作的历年概况，以及对外友好交往情况。

二、本章资料的统计范围和数据来源

1.对外贸易情况

对外贸易统计的范围是凡能引起北京市海关境内物质资源存量增加或减少的进出口货物，除制度另有规定者外，均列入该项统计，调查方法采用全面调查。主要内容包括北京地区进出口总值；主要产品进出口数量等。数据来源于中华人民共和国北京海关。

2.口岸运营情况

口岸运营情况的统计范围是北京首都国际机场空港口岸、北京丰台货运口岸、北京朝阳口岸、北京西站铁路口岸、北京平谷国际陆港、北京天竺综合保税区。主要内容包括旅客吞吐量、货邮吞吐量、监管货物的数量、征收关税等。数据来源于北京市人民政府口岸办公室。

3.利用外资情况

利用外资情况的统计范围是凡经工商行政管理机关核准登记，在中华人民共和国北京地域内所有使用外资（包括港澳台地区投资）的单位和部门，经批准设立的中外合资经营企业、合作经营企业、外资企业、外商投资股份制企业、合作开发项目等具有法人资格的独立核算企业(包括港澳台地区投资企业)，在华从事经营活动的外国及港澳台地区企业及外国公司在中国境内设立的分支机构。主要内容包括实际利用外商直接投资，外商投资企业经营情况，调查方法采用全面调查。数据来源于北京市商务委员会(原北京市商务局)和北京市统计局。

4.对外经济合作

对外经济合作的统计范围是经各级商务部门批准的从事对外承包、劳务合作和设计咨询业务并具有法人资格的对外承包劳务企业；调查方法采用全面调查。主要内容包括对外承包工程、劳务合作和设计咨询。数据来源于北京市商务委员会(原北京市商务局)。

5.友好城市

主要内容包括与北京市建立友好关系的城市名录。数据来源于北京市人民政府外事办公室。

Brief Introduction

I. Main Content

Data in this chapter show the development of foreign economic relations and trade in Beijing, including foreign trade, foreign capital utilization, and foreign economic cooperation in Beijing over the years, as well as friendly exchanges.

II. Scope of Statistical and Source of Data

1. Foreign trade

Foreign trade statistics apply for: any imports and exports that lead to increase or decrease in the stock of physical resources at Beijing customs, except for those otherwise stated in regulations, and were obtained through comprehensive survey. Foreign trade data include: total volume of import and export in Beijing, and quantity of main import and export products, and so on.. Foreign trade data are from Beijing Customs, P.R.C..

2. Statistics for Port Operation

The statistical scope of port operation covers the Port of Beijing Capital International Airport, Beijing Fengtai Cargo Transport Port, Beijing Chaoyang Transport Port, Railway Port at Beijing West Railway Station, Beijing Pinggu International Land Port, and Beijing Tianzhu Comprehensive Bonded Zone. Statistics in this chapter, which is sourced from Port Administration Office of the People's Government of Beijing Municipality, mainly include passenger throughput, cargo throughput, cargos under customs regulation and duties levied.

3. Foreign capital utilization

Scope of statistics: all entities and organizations registered with administration for industry and commerce upon approval, and using foreign capital (including investment from Hong Kong, Macao and Taiwan region) within the jurisdiction of Beijing, P.R.C, enterprises with legal person statues and independent accounting system (including enterprises invested by companies from Hong Kong, Macao and Taiwan region), including joint ventures, cooperative enterprises and foreign-invested enterprises, foreign-invested joint-stock enterprises, and cooperative development projects, and enterprises of foreign countries and Hong Kong, Macao and Taiwan region conducting operations in China as well as branch offices opened by foreign companies in China. Foreign capital utilization data include foreign direct investment, operation of foreign-invested enterprises, and were obtained through comprehensive survey. Data are sourced from Beijing Municipal Commission of Commerce (former Beijing Municipal Bureau of Commerce) and Beijing Municipal Bureau of Statistics.

4. Foreign economic cooperation

Statistics cover foreign labor service enterprises with legal person statues that are engaged in foreign contracting, labor service cooperation and design consulting with approval from departments of commerce at different levels. Comprehensive survey was used. Foreign economic cooperation statistics apply for: foreign contracting projects, labor service cooperation and design consulting. Data are sourced from Beijing Municipal Commission of Commerce (former Beijing Municipal Bureau of Commerce).

5. Sister cities

Data showing the detailed list of sister cities of Beijing are from Foreign Affairs Office of the People's Government of Beijing Municipality.

15-1 北京地区对外经济贸易(1980-2014年)
FOREIGN ECONOMIC RELATIONS AND TRADE (1980-2014)

年 份 Year	进出口总值(万美元) Total Value of Imports and Exports (USD 10000)	出 口 Exports	#高新技术产品 High-tech Products	#机电产品 Mechanical and Electrical Products	进 口 Imports	#高新技术产品 High-tech Products	#机电产品 Mechanical and Electrical Products
1980							
1981-1985							
1981							
1982							
1983	3059926	1468740			1591186		
1984	3559284	1751704			1807580		
1985	3254341	437398			2816943		
1986-1990	**13945243**	**1865234**			**12080009**		
1986	3060236	371282			2688954		
1987	2670466	354374			2316092		
1988	2988576	395887			2592689		
1989	2861489	302343			2559146		
1990	2364476	441348			1923128		
1991-1995	**14305670**	**3547263**			**10758405**		
1991	2424137	457114			1967023		
1992	2498241	561037		157835	1937204	271005	731359
1993	2791700	669930		151133	2121769	302965	885074
1994	2888079	834205		194937	2053873	421071	1121082
1995	3703513	1024977		281810	2678536	407176	1225200
1996-2000	**17397285**	**5011639**		**1609152**	**12385646**	**2242338**	**5049210**
1996	2931833	811975		254450	2119858	240903	733641
1997	3038852	961103		271119	2077749	346166	766288
1998	3050608	1051293		325390	1999315	347556	909222
1999	3435951	990352		320852	2445599	567687	1213857
2000	4940041	1196916	226549	437341	3743125	740026	1426202
2001-2005	**39258570**	**9270820**	**2525916**	**4291246**	**29987748**	**5318558**	**10501427**
2001	5149809	1177236	263382	477568	3972572	992797	1883151
2002	5250529	1261386	314174	570971	3989142	916363	1701504
2003	6850017	1688682	396489	715359	5161335	990357	1949077
2004	9457572	2056926	580929	970117	7400647	1053395	2271805
2005	12550643	3086590	970942	1557231	9464052	1365646	2695890
2006-2010	**113918161**	**24817747**	**8781469**	**14861935**	**89100414**	**11589524**	**25107110**
2006	15803663	3795398	1388925	2170700	12008265	1704997	3786847
2007	19299976	4892639	1797751	2862301	14407337	2360093	4477646
2008	27169290	5749961	1906381	3354179	21419329	2417936	4987666
2009	21479103	4835807	1751571	3080447	16643296	2357239	5194072
2010	30166129	5543942	1936840	3394308	24622187	2749258	6660878
2011	38958314	5899770	1811744	3523452	33058544	3145224	7667795
2012	40810735	5963212	1901750	3737918	34847523	2987939	7217809
2013	42994169	6309757	2035695	3894782	36684413	2923787	7167539
2014	41553810	6233597	1874973	3789748	35320213	2937309	7785199

注：进出口总值为海关统计的北京地区进出口数据(包括中央单位)。

资料来源：北京市商务委员会、中华人民共和国北京海关。

Note: Figures of "total value of imports and exports" were imports and exports of Beijing counted by Beijing Customs (including central entities).

Source: Beijing Municipal Commission of Commerce and Beijing Customs of People's Republic of China.

15-1 续表 Continued

年 份 Year	外商直接投资项目(合同)个数 (个) Number of Foreign Direct Investment Projects (Contracts) (unit)	实际利用外商直接投资额 (万美元) Actal Use of Foreign Direct Investment (USD10000)
1980	4	
1981-1985	**124**	
1981	3	
1982	4	
1983	5	
1984	29	
1985	83	
1986-1990	**709**	
1986	63	
1987	72	9534
1988	148	50278
1989	185	31846
1990	241	27696
1991-1995	**10912**	**410896**
1991	724	24482
1992	2208	34984
1993	3753	66693
1994	2675	144460
1995	1552	140277
1996-2000	**4100**	**989794**
1996	868	155290
1997	790	159286
1998	651	206415
1999	644	223004
2000	1147	245799
2001-2005	**7821**	**1231631**
2001	1147	177000
2002	1370	178964
2003	1362	214675
2004	1806	308354
2005	2136	352638
2006-2010	**9232**	**2818387**
2006	2106	455191
2007	2177	506572
2008	1897	608172
2009	1423	612094
2010	1629	636358
2011	1345	705447
2012	1360	804160
2013	1190	852418
2014	1318	904085

15-2 北京地区海关进出口贸易总值(按登记注册类型、贸易方式分)

TOTAL VALUE OF IMPORTS AND EXPORTS AT BEIJING CUSTOMS (BY REGISTRATION TYPE AND COMPOSITION)

项目	Item	金额(万美元) Value (USD 10000) 2014	2013	2014年为2013年% 2014as % of 2013	构成(%) Composition(%) 2014	2013
出口	**Local Exports**	**6233597**	**6309757**	**98.8**	**100.00**	**100.00**
按登记注册类型分	**By Registration Type**					
内资企业	Domestically-invested Enterprises	4159533	4042999	102.9	66.73	64.08
国有企业	State-owned Enterprises	3371995	3374852	99.9	54.09	53.49
集体企业	Collectively-owned Enterprises	8397	12156	69.1	0.13	0.19
其他	Others	779141	655990	118.8	12.50	10.40
外商投资企业	Foreign-invested Enterprises	2074064	2266758	91.5	33.27	35.92
中外合资	Joint Ventures	1223146	1458547	83.9	19.62	23.12
中外合作	Cooperatives	5661	4777	118.5	0.09	0.08
外商独资	Solely-funded Enterprises	845258	803434	105.2	13.56	12.73
按贸易方式分	**By Composition**					
#一般贸易	General Trade	2837416	2728270	104.0	45.52	43.24
来料加工装配贸易	Trade of Processing & Assembling Supplied Materials	722020	644232	112.1	11.58	10.21
进料加工贸易	Trade of Processing Imported Materials	1511197	1909468	79.1	24.24	30.26
对外承包工程货物	Contracted Foreign Goods and Projects	801066	654103	122.5	12.85	10.37
出料加工贸易	Trade of Processing Exported Materials	3719	3703	100.4	0.06	0.06
进口	**Imports**	**35320213**	**36684413**	**96.3**	**100.00**	**100.00**
按登记注册类型分	**By Registration Type**					
内资企业	Domestically-invested Enterprises	29458492	31472011	93.6	83.40	85.79
国有企业	State-owned Enterprises	24493991	24900054	98.4	69.35	67.88
集体企业	Collectively-owned Enterprises	95276	108791	87.6	0.27	0.30
其他	Other	4869226	6463167	75.3	13.79	17.62
外商投资企业	Foreign-invested Enterprises	5861721	5212401	112.5	16.60	14.21
中外合资	Joint Ventures	1208553	1194042	101.2	3.42	3.25
中外合作	Cooperatives	7420	5265	140.9	0.02	0.01
外商独资	Solely-funded Enterprises	4645748	4013095	115.8	13.15	10.94
按贸易方式分	**By Composition**					
#一般贸易	General Trade	30509017	32705792	93.3	86.38	89.15
来料加工装配贸易	Trade of Processing and Assembling Supplied Materials	1854276	1346798	137.7	5.25	3.67
进料加工贸易	Trade of Processing Imported Materials	653396	718996	90.9	1.85	1.96
外商投资企业进口设备、物品	Equipment and Goods Imported by Foreign-invested Enterprises	28924	31403	92.1	0.08	0.09
租赁贸易	Leasing Trade	190810	171932	111.0	0.54	0.47

资料来源：中华人民共和国北京海关。
Source: Beijing Customs of People's Republic of China.

15-3 北京地区海关进出口贸易总值(按国别、地区分)
TOTAL VALUE OF IMPORTS AND EXPORTS AT BEIJING CUSTOMS (BY COUNTRY AND REGION)

项　　目	Item	金额（万美元）Value (USD 10000) 2014	2013	2014年为2013年% 2014as % of 2013	构成(%) Composition(%) 2014	2013
出口合计	**Total Exports**	**6233597**	**6309757**	**98.8**	**100.00**	**100.00**
按国别(地区)分	**By Country (Region)**					
#中国香港	Hong Kong, China	507876	607756	83.6	8.15	9.63
中国澳门	Macao, China	36609	34501	106.1	0.59	0.55
中国台湾	Taiwan, China	133640	128041	104.4	2.14	2.03
日　本	Japan	470331	482935	97.4	7.55	7.65
新加坡	Singapore	192497	162107	118.7	3.09	2.57
韩　国	Korea	242991	226633	107.2	3.90	3.59
越　南	Vietnam	259906	202705	128.2	4.17	3.21
伊　朗	Iran	188560	110431	170.7	3.02	1.75
印　度	India	219417	215731	101.7	3.52	3.42
印度尼西亚	Indonesia	165677	202148	82.0	2.66	3.20
英　国	United Kingdom	117014	111990	104.5	1.88	1.77
德　国	Germany	133478	125896	106.0	2.14	2.00
法　国	France	80779	81682	98.9	1.30	1.29
意大利	Italy	52090	55666	93.6	0.84	0.88
匈牙利	Hungary	42505	95953	44.3	0.68	1.52
俄罗斯联邦	Russian Federation	161754	173167	93.4	2.59	2.74
美　国	United States	578246	571241	101.2	9.28	9.05
澳大利亚	Australia	73470	59823	122.8	1.18	0.95
进口合计	**Total Imports**	**35320213**	**36684413**	**96.3**	**100.00**	**100.00**
按国别(地区)分	**By Country (Region)**					
#中国香港	Hong Kong, China	143940	414933	34.7	0.41	1.13
日　本	Japan	1278859	1210041	105.7	3.62	3.30
新加坡	Singapore	200064	172814	115.8	0.57	0.47
韩　国	Korea	1142957	1290432	88.6	3.24	3.52
沙特阿拉伯	Saudi Arabia	2723621	3118808	87.3	7.71	8.50
英　国	United Kingdom	424411	368759	115.1	1.20	1.01
德　国	Germany	2246743	1818918	123.5	6.36	4.96
法　国	France	293808	326191	90.1	0.83	0.89
意大利	Italy	211268	205565	102.8	0.60	0.56
瑞　士	Switzerland	1874212	3373473	55.6	5.31	9.20
比利时	Belgium	82918	79254	104.6	0.23	0.22
俄罗斯联邦	Russian Federation	1275884	864664	147.6	3.61	2.36
加拿大	Canada	638306	423888	150.6	1.81	1.16
美　国	United States	2908354	2970023	97.9	8.23	8.10
澳大利亚	Australia	1281957	1483160	86.4	3.63	4.04
阿　曼	Oman	1530101	1648325	92.8	4.33	4.49
安哥拉	Angola	2503663	2658449	94.2	7.09	7.25

资料来源：中华人民共和国北京海关。
Source: Beijing Customs of People's Republic of China.

15-4 北京地区海关主要商品进口量及金额(2014年)
VOLUME & VALUE OF MAJOR COMMODITIES IMPORTED AT BEIJING CUSTOMS (2014)

项目		Item		进口数量 Import Volume	进口金额(万美元) Import Value (USD 10000)
粮食	(万吨)	Grain	(10000 tons)	892	401526
食用植物油	(万吨)	Edible Vegetable Oil	(10000 tons)	84	84268
食糖	(万吨)	Sugar	(10000 tons)	91	43756
酒类	(万升)	Alcohol	(10000 liters)	14697	36121
合成橡胶(包括胶乳)	(万吨)	Synthetic Rubber (Including Latex)	(10000 tons)	2	6003
纸浆	(万吨)	Paper Pulp	(10000 tons)	63	39578
羊毛	(万吨)	Wool	(10000 tons)	4	26697
棉花	(万吨)	Cotton	(10000 tons)	27	53669
纺织用合成纤维	(万吨)	Synthetic Fiber for Textile	(10000 tons)	3	7909
铁矿砂及其精矿	(万吨)	Iron Sand and Iron Ore Concentrates	(10000 tons)	11119	1074532
原油	(万吨)	Crude Oil	(10000 tons)	21706	16033350
成品油	(万吨)	Product Oil	(10000 tons)	728	562633
液化石油气及其他烃类气	(万吨)	LPG and Other Hydrocarbon Gas	(10000 tons)	622	561691
医药品	(万吨)	Medicines	(10000 tons)	1	394924
肥料	(万吨)	Fertilizers	(10000 tons)	656	238437
非泡沫塑料的板、片、膜、箔	(万吨)	Non-foam Plastic Plates, Sheets, Films and Foils	(10000 tons)	2	16026
纸及纸板(未切成形的)	(万吨)	Paper and Pressboard (Not Shaped by Cutting)	(10000 tons)	19	32401
纺织纱线、织物及制品		Textile Yarn, Fabric and Products			119894
服装及衣着附件		Clothes and Clothing Accessories			42830
钢材	(万吨)	Steel Products	(10000 tons)	51	103824
建筑及采矿用机械及零件		Building and Mining Machinery and Parts			28492
印刷、装订机械及零件		Printing and Binding Machinery and Parts			98762
自动数据处理设备及其部件		Automatic Data Processing Equipment and Their Components			205801
电动机及发电机	(万台)	Electromotors and Generators	(10000 sets)		36976
变压、整流、电感器及零件		Voltage Transformer, Rectifier, Inductor and Parts			105184
电视摄像机、数字照相机及视频摄录一体机	(万台)	Television Cameras, Digital Cameras and Integrated Video Cameras and Recorders	(10000 sets)	367	135996
印刷电路	(万块)	Printed Circuits	(10000 pieces)	138263	13182
集成电路	(万个)	Integrated Circuits	(10000 units)	866656	361228
电线和电缆	(万吨)	Wires and Cables	(10000 tons)	1	18667
汽车		Automobiles			2905035
汽车零件		Auto Parts			378463
飞机		Aircrafts			311221
船舶		Ships and Boats			19261
医疗仪器及器械		Medical Instruments and Devices			208235
计量检测分析自控仪器及器具		Automatically-controlled Measuring, Testing and Analyzing Instruments			501239

15-5 北京地区海关主要商品出口量及金额(2014年)
VOLUME & VALUE OF MAIN COMMODITIES EXPORTED AT BEIJING CUSTOMS (2014)

项目		Item		出口数量 Export Volume	出口金额 Export Value (万美元) (USD 10000)
粮食	(万吨)	Grain	(10000 tons)	27	24937
果蔬汁	(万吨)	Fruit and Vegetable Juice	(10000 tons)	7	10061
肥料	(万吨)	Fertilizers	(10000 tons)	484	148100
煤	(万吨)	Coal	(10000 tons)	195	22054
焦炭、半焦炭	(万吨)	Coke and Semi-coke	(10000 tons)	287	58082
原油	(万吨)	Crude Oil	(10000 tons)		
成品油	(万吨)	Product Oil	(10000 tons)	971	885200
医药品	(万吨)	Medicines	(10000 tons)	2	33342
纺织纱线、织物及制品		Textile Yarn, Fabric and Products			69370
铁合金	(万吨)	Ferroalloy	(10000 tons)	2	19230
钢材	(万吨)	Steel Products	(10000 tons)	386	314803
未锻造的铝及铝材	(万吨)	Non-forged Aluminum and Aluminum Products	(10000 tons)	4	12746
纺织机械及零件		Textile Machinery and Parts			22015
金属加工机床	(万台)	Metal Processing Lathe	(10000 sets)	1	16347
自动数据处理设备及其部件		Automatic Data Processing Equipment and Their Components			76143
液晶显示板	(万个)	LCD Plates	(10000 units)	2025	50100
电动机及发电机	(万台)	Electromotors and Generators	(10000 sets)	215	11814
变压器	(万个)	Voltage Transformers	(10000 units)	46	24136
蓄电池	(万个)	Storage Cells	(10000 units)	3437	12256
电话机	(万台)	Telephone Sets	(10000 sets)	10122	924092
二极管及类似半导体器件	(万个)	Diode and Similar Semiconductor Devices	(10000 units)	58142	17597
集成电路	(万个)	Integrated Circuits	(10000 units)	566228	180040
电线和电缆	(万吨)	Wires and Cables	(10000 tons)	5	50415
汽车(包括整套散件)	(万辆)	Automobiles (Including Complete Sets of Spare Parts	(10000 sets)	7	137639
汽车零件		Auto Parts			184301
船舶		Boats and Ships			116161
医疗仪器及器械		Medical Instruments and Devices			59735
家具及其零件		Furnitures and Their Parts			23603
服装及衣着附件		Clothes and Clothing Accessories			157985
鞋类	(万吨)	Footwear	(10000 tons)	2	20068
塑料制品	(万吨)	Plastic Products	(10000 tons)	5	27390

资料来源：中华人民共和国北京海关。
Source: Beijing Customs of People's Republic of China.

15-6 北京口岸运营情况
STATISTICS FOR PORT OPERATION IN BEIJING

项目		Item		2014	2013	2014年为2013年% 2014 as % of 2013
北京首都国际机场空港口岸		**Port of Beijing Capital International Airport**				
旅客吞吐量	(万人次)	Passenger Throughput	(10000 person-times)	8612.83	8371.24	102.9
进出境人员	(万人次)	Inbound/Outbound Visitors	(10000 person-times)	2204.85	2102.52	104.9
#外籍人员进出境	(万人次)	Inbound/Outbound Foreign Visitors	(10000 person-times)	789.91	822.36	96.1
货邮吞吐量	(万吨)	Cargos Carried	(10000 tons)	184.83	184.37	100.2
飞机起降	(架次)	Takeoff and Landing of Airplanes	(unit)	581953	567759	102.5
#进出境飞机起降	(架次)	Takeoff and Landing of Airplanes Inbound/Outbound	(unit)	125760	123562	101.8
海关监管货物	(万吨)	Cargos under Customs Regulation	(10000 tons)	49.05	50.59	97.0
海关征收关税及代征税	(万元)	Duties Levied and Collected by Customs	(10000 yuan)	3347288	3066200	109.2
北京丰台货运口岸		**Beijing Fengtai Cargo Transport Port**				
海关监管货物	(吨)	Cargos under Customs Regulation	(ton)	17336	17642	98.3
海关征收关税及代征税	(万元)	Duties Levied and Collected by Customs	(10000 yuan)	9699	5033	192.7
北京朝阳口岸		**Beijing Chaoyang Transport Port**				
海关监管货物	(标箱)	Cargos under Customs Regulation	(standard container)	114251	120920	94.5
海关监管货物	(吨)	Cargos under Customs Regulation	(ton)	1193909	900766	132.5
海关征收关税及代征税	(万元)	Duties Levied and Collected by Customs	(10000 yuan)	1258514	1173486	107.2
北京西站铁路口岸		**Railway Port at Beijing West Railway Station**				
进出境人员	(人次)	Inbound/Outbound Visitors	(person-times)	91996	98705	93.2
#外籍人员进出境	(人次)	Inbound/Outbound Foreign Visitors	(person-times)	5535	7487	73.9
北京平谷国际陆港		**Beijing Pinggu International Land Port**				
海关监管货物	(标箱)	Cargos under Customs Regulation	(standard container)	31142	27316	114.0
海关监管货物	(吨)	Cargos under Customs Regulation	(ton)	198586	198261	100.2
海关征收关税及代征税	(万元)	Duties Levied and Collected by Customs	(10000 yuan)	211451	202858	104.2
北京天竺综合保税区		**Beijing Tianzhu Comprehensive Bonded Zone**				
实际进出货物	(吨)	Cargos under Customs Regulation	(ton)	49592	40016	123.9
海关征收关税及代征税	(万元)	Duties Levied and Collected by Customs	(10000 yuan)	662750	720113	92.0

注：自2013年起，北京朝阳口岸海关监管货物统计口径调整为按实际报关量统计的监管货物表箱总量，2012年为同口径数据。
资料来源：北京市人民政府口岸办公室。
Note: Since 2013,the statistical basis of cargos under customs regulation of Chaoyang Transport Port has been changed as the actual number of cargoes that went through custom clearance.
Source: Port Administration Office of the People's Government of Beijing Municipality.

15-7 外商投资企业实际利用外资情况(2006-2014年)
ACTUAL USE OF FOREIGN CAPITAL BY FOREIGN INVESTED ENTERPRISES (2006-2014)

单位：万美元 (USD 10000)

项 目	Item	2006	2007	2008	2009	2010	2011	2012	2013	2014
实际利用外商直接投资额	**Actual Use of Foreign Direct Investment**	**455191**	**506572**	**608172**	**612094**	**636358**	**705447**	**804160**	**852418**	**904085**
按登记注册类型分	**By Registration Type**									
合资经营	Joint Ventures	80570	77887	90916	91049	91335	78983	191944	190667	154808
合作经营	Cooperatives	33039	18037	21372	32249	22890	15068	14184	22887	5166
独资经营	Solely-funded Enterprises	341367	408754	490252	448912	516766	594890	592310	593258	704367
外商投资股份制	Companies Limited by Shares	215	1894	5632	39884	5367	16506	5722	45606	39744
按产业分	**By Industry**									
第一产业	Primary Industry	544	4774	2032	3833	1246	214	733	1717	13947
第二产业	Secondary Industry	109380	93391	162515	88536	71899	80798	112326	149687	97254
第三产业	Tertiary Industry	345267	408407	443625	519725	563213	624435	691101	701014	792884
按行业分	**By Sector**									
农、林、牧、渔业	Agriculture, Forestry, Animal Production and Hunting, Fishing	544	4774	2032	3833	1246	214	733	1717	13947
制造业	Manufacturing	105590	89618	150056	75364	68496	63303	86378	106848	84226
建筑业	Construction	1254	878	1715	2493	411	2343	383	193	703
信息传输、计算机服务和软件业	Information Transmission, Computer Services and Software	44341	78470	105396	94752	95453	109246	135121	119547	115292
批发与零售业	Wholesale and Retail Trade	24378	33318	34677	55411	66032	115437	74311	92739	54792
住宿和餐饮业	Accommodation and Restaurants	1882	5824	3357	8427	3525	1705	2877	1822	2047
房地产业	Real Estate	72242	119476	78787	79682	141728	112539	87739	148057	136822
租赁和商务服务业	Renting and Leasing Activities, Business Services	174342	92896	132541	225888	175580	190363	161595	171079	339759
其他行业	Other Sectors	30618	81318	99611	66244	83887	110297	255023	210416	156497
按外商国别(地区)分	**By Country (Region) of Foreign Investors**									
#中国香港	Hongkong,China	86600	149291	173292	270295	312863	323041	440357	360481	541495
英属维尔京群岛	Virgin Islands	78445	104154	125045	123201	76255	112981	28882	51111	37592
开曼群岛	Cayman Islands	27596	68646	75463	41389	45209	35982	59320	43982	36835
日 本	Japan	67580	30386	47174	23905	40692	77196	59022	44781	31125
韩 国	Korea	35357	24420	27841	17601	14725	22372	70959	21029	18584
美 国	United States	20043	18280	17888	18628	21370	30221	21097	38882	15634
新加坡	Singapore	17616	15328	10520	12600	24888	12898	31656	19383	35631
巴巴多斯	Barbados	7278	13789	15803	2384	941	821	200	2839	3000
德 国	Germany	47797	11476	26654	14308	22344	17939	25763	107467	99968
毛里求斯	Mauritius	10166	8068	7780	5615	7179	1311	1392	3297	3586
百慕大	Bermuda	1658	7540	1699	4441	4860	813	1483	265	2005
萨摩亚	Samoan	1483	6189	2468	1310	1705	893	1163	589	311
荷 兰	Netherlands	4610	4876	28520	4906	10639	3677	8542	14619	12119
法 国	France	3578	3824	2583	6349	3700	6642	2286	1409	6284
英 国	United Kingdom	2977	3304	4897	4242	1120	6245	3828	2387	1738

资料来源：北京市商务委员会。
Source: Beijing Municipal Commission of Commerce.

15-8 外商投资企业基本情况

项 目	Item	企业单位数（个） Number of Enterprises (unit)	
		2014	2013
合 计	**Total**	**4107**	**4360**
按登记注册类型分	**By Registration Type**		
港澳台商投资企业	Hong Kong, Macao and Taiwan-invested Enterprises	1564	1615
与港澳台商合资	Joint Ventures	491	528
与港澳台商合作	Cooperatives	119	128
港澳台商独资	Solely-funded Enterprises	922	926
港澳台商投资股份有限公司	Companies Limited by Shares	31	33
其他港澳台投资企业	Others	1	
外商投资企业	Foreign-invested Enterprises	2543	2745
中外合资	Joint Ventures	743	808
中外合作	Cooperatives	104	114
外商独资	Solely-funded Enterprises	1657	1779
外商投资股份有限公司	Companies Limited by Shares	36	42
其他外商投资企业	Others	3	2
按国民经济行业分	**By Sector**		
农、林、牧、渔业	Agriculture, Forestry, Animal Production and Hunting, Fishing		
制造业	Manufacturing	838	875
建筑业	Construction	83	89
批发与零售业	Wholesale and Retail Trade	596	544
住宿和餐饮业	Accommodation and Restaurants	212	208
信息传输、软件和信息技术服务业	Information Transmission, Software and Information Technology Services	532	580
房地产业	Real Estate	394	424
租赁和商务服务业	Renting and Leasing Activities, Business Services	627	791
其他行业	Other Sectors	471	849
按三次产业分	**By Industry**		
第一产业	Primary Industry		
第二产业	Secondary Industry	928	970
第三产业	Tertiary Industry	3179	3390

注：1. 本表统计范围为限额以上法人企业。
2. 行业划分执行2011年国民经济行业分类标准(GB/T 4754-2011)。

STATISTICS FOR FOREIGN-INVESTED ENTERPRISES

从业人员平均人数(人) Average Number of Persons Employed (person)		主营业务收入（万元） Revenue from Main Businesses (10000 yuan)		利润总额（万元） Total Profits (10000 yuan)		应交税金合计（万元） Total Taxes Paid (10000 yuan)	
2014	2013	2014	2013	2014	2013	2014	2013
1355156	**1332263**	**258975400**	**242367954**	**32236919**	**29844224**	**8909118**	**9045355**
524962	488513	74163799	63622202	9131162	6835132	2337891	2207459
148350	150675	14026110	13918810	2242179	2134209	697805	777635
19324	22388	1574471	2515151	281993	618611	144474	227366
294757	258055	49034042	37553296	5977075	3653282	1463291	1110145
58178	57395	9246811	9634945	568441	429030	19490	92313
***	***	***	***	***	***	***	***
830194	843750	184811601	178745753	23105757	23009093	6571227	6837896
289432	293492	60652611	59543126	7408245	6413106	3009711	2873787
18438	19895	1670099	2084745	150736	367371	135494	140491
496025	493943	121303047	115351147	15221937	15899323	3349544	3686866
26008	31906	1182391	1530301	324977	312251	75333	124161
***	***	***	***	***	***	***	***
377470	392796	75733923	70656413	5453339	5270268	3428240	3420155
12189	11832	2052475	1955321	36114	45936	54039	53752
211082	189701	110247069	88557419	5220950	4308445	2358084	2365653
100346	95975	2984229	2872459	119170	167276	196744	182652
226801	215862	21365567	18164534	8501618	9397331	941568	793776
64851	63192	5848543	7917483	1295147	2229144	712169	966216
115361	120540	16263818	29824725	3152276	2891679	491769	572394
88708	242365	8421998	22419600	958472	5534145	345994	690758
393088	408005	80702840	74823199	6068379	5755038	3643803	3651295
962068	924258	178272560	167544756	26168541	24089187	5265315	5394060

Note: a) Statistics in this table cover corporate enterprises above designated size.
b) Sectors in this table are classified in accordance with the Standard for Classification of National Economic Sectors 2011 (GB/T 4754-2011).

15-9 境外投资情况(2003-2013年)
STATISTICS FOR OVERSEAS INVESTMENT (2003-2013)

单位：万美元 (USD 10000)

年 份 Year	中方投资额 Amount of Investment by China	截至到各年期末直接投资存量 Diret Investment Stock by the Year End
2003	30054	44844
2004	15739	70086
2005	11306	92940
2006	5612	91873
2007	15295	159195
2008	47299	251019
2009	45185	375865
2010	76614	480882
2011	117503	603380
2012	168900	757800
2013	413010	1276456

资料来源：北京市商务委员会。
Source: Beijing Municipal Commission of Commerce.

15-10 对外经济合作(1984-2014年)
STATISTICS FOR FOREIGN ECONOMIC COOPERATION (1984-2014)

年份 Year	合同数(份) Number of Contracts (unit)	#对外承包工程 Foreign Contracted Works	合同额(万美元) Contract Value (USD 10000)	#对外承包工程 Foreign Contracted Works	完成营业额(万美元) Turnover (USD 10000)	#对外承包工程 Foreign Contracted Works	年末在外人数(人) Year-end Workers Staying Abroad (person)	对外承包工程 Foreign Contracted Works	对外劳务合作 Foreign Labor Service Cooperation
1984	9	2	2801	2768	502	331	541	163	378
1985	12	2	852	736	2083	355	2401	18	2383
1986	30	7	446	319	1535	90	837	71	766
1987	37	5	547	354	696	186	690	20	670
1988	46	5	885	344	802	281	819	104	715
1989	111	7	1685	235	1018	459	600	83	517
1990	105	16	3756	2253	1056	625	336	25	311
1991	114	9	3202	1671	1897	1469	980	306	674
1992	130	16	8889	7762	3140	2543	952	264	688
1993	143	48	29397	27625	9748	8871	1555	532	1023
1994	114	34	15715	15089	18783	17822	2720	1694	1026
1995	116	35	15613	14014	12789	12156	2604	1297	1307
1996	116	49	67689	62945	43057	38124	2516	1559	957
1997	107	37	35640	23374	29629	17945	3122	1993	1129
1998	180	48	25526	19292	31009	24930	3647	2239	1408
1999	90	28	25232	18715	26167	19690	3476	2199	1277
2000	104	54	16285	9936	19799	13543	3205	1660	1545
2001	105	54	21439	14758	18628	11680	3494	2141	1353
2002	73	42	27949	19376	23160	14453	2134	1112	1022
2003	117	99	48271	30761	34926	17334	2097	1270	827
2004	128	116	81185	51136	59630	29241	2552	1629	923
2005	272	238	93732	56709	71281	35554	4424	2528	1896
2006	232	166	176752	160328	83518	70062	8962	6760	2202
2007	317	143	236881	211560	94077	71727	11299	7060	4239
2008	486	197	558714	520973	168416	131686	11422	6366	5056
2009	190	182	336223	296851	226893	185017	17121	11805	5316
2010	199	170	286179	251114	259794	222514	22499	17145	5354
2011	229	229	264019	262078	252951	249146	17821	12393	5428
2012	340	340	405885	403475	295639	289902	16747	12143	4604
2013	349	349	564383	562440	341046	335854	21036	16549	4487
2014	283	283	437463	429369	365358	357432	29457	21683	7774

注：1984-2008年，对外承包工程统计中含对外设计咨询统计数据。
资料来源：北京市商务委员会。
Note: In 1984-2008, statistics for foreign contracted projects included statistics for consultation on foreign design.
Source: Beijing Municipal Commission of Commerce.

15-11 北京市市级友好城市
MUNICIPAL-LEVEL SISTER CITIES OF BEIJING

顺序 No.	城市	City	所在国家	Contury	所属洲	Continent	缔结日期 Date of Conclusion
1	东京都	Tokyo	日本	Japan	亚洲	Asia	1979.03.14
2	纽约市	New York	美国	USA	北美洲	North America	1980.02.25
3	贝尔格莱德市	Belgrade	塞尔维亚	Serbia	欧洲	Europe	1980.10.14
4	利马市	Lima	秘鲁	Peru	南美洲	South America	1983.11.21
5	华盛顿特区	Washington, DC	美国	USA	北美洲	North America	1984.05.15
6	马德里市	Madrid	西班牙	Spain	欧洲	Europe	1985.09.16
7	里约热内卢市	Rio De Janeiro	巴西	Brazil	南美洲	South America	1986.11.24
8	巴黎大区	Greater Parisian Region	法国	France	欧洲	Europe	1987.07.02
9	科隆市	Cologne	德国	Germany	欧洲	Europe	1987.09.14
10	安卡拉市	Ankara	土耳其	Turkey	亚洲	Asia	1990.06.20
11	开罗省	Cairo	埃及	Egypt	非洲	Africa	1990.10.28
12	雅加达省	Jakarta	印度尼西亚	Indonesia	亚洲	Asia	1992.08.04
13	伊斯兰堡市	Islamabad	巴基斯坦	Pakistan	亚洲	Asia	1992.10.08
14	曼谷市	Bangkok	泰国	Thailand	亚洲	Asia	1993.05.26
15	布宜诺斯艾利斯市	Buenos Aires	阿根廷	Argentina	南美洲	South America	1993.07.13
16	首尔特别市	Seoul Special City	韩国	South Korea	亚洲	Asia	1993.10.23
17	基辅市	Kiev	乌克兰	Ukraine	欧洲	Europe	1993.12.13
18	柏林市	Berlin	德国	Germany	欧洲	Europe	1994.04.05
19	布鲁塞尔大区	Greater Brussels Region	比利时	Belgium	欧洲	Europe	1994.09.22
20	河内市	Hanoi	越南	Viet Nam	亚洲	Asia	1994.10.06
21	阿姆斯特丹市	Amsterdam	荷兰	Holland	欧洲	Europe	1994.10.29
22	莫斯科市	Moscow	俄罗斯	Russia	欧洲	Europe	1995.05.16
23	巴黎市	Paris	法国	France	欧洲	Europe	1997.10.23
24	罗马市	Rome	意大利	Italy	欧洲	Europe	1998.05.28
25	豪登省	Gauteng	南非	South Africa	非洲	Africa	1998.12.06
26	渥太华市	Ottawa	加拿大	Canada	北美洲	North America	1999.10.18
27	首都地区	The Capital Region	澳大利亚	Australia	大洋洲	Oceania	2000.09.14
28	马德里自治区	Madrid Autonomous Region	西班牙	Spain	欧洲	Europe	2005.01.17
29	雅典市	Athens	希腊	Greece	欧洲	Europe	2005.05.10
30	布达佩斯市	Budapest	匈牙利	Hungary	欧洲	Europe	2005.06.16
31	布加勒斯特市	Bucharest	罗马尼亚	Rumania	欧洲	Europe	2005.06.21
32	哈瓦那市	Havana	古巴	Cuba	南美洲	South America	2005.09.24
33	马尼拉市	Manila	菲律宾	Philippines	亚洲	Asia	2005.11.14
34	伦敦市	London	英国	UK	欧洲	Europe	2006.04.11
35	亚的斯亚贝巴市	Addis Abeba	埃塞俄比亚	Ethiopia	非洲	Africa	2006.04.17
36	惠灵顿市	Wellington	新西兰	New Zealand	大洋洲	Oceania	2006.05.10
37	赫尔辛基市	Helsinki	芬兰	Finland	欧洲	Europe	2006.07.14
38	阿斯塔纳市	Astana	哈萨克斯坦	Kazakstan	亚洲	Asia	2006.11.16
39	特拉维夫市	Tel Aviv	以色列	Israel	亚洲	Asia	2006.11.21
40	首都大区	The Greater Capital Region	智利	Chile	南美洲	South America	2007.08.06
41	里斯本市	Lisbon	葡萄牙	Portugal	欧洲	Europe	2007.10.22
42	地拉那市	Tirana	阿尔巴尼亚	Albania	欧洲	Europe	2008.03.21
43	多哈市	Doha	卡塔尔	Qatar	亚洲	Asia	2008.06.23
44	圣何塞市	San Jose	哥斯达黎加	Costarica	北美洲	North America	2009.10.17
45	墨西哥城	Mexican City	墨西哥	Mexico	北美洲	North America	2009.10.19
46	都柏林市	Dublin	爱尔兰	Ireland	欧洲	Europe	2011.06.02
47	哥本哈根市	Copenhagen	丹麦	Denmark	欧洲	Europe	2012.06.28
48	新南威尔士州	New South Wales	澳大利亚	Australia	大洋洲	Oceania	2012.08.03
49	德里邦	Delhi	印度	India	亚洲	Asia	2013.10.23
50	德黑兰	Teheran	伊朗	Iran	亚洲	Asia	2014.02.27
51	乌兰巴托	Ulaanbaatar	蒙古国	Mongolia	亚洲	Asia	2014.08.17

资料来源：北京市人民政府外事办公室。
Sourse: Foreign Affairs Office of the People's Government of Beijing Municipality.

主要统计指标解释

进出口总值 指实际进、出我国海关并能引起我国境内物质资源增加或减少的进出口货物总金额。包括我国境内法人和其他组织以一般贸易、易货贸易、加工贸易、补偿贸易、寄售代销贸易等方式进出口的货物、租赁期一年及以上的租赁进出口货物、边境小额贸易货物、国际援助物资或捐赠品、保税区和保税仓库进出口货物等的金额合计。进出口总值用以观察一个国家在对外贸易方面的总规模。我国规定出口货物按离岸价格统计，进口货物按到岸价格统计。

一般贸易 指我国境内有进出口经营权的企业单边进口或单边出口的货物。

来料加工装配贸易 指由外商提供全部或部分原材料、辅料、零部件、元器件、配套件和包装物料，必要时提供设备，由我方按对方的要求进行加工装配，成品交对方销售，我方收取工缴费；或对方提供的作价设备价款，我方用工缴费偿还的交易形式。

进料加工贸易 指我方用外汇购买进口的原料、材料、辅料、元器件、零部件、配套件和包装物料，加工成品或半成品后再外销出口的交易形式。

旅客吞吐量 指经乘航班进出北京民用运输机场的中国公民、港澳台同胞、华侨及外国人等旅客数量的总和。

货邮吞吐量 指通过民用运输机场的航班运输的货物、邮寄物品和随身携带的行李物品重量总和。

飞机起降架次 指进出民用运输机场的正常航班架次，不包括包机和其他非正常航班。

海关征收关税 指进出口商品在经过国家关境时，由政府设置的海关向进出口国所征收的税收。

批准外商直接投资企业项目个数 指外商直接投资中批准设立的外商投资企业个数、批准的合作开发项目个数。

实际利用外商直接投资额 指批准的合同外资金额的实际执行数，外国投资者根据批准外商投资企业的合同（章程）的规定实际缴付的出资额和企业投资总额内外国投资者以自己的境外自有资金实际直接向企业提供的贷款。

对外承包工程 指企业按照国际通行做法，在国（境）外承揽和实施各类工程项目的经济活动。企业承揽的我国对外经济援助项目、我国驻外使（领）馆等建设项目视同对外承包工程项目。

对外劳务合作 指企业按照与国（境）外政府有关机构、团体、企业、私人雇主所签合同规定，向国（境）外派遣各类劳务人员的经济活动。企业自带设备以提供技术服务的形式在国（境）外承揽的项目视同对外劳务合作项目。

对外设计咨询 指企业在国（境）外承揽的工程设计、工程监理、技术咨询和人员培训等经济活动。

Explanatory Notes on Main Statistical Indicators

Total Value of Imports and Exports refer to the total value of goods actually imported and exported at China's customs, which lead to increase or decrease in the physical resources in China, including goods imported/exported by China domestic legal persons and other organizations in such manners as general trade, barter trade, processing trade, compensation trade, commission-based sales trade, leasing imports/exports with a lease period of one year and more, small-sum border trade goods, international aid goods and donations, imports/exports in bonded zones and bonded warehouses. The indicator of the Total Value of Imports and Exports can be used to observe the total size of foreign trade in a country. In accordance with the stipulation of the Chinese government, imports are calculated at CIF, while exports are calculated at FOB.

General Trade means goods imported and exported unilaterally by domestic enterprises with import/export rights.

Trade of Processing and Assembling Supplied Materials is a form of transaction in which all or part of raw materials, auxiliary materials, parts and components, elements, fittings, and packaging materials, and equipment if necessary are provided by the foreign party, processed or assemble by Chinese party according to requirements of the foreign party, and the finished products are sold by the foreign party. The Chinese party charges processing fees and pays back the money of priced equipment provided by the foreign party with processing charges.

Trade of Processing Imported Materials is a form of transaction in which the Chinese party purchases raw materials, auxiliary materials, parts and components, elements, fittings, and packaging materials with foreign exchange, processing them into finished or semi-finished products and export them.

Passenger Throughput means the total number of Chinese citizens, compatriots form Hong Kong, Macao and Taiwan, oversea Chinese and foreigners that take off and land at civil airports in Beijing by flights.

Cargos Throughput means the sum of goods, mailed articles and luggage transported by flights taking off from and landing at civil airports in Beijing.

Takeoff and Landing of Airplanes means the number of regular flights taking off from and landing at civil airports in Beijing, excluding chartered flights and other non-regular flights.

Duties Levied and Collected by Customs mean the sum of duties actually levied from the imported and exported by customs established by the government when imported and exported goods are going through national borders.

Number of Direct Foreign-invested Enterprises Approved means the number of foreign-invested enterprises and joint development projects approved in foreign direct investment (FDI).

Actual Use of Foreign Capital means the value of approved contractual foreign investment actually used, the amount of actual capital contribution by foreign investors according to the contract (articles of incorporation) of the foreign-invested enterprise approved and, in the total investment of an enterprise, the amount of loans provided directly by foreign investor with its own overseas money.

Foreign Contracted Projects refer to economic activities in which enterprises undertake and implement various projects in foreign (overseas) countries in line with international practices. Foreign economic aid projects and construction projects of Chinese Embassies (Consulates) undertaken by enterprises are deemed as foreign contracted projects.

Foreign Labor Service Cooperation means any economic activity in which enterprises dispatch labors to foreign (overseas) countries as stated in contracts signed with foreign (overseas) government agencies, groups, enterprises, and private employers. Projects undertaken by enterprises in foreign (overseas) countries in a manner of providing technical service with their own equipment are deemed as foreign labor service cooperation projects.

Foreign Design Consulting means any economic activity of project design, project supervision, technical consulting and personnel training undertaken in foreign (overseas) countries by enterprises.

16

北京统计年鉴2015 BEIJING STATISTICAL YEARBOOK

旅游业
TOURISM

简要说明

一、本章资料的主要内容和统计范围

本章内容主要包括来京旅游者人数及其在京花费情况、星级饭店经营及接待住宿者情况、旅行社接待及出境旅游情况、A级及以上重点旅游景区活动情况等。

统计范围包括国际旅游和国内旅游。

二、本章资料的数据来源

本章中的旅游外汇收入、国内旅游者人数、国内旅游收入、在京旅游花费情况资料来源于北京市旅游发展委员会。入境旅游者人数根据北京市统计局的星级饭店、限额以上非星级饭店全面调查、限额以下饭店抽样调查，以及北京市旅游发展委员会的其他住宿设施抽样调查结果汇总得出。星级饭店、旅行社、A级及以上和重点旅游景区有关数据通过全面调查取得，由北京市统计局、国家统计局北京调查总队提供。

Brief Introduction

I. Main Content and Scope of Statistics

This chapter includes statistics for the number and cost of tourists to Beijing, operation and reception of star-rated hotels, reception and outbound tours made through travel agencies, activities at Level A-or-above key scenic spots, and so on.

Statistics include international and domestic tours.

II. Source of Data

Data of foreign exchange income from tourism, number of domestic tourists, domestic tourism income, and cost of tourists in Beijing are sourced from Beijing Municipal Commission of Tourism Development. The number of inbound tourists is summed from the results of comprehensive survey of star-rated hotels and non-star-rated hotels above designated size, sample survey of hotels below designated size conducted by Beijing Municipal Bureau of Statistics, as well as the results of sample survey of other accommodation facilities conducted by Beijing Municipal Commission of Tourism Development. Data concerning star-rated hotels, travel agencies, Level A-or-above key scenic spots were obtained through comprehensive survey, and provided by Beijing Municipal Bureau of Statistics and NBS Survey Office in Beijing.

16-1 国际、国内旅游情况(1978-2014年)
STATISTICS FOR INTERNATIONAL AND DOMESTIC TOURISM (1978-2014)

年份 Year	来京旅游者人数（万人次） Number of Tourists to Beijing (10000 person-times)	入境旅游者人数 Inbound Tourists	国内旅游者人数 Domestic Tourists	旅游外汇收入总额（万美元） Foreign Exchange Earnings of Tourism (USD 10000)	国内旅游收入（亿元） Revenue from Domestic Tourism (100 million yuan)
1978		18.7		10000	
1979		25.2		9000	
1980		28.6		12000	
1981-1985		**295.4**		**94000**	
1981		39.4		12000	
1982		45.7		13000	
1983		50.9		14000	
1984		65.7		23000	
1985		93.7		32000	
1986-1990		**492.0**		**280901**	
1986		99.0		46000	
1987		108.1		55000	
1988		120.4		67000	
1989		64.5		47195	
1990		100.0		65706	
1991-1995		**919.6**		**735519**	
1991		132.0		85001	
1992		174.8		107286	
1993		202.8		124128	
1994	6913.0	203.0	6710.0	200904	298.0
1995	6527.0	207.0	6320.0	218200	352.6
1996-2000	**45284.7**	**1203.3**	**44081.4**	**1214800**	**2388.4**
1996	7901.9	218.9	7683.0	225200	359.6
1997	8450.8	229.8	8221.0	224800	391.3
1998	8951.5	220.1	8731.4	238400	424.5
1999	9512.4	252.4	9260.0	249600	530.0
2000	10468.1	282.1	10186.0	276800	683.0
2001-2005	**57116.7**	**1459.7**	**55657.0**	**1475000**	**4968.7**
2001	11292.8	285.8	11007.0	295000	887.7
2002	11810.4	310.4	11500.0	311000	930.0
2003	8885.1	185.1	8700.0	190000	706.0
2004	12265.5	315.5	11950.0	317000	1145.0
2005	12862.9	362.9	12500.0	362000	1300.0
2006-2010	**77925.4**	**2107.4**	**75818.0**	**2247000**	**9712.9**
2006	13590.3	390.3	13200.0	402600	1482.7
2007	14715.5	435.5	14280.0	458000	1753.6
2008	14560.0	379.0	14181.0	446000	1907.0
2009	16669.5	412.5	16257.0	436000	2144.5
2010	18390.1	490.1	17900.0	504400	2425.1
2011	21404.4	520.4	20884.0	541600	2864.3
2012	23134.6	500.9	22633.7	514900	3301.3
2013	25189.0	450.1	24738.8	479468	3666.3
2014	26149.7	427.5	25722.2	460770	3997.0

资料来源：旅游外汇收入总额、国内旅游者人数、国内旅游收入来源于北京市旅游发展委员会。

Source: Data of "Foreign Exchange Earnings of Tourism, Number of Domestic Tourists, Revenue from Domestic Tourism" were provided by Beijing Municipal Commission of Tourism Development.

16-2 按客源地分入境旅游者人数(1978-2014年)
NUMBER OF INBOUND TOURISTS BY COUNTRY/REGION (1978-2014)

单位：万人次 (10000 person-times)

年份 Year	入境旅游者人数 Number of Inbound Tourists	港澳台同胞 Hong Kong, Macao and Taiwan Tourists	外国人 Foreigner	#香港 Hong Kong	#日本 Japan	#韩国 Korea	#美国 United States	#英国 United Kingdom	#法国 France	#德国 Germany	#俄罗斯 Russia
1978	18.7	3.3	15.4								
1979	25.2	4.1	21.1								
1980	28.6	5.8	21.7		6.0		3.7	1.3	0.9	0.9	
1981-1985	**295.4**	**47.5**	**233.0**		**68.3**		**47.1**	**10.1**	**9.2**	**10.6**	
1981	39.4	6.8	31.3		5.3		3.8	1.1	1.1	1.0	
1982	45.7	8.2	35.9		8.2		6.6	1.3	1.3	1.4	
1983	50.9	8.9	39.7		10.0		9.4	1.5	1.5	1.7	0.1
1984	65.7	10.0	52.1		17.2		12.5	2.3	2.1	2.5	0.1
1985	93.7	13.6	74.0		27.6		14.8	3.9	3.2	4.0	0.2
1986-1990	**492.0**	**117.7**	**357.0**		**110.0**		**63.8**	**18.1**	**15.7**	**22.4**	**3.8**
1986	99.0	15.8	79.0		25.5		14.7	4.1	3.1	4.6	0.3
1987	108.1	21.8	81.7		26.3		16.5	4.5	4.3	5.1	0.3
1988	120.4	28.8	86.5		27.8		16.7	4.2	4.2	5.4	0.7
1989	64.5	16.6	46.0		12.2		7.3	2.4	2.1	3.3	1.0
1990	100.0	34.7	63.8	11.4	18.2		8.6	2.9	2.0	4.0	1.5
1991-1995	**919.6**	**217.9**	**683.4**	**122.7**	**188.0**	**47.2**	**68.9**	**25.2**	**30.1**	**45.9**	**27.4**
1991	132.0	38.2	91.4	17.6	27.6	4.3	9.5	4.3	3.7	6.0	3.5
1992	174.8	51.2	120.5	24.6	37.6	5.6	12.3	4.4	6.6	9.4	5.1
1993	202.8	52.8	145.0	29.4	39.3	7.3	14.3	5.3	6.9	12.0	7.7
1994	203.0	39.4	160.0	25.7	41.1	12.7	15.4	5.4	6.7	9.7	4.9
1995	207.0	36.3	166.5	25.4	42.4	17.3	17.4	5.8	6.2	8.8	6.2
1996-2000	**1203.3**	**206.2**	**984.3**	**128.3**	**229.4**	**92.6**	**118.6**	**43.8**	**37.5**	**53.0**	**28.1**
1996	218.9	38.6	176.2	25.5	43.0	18.0	18.5	7.5	6.6	10.0	6.9
1997	229.8	40.3	186.9	26.3	43.0	19.4	21.7	9.0	6.5	9.1	6.5
1998	220.1	39.1	178.2	25.0	43.5	8.2	23.2	8.8	6.9	11.3	6.2
1999	252.4	44.1	205.0	26.5	45.6	19.2	24.1	8.8	7.9	10.5	4.6
2000	282.1	44.1	238.0	25.0	54.3	27.8	31.1	9.7	9.6	12.1	3.9
2001-2005	**1459.7**	**220.9**	**1238.8**	**133.2**	**233.7**	**182.9**	**173.8**	**57.8**	**51.7**	**56.9**	**33.2**
2001	285.8	45.9	239.9	26.9	50.7	32.7	33.1	11.1	10.2	12.3	4.9
2002	310.4	43.9	266.5	25.5	56.5	38.0	37.4	12.9	11.3	12.2	5.2
2003	185.1	32.4	152.7	21.7	29.2	24.5	19.4	8.1	5.5	6.3	5.2
2004	315.5	47.4	268.1	27.7	52.3	42.4	37.4	11.8	11.1	11.5	8.2
2005	362.9	51.3	311.6	31.4	45.0	45.3	46.5	13.9	13.6	14.6	9.7
2006-2010	**2107.4**	**286.2**	**1821.1**	**174.4**	**248.2**	**207.9**	**291.8**	**82.4**	**72.3**	**85.7**	**85.2**
2006	390.3	52.0	338.3	30.3	50.6	42.4	49.8	14.8	14.2	15.3	15.0
2007	435.5	52.9	382.6	31.3	58.8	44.4	60.3	17.0	16.4	17.5	18.3
2008	379.0	43.3	335.7	28.1	40.0	35.3	53.8	17.5	14.5	16.0	17.9
2009	412.5	69.6	342.9	44.4	46.2	35.2	57.9	16.3	12.9	16.8	15.0
2010	490.1	68.4	421.6	40.3	52.6	50.6	70.0	16.8	14.3	20.1	19.0
2011	520.4	73.0	447.4	43.4	51.0	53.4	78.9	18.8	15.0	22.2	20.5
2012	500.9	66.5	434.4	37.6	43.7	44.2	75.1	18.5	15.1	24.5	20.0
2013	450.1	62.5	387.6	35.4	24.9	37.7	74.7	17.5	13.4	23.0	16.7
2014	427.5	62.0	365.5	34.2	24.9	38.7	71.5	16.9	13.4	22.6	13.7

注：1. 1980-1999年的入境旅游者人数由外国游客、港澳台游客、华侨三部分组成。
2. 1990-1999年香港游客人数为香港、澳门合计。

Note: a) "Number of inbound tourists" in 1980-1999 consisted of foreign visitors, visitors from Hong Kong, Macao and Taiwan, and overseas Chinese.

b) Tourists from Hong Kong in 1990-1999 were the total number of tourists from Hong Kong and Macao.

16-3 来京旅游者人数
NUMBER OF TOURISTS TO BEIJING

单位：万人次 (10000 person-times)

项目	Item	2014	2013	2014年为2013年% 2014 as % of 2013
合计	**Total**	**26149.7**	**25189.0**	**103.8**
国内旅游人数	**Number of Domestic Tourists**	**25722.2**	**24738.8**	**104.0**
外地来京旅游者人数	Number of Tourists to Beijing from Outside Beijing	15615.8	14755.5	105.8
市民在京游人数	Number of Beijing Citizens Touring in Beijing	10106.4	9983.3	101.2
入境旅游者人数	**Number of Inbound Tourists**	**427.5**	**450.1**	**95.0**
港澳台同胞	Hong Kong, Macao and Taiwan Tourists	62.0	62.5	99.2
中国香港	Hong Kong, China	34.2	35.4	96.6
中国澳门	Macao, China	2.2	1.8	123.5
中国台湾	Taiwan, China	25.6	25.3	101.0
外国人	Foreigners	365.5	387.6	94.3
亚洲	Asia	130.4	139.0	93.8
#日本	Japan	24.9	24.9	100.1
韩国	Korea	38.7	37.7	102.6
菲律宾	Philippines	1.9	2.3	82.8
印度尼西亚	Indonesia	5.4	6.2	87.8
马来西亚	Malaysia	8.1	13.4	60.7
新加坡	Singapore	11.6	13.0	89.8
泰国	Thailand	5.3	5.8	90.9
印度	India	6.9	7.2	95.5
蒙古	Mongolia	5.5	6.3	86.9
美洲	America	94.8	102.0	92.9
#美国	United States	71.5	74.7	95.7
加拿大	Canada	14.0	15.9	88.2
欧洲	Europe	112.8	117.9	95.7
#英国	United Kingdom	16.9	17.5	96.4
法国	France	13.4	13.4	99.7
德国	Germany	22.6	23.0	98.1
意大利	Italy	6.4	6.7	95.3
西班牙	Spain	4.5	4.4	103.6
瑞典	Sweden	4.6	5.0	92.1
瑞士	Switzerland	3.5	3.4	102.8
俄罗斯	Russia	13.7	16.7	82.0
大洋洲	Oceania	17.5	18.4	95.2
#澳大利亚	Australia	14.6	15.5	94.1
新西兰	New Zealand	2.0	2.2	87.7
非洲	Africa	9.2	9.4	98.3
其他	Others	0.7	0.9	84.0

资料来源：表中“国内旅游人数”的相关资料来自北京市旅游发展委员会。
Source: Data related to "Number of Domestic Tourists" in this table were provided by Beijing Municipal Commission of Tourism Development.

16-4 在京旅游花费构成情况(2005-2014年)
COMPOSITION OF EXPENDITURES FOR TOURISM IN BEIJING (2005-2014)

单位：% (%)

项　　目	Item	2005	2006	2007	2008	2009	2010	2011	2012	2013	2014
入境旅游者花费构成	**Compositition of Expenditures for Inbound Tourists**	**100.0**	**100.0**	**100.0**	**100.0**	**100.0**	**100.0**	**100.0**	**100.0**	**100.0**	**100.0**
长途交通费	Long-distance Transportation Expenses	35.3	30.0	29.0	31.1	37.4	28.1	26.4	28.0	26.9	27.0
民　航	Air	30.9	29.6	24.4	25.3	27.1	19.8	20.5	22.3	21.2	21.4
铁　路	Railway	1.1	0.3	3.0	3.6	5.5	5.3	3.4	3.3	3.7	3.6
公　路	Highway	3.3	0.1	1.6	2.2	4.8	3.0	2.5	2.4	2.0	2.0
市内交通费	Local Transportation Expenses	1.1	1.7	2.6	2.4	2.7	3.4	3.5	3.5	2.5	2.6
住　宿	Accommodation	17.3	32.0	16.9	16.4	14.5	14.4	15.5	16.5	16.9	16.7
餐　饮	Restaurants	9.2	11.7	8.7	8.7	7.5	8.7	6.8	7.4	7.3	7.4
购　物	Shopping	19.9	15.9	22.5	19.1	20.4	25.1	25.3	23.5	27.6	26.7
邮电通讯	Post and Telecommunications	3.4	0.8	2.7	3.8	2.7	3.2	2.0	2.2	1.7	1.7
景区游览	Scenic Spot Sightseeing	4.7	2.3	4.2	4.8	3.9	4.7	4.2	5.0	4.2	4.3
文化娱乐	Culture and Entertainment	4.6	3.2	5.0	4.5	4.6	5.0	6.0	5.4	3.8	4.0
其　他	Others	4.5	2.4	8.4	9.2	6.3	7.4	10.3	8.5	9.1	9.6
外地来京游客花费构成	**Compositition of Expenditures for Tourists from Outside Beijing**	**100.0**	**100.0**	**100.0**	**100.0**	**100.0**	**100.0**	**100.0**	**100.0**	**100.0**	**100.0**
长途交通费	Long-distance Transportation Expenses	12.8	15.1	16.3	15.4	12.9	12.8	13.5	15.5	17.0	17.6
民　航	Air		8.0	9.2	9.1	6.6	6.0	6.2	7.7	7.5	7.1
铁　路	Railway		6.1	6.4	4.5	1.3	5.8	6.9	7.5	9.1	10.2
公　路	Highway		1.1	0.7	1.8	5.0	1.0	0.3	0.3	0.4	0.3
市内交通费	Local Transportation Expenses	5.7	5.1	5.5	5.6	4.9	5.0	4.5	4.0	3.8	3.8
住　宿	Accommodation	17.2	14.9	17.3	15.1	17.7	19.6	20.0	19.8	19.5	20.2
餐　饮	Restaurants	19.8	18.7	20.5	23.2	21.8	20.2	20.9	21.4	21.4	22.1
购　物	Shopping	24.1	22.2	25.8	32.7	34.5	34.5	34.3	32.1	30.9	28.2
邮电通讯	Post and Telecommunications	1.0	1.2	1.8	1.0	0.6	0.5	0.3	0.2	0.2	0.3
景区游览	Scenic Spot Sightseeing	9.1	9.5	7.2	4.5	6.1	6.2	5.7	6.1	6.6	6.5
文化娱乐	Culture and Entertainment	3.1	2.5	1.9	1.6	1.2	1.0	0.8	0.7	0.5	0.6
其　他	Others	7.1	10.8	3.7	0.9	0.3	0.2	0.1	0.1	0.1	0.7

资料来源：北京市旅游发展委员会。
Source: Beijing Municipal Commission of Tourism Development.

16-5 旅游服务设施情况(1978-2014年)
TOURISM SERVICE FACILITIES (1978-2014)

年 份 Year	饭店个数(个) Number of Hotels (unit)	五星 5-star	四星 4-star	三星 3-star	二星 2-star	一星 1-star	饭店客房数(万间) Number of Hotel Guest Rooms (10,000 rooms)	旅行社家数(个) Number of Travel Agencies (unit)	#国际社 International Travel Agencies	A级及以上景区个数(个) Number of Scenic Spots at Grade-A and Above (unit)	5A	4A	3A	2A	1A
1978	11						0.39								
1979	13						0.44								
1980	20						0.49								
1981	35						0.69								
1982	39						1.00								
1983	41						1.03								
1984	50						1.30								
1985	63						1.66								
1986	80						2.10								
1987	97						2.40								
1988	96						2.80	30							
1989	101						3.50	77							
1990	122						3.95	77							
1991	213						4.40	69							
1992	226						5.20	69							
1993	226						5.20	55							
1994	175	14	20	32	72	37	5.40	297	113						
1995	197	15	25	43	79	35	5.90	310	125						
1996	204	15	25	46	82	36	6.10	349	128						
1997	248	16	26	60	109	37	6.80	350	130						
1998	258	16	32	65	113	32	7.00	380	135						
1999	268	17	32	71	117	31	7.20	419	144						
2000	409	21	34	132	176	46	8.40	456	150						
2001	506	21	43	154	230	58	9.30	490	160	47		17	4	22	4
2002	572	26	56	175	252	63	10.30	505	161	86		25	9	43	9
2003	614	30	62	195	267	60	10.90	530	165	93		28	9	46	10
2004	613	34	70	207	260	42	9.10	585	170	93		28	9	46	10
2005	652	36	79	224	267	46	10.97	714	196	124		36	26	50	12
2006	700	37	91	228	292	52	11.20	790	212	124		36	26	50	12
2007	806	42	114	257	338	55	13.00	844	239	154	4	41	35	54	20
2008	836	52	127	272	334	51	13.40	860	266	158	4	44	36	54	20
2009	757	54	129	268	269	37	12.95	888	265	179	4	55	53	51	16
2010	729	64	139	262	237	27	13.05	819		201	4	66	72	44	15
2011	598	63	127	207	181	20	11.64	919		211	6	63	80	46	16
2012	612	62	130	207	191	22	11.71	1021		203	8	64	78	40	13
2013	614	62	131	207	193	21	11.64	1147		213	8	67	86	42	10
2014	581	65	133	205	165	13	11.38	1243		221	8	69	89	45	10

注：1. 1993年及以前饭店数为涉外饭店口径,1994年以后为星级饭店口径。

2. 1994-1996年国际旅行社为一、二类旅行社合计。从2010年起，旅行社不再按国际旅行社和国内旅行社分组。

资料来源：北京市旅游发展委员会。

Note: a) Number of hotels in 1993 and before was the number of hotels for foreign tourists, and after 1994,the number of star-rated hotels.

b) International travel agencies were the total number of travel agencies of categories I and II after 1994-1996. From 2010, statistics of travel agencies were no more grouped into international and domestic angencies.

Source: Beijing Municipal Commission of Tourism Development.

16-6 星级饭店接待及经营情况(1995-2014年)
RECEPTION AND OPERATION OF STAR-RATED HOTELS (1995-2014)

年份 Year	企业个数 (个) Number of Enterprises (unit)	接待住宿人数 (万人次) Tourists Received (10000 person-time)	接待住宿人天数 (万人天) Persons-Day Received (10000 person-day)	出租率 (%) Renting Rate (%)	平均房价 (元/间天) Average Prices (yuan/room.day)	营业收入 (万元) Business Income (10000 yuan)	利润总额 (万元) Total Profits (10000 yuan)	从业人员平均人数 (人) Average Number of Employed Persons (person)
1995	191	484.6	1843.4	67.0	491	1136136	188095	98535
1996-2000		**3168.1**	**10110.0**			**5388348**	**286868**	
1996	207	485.3	1691.6	63.0	483	1132827	153145	94352
1997	235	541.8	1801.4	59.0	463	1145884	104918	103255
1998	262	605.0	1867.7	55.0	397	1038991	-24239	104391
1999	263	681.5	1918.6	57.0	352	970907	22383	103827
2000	294	854.5	2830.6	61.0	394	1099739	30661	96115
2001-2005		**5931.5**	**14152.9**			**7243160**	**316031**	
2001	363	1038.5	3191.7	62.0	384	1202746	50466	105792
2002	390	1071.2	2437.6	62.0	392	1307094	27212	107091
2003	441	1007.4	2497.2	52.0	389	1227956	-33471	105994
2004	464	1270.8	2798.9	65.0	409	1654198	117541	107386
2005	594	1543.6	3227.5	62.0	425	1851166	154283	126817
2006-2010		**8761.5**	**17721.0**			**11799293**	**650440**	
2006	597	1578.5	3284.5	61.3	460	2055300	194460	126430
2007	638	1664.2	3403.6	60.2	494	2369964	219891	129523
2008	694	1566.1	3206.6	52.0	605	2504849	232746	130609
2009	815	1827.3	3652.8	49.2	430	2261411	-76121	134159
2010	729	2125.4	4173.5	56.4	450	2607769	79464	130050
2011	598	2111.1	4119.6	59.9	482	2853358	162374	128609
2012	612	2101.0	4085.2	60.0	523	3031116	179495	122379
2013	614	1958.8	3769.5	58.4	530	2727974	111669	112512
2014	581	1940.3	3664.6	57.6	513	2568185	12499	99258

注：1. 表中企业个数为全市星级宾馆饭店数，其余指标1995-1999年为涉外饭店数据，2000年及以后为星级宾馆饭店数据。
2. 从2011年开始北京市旅游发展委员会每年对全市星级饭店进行重新评定，对未达标饭店取消星级。

Note: a) Number of Enterprises refer to the number of star-rated hotels in Beijing, Other indicators covered hotels for foreign tourists for 1995-1999, and star-rated hotels after 2000.
b) From 2011, Beijing Municipal Tourism Development Commission reevalutaed star-rated hotels across the city , and cancelled the rating of hotels that did not meet the standard.

16-7 星级饭店经营情况
OPERATION OF STAR-RATED HOTELS

项 目	Item	企业个数(个) Number of Enterprises (unit)		出租率(%) Renting Rate (%)		平均房价(元/间天) Average Prices (yuan/room.day)	
		2014	2013	2014	2013	2014	2013
合 计	**Total**	**581**	**614**	**57.6**	**58.4**	**513**	**530**
四星、五星合计	**Hotels of 4 and 5 Star Grade**	**198**	**193**	**60.2**	**61.6**	**630**	**669**
五 星	5-Star	65	62	63.0	62.2	802	858
四 星	4-Star	133	131	58.1	61.0	489	500
一星至三星合计	**Hotels of 1 to 3-Star Grade**	**383**	**421**	**54.0**	**54.0**	**330**	**335**
三 星	3-Star	205	207	54.6	55.5	357	361
二 星	2-Star	165	193	54.0	51.6	268	252
一 星	1-Star	13	21	27.6	41.3	181	217

16-7 续表 Continued

项 目	Item	营业收入(万元) Business Income (10000 yuan)		利润总额(万元) Total Profits (10000 yuan)		从业人员平均人数(人) Average Number of Employed Persons (person)	
		2014	2013	2014	2013	2014	2013
合 计	**Total**	**2568185**	**2727974**	**12499**	**111669**	**99258**	**112512**
四星、五星合计	**Hotels of 4 and 5 Star Grade**	**1937983**	**2052400**	**32711**	**123904**	**67168**	**75875**
五 星	5-Star	1120181	1169186	42689	93325	32265	35947
四 星	4-Star	817802	883214	-9978	30579	34903	39928
一星至三星合计	**Hotels of 1 to 3-Star Grade**	**630202**	**675574**	**-20212**	**-12235**	**32090**	**36637**
三 星	3-Star	507979	548796	-22091	-13084	25497	29381
二 星	2-Star	120237	121045	1872	635	6404	6849
一 星	1-Star	1986	5734	7	214	189	407

16-8 星级饭店接待住宿者情况(按住宿者类别分)
TOURSITS RECEIVED BY STAR-RATED HOTELS (BY TYPE OF TOURISTS)

项目	Item	2014		2013		2014年为2013年%
		接待量 Tourists Received	构成(%) Composition (%)	接待量 Tourists Received	构成(%) Composition (%)	2014 as % of 2013
接待住宿人数 (万人次)	**Tourists Received (10000 person-times)**	**1940.3**	**100.0**	**1958.8**	**100.0**	**99.1**
国内住宿者	Domestic Tourists	1693.8	87.3	1693.6	86.5	100.0
外国人	Foreigners	215.5	11.1	233.5	11.9	92.3
香港同胞	Compatriots from Hong Kong, China	17.1	0.9	18.0	0.9	94.9
澳门同胞	Compatriots from Macao, China	0.8	0.0	0.8	0.0	110.7
台湾同胞	Compatriots from Taiwan, China	13.0	0.7	13.0	0.7	100.4
接待住宿人天数 (万人天)	**Persons-day Received (10000 persons-day)**	**3664.6**	**100.0**	**3769.5**	**100.0**	**97.2**
国内住宿者	Domestic Tourists	3127.5	85.3	3181.1	84.4	98.3
外国人	Foreigners	469.3	12.8	518.5	13.8	90.5
香港同胞	Compatriots from Hong Kong, China	35.8	1.0	38.1	1.0	94.1
澳门同胞	Compatriots from Macao, China	2.2	0.1	2.0	0.1	111.0
台湾同胞	Compatriots from Taiwan, China	29.8	0.8	29.8	0.8	100.1

16-9 星级饭店接待住宿者情况(按饭店星级分)
TOURSITS RECEIVED BY STAR-RATED HOTELS (BY STAR RATING)

单位：万人次 (10000 person-times)

项目	Item	2014		2013		2014年为2013年%
		接待量 Tourists Received	构成(%) Composition (%)	接待量 Tourists Received	构成(%) Composition (%)	2014 as % of 2013
接待住宿人数	**Tourists Received**	**1940.3**	**100.0**	**1958.8**	**100.0**	**99.1**
五星级	5-Star	516.9	26.6	541.6	27.6	95.4
四星级	4-Star	623.3	32.1	624.8	31.9	99.7
三星级	3-Star	541.7	27.9	563.0	28.7	96.2
二星级	2-Star	249.4	12.9	215.2	11.0	115.9
一星级	1-Star	9.0	0.5	14.1	0.7	64.0
接待入境住宿人数	**Inbound Tourists Received**	**246.5**	**100.0**	**265.2**	**100.0**	**92.9**
五星级	5-Star	139.5	56.6	150.4	56.7	92.8
四星级	4-Star	85.4	34.6	89.8	33.9	95.1
三星级	3-Star	16.1	6.5	18.4	6.9	87.6
二星级	2-Star	5.5	2.2	6.6	2.5	83.1
一星级	1-Star	0.02	0.01	0.1	0.04	14.6

16-10 旅行社接待及经营情况(1990-2014年)
RECEPTION AND OPERATION OF TRAVEL AGENCIES (1990-2014)

年 份 Year	企 业 个 数 (个) Number of Enterprises (unit)	外联(组团) 人 数 (万人次) Number of Inbound Tourists (Organized) (10000 person-times)	接 待 人 数 (万人次) Tourists Received (10000 person-times)	国内居民 出境人数 (万人次) Number of Outbound Chinese Tourists (10000 person-times)	营 业 收 入 (万元) Business Income (10000 yuan)	利 润 总 额 (万元) Total Profits (10000 yuan)	从业人员 平均人数 (人) Average Number of Employed Persons (person)
1990		32.5	54.7				
1991-1995		**355.6**	**451.7**				
1991		53.3	69.1				
1992		61.2	100.7				
1993		71.3	103.6				
1994		84.1	91.0	1.0			
1995	100	85.7	87.4	1.2	290987.9	107654.6	
1996-2000		**487.1**	**417.5**	**37.9**	**2187374.9**	**106167.0**	
1996	105	88.0	78.6	2.7	351634.7	13520.8	
1997	110	87.3	76.0	3.8	386254.1	16009.6	
1998	131	85.0	69.0	6.6	387562.7	21319.9	
1999	120	103.1	92.9	11.1	485678.8	26572.0	
2000	127	123.7	101.0	13.7	576244.6	28744.7	6280
2001-2005		**986.2**	**919.6**	**185.4**	**4453919.0**	**51899.5**	
2001	140	143.4	130.1	21.9	700529.0	18682.5	8259
2002	151	179.4	176.3	28.5	823551.0	23362.0	9350
2003	147	80.2	82.4	31.9	553787.0	-11829.0	8382
2004	147	274.8	252.6	51.4	1059989.0	11444.0	7760
2005	147	308.4	278.2	51.7	1316063.0	10240.0	8752
2006-2010		**2036.3**	**1852.4**	**515.9**	**11530195.8**	**82083.6**	
2006	147	343.9	315.7	79.2	1610265.0	7012.0	8659
2007	189	424.1	377.9	100.2	2101874.5	28409.2	11597
2008	245	359.6	310.1	102.0	2166898.1	18121.6	14369
2009	265	370.6	306.6	84.9	2134058.8	5904.6	15262
2010	819	538.1	542.2	149.6	3517099.4	22636.2	21454
2011	919	593.9	552.3	184.3	4436713.3	20879.2	23871
2012	1021	684.5	519.1	272.5	5415692.9	35274.4	28022
2013	1147	661.3	441.6	331.0	6103603.4	64177.5	31694
2014	1243	628.0	427.0	410.2	6989125.4	27881.7	33591

注：1. 本表2009年及以前为国际旅行社口径，从2010年起调整为全部旅行社口径。
2. 国内居民出境人数为旅行社组织出境游客的实际人次数，不重复统计。

Note: a) Figures in this table refer to international travel agencies in and before 2009, and all travel agencies after 2010.
b) Number of outbound Chinese visitors is the actual number of tourists going abroad that were organized by travel agencies, which has not been calculated repeatedly.

16-11 旅行社外联(组团)及接待情况
TOURISTS GROUPED (ORGANIZED) AND RECEIVED BY TRAVEL AGENCIES

项 目	Item	2014	2013	2014年为2013年% 2014 as % of 2013
外联(组团)人数 (万人次)	**Tourists Grouped (Organized) (10000 person-times)**	**628.0**	**661.3**	**94.9**
国内旅游者	Domestic Tourists	457.2	470.8	97.1
港澳同胞	Compatriots from Hong Kong and Macao, China	4.2	4.9	86.2
台湾同胞	Compatriots from Taiwan, China	4.3	4.0	109.7
外国人	Foreigners	162.2	181.7	89.3
接待人数 (万人次)	**Tourists Received (10000 person-times)**	**427.0**	**441.6**	**96.7**
国内旅游者	Domestic Tourists	317.2	319.5	99.3
港澳同胞	Compatriots from Hong Kong and Macao, China	8.5	6.5	131.4
台湾同胞	Compatriots from Taiwan, China	3.6	3.5	103.7
外国人	Foreigners	97.7	112.1	87.1
外联(组团)人天数(万人天)	**Persons-day of Tourists Grouped (Organized) (10000 persons-day)**	**2469.6**	**2435.1**	**101.4**
国内旅游者	Domestic Tourists	1693.0	1781.8	95.0
港澳同胞	Compatriots from Hong Kong and Macao, China	17.6	18.7	94.2
台湾同胞	Compatriots from Taiwan, China	23.5	19.3	121.7
外国人	Foreigners	735.5	615.3	119.5
接待人天数 (万人天)	**Persons-day of Tourists Received (10000 persons-day)**	**1656.8**	**1701.5**	**97.4**
国内旅游者	Domestic Tourists	1137.3	1161.6	97.9
港澳同胞	Compatriots from Hong Kong and Macao, China	41.7	29.0	143.7
台湾同胞	Compatriots from Taiwan, China	19.1	18.2	105.1
外国人	Foreigners	458.7	492.7	93.1

16-12 旅行社组织国内居民出境旅游情况
OUTBOUND CHINESE TOURISTS ORGANIZED BY TRAVEL AGENCIES

单位：万人次 (10000 person-times)

项 目	Item	2014	2013	2014年为2013年% 2014 as % of 2013
旅行社个数(个)	**Number of Travel Agencies (unit)**	**367**	**259**	**141.7**
国内居民出境人数	**Number of Outbound Chinese Tourists**	**410.2**	**331.0**	**123.9**
前往国别及地区	**Countries and Regions of Destination**			
#中国香港	Hong Kong, China	26.3	29.6	88.8
中国澳门	Macao, China	13.3	11.3	117.5
中国台湾	Taiwan, China	27.1	18.3	148.1
泰 国	Thailand	47.1	64.8	72.8
新加坡	Singapore	10.6	16.6	64.2
马来西亚	Malaysia	9.4	17.1	55.1
菲律宾	Philippines	3.5	3.7	93.5
韩 国	Korea	73.7	41.1	179.4
日 本	Japan	43.5	18.7	232.4
澳大利亚	Australia	11.2	11.3	99.0
新西兰	New Zealand	5.4	6.3	85.5

注：1. 本表统计范围为有特许经营出境旅游业务权的旅行社。
2. 国内居民出境人数为旅行社组织出境游客的实际人次数，不重复统计。
3. 前往国别及地区统计中，游客一次出境旅游去往多个国家及地区的，分别计入前往国家及地区。

Note: a) Figures in this table cover the travel agencies that are franchised to operate outbound travelling business.
b) Number of outbound Chinese tourists is the actual number of tourists going abroad who were organized by travel agencies,which has not been calculated repeatedly.
c) In the statistics for "countries and regions of destination", if a tourist went to several countries and regions, he/she would be included in each country and region.

16-13 旅行社经营情况
OPERATION OF TRAVEL SERVICES

单位：万元 (10000 yuan)

项目	Item	2014	2013	2014年为2013年% 2014 as % of 2013
企业个数 (个)	Number of Enterprises (unit)	1243	1147	108.4
营业收入	Business Income	6989125.4	6103603.4	114.5
主营业务成本	Main Business Cost	6514223.8	5684509.5	114.6
营业费用	Business Expenses	244497.5	193978.6	126.0
主营业务税金及附加	Main Business Tax and Surtax	28120.7	24865.8	113.1
主营业务利润	Main Business Profits	437225.4	389009.4	112.4
管理费用	Management Expenses	213697.3	186359.8	114.7
营业利润	Business Profits	20062.7	57391.3	35.0
利润总额	Total Profits	27881.7	64177.5	43.4
从业人员平均人数 (人)	Average Number of Employed Persons (person)	33591	31694	106.0

16-14 A级及以上和重点旅游景区活动情况
STATISTICS FOR KEY SIGHT SPOTS ABOVE GRADE A

项目	Item	2014	2013	2014年为2013年% 2014 as % of 2013
A级及以上和重点旅游景区数 (个)	Number of Key Sight Spots Above Grade (unit)	221	215	102.8
收入合计 (万元)	Total Income (10000 yuan)	656909	621561	105.7
门票收入	Ticket Income	417698	398495	104.8
商品销售收入	Commodity Sales	16750	13445	124.6
其他收入	Other Income	222462	209621	106.1
接待人数 (万人次)	Tourists Received (10000 person-times)	28685	26726	107.3
#入境旅游者人数	Inbound Tourists	897	947	94.7

主要统计指标解释

入境旅游者 指来中国（大陆）观光、度假、探亲访友、就医疗养、购物、参加会议或从事经济、文化、体育、宗教活动，且在中国（大陆）的旅游住宿设施内至少停留一夜的外国人、港澳台同胞等游客。入境旅游者不包括以下人员：（1）应邀来华访问的政府部长以上官员及其随行人员；（2）外国驻华使领馆官员、外交人员以及随行的家庭服务人员和受赡养者；（3）常住中国（大陆）一年以上的外国专家、留学生、记者、商务机构人员等；（4）乘坐国际航班过境不需要通过护照检查进入中国（大陆）口岸的中转旅客；（5）边境地区往来的边民；（6）回大陆定居的港澳台同胞；（7）已在中国（大陆）定居的外国人和原已出境又返回在中国（大陆）定居的外国侨民；（8）归国的中国（大陆）出国人员。

国内旅游者 指中国（大陆）居民离开惯常居住地在境内其他地方的旅游住宿设施内至少停留一夜，最长不超过12个月的国内游客。

旅游外汇收入 指入境游客在中国（大陆）境内旅行、游览过程中用于交通、参观游览、住宿、餐饮、购物、娱乐等全部花费。

国内旅游收入 指国内游客在国内旅行、游览过程中用于交通、参观游览、住宿、餐饮、购物、娱乐等全部花费。

外联（组团）入境旅游者人数 指报告期内旅行社自组外联的入境旅游者人数，反映旅行社对外招徕的能力。旅行社按以下要求统计外联人数：入境游客不论其停留时间多少、旅游线路长短，只统计一次；旅行社只统计本社自组外联团的实到人数，不包括非本社外联、仅由本社接受委托办理签证的人数。

接待入境旅游者人数 指报告期内本旅行社派地陪接待的入境人数。

出境旅游总人数 指中国（大陆）公民因公或因私出境前往其他国家、中国香港特别行政区、澳门特别行政区和台湾省观光、度假、探亲访友、就医疗养、购物、参加会议或从事经济、文化、体育、宗教活动的人数。统计时，出境游客按每出境一次统计1人次。

Explanatory Notes on Main Statistical Indicators

Inbound Tourists refer to tourists from foreign countries, Hong Kong, Macao and Taiwan to (mainland of) China for sightseeing, holidays, visiting relatives and friends, medical service and rehabilitation, shopping, conferences, or economic, cultural, sports and religious activities, and staying in a tour accommodation facility in (the mainland of) China for at least one night. They do not include: (1) officials above the rank of governmental ministers, and their accompanying persons who visit China upon invitation; (2) officials in foreign embassies and consulates in Beijing, diplomatic personnel, and their accompanying family service personnel and dependents; (3) foreign experts, students, reporters, and personnel in business institutions who have been in (the mainland of) China for more than one year; (4) transit passengers via (the mainland of) China by international flights without passport checking; (5) people living on the frontiers who pass through borders; (6) compatriots from Hong Kong, Macao and Taiwan who settle down in the mainland of China; (7) Foreigners that have settled down in China and foreign nationals that have left the country and then come back to settle down in (the mainland of) China; (8) Chinese (Mainland) people who have gone abroad and returned to China.

Domestic Tourists refer to domestic visitors as residents in (the mainland of) China who leave their regular dwelling places to stay at least one night and at most 12 months in a travel accommodation facility of other domestic places.

Foreign Exchange Earnings of Tourism means the total spending of international tourists on traffic, tour, accommodation, restaurants, shopping, entertainment and so on during their tour and travel in (the mainland of) China.

Revenue from Domestic Tourism means the total spending of domestic tourists on traffic, tour, accommodation, restaurants, shopping and entertainment, and so on during their tour and travel in China.

Number of Inbound Tourists Organized by Travel Agencies means the number of inbound tourists organized by travel agencies in the reporting period. It shows the capacity of travel agencies in attracting inbound tourists; travel agencies shall count the tourists organized as follows: an inbound tourist is regarded as one visit regardless of the duration and distance of the tour; only the actual tourists organized by travel agencies are included. Those organized by other travel agencies or those who have visa submitted by the travel agencies are not included.

Number of Inbound Tourists Received means the number of inbound tourists received by local guides dispatched by travel agencies in the reporting period.

Total Number of Outbound Tourists means the number of citizens from (the mainland of) China who visit other countries, Hong Kong Special Administrative Region of PRC, Macao Special Administrative Region of PRC, and Taiwan for sightseeing, holiday, visiting relatives and friends, medical service and rehabilitation, shopping, conferences, or economic, cultural, sport and religious activities for official or private purpose. One visit is calculated as one person-time.

17

金融和保险
FINANCE AND INSURANCE

简要说明

一、本章资料的主要内容

本章反映北京地区金融业发展情况。主要包括以下四个部分:

1. 金融机构信贷收支情况;
2. 证券市场交易情况;
3. 保险业务情况;
4. 上市公司基本情况。

二、本章资料的数据来源

1. 信贷收支数据来源于中国人民银行营业管理部。
2. 证券市场交易量数据来源于北京市统计局。
3. 银行、保险系统机构及人员数据来源于北京市统计局。
4. 保险业务数据来源于中国保险监督管理委员会北京监管局。
5. 上市公司数据来源于中国证券监督管理委员会北京证监局。

Brief Introduction

I. Main Content

This chapter reflects the development of the financial industry in Beijing, mainly consisting of four parts:

1. Balance of credit for financial institutions;
2. Transactions in securities market;
3. Insurance business;
4. Basic information of listed companies.

II. Source of Data

1. Figures of balance of credit are gathered from the Banking Management Department of the People's Bank of China.
2. Data of transactions in securities market are gathered from Beijing Municipal Bureau of Statistics.
3. Data of banks, insurance institutions and personnel are gathered from Beijing Municipal Bureau of Statistics.
4. Data of insurance business are gathered from Beijing Bureau of China Insurance Regulatory Commission.
5. Data of basic information of listed companies are gathered from Beijing Securities Regulatory Bureau of China Securities Regulatory Commission.

17-1 北京市金融机构(含外资)存贷款余额(1978-2014年)
DEPOSIT AND LOAN BALANCE OF FINANCIAL INSTITUTIONS (INCLUDING FOREIGN BANKS) (1978-2014)

单位：亿元 (100 million yuan)

年份 Year	金融机构本外币存款 Balance of Savings Deposit in Domestic and Foreign Currencies in Financial Institutions	#个人储蓄存款 Individual Saving Deposits	#人民币存款 RMB Deposits	#个人储蓄存款 Individual Saving Deposits	金融机构本外币存款 Deposits in Domestic and Foreign Currencies in Financial Institutions: 中资金融机构 Chinese Financial Institutions: 存款合计 Total Deposits	人民币存款 RMB Deposits	外汇(亿美元) Foreign Exchange (USD 100 million)	外资银行 Foreign-funded Financial Bank: 存款合计 Total Deposits	人民币存款 RMB Deposits	外汇(亿美元) Foreign Exchange (USD 100 million)
1978						114.7				
1979						139.1				
1980						168.0				
1981						220.5				
1982						279.2				
1983						321.3				
1984						375.5				
1985						411.0				
1986						508.8				
1987						610.8				
1988						609.9				
1989						717.6				
1990						893.9				
1991						1244.1				
1992						1528.3				
1993						1873.1				
1994						2677.3				
1995						3527.2				
1996						4378.9				
1997						5228.0				
1998						6666.8				
1999						8267.2				
2000	11526.0					9759.8	205.6			…
2001	14109.2	4599.8			14042.1	12223.4	219.8			7.3
2002	17438.4	5559.5			17369.9	15392.7	238.9			8.3
2003	20476.0	6441.4			20398.2	18321.9	250.9			9.4
2004	23781.3	7154.3	21625.9	6122.3	23679.3	21625.9	248.1			12.3
2005	28969.9	8315.8	26785.9	7477.7	28800.9	26731.3	256.4		54.6	14.2
2006	33793.3	9515.0	31313.8	8705.1	33484.1	31179.2	295.2		134.5	22.4
2007	37700.3	9743.5	35369.7	9155.3	37087.5	35014.1	283.8		355.6	35.2
2008	43980.7	12538.1	42107.6	11955.2	43094.4	41500.0	233.3	886.3	607.5	40.8
2009	56960.1	15329.2	54275.5	14672.1	55804.8	53428.8	348.0	1155.3	846.6	45.2
2010	66584.6	17585.2	64453.9	17003.1	64897.6	63025.2	282.7	1687.0	1428.7	39.0
2011	75001.9	19690.6	72655.4	19126.1	73018.9	70985.1	322.8	1983.1	1670.3	49.6
2012	84837.3	22298.6	81389.6	21644.9	82615.9	79620.6	476.5	2221.4	1769.1	72.0
2013	91660.5	23747.6	87990.6	23086.4	89187.4	85897.2	539.6	2473.1	2093.4	62.3
2014	100095.5	24855.7	95370.5	24158.4	97645.9	93326.0	706.0	2449.6	2044.5	66.2

资料来源：中国人民银行营业管理部。
Source: Banking Management Department of People's Bank of China.

17-1 续表 Continued

单位：亿元 (100 million yuan)

年份 Year	金融机构本外币贷款余额 Balance of Loans in Domestic and Foreign Currencies in Financial Institutions	#人民币贷款 RMB Loans	#中长期贷款 Medium-term &Long-term Loans	金融机构本外币贷款 Loans in Domestic and Foreign Currencies in Financial Institutions：中资金融机构 Chinese Financial Institutions：贷款合计 Total Loans	人民币贷款 RMB Loans	外汇(亿美元) Foreign Exchange (USD 100 million)	外资银行 Foreign-funded Financial Bank：贷款合计 Total Loans	人民币贷款 RMB Loans	外汇(亿美元) Foreign Exchange (USD 100 million)
1978					53.9				
1979					74.2				
1980					87.3				
1981					91.3				
1982					109.1				
1983					149.5				
1984					174.3				
1985					249.8				
1986					299.2				
1987					346.1				
1988					415.7				
1989					487.1				
1990					573.1				
1991					735.8				
1992					894.7				
1993					1128.1				
1994					1429.0				
1995					1779.1				
1996					2082.8				
1997					2720.7				
1998					3326.6				
1999					4007.8				
2000	6407.9		3106.7	6306.3	6008.2	27.7			9.0
2001	7612.2		3797.3	7514.9	7202.9	37.4			10.8
2002	9704.3		5026.9	9602.6	9230.8	44.9			12.1
2003	12057.7		6352.0	11884.4	11314.7	68.8			20.9
2004	13577.7		7506.4	13312.3	12600.2	86.0			32.0
2005	15335.5		8632.4	14996.6	13792.2	149.2		42.3	36.8
2006	18131.6	15632.7	11142.8	17631.7	15486.9	274.7		145.8	45.4
2007	19861.5	17812.5	12217.6	19053.9	17360.2	231.9	807.5	452.3	48.6
2008	23010.7	19985.0	14688.9	22160.5	19431.1	399.4	850.2	554.0	43.3
2009	31052.9	25421.8	21163.8	30151.6	24805.1	783.0	901.3	616.7	41.7
2010	36479.6	29563.8	26180.2	35352.0	28748.1	997.2	1127.6	815.6	47.1
2011	39660.5	33367.0	24886.3	38410.3	32434.6	948.4	1250.2	932.5	50.4
2012	43189.5	36441.3	26333.5	41839.8	35441.7	1017.9	1349.7	999.6	55.7
2013	47880.9	40506.7	28171.7	46539.5	39557.5	1145.2	1341.4	949.2	64.3
2014	53650.6	45458.7	30882.3	52254.3	44438.8	1277.3	1396.2	1019.9	61.5

资料来源：中国人民银行营业管理部。
Source: Banking Management Department of People's Bank of China.

17-2 北京市金融机构(含外资)本外币信贷收支表
BALANCE OF CREIT IN DOMESTIC AND FOREIGN CURRENCIES FOR FINANCIAL INSTITUTIONS (INCLUDE FOREIGN BANKS)

单位：万元，汇率：6.1190 （10000 yuan,at an exchange rate of 6.1190）

项目	Item	余额 Balance		比年初增减额(+、-) Increase or Decrease than the Beginning of the Year	
		2014	2013	2014	2013
各项存款	**Total Deposits**	**1000955390**	**916605365**	**84350042**	**65888214**
#人民币存款	RMB	953705350	879905968	73799399	63869315
单位存款	Corporate Deposits	633930504	576116247	57643740	59626838
个人存款	Individual Deposits	264966801	255520029	9446771	4837783
#储蓄存款	Saving Deposits	248557100	237475704	11081395	15134441
财政性存款	Fiscal Deposits	21903562	14008775	7894788	390090
临时性存款	Provisional Deposits	807434	1164507	-186539	166488
委托存款	Entrusted Deposits	6513867	5230118	1283749	-57881
其他存款	Other Deposits	72833221	64565688	8267533	924897
各项贷款	**Total Loans**	**536505634**	**478809245**	**56613609**	**45786988**
#人民币贷款	RMB Loans	454587067	405066994	48446782	39540595
境内贷款	Domestic Loans	505764907	450521555	54124580	45928488
短期贷款	Short-term Loans	176390052	156937975	18597130	28085372
中长期贷款	Medium-term & Long-term Loans	308822667	281717190	26841652	18568762
融资租赁	Financial Lease	1407680	439723	967956	-65132
票据融资	Bill Financing	18821833	11372481	7449352	-656380
各项垫款	Advances	322675	54186	268489	-4133
境外贷款	Oversea Loans	30740727	28287690	2489030	-141500

资料来源：中国人民银行营业管理部。
Source: Banking Management Department of People's Bank of China.

17-3 北京市中资金融机构本外币信贷收支表
BALANCE OF CREDIT IN DOMESTIC AND FOREIGN CURRENCIES FOR DOMESTICALLY-FUNDED FINANCIAL INSTITUTIONS

单位：万元，汇率：6.1190 （10000 yuan ,at an exchange rate of 6.1190）

项目	Item	余额 Balance		比年初增减额(+、-) Increase or Decrease than Year-beginning	
		2014	2013	2014	2013
各项存款	**Total Deposits**	**976459192**	**891873927**	**84585265**	**65397100**
#人民币存款	RMB	933259862	858972033	74287830	62458926
单位存款	Corporate Deposits	613651429	555774582	57706313	59214062
个人存款	Individual Deposits	262031633	252388346	9643287	4808788
#储蓄存款	Saving Deposits	246247170	235173334	11073835	15070962
财政性存款	Fiscal Deposits	21903562	14008775	7894788	390090
临时性存款	Provisional Deposits	791083	1151010	-189394	165188
委托存款	Entrusted Deposits	6513867	5230118	1283749	-57881
其他存款	Other Deposits	71567618	63321096	8246523	876853
各项贷款	**Total Loans**	**522543447**	**465395030**	**56065638**	**46001668**
#人民币贷款	RMB Loans	444388412	395575414	47739707	40175609
境内贷款	Domestic Loans	492451181	437801840	53530568	46173144
短期贷款	Short-term Loans	169564944	150488145	18237152	28569063
中长期贷款	Medium-term&Long-term Loans	303764023	276796332	26688567	18503870
融资租赁	Financial Lease	1407680	439723	967956	-65132
票据融资	Bill Financing	17394514	10023454	7371060	-830524
各项垫款	Advances	320019	54186	265833	-4133
境外贷款	Oversea Loans	30092267	27593189	2535070	-171476

资料来源：中国人民银行营业管理部。
Source: Banking Management Department of People's Bank of China.

17-4 银行、保险系统机构及人员(2014年)
INSTITUTIONS AND PERSONNEL OF BANKING AND INSURANCE SYSTEMS (2014)

项目	Item	银行系统 Banking System		保险系统 Insurance System	
		机构(个) Institutions (unit)	人员(人) Personnel (person)	机构(个) Institutions (unit)	人员(人) Personnel (person)
全市	**Total**	**4018**	**189776**	**645**	**119954**
首都功能核心区	Core Functional Area of the Capital	731	97330	170	41996
城市功能拓展区	Urban Function Extension Area	2052	72933	214	53858
城市发展新区	New Area of Urban Development	839	14003	179	17458
生态涵养发展区	Ecological Conservation Area	396	5510	82	6642

注：1. 本表口径为在北京地区经营的银行、保险公司的总行(总公司)、分行(分公司)及所属分支机构。
2. 保险系统人员构成中含营销员。

Note: a) Figures in this table cover the headquarters (head offices), branches banks (branch companies) and subsidiaries of banks and insurance companies operating in Beijing.
b) Personnel of insurance system includes marketing personnel.

17-5 上市公司基本情况(1993-2014年)
LISTED COMPANIES (1993-2014)

年份 Year	年末上市公司(家) Companies Listed by Year-end (unit)	上市公司总股本(万股) Total Equity of Listed Companies (10000 Shares)	股票首发数量(万股) Initial Public Offering Shares (10000 Shares)	首发募集资金(亿元) Funds Raised Through IPO (10000 yuan)	增发募集资金(亿元) Funds Raised Through Right Offerings (10000 yuan)	配股募集资金(亿元) Funds Raised Through Seasoned Equity Offerings (10000 yuan)
1993	3	24592	3924	58.0		28.8
1994	7	124038	20300	11.7		0.5
1995	7	133309				3.8
1996-2000			**439955**	**304.4**	**33.0**	**85.8**
1996	13	198956	29763	12.8		1.9
1997	26	470026	80200	52.2		7.0
1998	33	723561	52750	32.9		20.2
1999	43	1439894	121242	63.0	10.8	10.7
2000	54	2015049	156000	143.5	22.2	46.0
2001-2005			**764200**	**413.8**	**49.2**	**26.3**
2001	63	9764783	345500	191.6		17.0
2002	68	11929954	23800	16.8	14.9	
2003	74	11493598	373600	188.7	2.8	2.2
2004	83	12553074	21300	16.7	28.4	7.1
2005	83	13159721			3.1	
2006-2010			**11456582**	**6506.1**	**1665.5**	**852.8**
2006	92	58156652	2667911	1073.4	79.4	
2007	104	86151941	2428976	2433.3	304.7	12.1
2008	109	90486962	698853	546.9	502.0	63.8
2009	126	97911881	2179290	1154.2	430.7	
2010	165	137726461	3481552	1298.3	348.7	777.0
2011	194	143088054	420483	462.0	661.7	175.6
2012	217	146788089	211752	191.4	436.2	69.1
2013	219	151694399			183.9	32.5
2014	235	214359521	67787	74.9	1319.0	4.9

注：1. 此表数据统计口径为注册地统计。
2. 1995年、2005年和2013年没有新股发行。

资料来源：中国证券监督管理委员会北京证监局。

Note: a) Statistics in this table are counted in terms of registered area.
b) There were no shares issued in 1995, 2005 and 2013.

Source: Beijing Regulatory Bureau of China Securities Regulatory Commission.

17-6 证券市场交易额情况(1994-2014年)
TRADE VOLUME OF STOCK MARKETS (1994-2014)

单位：亿元 (100 million yuan)

年份 Year	证券市场交易额 Trading Volume of Stock Market	#股票交易 Stock Trading	#基金交易 Fund Trading	#债券交易 Bond Trading	年末证券市场累计开户数(万户) Total Investors in Stock Markets (year-end) (10000 investors)
1994	183.26	135.51		47.75	
1995	1619.04	520.48		152.31	
1996	5224.77	2900.63		2324.06	
1997	7934.42	3900.93		3844.82	
1998	10241.50	3426.37	187.02	6435.43	
1999	10694.46	5268.19	341.74	5005.52	88.93
2000	14456.98	9136.52	346.02	4825.91	115.18
2001	12596.50	5339.61	400.61	6729.69	148.95
2002	12565.91	3788.22	485.77	8216.53	154.99
2003	23369.83	5041.40	110.45	18048.37	162.39
2004	18512.92	7247.72	78.94	10928.92	166.21
2005	9322.49	4343.65	91.30	4567.28	169.83
2006	19557.06	14851.55	298.27	2075.20	189.37
2007	97978.66	77487.83	1534.96	2060.09	314.92
2008	62773.56	46231.27	1389.37	4052.52	373.62
2009	92148.02	78339.50	2253.54	1791.32	426.10
2010	87575.38	79843.07	1714.94	3384.28	475.14
2011	79103.13	61743.17	1494.81	15275.31	521.53
2012	85412.95	44993.38	2355.87	37388.61	551.50
2013	145932.74	61596.27	4104.79	69625.37	563.61
2014	232318.56	85714.54	7311.67	110657.53	587.47

17-7 证券市场交易额情况
TRADE VOLUME OF STOCK MARKETS

项目	Item	2014	2013	2014年为2013年% 2014 as % of 2013
成交额合计 (亿元)	**Total Trade Volume (100 million yuan)**	**232318.6**	**145932.7**	**159.2**
股票交易	Stock Trading	85714.5	61596.3	139.2
债券交易	Bond Trading	110657.5	69625.4	158.9
债券现货	Bonds in Stock	2867.5	1270.7	225.7
债券回购	Bond Repurchasing	107790.0	68354.7	157.7
募集资金交易	Trading of Funds Raised	345.5	92.9	372.0
基金交易	Fun Trading	7311.7	4104.8	178.1
其他交易	Other Tradings	28289.3	10513.4	269.1
年末证券市场累计开户数 (万户)	**Total Investors in Stock Markets (10000 investors)**	**587.5**	**563.6**	**104.2**

17-8 保险业务情况(1997-2014年) INSURANCE BUSINESS (1997-2014)

单位：亿元 (100 million yuan)

年份 Year	原保险保费收入 Premium Income of Original Insurance	人身险 Life Insurance	财产险 Property Insurance	赔付支出 Compensation Expenses	人身险 Life Insurance	财产险 Property Insurance
1997	102.5					
1998	88.6					
1999	91.8			29.9		
2000	93.4			28.4		
2001	141.3			32.0		
2002	234.1			46.9		
2003	282.5			48.0		
2004	279.3			55.3		
2005	498.2			75.4		
2006	411.5	327.2	84.4	84.0	45.1	38.9
2007	498.1	386.3	111.8	135.4	85.7	49.7
2008	585.9	451.8	134.1	188.9	121.0	67.9
2009	697.6	533.2	164.4	196.0	110.6	85.4
2010	966.5	754.2	212.3	199.7	105.9	93.7
2011	820.9	588.4	232.6	232.8	113.8	119.0
2012	923.1	656.1	267.0	286.2	133.9	152.3
2013	994.4	706.4	288.0	318.2	152.9	165.3
2014	1207.2	892.5	314.8	407.2	224.6	182.7

资料来源：中国保险监督管理委员会北京监管局。
Source: Beijing Regulatory Bureau of China Insurance Regulatory Commission.

17-9 保险业务情况 STATISTICS FOR INSURANCE BUSINESS

单位：亿元 (100 million yuan)

项目	Item	原保险保费收入 Premium Income of Original Insurance 2014	2013	赔付支出 Compensation Expenses 2014	2013
合计	**Total**	**1207.2**	**994.4**	**407.2**	**318.2**
人身险业务小计	**Subtotal of Life Insurance**	**892.5**	**706.4**	**224.6**	**152.9**
人寿保险	Life Insurance	708.7	570.8	164.7	108.1
非分红产品	Non-participating Products	246.5	53.0	17.1	18.3
分红产品	Participating Products	457.9	513.5	146.6	88.9
投资连接产品	Investment-linked Products	0.5	0.5	0.1	0.1
万能产品	Universal Products	3.8	3.9	1.0	0.9
意外伤害保险	Accident Insurance	34.6	29.9	9.2	6.6
健康保险	Health Insurance	149.2	105.7	50.7	38.2
财产险业务小计	**Subtotal of Property Insurance**	**314.8**	**288.0**	**182.7**	**165.3**
#企业财产保险	Enterprise Property Insurance	34.0	30.6	25.1	15.3
家庭财产保险	Household Property Insurance	0.9	0.7	0.3	0.2
机动车辆及第三者责任保险	Motor Vehicle and Third Party Liability Insurance	224.1	205.3	135.0	131.8
货物运输保险	Freight Transport Insurance	11.0	11.6	4.0	3.8
责任保险	Liability Insurance	18.8	15.0	6.6	5.9
工程险	Construction Insurance	7.8	7.2	2.4	1.9

资料来源：中国保险监督管理委员会北京监管局。
Source: Beijing Regulatory Bureau of China Insurance Regulatory Commission.

主要统计指标解释

存款 企业、机关、团体或居民根据可以收回的原则，把货币资金存入银行或其他信用机构保管并取得一定利息的一种信用活动形式。根据存款对象的不同可划分为企业存款、财政存款、机关团体存款、储蓄存款、农业存款等科目。它是银行信贷资金的主要来源。

贷款 银行或其他信用机构根据必须归还的原则，按一定利率，为企业、个人等提供资金的一种信用活动形式。我国银行贷款分为短期贷款、中长期贷款、委托及信托类贷款、其他类贷款等。

原保险保费收入 是指保险企业确认的原保险合同保费收入。是投保人根据保险合同的有关规定，为被保险人取得因约定危险事故发生所造成的经济损失补偿（或给付）权利，付给保险人的代价。包括财产险和人身险收入。

保险赔付支出 公司按保险合同约定支付给被保险人（或受益人）的赔款、保险金、给付等。包括赔款支出、死伤医疗给付、满期给付和年金给付。

股票交易额 指报告期投资者在各类证券交易场所进行股票买卖交易活动的金额。包括A股、B股、股份转让等。不含申购新股及申购中签交易额，也不含配股、分红、送股及转增交易额。

基金交易额 指报告期投资者在各类证券交易场所进行基金买卖交易活动的金额。包括封闭式基金、开放式基金中的ＥＴＦ、LOF 等。填报时，不在交易所挂牌交易的开放式基金的交易额不计在内。

债券交易额 指报告期投资者在各类证券交易场所进行债券买卖交易活动的金额。包括国债、地方政府债、金融债、企业债、公司债、分离债、可转债、私募债、资产支持类债券等。

债券现货交易额 指报告期投资者在各类证券交易场所进行债券买卖交易活动现货成交金额。

Explanatory Notes on Main Statistical Indicators

Deposit is a form of credit activity that enterprises, public institutions, groups or residents save their money, on a reclaimable basis, in banks or other credit institutions and receive certain interest. In terms of depositors, there are enterprise deposit, fiscal deposit, government agency deposit, savings deposit, agricultural deposit and so on, which constitute a main source of bank funds for extending credit..

Loan is a form of credit activity that banks or other credit institutions provide funds which must be repaid for enterprise and individuals at a given interest rate,. In China, bank loans are classified as short-,, medium-, and long-term loans, entrusted and trust loans, and others.

Premium Income means the income of insurance premium of original insurance contracts confirmed by insurance companies. It is the price paid by policy holders to the insurer for the right to receive compensation (claim settlement) for any economic loss caused by agreed dangerous accidents pursuant to relevant provisions in the insurance contract. There are property insurance and life insurance incomes.

Insurance Indemnity Payments refer to indemnity, insurance money, and claim settlement, etc. paid by the insurance company to the insurant (or beneficiary) as agreed in the insurance contract, including indemnity payment, claim settlement for medical costs of death and injury, maturity payment and annuity payment.

Stock Market Turnover means the value of shares traded by investors in various securities exchanges, including: A share, B share and share transfer, etc., excluding turnover related to IPO subscription, IPO lot-winning, allotment, dividend, share-granting and capital reserve converted into share capital.

Funds Turnover means the value of funds traded by investors in various securities exchanges during the reporting period, including ETF and LOF, etc. in the closed-end funds and open-end funds. The turnover of open-end funds not listed and traded in exchanges shall not be included in the funds turnover reported.

Bonds Turnover means the value of bonds traded by investors in various securities exchanges during the reporting period, including treasury bonds, local government bonds, financial bonds, enterprise bonds, corporate bonds, convertible bonds, warrants bonds, private placement bonds and asset-backed bonds.

Bonds Spot Turnover means the spot turnover of bonds traded by investors in various securities exchanges during the reporting period.

18

教育、文化
EDUCATION AND CULTURE

简要说明

一、教育部分的主要内容和资料来源

教育统计资料包括高等教育（研究生教育、普通本专科教育、成人本专科、其他各类高等学历教育）、中等教育(高中阶段、初中阶段)、小学教育、学前教育、特殊教育(盲聋哑和弱智儿童学校等)、工读学校等资料。主要指标包括学校数、在校学生数、招生数、毕业生数、教职工数、专任教师数等内容。

教育统计资料由北京市教育委员会提供。

二、文化部分的主要内容和资料来源

文化部分主要包括公共图书馆、博物馆、文化馆、档案馆、文化站、广播、电影、电视以及新闻等文化单位的机构、人员和业务活动情况。

文化部分数据中，公共图书馆和群众文化活动的资料主要来自北京市文化局；档案馆资料来自北京市档案局；博物馆资料来自北京市文物局；广播、电影和电视，报纸、期刊、图书出版资料来自北京市新闻出版广电局。

Brief Introduction

I. Main Content and Sources of Data for the Part of Education

Educational statistics include those for higher education (postgraduate education, undergraduate and junior college education, undergraduate and junior college education for adults, and other kinds of higher education for diplomas); secondary education (senior high school, junior high school); primary education; preschool education; special education (schools for the blind, deaf and mute, and mentally handicapped children, etc.); work-study schools for delinquent children. Main indicators include the number of schools, student enrollment, , number of new enrollment, number of teachers and staff, and number of full-time teachers, etc.

Educational data were provided by Beijing Municipal Commission of Education.

II. Main Content and Sources of Data for the Part of Culture

Cultural statistics include public libraries, museums, cultural centers, archives, broadcast, films, television and press, and other cultural organizations.

In Cultural data, libraries, and mass culture are from Beijing Municipal Bureau of Culture; data of archives are from Beijing Municipal Bureau of Archives; data of museums are from Beijing Municipal Administration of Cultural Heritage; radio, film and television, newspaper, magazine and book publications data are from Beijing Municipal Administration of Press, Publication, Radio, Film and Television.

18-1 教育基本情况(1978-2014年)
BASIC STATISTICS FOR EDUCATION (1978-2014)

年 份 Year	全市各类学校数(个) Total Number of Various Schools (unit)	#普通高等学校 General Institutions of Higher Education	#普通中等学校 General Middle Schools	#高中 Senior Middle Schools	#小学 Primary Schools	全市各类学校在校学生数(人) Enrolled Students in Various Schools (person)	#普通高等学校 General Institutions of Higher Education	#普通中等学校 General Middle Schools	#高中 Senior Middle Schools	#小学 Primary Schools
1978		35			4666		48618		415612	937336
1979		48			4534		55073		299974	968723
1980		50			4485		83032		312188	951763
1981		51			4445		98044		175180	900350
1982		51			4381		93878		92401	854516
1983		54			4269		90894		88657	838078
1984		57			4168		102962		110916	763204
1985		61			4059		122791		119876	733605
1986		66			3995		129647		109862	749101
1987		67			3875		136694		109023	777982
1988		67			3793		145134		108106	850577
1989		67			3703		141625		110745	934696
1990		67			3611		139646		100669	995831
1991	8496	67	1168	282	3482	2142085	136940	565357	93728	1013268
1992	8052	67	1150	279	3306	2194268	139978	617847	82894	1001762
1993	7789	66	1145	280	3190	2266932	158906	679821	78261	1022166
1994	7574	67	1150	280	3035	2348406	175203	758310	86584	1024503
1995	7158	65	1170	286	2867	2380096	182173	834903	102522	1007301
1996	7121	65	1189	296	2780	2388002	189953	881912	118476	999740
1997	6858	65	1181	288	2696	2361438	195842	887644	133461	977323
1998	6456	63	1190	282	2511	2325043	212984	895042	145966	919531
1999	5807	64	1182	275	2352	2297673	234033	931029	161473	836655
2000	5458	59	1159	302	2169	2299433	282585	972930	179002	743109
2001	4873	61	1111	289	1960	2297107	340284	988985	194283	664443
2002	4447	62	998	325	1824	2294947	398573	984117	220667	594241
2003	4158	74	977	329	1652	2299416	458898	968035	250959	546530
2004	3971	77	945	338	1504	2291594	500245	919178	274803	516042
2005	3782	79	917	335	1403	2264004	536724	859132	278358	494482
2006	3751	82	888	335	1310	2910228	554702	799074	259414	473275
2007	3593	83	863	328	1235	3195763	567875	839038	243818	666617
2008	3508	82	838	325	1202	3208704	575639	782866	219163	659500
2009	3425	88	804	305	1160	3214354	577154	740396	203477	647101
2010	3330	89	779	289	1104	3299555	577828	727741	198415	653255
2011	3367	89	769	290	1090	3426025	578633	711130	195072	680457
2012	3314	91	760	289	1081	3568273	581844	732224	193505	718655
2013	3439	89	757	291	1093	3736003	589234	706713	187586	789276
2014	3437	89	766	306	1040	3774868	594614	651443	177554	821152

注：1. 从2007年开始，普通中学、小学、工读学校、特殊教育、学前教育在校学生数包括外省市户口借读学生。
2. 1991-2005年，普通中等学校包括普通中专、技工学校、职业中学、普通中学和工读学校。2006年及以后普通中等学校为中等教育口径，包括普通中专、成人中专、技工学校、职业高中和普通中学。

资料来源：北京市教育委员会。

Note: a) From 2007, enrolled students in general high schools, primary schools, work-study schools for delinquent children, special education schools, and pre-school education included those from outside Beijing and studying in Beijing on temporary basis.
b) In 1991-2005, general middle schools included technical secondary schools, technician training schools, vocational schools, general high schools, and work-study schools. In and after 2006, middle schools included technical secondary schools, technical secondary schools for adults, technician training schools, vocational senior high schools and general high schools.

Source: Beijing Municipal Commission of Education.

18-1 续表 1 Continued 1

年 份 Year	全 市 各类学校 招 生 数 (人) New Enrollment in Various Schools (person)	#普 通 高 等 学 校 General Institutions of Higher Education	#普 通 中 等 学 校 General Middle Schools	#高 中 Senior Middle Schools	#小 学 Primary Schools	全 市 各类学校 毕业生数 (人) Number of Graduates in Various Schools (person)	#普 通 高 等 学 校 General Institutions of Higher Education
1978		17445		161288	199076		10881
1979		15848		160340	154809		8585
1980		17972		131961	138751		8233
1981		17921		54296	121744		2289
1982		21936		35212	104357		25753
1983		27988		40282	96028		31009
1984		31805		47068	103482		20110
1985		40670		35265	135048		21442
1986		35390		27863	160513		26953
1987		41163		41186	156954		34894
1988		42187		35429	184516		33066
1989		33557		33254	184609		35863
1990		36275		30596	161742		36171
1991	571685	37700	205107	28589	148300	487740	37702
1992	622142	41517	232765	25790	157145	520787	37075
1993	651729	52205	242274	26275	175853	526982	32888
1994	704933	51884	287642	34704	186315	528199	34855
1995	691972	52868	308786	40803	168903	554690	45094
1996	628772	55269	289612	42603	156898	575969	46471
1997	581091	56884	289719	49566	124231	584120	49973
1998	581786	62264	308157	52956	100415	600662	49322
1999	603332	78354	320731	56998	94358	603027	49936
2000	635328	99397	324862	65890	92002	604900	51556
2001	641432	116344	313257	69195	91230	617889	55831
2002	671956	128320	326835	84679	86406	624329	67621
2003	662877	143483	302071	94894	82631	610826	83816
2004	635842	147298	271396	93519	73577	614137	99637
2005	630515	156124	259133	88605	71020	622974	117367
2006	851808	154969	234524	76375	73138	787596	132488
2007	927144	156222	252709	71590	109203	851126	138834
2008	938891	157238	236714	68397	110440	832585	149459
2009	962648	158992	240937	65983	102414	865025	152336
2010	1002141	155228	238954	65649	113728	834340	150156
2011	1050131	157543	243754	64146	132719	838521	151277
2012	1108574	162042	254790	63381	141738	881804	152980
2013	1182301	163081	239010	59983	165807	923050	148689
2014	1113688	160056	202434	55184	153249	937209	147023

18-1 续表 2 Continued 2

年 份 Year	#普通中等学校 General Middle Schools	#高 中 Senior Middle Schools	#小 学 Primary Schools	学龄儿童入学率(%) Enrollment Rate of Children at School-age (%)	专任教师数(人) Full-time Teachers (person)	平均每一专任教师负担学生数(人) Average Number of Students Instructed by a Full-time Teacher(person) 高等学校 Institutions of Higher Education	普通中学 General Middle Schools	小 学 Primary Schools
1978		174899	151950	99.00			19.9	20.7
1979		239813	114047	98.50			16.1	21.3
1980		145501	144025	98.70			14.8	21.7
1981		170992	162306	98.90			13.4	19.7
1982		111153	135562	98.90			12.3	19.5
1983			95919	99.10			11.5	19.6
1984		24498	169251	99.30			13.2	18.2
1985		24720	156035	99.10			13.9	17.4
1986		36942	138350	99.50			14.1	17.3
1987		43589	121599	99.50			12.8	16.8
1988		36127	105948	99.50			11.4	17.6
1989		29267	97208	99.70			11.0	19.1
1990		40369	102782	99.50			10.1	18.6
1991		34428	132544	99.17	168485		10.5	18.0
1992		32471	156306	99.65	169249		11.3	17.4
1993		27428	157838	99.88	170361		12.1	17.4
1994		24112	184566	99.92	175025		13.1	16.9
1995		23353	183894	99.93	176591		13.6	16.5
1996		25170	162030	99.93	178006		13.7	16.1
1997		33010	146023	99.95	179080		13.2	15.7
1998		39683	156194	99.96	178210		12.8	14.9
1999		40660	175656	99.95	175496	12.0	13.2	13.7
2000		47569	185059	99.95	167040	14.0	14.1	12.8
2001		51263	167076	99.62	168080	17.0	14.3	12.1
2002		51180	156683	99.63	166490	19.0	14.2	11.2
2003		56601	123580	99.95	166510	19.0	13.7	11.0
2004		66556	100139	99.92	172055	17.1	12.9	10.6
2005		73260	93486	99.90	174589	17.0	11.8	10.3
2006	290047	78037	90799	99.96	191365	17.0	10.8	9.8
2007	272651	78408	112332	100.00	195568	15.4	11.5	13.8
2008	262871	78468	112268	100.00	199114	17.1	10.9	13.5
2009	253067	70132	110730	100.00	203825	16.5	10.0	13.0
2010	233837	62305	102971	99.96	206602	16.6	10.2	13.2
2011	223955	58275	101678	99.99	199789	17.1	9.8	13.4
2012	224938	55657	109492	99.99	204812	17.0	9.7	13.7
2013	240225	58072	111839	99.99	216463		9.5	14.4
2014	229640	57773	112819	99.99	225165		9.0	14.4

18-2 幼儿园基本情况(1978－2014年)
BASIC STATISTICS FOR KINDERGARTENS (1978-2014)

单位：人 (person)

年 份 Year	园数(所) Number of Kindergartens (unit)	班数(个) Number of Classes (unit)	离园人数 Children Leaving	入园人数 Children Entering	在园人数 Children Enrollment	教职工数 Teachers and Staff	#专任教师 Full-time Teachers
1978	5074				235923	39982	8369
1979	4623				237037	40424	8777
1980	3991				219407	38475	7765
1981	3888				233089	38832	8814
1982	3849				254458	42663	9271
1983	1999				306975	48666	8234
1984	3682				295427	47721	9499
1985	2955				316024	47033	10523
1986	3503				342824	52654	12690
1987	3732				364011	54211	14449
1988	3563				354367	52105	14705
1989	3509				344394	50280	17208
1990	3798				372555	49587	17972
1991	3761		133788	172884	402699	49472	18788
1992	3510		158740	181299	404779	48007	18513
1993	3369		165963	170580	372368	44741	18114
1994	3301		113652	167267	352979	42118	17413
1995	3024		103355	148272	315277	38549	16084
1996	3056		135376	112449	271752	33586	14792
1997	2892		110345	95140	253478	32811	14596
1998	2662		99279	93819	245046	30362	13841
1999	2180		91996	89463	237055	29367	13216
2000	2047		85301	91724	229012	27257	12595
2001	1719	8259	85842	87892	217521	26106	12479
2002	1540	8494	79447	91092	213794	25402	12127
2003	1430	7733	76879	86465	199390	26324	13056
2004	1422	8087	71677	86672	205532	28326	14208
2005	1358	8148	71926	83485	202301	28026	14813
2006	1361	8051	70400	68299	197546	28958	15632
2007	1306	8132	70681	83969	214423	30465	17013
2008	1266	8382	72119	85938	226681	32535	18176
2009	1253	9036	65684	89761	247778	34973	17952
2010	1245	9883	68135	105048	276994	37227	21677
2011	1305	11213	76790	115539	311417	44458	24170
2012	1266	11882	79131	115248	331524	48080	26330
2013	1384	12580	88322	128106	348681	53049	28806
2014	1426	13245	96478	133977	364954	57950	31692

资料来源：北京市教育委员会。
Source: Beijing Municipal Commission of Education.

18-3 各类学校基本情况
BASIC STATISTICS FOR VARIOUS SCHOOLS

单位：人 (person)

项　目	Item	校　数(所) Number of Schools (unit)		教职工数 Teachers and Staff		专任教师 Full-time Teachers	
		2014	2013	2014	2013	2014	2013
合　计	**Total**	**3437**	**3439**	**365318**	**354704**	**225165**	**216463**
高等教育	**Higher Education**	**177**	**177**	**148930**	**146264**	**71079**	**69625**
研究生培养机构(不计校数)	Institutions Providing Postgraduate Programs (Number of Schools Not Counted)	(136)	(136)			(51415)	(47841)
高等学校	Institutions of Higer Education	(56)	(56)			(41648)	(38747)
科研机构	Research Institutes	(80)	(80)			(9767)	(9094)
普通高等学校	General Institutions of Higher Education	89	89	140685	137825	67549	66026
成人高等学校	Adult Institutions of Higher Education	19	19	3273	3403	1551	1523
民办的其他高等教育机构	Privately-funded Institutions of Higher Education	69	69	4972	5036	1979	2076
中等教育	**Secondary Education**	**766**	**757**	**98766**	**96012**	**71799**	**68175**
高中阶段教育	Senior Secondary Education	429	410	98766	96012	51105	47704
普通高中	General Middle Schools	306	291	82224	80511	40349	38492
中等职业教育	Secondary Vocational Schools	123	119	16542	15501	10756	9212
普通中专	General Technical Secondary Schools	31	31	3614	3701	2002	1995
成人中专	Technical Secondary Schools for Adults	11	11	565	572	308	313
职业高中	Vocational Senior High Schools	52	55	7495	7653	4889	4872
技工学校	Technician Training Schools	29	22	4868	3575	3557	2032
初中阶段教育	Junior Secondary Education	337	347			20694	20471
小学教育	**Primary Schools**	**1040**	**1093**	**58108**	**57832**	**49434**	**48726**
工读学校	**Work-Study Schools for Delinquent Children**	**6**	**6**	**286**	**294**	**195**	**196**
特殊教育	**Special Education**	**22**	**22**	**1278**	**1253**	**966**	**935**
学前教育	**Pre-school Education**	**1426**	**1384**	**57950**	**53049**	**31692**	**28806**

注：1. 普通高中的教职工数中包含普通初中的教职工数。
2. 表中带()数据不计入“校数”的合计数据中。
资料来源：北京市教育委员会。

Note: a) Number of "Teachers and Staff" in general senior high schools includes those in general junior high schools.
b) In this table data with () were not be calculated in the total number of schools.
Source: Beijing Municipal Commission of Education.

18-3 续表 Continued

单位：人 (person)

项 目	Item	毕业生数 Graduates		招生数 New Enrollment		在校学生数 Total Enrollment	
		2014	2013	2014	2013	2014	2013
合 计	**Total**	**937209**	**923050**	**1113688**	**1182301**	**3774868**	**3736003**
高等教育	**Higher Education**	**495945**	**480612**	**622602**	**647871**	**1928977**	**1882237**
研究生	Postgraduates	77442	73357	92776	91399	274443	265656
高等学校	Institutions of Higher Education	72706	68965	87040	85759	257231	249225
科研机构	Scientific Research Institutions	4736	4392	5736	5640	17212	16431
普通本专科	General Undergraduates and College Students	147023	148689	160056	163081	594614	589234
中央部委属高校	Under Central Ministries and Commissions	72740	71725	79067	79225	307689	304179
市属高校	Under Municipal Government	74283	76964	80989	83856	286925	285055
公办高校	Public Colleges and Universities	56959	58149	62109	63877	218608	217293
民办高校	Privately-funded Colleges and Universities	17324	18815	18880	19979	68317	67762
成人本专科	Adult Undergraduates and College Students	93874	94519	88282	101654	237644	258278
成人高等学校	Adult Institutions of Higher Education	8964	9223	7923	9152	20412	23598
普通高等学校	General Institutions of Higher Education	84910	85296	80359	92502	217232	234680
在职人员攻读	Employees Enrolled in Graduate Programes						
硕士学位	Leading to Master Degrees			21974	22744	87157	80492
网络本专科生	Students Enrolled in Internet-based Courses	177606	164047	259514	268993	735119	688577
中等教育	**Secondary Education**	**229640**	**240225**	**202434**	**239010**	**651443**	**706713**
高中阶段教育	Senior Secondary	139500	147852	99741	132284	344654	396145
普通高中	General Middle Schools	57773	58072	55184	59983	177554	187586
#北京市户籍	Registered Residents of Beijing	53315	53837	50787	51730	158951	166221
中等职业教育	Secondary Vocational Schools	81727	89780	44557	72301	167100	208559
普通中专	General Technical Secondary Schools	16394	17002	12319	14029	51296	56275
成人中专	Technical Secondary Schools for Adults	33778	40786	11861	34392	40568	59871
职业高中	Vocational High Schools	16792	17999	5585	7162	34155	49255
技工学校	Technical Schools	14763	13993	14792	16718	41081	43158
初中阶段教育	Junior Secondary Education	90140	92373	102693	106726	306789	310568
#北京市户籍	Registered Residents of Beijing	67667	71077	65722	65697	204451	207098
小学教育	**Primary Education**	**112819**	**111839**	**153249**	**165807**	**821152**	**789276**
#北京市户籍	Registered Residents of Beijing	65555	65651	98016	90917	452651	419693
工读学校	**Work-study School for Delinquent Children**	**330**	**346**	**316**	**351**	**600**	**748**
特殊教育	**Special Education Schools**	**1997**	**1706**	**1110**	**1156**	**7742**	**8348**
学前教育	**Preschool Education**	**96478**	**88322**	**133977**	**128106**	**364954**	**348681**

18-4 全市高等教育学生情况(2014年)
STATISTICS FOR STUDENTS IN INSTITUTIONS OF HIGHER EDUCATION (2014)

单位：人 (person)

项目	Item	毕(结)业生人数 Number of Graduates	招生数 New Enrollment	在校学生数 Total Enrollment
普通本科、专科生	General Undergraduates and Junior College Students	147023	160056	594614
专　科	Enrolled in Specialized Courses Education	34129	34611	105322
本　科	Enrolled in Full Undergraduate Courses	112894	125445	489292
成人本科、专科生	Adult Undergraduates and Junior College Students	93874	88282	237644
专　科	Enrolled in Specialized Courses Education	41350	38122	93486
本　科	Enrolled in Full Undergraduate Courses	52524	50160	144158
网络本科、专科生	Students Enrolled in Internet-based Courses	177606	259514	735119
专　科	Enrolled in Specialized Courses	105357	151248	400526
本　科	Enrolled in Full Undergraduate Courses	72249	108266	334593
研究生	Postgraduates	77442	92776	274443
硕　士	Master Degree	63355	73932	198161
博　士	Doctor Degree	14087	18844	76282
在职人员攻读硕士学位	Employees Enrolled in Graduate Programes Leading to Master Degrees		21974	87157
自考助学班	Classes for Self-Learning Programs	745		1928
普通预科生	College Preparatory Courses			1652
研究生课程进修班	Postgraduate Courses for Advanced Study	8179		18743
进修及培训	In-Service Training Courses	725561		636372
留学生	Overseas Students	24950	27690	39379

资料来源：北京市教育委员会。
Source: Beijing Municipal Commission of Education.

18-5 普通高等学校本专科基本情况(2014年)
BASIC STATISTICS FOR GENERAL INSTITUTIONS OF HIGHER EDUCATION (2014)

单位：人 (person)

项目	Item	校数(所) Number of Schools (unit)	毕业生数 Graduates	招生数 New Enrollment	在校学生数 Total Enrollment	教职工数 Teachers and Staff	#专任教师 Full-time Teachers
合　计	**Total**	**89**	**147023**	**160056**	**594614**	**140685**	**67549**
#女　性	Females		75889	81795	306463	68150	30355
综合大学	Comprehensive Universities	5	18989	19302	73410	25744	12862
理工院校	Science and Engineering	29	60863	66677	247669	52484	26470
农业院校	Agriculture	3	6414	6400	23143	4905	2535
林业院校	Forestry	1	3187	3296	13235	1844	1186
医药院校	Medicine	4	2722	3796	14123	17515	3255
师范院校	Teacher Training	2	4646	5597	20663	5765	3473
语文院校	Literature	9	10772	11514	42853	7270	4056
财经院校	Finance and Economics	16	21198	22414	83398	11094	6443
政法院校	Politics and Law	8	9504	11494	39048	6659	2950
体育院校	Physical Culture	3	2562	3070	11665	1696	1048
艺术院校	Art	8	3424	3694	14097	3701	2074
民族院校	Minorities Colleges	1	2742	2802	11310	2008	1197

资料来源：北京市教育委员会。
Source: Beijing Municipal Commission of Education.

18-6 全市分学科研究生情况(2014年)
BASIC STATISTICS FOR POSTGRADUATES BY SUBJECT OF STUDY (2014)

单位：人 (person)

项 目	Item	毕业生 Graduates			招生数 New Enrollment			在校学生数 Student Enrollment		
		合 计 Total	硕 士 Master Degree	博 士 Doctor Degree	合 计 Total	硕 士 Master Degree	博 士 Doctor Degree	合 计 Total	硕 士 Master Degree	博 士 Doctor Degree
合 计	**Total**	**77442**	**63355**	**14087**	**92776**	**73932**	**18844**	**274443**	**198161**	**76282**
#女 性	Females	38802	33434	5368	45253	37776	7477	128945	100349	28596
学术型学位	**Academic Degree**									
哲 学	Philosophy	661	463	198	719	448	271	2299	1306	993
经济学	Economics	5380	4710	670	6466	5512	954	16376	12495	3881
法 学	Law	7479	6503	976	7967	6734	1233	22669	17808	4861
教育学	Education	2978	2681	297	3424	3017	407	9572	7924	1648
文 学	Literature	4572	4009	563	4985	4268	717	14090	11156	2934
历史学	History	606	444	162	771	549	222	2316	1486	830
理 学	Science	6884	3834	3050	9740	5415	4325	30949	15153	15796
工 学	Engineering	28579	23775	4804	34438	27671	6767	107107	76954	30153
农 学	Agriculture	2572	1960	612	3102	2375	727	8511	5848	2663
医 学	Medicine	4358	2835	1523	5251	3602	1649	15331	10084	5247
军事学	Military	32	24	8	26	23	3	107	64	43
管理学	Management	10756	9824	932	12666	11421	1245	35991	29954	6037
艺术学	Art	2585	2293	292	3221	2897	324	9125	7929	1196

资料来源：北京市教育委员会。
Source: Beijing Municipal Commission of Education.

18-7 高等教育外国留学生情况(2014年)
STATISTICS FOR FOREIGN STUDENTS STUDYING IN BEIJING FOR HIGHER EDUCATION (2014)

单位：人 (person)

项 目	Item	毕(结)业生数 Graduates	授予学位人数 Number of Students Conferred with Degree	招生数 New Enrollment	在校学生数 Total Enrollment
合 计	**Total**	**24950**	**4937**	**27690**	**39379**
#女 性	Females	12228	2004	13853	18063
按学历划分	**By Educational Background**				
专 科	Enrolled in Specialized Courses	95		134	192
本 科	Enrolled in Full Undergraduate Courses	3485	2865	4300	15425
硕 士	Master Degree	1874	1760	2382	5337
博 士	Doctor Degree	334	312	884	2803
培 训	Training	19162		19990	15622
按地区划分	**By Region**				
亚 洲	Asia	13644	3616	14305	25207
非 洲	Africa	1187	465	1696	2951
欧 洲	Europe	6188	464	7158	6944
北美洲	North America	2929	249	3282	2932
南美洲	South America	553	74	734	808
大洋洲	Oceania	449	69	515	537
按经费来源	**By Source of Funds**				
国际组织资助	From International Organizations	40	23	157	283
中国政府资助	From Chinese Government	2701	1247	4325	7605
本国政府资助	From the Government of the Students' Home Country	286	186	318	814
学校间交换	Interscholastic Exchange	2997	59	3335	2572
自 费	Self Funding	18926	3422	19555	28105

资料来源：北京市教育委员会。
Source: Beijing Municipal Commission of Education.

18-8 普通中专分科情况(2014年)
BASIC STATISTICS FOR SPECIALIZED SECONDARY SCHOOLS BY MAJOR (2014)

单位：人 (person)

项　目	Item	毕业生数 Graduates	招生数 New Enrollment	在校学生数 Total Enrollment
合　计	**Total**	**16394**	**12319**	**51296**
#女　生	Females	7553	5160	23780
按类别分	**By Category**			
农林牧渔类	Agriculture, Forestry, Animal Production and Hunting, Fishing	125	158	636
资源环境类	Resources and Environment	61	117	333
能源与新能源类	Energy and New Energy	320	56	553
土木水利类	Construction and Water Conservancy	884	637	2956
加工制造类	Processing and Manufacturing	1785	913	4543
石油化工类	Petroleum and Chemicals	54		48
轻纺食品类	Light Industry, Textile and Foods	154	102	359
交通运输类	Transportation	2601	2860	9631
信息技术类	IT	1273	794	3344
医药卫生类	Medicine and Health	3320	2340	10553
休闲保健类	Recreation and Healthcare			
财经商贸类	Finance, Business and Trade	1718	1195	5125
旅游服务类	Tourism Services	331	125	649
文化艺术类	Culture and Arts	1814	1612	7642
体育与健身	Sports and Fitness	536	418	1561
教育类	Education	450	257	1150
司法服务类	Judicial Services	207	142	433
公共管理与服务类	Public Management and Services	174	272	777
其　他	Others	587	321	1003

资料来源：北京市教育委员会。
Source: Beijing Municipal Commission of Education.

18-9 职业高中分科情况(2014年)
BASIC STATISTICS FOR VOCATIONAL SCHOOLS BY MAJOR (2014)

单位：人 (person)

项　目	Item	毕业生数 Graduates	招生数 New Enrollment	在校学生数 Total Enrollment
合　计	**Total**	**16792**	**5585**	**34155**
#女　生	Females	8548	2702	17108
按类别分	**By Category**			
农林牧渔类	Agriculture, Forestry, Animal Production and Hunting, Fishing	273	116	522
资源环境类	Resources and Environment			
能源与新能源类	Energy and New Energy			1
土木水利类	Construction and Water Conservancy	127	30	187
加工制造类	Processing and Manufacturing	921	210	1414
石油化工类	Petroleum and Chemicals			
轻纺食品类	Light Industry, Textile and Foods	66	18	190
交通运输类	Transportation	1752	1016	4033
信息技术类	IT	2650	642	4897
医药卫生类	Medicine and Health	392	140	656
休闲保健类	Recreation and Healthcare	636	53	1129
财经商贸类	Finance, Business and Trade	2522	859	5734
旅游服务类	Tourism Services	2137	708	4076
文化艺术类	Culture and Arts	1908	713	5284
体育与健身	Sports and Fitness	298	16	556
教育类	Education	2664	935	4561
司法服务类	Judicial Services	34	14	277
公共管理与服务类	Public Management and Services	395	95	588
其　他	Others	17	20	50

资料来源：北京市教育委员会。
Source: Beijing Municipal Commission of Education.

18-10 校外教育情况(2014年)
STATISTICS FOR AFTER-SCHOOL EDUCATION (2014)

单位：人 (person)

项　　目	Item	单位数(个) Number of Organizations(unit)	活动小组数(个) Activity Groups(unit)	参加小组学生数 Participating Students	教职工人数 Teachers and Staff	#专职辅导员 Full-time Coaches	兼职辅导员 Part-time Coaches
合　计	**Total**	**646**	**9553**	**562833**	**2668**	**1395**	**2308**
少年宫	Children's Palaces	22	6609	319266	1457	821	758
少年科技馆	Children's Scientific Museums	10	853	63121	395	214	232
少年之家	Children's Homes	30	1418	140843	500	258	480
少年活动站	Children's Clubs	584	673	39603	316	102	838

资料来源：北京市教育委员会。
Source: Beijing Municipal Commission of Education.

18-11 幼儿园基本情况(2014年)
STATISTICS FOR KINDERGARTENS (2014)

单位：人 (person)

项　　目	Item	总计 Total	#女 Females	城区 In City	镇区 In Counties and Towns	乡村 In Villages
园　数　(所)	Number of Kindergartens (unit)	1426		1031	197	198
班　数　(个)	Number of Classes (unit)	13245		10887	1458	900
在园幼儿数	Children Enrollment	364954	173629	303618	39862	21474
教职工数	Teachers and Staff	57950	52952	49842	5551	2557
#园　长	Headmasters	2179	2089	1752	254	173
专任教师	Full-time Teachers	31692	30945	26822	3275	1595
保健医	Health Workers	2291	2242	2017	191	83

资料来源：北京市教育委员会。
Source: Beijing Municipal Commission of Education.

18-12 高等教育自学考试情况
STATISTICS FOR HIGHER EDUCATION SELF-STUDY EXAMINATION

项　　目	Item	2014	2013
报考人次 (人次)	Number of Registered Person-times (person-time)	148711	137528
报考科次 (科次)	Number of Registered Subject-times (person-time)	439767	376699
发出专科毕业证书 (个)	Number of Junior College Diplomas Issued (unit)	2449	3803
发出本科毕业证书 (个)	Number of General College Diplomas Issued (unit)	3816	6764
开考专业 (个)	Number of Majors Examined (unit)	106	106

资料来源：北京市教育委员会。
Source: Beijing Municipal Commission of Education.

18-13 特殊教育情况(2014年)
STATISTICS FOR SPECIAL EDUCATION (2014)

单位：人 (person)

项　　目	Item	毕业生 Graduates	招生数 New Enrollment	在校学生数 Total Enrollment
合　计	**Total**	**1997**	**1110**	**7742**
#女　性	Females	696	449	2780
特殊教育学校	Special Education Schools	528	430	2755
小学附设特教班	Special Classes Attached to Primary Schools	28	14	142
小学随班就读	Studying in Primary Schools	625	154	2700
普通(职业)初中随班就读	Studying in General Junior Secondary (Vocational) Classes	816	512	2145

资料来源：北京市教育委员会。
Source: Beijing Municipal Commission of Education.

18-14 职业技术培训机构基本情况(2014年)
BASIC STATISTICS FOR VOCATIONAL AND TECHNICAL TRAINING INSTITUTIONS(2014)

项　目	Item	学校数(所) Schools (unit)	教学班(点、个) Teaching Classes (site,unit)	结业生数(人次) Students Completing Courses (person-time) 合计 Total	#女性 Females
合　计	**Total**	**3634**	**44234**	**2829188**	**1543590**
#少数民族	National Miniorities			19347	8578
按培训机构分	**By Training Institution**				
职工技术培训学校(机构)	**Technical Training Schools (Institutions) for Employees**	**31**	**579**	**69968**	**37467**
教育部门和集体办	Run by Education Authorities and Collectively-run	1	211	11530	7402
其他部门办	Run by Other Authorities	13	365	58247	30005
民　办	Privately-funded	17	3	191	60
农村成人文化技术培训学校(机构)	**Cultural and Technical Training Schools (Institutions) for Rural Adults**	**2137**	**8777**	**870443**	**511295**
#教育部门和集体办	Run by Education Authorities and Collectively-run	2132	8756	867662	509898
县　办	Run by Counties	13	364	71356	36063
乡　办	Run by Townships	164	4839	435283	255874
村　办	Run by Villages	1955	3553	361023	217961
其他培训机构(含社会培训机构)	**Other Training Institutions (Including Social Training Institutions)**	**1466**	**34878**	**1888777**	**994828**
教育部门和集体办	Run by Education Authorities and Collectively-run	70		79532	40249
其他部门办	Run by Other Authorities	187	163	710784	389854
民　办	Privately-funded	1209	34715	1098461	564725
按培训时间分	**By Training Duration**				
一个月以内	within 1 month			1361192	753494
一个月至三个月以内	1-3 months			432681	235020
三个月至半年以内	3-6 months			550957	296191
半年至一年以内	6 months to 1 year			354432	186403
一年及以上	over 1 year			129926	72482
按培训形式分	**Group by Form of Training**				
#资格证书培训	Qualification Certificate Training			327119	163754
岗位证书培训	Job Post Certificate Training			471560	214015

资料来源：北京市教育委员会。
Source: Beijing Municipal Commission of Education.

18-14 续表 Continued

单位：人 (person)

项目	Item	注册学生数 Student Enrollment 合计 Total	#女性 Females	教职工数 Teachers and Staff 合计 Total	#专任教师 Full-time Teachers	聘请校外教师 External Teachers Retained
合计	**Total**	**2548804**	**1322292**	**53316**	**19539**	**17252**
#少数民族	National Miniorities	20829	9260	108	60	67
按培训机构分	**By Training Institution**					
职工技术培训学校(机构)	**Technical Training Schools (Institutions) for Employees**	**58528**	**30984**	**400**	**257**	**160**
教育部门和集体办	Run by Education Authorities and Collectively-run	3767	2727	82	70	70
其他部门办	Run by Other Authorities	54570	28197	250	135	90
民办	Privately-funded	191	60	68	52	
农村成人文化技术培训学校(机构)	**Cultural and Technical Training Schools (Institutions) for Rural Adults**	**447763**	**250059**	**1499**	**811**	**2685**
#教育部门和集体办	Run by Education Authorities and Collectively-run	447763	250059	1499	811	2685
县办	Run by Counties	64575	31520	102	64	244
乡办	Run by Townships	224067	127480	661	416	1207
村办	Run by Villages	159121	91059	736	331	1234
其他培训机构(含社会培训机构)	**Other Training Institutions (Including Social Training Institutions)**	**2042513**	**1041249**	**51417**	**18471**	**14407**
教育部门和集体办	Run by Education Authorities and Collectively-run	101145	51471	2346	946	947
其他部门办	Run by Other Authorities	796473	400054	16070	5153	5051
民办	Privately-funded	1144895	589724	33001	12372	8409
按培训时间分	**By Training Duration**					
一个月以内	within 1 month	966994	490571			
一个月至三个月以内	1-3 months	424638	213231			
三个月至半年以内	3-6 months	564679	297411			
半年至一年以内	6 months to 1 year	444908	239303			
一年及以上	over 1 year	147585	81776			
按培训形式分	**Group by Form of Training**					
#资格证书培训	Qualification Certificate Training	290154	141191			
岗位证书培训	Job Post Certificate Training	447149	202523			

18-15 民办教育基本情况(2014年)
STATSTICS FOR PRIVATELY-FUNDED EDUCATION (2014)

单位：人 (person)

项目	Item	校数(所) Number of Schools (unit)	毕业生数 Graduates	招生数 New Enrollment	在校学生数 Total Enrollment	教职工数 Teachers and Staff	#专任教师 Full-time Teachers	聘请校外教师数 External Teachers Retained
合计	**Total**	**788**	**74226**	**83335**	**314225**	**48653**	**25802**	**3896**
民办高等教育	**Privately-funded Higher Education**	**84**	**17363**	**18948**	**68451**	**11313**	**5290**	**3521**
普通高校	General Institutions of Higher Education	15	17363	18948	68451	6371	3311	1694
民办高等教育机构	Other Privately-funded Higher Education Institutions	69				4942	1979	1827
民办中等教育	**Privately-funded Secondary Education**	**107**	**14607**	**12383**	**47315**	**10317**	**6387**	**296**
高中阶段教育	Senior High School Education	86	6555	3454	21229	10317	6387	296
民办普通高中	Privately-funded Senior High Schools	63	4926	3000	16809	9159	5779	50
民办中等职业教育	Privately-funded Secondary Vocational Education	23	1629	454	4420	1158	608	246
初中阶段教育	Junior High School Education	21	8052	8929	26086			
民办小学	**Privately-funded Primary Schools**	**65**	**10771**	**9372**	**71512**	**3011**	**2254**	
民办幼儿园	**Privately-funded Kindergartens**	**532**	**31485**	**42632**	**126947**	**24012**	**11871**	**79**

注：普通中学教职工数、专任教师及聘请校外教师数为初中高中合计数。
资料来源：北京市教育委员会。
Note: Number of teachers,staff,full-time teachers,substitutive and part-time teachers in regular secondary schools includes those in junior and senior middle schools.
Source: Beijing Municipal Commission of Education.

18-16 高校办学条件(2014年)
SCHOOL CONDITIONS OF HIGHER EDUCATION INSTITUTIONS (2014)

项目	Item	合计 Total	中央 Central	市属市管 Municipal
普通高校	**General Institutions of Higher Education**			
校舍建筑面积 (平方米)	Building Area (sq.m)	35214326	24177544	11036782
占地面积 (平方米)	Floor Space (sq.m)	49931051	33715781	16215270
图书 (万册)	Books (10000 volumes)	10991.67	7055.53	3936.14
电子图书藏量 (千兆字节)	E-books Collections (Gigabyte)	6208425.48	6041795.87	166629.61
拥有教学用计算机 (台)	Computers for Teaching (unit)	412327	212390	199937
成人高校	**Institutions of Higher Education for Adults**			
校舍建筑面积 (平方米)	Building Area (sq.m)	944342	311628	632714
占地面积 (平方米)	Floor Space (sq.m)	1299227	317317	981910
图书 (万册)	Books (10000 volumes)	222.21	43.72	178.49
电子图书藏量 (千兆字节)	E-books Collections (Gigabyte)	25704.88	17964.11	7740.77
拥有教学用计算机 (台)	Computers for Teaching (unit)	10694	1649	9045

资料来源：北京市教育委员会。
Source: Beijing Municipal Commission of Education.

18-17 基础教育办学条件(2014年)
SCHOOL CONDITIONS OF BASIC EDUCATION (2014)

单位：平方米 (sq.m)

项目	Item	普通中学 General Middle Schools	小学 Primary Schools
学校占地面积	Floor Space	22945723	14169639
校舍建筑面积	Building Area	12617591	6827432
#当年新增	Newly Added in the Year	858324	486576
#危房面积	Area of Dangerous Buildings		459
教学及辅助用房	Teaching and Auxiliary Houses	4700485	3197881
普通教室	Classrooms	2777707	2515188
实验室	Laboratories	791941	207003
图书室	Libraries	342014	160792
微机室	Computer Rooms	202020	140567
语音室	Language Labs	32985	17293
体育馆	Gymnasiums	553818	157038
行政办公用房	Administrative Houses	1400451	796098
生活用房	Houses for Life (Residencial Houses)	3549911	1156745
其他用房	Houses for Other Purposes	2966744	1676708
计算机 (台)	Computers (unit)	259716	219446
图书藏量 (册)	Books Collections (volume)	28154344	26737601
电子图书藏量（千兆字节）	E-book Collections (Gigabyte)	181053.84	166480.37

资料来源：北京市教育委员会

Source: Beijing Municipal Commission of Education.

18-18 非本市户籍、外国籍学生情况(2014年)
STATISTICS FOR STUDENTS FROM OTHER PROVINCES, MUNICIPALITIES AND AUTONOMOUS REGIONS ALONG WITH OTHER COUNTRIES (2014)

单位：人 (person)

项目	Item	非本市户籍学生数 Students from Other Provinces, Municipalities and Autonomous Regions	#民办学校 Privately-funded Schools	外国留学生 Overseas Students	#民办学校 Privately-funded Education
合计	**Total**	**649757**	**135969**	**6677**	**2830**
普通中学	General Middle Schools	120941	19442	2610	877
初中	Junior Secondary Schools	102338	14477	1033	341
高中	Senior Secondary Schools	18603	4965	1577	536
中等职业教育	Vocational Secondary Schools	58024	4249	94	
小学	Primary Schools	368501	62646	2447	865
特殊教育	Special Education Schools	695	35	6	
幼儿园	Kindergartens	101596	49597	1520	1088

资料来源：北京市教育委员会。

Source: Beijing Municipal Commission of Education.

18-19 图书馆、文化馆、档案馆情况(1978-2014年)
LIBRARIES, CULTURAL CENTERS AND ARCHIVES (1978-2014)

年份 Year	公共图书馆 Public Libraries				群众艺术馆、文化馆 Mass Art Centers, Cultural Centers		档案馆 Archiving Institutions			
	个数(个) Number (unit)	总藏数(万册、万件) Total Collections (10000 volumes)	建筑面积(万平方米) Building Area (10000 sq.m)	书刊文献外借人次(万人次) Person-times Borrowing Books, Magazines, and Documents (10000 person-times)	个数(个) Number (unit)	组织文艺活动(次) Art Activities Organized (times)	个数(个) Number (unit)	建筑面积(平方米) Building Area (10000 sq.m)	利用档案资料人次(万人次) Persons of Using Files (10000 person-times)	案卷(万卷件) Records (10000 rolls)
1978	18	1423		168.5	19	516				
1979	21	1502		173.7	19	1033				
1980	20	1606	1.8	210.4	19	778				
1981	21	1614	1.9	211.0	19	1131				
1982	21	1676	2.0	228.4	20	1334				
1983	21	1733	1.9	243.0	20	1015				
1984	22	1824	2.3	223.7	22	489				
1985	22	1860	3.0	219.9	23	469				
1986	23	1874	6.0	219.9	23	883				
1987	23	1959	20.6	169.8	23	1067	20	10695	1.30	86.13
1988	23	2050	23.4	300.4	23	647	20	21472	1.46	115.98
1989	23	2128	24.5		23	1411	20	31280	1.48	156.28
1990	23	2205	25.0		23	1429	20	23618	2.51	167.37
1991	23	2281	25.3		23	1128	20	33491	3.24	177.45
1992	23	2397	25.4	147.0	23	978	20	35950	2.64	181.31
1993	23	2461	25.5	212.0	23	764	20	37650	1.73	192.39
1994	23	2548	23.8	383.8	23	1034	20	42641	1.50	192.35
1995	23	2629	24.1	139.3	23	1127	20	65489	1.42	204.06
1996	22	2652	25.3	145.6	23	2277	20	62994	3.03	223.70
1997	23	2789	25.7	188.0	23	1875	20	64147	2.69	227.42
1998	24	2848	25.6	189.0	23	2554	20	67759	2.71	240.78
1999	24	2934	26.4	607.0	23	1490	20	72597	2.52	259.50
2000	26	3020	27.0	283.0	23	1809	20	72596	3.01	278.29
2001	26	3133	31.4	287.7	23	1822	20	72730	4.17	297.02
2002	26	3248	30.7	337.5	20	1817	20	72946	4.53	328.42
2003	26	3355	30.9	334.8	20	2023	20	81519	6.27	358.95
2004	26	3451	30.9	405.0	22	1826	20	83162	7.03	379.13
2005	26	3626	31.7	480.0	22	3697	20	84656	6.97	404.69
2006	25	3776	31.0	515.0	21	2200	20	93773	10.59	436.70
2007	25	3940	31.5	479.0	21	4752	20	93463	9.51	461.67
2008	25	4100	33.4	450.0	20	3007	20	97605	9.00	495.70
2009	25	4368	41.9	471.0	20	3470	20	97605	9.88	523.84
2010	25	4613	42.4	441.0	20	3564	18	97611	13.45	557.99
2011	25	5049	42.1	333.0	20	3401	18	97976	12.30	582.92
2012	25	5556	47.6	317.0	20	3848	18	98879	12.37	602.54
2013	25	5316	48.4	325.0	20	4769	18	101896	23.85	636.10
2014	25	5601	52.7	407.0	20	2158	18	98220	22.18	697.90

注：1978-1981年，群众艺术馆、文化馆数据不包括群众艺术馆。
资料来源：北京市文化局、国家图书馆、北京市档案局。
Note: In 1978-1981, the data of mass art centers and cultural centers didn't include those of mass art centers.
Source: Beijing Municipal Bureau of Culture, National Library of China, and Beijing Municipal Bureau of Archives.

18-20 博物馆情况(1982-2014年)
STATISTICS FOR MUSEUMS (1982-2014)

年 份 Year	北京地区 博物馆数 (个) Number of Museums in Beijing (unit)	文 物 藏品数 (万件) Cultural Relic Collections (10000 units)	博物馆及其他文物保护机构(文物局系统内) Museums and Other Cultural Relic Protection and Administration Organizations (under the jurisdiction of Beijing Municipal Administration of Cultural Heritage) 个 数 (个) Number (unit)	#博物馆 Museums	文物藏品数 (万件) Cultural Relic Collections (10000 units)	#一级品 (件) Grade-I Collections (unit)	参观人次 (万人次) Visitors (10000 person-times)
1982			28		8.4	294	9.7
1983			29		4.0		58.0
1984							
1985			32		9.0		20.0
1986			39	7	21.0		905.0
1987							
1988			42	11	21.0		1098.0
1989			46	12	14.0		992.0
1990							
1991			46	12	11.7	2901	6629.1
1992							
1993			50	16	17.4	479	2423.4
1994			51	17	16.7	447	955.0
1995			51	17	16.7	447	2100.3
1996			51	17	18.0	443	2009.3
1997			54	24	18.2	443	935.8
1998			56	26	18.3	387	697.8
1999			54	26	18.5	374	5641.8
2000			53	25	18.2	367	702.7
2001			58	26	17.3	366	99.1
2002			48	27	20.1	716	170.8
2003			55	27	112.4	716	119.2
2004			66	31	370.4	656	599.9
2005			73	34	115.1	620	1370.9
2006			70	33	115.5	643	1416.7
2007			69	34	113.5	439	1493.0
2008	148	331	71	37	116.0	678	1368.4
2009	151	331	76	40	117.0	722	1647.9
2010	156	332	79	41	117.0	725	1712.1
2011	162	430	78	41	117.0	852	1373.4
2012	165	430	78	41	117.0	903	1887.9
2013	167	430	78	41	117.0	903	1760.0
2014	171	430	78	41	128.0	891	1848.0

资料来源：北京市文物局。
Source: Beijing Municipal Administration of Cultural Heritage.

18-21 博物馆及其他文物保护管理机构情况(2014年)
STATISTICS FOR MUSEUMS AND OTHER CULTURAL RELIC PROTECTION AND ADMINISTRATION ORGANIZATIONS (2014)

项目	Item	合计 Total	市属 Under the Jurisdiction of the City	区县属 Under the Jurisdiction of a District/County
全市按行业管理登记的博物馆	**Museums Registered by Industry Administration**			
博物馆数 (个)	Museums (unit)	**171**	**43**	**42**
#免费开放的博物馆数 (个)	Museums Open for Free (unit)	79	23	23
文物藏品数 (万件)	Cultural Relic Collections (10000 units)	430		
参观人次 (万人次)	Visitors (10000 person-times)	3500		
文物古迹个数 (处)	Cultural Relics and Historical Sites (unit)	3840		
文物拍卖机构数 (个)	Organizations of Cultural Relic Auctions (unit)	137		
举办文物艺术品拍卖场次 (场)	Cultural Relic Auctions (time)	254		
文物拍卖标的数 (件、套)	Auction Targets (unit)	186251		
文物拍卖标的成交金额 (万元)	Turnover of Cultural Relic Auctions (10000 yuan)	2315746		
文物局系统内博物馆及文物保护管理机构 (个)	**Museums and Cultural Relic Protection and Administration Organizations under the Municipal Administration of Cultural Heritage (unit)**	**78**	**31**	**47**
#博物馆 (个)	Museums (unit)	41	17	24
博物馆按类别分	Grouped by Category			
综合性 (个)	Comprehensive (unit)	11	2	9
历史性 (个)	Historical (unit)	17	7	10
艺术性 (个)	Art (unit)	6	5	1
自然科技类 (个)	Natural Science (unit)	2	1	1
其他类 (个)	Others (unit)	5	2	3
从业人员 (人)	Employment (person)	6225	3140	3085
文物藏品数 (万件)	Cultural Relic Collections (10000 units)	128	122	6
#一级品 (件)	Grade-I Collections (unit)	891	629	262
参观人次 (万人次)	Visitors (10000 person-times)	1848	299	1549
本年收入 (万元)	Revenues in the Year (10000 yuan)	214175	90012	120163
#财政收入 (万元)	Fiscal Revenue (10000 yuan)	121057	51242	69815
门票收入 (万元)	Ticket Revenue (10000 yuan)	44533	1815	42718
本年支出 (万元)	Expenditures in the Year (10000 yuan)	197337	87141	110196

注：全市博物馆数为北京地区按行业管理登记的博物馆数。
资料来源：北京市文物局。
Note: Number of museums in the city means the number of museums registered by industrial administration in Beijing.
Source: Beijing Municipal Administration of Cultural Heritage.

18-22 公共图书馆(2014年)
PUBLIC LIBRARIES (2014)

项目		Item		合计 Total	中央属 Under Central Jurisdiction	市属 Under the Jurisdiction of the City	区县属 Under the Jurisdiction of a District/County
个数	(个)	Number	(unit)	25	1	1	23
从业人员	(人)	Employed Persons	(person)	3000	1722	364	914
总藏数	(万册、万件)	Total Collections	(10000 volumes)	5601	3378	733	1490
#图书	(万册、万件)	Books	(10000 volumes)	3156	1183	595	1378
建筑面积	(万平方米)	Building Area	(10000 sq.m)	52.7	27.8	9.4	15.5
阅览座席	(个)	Seating Capacity of Reading Rooms	(unit)	21063	5155	2924	12984
总流通人次	(万人次)	Total Number of Visitors	(10000 person-times)	1544	398	455	691
#书刊文献外借人次	(万人次)	Person-times Borrowing Books, Magazines and Documents	(10000 person-times)	407	12	68	327
#书刊文献外借册次	(万册次)	Volume-times of Borrowed Books, Magazines and Documents	(10000 volunme-times)	1061	108	283	670

资料来源：北京市文化局、国家图书馆。
Source: Beijing Municipal Bureau of Culture, and National Library of China.

18-23 群众艺术馆、文化馆和文化站情况(2014年)
STATISTICS FOR MASS ART CENTERS, CULTURAL CENTERS AND CULTURAL STATIONS(2014)

项目		Item		合计 Total	群众艺术馆 Mass Art Centers	文化馆 Cultural Centers	文化站 Cultural Stations
个数	(个)	Number	(unit)	346	1	19	326
从业人员	(人)	Employed Persons	(person)	2500	56	750	1694
举办展览个数	(个)	Exhibitions Held	(unit)	1804	5	187	1612
组织文艺活动	(次)	Art Activities Organized	(times)	26297	19	2139	24139

资料来源：北京市文化局。
Source: Beijing Municipal Bureau of Culture.

18-24 档案事业基本情况(2014年)
STATISTICS FOR ARCHIVING INSTITUTIONS (2014)

项目		Item		合计 Total	市属 Under the Jurisdiction of the City	区县属 Under the Jurisdiction of a District/County
档案馆个数	**(个)**	**Number of Archives**	**(unit)**	**18**	**2**	**16**
建筑面积	**(平方米)**	**Building Areas**	**(sq.m)**	**98220**	**30962**	**67258**
馆藏档案情况		**Files Colllected in Archives**				
全宗	(个)	Full Archives	(unit)	3240	827	2413
案卷	(万卷件)	Records	(10000 rolls)	6979	2986	3993
建国前档案	(万卷件)	Files Prior to the Foundation of PRC	(10000 rolls)	1004	988	16
建国后档案	(万卷件)	Files After the Foundation of PRC	(10000 rolls)	5975	1998	3977
录音、录像、影片档案	(盘)	Tape, Video, and Film Files	(piece)	43265	35028	8237
照片档案	(张)	Photo Files	(disc)	727446	335690	391756
缩微胶片		Microfiches				
平片、开窗卡	(张)	Flat and Window-open Microfiches	(disc)	289067	289067	
卷片	(万幅)	Rolled Microfiches	(10000 rolls)	5426	5376	50
档案利用情况		**File Utilization**				
本年利用档案人次	(人次)	Person-times Using Files in the Year	(person-times)	221359	15550	205809
本年利用档案	(万卷件次)	Files Used in the Year	(10000 roll.times)	181	55	126
本年利用资料册次	(册次)	Data Books Used in the Year	(volume-times)	2735	324	2411
本年利用资料人次	(人次)	Person-times Using Data in the Year	(person-times)	449	151	298
本年编研档案、资料	(万字)	Files and Data Edited and Studied in the Year	(10000 Chinese characters)	5019	2014	3005
档案馆网站来访IP次数	**(万次)**	**IPs Visiting Archive Websites**	**(10000 times)**	**296**	**46**	**250**

资料来源：北京市档案局。
Source: Beijing Municipal Bureau of Archives.

18-25 电影、电视、广播电台情况(1978-2014年)

年份 Year	电影 Films 放映场次 (万场次) Show Times (10000 Times)	观众人次 (万人次) Audience (10000 Person-times)	票房收入 (亿元) Ticket Revenue (100 million yuan)	电视 TVs 电视节目套数 (套) Number of TV Programs (unit)	平均每日电视节目播出时间 (小时) Daily Show Hours of TV Programs (hour)	电视综合覆盖率 (%) Comprehensive Coverage Rate of TVs (%)
1978	31.9	29924.1				
1979	35.5	34626.0				
1980	33.1	31189.5		1	4.25	
1981	31.9	30067.0		1	5.46	100.00
1982	32.8	28743.5		1	6.85	91.00
1983	30.1	27345.5		1	7.07	90.00
1984	27.8	23966.7		1	7.15	98.00
1985	23.0	18875.0		1	7.54	98.00
1986	20.6	15904.4		2	19.07	98.00
1987	19.0	13517.7		2	13.64	98.00
1988	19.2	13269.4		2	19.39	98.00
1989	21.5	14492.6		4	25.43	98.00
1990	20.7	12771.2		4	29.43	98.00
1991	21.3	12558.3		4	27.79	98.00
1992	22.1	11587.4		6	45.02	98.00
1993	11.9	5369.8		7	58.18	98.00
1994	10.6	2166.5	0.51	9	77.79	98.30
1995	9.2	1598.6	0.93	12	98.36	98.30
1996	11.5	1644.1	1.07	12	101.01	98.81
1997	12.6	1742.3	1.17	12	111.00	99.12
1998	12.3	1443.5	1.28	12	110.68	99.60
1999	11.7	964.7		12	118.36	99.80
2000	12.2	873.2		12	122.45	99.80
2001	12.6	804.7	0.92	16	200.15	99.91
2002	12.3	827.4	1.09	18	329.40	99.82
2003	11.8	683.0	1.35	19	259.32	99.90
2004	18.1	814.4	1.86	24	244.17	99.50
2005	22.6	873.8	2.29	25	329.81	99.99
2006	28.0	1221.0	3.02	25	294.23	99.99
2007	38.0	1711.0	3.70	25	309.12	99.99
2008	46.8	1767.3	5.37	24	309.06	99.99
2009	62.4	2451.5	8.19	26	319.13	99.99
2010	74.3	2923.3	11.81	26	319.24	99.99
2011	97.4	3235.9	13.52	25	334.22	100.00
2012	120.0	3954.6	16.23	26	343.68	100.00
2013	137.8	4288.5	18.60	26	347.89	100.00
2014	162.5	5184.6	22.82	26	344.02	100.00

资料来源：北京市新闻出版广电局。

STATISTICS FOR FILMS, TELEVISIONS, AND BROADCASTING STATIONS (1978-2014)

电 视 TVs				广播电台 Broadcasting Stations			
农村电视综合覆盖率 (%) Comprehensive Coverage Rate of TVs in Rural Area (%)	无线电视综合覆盖率 (%) Comprehensive Coverage Rate of Wireless TVs (%)	有线电视注册用户数 (万户) Subscnbers of Cable Televisions (10000 households)	有线广播电视入户率 (%) Access Rate of Cable Televisions (%)	广播节目套数 (套) Number of Radio Programs (unit)	平均每日广播节目播出时间 (小时) Daily Show Hours of Radio Programs (hour)	广播综合覆盖率 (%) Comprehensive Coverage Rate of Broadcast (%)	广告收入 (万元) Advertising Income (10000 yuan)
				4	56.08		
				4	57.22	100.00	139
				4	59.37	98.00	166
				5	61.97	98.00	117
				5	73.67	98.00	668
				5	65.87	98.00	645
				5	66.17	98.00	555
				6	68.75	98.00	771
				6	76.33	98.00	964
				7	78.67	98.00	1668
				7	77.87	98.00	2885
				7	77.87	98.00	5115
				10	94.75	98.00	9680
				12	134.75	98.00	15225
		52.71		12	134.85	98.00	26480
		82.21		13	148.25	91.00	45398
		182.97		13	150.25	96.97	93428
		202.75		15	156.05	98.44	100546
		230.97		16	174.67	99.98	106773
		165.78	43.24	16	178.20	99.96	115072
		175.71	45.80	16	188.90	97.7	149661
		205.95	51.76	16	192.43	99.91	136451
		231.24	57.05	16	197.43	99.88	154317
		243.00	58.39	16	197.86	99.91	157210
	97.57	265.50	62.09	16	229.55	100.00	212091
	99.99	282.00	64.12	17	281.88	100.00	236334
99.97	94.90	319.58	70.75	17	282.88	100.00	240146
99.97	93.13	345.06	74.43	17	288.92	99.98	317437
99.97	93.19	383.13	81.00	17	297.40	99.98	385231
99.97	94.38	413.50	85.90	18	316.58	99.99	453932
99.97	98.72	448.12	91.68	18	324.82	99.99	613672
100.00	99.74	475.92	95.90	18	329.56	100.00	796113
100.00	99.75	495.70	99.13	25	471.69	100.00	1081857
100.00	99.75	524.59	103.00	25	473.62	100.00	1689443
100.00	99.75	551.57	106.85	25	472.61	100.00	1753933

Source: Beijing Municipal Administration of Press, Publication, Radio, Film and Television.

18-26 电影、电视剧制作情况
STATISTICS FOR PRODUCTION OF FILMS AND TV PLAYS

项目		Item		2014 全国 National Total	2014 北京 Beijing	2014 占全国比重(%) As % of National Total	2013 全国 National Total	2013 北京 Beijing	2013 占全国比重(%) As % of National Total
生产故事片	(部)	Feature Films	(Piece)	618	270	43.7	638	222	34.8
制作电视剧	(部)	TV Plays	(Piece)	429	86	20.0	441	87	19.7
	(集)		(Episode)	15983	3129	19.6	15770	2952	18.7
电视剧出口量部	(部)	TV Plays Exported	(Piece)	296	47	15.9	243	40	16.5
	(集)		(Episode)	13824	1754	12.7	11180	1529	13.7
电视剧出口额	(万元)	Value of TV Plays Exported	(10000 yuan)	20795	5084	24.4	9250	2290	24.8

资料来源：北京市新闻出版广电局。
Source: Beijing Municipal Administration of Press, Publication, Radio, Film and Television.

18-27 电影放映单位情况(2014年)
STATISTICS FOR MOVIE PROJECTION ORGANIZATIONS (2014)

项目	Item	放映单位数(个) Number of Projection Organizations (unit)	总银幕数(块) Total Screens (Piece)	#3D银幕数 3D Screens	#IMAX巨幕数 IMAX Large Screens	放映场次(万场次) Show Times (10000 Times)	观影人次(万人次) Audience (10000 Person-times)	票房收入(亿元) Ticket Revenues (100 million yuan)
合计	**Total**	**169**	**963**	**576**	**11**	**162.75**	**5281.31**	**22.90**
院线影院	Cinema Chains	169	963	576	11	162.47	5184.57	22.82
二级市场	Secondary Market					0.28	96.74	0.08

资料来源：北京市新闻出版广电局。
Source: Beijing Municipal Administration of Press, Publication, Radio, Film and Television.

18-28 电视台情况
STATISTICS FOR TELEVISION STATIONS

项目		Item		2014 中央 Central	2014 地方 Local	2013 中央 Central	2013 地方 Local
基本情况		**Basic Statistics**					
电视台	(座)	Television Stations	(unit)	1	1	1	1
公共节目套数	(套)	Number of Public Programs	(unit)	35	26	34	26
全年公共节目播出时间	(小时)	Annual Broadcast Time of Public Programs	(hour)	291462	125569	270113	126983
播放节目情况		**Shows of TV Programs**					
新闻咨询类节目	(小时)	News and Consulting Programs	(hour)	80249	22905	69008	22538
专题服务类节目	(小时)	Special Service Programs	(hour)	85482	48160	81855	52342
综艺益智类节目	(小时)	Entertainment and Education Programs	(hour)	41140	9284	37647	6876
影视剧类节目	(小时)	Movie and TV Play Programs	(hour)	69645	28373	48976	26055
广告类节目	(小时)	Commercial Programs	(hour)	5020	9782	7490	9945
其他类节目	(小时)	Other Programs	(hour)	9927	7065	25137	9227

注：电视台数不包括区县电视台。
资料来源：北京市新闻出版广电局。
Note: Number of television stations excludes TV stations of districts and counties.
Source: Beijing Municipal Administration of Press, Publication, Radio, Film and Television.

18-29 广播电台情况
STATISTICS FOR BROADCASTING STATIONS

项目	Item	2014 中央 Central	2014 地方 Local	2013 中央 Central	2013 地方 Local
基本情况	**Basic Statistics**				
电台数 (座)	Number of Broadcasting Stations (unit)	2	1	2	1
公共节目套数 (套)	Number of Public Programs (unit)	22	25	34	25
全年公共节目播出时间 (小时)	Annual Broadcast Time of Public Programs (hour)	342365	172503	432014	172870
播放节目情况	**Shows of Radio Programs**				
新闻咨询类节目 (小时)	News and Consulting Programs (hour)	107856	18874	150206	18448
专题服务类节目 (小时)	Special Service Programs (hour)	135643	42422	163562	35423
综艺类节目 (小时)	Entertainment and Education Programs (hour)	58311	82288	92581	88267
广播剧类节目 (小时)	Radio Plays (hour)	10454	10738	4686	10512
广告类节目 (小时)	Commercial Programs (hour)	14555	11835	16518	12705
其他类节目 (小时)	Other Programs (hour)	15545	6346	4462	7515

注：1. 广播电台数不包括区县电台。
2. 公共节目套数中含县级广播电视台的广播节目套数。
资料来源：北京市新闻出版广电局。
Note: a) Number of broadcasting stations excluded those of districts and counties.
b) Public programs included broadcast programs of radio stations at county levels.
Source: Beijing Municipal Administration of Press, Publication, Radio, Film and Television.

18-30 广播电视综合覆盖率(2014年)
COMPREHENSIVE COVERAGE RATE OF BROADCASTS AND TELEVISIONS (2014)

项目	Item	2014
广播综合覆盖率 (%)	Comprehensive Coverage Rate of Broadcasts (%)	100.0
农村广播综合覆盖率 (%)	Comprehensive Coverage Rate of Broadcasts in Rural Areas (%)	100.0
无线广播综合覆盖率 (%)	Comprehensive Coverage Rate of Radios (%)	100.0
电视综合覆盖率 (%)	Comprehensive Coverage Rate of Televisions (%)	100.0
农村电视综合覆盖率 (%)	Comprehensive Coverage Rate of Televisions in Rural Areas (%)	100.0
无线电视综合覆盖率 (%)	Comprehensive Coverage Rate of Wireless Televisions (%)	99.75
有线广播电视入户率 (%)	Access Rate of Wire Broadcasting and Cable TVs (%)	106.85
有线电视注册用户数 (万户)	Registered Subscribers of Cable TVs (10000 households)	551.57
#高清交互数字电视用户数 (万户)	Subscribers of High-definition Interactive Digital Televisions (10000 households)	420.03
付费电视用户数 (万户)	Subscribers of Pay TVs (10000 households)	216.49
农村有线广播电视用户数 (万户)	Subscribers of Wire Broadcasting and Cable TVs in Rural Area: (10000 households)	75.83

资料来源：北京市新闻出版广电局。
Source: Beijing Municipal Administration of Press, Publication, Radio, Film and Television.

18-31 报纸、期刊、图书出版情况(1978-2013年)
NEWSPAPER, JOURNAL AND BOOK PUBLICATIONS (1978-2013)

年份 Year	报纸出版 Newspaper Publications				期刊出版 Journal Publications				图书出版 Books Publications		
	种数(种) Types (kind)	平均期印数(万份) Average Printed Copies Per Issue (10000 copies)	总印数(亿份) Total Printed Copies (100 million copies)	总印张(亿印张) Total Sheets Printed (100 million pieces)	种数(种) Types (kind)	平均期印数(万册) Average Printed Copies Per Issue (10000 copies)	总印数(亿册) Total Printed Copies (100 million copies)	总印张(亿印张) Total Sheets Printed (100 million pieces)	种数(种) Types (kind)	总印数(亿册、亿张) Total Sheets Printed (100 million copies)	总印张(亿印张) Total Sheets Printed (100 million pieces)
1978	11		68.50		468		4.50		5253	5.12	
1979	16		81.60		697		5.92		6723	5.91	
1980	41		84.50		839		5.80		9534	6.28	
1981	55		83.10		886		6.69		11139	7.84	
1982	57		78.30		882		6.67		13862	8.71	
1983	61		79.90		940		6.84		14384	8.49	
1984	73		83.00		987		7.89		15636	8.43	
1985	99		86.00		1098		8.21		17178	9.01	
1986	126		82.00		1206		7.95		19362	5.82	
1987	129		86.00		1409		8.24		21843	6.94	
1988	151		87.00		1514		8.23		23689	7.28	
1989	161		66.00		1580		6.24		25980	6.31	
1990	148		68.00		1415		5.90		27345	6.17	
1991	157		76.70		1499		6.83		29609	7.05	
1992	164	3886	81.38	88.39	1594	6043	7.79	22.30	31320	7.83	58.67
1993	170	3965	81.70	87.71	1597	6037	7.80	22.36	34393	8.60	70.96
1994	233	3759	69.98	92.59	1854	5328	6.29	19.11	38498	8.28	71.71
1995	240	3823	72.92	108.32	1884	5018	6.38	19.62	38819	8.33	70.15
1996	242		70.52		2129		6.13		41572	9.45	
1997	242	3624	71.80	122.17	2162	5396	6.61	22.87	45775	9.93	78.62
1998	247	3561	71.70	130.01	2274	5797	7.28	26.54	50155	10.95	86.05
1999	247	3520	71.65	144.65	2273	6116	8.04	35.18	54783	11.34	93.38
2000	240	3343	68.67	149.58	2352	5909	7.91	32.96	57821	9.63	92.98
2001	243	3339	69.35	153.22	2374	5761	8.09	32.61	63928	10.27	105.06
2002	247	3364	71.02	169.87	2377	5708	8.23	34.34	73836	12.16	127.48
2003	250	3393	72.45	190.35	2382	5702	8.18	34.25	85244	13.82	140.77
2004	253	3405	70.40	206.53	2791	5233	7.97	35.53	98312	15.22	157.17
2005	255	3169	66.16	227.22	2809	4957	7.72	40.80	108152	17.07	180.51
2006	256	3651	74.01	240.39	2809	5077	8.29	47.39	113232	17.19	186.10
2007	256	3454	73.09	218.55	2809	5340	9.17	54.21	125412	18.68	195.30
2008	259	3328	73.21	241.27	2898	5392	9.36	55.39	136284	20.78	220.00
2009	260	3232	71.63	232.50	3030	5373	9.70	59.35	144211	21.04	220.21
2010	262	3406	77.54	275.62	3063	5519	10.03	69.61	155209	21.45	251.18
2011	254	3453	83.07	293.72	3044	5991	10.19	76.74	167942	22.60	243.05
2012	257	3725	89.49	300.17	3064	5940	10.31	76.68	179634	22.54	250.70
2013	254	3737	91.72	298.20	3053	6094	10.36	78.02	192137	24.01	269.54

注：1991年及以前，报纸、期刊、图书为出版数；1992年及以后均为总印数。
资料来源：北京市新闻出版广电局。
Note: Figures on newspaper, journals and books in and before 1991 were figures of publications; after 1992, they were total sheet printed.
Source: Beijing Municipal Administration of Press, Publication, Radio, Film and Television.

18-32 报纸出版情况
NEWSPAPER PUBLICATION

项　目	Item	种数(种) Types of Publications (kind)		平均期印数(万份) Average Printed Copies Per Issue (10000 copies)		总印数 (亿份) Total Printed Copies (100 million copies)		总印张 (亿印张) Total Sheets Printed (100 million pieces)	
		2013	2012	2013	2012	2013	2012	2013	2012
合　计	**Total**	**254**	**257**	**3737**	**3725**	**91.7**	**89.5**	**298.2**	**300.2**
综合报	Comprehensive	30	30	1436	1382	47.2	46.0	177.3	178.2
专业报	Professional	224	227	2301	2343	44.5	43.5	120.9	121.9

资料来源：北京市新闻出版广电局。
Source: Beijing Municipal Administration of Press, Publication, Radio, Film and Television.

18-33 期刊出版情况
JOURNAL PUBLICATION

项　目	Item	种　数 (种) Types of Publications (kind)		平均期印数 (万册) Average Printed Copies Per Issue (10000 copies)		总 印 数 (亿册) Total Printed Copies (100 million copies)		总 印 张 (亿印张) Total Sheets Printed (100 million pieces)	
		2013	2012	2013	2012	2013	2012	2013	2012
合　计	**Total**	**3053**	**3064**	**6094**	**5940**	**10.36**	**10.31**	**78.02**	**76.68**
综　合	Comprehensive	70	70	150	167	0.37	0.40	2.67	3.19
哲学、社会科学	Philosophy and Social Sciences	906	906	3759	3484	6.43	6.20	34.61	32.82
自然科学技术	Natural Sciences and Technology	1568	1580	1280	1335	1.79	1.88	20.40	19.92
文化、教育	Culture and Education	368	369	712	761	1.37	1.46	17.46	18.14
文学、艺术	Literature and Art	141	139	194	193	0.40	0.38	2.87	2.61

资料来源：北京市新闻出版广电局。
Source: Beijing Municipal Administration of Press, Publication, Radio, Film and Television.

18-34 图书出版情况
BOOK PUBLICATION

项 目	Item	出版图书种数合计(种) Types of Publications (kind)		#新 书 New Publications		总印数(万册、万张) Total Printed Copies (10000 volumes, 10000 pieces)		总印张(万印张) Total Sheets Printed (10000 print sheets)	
		2013	2012	2013	2012	2013	2012	2013	2012
合 计	**Total**	**192137**	**179634**	**111865**	**107013**	**240142**	**225411**	**2695355**	**2506987**
书籍合计	**Books**	**192047**	**179569**	**111789**	**106971**	**238106**	**223445**	**2683793**	**2490769**
马列主义、毛泽东思想	Maxism, Leninism, Mao Zedong Thought	426	318	297	203	1175	969	23225	18408
哲 学	Philosophy	5183	4993	3599	3561	3172	3388	47664	51042
社会科学总论	General Social Sciences	3287	3140	2019	1974	1845	1923	32873	34300
政治、法律	Politics and Law	13180	12239	10122	9464	13550	11407	182810	155462
军 事	Military Science	986	760	802	603	540	542	7919	7452
经 济	Economics	21520	20775	13488	13635	10875	11360	189657	194531
文化、科学、教育、体育	Culture,Science,Education and Sports	38084	34881	18644	17958	126301	121643	1010837	942051
语言、文字	Languages	12706	11979	5906	5853	21447	12809	322320	222689
文 学	Literature	15512	13938	11761	10559	14450	14615	191311	193013
艺 术	Art	8051	7408	5560	5065	4861	4732	46411	62674
历史、地理	History and Geography	8263	8029	5936	6112	8461	6282	93373	78955
自然科学总论	General Natural Sciences	381	296	257	157	252	202	2849	2589
数学科学、化学	Mathematics and Chemistry	5326	4736	2001	1870	3016	2885	49736	50102
天文学、物理科学	Astronomy and Physics	1608	1434	1129	972	555	598	7253	7375
生物科学	Biology	1629	1516	917	882	871	997	12581	12474
医药、卫生	Medicine and Healthcare	11687	10483	6726	6078	7019	7948	132823	126241
农业科学	Agricultural Sciences	3269	3453	1931	1997	1316	2060	16174	21294
工业技术	Industrial Technologies	34462	33321	16911	16609	14657	15520	261873	261673
交通运输	Transportation	3892	3334	1982	1664	2588	2059	35118	28466
航空、航天	Aeronautics and Aerospace	305	301	236	212	107	113	1545	1565
环境科学	Environmental Sciences	1289	1269	868	883	456	566	6257	7299
综合性图书	General Books	1001	966	697	660	593	827	9181	11116
图片及小件印品合计	**Pictures and Small Printed Publications**	**90**	**65**	**76**	**42**	**2036**	**1966**	**11563**	**16218**

资料来源：北京市新闻出版广电局。
Source: Beijing Municipal Administration of Press, Publication, Radio, Film and Television.

18-35 录音制品出版情况
PUBLICATION OF AUDIO PRODUCTS

项目 Item	录音带 Audio-tapes				激光唱盘 CDs				高密度激光唱盘 DVDs-A			
	种数(种) Types (kind)		数量(万盒) Number (10000 cassettes)		种数(种) Types (kind)		数量(万张) Number (10000 pieces)		种数(种) Types (kind)		数量(万张) Number (10000 pieces)	
	2013	2012	2013	2012	2013	2012	2013	2012	2013	2012	2013	2012
合　计 Total	**1310**	**1267**	**15243.3**	**13904.0**	**2128**	**2014**	**2345.1**	**1345.1**	**917**	**965**	**738.7**	**1070.8**
#市　属 Municipal	69	17	7.8	4.2	64	56	60.6	59.3	10	44	2.4	12.4

资料来源：北京市新闻出版广电局。
Source: Beijing Municipal Administration of Press, Publication, Radio, Film and Television.

18-36 录像制品出版情况
PUBLICATION OF VIDEO PRODUCTS

项目 Item	录像带 Videotapes				激光视盘 VCDs				高密度激光视盘 DVD-Vs			
	种数(种) Types (kind)		数量(万盒) Number (10000 cassettes)		种数(种) Kind (kind)		数量(万张) Number (10000 pieces)		种数(种) Types (kind)		数量(万张) Number (10000 pieces)	
	2013	2012	2013	2012	2013	2012	2013	2012	2013	2012	2013	2012
合　计 Total	**117**	**46**	**49.8**	**20.3**	**1003**	**964**	**2590.7**	**3261.7**	**2703**	**3282**	**3459.7**	**3421.8**
#市　属 Municipal	5		38.5		1	4	…	0.5	83	124	201.1	133.4

资料来源：北京市新闻出版广电局。
Source: Beijing Municipal Administration of Press, Publication, Radio, Film and Television.

18-37 电子出版物出版情况(2013年)
PUBLICATION OF E-PUBLICATIONS (2013)

项目 Item	只读光盘 CD-ROMs		交互式光盘 CD-Is		高密度只读光盘 DVD-ROMs	
	种数(种) Types (kind)	数量(万盒) Number (10000 cassettes)	种数(种) Types (kind)	数量(万张) Number (10000 pieces)	种数(种) Types (kind)	数量(万张) Number (10000 pieces)
合计 Total	**4455**	**22097.8**	**1071**	**1601.4**	**2603**	**3574.1**
#市属 Municipal	19	14.96	17	0.1	35	23.6

资料来源：北京市新闻出版广电局。
Source: Beijing Municipal Administration of Press, Publication, Radio, Film and Television.

18-38 引进版权量情况
NUMBER OF IMPORTED COPYRIGHTS

项目	Item	2013	2012
引进版权量 (件)	**Number of Imported Copyrights (set)**	**9391**	**9587**
软件和电子出版物 (件)	Softwares and E-Publications (set)	176	233
图书 (件)	Books (set)	9215	9354

注：2012年引进图书版权量含期刊。
资料来源：北京市新闻出版广电局。
Note: Data on number of imported copyrights in 2012 includes journals.
Source: Beijing Municipal Administration of Press, Publication, Radio, Film and Television.

主要统计指标解释

教　育

研究生培养机构 指经国家批准按国家计划招收和培养硕士、博士和其他研究生的高等学校和科学研究机构。

普通高等学校 指按国家规定的设置标准和审批程序批准举办的，通过国家统一招生考试，招收高中毕业生为主要培养对象，实施高等教育的全日制大学、独立设置的学院和高等专科学校、短期职业大学。

成人高等学校 指按国家规定的设置标准和审批程序批准举办的，通过全国成人高等教育统一招生考试，招收具有高中毕业或同等学历的人员为主要培养对象，利用函授、业余、脱产等多种形式对其实施高等学历教育的学校。包括：职工高等学校、农民高等学校、管理干部学院、教育学院、独立函授学院、广播电视大学和其他机构。

高等教育机构 指经省、自治区、直辖市教育行政部门审批并颁发办学许可证，不具有颁发学历文凭资格的实施高等教育的单位。

民办学校 指经有关主管部门批准，公民个人、社会团体及其他社会组织等利用非国家财政性教育经费，面向社会举办的学校及其他教育机构。

学历文凭考试机构 经教育行政部门专门批准，进行全日制高等教育的民办其他高等教育机构。

专科教育 应当使学生掌握本专业必备的基础理论、专门应用技术知识，具有从事本专业实际工作的基本技能和技术应用能力。全日制专科教育的基本修业年限为二至三年。

本科教育 应当使学生比较系统地掌握本学科、专业必需的基础理论、基本知识，掌握本专业必要的基本技能、方法和相关知识，具有从事本专业实际工作和研究工作的初步能力。全日制本科教育的基本修业年限为四至五年。

硕士研究生教育 应当使学生掌握本学科坚实的基础理论、系统的专业知识，掌握相应的技能、方法和相关知识，具有从事本专业实际工作和科学研究工作的能力。硕士研究生教育的基本修业年限为二至三年。

博士研究生教育 应当使学生掌握本学科坚实宽广的基础理论、系统深入的专业知识、相应的技能和方法，具有独立从事本学科创造性科学研究工作和实际工作的能力。博士研究生教育的基本修业年限为三至四年。

网络学生 指经教育部批准的现代远程教育试点学校设立的网络教育学院，基于互联网上实施高等学历教育所招收的普通和成人本科、专科学生。

在职人员攻读博士、硕士学位学生 指经国务院学位委员会批准的，为提高在职人员业务水平，通过攻读博士、硕士学位入学全国联考所招收的学生。培养的学生只有学位没有学历。

证书教育 指由各类高等教育机构举办的，招收具有高中毕业文化程度，从事专业技术工作或专业性较强的管理工作人员，经过学校学习及考试合格，取得达到岗位要求的专业知识水平证明的非学历教育。证书教育形式包括单科班和专业证书班。

单科班 指学生在学校只学一个科目中的一门或几门课程，考试合格可获得单科结业证书。

专业证书班 学生在学校学习 8 至 10 门课程，考试合格可获得岗位要求的大专层次专业知识水平的证书。

岗位培训 指由各类高等教育机构举办的，以提高本职工作能力为目的的非学历教育和培训活动。接受培训的各类人员按要求经考核合格，颁发岗位合格证书和上岗任职聘任书。岗位培训形式包括资格性培训和适应性培训。

资格性培训 指学生按照岗位规范要求取得上岗(在岗)、转岗、晋升等资格的培训。

适应性培训 指学生根据本岗位工作的发展需要而进行各种适应性的培训。

进修及培训 指对具有大学专科以上学历和中级以上职称的专业人员和管理人员进行扩展知识，提高技能的非学历教育。

外国留学生 指接受来中国学习的外籍学生。

毕业生数 指上学年度内，具有学籍的学生学完教学计划规定的全部课程，考试及格，取得毕业证书，实际毕业的学生数。不包括结业生和肄业生数。

招生数 指新学年开始时，按照国家计划实际招收入学的新生数。不包括留级生和复读学生数。

在校学生数 指学年初开学以后，具有学籍的注册学生数。

结业生数 指具有学籍的学生学习期满，有一门以上主要课程(包括毕业论文或毕业设计)不及格或其他方面不合格，未予毕业而发给结业证书的学生数。不包括短训班和单科结业学生。

教职工数 指在学校(机构)工作并由学校(机构)支付工资的教职工人数。教职工数包括校本部教职工、科研机构人员、校办企业职工、其他附设机构人员。

专任教师 指主要从事教育工作的人员。包括临时（一年以内）调去帮助做其他工作的教学人员。不包括调离教学岗位，担任行政领导工作或其他工作的原教学人员；不包括兼任教师和代课教师。

特殊教育学校 指招收盲聋哑青少年进行初中等教育的学校。

校舍建筑面积 指产权归学校所有，已经使用的各种用房的建筑面积。不包括尚未竣工的在建工程和借用、租用的房舍或临时搭用的棚舍。

危房面积 指年久失修、结构构件受到严重损坏，有倒塌危险，经房管部门鉴定属于危房的面积。

学校占地面积 指学校校园内的土地面积，不包括校园外学校拥有的农场、林场及校办工厂等的土地面积。

文 化

公共图书馆藏书 指各级文化部门举办的面向社会服务的独立的图书馆（不包括文化馆的图书室，也不包括文化系统以外的图书馆）藏书数量。

广播综合覆盖率 根据国家广电总局制定的《广播电视人口覆盖率统计技术标准和方法》进行统计调查的，在对象区内能接收到广播节目的覆盖人口数占本行政区域内人口总数的比率。

农村广播综合覆盖率 根据国家广电总局制定的《广播电视人口覆盖率统计技术标准和方法》进行统计调查的，在对象区内能接收到广播节目的农村人口数占本行政区域内农村人口总数的比率。农村是指经国家批准设立的乡镇人民政府的乡和农村建制镇所辖区，不包括县政府驻地镇。

无线广播综合覆盖率 根据国家广电总局制定的《广播电视人口覆盖率统计技术标准和方法》进行统计调查的，在对象区内能接收到用中、短波、调频等无线传输技术发射转播的广播节目的人口数占本行政区域内人口总数的比率。包括中央、省、地市、县四级无线广播综合覆盖人口。

电视综合覆盖率 根据国家广电总局制定的《广播电视人口覆盖率统计技术标准和方法》进行统计调查的，在对象区内能接收到电视节目的人口数占本行政区域内人口总数的比率，包括中央、省、地市、县电视节目综合覆盖人口。

农村电视综合覆盖率 根据国家广电总局制定的《广播电视人口覆盖率统计技术标准和方法》进行统计调查的，在对象区内能接收到电视节目的农村人口数占本行政区域内农村人口总数的比率，包括中央、省、地市、县电视节目综合覆盖农村人口。农村是指经国家批准设立的乡镇人民政府的乡和农村建制镇所辖区，不包括县政府驻地镇。

无线电视综合覆盖率 根据国家广电总局制定的《广播电视人口覆盖率统计技术标准和方法》进行统计调查的，在对象区内能接收到用中、短波、调频等无线传输技术发射转播的电视节目的人口数占本行政区域内人口总数的比率。包括中央、省、地市、县四级无线电视综合覆盖人口。

有线电视入户率 指通过广播电视有线传输网收看电视节目的家庭用户数（包括接收模拟信号和接收数字信号的有线电视用户数，不包括宾馆、单位、写字楼等集体用户）与本行政区域内总户数的比率。

数字电视用户数 指通过广播电视有线传输网收看数字信号电视节目的家庭用户数。

付费电视用户数 指通过广播电视有线传输网收看数字信号的电视节目，并交纳收看费的有线电视家庭用户数。

Explanatory Notes on Main Statistical Indicators

Education

Institutions Providing Postgraduate Programs refer to colleges and universities, research institutions recruiting and educating postgraduates of master's degree, doctor's degree and other degree upon approval by the government and under the State Plan.

Regular Institutions of Higher Education refer to educational establishments set up according to the government evaluation and approval procedures, recruiting graduates from senior secondary schools as the main target by National Matriculation Test. They include full-time universities, independent colleges and higher professional schools, short-term vocational colleges.

Adult Institutions of Higher Education refer to educational establishments, set up in line with relevant rules approved by the government, recruiting personnel with senior high school or equivalent educational diploma through national college entrance test for adults, and providing higher education courses in many forms of correspondence, spare-time, or full-time teaching for adults. Institutions of higher learning for adults include schools of higher education for staff and workers, schools of higher education for farmers, colleges for management cadres, pedagogical colleges, independent correspondence colleges, Radio and TV universities and other educational establishments.

Higher Education Institutions refer to institutions offering higher education upon examination and approval by administrative departments in charge of education in provinces, autonomous regions and municipalities, with an education license, which are not eligible for conferring diploma.

Civilian-run Schools refer to schools and other educational institutions run by individuals, social groups and other social organizations upon approval by relevant competent authorities, by using educational funds not from state revenues.

Diploma Test Institutions refer to other civilian-run higher education institutions offering full-time higher education upon special approval by educational administration.

Secondary Technical Education shall enable students to understand necessary basic theories and special knowledge on applied technologies of a specialty, have basic skills and technical application ability for practice of the specialty. Full-time secondary technically education offers a basic study term of 2-3 years.

Undergraduate Education shall enable students to understand necessary basic theories and knowledge of a subject or specialty, have necessary basic skills, methodology and relevant knowledge of the specialty, and have preliminary skills for practical work and research of the specialty. Full-time undergraduate education offers a basic study term of 4-5 years.

Master's-degree Postgraduate Education shall enable students to understand solid basic theories, systematic professional knowledge of a subject, have relevant skills, methodology and relevant knowledge of the specialty, and have preliminary skills for practical work and research of the specialty. Master's-degree postgraduate education offers a basic study term of 2-3 years.

Doctor's-degree Postgraduate Education shall enable students to understand solid and extensive basic theories, systematic and in-depth professional knowledge, relevant skills and methodology of a subject, have relevant skills, methodology and relevant knowledge of the specialty, and have preliminary skills for independent creative research and practical work of the specialty. Doctor's-degree postgraduate education offers a basic study term of 3-4 years.

Online Students refer to students for Internet-based general higher courses, undergraduate courses for adults, and secondary technical courses recruited in online education colleges opened in schools as modern remote education pilots approved by the Ministry of Education.

Employees Enrolled in Graduate Programs refer to students recruited through national joint test for studies of Doctor's and Master's degrees approved by the Academic Degree Commission of the State Council, in order to improve the practical skills of on-the-job personnel. Graduated students will be conferred academic degree only, without academic credentials.

Certificate Education refers to education not for academic credentials, run by various higher education institutions that recruit management personnel who are graduated from senior high schools and engaged in professional technical work or strongly professional management work, and receive a certificate for professional knowledge level meeting the requirements of their job position after studying in the school and pass the test. It consists of single-subject program and professional certificate program.

Single-subject Program means that students study only one or more courses of one subject, and will be awarded a certificate of completion of single subject.

Professional Certificate Program means that students study 8-10 courses in the school, and will be awarded a certificate for professional knowledge at junior college level required for their job.

Occupational Training refers to educational and

training activities not for academic credentials, aiming to improve the competence, run by various higher education institutions. Various trainees will be awarded Occupational Incumbency Certification and Engagement Certification. The occupational training is in the form of qualification training and adaptability training.

Qualification Training means any training for students to become qualified for being employed (reemployed) on a job, transfer of job, and promotion as required by job criterion.

Adaptability Training means that students receive training for adaptability in line with needs of their own job.

Advanced Studies and Trainings means education not for academic credentials, offered for professional and managers with educational background of college and above, and technical title above middle rank, to expand their knowledge and improve their skill.

Foreign Students Studying in China refers to foreign students who study in China.

Number of Graduated Students means the number of enrolled students who are actually graduated after passing all exams and receiving a diploma upon completing all courses stated in the teaching plan within the last academic year. This does not include the number of students completing all courses with any one course not passed, and students not completing all courses or discontinuing their schooling.

Number of New Students refers to the number of students actually recruited at the beginning of an academic year in line with State plan, excluding the number of students failing to go up to the next grade and those resuming their interrupted studies.

Number of Enrolled Students means the number of students enrolled at the beginning of a new academic year.

Number of Students Completing Courses means the number of enrolled students completing their schooling with one and more courses not passed (including the graduation paper or graduation design) or other aspects not passed, who are not granted for graduation and awarded a certificate of completion, excluding the number of students completing short-term training courses and single-subject programs.

Faculty Number means the number of faculty working in and paid by schools (institutions). It includes the number of teachers and workers in the principal campus, in research institutions, school-run enterprises and other subsidiaries.

Full-time Teachers refer to personnel mainly engaged in teaching, including persons temporarily (within one year) transferred to other jobs, excluding persons transferred from teaching to administrative leadership or other jobs; excluding part-time teachers and teachers taking over a class for absent teachers.

Schools for Special Education mean schools recruiting blind, deaf and mute teenagers for primary and secondary education.

Floor Space of Schoolhouse refers to the building area of various houses of which the property right is owned by the school and which have been used, excluding houses not completed and under construction, borrowed and rented, or temporarily built sheds and houses.

Area of Dilapidated Houses refers to the area of those houses that have not been repaired for many years, have seriously damaged components, are at the risk of collapse, and are identified by the house administration authority as dilapidated houses.

Area of Land Occupied by School means the area of land within campus, excluding the area of land for farms and forest land outside schools and school-run factories.

Culture

Collection of Books in Public Libraries means the number of books collected in independent libraries open to the public and run by all-level cultural bodies (excluding book rooms in culture centers, and books collected in libraries not included in the cultural system).

Comprehensive Coverage Rate of Broadcast means the share of population who can receive broadcasting programs in the target area, calculated in line with *Statistical Standard and Method on Television and Radio Coverage of Population* established by the State Administration of Broadcasting, Film and Television, of the total population in the administrative area.

Comprehensive Coverage Rate of Broadcast in Rural Area means the share of rural population who can receive broadcasting programs in the target area, calculated in line with *Statistical Standard and Method on Television and Radio Coverage of Population* established by the National Administration of Broadcasting, Film and Television, of the total rural population in the administrative area. Rural area means villages of towns with people's governments approved by the State and areas under the jurisdiction of rural towns with organizational system, excluding towns where people's governments of counties are located.

Comprehensive Coverage Rate of Radio means the share of population who can receive broadcasting programs transmitted with short-wave, medium-wave, FM and other radio transmission technologies in the target area, calculated in line with *Statistical Standard and Method on Television and Radio Coverage of Population* established by the National Administration of Broadcasting, Film and Television, of the total population in the administrative area, including the population covered by broadcasting programs from central, provincial, prefectural cities and county radio stations.

Comprehensive Coverage Rate of TV means the share of population who can receive TV programs in the target area, calculated in line with *Statistical Standard and Method on Television and Radio Coverage of Population* established by the National Administration of Broadcasting, Film and Television, of the total population in the administrative area, including the population covered by TV programs from central, provincial, prefectural cities and county TV stations.

Comprehensive Coverage Rate of TV in Rural Area means the share of rural population who can receive TV programs in the target area, calculated in line with *Statistical Standard and Method on Television and Radio Coverage of*

Population established by the National Administration of Broadcasting, Film and Television, of the total rural population in the administrative area, including the population covered by TV programs from central, provincial, prefectural cities and county TV stations. Rural area means villages of towns with people's governments approved by the State and areas under the jurisdiction of rural towns with organizational system, excluding towns where people's governments of counties are located.

Comprehensive Coverage Rate of Wireless TV means the share of population who can receive TV programs transmitted with short-wave, medium-wave, FM and other radio transmission technologies in the target area, calculated in line with *Statistical Standard and Method on Television and Radio Coverage of Population* established by the National Administration of Broadcasting, Film and Television, of the total population in the administrative area, including the population covered by radio television programs from central, provincial, prefectural cities and county TV stations.

Access Rate of CATV refers to the percentage of households which can watch television programs by cable broadcasting and television transmission network (including cable TV households receiving analog signals and digital signals, excluding collective subscribers such as hotels, companies and entities, office buildings), to the total households in the administrative area).

Number of Digital Broadcast/TV Subscribers means the number of households watching digital-signal TV programs through the TV and radio cable transmission network.

Number of Pay TV Subscribers means the number of cable TV households watching digital-signal TV programs through the TV and radio cable transmission network and paying fees for watching.

19

科 技
SCIENCE AND TECHNOLOGY

简 要 说 明

一、本章资料的主要内容

本章主要包括：研究与试验发展（R&D）人员情况，研究与试验发展（R&D）经费情况，研究与试验发展（R&D）项目（课题）情况，研究机构情况，规模以上工业企业 R&D 活动基本情况，限额以上信息传输、软件和信息技术服务业企业研究与试验发展(R&D)活动基本情况，规模以上高技术制造业主要科技指标，高等学校科技活动情况、研究与开发机构研发活动、专利申请及授权情况等。

二、本章资料的统计范围

国民经济中研究与试验发展（R&D）活动相对密集行业的法人单位，主要数据包括：农、林、牧、渔业，采矿业，制造业，电力、热力、燃气及水的生产和供应业，建筑业，交通运输、仓储和邮政业，信息传输、软件和信息技术服务业，金融业，租赁和商务服务业，科学研究和技术服务业，水利、环境和公共设施管理业，教育，卫生和社会工作，文化、体育和娱乐业，公共管理、社会保障和社会组织等。

三、本章资料的数据来源

本章由北京市统计局、北京市科学技术委员会、北京市教育委员会、北京市经济和信息化委员会、北京市人力资源和社会保障局、北京市知识产权局、北京市科学技术协会、北京技术市场管理办公室等部门提供。

四、有关统计标准的变化说明

（一）关于行业划分。根据国家统计局规定，自 2012 年开始执行《国民经济行业分类》（GB/T 4754-2011）标准。

（二）关于三次产业划分。根据国家统计局《三次产业划分规定》（国统字[2012]108 号），该规定对三次产业的范围进行了调整。其中第一产业是指农、林、牧、渔业（不含农、林、牧、渔服务业）；第二产业是指采矿业（不含开采辅助活动），制造业（不含金属制品、机械和设备修理业），电力、热力、燃气及水生产和供应业，建筑业；第三产业是指除第一产业、第二产业以外的其他行业。自 2012 年开始执行此规定。

（三）关于高技术制造业。根据国家统计局《关于印发高技术产业（制造业）分类（2013）的通知》（国统字〔2013〕55 号），本分类在《高技术产业统计分类目录》（国统字〔2002〕33 号）的基础上修订完成，采用了原分类的基本结构框架。自 2013 年开始执行此标准。

Brief Introduction

I. Main Content

Data in this chapter reflect the situation of scientific and technological activities and patents, R&D personnel, R&D funds, R&D projects (tasks), research institutions, basic information on R&D of industrial enterprises above the designated size, basic information on R&D of information transmission, software and information technology service enterprises, scientific and technological activities of colleges and universities, R&D of research institutions and personnel, patent application and licensing, etc.

II. Scope of Statistics

Included in this chapter are the corporate entities in sectors with relatively intensive R&D activities in national economy, such as agriculture, forestry, animal production and hunting, fishing, mining, manufacturing, generation and distribution of electricity, heating, gas and water, construction, transport, storage and post, scientific research and development, technology services, information transmission, software and information technology services, finance, renting and leasing activities and business services, management of water conservancy, environment and public facilities, education, healthcare and social works, culture, sports and entertainment, public administration, social security and social organizations, etc.

III. Source of Data

Data in this chapter are from Beijing Municipal Bureau of Statistics, Beijing Municipal Science & Technology Commission, Beijing Municipal Commission of Education, Beijing Municipal Commission of Economy and Information Technology, Beijing Municipal Bureau of Human Resources and Social Security, Beijing Intellectual Property Bureau, Beijing Municipal Association of Science and Technology, and Beijing Technical Market Management Office, etc.

IV. Changes in Relevant Statistical Standards

(I) Classification of Sectors. According to relevant provisions of National Bureau of Statistics, the Standard for *Classification of National Economic Sectors* (GB/T4754-2011) became effective in 2012.

(II) Classification of Primary, Secondary, and Tertiary Industries. According to the *Provision of Classification of Three Industries* (G.T.Z. [2012] No. 108) issued by National Bureau of Statistics, the scope of three industries has changed. The primary industry includes agriculture, forestry, animal production and hunting, fishing (excluding agricultural, forestry, animal production and hunting, fishing services); the secondary industry includes mining (excluding mining support activities), manufacturing (excluding metal products, machinery and equipment repairing), production and distribution of electricity, heating, natural gas and water and construction industry; the tertiary industry means industries other than the primary and secondary industries. The *Provisions of Classification of Three Industries* (G.T.Z. [2012] No. 108) came into effect in 2012.

(III) High-tech Manufacturing. According to the *Circular of National Bureau of Statistics on Printing and Issuing the Classification of High-tech Industry (Manufacturing) 2013* (G.T.Z. [2013] No. 55). This Classification is revised on the basis of *Classified Catalog of High-tech Industry Statistics* (G.T.Z. [2002] No. 33), following the structure of the original classification. The standard has been put in place since 2013.

19-1 科技活动及专利情况(1985-2014年)
SCIENCE AND TECHNOLOGY ACTIVITIES AND PATENTS (1985-2014)

年份 Year	科技活动人员 (人) Personnel Engaged in Science and Technology Activities (person)	研究与试验发展(R&D)人员折合全时当量 (人年) Full-time Equivalent of R&D Professionals (person-year)	研究与试验发展(R&D)经费内部支出 (万元) Internal R&D Expenditures (10000 yuan)	研究与试验发展(R&D)经费内部支出相当于地区生产总值比例(%) Internal R&D Expenditures as Percentage of GDP (%)
1985				
1986-1990				
1986				
1987				
1988				
1989				
1990				
1991-1995				
1991	228167			
1992	247525			
1993	252811			
1994	240386			
1995	252232			
1996-2000			**4307457**	
1996	265552	84793	418614	2.34
1997	273161	84913	532257	2.56
1998	237127	86602	861138	3.62
1999	229584	85740	938437	3.50
2000	261113	98723	1557011	4.92
2001-2005			**13434129**	
2001	240609	95255	1711696	4.62
2002	257326	114919	2195402	5.09
2003	270921	110358	2562518	5.12
2004	301202	152132	3169064	5.25
2005	383153	177765	3795450	5.45
2006-2010			**30706037**	
2006	382756	168875	4329878	5.33
2007	450331	204668	5270591	5.35
2008	450147	200080	6200983	5.58
2009	529985	191779	6686351	5.50
2010	529811	193718	8218234	5.82
2011	605980	217255	9366440	5.76
2012	651003	235493	10633640	5.95
2013	681346	242175	11850469	5.98
2014	726792	245384	12687953	5.95

资料来源：北京市统计局、北京市科学技术委员会、北京市教育委员会、北京市经济和信息化委员会、北京市知识产权局。
Source: Beijing Municipal Bureau of Statistics, Beijing Municipal Science & Technology Commission, Beijing Municipal Commission of Education, Beijing Municipal Commission of Economy and Information Technology, Beijing Intellectual Property Office.

19-1 续表 Continued

年份 Year	专利申请量(件) Patent Applications (unit)	发明 Inventions	实用新型 Utility Models	外观设计 Industrial Designs	专利授权量(件) Patents Granted (unit)	发明 Inventions	实用新型 Utility Models	外观设计 Industrial Designs
1985	1540	754	720	66				
1986-1990	**15087**	**3332**	**11003**	**752**	**6700**	**737**	**5614**	**349**
1986	1692	535	1091	66	491	43	408	40
1987	2425	523	1796	106	776	102	630	44
1988	3342	702	2494	146	1376	169	1147	60
1989	3344	742	2408	194	1789	207	1497	85
1990	4284	830	3214	240	2268	216	1932	120
1991-1995	**31126**	**6604**	**21787**	**2736**	**19379**	**1801**	**15835**	**1743**
1991	4624	1023	3324	277	2369	263	1917	189
1992	6316	1340	4493	483	3265	312	2724	229
1993	6972	1483	4931	558	5806	530	4780	496
1994	6852	1506	4666	680	3914	368	3245	301
1995	6362	1252	4372	738	4025	328	3169	528
1996-2000	**37296**	**10344**	**20395**	**6557**	**22156**	**2483**	**14836**	**4837**
1996	6595	1441	4255	899	3295	246	2563	486
1997	6313	1678	3667	968	3327	281	2340	706
1998	6321	1754	3444	1123	3800	309	2522	969
1999	7723	2062	4045	1616	5829	573	3948	1308
2000	10344	3409	4984	1951	5905	1074	3463	1368
2001-2005	**83993**	**39312**	**30960**	**13721**	**39944**	**10960**	**20019**	**8965**
2001	12174	4984	5114	2076	6246	946	3600	1700
2002	13842	5785	5920	2137	6345	1061	3721	1563
2003	17003	7833	6665	2505	8248	2261	4244	1743
2004	18402	8608	6321	3473	9005	3216	3956	1833
2005	22572	12102	6940	3530	10100	3476	4498	2126
2006-2010	**209275**	**124175**	**62237**	**22863**	**100371**	**35532**	**48350**	**16489**
2006	26555	14226	8200	4129	11238	3864	5490	1884
2007	31680	18763	8819	4098	14954	4824	7364	2766
2008	43508	28394	11157	3957	17747	6478	8776	2493
2009	50236	29326	15424	5486	22921	9157	10141	3623
2010	57296	33466	18637	5193	33511	11209	16579	5723
2011	77955	45057	26615	6283	40888	15880	19628	5380
2012	92305	52720	32609	6976	50511	20140	24672	5699
2013	123336	67554	47586	8196	62671	20695	36301	5675
2014	138111	78129	48228	11754	74661	23237	44071	7353

19-2 研究与试验发展(R&D)活动人员情况

项 目	Item	研究与试验发展(R&D)人员(人) R&D Personnel (person)		#本科及以上学历 Bachelor Degree or above	
		2014	2013	2014	2013
合 计	**Total**	**343165**	**334194**	**231650**	**217982**
按执行部门分	**By Executive Department**				
企 业	Enterprises	145430	142522	58903	52478
工业企业	Industrial Enterprises	79915	79368	29171	25869
非工业企业	Non-industrial Enterprises	65515	63154	29732	26609
科研机构	Scientific Research Institutions	109363	107796	95511	93649
高等学校	Institutions of Higher Education	77255	72905	71892	66780
事业单位	Public Institutions	11117	10971	5344	5075
按隶属关系分	**By Affiliation**				
中 央	Central	204527	200192	164052	159131
地 方	Local	138638	134002	67598	58851
按行业门类分	**By Sector**				
#制造业	Manufacturing	76427	73710	28133	25045
信息传输、软件和信息技术服务业	Information Transmission, Software and Information Technology Services	31872	36242	9425	10652
科学研究和技术服务业	Scientific Research and Development, Technical Services	133074	126994	116972	111032
教 育	Education	77255	72905	71892	66780

注：行业划分执行2011年国民经济行业分类标准(GB/T 4754-2011)。

资料来源：北京市统计局、北京市科学技术委员会、北京市教育委员会、北京市经济和信息化委员会。

RESEARCH AND EXPERIMENTAL DEVELOPMENT PERSONNEL

研究与试验发展(R&D)人员折合全时当量(人年) Full-time Equivalent of R&D Professionals (person-year)		基础研究 Basic Research		应用研究 Applied Research		试验发展 Experimental Development	
2014	2013	2014	2013	2014	2013	2014	2013
245384	**242175**	**39042**	**35933**	**59082**	**59253**	**147263**	**146991**
108612	107245	403	487	3029	3125	105182	103636
57761	58036	27	120	578	578	57156	57337
50851	49209	376	366	2451	2547	48026	46299
97130	96249	24731	22432	34277	34834	38122	38983
33557	32307	13058	12212	19651	19076	847	1020
6086	6373	850	803	2125	2218	3112	3353
149620	150139	34336	31491	48495	49085	66790	69563
95764	92036	4706	4442	10588	10168	80473	77428
55090	54158	25	118	559	578	54506	53462
25264	28324			943	848	24322	27476
117007	112978	25391	23053	36428	37235	55188	52690
33557	32307	13058	12212	19651	19076	847	1020

Note: Sectors in this table are classified in accordance with the Standard for Classification of National Economic Sectors 2011 (GB/T 4754-2011).
Source: Beijing Municipal Bureau of Statistics, Beijing Municipal Science & Technology Commission, Beijing Municipal Commission of Education, Beijing Municipal Commission of Economy and Information Technology.

19-3 研究与试验发展(R&D)经费情况

单位：万元

项 目	Item	研究与试验发展(R&D)经费内部支出 Internal R&D Expenditures		按活动类型分 Group by Type of Activity			
				基础研究 Basic Research		应用研究 Applied Research	
		2014	2013	2014	2013	2014	2013
合 计	**Total**	**12687953**	**11850469**	**1594874**	**1372366**	**2749447**	**2580388**
按执行部门分	**By Executive Department**						
企 业	Enterprises	4634972	4283298	32777	28035	193078	182563
工业企业	Industrial Enterprises	2335010	2130618	243	3086	27751	22176
非工业企业	Non-industrial Enterprises	2299962	2152681	32534	24950	165327	160387
科研机构	Scientific Research Institutions	6409252	6023924	992537	841732	1669940	1545116
高等学校	Institutions of Higher Education	1456552	1366460	546908	481664	836295	805499
事业单位	Public Institutions	187177	176787	22651	20934	50134	47210
按隶属关系分	**By Affiliation**						
中 央	Central	9128156	8815089	1489670	1305688	2454637	2351800
地 方	Local	3559797	3035380	105204	66678	294810	228588
按行业门类分	**By Sector**						
#制造业	Manufacturing	2247003	2035064	175	2911	27151	22176
信息传输、软件和信息技术服务业	Information Transmission, Software and Information Technology Services	1121101	1103590			67197	43565
科学研究和技术服务业	Scientific Research and Development, Technical Services	7432375	6949711	1040824	880682	1795065	1683657
教 育	Education	1456552	1366460	546908	481664	836295	805499

注：行业划分执行2011年国民经济行业分类标准(GB/T 4754-2011)。
资料来源：北京市统计局、北京市科学技术委员会、北京市教育委员会、北京市经济和信息化委员会。

RESEARCH AND EXPERIMENTAL DEVELOPMENT FUNDS

(10000 yuan)

试验发展 Experimental Development		按支出用途分 Group by Purpose of Payment							
		日常性支出 Routine Expenses		#人员劳务费 Labor Cost		资产性支出 Expenditures for Assets		#仪器和设备 Instruments and Equipment	
2014	2013	2014	2013	2014	2013	2014	2013	2014	2013
8343632	**7897716**	**10738643**	**10020407**	**3535287**	**3222578**	**1949310**	**1830062**	**1356112**	**1340780**
4409116	4072700	4309758	3907659	2173860	1969387	325213	375639	303662	348254
2307016	2105356	2237692	2032446	930509	808964	97319	98172	93892	95693
2102100	1967344	2072067	1875214	1243351	1160423	227895	277467	209770	252562
3746776	3637076	5037747	4775244	1106064	1037646	1371506	1248680	829442	794287
73349	79296	1243993	1179844	197902	156457	212560	186616	183833	180260
114391	108643	147146	157660	57461	59089	40031	19127	39175	17979
5183850	5157602	7441103	7218325	1769122	1686837	1687054	1596765	1120926	1115950
3159782	2740114	3297541	2802082	1766165	1535741	262256	233298	235186	224830
2219677	2009977	2152902	1942951	895355	778704	94101	92113	90875	89675
1053904	1060025	1041285	999386	791157	780215	79816	104204	79548	102685
4596486	4385372	5918857	5552943	1479613	1355924	1513518	1396768	954003	919061
73349	79296	1243993	1179844	197902	156457	212560	186616	183833	180260

Note: Sectors in this table are classified in accordance with the Standard for Classification of National Economic Sectors 2011 (GB/T 4754-2011).
Source: Beijing Municipal Bureau of Statistics, Beijing Municipal Science & Technology Commission, Beijing Municipal Commission of Education, Beijing Municipal Commission of Economy and Information Technology.

19-3 续表 Continued

单位：万元 (10000 yuan)

项 目	Item	按资金来源分 Group by Fund Source							
		政府资金 Governmental Funds		企业资金 Enterprise Funds		国外资金 Foreign Funds		其他资金 Others	
		2014	2013	2014	2013	2014	2013	2014	2013
合 计	**Total**	**7000675**	**6795421**	**4346862**	**4011290**	**405612**	**381571**	**934803**	**662188**
按执行部门分	**By Executive Department**								
企 业	Enterprises	391766	409748	3789590	3446361	358482	338223	95134	88967
工业企业	Industrial Enterprises	222348	227527	2022384	1819635	18128	16765	72150	66691
非工业企业	Non-industrial Enterprises	169418	182220	1767206	1626726	340355	321458	22984	22277
科研机构	Scientific Research Institutions	5471283	5317749	124089	156745	18421	19098	795459	530332
高等学校	Institutions of Higher Education	974566	925233	427589	397842	27232	22680	27165	20705
事业单位	Public Institutions	163060	142691	5594	10342	1477	1570	17046	22183
按隶属关系分	**By Affiliation**								
中 央	Central	6550678	6442980	1651777	1705465	49496	45100	876205	621545
地 方	Local	449997	352441	2695085	2305825	356116	336471	58599	40643
按行业门类分	**By Sector**								
#制造业	Manufacturing	215678	220221	1945073	1731395	18128	16757	68124	66691
信息传输、软件和信息技术服务业	Information Transmission, Software and Information Technology Services	19577	25395	843023	808298	247891	256185	10609	13712
科学研究和技术服务业	Scientific Research and Development, Technical Services	5754802	5587077	746623	723820	108369	80124	822581	558690
教 育	Education	974566	925233	427589	397842	27232	22680	27165	20705

19-4 单位内部办研发机构情况
STATISTICS FOR IN-HOUSE RESEARCH AND DEVELOPMENT INSTITUTIONS

项 目	Item	机构数 (个) Number of Institutions (unit)		机构研究与试验发展(R&D)人员 (人) R&D Personnel (Person)		机构研究与试验发展(R&D)经费支出 (万元) R&D Expenditures (10000 yuan)	
		2014	2013	2014	2013	2014	2013
合 计	**Total**	**2601**	**2362**	**181967**	**175098**	**8991229**	**8570151**
按机构所属学科分	**By Subject of Institution**						
自然科学	Natural Science	152	151	27779	28698	1226659	1091631
农业科学	Agricultural Science	79	75	5910	5427	237400	205308
医药科学	Medical Science	106	104	10270	9753	316804	263555
工程与技术科学	Engineering and Techical Science	1897	1689	126696	120352	7014381	6815392
人文与社会科学	Humanities and Social Science	367	343	11312	10868	195985	194265
按机构组成类型分	**By Institution Composition**						
政府部门办	Run by Government Agency	558	531	121240	119291	6922877	6638914
与国内高校合办	Jointly Run with Domestic Colleges and Universities	31	29	586	568	40411	35590
与国内独立研究机构合办	Jointly Run with Domestic Independent Research Institutions	10	13	188	242	741	1361
与境外机构合办	Jointly Run with Overseas Institutions	9	10	107	110	979	3514
与境内注册外商独资企业合办	Jointly Run with Solely Foreign-invseted Enterprises Registered in China						
与境内注册其他企业合办	Jointly Run with Other Enterprises Registered in China	62	62	1304	1186	50323	31968
单位自办	Self Run	1928	1714	58451	53620	1975627	1858526
其 他	Others	3	3	91	81	271	279

资料来源：北京市统计局、北京市科学技术委员会、北京市教育委员会、北京市经济和信息化委员会。

Source: Beijing Municipal Bureau of Statistics, Beijing Municipal Science & Technology Commission, Beijing Municipal Commission of Education, Beijing Municipal Commission of Economy and Information Technology.

19-5 研究与试验发展(R&D)项目(课题)情况
RESEARCH AND EXPERIMENTAL DEVELOPMENT PROJECTS (TASKS)

项　目	Item	项目(课题)数 (项) Number of Projects (Tasks) (unit)		项目(课题)人员折合全时当量 (人年) Full-time Equivalent of Project (Task) Personnel (person-year)		项目(课题)经费内部支出 (万元) Internal Project (Task) Expenditures (10000 yuan)	
		2014	2013	2014	2013	2014	2013
合　计	**Total**	**128179**	**118710**	**231280**	**221745**	**9647685**	**8976148**
按项目(课题)来源分	**By Source**						
国家科技项目	National Science and Technology Projects	54619	50858	95925	99271	4782961	4824349
地方科技项目	Local Science and Technology Projects	12524	10741	10972	10661	209303	204324
企业委托科技项目	Science and Technology Projects Entrusted by Enterprises	29679	27103	21866	18460	812070	713566
自选科技项目	Self-chosen Science and Technology Projects	25476	24926	79581	72307	2706193	2178371
来自国外的科技项目	Science and Technology Projects from Foreign Countries	2037	1983	8632	9649	470541	486664
其它科技项目	Other Science and Technology Projects	3843	3098	14304	11398	666617	568875
按项目(课题)合作形式分	**By Form of Cooperation**						
与境外机构合作	Cooperating with Overseas Institutions	1706	1693	5774	7142	326880	294901
与国内高校合作	Cooperating with Domestic Colleges and Universities	6894	6517	11806	14378	431616	465650
与国内独立研究机构合作	Cooperating with Domestic Independent Research Institutions	8443	8419	18681	17846	788032	672088
与境内注册外商独资企业合作	Cooperating with solely Foreign-invested Enterprises Registered in China	239	273	386	544	15779	19835
与境内注册其他企业合作	Cooperating with Other Enterprises Registered in China	6262	6036	10732	11125	538965	494328
独立完成	Independent	101611	92661	176254	163614	7237575	6727168
其　他	Others	3023	3110	7647	7098	308838	302179
按项目(课题)活动类型分	**By Type of Project (Task) Activity**						
基础研究	Basic Research	43529	38584	36326	33562	1084606	981414
应用研究	Applied Research	61997	57202	56256	55987	2018892	1926244
试验发展	Experimental Development	22653	22924	138698	132196	6544187	6068491
按项目(课题)社会经济目标分	**By Social and Economic Objective**						
#环境保护及污染防治	Environmental Protection and Pollution Prevention and Control	6404	5309	7724	7237	263147	214590
促进能源的生产、分配和合理利用	Promotion of Production, Allocation and Reasonable Utilization of Energy	8636	6990	15560	12026	649328	518601
促进卫生事业的发展	Promotion of Public Health	9161	8074	16763	15742	262895	218153
促进教育事业的发展	Promotion of Education	10910	9832	3074	2878	58540	47538
基础设施以及城市和农村规划	Infrastructure,Urban and Rural Planning	6916	6750	10040	10196	337616	341234

资料来源：北京市统计局、北京市科学技术委员会、北京市教育委员会、北京市经济和信息化委员会。

Source: Beijing Municipal Bureau of Statistics, Beijing Municipal Science & Technology Commission, Beijing Municipal Commission of Education, Beijing Municipal Commission of Economy and Information Technology.

19-5 续表 Continued

项　目	Item	项目(课题)数 (项) Number of Projects (Tasks) (unit)		项目(课题)人员折合全时当量 (人年) Full-time Equivalent of Project (Task) Personnel (person-year)		项目(课题)经费内部支出 (万元) Internal Project (Task) Expenditures (10000 yuan)	
		2014	2013	2014	2013	2014	2013
社会发展和社会服务	Social Development and Social Service	14535	13908	9057	9274	215249	228562
地球和大气层的探索和利用	Exploration and Exploitation of Earth and Aerosphere	3427	3273	5369	5948	158387	173489
民用空间的探测及开发	Exploration and Exploitation of Civil Space	861	833	1229	1158	100983	69894
促进农林牧渔业发展	Promotion of Agriculture, Forestry, Animal Production and Hunting, Fishing	6329	6569	7009	6870	211719	223512
促进工商业发展	Promotion of Industry and Commerce	23518	24312	86119	85126	3257025	2958249
非定向研究	Non-oriented Research	28097	24374	23029	21442	772025	730887
按项目(课题)服务的国民经济行业分	**By Sector of National Economy Served**						
农、林、牧、渔业	Agriculture, Forestry, Animal Production and Hunting, Fishing	6735	5891	6082	5838	195991	189682
采矿业	Mining and Quarrying	3322	2803	6361	6490	284711	262905
制造业	Manufacturing	23772	23094	61970	60229	2425426	2183949
电力、热力、燃气及水生产和供应业	Production and Distribution of Electricity, Heating Power, Gas, Water	2325	1919	2660	2934	112133	83077
建筑业	Construction	3015	2826	6569	6642	208059	182137
批发和零售业	Wholesale and Retail Trade	183	255	68	167	2822	7053
交通运输、仓储和邮政业	Transport, Storage and Post	3089	2664	2849	2452	68978	85699
住宿和餐饮业	Accommodation and Restaurants	99	173	32	48	1289	650
信息传输、软件和信息技术服务业	Information Transmission,Software and Information Technology Services	5047	4196	26670	28150	1115301	1029484
金融业	Finance	1087	1077	299	355	4423	6633
房地产业	Real Estate	134	438	37	116	1077	1937
租赁和商务服务业	Renting and Leasing Activities and Business Services	2242	2672	1984	2068	83924	81412
科学研究和技术服务业	Scientific Research and Development, Technical Services	44579	40856	88560	80909	4612744	4401848
水利、环境和公共设施管理业	Management of Water Conservancy, Environment and Public Falicities	3927	3909	5693	4651	194051	155291
居民服务、修理和其他服务业	Resident Services, Repair and Other Services	1186	2217	504	709	13604	11923
教　育	Education	9771	8035	2877	2495	65701	55278
卫生和社会工作	Healthcare and Social Works	7411	6506	12218	11520	171674	144923
文化、体育和娱乐业	Culture, Sports and Entertainment	4830	4875	3739	3883	35384	33616
公共管理、社会保障和社会组织	Public Management, Social Security and Social Organizations	5285	4198	2078	2056	49887	57395
国际组织	International Organizations	140	106	33	34	506	1258

注：行业划分执行2011年国民经济行业分类标准(GB/T 4754-2011)。
Note: Sectors in this table are classified in accordance with the Standard for Classification of National Economic Sectors 2011 (GB/T 4754-2011).

19-6 规模以上工业企业研究与试验发展(R&D)活动基本情况(2014年)

项目	Item	企业数(个) Number of Enterprises (unit)	#有研究与试验发展(R&D)活动的企业数 Enterprises with R&D Activities	研究与试验发展(R&D)人员(人) R&D Personnel (person)	研究与试验发展(R&D)人员折合全时当量(人年) Full-time Equivalent of R&D Personnel (person-year)	研究与试验发展(R&D)经费内部支出(万元) Internal R&D Expenditures (10000 yuan)
合计	**Total**	**3686**	**1140**	**79915**	**57761**	**2335010**
按企业规模分	**By Size of Enterprise**					
#大中型企业	Medium and Large-sized	748	377	58772	43115	1891375
按隶属关系分	**By Affiliation**					
中央	Central	237	138	15901	11610	604752
地方	Local	3449	1002	64014	46151	1730258
按登记注册类型分	**By Registration Type**					
内资企业	Domestically-invested Enterprises	2834	927	61639	45832	1608752
#国有企业	State-owned Enterprises	83	25	3507	2919	101867
港澳台商投资企业	Hong Kong, Macao and Taiwan-invested Enterprises	209	58	5563	3426	264383
外商投资企业	Foreign-invested Enterprises	643	155	12713	8504	461875
按重点产业分	**By Key Sector**					
#高技术制造业	High-tech Manufacturing	805	450	32779	23741	1107598
#现代制造业	Modern Manufacturing	609	319	21478	15344	630613

BASIC INFORMATION ON RESEARCH AND EXPERIMENTAL DEVELOPMENT ACTIVITIES OF INDUSTRIAL ENTERPRISES ABOVE DESIGNATED SIZE (2014)

				专利		新产品	新产品	
政府资金 Governmental Funds	企业资金 Enterprise Funds	国外资金 Foreign Funds	其他资金 Others	申请数(件) Patent Applications (unit)	#发明专利 Inventions	产值(万元) Output Value of New Products (10000 yuan)	销售收入(万元) Sales Income of New Products (10000 yuan)	#出口 Exports
222348	**2022384**	**18128**	**72150**	**19916**	**9835**	**42651776**	**42470008**	**4604212**
197005	1612005	16182	66184	15050	8010	33685115	33478587	4280864
136002	408473	848	59429	4146	2173	8261013	8312851	91986
86346	1613912	17280	12721	15770	7662	34390763	34157157	4512227
195795	1342735	969	69253	13980	6537	22604730	22508508	573969
7595	79573		14699	820	411	1516589	1402688	2828
5779	247869	9711	1024	3900	2927	9896943	9875585	737853
20774	431780	7448	1874	2036	371	10150103	10085915	3292391
177454	869408	10009	50727	8906	5845	18813343	18651122	3626776
24511	577772	8207	20124	5777	4064	16429763	16181140	2894316

19-7 规模以上工业企业研究与试验发展(R&D)活动基本情况(按行业分)(2014年)

项目	Item	企业数(个) Number of Enterprises (unit)	#有研究与试验发展(R&D)活动的企业数 Enterprises with R&D Activities	研究与试验发展(R&D)人员(人) R&D Personnel (person)
合计	**Total**	**3686**	**1140**	**79915**
采矿业	**Mining and Quarrying**	**24**	**11**	**2527**
煤炭开采和洗选业	Mining and Washing of Coal	4	3	1205
石油和天然气开采业	Extraction of Petroleum and Natural Gas	2	2	209
黑色金属矿采选业	Mining and Processing of Ferrous Metal Ores	7	1	420
有色金属矿采选业	Mining and Processing of Non-Ferrous Metal Ores			
非金属矿采选业	Mining and Processing of Nonmetal Ores	5		
开采辅助活动	Mining Support Service Activities	6	5	693
其他采矿业	Mining of Other Ores			
制造业	**Manufacturing**	**3557**	**1118**	**76427**
农副食品加工业	Processing of Food from Agriculture Products	144	25	810
食品制造业	Manufacture of Foods	125	20	1047
酒、饮料和精制茶制造业	Manufacture of Wine, Beverage and Refined Tea	42	6	1002
烟草制品业	Manufacture of Cigarettes and Tobacco	1	1	***
纺织业	Manufacture of Textile	27	6	85
纺织服装、服饰业	Manufacture of Textile Wearing Apparel and Ornament	141	5	392
皮革、毛皮、羽毛及其制品和制鞋业	Manufacture of Leather, Fur, Feather and Its Products, and Footwear	15		
木材加工和木、竹、藤、棕、草制品业	Processing of Timbers, Manufacture of Wood, Bamboo, Rattan, Palm, and Straw Products	16		
家具制造业	Manufacture of Furniture	70	2	374
造纸和纸制品业	Manufacture of Paper and Paper Products	41	2	89
印刷和记录媒介复制业	Printing, Reproduction of Recording Media	118	11	869
文教、工美、体育和娱乐用品制造业	Manufacture of Articles for Culture,Education, Artwork, Sport and Entertainment Activities	35	3	60
石油加工、炼焦和核燃料加工业	Processing of Petroleum, Coking, Processing of Nuclear Fuel	23	2	136
化学原料和化学制品制造业	Manufacture of Raw Chemical Materials and Chemical Products	215	79	2390
医药制造业	Manufacture of Medicines	193	105	7776
化学纤维制造业	Manufacture of Chemical Fibers	3	3	215
橡胶和塑料制品业	Manufacture of Rubber and Plastics Products	124	21	587
非金属矿物制品业	Manufacture of Non-Metallic Mineral Products	251	45	2766
黑色金属冶炼和压延加工业	Smelting and Pressing of Ferrous Metals	26	4	234
有色金属冶炼和压延加工业	Smelting and Pressing of Non-Ferrous Metals	38	13	1087
金属制品业	Manufacture of Fabricated Metal Products	228	37	2200
通用设备制造业	Manufacture of General-Purpose Machinery	252	110	6432
专用设备制造业	Manufacture of Special-Purpose Machinery	328	159	7374
汽车制造业	Manufacture of Motor Vehicles	237	44	9863
铁路、船舶、航空航天和其他运输设备制造业	Manufacture of Railway Locomotives, Building of Ships and Boats, Manufacture of Air and Spacecrafts and Other Transportation Equipment	72	35	4653
电气机械和器材制造业	Manufacture of Electrical Machinery and Equipment	267	96	5963
计算机、通信和其他电子设备制造业	Manufacture of Computers, Communication Equipment and Other Electronic Equipment	300	158	13668
仪器仪表制造业	Manufacture of Measuring Instruments and Meters	176	106	4812
其他制造业	Other Manufacturing	25	11	602
废弃资源综合利用业	Recycling and Disposal of Waste	8	1	4
金属制品、机械和设备修理业	Repair of Fabricated Metal Products, Machinery and Equipment	16	8	898
电力、热力、燃气及水的生产和供应业	**Production and Distribution of Electricity, Heating Power, Gas and Water**	**105**	**11**	**961**
电力、热力生产和供应业	Production and Distribution of Electricity and Heating Power	63	6	238
燃气生产和供应业	Production and Distribution of Gas	22	1	436
水的生产和供应业	Production and Distribution of Water	20	4	287

注：行业划分执行2011年国民经济行业分类标准(GB/T 4754-2011)。

BASIC INFORMATION ON RESEARCH AND EXPERIMENTAL DEVELOPMENT ACTIVITIES OF INDUSTRIAL ENTERPRISES ABOVE ESIGNATED SIZE (BY SECTOR) (2014)

研究与试验发展(R&D)人员折合全时当量(人年) Full-time Equivalent of R&D Personnel (person-year)	研究与试验发展(R&D)经费内部支出(万元) Internal R&D Expenditures (10000 yuan)	政府资金 Governmental Funds	企业资金 Enterprise Funds	国外资金 Foreign Funds	其他资金 Others	专利申请数(件) Applications Patents (unit)	#发明专利 Inventions	新产品产值(万元) Output Value of New Products (10000 yuan)	新产品销售收入(万元) Sales Income of New Products (10000 yuan)	#出口 Exports
57761	**2335010**	**222348**	**2022384**	**18128**	**72150**	**19916**	**9835**	**42651776**	**42470008**	**4604212**
1985	**73423**	**5515**	**63887**		**4020**	**318**	**237**	**3081162**	**3081162**	
911	11827		11827					3081162	3081162	
159	8760	4849	3911			9	6			
420	12674	110	12564			226	187			
495	40161	556	35585		4020	83	44			
55090	**2247003**	**215678**	**1945073**	**18128**	**68124**	**18054**	**8953**	**39554296**	**39374709**	**4604212**
586	26288	815	25389		84	139	106	308732	303459	5804
757	26755	886	25827		43	61	43	227908	242373	24429
841	13620	281	13340			36	6	250483	288722	3018
***	***	***	***	***	***	***	***	***	***	***
51	1992	136	1856			33	20	57142	95148	814
188	9561	229	9332			35	1	212255	201202	252
183	2932		2932			308	11	52137	55904	10
14	1254		1254			17	7	57674	59438	16213
504	10863	60	9966		837	51	6	180334	175731	2042
45	1523	2	1520			17	1	17522	24640	1821
100	2280	82	2199					197328	378865	
1443	39499	697	38712		90	349	273	746327	709512	64026
5459	170705	8676	159826		2203	479	364	1614400	1644403	13961
93	710	72	638			16	8	4240	3817	
398	10104	35	9782		287	99	18	230443	230743	9322
1916	61810	4205	57604			675	248	1051636	1171740	34363
116	4635	850	3786			42	22	101839	101017	1902
806	20026	2623	16862		541	139	112	336549	311802	61619
1197	47165	2450	44531		184	313	123	704595	720053	72260
4552	149538	5337	143750	121	331	631	169	2235996	2251759	490329
4942	178077	9474	168494		110	1726	819	2275953	2143013	186973
8242	344829	8205	336625			3375	909	6245245	6377417	14519
3873	274994	107477	114827	289	52401	713	351	1850323	1694936	2514
4881	182862	2438	171250	7998	1176	1239	380	3983304	3906075	160435
9827	543595	50384	480474	8216	4521	6763	4656	15353851	15040179	3389249
3360	88351	7065	76593	1504	3190	624	236	1108075	1110883	47774
291	17833	3193	12749		1891	160	63	135964	116631	
3	103		103			3		9053	9794	343
384	12181	8	11937		237	11	1	2315	2778	
686	**14585**	**1155**	**13424**		**6**	**1544**	**645**	**16318**	**14138**	
189	4373	576	3792		6	1443	609			
248	5385	63	5322			38	12	6596	6596	
249	4827	516	4310			63	24	9722	7542	

Note: Sectors in this table are classified in accordance with the Standard for Classification of National Economic Sectors 2011 (GB/T 4754-2011).

19-8 规模以上高技术制造业主要科技指标

项　目	Item	R&D人员折合全时当量（人年）Full-time Equivalent of R&D Personnel (person-year)	
		2014	2013
高技术制造业	**High-tech Manufacturing**	**23741**	**23707**
医药制造业	Manufacture of Medicines	5459	4930
#化学药品制造	Manufacture of Chemical Medicine	2290	2166
生物药品制造	Manufacture of Biological Medicine and Biochemical Chemical Products	1475	1447
航空、航天器及设备制造业	Manufacture of Aircrafts and Spacecrafts	3291	3055
#航空航天器修理	Repair of Air and Spacecrafts	367	460
电子及通信设备制造业	Manufacture of Electronic Equipment and Communication Equipment	8303	9580
#通信设备制造	Manufacture of Communication Equipment	2951	4328
电子器件制造	Manufacture of Electronic Appliances	2604	2379
电子元件制造	Manufacture of Electronic Components	797	893
其他电子设备制造	Manufacture of Other Electronic Equipment	1131	1231
计算机及办公设备制造业	Manufacture of Computers and Office Equipments	1880	1416
#计算机整机制造	Manufacture of Entired Computer	1328	888
医疗仪器设备及仪器仪表制造业	Manufacture of Medical Equipments and Meters	4809	4727
医疗仪器设备及器械制造	Manufacture of Medical Equipment and Appliances	1449	1485
仪器仪表制造	Manufacture of Measuring Instrument and Meter	3360	3242

注：本表高技术行业中不包括信息化学品制造业。

MAJOR SCIENCE AND TECHNOLOGY INDICATORS OF HIGH-TECH MANUFACTURING ABOVE DESIGNATER SIZE

R&D经费支出 (亿元) R&D Expenditures (100 million yuan)		新产品销售收入 (亿元) Sales Income of New Products (100 million yuan)		专利申请数 (件) Patent Applications (unit)		#发明专利 Inventions	
2014	2013	2014	2013	2014	2013	2014	2013
110.8	**106.5**	**1865.1**	**1584.5**	**8906**	**8308**	**5845**	**5358**
17.1	13.4	164.4	169.1	479	465	364	333
8.3	6.1	51.8	55.6	211	154	170	131
5.3	4.4	47.9	47.7	118	145	90	102
23.8	20.8	33.5	35.3	385	262	236	139
1.1	1.2			10	10	1	
40.2	42.4	1210.9	900.6	3463	3649	2114	2273
13.6	15.8	906.1	705.2	688	779	553	643
18.6	15.9	190.4	118.0	1813	2081	897	1157
1.7	2.5	25.2	24.4	96	95	28	40
4.0	4.6	46.9	24.9	601	458	500	322
15.2	13.0	327.4	349.3	3456	2687	2642	2103
13.2	11.3	248.7	311.1	3065	2339	2482	1941
14.5	16.9	128.9	130.2	1123	1245	489	510
5.7	7.4	17.8	18.9	499	596	253	272
8.8	9.5	111.1	111.2	624	649	236	238

Note: Information chemical manufacturing is not included in the high-tech sector stated in this table.

19-9 限额以上信息传输、软件和信息技术服务业企业研究与试验发展(R&D)活动基本情况(2014年)

项目	Item	企业数(个) Number of Enterprises (unit)	#有研究与试验发展(R&D)活动的企业数 Enterprises with R&D Activities	研究与试验发展(R&D)人员(人) R&D Personnel (person)	研究与试验发展(R&D)人员折合全时当量(人年) Full-time Equivalent of R&D Personnel (person-year)
合计	**Total**	**2704**	**353**	**31872**	**25264**
按隶属关系分	**By Affiliation**				
中央	Central	128	35	3086	2228
地方	Local	2576	318	28786	23037
按登记注册类型分	**By Registration Type**				
内资企业	Domestically-invested Enterprises	2175	312	17898	12445
#国有企业	State-owned Enterprises	22	4	685	450
港澳台商投资企业	Hong Kong, Macao and Taiwan-invested Enterprises	180	16	2585	1861
外商投资企业	Foreign-invested Enterprises	349	25	11389	10958
按行业分	**By Sector**				
电信、广播电视和卫星传输服务	Telecommunications, Broadcasting, Television and Satellite Transmission services	212	30	5497	5017
互联网和相关服务	Internet and Related Services	258	16	4483	3856
软件和信息技术服务业	Software and Information Technology Services	2234	307	21892	16391

注：行业划分执行2011年国民经济行业分类标准(GB/T 4754-2011)。

BASIC INFORMATION ON R&D ACTIVITIES OF INFORMATION TRANSMISSIOM, SOFTWARE AND INFORMATION TECHNICIAL SERVICE ENTERPRISES ABOVE DESIGNATED SIZE (2014)

研究与试验发展(R&D)经费内部支出(万元) Internal R&D Expenditures (10000 yuan)	政府资金 Governmental Funds	企业资金 Enterprise Funds	国外资金 Foreign Funds	其他资金 Others	专利申请数(件) Patent Applications (unit)	#发明专利 Inventions
1121101	**19577**	**843023**	**247891**	**10609**	**13347**	**9958**
89079	4491	78879	865	4845	2644	2508
1032022	15086	764144	247027	5765	10703	7450
441356	17034	413308	865	10149	8974	7226
22685	979	17763	865	3079	1313	1278
68058	335	67724			994	702
611687	2208	361991	247027	461	3379	2030
285398	1774	175689	106171	1764	1928	1840
210387	464	209899		23	2979	2238
625317	17339	457436	141721	8822	8440	5880

Note: Sectors in this table are classified in accordance with the Standard for Classification of National Economic Sectors 2011 (GB/T 4754-2011).

19-10 研究与开发机构研发活动情况(2007-2014年)

项目		Item		2007
研究与开发机构基本情况		**Basic Information on R&D Institutions**		
机构数	(个)	Number	(unit)	265
中　央	(个)	Central	(unit)	221
地　方	(个)	Local	(unit)	44
研究与试验发展(R&D)投入情况		**R&D Input**		
R&D人员	(万人)	R&D Personnel	(10000 persons)	4.6
按隶属关系分		By Affiliation		
中　央	(万人)	Central	(10000 persons)	4.4
地　方	(万人)	Local	(10000 persons)	0.2
R&D人员折合全时当量	(万人年)	Full-time Equivalent of R&D Personnel	(10000 persons-year)	3.8
基础研究	(万人年)	Basic Research	(10000 persons-year)	1.2
应用研究	(万人年)	Applied Research	(10000 persons-year)	1.6
试验发展	(万人年)	Experimental Development	(10000 persons-year)	1.0
R&D经费内部支出	(亿元)	Internal R&D Expenditures	(100 million yuan)	103.1
按隶属关系分		By Affiliation		
中　央	(亿元)	Central	(100 million yuan)	99.0
地　方	(亿元)	Local	(100 million yuan)	4.1
按活动类型分		By Type of Activity		
基础研究	(亿元)	Basic Research	(100 million yuan)	26.4
应用研究	(亿元)	Applied Research	(100 million yuan)	45.2
试验发展	(亿元)	Experimental Development	(100 million yuan)	31.5
按资金来源分		By Source of Funds		
政府资金	(亿元)	Governmental Funds	(100 million yuan)	88.6
企业资金	(亿元)	Enterprise Funds	(100 million yuan)	3.2
境外资金	(亿元)	Foreign Funds	(100 million yuan)	1.3
其他资金	(亿元)	Others	(100 million yuan)	10.0
研究与试验发展(R&D)项目(课题)情况		**R&D Projects (Tasks)**		
R&D项目(课题)数	(项)	Number of R&D Projects (Tasks)	(unit)	15079
R&D项目(课题)人员折合全时当量	(万人年)	Full-time Equivalent of R&D Personnel	(10000 persons-year)	2.2
R&D项目(课题)经费内部支出	(亿元)	Internal R&D Expenditures	(100 million yuan)	57.1
科技产出及成果情况		**Science & Technology Output and Achievement**		
发表科技论文	(篇)	Published Articles on Science and Technology	(unit)	37232
#国外发表	(篇)	Published Abroad	(unit)	9005
出版科技著作	(种)	Published Writings on Science and Technology	(Sort)	1489
专利申请数	(件)	Number of Patents Applications	(unit)	1993
#发明专利	(件)	Invention Patents	(unit)	1784
专利授权数	(件)	Number of Patents Granted	(unit)	985
#发明专利	(件)	Invention Patents	(unit)	752

注：研究与开发机构范围是北京市政府部门属的科学研究与技术开发机构、科技情报与文献机构。

资料来源：北京市科学技术委员会。

STATISTICS FOR R&D ACTIVITIES IN RESEARCH AND DEVELOPMENT INSTITUTIONS (2007-2014)

2008	2009	2010	2011	2012	2013	2014
266	275	281	280	288	287	299
225	228	231	231	238	237	248
41	47	50	49	50	50	51
4.8	5.2	5.7	5.9	6.3	6.6	6.6
4.5	4.9	5.4	5.6	5.9	6.2	6.2
0.3	0.3	0.3	0.3	0.4	0.4	0.4
3.9	4.2	4.6	4.7	5.3	5.5	5.5
1.3	1.4	1.5	1.6	1.8	1.9	2.0
1.6	1.7	2.0	2.1	2.2	2.3	2.3
1.0	1.1	1.1	1.0	1.3	1.3	1.2
123.8	150.3	187.0	195.1	222.0	246.8	271.2
117.4	143.9	178.9	185.1	211.5	236.3	253.6
6.4	6.4	8.1	10.0	10.5	10.5	17.6
28.3	39.2	49.9	58.5	65.1	73.6	86.5
49.0	61.5	78.0	84.0	92.0	102.2	108.9
46.5	49.6	59.1	52.6	64.9	71.0	75.8
106.6	126.3	164.4	168.0	192.6	220.0	244.6
4.0	4.4	3.6	6.6	6.5	8.2	8.2
1.8	2.0	1.5	2.5	1.5	1.9	1.8
11.4	17.6	17.5	18.0	21.4	16.7	16.6
16383	17816	19545	20333	22842	23949	25550
2.3	3.8	4.1	4.3	4.9	5.0	5.0
70.9	87.1	107.2	115.0	142.7	156.8	161.0
37149	39380	39384	41442	44218	45509	48040
9184	12011	11696	13361	14003	17216	17905
1636	1873	1601	1828	1670	1921	2058
2488	3182	3879	4880	5456	6192	6004
2119	2772	3450	4373	4798	5144	5115
1146	1574	1879	2260	3251	3646	3932
922	1299	1455	1756	2635	2763	3001

Note: R&D institutions cover scientific research and technological development institutions, scientific and technological information institutions subordinate to government authorities of Beijing.

Source: Beijing Municipal Science & Technology Commission.

19-11 高等学校研发活动情况
STATISTICS FOR R&D ACTIVITIES IN COLLEGES & UNIVERSITIES

项目		Item		2014	2013
高等学校基本情况		**Basic Information of Colleges & Universities**			
学校数	(个)	Number of Colleges and Universities	(unit)	99	95
#理工农医	(个)	Colleges & Universities of Science, Engineering, Agriculture, Medical Science	(unit)	69	65
#人文社科	(个)	Colleges & Universities of Arts and Social Sciences	(unit)	66	65
研究与试验发展(R&D)机构数	(个)	Number of R&D Institutions	(unit)	833	776
研究与试验发展(R&D)投入情况		**R&D Input**			
R&D人员	(万人)	R&D Personnel	(10000 person)	7.73	7.29
R&D人员折合全时当量	(万人年)	Full-time Equivalent of R&D Personnel	(10000 persons-year)	3.36	3.23
基础研究	(万人年)	Basic Research	(10000 persons-year)	1.31	1.22
应用研究	(万人年)	Applied Research	(10000 persons-year)	1.97	1.91
试验发展	(万人年)	Experimental Development	(10000 persons-year)	0.08	0.10
R&D经费内部支出	(亿元)	Internal R&D Expenditures	(100 million yuan)	145.66	136.65
按活动类型分		By Type of Activity			
基础研究	(亿元)	Basic Research	(100 million yuan)	54.69	48.17
应用研究	(亿元)	Applied Research	(100 million yuan)	83.63	80.55
试验发展	(亿元)	Experimental Development	(100 million yuan)	7.34	7.93
按资金来源分		By Source of Funds			
#政府资金	(亿元)	Governmental Funds	(100 million yuan)	97.46	92.52
企业资金	(亿元)	Enterprise Funds	(100 million yuan)	42.76	39.78
研究与试验发展(R&D)项目(课题)情况		**R&D Projects (Tasks)**			
R&D项目(课题)数	(项)	Number of R&D Projects (Tasks)	(unit)	83455	76331
R&D项目(课题)人员折合全时当量	(万人年)	Full-time Equivalent of R&D Personnel	(10000 persons-year)	3.35	3.22
R&D项目(课题)经费内部支出	(亿元)	Internal R&D Expenditures	(100 million yuan)	118.94	112.93
科技产出及成果情况		**Science & Technology Output and Achievement**			
发表科技论文	(篇)	Published Articles on Science and Technology	(unit)	115143	113220
#国外发表	(篇)	Published Abroad	(unit)		
出版科技著作	(种)	Published Writings on Science and Technology	(Sort)	5357	5410
专利申请数	(件)	Number of Patent Applications	(unit)	11503	12024
#发明专利	(件)	Invention Patents	(unit)	10025	10291
专利授权数	(件)	Number of Patents Granted	(unit)	7279	7745
#发明专利	(件)	Invention Patents	(unit)	5829	5919

资料来源：北京市教育委员会。
Source: Beijing Municipal Commission of Education.

19-12　科学技术协会及所属学会工作情况(2014年)
STATISTICS FOR SCIENCE AND TECHNOLOGY ASSOCIATION AND SUBORDINATE INSTITUTES (2014)

项　目		Item		合计 Total	市科协 Municipal Science and Technology Association	市级学会 Institutes at Municipal Level
基本情况		**Basic Information**				
机构数	(个)	Number of Institutions	(unit)	171	1	170
机构从业人员	(人)	Number of Employed Persons in the Institutions	(person)	1200	392	808
学术交流活动		**Academic Exchange Activities**				
国内学术会议	(次)	Domestic Academic Meetings	(time)	1090	2	1088
参加人数	(人次)	Number of Participants	(person-time)	323974	200	323774
交流论文	(篇)	Number of Papers Exchagned	(unit)	19762	20	19742
境内国际学术会议	(次)	Domestically-held International Academic Meetings	(time)	87		87
参加人数	(人次)	Number of Participants	(person-time)	10317		10317
交流论文	(篇)	Number of Papers Exchagned	(unit)	2295		2295
港澳台地区学术会议	(次)	Academic Meetings Held in Kong Kong, Macao and Taiwan	(time)	10		10
参加人数	(人次)	Number of Participants	(person-time)	1131		1131
交流论文	(篇)	Number of Papers Exchagned	(unit)	336		336
科技期刊		**Science and Technology Journals**				
主办科技期刊种数	(种)	Types of Science and Technology Journals Sponsored	(sort)	31	1	30
科技期刊总印数	(万册)	Number of Total Printings of Science and Technology Journals	(10000 copies)	110.22	2.25	107.97
科技期刊发表论文数	(篇)	Papers Published on Science and Technology Journals	(unit)	5484	23	5461
科普活动		**Activities to Popularize Scientific Knowledge**				
举办科普宣讲活动	(次)	Scientific Knowledge Lectures	(time)	5824	1700	4124
播放科技广播、影视节目	(分钟)	Playing Radio, Films and TV Programs on Science and Technology	(minute)	7953	1918	6035
举办实用技术培训	(次)	Holding Practical Technology Trainings	(time)	681	218	463
推广新技术、新品种	(项)	Promoting New Technologies and New Varieties	(unit)	316	51	265
参加活动科技人员总数	(人次)	Participating in Science and Technology Personnel	(person-time)	41554	15539	26015
参加活动的学会、协会、研究会	(个次)	Participating in Socieities, Associations and Research Institutes	(unit-time)	1230	670	560
科技传播		**Science and Technology Dissemination**				
主办科技报纸种数	(种)	Types of Science and Technology Newspaper Sponsored	(sort)	1	1	
制作科普挂图种数	(种)	Types of Scientific Knowlede Flip Charts Produced	(sort)	203	14	189
制作科技广播、影视节目套数	(套)	Science and Technology Raido, Films and TV Programs Produced	(unit)	56	26	30
制作科技光盘种数	(种)	Types of Science and Technology CDs Produced	(sort)	113	58	55
制作科普动漫作品套数	(套)	Scientific Knowledge Animation Works Produced	(unit)	4005	4001	4
主办科技网站	(个)	Science and Technology Websites Sponsored	(unit)	59	10	49
科技开放与交流		**Science and Technology Opening-up and Exchange**				
加入国际民间科技组织	(个)	International Cilvilian Science and Technology Organizations Joined	(unit)	11		11
促成科技合作项目	(项)	Scientific and Technological Cooperation Projects Facilitated	(unit)	4		4
参加国外科技活动人数	(人次)	Number of Persons Participating in Foreign Science and Technology Activities	(person-time)	493	84	409
参加港澳台地区科技活动人数	(人次)	Number of Persons Participating in Science and Technology Activities in Hong Kong, Macao and Taiwan	(person-time)	183	11	172
接待国外专家学者	(人次)	Foreign Experts and Scholars Received	(person-time)	634	316	318
接待港澳台地区专家学者	(人次)	Experts and Scholars from Kong Kong, Macao and Taiwan Received	(person-time)	335	130	205
科技服务		**Science and Technology Service**				
提供决策咨询报告	(篇)	Providing Policy-making Consulting Reports	(unit)	192	57	135
举办决策咨询活动	(次)	Holding Policy-making Consulting Activities	(time)	206	23	183

注：本表统计范围是北京市科学技术协会所属学会、研究会。
资料来源：北京市科学技术协会。
Note: Figures in this table cover societies and research institutes affiliated with Beijing Association for Science & Technology.
Source: Beijing Association for Science & Technology.

19-13 公有经济企事业单位专业技术人员(2014年)
NUMBER OF PORFESSIONAL TECHNICAL PERSONNEL IN PUBLIC ENTERPRISES AND INSTITUTIONS (2014)

单位：人 (person)

项 目	Item	合 计 Total	#高 级 Senior	#中 级 Intermediate	#初 级 Junior
合 计	**Total**	**517547**	**66127**	**172813**	**193608**
#工程技术人员	Engineering Technicians	129352	13576	32436	40296
农业技术人员	Agricultural Technicians	4552	508	1300	2125
科学研究人员	Science Research Personnel	8332	1895	3086	1257
卫生技术人员	Medical Technicians	95943	10953	32230	49259
教学人员	Teaching Personnel	168685	31210	75767	57773
经济人员	Economic Personnel	58022	3466	13440	19094
会计人员	Accountants	25379	1457	6163	12396
统计人员	Statisticians	3125	108	665	1361

注：公有经济是指北京市属国有和集体企事业单位,不包含在京中央属企事业单位。

资料来源：北京市人力资源和社会保障局。

Note: Public sector means state-owned and collectively-owned enterprises and institutions in Beijing, excluding central enterprises and institutions located in Beijing.

Source: Beijing Municipal Bureau of Human Resources and Social Security.

19-14 技术合同成交情况(1990-2014年)
STATISTICS FOR CONCLUSION OF TECHNOLOGICAL CONTRACTS (1990-2014)

年 份 Year	合同数 (项) Number of Contracts (unit)	技术合同成交总额 (亿元) Total Volume of Transaction of Technological Contracts Concluded (100 million yuan)	#技术交易额 Total Volume of Transaction of Technology	#流向外省市技术合同额 Amount of Transaction Flowing to Other Provinces and Municipalities	实现合同总金额 (亿元) Total Volume of Transaction Achieved in Contracts (100 million yuan)	#技术交易实现金额 Amount of Technological Transactions Achieved
1990	18588	20.3	10.5		15.4	8.4
1991-1995	**93970**	**167.7**	**120.0**		**115.4**	**83.8**
1991	18547	22.4	13.1		15.3	9.1
1992	23395	31.3	22.2		20.0	14.4
1993	20461	35.6	25.6		24.9	17.6
1994	15220	37.2	26.9		26.9	20.4
1995	16347	41.2	32.2		28.4	22.3
1996-2000	**91421**	**414.2**	**375.9**		**206.7**	**188.1**
1996	14850	45.8	39.2		29.6	25.4
1997	13866	54.3	48.1		31.1	27.8
1998	20724	81.6	73.9		42.1	37.6
1999	20711	92.2	88.5		43.6	41.0
2000	21270	140.3	126.3	65.5	60.3	56.3
2001-2005	**156114**	**1443.8**	**1217.2**	**688.9**	**669.5**	**628.1**
2001	23921	191.0	164.8	85.4	97.6	93.0
2002	27037	221.1	181.0	100.4	101.9	97.2
2003	32173	265.5	226.8	132.4	119.9	113.9
2004	35478	331.8	294.3	165.8	148.7	143.4
2005	37505	434.4	350.4	204.9	201.4	180.6
2006-2010	**256074**	**5422.8**	**3984.7**	**2372.7**	**2226.7**	**2006.7**
2006	51575	697.3	572.6	325.3	349.5	319.7
2007	50972	882.6	660.3	407.4	418.1	353.5
2008	52742	1027.2	778.1	487.0	406.2	375.0
2009	49938	1236.2	906.9	498.2	516.8	452.9
2010	50847	1579.5	1066.7	654.8	536.0	505.6
2011	53552	1890.3	1268.3	635.9	580.4	563.3
2012	59969	2458.5	2048.6	1385.0	739.8	707.0
2013	62743	2851.2	2252.4	1615.9	684.0	659.3
2014	67278	3136.0	2531.5	1722.0	708.2	675.1

资料来源：北京技术市场管理办公室。
Source: Beijing Technical Market Management Office.

19-15 技术合同成交情况
CONCLUSION OF TECHNICAL CONTRACTS

项目	Item	合同数(项) Number of Contracts (unit) 2014	2013	成交额(万元) Volume of Transaction (10000 yuan) 2014	2013
合计	**Total**	**67278**	**62743**	**31359985.3**	**28511954.3**
按合同类别分类	**By Type of Contract**				
技术开发合同	Technological Development	24938	24000	6833184.3	6104492.5
技术转让合同	Technology Transfer	1296	1570	647595.2	579535.1
技术咨询合同	Technical Consultation	4302	4938	395252.3	488438.2
技术服务合同	Technical Service	36742	32235	23483953.5	21339488.4
按合同卖方类别分类	**By Type of Seller**				
机关法人	Government Organisations	21	8	5017.4	2545.0
事业法人	Public Institutions	11122	10274	1098148.6	1024315.5
社团法人	Mass Organisations	15	23	1095.5	1999.0
企业法人	Enterprises	56069	52388	30233204.0	27460488.6
自然人	Natural Persons	28	32	6573.7	9623.7
其他组织	Other Organizations	23	18	15946.2	12982.5
按合同买方类别分类	**By Type of Buyer**				
机关法人	Government Organisations	5280	5133	1787487.3	2119154.5
事业法人	Public Institutions	12066	10625	1643707.5	1932410.8
社团法人	Mass Organisations	313	270	24959.3	48030.3
企业法人	Enterprises	48527	45448	25230280.1	21828387.3
自然人	Natural Persons	404	457	102228.4	18822.6
其他组织	Other Organizations	688	810	2571322.7	2565148.7
按服务社会经济目标分类	**By Social and Economic Service Objectives**				
环境保护、生态建设及污染防治	Environmental Protection, Ecological Development and Pollution Control	3386		3660854.0	
能源生产、分配和合理利用	Energy Production, Allocation and Reasonable Utilization	5420		5647012.1	
卫生事业发展	Health Services	1950		352179.8	
教育事业发展	Education Development	1864		272018.5	
基础设施以及城市和农村规划	Infrastructure and Rural and Urban Planning	7563		8565501.5	
社会发展和社会服务	Social Development and Social Services	24763		6934936.6	
地球和大气层的探索与利用	Exploration and Utilization Of The Earth and Atmosphere	167		473492.8	
民用空间探测及开发	Private Space Exploration and Development	700		108175.8	
农林牧渔业发展	Development in Agriculture, Forestry, Animal Production and Hunting, Fishing	1926		297670.6	
工商业发展	Industrial and Commercial Development	3185		754497.4	
非定向研究	Non-Directional Research	1590		666005.6	
其他民用目标	Other Cvilian Target	11741		3069743.1	
国防	National Defense	3023		557897.6	
按技术流向分类	**By Spread Area of Technology**				
流向本市	To Beijing	28830	28059	7172432.0	5817097.7
流向外省市	To Other Provinces and Municipalities	37212	33538	17219865.4	16158755.0
技术出口	Exports	1236	1146	6967687.9	6536101.6

资料来源：北京技术市场管理办公室。
Source: Beijing Technical Market Management Office.

19-16 科技成果及获奖情况(2001-2014年)
STATISTICS FOR SCIENTIFIC AND TECHNOLOGICAL ACHIEVEMENTS AND AWARDS (2001-2014)

单位：项 (unit)

年 份 Year	科技成果登记数 Registered Number of Scientific and Technological Achievements	#国家技术发明奖 National Awards of Technical Invention	#国家科学技术进步奖 National Awards of Scientific and Technological Advancement
2001-2005	**3063**	**25**	**233**
2001	326	1	38
2002	275	5	48
2003	468	5	52
2004	976	6	43
2005	1018	8	52
2006-2010	**5081**	**56**	**257**
2006	1002	12	64
2007	1010	9	44
2008	1016	13	42
2009	1023	11	54
2010	1030	11	53
2011	1035	5	56
2012	1040	22	53
2013	1043	19	38
2014	1042	15	49

资料来源：北京市科学技术委员会。
Source: Beijing Municipal Science & Technology Commission.

19-17 专利申请及授权情况
APPLICATIONS AND GRANTING OF PATENTS

单位：件 (unit)

项　　目	Item	申请量 Patent Applications		授权量 Patents Granted	
		2014	2013	2014	2013
合　　计	**Total**	**138111**	**123336**	**74661**	**62671**
按种类分	**By Type**				
发　　明	Inventions	78129	67554	23237	20695
实用新型	Utility Models	48228	47586	44071	36301
外观设计	Industrial Designs	11754	8196	7353	5675
按对象分	**By Applicant**				
工矿企业	Industrial and Mining Enterprises	94998	79698	52181	40538
大专院校	Universities & Colleges	13574	13028	6823	6731
科研单位	Scientific Research Institutes	12884	12287	7165	6423
机关团体	Government Organizations	1556	1308	777	658
个　　人	Individuals	15099	17015	7715	8321

资料来源：北京市知识产权局。
Source: Beijing Intellectual Property Office.

19-18 有效发明专利情况
STATISTICS FOR VALID INVENTION PATENTS

单位：件 (unit)

项　　目	Item	2014	2013
合　计	**Total**	**103638**	**85434**
按对象分	**By Applicant**		
工矿企业	Industrial and Mininig Enterprises	54574	42992
大专院校	Universities & Colleges	22069	19623
科研单位	Scientific Research Institutes	20090	16373
机关团体	Government Organizations	1086	847
个　　人	Individuals	5819	5599

资料来源：北京市知识产权局。
Source: Beijing Intellectual Property Office.

主要统计指标解释

科技活动人员　指报告年度调查单位直接从事科技活动、以及从事科技活动管理和为科技活动提供直接服务的人员。直接从事科技活动人员包括：在单位办的研究室、实验室、技术开发中心及中试车间（基地）等机构中从事科技活动的人员；虽不在上述机构工作，但编入科技活动项目（课题）组的人员等。从事科技活动管理和为科技活动提供直接服务的人员包括：与科技活动相关的行政管理人员，以及直接为科技活动提供资料文献、材料供应、设备维护等服务的人员。

研究与试验发展（R&D）　指在科学技术领域，为增加知识总量、以及运用这些知识去创造新的应用而进行的系统的创造性的活动，包括基础研究、应用研究、试验发展三类活动。

研究与试验发展（R&D）人员　指单位内部从事基础研究、应用研究和试验发展三类活动的人员。包括直接参加上述三类项目活动的人员以及这三类项目的管理人员和直接服务人员。为研发活动提供直接服务的人员包括直接为研发活动提供资料文献、材料供应、设备维护等服务的人员。

研究与试验发展（R&D）人员折合全时当量　是国际上通用的、用于比较科技人力投入的指标。指 R&D 全时人员（全年从事 R&D 活动累积工作时间占全部工作时间的 90% 及以上人员）工作量与非全时人员按实际工作时间折算的工作量之和。

研究与试验发展（R&D）内部支出　指调查单位在报告年度用于内部开展 R&D 活动（基础研究、应用研究和试验发展）的实际支出。包括用于 R&D 项目（课题）活动的直接支出，以及间接用于 R&D 活动的管理费、服务费、与 R&D 有关的基本建设支出以及外协加工费等，不包括生产性活动支出、归还贷款支出以及与外单位合作或委托外单位进行 R&D 活动而转拨给对方的经费支出。

专业技术人员　指从事专业技术工作的人员以及从事专业技术管理工作且已在 1983 年以前评定了专业技术职称或在 1984 年以后聘任了专业技术职务的人员。从事专业技术工作的人员具体指工程技术人员，农业技术人员，科学研究人员（含自然科学研究及实验技术人员），卫生技术人员，教学人员（含高等院校、中等专业学校、技工学校、中学、小学），民用航空飞行技术人员，船舶技术人员，经济专业人员，会计人员，统计人员，翻译人员，图书资料、档案、文博人员，新闻、出版人员，律师、公证人员，广播电视播音人员，工艺美术人员，体育人员，艺术人员及企业政治思想工作人员。从事专业技术管理工作的人员是指企业、事业单位领导；企业、事业单位下设的职能机构、企业的生产车间的辅助车间（或附属辅助生产单位）中从事生产、技术、经济管理和政治工作的人员；按照公务员管理或参照公务员管理的人员不统计为专业技术人员。

专利　是专利权的简称，是对发明人的发明创造经审查合格后，由专利局依据专利法授予发明人和设计人对该项发明创造享有的专有权。包括发明、实用新型和外观设计。

发明专利　指专利法及其实施细则所称的发明，指对产品、方法或者改进所提出的新的技术方案。

实用新型专利　指专利法及其实施细则所称的实用新型，指对产品的形状、构造或者其结合所提出的适于实用的新的技术方案。

外观设计专利　指专利法及其实施细则所称的外观设计，指对产品的形状、图案、色彩或者其结合所做出的富有美感并适于工业上应用的新设计。

Explanatory Notes on Main Statistical Indicators

Personnel Engaged in Science and Technology Activities refer to persons directly engaged in science and technology activities as well as persons engaged in science and technology management and persons offering direct services to science and technology activities in the surveyed entities in the reporting year. Persons directly engaged in science and technology activities include: persons engaged in science and technology activities in such institutions as research labs of entities, laboratories, technical development centers and middle-stage test workshops (bases); persons not working in the above-mentioned institutions but included in the science and technology activity project (task) team, etc. Persons engaged in science and technology management and persons offering direct services for science and technology activities include administrative staff related to science and technology activities, as well as persons directly providing information and literature, supply of materials, equipment maintenance and other services.

R&D refers to systematic and creative activities in the field of science and technology to increase the total knowledge, and apply such knowledge to create new applications, including three kinds of activities, i.e. basic research, applied research, and experimental development.

R&D Personnel refer to persons in the surveyed entities who are engaged in three kinds of activities, i.e. basic research, applied research and experimental development. They include those who participate in the above-mentioned three kinds of activities directly, research management personnel and persons directly serving these activities. Persons providing direct services include those who provide information and literature, supply of materials, equipment maintenance and other services.

Full-Time Equivalent of R&D Personnel is an indicator globally used to compare input of scientific talents. It refers to the sum of workload of full-time R&D personnel (the personnel whose accumulative annual working time involved in R&D activities takes 90% and above of the whole working time) plus the workload of non-full time personnel that is equivalent of the actual working time.

Internal R&D Expenditure means the actual disbursement of investigated entities on internal R&D activities (basic research, applied research, and experimental development) in the reporting year, including direct spending on R&D project (task) activities, and management expenses and service fees indirectly spent on R&D activities, R&D related basic construction expense and external assisting processing charges, etc., excluding production-based activity expense, loan repayment expense and fund transferred to external institution cooperated or entrusted to conduct R&D activities.

Professional Technical Personnel refer to persons engaged in professional technological work and professional technological management whose professional technological titles were assessed and granted before 1983 or who have been retained at professional technological positions after 1984. Persons engaged in professional technological work refer to engineering technicians, agricultural technicians, research personnel (including natural science research and experiment technicians), medical technicians, teaching staff (including those in colleges and universities, technical secondary schools, vocational schools, high schools, and elementary schools), civil aviation flight technicians, watercraft technicians, economics professionals, accountants, statisticians, translators and interpreters, librarians, archivists, cultural expo personnel, journalists, publishers , lawyers, notaries, TV and radio broadcasters, industrial arts staff, sportspersons, artists, as well as personnel responsible for political ideology work in enterprises.. The professional technological management refer to leaders of enterprises and public institutions; persons engaged in management of production, technology and economy as well as political work in functional organs under enterprises and public institutions, auxiliary workplaces (or affiliated auxiliary production entities) of production workplaces of enterprises; persons managed as civil servants or with reference to civil servants are not counted as professional technicians.

Patent is the abbreviation of patent right, referring to the exclusive right granted by patent authorities upon examination and approval of inventions and creations to the inventors and designers with regard to the invention, including inventions, utility models and industrial designs.

Invention means the invention mentioned in the Patent Law and its detailed rules for implementation, i.e. the new technological solutions presented for the product, methodology, or improvement.

Utility Model means the utility model mentioned in the Patent Law and its detailed rules for implementation, i.e. the new practical technological solutions presented for the product shape, structure, color or combination.

Industrial Design means the industrial design mentioned in the Patent Law and its detailed rules for implementation, i.e. new designs of product shape, pattern, color or combination which are aesthetic and suitable for industrial applications.

20

卫生、体育
HEALTH CARE AND SPORTS

简要说明

一、本章资料的主要内容

本章主要反映卫生、体育的发展情况。

卫生部分主要内容包括卫生总费用、卫生机构、卫生技术人员、床位数，医院诊疗人次及入院人数，主要疾病死亡原因及构成，全市主要健康指标等情况。体育部分主要包括群众体育活动情况、体育场地情况、运动员获奖情况、体育彩票情况等。

二、本章资料的数据来源

卫生部分的资料由北京市卫生和计划生育委员会提供，体育部分的资料由北京市体育局提供。

Brief Introduction

I. Main Content

This chapter mainly reflects the development of health and sports.

Health statistics include the total health expenditures, the number of health institutions, health technicians, ward beds, patients treated and hospitalized persons, major causes of death and composition, main health indicators of Beijing, and so on. Sports statistics include public sports and sports venues, awards received by athletes, and sports lottery tickets, etc.

II. Source of Data

Health data are from Beijing Municipal Commission of Health and Family Planning. Sports data are from Beijing Municipal Bureau of Sports.

20-1 卫生事业基本情况(1978-2014年)
BASIC STATISTICS ON HEALTH CARE (1978-2014)

年 份 Year	卫生机构 (个) Healthcare Institutions (unit)	#医院(卫生院) Hospitals (Health Centers)	#医 院 Hospitals	#疾病预防控制中心(防疫站) Centers for Disease Control and Prevention	#妇幼保健院(所、站) Maternity and Child Care Centers (Stations)	#社区卫生服务中心(站) Community Health Services Centers (Stations)
1978	3263	389		22	15	
1979	3614	387		22	17	
1980	3818	393		22	19	
1981	4135	403		22	19	
1982	4389	413		22	18	
1983	4312	412		22	19	
1984	4173	423		22	18	
1985	4248	376		22	18	
1986	4483	371		22	20	
1987	4744	398		22	19	
1988	4342	445		22	17	
1989	4398	470		22	17	
1990	4953	512		22	17	
1991	4970	525	337	22	17	
1992	4868	535	345	22	16	
1993	4962	548	364	32	16	
1994	4958	629	387	33	16	
1995	4955	629	387	33	15	
1996	6470	645	405	33	13	
1997	6577	673	435	33	13	
1998	5723	676	449	32	11	
1999	5990	686	460	32	8	
2000	6176	674	458	30	8	
2001	5969	673	458	30	9	
2002	4998	647	461	24	19	35
2003	5075	646	459	29	19	36
2004	4835	657	503	29	19	43
2005	4818	692	519	28	18	93
2006	4878	705	541	28	18	90
2007	6189	686	535	31	18	1126
2008	6523	660	537	31	19	1282
2009	6603	638	522	31	19	1395
2010	6539		550	31	19	1587
2011	9699		569	32	19	1744
2012	9974		608	32	19	1897
2013	10141		647	32	19	1926
2014	10265		672	32	19	1958

注：1. 2010年及以前，本表中所有数据都不包含村卫生室及驻京部队医院情况。2011年开始，包含村卫生室情况。2012年开始，除床位数外均包含驻京部队医院数据（下表同）。

2. 2010年开始，原卫生院数据并入到社区卫生服务中心(站)等其他卫生机构。

资料来源：北京市卫生和计划生育委员会。

Note: a) In and before 2010, figures in this table did not include village health clinics and hospitals of troops stationed in Beijing. From 2011, figures included village health clinics. From 2012,figures in this table include troops stationed in Beijing with the bed number excluded. stationed in Beijing (the same to the follow tables).

b) From 2010, data on health centers were incorporated into other health institutions such as community health service centers (stations).

Source: Beijing Municipal Commission of Health and Family Planning.

20-1 续表 Continued

年 份 Year	卫生机构人员(人) Employed Persons in Healthcare Institutions (person)	#卫生技术人员 Medical Technical Personnel	#执业(助理)医师 Certified (Assistant) Physicians	#注册护士 Registered Nurses	实有床位数(张) Beds (unit)	#医院(卫生院) Hospitals (Health Centers)	#医院 Hospitals	每千户籍人口执业(助理)医师数(人) Certified Physicians Per 1000 Persons (person)	每千户籍人口注册护士数(人) Registered Nurses Per 1000 Persons (person)	每千户籍人口医院床位数(张) Beds Per 1000 Persons (unit)
1978	90174	65943	28435	16085	29767	26432		3.35	1.89	3.11
1979	97942	72131	31842	17398	30231	26808		3.66	1.87	3.08
1980	102601	74753	34365	17492	32453	28495		3.88	1.97	3.22
1981	110774	81183	37886	20025	33666	29783		4.20	2.20	3.30
1982	114420	83843	39385	20389	34574	30940		4.30	2.23	3.40
1983	119222	86593	41216	21181	35987	32242		4.40	2.26	3.50
1984	124664	89362	42112	22286	38580	34602		4.40	2.33	3.70
1985	127771	90831	42216	23782	41603	38180		4.44	2.48	3.99
1986	132865	94433	43403	25383	43956	40903		4.47	3.72	4.21
1987	142556	101829	46007	27786	47538	44407		4.66	2.81	4.49
1988	145362	105237	48216	30250	53078	48711		4.82	3.02	4.87
1989	150062	108108	49361	32056	55623	51877		4.83	3.14	5.08
1990	156304	111614	50934	34565	59036	55474		4.93	3.35	5.37
1991	161103	114342	52309	35714	61744	58744	54888	5.03	3.44	5.65
1992	164213	115825	53254	36768	63230	59833	55858	5.10	3.52	5.73
1993	165170	116173	53906	36687	65621	62340	58605	5.13	3.49	5.93
1994	164867	116818	53865	36608	67112	64416	60661	5.07	3.45	6.07
1995	164436	115967	54114	36719	66925	64211	60337	5.06	3.43	6.00
1996	164981	116849	54091	37712	66760	64902	60997	5.02	3.50	6.02
1997	167090	119256	54909	38630	67946	65826	61865	5.06	3.56	6.06
1998	162609	115976	51902	38883	69095	66954	63144	4.76	3.56	6.13
1999	161823	116597	52646	39625	69465	67684	63660	4.79	3.60	6.15
2000	160258	115510	51570	39900	71245	69183	65138	4.66	3.60	6.25
2001	158185	115935	52100	40537	73053	70837	66537	4.64	3.61	6.31
2002	144021	109564	47236	38879	75188	71967	67750	4.18	3.44	6.46
2003	148406	112212	47887	39912	74298	71173	66990	4.21	3.51	5.89
2004	153154	116610	48988	41547	77359	73811	69850	4.25	3.60	6.54
2005	157133	119874	50617	42897	79067	76031	72329	4.32	3.66	6.65
2006	166278	126904	52795	45647	81440	78588	74762	4.41	3.84	6.77
2007	182475	139275	54989	50890	83736	80158	76915	4.53	4.19	6.34
2008	193799	149916	58773	55349	86196	81937	79089	4.78	4.50	6.43
2009	208156	160435	62348	61604	90100	84896	82471	5.00	4.94	6.62
2010	219762	171093	65954	67308	92871		85935	5.24	5.35	6.83
2011	235708	181938	69749	72812	94735		87596	5.46	5.70	6.85
2012	276654	219714	82192	95202	100167		92610	6.33	7.34	7.14
2013	294012	229720	85819	100652	104034		96558	6.52	7.65	8.76
2014	304990	242923	89590	106167	109789		102851	6.72	7.96	7.71

注：表中每千户籍人口执业(助理)医师数、每千户籍人口注册护士数、每千户籍人口医院床位数均按年末户籍人口计算。2014年上述指标按年末常住人口计算分别为4.16人、4.93人和4.78张。

Note:The data of "Certified Physicians per 1000 Persons", "Registered Nurses per 1000 Persons", "Beds per 1000 Persons" were calculated by year-end registered population. These indicators for 2014 calculated by year-end permanent population were 4.16 persons, 4.93 persons and 4.78 units.

20-2 卫生总费用(2000-2013年)
TOTAL HEALTH EXPENDITURES (2000-2013)

年份 Year	卫生总费用(亿元) Total Health Expenditures (100 million yuan)	政府卫生支出 Health Expenditures by Governments		社会卫生支出 Social Health Expenditures		个人现金卫生支出 Health Expenditures in Cash by Individuals		相当于地区生产总值比例(%) Total Health Expenditure as % of GDP Total (%)
		绝对数(亿元) Absolute Number (100 million yuan)	占卫生总费用比重(%) As % of Total (%)	绝对数(亿元) Absolute Number (100 million yuan)	占卫生总费用比重(%) As % of Total (%)	绝对数(亿元) Absolute Number (100 million yuan)	占卫生总费用比重(%) As % of Total (%)	
2000	166.72	34.70	20.81	61.78	37.05	70.25	42.13	5.27
2001	201.12	45.28	22.52	73.18	36.39	82.65	41.10	5.42
2002	262.36	48.51	18.49	99.61	37.97	114.23	43.54	6.08
2003	314.16	65.80	20.94	132.04	42.03	116.33	37.03	6.27
2004	357.19	69.35	19.41	150.72	42.20	137.12	38.39	5.92
2005	432.80	85.73	19.81	187.84	43.40	159.22	36.79	6.21
2006	497.41	115.89	23.30	208.00	41.82	173.52	34.88	6.13
2007	523.20	142.03	27.15	212.00	40.52	169.17	32.33	5.31
2008	668.52	180.01	26.93	271.26	40.58	217.25	32.50	6.01
2009	689.60	201.14	29.17	296.25	42.96	192.21	27.87	5.67
2010	814.74	226.84	27.84	385.10	47.27	202.80	24.89	5.77
2011	977.26	275.48	28.19	453.16	46.37	248.62	25.44	6.01
2012	1190.01	320.40	26.92	600.96	50.50	268.65	22.58	6.66
2013	1349.62	356.42	26.41	717.75	53.18	275.45	20.41	6.38

资料来源：北京市卫生和计划生育委员会。
Source: Beijing Municipal Commission of Health and Family Planning.

20-3 卫生机构基本情况
BASIC STATISTICS FOR HEALTH CARE INSTITUTIONS

项　　目	Item	2014	2013	构成(%) Composition (%) 2014	构成(%) Composition (%) 2013
卫生机构　（个）	**Health Care Institutions (unit)**	**10265**	**10141**	**100.0**	**100.0**
#医　院	Hospitals	672	647	6.5	6.4
社区卫生服务中心(站)	Health Service Centers (Stations) for Community	1958	1926	19.1	19.0
门诊部	Outpatient Departments	1016	946	9.9	9.3
妇幼保健院(所、站)	Maternity and Child Care Hospitals	19	19	0.2	0.2
疾病预防控制中心(防疫站)	Disease Prevention and Control Center (Epidemic Prevention Station)	32	32	0.3	0.3
专科疾病防治院(所、站)	Specific Disease Prevention and Cure Centers	27	28	0.3	0.3
诊所、卫生所、医务室、护理站	Clinics, Health Centers, Infirmaries, Nursing Stations	3529	3471	34.3	34.2
床　位　（张）	**Beds (unit)**	**109789**	**104034**	**100.0**	**100.0**
#医　院	Hospitals	102851	96558	93.7	92.8
社区卫生服务中心(站)	Health Service Centers (Stations) for Community	4515	4548	4.1	4.4
妇幼保健院(所、站)	Maternity and Child Care Hospitals	1939	1912	1.8	1.8
专科疾病防治院(所、站)	Specific Disease Prevention and Cure Centers	484	539	0.4	0.5
卫生技术人员　（人）	**Medical Technical Personnel (person)**	**242923**	**229720**	**100.0**	**100.0**
#医　院	Hospitals	182567	170571	75.2	74.3
社区卫生服务中心(站)	Health Service Centers (Stations) for Community	25561	25122	10.5	10.9
妇幼保健院(所、站)	Maternity and Child Care Hospitals	5000	4662	2.1	2.0
专科疾病防治院(所、站)	Specific Disease Prevention and Cure Centers	588	622	0.2	0.3
#执业(助理)医师	Certified Doctors	89590	85819	36.9	37.4
注册护士	Registered Nurses	106167	100652	43.7	43.8

注：本表数据除床位数外均包含驻京部队医院数据。
资料来源：北京市卫生和计划生育委员会。
Note: Figures in this table include troops stationed in Beijing with the bed number excluded.
Source: Beijing Municipal Commission of Health and Family Planning.

20-4 全市医院基本情况(2014年)
BASIC STATISTICS ON HOSPITALS (2014)

项目	Item	医院数(个) Hospitals (unit)	床位数(张) Beds (unit)	职工人数(人) Employed Persons (person)	#卫生技术人员 Medical Technical Personnel	#执业医师 Certified Doctors	#中医 Doctors of Traditional Chinese Medicine
合计	**Total**	**672**	**102851**	**225630**	**182567**	**60940**	**8896**
按隶属关系分	**By Affiliation**						
#市级	Municipal	30	22569	43961	35651	11502	764
区县	Districts and Counties	99	30245	54477	43902	15260	2802
按专业分	**By Specialty**						
#综合医院	General Hospitals	328	62500	155952	129659	43102	2299
中医医院	Hospital Specialized in Traditional Chinese Medicine	154	13150	24984	19696	7792	5370
中西医结合医院	Hospitals Combining Western Medicine with Traditional Chinese Medicine	21	5453	6595	5393	1997	740
民族医院	Nationality Hospitals	3	177	463	270	95	44
口腔医院	Stomatology Hospitals	18	369	4074	3251	1246	5
眼科医院	Ophthalmology Hospitals	10	456	707	435	149	6
肿瘤医院	Tumor Hospitals	9	3237	5230	3821	1100	49
心血管病医院	Hospitals for Cardiovascular Diseases	2	1058	3113	2608	651	4
胸科医院	Thorax Hospitals	1	533	809	609	138	1
妇(产)科医院	Hospitals for Gynecology and Obstetrics	13	900	3165	2217	657	26
儿童医院	Children's Hospitals	8	1770	4224	3335	965	50
精神病医院	Psychiatric Hospital	21	7584	5732	4155	913	47
传染病医院	Infectious Disease Hospitals	3	1338	2916	2278	716	34
骨科医院	Hospitals of Orthopedics	9	792	1122	797	225	51
整形外科医院	Orthopaedics Hospitals	1	328	737	520	164	
其他专科医院	Other Specialized Hospitals	65	3106	5749	3485	1018	168
护理院	Nursing Hospitals	6	100	58	38	12	2

注：本表数据除床位数外均包括驻京部队数据。
资料来源：北京市卫生和计划生育委员会。
Note: Figures in this table include troops stationed in Beijing with the bed number excluded.
Source: Beijing Municipal Commission of Health and Family Planning.

20-4 续表 Continued

单位：人 (person)

项　目	Item	#执业助理医师 Certified Assistant Doctors	#中医 Doctors of Traditional Chinese Medicine	#注册护士 Registered Nurses	#药师(士) Pharmacists (Assistant Pharmacists)	#技师(士) Technicians (Assistant Technicians)	#检验师(士) Laboratorians (Assistant Laboratorians)
合　计	**Total**	**1407**	**309**	**88636**	**8341**	**7896**	**5011**
按隶属关系分	**By Affiliation**						
#市　级	Municipal	42	2	17254	1736	1929	1133
区　县	Districts and Counties	607	92	20022	2579	2093	1475
按专业分	**By Specialty**						
#综合医院	General Hospitals	806	114	65064	4959	5292	3318
中医医院	Hospital Specialized in Traditional Chinese Medicine	261	129	7402	1943	974	633
中西医结合医院	Hospitals Combining Western Medicine with Traditional Chinese Medicine	94	33	2319	318	234	167
民族医院	Nationality Hospitals	10	3	108	15	17	10
口腔医院	Stomatology Hospitals	24		1404	36	82	24
眼科医院	Ophthalmology Hospitals	10	3	210	19	25	16
肿瘤医院	Tumor Hospitals	8	1	1930	151	232	102
心血管病医院	Hospitals for Cardiovascular Diseases	1		1464	61	67	47
胸科医院	Thorax Hospitals			365	31	53	24
妇(产)科医院	Hospitals for Gynecology and Obstetrics	8	1	1043	80	157	97
儿童医院	Children's Hospitals	7	2	1413	193	234	168
精神病医院	Psychiatric Hospitals	79	6	2351	203	137	114
传染病医院	Infectious Disease Hospitals	3		1183	105	150	127
骨科医院	Hospitals of Orthopedics	17	3	367	36	40	24
整形外科医院	Orthopaedics Hospitals			255	9	15	8
其他专科医院	Other Specialized Hospitals	76	12	1743	179	183	130
护理院	Nursing Hospitals	3	2	15	3	4	2

资料来源：北京市卫生和计划生育委员会。
Source: Beijing Municipal Commission of Health and Family Planning.

20-5 医院工作情况(2014年)
WORKS OF HOSPITALS (2014)

项目	Item	诊疗人次数(千人次) Patients Treated (1000 person times)	#门诊 Out-patients	健康检查人数(千人次) Health Check (1000 person times)	平均开放病床数(张) Beds in Use (unit)	入院人数(千人次) In-patients (1000 person times)	出院人数(千人次) Discharged Patients (1000 person times)
合计	**Total**	**157509.2**	**132351.5**	**3223.4**	**96941.9**	**2562.3**	**3084.8**
#综合医院	General Hospitals	106365.2	83323.9	2572.4	58236.5	1764.1	2289.2
中医医院	Hospital Specialized in Traditional Chinese Medicine	29461.4	28486.0	282.5	12349.7	244.4	244.1
中西医结合医院	Hospitals Combining Western Medicine with Traditional Chinese Medicine	5041.7	4687.3	174.2	5435.3	65.2	65.0
民族医院	Nationality Hospitals	164.8	164.8	3.4	119.9	1.5	1.5
口腔医院	Stomatology Hospitals	2376.5	2286.6	12.8	350.5	9.0	9.1
眼科医院	Ophthalmology Hospitals	231.1	230.5	30.8	453.0	10.8	10.6
肿瘤医院	Tumor Hospitals	1307.3	1293.1	89.4	3167.3	104.6	104.5
心血管病医院	Hospitals for Cardiovascular Diseases	648.0	620.6	2.2	1028.9	53.5	53.6
胸科医院	Thorax Hospitals	237.1	232.5		533.0	11.5	11.5
妇(产)科医院	Hospitals for Gynecology and Obstetrics	1631.7	1590.6	7.6	886.4	52.0	52.0
儿童医院	Children's Hospitals	6108.1	5644.8	15.6	1638.8	105.5	104.0
精神病医院	Psychiatric Hospitals	1193.1	1180.4	5.9	7460.8	18.8	18.5
传染病医院	Infectious Disease Hospitals	1170.4	1091.4		1330.0	46.2	46.3
骨科医院	Hospitals of Orthopedics	297.9	287.8	16.6	784.3	15.7	15.5
整形外科医院	Orthopaedics Hospitals	126.5	122.9	0.2	328.0	12.8	12.8
其他专科医院	Other Specialized Hospitals	1147.2	1107.0	9.7	2781.2	46.7	46.7
护理院	Nursing Centers	1.3	1.3		58.4	…	…

资料来源：北京市卫生和计划生育委员会。
Source: Beijing Municipal Commission of Health and Family Planning.

20-5 续表 Continued

项　目	Item	病死率 (%) Case Fatality Rate (%)	病床周转次数 (次) Turnover Beds (time)	病床使用率 (%) Utilization Rate of Beds (%)	出院者平均住院日 (日) Average Hospitalization Period (day)
合　计	**Total**	**1.16**	**26.4**	**80.0**	**10.3**
#综合医院	General Hospitals	1.24	30.2	83.8	9.9
中医医院	Hospital Specialized in Traditional Chinese Medicine	1.46	19.8	73.1	13.2
中西医结合医院	Hospitals Combining Western Medicine with Traditional Chinese Medicine	2.26	12.0	75.3	20.3
民族医院	Nationality Hospitals	1.39	12.6	65.6	19.0
口腔医院	Stomatology Hospitals	0.04	25.8	57.8	8.2
眼科医院	Ophthalmology Hospitals	0.01	23.3	61.2	8.0
肿瘤医院	Tumor Hospitals	0.39	33.0	83.3	9.4
心血管病医院	Hospitals for Cardiovascular Diseases	0.25	52.1	104.3	7.3
胸科医院	Thorax Hospitals	1.23	21.7	100.4	17.0
妇(产)科医院	Hospitals for Gynecology and Obstetrics	…	58.6	75.8	4.6
儿童医院	Children's Hospitals	0.14	63.5	112.3	6.0
精神病医院	Psychiatric Hospital	0.86	2.5	97.5	125.4
传染病医院	Infectious Disease Hospitals	1.93	34.8	110.0	11.6
骨科医院	Hospitals of Orthopedics	0.29	19.7	79.6	14.9
整形外科医院	Orthopaedics Hospitals		39.2	63.3	5.9
其他专科医院	Other Specialized Hospitals	1.43	16.8	58.8	10.9
护理院	Nursing Centers			2.1	455.0

20-6 全市居民前十位死因顺位、死亡率及构成(2014年)
DEATH RATE AND COMPOSITION OF 10 MAJOR DISEASES (2014)

顺 位 No.	死因名称	Cause of Death	死亡率(1/10万) Death Rate (1/100 thousands)	构 成(%) Composition (%)
	全 市	**Total**		
1	恶性肿瘤	Malignant Tumour	168.90	27.08
2	心脏病	Heart Disease	158.28	25.37
3	脑血管病	Cerebrovasular Disease	128.99	20.68
4	呼吸系统疾病	Disease of the Respiratory System	63.03	10.10
5	损伤和中毒	Trauma and Toxicosis	23.04	3.69
6	内分泌、营养、代谢及免疫疾病	Endocrine, Nutrition, Metabolite and Immunity Disease	18.02	2.89
7	消化系统疾病	Disease of the Gigestive System	15.70	2.52
8	神经系统疾病	Neurological Disease	7.37	1.18
9	泌尿生殖系统疾病	Disease of the Genitourinary System	5.36	0.86
10	传染病	Infectious Disease	4.36	0.70
	男 性	**Male**		
1	恶性肿瘤	Malignant Tumour	200.27	28.78
2	心脏病	Heart Disease	166.58	23.94
3	脑血管病	Cerebrovasular Disease	144.12	20.71
4	呼吸系统疾病	Disease of the Respiratory System	70.92	10.19
5	损伤和中毒	Trauma and Toxicosis	28.12	4.04
6	消化系统疾病	Disease of the Gigestive System	17.94	2.58
7	内分泌、营养、代谢及免疫疾病	Endocrine, Nutrition, Metabolite and Immunity Disease	16.87	2.43
8	神经系统疾病	Neurological Disease	8.05	1.16
9	传染病	Infectious Disease	6.32	0.91
10	泌尿生殖系统疾病	Disease of the Genitourinary System	5.49	0.79
	女 性	**Female**		
1	心脏病	Heart Disease	149.93	27.19
2	恶性肿瘤	Malignant Tumour	137.35	24.91
3	脑血管病	Cerebrovasular Disease	113.78	20.64
4	呼吸系统疾病	Disease of the Respiratory System	55.08	9.99
5	内分泌、营养、代谢及免疫疾病	Endocrine, Nutrition, Metabolite and Immunity Disease	19.18	3.48
6	损伤和中毒	Trauma and Toxicosis	17.93	3.25
7	消化系统疾病	Disease of the Gigestive System	13.44	2.44
8	神经系统疾病	Neurological Disease	6.68	1.21
9	泌尿生殖系统疾病	Disease of the Genitourinary System	5.22	0.95
10	肌肉骨骼和结缔组织病	Diseases of musculoskeletal and connective tissue	3.07	0.56

资料来源：北京市卫生和计划生育委员会。
Source: Beijing Municipal Commission of Health and Family Planning.

20-7 全市主要健康指标情况(1978-2014年)
MAJOR HEALTH INDICATIONS OF BEIJING (1978-2014)

年 份 Year	婴 儿 死亡率 (‰) Infant Mortality (‰)	城 郊 Suburban Districts	远 县 Counties	新生儿 死亡率 (‰) Newborn Baby Mortality (‰)	城 郊 Suburban Districts	远 县 Counties	孕产妇 死亡率 (1/10万) Pregnant & Lying-in Women Mortality (1/100000)	城 郊 Suburban Districts	远 县 Counties	甲乙类传染病发病率 (1/10万) Incidence Rate of Catogory A and B Epidemics (1/100000)
1978	17.11	10.34	21.15	12.21	7.35	15.60	31.00	5.00	53.00	
1979	16.97	12.81	19.43	10.08	8.00	12.77	34.70	13.10	41.30	1584.25
1980	14.79	10.40	17.73	10.24	7.12	12.81	26.30	12.50	34.60	2165.23
1981	13.84	9.69	17.26	9.22	6.00	11.85	48.50	18.70	76.10	2225.71
1982	12.97	9.95	15.19	8.02	6.20	9.76	24.50	21.70	32.60	2193.16
1983	13.79	10.54	17.24	8.78	6.22	11.84	28.10	24.30	45.10	1904.55
1984	10.98	10.33	12.49	7.78	6.72	9.20	16.80	11.40	41.50	1666.68
1985	13.94	10.02	18.85	10.41	6.40	15.97	22.90	24.30	35.10	1335.23
1986	16.05	13.42	19.24	12.13	8.97	15.41	30.50	22.90	43.10	1120.19
1987	15.56	12.63	18.23	11.08	8.01	14.02	26.60	14.80	33.30	826.51
1988	14.98	11.71	17.92	10.48	7.96	13.20	24.80	25.40	32.40	640.98
1989	14.96	11.59	18.30	10.53	8.08	13.23	34.50	3.90	55.80	547.61
1990	11.66	10.12	12.55	8.49	7.43	9.38	25.00	13.00	30.50	509.55
1991	12.46	11.94	13.11	8.56	7.83	9.47	24.00	23.80	24.20	448.23
1992	12.12	10.81	14.43	8.93	7.72	11.18	30.10	30.20	29.80	385.98
1993	10.38	10.68	9.93	7.21	7.28	7.10	16.50	21.10	9.60	356.66
1994	10.93	12.09	9.43	7.29	7.57	6.94	18.94	21.02	16.26	374.31
1995	11.45	14.23	8.20	7.52	8.91	5.90	22.27	23.89	20.36	309.99
1996	10.05	11.57	8.13	6.97	7.61	6.17	15.32	11.45	20.19	340.24
1997	9.45	10.49	8.05	6.36	6.75	5.83	23.69	25.25	21.60	294.41
1998	7.58	9.07	5.75	5.53	6.46	4.39	10.46	10.87	9.97	306.37
1999	7.95	7.78	8.38	5.94	5.74	6.45	17.53	15.69	22.06	308.10
2000	5.36	6.29	4.05	3.70	4.26	2.91	9.70	7.10	13.38	301.19
2001	6.01	6.26	5.62	4.05	4.16	3.89	11.71	13.85	8.45	276.85
2002	5.56	5.57	5.54	3.70	3.65	3.77	15.12	16.24	13.29	282.95
2003	5.89	5.91	5.83	3.83	3.56	4.33	15.60	6.92	31.35	228.00
2004	4.61	4.51	4.79	3.49	3.42	3.62	15.19	17.69	10.66	408.03
2005	4.35	4.08	4.84	3.29	3.03	3.79	15.91	7.33	31.95	445.91
2006	4.66	3.96	6.04	3.42	2.99	4.26	7.87	7.12	9.36	448.70
2007	3.89	3.50	4.72	2.65	2.31	3.39	16.74	18.92	12.10	421.02
2008	3.70	3.49	4.21	2.45	2.41	2.52	18.52	15.86	24.76	312.99
2009	3.49	3.28	4.02	2.47	2.37	2.73	14.55	12.56	19.49	339.89
2010	3.29	2.95	4.25	2.06	1.94	2.42	12.14	8.95	21.23	268.99
2011	2.84	2.62	3.43	1.88	1.77	2.17	9.09	9.99	6.67	226.76
2012	2.87	2.48	3.87	1.91	1.65	2.60	6.05	4.20	10.82	174.45
2013	2.33	2.19	2.69	1.52	1.48	1.63	9.45	6.51	17.20	155.87
2014	2.33	2.23	2.57	1.50	1.46	1.58	7.19	5.53	11.27	165.49

注：城郊包括东城区、西城区、朝阳区、丰台区、石景山区、海淀区、门头沟区、房山区；远县包括通州区、昌平区、顺义区、大兴区、怀柔区、平谷区、密云县、延庆县。

资料来源：北京市卫生和计划生育委员会。

Note: Suburban districts include Dongcheng, Xicheng, Chaoyang, Fengtai, Shijingshan, Haidian, Mentougou, and Fangshan Districts. Counties include Tongzhou, Changping, Shunyi, and Daxing Districts, Huairou, Pinggu, Miyun and Yanqing Counties.

Source: Beijing Municipal Commission of Health and Family Planning.

20-8 主要年份体育场地情况
SITUATION OF THE GYMNASIUMS AND STADIUMS IN MAIN YEARS

单位：个 (unit)

年份 Year	合计 Total	#体育场 Stadiums	#体育馆 Gymnasiums	#游泳场馆 Natatoriums	#室内 Indoor	#各种训练房 Exercise Rooms
1950	19	1				2
1955	61	1		2	2	10
1960	124	2		4	3	19
1970	188	2	2	8	3	24
1975	234	3	2	11	4	28
1980	293	3	2	12	4	32
1985	405	4	2	20	8	54
1990	780	12	12	49	26	153
1995	1381	18	18	88	56	291
2000	2815	35	24	214	161	863
2001	3500	42	27	283	216	1101
2002	4176	57	33	334	263	1358
2003	6100	93	36	443	371	1729
2004	6104	93	36	443	371	1729
2005	6112	93	36	446	374	1731
2006	6122	93	36	446	374	1734
2007	6146	94	37	446	374	1736
2008	6149	94	37	446	374	1739
2009	6149	94	37	446	374	1739
2010	6151	94	37	446	374	1741
2011	6151	94	37	446	374	1741
2012	6156	94	37	447	375	1742
2013	20075	131	70	590	548	2836

注：本表2013年数据口径为第六次全国体育场地普查数据资料，此次普查时点为2013年12月31日。
资料来源：北京市体育局。

Note: The data in the table of 2013 is collected according to the sixth national census on gymnasiums and stadiums. The date of this census is December 31st, 2013.

Source: Beijing Municipal Bureau of Sports.

20-9 群众体育活动情况
ACTIVITIES OF MASS SPORTS

项目	Item	2014	2013
晨晚练辅导站 （个）	Instruction Stations of Morning and Evening Exercises (unit)	7981	6360
青少年体育俱乐部数 （个）	Number of Teenager Sport Clubs (unit)	211	203
社会体育指导员 （人）	Social Sport Instructors (person)	45522	38915
社区健身俱乐部 （个）	Community Fitness Clubs (unit)	144	129
体育生活化社区 （个）	Life-oriented Sports Communities (unit)	2113	1453

资料来源：北京市体育局。
Source: Beijing Municipal Bureau of Sports.

20-10 运动员、裁判员情况
ATHLETES AND REFEREES

单位：人 (person)

项目	Item	2014	#女性 Females	2013	#女性 Females
分等级运动员发展人数	**Number of Graded Athletes**	**1826**	**793**	**1676**	**612**
国际级运动健将	World-class Athletes	12	3	5	2
国家级运动健将	National Grade Athletes	93	38	69	26
一级	First Grade Athletes	528	274	325	129
二级	Second Grade Athletes	1193	478	1277	455
分等级裁判员发展人数	**Number of Graded Referees**	**1468**	**437**	**1122**	**335**
国家级	National Grade Referees	36	9		
一级	First Grade Referees	282	112	289	99
二级	Second Grade Referees	1150	316	833	236

资料来源：北京市体育局。
Source: Beijing Municipal Bureau of Sports.

20-11 运动员获奖牌情况(2014年)
STATISTICS FOR MEDALS WON (2014)

单位：块 (piece)

项目	Item	金牌 Gold	银牌 Silver	铜牌 Copper
合计	**Total**	**69**	**47**	**62**
国际比赛	International Competitions	26	10	9
国内比赛	Domestic Competitions	43	37	53

资料来源：北京市体育局。
Source: Beijing Municipal Bureau of Sports.

20-12 体育彩票
SPORTS LOTTERY

项目	Item	2014	2013
电脑体育彩票销售个数（个）	Number of Computer Sports Lottery Tickets Sold (unit)	2420	2607
体育彩票发行额（万元）	Circulation of Sports Lottery (10000 yuan)	624258	538876
体育彩票公益金提取额（万元）	Public Welfare Funds Drawn from Sports Lottery (10000 yuan)	153617	131328

资料来源：北京市体育局。
Source: Beijing Municipal Bureau of Sports.

主要统计指标解释

卫 生

卫生机构 指从卫生行政部门取得《医疗机构执业许可证》，或从民政、工商行政、机构编制管理部门取得法人单位登记证书，为社会提供医疗保健、疾病控制、卫生监督服务或从事医学科研和医学在职培训等工作的单位。

卫生技术人员 指由卫生机构支付工资的全部固定职工和合同制职工中现任职务为卫生技术工作的专业人员，不包括从事管理工作的人员。

执业医师和注册护士 指领取医师执业证书和注册护士证书的人员，不包括从事管理工作的医师和护士。

死亡率（死因死亡率） 是指某种原因（如疾病）所致的死亡人数占户籍人口比重。

婴儿死亡率 指某地区一年内每 1000 名活产婴儿与未满 1 岁的婴儿死亡人数之比。婴儿死亡率可以衡量一个国家或地区经济文化、居民健康状况和卫生保健事业发展情况，同时也是人口平均期望寿命研究的重要内容。

5岁以下儿童死亡率 指某地区一年内每1000名活产婴儿与未满 5 岁儿童死亡人数之比。5 岁以下儿童死亡率是目前国际上公认的反映儿童生存状况的重要指标。

孕产妇死亡率 指某年某地每十万活产中的孕产妇死亡比例。同婴儿死亡率一样，孕产妇死亡率是评价某一地区社会发展状况的重要指标，它的高低与社会经济状况、孕产妇社会环境及卫生保健服务有直接的联系。

体 育

体育场地 指专门用于体育训练、比赛和健身活动的，有一定投资的公益性或经营性体育建筑设施，包括必要的附属功能用房。

晨晚练辅导站 是指本市公民自愿参加，在本市体育场馆、公园、街道、街心花园等公共场所设立的，利用早晚时间，以开展健身活动为目的的群众体育健身场所。

青少年体育俱乐部数 指创建单位利用自己所拥有的体育场馆、人才等资源建立起来的具有社会公益性的新型社会化青少年体育组织。

社会体育指导员 指在竞技体育、学校体育、部队体育以外的群众性体育活动中从事技能传授、锻炼指导和组织管理的工作人员。

专项球类活动场地 为满足不同人群特别是青少年的健身需求，而建设的专项球类活动场地，分篮球广场、笼式多功能球场、乒乓球长廊三种类型。

社区健身俱乐部 指“城市社区居民根据共同的目的和兴趣自愿组成的，以辖区内特定的体育场地设施为依托，经常开展体育活动，且隶属于街道办事处或社区居委会的公益性群众体育组织。”

等级运动员人数 指经考核正式批准授予等级运动员称号的人数。运动员等级分为国际级运动健将、国家级运动健将、一级运动员、二级运动员、三级运动员、少年级运动员。

等级裁判员人数 指经考核正式批准授予等级裁判员称号的人数。裁判员等级分为国际级裁判、国家级裁判、一级裁判、二级裁判、三级裁判。

运动员获奖牌情况 指当年北京市运动员在世界比赛、亚洲比赛、全国比赛中获得金、银、铜牌的数量。

Explanatory Notes on Main Statistical Indicators

Health

Healthcare Institutions refer to institutions granted with *License for Medical Institution* by the health administration authority, or granted with certificate of corporate unit by the civil affair, administration for industry and commerce, management authority of institutional organization, and providing medical service and healthcare, disease control, health supervision service or carrying out medical research and education, and so on.

Medical Technical Personnel refer to all fixed employees and of contract-based employees, professional personnel in health technology, who receive pays from health institutions, excluding personnel engaged in management.

Certified Doctors and Registered Nurses refer to personnel who have received a physician practicing certificate and certified nurse certificate, excluding physicians and nurses engaged in management.

Mortality (Cause-specific Death Rate) means the proportion of persons dead due to certain cause (such as disease) in the permanent population.

Infant Mortality means the rate of dead infants under 1 year old to 1,000 live infants in an area in a year. Infant death rate measures the development of economy, culture, citizen health and health care in a country or region. It is also an important component of study on average life expectancy of population.

Mortality of Children under 5 means the rate of dead children under 5 years old to 1,000 live infants in an area in a year. This is an important indicator now internationally recognized to reflect the survival status of children.

Pregnant and Lying-in Women Mortality refers to the rate of dead pregnant and lying-in women to 100,000 live pregnant and lying-in women in an area in a year. This is an important indicator to evaluate the social development status in an area. The figure of this indicator is directly related to the social and economic status, social environment and health care service for pregnant and lying-in women.

Sports

Sports Venues refer to sports building facilities for public welfare or operating purpose, specially used for sports training, games and fitness activities, and with certain investment.

Instruction Station of Morning and Evening Exercise refer to public sports and fitness sites located in sports gyms and stadiums, parks, streets, street parks and other public sites in a city, where the citizens in the city participate in voluntarily fitness activities in the morning or evening.

Number of Teenager Sports Clubs means the number of new-type social sports organizations for teenagers in the nature of socialistic public welfare, which are established by the builder with its own resources such as sports gyms and stadiums and human resource.

Social Sports Instructors refer to working personnel who carry out skill teaching, exercise instruction, organization and management in mass sports activities other than athletic sports, school sports and army sports.

Special Ball Game Venue and Facilities are special venues for ball activities built to meet the fitness need of different population, especially teenagers, consisting of three types, i.e. basketball squares, multi-purpose cage-shaped courts, and table tennis corridors.

Community Fitness Clubs refer to "mass sports organizations in the nature of public welfare, which are formed by residents in urban communities voluntarily according to their common purpose and interest, based on specific sports venue facilities in the jurisdiction, for frequent sports activities, and under the jurisdiction of sub-district administrative office or community neighborhood committee."

Number of Graded Athletes means the number of athletes formally granted with the title of graded athlete upon examination. Grades of athletes include international master sportsman, national maser sportsman, grade-I athlete, grade-II athlete, grade-III athlete and juvenile athlete.

Number of Graded Referees means the number of referees formally granted with the title of graded referees upon examination. Grades of referees include international referee, national referee, grade-I referee, grade-II referee and grade-III referee.

Medals Won by Athletes mean the number of gold, silver and copper medals won by athletes of Beijing in world games, Asian games and national games.

21

北京统计年鉴2015　BEIJING STATISTICAL YEARBOOK

社会福利、社区、政法及其他
SOCIAL WELFARE, COMMUNITY, LAW AND OTHERS

简要说明

一、本章资料的主要内容

本章资料主要包括社会活动参与、公检法司、民政事业、劳动保障、残疾人事业、妇女及儿童发展规划监测情况等内容。

二、本章资料的数据来源

1.社会活动参与的内容主要包括历届北京市人大代表和政协委员人数及议案情况、妇联组织和工会组织情况等。资料分别由北京市人民代表大会常务委员会、中国人民政治协商会议北京市委员会、北京市妇女联合会和北京市总工会提供。

2.公检法司的资料主要包括公安机关的刑事案件立案情况和治安案件查处情况，交通、火灾事故情况，检察机关的办案情况，人民法院审理案件和收结案情况，以及司法局提供的律师、公证、调解工作等情况。资料分别由北京市公安局、北京市高级人民法院、北京市人民检察院和北京市司法局提供。

3.民政事业和劳动保障统计资料主要包括社会福利企事业机构、人员、优抚和社会救济情况、婚姻登记情况。资料分别由北京市民政局、北京市人力资源和社会保障局提供。

4.残疾人资料主要包括残疾人康复、教育、就业、扶贫和残联组织建设等情况。资料由北京市残疾人联合会提供。

5.妇女与儿童发展规划监测资料主要包括妇女参与决策和管理、就业、教育、健康、法律保护等情况；儿童的健康、教育、法律保护社会生活环境等情况。资料由北京市统计局依据部门统计报表资料整理提供。

6.安全生产情况由北京市行政工商管理局、北京市食品药品监督管理局、北京市公安交通管理局、北京市安全生产监督管理局提供。

Brief Introduction

I. Main Content

This chapter consists of statistics for social activity participation, public security institutions, procuratorates, courts, judicial authorities, civil affairs, labor security, undertakings for disabled people, women and children development planning and monitoring.

II. Data Sources

1. Statistics for social activity participation consist of the numbers of deputies and proposals at people's congress and political consulting conferences of Beijing in previous years, women's federation and organizations, and labor unions. Data were provided respectively by the Standing Committee of Beijing Municipal People's Congress, Beijing Committee of CPPCC, Beijing Women's Federation, and Beijing Federation of Labor Unions.

2. Statistics for public security institutions, procuratorates, courts, and judicial authorities cover criminal cases put on the record of public security organs as well as public security investigation and punishments, traffic accidents and fires, case settlements in procuratorates, cases accepted and settled by people's courts, information on lawyers, notary, mediation provided by juridical bureaus. Data were provided by Beijing Municipal Bureau of Public Security, People's High Court of Beijing, People's Procuratorate of Beijing, and Beijing Municipal Bureau of Justice.

3. Statistics for civil affairs and labor security mainly consist of social welfare institutions, personnel, social relief, special care, and marriage registration. Data were provided by Beijing Municipal Bureau of Civil Affairs, and Beijing Municipal Bureau of Human Resources and Social Security.

4. Statistics for disabled persons mainly include information on rehabilitation, education, employment and poverty reduction, and building of federations for disabled persons, etc. Data were provided by Beijing Disabled Persons' Federation.

5. Supervision data on women and children development are composed of women's participation in decision making and management, employment, education, health, legal protection, and so on; children's health, education, legal protection, social living environment, etc. Data were provided respectively by Beijing Municipal Bureau of Statistics in accordance with statistic reporting system of different departments.

6. Safe production data were provided by Beijing Administration for Industry and Commerce, Beijing Municipal Food and Drug Administration, Beijing Municipal Bureau of Traffic Management, Beijing Administration of Work Safety.

21-1 北京市历年社会保障相关待遇标准(1994-2014年)
HISTORICAL LEVEL ON SOCIAL WELFARE IN BEIJING (1994-2014)

单位：元/月 (yuan/month)

年份 Year	标准 Standard	职工最低工资 Minimum Wages of Employed Persons	失业保险金最低标准 Minimum Unemployment Insurance	城市居民最低生活保障标准 Minimum Subsistence for Allowance Urban Residents	企业退休人员基本养老金最低标准 Minimum of Basic Pensions for Retired Persons	企业退职人员基本养老金最低标准 Minimum of Basic Pensions for Resigned Persons	企业退养人员基本养老金最低标准 Minimum of Basic Pensions for Early-retired Persons
1994		210					
1995		240	174				
1996		270	189	170	263	202	170
1997		290	203	190	293	232	200
1998		310	217	200	336	265	233
1999年第一次	First-time in 1999	320	224	210			
1999年第二次	Second-time in 1999	400	291	273	396	335	288
2000		412	300	280	421	360	308
2001		435	305	285	441	380	317
2002		465	326	290	466	405	367
2003		465	326	290	466	405	367
2004年第一次	First-time in 2004	495					
2004年第二次	Second-time in 2004	545	347	290	510	443	402
2005		580	382	300	563	488	443
2006		640	392	310	620	537	487
2007		730	422	330	675	592	527
2008		800	502	390	775	682	607
2009		800	562	410	900	800	700
2010		960	632	430	1000	900	800
2011		1160	782	500	1100	1000	900
2012		1260	842	520	1210	1100	1000
2013		1400	892	580	1330	1210	1100
2014		1560	1012	650	1463	1331	1210

资料来源：城市居民最低生活保障标准由北京市民政局提供，本表其他资料由北京市人力资源和社会保障局提供。

Source: Data on minimum subsistence allowance for urban residents was provided by Beijing Municipal Bureau of Civil Affairs,others were provided by Beijing Municipal Bureau of Human Resources and Social Security.

21-2 北京市历年参加社会保障情况(1995-2014年)

单位：万人

年 份 Year	参加基本养老保险人数 Employed Persons Participating in Basic Pension Insurance	参加基本医疗保险人数 Staff and Workers Participating in Basic Medical Care Insurance	参加失业保险人数 Employed Persons Participating in Unemployment Insurance	参加工伤保险人数 Employed Persons Participating in Work-related Injury Insurance	参加生育保险人数 Employed Persons Participating in Maternity Insurance
1995	261.1		219.8		
1996	252.0		214.5		
1997	264.3		214.0		
1998	359.2		222.9		
1999	379.0		289.0		
2000	391.6		287.8	212.0	
2001	425.9	210.2	287.2	212.7	
2002	436.2	353.8	299.5	221.0	
2003	448.5	436.1	306.6	242.9	
2004	460.0	484.0	308.0	259.0	
2005	520.0	574.8	394.6	328.9	226.1
2006	604.1	679.5	482.2	465.3	263.3
2007	671.7	783.0	535.3	609.2	290.6
2008	758.1	871.0	614.3	666.5	324.1
2009	827.7	938.4	675.7	747.1	346.8
2010	982.5	1063.7	774.2	823.8	372.2
2011	1091.9	1188.0	881.0	862.4	395.3
2012	1206.4	1279.7	1006.7	897.2	844.7
2013	1311.3	1354.8	1025.1	920.3	883.2
2014	1392.6	1431.3	1057.1	961.0	915.6

注：1. 2001年开始设置基本医疗保险指标，以前年份称为大病统筹，2000年参加大病统筹人数为232.6万人。
2. 2005年7月1日《北京市企业职工生育保险规定》开始实施。全市农村社会养老保险1992年试点，1996年全市正式实施。
3. 从2006年起，农村最低生活保障人数不含农村五保供养人员。
4. 农村居民参加城乡居民养老保险人数在2007年及以前为参加农村社会养老保险人数口径；2008年为参加新型农村社会养老保险人数；2009年及以后为参加城乡居民养老保险人数中农村参保人数。

资料来源：城乡居民享受最低生活保障人数来源于北京市民政局；参加农村新型医疗人数和参合率来源于北京市卫生和计划生育委员会；其他资料来源于北京市人力资源和社会保障局。

SOCIAL SECURITY PARTICIPATION IN BEIJING (1995-2014)

(10000 persons)

参加城乡居民养老保险人数 Residents Participating in Basic Pension Insurance	#农村居民 Rural Residents	参加城镇居民医疗保险人数 Residents Participating in Basic Urban Medical Insurance	参加新型农村合作医疗人数 Residents Participating in New-type Rural Cooperative Medicare	城市居民最低生活保障人数 Persons Receiving Subsistence Allowances in Urban Areas	农村最低生活保障人数 Persons Receiving Subsistence Allowances in Rural Areas	新型农村合作医疗参合率 (%) Percentage of Persons Participating in New-type Rural Cooperative Medicare
	29.2			0.9		
	37.4			0.9		
	41.2			2.8		
	34.4			4.3	1.2	
	38.5			6.7	1.6	
	34.7			7.6	1.8	
	32.0			12.0	5.4	
	33.6			16.1	6.7	
	36.8		234.0	16.1	7.5	71.9
	40.6		250.4	15.5	7.8	80.3
	44.8		261.0	15.2	7.6	86.9
	49.1		268.5	14.8	7.8	88.9
	127.5		272.5	14.5	7.9	92.9
	153.9		274.9	14.7	8.0	95.7
168.5	159.3	143.7	278.5	13.7	7.7	96.7
173.4	163.7	159.8	276.8	11.7	7.0	97.7
177.3	167.0	151.9	267.5	11.0	6.3	98.1
180.1	168.7	160.1	254.4	10.4	6.0	98.0
186.2	173.4	173.0	242.6	8.9	5.1	99.6

Note: a) The basic medicare indicator was set from 2001. Before that it was called general healthcare program for major diseases which covered 2.326 million people in 2000.

b) Regulations of Beijing on Maternity Insurance for Enterprise Employed Persons became effective from July 1st, 2005. Pilots were made for social pension program in rural area of Beijing in 1992. The program was formally effective in 1996 across the city.

c) Rural persons receiving minimum subsistence allowance excluded rural persons enjoying five guarantees from 2006.

d) In and before 2007, the number of rural people participating in urban and rural pension insurance covered the people participating in rural social pension insurance; in 2008, this figure covered the people participating in new-type rural social pension insurance; since 2009, this figure covered the rural people of those participating in the urban and rural pension insurance.

Source: Figures on persons receiving subsistence allowances in urban and rural areas are from Beijing Municipal Bureau of Civil Affairs; Figures on persons participating in new-type rural medicare and percentage of these persons are from Beijing Municipal Commission of Health and Family Planning; other data are from Beijing Municipal Bureau of Human Resources and Social Security.

21-3 城镇职工参加社会保险情况(2014年)
PARTICIPATION OF EMPLOYED PERSONS FOR SOCIAL SECURITY INSURANCE PROGRAMS IN THE URBAN AREA (2014)

项目	Item	基本养老保险 Basic Pension Insurance		基本医疗保险 Basic Medical Insurance	
		单位个数(个) Number of Entities (unit)	人数(人) Number of Persons (person)	单位个数(个) Number of Entities (unit)	人数(人) Number of Persons (person)
合　计	**Total**	**369141**	**13926052**	**364868**	**14312611**
按登记注册类型分	**By Registration Type**				
国　有	State-owned	6909	2044675	5690	1943648
集　体	Collectively-owned	6358	266338	5376	254943
其　他	Others	355874	11615039	353802	12114020
按隶属关系划分	**By Affiliation**				
中央单位	Central	7316	1876347	6636	1797184
地方单位	Local	361825	12049705	358232	12515427

资料来源：北京市人力资源和社会保障局。
Source: Beijing Municipal Bureau of Human Resources and Social Security.

21-3 续表 Continued

项目	Item	失业保险 Unemployment Insurance		工伤保险 Industrial Injury Insurance		生育保险 Maternity Insurance	
		单位个数(个) Number of Entities (unit)	人数(人) Number of Persons (person)	单位个数(个) Number of Entities (unit)	人数(人) Number of Persons (person)	单位个数(个) Number of Entities (unit)	人数(人) Number of Persons (person)
合　计	**Total**	**368954**	**10571258**	**381226**	**9610240**	**366566**	**9155717**
按登记注册类型分	**By Registration Type**						
国　有	State-owned	6413	1029763	6602	1029718	6467	994524
集　体	Collectively-owned	6035	133283	6409	134740	6168	123199
其　他	Others	356506	9408212	368215	8445782	353931	8037994
按隶属关系划分	**By Affiliation**						
中央单位	Central	7111	1460548	7456	1391404	7242	1227077
地方单位	Local	361843	9110710	373770	8218836	359324	7928640

资料来源：北京市人力资源和社会保障局。
Source: Beijing Municipal Bureau of Human Resources and Social Security.

21-4 城乡居民参加社会保险情况(2010-2014年)
PARTICIPATION OF RURAL AND URBAN RESIDENTS FOR SOCIAL SECURITY INSURANCE PROGRAMS (2010-2014)

单位：万人　　(10000 persons)

年 份 Year	城乡居民基本养老保险人数 Basic Pension Insurance		城镇居民医疗保险人数 Basic Medical Care Insurance			
	合 计 Total	#农村居民 Rural Residents	合 计 Total	学生儿童 Students and Children	无保障老人 Unguaranteed Aged Persons	无业居民 Unemployed Residents
2010	168.5	159.3	143.7	121.3	17.7	4.7
2011	173.4	163.7	159.8	135.5	19.1	5.3
2012	177.3	167.0	151.9	128.6	18.5	4.8
2013	180.1	168.7	160.1	137.5	18.8	3.7
2014	186.2	173.4	173.0	149.8	19.7	3.6

资料来源：北京市人力资源和社会保障局。
Source: Beijing Municipal Bureau of Human Resources and Social Security.

21-5 优抚及主要救助对象情况
STATISTICS FOR PERSONS RECEIVING SPECIAL CARE AND RELIEF

单位：人　　(person)

项 目	Item	人数 Number of Persons 2014	2013	2014年为2013年% 2014 as % of 2013
抚恤、补助优抚对象总人数	**Total Number of Persons Receiving Pensions, Subsidies, and Special Care Treatment**	**44537**	**43427**	**102.6**
定期抚恤人数	Number of Persons Receiving Regular Pensions	1708	1775	96.2
定期补助人数	Number of Persons Receiving Regular Subsidies	31392	30477	103.0
伤残人数	Total Number of Disabled Persons	11437	11175	102.3
医疗救助人次数	**Total Number of Persons Receiving Medical Assistance**	**88873**	**143196**	**62.1**
城市医疗救助人次数	Number of Persons Receiving Medical Assistance in the Urban Area		81730	
农村医疗救助人次数	Number of Persons Receiving Medical Assistance in the Rural Area		61466	
社会救助对象总人数	**Total Number of Persons Receiving Social Relief**	**144653**	**167333**	**86.4**
城市居民最低生活保障人数	Number of Persons Receiving Subsistence Allowances in Urban Areas	89135	103682	86.0
农村居民最低生活保障人数	Number of Persons Receiving Subsistence Allowances in Rural Areas	51324	59575	86.2
农村五保供养人数	Rural Residents Enjoying Five Guarantees	4194	4076	102.9
农村集中五保供养人数	Collective Rural Residents Enjoying Five Guarantees	1964	2039	96.3
农村分散五保供养人数	Scattered Rural Residents Enjoying Five Guarantees	2230	2037	109.5

注：“农村最低生活保障人数”不含“农村五保供养人数”。
资料来源：北京市民政局。
Note: Number of persons receiving subsistence allowances in rural areas excludes "Rural Residents Enjoying the Five Guarantees".
Source: Beijing Municipal Bureau of Civil Affairs.

21-6 社会福利事业、社区情况情况
STATISTICS FOR SOCIAL WELFARE AND CMMUNITY

项目		Item		2014	2013	2014年为2013年% 2014 as % of 2013
社区服务机构数	(个)	Number of Service Facilities in Urban Communities	(unit)	6783	6525	104.0
#社区服务中心	(个)	Community Service Centers	(unit)	193	192	100.5
社区服务志愿者组织数	(个)	Number of Community Service Volunteer Organizations	(unit)	10253	11090	92.5
城市便民利民服务网点数	(个)	Number of Urban Convenient Service Outlets	(unit)	10372	11004	94.3
社会福利企业单位数	(个)	Number of Social Welfare Enterprises	(unit)	574	612	93.8
社会福利企业年末职工人数	(人)	Year-end Employed Persons in Social Welfare Enterprise	(person)	26179	28384	92.2
#残疾职工	(人)	Disabled Employed Persons	(person)	10443	11200	93.2

资料来源：北京市民政局。
Source: Beijing Municipal Buresu of Civil Affairs.

21-7 收养性单位情况(2014年)
STATISTICS ON ADOPTING INSTITUTIONS (2014)

项目		Item		合计	#光荣院 Homes for Disabled Veterans	#社会福利院 Social Welfare Institutions	#儿童福利院 Children's Welfare Institutions	#福利类精神病院和医院 Welfare Mental Hospitals and Hospitals	#城市养老服务机构 Urban Elderly Care Agencies	#农村养老服务机构 Rural Elderly Care Agencies
单位数	(个)	Institutions	(unit)	472	10	9	11	2	162	275
职工人数	(人)	Employed Persons	(person)	12608	188	1085	514	354	5097	5214
床位数	(张)	Beds	(unit)	93183	683	3337	1510	654	33202	52919
年末在院人数	(人)	Persons Received	(person)	37037	147	2653	1423	422	14341	17702
#自费	(人)	Self-supported	(person)	31330	17	1915	15	105	13747	15186

资料来源：北京市民政局。
Source: Beijing Municipal Buresu of Civil Affairs.

21-8 离婚、青少年刑事案犯情况
STATISTICS FOR DIVORCE AND JUVENILE CRIMINAL CASES

项目		Item		2014	2013
婚姻家庭纠纷案件数(结案)	(件)	Marriage and Family Disputes (Closed)	(case)	30542	28592
#离婚案件数	(件)	Divorce Cases	(case)	20159	20607
#调离案件数	(件)	Cases of Divorce Reconciled	(case)	6464	7505
#判离案件数	(件)	Cases of Divorce Judged	(case)	2971	2977
建立少年法庭个数	(个)	Juvenile Courts Established	(unit)	20	20
青少年罪犯人数	(人)	Teenager Offenders	(person)	6372	9342
14周岁以上不满16周岁罪犯人数	(人)	Teenager Offenders 14-16	(person)	73	79
16周岁以上不满18周岁罪犯人数	(人)	Teenager Offenders 16-18	(person)	772	974
18周岁以上不满25周岁罪犯人数	(人)	Teenager Offenders 18-25	(person)	5527	8289
青少年刑事案犯占全部刑事案犯的比重	(%)	Teenager Criminal Offenders as % of Total Criminal Offenders	(%)	24.64	32.04

资料来源：北京市高级人民法院。
Source: The People's High Court of Beijing.

21-9 婚姻登记(1981-2014年)
BASIC STATISTICS FOR MARRIAGE AND DIVORCE REGISTRATIONS (1981-2014)

年 份 Year	结 婚 对 数 (对) Registered Marriages (couple)	#涉外及华侨、港澳台居民登记结婚对数 Registered Marriages Involving Foreigners and Citizens of Hong Kong, Macao and Taiwan	初 婚 总人数 (人) First Marriages (person)	离 婚 对 数 (对) Registered Divorces (couple)	#民政部门 登 记 离婚对数 Divorces Registered in the Civil Affair Department (couple)
1981	200352		392855	5170	1780
1982	141253		265834	5359	1581
1983	117976			5322	1465
1984	113362		218009	5654	1387
1985	134462		258256	5874	1746
1986	143105		273634	7541	2474
1987	149952		285803	8916	3218
1988	113333		212070	10664	4198
1989	103829		190978	12515	5174
1990	92988		168304	14748	5791
1991	91979		166579	15287	6483
1992	89095		159588	15567	6477
1993	89938		160127	17829	7589
1994	90379		161972	19928	8327
1995	85511		149878	20160	8096
1996	86803		147855	20716	8225
1997	84208		145099	22257	8628
1998	85534		148026	23708	9381
1999	83312		141740	23922	8502
2000	80212		135620	26616	6384
2001	79385	873	133259	27683	5425
2002	76136	606	126371	27691	5810
2003	93526	761	158729	30637	10142
2004	126436	974	214443	32657	21013
2005	96596	937	158736	34244	23991
2006	171286	1172	294223	35505	24954
2007	117926	991	193387	36622	26432
2008	147516	1165	246309	37619	27277
2009	181771	1176	305803	41299	29998
2010	138104	1085	222269	43970	32595
2011	173238	1260	288406	43521	32999
2012	174114	1242	287436	48575	38243
2013	163676	1070	251636	64610	54536
2014	170027	1149	253774	76351	56192

注：离婚对数包括在民政部门登记的对数和经法院调离和判离的对数。
资料来源：北京市民政局、北京市高级人民法院。
Note: Registered divorces include those registered in the civil affair department and those mediated and judged in courts.
Source: Beijing Municipal Bureau of Civil Affairs, and The People's High Court of Beijing.

21-10 婚姻登记情况
BASIC STATISTICS ON MARRIAGE AND DIVORCE REGISTRATIONS

项　　目		Item		2014	2013	2014年为2013年% 2014 as % of 2013
登记结婚对数	**（对）**	**Registered Marriages**	**(couple)**	**170027**	**163676**	**103.9**
按婚前状况分		**By Pre-marriage Status**				
初婚人数	（人）	First Marriages	(person)	253774	251636	100.8
再婚人数	（人）	Remarriages	(person)	86280	75716	114.0
#女　性	（人）	Females	(person)	41213	35954	114.6
按居住地分		**By Place of Residence**				
内地居民登记结婚对数	（对）	Registered Marriages in Mainland	(couple)	168878	162606	103.9
涉外及华侨、港澳台居民登记结婚对数	（对）	Registered Marriages with involving Foreigner and the Citizens of Hong Kong, Macao and Taiwan	(couple)	1149	1070	107.4
内地居民	（人）	Mainland Residents	(person)	1052	1002	105.0
#女　性	（人）	Females	(person)	733	725	101.1
香港居民	（人）	Hong Kong Residents	(person)	45	59	76.3
澳门居民	（人）	Macao Residents	(person)	4	8	50.0
台湾居民	（人）	Taiwan Residents	(person)	158	129	122.5
华　侨	（人）	Overseas Chinese	(person)	40	28	142.9
外国人	（人）	Foreigners	(person)	999	914	109.3
离婚登记对数	**（对）**	**Registered Divorces**	**(couple)**	**56192**	**54536**	**103.0**
内地居民登记离婚对数	（对）	Mainland Residents	(couple)	55989	54363	103.0
涉外及华侨、港澳台居民登记离婚对数	（对）	Overseas Chinese,Hongkong,Macao, Taiwan Residents	(couple)	203	173	117.3

注：离婚对数不含法院判离数。

资料来源：北京市民政局。

Note: Number of registered divorces excludes the divorces ruled by courts.

Source: Beijing Municipal Bureau of Civil Affairs.

21-11 残疾人事业基本情况
BASIC INFORMATION OF UNDERTAKINGS FOR DISABLED PERSONS

项 目		Item		2014	2013
康 复		**Rehabilitation**			
0-6岁残疾儿童享受康复政策人数	(人)	Number of Disabled Children of 0 to 6 Years Old Enjoying Rehabilitation Policies	(person)	813	
7-15岁残疾儿童少年享受康复政策人数	(人)	Number of Disabled Children and Teenagers of 7 to15 Years Old Enjoying Rehabilitation Policies	(person)	908	
残疾人接受辅助器具服务人数	(人)	Number of Disabled Persons With Assistive Devices	(person)	15778	
精神残疾人接受免费服药人数	(人)	Number of Mentally Disabled Persons Receiving Free Drug Treatment	(person)	22000	
贫困白内障患者接受减免费复明手术人数	(人)	Number of Poor Cataract Patients Receiving Free Cataract Surgery or That of Preferential Price	(person)	1626	
盲人接受定向行走训练人数	(人)	Number of Blind Persons Receiving Mobility and Orientation Training	(person)	835	
肢残人在社区接受康复训练人数	(人)	Number of The Physical Disabled Receiving Rehabilitation Training In Communities	(person)	7425	
智障人在社区接受康复训练人数	(人)	Number of Retarded Persons Receiving Rehabilitation Training In Communities	(person)	7269	
精神残疾人在社区接受康复训练人数	(人)	Number of Mentally Disabled Persons Receiving Rehabilitation Training In Communities	(person)	3341	
家庭康复培训残疾人亲友、家属总人数	(人)	Total Number of Family Members and Friends of Disabled Persons Receiving Family Rehabilitation Training	(person)	50000	
教 育		**Education**			
未入学适龄残疾儿童少年	(人)	School-age Disabled Children Without Schooling	(person)	76	243
培 训		**Training**			
职业教育与培训机构数(残联认定)	(个)	Number of Vocational Education and Training Institutions (recognized by China Disabled Persons' Federation)	(unit)	64	62
职业技能培训人数	(人次)	Number of Persons Receiving Vocational Skill Training	(person-time)	9260	10471
就 业		**Employment**			
城镇残疾人就业状况		Employment of Urban Disabled Persons			
当年安排就业人数	(人)	Persons Employed by Arrangement in the Year	(person)	4285	3244
#按比例就业人数	(人)	Employed by Quota Scheme	(person)	1805	1221
集中就业人数	(人)	Disabled Persons Employed in Concentrated Way	(person)	190	75
个体就业人数	(人)	Self-employed	(person)	1918	1233
残疾人就业服务机构数	(个)	Employment Placement Service Facilities for Disabled Jobseekers	(unit)	17	17
盲人按摩		Massage by Persons with Visual Disability			
保健按摩机构	(家)	Healthcare Massage Institutions	(unit)	396	409
医疗按摩机构	(家)	Medical Massage Institutions	(unit)	4	2
保健按摩员培训人次	(人次)	Massage Therapists Training	(person-time)	1491	1115
医疗按摩员培训人次	(人次)	Keep-fit Massager Training	(person-time)	279	23
扶 贫		**Poverty Alleviation**			
享受城镇廉租住房的残疾人户数	(户)	Number of Households with Disabled Persons Enjoying Low-cost Urban House Leasing	(household)	1629	1185
扶持农村残疾人数	(人)	Number of Disabled Persons Supported in Rural Areas	(person)	3824	9197
社会保障		**Social Security**			
城 镇		Urban Areas			
已纳入最低生活保障范围人数	(人)	Covered by the Basic Living System	(person)	20875	19887
享受失业且无稳定收入生活补助重残人数	(人)	Number of Severely Disabled Persons Enjoying Allowance For Unemployment and Unsteady Income	(person)	13908	
享受失业且无稳定收入生活补助非重残人数	(人)	Number of Non-Severely Disabled Persons Enjoying Allowance For Unemployment and Unsteady Income	(person)	8408	
参加城乡居民养老保险残疾人数	(人)	Number of Disabled Persons Insured by Urban Resident Pension Insuranc	(person)	26817	
参加城镇居民医疗保险残疾人数	(人)	Number of Disabled Persons Insured by Urban Resident Medical Insuranc	(person)	45000	
其他救助救济人数	(人)	Number of Other Persons Assisted and Supported	(person)	14516	7333
农 村		Rural Areas			
已纳入最低生活保障范围人数	(人)	Covered by The Basic Living System	(person)	20416	19887
享受失业且无稳定收入生活补助重残人数	(人)	Number of Severely Disabled Persons Enjoying Allowance For Unemployment and Unsteady Income	(person)	23555	
享受失业且无稳定收入生活补助非重残人数	(人)	Number of Non-severely Disabled Persons Enjoying Allowance For Unemployment and Unsteady Income	(person)	30452	
参加城乡居民养老保险残疾人数	(人)	Number of Disabled Persons Insured by Urban Resident Pension Insuranc	(person)	71413	
参加新型农村合作医疗保险残疾人数	(人)	Number of Disabled Persons Insured by New Rural Cooperative Medical Service	(person)	121977	
其他救助救济人数	(人)	Number of Other Persons Assisted and Supported	(person)	14226	7333
残联组织建设		**Organization Building of Disabled Persons' Federation**			
残疾人工作者数	(人)	Workers for Disabled Persons	(person)	1214	1202

资料来源：北京市残疾人联合会。
Source: Beijing Disabled Persons' Federation.

21-12 残疾人就业、维权援助情况
STATISTICS FOR EMPLOYMENT AND AID FOR RIGHT PROTECTION OF DISABLED PERSONS

项目		Item		2014	2013
残疾人职业培训人数	(人)	Number of Disabled Persons Trained for Employment	(person)	16283	12989
#女性	(人)	Females	(person)	6918	5591
新安置残疾人员就业人数	(人)	New Employment of Disabled Persons	(person)	3812	3885
#女性	(人)	Females	(peoson)	2566	1270
维权信访咨询件数	(件)	Right Protection Letters, Visits and Consulting	(case)	23066	18856
维权法律服务件数	(件)	Right Protection Legal Aid	(case)	2840	4251

资料来源：北京市残疾人联合会。
Source: Beijing Disabled Persons Federation.

21-13 律师工作
STATISTICS FOR LAWYERS

项目		Item		2014	2013	2014年为2013年% 2014 as % of 2013
律师事务所	(个)	Law Firms	(unit)	1924	1782	108.0
执业律师	(人)	Number of Practicing Lawyers	(person)	24467	23761	103.0
专职律师	(人)	Full-time Lawyers	(person)	23067	22222	103.8
兼职律师	(人)	Part-time Lawyers	(person)	928	1068	86.9
公司律师	(人)	Company Lawyers	(person)	345	349	98.9
公职律师	(人)	Government Lawyers	(person)	62	62	100.0
法律援助律师	(人)	Legal Aid Lawyers	(person)	65	60	108.3
担任法律顾问	(家)	Legal Counsel	(unit)	22872	21713	105.3
民事诉讼代理	(件)	Civil Case Litigation Agencies	(case)	90115	98630	91.4
行政诉讼代理	(件)	Administrative Case Litigation Agencies	(case)	4384	4815	91.0
刑事诉讼辩护及代理	(件)	Criminal Case Litigation Agencies	(case)	25144	28062	89.6
非诉讼法律事务	(件)	Off-court Cases	(case)	86884	72530	119.8

资料来源：北京市司法局。
Source: Beijing Municipal Bureau of Justice.

21-14 调解工作
MEDIATION

项　　目		Item		2014	2013	2014年为2013年% 2014 as % of 2013
人民调解委员会个数	(个)	People's Mediation Committees	(unit)	7722	7646	101.0
调解员人数	(万人)	Mediators	(10000 persons)	8.22	7.75	106.1
调解各类纠纷件数	(万件)	Disputes Mediated	(10000 cases)	19.41	22.85	84.9
#调解各类纠纷成功件数	(万件)	Succeed Disputes Mediated	(10000 cases)	18.86	21.71	86.9
防止民间纠纷激化件数	(件)	Civil Disputes Prevented from Intensifi	(case)	1627	1036	157.0
防止民间纠纷激化人数	(人次)	Persons Involved in Civil Disputes Prev	(person)	15092	16071	93.9

资料来源：北京市司法局。
Source: Beijing Municipal Bureau of Justice.

21-15 公证工作
NOTARIZATIONS

项　　目		Item		2014	2013	2014年为2013年% 2014 as % of 2013
公证机构个数	(个)	Notary Offices	(unit)	25	25	100.0
执业公证员人数	(人)	Certified Notaries	(person)	327	274	119.3
总办证数	(件)	Certificates Issued	(case)	940373	814088	115.5
国内公证业务	(件)	Domestic Notarial Services	(case)	431105	382217	112.8
涉外公证业务	(件)	Foreign-Relatesd Notarial Docummbents	(case)	501173	423688	118.3
涉港澳公证业务	(件)	Hongkong,Macao affairs	(case)	4598	4947	92.9
涉台公证业务	(件)	Naiwan Notarial Services	(case)	3497	3236	108.1

资料来源：北京市司法局。
Source: Beijing Municipal Bureau of Justice.

21-16 法律援助工作情况
STATISTICS FOR LEGAL AID

项　目		Item		2014	2013	2014年为2013年% 2014 as % of 2013
法律援助机构个数	（个）	Number of Legal Aid Agencies	(unit)	25	26	96.2
法律援助机构人员数	（人）	Number of Legal Aid Persons	(person)	286	260	110.0
承办民事法律援助案件数	（件）	Civil Cases Aided	(case)	15420	15760	97.8
承办刑事法律援助案件数	（件）	Criminal Cases Aided	(case)	2822	4421	63.8
承办行政法律援助案件数	（件）	Administrative Cases Aided	(case)	31	24	129.2
法律援助机构接待咨询人次	（万人次）	Consultations by Legal Aid Agencies	(10000 person-times)	13.2	23.5	56.2
得到法律援助机构援助的妇女人数	（人次）	Females Receiving Aids from Legal Aid Agencies	(person-times)	6132	4928	124.4
得到法律援助机构援助的儿童人数	（人次）	Children Receiving Aids from Legal Aid Agencies	(person-times)	2111	2453	86.1

资料来源：北京市司法局。
Source: Beijing Municiapl Bureau of Justice.

21-17 司法鉴定工作情况
STATISTICS FOR JUDICIAL APPRAISAL

项　目		Item		2014	2013
司法鉴定机构个数	（个）	Judicial Appraisal Organizations	(unit)	108	111
司法鉴定人员数	（人）	Judicial Appraisal Personnel	(person)	1680	1740
司法鉴定业务量	（件）	Judicial Appraisal Cases Proceeded	(case)	71157	48348

注：本表中司法鉴定机构数为“北京市司法局审核登记的全部司法鉴定机构”个数。
资料来源：北京市司法局。
Note: In the table, the number of judicial appraisal organizations is the number of "all judicial appraisal organizations approved by and registered with Beijing Municipal Bureau of Justice".
Source: Beijing Municipal Bureau of Justice.

21-18 公安、法院、检察院收案、结案情况(2005-2014年)
CASES ACCEPTED AND SETTLED BY PUBLIC SECURITY DEPARTMENTS, COURTS AND PROCURATORATES (2005-2014)

项目		Item		2005	2006	2007
公安部门侦破刑事案件		**Criminal Cases Detected by Public Security Departments**				
立案	(起)	Cases Put on File	(case)	107988	120554	127446
破案	(起)	Cases Settled	(case)	59035	66399	74232
法院刑事案件收、结案情况		**Criminal Cases Accepted and Settled in Courts**				
收案	(件)	Cases Accepted	(case)	17488	17725	19592
结案	(件)	Cases Settled	(case)	17624	17701	19536
法院婚姻家庭、继承纠纷案件收、结案情况		**Marriage and Inheritance Dispute Cases Accepted and Settled in Courts**				
收案	(件)	Cases Accepted	(case)	26739	27860	28089
结案	(件)	Cases Settled	(case)	27002	27845	27916
法院合同纠纷案件收、结案情况		**Contract Dispute Cases Accepted and Settled in Courts**				
收案	(件)	Cases Accepted	(case)	133534	141485	135099
结案	(件)	Cases Settled	(case)	135612	141439	134829
法院权属、侵权纠纷及其他民事案件收、结案情况		**Ownership, Infringement Dispute and Other Civil Cases Accepted and Settled in Courts**				
收案	(件)	Cases Accepted	(case)	42690	44890	46892
结案	(件)	Cases Settled	(case)	43166	45005	46372
检察机关查办反贪污贿赂案件		**Anti-Corruption and Bribery Cases Handled by Procuratorates**				
受案	(件)	Cases Accepted	(case)	1202	1330	1276
立案		Cases Put on File				
件数	(件)	Number of Cases	(case)	292	321	322
人数	(人)	Number of Persons Involved	(person)	356	363	372
挽回经济损失	(万元)	Economic Losses Redeemed	(10000 yuan)	30701	29545	14703
检察机关办理渎职侵权案件		**Misconduct and Infringement Cases Handled by Procuratorates**				
受案	(件)	Cases Accepted	(case)	218	162	205
立案		Cases Put on File				
件数	(件)	Number of Cases	(case)	37	30	34
人数	(人)	Number of Persons Involved	(person)	38	31	36
挽回经济损失	(万元)	Economic Losses Redeemed	(10000 yuan)	1320	458	71

资料来源：北京市公安局、北京市人民检察院、北京市高级人民法院。
Source: Beijing Municipal Bureau of Public Security, the People's Procuratorate of Beijing, and the People's High Court of Beijing.

21-18 续表 Continued

项 目	Item	2008	2009	2010	2011	2012	2013	2014
公安部门侦破刑事案件	**Criminal Cases Detected by Public Security Departments**							
立 案 (起)	Cases Put on File (case)	90045	98750	104327	142835	145724	140498	153334
破 案 (起)	Cases Settled (case)	63294	71950	80401	89156	101776	112594	122383
法院刑事案件收、结案情况	**Criminal Cases Accepted and Settled in Courts**							
收 案 (件)	Cases Accepted (case)	20024	18819	19824	19574	22168	19109	20556
结 案 (件)	Cases Settled (case)	20004	18773	19870	19423	22084	19012	20357
法院婚姻家庭、继承纠纷案件收、结案情况	**Marriage and Inheritance Dispute Cases Accepted and Settled in Courts**							
收 案 (件)	Cases Accepted (case)	30402	33056	36799	35251	35418	37347	39390
结 案 (件)	Cases Settled (case)	29499	32902	37160	35149	35201	35296	38565
法院合同纠纷案件收、结案情况	**Contract Dispute Cases Accepted and Settled in Courts**							
收 案 (件)	Cases Accepted (case)	144948	153766	148655	144433	145017	149237	162893
结 案 (件)	Cases Settled (case)	140512	152128	153130	144766	143153	141642	155472
法院权属、侵权纠纷及其他民事案件收、结案情况	**Ownership, Infringement Dispute and Other Civil Cases Accepted and Settled in Courts**							
收 案 (件)	Cases Accepted (case)	53864	58057	64379	65972	62736	64747	69541
结 案 (件)	Cases Settled (case)	51668	57135	65763	66405	62235	61688	67444
检察机关查办贪污贿赂案件	**Anti-Corruption and Bribery Cases Handled by Procuratorates**							
受 案 (件)	Cases Accepted (case)	1060	1113	1138	988	1070	871	1087
立 案	Cases Put on File							
件 数 (件)	Number of Cases (case)	282	319	356	343	379	299	382
人 数 (人)	Number of Persons Involved (person)	333	369	418	425	459	357	429
挽回经济损失 (万元)	Economic Losses Redeemed (10000 yuan)	21148	62542	14634	36469	29955	16171	9050
检察机关办理渎职侵权案件	**Misconduct and Infringement Cases Handled by Procuratorates**							
受 案 (件)	Cases Accepted (case)	150	206	213	193	351	443	291
立 案	Cases Put on File							
件 数 (件)	Number of Cases (case)	29	48	57	55	77	74	75
人 数 (人)	Number of Persons Involved (person)	31	53	60	66	94	81	78
挽回经济损失 (万元)	Economic Losses Redeemed (10000 yuan)	3019	25	16	58	735	962	210

21-19 法院行政案件收、结案情况(2014年)
STATISTICS FOR ADMINISTRATIVE CASES ACCEPTED AND SETTLED BY COURT (2014)

单位：件 (case)

项　　目	Item	收　案 Cases Accepted	结　案 Cases Settled	#判　决 Judgment	#裁　定 Mediation
合　计	**Total**	**15649**	**10391**	**6716**	**3672**
公　安	Public Security	381	393	239	154
资　源	Resources	151	154	42	113
城　建	City Construction	613	604	283	331
工　商	Industry and Commerce	160	150	82	69
专　利	Patents	562	425	392	41
劳动和社会保障	Labor and Social Security	102	119	96	23
教　育	Education	5	5	1	4
其　他	Others	13675	8541	5581	2937

资料来源：北京市高级人民法院。
Source: The People's High Court of Beijing.

21-20 法院刑事案件收、结案情况(2014年)
STATISTICS FOR CRIMINAL CASES ACCEPTED AND SETTLED BY COURT (2014)

项　　目	Item	收　案 (件) Cases Accepted (case)	结　案 (件) Cases Settled (case)	判决发生法律效力 Judgment with Legal Forces 件　数 (件) Number of Cases (case)	判决发生法律效力 Judgment with Legal Forces 人　数 (人) Number of Persons (person)
合　计	**Total**	**20556**	**20357**	**20251**	**24798**
#危害公共安全罪	Offences against Public Security	3038	3024	2870	2937
破坏社会主义市场经济秩序罪	Offences against the Socialist Market Economy Order	2646	2602	2747	3286
侵犯公民人身权利、民主权利罪	Offences against Civil Personal Rights and Democratic Rights	3887	3852	3824	4572
侵犯财产罪	Offences against Property	6280	6226	6370	7908
妨害社会管理秩序罪	Offences against Social Administration	4393	4333	4151	5731
危害国防利益罪	Offences against National Defense Interest	22	19	19	25
贪污贿赂罪	Crimes of Corruption and Bribery	252	263	238	304
渎职罪	Crimes of Misconduct in Office	34	34	22	23

资料来源：北京市高级人民法院。
Source: The People's High Court of Beijing.

21-21 法院婚姻家庭、继承纠纷案件收、结案情况(2014年)

STATISTICS FOR MARRIAGE AND FAMILY AND INHERITANCE DISPUTE CASES ACCEPTED AND SETTLED BY COURT (2014)

单位：件 (case)

项目	Item	收案 Cases Accepted	结案 Cases Settled	#判决 Judgment	#调解 Mediation
合计	**Total**	**39390**	**38565**	**11536**	**16132**
婚姻家庭纠纷	**Marriage and Family Disputes**				
离婚	Divorces	20159	19688	6666	6799
解除非法同居关系	Relieving the Relation of Illicit Cohabitation	320	312	101	124
抚养、扶养关系纠纷	Child-support Disputes	1044	1043	264	521
抚育费纠纷	Child-support Payment Disputes	1148	1148	505	348
赡养纠纷	Support Disputes	1121	1118	496	248
分家析产	Family Property Division	4316	4229	593	2754
其他	Others	2434	2400	889	657
继承纠纷	**Inheritance Disputes**				
法定继承	Legal Inheritance	5719	5626	1056	3369
遗嘱继承	Testamentary Inheritance	953	918	346	364
继承权确认纠纷	Inheritance Right Dispute				
其他	Others	2176	2083	619	948

资料来源：北京市高级人民法院。
Source: The People's High Court of Beijing.

21-22 法院合同纠纷案件收、结案情况(2014年)

STATISTICS FOR CONTRACT CASES ACCEPTED AND SETTLED BY COURT (2014)

单位：件 (case)

项目	Item	收案 Cases Accepted	结案 Cases Settled	#判决 Judgment	#调解 Mediation
合计	**Total**	**162893**	**155472**	**59474**	**27880**
#买卖合同纠纷	Trade Contracts	18533	17334	6813	3794
房地产开发经营合同纠纷	Real Estate Development & Operation Contracts	5896	5758	3075	1389
供用电、水、气、热力合同纠纷	Electricity, Water, Gas, Heating Supply contracts	13944	13766	1545	2331
借款合同纠纷	Loan Contracts	21649	19520	9518	3889
租赁合同纠纷	Lease Contracts	13512	12675	5430	1828
建设工程合同纠纷	Construction Contracts	4533	4292	1727	850
承揽合同纠纷	Contracts for Hire of Work	2477	2321	733	541
运输合同纠纷	Transportation Contracts	802	789	367	174
经营合同纠纷	Management Contracts	1175	1096	451	166
农村承包合同纠纷	Rural Contracts	125	122	56	18
劳动争议	Labor Disputes	20235	19286	9723	4348

资料来源：北京市高级人民法院。
Source: The People's High Court of Beijing.

21-23 法院权属、侵权纠纷及其他民事案件收、结案情况(2014年)
STATISTICS FOR OWNERSHIP, TORTIOUS DISPUTES AND OTHER CIVIL CASES ACCEPTED AND SETTLED BY COURT (2014)

单位：件 (case)

项目	Item	收案 Cases Accepted	结案 Cases Settled	#判决 Judgment	#调解 Mediation
合计	**Total**	**69541**	**67444**	**28216**	**13589**
所有权及与所有权相关权利纠纷	Ownership and Related Rights	18851	18169	6352	4776
票据、证券权益纠纷	Bill and Securities Rights	363	323	126	54
股东权纠纷	Shareholder's Rights	1226	993	432	72
不正当竞争纠纷	Unfair Competition	190	169	85	15
人身权纠纷	Personal Rights	10557	10117	5231	2181
特殊侵权纠纷	Special Infringements	19967	19424	11033	4490
适用特别程序案件	Special-poceeding Cases	6742	6634	2316	
其他	Others	11645	11615	2641	2001

资料来源：北京市高级人民法院。
Source: The People's High Court of Beijing.

21-24 检察机关办理各类案件情况(2014年)
STATISTICS FOR CASES HANDLED BY PROCURATORIAL ORGANS (2014)

项目	Item	受案(受理) Cases Accepted		审结案合计 Cases Settled	
		件 Case	人 Person	件 Case	人 Person
审查逮捕	**Arrests to Be Examined and Approved**	**16594**	**21352**	**16606**	**21364**
批准逮捕	Approved			12923	16085
不批准逮捕	Disapproved			3683	5279
审查起诉	**Prosecution to Be Reviewed and Made**	**22251**	**27748**	**22455**	**27784**
起诉	Prosecuted			20643	25194
不起诉	Non-prosecution			1767	2537
附条件不起诉	Conditional Non-prosecution			45	53
举报案件	**Reported Cases**	**3180**		**3139**	
控告案件	**Complaints**	**2137**		**2133**	
申诉案件	**Appeal Cases**	**2437**		**2436**	
民事、行政案件	**Civil and Administrative Cases**				
民事检察案件	Civil Cases	1202		1097	
行政检察案件	Administrative Cases	222		218	

资料来源：北京市人民检察院。
Source: The People's Procuratorate of Beijing.

21-25 查办贪污贿赂、渎职侵权案件情况(2014年)
STATISTICS FOR CORRUPTION, BRIBERY, MALPRACTICE AND INFRINGEMENT CASES (2014)

项目		Item		查办贪污贿赂案件 Corruption and Bribery Cases	贪污案 Corruption Cases	贿赂案 Bribery Cases	挪用公款案 Misappropriation of Public Funds	其他 Others	渎职侵权案件 Malpractice and Infringement Cases
受案	**(件)**	**Cases Accepted**	**(case)**	**1087**	**349**	**674**	**40**	**24**	**291**
立案		**Cases Registered**							
件数	(件)	Number of Cases	(case)	382	81	279	17	5	75
人数	(人)	Persons involved	(person)	429	99	306	18	6	78
大案	**(件)**	**Major Cases**	**(case)**						
按查办贪污贿赂案件类型分		**By Type of Corruption and Bribery Case**							
5至10万元(不含)	(件)	50000-100000 Yuan	(case)	34	13	21			
10至50万元(不含)	(件)	100000-500000 Yuan	(case)	117	26	85	6		
50至100万元(不含)	(件)	500000-1000000 Yuan	(case)	64	8	56			
100至1000万元(不含)	(件)	1000000-10000000 Yuan	(case)	108	25	76	7		
1000万元及以上	(件)	Above 10000000 Yuan	(case)	12	1	8	3		
按查办渎职侵权案件类型分		**By Type of Malpractice and Infringement Case**							
重大	(件)	Serious Cases	(case)						20
特大	(件)	Extraordinary Serious Cas	(case)						11
要案	**(人)**	**Important Cases**	**(person)**						
县处级	(人)	County Level	(person)	78	21	50	2	5	15
地厅级	(人)	Departmental Level	(person)	43	5	36	2		
省部级以上	(人)	Above Provincial Level	(person)	2		2			
侦结		**Cases Closed**							
件数	(件)	Number of Cases	(case)	278	86	169	18	5	69
人数	(人)	Number of Persons	(person)	314	102	186	18	8	69
#移送起诉		Handed over to Law Suit							
件数	(件)	Number of Cases	(case)	271	83	166	17	5	65
人数	(人)	Number of Persons	(person)	307	99	183	17	8	65
#移送不起诉		Handed over yet Immunity from Suit							
件数	(件)	Number of Cases	(case)						4
人数	(人)	Number of Persons	(person)						4
挽回经济损失	**(万元)**	**Economic Losses Redeemed**	**(10000 yuan)**	**9050**	**3462**	**4453**	**903**	**232**	**210**

资料来源：北京市人民检察院。
Source: The People's Procuratorate of Beijing.

21-26 刑事案件情况
STATISTICS FOR CRIMINAL CASES

单位：起 (case)

项 目	Item	2014	2013	2014年为2013年% 2014 as % of 2013
刑事案件	**Criminal Cases**			
立 案	Cases Registered	153334	140498	109.1
破 案	Cases Settled	122383	112594	108.7

资料来源：北京市公安局。
Source: Beijing Municipal Bureau of Public Security.

21-27 消防建设情况(1996-2014年)
STATISTICS FOR FIRECONTROL (1996-2014)

年 份 Year	公安消防队数 (支) Number of Fire Brigades of Public Security (unit)	公安消防车辆 (辆) Number of Fire-fighting Vehicles of Public Security (unit)	企业专职消防队队数 (支) Number of Full-time Fire Brigades in Enterprises (unit)	企业专职消防队人数 (人) Persons of Full-time Fire-fighters in Enterprises (person)
1996	36	180	101	1865
1997	38	190	104	1885
1998	41	210	108	1993
1999	44	236	120	2447
2000	47	259	120	2447
2001	50	266	120	2447
2002	52	296	112	2228
2003	56	303	112	2147
2004	57	381	120	2477
2005	57	342	120	2477
2006	64	357	109	2269
2007	69	401	109	2269
2008	77	558	109	2269
2009	86	572	109	2269
2010	91	664	109	2269
2011	98	604	87	1766
2012	107	670	76	1405
2013	122	735	76	1405
2014	125	799	76	1405

资料来源：北京市公安局消防局。
Source: Fire Department of Beijing Municipal Bureau of Public Security.

21-28 火灾及损失
FIRE ACCIDENTS AND LOSSES

项目	Item	数量 Number 2014	数量 Number 2013	直接经济损失(万元) Direct Economic Losses (10000 yuan) 2014	直接经济损失(万元) Direct Economic Losses (10000 yuan) 2013
火灾起数 (起)	**Fire Accidents (case)**	**4477**	**4214**	**6854.9**	**5265.9**
特别重大火灾	Extraordinarily Serious				
重大火灾	Serious		1		200.0
较大火灾	Big Fire		3		1434.5
一般火灾	Relatively Big Fire	4477	4210	6854.9	3631.4
起火原因	**Cause of Fire**				
电气	Electricity and Gas	1321	1348	4292.8	3110.8
生产作业	Violation of Operation	114	165	452.8	526.2
生活用火不慎	Carelessness in Fire Use	704	634	611.0	179.9
吸烟	Smoking	100	105	43.5	74.7
玩火	Fire Playing	47	56	30.3	40.1
自燃	Spontaneous Combustion	117	111	344.7	87.1
雷击	Thunderstroke	3	14	2.8	9.5
静电	Static	2	3	2.5	3.2
放火	Incendiarism	107	135	119.5	211.8
其他	Others	1962	1643	955.0	1022.7
受伤人数 (人)	**Number of Injuries (person)**	**15**	**18**		
死亡人数 (人)	**Number of Deaths (person)**	**51**	**53**		

资料来源：北京市公安局消防局。
Source: Fire Department of Beijing Municipal Bureau of Public Security.

21-29 安全生产情况
STATISTICS FOR SAFE PRODUCTION

项目	Item	2014	2013
亿元地区生产总值安全生产事故死亡率 (人/亿元)	Death Rate of Work Accidents Per 100 million yuan GDP (person/100 million yuan)	0.051	0.053
工矿商贸企业从业人员10万人生产安全事故死亡率 (人/10万人)	Death Rate of Work Accidents in the Mining, Commercial and Trade Industries Per 100,000 Persons (1/100000)	0.94	0.94
煤矿百万吨死亡率 (人/百万吨)	The Death Rate of Coal Mines Per Million Tons (Person/million tons)	0.91	0.40
道路交通万车死亡率 (人/万车)	Road Traffic Death Rate Per 10000 Vehicles (person/10000 vehicles)	1.65	1.58
65大类食品检验合格率 (%)	Up-to -standard Rate in Inspection on 65 Categories of Food (%)	97.46	97.41
#重点食品安全监测抽检合格率 (%)	Up-to-standard Rate of Key Foods Security Monitor Spot Checks (%)	98.39	98.35
药品抽验合格率 (%)	Up-to-standard Rate of Drug Spot Checks (%)	99.88	99.88

数据来源：北京市食品药品监督管理局、北京市公安交通管理局、北京市安全生产监督管理局。
Source: Beijing Municipal Food and Drug Administration, Beijing Municipal Bureau of Traffic Management, Beijing Administration of Work Safety.

21-30 交通事故及损失
STATISTICS FOR TRAFFIC ACCIDENTS AND LOSSES

项目	Item	2014	2013	2014年为2013年% 2014 as % of 2013
交通事故	**Traffic Accidents**			
交通事故发生数 (起)	Number of Traffic Accidents (case)	3268	3063	106.7
受伤人数 (人)	Number of Injuries (person)	3362	3359	100.1
死亡人数 (人)	Number of Deaths (person)	923	860	107.3
机动车事故	**Motor Vehicle Accidents**			
机动车事故发生数 (起)	Number of Motor Vehicle Accidents (case)	2754	2477	111.2
受伤人数 (人)	Number of Injuries (person)	2498	2357	106.0
死亡人数 (人)	Number of Deaths (person)	763	668	114.2
直接经济损失 (万元)	**Direct Economic Losses (10000 yuan)**	**3129.2**	**2805.2**	**111.5**
每万辆机动车死亡人数 (人)	**Persons Died Per 10,000 Motor Vehicles (person)**	**1.65**	**1.58**	**104.4**

资料来源：北京市公安局公安交通管理局。
Source: Beijing Municipal Bureau of Traffic Management.

21-31 地震应急避难场所情况
EMERGENT EARTHQUAKE REFUGES

项目	Item	2014	2013
地震应急避难场所累计个数 (个)	Total Number of Emergent Earthquake Refuges (unit)	94	92
地震应急避难场所累计面积 (万平方米)	Total Area of Emergent Earthquake Refuges (10000 sq.m)	1644	1648

资料来源：北京市地震局。
Source: Beijing Municipal Bureau of Earthquake.

21-32 妇联组织状况
STATISTICS FOR WOMEN'S FEDERATIONS AND ORGANIZATIONS

单位：个，人 (unit,person)

项目	Item	2014	2013	2014年为2013年% 2014 as % of 2013
妇联组织状况	**Status of Women's Federations and Organizations**			
区妇联数	Number of Women's Federations in Districts	14	14	100.0
县妇联数	Number of Women's Federations in Counties	2	2	100.0
乡、镇妇联组织数	Number of Women's Federations in Townships	182	115	158.3
街道妇联组织数	Number of Women's Federations in Subdistricts	145	214	67.8
妇联干部状况	**Status of Cadres in Women's Federation**			
区妇联干部数	Cadres in Women's Federations in Districts	250	253	98.8
县妇联干部数	Cadres in Women's Federations in Counties	33	35	94.3
乡、镇、街道妇联干部数	Cadres in Women's Federations in Townships, Towns and Subdistricts	327	321	101.9
妇联基层妇代会组织个数	**Number of Grass-root Women Congresses of Women's Federations**			
城市	Urban	2951	2719	108.5
农村	Rural	3709	3941	94.1
各类妇女联谊组织数	**Women's Sodalities**	**31**	**31**	**100.0**

资料来源：北京市妇女联合会。
Source: Beijing Women's Federation.

21-33 工会组织建设情况(2014年)
STATISTICS FOR LABOR UNIONS (2014)

项 目	Item	基层工会组织 (个) Grassroot Labor Unions (unit)	职工人数 (人) Number of Employed Persons (person)	会员人数 (人) Number of Members (person)
合 计	**Total**	**33687**	**4698528**	**4190760**
按单位类别划分	**By Registration Type**			
国有企业	State-owned Enterprises	1463	616321	591850
集体企业	Collectively-owned Enterprises	1631	135140	122170
股份合作企业	Joint-equity Cooperative Enterprises	621	79830	65400
联营企业	Associated Enterprises	62	4087	3978
国有独资公司	Solely State-owned Enterprises	397	177056	160746
其他有限责任公司	Other Limited-Liability Companies	10358	1022732	836060
国有控股公司	State-holding Companies	387	339553	323513
其他股份有限公司	Other Holding Companies	1064	194647	164840
私营企业	Private Enterprises	6617	497675	385921
其他内资企业	Other Domestically-invested Enterprises	62	3990	3316
港澳台商投资企业	Hong Kong, Macao and Taiwan-invested Enterprises	374	99036	81422
外商投资企业	Foreign-invested Enterprises	888	308662	283568
事业单位	Public Institutions	4304	630164	598841
机 关	Governmental Agencies and Organizations	1486	233907	228773
其 他	Others	3973	355728	340362
按系统分	**By System**			
工业国防工会	Labor Unions for Industry and National Defence	761	381890	364702
工 业	Industry	17	11811	11694
国 防	National Defence	744	370079	353008
建筑工会	Construction	1545	709649	538661
本 市	Local	458	213736	202592
市 外	Non-local	1087	495913	336069
服务业工会	Services	760	260103	240670
交通运输工会	Transportation	206	300699	299823
机关事业部	Governmental Institutions	307	115644	113600
教育工会	Education	86	149547	136238
金融工会	Finance	69	121660	117177
市直机关工会	Institutions under Direct Municipal Leadership	387	49255	46750
区县工会	Labor Unions in Districts and Counties	29566	2610081	2333139

资料来源：北京市总工会。
Source: Beijing Federation of Labor Unions.

21-34 北京市妇女发展规划监测统计资料
SUPERVISORY STATISTICS ON WOMEN DEVELOPMENT PROGRAMS OF BEIJING

项目		Item		2014	2013
城镇单位就业人员数	(万人)	Employed Persons in Urban Entites	(10000 persons)	755.9	742.3
#女性		Females		303.3	298.3
城镇登记失业人员总数	(万人)	Urban Registered Unemployment	(10000 persons)	25.2	24.8
#女性		Females		10.2	9.9
城镇登记失业人员就业人数	(万人)	Employed Persons from Urban Registered Unemployment	(10000 persons)	16.9	16.9
#女性		Females		6.9	6.8
参加基本养老保险人数	(万人)	Number of Participants in Basic Pension Insurance	(10000 persons)	1392.6	1311.3
#女性		Females		633.2	595.5
参加基本医疗保险人数	(万人)	Number of Participants in Basic Medical Insurance	(10000 persons)	1431.3	1354.8
#女性		Females		660.8	624.8
参加失业保险人数	(万人)	Number of Participants in Unemployment Insurance	(10000 persons)	1057.1	1025.1
#女性		Females		464.4	450.1
参加工伤保险人数	(万人)	Number of Participants in Work Injury Insurance	(10000 persons)	961.0	920.3
#女性		Females		407.7	388.5
城乡居民养老保险参保人数	(万人)	Number of Urban and Rural Residents Participating in Basic Pension Insurance for Urban and Rural Residents	(10000 persons)	186.2	180.1
#女性		Females		96.7	92.8
市人大女代表领衔提出的议案数	(件)	Number of Proposals Put Forward by Women Deputies of Beijing Municipal People's Congress(BMPC)	(case)	19	8
市政协女委员提出的提案数	(件)	Number of Proposals Put Forward by Women Deputies of Beijing Committee of Chinese People's Political Consultative Conference	(case)	401	585
普通高校在校学生人数	(万人)	Enrollment in Institutions of Higher Education	(10000 persons)	59.5	58.9
#女性		Females		30.6	30.4
在读研究生人数	(万人)	Number of Enrolled Postgraduates	(10000 persons)	27.4	26.6
#女性		Females		12.9	12.5
成人本专科在校生人数	(万人)	Enrollment of Technical Higher and Secondary Education for Adults	(10000 persons)	23.8	25.8
#女性		Females		13.2	14.5
妇科病普查率	(%)	Rate of Gynaopathy General Surveys	(%)	50.7	15.6
乳腺癌检出率	(1/10万)	Detection Rate of Breast Cancer	(1/100000)	30.0	20.0
宫颈癌检出率	(1/10万)	Detection Rate of Cervical Cancer	(1/100000)	4.9	5.0
高危孕产妇住院分娩率	(%)	Birth-giving Rate of High-risk Lying-in Women in Hospitals	(%)	100.0	100.0
已婚育龄妇女综合避孕率	(%)	Practising Contraception Rate of Married Women of Child Bearing Age	(%)	77.3	77.1
抓获刑事作案成员中女性比例	(%)	Share of Females in Criminal Suspects Captured	(%)	18.5	17.7
得到法律援助机构援助的妇女人数	(人)	Number of Women Receiving Aids from Law Aid Institutions	(person)	6132	4928

21-35 北京市儿童发展规划监测统计资料
SUPERVISORY STATISTICS FOR CHILDREN DEVELOPMENT IN BEIJING

项目		Item		2014	2013
婚前医学检查率	(%)	Rate of Premarital Medical Checks	(%)	6.8	7.2
新生儿遗传代谢性疾病筛查率	(%)	Screening Rate of Genic Metabolic Diseases for Newborn	(%)	98.6	99.8
出生缺陷监测率	(%)	Monitoring Rate of Birth Deficiencies	(%)	100.0	100.0
新生儿听力筛查率	(%)	Screening Rate of Hearing for Newborns	(%)	96.54	96.95
出生缺陷发生率	(‰)	Rate of Birth Deficiencies	(‰)	14.02	14.70
7岁以下儿童保健管理率	(%)	Rate of Health Management for Children Under 7 Years Old	(%)	97.88	98.37
0-6个月婴儿纯母乳喂养率	(%)	Rate of Exclusive Breast Breeding for Infants of 0-6 Months	(%)	71.22	70.01
婴儿死亡率	(‰)	Mortality Rate of Infants	(‰)	2.33	2.33
5岁以下儿童死亡率	(‰)	Mortality Rate of Children below 5 Years Old	(‰)	2.89	2.89
儿童肥胖率	(%)	Rate of Obesity for Children	(%)	5.08	5.06
儿童龋齿率	(%)	Rate of Decayed Teeth for Children	(%)	37.55	36.74
卡介苗疫苗接种率	(%)	Rate of Inoculation of BCG Vaccines	(%)	99.86	99.84
脊髓灰质炎疫苗接种率	(%)	Rate of Inoculation of Poliomyelities Polio Vaccines	(%)	99.55	99.87
百白破疫苗接种率	(%)	Rate of Inoculation of Pertussis, Diphtheria and Tetanus Vaccines	(%)	99.55	99.87
含麻疹成分疫苗接种率	(%)	Rate of Inoculation of Vaccines with Measle Ingredients	(%)	99.64	99.84
孕产妇系统管理率	(%)	Rate of Systematic Management for Pregnant and Lying-in	(%)	97.43	97.06
城市		Urban		96.99	96.57
农村		Rural		98.26	98.03
孕产妇健康教育普及率	(%)	Popularization Rate of Health Education for Pregnant and Lying-in Women	(%)	99.97	99.94
孕产妇住院分娩率	(%)	Birth-giving Rate of Pregnant and Lying-in Women in Hospital	(%)	100.0	100.0
孕产妇死亡率	(1/10万)	Mortality Rate of Pregnant and Lying-in Women	(1/100000)	7.19	9.45

21-36 北京市历届人代会代表人数性别构成及议案、建议数
NUMBER AND SEX COMPOSITION OF DEPUTIES、NUMBERS OF PROPOSALS AND SUGGESTIONS AT PREVIOUS SESSIONS OF PEOPLE'S CONGRESS OF BEIJING

单位：人、%、件 (person,%,case)

项目 Item	代表人数 Number of Deputies			性别比例 Sex Percentage		议案立案数 Number of Proposals on Record	建议数 Suggestions
	合计 Total	女性 Females	男性 Males	女性 Females	男性 Males		
第一届 1st	564	106	458	18.8	81.2		
第二届 2nd	619	142	477	22.9	77.1		
第三届 3rd	618	162	456	26.2	73.8		
第四届 4th	745	202	543	27.1	72.9		
第五届 5th	751	203	548	27.0	73.0		
第七届 7th	1195	325	870	27.1	72.9		
第八届 8th	973	252	721	25.9	74.1	55	6644
第九届 9th	880	217	663	24.7	75.3	86	7921
第十届 10th	885	224	661	25.3	74.7	156	7281
第十一届 11th	763	197	566	25.8	74.2	166	9717
第十二届 12th	762	235	527	30.8	69.2	276	9859
第十三届 13th	779	237	542	30.4	69.6	153	7576
第十四届 14th	771	257	514	33.3	66.7	64	2539

注：1. 北京市人大常委会是经北京市七届三次人民代表大会选举成立的，故一至七届人代会无议案及建议数。
2. 代表人数为届首选举数，议案及建议数均是本届五年会上及平时议案及建议的合计数。
3. 第十四届议案立案及建议数截止到2014年12月底。

资料来源：北京市人民代表大会常务委员会。

Note: a) Standing Committee of Beijing People's Congress was established upon election at the 3rd Session of Beijing 7th People's Congress. As a result, there were no proposals and suggestions at the 1st-7th People's Congresses.
b) Deputies were those first elected for that term. Proposals and suggestions at other terms of Congress included those at the meeting of the term and/or at ordinary times.
c) Data of proposals and suggestions of 14th Congress was counted by the end of december of 2014.

Source: Standing Committee of Beijing Municipal People's Congress (BMPC).

21-37 北京市历届政协会委员人数及提案立案数
NUMBER OF MEMBERS AND PROPOSALS AT HISTORICAL BEIJING CPPCC

单位：人、件 (person,case)

届别 Term	起止年月 Beginning-ending Month	委员人数 Number of Members			提案立案数 Number of Proposals on Record
		合计 Total	女性 Females	男性 Males	
第一届 1st	1955.04-1959.09	270	40	230	37
第二届 2nd	1959.09-1962.12	463	84	379	13
第三届 3rd	1962.12-1965.09	519	92	427	884
第四届 4th	1965.09-1977.11	529	88	441	23
第五届 5th	1977.11-1983.03	779	161	618	1610
第六届 6th	1983.03-1988.01	766	168	598	3122
第七届 7th	1988.01-1993.01	703	179	524	4276
第八届 8th	1993.01-1998.01	740	185	555	4975
第九届 9th	1998.01-2003.01	782	203	579	6240
第十届 10th	2003.01-2008.01	824	226	598	6871
第十一届 11th	2008.01-2013.01	737	233	504	5354
第十二届 12th	2013.01-2014.12	758	236	522	1693

资料来源：中国人民政治协商会议北京市委员会。

Source: The Chinese People's Political Consultative Conference Beijing Committe.

主要统计指标解释

优抚对象 依照法律和政策的规定，享受国家、社会和群众抚恤优待的人员，包括中国人民解放军（包括中国人民武装警察部队）现役军人、革命伤残人员、复员退伍军人、革命烈士家属、因公牺牲军人家属、病故军人家属、现役军人家属。

社会救助对象总人数 指在报告期末生活在当地规定的最低生活保障线以下的家庭人员及国家规定由民政部门救济的特殊人员和60年代精简退职老职工救济人员等。

城市居民最低生活保障人数 指报告期末家庭平均收入在当地规定的最低生活保障线以下的城镇居民数。包括“三无”对象、失业人员和在职、下岗、退休人员等。

农村居民最低生活保障人数 指报告期末在建立农村最低生活保障制度的地区，得到当地政府或集体给予最低生活保障的农业人口家庭人数。

参加基本养老保险人数 指报告期末按照国家法律、法规和有关政策规定参加基本养老保险并在社保经办机构已建立缴费记录档案的职工人数，包括中断缴费但未终止养老保险关系的职工人数和参加基本养老保险的离休、退休和退职人员的人数。不包括只登记未建立缴费记录档案的人数。

参加基本医疗保险人数 指报告期末按国家有关规定参加基本医疗保险的人数。包括参加保险的职工人数和退休人员数。

参加失业保险人数 指报告期末按照国家法律、法规和有关政策规定参加了失业保险的城镇企业事业单位的职工及地方政府规定参加失业保险的其他人员的人数。参加失业保险人数为参加失业保险的职工人数。

参加工伤保险人数 指报告期末参加工伤保险的职工人数。

参加生育保险人数 指报告期末参加生育保险的职工人数。

农村居民参加城乡居民养老保险人数 指截止报告期末参加城乡居民养老保险的农村居民人数。

参加农村新型合作医疗人数 指截止报告期末乡镇已参加农村新型合作医疗的总人数。农村新型合作医疗制度是由政府组织、引导、支持，农民自愿参加，集体、个人和政府多方筹资，以大病统筹为主的农民医疗互助共济制度。

社区服务机构数 指报告期末社区服务站、社区服务中心、其它社区服务设施的总和。

律师 指受聘参加律师事务所工作，提任法律顾问、刑（民）事代理人、刑事辩护人，办理非诉讼事件、解答法律询问，代写法律事务文书等主要从事律师业务的专职法律工作者和兼职律师。

公证人员 指在国家公证机关依法办理公证事务的司法人员。包括公证员、助理公证员和在公证处工作的其他人员。

办理公证文书 指公证处在一定时期内办结的公证文书件数。公证文书系按司法部规定或批准的格式制作。

调解人员 指人民调解委员会担负调解民间一般民事纠纷和轻微违法行为所引起的纠纷的工作人员。包括调解委员会的委员和调解小组调解员。

调解民间纠纷 指调解委员会依照法律规定，根据自愿原则，用说服教育的方法调解民间发生的有关民事权利和义务的争执，促成当事双方达到协议和谅解，解决纠纷。包括婚姻家庭纠纷，财产权益纠纷等。不包括法院受理调解的民事案件数。

地震应急避难场所 指适用于地震等自然灾害，也适用于其他事件应急状态下，供居民紧急疏散的公园、公共绿地、城市广场、体育场、学校运动场等场地数量。

Explanatory Notes on Main Statistical Indicators

Persons Receiving Special Care refer to persons receiving special treatment from the country, society and the public in accordance with provisions in laws and policies, including active servicemen of PLA (including the People's Armed Policy Army), persons wounded and disabled due to revolution, veterans, military dependents of revolutionary martyrs, military dependents of servicemen who sacrificed on duty, military dependents of servicemen who died of illness, military dependents of active servicemen.

Total Number of Persons Receiving Social Relief refer to the number of family members living under the minimum living standard provided by local governments, special persons receiving relief by civil affair authorities in line with national regulations, as well as employed persons retired because of streamlining in the 1960s, at the end of the reporting period.

Number of Persons Receiving Subsistence Allowances in Urban Areas refers to the number of urban residents whose average family income is below locally provided minimum living standard, including elderly persons, minors, psychotic patients and disables who have no statutory guardian, no fixed pocketbook, no labor ability, unemployed persons, on-the-job persons, laid-off persons, and retired persons, etc.

Number of Persons Receiving Subsistence Allowances in Rural Areas refers to the number of persons in agricultural families covered by subsistence allowances of local government or collective entities in an area where rural minimum living standard guarantee system is established, at the end of reporting period.

Number of People Participating in Basic Pension Insurance refers to the number of employed persons participating in basic pension insurance and keeping insurance premium payment records with social security organizations in accordance with provisions in national laws, rules and relevant policies at the end of reporting period, including the number of employed persons suspending the payment of insurance premium without terminating the pension insurance relation as well as retired employed persons participating in basic endowment insurance, excluding the number of persons only registered but having no insurance premium payment records.

Number of People Participating in Basic Medical Insurance refers to the number of persons participating in medical insurance programs at the end of the reporting period in accordance with relevant national regulations, including the number of employed persons and retired persons participating in the insurance.

Number of People Participating in Unemployment Insurance refers to the number of employed persons in urban enterprises and public institutions participating in unemployment insurance programs at the end of the reporting period in accordance with provisions in national laws, rules and relevant policies, as well as other persons specified by local governments to participate in unemployment insurance. The number of persons participating in unemployment insurance program is the number of employees who participate in unemployment insurance.

Number of People Participating in Work-related Injury Insurance refers to the number of persons participating in work injury insurance programs at the end of the reporting period.

Number of People Participating in Maternity Insurance refers to the number of persons participating in maternity insurance programs at the end of the reporting period.

Number of People Participating in Rural Basic Pension Insurance refers to the number of rural residents who had participated in urban and rural pension insurance programs by the end of the reporting period.

Number of People Participating in New-type Rural Cooperative Medicare refers to the total number of persons who had participated in the rural new-type cooperative medical service by the end of reporting period. The rural new-type cooperative medical service system is a mutual aid medical system for farmers, focusing on general health care programs for major diseases, organized, guided and supported by government, with farmers' voluntary participation.

Number of Service Facilities in Urban Communities refers to the total number of community service stations, service centers, and other service facilities, by the end of reporting period.

Lawyer refers to a full-time legal worker and part-time lawyer joining a law firm, serving as a legal consultant, criminal (civil) proxy, criminal counsel, handling non-lawsuit events, answering legal questions, writing legal documents for others, and other lawyer business.

Notary refers to any judicial person handling notarization matters in national notarization agencies according to laws, including notaries, assistant notaries, and other personnel working in notarization offices.

Notarization Documents Executed refers to the number of notarization documents executed at notarization offices within a given period of time. Notarization documents are prepared in the format specified or approved by the Ministry of Justice.

Mediator refer to working personnel responsible for mediating general civil disputes as well as disputes caused by slightly illegal acts in any people's mediation committee, including members of people's mediation committees and mediators of mediation teams.

Mediation of Civil Disputes refers to the mediation of disputes against civil rights and obligations by mediation committees on voluntary basis and in accordance with provisions in laws in order to urge both parties to reach an agreement and understanding to resolve the dispute, including marriage and family disputes, property rights and interest disputes, etc., excluding the number of civil cases accepted by courts.

Emergent Earthquake Refuges refer to the number of parks, public green land, city squares, gyms, school playgrounds for residents' emergent evacuation in the event of natural disasters such as earthquake, and under the condition of other emergent events.

22

第三产业
TERTIARY INDUSTRY

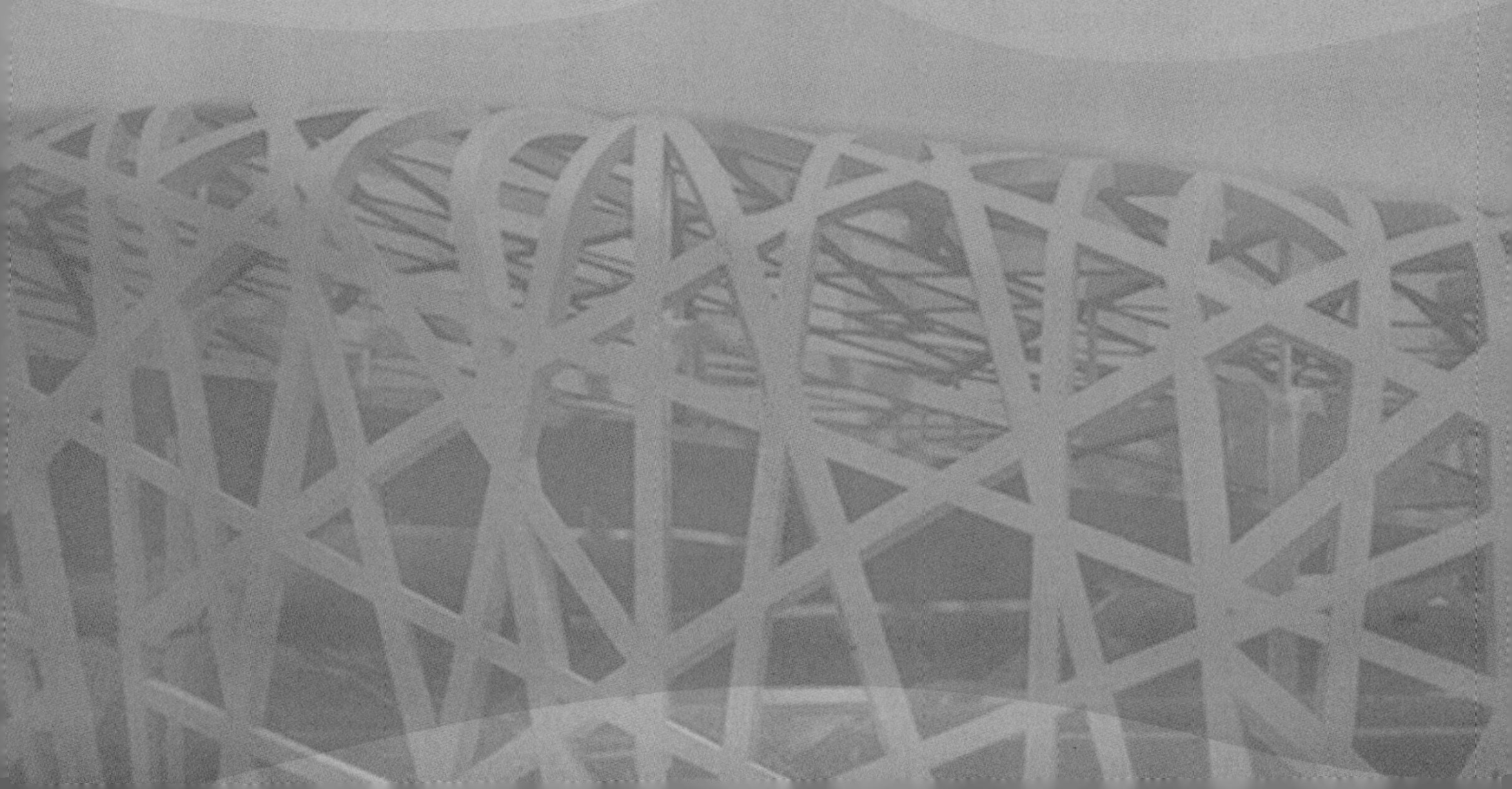

简要说明

一、本章资料的主要内容

本章主要内容包括第三产业主要指标、规模以上第三产业主要指标、规模以上第三产业企业财务状况、北京地区服务贸易、文化创意产业、物流业、会展活动和体育及相关产业活动情况等。

二、本章资料的数据来源

本章除北京地区服务贸易情况由北京市商务委员会提供外，其他资料由北京市统计局、国家统计局北京调查总队提供。

三、本章资料的统计范围

本章规模以上第三产业是指除国际组织以外的各行业限额以上的法人单位。2014 年具体为房地产开发业的全部法人单位；金融业为全部金融监管法人单位及年营业收入 500 万元及以上的非金融监管的金融业法人单位；批发业为年主营业务收入 2000 万元及以上的企业；零售业为年主营业务收入 500 万元及以上的企业；住宿业为星级饭店和星级以外年主营业务收入 200 万元及以上企业；餐饮业为年主营业务收入 200 万元及以上的企业；居民服务、修理和其他服务业，文化、体育和娱乐业为年营业收入 500 万元或从业人员期末人数 50 人及以上的企业；其余行业为年营业收入 1000 万元及以上或从业人员期末人数 50 人及以上的企业；执行行政事业、民间非营利组织会计制度收入合计 1000 万元及以上的法人单位。

文化创意产业资料根据文化创意产业法人单位的统计年报等有关资料测算取得。

物流业统计范围主要涉及铁路运输业、道路运输业、水上运输业、航空运输业、管道运输业、装卸搬运和运输代理业、仓储业、邮政业、包装服务业、批发业、零售业和工业企业。

会展业统计对象涉及会展活动的举办服务单位和接待单位。具体包括星级宾馆饭店及星级以外年主营业务收入 200 万元及以上的宾馆饭店、从事各种会展活动的场馆、大型会展活动的举办单位（名单主要由北京市公安局提供）以及为会展活动提供各类专业服务的规模以上单位和旅行社。由于每年的统计对象单位范围不完全相同（有新增或撤消单位），为保持数据的可比性，同时列出统计对象本年和上年数据。

体育及相关产业情况根据体育及相关产业单位的统计年报等有关资料汇总计算，执行 2008 年国家体育总局、国家统计局颁布的《体育及相关产业分类（试行）》标准。

四、有关统计标准的变化说明

（一）关于行业划分。根据国家统计局规定，自 2012 年开始执行《国民经济行业分类》GB/T 4754-2011 标准。

（二）关于三次产业划分。根据国家统计局《三次产业划分规定》(国统字[2012]108 号)，该规定对三次产业的范围进行了调整。其中第一产业是指农、林、牧、渔业（不含农、林、牧、渔服务业）；第二产业是指采矿业（不含开采辅助活动），制造业（不含金属制品、机械和设备修理业），电力、热力、燃气及水生产和供应业，建筑业；第三产业是指除第一产业、第二产业以外的其他行业。自 2012 年开始执行此规定。

Brief Introduction

I. Main Content

This chapter includes: main indicators for tertiary industry, main indicators for tertiary industry above designated size, financial status of tertiary industry above designated size, service trade, cultural and creative industry, logistics industry, exhibition activities, sports and activities in related sectors in Beijing.

II. Date Source

Except for the data on service trade in Beijing, which are acquired from Beijing Municipal Commission of Commerce, other data are provided by Beijing Municipal Bureau of Statistics, and NBS Survey Office in Beijing.

III. Scope of Statistics

In this chapter, the tertiary industry above designated size refers to corporate enterprises above designated size other than international organizations. In 2014, it includes all corporate enterprises in real estate development sectors, all corporate enterprises under financial regulation and the ones without financial regulation whose annual business income hitting RMB 5 million and more in finance, enterprises with annual main business income of RMB 20 million and more in wholesale trade, enterprises with annual main business income of RMB 5 million and more in retail trade, star-level hotels and non-star-level enterprises with annual main business income of RMB 2 million and more in accommodation, enterprises with annual main business income of RMB 2 million and more in restaurants, enterprises with annual business income of RMB 5 million and above or with period-end employees of 50 and above in resident service, repair, other services, culture, sports and entertainment, enterprises with annual business income of RMB 10 million and above or with period-end employees of 50 and above in other sectors, and corporate enterprises with total income of RMB 10 million and more following accounting system designed for administrative institutions and non-profit private organizations.

Data on cultural and creative industry were calculated based on annual statistical reports and other related materials of corporate enterprises in cultural and creative sector.

The statistical scope of logistics include enterprises in railway transport, road transport, water transport, air transport, transport via pipelines, loading, unloading, portage, storage, post, packaging services, wholesale trade, retail trade and industrial enterprises above designated size.

Statistical scope of MICE industry covers service companies and reception companies holding the exhibitions, in details, including: star-level hotels and those hotels with annual main business income of RMB 2 million and more; venues for exhibitions; sponsors of large exhibitions (with the list provided by Beijing Municipal Bureau of Public Security) together with organizations providing various professional services to exhibitions. Statistics for MICE in 2013 are calculated after collecting data from annual statistical report and relevant departments. As the scope of companies under survey is not completely the same (there are companies newly added and phasing out), data in both the current year and previous year are collected from the surveyed companies to keep the data comparable.

Data on sports and related industry were calculated according to the data in annual statistical reports and other related materials. As for the scope of statistics, the standards in the *Classification of Sports and Related Industry (Temporary)* issued by the State Administration for Sports and National Bureau of Statistics were applied.

IV. Changes in Relevant Statistical Standards

(I) Classification of Sectors. According to relevant provisions of National Bureau of Statistics, the *Classification of National Economic Sectors* (Standard GB/T4754-2011) came into effect in 2012.

(II) Classification of Three Industries. According to the *Regulations on Three Industries Classification* (G.T.Z. [2012] No. 108) of National Bureau of Statistics, the scope of three industries has been adjusted. The primary industry refers to agriculture, forestry, animal production and hunting, fishing (excluding service activities for agriculture, forestry, animal production and hunting, fishing); secondary industry refers to mining and quarrying (excluding mining support service activities), manufacturing (excluding repair of fabricated metal products, machinery and equipment), production and distribution of electricity, heating power, gas and water and construction; the tertiary industry refers to others excluding the primary and secondary industries. The Provisions of the National Bureau of Statistics on *Regulations on Three Industries Classification* (G.T.Z. [2012] No. 108) came into effect in 2012.

22-1 第三产业主要指标及占全市比重(2000-2014年)

项 目		Item		2000	2001	2002	2003
增加值	(亿元)	Value Added	(100 million yuan)	2049.1	2484.8	2982.6	3435.9
占全市比重	(%)	Percentage of the Total	(%)	64.8	67.0	69.1	68.6
劳动生产率	(元/人)	Overall Labor Productivity	(yuan/person)	61525	73082	83069	86864
相当于全市比例	(%)	Percentage of the Total	(%)	120.4	123.0	125.9	119.9
从业人员年末人数	(万人)	Year-end Employed Persons	(10000 persons)	338.2	341.8	376.3	414.8
占全市比重	(%)	Percentage of the Total	(%)	54.6	54.4	55.4	59.0
固定资产投资	(亿元)	Investment in Fixed Assets	(100 million yuan)	510.3	1367.9	1621.8	1875.4
占全市比重	(%)	Percentage of the Total	(%)	39.3	89.3	89.4	86.9
实际利用外资金额	(亿美元)	Actual Use of Foreign Capital	(USD 100 million)	22.2	12.8	12.5	14.0
占全市比重	(%)	Percentage of the Total	(%)	90.5	72.4	69.8	65.3
能源消费总量	(万吨标准煤)	Energy Consumption	(10000 tons of SCE)	1080.9	1196.2	1334.5	1391.0
占全市比重	(%)	Percentage of the Total	(%)	26.1	28.3	30.1	29.9

22-2 北京地区服务贸易情况(2003-2014年)

单位：亿美元

项 目	Item	2003	2004	2005
服务贸易总额	**Total Volume of Service Trade**	**162.24**	**235.70**	**300.74**
运 输	Transportation	42.73	66.79	80.06
旅 游	Tourism	30.87	48.60	54.93
通讯服务	Communication Services	8.71	7.41	8.55
建筑服务	Construction Services	10.66	11.90	19.56
保险服务	Insurance Services	8.91	11.90	14.91
金融服务	Financial Services	0.53	0.47	0.53
计算机和信息服务	Computer and Information Services	9.00	9.76	11.60
专利使用费和特许费	Patent and Royalty Fee	5.27	7.38	9.40
咨 询	Consultation	12.22	18.94	28.33
广告、宣传	Advertisements and Publicity	3.19	5.16	6.26
电影、音像	Movies and Audio-video Products	0.74	1.33	1.95
其他商业服务	Other Commercial Services	29.41	46.06	64.66

资料来源：北京市商务委员会。
Source: Beijing Municipal Commission of Commerce .

MAIN INDICATORS OF THE TERTIARY INDUSTRY AND THEIR PERCENTAGES OF BEIJING'S TOTAL (2000-2014)

2004	2005	2006	2007	2008	2009	2010	2011	2012	2013	2014
4092.2	4854.3	5837.6	7236.1	8375.8	9179.2	10600.8	12363.1	13669.9	14986.5	16627.0
67.8	69.6	71.9	73.5	75.4	75.5	75.1	76.1	76.5	76.9	77.9
83977	84828	95800	112388	122794	126872	140968	158613	167852	175066	187972
108.4	105.4	106.1	106.3	106.3	103.3	101.4	102.5	102.2	100.9	101.2
559.8	584.7	634.0	653.7	710.5	736.5	767.5	791.4	837.4	874.7	894.4
65.5	66.6	68.9	69.3	72.4	73.8	74.4	74.0	75.6	76.7	77.3
2112.7	2405.6	2993.8	3465.8	3434.4	4389.5	4922.3	5101.3	5597.5	6101.7	6681.6
83.6	85.1	88.8	87.4	89.2	90.3	89.6	86.3	86.6	86.8	88.4
19.2	23.0	34.5	40.8	44.4	52.0	56.3	62.4	69.1	70.1	79.3
62.4	65.2	75.8	80.6	72.9	84.9	88.5	88.5	85.9	82.2	87.7
1638.0	1918.7	2129.3	2389.5	2610.5	2760.3	2897.4	3100.5	3252.1	3423.0	3236.5
31.9	34.7	36.1	38.0	41.3	42.0	41.7	44.3	45.3	46.5	47.4

STATISTICS FOR SERVICE TRADE (2003-2014)

(USD 100 million)

2006	2007	2008	2009	2010	2011	2012	2013	2014
393.23	**503.06**	**691.92**	**644.10**	**798.29**	**895.40**	**1000.20**	**1023.30**	**1106.10**
107.29	110.96	144.38	140.50	177.11	196.30	223.21	215.40	223.60
68.22	94.13	88.66	92.90	108.68	136.10	155.48	195.90	327.10
11.49	18.39	24.28	17.20	17.62	21.50	26.15	24.20	31.00
23.69	46.28	79.56	74.30	87.16	92.40	85.23	59.80	116.30
19.85	23.54	72.85	58.60	92.22	133.10	132.14	152.90	70.40
0.53	1.79	1.93	4.70	8.09	11.70	22.16	1.60	12.20
18.32	24.74	29.25	28.80	39.83	52.00	60.19	74.20	89.40
14.39	16.80	20.38	16.40	21.11	22.60	28.40	35.70	30.80
43.28	57.91	84.38	81.10	89.47	99.10	116.36	142.30	144.30
7.40	10.02	12.90	10.80	13.19	17.80	19.61	20.30	15.40
1.82	3.85	5.51	2.70	3.56	3.40	4.91	5.90	10.80
76.95	94.65	127.82	116.00	140.27	109.50	126.36	95.10	34.80

22-3 北京地区服务贸易情况
STATISTICS FOR SERVICE TRADE

单位：亿美元 (USD 100 million)

项　目	Item	服务贸易总额 Total Turnover of Service Trade		外汇收入 Forex Income		外汇支出 Forex Payment		顺(逆)差 Surplus (Deficit)	
		2014	2013	2014	2013	2014	2013	2014	2013
合　计	**Total**	**1106.10**	**1023.30**	**435.00**	**426.90**	**671.10**	**596.40**	**-236.10**	**-169.50**
运　输	Transportation	223.60	215.40	51.50	50.80	172.10	164.60	-120.60	-113.80
旅　游	Tourism	327.10	195.90	46.30	47.90	280.80	148.00	-234.50	-100.10
通讯服务	Communication Services	31.00	24.20	11.80	12.20	19.20	12.00	-7.40	0.20
建筑服务	Construction Services	116.30	59.80	92.60	44.10	23.70	15.70	68.90	28.40
保险服务	Insurance Services	70.40	152.90	29.80	27.40	40.60	125.50	-10.80	-98.10
金融服务	Financial Services	12.20	1.60	1.20	0.30	11.00	1.30	-9.80	-1.00
计算机和信息服务	Computer and Information Services	89.40	74.20	53.50	51.60	35.90	22.60	17.60	29.00
专利使用费和特许费	Patent or Royalty Fee	30.80	35.70	2.40	3.90	28.40	31.80	-26.00	-27.90
咨　询	Consultation	144.30	142.30	100.40	103.90	43.90	38.40	56.50	65.50
广告、宣传	Advertisements and Publicity	15.40	20.30	10.40	12.70	5.00	7.60	5.40	5.10
电影、音像	Movies and Audio-video Products	10.80	5.90	0.90	0.60	9.90	5.30	-9.00	-4.70
其他商业服务	Other Commercial Services	34.80	95.10	34.20	71.50	0.60	23.60	33.60	47.90

资料来源：北京市商务委员会。
Source: Beijing Municipal Commission of Commerce .

22-4 规模以上第三产业主要指标(2004-2014年)
MAIN INDICATORS FOR TERTIARY INDUSTRY ENTERPRISES ABOVE DESIGNATED SIZE (2004-2014)

项 目		Item		2004	2005	2006	2007	2008
单位数	(个)	Number of Enterprises	(unit)	25725	23661	24921	25651	34820
从业人员平均人数	(万人)	Average Number of Employed Persons	(10000 persons)	301.4	323.3	340.4	373.5	443.6
资产总计	(亿元)	Total Assets	(100 million yuan)	184985.5	274180.3	336485.9	422458.7	579095.5
收入合计	(亿元)	Income	(100 million yuan)	21467.2	24444.6	29468.7	38361.8	47524.3
应交税金合计	(亿元)	Total Tax Payable	(100 million yuan)	908.1	1004.0	1376.0	2360.9	1855.2
企业利润总额	(亿元)	Total Profits	(100 million yuan)	1544.8	2696.1	2967.2	4511.2	4577.6

注：应交税金合计主要包括应交增值税、应交所得税、营业税金及附加和管理费用中的税金等。
Note: Total tax payable mainly includes VAT payable, income tax payable, business tax and surtax, and tax in management expenses, etc.

22-4 续表 Continued

项 目		Item		2009	2010	2011	2012	2013	2014
单位数	(个)	Number of Enterprises	(unit)	36177	36064	36102	36616	36504	36361
从业人员平均人数	(万人)	Average Number of Employed Persons	(10000 persons)	472.1	487.9	509.9	545.0	565.2	586.6
资产总计	(亿元)	Total Assets	(100 million yuan)	712313.4	798485.4	909953.5	1022849.7	1093973.1	1242344.8
收入合计	(亿元)	Total Income	(100 million yuan)	55390.3	69106.8	79246.0	92138.2	103398.8	110308.2
应交税金合计	(亿元)	Total Tax Payable	(100 million yuan)	2560.8	3122.4	4018.9	4652.8	5415.4	5998.0
企业利润总额	(亿元)	Total Profits	(100 million yuan)	10540.8	10236.3	11413.1	14248.4	18410.6	20601.7

22-5 规模以上第三产业单位主要经济指标(2013年)
MAIN INDICATORS FOR TERTIARY INDUSTRY ENTERPRISES ABOVE DESIGNATED SIZE (2013)

项目	Item	单位数 (个) Enter -prises (unit)	从业人员平均人数 (万人) Average Number of Employed Persons (10000 persons)	资产总计 (亿元) Total Assets (100 million yuan)	收入合计 (亿元) Total Incomes (100 million yuan)	应交税金合计 (亿元) Total Tax (100 million yuan)	利润总额 (亿元) Total Profits (100 million yuan)
合计	**Total**	**36504**	**565.2**	**1093973.1**	**103398.8**	**5415.4**	**18410.6**
按隶属关系分	**By Affiliation**						
中央	Central	4245	126.0	877666.6	47402.7	2920.4	13463.8
地方	Local	32259	439.2	216306.4	55996.1	2495.0	4946.8
按行业分	**By Sector**						
批发和零售业	Wholesale and Retail Trade	7462	71.8	32025.7	49352.5	777.7	1053.1
交通运输、仓储和邮政业	Transport, Storage and Post	1089	59.7	13161.6	4540.3	68.9	288.8
住宿和餐饮业	Accommodation and Restaurants	2927	39.1	1645.2	883.1	67.2	-1.3
信息传输、软件和信息技术服务业	Information Transmission,Software and Information Technology Services	2795	62.0	24904.6	5055.1	477.2	1889.7
金融业	Financial Intermediation	1783	37.6	870054.9	16079.1	2639.7	10612.6
房地产业	Real Estate	4622	40.6	42400.9	4701.7	669.9	819.4
租赁和商务服务业	Leasing and Business Services	6213	69.2	82185.1	8630.2	400.2	3072.2
科学研究和技术服务业	Scientific Research and Technical Services	3396	54.8	13966.7	6160.0	205.9	525.8
水利、环境和公共设施管理业	Management of Water Conservancy, Environment and Public Facilities	543	9.0	1535.3	457.4	12.4	21.7
居民服务、修理和其他服务业	Resident Services, Repair and Other Services	479	8.5	178.9	190.9	10.2	5.1
教育	Education	1538	38.1	3296.9	1481.5	14.4	14.2
卫生和社会工作	Health Care and Social Works	619	22.0	1171.0	1294.5	2.0	6.1
文化、体育和娱乐业	Culture, Sports and Entertainment	1285	15.8	3224.9	1344.0	67.5	103.2
公共管理、社会保障和社会组织	Pulic Administration,Social Security and Social Organizations	1753	37.1	4221.4	3228.3	2.2	
按登记注册类型分	**By Registration Type**						
内资	Domestic Investment Economy	33124	473.5	1050142.7	85566.5	4564.6	16006.6
国有	State-owned Units	6460	156.1	291757.5	16540.6	455.4	2365.6
集体	Collective-owned Units	570	5.9	1270.3	281.3	10.8	16.9
股份合作	Share Holding	387	3.0	553.8	160.1	5.3	2.5
联营	Joint Ownership Units	41	0.3	48.8	28.6	0.7	1.3
有限责任公司	Limited-Liability Corporations	11684	161.2	175045.9	46347.0	1465.8	8483.9
股份有限公司	Share Holding Corporations Ltd.	899	54.4	571529.4	14350.5	2378.3	4975.5
私营	Private Units	12680	86.3	9249.1	7490.9	245.6	157.3
其他	Others	403	6.3	687.9	367.3	2.6	3.5
港澳台商投资	Hong Kong, Macao and Taiwan-invested Enterprises	1344	39.3	13280.9	4910.3	327.0	632.4
外商投资	Foreign Funded Units	2036	52.4	30549.4	12922.1	523.8	1771.6

注：1. 行业划分执行2011年国民经济行业分类标准(GB/T 4754-2011)。
2. 应交税金合计主要包括应交增值税、应交所得税、营业税金及附加和管理费用中的税金等。
3. 本表数据为第三次全国经济普查数据。

Note: a) Sectors in this table are classified in accordance with the Standard for Classification of National Economic Sectors 2011 (GB/T 4754-2011).
b) Total Tax mainly includes payable VAT,payable income tax, business tax and surtax, and tax in management expenses, etc.
c) Data for the table were collected from the third national economic census.

22-6 规模以上第三产业单位主要经济指标(2014年)
MAIN INDICATORS FOR TERTIARY INDUSTRY ENTERPRISES ABOVE DESIGNATED SIZE (2014)

项 目	Item	单位数 (个) Enter-prises (unit)	从业人员平均人数 (万人) Average Number of Employed Persons (10000 persons)	资产总计 (亿元) Total Assets (100 million yuan)	收入合计 (亿元) Total Incomes (100 million yuan)	应交税金合计 (亿元) Total Tax (100 million yuan)	利润总额 (亿元) Total Profits (100 million yuan)
合 计	**Total**	**36361**	**586.6**	**1242344.8**	**110308.2**	**5998.0**	**20601.7**
按隶属关系分	**By Affiliation**						
中 央	Central	4092	127.2	981529.7	48738.6	3274.9	14680.1
地 方	Local	32269	459.4	260815.0	61569.6	2723.1	5921.6
按行业分	**By Sector**						
批发和零售业	Wholesale and Retail Trade	8589	74.1	35723.0	51596.5	764.8	1012.5
交通运输、仓储和邮政业	Transport, Storage and Post	1002	59.8	14133.7	4485.0	139.1	343.2
住宿和餐饮业	Accommodation and Restaurants	3029	36.8	1666.3	878.4	65.8	-18.6
信息传输、软件和信息技术服务业	Information Transmission,Software and Information Technology Services	2785	65.8	27225.7	5850.2	337.3	1724.0
金融业	Financial Intermediation	2088	41.1	990873.8	18991.8	3268.0	12760.6
房地产业	Real Estate	4236	40.5	47623.0	4764.2	683.8	792.3
租赁和商务服务业	Leasing and Business Services	5336	79.2	93529.8	7985.4	395.2	3341.8
科学研究和技术服务业	Scientific Research and Technical Services	3202	56.1	15657.7	6959.1	220.6	480.8
水利、环境和公共设施管理业	Management of Water Conservancy, Environment and Public Facilities	533	9.4	1722.7	508.2	15.1	22.0
居民服务、修理和其他服务业	Resident Services, Repair and Other Services	477	8.7	192.2	189.2	9.6	4.4
教 育	Education	1487	38.6	3919.5	1651.6	18.0	18.6
卫生和社会工作	Health Care and Social Works	654	23.2	1321.8	1466.6	2.7	7.3
文化、体育和娱乐业	Culture, Sports and Entertainment	1267	15.5	3771.6	1431.3	74.9	113.0
公共管理、社会保障和社会组织	Pulic Administration,Social Security and Social Organizations	1676	37.6	4983.9	3550.9	3.2	
按登记注册类型分	**By Registration Type**						
内 资	Domestic Investment Economy	33190	492.6	1192453.8	90853.1	5137.8	17990.9
国 有	State-owned Units	6116	156.8	320833.0	16945.2	303.7	2693.4
集 体	Collective-owned Units	529	6.0	1316.9	282.6	11.0	18.2
股份合作	Share Holding	344	2.8	597.5	157.0	5.1	4.8
联 营	Joint Ownership Units	32	0.3	40.9	17.4	0.6	1.2
有限责任公司	Limited-Liability Corporations	12012	169.7	204865.0	48129.5	1641.2	9491.5
股份有限公司	Share Holding Corporations Ltd.	920	56.0	652551.6	15999.7	2891.2	5555.3
私 营	Private Units	12855	95.0	11469.8	8854.0	280.3	220.0
其 他	Others	382	6.1	779.0	467.7	4.7	6.5
港澳台商投资	Hong Kong, Macao and Taiwan-invested Enterprises	1313	41.3	17354.5	5565.4	326.0	816.5
外商投资	Foreign Funded Units	1858	52.7	32536.5	13889.8	534.2	1794.3

注：1. 行业划分执行2011年国民经济行业分类标准(GB/T 4754-2011)。
2. 应交税金合计主要包括应交增值税、应交所得税、营业税金及附加和管理费用中的税金等。

Note: a) Sectors in this table are classified in accordance with the Standard for Classification of National Economic Sectors 2011 (GB/T 4754-2011).
b) Total Tax mainly includes payable VAT,payable income tax, business tax and surtax, and tax in management expenses, etc.

22-7 规模以上第三产业企业财务状况(按登记注册类型分)(2014年)

单位: 万元

项目	Item	企业单位个数(个) Number of Enterprises (unit)	资产负债 资产总计 Total Assets	流动资产合计 Total Current Assets	#应收账款 Accounts Receivable
合计	**Total**	**31450**	**10120948527**	**1193462503**	**111558849**
按隶属关系分	**By Affiliation**				
中央	Central	2653	7573890801	434538860	38352028
地方	Local	28797	2547057725	758923643	73206821
按登记注册类型分	**By Registration Type**				
内资企业	Domestically-invested Enterprises	28282	9622073444	1018226854	86953607
国有企业	State-owned Enterprises	1662	914434237	157681917	7783916
集体企业	Collectively-owned Enterprises	450	12092544	7465933	249439
股份合作企业	Joint-equity Cooperative Enterprises	338	5954334	3853240	459124
联营企业	Associated Enterprises	27	366340	184067	8120
有限责任公司	Limited-Liability Companies	12007	2048175198	613057633	54272663
股份有限公司	Companies Limited by Shares	920	6525516096	153271876	10095251
私营企业	Private Enterprises	12820	114501453	81957548	14054342
其他企业	Others	58	1033242	754639	30752
港澳台商投资企业	Hong Kong, Macao and Taiwan-invested Enterprises	1313	173545199	71323401	7301819
外商投资企业	Foreign-invested Enterprises	1855	325329883	103912249	17303423

注: 1. 行业划分执行2011年国民经济行业分类标准(GB/T 4754-2011)。
2. 应交税金合计主要包括应交增值税、应交所得税、营业税金及附加和管理费用中的税金。
3. 执行《2006年会计准则》的银行、证券、保险业企业, 其"主营营业税金及附加"用"营业税金及附加"代替,"营业成本"和"主营业务成本"用"营业支出-营业税金及附加"代替。

FINANCIAL STATUS OF TERTIARY INDUSTRY ENTERPRISES ABOVE DESIGNATED SIZE(BY REGISTRATION TYPE) (2014)

(10000 yuan)

Assets and Liabilites						
固定资产合计 Total Fixed Assets	固定资产原价 Total Original Value of Fixed Assets	负债合计 Total Liabilities	#流动负债合计 Total Current Liabilities	#应付账款 Accounts Payable	所有者权益合计 Total Owner's Equity	#实收资本 Paid-up Capital
169984226	**242368680**	**7693454716**	**944840572**	**146979529**	**2427493064**	**1163153943**
71152837	103090994	5759115181	370123904	61512473	1814775621	848341236
98831388	139277687	1934339535	574716668	85467056	612717443	314812707
137109190	186309452	7416405826	817871442	117716410	2205666871	1073259809
27342831	39734545	530256423	107627160	9252863	384177814	211171499
1877616	2572094	8548299	6325219	303966	3544245	674904
719084	1018903	4295919	3805152	271375	1658415	575141
51810	95635	181680	121300	23722	184660	203008
61291249	84601193	1162147626	496075505	81645844	886026825	533651134
40539754	50105228	5629635906	131158803	12318949	895880190	296898098
5055100	7896377	80734779	72184287	13769519	33766674	30021436
231746	285477	605194	574015	130173	428049	64589
26140456	43805671	99021336	51305181	10710437	74523863	51437000
6734580	12253557	178027554	75663949	18552683	147302329	38457135

Note:a) Sectors in this table are classified in accordance with the Standard for Classification of National Economic Sectors in 2011(GB/T 4754-2011).
b) Total taxes payable mainly include VAT payable, income tax payable, business tax and surtax, and tax in management expenses, etc.
c) For banks, security and insurance enterprises implementing 2006 Standard of Accounting System, the indicator of "Main Business Tax and Surtax" is replaced with "Business Tax and Surtax" and indicators of "Business Cost" and "Main Business Cost" are replaced with "Business Cost-Busniess Tax and Surtax".

22-7 续表

单位：万元

项目	Item	损益及分配 营业收入 Revenue from Main Businesses	#主营业务收入 Main Business Income	营业成本 Business Cost	#主营业务成本 Main Business Cost
合计	**Total**	**1011296915**	**994871935**	**755099832**	**746193512**
按隶属关系分	**By Affiliation**				
中央	Central	437026202	429384117	305854210	301204009
地方	Local	574270713	565487817	449245622	444989503
按登记注册类型分	**By Registration Type**				
内资企业	Domestically-invested Enterprises	816769529	803881681	610320049	603027880
国有企业	State-owned Enterprises	82548204	80139155	73947838	73377068
集体企业	Collectively-owned Enterprises	2193457	2104045	1541586	1519061
股份合作企业	Joint-equity Cooperative Enterprises	1545495	1507491	1132523	1129548
联营企业	Associated Enterprises	158583	156819	119568	119147
有限责任公司	Limited-Liability Companies	481282102	472526260	366400874	360108645
股份有限公司	Companies Limited by Shares	159996527	159133961	95923780	95711028
私营企业	Private Enterprises	88415770	87695342	70931137	70745612
其他企业	Others	629392	618606	322744	317773
港澳台商投资企业	Hong Kong, Macao and Taiwan-invested Enterprises	55653656	54667164	36498373	35943716
外商投资企业	Foreign-invested Enterprises	138873730	136323090	108281410	107221916

22-7 continued

(10000 yuan)

Profits and Losses							
销售费用 Sales Expenses	管理费用 Management Expenses	财务费用 Financial Expenses	利润总额 Total Profits	应交税金合计 Total Tax Payable	#营业税金及附加 Business Tax and Surtax	#主营业务税金及附加 Business Tax and Surtax	#应交所得税 Income Tax Payable
42569755	**47912835**	**13935706**	**206017002**	**59479022**	**12801698**	**12390542**	**36926912**
5689382	11386457	6041283	146801197	32327646	3951236	3713445	26172223
36880372	36526377	7894423	59215804	27151376	8850462	8677097	10754689
24869070	33673782	12913906	179909040	50877284	11026008	10637634	33570379
1445553	5364272	1289035	26934135	2558906	1041034	882541	1151372
164042	355145	-9907	182412	108172	46315	42584	31883
135760	225169	3995	47945	50812	22919	22053	12053
12393	23870	-1447	11552	5959	1294	1233	1064
13008589	16720845	7714654	94915190	16411578	5283719	5111084	7583227
2847854	3512662	3027915	55553032	28912485	3803039	3763226	24214756
7165310	7311527	906762	2200050	2801037	811167	798583	569168
89569	160293	-17101	64724	28336	16520	16331	6858
5541337	5297790	748405	8164505	3259555	828503	820630	1390220
12159349	8941262	273395	17943457	5342183	947188	932278	1966313

22-8 规模以上第三产业企业财务状况(按行业分)(2014年)

单位：万元

项目	Item	企业单位个数(个) Number of Enterprises (unit)	资产负债	
			资产总计 Total Assets	流动资产合计 Total Current Assets
合计	**Total**	**31450**	**10120948527**	**1193462503**
批发和零售业	**Wholesale and Retail Trade**	**8589**	**357230450**	**263863656**
批发业	Wholesale	5780	315443628	232081225
零售业	Retail Trade	2809	41786822	31782431
交通运输、仓储和邮政业	**Transport, Storage and Post**	**1002**	**141336761**	**48058552**
铁路运输业	Railway Transport	15	48704631	6592463
道路运输业	Road Transport	479	19282294	5007940
水上运输业	Water Transport	4	55719	18138
航空运输业	Air Transport	21	24705342	4330664
管道运输业	Transport Via Pipelines	3	***	***
装卸搬运和运输代理业	Loading, Unloading, Portage and Other Transport Services	341	6575069	4019703
仓储业	Storage	105	23469102	22717747
邮政业	Post	34	5507575	3661386
住宿和餐饮业	**Accommodation and Restaurants**	**3029**	**16662699**	**6546060**
住宿业	Accommodation	1161	12401680	4235080
餐饮业	Restaurants	1868	4261019	2310980
信息传输、软件和信息技术服务业	**Information Transmission, Software and Information Technology Services**	**2739**	**270085262**	**94189824**
电信、广播电视和卫星传输服务	Telecommunications, Broadcasting, Television and Satellite Transmission Services	213	200260704	44585539
互联网和相关服务	Internet and Related Services	265	12457706	8828708
软件和信息技术服务业	Software and Information Technology Services	2261	57366853	40775577
金融业	**Finance**	**2072**	**7776329149**	**50319895**
货币金融服务	Monetary Financial Services	630	6365515658	9154934
资本市场服务	Capital Market Services	563	218570445	11026904
保险业	Insurance	508	382530070	897312
其他金融业	Other Financial Services	371	809712975	29240745

FINANCIAL STATUS OF TERTIARY INDUSTRY ENTERPRISES ABOVE DESIGNATED SIZE(BY SECTOR) (2014)

(10000 yuan)

Assets and Liabilites							
#应收账款 Accounts Receivable	固定资产合计 Total Fixed Assets	固定资产原价 Total Original Value of Fixed Assets	负债合计 Total Liabilities	#流动负债合计 Total Current Liabilities	#应付账款 Accounts Payable	所有者权益合计 Total Owner's Equity	#实收资本 Paid-up Capital
111558849	**169984226**	**242368680**	**7693454716**	**944840572**	**146979529**	**2427493064**	**1163153943**
45103740	**9348460**	**14971316**	**258062964**	**230994353**	**68227812**	**99166739**	**51502280**
41405720	6437787	10061345	225883640	200247544	60276552	89560039	45572256
3698020	2910673	4909972	32179323	30746809	7951261	9606700	5930024
4717784	**71035174**	**93232496**	**75453058**	**50328587**	**8209833**	**65883703**	**53409795**
1623074	34384784	43003940	16627981	9007740	3187420	32076651	34613800
671161	11946013	15740808	12095649	6005923	824773	7186645	5707627
4247	36241	71106	30104	14554	2721	25615	11788
808357	14335772	20938847	16177961	6141250	2422320	8527380	3189373
***	***	***	***	***	***	***	***
1028180	509528	830516	3265714	2942687	912661	3309355	1759788
59101	479506	666023	22719142	22349023	63138	749960	369655
495299	463618	928128	3063112	2712084	356742	2444463	1529580
300693	**5456602**	**9416999**	**12948732**	**9563829**	**1014765**	**3713966**	**4488949**
166385	4854118	8240768	9407954	6451354	415254	2993726	3633466
134308	602484	1176231	3540778	3112476	599511	720240	855483
16451878	**13868227**	**29998182**	**69874859**	**57822681**	**13558356**	**200210403**	**103053771**
4019744	8742511	20509723	35571381	26142662	5665986	164689323	89679298
1104917	1354276	2596416	6101272	5734601	1113465	6356434	1630509
11327217	3771440	6892043	28202206	25945417	6778905	29164647	11743965
5114835	**18855478**	**23602440**	**6428680721**	**37529844**	**1818650**	**1347648428**	**610920920**
2991228	13615491	18020266	5750413310	9475192	379563	615102348	208789840
956876	925103	1415709	148741843	7864734	803500	69828602	34716226
91758	3347218	2616249	256238121	290624	74780	126291949	51096720
1074973	967667	1550216	273287447	19899294	560807	536425528	316318134

22-8 续表 1

单位：万元

项 目	Item	损益及分配 营业收入 Business Income	#主营业务收入 Revenue from Main Business	营业成本 Business Cost
合 计	**Total**	**1011296915**	**994871935**	**755099832**
批发和零售业	**Wholesale and Retail Trade**	**515965426**	**506767557**	**478798730**
批发业	Wholesale	439269563	431766167	411430543
零售业	Retail Trade	76695863	75001390	67368187
交通运输、仓储和邮政业	**Transport, Storage and Post**	**44850299**	**43911252**	**38092725**
铁路运输业	Railway Transport	10193177	9751665	8552305
道路运输业	Road Transport	5002462	4904268	5750483
水上运输业	Water Transport	26255	26254	14513
航空运输业	Air Transport	10791612	10504292	8981241
管道运输业	Transport Via Pipelines	***	***	***
装卸搬运和运输代理业	Loading, Unloading, Portage and Other Transport Services	8266283	8216763	7263885
仓储业	Storage	4711225	4700488	4417302
邮政业	Post	3022853	2996302	1979762
住宿和餐饮业	**Accommodation and Restaurants**	**8783826**	**8691752**	**3143418**
住宿业	Accommodation	3438789	3405588	907069
餐饮业	Restaurants	5345038	5286163	2236349
信息传输、软件和信息技术服务业	**Information Transmission, Software and Information Technology Services**	**57809440**	**56888436**	**35050793**
电信、广播电视和卫星传输服务	Telecommunications, Broadcasting, Television and Satellite Transmission Services	11555861	11156027	7702714
互联网和相关服务	Internet and Related Services	8738925	8679503	4337144
软件和信息技术服务业	Software and Information Technology Services	37514655	37052907	23010935
金融业	**Finance**	**189646263**	**189334963**	**57456946**
货币金融服务	Monetary Financial Services	67226367	67122768	25667628
资本市场服务	Capital Market Services	11636232	11538530	3174502
保险业	Insurance	46865987	46860131	25492047
其他金融业	Other Financial Services	63917677	63813534	3122769

22-8 Continued 1

(10000 yuan)

Profits and Losses								
#主营业务成本 Main Business Cost	销售费用 Sales Expenses	管理费用 Management Expenses	财务费用 Financial Expenses	利润总额 Total Profits	应交税金合计 Total Tax Payable	#营业税金及附加 Business Tax and Surtax	#主营业务税金及附加 Business Tax and Surtax	#应交所得税 Income Tax Payable
746193512	**42569755**	**47912835**	**13935706**	**206017002**	**59479022**	**12801698**	**12390542**	**36926912**
472977165	**19420653**	**8874589**	**2090554**	**10124902**	**7648204**	**949034**	**896424**	**2395582**
405909620	13656814	6610954	1750129	8693420	5857299	667516	637136	2012970
67067545	5763840	2263635	340426	1431482	1790906	281518	259288	382612
37262867	**1745608**	**2974319**	**1093811**	**3431580**	**1390583**	**180998**	**160401**	**829721**
8123167	9116	1008772	413971	278487	493959	36224	26935	209379
5703710	189050	540247	355022	135991	201432	56769	53218	50452
14513	1979	5105	1358	3936	1204	14	14	1009
8824263	750111	344536	376134	582777	76125	26169	25034	128928
***	***	***	***	***	***	***	***	***
7230387	294370	487704	16725	260453	195983	14702	14081	72739
4414401	76916	89272	9229	148300	-282447	5482	5260	6700
1843837	399357	409642	-7002	252804	140679	8724	8582	76591
3120825	**3301489**	**1872452**	**241949**	**-186167**	**657748**	**472876**	**471175**	**91195**
900286	1095440	1226440	191473	-108418	316746	190787	190230	50542
2220538	2206049	646012	50475	-77749	341003	282089	280945	40653
34493147	**7539091**	**9106215**	**-316402**	**17239722**	**3367234**	**545951**	**535785**	**904873**
7382456	1632653	1260565	-223448	11185187	467285	152226	144359	45819
4331780	1585975	1302137	-152178	1640046	635125	144096	143596	257748
22778912	4320463	6543513	59224	4414489	2264824	249629	247830	601307
57334636	**411889**	**1579793**	**494721**	**127605772**	**32679396**	**4580124**	**4560469**	**27860753**
25621825	53689	165351	151091	37186782	26217973	3535047	3534203	22576605
3128928	39221	471630	143802	8696142	2145606	355485	353386	1767218
25489879	63035	183672	-2102	20818270	2626634	430729	430441	2133877
3094003	255944	759140	201930	60904578	1689184	258863	242440	1383053

22-8 续表 2

单位：万元

项 目	Item	企业单位个数(个) Number of Enterprises (unit)	资产负债 资产总计 Total Assets
房地产业	**Real Estate**	**4215**	**475946233**
租赁和商务服务业	**Renting and Leasing Activities, Business Services**	**5071**	**928852970**
租赁业	Renting and Leasing	104	7145789
商务服务业	Business Services	4967	921707182
科学研究和技术服务业	**Scientific Research and Development, Technical Services**	**2646**	**115295455**
研究和试验发展	Research and Experimental Development	269	21216298
专业技术服务业	Professional Technical Services	1386	67722034
科技推广和应用服务业	Technique Generalization and Application Services	991	26357123
水利、环境和公共设施管理业	**Management of Water Conservancy, Environment and Public Facilities**	**321**	**14938058**
水利管理业	Management of Water Conservancy	12	773849
生态保护和环境治理业	Ecological Protection and Environmental Control	49	2408097
公共设施管理业	Management of Public Facilities	260	11756111
居民服务、修理和其他服务业	**Resident Services, Repair and Other Services**	**431**	**1552942**
居民服务业	Resident Services	120	573863
机动车、电子产品和日用产品修理业	Repair of Motor Vehicles, Electronics and Household Appliances	144	563237
其他服务业	Other Services	167	415842
教 育	**Education**	**176**	**2331612**
卫生和社会工作	**Healthcare and Social Works**	**170**	**1188722**
卫 生	Healthcare	167	1160054
社会工作	Social Works	3	28668
文化、体育和娱乐业	**Culture, Sports and Entertainment**	**989**	**19198216**
新闻和出版业	Journalism and Publishing	453	10453825
广播、电视、电影和影视录音制作业	Radio Broadcasting, Television, Movies, Videos and Sound Recording	200	5917886
文化艺术业	Culture and Arts	116	806450
体 育	Sports Activities	136	1509376
娱乐业	Entertainment	84	510679

22-8 Continued 2

(10000 yuan)

Assets and Liabilites								
流动资产合计 Total Current Assets	#应收账款 Accounts Receivable	固定资产合计 Total Fixed Assets	固定资产原价 Total Original Value of Fixed Assets	负债合计 Total Liabilities	#流动负债合计 Total Current Liabilities	#应付账款 Accounts Payable	所有者权益合计 Total Owner's Equity	#实收资本 Paid-up Capital
366252710	**9934474**	**17833215**	**23541765**	**365116937**	**259909112**	**17759710**	**110829296**	**66681500**
272078110	**14125032**	**21186130**	**29116644**	**391960790**	**224781264**	**14482935**	**536892181**	**244833122**
2510305	379910	2697836	3359280	4862150	1823258	324860	2283639	1374491
269567805	13745123	18488294	25757364	387098640	222958006	14158075	534608542	243458630
72001951	**12865359**	**6279045**	**9847742**	**69639625**	**60230306**	**18498638**	**45655830**	**20981686**
16027489	849515	1541095	2274535	15129447	12361449	4490197	6086851	2808074
39722967	8070142	3054728	5037430	39096373	34317940	9667123	28625660	12344608
16251495	3945703	1683222	2535776	15413805	13550918	4341318	10943318	5829005
5093059	**1221498**	**2604557**	**3079627**	**10003118**	**3596456**	**1205127**	**4934940**	**1696792**
151490	14524	132083	217260	427085	214430	19396	346764	207968
1598947	514411	345679	401960	1423044	1073404	509248	985054	545739
3342622	692564	2126795	2460407	8152989	2308621	676483	3603123	943085
1112780	**184560**	**171044**	**316840**	**1221983**	**1118480**	**176613**	**330959**	**328733**
384177	23693	67430	119421	513574	471927	43669	60289	76523
416062	78214	71548	131453	412320	386252	76398	150917	141678
312541	82654	32066	65966	296089	260301	56546	119753	110532
1715563	**87572**	**320895**	**556651**	**1540132**	**1468527**	**169516**	**791481**	**271149**
662657	**102521**	**364599**	**580922**	**691375**	**639312**	**248249**	**497346**	**387272**
650006	102521	349027	546226	677309	625245	248249	482745	386563
12651		15572	34696	14067	14067		14601	709
11567688	**1348903**	**2660800**	**4107058**	**8260424**	**6857822**	**1609325**	**10937792**	**4597974**
6776695	489008	1462168	2143484	3671510	2979113	725347	6782315	2378753
3418764	741037	499495	806797	2370852	2107881	682114	3547034	1450637
478947	59754	105249	158674	435613	398479	47420	370837	278459
632638	43181	482349	803913	1487530	1169347	108405	21846	341314
260645	15923	111539	194190	294919	203003	46039	215760	148811

22-8 续表 3

单位：万元

项目	Item	损益及分配 营业收入 Business Income	 #主营业务收入 Revenue from Business Income
房地产业	**Real Estate**	**47030672**	**45970282**
租赁和商务服务业	**Renting and Leasing Activities, Business Services**	**78194065**	**75231839**
租赁业	Renting and Leasing	1455825	1419341
商务服务业	Business Services	76738240	73812498
科学研究和技术服务业	**Scientific Research and Development, Technical Services**	**53030379**	**52507014**
研究和试验发展	Research and Experimental Development	3409838	3303265
专业技术服务业	Professional Technical Services	36420613	36145902
科技推广和应用服务业	Technique Generalization and Application Services	13199928	13057847
水利、环境和公共设施管理业	**Management of Water Conservancy, Environment and Public Facilities**	**3457551**	**3430819**
水利管理业	Management of Water Conservancy	89698	86199
生态保护和环境治理业	Ecological Protection and Environmental Control	1087024	1083717
公共设施管理业	Management of Public Facilities	2280829	2260903
居民服务、修理和其他服务业	**Resident Services, Repair and Other Services**	**1665938**	**1631828**
居民服务业	Resident Services	395988	388099
机动车、电子产品和日用产品修理业	Repair of Motor Vehicles, Electronics and Household Appliances	732171	711532
其他服务业	Other Services	537780	532197
教育	**Education**	**1587132**	**1569671**
卫生和社会工作	**Healthcare and Social Works**	**1306406**	**1301434**
卫生	Healthcare	1300057	1296569
社会工作	Social Works	6349	4865
文化、体育和娱乐业	**Culture, Sports and Entertainment**	**7969517**	**7635089**
新闻和出版业	Journalism and Publishing	3938031	3659873
广播、电视、电影和影视录音制作业	Radio Broadcasting, Television, Movies, Videos and Sound Recording	2875437	2836614
文化艺术业	Culture and Arts	426111	421902
体育	Sports Activities	474192	462330
娱乐业	Entertainment	255746	254369

22-8 continued 3

(10000 yuan)

Profits and Losses									
营业成本 Business Cost	#主营业务成本 Main Business Cost	销售费用 Sales Expenses	管理费用 Management Expenses	财务费用 Financial Expenses	利润总额 Total Profits	应交税金合计 Total Taxes Payable	#营业税金及附加 Business Tax and Surtax	#主营业务税金及附加 Main Business Tax and Surtax	#应交所得税 Income Tax Payable
29057950	**28626120**	**1922092**	**4414335**	**2719002**	**7923339**	**6837795**	**4539870**	**4446506**	**1965438**
59960483	**59323376**	**4880659**	**11401088**	**7335447**	**33417877**	**3903005**	**924267**	**726375**	**1837468**
806296	772442	53895	215014	45280	337929	125336	13390	13305	74831
59154187	58550934	4826765	11186074	7290167	33079948	3777669	910877	713071	1762638
42984601	**42663650**	**1683954**	**5027530**	**247934**	**4807828**	**2080873**	**353199**	**344213**	**744122**
2404362	2341949	189803	729710	-62422	444437	203764	21039	18024	74151
30044617	29894550	897282	2973752	158422	3345690	1368080	244771	239948	500955
10535622	10427151	596869	1324069	151935	1017701	509029	87389	86241	169016
2701239	**2692560**	**98557**	**347393**	**69255**	**220233**	**142878**	**73266**	**71751**	**36190**
52170	51710	551	30379	9049	11221	2203	1112	346	1239
853647	852877	26874	84287	23368	99800	51091	10239	10205	16415
1795422	1787973	71132	232727	36838	109212	89583	61915	61200	18536
1013605	**1002388**	**301272**	**265699**	**7488**	**43666**	**94585**	**40024**	**39313**	**20528**
145411	142902	120727	96433	2119	16155	25462	14641	14533	7451
521882	517649	107977	72385	3146	23237	37427	5982	5760	7818
346312	341837	72569	96881	2224	4275	31695	19401	19020	5259
752134	**744079**	**269043**	**372019**	**-22009**	**185643**	**103046**	**46388**	**46193**	**42780**
863714	**862584**	**136995**	**265595**	**3074**	**72569**	**22094**	**840**	**747**	**19818**
859981	858850	136955	260540	3141	72925	21824	826	733	19816
3734	3734	40	5056	-67	-356	270	14	14	2
5223494	**5090117**	**858452**	**1411806**	**-29119**	**1130038**	**551581**	**94863**	**91191**	**178444**
2310718	2197173	483144	904736	-45633	663383	340032	40998	38756	91564
2216274	2201572	169950	244710	4391	477463	130945	15390	14553	66310
291972	289081	39407	72264	3319	35129	23039	5600	5553	8232
256217	254064	120415	152478	7328	-57930	38188	21857	21467	7065
148314	148228	45536	37618	1476	11993	19378	11017	10862	5273

22-9 文化创意产业活动单位基本情况
STATISTICS FOR CULTURAL AND CREATIVE INDUSTRY

单位：亿元 (100 million yuan)

项目	Item	资产总计 Total Assets		收入合计 Total Income		从业人员平均人数（万人） Average Number of Employed Persons (10000 persons)	
		2014	2013	2014	2013	2014	2013
合计	**Total**	**26441.8**	**20594.7**	**13982.0**	**12377.4**	**191.6**	**183.6**
文化艺术	Culture and Arts	1284.4	1054.9	410.1	349.5	11.2	10.9
新闻出版	Journalism and Publications	2257.3	1866.8	1034.8	973.7	15.7	15.9
广播、电视、电影	Radios, Televisions amd Movies	2433.1	2091.6	859.4	771.9	7.2	7.0
软件、网络及计算机服务	Software, Network & Computer Services	11143.7	8935.6	5380.0	4587.7	90.8	84.8
广告会展	Advertisements & Exhibitions	1922.5	1717.1	1835.0	1646.4	17.3	17.5
艺术品交易	Transaction of Artworks	892.8	790.6	1094.5	1056.2	2.7	2.8
设计服务	Design Services	1053.6	948.1	576.1	536.3	16.7	15.6
旅游、休闲娱乐	Tourism and Enterainment	1678.8	1380.7	1054.7	984.3	13.0	12.7
其他辅助服务	Other Auxiliary Services	3775.5	1809.2	1737.5	1471.4	17.0	16.2

注：2013年数据为第三次全国经济普查数据。
Note: Data for 2013 were collected from the third national economic census.

22-10 物流业活动情况
STATISTICS FOR LOGISTICS

项目	Item	2014	2013	2014年为2013年% 2014 as % of 2013
物流业务收入（亿元）	**Business Income of Logistics Sector (100 million yuan)**	**2482.5**	**2267.6**	**109.5**
运输收入	Transportation Income	1757.9	1618.8	108.6
保管收入	Storage Income	659.2	596.2	110.6
一体化物流业务收入	Integrated Logistics Income	65.3	52.7	123.9
社会物流总额（亿元）	**Total Amount of Social Logistics (100 million yuan)**	**75923.6**	**72440.0**	**104.8**
农产品	Agricultural Products	358.2	360.0	99.5
工业品	Industrial Products	17911.6	13875.4	129.1
进口货物	Imported Goods	21695.5	22656.4	95.8
再生资源	Renewable Resources	201.7	129.7	155.6
外省市流入物品	Goods from Other Provinces and Cities	35508.4	35230.3	100.8
单位与居民物品	Entities and Residents' Goods	248.2	188.3	131.8
物流业从业人员平均人数（万人）	**Employment in Logistics Sector (10000 persons)**	**50.8**	**51.0**	**99.6**
交通运输、邮政、仓储业	Transportation, Post, Storage	35.2	35.0	100.6
采掘业、制造业、批发和零售业	Excavation, Manufacturing, Wholesale and Retail Trade	15.6	16	97.5

22-11 会展业活动情况
STATISTICS FOR MICE INDUSTRY IN BEIJING

项目		Item		2014	2013	2014年为2013% 2014 as % of last year
人员情况		**Employed Persons**				
从业人员平均人数	(万人)	Year-end Employed Persons	(10000 person)	20.3	20.0	101.7
接待设施情况		**Facilities**				
接待场所会议室个数	(个)	Number of Meeting Rooms	(unit)	5593	5604	99.8
#座位数超过500座的会议室	(个)	Number of Meeting Rooms with More Than 500 Seats	(unit)	194	193	100.5
接待场所会议室使用面积	(万平方米)	Usable Area of Meeting Rooms	(10000 sq.m)	81.7	82.2	99.4
接待场所会议室可容纳人数	(万人)	Capacity of Meeting Rooms	(10000 person)	48.8	48.4	100.8
会议情况		**Meetings**				
接待会议个数	(万个)	Number of Meetings Held in Beijing	(10000 unit)	23.1	23.7	97.5
#国际会议	(万个)	International Meetings	(10000 unit)	0.7	0.6	105.2
接待会议人数	(万人次)	Number of Meeting Participants	(10000 person-times)	1639.3	1622.7	101.0
#国际会议	(万人次)	International Meeting Participants	(10000 person-times)	64.4	62.1	103.8
展览情况		**Exhibitions**				
接待展览个数	(个)	Number of Exhibitions Held in Beijing	(unit)	733	769	95.3
#国际展览	(个)	International Exhibitions	(unit)	196	193	101.6
#展览面积1万(不含)平方米以下的展览个数	(个)	Number of Exhibitions with Exhibition Area under 10,000 sq.m (10,000 sq.m excluded)	(unit)	529	570	92.8
展览面积1万平方米及以上的展览个数	(个)	Number of Exhibitions with Exhibition Area of 10,000 sq.m and over	(unit)	204	199	102.5
接待展览累计面积(含室外展览面积)	(万平方米)	Total Exhibition Area (including outdoor exhibition area)	(10000 sq.m)	673.9	677.4	99.5
#国际展览累计面积	(万平方米)	International Exhibition Area	(10000 sq.m)	382.2	343.1	111.4
接待展览观众人数	(万人次)	Number of Exhibition Visitors	(10000 person-times)	946.4	843.4	112.2
#国际展览观众人数	(万人次)	International Exhibition Visitors	(10000 person-times)	430.8	386.8	111.4
奖励旅游情况		**Incentives**				
服务奖励旅游人数	(万人次)	Number of Incentive Tourists	(10000 person-times)	24.3	19.6	124.3
收入情况		**Revenues**				
会展收入	(亿元)	Total Revenues from MICE Industry	(100 million yuan)	202.8	206.0	98.4
会议收入	(亿元)	Revenues from Meetings	(100 million yuan)	102.2	110.2	92.8
#国际会议收入	(亿元)	Revenues from International Meetings	(100 million yuan)	10.3	9.4	109.5
展览收入	(亿元)	Revenues from Exhibitions	(100 million yuan)	92.5	86.2	107.5
#国际展览收入	(亿元)	Revenues from International Exhibitions	(100 million yuan)	35.8	34.4	104.2
奖励旅游收入	(亿元)	Revenues from Incentives	(100 million yuan)	8.1	9.7	83.7

注：会展业统计范围包括会展场馆、星级饭店、会展举办单位以及规模以上会议及展览服务业法人单位和旅行社等。由于统计范围内的单位名录每年均有变化,为保证数据的可比性，需要调整上年同期数据以计算可比增速。

Note: Statistical scope in MICE industry includes MICE venue, star-level hotel and main organizer of MICE, etc. As items in the said statistical scope change every year, so in order to ensure figure comparability, figures of the same period in the previous year need to be adjusted to calculate comparable growth rate.

22-12 体育及相关产业情况
STATISTICS FOR SPORTS INDUSTRY

项目	Item	收入合计(亿元) Total Income (100 million yuan) 2014	2013	从业人员平均人数(万人) Average Number of Employed Persons (10000 persons) 2014	2013
合计	**Total**	**958.6**	**863.6**	**13.5**	**13.2**
体育组织管理活动	Sports Organization and Management Activities	131.6	126.4	1.8	1.8
体育场馆管理活动	Gym Management Activities	17.2	22.2	0.6	0.6
体育健身休闲活动	Sports, Body Building and Entertainment Activities	37.1	39.5	3.2	3.5
体育中介活动	Sports Agency Activities	27.6	25.4	0.5	0.6
其他体育活动	Other Sports Activities	115.9	93.2	1.5	1.4
体育用品、服装、鞋帽及相关体育产品的制造	Manufacturing of Sports Supplies, Clothes, Shoes and Caps, and Related Sports Products	52.9	60.4	0.7	0.8
体育用品、服装、鞋帽及相关体育产品的销售	Sales of Sports Supplies, Clothes, Shoes and Caps, and Related Sports Products	552.1	483.8	5.0	4.5
体育场馆建筑活动	Gymnasium Building Activities	24.3	12.6	0.1	0.1

主要统计指标解释

物流业务收入 指通过物流业务活动取得的收入。包括企业完成运输、存储、装卸、搬运、包装、流通加工、配送、信息等物流业务取得的收入之和。反映物流相关行业物流活动的总规模。

物流业从业人员 指企业中直接或间接从事物流活动的人数。直接从事物流活动的人员包括在企业中从事运输、配送、装卸搬运、仓储保管等物流活动并取得劳动报酬的从业人员；间接从事物流活动的人员包括在企业中从事物流管理活动并取得劳动报酬的从业人员，包括采购、销售部门的主管人员，但不包括采购、销售部门内部办事人员。

社会物流总额 指第一次进入市内需求领域，产生从供应地向接受地实体流动的物品的价值总额。包括六个方面的内容：进入需求领域的农产品物流总额、工业品物流总额、进口货物物流总额、外省市调入物品物流总额、再生资源物流总额、单位与居民物品物流总额。.

接待会议个数 指报告期内，接待的各种类型会议的个数。包括国际会议和国内会议。

接待国际会议个数 指报告期内，接待的国际会议的个数。国际会议是指在我国境内举办的，与会者来自 3 个或 3 个以上中国大陆以外国家和地区（含港、澳、台地区）的会议、论坛、研讨会、报告会、交流会等。

接待展览个数 指报告期内，接待的各种类型展览的个数。包括国际展览和国内展览。

接待国际展览个数 指报告期内，接待的国际展览的个数。国际展览指中国大陆以外国家和地区（含港、澳、台地区）的参展商参展面积达到该次展出面积 20%以上的展览个数。

服务奖励旅游人数 指报告期内，服务的奖励旅游人数的总和（含接待）。

服务贸易 服务贸易包括跨境提供、境外消费、商业存在和自然人移动等内容。

跨境提供 是指服务提供者从中国境内向任何其他国家或地区的服务消费者提供服务以及服务提供者从其他国家或地区向中国境内的服务消费者提供服务。

境外消费 是指在中国境内向其他国家或地区的服务消费者提供服务以及在其他国家或地区向中国境内的服务消费者提供服务。

商业存在 是指中国境内的服务提供者通过在任何其他国家或地区设立的企业或分支机构提供服务以及其他国家或地区的服务提供者通过在中国境内设立企业或分支机构提供服务。

自然人移动 是指中国境内的服务提供者通过在其他国家或地区的自然人提供服务以及其他国家或地区的服务提供者通过在中国境内的自然人提供服务。

体育组织管理活动 指专门为社会公众提供比赛、训练、辅导和管理的组织的活动，如群众性体育组织、专项性体育管理组织的活动。

体育场馆管理活动 指为社会公众提供观赏比赛和专业训练的体育场馆管理活动，如综合性体育场馆，训练用场地的管理活动。

体育健身休闲活动 指社会公众提供的可供参与和选择的各种健身休闲活动场所的管理活动。

体育中介活动 指为社会公众提供的体育中介活动，如各种体育商务代理、经纪、咨询活动。

其他体育活动 指为社会公众提供的其他体育服务活动。包括体育培训服务、体育科研服务、体育彩票服务、体育传媒服务、体育展览服务、体育市场管理服务、体育场馆设计服务、体育场所保洁服务和体育文物及文化保护服务。

体育用品、服装、鞋帽及相关体育产品的制造 指提供体育服务所必须的体育用品、服装、鞋帽及相关体育产品的制造活动。

体育用品、服装、鞋帽及相关体育产品的销售 指提供体育服务所必须的体育用品、服装、鞋帽及相关体育产品的销售活动。

体育场馆管理活动 指提供体育服务所必须的体育场馆建筑活动。

Explanatory Notes on Main Statistical Indicators

Business Income of Logistics Sector refers to the income earned from logistics business activities, which is equal to the sum of incomes from such logistics operations completed by enterprises as transportation, storage, loading and unloading, handling, package, circulation and processing, delivery, and information. It reflects the overall scale of logistics activities in logistics related sector.

Employees in Logistics Sector refers to the number of persons directly and indirectly engaged in logistics activities in enterprises. Persons directly engaging in logistics activities are those engaging in logistics activities such as transportation, delivery, loading and unloading, handling, storage and warehouse keeping in enterprises and receiving labor remuneration; persons indirectly engaging in logistics activities are those engaging in management activities in enterprises and receiving labor remuneration, including executives in purchase and sales departments, but excluding clerks in purchase and sales departments.

Total Amount of Social Logistics refers to the total value of goods entering the demand area in the city for the first time and having physical flow from the supply place to the receiving place, consisting of value on six aspects: total logistics amount of agricultural products, total logistics amount of industrial products, total logistics amount of imported goods, total logistics amount of goods transferred from other provinces and cities, total logistics amount of recycled resources, and total logistics amount of corporate and household supplies entering the demand field.

Number of Meeting Held in Beijing refers to the number of various types of conference held in Beijing in the reporting period, including international and domestic conferences.

Number of International Meeting refers to the number of international conferences held in Beijing in the reporting period. International conference means any conference, forum, seminar, report conference, and workshops, etc. held in our country, with participants coming from 3 or more countries and regions (including Hong Kong, Macao and Taiwan) outside Chinese mainland.

Number of Exhibitions Held in Beijing refers to the number of various types of exhibitions held in Beijing in the reporting period, including international and domestic exhibitions.

Number of International Exhibitions Received refers to the number of international exhibitions received in the reporting period. International exhibition means any exhibition with participants from countries and regions (including Hong Kong, Macao and Taiwan) outside Chinese mainland whose exhibition floorage accounts for more than 20% of the exhibition.

Number of Incentive Tourists refers to the sum of persons of incentive tour served in the reporting period.

Service Trade includes overseas provision, overseas consumption, commercial existence, movement of natural persons, and so on.

Overseas Provision refers to any service provider provides service within China for service consumers in any other country or region, and any service provider provides service in any other country or region to service consumers within China.

Overseas Consumption refers to provision of service in China for service consumers in any other country or region, and provision of service in any other country or region for service consumers in China.

Commercial Existence refers to that any service provider in China provides service through its business or branch set up in any other country or region, and any service provider in any other country or region provides service through its business or branch set up in China.

Movement of Natural Persons means that any service provider in China provides service through any natural person in any other country or region, and any service provider in any other country or region provides service through any natural person in China.

Sports Organization and Management Activities mean activities organized specially for providing games, training, coaching and management for the public, such as activities organized for mass sport organizations and special sport management.

Gym Management Activities mean management activities in gym providing games for view and special trainings for the public, such as management activities in comprehensive sports venues and training fields and courts.

Sports, Body Building and Entertainment Activities mean management activities provided for the public at Sports bodybuilding and entertainment sites, which are to be participated in and chosen.

Sports Agency Activities refer to sport agency activities provided for the public, such as various sports business agency, broker and consulting activities.

Other Sports Activities refer to activities of other sports service provided for the public, including sports training service, sports research service, sports lottery service, sports communication service, sports exhibition service, sports market management service, sports venue design service, sports site cleaning service, sports cultural relics and cultural protection service.

Manufacturing of Sports Supplies, Clothes, Shoes and Caps, and Related Sports Products refers to manufacturing of sports supplies, clothes, shoes and caps, and related sports products necessary for provision of sports service.

Sales of Sports Supplies, Clothes, Shoes and Caps, and Related Sports Products refers to sales of sports supplies, clothes, shoes and caps, and related sports products necessary for provision of sports service.

Gymnasium Building Activities refer to activities of construction of sports venues necessary for provision of sports service.

23

开发区
DEVELOPMENT ZONES

简 要 说 明

一、本章资料的主要内容

本章资料主要反映北京市开发区的基本情况，招商、入资，企业生产经营、财务、科技活动和人力资源情况，重点介绍了北京经济技术开发区、中关村国家自主创新示范区及北京天竺综合保税区的主要情况。其中，中关村国家自主创新示范区亦庄园在中关村国家自主创新示范区与北京经济技术开发区中为重叠部分。

二、本章资料的数据来源

本章中关村国家自主创新示范区的统计资料由北京市统计局提供；其他各开发区中涉及招商、土地、投资的统计资料由各开发区管委会提供，财务资料由北京市统计局提供；北京经济技术开发区的统计资料由北京经济技术开发区统计局、调查队提供；北京天竺综合保税区中涉及招商、土地、投资等方面的统计资料由北京天竺综合保税区管委会提供，财务资料由北京市统计局提供。

三、本章的有关变化说明

根据 2012 年《国务院关于同意调整中关村国家自主创新示范区空间规模和布局的批复》，自 2013 年起，中关村国家自主创新示范区的统计范围在原有的海淀园、丰台园、昌平园、电子城科技园、亦庄园、德胜园、雍和园、石景山园、通州园和大兴生物医药产业基地的基础上，增加了平谷园、门头沟园、顺义园、房山园、密云园、怀柔园和延庆园七个园区。同时，“电子城科技园”更名为“朝阳园”；“德胜园”更名为“西城园”；“雍和园”更名为“东城园”。

Brief Introduction

I. Main Content

Data in this chapter mainly shows the basic condition of development zones in Beijing, business invitation, investment, production and operation of enterprises, financial status, scientific and technological activities, and human resources. This chapter mainly focuses on the situation of Beijing Economic-Technological Development Area, Zhongguancun National Innovation Demonstration Zone and Beijing Tianzhu Bonded Zone. Data of Zhongguancun Yizhuang Sub-park is counted in both Zhongguancun National Innovation Demonstration Zone and Beijing Economic-Technological Development Area.

II. Source of Data

Data of Zhongguancun National Innovation Demonstration Zone in this chapter are sourced from Beijing Municipal Bureau of Statistics; statistics for other development zones in terms of business innovation, land and investment are gathered and provided by Beijing Municipal Commission of Economy and Information Technology and financial data are provided by Beijing Municipal Bureau of Statistics; data for Beijing Economic- Technological Development Area are from the Statistics Bureau and Survey Team of Beijing Economic-Technological Development Area; data for business invitation and land in Beijing Tianzhu Bonded Zone are provided by the Administrative Committee of the Bonded Zone, while other data are from Beijing Municipal Bureau of Statistics.

III. Notes on Changes in This Chapter

According to the *Official Reply of the State Council on Approving the Adjustment of Spatial Scale and Layout of Zhongguancun National Innovation Demonstration Area* issued in 2012, the statistic scope of Zhongguancun Area has been enlarged to include Pinggu Sub-park, Mentougou Sub-park, Shunyi Sub-park, Fangshan Sub-park, Miyun Sub-park, Huairou Sub-park and Yanqing Sub-park to supplement Haidian Sub-park, Fengtai Sub-park, Changping Sub-park, Electronic Park, Yizhuang Sub-park, Deshengyuan Sub-park, Yonghe Sub-park, Shijingshan Sub-park, Tongzhou Sub-park and Daxing Ecological Sub-park Pharmaceutical Base. At the same time, Electronic Park is changed into Chaoyang Sub-park, Deshengyuan Sub-park into Xicheng Sub-park and Yonghe Sub-park into Dongcheng Sub-park.

23-1 开发区基本情况(2014年)
STATISTICS ON DEVELOPMENT ZONES (2014)

项目		Item		国家级 National	市级 Municipal
开发区个数	(个)	Number of Development Zones	(unit)	3	16
区规划总面积	(公顷)	Total Planned Area of Development Zones	(hectare)	41207.3	8068.9
累计已开发土地面积	(公顷)	Accumulated Area of Developed Land	(hectare)	26650.0	6106.9
累计已供应土地面积	(公顷)	Accumulated Area of Supplied Land	(hectare)	14837.2	4896.8
累计已建成城镇建设用地面积	(公顷)	Accumulated Area of Land for Urban Development	(hectare)	20864.6	4731.5
累计招商项目企业个数	(个)	Accumulated Number of Enterprises of Business Inviting Programs	(unit)	43861	17398
累计招商项目总投资	(亿元)	Accumulative Total Investment of Business Inviting	(100 million yuan)	14326.0	2368.6
累计招商项目注册资本	(亿元)	Accumulative Registered Capital of Business Inviting Programs	(100 million yuan)	12616.6	1354.0
#三资企业	(亿元)	Three Kinds of Foreign-funded Enterprises	(100 million yuan)	1997.3	364.7
累计招商项目合同外资金额	(亿美元)	Accumulative Contracted Foreign Capital of Business Inviting Programs	(USD 100 million)	246.7	49.8
累计招商项目外商实际投资	(亿美元)	Accumulated Actual Foreign Investment of Business Inviting Programs	(USD 100 million)	187.3	59.0
固定资产投资	(亿元)	Investment in Fixed Assets	(100 million yuan)	936.2	111.6
总收入	(亿元)	Total Revenue	(100 million yuan)	38067.0	5033.8
工业总产值(当年价格)	(亿元)	Gross Output Value Of Industry (at current prices)	(100 million yuan)	9523.8	1317.9
工业销售产值(当年价格)	(亿元)	Sales Value of Industry (at current prices)	(100 million yuan)	9326.2	1317.4
利润总额	(亿元)	Total Profits	(100 million yuan)	3056.1	234.9
应缴税金	(亿元)	Total Taxes Payable	(100 million yuan)	1570.6	149.4

注：1. 本表所指开发区包括北京市级及国家级开发区情况。
2. 表内“累计”指自开始至年末的累计数。
3. 本表“总收入”、“工业总产值(当年价格)”、“工业销售产值”(当年价格)、“利润总额”和“应缴税金”数据的统计范围为注册在开发区内的规模(限额)以上法人单位。

Note: a) Development zones in this table include those at Beijing municipal level and national level.
b) Accumulative data in this table refer to the accumulation from the beginning to the end of this year.
c) The statistical scope of total revenue, gross output value of industry (at current prices), sales value of industry (at current prices), total profits and total taxes payable in this table cover legal entities above designated size that are registered in the development zones.

23-2 开发区土地开发情况(2014年)
LAND EXPLOITATION OF DEVELOPMENT ZONES(2014)

单位：公顷 (hectare)

名　　称	Item	规划总面积 Total Planned Area	累计已开发土地面积 Accumulated Area of Developed Land	累计已供应土地面积 Accumulated Area of Supplied Land	累计已建成城镇建设用地 Accumulated Area of Land for Urban Development
国家级开发区	**State-level Development Zone**				
北京经济技术开发区	Beijing Economic-Technological Development Area	4680.0	3700.0	3873.9	3700.0
中关村国家自主创新示范区	Zhongguancun National Independent Innovation Demonstration Zone	38610.9	25278.5	10642.8	19663.8
中关村示范区海淀园	Zhongguancun Haidian Sub-park	13242.2	10683.9	697.8	9986.2
中关村示范区丰台园	Zhongguancun Fengtai Sub-park	1763.0	289.0	200.0	166.6
中关村示范区昌平园	Zhongguancun Changping Sub-park	5140.0	2068.9	1952.9	1719.7
中关村示范区朝阳园	Zhongguancun Chaoyang Sub-park	2610.0	1471.9	1447.1	1240.0
中关村示范区亦庄园	Zhongguancun Yizhuang Sub-park	2678.0	2678.0		2678.0
中关村示范区西城园	Zhongguancun Xicheng Sub-park	1000.0	1000.0	1000.0	
中关村示范区东城园	Zhongguancun Dongcheng Sub-park	603.0	288.8		288.8
中关村示范区石景山园	Zhongguancun Shijingshan Sub-park	1334.0	127.6	41.0	127.6
中关村示范区通州园	Zhongguancun Tongzhou Sub-park	3434.5	2158.2	2007.6	1508.8
中关村示范区大兴生物工程与医药产业基地	Zhongguancun Daxing Ecological Sub-park and Pharmaceutical Base	1124.7	710.2	472.8	297.6
中关村示范区平谷园	Zhongguancun PingGu Sub-park	508.0	329.0	103.4	85.2
中关村示范区门头沟园	Zhongguancun MenTouGou Sub-park	189.0	120.0	120.0	120.0
中关村示范区房山园	Zhongguancun FangShan Sub-park	1573.0	1205.4	1013.7	550.2
中关村示范区顺义园	Zhongguancun ShunYi Sub-park	1208.5	912.1	574.8	224.3
中关村示范区密云园	Zhongguancun MiYun Sub-park	1000.8	699.3	597.0	462.4
中关村示范区怀柔园	Zhongguancun HuaiRou Sub-park	711.0	266.3	165.3	17.9
中关村示范区延庆园	Zhongguancun YanQing Sub-park	491.2	270.0	249.6	190.6
北京天竺综合保税区	Beijing Tianzhu Bonded Area	594.4	349.5	320.5	178.8
市级开发区	**Municipal-level Development Zone**				
北京石龙经济开发区	Shilong Economic Development Zone	189.0	120.0	120.0	120.0
北京良乡经济开发区	Liangxiang Economic Development Zone	240.9	136.1	132.7	109.2
北京大兴经济开发区	Daxing Economic Development Zone	414.8	278.5	272.2	261.9
北京通州经济开发区	Tongzhou Economic Development Zone	767.0	540.6	507.4	261.5
北京雁栖经济开发区	Yanqi Economic Development Zone	1096.0	942.4	712.9	659.5
北京兴谷经济开发区	Xinggu Economic Development Zone	503.2	437.0	310.0	437.0
北京密云经济开发区	Miyun Economic Development Zone	1246.4	1246.4	993.5	910.0
北京林河经济开发区	Linhe Economic Development Zone	416.0	385.0	260.0	349.0
北京天竺空港经济开发区	Tianzhu Economic Development Zone	660.0	660.0	449.0	405.4
北京八达岭经济开发区	Badaling Economic Development Zone	480.8	318.6	209.6	291.6
北京永乐经济开发区	Yongle Economic Development Zone	459.8	219.3	137.1	137.1
北京延庆经济开发区	Yanqing Economic Development Zone	418.6	173.2	143.0	221.0
北京昌平小汤山工业园区	Changping Xiaotangshan Industrial Park	257.3	14.3	14.3	45.3
北京采育经济开发区	Caiyu Economic Development Zone	355.0	327.1	327.1	299.3
北京房山工业园区	Fangshan Industrial Park	218.5	159.5	159.5	112.3
北京马坊工业园区	Mafang Bonded Area Industrial Park	345.6	149.0	148.4	111.5

注：1. 本表所指开发区包括北京市级及国家级开发区情况。
2. 中关村国家自主创新示范区亦庄园数据在中关村国家自主创新示范区与北京经济技术开发区中为重叠部分。
3. 自2013年起，平谷园、门头沟园、房山园、顺义园、密云园、怀柔园和延庆园七个园区纳入中关村国家自主创新示范区统计范围，后表同(详见简要说明)。
4. 除中关村国家自主创新示范区海淀园外，中关村国家自主创新示范区各园“规划总面积”指标均填报批复土地面积，范围较2012年有所变化。
5. 表内“累计”指自开始至年末的累计数。

Note: a) Development zones in this table include those at Beijing municipal level and national level.
b) Data on Yizhuang Sub-park of Zhongguancun Demonstration Zone are overlapped in Zhongguancun National Innovation Demonstration Zone and Beijing Economic and Technological Development Area.
c) Since 2013, the Pinggu Sub-park, Mentougou Sub-park, Fangshan Sub-park, Shunyi Sub-park, Huairou Sub-park and Yanqing Sub-park are incorporated into the statistical scope of Zhongguancun National Independent Innovation Demonstration Zone (the same in the following tables). (For details, please refer to the Brief Introduction to this chapter.)
d) Apart from Haidian Sub-park, the total planned area of all sub-parks of Zhongguancun National Independent Innovation Demonstration Zone refers to the approved area of land. The statistical scope is slightly different from that of 2012.
e) "Accumulated" in this table refers to the accumlation from the beginning to the end of the year.

23-3 开发区招商、入资情况(2014年)

名　称	Item	招商项目企业个数(个) Number of Enterprises Involved in Business Inviting Programs (unit)
国家级开发区	**State-level Development Zone**	
北京经济技术开发区	Beijing Economic-Technological Development Area	9350
中关村国家自主创新示范区	Zhongguancun National Independent Innovation Demonstration Zone	35026
中关村示范区海淀园	Zhongguancun Haidian Sub-park	20247
中关村示范区丰台园	Zhongguancun Fengtai Sub-park	5303
中关村示范区昌平园	Zhongguancun Changping Sub-park	2576
中关村示范区朝阳园	Zhongguancun Chaoyang Sub-park	1434
中关村示范区亦庄园	Zhongguancun Yizhuang Sub-park	720
中关村示范区西城园	Zhongguancun Xicheng Sub-park	473
中关村示范区东城园	Zhongguancun Dongcheng Sub-park	1084
中关村示范区石景山园	Zhongguancun Shijingshan Sub-park	2429
中关村示范区通州园	Zhongguancun Tongzhou Sub-park	200
中关村示范区大兴生物工程与医药产业基地	Zhongguancun Daxing Ecological Sub-park and Pharmaceutical Base	74
中关村示范区平谷园	Zhongguancun PingGu Sub-park	60
中关村示范区门头沟园	Zhongguancun MenTouGou Sub-park	86
中关村示范区房山园	Zhongguancun FangShan Sub-park	58
中关村示范区顺义园	Zhongguancun ShunYi Sub-park	142
中关村示范区密云园	Zhongguancun MiYun Sub-park	84
中关村示范区怀柔园	Zhongguancun HuaiRou Sub-park	29
中关村示范区延庆园	Zhongguancun YanQing Sub-park	27
北京天竺综合保税区	Beijing Tianzhu Bonded Area	205
市级开发区	**Municipal-level Development Zone**	
北京石龙经济开发区	Shilong Economic Development Zone	9692
北京良乡经济开发区	Liangxiang Economic Development Zone	81
北京大兴经济开发区	Daxing Economic Development Zone	2064
北京通州经济开发区	Tongzhou Economic Development Zone	80
北京雁栖经济开发区	Yanqi Economic Development Zone	1695
北京兴谷经济开发区	Xinggu Economic Development Zone	198
北京密云经济开发区	Miyun Economic Development Zone	242
北京林河经济开发区	Linhe Economic Development Zone	282
北京天竺空港经济开发区	Tianzhu Economic Development Zone	634
北京八达岭经济开发区	Badaling Economic Development Zone	1224
北京永乐经济开发区	Yongle Economic Development Zone	26
北京延庆经济开发区	Yanqing Economic Development Zone	962
北京昌平小汤山工业园区	Changping Xiaotangshan Industrial Park	78
大兴采育经济开发区	Caiyu Economic Development Zone	59
北京房山工业园区	Fangshan Industrial Park	25
北京马坊工业园区	Mafang Industrial Park	56

注：1.中关村国家自主创新示范区亦庄园数据在中关村国家自主创新示范区与北京经济技术开发区中为重叠部分。
2.本表中关村国家自主创新示范区统计口径为注册在园区内的法人单位，其他开发区统计口径为经营在开发区内的法人单位，部分开发区范围较2012年有所变化。

STATISTICS FOR BUSINESS INVITATION AND INVESTMENT IN DEVELOPMENT ZONES (2014)

自开始至报告期累计 Accumulative Number from Beginning				
项目总投资(万元) Total Investment (10000 yuan)	注册资本(万元) Registered Capital (10000 yuan)	#三资企业 Foreign-funded Enterprises	合同外资金额(万美元) Contracted Foreign Capital (USD 10000)	外商实际投资(万美元) Actual Foreign Investment (USD 10000)
37417718	28100354	7046542	826865	674801
119829035	105350075	16878610	1936643	1532869
45046850	39296691	8306367	1167502	763653
13965808	13965808	227253	26905	33239
20125765	20022781	902200	68643	68643
9271027	9271027	1229885	103550	103550
15685308	8202637	4271020	341453	338956
5617476	5617476	447090	73293	73293
1112380	1112380	101275	3293	3142
2862123	2862123	203505	31308	34210
1386947	641504	304009	16384	16384
206809	200000	16000	5200	4750
54669	54669			
908731	908731	10372	1019	319
28860	716175	221863	75	1451
2400468	2017576	609657	94653	87891
586500	359935	25498	3003	3003
526365	65977			
42948	34584	2616	363	386
1698062	918043	318822	44796	4533
2888137	2888137	41265	7997	6423
328327	107545	12057	1532	1532
478512	817148	148943	10675	9491
2839846	657345	213306	44370	41208
3113958	925292	460489	240471	252780
799886	315676	560325	4948	50918
2666371	519067	131210	24807	48497
902107	588209	94469	12597	7864
5494036	3756030	1950481	142203	161679
662045	657986	19981	60	60
193769	47139	1000		1487
2003533	1736076		5857	6494
52800	34731	6242	989	655
753971	130317	6981	1735	780
278946	129349			
230141	230141			

Note: a) Data on Yizhuang Sub-park of Zhongguancun Demonstration Zone are overlapped in Zhongguancun National Innovation Demonstration Zone and Beijing Economic and Technological Development Area.

b) The statistical scope of Zhongguancun Demonstration Zone covers all legal entities registered in the zone, while the scope for other development zones covers all legal entities operating in them. The scope for some development zones is modified from that of 2012.

23-4 开发区投资、生产情况(2014年)
INVESTMENT AND PRODUCTION OF DEVELOPMENT ZONES (2014)

名称	Item	自年初累计 Accumulative Number from Year-beginning		
		固定资产投资(万元) Investment in Fixed Assets (10000 yuan)	总收入(万元) Total Revenue (10000 yuan)	利润总额(万元) Total Profits (10000 yuan)
国家级开发区	**State-level Development Zone**			
北京经济技术开发区	Beijing Economic-Technological Development Area	3910369	55953685	2495710
中关村国家自主创新示范区	Zhongguancun National Independent Innovation Demonstration Zone	6677894	360575733	30315111
中关村示范区海淀园	Zhongguancun Haidian Sub-park	972816	144494589	11422645
中关村示范区丰台园	Zhongguancun Fengtai Sub-park	739349	36993851	2193685
中关村示范区昌平园	Zhongguancun Changping Sub-park	275038	31836041	2663048
中关村示范区朝阳园	Zhongguancun Chaoyang Sub-park	340000	40901144	4903686
中关村示范区亦庄园	Zhongguancun Yizhuang Sub-park	1324696	37222959	2334553
中关村示范区西城园	Zhongguancun Xicheng Sub-park	114223	18747680	1987501
中关村示范区东城园	Zhongguancun Dongcheng Sub-park	862227	15019392	1464787
中关村示范区石景山园	Zhongguancun Shijingshan Sub-park	14847	15259599	1675324
中关村示范区通州园	Zhongguancun Tongzhou Sub-park	1255349	3835649	328829
中关村示范区大兴生物工程与医药产业基地	Zhongguancun Daxing Ecological Sub-park and Pharmaceutical Base	211764	2633186	209013
中关村示范区平谷园	Zhongguancun PingGu Sub-park	4676	800251	42508
中关村示范区门头沟园	Zhongguancun MenTouGou Sub-park	8409	1039420	71244
中关村示范区房山园	Zhongguancun FangShan Sub-park	383042	1932637	15902
中关村示范区顺义园	Zhongguancun ShunYi Sub-park	74182	5652372	572725
中关村示范区密云园	Zhongguancun MiYun Sub-park	28639	1649237	170646
中关村示范区怀柔园	Zhongguancun HuaiRou Sub-park	51352	1903318	198533
中关村示范区延庆园	Zhongguancun YanQing Sub-park	17285	654410	60481
北京天竺综合保税区	Beijing Tianzhu Bonded Area	98000	1419041	88975
市级开发区	**Municipal-level Development Zone**			
北京石龙经济开发区	Shilong Economic Development Zone	90947	6625760	37605
北京良乡经济开发区	Liangxiang Economic Development Zone	12944	2794208	27390
北京大兴经济开发区	Daxing Economic Development Zone	69550	1939455	58531
北京通州经济开发区	Tongzhou Economic Development Zone	79151	1022455	221936
北京雁栖经济开发区	Yanqi Economic Development Zone	148085	3630877	323219
北京兴谷经济开发区	Xinggu Economic Development Zone	85061	2318314	145572
北京密云经济开发区	Miyun Economic Development Zone	126674	3381768	253067
北京林河经济开发区	Linhe Economic Development Zone	260040	1666175	64216
北京天竺空港经济开发区	Tianzhu Economic Development Zone	138920	23693482	1029203
北京八达岭经济开发区	Badaling Economic Development Zone	2228	1217984	83675
北京永乐经济开发区	Yongle Economic Development Zone	27433	44385	662
北京延庆经济开发区	Yanqing Economic Development Zone	22265	1219931	118335
北京昌平小汤山工业园区	Changping Xiaotangshan Industrial Park		11336	93
大兴采育经济开发区	Caiyu Economic Development Zone	12395	567288	-8425
北京房山工业园区	Fangshan Industrial Park	20762	173573	-6247
北京马坊工业园区	Mafang Industrial Park	19627	30884	97

注：1.中关村国家自主创新示范区亦庄园数据在中关村国家自主创新示范区与北京经济技术开发区中为重叠部分。
2.北京经济技术开发区、市级各开发区“总收入”、“利润总额”指标的统计范围为规模(限额)以上法人单位。

Note: a) Data on Yizhuang Sub-park of Zhongguancun Demonstration Zone are overlapped in Zhongguancun National Innovation Demonstration Zone and Beijing Economic and Technological Development Area.
b) The statistical scope of total revenue and total profits for Beijing Economic-Technological Development Area and other municipal-level development zones covers legal entities above designated size.

23-5 北京经济技术开发区主要经济指标 MAIN ECONOMIC INDICATORS FOR BEIJING ECONOMIC-TECHNOLOGICAL DEVELOPMENT AREA

项　目		Item		2014	2013	2014年为2013年% 2014 as % of 2013
规划面积	(公顷)	Area Planned	(hectare)	4680.0	4680.0	100.0
开发区生产总值	(亿元)	Gross Output Value	(100 million yuan)	997.4	913.5	109.2
工业总产值（当年价格）	(亿元)	Gross Output Value of Industry (at current prices)	(100 million yuan)	2421.0	2292.9	105.6
#高新技术企业	(亿元)	High and New Technology Enterprises	(100 million yuan)	2201.7	2129.0	103.4
销售(营业)收入	(亿元)	Sales(Business)Revenue	(100 million yuan)	5589.9	4786.2	116.8
利润总额	(亿元)	Total Profits	(100 million yuan)	249.2	276.6	90.1
进出口总值	(亿美元)	Total Value of Imports and Exports	(USD 100 million)	190.0	210.8	90.1
出　口	(亿美元)	Exports	(USD 100 million)	88.6	109.4	81.0
进　口	(亿美元)	Imports	(USD 100 million)	101.4	101.4	100.0
公共财政预算收入	(亿元)	Local Public Finance Budget Revenue	(100 million yuan)	120.0	100.3	119.7
公共财政预算支出	(亿元)	Local Public Finance Budget Expenditure	(100 million yuan)	112.1	102.0	109.9
批准企业个数	(个)	Number of Enterprises Ratified	(unit)	2736	1414	193.5
入区企业投资额	(亿美元)	Investment of Enterprises Entering the Area	(USD 100 million)	119.5	93.8	127.4
注册资本	(亿美元)	Registered Capital	(USD 100 million)	113.5	56.0	202.8
合同外资金额	(亿美元)	Contracted Foreign Capital	(USD 100 million)	5.0	8.0	62.7
实际利用外资	(亿美元)	Actual Use of Foreign Capital	(USD 100 million)	6.4	6.3	102.1
固定资产投资	(亿元)	Investment in Fixed Assets	(100 million yuan)	391.0	375.2	104.2
从业人员期末人数	(人)	Number of Employed Persons	(person)	286133	279462	102.4
从业人员工资总额	(万元)	Total Wages of Employed Persons	(10000 yuan)	2885362	2597521	111.1

注：1．工业总产值(当年价格)、销售(营业)收入和利润总额指标的统计范围是规模(限额)以上法人单位。
2．2013年进出口总值根据海关数据进行调整。
资料来源：北京经济技术开发区统计局、调查队。
Note: a) The statistical scope of gross output value of industry (at current prices), sales (business) revenue and total profits covers legal entities above designated size.
b) Total value of imports and exports in 2013 are adjusted according to customs data.
Source: Statistics Bureau and Survey Team of Beijing Economic-Technological Development Area.

23-6 中关村国家自主创新示范区企业经营及科技活动情况(2008-2014年) OPERATING ACTIVITIES AND SCIENCE ACTIVITIES OF ENTERPRISES IN ZHONGGUANCUN NATIONAL INNOVATION DEMONSTRATION ZONE (2008-2014)

项　目		Item		2008	2009	2010	2011	2012	2013	2014
总收入	**(亿元)**	**Total Revenue**	**(100 million yuan)**	**10222.4**	**13004.6**	**15940.2**	**19646.0**	**25025.0**	**30497.4**	**36057.6**
技术收入	(亿元)	Technological Revenue	(100 million yuan)	1693.4	2093.6	2478.3	2845.9	3403.1	4032.43	4837.7
产品销售收入	(亿元)	Products Sales Revenue	(100 million yuan)	5229.2	5923.6	6889.6	7809.4	8741.2	10788.4	12474.2
#新产品销售收入	(亿元)	Sales Revenue of New Products	(100 million yuan)	3327.0	3203.7	3949.2	3405.1	3352.1	4070.4	4614.83
商品销售收入	(亿元)	Commodity Sales Revenue	(100 million yuan)	2398.9	3689.4	5032.2	7161.9	10077.4	11339.6	12832.6
其他收入	(亿元)	Other Revenues	(100 million yuan)	900.9	1298.0	1540.1	1828.9	2803.4	4336.96	5913.1
出口总额	(亿美元)	Total Exports	(USD 100 million)	207.4	208.2	227.4	237.3	261.7	336.2	337.3
实缴税费总额	(亿元)	Total Tax Paid	(100 million yuan)	504.0	658.7	767.2	925.8	1445.8	1506.6	1857.6
利润总额	(亿元)	Total Profits	(100 million yuan)	726.3	1122.4	1298.9	1533.9	1788.6	2264.8	3031.5
获奖成果情况		**Statistics on Prize-winning Achievements**								
获奖成果个数	(个)	Number of Prize-winning Achievements	(unit)	1448	1909	1811	2329	2509	2852	2636
#国家级	(个)	National	(unit)	282	276	256	323	377	450	364
省部级	(个)	Provincial	(unit)	641	1044	1015	1351	1318	1652	1522
专利情况		**Statistics on Patents**								
专利申请数	(件)	Number of Patents Applied	(unit)	17219	17226	18515	24894	34192	44275	55009
拥有有效发明专利数	(件)	Number of Patents in Force	(unit)	9836	11611	13988	15232	23198	35000	44870
专利授权数	(件)	Number of Patents Licensed	(unit)	9050	10512	13151	12951	17969	22308	25065

23-7 中关村国家自主创新示范区企业经营活动情况
OPERATING ACTIVITIES OF ENTERPRISES IN ZHONGGUANCUN NATIONAL INNOVATION DEMONSTRATION ZONE

单位：亿元 (100 million yuan)

项 目	Item	2014	2013
工业总产值(当年价格)	Gross Output Value of Industry (at current prices)	9289.0	7890.3
工业销售产值(当年价格)	Sales Value of Industry (at current prices)	9102.0	7769.2
#出口交货值	Delivery Value of Exports	963.2	929.9
总收入	Total Revenue	36057.6	30497.4
技术收入	Technological Revenue	4837.7	4032.4
产品销售收入	Products Sales Revenue	12474.2	10788.4
#新产品销售收入	Sales Revenue of New Products	4614.8	4070.4
#出口收入	Export Revenue	1023.7	1067.7
商品销售收入	Commodity Sales Revenue	12832.6	11339.6
其他收入	Other Revenues	5913.1	4337.0
利润总额	Total Profits	3031.5	2264.8
实缴税费总额	Total Tax Paid	1857.6	1506.6
#增值税	Value Added Tax	830.2	584.7
营业税	Business Tax	138.7	116.5
所得税	Corporate Income Tax	493.4	403.5
本年实缴关税	Duties Paid in the Year	184.1	143.2
减免税总额	Reduced and Exempted Tax	315.0	224.3
#增值税	Value Added Tax	105.6	90.8
营业税	Business Tax	1.2	4.3
所得税	Corporate Income Tax	202.2	121.7
应交增值税	Value Added Tax Payable	647.8	410.1
出口总额（亿美元）	Foreign Exchange Created by Export (USD100 million)	337.3	336.2

23-8 中关村国家自主创新示范区企业科技活动情况
SCIENTIFIC ACTIVITIES OF ENTERPRISES IN ZHONGGUANCUN NATIONAL INNOVATION DEMONSTRATION ZONE

项目	Item	2014	2013
科技活动情况	**Statistics on Scientific and Technological Activities**		
科技活动人员合计 (人)	Total Number of Personnel Engaged in Scientific and Technological Activities (person)	531609	499870
#全时人员	Full-time Personnel	476858	445849
企业内部用于科技活动的经费支出 (亿元)	Total Expenditures on Research Activities Inside Enterprises (100 million yuan)	1224.099	1032.6
#人员人工费(包括各种补贴)	Labor Cost (Including Various Subsidies)	662.0	560.5
原材料费	Cost of Raw Materials	215.3	185.8
委托外单位开展科技活动经费支出 (亿元)	Expenditures on Scientific and Technological Activities Institutions Conducted by External Institutes Entrusted (100 million yuan)	131.9	132.5
#对境内研究机构及高等学校的支出	Spending on Domestic Research Institutes and of Higher Education	92.3	85.5
对境外支出	Overseas Spending	6.1	4.2
企业科技活动产出情况	**Scientific and Technological Output**		
获奖成果情况	**Statistics on Prize-winning Achievements**		
获奖成果个数 (个)	Number of Prize-winning Achievements (unit)	2636	2852
#国家级 (个)	National (unit)	364	450
省部级 (个)	Provincial (unit)	1522	1652
地市级 (个)	Prefecture and City-level (unit)	750	747
专利情况	**Statistics on Patents**		
专利申请数 (件)	Number of Patents Applied (case)	55009	44275
#发明专利 (件)	Invention Patents (case)	34523	26737
拥有有效发明专利数 (件)	Number of Patents in Force (case)	44870	35000
专利授权数 (件)	Number of Patent Licensed (case)	25065	22308
论文、著作情况	**Statistics on Papers and Writings**		
发表科技论文篇数 (篇)	Number of Published Scientific Papers (unit)	14744	13227
技术改造和技术获取情况	**Technical Rennovation and Acquisition**		
技术改造经费支出 (亿元)	Expenditures on Technical Rennovation (100 million yuan)	37.9	13.4
引进国外技术经费支出 (亿元)	Expenditures on Introduction of Foreign Technologies (100 million yuan)	13.4	16.1
引进技术的消化吸收经费支出 (亿元)	Expenditures on Absorption of Imported Technologies (100 million yuan)	7.7	5.7
购买国内技术经费支出 (亿元)	Expenditures on Purchasing Domestic Technologies (100 million yuan)	9.7	14.7

23-9 中关村国家自主创新示范区企业人力资源情况
HUMAN RESOURCES OF ENTERPRISES IN ZHONGGUANCUN NATIONAL INNOVATION DEMONSTRATION ZONE

单位：人 (person)

项　目	Item	2014	2013
企业人力资源情况	**Statistics on Human Resource**		
从业人员年末人数	**Number of Employeed Persons at the Year End**	**2010448**	**1898756**
#工程技术人员	Engineering Technician	572664	578860
#留学归国人员	Returned Students Studying Abroad	21521	19763
#在岗长期职工	On-the-post Long-term Employed Persons	1835847	1723520
按文化程度分	**By Educational Background**		
博士及以上	Doctor Degree and Above	19774	18426
#留学归国人员	Returned Students Studying Abroad	2237	2185
硕　士	Masters	198237	183350
#留学归国人员	Returned Students Studying Abroad	14363	12613
大　本	Undergraduates	810731	747026
大　专	Junior College	433752	412466
按技术职称分	**By Technical Post**		
高　级	Senior	122111	108358
中　级	Middle	223465	196578
初　级	Junior	240694	219991
按年龄分	**By Age**		
#29岁及以下	Age 29 and Below	899410	881781
30-39岁	30-39	690093	632065
40-49岁	40-49	282530	258292
从业人员平均人数	**Average Number of Empolyed Persons**	**1972084**	**1844792**
在岗职工参加社会保险人数	**Number of Employees Covered by the Social Insurance**	**1761881**	**1638578**

23-10 中关村国家自主创新示范区企业财务状况
FINANCIAL STATUS OF ENTERPRISES IN ZHONGGUANCUN NATIONAL INNOVATION DEMONSTRATION ZONE

单位：亿元 (100 million yuan)

项　目	Item	2014	2013
资产总计	Total Assets	64770.8	50814.4
流动资产合计	Total Current Assets	35648.9	29545.1
固定资产合计	Total Fixed Assets	7495.2	6580.7
固定资产原价	Original Value of Fixed Assets	10997.0	9106.2
累计折旧	Accumulative Depreciation	3731.0	2595.7
负债合计	Total Liabilities	36105.7	28472.4
所有者权益合计	Total Owner's Equity	28665.1	22342.0
实收资本	Paid-up Capital	15010.2	11464.4
主营业务收入	Operating Income	34857.1	29877.8
主营业务成本	Main Business Cost	28601.9	24513.1
主营业务税金及附加	Main Business Tax and Surtax	283.5	245.2
利润总额	Total Profits	3031.5	2264.8

主要统计指标解释

已开发土地面积 指在规划范围内达到“七通一平”标准的，具备进行房屋建筑物施工或出让条件的土地面积。

已供应土地面积 指开发区内通过各种方式获得土地使用权的土地面积，包括出让、划拨、租赁等。

已建成城镇建设用地面积 截至报告期，已经建设并通过竣工验收的国有建设用地。包括已建成的住宅用地、工矿仓储用地、多功能用地、交通运输用地、商服用地、公共管理与公共服务用地，以及其他城镇建设用地等。海关特殊监管区域的已建成城镇建设用地包括现状围网范围内已建成的城镇建设用地，及开发区四至范围与围网范围间的海关专属办公用地。

累计招商项目企业个数 指自开始至报告期末累计招商入区，并经工商管理机关注册取得法人营业执照的企业个数。

累计招商项目总投资 指自开始至报告期末累计批准的合同（章程）规定的投资总额。

累计招商项目注册资本 指自开始至报告期末累计为设立经营企业在工商行政管理机关注册的资本总额。

累计招商项目合同外资金额 指自开始至报告期末累计批准的合同（章程）中，外商和港、澳、台商的出资额。

累计招商项目外商实际投资 指自开始至报告期末累计按合同规定的外方和港、澳、台方以现金、实物、工业产权及专有技术的计价实缴资本投资额。

总收入 指企业全年的生产产品销售收入、技术性收入和与本企业产品相关的商品的销售收入、其它收入等各种收入的总和，总收入等于主营业务收入加上其他业务收入。总收入应按不含增值税的价格计算，不包括补贴收入、营业外收入、投资收益。

出口总额 指出售给外贸部门或直接出售给外商的产品或商品的总金额。包括来料加工装配出口，境外技术合同实现金额及在国内以外汇计价的商品出售和技术服务的总额等。

留学归国人员 指出国学习，取得学位的归国人员。

Explanatory Notes on Main Statistical Indicators

Area of Developed Land refers to the area of land that meets the standard of "seven connections and one leveling" and is qualified for construction or sale.

Area of Supplied Land refers to the area of land whose right of use is acquired in the development zones by various means including sale, transfer, and lease.

Area of Land for Urban Development refers to state-owned construction land that has already gone through construction and acceptance check by the end of the reporting period. It includes land for complete residential buildings, land for industrial, mining and storage use, multi-functional land, land for transportation, land for commercial services, land for public administration and services and other lands for urban development. Land for urban development under special administration of customs includes urban development land completed inside the current seine and land for office buildings of customs inside the development zones and between the seines.

Accumulated Number of Enterprises Involved in Business Inviting Programs refers to the total number of enterprises invited to development zones and awarded with business licenses for legal persons from the administration for industry and commerce from the beginning to the end of the reporting period.

Accumulative Investment of Business Inviting Programs refers to the total investment of contracts (articles of incorporation) approved from the beginning to the end of the reporting period.

Accumulative Registered Capital of Business Inviting Programs refers to the total capital registered with the administration for industry and commerce for the purpose of establishment of operating enterprises from the beginning to the end of the reporting period.

Accumulative Contracted Foreign Capital of Business Inviting Programs refers to the cumulative capital contribution of investors from foreign countries, Hong Kong, Macao and Taiwan as approved in contracts (articles of incorporation) from the beginning to the end of the reporting period.

Accumulative Actual Foreign Investment of Business Inviting Programs refers to the cumulative amount of paid-up capital investment from foreign countries, Hong Kong, Macao and Taiwan made in cash, in physical material, industrial property right and proprietary technology, as stated in contracts, from the beginning to the end of the reporting period.

Total Revenue refers to the sum of income earned by enterprises from sales of their own products, technological income, and income from selling commodities related to their own products, and other income. Total revenue is the sum of main business income and other business income. Total revenue shall be calculated at VAT-excluded prices, and exclude subsidies, non-operating income and return on investment across the year.

Total Exports refers to the total amount of products or commodities sold to foreign trade organizations or directly sold to foreign traders. It includes the value of export of investor's raw materials processed, the value of technical contracts completed at home and abroad, and the total value of domestic commodity sales and technical services measured in foreign currency.

Returned Students Studying Abroad refer to persons who have come home after studying abroad and been conferred with academic degrees.